DATE DUE

DEMCO 38-296

ENCYCLOPEDIA OF ARMS CONTROL AND DISARMAMENT

Encyclopedia of Arms Control and Disarmament

RICHARD DEAN BURNS

Editor in Chief

Volume II

CHARLES SCRIBNER'S SONS • NEW YORK
Maxwell Macmillan Canada • TORONTO
Maxwell Macmillan International • NEW YORK   OXFORD   SINGAPORE   SYDNEY

Charles Scribner's Sons   Maxwell Macmillan Canada, Inc.
Macmillan Publishing Company   1200 Eglinton Avenue East
866 Third Avenue   Suite 200
New York, New York 10022   Don Mills, Ontario M3C 3N1

Macmillan Publishing Company is part of the Maxwell Communication Group of Companies.

Library of Congress Cataloging-in-Publication Data

Encyclopedia of arms control and disarmament / Richard Dean Burns,
    editor in chief.
        p.   cm.
    Includes bibliographical references and index.
    ISBN 0-684-19281-0 (set : alk. paper) : $280.00. — ISBN
0-684-19603-4 (vol. 1 : alk. paper). — ISBN 0-684-19604-2 (vol. 2 :
alk. paper). — ISBN 0-684-19605-0 (vol. 3 : alk. paper)
    1. Arms control—Encyclopedias.   2. Disarmament—Encyclopedias.
I. Burns, Richard Dean.
JX1974.E57   1993
327.1′74′03—dc20   92-36167
                                                   CIP

  1   3   5   7   9   11   13   17   19   V/C   20   18   16   14   12   10   8   6   4   2

PRINTED IN THE UNITED STATES OF AMERICA

The paper used in this publication meets the minimum requirements
of American National Standard for Information Sciences—Permanence
of Paper for Printed Library Materials. ANSI Z3948-1984. ∞™

CONTENTS

PART

3

HISTORICAL DIMENSIONS TO 1945

Restraining Violence in Early Societies

NETA C. CRAWFORD

See also Arms Control in Antiquity; Disarmament and Development in the Third World; Medieval Arms Control Movements and the Western Quest for Peace; *and* Psychological Dimensions of Nuclear Arms Control.

It is widely believed that violence and warfare within and between groups in "primitive" societies were common. This view is articulated by Hobbes, who in *Leviathan* (1651) described a "war of all against all" in the state of nature. The view that non-European "primitive" peoples were universally violent is probably related to the belief that humans are instinctually aggressive. This perspective has been articulated by such scholars as Sigmund Freud; international-affairs expert Hans Morgenthau, who believed that humans had a psychobiological drive for power; and Konrad Lorenz, who in his 1966 work *On Aggression* proposed the notion that aggression was universal in both the animal and human kingdoms. In his *The Evolution of War: A Study of Its Role in Early Societies* (1929), Maurice R. Davie argued, "in general, the more primitive and undeveloped the groups, the greater is the hostility and the fewer are the restraining influences" (p. 196).

Thus while much has been written surveying conflict and war among groups, much less has been written about methods of restraining violence and war in these societies. The difference in coverage may be due to three important historical conditions. First, these early societies often left little in the way of recorded histories, so their social and political relations are frequently interpreted through the lenses of another culture. Second, many of the practices of these groups changed dramatically upon contact with more politically and technically sophisticated, especially European, societies, mostly as a result of their introduction to more destructive weaponry. Therefore, it is difficult to determine the precise nature of social relations among so-called primitive societies prior to their contact with Western societies by the nature of the archaeological evidence. Third, it is possible that scholars have been biased in their analyses of violent versus nonviolent societies. Thousands of years may have erased all but the most resilient of artifacts; the stone and iron tools of war may be more durable than the verbal and cultural tools of peace.

The focus of this essay is on both partial and comprehensive systems of restraining violence among early societies. Several groups studied by modern anthropology appear to have developed successful methods for restraining violence. Those methods may be grouped into three types: (1) partial prohibitions or limitations on the use of force (analogous to modern arms control); (2) comprehensive domestic socialization, including conflict resolution and de-escalation practices; (3) international organization in a security regime. After discussing the general causes of conflict in preliterate and precolonial societies and reviewing the patterns of peaceful and violent relations in those societies, this essay will examine both the partial and the comprehensive systems of restraining violence. Particularly, the Kalihari !Kung and the North American Iroquois provide examples of socialization and security regimes.

DIFFERING SOCIETAL RESPONSES

Potentially violent conflicts among early peoples arose from several sources: economic issues, in particular access to resources including land, water, and game, and workers, who could be captured and enslaved or perhaps fully integrated into society; social issues, including jealousy, disagreements about the status of mates, and blood feuds; religious or ritual reasons, whereby war was undertaken to placate deities; and political reasons resulting from competition for leadership among groups. Feuds, originally begun for economic, social, religious, or political reasons, sometimes would continue over several generations with little or no relation to the original source of the antagonism, as raids and counterraids perpetuated the conflict.

Societies varied widely in their response to these potentially conflictual situations, from peaceful to violent. These extremes are defined below.

A peaceful or nonaggressive society prefers nonviolent methods of conflict resolution over violent means, valuing peaceful relations between individuals and groups and discouraging unresolved, perpetual antagonism. In peaceful societies, the resort to force is rare or nonexistent, and when violence does occur, it is strictly limited by the group. In peaceful societies, socially recognized norms of nonviolent conflict resolution are the dominant means of preserving the peace.

Violent peoples are characterized by both in-group and intergroup violence, manifesting a high incidence of brute-force coercion as a method of conflict resolution. In violent societies the use of brute force within or between groups is legitimate, if not directly encouraged. Individuals are kept under control within the group by implicit or explicit threats of physical punishment. Internally violent societies have a high incidence of violent acts among members of the same group. For example, wife beating, child abuse, incest, murder, mugging, and rape are common in violent societies. These acts are either socially sanctioned, or the prohibitions against them are minimal.

Violent societies may also engage in intergroup war—organized violence between groups manifesting a "commitment" or tendency to use brute force to settle disagreements between groups. One measure of a commitment to the use of brute force is the development of special technologies—weaponry—which have as their primary function the injuring or killing of adversaries. Further, when violent societies engage in war, there may be rules for the conduct of war, but the use of force ultimately determines the outcome of the dispute—with or without limit on the type of legitimate target (combatant versus noncombatant), on the number of casualties, or upon the use of certain weapons.

It should be understood that if simple dichotomous definitions of *peaceful* and *violent* are applied, possibly no precolonial society would fall neatly and exclusively into either category. In the continuum between peaceful and violent societies there are communities in which violence was praised or encouraged between groups but discouraged within the group, and other societies in which intergroup violence was limited while at the same time highly regularized or ritualized (as among the Yanamamö of Brazil).

These early societies, therefore, may fall into one of four broad categories. There may be peaceful relations within and between groups; peaceful relations within the group but violence between groups, with or without partial prohibitions on the use of force; the sanctioning of violent relations within the group but discouragement of violence with out-groups; and the sanctioning of violent relations with both in-groups and out-groups.

PARTIAL PROHIBITIONS: ARMS CONTROL TECHNIQUES EMPLOYED

Partial prohibitions on the use of force were frequently employed among even violent societies, and these prohibitions were analogous to modern arms control practices. Many peoples who frequently engaged in military combat appear to have controlled the violence of their wars through: 1) limits on the number killed; 2) ritualized combat; 3) protection for noncombatants; and 4) prohibitions on the use of certain weapons. The following paragraphs illustrate the widespread nature of these partial prohibitions.

Limiting Casualties   The battles of the Indian tribes of British Columbia apparently resulted in few casualties; while in the battles of the Arapesh of Papua New Guinea the loss of a man or two was generally sufficient to prompt the withdrawal of one group of warriors. When some Native American groups in the Pacific Northwest found that they could not settle their differences, they would often set a day aside for battle. The issues were considered decided when one or two prominent tribesmen fell in the fighting.

Ritualized Warfare   Ritual or ceremonial battles were not uncommon in precolonial societies. Throughout Oceania, for example, there were rules that, although they varied from one group to another, "included a formal declaration of hostilities, the use of a prearranged fighting ground, restrictions as to weapons and the manner of their use, and a formal peacemaking ceremony to conclude the fighting" (Wedgwood, "Some Aspects of Warfare in Melanesia," *Oceania* 1 [April 1930]: 13). On islands near Malekula, local villagers "had a special fighting ground on the beach at the junction of their respective territories, but the beach was furnished with a stone fort where it was the custom of the defenders to await attack.... When the two sides met at the stone fort, the fighting consisted of hurling insults and recitations of present and past grievances interspersed with occasional volleys of stones" (J. W. Layard, *Stone Men of Malekula,* 1942, p. 597).

Dueling—highly regulated combat by individuals or small groups—was another ritualized means of resolving intergroup disputes. For example, some Eskimo groups used duels to resolve conflicts. In Siberia and Alaska, individuals would sometimes wrestle, with the winner and loser of a dispute determined not by right but by physical prowess. On occasion, antagonistic eastern Greenland Eskimo engaged in song duels in which, by popular acclaim, the best performer won the dispute. If the Botocudo of Brazil had a dispute that arose from the encroachment of one group on another's hunting grounds, the conflict was usually resolved by a duel between tribal champions. These warriors would strike at each other with staves until one conceded; however, if the losing tribe picked up their bows and arrows a full-scale battle would take place.

Protection for Noncombatants   Some precolonial groups recognized specific individuals, most commonly women, as being noncombatants

and therefore immune from martial violence. Precolonial Samoans apparently considered killing women in war cowardly. The Kapauku Papuans of western New Guinea also exempted married women as targets in war (even though they sometimes retrieved stray arrows or scouted for their males engaged in battle). According to Leopold Pospisil, it was considered "highly immoral for a man to shoot at a female during a battle. He is ... taunted even by his own people and relatives: 'You better stay home and don't fight; all you can do is shoot a woman.'" Sometimes the women exploited this situation: on occasion they would use their walking sticks to strike enemy warriors. Pospisil also notes that several women "even climbed a hill behind the enemy's lines, and from there, shouted advice concerning the enemy's movements to their fighting husbands. The annoyed and embarrassed enemy could only try to chase the women away by pushing them or beating them with bows and fists" (*The Kapauku Papuans of West New Guinea*, 1963, p. 59).

Occasionally, other groups were given noncombatant immunity. The Lushais, from near the Malay Peninsula, who carried out their campaigns by raiding the villages of their enemies, regarded the practice of waylaying farmers who were cultivating crops as unfair. One chief expounded: "How can people live if cultivation is impossible?" (quoted in Davie, *Evolution of War,* p. 181).

Outlawing the Use of Specific Weapons
Some groups prohibited the use of certain weapons or restricted the way that a weapon could be used in combat. For example, on the Small Islands, adjacent to Malekula, where conflicts between villages led to ceremonial battles, it was agreed that spears would not be used—only clubs and stones. However, when these same villagers fought with warriors from other islands, there was no restriction on weapons. According to Pospisil, when the Kapauku Papuans of western New Guinea met in ritualized battle, they fought "exclusively with bows and arrows" (*The Kapauku Papuans of West New Guinea,* p. 58).

In several instances, "poison" weapons were not employed in battles. The Tangale of western Africa, for example, poisoned their weapons for hunting elephants but did not use poison in their warfare. The Naga of the Indian subcontinent seldom employed poisoned arrows when engaged in combat because they thought it showed no respect for their opponents; however, since they had no concept of noncombatancy, they might fire them at a woman.

COMPREHENSIVE METHODS FOR RESTRAINING VIOLENCE

Nonviolent or peaceful precolonial societies used several means to restrain violence that were both structural and conflict-specific. Peace-maintaining mechanisms were embedded in the social practices and structure of some societies. Conflict-specific practices were also employed, via conflict-resolution techniques and methods of de-escalation.

Maintaining Peace: Social Practices and Structure

In the realm of social structure, perhaps the most important peace-maintaining mechanism was socialization. Socialization of the norms of nonviolent dispute resolution occurred during childhood and was reinforced throughout adulthood. In the case of several peaceful peoples, child-rearing practices were nonviolent, tolerant to the point of being overindulgent from a modern European/North American perspective, and openly affectionate. This has been particularly well documented in research on the Semai, Inuit, and !Kung.

A second structural aspect of maintaining peace within precolonial societies involved patterns of mutual obligation. In some societies this took the form of the male or female moving to the household of his or her spouse upon marriage for a period of limited or unlimited service. In some cases this mutual obligation revolved around ritualized patterns of gift giving or wealth sharing. However patterns of mutual obligation were established, those obligations served to bind people to one another within and across extended families.

A third structural feature often associated with peaceful precolonial societies is a lack of rigid hierarchies of power and a norm of egalitarianism. There were not huge differentials in wealth or power among these groups. Moreover, while there were often fairly circumscribed gender roles, there were not extreme differences in the power wielded by the two sexes in social and political relations. For example, both the Mbuti of Africa and Copper Eskimo of the Canadian Arctic appear to have been entirely egalitarian, with no hierarchies of political power evident within the group across gender or other lines: decision making was consensual.

Conflict Resolution and De-escalation

Of the methods of restraining violence that appeared focused specifically upon the problem of conflict, several precolonial societies had similar conflict-resolution and de-escalation practices.

The most common tool for conflict resolution among nonviolent groups was verbal argumentation between the conflicting parties. When this failed, conflict was often resolved through adjudication by third parties, most often by elders or family members not directly involved in the dispute. In many precolonial societies, complex informal and formal legal systems existed, as among the Yurok Indians of Northern California, where precise codes for the compensation of wrongs were enforced by public pressure. On the formal end of the spectrum, the Lozi of southern Africa developed a judicial system involving courts, or "kuta," several levels of judges, and a style of adversarial litigation where the norms of the society were articulated and applied.

When conflict escalated beyond the ability of the disputants to resolve the issue themselves and violence appeared imminent, several methods were employed to de-escalate the tension in peaceful societies. Observers would often intervene with a joke or make light of the confrontation by ridiculing parties to the dispute. In some cases, particularly when the conflict led to nasty shouts or blows, antagonists were physically separated by third parties until the disputants calmed down. Finally, in some cases, for example among the Semai of Malaysia, the approbation of deities was invoked by observers to cause the conflicting parties to behave.

To limit war and violence between groups, early peoples also practiced diplomacy. In some cases, most notably in North America, security regimes known as "confederacies" were established to reduce conflict between neighboring Native American groups. Thus "international" law in the form of negotiated settlement and treaty making may often have been the first recourse for resolving disputes between some Native American nations.

Examples from two societies are discussed in greater detail below to illustrate the means by which conflict was resolved and peace maintained within and between groups. First, the !Kung illustrate mechanisms of maintaining peace within a hunter-gatherer society. Second, the Iroquois League illustrates the security regime mechanism for maintaining peace among Native American nations.

RESTRAINING VIOLENCE WITHIN THE GROUP: THE KALAHARI !KUNG

The traditional !Kung of southern Africa were (and in some cases remain) a nonliterate, hunter-gatherer society, characterized by peaceful intra-group and intergroup relations. !Kung society used three methods of restraining violence: social practices and structures helped maintain peaceful relations; conflict was resolved through a system of verbal dispute and argumentation procedures; and violent interactions were often de-escalated through bystander intervention.

The traditional !Kung lived in the Kalahari Desert regions of the modern states of Zimbabwe, Botswana, and Namibia. They were (and in some locations remain) seminomadic hunter-gatherers who did not practice any form of agricultural food production. The largest group structure of the traditional !Kung was the band, an autonomous collection of extended families who lived and worked together. The division of labor ran along gender lines. Men hunted together using poisoned arrows in order to track and kill both large and small game. Women gathered food by foraging through the bush for edible plants. Both men and women brought home the food they obtained in the bush to share with other members of the band.

Climatic and geographical conditions in the region were not overly hospitable. The Kalahari Desert is a delicate ecosystem where plant and animal resources are scarce and valuable. Water resources may be replenished regularly but vegetable resources, once harvested, were not available again until the next season. Hence, one might have expected frequent conflicts among members of bands or between bands over food and water resources. Yet, while conflict among the !Kung was frequent, violent conflict was rare and disputes were, as a general practice, resolved peacefully.

Maintaining Peace   Peaceful relations were maintained through socialization and patterns of mutual obligation. The primary method of socialization was child rearing, while patterns of mutual obligation were developed in the institutions of bride service, gift giving, and sharing. Moreover, there was a norm of constant communication that helped to maintain peace.

There was no formal education of children in traditional !Kung society. Children learned social expectations and the techniques necessary to live in the bush through observation and informal teaching by older children and adults. Children were never struck by their parents or other adults. Rather they, especially the very young, accompanied adults almost everywhere (though they were not involved in the hunt), and their needs were attended to almost as soon as they were expressed.

The constant supervision of children ensured that the child's needs were met. More important, conflict between children or between adults and children never got far out of control before someone intervened. Parents who were frustrated with their children had many other adults nearby to turn to for support, so child abuse was rare. Any violence between children was halted quickly by separation of the antagonists, and violent acts were often ignored by adults, so as not to reward the violent child.

In this way, !Kung children were incorporated into nonaggressive or peaceful relations from their first, primary relationships and throughout their childhood. There were no models of violent behavior, nor were children taught that the use of force brought social approbation. Rather children, from the very beginning of awareness, observed the nonviolent ways that adults managed disagreements with one another.

Other social institutions encouraged peaceful relations. Among the !Kung, bride service and patterns of gift giving and sharing established cross-cutting family ties and a web of mutual obligation or reciprocity. Bride service occurred after marriage when the male moved into the female's family for an indefinite period, usually long enough for the birth of three children, in order to provide meat for her parents and their dependents.

Sharing was the norm in !Kung society; both men and women brought food they gathered or captured home to share with other members of the band. The expectation that people would share their good fortune was strong and reinforced by the knowledge that others would share when they were fortunate in hunting or gathering. Further, the individual who did not share to the expected degree was charged with stinginess and neglect of friendship.

Gift giving among the !Kung, known as "hxaro," fulfilled the social expectation that valuables were shared. Gifts could not be refused, and the recipient was obligated, after a delay, to give the donor a different gift. The delayed nature of the gift giving ensured that gift giving was not seen as trade or barter and that the exhange never ended. Hxaro also served to prevent extreme differentials of wealth from accumulating and provided an occasion for individuals to visit relatives and friends who lived with other bands. Thus, the gift giving reinforced relationships with distant groups.

Moreover, while the !Kung had concepts of territory, that is, that bands control an area's resources through use and inheritance, custom required that food was shared with visiting individuals and bands. Bands traveling outside their territory were required to receive permission to use the resources of the area, and visitors were expected to reciprocate by returning access to resources within their home area at another time. If disputes arose over resources, they were argued between bands and resolved by references to past sharing, recalling the norm of reciprocity.

Finally, peaceful relations were maintained through constant communication within the group and through visits to other bands. Conversation kept lines of communication open, was an outlet for immediate venting of emotion, and was the principal way that the community rewarded and disciplined its members. If someone in the band had a grievance, verbal communication was used to make the point: the aggrieved individual may have carried on a monologue in the form of a story addressed to the community at large hoping that someone would satisfy his need, or he may have directly communicated to the person with whom he had a grievance.

Conflict Resolution and De-escalation Among the !Kung

Talk, appealing especially to norms of reciprocity and fairness, was the way in which the !Kung most often attempted to resolve disputes. In a direct conflict between individuals, an argument may have ensued whereby someone accused another of wrongdoing. At this point, the conflict may have escalated into shouting and the exchange of insults. The argument may then have been resolved gradually by the participants through animated negotiation. In addition, to help resolve a dispute, individuals could appeal to public opinion in hopes of getting the support of their peers.

This leads into another method of restraining violence, namely, techniques for the de-escalation of fights. Disagreements and fights among the !Kung were often kept at a low level or de-escalated through the intervention of bystanders. For instance, if arguments and shouting led to blows, members of the community would step in, even in cases in which the fights were between spouses or involved the poisoned arrows and spears used for hunting. Intervention could be verbal or physical. Verbal intervention included insulting or joking with antagonists to diffuse tension or to distract them, while physical intervention included blocking individuals from each other by stepping in between them or by holding the antagonists apart from each other. Physical separation of antagonists could occur voluntarily as well. These intervention techniques were practiced at all levels of social interaction; among bands, between peers, in married couples, and among children.

Gifts were often given to someone with whom the giver had had a quarrel. According to custom, the recipient had to accept the gift, helping to bring peace between antagonists. In situations of intense disagreement within the band or between spouses, long-term or permanent separation was not uncommon. Thus, gift giving and separation of antagonists were often successful methods of de-escalation.

Homicide and Infanticide Observers have noted that murder was not unheard of among the !Kung. For instance, anthropologist Richard Lee recorded twenty-two homicides among a population of 1,500 !Kung in the period 1920–1955. According to Lee in his 1984 *The Dobe !Kung*, homicide "ceased" between the mid-1950s and the mid-1970s; but homicide among the !Kung resumed in the mid-1970s as some !Kung were drawn into the war between the South African Defense Forces and the Namibian independence movement (p. 383). Moreover, it is known that infanticide was occasionally practiced among the !Kung. How are murder and infanticide accounted for among a "peaceful" people?

The !Kung explained infanticide in terms of birth spacing and mobility. Children were breast-fed up to the age of three or four because mother's milk, the only milk available to the traditional !Kung, was thought to ensure that children were strong enough to survive in the bush. !Kung mothers argued that birth spacing was essential to the health of their children; mothers could not adequately breast-feed two infants at the same time or both would be weak. There was no birth control available to traditional !Kung apart from postpartum abstinence, which was difficult to practice in a society that appeared to stress sexual activity. Moreover, small children and all possessions had to be carried by hand or on the backs of the !Kung people when they moved to find food. The group became less able to sustain themselves in the bush if they were immobilized by small children. Thus, in the context of birth spacing and the need to be mobile, the !Kung's own explanations of infanticide appear to be consistent with their gentle and nurturing child-rearing practices.

But how should the reports of homicide among the !Kung be understood? Observers of the !Kung have noted that most fights that led to wounding or death were spontaneous, escalating too rapidly for effective bystander intervention. The duration of the actual exchange of blows was usually under five minutes. Most fights that led to injury or death were caused by adultery. Nearly 50 percent of the deaths resulting from those fights were to innocent bystanders or peacemakers who intervened in the disputes. Richard Lee observed that four of the twenty-two homicides he documented were executions by the community of those who had killed others. Thus, !Kung homicides, nearly half of which appeared to be the unpremeditated deaths of bystanders or intervening peacemakers, may be understood as the failure of the conflict-resolution and de-escalation systems to be implemented quickly enough to halt the immediate anger of an individual from leading to deadly blows.

Summary The traditional !Kung of southern Africa developed an elaborate system of maintaining peace, resolving conflict, and de-escalation. The system relied on socialization, patterns of mutual obligation and norms of argumentation, and intervention to resolve disputes and halt violent conflict. The system appeared to work well, although the existence of homicide proves that violence was not entirely eliminated.

RESTRAINING WAR BETWEEN GROUPS: THE IROQUOIS LEAGUE

The League of the Iroquois constituted a security regime in precolonial North America for over three centuries. There were wars between other native nations, and specialists of violence among the Iro-

quois League member nations, that is, males who served as warriors, but the league was a system that kept member nations from fighting each other. (After contact with European colonial powers the operations of the league greatly changed.) Each league-member nation sent representatives to a Great Council meeting that set policy for the league and functioned to renew their pledge not to fight each other.

The Iroquois League was a security regime, in the sense that scholar Robert Jervis describes, of principles, rules, and norms that permit nations to be more restrained in their behavior toward other groups in the belief that others will reciprocate. Jervis describes four conditions for the formation of a security regime. First, the actors must want to establish the regime. Second, the actors must believe that others share the (high) value that they place on security. Third, a regime cannot form when one or more actors believes that security is best achieved by expansion. Fourth, the individual pursuit of security and the waging of war must be understood as costly.

The League of the Iroquois met all of the criteria for a security regime. The history of the formation of the league as told in Iroquois tradition demonstrates that the beliefs about the undesirability of conflict and war between regime members were present. The traditional accounts state that warfare between the five nations was frequent and costly before the league was established in around 1450.

The history of the functioning of the league demonstrates that it worked to maintain the peace between the five, and later six, nations for more than three hundred years, even while under the pressures of Dutch, British, French, and early United States colonial expansion, which included bribes, threats, and warfare. Although individual Iroquois League members occasionally disagreed with one another, at times setting policies toward outside groups that were the direct opposite of each other's, their security regime held. Even when they agreed to dissolve the league because of differences over who to support in the American Revolution, they parted company without resorting to war with one another.

Background Prior to contact with European settlers, the Iroquois League was a group of five Native American nations based in what is now upstate New York. The original five nations of the league (also known as the Iroquois Confederacy), Mohawk, Oneida, Onondaga, Cayuga, and Seneca, were ranged in the above order from east to west. The Tuscarora Nation, fleeing colonial expansion in the Carolinas, joined the league in the early eighteenth century.

There is evidence that these nations were living in that region as early as A.D. 800 or 1000. Although estimates of the number of people in the league vary widely, there were perhaps seventy-five thousand total in the original five nations before substantial contact was made with Europeans. The member nations were autonomous within the league. In addition to having different but related languages, they had certain unique social practices.

The Iroquois nations were agriculturally based societies: their most important crop was maize, although many other types of crops were produced. The people lived in villages with members of their extended families in buildings known as longhouses, near large fields of produce. Villages consisted of several hundred people, and towns appear to have been quite large, consisting of perhaps 150 longhouses surrounded by a palisade. In each nation there were two groups of several distinct clans (a moiety) with rules about intermarriage between these groups of clans.

Social and Political Relations   The five nations were matrilineal, and this matrilineal extended-family system was the basis of Iroquois political order. Women were heads of households, the keepers/owners of the land, and the designators of political leaders. Women and men appear to have had nearly equal political power although their roles were different. Women were charged with nominating sachems, the male spokespersons who represented the village within the nation and also within the league. The sachems were located in specific maternal households. The elder woman of the lineage led the meeting that nominated or recalled a sachem. Elected spokespersons could obtain their position by heredity or merit and those appointed on the basis of merit could also serve in the Great Council of the league. Sachems were prohibited from assuming military leadership roles; separate military chiefs achieved their status by merit. Military chiefs were prohibited from serving in the Great Council.

As with political organization, labor was divided along gender lines. Men were charged with diplomacy, hunting, and leading warfare, and women with making political appointments, farming, caring

for children, and running the household. It was also not unusual for women to take part in warfare, although it appears that all military chiefs were male.

The Iroquois were relentlessly democratic. Early observers were impressed with the fact that slavery was nonexistent among them and indeed, no one could compel another to do anything except by persuasion. In villages (and among nations in the league council) decision making was consensual. If a family member had a matter to take up with the village or nation, or even the Great Council of the league, that person would first bring up the matter within his or her family. The issue would then be taken up with the clan, next with the four related clans, then the nation, and then it would be discussed in the Great Council. However, once the league came to a decision, that decision went back through the chain for approval by each nation. Action could only then be taken if a consensus was reached by all concerned.

To simplify the organization of political decision making, the political organization of each nation consisted of roughly five clusters: fireside (immediate nuclear family); matriarchal household; tribe/clan (with more than one clan residing in each village); village; and nation. It is important to stress that the political organization was not hierarchical in a European sense. Iroquois decision making could be considered as a series of concentric circles, with the number of persons involved increasing as a proposal moved from fireside to nation.

The Iroquois did not use writing as we know it, but prized public speaking and oral history. They used wampum beads (made from shells) arranged on strings or woven into belts as an aid to memory during meetings or as a way to send messages to other groups. Wampum was a way of keeping the oral tradition faithful; it was also used as a symbol of formal statements and negotiation and also as a mnemonic device by which the agreements were remembered. Wampum beads, as well as songs made to memorialize an event, were important as records of formal statements, and wampum was the official record of agreements concluded between the league nations.

Origin of the League   It is difficult to determine and often disputed exactly how and when the League of the Iroquois was founded. Traditional accounts of the formation of the league trace its founding back to a period of intense warfare among the original five nations. The oral tradition recalls that Dekanawidah proposed the idea of a league to stop intertribal warfare and the formation of the league was negotiated by a Mohawk chief, Hiawatha, over several years. According to the tradition, the Seneca were the last of the original five nations to be convinced of the merits of a league and to decide to join. It also appears that other Iroquoian-speaking nations were asked to join the league upon its formation, notably the Cherokee, Erie, and Delaware, but they declined.

The League of the Iroquois was probably formed before the five original nations came into contact with European explorers and settlers. Indeed, the league may have been a reconfiguration of an older, less formal confederation that was not working to keep the peace among the five nations, rather than an entirely new political organization. In any case, it appears likely that the negotiations for the formation of the league were probably concluded around 1450, about eighty-five years before the Mohawks met the French explorer Jacques Cartier on the Saint Lawrence River.

The Great Law The constitution of the league was codified in the Great Law of Peace (or the Great Binding Law), which outlined the organization, membership, and procedures of the league. The philosophical orientation of the Great Law was framed in terms of general peace, where the image is of nations sitting together under a tree of peace, having cast their weapons into a pit. The Great Law was, according to Iroquois oral tradition, narrated by Dekanawidah, memorized and told over the generations; it was not translated and written down until the late nineteenth and early twentieth centuries.

In terms of the relationships between members of the league, the Great Law clearly states that the five nations were to remain autonomous. Moreover, the rights of each nation, that is, their cultural as well as political autonomy, were not changed by their membership in the league. But although the nations were formally equal and autonomous, the Great Law outlined different roles for each. For instance, the Onondaga were designated the keepers of the fire (meeting place) and the wampum-bead records of the league. The Mohawk and the Seneca were known as the older brothers, while the Cayuga and the Oneida were younger brothers. There was a ritual protocol assigning different roles to the league members for decision making. Each

"brotherhood" talked separately about an issue and came to consensus before consulting the other members. The decisions of the Great Council were then to be confirmed by going back to the people of each nation, even in times of great threat.

In terms of relationships between league and nonleague nations, the Great Law provided that all were welcome under the metaphorical tree of peace if they were willing to abide by the laws of the league. The Great Law also provided that a proposition to establish the Great Peace between the league and outsiders would be made in councils between the Iroquois and the outsider nation. The nation should be persuaded by reason, and the request to join should be made several times if the nation did not immediately agree to join the league.

When the league decided to offer membership to an outsider nation and that nation declined, the Great Law provided that war should be waged. It is not clear from the Great Law or historical accounts under what circumstances the invitation to other states was made to join the league. Specifically, was an invitation made only if the outside nation had attacked an Iroquois league nation or was an invitation made to neighboring nations as part of a policy of expansion?

Whether a nation joined the league of its own free will or as the result of conquest, it was to be disarmed, but it could continue its own system of internal government. Once in the league the nation was required to halt all war against others and observe the provisions of the Great Law. Newly admitted nations were not to have a right to participate equally in the league councils. In addition, individuals were free to join and to leave the individual nations of the league. The Great Law also provided for expelling those nations that did not follow the law of the five nations.

Functioning of the League The league's Great Council met annually in the fall (or at other times when necessary) at Onondaga, where it discussed alliance formation and peacemaking, and made decisions on major wars. Each nation sent a number of sachems, or spokespersons, to the Great Council; a total of fifty sachems were present. Again, the sachems themselves were not allowed to take part in warfare as leaders; there were separate military chiefs for war.

In practice, the five nations, and later the Tuscarora, made decisions in the Great Council by consensus, although the council also functioned as an information and communication center as well as a decision-making body. In local matters of revenge warfare against nonleague tribes, the Great Council of the league would sometimes remain silent, and nations were allowed to make separate alliances with other nations. Other nations not formally in the league were consulted in accordance with their relationship with or status in the league. Formal allies were treated as equals in discussions, and attempts were made to persuade via league oratory. When allies were not persuaded, the five nations apparently assented to their right to hold a different position.

Precolonial Warfare   War as a result of boundary disputes appears to have been uncommon, although there is good evidence that the Iroquois and other groups did have clear notions of territory and sovereignty. The dominant type of warfare among precolonial Iroquois nations and other Native American nations was the blood feud. Blood feuds are ritualized and involve almost certain revenge for an attack where life is lost. The feuds were conducted by forest-raiding parties composed of male warriors. Rather than kill in revenge, the Iroquois often captured and repatriated individuals into their group, giving them full rights and privileges as members of the nation. While the ratio between those killed in raids versus those captured and repatriated into Iroquois life is not known, this institution was practiced on a large scale and many appear to have been repatriated rather than killed.

The myth/story of Dekanawidah and the founding of the league holds that warfare was widespread among the five nations before the league's formation. The existence of the league itself suggests that war between the five nations significantly declined or was entirely eliminated; thus, as a security regime, the league appears to have worked.

The next question involves the pattern of warfare between league and nonleague nations before European contact. It appears that the five nations did not use the league as a war-making alliance but that the council of the league would urge restraint, and then pursue noninterference while an individual member nation of the league went to war.

The league was not simply an alliance directed toward external threats; its history shows that the Iroquois made alliances for specific threats at specific times and dropped or renewed those alliances when necessary. So, although the league was not an alliance specifically formed and functioning to

make war against league neighbors, peace between members may have allowed individual member nations to wage war against others with the knowledge that at least one of its immediate borders was secure.

Iroquois War After Contact with Europeans
The pattern and scale of Iroquois war and diplomatic activity appears to have changed dramatically soon after the first Europeans began to settle in the Northeast and trade with the Iroquois and other nations. Whereas precolonial Iroquois warfare primarily consisted of blood feuds, several new motives for war were introduced. With European settlement of the Northeast, the Iroquois began to fight for access to trade goods, to retain their influence in the region among other native groups and between themselves and the Europeans, and to protect their land from encroachment by the settlers and traders.

In addition, twice during the eighteenth century (in 1721 and in the early 1760s), the league proposed that all native nations combine to rid North America of the European colonists who were seizing their territory at alarming rates. Obviously, neither effort was successful: in the first attempt, the league was unable to convince other native nations to join the fight and their effort was abandoned; in the second case, after some short-term military successes against the English, the Iroquois were defeated.

The Iroquois League also used diplomacy to secure those same ends. Numerous agreements and alliances, part of what was known as the Covenant Chain, were made between the league and colonial powers. The Covenant Chain extended to alliances between the league and other Native American nations and confederacies. Moreover, apart from league treaties, the five and, later, six Iroquois nations made separate treaties with other Native American nations and the Europeans.

The league survived until the late eighteenth century, when it dissolved due to a disagreement between member nations over whom to support in the American Revolution. Both the English and colonial rebels requested Iroquois support. Upon the league's dissolution, wampum was divided between the two sides, and the Iroquois supported the colonial rebels and the English, respectively. Some decades after the revolution, the young United States pushed many Iroquois onto reservations in New York, Wisconsin, Oklahoma, and Canada. Later the league was reconstituted on the reservations as a form of intertribal government.

Summary The League of the Iroquois is an example of a security regime functioning to decrease conflict among several Native American nations in precolonial North America. Social relations within the league were egalitarian and noncoercive. Relations between the member nations of the league were similarly based on consensus, although league member nations were not of equal strength.

That the League of the Iroquois was also at times an offensive alliance and increasingly a defensive alliance after contact with Europeans does not reduce the league's importance as a regime to decrease conflict. If accounts of the formation and functioning of the League of the Iroquois are accurate, the league functioned to restrain violence among the Iroquois nations for more than three hundred years.

BIBLIOGRAPHY

Several overviews provide useful orientations to the subjects of violence and methods of restraining violence in precolonial societies. For analysis of the patterns of conflict in precolonial societies and some of the partial sanctions against violence in war see MAURICE R. DAVIE, *The Evolution of War: A Study of Its Role in Early Societies* (New Haven, Conn., 1929); MARGARET MEAD, ed., *Cooperation and Competition Among Primitive Peoples* (New York and London, 1937); and QUINCY WRIGHT, *A Study of War,* 2d ed. (Chicago, 1965).

The view that precolonial societies were highly conflictual is disputed in PAUL BOHANNAN, ed., *Law and Warfare: Studies in the Anthropology of Conflict* (Garden City, N.Y., 1967); RIANE EISLER, *The Chalice and the Blade: Our History, Our Future* (San Francisco, 1987); SUE MANSFIELD, *The Gestalts of War: An Inquiry into Its Origins and Meanings as a Social Institution* (New York, 1982); OFUR ZUR, "The Psychohistory of Warfare: The Co-Evolution of Culture, Psyche and Enemy," *Journal of Peace Research* 24 (June 1987): 125–134; ANDREW BARD SCHMOOKLER, *The Parable of the Tribes: The Problem of Power in Social Evolution* (Berkeley, Calif., 1984). On security regimes see ROBERT JERVIS, "Security Regimes," in STEPHEN D. KRASNER, ed., *International Regimes* (Ithaca, N.Y., 1983): 173–194.

Several important survey studies on restraining violence in precolonial societies are available. See ROBERT A. LEVINE, "Anthropology and the Study of Conflict," *Journal of Conflict Resolution* 5 (March 1961): 3–15; DAVID FABBRO, "Peaceful Societies: An Introduction," *Journal of Peace Research* 15 (1978): 67–83; and MARC HOWARD ROSS, "Internal and External Conflict and Violence, Cross-Cultural Evidence and a New Analysis," *Journal of Conflict Resolution* 29 (December 1985): 547–579.

Studies of Specific Groups and Cultures
See ASHLEY MONTAGU, ed., *Learning Non-Aggression: The Experience of Non-Literate Societies* (New York, 1978) for articles about the child-rearing practices of the New Guinea Fore, the !Kung, the Inuit, the Semai, Australian Aborigines, the Mbuti, and native Tahitians. On the Semai, see ROBERT K. DENTAN, *The Semai: A Nonviolent People of Malaya* (New York, 1984). On the Mbuti, see COLIN M. TURNBULL, *The Forest People: A Study of the Pygmies of the Congo* (New York, 1962).

Readers interested in more detailed discussions of the traditional !Kung will find several anthropological accounts useful. RICHARD BORSHAY LEE, *The !Kung San: Men, Women, and Work in a Foraging Society* (Cambridge and New York, 1979); RICHARD BURSHAY LEE, *The Dobe !Kung* (New York, 1984); LORNA MARSHALL, *The !Kung of Nyae Nyae* (Cambridge, Mass., 1976); and MARJORIE SHOSTAK, *Nisa, The Life and Words of a !Kung Woman* (Cambridge, Mass., 1981). An important and controversial revisionist work on the San people of the Kalihari is EDWIN N. WILMSEN, *Land Filled with Flies: A Political Economy of the Kalihari* (Chicago, 1989).

On the Iroquois, several classics provide good introductions. See CADWALLADER COLDEN, *The History of the Five Indian Nations of Canada, which are Dependent on the Province of New York, and are a Barrier Between the English and the French in that Part of the World,* 2 vols. (New York, 1747/1904); LEWIS H. MORGAN, *League of the Ho-De'-No-Sau-Nee, or Iroquois,* 2 vols. (Rochester and New York, 1851/1901); ELY PARKER, *The Constitution of the Five Nations, or the Iroquois Book of the Great Law* (Syracuse, N.Y., 1916), reprinted in ARTHUR CASWELL PARKER, *Parker on the Iroquois,* edited by William N. Fenton (Syracuse, N.Y., 1968); and GEORGE T. HUNT, *The Wars of the Iroquois: A Study in Intertribal Trade Relations* (Madison, Wis., 1940). Good later treatments include GEORGE S. SNYDERMAN, *Be-*

hind the Tree of Peace: A Sociological Analysis of Iroquois Warfare (New York, 1948/1978); ANTHONY F. C. WALLACE, The Death and Rebirth of the Seneca (New York, 1970); FRANCIS JENNINGS, The Ambiguous Iroquois Empire: The Convenant Chain Confederation of Indian Tribes with English Colonies from Its Beginnings to the Lancaster Treaty of 1744 (New York, 1984); FRANCIS JENNINGS, WILLIAM N. FENTON, and MARY A. DRUKE, eds., The History and Culture of Iroquois Diplomacy: An Interdisciplinary Guide to the Treaties of the Six Nations and Their League (Syracuse, N.Y., 1985); and ELISABETH TOOKER, "The League of the Iroquois: Its History, Politics, and Ritual," in BRUCE G. TRIGGER ed., Northeast, vol. 15 of Handbook of North American Indians (Washington, D.C., 1978–): 418–441.

Arms Control in Antiquity

○

STANLEY M. BURSTEIN

See also Medieval Arms Control Movements and the Western Quest for Peace *and* Restraining Violence in Early Societies. *Most of the treaties discussed in this essay are excerpted in Volume III.*

In 230 B.C. a Roman embassy complained to Queen Teuta, ruler of the Illyrians in what is roughly present-day Yugoslavia, of piratical raids on Italian merchantmen conducted by her subjects in the Adriatic. The queen replied that she could not interfere with the reprisal rights of the Illyrians. Ultimately, of course, Rome solved the problem militarily in the First Illyrian War (229 B.C.). The episode is of minor consequence, but instructive because it highlights an important fact. Anthropologists have documented numerous examples of devices employed by "primitive" peoples to limit the magnitude of violence in war; to the extent that only states can enter into mutually binding agreements, however, these devices were largely unsuccessful. For this reason, the history of formal arms control begins with the appearance of the first state-level societies, during the fourth millennium B.C. in southern Mesopotamia and Egypt.

The literature of ancient civilization is replete with eulogies of the blessings of peace, of the benefits of "beating swords into ploughshares," and of the agony of war, in which the normal moral order is inverted and fathers bury sons. Despite the ubiquity of these themes, however, nothing like a modern peace movement developed in the ancient world. All ancient states operated on the principle independently enunciated in the fourth century B.C. by the Greek philosopher Plato and the Indian political theorist Kauṭilya, namely that war, hot or cold, is the natural state of relations between states. Not surprisingly, therefore, the sole example of a general peace conference in antiquity, a session held in 546 B.C. by the states of north China, achieved little more than a temporary pause in the almost chronic state of war that characterized the history of pre-Han China. Similarly, literary protests against war, such as Aristophanes' comedy *Lysistrata* in 411 B.C., or the works of the Roman elegiac poets in the 20s B.C., were cries of despair during unusually brutal conflicts, or expressions of relief at their end, not statements of principled pacifism; and they were quickly forgotten when hostilities subsided. If war was the norm in antiquity, a rich variety of devices to resolve conflicts diplomatically and to restrain violence during war nevertheless did evolve.

THE ANCIENT NEAR EAST

The uncovering of the history of the Ancient Near East is one of the great triumphs of modern historical scholarship, albeit a grim one. From the emergence of the first Sumerian states in southern Mesopotamia in the fourth millennium B.C. to the destruction of the Persian Empire, the last of the great imperial powers of the Ancient Near East, by the forces of Alexander the Great in the 330s B.C., war was one of the enduring facts of Ancient Near Eastern history. The persistence of war was accompanied by major increases in the scale and sophistication of war-making potentials of states in the region, beginning with the appearance of well-organized armored infantry and chariot forces in the third millennium B.C. and ending with specialized cavalry and engineering units in the first millennium B.C. Almost simultaneous with the appearance of organized warfare came efforts to limit the incidence and severity of hostilities.

551

Although our sources do not provide a continuous history of arms control in the Ancient Near East, the general picture is clear. Efforts to reduce people's ability to wage war by imposing formal restraints on war-making capacity were minimal, the only known example being the ban on ironworking—which indirectly restricted the possession of iron weapons—imposed on the Israelites by the Philistines in the eleventh century B.C. The technical simplicity of Ancient Near Eastern weaponry, primarily cutting and concussion weapons, and the general availability of the metallurgical technology and resources required to produce it, made it unlikely that such a ban could be effective for long. Absent also from the sources available to us is evidence of efforts to limit the use of particular types of weapons or to establish a set of rules governing behavior in war that went beyond such generally accepted customs as ransoming prisoners of war and sparing surrendering cities the rigors of a sack. On the contrary, the belief shared by peoples of the Ancient Near East throughout antiquity, that military defeat reflected condemnation by the gods, legitimized infliction of the most extreme violence not only on one's military opponents but on their entire populations. Not surprisingly, therefore, the main focus of Ancient Near Eastern diplomacy was not arms control, but conflict avoidance or resolution. Both diplomatic and religious means were employed to achieve these goals.

Ancient Near Eastern diplomats developed a variety of instruments, including conflict avoidance, to deal with the various problems of interstate relations. Unfortunately, only a single example survives today, the peace and nonaggression treaty concluded ca. 1280 B.C. between the Egyptian king Ramesses II and the Hittite ruler Hattusilis III following the inconclusive battle of Qadesh. Since both the Egyptian and Hittite copies of the treaty are extant, scholars have been able to completely reconstruct its terms. The treaty begins with an historical introduction outlining the background of the treaty and clearly indicating its purpose, namely, to "not permit hostility to occur between them forever" (Pritchard, pp. 199–203). Detailed clauses follow, defining the terms of the peace and the obligations undertaken by each of the parties. These clauses include pledges of mutual nonaggression and defense against attack by third parties; rules for the repatriation of exiles by Egypt to the Hittites and vice versa; promises that returning refugees will suffer no reprisals; invocations to the gods of both countries to be witnesses and guarantors of the treaty; and finally, formal descriptions of the treaty documents and their seals. Weaknesses in this document are readily apparent, most notably the lack of a clear demarcation of the boundary of the Egyptian and Hittite spheres of influence in Syria and the lack of effective sanctions should its terms be violated. The clarity and economy with which its goals and terms are set out, however, and the fact that the peace established by it between Egypt and the Hittites lasted for almost a century, until the destruction of the Hittite empire ca. 1200 B.C., make it an eloquent witness to the sophistication of Ancient Near Eastern diplomacy in the second millennium B.C.

Divine sanction was not only invoked to guarantee peace treaties; divine aid was also sought in the hope of resolving disputes before they led to full-scale hostilities. Divine conflict resolution is attested to as early as the twenty-fifth century B.C., when the Sumerian cities of Lagash and Umma in southern Mesopotamia referred a boundary dispute, the most common pretext for war in Sumer, to the oracle of the storm god Enlil—the chief god of the Sumerian pantheon at the holy city of Nippur. Enlil's decision and its implementation are recorded in a cuneiform inscription that must count as the earliest record of a formal arbitration between states: "Enlil, by his authoritative command, demarcated the boundary between Ningirsu and Shara. Mesalim, king of Kish, at the command of Ishtaran, measured it off and erected a monument there" (as quoted in Jerrold S. Cooper, *Reconstructing History from Ancient Inscriptions: The Lagash-Umma Border Conflict*, p. 48). Although the document leaves unspecified the manner of consulting the oracle, the arbitration procedure itself is clear. After the god's decision had been rendered, a neutral third party, Mesalim, the king of Kish and titular overlord of all Sumer, was commissioned to implement the oracle's decision by formally marking out the disputed boundary and publicizing it on an inscribed monument. Unfortunately, the result was less satisfactory than the procedure itself, since the lack of effective sanctions to enforce Enlil's decision encouraged the losing city, Umma, to disregard it and to force its own views on Lagash under cover of a new oracular decision obtained from a different deity.

Alternatively, if hostilities could not be avoided, the extent of their violence could be minimized through the device of a "battle of champions," in which the gods' decision would favor the survivor or victor, and the subsequent demoralization and rout of the army of the defeated champion or team of champions. The best known instance of a battle of champions, of course, is the biblical story of David and Goliath; but the discovery of a Hittite example, and references to actual instances of such combats or treaty provisions for such combats in Greece as late as the fifth century B.C. and in early Rome suggests that the device may have been more widely employed by the peoples of the Mediterranean and the Ancient Near East than was previously believed. The range of devices employed by the civilizations of the Ancient Near East to avoid or limit war is clearly impressive, but so is the apparent rarity of their use. As the steady increase in the volume of sources for the history of the Ancient Near East has not materially changed this situation, its explanation must lie not in the deficiencies of the evidence but in the role of warfare in Ancient Near Eastern culture.

Implicit in the practice of arms control and its related activities is the acceptance of a multicentered political universe of independent states. Conflict avoidance or limitation devices such as arbitration or decision by battle of champions are attested precisely in periods when such multipolar political systems were dominant. That was the case in early third millennium B.C. Sumer and in late second and early first millennium B.C. western Asia. For much of the history of the Ancient Near East, however, the dominant political model was not that of the coexistence of a multiplicity of independent states but the so-called World Empire in which a particular ruler—claiming to act as the chosen representative of a particular deity—attempted to bring under his and his people's control as much of the civilized world as possible. Imperial expansion was the raison d'être of such states and needed no justification. Arms control devices would be resorted to, and then only grudgingly, when the spheres of two such empires intersected and neither could gain a decisive advantage.

This was the situation, for instance, in the case of the nonaggression treaty between Egypt and the Hittites. Not surprisingly, the device for limiting conflict employed by such states was not the rarely documented arbitration or nonaggression agreement, but the vassal treaty. It eliminated conflicts within the territory controlled by an imperial state and defined the relationship between it and its subject states through the unilateral imposition of restrictions on the latter's ability to employ military force or establish ties with other political entities. So the Persians demanded that their Greek subjects demolish part of their defensive walls, abjure war, and submit their disputes to the decision of the local governor (satrap) while providing military forces to the Persian king on demand. Thus, despite some apparently promising first steps, arms control never played a significant role in the history of the Ancient Near East. A similar pattern is evident in the better-documented history of arms control in ancient Greece and Rome.

ANCIENT GREECE

Greek-speaking peoples have inhabited the southern portion of the Balkan Peninsula since at least the first half of the second millennium B.C. Because our sources are limited, evidence relevant to the history of arms control becomes available only in the second quarter of the first millennium B.C., but it then increases in volume, variety, and clarity for the rest of antiquity. Equally clear is the picture that emerges from the sources. Until the Roman conquest of Greece in the second century B.C. permanently ended Greek independence, war is the central fact of Greek history. Greek literature begins with a celebration of war, Homer's *Iliad,* and war is the great theme of Greek historiography. So accepted was the normalcy of war that Greek thinkers felt no need to seriously examine the causes of war and Greek diplomacy lacked even the concept of peace before the fourth century B.C. What historians call peace treaties were in actuality armistices that specified the length of time before hostilities could resume. Not without reason was Greece rated as one of the most warlike cultures in history in Quincy Wright's famous general study of war as a historical phenomenon, *A Study of War* (Chicago, Ill., 1942). Paradoxically, however, a large part of the reason for the prevalence of war in Greek history was the Greeks' success for much of their history in containing and limiting the extent and scale of the violence of war. As a result, warfare posed no threat to the survival and growth of Greek society despite its frequent occurrence.

As was true of the Ancient Near East, agreements to ban or limit the use of particular classes of weapons contributed little to this outcome. One such accord is known, a treaty dating to the late eighth or early seventh century B.C. banning the use of missile weapons, presumably slings and bows and arrows, on the Greek island of Euboea. The existence of this treaty has been doubted, but on insufficient grounds. Like the ban on crossbows in late Medieval Europe and that on firearms in early modern Japan, the probable goal of the treaty was to protect the social order by insulating the aristocracy from the threat posed by the emergence of specialized lower class military forces armed with effective weaponry. Greece, however, was not an isolated and homogeneous society like Japan in which such a ban could be enforced, and so the treaty failed and was remembered only as a quaint example of archaic military ideals. Hardly more effective was the condemnation of the use of poisoned weapons suggested by a passage of the *Odyssey* (1: 260–263) in which Odysseus is refused arrow poison because of fear of the gods, since fourth century B.C. military theorists were still discussing the relative merits of various venomous serpents as sources of poison. In the final analysis, the limits on the extent and violence of Greek warfare were not legal, but structural.

Like early Sumer, the key to the paradox is the multipolar nature of the classical Greek political system, which was composed of a multitude of independent and often mutually hostile ministates called poleis. Over a thousand of these, by some counts, were scattered throughout the southern Balkan Peninsula and the coasts of the Mediterranean and Black Sea. Despite the frequency of war between poleis, and the ferocity permitted by the rules of Greek warfare—which allowed the general massacre of the men and the sale of the women and children of a captured city—the grounds for war were few, and the goals of combat were limited. Overwhelmingly, Greek wars prior to the mid-fifth century B.C. were retaliatory in character, originating in claims of the unjust occupation of disputed territory or damage inflicted on the property or citizens of one state by those of another. Greek legend spoke of the destruction of poleis and examples of such catastrophes, the ultimate horror in Greek thought, can be cited from historical times. Still, the Greek view of war assumed the illegitimacy of such total war, a fact well illustrated by the oath taken by the twelve members of the Delphic Amphictyony that they would not destroy any member city nor shut off its water supply either in war or peace. Such was the ideal, but it was an ideal supported by the rules of Greek diplomacy and the practice of Greek warfare.

Classical Greek warfare consisted of set battles between citizen militias equipped as heavy armored infantry, or hoplites. The horror of such conflicts should not be underestimated, but more relevant to the theme of this essay are the limitations of this type of warfare. Lacking effective cavalry, field artillery, and the capacity to conduct either extended campaigns at a distance from home base or to capture fortified centers, the Greeks did not normally pursue the modern military goal of victory through the total destruction of the enemy. Combined with the retaliatory character of Greek justifications for war, these constraints gave Greek battles much of the character of ritualized duels.

Indeed, wars occasionally were settled by duels of champions, as was done in the case of a seventh century B.C. dispute between Argos and Sparta in which each side fielded a team of three hundred selected warriors. Failing such a solution—and such duels of champions are not attested after the end of the seventh century B.C.—a war normally began with an invasion of an enemy's territory intended to threaten an enemy's crops and rural property, and was decided by a single battle on a piece of level ground not far from the city. The encounter itself was brief, with victory decided by the flight of the defeated army from the battlefield and its request for a truce to collect its dead and wounded and withdraw. The victor publicly commemorated his victory by setting up a trophy on the site of the battle. Victor Hanson, in *The Western Way of War,* has well characterized Greek warfare as a system in which disputes over agricultural land were settled by "struggles between small landholders who by mutual consent sought to limit warfare (and hence killing) to a single, brief, nightmarish occasion." Horrible though any particular battle might be, the endemic state of low-level conflict encouraged by this kind of warfare posed no threat to the survival of the Greek polis system, especially since the systemic restraints on its destructiveness were reinforced by the rules of Greek diplomacy.

The basic principle of Greek diplomacy was that only a direct assault by the citizens of one city on the citizens or property of another counted as a *casus belli.* Aid of any sort rendered to either side by third parties did not ipso facto involve them in the conflict, which remained confined to the original combatants. At the same time, the quasi-judicial character of Greek warfare as being essentially a device for deciding territorial disputes between states or inflicting reprisals for alleged felonies against a state's citizens or their property facilitated the development of diplomatic devices for avoiding war by limiting the occasions that might lead to disputes or by providing for their peaceful resolution.

The principal mechanisms for conflict avoidance available to the Greek cities were *asyleia,* the practice by which a state protected the citizens of another state from assault by its own citizens by a grant of immunity from reprisal in satisfaction of personal grievances; and *proxenia,* the designation of a citizen of one city as representative of the interests of another. The practice of designating major temples and festival sites as asylums, safe havens from reprisals, and proclaiming sacred truces at the time of major festivals, such as the Olympic and other Panhellenic games, served the same purpose on an international scale since it ensured that conflicts remained local by preventing them from spreading to uninvolved cities through accidental assaults on their citizens passing through the territories of the combatants on their way to the festival or during their stay at a sanctuary or festival site.

As in early Sumer, the main device employed by the Greeks for the peaceful resolution of potential conflicts was arbitration. Unlike the Sumerian system, however, Greek arbitration was essentially a secular process in which the contesting states submitted their dispute to a mutually acceptable third party. This might be either another state or a ruler, as when the case of the mid–seventh century B.C. dispute between Athens and Mytilene over the possession of the northwest Anatolian port of Sigeum was settled in Athens' favor by the tyrant of Corinth. Little is known concerning the procedures involved in such arbitrations, although the sources suggest that the disputants had wide latitude regarding the nature of the evidence they could submit in support of their case. Nor, in the absence of effective enforcement mechanisms, were adverse decisions invariably accepted. A good example is the case of the dispute between Athens and Megara over the island of Salamis. It was ultimately settled militarily after Megara rejected a Spartan arbitration decision favoring Athens on the grounds that the Athenians had falsified the historical evidence by interpolating a line supposedly supporting their case into the text of the *Iliad!* Despite its limitations, however, the principle that states should attempt to resolve their disputes through arbitration was generally accepted and employed—one study records sixty-one examples of interstate arbitration prior to the beginning of the reign of Alexander the Great in 336

B.C. Arbitration provisions were a normal feature of Greek treaties, and offers to arbitrate disputes were standard ploys in Greek diplomacy, the refusal of which was considered to undermine the moral legitimacy of one's cause.

Should efforts to avert the outbreak of war fail, however, then Greek diplomacy also possessed effective devices for limiting the actual cost of war by providing for the ransom of prisoners, sometimes even specifying in advance by mutual agreement the scale of ransom charges for prisoners of war and for the negotiation of multi-year armistices that would allow the defeated city to rebuild its resources in relative security. Greek diplomacy, however, was successful because its principles were ideally suited to a fragmented political world with limited military potential, and this pre-condition changed radically in the fifth century B.C.

The disunity of early Greece was replaced by an imperfect but nevertheless real political integration of the Aegean Greek world as a result of the emergence, after the Greek victory over Persia in 480/79 B.C., of two great power blocs, the Athenian empire and its rival, the Peloponnesian League. At the same time, the adoption of the trireme, which required crews of two hundred men, as the standard Greek warship increased both the economic and human costs of naval warfare to the point that the loss of a single warship could threaten the very survival of a small polis. The results were similar to those resulting from the increasingly high cost of weaponry in the twentieth century. Consequently, the number of states capable of undertaking independent military action dropped dramatically. And so also did the number of major wars, only two occurring between 479 and 400 B.C., namely, the so-called First Peloponnesian War that lasted from ca. 457 to 445 B.C. and the Peloponnesian War fought between 431 and 404 B.C. Unfortunately, the reduction in the number of wars was matched by a significant increase in their violence and destructiveness—as was noted by the historian Thucydides, who observed in his great *History of the Peloponnesian War* (1.23) that that war "not only lasted for a long time, but throughout its course brought with it unprecedented suffering for Hellas."

New arms control devices also appeared in the fifth century B.C.—devices that were both unilateral and bilateral. The former are always attractive to imperial powers. So the Athenians sought to curb the ability of the member states of the Athenian empire to conduct independent military action by compelling rebellious allies to demobilize their fleets and dismantle their defensive walls. The relatively tightly integrated structure of the Athenian empire facilitated the imposition of such measures, but their use was not limited to Athens as is illustrated by the terms imposed on Athens by Sparta at the end of the Peloponnesian War in 404 B.C.: destruction of Athens' long walls and those of her port, Piraeus, the surrender of all but twelve of her warships, and the obligation to follow Sparta's lead in foreign affairs.

There were also efforts to eliminate the pretexts for war by requiring disputes between allies to be submitted to arbitration, with the decisions to be enforced by Athens, as was done in the case of a dispute between the cities of Samos and Miletus in 440/39 B.C. The principal bilateral device employed in the fifth century B.C. was the multi-year truce. Examples are the Peace of Callias, concluded between Athens and Persia in the 460s B.C., the Thirty Years Peace of 446/45 B.C. that ended the First Peloponnesian War, and the Peace of Nicias of 421 B.C. that concluded the first phase of the Peloponnesian War proper. Their specific terms varied, but common to all these diplomatic instruments was the attempt to avert conflict by defining both the spheres of influence of each imperial state and what would constitute an infraction of those spheres of influence. So the Peace of Callias provided for demilitarized buffer zones into which neither Athens nor Persia could send military forces and apparently also pledges of nonintervention in the internal relations of either empire. The terms of the Thirty Years Peace and Peace of Nicias included recognition of the hegemony of Athens and Sparta over the member states of each other's alliance, mutual pledges of nonaggression, requirements for the submission of disputes between them to arbitration, and guarantees of the rights of autonomy and neutrality for nonaligned states.

Clearly, it would be incorrect to say that Greek diplomacy failed to cope with the new diplomatic conditions of the fifth century B.C. As already mentioned, these measures did succeed in dramatically reducing the number of major wars that were actually fought. Unfortunately, they did not also contain the violence of wars between imperial blocs within bearable limits as was proved by the Peloponnesian War and the series of debilitating wars between rival contenders for the position of successor to Athens as hegemon of Greece that mark Greek history until the Macedonian conquest of Greece in 338 B.C. effectively ended Greek independence for the rest of antiquity.

This failure of Greek diplomacy to arrest the escalation of the destructiveness of war in the fifth century B.C. resulted in the only significant attempt to limit its incidence in Greek history, the Common Peace movement of the fourth century B.C. In the face of the chronic political and social instability created by endemic warfare in the fourth century, Greek thinkers attempted to redefine the place of war in Greek life. To be sure, the extent of this redefinition was limited. In particular, the legitimacy of war itself was not challenged but the extent of that legitimacy was scaled back so that only war against barbarians was henceforth to be considered just and, perhaps, even desirable as a safety valve for the release of tensions within Greece itself. So the orator Isocrates repeatedly urged that the Greeks redirect their military activities toward the conquest of some portion of the Persian empire that could provide homes for economically deprived and politically embittered elements within Greek cities. Thinkers such as Isocrates considered war between Greeks, however, civil war and, as such, inherently unjust and to be avoided if at all possible. The parallel with the Medieval Crusade movement, which also originated as a device to reduce conflict within Europe by redirecting military activity toward the Muslim world in the name of liberating the holy land, is striking. It is ironic, therefore, in view of the xenophobic character of these ideas that the first attempt to establish the sort of general peace in Greece desired by Isocrates and similarly minded reformers was the "King's Peace." It was so named from the fact that it was imposed on the Greeks by their arch enemy, the King of Persia, in 387/86 B.C. for the purpose of bringing to end a war between Sparta and a coalition of her enemies led by Athens that had lasted for almost a decade. The terms of the King's Peace as stated by the first-century B.C. historian Diodorus were simple: "the Greek cities in Asia were made subject to the King, but all other Greek cities were autonomous; he [the king] would act through those who accepted the terms to attack those who rejected the treaty" (Diodorus, *Library of History* 14.110.3).

Not surprisingly, Greeks bitterly resented the fact that the peace resulted from the Great King's initiative and, even more important, that acceptance of its terms implied recognition of his claim to rule the Greeks of Asia and his right to enforce the peace. Nevertheless, the principle of explicit recognition of the autonomy, that is, the freedom, of all Greek cities first clearly enunciated in the King's Peace became the lynch pin of fourth century B.C. Greek diplomacy, reappearing in a series of important treaties including the foundation documents of both the Second Athenian League in 374 B.C., which marked the reappearance of Athens as a major Greek power, and the League of Corinth, which was organized by King Philip II of Macedon in 338 B.C. to give institutional form to his conquest of Greece two years earlier. The League of Corinth was the most elaborate of the fourth century Common Peaces. Included in its constitution were clauses guaranteeing the independence of all Greek states sharing the peace, pledges of mutual nonaggression, collective security guarantees for any city menaced by attack or internal subversion, and authorization for the general council of the league to arbitrate disputes between members. With its detailed provisions for conflict avoidance and resolution, the League of Corinth clearly illustrated both the strengths and weaknesses of Common Peace diplomacy. On the one hand, its terms clearly reflected the ideals of civic autonomy and security for all Greek cities proclaimed by fourth century intellectuals and seemingly provided guarantees for securing them. On the other hand, like its predecessors, the primary purpose of the League of Corinth was not to bring peace to Greece but to advance the goals of its organizer, King Philip II of Macedon, who used his position as chief executive of the league to enforce his authority in Greece and to mobilize the resources of Greece for a "just" war, that is, a war against a non-Greek power, namely, Persia. As the reign of Philip's son Alexander the Great (336–323 B.C.) was to demonstrate, however, that war would render meaningless the ideal of general peace among Greeks that the League was supposed to foster, leaving only the slogan of Greek freedom to be exploited by the Macedonian and Roman conquerors of Greece in their attempts to establish their hegemony over the states of the Aegean basin.

The Greeks developed no further arms control devices after the Common Peace. War remained a central fact of the history of the Greeks until the Romans stripped from them in 146 B.C. the last vestiges of independence and with it the ability itself to wage war. Nevertheless, judged by the pragmatic standard of whether or not the incidence and destructiveness of war was reduced, the Greek achievement in arms control was considerable. Liv-

ing in a multipolar political universe in which the juxtaposition of numerous ministates gave rise to numerous disputes that could lead to war, the Greeks developed and used a wide variety of diplomatic instruments and procedures to avert war or moderate its effects that included truces, asylum rights, interstate arbitration, the establishment of demilitarized zones, and the Common Peace treaty. Equally important, they employed these devices with considerable success. Thus, while the number of wars known to have occurred in Greek history is high, most, thanks to the isolating tendencies of Greek diplomacy, were of brief duration with their effects confined to the parties directly involved in them and, hence, posed no danger to the Greek political system as a whole. Also, and perhaps still more significant, is the fact illustrated by the well over 100 known examples of interstate arbitration of disputes between the seventh and first centuries B.C.—and more examples are continually discovered—namely, that the prevention of war by the use of quasi-judicial devices was a recognized and widely employed feature of Greek diplomacy.

ROME

At first glance, Roman history suggests that, contrary to the experience of Greece, arms control played a small role in the history of the ancient Romans. This impression is not wholly unjustified. Roman history can be divided roughly into three periods: (1) the monarchy, extending from the legendary founding of the city of Rome in 753 B.C. to the establishment of the Republic in 509 B.C.; (2) the Republic, which lasted from 509 B.C. to the reappearance of monarchic government as a result of the civil wars of the mid-first century B.C.; and (3) the Empire, the beginning of which is conventionally dated to the defeat of the forces of Mark Antony and Cleopatra VII of Egypt at the Battle of Actium by those of the later Emperor Augustus in 31 B.C. and the end of which is traditionally equated with the cessation of the line of emperors resident in Italy in A.D. 476. The dominant theme of this almost fifteen-hundred-year-long history is imperial expansion. From a small city-state in west central Italy with institutions not unlike those of a Greek polis, Rome expanded through almost constant warfare to become, by the mid-third century B.C., ruler of the Italian peninsula. A little over a century later it was in control of the Mediterranean basin, and finally by the early second century A.D. it ruled most of Western and Eastern Europe, North Africa, and the Near East, a territory almost as large as the continental United States.

Roman historians have often tried to explain the remarkable ascent of Rome, from an isolated city-state to ruler of the greatest empire in Western history, as unintentional, as the unanticipated result of a policy of preemptive defense followed by the Roman Senate. Supporters of this interpretation have relied on two main pieces of evidence: (1) the *fetial* ritual, a complex procedure that required that a declaration of war be preceded by a formal presentation of grievances to an enemy who was given the opportunity of avoiding war by granting satisfaction to Rome; and (2) the repeated statements by Roman authors of the late Republic who insisted that Rome only fought just wars and, writing under the influence of Stoicism, insisted that only defensive wars were just.

But recognition of the deliberately expansionist character of Roman policy has become increasingly common among Roman historians. The reasons behind this revision of scholarly opinion are threefold. First, the grievances presented in the fetial procedure took the form of a nonnegotiable ulti matum intended to satisfy the Roman religious requirement that an enemy in a just war be clearly seen to have refused an opportunity for peaceful settlement. Second, Rome was the sole arbiter of what constituted a threat requiring a "defensive" response; and, as Julius Caesar's *Commentaries on the Gallic Wars* clearly reveal, such responses were often based more on calculations of Roman interest and advantage than on the perception of a real danger to Rome or its allies.

Third and most important, imperialism was not only sanctioned, but strongly encouraged by the value system of the ruling Senatorial aristocracy—a value system that defined success for a man in terms of glory won in war and service to the state through the holding of political offices. Clear evidence of the pervasive impact of these on the conduct of Roman foreign policy is provided by the prayer offered by the chief priest of Rome for the expansion of the empire of the Roman people that traditionally began the Roman year. It was, therefore, entirely consistent with the most fundamental traditions of Rome that Roman intellectuals condemned as cowardly the policy of imperial restraint, praised by modern historians, that the emperor Augustus recommended to his successors at the end of his long reign in A.D. 14. Equally unsurprising is their applause for the brief resumption of an expansionist policy by the emperor Trajan in the early second century A.D., which they viewed as the return of glory despite the fact that the disastrous failure of that policy placed the very survival of the empire in danger.

Not surprisingly, the worldview of Roman statesmen did not include the concept of a multipolar political universe that underpinned arms control in early Sumer and Greece. The very different attitude of the men who formulated and carried out Roman diplomacy was well summed up in two famous passages of the late first century B.C. poet Virgil's *Aeneid,* in which Rome is promised by the gods "empire without limit," (1:278) and the poem's hero, Aeneas, the legendary Trojan founder of Rome, is told that Rome's purpose is to "spare the defeated and tame the arrogant in war." In accordance with such ideas, Roman wars were conducted with a ferocity unique in the ancient world. All too often Rome's enemies were offered the stark alternatives of unconditional surrender or total destruction. The cruel fate of the cities of Corinth and Carthage in 146 B.C. bore witness to the reality of the latter possibility. Many of Rome's contemporaries would have agreed with the cynical assessment of Roman imperialism placed in the mouth of a British chieftain by the early second century A.D. historian Tacitus (*Agricola* 30.6): "the Romans make a desert and call it peace."

Clearly, arms control as practiced by the Greeks could have no place in the Roman scheme of things. True, the Roman Senate might agree to arbitrate disputes between Greek states; that was a welcome confirmation of Rome's political preeminence. That the validity of Roman grievances might be judged and found wanting by a neutral third party was unthinkable, and Rome regularly refused to submit its claims to arbitration when offered the opportunity. More important, however, the basic goal of Roman arms control diplomacy was different from that of most of the other peoples already considered. However imperfect the result, the purpose of Greek and probably Sumerian arms control was conflict resolution, that is, the avoidance of war through peaceful resolution of the disputes that might lead to it. The purpose of Roman arms control was only secondarily the avoidance of war; its primary goal was the reduction of the ability of real or potential enemies to wage war against them. To that end Rome employed both unilateral and bilateral approaches to arms control.

The use of both approaches is attested from the beginning of Roman history. A good example of a bilateral diplomatic instrument is the treaty concluded in 508 B.C. with the powerful North African city of Carthage, which marked the beginning of the diplomatic history of the Roman Republic. Fortunately, a detailed summary of its provisions by the second century B.C. Greek historian of Roman imperialism, Polybius (3.22.4–13), makes clear that the purpose of the treaty was conflict avoidance through the delineation of the respective spheres of influence of the two cities. Included in its provisions were geographical limits on the movement of naval forces, precise identification of areas protected under the treaty, rules for the peaceful evacuation of military forces that inadvertently intruded into territory claimed by the other partner, and for the treatment of foreign merchants. Although two renewals of this treaty are attested as well as a similar treaty with the south Italian Greek city of Tarentum, such treaties were rare, since their explicit recognition of the independence of other states and limitations on the free exercise of Roman power conflicted with basic Roman values. Equally important, they were readily broken whenever the growth of Roman power made such action seem safe and possible advantage made it expedient as both Tarentum and Carthage learned to their cost in the third century B.C. More suited to the expansionist goals of Roman policy and, therefore, more widely employed during the Republican period was a unilaterally imposed arms control device the Romans called a *foedus inaequum,* an "unequal treaty."

The foedus inaequum was similar in its goals and character to ancient near eastern vassal treaties and like them, it was normally imposed on an enemy that had just suffered a decisive military defeat. In its simplest form the terms of a foedus inaequum left a defeated state autonomy in internal affairs while stripping from it the ability to conduct an independent foreign policy by forbidding it from concluding alliances with any state other than Rome and requiring it "to have the same friends and enemies as the Roman people," that is, it had to defer to Rome the decision as to when and with whom it would go to war. Developed originally to deal with Italian states defeated by Rome in the fifth and fourth centuries B.C., the foedus inaequum

became increasingly sophisticated and complex as Roman power expanded throughout the Mediterranean basin. Its basic purpose of neutralizing the military potential of formally independent states never changed as is clearly revealed by the terms of the three most important such treaties, namely, those concluded with Carthage at the end of the Second Punic War (218–201 B.C.), with Macedon after the Second Macedonian War (200–196 B.C.), and with the Seleucid king Antiochus III in 188 B.C.

These treaties share three fundamental characteristics. First, they all contain significant disarmament provisions. So all three states were required to surrender or destroy all but a token number of warships. In addition, Carthage and Antiochus III were required to also destroy all war elephants and the latter was forbidden to recruit mercenary troops in Greece. Second, their freedom to wage war in the future was restricted by the establishment of security zones. Thus, Carthage was barred from campaigning beyond her city limits in the territories of her former North African subjects while Macedon and Antiochus III were similarly required to desist from military action in regions formally controlled by them in Greece and Anatolia. In addition, Carthage had to obtain permission from Rome before it could even conduct defensive operations within the borders guaranteed it under its peace treaty with Rome. Third, an effort was made to limit their capacity to rebuild their military forces by assessing severe reparations much as was attempted against Germany in the Treaty of Versailles. Unfortunately, the outbreak of the Third (171–167 B.C.) and Fourth Macedonian Wars (149–148 B.C.) and the Third Punic War (149–146 B.C.) demonstrated that, like the Treaty of Versailles, the peace and security provided by these treaties was only temporary.

A new approach to arms control becomes evident with the transition from the Republic to the Empire, albeit not because of a change in fundamental Roman values. Thus, the celebration of peace that is so striking a feature of early Augustan literature and art immediately after the end of the civil wars that destroyed the Republic quickly yielded to renewed glorification of military success as imperial expansion resumed on a large scale in the last decade of the first century B.C. and the first decade of the first century A.D. Instead, the change resulted from the imperial government's recognition that maintenance of the new enlarged frontiers exceeded the empire's economic and military resources. The most visible evidence of this new reality was the delineation of fixed borders marked out by heavily fortified defensive positions.

In dealing with this new situation, Rome continued to employ some unilateral arms control measures, most notably the attempt to limit the military capacity of less economically developed peoples beyond the Roman frontiers by imposing strict controls on the export of militarily valuable products such as iron and bronze and arms and armor. More important and more effective, however, was the formulation of a new diplomacy based for the first time on the assumption of long term coexistence between Rome and its various neighbors. This diplomacy continued to evolve and change throughout the whole of imperial history, but the details of that evolution cannot be dealt with here.

One feature of that diplomacy is, however, relevant to the theme of this study, the establishment by mutual agreement of buffer zones or states between the territory of Rome and its neighbors. The first example of such a device was in northeast Africa, where a seventy mile stretch of the Nile Valley south of the present Aswan high dam was neutralized in 20 B.C. by following Ptolemaic precedent and having title to it assigned to a religious entity, the temple of Isis at Philae after the establishment of peace between Rome and the central Sudanic kingdom of Meroe. The most important such arrangement, however, was on Rome's eastern frontier, where war between Rome and her powerful Iranian neighbors, the Parthians and then from the third century A.D. the Sassanid Persians, was averted for long periods of time by the neutralization of the buffer state of Armenia. This was accomplished first by the negotiation of a convention according to which Armenia would be ruled by kings related to the Parthian royal family but approved and crowned by the Roman government and then by the partition of Armenia by Rome and Sassanid Persia in a manner reminiscent of the partition of Poland by Russia and Prussia in the eighteenth century A.D.

CONCLUSION

The buffer system was the last major development in the long history of arms control in antiquity, and like ancient arms control in general it was imperfect. Wars between Rome and her eastern neighbors were not eliminated, nor was the intensity of those that occurred materially reduced. It did, however, provide a framework within which frictions between the powers involved could be contained. For much of the almost six and half centuries of its use, therefore, an uncertain state of peace—but a state of peace nevertheless—reigned on Rome's eastern frontier.

The balance sheet of ancient arms control in general is similarly mixed. To the end of antiquity, war remained a central fact of ancient life, but so also did the effort to find ways of resolving the conflicts that led to it. In that search the peoples of the Ancient Near East and Greece and Rome invented and employed most of the arms control devices still being considered today. It is this fact that makes the history of ancient arms control of interest to all who are concerned with the problems of finding practical means of limiting violence in the modern world.

BIBLIOGRAPHY

The Ancient Near East   Arms control was not explicitly recognized as a diplomatic category in antiquity and no comprehensive modern study of the subject exists. Consequently, anyone interested in the topic must consult a wide variety of ancient and modern sources. The situation is particularly difficult with regard to the Ancient Near East. Useful case studies of problems related to arms control, however, are JERROLD S. COOPER, *Reconstructing History from Ancient Inscriptions: The Lagash-Umma Border Conflict* (Malibu, Cal., 1983); and HARRY A. HOFFNER, JR., "A Hittite Analogue to the David and Goliath Contest of Champions?" *Catholic Biblical Quarterly* 30 (April 1968): 220–225. Excellent translations of the most important diplomatic texts can be found in JAMES B. PRITCHARD, *Ancient Near Eastern Texts Relating to the Old Testament*, 3d ed. (Princeton, N.J., 1969).

Ancient Greece and Rome   The problems of war and peace in the classical civilizations of Greece and Rome are the subject of an extensive scholarly literature. Classical ideas concerning peace are surveyed in GERARDO ZAMPAGLIONE, *The Idea of Peace in Antiquity* (Notre Dame, Ind., 1973); and IVO SCHALBROECK, "Peace in the Ancient World," in *World Encyclopedia of Peace,* vol. 2, edited by Linus Pauling (Oxford and New York, 1986): 197–

212. An uneven but useful attempt to assess the extent of peace in the ancient world is MATTHEW MELKO and RICHARD D. WEIGEL, *Peace in the Ancient World* (Jefferson, N.C., 1981). Understandably, however, most attention has been devoted to the place of war in Greek and Roman history.

The social context of classical warfare is clearly analyzed in YVON GARLAN, *War in the Ancient World: A Social History* (New York, 1975), and VICTOR DAVIS HANSON, *The Western Way of War: Infantry Battle in Classical Greece* (New York, 1989). The Greek acceptance of war is the subject of an important essay by ARNALDO MOMIGLIANO, "Some Observations on Causes of War in Ancient Historiography," *Studies in Historiography* (London, 1966): 112–126. Roman attitudes to war are treated in WILLIAM V. HARRIS, *War and Imperialism in Republican Rome 327–70 B.C.* (New York, 1979). Valuable for understanding the diplomatic framework for classical arms control are ELIAS J. BICKERMAN, "The Greek Experience of War and Peace," in *Approaches to World Peace: Fourth Symposium of the Conference on Science, Philosophy and Religion* edited by L. Bryson et al. (New York, 1944): 203–214; and SIR FRANK ADCOCK and D. J. MOSELEY, *Diplomacy in Ancient Greece* (New York, 1975).

Interest in specific Greco-Roman arms control devices has risen and fallen in tandem with twentieth century concerns for arms control. Thus, the negotiation of the 1907 Hague Treaty inspired a number of important studies of Greek arbitration of which the most useful are A. RAEDER, *L'Arbitrage international chez les Hellènes* (Kristiania and New York, 1912) and MARCUS NIEHBUHR TOD, *International Arbitration Amongst the Greeks* (Oxford, 1913). The Cold War and its peace diplomacy resulted in a similar renewal of interest in classical arms control precedents including arbitration, as evidenced by the appearance of the first volume of a complete collection of Greek arbitration documents edited by LUIGI PICCIRILLI, *Gli Arbitrati Interstatali Greci* (Pisa, 1973). The conflict avoidance function of asylum is considered in DENIS VAN BERCHEM, "Trois cas d'asylie archaïque," *Museum Helveticum* 17 (January 1960): 21–33. A fundamental study of fifth century B.C. Athenian peace diplomacy is found in E. BADIAN, "The Peace of Callias," *Journal of Hellenic Studies* 107 (1987): 1–39. Greek collective security experiments are studied in TIMOTHY THOMAS B. RYDER, *Koine Eirene: General Peace and Local Independence in Ancient Greece* (London and New York, 1965). Finally, the history of Rome's attempt to avert conflict with Persia through diplomatic means is surveyed in VERN L. BULLOUGH, "The Roman Empire vs. Persia, 363–502: a Study of Successful Deterrence," *The Journal of Conflict Resolution* 7 (March 1963) 55–68; and ROGER BLOCKLEY, *Rome and Persia: International Relations in Late Antiquity* (Ottawa, 1985).

Medieval Arms Control Movements and the Western Quest for Peace

UDO HEYN

See also The Law of War; Transnational Peace Movements and Arms Control: The Nineteenth and Twentieth Centuries; *and* Unilateral Initiatives. *Most of the treaties discussed in this article are excerpted in Volume III.*

In Western culture the quest for peace has developed through three traditions representing three different perspectives on history, morality, and politics and, implicit within these, three different perceptions of justice and order and three different approaches to the control of violence and the use of arms. We are speaking of the "just war" tradition of acknowledging, but limiting, the conflicts of this world; the pacifist tradition of withdrawing from these conflicts; and the utopian tradition of restructuring the world so that the causes of the conflicts will wither away. As James Turner Johnson argued so persuasively in *The Quest for Peace* (1987), these traditions did not coalesce until the Middle Ages, when they emerged from a growing cultural consensus on the justification and limitation of the use of force. Subsequently, this body of theory and practice was extended into modern times through religious indoctrination and military custom as well as the work of jurists, secular moralists, and legal and political thinkers.

The movements that came to dominate the practice and ideology of peacemaking in the West squarely fall under the first of these traditions and took the form of a series of campaigns launched by church and state in the Middle Ages to control the availability and permissibility of arms and to suppress crime, feud, and war. They evolved from the tenth to the sixteenth centuries through three distinct, yet interrelated phases known as the Peace of God (*Pax Dei*), the Truce of God (*Treuga Dei*) and the Peace of the Prince (in German, *Landfriede,* or "Peace of the Realm"). In an era of predominantly private violence, these official programs not only countered feud and crime directly but also stimulated broader efforts to define, legalize, and restrain the use of public force. The outcome was as novel as it was unforeseen. Of limited impact over the short run, the campaigns turned into the longest and most comprehensive law-and-order movement known to man, instrumental in the rise of the nation-state, the separation of private from public violence, and the restriction of war to international conflict. What is more, they revalued man's notions of disarmament and arms control, redefined peace, and pioneered institutions suitable for attaining and preserving it.

THE RISE OF THE JUST-WAR TRADITION

The roots of these programs reach back to the Hebrews, Greeks, and Romans, who agreed in principle that peace (*shalom, eirene, pax*) should aim at

563

the well-being of society, which is to say, a state of order and justice. This thinking eventually entered Western culture in the form of just-war and utopian concepts. But there was also the Germanic notion of peace, which centered on the preservation of tribal custom and featured the use of violence as part of the judicial process. Lastly, Christianity contributed a powerful ideological element with its implied mission to bring the kingdom of God to man on earth, and its resultant pacifist bent. Thus, Latin Christendom and, eventually, Western civilization were to face a series of agonizing choices regarding the nature and implementation of peace, both within and between their member groups.

This dilemma began with early Christianity, which tended to reject the political use of force in the form of war, military service, or even judicial punishment. But it did so more in the imminent expectation of the Second Coming of Christ than in an outright rejection of violence, and when, by the end of the second century, it became obvious that a new and purer world order was not at hand, Christians in various parts of the Roman Empire reacted in dissimilar ways. While a minority developed divergent doctrinal positions or withdrew entirely from worldly life, the majority began to participate in affairs of the state (including military service) and accepted a limited justification for violence in the pursuit of order and justice. Spelled out in the writings of such church fathers as Clement of Alexandria and his pupil Origen, that view was turning into the normative position of the church by the fourth century and, by the beginning of the fifth, found its place in one of the seminal texts of world history, *De civitate Dei* (*The City of God*) of Augustine, bishop of Hippo.

Augustine wrote *The City of God* in the aftermath of a catastrophe that shook the foundations of his own world, Alaric's sack of Rome in 410. Trying to rebut the charges of pagan critics that Christian pacifism had led to the collapse of the empire, Augustine set out to examine the flaws in human civilization and arrived at a detailed philosophy of history that encompassed, for the first time, a consistent, coherent argument that war serves the end of restoring peace and is subject to human control. Discussed most fully in chapters XV.4 and XIX.7 of *The City of God,* Augustine's notions on war did not become authoritative church doctrine until after the twelfth century, and then only as elaborated and refined by canonists such as Gratian, theologians such as Thomas Aquinas, and the theorists of the

secular *ius gentium* (the body of "common law," thought to reflect the customary relationships binding all men); in addition, they were modified by the chivalric *loi d'armes* (law of arms) and the habits of relations among princes.

Augustine's role was crucial for three reasons. First, he promulgated a notion of peace that reached back to Plato and Aristotle and was shared by the Stoics and Neoplatonists of his day: peace defined not necessarily as the absence of violence but as a state of communal harmony rooted in order and justice. This concept was, indeed, well established in Roman law and practice and ritualized in the prerequisites for sanctioning a *bellum iustum*—a just cause and proper authority to legitimize the use of arms. Second, Augustine added to these Roman terms for waging a just war a new prerequisite, right intent; tied to the effects of cupidity and charity on the human soul, it made the concept of peace and justice explicit in Christian terms. Although augmented by Augustine with other provisions drawn from Roman law, these three ideas were to constitute the key elements of what would eventually be known as the *ius ad bellum* (the law defining a justifiable war). In addition, they would bear implications to which, in the late Middle Ages, the *ius in bello* (the law governing the proper conduct of war) could be related. And third, Augustine imbued these concerns with a powerful transcendental element in the admonition that even the temporal peace of the Earthly City (*civitas terrenae*) be considered but a prologue to the happiness of eternal peace, to be found in the City of God.

The *civitas divina* and the *civitas terrenae* symbolized not only the central hope but the central problem of the Middle Ages: how to bridge the gap between their two kinds of peace and make them one. To Augustine, the link was the "well-ordered concord of civic obedience and civic rule" (XIX.16–17), which would mitigate man's *cupiditas* and draw him toward God's love (*caritas*). This was to remain the model for Latin Christendom throughout the Middle Ages; initially, it hardly impressed the Germanic chieftains, who were transforming the ruins of the western Roman Empire into independent kingdoms. By the sixth century, western Europe was under the control of more than two dozen tribal groups that made no distinction between warrior and civilian and maintained order by the private and public resort to arms. Whereas Rome had conceived of violence as a means to an end—the protection of state and society—Germanic culture glorified war and warrior in and of themselves, an attitude reinforced by an elite that lived by violence and based its power on it.

Thus, Augustine's nascent just-war theory languished even as the moral precepts contained in the Bible and the writings of the early church fathers came to be merged with the canons and decrees of church councils and synods, the edicts and decisions of individual bishops, the laws of Christian emperors and kings, and the priests' penitentials to constitute a common body of theological doctrine that very slowly transformed Germanic ways of life. In the fifth century, Augustine's teachings inspired a number of spurious works, such as the letter *Gravi de pugna,* that managed to reconcile Christian notions of violence with Germanic ones by claiming that the proof of justice lay in a test of arms, thus strengthening the Germanic practice of the ordeal. In the seventh century Isidore of Seville, in transmitting Roman ideas of the just war to the High Middle Ages, added to Augustine's criteria for a *iustum bellum*—which were held to imply that defensive wars were just by definition—a potential justification for offensive wars. And by the twelfth century, the degree to which a then-developed "Augustinian position" on just war was holding sway was exemplified by Ivo of Chartres, who drew extensively on Augustine and Isidore even while considered an authority in his own right. In this fashion, Augustine's concept of a Christian commonwealth—and, in particular, his notion that any hostile act was justified if motivated by Christian charity—hardened into a foundation of universal thought that became the common heritage of medieval thinkers and lawyers and, reduced to a few rudimentary statements and ideas, was the basis of the actions of medieval men. Eventually, these ideas were to resurface in Gratian's canon law and become systematized in the Thomistic just-war doctrine, but more immediately, they came to provide the ideology that suggested the strategy for the official peace campaigns.

THE PEACE CAMPAIGNS OF CHURCH AND STATE

Violence was pervasive throughout the Middle Ages; as Richard W. Kaeuper observed, in *War, Justice, and Public Order* (1988), "the warfare of great kingdoms was only the massive and elaborate end-point on a scale of violent action reaching down through the private wars and feuds of great lords, knights, and townsmen to the tavern murders and midnight robberies of village society" (p. 6). Collective violence, in particular, was habitual among three groups: the nobles, both great and lesser; their mercenaries and personal retainers; and gangs of roving bandits. Because lines between the private and public use of force were blurred, none of these categories were mutually exclusive or exempt from criminal intent. But while there was no lack of wars fought for political and dynastic ends or periodic rebellions, most of the organized fighting in the Middle Ages was an expanded version of the old Germanic habit of settling judicial disputes quasi-privately, through the feud. In *The Forgotten Victim* (1982), Richard Shelly Hartigan noted that "any crime was considered a *Friedensbruch,* a rupture of the peace; the execution of a sanction against the wrongdoer was the *faida* or, in German, *Fehde*" (p. 59). While every freeman had originally been entitled to invoke the feud, the Carolingian monarchy had taken this privilege from the peasants and severely limited their right to bear arms. The prerogative to pursue disputes through the *Fehde,* out of court and without objective constraint, thus came to rest with the arms-bearing nobles (and, eventually, burghers), who typically settled their disputes by taking their opponents hostage, terrorizing each other's serfs and freemen, and laying waste to each other's villages and fields.

While major wars were relatively short and limited—armies would come together in early summer and go home again in the fall—and some knights and mercenaries might continue pillaging even after the armies were disbanded, personal and family feuds festered without respite and, seemingly, without end. At the same time, gangs of bandits struck from the fringes of the settled regions and bands of beggars, thieves, and cutthroats roamed the countryside and towns. In general, a strong central government, backed by powerful local magnates would keep most of these troublemakers at bay; but where these authorities faltered, anarchy quickly spread.

That was, in fact, the case throughout most of western Europe from the ninth century onward. Christian Europe was falling into chronic, widespread chaos because of Viking, Muslim, and Magyar invasions and the collapse of Carolingian rule. Ensconced in their new motte and bailey castles, local magnates and their vassals became the sole source of justice and defense, treating their political power as their private possession. Even the papacy, deprived of its secular protection, fell prey to political intrigue and corruption, which, from the tenth into the first half of the eleventh centuries, prompted mounting calls for reform.

PEACE OF GOD AND TRUCE OF GOD

Despite its enthusiasm for wars motivated by religion (such as Charlemagne's campaigns against pagans and infidels), Carolingian society had been deeply suspicious of killing even in a justifiable war, and as the writers, canonists, councils, and formulae of the royal and pontifical chanceries of the time attest, Augustine's ideal of a peaceful Christian commonwealth attainable in this world remained very much alive in the tenth century. Thus, the ecclesiastic authorities decided to counter the violence around them by enforcing societal behavior appropriate to Augustine's vision. Prefiguring later papal efforts, the abbots of Cluny and Gorze devised programs of monastic reform centered on a concept of spirituality endorsed by Louis the Pious and his religious adviser, Benedict of Aniane, that encouraged the monks (drawn from the warrior class) to surrender their weapons and make themselves voluntarily weak (or, 'poor')," as Lester K. Little put it in *Religious Poverty and the Profit Economy in Medieval Europe* (1978, p. 68). Yet, as quickly as these monasteries grew in reach and influence, ecclesiastics in southern France continued to face violence and chaos, especially at the hands of lesser lords and their retainers. In time, a number of bishops and abbots decided to pursue peace more directly by strengthening the powers of lay and ecclesiastical magnates and, with the support of local nobles, began to call special "councils" of the faithful to proclaim legislation designed to protect the properties and noncombatants in their care. In 975 at Le Puy, Bishop Guy of Anjou assembled the knights and peasants of his diocese in an open field "to hear from them what their advice was for the maintenance of peace" and then imposed on the *milites* (knights) an oath "to respect the Church's possessions and those of the peasants" (Johnson, *The Quest for Peace*, pp. 79–80). When some knights resisted, they were put down by the forces of two powerful relatives of the bishop, the counts of

Brioude and Gévaudan. But the first solid evidence of this program, to be known in time as the *Pax Dei* (Peace of God), dates from the Synod of Charroux (June 989) at which Archbishop Gombaud of Bordeaux and his suffragans anathematized in three canons all those who would break into churches, attack unarmed clerics, or pillage the poor (meaning, mostly, peasants). While these provisions were eventually to furnish the core of the idea of noncombatant immunity in the classic just-war doctrine, the event was even more remarkable for the emergence of a collective consciousness that was soon to grow into a widespread public movement strong enough to challenge the Germanic tradition of private war.

These councils drew initially on laws and regulations in force in Carolingian times, but soon began to seek their sanction in a "new" canon law (*ius novum*) backed by formal oaths to observe the Peace of God, often sworn by fighting men on religious relics before a crowd. As the canonical records attest, the sponsors of the Peace of God looked upon these commitments with extreme seriousness, invoking excommunication and interdict against individuals and communities that violated the status of noncombatants. In 990 the Council of Narbonne declared against nobles who attacked the goods and persons of ecclesiastics, and four years later, at Anse, the bishops specifically forbade the lay nobility to violate, or build castles and fortifications to threaten, the lands, churches, and livestock of the monastery at Cluny. In 998, Widon, bishop of Prey, and Theobald, archbishop of Vienne, promulgated a written "Pact of Peace" between the lords and bishops that provided for the protection of merchants, laborers, and the weak. Subsequent councils in or near Aquitaine (e.g., Poitiers in 1011–1014, Limoges in 1028, Bourges in 1031) and Burgundy (Verdun-sur-le-Doubs in 1019–1021 and Anse in 1025) spread the Peace of God until it covered most of France (including the royal demesne) and Catalonia. In Flanders the Peace of God also appeared in the eleventh century, with the most important proclamations occurring in 1034 and 1099. Even relations between princes were affected, as happened in 1024 when the Capetian king Robert II ("the Pious") and the German emperor Henry II met on the border of their empires to proclaim a universal peace.

According to the chronicler Raoul Glaber, the Peace of God reached its peak by 1033, the millennium of Christ's Passion; not only did the French king call for councils to be held throughout France, but "bishops and lay rulers enacted a great deal of legislation, including regulations of weekly diets; and the huge and wildly enthusiastic crowds experienced the assemblies as a covenant of peace between God and men" (R. Landes and F. Paxton, "Pax Dei," *World Encyclopedia of Peace,* 1986). Still, the violence continued, especially once the fears and hopes associated with the Apocalypse began to wane. As a result, the bishops found it necessary to supplement the perpetual protection of certain types of persons and possessions sought in the Peace of God with measures aimed at the temporary suspension of all hostilities—the *Treuga Dei* (Truce of God).

The notion of a truce to curb private violence had long been part of the cultural heritage of the nobility that occupied the seats of ecclesiastical power. In Germanic society, violence had been forbidden during religious festivals, at the assemblies of the free men of the tribe, and during military expeditions, and failure to observe the peace at these times could result in the trial of the offender and his banishment or execution. Now that concept reemerged, especially among Cluny's followers, again with the aim of securing an ordered Christian peace. At first, Peace of God councils in Burgundy (Verdun-sur-le-Doubs, 1016) and Catalonia (Toulouges, 1020) enjoined the knights to lay down their arms during the Easter season. Then, in 1027, the Council of Toulouges (in the diocese of Elne and the county of Roussillon) provided in a *pactum vel treuga* that no one should attack his enemy between Saturday evening and Monday morning, "in order to enable every man to show proper respect for the Lord's Day" (H. E. J. Cowdrey, "The Peace and Truce of God in the Eleventh Century," *Past and Present,* 1970, p. 44). The Truce of God also covered Septimania and Provence, and when fully developed at a Council at Arles (c. 1041–1043), it sought to restrict warfare year-round to three days a week. When the bishops of Provence, in 1041, sent a letter to the Italian bishops, asking them to "receive" and maintain "peace and this truce of God which has been handed down from Heaven," they defined the truce as extending from vespers on Wednesday until sunrise on Monday, and commended it to "all Christians, friend and foe" (Johnson, *The Quest for Peace,* p. 87).

The Truce of God backed the spiritual sanctions of the Peace of God with secular prosecution and, eventually, sought to cover entire seasons of the ec-clesiastical year—Christmas, Lent, the period from Rogations to Pentecost, the feasts and vigils of the Virgin, and some festivals of saints. Finally, by the middle of the eleventh century, elements of the Peace and Truce seem to have been merged in practice and enforced by special tribunals (*audientiae pacis, iustitiae pacis*) and peace leagues or militias (*militiae pacis*). While the earliest example, a league of nobles under the leadership of the duke of Aquitaine (c. 1000), still resembled conventional peacekeeping forms, the league founded in 1038 at the initiative of Aimon, archbishop of Bourges, enlisted the entire male population in a broad-based popular (though abortive) effort to battle peace-breaking nobles. Such popular armies of peasants and townsmen (at times supported by a "peace tax") became a standing feature in most of France for the next century and a half and, led by clergy or laymen, replaced any central authorities unable or slow to preserve the peace. Finally, in 1054, the Council of Narbonne joined the Peace and the Truce in canon law; ordaining that "no Christian should kill another Christian, for whoever kills a Christian undoubtedly sheds the blood of Christ," it seemed to offer the prospect of a pacified Christian world (Cowdrey, p. 53).

PEACE OF PRINCE AND PEACE OF REALM

Subsequently the Truce of God and, by common understanding, the Peace of God were to be reaffirmed, without detailed comment, at the First Lateran Council in 1123; and the Truce was reaffirmed, once more, at the Second and Third Lateran Councils in 1139 and 1179, respectively. But after the second half of the eleventh century, the Peace and Truce had, in effect, lost their driving force; as Kaeuper commented, "further progress depended on the active appropriation of the peace movement by . . . temporal rulers who could make use of its principles as they created new and lasting political and legal structures in their domains" (p. 147). And indeed, the programs at that point entered a new phase in which the direct involvement of clergy and populace waned and the control of violence devolved upon public institutions headed by papacy, monarchy, high nobility, and commune. Even while competing among themselves, all of them agreed on the need to wrest the authority to use force from the lesser feudal ranks and from social and ideological dissidents and to apply it with renewed vigor in support of their own particular ends.

Again it was the church that was to provide the first and vital impetus. In the second half of the eleventh century, monastic reform was followed by reform of the papacy and the reemergence of the Holy See as a preeminent political and ecclesiastical institution. Pope Leo IX considered the encroachment of the secular on the sacred the greatest evil of his day and initiated what was to become known (after Gregory VII, the most famous of his immediate successors) the great Gregorian Reform. Thus, Leo not only sought to prohibit simony and clerical marriage but in 1049, at the Council of Reims, decreed that clerics in holy orders (and the poor) should be immune from violence. In 1059, Pope Nicholas II issued a bull stating that pilgrims should be exempt from attack as well, and at the Council of Clermont in 1095, Urban II—a former prior of Cluny—threw the full authority of the church behind the Peace and Truce. The council's canons confirmed the immunity of clerics, monks, and women; proscribed violence against the church; and prescribed anathema against those who would kill clerics or steal their goods. Even more important for the future, however, was Urban's simultaneous call for the First Crusade. Following the final schism (1054) between the eastern (Orthodox) and western (Roman) churches, the papacy asserted its supremacy over all of Christendom by proclaiming an eternal peace in the Latin West, seeking to extend the papal reform to the Christian East, and declaring war upon Islam.

With these measures, the constraint of internal violence was now clearly linked to the use of force abroad; but if the Crusades did indeed reduce some types of violence in western Europe, the concept of holy war gave rise to new ones, as well. Trying to Christianize warfare by championing the feudal knight and his code of honor, the papacy introduced an element of militancy into the peace campaigns that served the church's hierocratic aims and a Pan-Christian expansionism, but negated a thousand years of Christian tradition. Even if medieval jurists did view the holy war as a specific subset of *bellum iustum*—a war fought by Christians in defense of the Holy Cross "to recover what was rightfully theirs" (Hans Eberhard Mayer, *The Crusades,* 1988, p. 15)—it was only with the age of Gregory VII and Urban II that unrestricted warfare became

accepted as meritorious when directed against dissidents both inside and outside the Christian world. At the Third Lateran Council the church extended the indulgences granted to crusaders in the Holy Land to those who joined expeditions against heretics, and in 1208, Pope Innocent III launched the Albigensian Crusade in a conciliar decree. It was only after the Battle of Lepanto (1571) and the Counter-Reformation that foreign and domestic crusades began to fade from history, and not before they had been used to target such diverse groups as the Muslims in Spain and the Holy Land, pagans in the Baltics, and the Holy Roman Emperor Frederick II and his family, and invoked as a pretext to serve a variety of personal, political, and even fiscal needs.

Meanwhile, the Second Lateran Council had seen the birth of yet another canonical initiative, a ban on tournaments and specific weapons. Between the middle of the twelfth and fourteenth centuries, tournaments tended, with distressing frequency, to turn into real battles, and as temporal rulers equivocated, the church undertook to restrict this form of mock combat itself. Repeating canon 9 of the Synod of Clermont (1130), which had condemned jousts and tournaments, the Second Lateran Council forbade participation in tournaments once again; when that edict proved ineffective, the Third Lateran Council denied Christian burial to all slain in simulated combat. While this move did not halt tournaments either, it did bring about the use of blunted weapons and the reduction of these events to relatively harmless social pageants by the mid-fourteenth century.

Less successful, though in principle more important, was the weapons ban of the Second Lateran Council, applied to the use of crossbow (*arbalest*), bow and arrow, and *ballista* among warring Christians. Directed primarily against the mercenary companies formed around the skilled use of these weapons, it was no less an attempt to check a social challenge to the aristocracy than it was a tool to limit a military threat. The ban was reaffirmed several times, but foundered ultimately when the authorities found the mercenaries and their weapons useful for their own purposes, which by now encompassed peace campaigns, for the initiative for the control of arms and violence had begun to pass from church to secular authorities. And it was the latter that were to become responsible for the third and final phase of the peace campaigns, as the programs turned their attention, once again, to controlling the permissibility (rather than the availability) of arms.

When Charlemagne, an avid student of *The City of God,* had renewed the Roman *imperium,* he had given life to one of the most cherished ideals of medieval man, the notion of a peaceful commonwealth divinely ordained and placed under the secular rule of the emperor and the spiritual leadership of the pope. In practice, however, the dissolution of the Roman Empire had brought a merging of imperial and ecclesiastic institutions that made it difficult to separate the jurisdictions of state and church; and as bishops and abbots had usurped the peacekeeping functions of the monarchy in the tenth century, so kings and high nobility began to use the church for their dynastic designs in the eleventh. Building on *Pax* and *Treuga,* territorial rulers now established legal orders in which their own justice became the cornerstone of public peace. Thus, William, Duke of Normandy, who "was sufficiently strong to call councils himself along with the archbishop" (Landes and Paxton), established his Peace of the Prince in 1061 and 1064, while Count Ramon Berenguer I promulgated his *Usatges de Barcelona* between 1061 and 1063. A compilation of laws and customs from Visigothic and Roman, secular and ecclesiastic, judicial and legislative sources, the latter included several provisions that set sanctions for the breach of the Peace and Truce of God. In the twelfth century, the Peace of God was followed in Catalonia by an era of secular edicts, which appeared also in Aragon, and "these developed in a manner similar to that of the German peace statutes, the earlier ones being patterned after the Peace of God proclamations, the later ones taking a more legislative than contractual form and dealing with new areas of procedure, marriage, debt, and public crimes" (Harold Joseph Berman, *Law and Revolution,* 1983, p. 512).

In Castile and León, such efforts materialized somewhat later, but were also patterned on the Peace, as was the case in the covenanted, sworn communities (*communia pro pace,* "communes for peace") that typically gained their independence in the late eleventh century and the twelfth century through militias modeled on the *Pax.* In Flanders, the Truce appeared about 1071 and was promptly adapted to help the prince assume control over the administration of justice. The first sec-

ular peace statute (*Landfriede*) was proclaimed there in 1111; renewed in 1119, 1138, and frequently thereafter, it was to be of major importance for the future development of Flemish urban and territorial law. In Italy the Truce commended to the Lombard clergy in 1041 also seems to have served the ends of the high nobility, and in Norman Sicily, Roger II used the *Treuga* to establish a general peace very similar to that developed in Normandy by William I and Henry I. Only England, which before the Conquest had been the most highly centralized monarchy in western Europe and which, in the eleventh century, was still being ruled by a Germanic monarchy of the Carolingian type, was able to chart a different course. The early assertion of royal jurisdiction over serious breaches of the peace and the capacity of the crown to enforce this jurisdiction, coupled with timely innovations in civil law, prevented both the growth of the right, and the actual spread, of private war. Except for a brief appearance of the Peace and Truce during the anarchy of Stephen of Blois's reign, the peace movements of the Continent barely affected the island realm.

In France the ancient practice of the feud had been formally acknowledged for the noble classes in a *droit de guerre,* so that any change toward a monopoly of force gathered in the hands of a sovereign king was bound to be slow. By the mid-eleventh century the Capetians were using the Peace to build their authority on their demesne, and in the twelfth century, coinciding with papal efforts to strengthen the Peace in France at the councils of Clermont (1130) and Reims (1119 and 1148), Louis VI and Louis VII enlisted the Truce to establish what was in effect a King's Peace.

Indeed, during Louis VII's absence on the Second Crusade, the entire kingdom came under the protection of the church (and, in effect, the governance of Abbot Suger of St. Denis). Upon his return, Louis continued this trend, most notably through judicial interventions, exemplified by the Council of Soissons (1155). There a great assembly that included the archbishops of Reims and Sens and their suffragans, the duke of Burgundy, and the counts of Flanders, Champagne, Nevers, and Soissons promulgated edicts similar to the conciliar decrees that had shaped the peace programs for generations; but in this assembly the phrase "Peace of the Realm" significantly replaced the traditional "Peace of God." Since the great vassals swore to maintain the peace for ten years, this pact was more a commitment to a truce than a true peace; yet, the long-range meaning was clear. The Capetians had moved from seeking protection behind the shield of the peace movement to directing the movement and legislating peace measures in their own right.

Between the death of Louis VII (1180) and that of Louis IX (1270), the French monarchy kept building on these foundations, so that by the second half of the thirteenth century it had secularized the peace programs and their ecclesiastical notion of peace and established central and local courts on which a system of appeals and supervision of inferior jurisdictions could be based. To be sure, as Kaeuper points out, "the sum total of these measures did not vastly reduce private warfare, which Beaumanoir considered quite normal in the 1280s, albeit regulated by an elaborate code and occasionally obviated by *asseurements*" (assurances of peaceful behavior between specified parties); but there is evidence to show that the royal government's willingness—and capacity—to control private warfare kept increasing at a steady pace. As Kaeuper continues,

offenders were brought into royal courts for offences specifically stated to be violations of the king's ordinances against private war, but whether or not such legislation had been recently enacted, the king's officers could bring charges of *port d'armes* [the carrying of arms with offensive intent], *chevauchée* [cavalry raid], and ambush; and cognizance of violations of the king's safeguard given to an individual or institution, or of violation of a peace or assurement sworn before a king's justice were independent of any ordinance on private war. (pp. 234, 236)

These efforts reached a peak in the reigns of Philip the Fair and his son, Philip V; *ordonnances* kept prohibiting and regulating feuds periodically, and the number of cases of private warfare heard in royal courts continued to grow. A prohibition of judicial duels and tournaments as well as private wars late in the thirteenth century lasted through the war in Gascony, while an ordinance of 1311 forbade private war throughout the realm, even where ancient custom had allowed the practice. In 1313, near the end of Philip the Fair's reign, the Parlement of Paris opened a separate register for criminal cases, and the number of complaints brought before it because of violations of royal safeguards (*panonceaux*) also kept swelling across the rest of the century. Finally, Philip V crowned his father's

work by extending efforts to restrain private warfare among the high nobility to the feuds, riots, and reciprocal manslaughter of the lesser nobles and by tailoring his peacekeeping policies explicitly to the needs of the provinces of France.

It was a policy that, in Kaeuper's words, "meant a more active crown effort in peace measures than at any previous time" (p. 258), but it could not be sustained, because of the uncertainties caused by the end of the Capetian dynasty and the accession of the Valois (1328) and the outbreak of the Hundred Years' War (1337). The war was to preempt internal issues of justice and order for more than one hundred years; indeed, the late fourteenth century was destined to see a number of setbacks in the Crown's peacekeeping efforts. An attempt, in 1361, to prohibit all feuds in peacetime was followed by an ordinance (1363) that accepted the nobles' view that only in wartime could their private quarrels be forbidden; and Charles V, in 1378, had to recognize private wars when the adversaries agreed to, and followed, proper form. Then as before, moreover, entire regions of France continued to escape the king's jurisdiction over private warfare altogether.

Thus, it was in Germany that this phase of the peace campaigns reached its most elaborate and extensive form, in the guise of the *Landfriede* (Peace of the Realm). While imperial power was seriously impaired throughout the late eleventh, twelfth, and early thirteenth centuries, the peace edicts of the German emperors did, nonetheless, lay the foundations for a German common law, which is to say, "a common body of legal institutions, concepts, principles, rules, which was universally accepted in the imperial and the territorial and the urban polities" (Berman, p. 503). But more to the point, the German principalities themselves "became modern states, or prototypes of modern states, surpassing the empire in this respect" (Berman, p. 491). Each *Land* was, in effect, a kingdom unto itself, so that the *Landfrieden* came to resemble modern international treaties that, from the subject's point of view, carry the force of law. The result was an approach to peace that promoted not only the political and legal identity and integrity of each constituent German territory but the ultimate triumph of "the postulate that the authority to rule—sovereignty, as it would later be called—was grounded in control over adjudication" (Berman, p. 492). With this breakthrough, the axiom that law was the ruler's principal tool for justice and order moved to the core of the Western legal tradition, and on its strength, the *Landfrieden* emerged as not only the principal German variant, but the European culmination, of the peace campaigns.

Filtered through the Cluniac movement, the *Pax* and *Treuga* of Aquitaine and Burgundy had gradually found their way into a Germany whose emperors for almost a century—from the coronation of Otto I in 962 to the death of Henry III in 1056—routinely interfered in the papacy's affairs, especially the appointment of bishops and abbots. Not surprisingly, then, these rulers also tended to bend the peace campaigns to their own ends. Henry II, for instance, envisaged a permanent state of peace anchored in his role as *rex et sacerdos* (king and priest), and Henry III aimed at nothing less than an imperial theocracy, as attested by his removal from office of three rival popes at the Synod of Sutri (1046). Although deeply religious and committed to peace, both emperors merged temporal and spiritual motives in their quest to protect and promote a Christian commonwealth they saw threatened by the particularistic tendencies of their feudal lords.

In the second half of the eleventh century, however, this precipitated an open struggle with a papacy taken over by monastic reformers who drew on the Peace for its theme (the purification of the church), methods (interdict and excommunication), and popular support. Among Leo IX's reformist associates was a former Cluniac prior, Hildebrand, who in 1073 ascended the papal throne as Gregory VII. Within two years, Gregory was in open conflict with the Holy Roman Emperor–elect, Henry IV, over the issue of lay investiture, and their struggle plunged Germany into a civil war that lasted for almost two generations. The result was the strengthening of the powers of the great lords over those of the emperor and Germany's conversion from a hereditary into an electoral monarchy. But, even more important, the deposition of Henry IV by Gregory VII (1076) and his humiliation at Canossa (1077) brought home the message that individual rulers were only the temporary and interchangeable trustees of their realms, and spelled the end of any theocratic notions Europe's monarchs might still have held. In France, the contest between monarchy and papacy fell into the reign of Philip I and was resolved by compromise, without a formal agreement, in 1098; in England and Normandy, which belonged to England, Henry I renounced investiture in 1107 in the

Concordat of Bec. Although a final compromise in Germany had to await the Concordat of Worms (1122), and in England the martyrdom of Thomas à Becket (1170), the separation of church and state had become an accomplished fact.

In Germany the expansionism of the church seriously undermined the capacity of the German emperors to develop a consistent policy, let alone a body of laws, for dealing with internal strife. Once more, the bishops intervened to restore public order, proclaiming the Peace of God in councils at Liège (1082), Cologne (1083), and Bamberg (1085); then, from 1083 (Swabia) and 1094 (Bavaria), a number of secular princes (and a provincial assembly in Alsace) launched their own local *Landfrieden,* soon to be emulated in municipal peace edicts (*Stadtfrieden*) as well. Both predated (as they were to outlive) the peace efforts of the *Reich;* the *Reichslandfriede* put forward by Henry IV in 1103 and embodying a coherent plan to subject all social classes to a common criminal code was to be patterned after the Peace of God of Mainz (1085).

The imperial edict of 1103 was followed by at least seventeen additional imperial peace statutes, in 1119, 1121, 1125 (two), 1135, 1147, 1152, 1158, 1179, 1186, 1207, 1208, 1221, 1223, 1224, 1234, and 1235. But just as Henry's attempt to establish a royal judiciary to enforce his edict of 1103 failed, so his successors from Henry V through Frederick II were unable to summon the strength and authority to mandate a general peace. Instead, the search for peace in Germany was to remain focused—de facto, if not de jure—on the *Stadtfrieden* of the local communities and the *Territoriallandfrieden* of the autonomous dukes, kings, and princes of the *Länder* and territorial leagues. Thus, there were at least eight additional territorial peace statutes, issued in 1104, 1127, 1152, 1156, 1171, 1200, 1229, and 1233, in Swabia, Bavaria, Saxony, Brixen (Bressanone), Hennegau, and Alsace.

Rudolf His, in a classic definition, saw the *Landfriede* as "the promulgation, through secular law or contract, of extraordinary norms intended to fight or check the knights' feud (*Ritterfehde*) and to suppress pillage and other crimes likely to imperil the commonweal" (*Das Strafrecht des deutschen Mittelalters,* 1920, vol. 1, p. 7). Evolving from *Landfriedensgebot* (peace statute) into *Landfriedensbündnis* (i.e., pacts between imperial estates), the Peace of the Realm eventually came to address the most common threats to life and property (e.g., murder, arson, and rape) as defined in terms of traditional notions of peace (especially the *Pax*) as well as local law enforcement (and fiscal) needs. Thus, the *Landfrieden* assumed a variety of guises aimed at reducing the resort to violence, ranging from the pacification of certain persons, places, and times to the proscription of certain categories of arms and acts of war, the technical regulation of the conduct of the feud, and administrative measures dealing with coinage, customs duties, and income levies on craftsmen and millers.

Medieval legislation, in general, and imperial legislation, in particular, anticipated persistent violation of their edicts and therefore reiterated, again and again, the prohibition of the same offense; in this fashion the *Landfrieden,* too, were routinely renewed into the late fifteenth century. In the process, as Berman pointed out, the programs extended significantly the scope and content of the Peace and Truce. Binding all people within a ruler's jurisdiction without a time limit, they caused the idea of the sworn peace to disappear; instead of asking their subjects to consent to renounce various forms of violence, rulers now demanded that they obey a series of new laws that systematized and reformed the preexisting legal order. Moreover, the programs' sanctions were made identical, whether tied to feud or crime, and as they came to include an ever-increasing variety of criminal penalties and civil and administrative rules, the edicts developed into comprehensive legislative acts that, by the mid-twelfth century, were finding their way into compilations of urban and territorial law, as well as Gratian's *Decretals.*

Typical, and by far the most important, of these collections was the *Sachsenspiegel* (*Saxon Mirror*), which, in the 1220s, channeled earlier peace statutes into German common law in a two-part opus consisting of *Landrecht* (territorial law) and *Lehn-recht* (feudal law). Essentially the private effort of an East Saxon knight, Eike von Repgow, the *Saxon Mirror* was the earliest major prose work written in German and covered private and penal as well as procedural and public law. It was used not only throughout northern Germany, but widely disseminated, from the Low Countries to Poland and Russia, imitated by other "mirrors of the law"—the *Schwabenspiegel, Frankenspiegel, Deutschenspiegel*—and emulated by towns in France and Germany that adopted each others' laws to augment their local customs. In similar fashion, the first modern code of royal law in Western history, King

Roger II's *Assizes of Ariano* of 1140, grew into the far more comprehensive *Constitutions of Melfi* (or *Liber Augustalis*) of 1231. In England, Ranulf de Glanville's *Tractatus de legibus et consuetudinibus regni Angliae* (*Treatise on the Laws and Customs of the Kingdom of England*) of 1187 summarized Henry II's reforms and became the first systematic treatise on the English common law; it was to be followed in the thirteenth century by a more extensive work, Henry de Bracton's *De legibus et consuetudinibus Angliae* (*Treatise on the Laws and Customs of England*). In 1283, Philippe de Beaumanoir's *Coutumes de Beauvaisis* (*Books of the Customs and Usages of Beauvaisians*) summarized the customary law applied in the French royal courts. With systems of royal (or princely) law comparable to those of France, Germany, and England firmly established in Normandy, Sicily, Catalonia, Aragon, and Castile and Léon, the principle of royal control over criminal justice had reasserted itself by the end of the thirteenth century throughout most of Europe.

As Kaeuper noted, "on both sides of the [English] Channel royal action for public order took two forms": the provision of courts and judicial mechanisms for the resolution of private disputes, and the official prosecution and suppression of extra-legal violence (p. 199). In Germany the imperial statutes (*Reichslandfrieden*) of 1234 and 1235 decreed that the feud could only be invoked if the state's judiciary failed to act, and in 1495 the Imperial Diet at Worms not only banned the feud entirely but proclaimed a Perpetual Peace of the Realm (*Ewiger Landfriede*), which became, in turn, the basis for Germany's first modern criminal code, the *Constitutio criminalis carolina,* promulgated at the Imperial Diet of Regensburg in 1532. In 1539, France followed suit by establishing the principle of equality and accountability in criminal proceedings in its *ordonnance royal,* the *Ordinance of Villers-Cotterets.*

THE EMERGENCE OF THE RULES OF WAR

Backed by a graded system of courts and an armed (police) force, the sovereign state and its ruler were now clearly the sole and undisputed source and authority of the law. Yet this did not necessarily mean the end of what had come increasingly to be seen as a European body of "common" law. Augmented by customary, feudal, canon, urban, and commercial law, that body had kept growing right into the fifteenth century, and even then the state continued to draw on it for its substance, especially in the areas of criminal law and procedure. There, in turn, the influence of the canon law remained decisive. Both the *Ordinance* and the *Carolina* had relied on the *Inquisitionsprozess,* a system of legal proof that was an amalgam of canon law and Roman civil law refined in the prosecution of heretics, and as that process gradually replaced the trial by ordeal and battle, it proved central to what John H. Langbein, in *Prosecuting Crime in the Renaissance: England, Germany, France* (Cambridge, Mass., 1974) called the "officialization of crime repression" (p. 146). Right through the sixteenth century, criminal justice systems with new procedural devices continued to emerge in nearly every country in Europe, transforming the accusatorial system of the feudal era into either the jury system adopted in England or the inquisitorial system characteristic of the Continent.

Yet, even as the state was taking the prosecution of crime out of private hands, public violence in the form of warfare was on the rise. Kingdoms, principalities, and chartered cities were consolidating their territories and jurisdictions into more-powerful political units, which provoked international conflicts and forced Europe's rulers to raise, and find the means to support, increasingly massive military forces. To obtain the needed revenues required the consent of the newly emerging middle classes, which, in turn, pushed for representative institutions: the Spanish Cortes and the German Reichstag of the late thirteenth century, the States General of France of 1302, and Edward I's Model Parliament of 1295. At the same time, the heavy cavalry of the armored knights and their men-at-arms was giving way to an infantry drawn from the common people, and military tactics were changing from siege warfare to pitched battles. Coupled with related advances in technology, such as gunpowder, cannon, and musket, these developments greatly expanded the scope and level of violence, increased lethality and destruction, and helped set the stage for the great European economic depression of the later Middle Ages.

Thus, the need to constrain war became more pressing, and legal theorists, political thinkers, and theologians turned with renewed urgency to the notion of *iustum bellum.* Drawing on Augustine via Isidore and Ivo of Chartres, the canonists merged just-war precepts with those of canon law and the law of arms, and a Camaldolese monk, Gratian, consolidated the results in the form of a textbook around 1140. In keeping with the aim of Scholasticism to harmonize secular and religious thought, Gratian gave his work the title *Concordantia discordantium canonum* (*A Concordance of Discordant Canons*); better known as the *Decretum Gratiani* or *Decreta,* it offered general tenets (*distinctiones*), presented fictitious legal cases (*causae*), and discussed legal problems (*quaestiones*). As Frederick H. Russell noted in *The Just War in the Middle Ages* (1975), the appearance of the work "marked a watershed in the history of canon law, for it climaxed the development of early medieval canon law collections and inaugurated the period of systematic canonical jurisprudence" (p. 55). In 1580, supplemented with a collection of papal decretals, it became the first part of the *Corpus iuris canonici,* the name by which it was subsequently cited and known. For the rest of the twelfth century, the *Decretum* became a starting point for canon lawyers–notably the Decretists and Decretalists—who kept developing an explicit, coherent and consensual body of thought and practice that, through the thirteenth and fourteenth centuries, was to turn into the Western church's normative doctrine on war. Carried forward was the theme elaborated in the peace campaigns, that violence was an instrument to be used for good and evil, and the scrutiny of the church's relationship to the emerging state. Debating the role of government in both *ius ad bellum* and *ius gentium* terms, theologians and jurists eventually redefined the concept of right authority to refer to the secular ruler, and the concept of just cause to the ruler's need to guarantee internal order and external defense. Once those issues had been resolved, the debate moved on to the rules of war, with the aim of incorporating them fully into the just-war doctrine. The restraints that canon law, common law, and the law of arms imposed on the pursuit of violence were linked to Augustine's prohibition of evil intent, and this brought to the fore two principles that came to constitute the heart of the *ius in bello.* One was the concept of proportionality (concerning the relationship of means to ends), and the other, the concept of discrimination (concerning the level of undesirable secondary effects associated with a warlike act). Thus, by the end of the Middle Ages, the doctrine of *iustum bellum* finally emerged in its classic form, composed of both a *ius ad bellum* (whose major terms required that a war be fought on proper authority, for a just cause, and with right intent) and, of equal importance, a *ius in bello* (which focused on discrimination and proportionality and was to affect, in particular, noncombatant immunity and arms control).

The crowning formulation of the just-war doctrine is usually attributed to Thomas Aquinas, whose most extensive discussion of war is to be found in the "Pars Secunda Secundae" of his *Summa theologica* (1265–1274). Still, it is worth noting that "the just war tradition has resulted from interplay among several churchly and secular sources of moral and legal norms, not all of which always agree and the result of which does not look exactly the same in all ages of history" (Johnson, p. 199). In Aquinas's case, it seems that neither the official peace programs nor the deliberations of canon and civil lawyers left much of an imprint, for Thomistic thought continued to favor (following Augustine via Gratian) the *ius ad bellum*. Instead, Aquinas's major contribution to the just-war doctrine lies in his use of political postulates, derived from Aristotle, to justify the authority of the prince to wage war. In any case, by the late fourteenth century, the just-war doctrine had gone far beyond its theological and canonical origins and absorbed much of chivalric tradition, not to mention many precepts of common law. For proof, one need only look to Honoré Bonet's *L'Arbre des batailles* (*The Tree of Battles*), a handbook for the knightly classes, and Christine de Pizan's *Livre des faits d'armes et de chivalrie* (*The Book of Fayttes of Armes and of Chivalrie*) and, in particular, their stress on noncombatant immunity.

Although the issue of civilian safety had been addressed implicitly since the Peace of God campaigns, the landmark official pronouncement on noncombatant immunity had been the treatise *De treuga et pace* (*Of Truces and Peace*) of the thirteenth century, added to the growing body of canon law under Pope Gregory IX. In it, the church had identified noncombatants by function, listing eight categories of persons to be protected from the ravages of war: clerics, monks, friars, other religious, pilgrims, travelers, merchants, and peasants cultivating the soil (as opposed to peasants fighting in feudal armies). Collaterally, animals and goods belonging to the innocent were protected as well, as was the land on which the peasants worked. By Bonet's time, the list was augmented with the cate-

gories favored in the chivalric code that identified noncombatants by their inability, as well as ineligibility, to bear arms. *L'Arbre des batailles,* accordingly, added women and children, the aged, and the infirm to *De treuga et pace* and treated the two lists as one. Pisan's work went even further, merging elements of canon law, civil law, and chivalric law in one unified and widely publicized account. Thus, when, in the early sixteenth century, Franciscus de Victoria came to modify the Thomistic view of war as divine retribution and the enemy as subjectively guilty, it proved comparatively easy to apply the principles of Christian charity to other cultures. By 1542, Charles V's *New Laws of the Indies,* relying heavily on Victoria's *De Indis* (*On the Indians*) and *De iure belli* (*On the Law of War*) signaled the transformation of a secularized just-war doctrine into international law.

SUMMARY AND EVALUATION

A product of the German historical school, the study of the medieval peace movements began with the collection and classification of individual peace edicts in the years before World War I and progressed to sweeping legal studies in the period between the wars. Since World War II the emphasis has shifted to more-general inquiries seeking to reassess the Middle Ages from an intercultural perspective or more-limited inquiries using a combination of methods and approaches borrowed from all the social sciences. In either case, the result has been a proliferation of historical schools plagued by a variety of interpretations, both substantive and semantic, and a good deal of controversy surrounding the meaning and efficacy of the movements. Hence, there is no standard definition of either Peace or Truce of God (the terms were, indeed, used interchangeably in the Middle Ages), no standard English term for *Landfriede,* no agreement on how to differentiate between the Peace of the Prince and the Peace and Truce of God, and no accord on what constitutes a peace "council" or a peace "league." Not surprisingly, historians from Edward Gibbon to Roland Bainton and M. H. Keen, as well as peace activists and textbook writers, have insisted that these peace programs cannot be judged with any certainty, questioned their observance, or dismissed them altogether with a cynicism bordering on contempt.

Results and Repercussions   There is little disagreement among historians that the immediate, direct effect of the peace campaigns on the control of violence was disappointing. Of the three canonical attempts to restrain the resort to force, the concept of noncombatant immunity advanced in the Peace of God left the most enduring mark; indeed, Hartigan called the movement's contribution to the notion of civilian safeguards "enormous" (p. 77). But that development came essentially after the concept had been reoriented from its Augustinian base in Christian charity to a secular foundation in "humanity," in which form Grotius turned it into the key component of the modern just-war doctrine. As far as the Truce of God is concerned, it is, in Barber's words, "hard to find a single instance where a battle was postponed because of the day" (p. 215), although truces seem to have been rather common during the sieges that dominated large-scale fighting. The ban on the use of lethal weapons at the Second Lateran Council applied only to conflicts among Christians—heretics and infidels were excluded—and may well be viewed as an effort to restrict the availability of arms to the knightly classes. Significantly, Gratian did not include the prohibition in his *Decretum,* and while later compilers included it in *Compilatio Prima* and the Gregorian decretals, most canonistic commentaries followed Gratian's lead. Last but not least, there are no known acts or decrees of synods or councils in which disarmament was ever ordered, let alone enforced.

Thus, it would appear that the official peace campaigns, in the short run, served not so much to limit violence and outlaw arms as to delineate who might legitimately use force and to what ends. By and large, the programs tended to address the permissibility of arms rather than their availability, and the net effect was to consolidate and enhance the right of the central authorities to use force on their own behalf. This undoubtedly resulted in a reduction of private violence and the eradication of dissident groups, but its impact on wars between the great nobles is far more uncertain.

Yet, by measuring these results against the programs' quasi-messianic goals, such analyses tend to miss the indirect, unintended, yet very tangible long-term results of the peace campaigns. Thus, for example, social historians have only recently come to appreciate the programs' central place in Europe's transformation from a Mediterranean culture into Western civilization, and political scientists,

their crucial role in making the people an autonomous factor in European history. Most important, legal historians—the earliest and most perceptive students of the peace campaigns—have at last come to acknowledge the "enormous" importance of the movements for the legal systems and the administration of justice in not only the West, but the rest of the world (Berman, p. 90). All of these trends were, in fact, well under way by the tenth century, as the monastery at Cluny led "the effective establishment of an order which would be conducive to . . . a full Christian peace" (Lubomir Gleiman, "Some Remarks on the Origins of the Treuga Dei," *Études d'histoire litteraire et doctrinale,* 1962, p. 122). It did this not only by providing the impetus for peace programs and papal reform, but by influencing secular politics through its many members who became abbots and bishops or tutors and advisers to lords and kings. The immediate result was an unending stream of legislation pouring from church councils and synods and the Holy See, to be joined eventually by a profusion of territorial and municipal regulations promulgated, typically, in the form of peace edicts originating in the chanceries of lay and ecclesiastic rulers, drafted by successive generations of lawyers trained in the new universities and drawing on the canons, glosses, and decretals collected and explicated by another group of rising professionals, the legal scholars.

The juristic base for western Europe throughout the Middle Ages was the Code of Justinian, the first part of which (the *Digest*) had been published in 533. In it, the "glossators," or "civilian" lawyers (as distinguished from the church, or canon, lawyers), had sought to edit and explain the traditional statutes and principles of Roman law. In the twelfth century, the code was rediscovered in the West, and spurred on by the peace campaigns, a second generation of commentators (the "post-glossators"), strove to adapt its civil law to their vastly different native cultures. In the event, these jurists came to shape the fused civil law tradition of France and Germany, whose influence on "the law of specific nations, the law of international organizations, and international law" is, in John Henry Merryman's words, "difficult to overstate" (*The Civil Law Tradition,* 1985, p. 3). Both older and more influential than the common law tradition, it now dominates the legal systems of most of western Europe; many parts of Africa, Asia, and the Middle East; and even a few enclaves (Louisiana, Puerto Rico, Quebec) in the common law world. In addition, it controlled legal tradition in the Soviet Union and its satellites until replaced by the socialist legal tradition (which it still affects). Finally, French and German civil law informed and inspired the European scholars who, in the sixteenth and seventeenth centuries, moved the just-war theory from its grounding in theology and cultural consensus to a new base in presumed patterns of "natural" behavior and established rules of war. Thus, when Hugo Grotius, early in the seventeenth century, saw the great states of Europe bound together, not by one common superior, but by the social requirements of an international community articulated in a "law of nations," he created, in Michael Howard's words, nothing less than "the framework of thinking about international relations, about war and peace, within which consciously or unconsciously we still function" (*War in European History,* 1976, p. 24).

More specifically, as Johnson said, Grotius (joined by John Locke and Emmerich von Vattel) was laying down "the main lines of what remains today the controlling theory of war and its limitation, not just for the West but for the world" (p. 253). Still, it is instructive and, indeed, necessary for the success of modern arms control efforts, to try to understand why the peace campaigns did fall short of their elementary, universal, and admittedly idealist goals. And here one indisputable fact stands out: the pacification of western Europe came about as the result of the interaction of innumerable legal, social, and political initiatives and forces, in which the peace programs played a key, catalytic role but had, from the very beginning, to contend with outright rejection, internal contradictions, and a unique historical milieu.

In fact, it was the concept of *iustum bellum* that provided the intellectual background against which the advocates of the other Western peace traditions, the pacifists and utopians, developed their own, divergent, peace prescriptions. Like the former, both traditions found their roots deep within the classical age; but these beginnings, too, had been neglected until revived within the context of pressing contemporaneous problems. Yet, unlike the just-war theory, these traditions did not sacrifice part of Augustine's ideal so that they could work within the bounds set by the emerging system of nation-states. Both traditions were idealist, designed explicitly by their followers to aim for an imaginary commonwealth to which its real-world counterpart was expected to aspire.

Still evolving by the thirteenth century, the pacifist position was exemplified by such dissident sects as the Cathari (also known as Albigensians) and Waldenses; denounced, respectively, as heretics and schismatics, they challenged not only society's deviation from the monastic way of life but its ties to the emerging profit economy and the centralizing tendencies of church and state. By the early fourteenth century, the rivalry between emperor and pope also revived the utopian tradition, but with opposite results. Seeking, not unlike the canon lawyers, to restrict the use of force to some central authority, intellectuals like Dante (*De monarchia,* 1310–1311?) and Marsilius of Padua (*Defensor pacis,* 1324) advocated a peace that would be defined in strictly secular terms and entrusted to an ideal state or monarch who would wield the sword against both internal and external foes. Eventually, the sectarian pacifists came to accept the utopian position that the rejection of violence was within man's historical potential, and in the modern era, the two traditions have moved into an alliance in support of the political activism of peace churches and world-order movements alike. But tied to a moral tradition that insisted on the persistence of evil and the need to curb it by force, the advocates of the just-war doctrine held with neither the separatism from an evil world pursued in sectarian pacifism nor the utopian notion that there would ultimately be no place for force in a perfectly structured universal state. Both church and secular authorities perceived the two traditions as rivals, with the pacifist sects, in particular, seen as deadly threats from the lay community. These threats had to be co-opted or eliminated, if necessary through the police actions of the peace campaigns.

As to the programs' inherent limitations, one must remember, first, that Germanic custom defined political status in terms of a man's right to bear arms. Thus, the nobles' claim on the use of force legitimized not only their social position and chivalric code but medieval government itself. The rise of a new merchant class only added to this tradition the practical need to arm the burghers (as earlier, the peasants) in the pursuit of war *or* peace. Second, the movements reached only parts of Europe—primarily the remnants of the Carolingian Empire—and their immediate impact was variable, at best. In consequence, they had to be complemented by other social mechanisms and control devices that ranged from the internalization of morality and the substitution of trading for "raiding" to the more obvious arbitration, *veme,* and inquisition, and extended, lastly, to a tightening of military discipline, internal and external colonization, poor laws, marriage alliances, and the formalization of relations between states. (The role of the *veme* remains controversial and unexplored. The *veme* constituted an initially open, and later clandestine, organization of Westphalian freeholders who, by the thirteenth century, were imposing and executing their judgments—primarily in capital cases— where they deemed official prosecution to have broken down. The *veme* thus served as a typical surrogate for the state's failing power to enforce the law.) Finally, one must realize that the official peace campaigns were never meant, or claimed, to be the equivalent of the social reform and peace movements the West has come to expect since the nineteenth century. Knights and priests coexisted in a symbiotic relationship, and their notions of justice and order remained delimited within the confines of feud, penance, and just war. Thus, the programs were seen as a tool to buttress the social and political status quo and to strengthen the hands of the secular powers, if need be through holy war.

Lastly, the campaigns were circumscribed by the impact and exigencies of the "medieval renewal" of which they were so integral a part. Between the eleventh and thirteenth centuries, Europe ended its period of gestation and, in a series of cultural, political, and socioeconomic transformations, changed from a Mediterranean culture into Western civilization. Against a background of population growth, intellectual and artistic ferment, expanding trade, technological innovation and improving material conditions, classical, Germanic, and Christian traditions coalesced to bring into being new social classes and new economic and political institutions, together with the new ways of life and legal systems these entailed. More secular, more innovative and, above all, more dynamic, this new society found its most characteristic and most potent expression in the concept of an independent, systematized, and rational jurisprudence integrated into a sovereign, centralized, and hierarchic state.

The Crucial Catalyst It was against the background of these competing and often conflicting forces that the peace campaigns became a constituent part of historical change, the conduit for the

modern world's dominant concepts of justice and order, its civil law tradition, the law of international organizations, and international law. They did so, in essence, in two stages. Confronted, in the tenth century, with the problem of limiting the availability and permissibility of arms, the ecclesiastical authorities opted for building on the established legal order to integrate their concept of peace into Europe's broadly evolving social system. That concept was defined by Augustine's "well-ordered concord of civic obedience and civic rule," and its instrument was to be the peace campaigns. The programs were to provide a "new way to God" by pursuing the service of God (implying a close association with ecclesiastic interests, whether pastoral, liturgical, economic, or political in nature) and the service of the king (which was closely associated with the political and economic interests of the princes). Implemented in conjunction with Augustine's notion of the justified use of force, this approach not only dictated the sanctions—ecclesiastical and temporal—imposed under the peace campaigns but also gave the latter a key role in bringing about the merger of Germanic and Christian notions of justice and order, raising public and individual consciousness, teaching nobles and commoners to internalize peaceful values, and awakening the lay populace to the possibilities of self-help.

But then, from the late eleventh into the fourteenth centuries, the peace programs became themselves tools of that wide-ranging institutionalization of superior authority that was the political hallmark of the medieval renewal. With the quickening of social and geographic mobility, new secular forces and values came into being, above all stirrings of class consciousness, egalitarian attitudes, and new contests over legal and political control; and as successive generations of jurists and bureaucrats used the peace campaigns to interfere in "received" law and legal systems, the notion that the law is a living body, consciously created and distinct from custom and religious doctrine, began to gain in credibility. Extralegal violence slowly gave way to lawsuits and courtroom pleadings, while the maintenance of peace through the control of violence and government through the administration of justice came to be universally accepted as the ruler's principal tasks. Peace, in short, came to be redefined and managed in political terms as orderly sociocultural change entrusted to a legal system designed and guaranteed by a superior authority to facilitate the ongoing, mutual accommodation of society's cultures and interest groups.

Thus, the new elites and their constituents finally gained the control their interests required—"leadership in war, protection of property, mechanisms for resolution of disputes, some minimal level of peace and personal security," even as they had to abandon their search for a "higher" order and justice, and freedom from arms and strife (Kaeuper, p. 120). Both sets of ideals were found to be unattainable, if not undesirable, and while the first yielded to the principle of equality before the law, the second was all but abandoned. By the late sixteenth century, all leading European jurists—Jean Bodin in France, Alberico Gentili in England, Franciscus de Victoria in Spain—were coming to endorse the notion that the state was the supreme judge of its interests ("A war is just when it is necessary," as Machiavelli had put it), and as the *ius ad bellum* was turning into *compétence de guerre,* the precepts of right cause, right authority, and right intent were compromised beyond repair. Moreover, the balance that had prevailed between *ius ad bellum* and *ius in bello* from the late Middle Ages through the neo-scholastic just-war theorists saw a decisive shift. Instead of focusing on the legitimacy of war itself, the nascent theories of international law concentrated on the restraints to be observed once war broke out. In addition, Vattel took up the tradition of noncombatant immunity, stating it in terms of secular values, and elaborated it into a broadened *ius in bello* that extended the immunity of noncombatant status to the conditions of civil life.

This, then, was essentially the form in which the doctrine of *iustum bellum* has come down through the last three hundred years, to dominate both Christian ethics and international law. To be sure, there have been efforts to recover a truncated *ius ad bellum* in the twentieth century, via the League of Nations Covenant, the Kellogg-Briand Pact, and the United Nations Charter; but taken together, these have done little more than resolve the question of justifiable war into one of first (aggressive) versus second (defensive) use of force. In the main, the quest for peace continues to focus on the question of what weapons may be permissible in warfare and against whom they may be employed—an issue pursued assiduously from the General Orders no. 100 of the Union army in the Civil War, through the Geneva Conventions defining a "humanitarian" law of war and the Hague conferences, with their restraints on the use of certain weapons and means of war, to the arms control and disarmament conferences of the present. And it is here, still in the realm of *ius in bello,* that the modern just-war doctrine continues to find its vindication and most palpable success, most notably in a broadening, worldwide consensus based on the principle of discrimination (with emphasis on the treatment of prisoners of war, the sick and wounded, and civilians) and the principle of proportionality (especially with regard to keeping local conflicts from escalating toward nuclear war).

BIBLIOGRAPHY

Among the works drawn on most extensively in this study, the following are especially well suited to serve as points of departure for the examination of medieval warfare, peace movements, and arms control.

Basic References At the core of any inquiry into the historical dimensions of the peace campaigns stand five massive surveys: DOLOROSA KENNELLY, *The Peace and Truce of God: Fact or Fiction?* (Ph.D. diss., Berkeley, Calif., 1962) and HARTMUT HOFFMANN, *Gottesfriede und Treuga Dei* (Stuttgart, 1964) for the early centuries; JOACHIM GERNHUBER, *Die Landfriedensbewegung in Deutschland bis zum Mainzer Landfrieden von 1235* (Bonn, 1952), HEINZ ANGERMEIER, *Königtum und Landfriede im deutschen Spätmittelalter* (München 1966) and RICHARD W. KAEUPER, *War, Justice, and Public Order* (Oxford, 1988) for the later Middle Ages. Another four works are basic to an evaluation of the just war theory and its role within the Western moral tradition: JAMES TURNER JOHNSON, *Ideology, Reason, and the Limitation of War* (Princeton, 1975), *Just War Tradition and the Restraint of War* (Princeton, 1981), and *The Quest for Peace* (Princeton, 1987); and FREDERICK H. RUSSELL, *The Just War in the Middle Ages* (Cambridge, 1975). HAROLD JOSEPH BERMAN, *Law and Revolution* (Cambridge, Mass., 1983) and PHILIPPE CONTAMINE, *War in the Middle Ages* (New York, 1984) are indispensable for exploring the legal and military institutions of medieval Europe.

Specialized Sources A second group of works is valuable for providing an introduction to some of the more specialized aspects of this study. On the cultural, political, and socioeconomic features of medieval life, see KARL BOSL, *Die Grundlagen der* *modernen Gesellschaft im mittelalterlichen Europa* (Stuttgart, 1972); DONALD S. DETWILER, *Germany: A Short History* (Carbondale, Ill., 1976); GEORGES DUBY, *The Chivalrous Society,* Cynthia Postan, trans. (Berkeley, Calif., 1977); ROLF SPRANDEL, *Verfassung und Gesellschaft im Mittelalter* (2d ed., Paderborn, 1978); ROBERT FOSSIER, *Enfance de l'Europe* (Paris, 1982); WILLIAM R. COOK and RONALD B. HERZMAN, *The Medieval World View* (New York, 1983); and PATRICK J. GEARY, *Before France and Germany* (New York, 1988). On legal and judicial matters, see MICHAEL R. WEISSER, *Crime and Punishment in Early Modern Europe* (rev. ed., Brighton, Sussex, 1982) and JOHN HENRY MERRYMAN, *The Civil Law Tradition* (2d ed., Stanford, Calif., 1985); and on doctrinal aspects of military strategy, see THOMAS PATRICK MURPHY, ed., *The Holy War* (Columbus, Ohio, 1976). On issues affecting the civilian and clerical/monastic sectors of medieval society, see FRIEDRICH PRINZ, *Klerus und Krieg im früheren Mittelalter* (Stuttgart, 1971); LESTER K. LITTLE, *Religious Poverty and the Profit Economy in Medieval Europe* (Ithaca, N.Y., 1978); and RICHARD S. HARTIGAN, *The Forgotten Victim* (Chicago, 1982). On officially sanctioned violence against deviants and dissidents, see R. I. MOORE, *The Formation of a Persecuting Society: Power and Deviance in Western Europe 950–1250* (New York, 1987). Still stimulating remains the work of BERNHARD TÖPFER, especially *Volk und Kirche zur Zeit der beginnenden Gottesfriedensbewegung in Frankreich* (Berlin, 1957), which explored the intellectual and social dimensions of the peace campaigns from a Marxist point of view; and that of ROGER BONNAUD-DELAMARE, from which only an unpublished doctoral thesis, *L'idée de paix au XIe et XIIe siècle* (Paris, 1945) and scattered essays have emerged.

Synopses For synoptic purposes, the following articles have proven particularly helpful: LUBOMIR GLEIMAN, "Some Remarks on the Origin of the Treuga Dei," *Études d'histoire litteraire et doctrinale* 17 (1962): 117–137; H. E. J. COWDREY, "The Peace and Truce of God in the Eleventh Century," *Past and Present* 46 (February 1970): 42–67; R. A. MARKUS, "Saint Augustine's Views on the Just War," in W. J. SHEILS, ed., *The Church and War* (Oxford,

1983): 1–14: R. LANDES and F. PAXTON, "Pax Dei," in *World Encyclopedia of Peace* (Oxford, 1986): 168–171; R. I. MOORE, "Family, Community, and Cult on the Eve of Gregorian Reform," *Transactions of the Royal Historical Society,* ser. 5, 30 (1980): 49–69; and UDO HEYN, "Pax et Iustitia: Arms Control, Disarmament, and the Legal System in the Medieval Reich," *Peace and Change* 8, no. 1 (Spring 1982): 23–35; "Arms Limitation and the Search for Peace in Medieval Europe," *War and Society* 2, no. 2 (September 1984): 1–18, and "Peace Movements in Medieval Europe: A Reappraisal," *Interdisciplinary Peace Research* 2, no. 2 (October/November 1990): 23–35 (expanded reprint in *Occasional Paper* 20 [1992], Center for the Study of Armament and Disarmament, CSULA, Los Angeles, Calif.), which contain extensive bibliographies.

Primary Sources Primary materials for the Peace and Truce of God are sparse, in contrast to the abundance that is still in existence from the high and late Middle Ages and, in particular, the Peace of the Realm. Most of these sources may now be found in collections of conciliar acts, peace edicts, declarations of feuds, and the correspondence between emperors, nobility, cities and estates; among these, J. D. MANSI ET AL., *Sacrorum Conciliorum Nova Et Amplissima Collectio* (Florence, Venice, Paris, and Arnhem, 1759–1927) and the *Constitutiones et acta publica imperatorum et regum* of the *Monumenta Germaniae Historica* (Hannover/Berlin 1826–) stand out. In addition, the reader may want to consult hagiographies, collections of sermons, and, above all, chronicles and legal textbooks as exemplified by ADHEMAR DE CHABANNES, *Chronique,* J. CHAVANON ed. (Paris, 1897), RAOUL GLABER, *Les Cinq Livres de ses histoires,* 900–1044, M. PROU, ed. (Paris, 1886), or Gratian, *Decretum,* in E. FRIEDBERG, ed., *Corpus Iuris Canonici,* vol. 1 (1879, repr. Graz, 1959). LUDWIG HUBERTI, *Die Friedensordnungen in Frankreich* (Ansbach, 1892) remains the most useful compilation of original canons, resolutions, and oaths passed at the Peace councils and assemblies, although its chronology should be checked against the more reliable dates in Gernhuber's and Toepfer's works.

The Rush-Bagot Agreement

Demilitarizing the Great Lakes, 1817 to the Present

—————————————— ◯ ——————————————

RON PURVER

See also Canada; Demilitarization and Neutralization Through World War II; Great Britain; *and* The United States. *The* Rush-Bagot Agreement *is excerpted in Volume III.*

The Rush-Bagot Agreement is one of the longest-lasting arms control arrangements in history. In its original form, it called for the virtual removal of armed warships belonging to the United States and Great Britain (and later, Canada) from the Great Lakes. Despite several rocky episodes, the spirit of the pact still exists.

In recent times, however, the agreement has undeservedly acquired a rather poor reputation among many historians and strategic analysts on the grounds that it was repeatedly violated and may have been unnecessary, given the "natural" friendly relations between the United States and Great Britain/Canada. Some of this criticism was a reaction to traditional exaggeration of its beneficial impact, by early historians and especially by peace groups who frequently invoked it as a shining example for the rest of the world to emulate.

Charles P. Stacey effectively demolished the myth that the Rush-Bagot Agreement more or less single-handedly inaugurated an era of unrelenting good-will between the United States and Great Britain, bringing an abrupt end to competitive arming in the Great Lakes region, on land as well as in the water. Stacey pointed out that, in fact, the building of land fortifications along the United States–Canadian border actually accelerated in the years after the signing of the agreement and did not end until about 1871, over a half century later.

Nevertheless, given their own predilections, critics may have overreacted—much as did the earlier peace groups—in their modern negative assessments. For as Richard Van Alstyne has written: "The Agreement did . . . remove the threat of sudden, offensive operations that the presence of a naval force would have facilitated" (pp. 95–96).

EARLY PROPOSALS FOR DEMILITARIZATION

Proposals for demilitarization of the Great Lakes were advanced diplomatically on at least three separate occasions prior to the negotiations that resulted in the Rush-Bagot Agreement of 1817. In 1783, U.S. diplomat John Adams raised the idea during the Paris talks that ended the Revolutionary War. John Jay, at the suggestion of Secretary of the Treasury Alexander Hamilton, reintroduced the notion during negotiations on an Anglo-American "Treaty of Amity and Commerce" in September 1794. The Jay Treaty, as it was named, was advanced again during the negotiations in Ghent, Belgium, to end the War of 1812.

The British appear to have rejected the idea in the first two instances. In the third, each side initially sought exclusive military control of the Great Lakes, the Americans by an outright cession of Canada and the British by one-sided disarmament of the Americans. The latter proposal led to a lengthy debate, with the British arguing that they were the weaker power on the North American continent; consequently, they were less capable of acting offensively and more exposed to sudden invasion. The Americans in turn denied that they enjoyed any local military superiority or had any designs on Canada; in any event, they insisted that their commerce—hostage to a superior British oceanic fleet—was sufficient to deter any such action. Throughout this period, and well into the nineteenth century, the British had exclusive responsibility for foreign and defense relations affecting Canada, which achieved a quasi-independent government only in 1849, when it assumed responsibility for domestic affairs.

In the end, both negotiating teams at Ghent appear to have been moving toward a mutual demilitarization of the area. In fact, in a draft of instructions written in July 1814 but marked "not used," British Foreign Secretary Lord Castlereagh had proposed a mutual undertaking not to construct any warships on the Great Lakes and to "entirely dismantle" those already in commission or under construction. This appears to have been the British fallback position hinted at in conversations with the Americans but never formally offered during the negotiations. As a result, the Treaty of Ghent, ratified by the U.S. Congress on 17 February 1815, contained no such provisions.

NEGOTIATION OF THE 1817 AGREEMENT

The War of 1812 had demonstrated the critical strategic significance of the Great Lakes for both Canada and the United States. The war had also witnessed, especially toward its end, a tremendous buildup of naval power in the area by both sides. The British flagship on the lakes was a "three-decker" more powerful than the *Victory,* Admiral Lord Nelson's flagship in the Battle of Trafalgar during the Napoleanic Wars. Meanwhile, two even larger vessels were under construction at Kingston. For their part, the Americans were building two warships that would have been the largest in the world.

Nevertheless, the drive to economize made itself felt immediately upon signature of the peace treaty. On 27 February 1815, the U.S. Congress authorized the president "to cause all armed vessels of the United States on the lakes to be sold or laid up, except such as he may deem necessary to enforce

proper execution of revenue laws; such vessels being first divested of their armament, tackle, and furniture, which are to be carefully preserved" (Callahan, "Agreement of 1817," p. 374). Accordingly, construction was stopped on the two U.S. "three-deckers," the *New Orleans* and *Chippewa,* at Sackett's Harbor on Lake Ontario, although they were carefully protected by shiphouses so that they could be completed in the future if necessary. According to one source, by late 1816 all the U.S. vessels were laid up or dismantled except for a brig of eighteen guns and three small schooners used for transport.

A considerable, though less sweeping, reduction followed on the British side. By the spring of 1816, the largest warships had been "laid up and housed over" at Kingston on Lake Ontario; construction of the two new ships of the line had been stopped; and the remaining vessels—including six small schooners used for transport—had few, if any, guns mounted.

Despite the peace treaty, a number of contentious issues continued to plague Anglo-American relations in the Great Lakes region, including unrest among the Indians and the desertion of British soldiers to the U.S. side. The result was a series of unhappy incidents, some involving naval vessels. The U.S. ambassador in London, John Quincy Adams, reported in August 1815 that the British were determined to increase their naval strength on the lakes. Although some historians believe this threat to have been largely exaggerated, Secretary of State James Monroe's subsequent initiative for demilitarization of the lakes is usually attributed to it. Thus, on 16 November 1815, Monroe told Adams that the president wished him to propose an "arrangement" by which the two governments would confine their naval forces on the lakes "to a certain moderate number, of armed vessels, and the smaller the number, the more agreeable to him; or to abstain altogether from an armed force beyond that used for the revenue" (Manning, vol. 1, p. 235). In Monroe's words: "It is evident, if each party augments it's [sic] force there, with a view to obtain the ascendancy over the other, that vast expence will be incurred, and the danger of collision augmented in like degree" (Manning, vol. 1, p. 235).

Adams accordingly approached Castlereagh on 25 January 1816, referring to "the increase of the British Armaments upon the Canadian Lakes, since the Peace" as one of the most dangerous sources of disagreement between the two countries, and conveying his government's proposal for a mutual reduction of forces, the greater the better. Castlereagh in reply appeared somewhat ambivalent on the question. He agreed that warships on the lakes during peacetime were "ridiculous and absurd" but invoked the British argument during the Ghent negotiations about their need for exclusive military control. Although Castlereagh promised to submit the proposal to the cabinet, Adams was pessimistic about its chances.

Thus, he was surprised when, at a meeting on 9 April, Castlereagh accepted in principle the U.S. proposal. Specifically, the British minister proposed to "lay up in Ordinary" all the armed vessels then on the Lakes, except those "necessary to convey troops occasionally from Station to Station" (Manning, vol. 1, p. 794). Castlereagh suggested concluding an agreement then and there, but Adams declined, pleading the need for further instructions. However, the American did state his understanding that it was "now agreed that no new or additional force should be commenced upon the Lakes on either side for the present" (Manning, vol. 1, pp. 794–5). The two men also agreed that the formulation of an "express Article" on the subject of naval armaments should be referred to negotiators in Washington.

On 23 April 1816, Castlereagh wrote the British minister in Washington, Charles Bagot, informing him of the conversations, authorizing him to take "ad referendum" any precise U.S. proposal, and suggesting that an informal understanding to "abstain from exertion in that quarter" might be easier to achieve than "positive stipulations" (Cruikshank, p. 162). Still ignorant of the British acceptance of the earlier proposal, President James Madison wrote Adams on 10 May that Congress would almost certainly order new U.S. construction if Britain did not give up her (nonexistent) building program. A few days later Monroe wrote Adams that the president would be satisfied with a mere freeze on the existing levels of force on both sides.

After receiving his instructions from London, Bagot passed on Castlereagh's suggestion of an informal understanding and suggested to Monroe that the subject be dealt with only after a "more important" Atlantic fisheries agreement had first been concluded. However, Monroe insisted on a formal agreement and gained President Madison's concurrence that it should be given priority over the fisheries question.

Monroe had several conversations with Bagot during July 1816, leading to a proposal embodied in a letter from the American on 2 August 1816. It called for a limit on naval forces of one vessel each on Lakes Ontario and Champlain, and two vessels for each side on the upper lakes (though not named, these were later understood to include Erie, Huron, Michigan, and Superior). Each vessel was not to exceed 100 tons or carry armament of more than one eighteen-pound cannon; all other "armed vessels on those Lakes" would be "forthwith dismantled," and neither party would "build or arm any other vessel on the Shores of those Lakes." The naval force retained would be "restricted in its duty, to the protection of its Revenue Laws, the transportation of troops, and goods, and to such other Services, as will in no respect interfere with the armed vessels of the other party" (Manning, vol. 1, p. 248).

It was not until early in the new year that Castlereagh notified Bagot of the government's acceptance of the U.S. terms and authorized a formal exchange of notes on the subject, incorporating the U.S. proposals of 2 August. By the time this dispatch had arrived from England (in late April), Monroe had become president and Richard Rush was acting secretary of state awaiting the return of Adams from London to assume that post.

The exchange of notes that came to be known as the "Rush-Bagot Agreement" took place on 28 and 29 April 1817. Monroe, unsure of the constitutional status of the documents, neglected to submit them to the Senate until almost a year later, on 6 April 1818, after some prodding by the British (who evidently believed it necessary under the U.S. Constitution). The Senate gave its unanimous consent on 16 April 1818, and the agreement was officially proclaimed by the president on 28 April of that year.

ISSUES OF COMPLIANCE

The agreement was put into effect almost immediately upon the formal exchange of notes in 1817. The British neglected to maintain in commission even the small fleet permitted by the agreement, and the United States had reduced its designated four vessels to just two by 1820. However, the agreement had called only for the dismantling, not the outright destruction, of the existing naval vessels. Accordingly, those major vessels, most of which had already been "laid up," were left in that state, ready to be refitted and rearmed if necessary, while the unfinished three-deckers also remained, subject to future completion if desired. Well-provisioned naval dockyards were also maintained on both sides for some years, the U.S. one at Sackett's Harbor being the second most expensive of the navy's thirteen yards nationwide. The British continued to repair their vessels at Kingston until 1831 and to maintain its dockyard until 1834. According to one source, in 1825 all the U.S. vessels were sold except the *New Orleans* and *Chippewa,* which were on the stocks, under cover, at Sackett's Harbor. The latter had been sold by 1834, but the former remained on the U.S. Navy list until 1882.

The Canadian Rebellions

The first major challenge to the Rush-Bagot Agreement came during the Canadian Rebellions of 1837–1838. By this time, although Canada had not yet achieved full self-government or control over foreign policy and defense matters, Canadian voices, often in the form of officials appointed by London, were beginning to be heard in the debates regarding the Rush-Bagot Agreement. In order to help put down the unrest, which included border raids aided and abetted by U.S. sympathizers, the British authorized the procurement of a number of armed steamers and schooners exceeding the Rush-Bagot limits. While seeking to reassure the Americans that the vessels were intended strictly for defensive (counterinsurgency) purposes, the Canadian governor-in-chief, Lord Durham, complained to London about the restrictiveness of the agreement. The colonial secretary replied that the termination or modification of the accord was under consideration but that it should not be violated in the meantime. By this time, however, the British naval force on Lake Ontario alone already consisted of two armed-steamers and three armed-schooners.

Secretary of State John Forsyth complained of British disregard for the agreement, although he did not issue a formal protest. On 25 November 1838, the British minister in Washington, Henry Fox, assured him that the additional force would "be discontinued at the earliest possible period" after the disturbances had ceased (Manning, vol. 3, p. 475). The Americans appeared satisfied with this explanation and issued no formal reply to it. Given the lack of U.S. protest, London decided it was better not to raise the issue of the possible modification or termination of the agreement.

The Americans let the matter rest until the fall of 1839, when Forsyth verbally informed Fox that, given the end of the rebellion, the president expected the British force to be reduced once again. Fox promised to pass on the message, observing that if the winter passed without further rebel activity, there would be no need for either government to maintain a force beyond the Rush-Bagot limits. Meanwhile, the British naval preparations had stirred considerable alarm in Congress, resulting in a flurry of calls for corresponding U.S. action. The Van Buren administration fended these off by producing Fox's assurances of November 1838, together with reports by American military commanders (one of whom confessed that he had never heard of the Rush-Bagot Agreement, and might himself have been guilty of technically violating it) suggesting that the British "threat" was greatly exaggerated.

In May 1840, however, the Americans discovered that a 500-ton ship, the *Minos,* was to be launched at Chippewa in Upper Canada in June, with construction of a second ship to follow. In September 1841, Governor William H. Seward of New York complained to Secretary of State Daniel Webster that the United States should reply in kind, evidently prompting Webster to write Fox on 25 September 1841. He reminded him of his assurances of November 1838; raised the issue of the latest British construction, which he described as "far exceeding" the Rush-Bagot limits; and asked for assurances that the new vessels would be used for strictly defensive purposes only. Fox confirmed that the assurances of 1838 still applied, but this did not prevent Webster from writing the British minister again on 29 November 1841. This time the American took a harder line, declaring that "rigid compliance with the terms of the Convention, by both Parties, can alone accomplish the purposes intended by it" and that "it cannot be expected that either party should acquiesce in the preparation by the other, of naval means beyond the limit fixed in the stipulation, and which are of a nature fitting them for offensive as well as defensive use, upon the ground of a vague and indefinite apprehension of future danger" (Manning, vol. 3, p. 158). It was surely no coincidence that, just two days earlier, the U.S. secretary of the navy had ordered the construction of a new, 500-ton steamer for service on Lake Erie.

London did not reply to the U.S. demarche until March the following year, when Foreign Secretary Lord Aberdeen explained to Webster that the unsettled conditions in Canada required continued temporary deviation from the agreement, but that

Britain would return to faithful compliance "as soon as it could be done with safety to Canada" (Callahan, p. 122).

According to historian James Callahan, the British force had probably been reduced to the Rush-Bagot limits by 1843. In that same year, however, the U.S. Navy launched the 498-ton "iron, side-wheel bark," the *Michigan,* in Erie, Pennsylvania. The ship was designed to carry two eight-inch guns and four thirty-two-pound cannons. This time it was Britain's turn to protest. On 23 July 1844, the British minister in Washington, Richard Pakenham, wrote to Secretary of State John Calhoun complaining that the U.S. naval force on Lakes Ontario, Erie, and Huron "at this moment considerably exceeds" the limits of Rush-Bagot. In reply, Calhoun on 5 September passed on a letter he had received from navy secretary John Young Mason that, while insisting that the United States had not intended to violate the agreement, charged that the British continued to maintain a force in excess of its limits. Mason's letter suggested that the Rush-Bagot Agreement was technologically obsolete—given the introduction of steam vessels, which could not be limited to only 100 tons—and that it might therefore be revised.

Meanwhile, the British government had been considering how to respond to the launching of the *Michigan.* Lord Aberdeen apparently favored replying in kind by building up to the U.S. level, and then negotiating a new agreement that would presumably freeze forces at the higher level. Colonial Secretary Lord Stanley questioned whether the agreement extended to steamers but believed the U.S. action had violated at least the spirit of the agreement. He proposed accepting an offer from a shipbuilding company to construct a certain number of trading steamers that could be readily converted to warships in time of emergency, and Prime Minister Sir Robert Peel agreed. It is unclear whether the British went ahead with this plan, but both sides evidently intended to convert merchant ships in the event of war. When the *Michigan* began cruising in 1844, it was armed with only one of the six guns her plans called for, reportedly to meet the conditions of the Rush-Bagot Agreement and to satisfy the British minister.

British ministers raised the issue of the *Michigan* with the American authorities on at least two later occasions. In December 1856 they elicited the admission that the ship "exceeded a little" the size limitation of the agreement but was still restricted to a single eighteen-pound gun. In April 1857, in response to another British demarche about the *Michigan,* Secretary of State Lewis Cass contended that "the ship in question was not, in fact, a vessel of war" (Callahan, p. 133).

In August 1861 the *Michigan* was the subject of one final British protest. Secretary of State Seward replied that the vessel was used only for recruiting and training purposes and therefore was not considered a violation of the Rush-Bagot Agreement. He nevertheless invited British views on the subject, but the latter were not forthcoming. Historians have speculated that London decided to overlook the excess tonnage of the *Michigan* in view of the fact that it remained the sole U.S. warship on the lakes. As it turned out, the vessel (later renamed the *Wolverine*) operated on the Great Lakes until 1923, was not stricken from the navy list until 1943, and was scrapped only in 1949.

The Civil War Years   The United States Civil War brought new challenges to the Rush-Bagot Agreement. Whereas the Canadian authorities in 1838–1839 had been harassed by raids originating on the other side of the border, in the 1860s the tables were turned and the Union found itself subject to similar attacks from Confederate sympathizers making use of Canadian territory. Also at this time, some Americans argued that the opening of ship canals at Welland, Ontario, and Lachine, Quebec—for the first time enabling small ocean-going vessels to enter the Great Lakes—had upset the Anglo-American naval balance of power in the region.

The construction of several new U.S. revenue cutters (small, one-masted sailing vessels) for service on Lake Erie prompted a British inquiry in May 1864. Secretary of State Seward replied that the cutters did not belong to the navy and were intended solely to prevent smuggling, but the British minister, Lord Lyons, was not satisfied. His contention that the vessels would still violate the agreement was met with the threat of U.S. abrogation on account of the smuggling problem.

Invoking the alleged threat posed by the Canadian canals, the U.S. House of Representatives on 18 June 1864 passed a resolution authorizing and directing the president to give the required formal notice of his intention to terminate the Rush-Bagot Agreement. The Senate at first failed to consider the resolution, however, and Seward assured the British that there was no present intention to do so. The official American attitude soon changed, however, after a group of Confederates from Canada commandeered a steamer on Lake Erie in a vain attempt to capture the *Michigan*. On 26 September 1864, Seward informed the British that the United States deemed it necessary to increase temporarily its "observing force" on the Great Lakes. The following month, another group raided St. Albans, Vermont, from across the Canadian border.

Finally, in November 1864, the Americans gave notice that at the end of six months, they would "deem themselves at liberty to increase the naval armament upon the lakes, if, in their judgment, the condition of affairs in that quarter shall require it" (U.S. Congress, p. 51). As several historians have noted, this fell somewhat short of a formal denunciation of the agreement. Seward evidently hoped that the British would good-naturedly accept its "temporary suspension," and in fact Foreign Secretary Lord Russell, while reminding Washington that Britain, too, would be free to exceed the limits after the expiry of six months, called for the agreement to be renewed once peace was restored. For its part, Congress insisted on passing a resolution (signed by the president on 9 February 1865) approving the notice of termination. However, many congressmen hoped for an early renewal, while the U.S. minister in London, Charles Francis Adams, assured the British that, by this time, the contemplated increase had been rendered unnecessary. Only a month later, on 8 March 1865, immediately after hearing that Confederate commissioners had been recalled from British North America and that the Canadian Parliament had appropriated money to compensate for the losses at St. Albans suffered in the confederate raid of the previous October, Seward instructed Adams to withdraw the notice of termination.

First Attempts at Revision Little more was heard of the agreement for over two decades. The British complained in late 1865 about a new U.S. deployment of revenue cutters but were assured that their armament would not exceed the Rush-Bagot limit. In response to raids against Canada by the Irish-American Fenians, in the late 1860s the Canadian authorities brought small British gunboats up the St. Lawrence canals and converted some lake steamers into improvised fighting ships. This temporarily created a force in excess of that allowed by the agreement, but apparently the United States did not protest. In 1878, R. W. Thompson, secretary of the Navy, proposed to replace the *Michigan* with a more modern vessel but was turned down on the grounds that a new vessel might infringe upon the Rush-Bagot Agreement.

In the early 1890s, Washington came under pressure from Great Lakes shipbuilding interests to modify or abrogate the agreement in order to allow them to compete in what was becoming a rapid expansion of the U.S. Navy. On 2 May 1892, Secretary of State James G. Blaine proposed to the British Minister in Washington, Sir Julian Pauncefote, that an "explanatory article" be added to the agreement permitting unrestricted shipbuilding on the Great Lakes as long as all revenue cruisers or warships remained unarmed and unarmored while in the area and provided that such vessels be removed from the lakes within a specified time after completion of their hulls.

The Canadian minister of marine and fisheries objected and the British Admiralty, reluctant to commit itself to the defense of the lakes, also favored preserving the original agreement. Thus, Washington was persuaded to drop the subject for the time being. However, in a report to the U.S. Congress on 7 December 1892, Secretary of State John Foster claimed that it was "tacitly understood on both sides" that revenue cutters did not fall within the Rush-Bagot limitations, since Britain had not raised any question in this regard since November 1865. Although his report ended with another call for a formal revision of the agreement, Congress was opposed on the grounds that it might lead to its abrogation. The United States, with its larger population and higher proportion of commerce in the Great Lakes region, had more to lose from the unbridled arms race that could result.

In 1895, a deterioration in Anglo-American relations over the British-Venezuelan boundary dispute and reports that Canada was building vessels for easy conversion in case of war led some Americans, including the mayor of Detroit, to call for outright abrogation of the agreement and the creation of a full-fledged Great Lakes fleet. The storm soon passed, as the British backed down over Venezuela at the beginning of 1896. The dispute was finally settled in 1899.

The Ill-fated Joint High Commission Proposals Canadian concern arose again in early 1896 after London learned that Congress had authorized the construction of two steam revenue cutters of the first class (700–800 tons each, bearing modern guns) for service on the Great Lakes. Subsequently, in October 1897, the Canadian government learned that the U.S. Navy had deployed a second training vessel—the 900-ton *Yantic*—to join the *Michigan* on the lakes. And early the following year Congress appropriated funds for a new gunboat to replace the *Michigan*. The Senate Naval Affairs Committee considered that the proposed vessel would not violate the Rush-Bagot Agreement since it would take the place of one that had not been used for offensive purposes and had not disturbed the agreement since it was launched on the lakes in 1843. In London, the Colonial Defence Committee recommended "an amicable representation" to Washington, and Lord Pauncefote was authorized to raise the matter at a time of his own choosing.

Meanwhile, however, the U.S. Navy secretary was appealing to the secretary of state to relax the restrictions on Great Lakes shipbuilders. When Pauncefote raised the matter of the new gunboat in June, the secretary of state suggested that the continuation of the Rush-Bagot agreement be referred to an impending Joint High Commission on United States–Canadian relations. Although elements of Canadian public opinion vehemently objected to the idea of revising the agreement and subsequently allowing the transit of U.S. warships to the Atlantic, Prime Minister Sir Wilfrid Laurier was persuaded by the British that a treaty that put some restraints on the United States would be better than no treaty at all.

By December 1898, a draft agreement had been reached and approved by the Colonial Defense Committee. Under this agreement, each nation would have been permitted to maintain two 1,000-ton training vessels, each with no more than two four-inch guns and six lesser guns; and six 900-ton revenue cutters armed with a single 6-pounder rapid fire gun. In addition, naval vessels for the high seas could be built on the lakes as long as they were not armed while on the lakes; not more than one was completed at the same time; and they were transferred to the Atlantic "at as early a date as practicable," for which purpose they would "have passage through all intermediate waterways" (Canada, *Naval Vessels,* p. 86). As it turned out, however, the agreement fell victim to the general collapse of the Joint High Commission as a result of its failure to

resolve the Alaska boundary dispute. The United States was informed in May 1899 that Canada was unwilling to proceed further until the latter had been settled.

Era of the Training Vessels   Meanwhile, the United States had begun a long series of individual requests for the passage of naval training vessels through the Canadian canals in order to take up station on the lakes. By this time, although Canada still maintained no separate diplomatic representation abroad and did not possess its own Department of External Affairs, it had assumed de facto responsibility for some of its external relations, particularly with the United States. Thus, U.S. requests for passage were routed through the British ambassador in Washington and the authorities in London, but the latter considered themselves bound by the decisions of the Canadian cabinet. In January 1900, the U.S. asked that the 607-ton *Frolic* be allowed to pass through the Canadian canals unarmed to join the Ohio National Guard. After the Canadian minister of railways and canals judged that there appeared to be no "intention of using the yacht in contravention of the [1817] Convention," the cabinet granted the U.S. request, on condition that the vessel pass through the canals unarmed and its later use be confined to drills. Subsequent requests, in January 1901, April 1904, and June 1905, met with the same response. Thus, by the end of 1905, the United States maintained a Great Lakes fleet of no fewer than five training vessels. These vessels had a combined displacement of over 4,000 tons, and three of them were well armed: four were revenue cutters, all exceeding the Rush-Bagot limits; the fifth was the *Michigan*.

The United States made another halfhearted attempt at formal revision of the agreement in 1906 under the prodding of Secretary of State Elihu Root, who proposed to allow the construction of naval vessels for use elsewhere. Root's proposal was opposed by both British intelligence and Canadian Prime Minister Laurier, however, and the subject was dropped early the next year.

The year 1907 saw three separate U.S. requests for the transit of unarmed training vessels through the Canadian canals to join state militias. The first two requests were routinely approved, but the third—for a modern, heavily-armed vessel (with eight four-inch guns), the 1,371-ton *Nashville*—caused the British Foreign Office to take notice. The

British realized that the *Nashville* would make a total of nine U.S. warships on the lakes, as against just one Canadian training vessel. The Canadian cabinet granted its permission for the passage of the *Nashville,* on the usual conditions, but questions were beginning to be raised for the first time in the Canadian House of Commons.

When the U.S. State Department in April 1908 sought approval for "continuing permission" for one of the training vessels to alternate between Lakes Erie and Ontario through the Welland Canal, the cabinet in Ottawa refused, insisting that permission be sought on a case-by-case basis. Moreover, it asked the British ambassador in Washington, James Bryce, to call to the attention of the secretary of state, Elihu Root, the number of warships that had received such permission since 1900. Subsequently, in July, the British were informed that, in view of the Canadian attitude as conveyed by Bryce to Root, the State Department had begun refusing to pass on requests from the Great Lakes states for the establishment of new militia-training ships on the lakes.

The Canadians were thus mollified to some extent, but not for long. The *Nashville,* as it turned out, had never made it to the Great Lakes during 1908. When the United States renewed its request in April 1909, it—inexplicably—further requested permission for the ship's armament to be installed after her arrival at Chicago (previous requests had never mentioned the rearmament of vessels after they had transited the canals, although this was routinely done). Meanwhile, alarmed by reports of impending American naval maneuvers involving nine warships on Lake Erie, Prime Minister Laurier called on Ambassador Bryce to protest strongly. And, in the absence of a quick Canadian reply to the second *Nashville* request, the United States went ahead and sent the vessel through the canals, having it stop in Buffalo to be rearmed on its way to Chicago. The vessel's passage created a sensation among the Canadian public.

When the Canadian cabinet finally discussed the issue on 6 July, unaware of what had transpired, it decided to refuse the U.S. request to rearm the *Nashville.* However, arguing that the Americans had taken Canadian silence as tacit consent to the vessel's passage (and by implication, its arming), Ambassador Bryce stalled, pleading for the cabinet to reconsider. After he finally informed Ottawa that the rearming had already taken place, Laurier backed away from the notion of a formal protest

and asked Bryce merely to discuss the question of violations of the agreement with Philander Knox, the secretary of state, pointing out that "the Treaty [sic] must be not only maintained but lived up to" (Eayrs, p. 381). In November, Bryce reported back that he had spoken to President William Howard Taft, who had expressed complete understanding for the Canadian position and agreed not to request any more warships in excess of the Rush-Bagot limits.

In early 1911, the Americans dropped a request for an additional training vessel after Laurier had objected to it. Later that year Canadian permission was requested, and granted, for the substitution of one training ship by another, less capable vessel, but Laurier objected to U.S. plans for naval maneuvers on the Great Lakes and succeeded in having them cancelled. In March 1912 the Americans tested the waters again by advising Bryce that the navy proposed to allow Great Lakes shipbuilders to compete on a contract for a small gunboat that would be disassembled and shipped overland for reassembly and armament at a foreign port without actually being launched on the lakes at all. The State Department concurred in the navy's view that such construction would not violate the 1817 agreement. However, after Canadian Prime Minister Robert Laird Borden objected on the grounds that such vessels could be kept on the stocks for a number of years ready for use in case of war, Bryce was able to report that he had persuaded the navy not to open the competition to Great Lakes shipbuilders.

During World War I, but before the United States entered, Washington on two occasions requested changes in the status of its naval forces on the Great Lakes. In early 1916, a request for the stationing of two additional training vessels was dropped after the British ambassador correctly anticipated Canadian objections, while early the following year, the State Department withdrew a similar proposal for the introduction of two new militia vessels. However, according to James Eayrs, after the United States became a belligerent the request for increased armament was submitted and granted. In May 1917, the tables were turned as the Canadian authorities were forced to seek U.S. permission to install gun seatings and magazines in merchant vessels being built on the Great Lakes. The United States agreed, on condition that it not prejudice the Rush-Bagot Agreement or be considered a precedent, that it last only for the duration of the war, and that the vessels in question not be retained on the Great Lakes. During the war, the United States engaged in naval shipbuilding on the Great Lakes for the first time since 1817, with Henry Ford mass producing no fewer than fifty-five "eagle boats" on the River Rouge near Detroit.

Post–World War I Developments Soon after the end of World War I, the Canadian authorities again became concerned about American activities that appeared to violate the Rush-Bagot Agreement. Large numbers of U.S. warships were passing through the Great Lakes and the Canadian canals without Canadian permission having been obtained or sought. The cabinet considered the issue on 16 February 1921 and recommended that no armed vessels or unarmed warships be permitted to transit Canadian canals without permission. However, it decided not to protest formally the U.S. actions or the continued infringements of the Rush-Bagot Agreement's limits on the numbers, tonnage, and armament of stationed vessels. The Canadian decision was based on intelligence reports that the ships in question were of little naval value; the technical obsolescence of the agreement; and the fear that the Americans might in turn either abrogate, or demand a revision of, the accord—either of which would result in an increase of U.S. forces and stimulate public demands for corresponding action on the Canadian side.

By this time, Canadian autonomy in foreign and defense policy was well established, and the Canadian authorities were accustomed to dealing directly with their U.S. counterparts without the use of British intermediaries. Shortly after becoming Canadian prime minister in 1921, William Lyon Mackenzie King decided that it was time to revise and upgrade the agreement. He and his defense minister, George Graham, accordingly traveled to Washington for talks with Secretary of State Charles Evans Hughes on 12 July 1922. King explained that Canadians viewed with alarm the increase of U.S. warships on the Great Lakes to about sixteen, apart from revenue cutters. He warned that his government would be hard-pressed to resist the demand for a matching naval force of its own and proposed that the 1817 agreement be revised in the form of a new treaty. Canada, he said, would not object to (and, Graham added, might itself be interested in) the construction of warships on the Great Lakes for

use elsewhere, provided that they were unarmed until they had left the area.

Secretary Hughes, while expressing surprise at the Canadian concern, welcomed the initiative and asked for a draft of the proposed treaty. The latter was prepared almost immediately and forwarded to Washington in November 1922. The Americans responded in May 1923 with a counterdraft, which differed significantly from the Canadian proposal.

The Canadian draft prohibited all armed vessels except those used for "revenue and police duties"; no vessel designed, built, or used for naval purposes could enter the Great Lakes without prior permission; and the numbers, specifications, and armament of revenue and police craft would be subject to prior agreement. No limits on the numbers and specifications of unarmed training vessels were proposed.

The U.S. draft, on the other hand, permitted naval training vessels to be armed, but such vessels were never to "be used for hostile purposes on the Great Lakes—even in time of war" and their number, specifications, and armament were to be agreed upon mutually. By contrast, the number, specifications, and armament of revenue and police craft were not to be subject to prior agreement, although their armament was to be limited to that "appropriate to [their] purpose," and they, too, were never to "be used for hostile purposes—even in time of war." Finally, neither revenue and police craft nor naval training vessels were required to seek permission before entering the lakes.

The Canadian and U.S. drafts agreed that any new naval vessels built on the lakes for use elsewhere could not be armed until after they had left the area, which was to occur within six months of their launch date, and that information about the signing of the contract, their launch date, and their main dimensions would be made available promptly.

It was not until 8 October 1924 that the Canadian cabinet considered the U.S. draft. The Canadian chief of the defense staff, General J. H. MacBrien, characterized the pledge regarding nonuse in time of war as "not ... worth the paper it was written on" (Eayrs, p. 398), and he objected to the right of shipbuilding for use elsewhere. However, despite the U.S. refusal to disarm their naval training vessels or to subject their entry into the lakes to prior agreement, the Canadian Department of National Defense had practically no objection to the American draft. Accepting as well the U.S. refusal to subject the numbers, specifications, and armament of revenue or police vessels to prior agreement, it asked only for a confidential exchange of information on such parameters on a case-by-case basis.

With this sole amendment, the Canadian cabinet on 8 October 1924 agreed to return the draft to Washington "as being in the form acceptable to the Canadian Government." However, the following day the minister of national defence requested a delay in transmission of the draft, which was granted. Nothing further is found in the published diplomatic correspondence except a June 1925 note from Hughes's successor as secretary of state, Frank B. Kellogg, requesting a Canadian response to the American draft treaty of May 1923. It is unclear why the treaty project died at this point. When asked to look into the matter in 1932, the Canadian director of naval intelligence noted that Canada had made considerable concessions to the United States without getting anything in return, and that, in addition, there appeared to be no reason for drawing attention to a dormant question.

World War II Interpretations   During the World War II era, the Rush-Bagot Agreement found itself subjected to a series of interpretations relaxing its terms for purposes of the war effort. Secretary of State Cordell Hull believed that actual modification or replacement of the agreement was undesirable in view of its longstanding importance as a symbol of friendly bilateral relations between the two countries, and the Canadian authorities agreed. In June 1939, Hull sought and won Canadian support for the following points: that the United States be allowed to maintain all five existing training vessels on the Great Lakes, without increasing their number (except for those used as "immobile" floating barracks); that the Rush-Bagot provisions limiting numbers of ships in specific lakes be relaxed, allowing freedom of stationing and movement throughout the basin; that the United States be allowed to place two four-inch guns on each of three of its training vessels for target practice (which would be restricted to its own territorial waters) provided that it removed all other armaments and dismantled the guns except in the summer training period; and that naval construction for use elsewhere be permitted, provided that full information was exchanged and that the ships were immediately removed from the Great Lakes on completion and remained unarmed while in the area. Canada insisted on reciprocal rights

and also that the United States ask permission in each case for passage through Canadian waters to the sea.

A little over a year later, on 30 October 1940, it was Canada's turn to play the supplicant. Given the wartime congestion in its Atlantic shipyards, it wished to have its ships being built on the Great Lakes completed as far as possible. Accordingly, it proposed allowing armament to be installed on such vessels while on the lakes provided that it was rendered incapable of immediate use while the vessels remained in the area. The United States readily agreed.

The Rush-Bagot Agreement was subject to one other agreed "interpretation" before the end of World War II. In February 1942, the United States proposed that warships built on the lakes be permitted to have their armament placed in complete readiness for action and to test fully all machinery and armament while still on the Great Lakes in order to prepare for immediate combat upon their arrival in the open sea. The Canadians, aware of the activity of German submarines in the Gulf of St. Lawrence at the time, readily agreed. In the end, large numbers of warships—at least 600,000 tons on the U.S. side alone—were built in Great Lakes shipyards during the war.

In March 1946 the American representative on the Permanent Joint Board on Defense raised the issue of training vessels once again. The U.S. Navy wanted to have a small number of operative minor war vessels for training purposes. Canada's External Affairs Department believed that a formal interpretation of the existing agreement was desirable and drafted a note proposing the unlimited stationing of naval-training vessels on the lakes provided that full notification of the number, disposition, functions, and armament of the vessels was made in advance. Notes to this effect were duly exchanged in November–December 1946. This alteration became the last formal interpretation of the Rush-Bagot Agreement.

EVALUATION OF THE AGREEMENT

A number of authors have speculated on the possible motives of both Great Britain and the United States in concluding the Rush-Bagot Agreement when they did. There is little reason to doubt that the American overture in late 1815 was prompted by precisely those considerations put forward to the British—the saving of money on what could otherwise be an expensive naval arms race and the desire to improve political relations (and avoid a recurrence of armed conflict) by removing potential irritants in the bilateral relationship. Figuring prominently in the administration's view at this time was Congress's action in reducing military expenditures.

It is true that the Rush-Bagot Agreement was also very much to the U.S. military advantage in the event of war with Canada or Great Britain, since the United States could build a force from scratch much more quickly and easily than could the British. Initial British skepticism and resistance to the U.S. proposal can probably be attributed to fear that military calculations of this nature lay behind it, but the U.S. desire to reduce defense efforts and at the same time cultivate good relations with Britain was undoubtedly the driving force.

There can be little doubt that Britain was motivated by largely the same considerations as those presented by Monroe. In the British case, however, an additional and highly significant factor was the realization that it was unlikely to win any sustained naval arms race on the Great Lakes, given the U.S. advantages of proximity and the preponderance of population and commerce on the U.S. side of the lakes. Furthermore, both nations were eager to avoid spending money on warships that would be useful only in the Great Lakes and that could not be employed on the high seas.

By the mid-nineteenth century, the Royal Navy had ceased considering the naval defense of the Great Lakes to be a viable proposition at all. It came to rely on the Rush-Bagot Agreement to forestall any demands for the peacetime stationing of forces there as well as to help prevent the occurrence of any occasion for their use. Subsequently, both Great Britain and the United States appear to have been motivated almost exclusively by politico-diplomatic, rather than military-strategic, considerations. The Canadians felt the latter aspect most keenly, even well into the twentieth century. However, it was the U.S. desire not to provoke controversy with Great Britain or to upset the generally friendly tenor of relations with Ottawa that led the Americans to preserve the agreement.

The immediate impact of the agreement in causing massive reductions of armaments has been exaggerated somewhat by some historians. By 1817,

the building programs on both sides had already ceased and the process of disarmament begun, even before the agreement was signed. Furthermore, significant forces remained "in being," able to be called upon in an emergency, long after the agreement had taken effect. From an arms control point of view, the greatest contribution of the agreement lay in helping to avert a new round of competitive building rather than immediately reducing or eliminating forces-in-being.

The chicken-and-egg argument about the relationship between arms control and improved political relations between former adversaries also applies to the Rush-Bagot case. Some would argue that the improvement of Anglo-American political relations across a broad front after the War of 1812 rendered superfluous or irrelevant the conclusion of a formal arms control agreement between them, just as the same analysts would argue that it was only this improved political climate that made possible—or even guaranteed—the achievement of the arms control agreement in the first place. The agreement was hardly considered superfluous or irrelevant at the time that it was first negotiated, however. Such a deterministic view of history seriously underestimates the difficulties faced by the negotiators, discounting the very real possibility that—for a host of reasons—they might have failed to achieve an agreement.

A more balanced view of the relationship between the political climate and arms control would suggest its interactive nature. While the Rush-Bagot Agreement can hardly be credited for single-handedly bringing about an Anglo-American détente in the wake of the War of 1812, it both benefited from and contributed to the improvement in overall relations between the two nations. It also had an important restraining effect during subsequent crises in the relationship, of which there were many.

Even one of the most critical historians, Charles P. Stacey, writing in the *Niagara Frontier,* acknowledged that "during the long period after the Treaty of Ghent when another Anglo-American war was possible and sometimes even probable, the Rush-Bagot Agreement, by preventing large-scale naval competition, was one of the factors operating to reduce tensions along the border. It helped to bring us through that dangerous era" (p. 29). Similarly, Charles Levermore wrote of the Venezuelan boundary crisis: "Surely hostilities in 1895 would have been far more imminent if the Great Lakes had held powerful British and American war fleets patrolling the waters and watching each other suspiciously" (pp. 27–28). Even later, once the military-strategic significance of the agreement had largely diminished due to the practical inconceivability of a war between Canada and the United States, it served an important political restraining function in smoothing over the still occasionally rocky relationship between the two nations.

Despite a history of repeated technical violations of the agreement, it is remarkable, given the revolution in technologies and the long passage of time, the extent to which the agreement has nevertheless been upheld, in spirit if not in letter. The U.S. representative on the Permanent Joint Board on Defense, J. Graham Parsons, may have put it best when he wrote, in 1946, that "both the United States and Canada have worked on the basis that the spirit of the agreement was observed when any deviation from its terms was made by mutual consent" (p. 1746). By this standard, the Rush-Bagot Agreement has been a very successful example of arms control indeed.

BIBLIOGRAPHY

Secondary Sources Related events preceding the agreement—the unsuccessful attempts of 1783, 1794, and 1814—are covered in CALLAHAN (1898). SAMUEL FLAGG BEMIS, *Jay's Treaty: A Study in Commerce and Diplomacy,* rev. ed. (New Haven, 1962) deals with the second of these attempts, and CALLAHAN (1937) and PERKINS (1964) extensively with the third.

The most detailed secondary accounts of the origin and negotiating history of the Rush-Bagot Agreement are found in JAMES MORTON CALLAHAN, *The Neutrality of the American Lakes and Anglo-American Relations* (Baltimore, 1898); E. A. CRUIKSHANK, "The Negotiation of the Agreement for Disarmament of the Lakes," *Royal Society of Canada Transactions* 30 (May 1936): 151–184; TERENCE JAMES FAY, "Rush-Bagot Agreement: A Reflection of the Anglo-American Détente 1815–1818" (Ph.D. diss., Georgetown University, 1974); and CHARLES H. LEVERMORE, *The Anglo-American Agreement of 1817 for Disarmament on the Great Lakes* (Boston, 1914).

JAMES MORTON CALLAHAN—the most prolific of all writers on the agreement—actually covers the period up to 1896; a shorter version of his study (up to 1892) is "Agreement of 1817: Reduction of Naval Forces Upon the American Lakes" in *Annual Report of the American Historical Association for the Year 1895* (1896): 369–392. He updated the subject to 1911 in his *American Foreign Policy in Canadian Relations* (New York, 1937). CRUIKSHANK provides long excerpts (without full citations, unfortunately) from various primary sources, including some on the British side not available in published form elsewhere. Much of CRUIKSHANK's work is in turn reproduced in WILBUR H. GLOVER, "Documents Relating to the Rush-Bagot Agreement," *Niagara Frontier* 14 (Spring 1967): 30–41. FAY does not break any new ground on the negotiating history, but does help place the agreement in its broader context. HENRY SHERMAN BOUTELL, "Is the Rush-Bagot Convention Immortal?" *North American Review* 173 (September 1901): 331–348, though an advocacy piece, provides a good summary and is especially solid on United States congressional action.

The period of the Canadian rebellions is well covered in ALBERT B. COREY, *The Crisis of 1830–1842 in Canadian-American Relations* (New Haven, 1941). For the American Civil War era see ROBIN W. WINKS, *Canada and the United States: The Civil War Years,* rev. ed. (Montreal, 1971). For the Joint High Commission of 1898–1899 see ROBERT CRAIG BROWN, *Canada's National Policy, 1883–1900: A Study in Canadian-American Relations* (Princeton, N.J., 1964). ALVIN C. GLUEK, "The Invisible Revision of the Rush-Bagot Agreement, 1898–1914," *Canadian Historical Review* 60 (December 1979): 466–484, makes extensive use of Canadian and British archival sources.

JAMES EAYRS, "Arms Control on the Great Lakes," *Disarmament and Arms Control* 2:4 (1964): 372–404, treats the fate of the agreement after its signature, from the late 1830s to World War II. DON COURTNEY PIPER, *The International Law of the Great Lakes* (Durham, N.C., 1967) also focuses on the issues of compliance and revision.

Finally, essential background to the fate of the Rush-Bagot Agreement during the nineteenth and early twentieth centuries can be found in KENNETH BOURNE, *Britain and the Balance of Power in North America, 1815–1908* (Berkeley, 1967); J. MACKAY HITSMAN, *Safeguarding Canada, 1763–1871* (Toronto, 1968); and RICHARD A. PRESTON, *The Defence of the Undefended Border: Planning for War in North America, 1867–1939* (Montreal, 1977).

Shorter accounts of the agreement, some of which are more critical, include ESTHER RICE BATTENFELD, "150 Years of Peace Under a Six-Month

Pact: The Great Lakes Armament Arrangement," *Inland Seas* 23 (Summer 1967): 137–148; A. L. BURT, *The United States, Great Britain, and British North America: From the Revolution to the Establishment of Peace After the War of 1812* (New York, 1940); STANLEY L. FALK, "Disarmament on the Great Lakes: Myth or Reality?" *U.S. Naval Institute Proceedings* 87 (December 1961): 69–74; BRADFORD PERKINS, *Castlereagh and Adams: England and the United States, 1812–1823* (Berkeley, 1964); C. P. STACEY, "The Myth of the Unguarded Frontier, 1815–1871," *American Historical Review* 56 (October 1950): 1–18. STACEY covers the entire period up to the time of his writing in *The Undefended Border: The Myth and the Reality* (Ottawa, 1953), and "The Rush-Bagot Agreement, 1817–1967," *Niagara Frontier* 14 (Spring 1967): 26–29. See also MERZE TATE, *The United States and Armaments* (Cambridge, Mass., 1948); and RICHARD W. VAN ALSTYNE, *American Diplomacy in Action* (Stanford, 1944).

Documentary Sources The published diplomatic correspondence relating to the agreement on the U.S. side, up to 1860, is contained in WILLIAM R. MANNING, *Diplomatic Correspondence of the United States: Canadian Relations, 1784–1860,* 4 vols. (Washington, D.C., 1940–1945). JOHN W. FOSTER, *Limitation of Armament on the Great Lakes* (Washington, D.C., 1914)—a reprint of the 1892 Report, U.S. Secretary of State to the U.S. Senate, Senate Ex. Doc. No. 9, 52nd Cong., 2nd sess.—provides a detailed account of the agreement's negotiating history and subsequent treatment, including extensive quotations from the diplomatic correspondence and internal U.S. documents. U.S. CONGRESS, HOUSE OF REPRESENTATIVES, *War Vessels on the Great Lakes* (56th Cong., 1st sess., 1900. H. Doc. 471), in addition to containing Foster's 1892 report, appends the full texts of internal U.S. documents and diplomatic correspondence for the years 1840–1865 and 1895–1898. Some interesting Anglo-Canadian correspondence dealing with the reaction to the launching of the *Michigan* is reprinted in PAUL KNAPLUND, "Documents: The Armaments on the Great Lakes, 1844," *American Historical Review* 40 (1934–1935): 473–476.

Canada, Naval Vessels on the Great Lakes: Correspondence, 1892–1917 (1918?), found in the Parliamentary Library of Canada, reprints Anglo-Canadian and Anglo-American diplomatic correspondence as well as internal Canadian documents dealing with the agreement during this period. Much of the later documentation is also found in CANADA, DEPARTMENT OF EXTERNAL AFFAIRS, *Documents on Canadian External Relations,* Vol. 1: *1909–1918* (Ottawa, 1967). Documentation of Canadian policy in the interwar period is found in LOVELL C. CLARK, ed., *Documents on Canadian External Relations,* vol. 3: *1919–1925* (Ottawa, 1967). The equivalent on the U.S. side is contained in U.S. DEPARTMENT OF STATE, *Papers Relating to the Foreign Relations of the United States, 1923,* Vol. 1 (1938). "Naval Vessels on the Great Lakes," *The Department of State Bulletin* 4:92 (1941): 366–372, reprints the United States–Canadian exchange of correspondence covering the reinterpretations of 1939 and 1940. DONALD M. PAGE, ed., *Documents on Canadian External Relations,* Vol. 12: *1946* (Ottawa, 1977), reprints internal Canadian documents and diplomatic correspondence regarding the proposed revision (and eventual reinterpretation) of the agreement in 1946.

Chile and Argentina

Entente and Naval Limitation, 1902

— ◯ —

ANDREW D. FARRAND

See also Demilitarization and Neutralization Through World War II; Disarmament and Development in the Third World; *and* Latin America. *The* Argentine-Chilean Naval Limitation Convention *is excerpted in Volume III.*

The Pactos de Mayo, or Pacts of May of 1902 between Chile and Argentina, have held great significance in the relations between these two nations. The four agreements that comprised the Pacts of May formed a bridge between the nineteenth and twentieth centuries and ended, at least temporarily, a fifty-year period of deteriorating relations that could well have resulted in war. The first of the four agreements was a protocol stating the international policy of both sides; the second was a general treaty of arbitration; the third was a convention limiting naval armaments; and the last hastened marking the boundary between the two nations. As a result there emerged an Argentine-Chilean pattern of interaction characterized by cooperation and cordiality.

The disputes between Chile and Argentina were long-standing and serious and could have brought the two, as the Chilean foreign minister Eliodoro Yáñez said in 1902 after the Pacts of May had been signed, "to the extreme of war" (Great Britain, Foreign Office, *General Correspondence: Argentina and Chile, 1896–1904,* p. 323). It was, then, "as wise as it was imperative" to settle all outstanding issues between both countries peacefully. The diplomacy of this era was marked by this sense of reality and by the belief that, no matter how valid the leaders of one nation thought their claims against the other to be, a war would be disastrous for both. In short, no matter the nature of Argentine-Chilean relations up until then, it was understood that there was more to gain by peace than by war.

ORIGINS OF THE DISPUTES

In large part, disputes between Chile and Argentina had their origins in the evolution of the South American continent following independence. This was not an easy process, as the Spanish system of administration and territorial division was not intended to prepare the people for eventual self-rule. For example, the former viceroyalties—Argentina, Colombia, and Peru—sought to maintain their hegemony in the affairs of the continent. Yet smaller colonial administrative units—Santiago, Quito, Caracas, and Montevideo—wanted to be free of outside control and establish independent countries of which they could serve as capital cities. As Robert N. Burr has explained in his 1965 text *By Reason or Force,* by 1830 these cities prevailed and Chile, Ecuador, Venezuela, and Uruguay became independent nations. Buenos Aires, Bogotá, and Lima, however, continued to demonstrate attitudes of superiority and preeminence which, Burr notes, "inspired the fear and distrust of lesser nations, and provided elements of future discord" (p. 4).

Newly independent nations had to establish exact boundaries with their neighbors, something the legacy of colonial rule made difficult at best. Boundaries that did exist were often vague and/or overlapped from one colonial possession to another. The new countries took as their borders those which existed during colonial rule, thereby increasing the possibilities of controversy. This can be seen in the relations between Chile and Argentina in the years leading up to the signing of the Pacts of May in 1902.

Both Chile and Argentina viewed the other with suspicion. Each was fearful of the growth and power of the other; each jealously guarded what it believed to be its right to predominate in its area of influence; and each believed in the zeitgeist of its own development and that this gave it the right to direct Latin American affairs. To extend its influence and protect its position on the continent, each nation relied on the armed forces, particularly the navy. This reliance, and the ruinous arms race it engendered, exacerbated tensions and threatened the respective treasuries with bankruptcy. It was only the wisdom of "sensible people," as Chilean foreign minister Yáñez put it, that brought about negotiation of the Pacts of May.

Building upon the cultural heritage of Europe, Latin American leaders adopted the principles of international politics they had learned under colonial rule. The essence of this political environment was "power politics," with its notion of competition between states, the goal being to attain maximum advantage over neighbors. This competition, many in Latin America believed, was best carried out by peaceful means. But states did not shrink from employing force or the threat of force to obtain their objectives.

The War of the Pacific

The War of the Pacific between Chile and a Peruvian-Bolivian coalition that began in 1879, and the Argentine-Chilean rivalry in the southern part of the continent over boundary demarcation are proof of this. What is also true is that a people, seeing the devastating effects war will have, can halt a slide toward hostilities and take actions that will ensure that peace will prevail. It is this higher wisdom that characterizes the negotiations leading to the Pacts of May.

Chile's desire for territorial expansion coincided with the wish to increase the extent of its international prestige and wealth. An early attempt was in the Atacama Desert, where Chileans, backed by British capital, sought to develop the area's rich deposits of nitrates. At first Lima and La Paz, which also claimed the desert, welcomed this Chilean interest, as they did not have the resources to devote to the venture themselves. However, it soon became apparent that cooperation was impossible, and that Peruvian and Bolivian national interests were incompatible with those of Chile, and in 1879 the War

of the Pacific resulted. Although fought between Chile and a Peruvian-Bolivian coalition, the war was to have a profound impact on Chilean-Argentine relations for the remainder of the century.

Militarily, the war went well for Chile. By October 1883, Peru signed the Treaty of Ancón, and thirteen months later Bolivia was forced to sign a truce. Chile, by virtue of its success, was in a particularly powerful position in Latin America. Victory, however, was to bring Chile's conflicts with Argentina into sharper focus and eventually change the nature of its foreign policy. As the historian Frederick B. Pike has shown, Chile suspected Argentina's support for United States' mediation to end the War of the Pacific to be an attempt to curb Chile's territorial expansion in the north, a suspicion exacerbated by activities to settle the southern boundary dispute between the two nations on terms Chilean leaders thought inimical to their interests.

Demilitarizing the Strait of Magellan

To the south, Chile and Argentina could not determine their boundary line. In 1843 Chile moved into the Strait of Magellan, founded the town of Punta Arenas, and claimed the strait, the Patagonia, and the Tierra del Fuego. Buenos Aires was too involved with European powers and the Paraguayan war to protest actively. However, by 1870 the situation had changed and Argentina was free to pursue its interests in the area and conducted negotiations with Chile to determine jurisdiction of the disputed land. In 1881, with the mediation of the United States, they signed a boundary treaty by which Chile accepted Argentinean dominion over Patagonia while Chile was granted sovereignty over the Strait of Magellan. Chile also agreed to the neutralization of the strait, while Argentina agreed not to block its entrance and exits. The Tierra del Fuego was to be divided, and the north-south boundary between the two nations would be set at the *divortium aquarum*. Finally, disputes arising from the agreement were to be submitted to arbitration.

The Treaty of 1881 between Chile and Argentina established the principle that Chilean interests would be protected on the Pacific side of the continent and those of Argentina on the Atlantic side. In practical terms, this meant the Andean boundary between the two nations was to be drawn along "las más altas cumbres que dividan las aquas" [the highest peaks that divide the waters]. That is, the boundary was to be drawn along the *divortium aquarum* in the cordillera separating the two countries; in short, a line drawn along the continental watershed.

When it came time to lay the boundary, experts found that the watershed did not correspond to the highest peaks. If the latter, that is the highest peak, definition prevailed, then Argentina's boundary could, in some instances, have extended into the Pacific Ocean. Chile resisted this interpretation as it meant that its rival would become a Pacific power.

Boundary Disputes   The ambiguity of the phrase *divortium aquarum* was to produce tension and threats of war that the Pacts of May finally ended. As the historian Robert N. Burr has described, the real concern was not so much the size of the territory under dispute as the benefits accruing to one country or the other depending upon which definition was enforced. If Chile's claims were accepted she would gain possession of Patagonia, and if Argentina's were acceded to she would become a Pacific power, scenarios unthinkable for the respective rivals of either country. Thus, although it appeared as though the 1881 accord would resolve boundary issues in the south, in the long run it served as a prelude to further difficulties.

One of the successful outcomes of the War of the Pacific for Chile was the increase in the size of the nation—by more than one-third. Because of this, and to protect the nation from Argentine ambitions, many in Santiago believed their nation's foreign policy should be less aggressive; it became more defensive in nature. As the historian Frederick Pike observed in *Chile and the United States, 1880–1962* (1963), by 1889 the Chilean "ambition to direct [South] American affairs had given way to a merely defensive mechanism" (p. 99). As Chilean President José Manuel Balmaceda explained, "I desire that Chileans . . . may prove, upon a strong military base and a navy in keeping with their wealth, that there is no possible profit in undertaking war against the Republic of Chile" (Burr, p. 176). This desire set the nation on a course of arms procurement that would make its army and navy the strongest on the continent, arms paid for in large part by the economic resurgence that followed the war's conclusion and, as J. Fred Rippy has attested, by British investments.

The perceived threat of Argentine ambition increased proportionately with the growth of Argentina's navy, a buildup necessitated, Buenos Aires felt, by the contentious relationship with Santiago and to offset the gains their rivals to the west had made. Chileans became especially alarmed when they learned in May 1898 that Argentina was contracting for the purchase of the Italian cruiser *Garibaldi;* shortly thereafter they learned further purchases were being made. In addition, German army personnel were modernizing Argentina's army. In his study of arms and influence in Latin America, Edwin Lieuwen stated that even though Chile protested that these activities would endanger relations between the two nations, Argentina asserted that strengthening the nation's military posture was necessary to offset recent purchases of naval vessels by Chile. This beginning to the naval arms race was one each nation could reasonably afford at the beginning, but as it proceeded it threatened to bankrupt each nation.

Chileans, at least from their perspective, had reason to fear the growth in importance of Argentina in the affairs of the continent. Argentina's economy had lagged behind that of Chile until the 1880s only to catch up and surpass its neighbor after that time, as Isaac Cox has pointed out in his edition of Luís Galdames's history of Chile. Argentina's population also expanded substantially, as did its control of land whose ownership had previously been in dispute. In part, Argentina's expansion was also fueled by British investments, especially in railroads, as Rippy has recorded, causing remote areas to be opened up for settlement and economic activity. Thus, when the boundary dispute between the two nations remained unsettled even with the 1881 accord, Chileans believed Argentina's challenge was not only to land rightfully theirs, but to their rightful place as the leaders of Latin American affairs.

As the end of the century approached, it was clear that each nation feared the growth in power of the other, and interpreted the activities of its adversary as a threat. This brought them closer to war than ever before. Neither side, however, was willing to take the final steps that would result in hostilities, and sought ways to settle disputes amicably; many in both nations were coming to realize that war would be catastrophic. In an attempt to lessen increasingly strident nationalist voices and the attendant war scare, leaders in both capitals wanted to settle boundary disputes between the two nations, including those in the south and the Puna de Atacama, which had been derived from Bolivia, claimed by both Chile and Argentina and referred to the United States Minister to Argentina, William I. Buchanan, for arbitration; he worked out a settlement in 1899 in which the Puna was essentially divided between Chile and Argentina. Citing Article VI of the 1881 accord concerning the southern territories in dispute, they asked Great Britain to arbitrate the issue and render a final settlement.

This London willingly did, as the British government was increasingly concerned that leaders in the two nations would eventually be unable to prevent hostilities. The threat of war was already having an impact on British (and other) investments, and only a continuation of peace could secure for investors a climate in which to conduct business. It was for this reason that England continued to play such an important role in helping to arrange the Pacts of May.

The entente seemed to establish a new, more peaceful relationship between the competing nations. It was symbolized by a meeting between Presidents Julio Argentino Roca and Federico Errázuriz Zañartu of Argentina and Chile in February 1899, known as the "Abrazo del Estrecho," when they met on shipboard in the Strait of Magellan. They pledged their peoples to peace and settlement of future accords in a spirit of cordiality. Yet, as events were to prove, this pledge would have to wait for some time before it would become anything more than empty words.

DISPUTES CONTINUED

The entente did not last long. The causes of contention in the first part of the twentieth century were, in reality, a continuation of those left unresolved from the nineteenth—the continuation of "the Pacific question"; disputes over territory in the southern tip of the continent; the "armed peace"; the role of Great Britain in effecting peace; and the Pacts of May.

The continuation of the Pacific question into the early years of the twentieth century proved to be particularly destabilizing. The "Pacific question" was the name given to the Chilean-Argentine confrontations over the disputed areas in the north. This included the controversies flowing from the Treaty of Ancón that ended the War of the Pacific (that is, the disputes between Chile and Peru/Bolivia, which Chile believed Argentina was trying to

exploit for its own advantage) and between Chile and Argentina in the Puna de Atacama. Chile still faced contentious issues related to Bolivia's desire for a port on the Pacific and with Peru over the ownership of the cities of Tacna and Arica. The welter of diplomatic activity over these issues served not only to strain Santiago's relations with La Paz and Lima, but created a situation in which Argentina's meddling seemed almost certain. Chile believed that any settlement of the Pacific question on unfavorable terms would present Argentina with an opportunity to enter the area and establish itself as a Pacific power and a direct threat to Chilean interests in the west.

Even though Argentina was not pursuing an aggressive diplomacy to settle outstanding questions between Chile, Bolivia, and Peru, leaders in Buenos Aires suggested their country had an obligation to use its influence (and force, if necessary) in the region. Communicating with the British Foreign Office in August 1901, William Barrington, British envoy in Buenos Aires, informed London that Argentina did not contemplate hostile action to fulfill the provisions of the Treaty of Ancón as they pertained to Tacna and Arica. However, he continued, Argentine leaders had informed him that they could not look on with indifference at any further Chilean encroachments on the Pacific Coast. He concluded by observing that "the [Argentine] papers arc dissatisfied . . . and continue sounding the note of alarm. The existence of a feeling of anxiety cannot be denied, and the situation is somewhat similar to that which existed some three years ago" (Great Britain, Foreign Office, p. 313).

Chile, for its part, would not permit Buenos Aires to meddle in her affairs with Peru and Bolivia and thus project its influence to the Pacific coast at Santiago's expense. Argentine President Roca stated that Chile's

eventual designs on [Peru and Bolivia] are regarded with the utmost suspicion. Their relative weakness is looked upon as a standing temptation to aggression on the part of Chile, and should she succeed in establishing a secure footing by enlarging her territory at the cost of Bolivia, she would then turn her eyes on this country with the view of constituting herself the predominant Power in Spanish South America. (Great Britain, Foreign Office, p. 27)

These were sentiments that concerned many in Chile and convinced them of Argentina's hostile intent. Things in the south were also unresolved, and although the disputes that erupted there were different from those that separated the two nations in the north, in reality the ingredients of the controversy were the same. Both feared the other's growth of power because of the effect this would have on the balance of power in South America.

The basis for discord in the south resulted from Chilean road building in the area under arbitration by Great Britain and Argentine incursions into the Chilean-claimed Inlet of Last Hope. In the early part of the new century Chile began building roads and military barracks in the disputed land, and Argentina did not accept the Chilean explanation that this activity was designed to facilitate the work of the British team and had no military value whatsoever. From Santiago's perspective, the question about road construction did not have the same weight as Argentina's intrusion in the Inlet of Last Hope. In the summer of 1901 Argentine border guards had occupied the region surrounding the inlet, something that alarmed Chile due to the inlet's proximity to the Strait of Magellan. In an effort to defuse this controversy, both sides agreed to meet in Santiago to negotiate a settlement.

The discussions did not go as smoothly as planned. Indeed, by November 1901 the British envoy to Santiago reported to the Foreign Office that the situation had deteriorated to such a degree that the two nations had broken off relations. By the end of the year, even though Buenos Aires instructed its envoy to remain in Chile, tensions remained high and both sides increased military preparations. As the U.S. envoy to Santiago Henry Lane Wilson informed Washington in December 1901:

In government, business and military circles, and among the people at large, the opinion is now almost unanimous that the differences between this country and the Argentine can be only settled by the arbitrement of the sword. (*Diplomatic Dispatches from United States Ministers in Chile,* National Archives microfilm, vol. 48)

Had Wilson waited slightly longer to communicate with the State Department, he could have reported that the impasse had been resolved. The Argentine minister to Chile followed his instructions and remained in the Chilean capital and sought ways to settle things peacefully. Argentina proposed that its police forces in the Inlet of Last Hope be withdrawn, declaring that the incursion occurred without the knowledge of the govern-

ment. Chile, for its part, declared that the construction of roads and barracks in the disputed territory would not be used to effect permanent possession, and both agreed to revert to the territorial status quo of 1898 when the frontier question was submitted to Great Britain for arbitration.

A Naval Arms Race Looms Diplomacy was backed by an arms buildup that began in the latter stages of the nineteenth century and accelerated in the first two years of the twentieth. In large part this arms race was naval in nature, as the continent's topography made a land conflict between the two nations unlikely. As one contemporary observer stated, Chile and Argentina "poured out their wealth into the coffers of European shipbuilders" as one tried to gain advantage over the other (Enrique Tagle, *Tratados de paz entre la república argentina y Chile,* 1902, p. 8). In late 1901 Argentina learned that Chile had contacted the House of Rothschild in London concerning a loan in the amount of 2.5 million pounds to be used partly for arms. That nation had already placed orders with English shipyards for a cruiser and several destroyers, an increase Argentina interpreted as a threat to its security. In order to maintain parity, Argentina ordered the construction of two heavy cruisers from shipyards in Genoa at a cost of $6.6 million. Chile responded in kind by placing additional orders in England totaling nearly $10 million, after which her rival placed an additional order with the Ansaldo Brothers shipyards in Genoa.

As this buildup in armaments continued into early 1902, leaders in Buenos Aires became increasingly apprehensive about the cost of an "armed peace." Although such influential Argentineans as Carlos Pellegrini and General Bartolomé Mitre, both former presidents, stated they supported arms for national defense, they wanted to ease tensions with Chile concerning the Pacific question, the one issue that had the potential to ignite war. On 9 April 1902, Mitre's influential newspaper, *La Nación,* editorialized that the affairs surrounding the Pacific question were not those of Argentina, and enjoined the people to examine their own destiny "before making ourselves soldiers for foreign causes." War with Chile "would be stupidity." Argentina, the editorial went on, "does not share in the affairs of the Pacific, nor has it anything to do with them while her own security . . . is not threatened."

The tone of the editorial was followed shortly thereafter in *El País* and *El Tiempo.* The latter editorialized that "the dispute to the Pacific is not ours. It is necessary to speak out, to put an end to the international equivocation that ... makes us lead a dangerous and ... agitated life [instead of one at] peace with ourselves and with those who surround us" (10 April 1902). Chile's disputes with Bolivia and Peru, the paper said five days later, are not ones in which Argentina has a right to intervene.

The Chilean people reacted favorably to these moderate Argentinean statements, and to the moderate course followed thereafter by other leaders in that country. In Santiago, Julio Zegers, a former member of the legislature, denounced those citizens who continually argued for war with Argentina. He saw no reason for war and abhorred munitions makers who helped to prolong the armed peace for their own profit. He implored his fellow citizens to pursue a policy of peace as this was the only way that Chile could advance into the front ranks of nations. These sentiments began the lessening of relations between the two countries, a situation that would end the drift toward war and financial paralysis that the arms buildup had produced. Indeed, this reasonable course pursued by both nations in early April of 1902 was instrumental in establishing the spirit of cordiality that culminated in the Pacts of May.

Economic Consequences   The moderation was also caused by the economic conditions in each country, which threatened disaster. In the first part of the twentieth century Argentina began to suffer the effects of a drought that severely crippled agricultural production. English newspapers were reporting that crop failures in the wheat and linseed industries produced the lowest tonnage for export in thirty years. As a result, foreign exchange fell off and the balance of trade was unfavorable. Businessmen were afraid to invest due to the high rate of business failures, and the extraordinary sum of thirty million pounds sterling on ships of war under construction raised doubts in the money markets as to how the sum was to be paid. The money could not be borrowed from foreign banks because foreign financiers, principally from Great Britain and the United States, were apprehensive about the political and economic stability of the continent. No matter what economic course the Argentine government pursued during this period, there was no hiding the fact that the economy was grinding to a halt, and few businessmen had confidence that things would change as long as the armed peace continued.

Things were not much better in Chile, and the expenditures for arms had equally debilitating effects there, although for different reasons. Whereas the Argentine economy was basically agricultural, that of Chile was based principally on the exports of nitrates extracted from the Atacama Desert. Even though many in the nation had encouraged economic diversification, nitrates became the nation's principal export commodity and the basic means of earning foreign exchange. But by the end of the nineteenth century Chile's nitrate markets became glutted and exports sharply declined; other forms of foreign commerce also fell off sharply, and commodity prices declined. The government found it virtually impossible to secure foreign loans due to the economic conditions in the country and the possibility of war with Argentina. Indeed, due to the fear of war, foreign capital fled the country, not to be reinvested until after the Pacts of May.

The economic effects of the armed peace on the Argentine and Chilean economies worried not only businessmen in both countries but foreign investors who had extensive holdings there. The fragility of the situation worried Great Britain. The threat of war produced economic stagnation and prevented English investors from making satisfactory profits. If war did break out, it was not inconceivable that it could spread to other parts of the continent, thereby threatening British investments in the entire area. It was to help bring a period of political and diplomatic calm and economic revival that Great Britain intervened and sought to bring about a resolution of all outstanding issues separating these two rivals.

NEGOTIATIONS BEGIN

England was fully aware that swift action was needed to settle the outstanding issues between Chile and Argentina relating to the southern border before the arms race ended in war. In order to expedite a settlement, in early 1902 the Foreign Office sent a commission headed by Sir Thomas Holdich to survey the situation. Landing first in Buenos Aires, Holdich chatted with Argentine officials and asked if a direct settlement between the competing nations was possible; he found them amenable to this course. However, officials in Chile were not so conciliatory, believing that both sides should abide by the treaty of 1881; they informed Holdich that under this treaty they had been deprived of the Patagonia in compensation for which the boundary line was established at the *divortium aquarum.* It appeared as though this rejection of a direct settlement of the boundary question would prolong a dispute that had already resulted in strained relations and the armed peace.

British officials realized that the armed peace was jeopardizing their role as arbitrators. Thus, they sought ways to bring it to an end. Yet they were not the only ones interested in ending the ruinous arms race. Ernesto Tornquist, an Argentine banker, knew full well that both countries could not sustain the outlay of resources much longer. In March he sought to enlist the good offices of the British government by appealing to the British bankers Rothschild and Baring, to pressure both sides to end the acquisition of new vessels of war. Tornquist wrote that it was very important for the British government to influence cancellation of current orders and discourage new ones. He concluded by saying that he was "quite certain any intervention of this kind will be accepted by [both] parties concerned" (Huneeus y Gana, p. 73). Yet the Foreign Office refused to step in unless officially requested by both governments to do so.

In early April, when the new British envoy to Santiago, Gerald Lowther, presented his credentials to the Chilean foreign minister, he reiterated his government's opposition to the arms race while the arbitration award was still pending. He urged Chile to accept the good offices of Great Britain in settling all questions, and told him that his colleague in Buenos Aires was prodding Argentina to accept this offer of British assistance as well. Foreign Minister Yáñez replied by saying that his nation's navy was only big enough for self-defense, whereas the size and composition of the Argentine navy was such that it could have only aggressive purposes. Moreover, Yáñez reasserted the contention that solutions to Chile's affairs in the north with Bolivia and Peru were being hindered by Argentine interference. Until such intrusions were halted, no accommodations of any kind could be reached. However, because Chile desired peace, Yáñez concluded, his government would not object if the British intervened to help achieve this goal.

On 21 April British foreign secretary Lord Lansdowne (Henry William Edmund Petty-Fitzmaurice) sent instructions to the envoys in Buenos Aires and Santiago about how to effect peace. He stated that "the competition for naval supremacy is not only financially disastrous to the countries concerned, but calculated to provoke a rupture, the effects of which would be widespread and calamitous." He went on to say that he believed the British government, because of its role as arbiter of the boundary question, had a right to ask both nations to refrain from making further naval purchases until an award had been made. Explain to them, he said "that this friendly warning is one which we cannot allow the Argentine and Chilean Governments to disregard" (Great Britain, Foreign Office, p. 4). Chile accepted this offer of British assistance on 22 April, and Argentina followed the next day. After several more days of intense negotiations about the language any final settlement must contain, particularly relating to a declaration of reciprocal neutrality in any questions that one contracting party might have with another country, both sides reached a mutually satisfactory accord.

The increasing influence of the moderate camp in Argentina was manifested by the appointment of José Antonio Terry as the new envoy to Chile. Terry's instructions did not indicate, however, any retreat from its former positions on the issues separating the two nations; Argentina would do nothing to compromise its position in advance. Two days after his arrival in Santiago, a governmental crisis occasioned by disputes about how to fund the armaments under contract left Chile bereft of a foreign minister with whom Terry could deal; it was not until 9 May that José Francisco Vergara Donoso was appointed to that post. During this two week period, Terry conversed with President Germán Riesco about the critical state of relations between their two countries, conversations that became the basis for a settlement between the republics. The new Argentine envoy gave assurances that his government would be agreeable to an arbitration treaty and that it had no desire for further territorial expansion. When the language Chile had demanded for a declaration of reciprocal neutrality in any questions that one contracting party might have with another was changed to suit Argentina, Terry and Riesco, with the assistance of Vergara and Lowther, wrote a statement of international policy for both nations, a policy of good intentions by Chile and Argentina. After this preliminary act was signed, which was to serve as a preamble to the arbitration treaty, Chile and Argentina agreed to a treaty of general arbitration in which all future disputes would be mediated by Great Britain.

The negotiations between Chile and Argentina relative to a naval accord were carried out over several weeks, and dealt with such issues as the "Pacific question," the method for attaining naval parity and the attendant issues of the disposition of ships already in the fleets and the cancellation of existing contracts, and arbitration of outstanding issues between the two nations. Hanging over all of these efforts was how they would be received by the legislative and public opinion leaders in each nation. Even though each side wanted to resolve outstanding issues, each also recognized that the legacy of mistrust and suspicion circumscribed their freedom of maneuver. Thus, in this effort to find a solution, negotiations were conducted privately as well as officially, and resulted in the convention on naval armaments.

THE PACTS OF MAY

The convention signed on 28 May 1902 provided stipulations that both countries desist from acquiring the ships under construction in Europe; that navies be reduced until equally balanced; that the strength of the navies be agreed upon within one year of ratification; that the parties not increase naval armaments for five years without first giving the other eighteen months' advance notice; and one party could not sell ships to a government in dispute with the other. In addition, any disputes arising over how to reach naval parity would be submitted to arbitration under provisions of the arbitration treaty. The last part of the Pacts of May was a provision to speed up the final demarcation of the boundary line between the two republics by the British team of experts.

Despite the fact that the publication of the Pacts quickly eased tensions in the two nations, opposition to them began to develop in both nations. Charges that national sovereignty and dignity had been sacrificed were bandied about in the respective legislatures. As Robert Burr has demonstrated, Chilean nationalists argued that the country did not have sufficient guarantees against Argentine interference in their affairs and that the nation had renounced territorial expansion except that which might arise out of carrying out existing treaties. For its part, in early June the Argentine government advised Terry that he try to obtain revision of that part of the agreement by which Argentina agreed to submit problems in arranging a "just" naval balance to arbitration. Terry and Vergara, in an effort to allay congressional objections by either nation, drew up a new protocol, which was signed on 10 July. It stated that "the execution of the Treaties in force or

of those resulting from them, and referenced to in the preamble of the Treaty of Arbitration, cannot be a matter for arbitration between the Parties, and in consequence neither of the Contracting governments has a right to interfere in the form which the other may adopt for giving effect to those Treaties." Thus, Chile could pursue her interests in the north with Peru and Bolivia free from fear of Argentine meddling.

With regard to the Argentine objections to the questions involving naval parity, the 10 July protocol stipulated that a "just balance" does not require the sale of vessels. "A just balance," the second article reads, "may be sought in disarmament or other means to the extent required in order that both Governments may retain the necessary fleets—the one for the natural defense and permanent security ("destino") of the Republic of Chile on the Pacific, and the other for the natural defense and permanent security ("destino") of the Argentine Republic on the Atlantic and the River Plate." Thus, as Burr points out, leaders in both countries could take satisfaction from the fact that each had granted to the other virtual hegemony in its sphere of influence. It was a protocol that eased resistance to the Pacts of May, although residual opposition existed in both nations for some months thereafter. However, ratification of the pacts was exchanged on 18 September 1902.

The rapprochement symbolized by the Pacts of May brought to a conclusion a period of contention between Chile and Argentina. Yet the new era of cordiality was tested early on by the arbitration award, one that satisfied neither Chile nor Argentina; the British took the middle ground between the positions each nation had set as the proper demarcation. In January both nations signed an agreement requesting Britain to physically mark the boundary line. A second test came as the two nations negotiated the naval disarmament protocol in the Pacts of May. In the January 1903 agreement, Chile and Argentina agreed to sell the ships under construction in Europe and, if they could not be sold, "in no case shall they be added to the respective fleets—not even with the previous notice of eighteen months required for the increase of naval armaments by Article II [of the 28 May 1902] agreement." Under Article IV, in order to establish the just balance between the two fleets," Chile also agreed to disarm the battleship *Capitán Prat* and Argentina reciprocated by disarming the battleships *Garibaldi* and *Pueyrredón*.

CONCLUSION

The new era was best symbolized by the delegation of distinguished and high-ranking military and naval officers sent by Argentina to Chile in September 1902 to exchange ratifications and to help Chile celebrate its Independence Day. The good feelings of this gesture sparked a discussion in the Chilean congress to send a similar delegation in May 1903 to Buenos Aires to help celebrate Argentina's independence.

That the conciliatory path pursued by both nations was both wise and patriotic, one observer noted, "is shown by the pleasure and enthusiasm with which the May treaties have been received in both countries" (Great Britain, Foreign Office, p. 323). What was particularly noteworthy in the disputes between Chile and Argentina was that, even when emotions in both nations seemed to be propelling them toward conflict, leaders turned away and actively sought the assistance of others in helping avert war. The diplomacy was marked, ultimately, by a desire for peace in which both nations and the entire continent could progress.

BIBLIOGRAPHY

General Accounts There are several studies that broadly survey the countries of the "southern cone," including A. CURTIS WILGUS, ed., *Argentine, Brazil and Chile Since Independence* (1935; repr. New York, 1963); LUÍS GALDAMES, *A History of Chile,* translated and edited by ISAAC J. COX (Chapel Hill, N.C., 1941); F. A. KIRKPATRICK, *A History of the Argentine Republic* (Cambridge, England, 1931); and RICARDO LEVENE, *A History of Argentina,* translated and edited by WILLIAM S. ROBERTSON (Chapel Hill, N.C., 1937).

Military attitudes and influence are examined by EDWIN LIEUWEN, *Arms and Politics in Latin America* (New York, 1965); while J. FRED RIPPY's *British Investments in Latin America, 1822–1949: A Case Study in the Operations of Private Enterprise in Retarded Regions* (Minneapolis, Minn., 1959) reviews the impact of economic affairs on Latin American politics.

Arms Control and Diplomacy FREDERICK B. PIKE studies diplomatic relationships in his *Chile and the United States, 1880–1962: The Emergence of Chile's Social Crisis and the Challenge to United States Diplomacy* (Notre Dame, Ind., 1963); and Argentina's diplomacy is related in ISIDORO RUIZ MORENO, *Historia de las Relaciones Exteriores Argentinas, 1810–1955* (Buenos Aires, 1961).

The arbitrations and mediations are told in THOMAS H. HOLDICH, *The Countries of the King's Award* (London, 1904); and PAUL D. DICKENS, "Argentine Arbitration and Mediations with Reference to United States Participation Therein," *Hispanic American Historial Review* 11 (November 1931): 464–484. Contemporary accounts quoted in this essay can be found in GREAT BRITAIN, FOREIGN OFFICE, *General Correspondence: Argentina and Chile, 1896–1904* (London, Public Records Office, F016-357).

More specific to the Pacts of May are ROBERT N. BURR, *By Reason or Force: Chile and the Balancing of Power in South America, 1830–1905* (Berkeley, Calif., 1965); and JORGE HUNEEUS Y GANA, *La amistad chileno-argentina: el verdadero origen de los Pactos de Mayo* (Santiago de Chile, 1908).

The League of Nations and Disarmament

○

JAMES BARROS

See also Demilitarization and Neutralization Through World War II; The Kellogg-Briand Pact and the Outlawry of War; Regulating Arms Sales Through World War II; *and* The United Nations and Disarmament. *The* League Covenant *and other agreements discussed in this essay are excerpted in Volume III.*

During the League of Nations' relatively short life-span, 1920 to 1946, the negotiations—discussions, debates, arguments, and rebuttals—that took place within its confines raised most of the basic issues related to arms control. These issues included attempts to define aggression, national and collective security, arms parity, verification, and compliance. One of the most important lessons that League diplomats eventually learned was that at its core the fundamental determining factors in arms control and disarmament were political, not technical.

BACKGROUND

In May 1862 British political leader and future prime minister Benjamin Disraeli complained that there had to be an end to "these bloated armaments." Europe's increasing military expenditure at that time and in the decades that followed was only a surface manifestation of a deeper malaise in interstate relations—namely, a lack of political consensus, especially among the great powers (England, France, Germany, Austria-Hungary, Italy, and Czarist Russia). The feelings of insecurity flowing from this situation inexorably led to competing political alliances and military buildups seeking countervailing power.

Like it or not, armaments were an unavoidable feature of an amoral political landscape and their expansion or diminution responded little to criticism or goodwill. There was, however, an abatement of political tension and an achievement of political accommodation among the competing states based on considerations of countervailing power, converging interests, and a desire to avoid conflict.

The last years of the nineteenth century and the first years of the twentieth century were devoid of any sophisticated international machinery capable of acting as a catalyst in fostering political accommodation among competing states and alliances. Rather than slackening, Europe's political tensions and competition increased, as did government expenditure on military establishments and armaments for use on both land and sea.

Nonetheless, for a period of about ninety-nine years Europe had enjoyed comparative peace. Then World War I erupted, and the new weapons made possible by advances in science and technology took their terrible toll. The ferocity of the war unleashed in the summer of 1914, the large number of states involved, its duration, the military and civilian casualties suffered, and the social and political dislocation the war generated affected the world community and political leadership enormously. In the minds of many well-meaning people, this tragedy was precipitated, in part, by the unrestrained armaments race among the powers. Accordingly it was argued that disarmament and arms control, along with the establishment of some sort of super-association of states, would go far in preventing a repetition of what had occurred.

By late 1917 it was obvious that some sort of superassociation of states would emerge from the war, provided the Anglo-French-Italian-U.S. coalition was victorious. Even British Prime Minister David Lloyd George, no proponent of the superassociation idea, in discussing the government's war aims assured the Trade Unions Conference at Caxton Hall in early January 1918 that London sought the establishment of an international organization to restrict the armaments burden and lessen the danger of another war. Several days later President Woodrow Wilson, in his address to the United States Congress on 8 January, enunciated his Fourteen Points, which formed the basis of America's postwar aims. The fourth point called for the reduction of armaments, while the last point spoke of the formation of a "general association of nations" to offer to all states, regardless of size, "mutual guarantees of political independence and territorial integrity."

THE LEAGUE COVENANT

The November 1918 armistice, and the Paris peace negotiations that began in early 1919 and led to the establishment of the League of Nations, attempted to flesh out through the clauses of the League Covenant the promises and objectives that the British prime minister, the U.S. president, and others had made pertaining to disarmament. This would be accomplished, to use Wilson's phrase, through a "general association of nations." The disarmament question was touched upon in several of the Covenant's articles, starting with Article 1, which provided that any new League member had to accept "such regulations" as the League might prescribe relating to its land, naval, air forces, and armaments.

Article 8 of the Covenant was the key disarmament article. It stipulated in its first paragraph that League members recognized that the maintenance of peace required "the reduction of national armaments to the lowest point consistent with national safety and the enforcement by common action of international obligations." The next two paragraphs described the methods to be followed. The League Council (the organization's primary peacekeeping body) was to take account of each state's geographical situation and circumstances and to formulate plans for the reduction of national armaments for the consideration and action of the League's mem-

bership. Since international relations are never static it also provided for the adjustment of disarmament plans every ten years at a minimum. To prevent armaments competition once disarmament plans were adopted by the member states, the armaments limits agreed upon would not be exceeded without the Council's concurrence.

Subsequent paragraphs of the Covenant attempted to eliminate secret military preparations by requiring League members to undertake to exchange fully and frankly information as to the scale of their land, naval, and air programs as well as their armaments and the state of those industrial processes that could be adopted to "warlike purposes." Moreover, League members agreed that the manufacture by private interests of armaments and weapons was "open to grave objections." The Council was to investigate how such armaments manufacture could be prevented, consideration being given to the needs of those member states unable to manufacture munitions and implements of war necessary for their own security. To advise on the execution of Articles 1 and 8 of the Covenant, the Council under Article 9 was to establish a permanent commission on military, naval, and air questions. The article's lack of clarity in spelling out what was expected of the permanent commission as well as its structure and composition gave an unintended advantage to those states and individuals interested in either delaying disarmament or undermining it altogether.

Article 23 of the Covenant entrusted the League with the task of supervising the trade in weapons and munitions with states "in which control of this traffic [was] necessary in the common interest." These strictures in the Covenant, the obligations assumed by League members to maintain the peace and take joint action against an aggressor state, and the organization's procedures for peaceful settlement of international questions, gave disarmament a sharper public focus than it had enjoyed prior to World War I. Prewar disarmament had been vitiated by a lack of any permanent superassociation of states capable of coordinating international efforts and any sophisticated international machinery capable of tackling the disarmament question. Seemingly all these drawbacks had now disappeared with the establishment of the League and its assigned task under the Covenant to affect disarmament in world affairs.

At first glance the League's disarmament burden appears to be relatively easy. Aside from the Covenant's provisions, somewhat analogous stipulations dealing with military, naval, and air questions were raised in Part 5 of all the peace treaties terminating the war—Versailles with Germany, Saint Germain with Austria, Trianon with Hungary, Sèvres with Turkey, and Neuilly with Bulgaria. The preamble to Part 5 specifically recalled the intention of the signatories to prepare to limit armaments and to observe the military and air clauses imposed by the treaties. The last article of Part 5, which was identical in all the treaties, conferred on the League Council a right of investigation. The signatories agreed to submit to it, provided the treaty remained in force and the Council thought the investigation necessary, even if it acted only by majority vote.

Likewise, the question of disarmament appeared easy to resolve in view of the postwar euphoria and the ardent universal desire for a lasting peace. By the time the League officially came into being on 10 January 1920, the situation had changed drastically. Peace in many areas was elusive and there were open hostilities in eastern Europe and the Balkans. Acute economic and financial dislocation, however, led to the need to reduce military budgets. But reductions entailed negotiations with the British, French, Italian, and Japanese, and in early 1920 these states had pressing reasons for postponing disarmament. This situation no doubt helped inspire the 8 March 1920 appeal from the Supreme Council of the Allies, composed of England, France, Italy, Japan, and initially the United States, to the League, in which the Supreme Council maintained that military forces everywhere should be reduced to peacetime levels and armaments limited to the lowest possible level compatible with national security, and it asked the League to tender proposals in this direction.

The Permanent Advisory Commission

The Supreme Council's March appeal was followed on 19 May 1920 by the League Council's decision in Rome to organize the advisory commission provided for in Article 9. The decision was based on a report drawn up by Léon Bourgeois, the French representative. His selection as the rapporteur reflected the status that France enjoyed in European disarmament matters based on its position as a leading member of the victorious coalition. During this early period the French Ministry of War and the French general staff enjoyed an enormous advantage over other states in the League Council's disarmament proceedings.

France's unique position was enhanced by the composition of the Council's Permanent Advisory Commission on Military, Naval, and Air Questions. Each Council member could appoint three experts in military, naval, and air questions to this commission. These three officers, along with the state's permanent Council representative, would compose the national delegation to the commission. In turn, the national delegations would be placed at the Council's disposal in order to advise it on the execution of Articles 1 and 8 as stipulated in Article 9 of the Covenant.

The officers of the Permanent Advisory Commission would be selected and paid by their individual states and so would be "responsible to their respective Governments and General Staffs," Bourgeois wrote. Thus they would "present the true wishes and plans of their respective nations at the discussions and enquiries of the Commissions." What Bourgeois left unsaid was that the commission would really be a mere appendage of the general staffs of the members of the League Council, especially its permanent members (Great Britain, France, Italy, and Japan). Its value to the League would be minimal, as proved to be the case except when the Council solicited a strictly technical assessment of some military question.

The Permanent Advisory Commission itself would be divided into three subcommissions to tackle military, naval, and air questions. The subcommissions' reports would be forwarded to the Council by the full Permanent Advisory Commission with its remarks appended. The commission's secretariat would be composed of three technical officers (army, naval, and air) representing each of the three subcommissions. Since these three officers were active members of their respective armed forces and had been named to the Permanent Advisory Commission only for three-year periods, they were not considered regular members of the League Secretariat (the body that coordinated all League activities). It was informally understood that, in order to continue the consensus that had won the war, the Secretariat's military secretary would be selected from the French army, the naval secretary from the British navy, and the air secretary from the Italian air force.

One of the first tasks assigned by the Council to the Permanent Advisory Commission was to study the technical questions flowing from Articles 1 and 8 of the Covenant and in particular to consider draft regulations under Article 1 regarding the armies, navies, air forces, and armaments of a number of states (Estonia, Georgia, Iceland, Luxembourg, San Marino, and Ukraine) that had applied for admission to the League.

One of the first decisions of the Permanent Advisory Commission was to ask the Council to consider favorably a suggestion by its British member that the United States, which had rejected the Versailles Treaty and with it the League Covenant, be approached and asked to be represented on the commission. The nonmembership of the United States and, until 1934, of Soviet Russia, did little to enhance the disarmament process and was a heavy burden that both the Permanent Advisory Commission and the League had to carry.

The Council in a cautiously worded communication invited Washington to appoint a representative to attend "in a consultative capacity" the commission's sessions dealing with disarmament, but the offer was rejected by U.S. President Woodrow Wilson. The Council's quick action on the commission's proposal was a clear message that it intended to act vigorously to promote the reduction of armaments.

The commitment of the Permanent Advisory Commission was more problematic. Certainly the structure of the commission, especially its military component, indicated that it could not be relied upon to reach prompt disarmament decisions. Aside from being asked to liquidate their own profession, the military assigned to the Permanent Advisory Commission and its three subcommissions were also expected to take steps that could threaten the safety and survival of their states. Most military professionals, rather than seeing disarmament policy in general and abstract terms, tend to focus on how a disarmament proposal will either strengthen their own military posture and that of their allies, or weaken their opponents.

Hence the performance of the Permanent Advisory Commission was, at best, lackluster. In its report of 12 December 1920 to the Council the Permanent Advisory Commission did not consider that armaments reduction could "be profitably considered and effectively assured" in view of the world's present state and the League's actual composition. Armaments reduction, the commission argued, depended not only on the "faithful execution" by the vanquished powers of the disarmament clauses stipulated in the various treaties, but also on the League's "practical and early organisation of cooperative action." This attitude clearly reflected the French security view, that is, that it had received no territorial guarantees against Germany, that it had no military arrangements with the United States and Great Britain which had been promised in exchange for such guarantees, and that it was left virtually abandoned to contend with a vindictive Germany whose population was considerably larger than France's and whose industrial base was measurably greater.

The League's Italian delegate labeled the Permanent Advisory Commission's report "dogmatic," adding that it would be "unfortunate" if the Council either approved the report or published it. In following this advice, the Council noted, but did not adopt, that part of the report pertaining to armaments reduction, and requested that the commission continue to study the disarmament question.

THE TEMPORARY MIXED COMMISSION

Obviously the stultification of Article 9 by the Council's creation of a Permanent Advisory Commission largely staffed by military men dictated that something had to be done. Under the Covenant the League Assembly (composed of all member nations, each having one vote) had been given no responsibility in disarmament matters, but by mid-1920 it had been thrust front and center on this vital question. As the organization's constitutionally weaker body, after the Council, the Assembly harbored for the most part small states that were militarily weak and that shrank from the need to spend public funds on national defense. These states believed that the more powerful members of the international community should relinquish a sizable portion of their military forces. Unlike the Council, the Assembly was more often than not impatient for action in the disarmament field.

The move to fuse the disarmament question with Assembly initiatives neatly dovetailed with public concerns that had been expressed on the issue of arms reduction. The views of the Supreme Council of the Allies on this matter, first voiced in March, were repeated in late August during a conference in Copenhagen by the foreign ministers and ministers of state of Denmark, Norway, and Sweden. The work of the Permanent Advisory Commission, the ministers said, should go forward "without delay" so that a basis of agreement could be devised regarding "an effective limitation" for arms reduction without which peace in the world community could not be assured. Somewhat analogous comments were raised in early October 1920 during the Brussels Financial Conference, which recommended that the League Council confer immediately with the governments concerned in order to secure an agreed reduction of the enormous burden that armaments continued to impose on the world's impoverished. According to the conference's representatives, the need to remain militarily prepared sapped the resources of war-damaged nations and imperiled "their recovery from the ravages of war."

At the request of the Scandinavian states the disarmament question was placed on the League Assembly's agenda at its first session in the autumn of 1920. The issue was referred to the Assembly's Sixth Committee (Armaments, Mandates, and the Economic Weapon), chaired by the Swedish Social Democratic leader and former prime minister Karl Hjalmar Branting. At Branting's urging the committee heard Christian Lange, the Norwegian general secretary of the Inter-Parliamentary Union, who was considered an expert on the subject of disarmament. Basing his address largely on the work of the Inter-Parliamentary Union in 1914, the Covenant's articles on disarmament, and the Council's endeavors up to that point, Lange proposed that the Assembly establish a commission—half of whose members would be selected by the Council and the other half by the Assembly. The commission's task would be to tender to the Council "as early as practicable all its preliminary studies and schemes for the reduction of armaments for the various States." Lange's proposal was submitted to extensive scrutiny during the closing months of 1920 by Branting's committee, by a subcommittee specifically established for this purpose, and by the full Assembly.

The Sixth Committee recommended that the commission be temporary and composed of individuals possessing the "requisite competence in matters of a political, social and economic nature, to prepare for submission to the Council" disarmament proposals as provided in Article 8 of the Covenant. Though the Sixth Committee's recommendation was unanimously adopted by the Assembly, the French did so grudgingly. The Assembly's call for what was to be entitled the Temporary Mixed Commission was not actually implemented by the Council until February 1921.

Lange's proposal that the commission be composed of civilians serving in an unofficial capacity was retained and six were included. They were free to tender plans and make proposals that would have been virtually impossible if they sat as official representatives. The civilian component, which might partially explain the tepid French reaction to the new commission, was offset by the inclusion of six members from the Council's Permanent Advisory Commission, four members from the League's Provisional Economic and Financial Commission, and six members from the governing body of the International Labour Organization, three of whom would be employers and three labor representatives selected by the governing body. The dilution of the mixed commission's civilian component, especially by the addition of six members from the Permanent Advisory Commission, was probably French inspired and if not, it was certainly enthusiastically endorsed by Paris. Concurrently a disarmament section was constituted within the League Secretariat and the secretariats of both the Permanent Advisory Commission and the mixed commission were amalgamated.

The appointment of former French Prime Minister René Viviani to preside over the mixed commission reflected Paris's desire to influence the work of the commission along lines that supported, or at least understood, France's fears and security considerations. The two commissions—the Permanent Advisory Commission, which dealt with the technical aspects of disarmament, and the Temporary Mixed Commission—moved in tandem. Their joint endeavors were instrumental in influencing the League's work in the disarmament arena.

From its inception the Temporary Mixed Commission undertook to exchange information regarding existing armaments. In mid-July 1921 it established a subcommittee to delve into the question. It was to inquire not only into matters of a statistical nature but also into questions general in scope and political in substance. On the basis of this work the subcommittee drew up a program that was approved in September 1921 by the League's Second Assembly. Although the statistical information covering the period 1921–1922 was compiled by the Secretariat, the general and political aspects of the subcommittee's investigations were conducted through a special questionnaire sent to all League members. The following year, 1922, the Third Assembly limited the 1922–1923 statistical inquiry to peacetime armaments and budgetary expenditure on national armaments. The end result was a proposal by the Temporary Mixed Commission to the League's Fourth Assembly in 1923 that a comprehensive yearbook be published based on information culled from published official sources. Its contents would be within the limits imposed by the final paragraph of Article 8 of the Covenant, namely to interchange full and frank information on the scale of armaments and the conditions of industries that were adaptable to warlike purposes. The Council adopted the proposal in early July 1923, but getting so mundane a matter accepted had required a long trek.

The question of private arms manufacturing was also tackled by the Temporary Mixed Commission and the Permanent Advisory Commission. While the advisory commission concluded that private entrepreneurs were probably beyond the reach of the League of Nations, the mixed commission held that the problem might best be approached by targeting international arms traffickers. Though stymied at first, the Assembly again addressed this issue during its fourth session in 1923. On the Assembly's recommendation the Council in December authorized a joint investigation by the mixed commission and the League's Economic Committee into the question of drawing up a draft treaty to control private arms manufacturing in the hope that an international conference could be called to deal with the matter. In the end, private arms manufacturing was not prohibited or even regulated, and arms traffic was never placed under League control. Likewise the exchange of information among members about their military forces and industrial war base was viewed as impracticable.

Aside from the actions of the two commissions the disarmament question was likewise delved into by the Assembly. By 1923 the Assembly had adopted thirteen resolutions dealing with various aspects of disarmament, some of which recommended limiting defense budgets and private arms manufacturing, and controlling the traffic in arms. The Assembly also investigated the possibilities of limiting the use of poisonous gases in war and attempted to publish new discoveries pertaining to the use of poisonous gases in order to diminish the military value that chemical warfare offered. Neither of these approaches proved particularly fruitful.

Despite these meager results, guarded optimism on disarmament percolated below the surface of the international community thanks to the qualified success of the Washington Naval Conference (November 1921–February 1922). Although the conference was in no way associated with the League's disarmament endeavors, the signatories (United States, Great Britain, Japan, France, and Italy) placed quantitative limits on capital ships and aircraft carriers. They also agreed on a ten-year moratorium on new capital ship construction and established a ratio formula on capital ships as well as qualitative restrictions on future construction. The signatories failed, however, to achieve prohibitions on auxiliary warships, especially submarines.

Moreover, France's attitude on disarmament had become less rigid and its stance in the proceedings of the Temporary Mixed Commission more accommodating. This could be traced to Paris's desire to handle disarmament questions with Germany and Soviet Russia through the League. By doing so France could avoid direct negotiations with either state.

The most beneficial outcome of the Washington Naval Conference was that the Americans, who had initiated and hosted the conference, imposed on themselves naval limitations through an international agreement without any request that they be offered some sort of protection in return. It was the clearest application since the war's end of direct arms control. The French, still fearing a resurgent Germany, had assiduously avoided direct disarmament if it was unlinked to mutual security considerations.

Limiting Military Forces: The Esher Plan

The impact of the Washington Naval Conference reverberated through the corridors of the League and on 20 February 1922, two weeks after the signing of the Washington naval treaty, Lord Esher, a member of the Temporary Mixed Commission and a former member of the Committee of Imperial Defense, proffered a plan to solve the general disarmament impasse. Under Esher's plan, clearly based on the naval conference's success, the European powers would institute an immediate and large-scale reduction in their peacetime land and air forces. Peacetime forces would be limited to a fixed ratio analogous to the formula dealing with capital ships agreed upon during the Washington Naval Conference. This fixed ratio served British interests in that it specified that forces for colonial and overseas defense would be determined by each state.

In a concession to the French the Permanent Advisory Commission would be reconstituted under a French-appointed chairman. The commission would have the task of reporting to the League infringements of the treaty and developing an enforcement mechanism. In addition, the Permanent Advisory Commission could nominate service attachés who would be authorized to receive information on "facilities and information regarding armaments" as might from time to time be required by the commission.

Last and most important, 30,000 men of all ranks from the army and air force would constitute a unit, and as such France would be entitled to six units (180,000 men), Great Britain to three units (90,000 men), Italy to four units (120,000 men), Holland to three units (90,000 men), Portugal to one unit (30,000 men), and so on. Numerically German, Austrian, Bulgarian, and Hungarian forces were to remain the same as defined in the peace treaties.

The Temporary Mixed Commission, the Permanent Advisory Commission, and a special subcommittee established specifically to examine Esher's proposal all found it inadequate. Specifically, it was felt that Esher's scheme dealt with peacetime effectives—that it failed to consider trained reserves, war matériels, colonial forces, and other defense imperatives of modern nations. Because of the Washington naval treaty it did not touch on naval reduction, thus reinforcing Britain's privileged position in that area. The objections directed at the technical aspects of Esher's proposal were not without merit, but the plan was rejected purely for political reasons.

What Esher failed to appreciate was that if the success of the Washington conference was due largely to the willingness of the United States to make major concessions, this was because in 1922 the United States was a world power that was satiated territorially and not threatened militarily. The European arena was far different. Germany, Europe's potentially most powerful state, had been defanged by the Versailles Treaty, a settlement that most Germans viewed as needlessly harsh. France, elevated to the status of most powerful state in the wake of Germany's defeat, and *primus inter pares* (first among equals) among the World War I victors, feared that Germany would reclaim its preeminence at the first opportunity. The direct method of arms limitation, as reflected in the Washington naval treaty, was due to a unique combination of factors not to be found in dealing with European national defenses. Disarmament in Europe, many observers agreed, if it was possible at all, could only

be accomplished indirectly: through a combination of armaments reduction concurrent with or linked to the development of some sort of international security system.

THE DRAFT TREATY OF MUTUAL ASSISTANCE

It was not until July 1922 that the Temporary Mixed Commission attempted to bridge the gap between the direct and indirect methods of arms reduction. The clash that ensued took a year to resolve and led to a draft treaty of mutual assistance, which it was hoped would bring about arms reduction. Mixed commission member Lord Robert Cecil, targeting the political aspects of arms reduction, offered four propositions: no scheme for arms reduction could succeed unless it was general; the world's present posture prevented this since most governments were unable to execute an arms reduction program unless they had assurances guaranteeing the safety of their states; any such treaty guarantee should also be general in character; and no such general treaty guarantees would be provided unless there was a definite commitment to arms reduction. Though not implicit in Cecil's propositions, the former director of the League's Disarmament Section, Salvador de Madariaga, said in the 1920s that the general treaty of guarantee would have acted "as a rider to the Covenant."

The French, in particular, disapproved of Cecil's third proposition—that any treaty guarantee be general in character. This would have required French commitment in areas of the world, Latin America, for example, where Paris felt it had no interests to protect. France's vigilance was centered across the Rhine, for it was Germany that threatened the Third Republic's immediate security and monopolized its attention. Hostility to the proposal of a general treaty guarantee was especially strong in the ranks of the French general staff.

In forwarding Cecil's four propositions to the League Council the mixed commission made it clear that its purpose was to allow states to reduce their armaments, while at the same time maintaining security equivalent to what they had enjoyed in the past. In view of French opposition, difficulties soon developed. The mixed commission now faced two contradictory proposals: either it could, as per Cecil's suggestion, draw up the draft of a general treaty, or some other well-defined plan; or it could endorse regional treaty arrangements.

There was no consensus on this question, even within British ranks. Cecil, who often outpaced both the British government and the Foreign Office on policy matters, collided with Britain's League of Nations Assembly representative Herbert A. L. Fisher, former Oxford don and minister of education. Fisher, who noted that the nonparticipation of the United States and Soviet Russia in the League made a general treaty unfeasible, was supported on the desirability of regional treaty arrangements by Branting. Sweden's influential representative argued that such arrangements were valuable because they made it possible to weigh the varied conditions of certain groupings of states—an undisguised allusion to Europe's Scandinavian bloc.

Despite the disagreement over a general treaty versus regional treaty arrangements, the substance of Cecil's propositions was adopted by the mixed commission. The Council's Permanent Advisory Commission, however, was not as accommodating. It emphasized that any general treaty guarantee offered to induce a state to reduce its armaments would be ineffective unless the guarantee was spelled out beforehand by the parties.

The permanent commission's criticism was cogent and caused some members of the mixed commission to withdraw their support for a general treaty because such an accord would present enormous technical problems. How would the general staffs, for example, devise plans leading to military cooperation that would cover every contingency and change for every state or combination of states? Those opposed to a general treaty wanted to scale down the treaty guarantee to a small group of states sharing a common fear (of Germany) buttressed by the technical military agreements emphasized by the Permanent Advisory Commission.

The notion of such a treaty arrangement was anathema to Cecil and those who supported his propositions. Their opposition was based on the argument that what was being forwarded would lead neither to a local nor to a general armaments reduction. On the contrary, the proposed arrangement would resuscitate, under the League's umbrella, the system of competing military alliances—the very setup that had led to World War I.

The two approaches—Cecil's desire for a general treaty guarantee and his critics' desire for regionally limited ones—were joined in debate during the Assembly's third session in the autumn of 1922. The inability to come to a consensus on this matter was illustrative of the deep split that divided the World War I victors, especially England and France. Insulated by a navy that was second to none and that enjoyed prerogatives under the provisions of the Washington naval treaty, Britain perceived disarmament problems in a manner that was generous at France's expense. Unlike the French, the British shared no common frontier with Germany, and Britain's worldwide empire gave it an edge in industrial potential and manpower.

France, however, as well as states like Belgium and Poland, perceived a more hostile European environment and held to the line that the peace could be kept only if the World War I victors enjoyed a measure of military predominance over Germany and her former allies. The French desire was not to reject Cecil's scheme outright, but to reshape it and emphasize the regional and security approach and do so in a manner that best served Paris's perceived interests. Henry de Jouvenel, the Assembly's French representative, offered a compromise, known as Assembly Resolution XIV, that was eventually accepted. The resolution promoted the principle that arms reductions depended upon regional and security considerations.

The opening clauses of this resolution left unchanged Cecil's scheme that arms reduction had to be general and that the consideration to do so would be a security guarantee. His proposition for a general treaty guarantee, in line with the criticisms of the Council's Permanent Advisory Commission, was amended to read that any state offering such guarantees was duty bound to render immediately and effectively any assistance based on a previously agreed plan. Bowing to the pressure of those who supported regional treaty arrangements, the obligation to furnish assistance to an attacked state was in principle to be restricted to states falling within the same geographic area. To quell French and Belgian fears it was also stipulated that should a particular state, based on historical, geographic, or other considerations, be especially exposed to possible attack, detailed schemes were possible for that state's defense in line with Cecil's original propositions and the modifications offered.

Lastly, Cecil's proposition that no general treaty guarantee would be provided unless there was a definite commitment to arms reduction was expanded by introducing the notion of limited treaties of guarantee as optional and supplementary measures. The arms reduction, according to the Assembly, could be achieved either through a general treaty, which was the desirable manner, or through partial treaties meant to be extended and opened to all states.

In the case of a general treaty there would be arms reduction. Should there be a partial treaty the arms reduction would be proportionate to the guarantee provided by the treaty. According to the Assembly, the mixed commission would examine how the two arms reduction systems could be carried out, and the Council would devise and submit to states for their consideration "the plan of the machinery, both political and military, necessary to bring them clearly into effect."

The Assembly request that each League member render its opinion on Resolution XIV provoked a flow of observations. Some states, in arguing that Resolution XIV went too far, held that they could not assume additional obligations beyond those stipulated in the Covenant. Other states declared that Resolution XIV did not go far enough, and that the kind of general treaty arrangement it proposed could not ensure their security. Sufficient security, they maintained, could be achieved only through special treaty arrangements that provided for immediate and joint actions with other states based on plans designed by military experts. Half the League's members tendered no reply at all. This was perhaps understandable in the case of the Latin American states, whose military potential was unimportant to European states. The silence was ominous in the case of Great Britain and the British Commonwealth states—with the exception of Canada, which rejected participation in a treaty of mutual guarantee.

The Permanent Advisory Commission, asked for its technical military view, replied that no general treaty guarantee justified any state action to reduce its armed forces. A reduction could occur only if it was in strict proportion to the reinforcements that could be expected to arrive immediately following an attack. Such an assurance could never be guaranteed by any general or regional treaty, even one that was open to all states within a given area. An assurance could flow only from a military alliance, grounded on mutual interest and organized for common action during a period of military crisis. The commission's British representatives maintained their stony silence.

The Italians and the Spaniards said that the alliance arrangements advocated by the commission would merely rekindle the pre-1914 armaments race. Conceivably, it might permit individual states to reduce their armed forces, but it would compel neighboring states to match the combined military forces of the alliance that had excluded them. The Permanent Advisory Commission's members agreed that there were difficulties in deciding when and how allied nations would go to the assistance of a member state. There was no problem in a state's committing itself to resist aggression, but in fact aggression had no universal definition. Moreover, if the attacked state went unsupported until the Council convened and gave its verdict, the victim might be overwhelmed before assistance arrived. Conversely, if states could unilaterally decide that a breach of the provisions of the treaty arrangements had occurred, was this not a retrogressive step and a return to the anarchy of the pre-1914 period?

Despite these criticisms Cecil prepared a draft treaty for the mixed commission based on Assembly Resolution XIV. He proposed that a general treaty be concluded guaranteeing that an attacked state would receive the support of the League's member states. Likewise, special treaties would be possible provided the League Council, by a three-quarters majority, agreed to negotiate a complementary defensive arrangement on behalf of a state that found itself in a dangerously exposed position. Should hostilities erupt, the League Council had four days to decide by a three-quarters majority which was the aggressor state, whether or not the states were signatories of the treaty. The treaty's signatories were bound by the Council's decision and obligated to supply immediate assistance to the victim of the aggression.

Cecil's proposals were savaged by the permanent commission's military experts, who argued that his draft did not constitute a basis for limiting national armaments. Effective assistance, they said, had to be prepared beforehand and had to be rendered immediately. And according to the Permanent Advisory Commission, drafting the requisite plans within the framework of a general treaty would prove very difficult.

The French, led by Jouvenel, had helped forge Resolution XIV and were keen on going forward with a plan that emphasized the regional and security approach. They were helped in this endeavor by their representative on the mixed commission, Colonel Édouard Réquin, who offered an alternate draft treaty. An influential member of the French general staff, Réquin had been the main critic of

Cecil's initial propositions, especially the one specifying that any treaty guarantee should be general in character. His alternative draft provided that signatories of the treaty would mutually come to each other's assistance if one of them were the victim of aggression. It also provided that to implement this general assistance the signatories might conclude agreements establishing purely defensive groups. They could agree beforehand what assistance they would extend to each other in accordance with the Covenant should there be an act of aggression against any of them.

Between January and September 1923 the mixed commission and its Special Committee established to study proposals on the subject sat for six weeks and considered a number of possible drafts. Their discussions of the Cecil-Réquin schema, from which the draft treaty of mutual assistance developed, largely focused on the two major problems upon which arms reduction hinged: war prevention and mutual guarantees. These long and tortuous negotiations succeeded in fusing—after a number of amendments—a single coordinated proposal that the mixed commission presented to the Assembly at its fourth session in September 1923.

In its proposal for a treaty of mutual assistance the mixed commission declared that aggressive war was an international crime that the parties would not commit. This was followed by language defining when a war would not be viewed as a war of aggression. Article 2 committed all parties to come to the assistance of members who were victims of a war of aggression. Council action was provided for in the event the League was notified of any threats of aggression. The parties were to give assistance as determined by the Council, and half a dozen courses of action by the Council were spelled out. For example, the Council could apply economic sanctions. It could also invoke the name of the parties whose assistance it required, although no party outside the continent where operations would take place could in principle be required to cooperate in military, naval, or air operations. The Council could determine the force that states had to place at its disposal, though states had the right of veto; and it could arrange for cooperation in financial and other areas and appoint a military high command. Likewise, to prevent war the Council was given extensive powers to initiate action on any appeal. Should fighting commence the Council had four days to decide which states were the objects of the aggression and whether these states were enti-

tled to claim the assistance that the treaty afforded. All parties agreed in advance to accept the Council's decision.

States might conclude bilateral or multilateral agreements that complemented the present treaty. This was acceptable provided that these agreements were solely for mutual defense and served to facilitate executing the stipulations enumerated in the treaty and to determine beforehand the assistance that states would offer to each other should there be an act of aggression. When these complementary agreements were reviewed and accepted by the Council they would be registered under Article 16 of the Covenant. If aggression occurred and allied states decided to provide immediate assistance, the League Council would be apprised of the specific course of action. If the Council determined that states had responded improperly to an act of aggression, these states themselves would be regarded by the Council as aggressors and be open to the sanctions outlined in the treaty.

Other articles dealt with demilitarized zones; reparation payments by the aggressor state; arms reduction or limitation; and cooperation in preparing any general plan for arms reduction proposed by the Council. It was also proposed that any arms reduction plan proffered by the Council and accepted by the states be fulfilled within two years, with no subsequent increments except by Council consent. States were to comply with requests for information from the Council; armaments quotas were to be revised every five years; and the validities of the peace treaties and all other treaties registered with the League were to be reserved.

The end result of these arduous negotiations was that in the coordinated text finally agreed to by the mixed commission, Cecil had succeeded in embodying the substance, but not the form of the draft he had originally submitted to the commission. The draft treaty, however, was not passed on by the Assembly because many delegations had qualms about its contents and others asked for time to examine the document before committing their governments to its acceptance. Accordingly, in late September 1923 Secretary-General Sir Eric Drummond forwarded the draft text to the members of the League. In mid-December the governments of states that were not League members also received the draft text. Of fifty-four member states, twenty-nine responded; of these, eighteen acceded to the suggested draft text, but many vitiated their consent by proposing amendments and changes.

Not surprisingly, the replies to the Council on the draft Treaty of Mutual Assistance hinged on how individual states viewed their security status, and whether the draft treaty could be expected to improve that status. Vulnerable states like Estonia and Latvia greeted the draft treaty with a sense of relief. Czechoslovakia, relatively secure because of its treaty ties to France, supported the draft treaty, although with reservations and suggestions. France, now governed by a moderate left coalition under Prime Minister Édouard Herriot, gave its unqualified approval. Belgium supported the treaty, but with conditions.

Acceptance by France and Belgium was to be expected in view of the major role their representatives had played in drawing up and shaping the draft treaty. On the other hand, France's client states in eastern Europe withheld their acceptance or flatly rejected the draft treaty, arguing that it did not increase their security enough to justify any national arms reduction.

The main blow against the draft treaty was delivered by the western states and those states that remained neutral during the world war. Great Britain, the British Commonwealth states, and other states that had unilaterally reduced their arms suplies contended that the accord involved a broad extension of their ongoing international obligations. Though Italy and Japan did not reject the draft treaty they offered reservations regarding the definition of aggression, special treaty agreements, and other important points.

Germany maintained that it could not assume the obligations stipulated in the draft treaty because of the disarmament provisions imposed on it by the Versailles settlement. Soviet Russia, a nonmember of the League and the foremost pariah of the international community, railed at some length against the draft treaty, denying that there was any interconnection between arms reduction and national security concerns. What was needed, Moscow argued, was universal and immediate arms reduction. Washington's reaction was in line with its rejection of the League Covenant: firm but polite refusal to consider participation in any treaty of mutual assistance. With the exception of Uruguay, no Latin American state responded to the Council's circulation of the draft treaty, although most Latin American leaders were in agreement with Britain and the British Commonwealth states.

Thus in attempting to limit national armaments the League had discovered that meaningful propos-als toward this end were inseparable from questions of state security. Yet the draft treaty of mutual assistance, which had been so painfully hammered out to resolve this problem, was obviously unacceptable to many of the League's most important members.

In its unfavorable response to the draft treaty, London intimated that a new approach might be in order; for instance, the convening of a League-sponsored arms reduction conference to include nonmember states. In view of the unique conditions that made the Washington Naval Conference a success, few observers were optimistic that a new conference would repeat this success in land armaments.

THE GENEVA PROTOCOL

When the Fifth Assembly convened in the autumn of 1924, its most urgent order of business was replacing the draft Treaty of Mutual Assistance with a viable alternative. Even those governments that had been critical of the draft treaty had voiced their concern that a resolution of the arms reduction-security problem pursued in the draft treaty was imperative.

Taking a new, indirect approach, negotiators reasoned that if the principle of compulsory arbitration could be extended in such a way as to enable the League to handle all international disputes, the vexing issue of security and disarmament might be bridged. In their replies to the League Council regarding the draft Treaty of Mutual Assistance most governments had noted that Council action would never be immediate and certain unless there was a foolproof method of determining which warring state was the aggressor.

Led by Britain's Prime Minister James Ramsay MacDonald and France's Prime Minister Édouard Herriot, who were united by their socialist idealism, the Assembly resolved to prepare for a forthcoming disarmament conference by reviewing the Covenant and the stillborn Treaty of Mutual Assistance and other plans subsequently submitted to Secretary-General Drummond. The Assembly's First Committee (Constitutional and Organizational) with Greece's Nikolaos Politis as rapporteur, investigated compulsory arbitration, while the Third Committee (Legal) with Czechoslovakia's Eduard Beneš as rapporteur, investigated security and arms reduction. Following a month of intense discussions the two rapporteurs on 1 October 1924 submitted to the Assembly the committees' joint recommendations for a draft "Protocol for the Pacific Settlement of International Disputes," thereafter called the Geneva Protocol. Attached to the committees' recommendations was a clear and cogent report analyzing both schemes. The Assembly quickly and unanimously recommended the protocol's adoption by the League's membership.

Like the draft treaty of mutual assistance, the Geneva Protocol denounced war, and no signatories would be entitled to resort to it against other signatories or against nonsignatory states that had accepted all the protocol's obligations. The protocol's principal purpose was to establish a connection between arbitration, security or sanctions, and disarmament. By doing so the protocol would strengthen the Covenant's system for pacific settlement of disputes and also close gaps that allowed League members to resort to war under certain conditions.

The first stone in the protocol's arch—the question of compulsory arbitration—stipulated that every signatory had to adhere to the Permanent Court of International Justice's optional clause, which gave the court compulsory jurisdiction on justiciable cases. Either party could refer a dispute to the court. Disputes that did not go to the court or to voluntary arbitration were to be brought before the League Council. If the Council's decision was unanimous it was binding on the parties. A divided Council would refer the dispute to arbitrators whose decision was binding.

The second stone in the protocol's arch was security, or sanctions. The state that decided on war rather than submit the dispute to arbitration, or refused to execute the arbitrators' decision, would automatically be considered the aggressor state unless the Council unanimously decided otherwise. Thus the protocol's signatories were duty bound to support the Covenant, to resist the aggressor state, and to help the state that had been attacked, provided their geographical location and their military prowess allowed it. However, League members could make special arrangements with the Council spelling out what forces they would hold in readiness and activate in support of the League Covenant and the Geneva Protocol.

The last stone in the arch was a disarmament conference to be convened by the Council in mid-June 1925 to which all signatory states would be invited as well as all other states regardless of whether or not they were League members. Until then the Council would prepare a program of arms reduction and limitation for the conference's approval. When the conference adopted a general arms reduction plan the protocol would then come into force; should the Council discover that the arms reduction plan was being circumvented, it would have the power to declare the protocol invalid.

The Geneva Protocol represented the high point in the League's attempt to institute arms reduction in line with Covenant objectives and world community desires.

Reflecting the euphoria of the day following its unanimous adoption by the Assembly it was signed immediately by fourteen states, including France, Poland, and Yugoslavia. After several states quickly followed suit, and Czechoslovakia went so far as to ratify the protocol, the League awaited Britain's reaction, which hinged on the results of the November 1924 national elections. In those contests British voters rejected MacDonald's minority Labour government in favor of a majority Conservative Party government under Stanley Baldwin, with Austen Chamberlain as foreign secretary. Though Chamberlain wanted to move in tandem with the French as much as possible, and the protocol was supported by the British delegation at Geneva, he nevertheless rejected the protocol. His decision was based in part on the British Commonwealth states' hostile reaction to the protocol, U.S. and Russian nonparticipation in the League's endeavors, London's reluctance to guarantee the status quo in eastern Europe, as well as its longtime enmity to the concept of compulsory arbitration. Especially important was London's opposition to assuming military obligations that were indefinite in nature, although British leaders were prepared to offer guarantees in particular areas where they perceived their interests lay. With the British rejection of the Geneva Protocol, the disarmament process was stymied.

THE PREPARATORY COMMISSION

No sooner had the Geneva Protocol been defeated than the French began pushing for its resurrection in revised form. Austen Chamberlain, however, hesitated. He was anxious that nothing jeopardize the ongoing British negotiations with Germany that would lead to the Locarno Pacts, a series of agreements reached at Locarno, Switzerland, to guarantee existing territorial boundaries in Europe and to provide for the arbitration of disputes among the signatories (Great Britain, Germany, France, Belgium, Italy, Czechoslovakia, and Poland). The disarmament compromise hammered out by the Sixth Assembly in late 1925 was an Assembly request to the Council to undertake a preparatory study for a disarmament conference. No time limit was set, but it was made clear that Council inactivity on this point "would fail to meet the ideas of the Sixth Assembly." In light of the rejection of the draft Treaty of Mutual Assistance and the Geneva Protocol, the Council in its preparatory study reverted to the direct method of disarmament discussion, that is, it eschewed the question of the political setting that might eventually bring about arms reduction and focused attention on armaments themselves. The hope, according to one authority, was that such an approach might disclose, as the Washington naval discussion had, "the possibility of immediate and proportionate reduction in the existing figures" (Walters, p. 362). The new organ devised by the Council to mark the trail was the Preparatory Commission for the Disarmament Conference. It was composed of all Council members, plus six other League members. Additional participants were Germany, the United States, Soviet Russia, and subsequently Turkey.

For the next five years the Preparatory Commission was the League's mainstay on the disarmament question, and despite its often slow work pace and intermittent adjournments it held the world's attention and generated heated debates. The technical experts on the Preparatory Commission were service officers attached to their delegations, as well as personnel selected by the League's Financial, Economic, and Communications Committee and by the workers' and employers' groups in the International Labour Organization.

Understandably in view of the Preparatory Commission's narrow mandate to concentrate on direct methods of arms reduction, its endeavors in large measure focused on technical aspects of the question, especially methods and general guidelines. It eschewed specific obligations for individual states until the disarmament conference convened, but it did examine limitations on serving forces, reserves, armaments expenditure, naval airplanes, warships by classes, and so on.

Throughout these discussions the French continued to insist that any disarmament convention would be unsatisfactory unless it contained provisions for an ironclad supervisory system that ensured that the signatories assumed their obligations under the treaty. In line with this, the Assembly instructed the commission to establish an arbitration and security committee to propose steps that, by providing security guarantees, might allow states to accept the lowest possible armaments limits.

The draft disarmament conventions tabled separately by the British and French in the spring of 1927 highlighted the wide variances that divided both states on the issues in question. To the British, the French demands for security pledges were only pretexts to disguise their intentions to maintain a paramount military position in Europe. To the French, the British were doing everything possible to unload their peacekeeping obligations, including those stipulated in the League Covenant. It was a replay of their political bickering prior and subsequent to the rejection of the draft Treaty of Mutual Assistance and the Geneva Protocol. Though there had been governmental changes in both states since 1919, their national interests on disarmament and security matters were unbridgeable and they held to their separate and divergent policies. The disarmament question spotlighted as nothing else could that perceived national interests prove more enduring than the transient governments that follow each other like the seasons.

As the Preparatory Commission's work was winding down, Moscow's proposal that all armed services be dissolved and all arms destroyed, and that the only weapons allowed be those possessed by the police and customs service, was received with derision and did not contribute substantively to the commission's task. Official conversations offstage to hasten the commission's work led nowhere. Optimism was generated by the 1928 Pact of Paris, the so-called Kellogg-Briand Pact, which, although negotiated outside the League's framework, renounced war as an instrument of national policy. Likewise in 1930 the London Naval Treaty extended the 1922 Washington naval arrangements to cover cruisers, destroyers, and submarines, thus lessening naval tension between Washington and London.

By late autumn 1930, and despite these two extra-League successes at arms control, the Preparatory Commission had made no real progress. Indeed, one article in the commission's draft convention stipulated that the proposed arms reduction arrangement would leave unaffected the obligations that already bound the signatory states. This was acceptable to France, which took it to mean that the disarmament provisions of the Versailles Treaty would be maintained, but it was totally insupportable to Germany.

THE DISARMAMENT CONFERENCE, 1932–1934

After numerous delays, the Disarmament Conference convened on 2 February 1932 and adjourned in mid-December with the understanding that it would reconvene in late January 1933. During these months the negotiations were influenced by fighting in Manchuria (which Japan had invaded in 1931), rising nationalism in Germany, and the spreading worldwide economic collapse. The positions previously voiced by various states were echoed during these months of seemingly endless logomachy, offstage maneuvers, and closeted discussions. Germany, for one, insisted that the proposed disarmament convention agreement should replace the disarmament provisions of the Versailles settlement, thereby ending the postwar division of the world community into victors and vanquished. France, supported by Belgium, Poland, and the states of the Little Entente (Czechoslovakia, Romania, and Yugoslavia), demanded that security guarantees precede arms reduction. Italy, whose opinion was shared by Britain and the United States, acquiesced to Germany's claim to equality and also pressed for the complete prohibition of powerful weaponry whether land-based, naval, or airborne. Militarily engaged in Manchuria, Japan was disinterested in arms control, while Soviet Russia opposed France's desires for security guarantees and appealed either for total disarmament or, at the least, for the abolition of the most aggressive weaponry.

Germany withdrew from the conference in mid-September, prompting the United States and the principal European powers to agree on 11 December 1932 that the conference's aim was to devise a disarmament convention in which Germany would enjoy equality in a system meant to provide security for all. In addition, states would renounce force as a means of settling their differences. The formula was a clear declaration that the convention would replace the disarmament clauses of the Versailles settlement. The arrangement was all things to all states: it induced Germany to return to the conference, while simultaneously allowing France to maintain her security demand. Great Britain in turn could insist that the concession granted prevented any state from raising new claims supported by threats.

The Disarmament Conference nonetheless ended in a stalemate. By the time it reconvened in late January 1933 the world situation had changed for the worse. On 30 January, Adolf Hitler was appointed German chancellor. In late March, Japan announced her intention to withdraw from the League in two years' time. The conference's initial discussions involved difficult talks between the French and the Germans on implementing the formula devised the previous December. Confronted by a resurgent Germany and by an Italy inclined, like Germany, toward revising the 1919 treaties, Paris found it virtually impossible to implement the policies required by the 11 December agreement. Unable to disavow the agreement, the French sought to use its ambiguities to raise procedural and substantive difficulties and revert once again to their oft-repeated desire for security guarantees. Deadlock on this issue moved the British in mid-March to offer a draft disarmament convention whose stipulations would supersede the disarmament clauses imposed on Germany by the Versailles Treaty and also accommodate Berlin in other matters. Concurrently, the draft treaty sought to placate France by offering some of the guarantees Paris desired against aggression; for example, it invoked U.S. Secretary of State Henry Stimson's doctrine that Washington's acceptance of the Kellogg-Briand Pact obligated it to consult with other signatory states if there was ever a breach of the treaty. The United States, Italy, and—apparently—Germany were supportive, but Japan raised reservations about naval limitations while France again returned to the theme that inspection and investigation procedures should be strengthened. Fearful of the Germans, Moscow drew closer to the French position and spoke less of disarmament and more about a regional security system.

In an attempt to modify the British plan, France offered to disarm and reach equality with Germany over an eight-year period, rather than a five-year period as suggested in the British draft. The first four years would see no actual disarmament, and if this first period proved satisfactory the reductions envisaged in the British draft would be implemented during the second period. London, Rome, and Washington accepted Paris's modifications. Hitler's riposte was to withdraw from the discussions of the Disarmament Conference and the League of Nations.

Extra-League negotiations between Britain, France, and Germany foundered because of Paris's refusal to reduce its arms or agree to German rearmament that exceeded the limits imposed by the Versailles Treaty. The talks collapsed completely when the 1934–1935 German budget showed an enormous increase in military expenditures, especially for aviation, which was expressly forbidden by the Versailles Treaty. French officials, convinced that Germany had begun to rearm in violation of the 1919 settlements, held that France had to look to her own security.

The French wanted to continue the Disarmament Conference, but insisted that the conference should not agree to Germany's rearmament or ask France to reduce its weapons supply. The British disagreed. The conference, London argued, could not continue without Germany. It believed that a convention was feasible, but Germany's rearmament had to be accepted. As to French security desires, London was not prepared to assume additional obligations. Italy refused to partake in the conference unless Germany returned to the negotiating table. The remaining states lacked a consensus, and the conference adjourned on 11 June 1934.

CONCLUSION

The years that followed were, contrary to the League Covenant's strictures, years of rearmament that saw states like Nazi Germany and Fascist Italy in Europe and Imperial Japan in the Far East gain the upper hand. The League's interwar endeavors show clearly that arms control and disarmament are largely political—not technical—questions. The absence of a political consensus leads to unending logomachy and stillborn, or rejected, proposals.

The tragedy of the interwar period was that although England and France both were committed to the maintenance of the European status quo as legitimized in the peace settlements of 1919, their means of achieving this end conflicted. France's persistent search for security guarantees, for airtight disarmament inspection, and so on mirrored its perceived military, demographic, and industrial weaknesses. The British resistance to these guarantees was based in part on a false reading of Eu-

ropean balance of power relations and the role of a revitalized Germany. The League's disarmament discussion that terminated in June 1934 did not fail because of a lack of imagination or goodwill, but because of political factors of enormous complexity little appreciated or understood at the time. Those who partook in the disarmament negotiations following World War II soon discovered that political factors stymied their own labors as it had their predecessors' except in areas where marginal arms control agreements did not threaten the perceived security interests of either side in the Cold War.

BIBLIOGRAPHY

The official view of the League of Nations' disarmament odyssey is recounted in LEAGUE OF NATIONS, *Ten Years of World Co-Operation* (Geneva, 1930). The unofficial view of the world organization's endeavors is described in detail and with clarity in the multivolumed *Survey of International Affairs* (1920–1963), published by London's Royal Institute of International Affairs. These volumes, which extend through the interwar period, were largely edited by ARNOLD J. TOYNBEE.

General Accounts   By far the best general history of the League, detailed but partial in its treatment of the organization, is FRANCIS PAUL WALTERS, *A History of the League of Nations,* 2 vols. (London, 1952). Other general histories of the League, though helpful and valuable, fall far short of Walters's classic, for example, GEORGE SCOTT, *The Rise and Fall of the League of Nations* (London, 1973).

The best work on the disarmament question as viewed from within the confines of the League Secretariat is SALVADOR DE MADARIAGA, *Disarmament* (London, 1929); de Madariaga correctly observed that disarmament was not a technical question and could not be divorced from security considerations. Lord Robert Cecil's linkage of disarmament and security guarantees is found in DAVID CARLTON, "Disarmament with Guarantees: Lord Cecil 1922–1927," *Disarmament and Arms Control* 3:2 (1965): 143–164. The divergent Anglo-French positions are cogently presented in ARNOLD WOLFERS, *Britain and France Between Two Wars* (New York, 1966).

Geneva Protocol   The League's endeavors at disarmament during the 1920s is tackled in a large number of works of which the following is a small sampling: "The Draft Treaty of Mutual Assistance," *International Affairs* 3 (March, 1924): 45–82; DAVID HUNTER MILLER, *The Geneva Protocol* (New York, 1925); PHILIP JOHN NOEL-BAKER, *The Geneva Protocol for the Pacific Settlement of International Disputes* (London, 1925); JOHN FISCHER WILLIAMS, *The Geneva Protocol of 1924* (London, 1925); and JOHN FISCHER WILLIAMS, "Model Treaties for the Pacific Settlement of Disputes—Mutual Assistance and Non-Aggression," *International Affairs* 7 (November 1928): 407–421. The best study of the Locarno Pacts is JON JACOBSON, *Locarno Diplomacy: Germany and the West, 1925–1929* (Princeton, N.J., 1972).

Arms Control Efforts   The work of the Preparatory Commission is very ably examined in JOHN W. WHEELER-BENNETT, *Disarmament and Security Since Locarno 1925–1931* (London, 1932). His other works on the Disarmament Conference are indispensable for those delving into the negotia-tions that led to its failure; for example, *The Disarmament Deadlock* (London, 1934) and *The Pipe Dream of Peace* (London, 1935). Perhaps one of the most important works is the memoir of PHILIP JOHN NOEL-BAKER, *The First World Disarmament Conference 1932–1933 and Why it Failed* (Oxford, 1979). The memoir of ARTHUR C. TEMPERLEY, *The Whispering Gallery of Europe* (London, 1938), recounts the opinions of the British military adviser at Geneva.

Reference Works   Equally valuable in tracing the world organization's disarmament work is the sixteen-volume LEAGUE OF NATIONS, *Armaments Year-Book* (Geneva, 1923–1939/40) and the fourteen-volume LEAGUE OF NATIONS, *Statistical Yearbook of the Trade in Arms and Ammunition* (Geneva, 1924–1938). For a fuller glimpse into the literature see VICTOR-YVES GHEBALI, *Bibliographical Handbook on the League of Nations,* 3 vols. (Geneva, 1980).

The Versailles Treaty

Imposed Disarmament

NEAL H. PETERSEN

See also Demilitarization and Neutralization Through World War II; The Disarming and Rearming of Germany; France; Germany; *and* The League of Nations and Disarmament. *The* Treaty of Versailles *is excerpted in Volume III.*

Few treaties in history have been as controversial and little understood as the Treaty of Versailles. This pertains especially to the clauses designed to insure the disarmament of Germany. Contemporary observers and subsequent historians have disagreed over the effectiveness and wisdom of the main thrust of the Versailles treaty—to impose unilateral disarmament on Germany as a means of achieving European security.

The treaty's arms control clauses employed a wide variety of mechanisms—the limitation of forces and weapons, the demilitarization of specific geographic areas, the restricting of arms manufacture and traffic, and the outlawing of specific weapons. Additionally, for the first time in history an organization employing on-site inspectors was established, charged with verifying German compliance. The successes and failures of these mechanisms are also a matter of disagreement.

While the treaty did not eliminate the threat of German aggression or prevent a new war, it did render Germany militarily impotent for a decade. The proportion of blame properly assigned to the Paris peacemakers of 1919 and their successor statesmen for failing to achieve lasting European security will never be decided to the satisfaction of all.

The formulation, implementation, and demise of the arms control terms of the Versailles treaty are instructive in the context of the tragic course of events of the 1930s. Even more important, however,

is what the history of the Versailles treaty can teach us about the role of arms control in international relations and about the technicalities of weapons inventory, destruction, and inspection. Certainly the Versailles experience suggests that it is futile to expect disarmament—either imposed or negotiated—to result in lasting security, unless it rests on a firm political foundation of equity and adaptability.

The travails of the drafters of the Versailles armaments clauses and the control commissions that sought to put them into effect are relevant to the arms control treaties of the late twentieth century, including the Intermediate-Range Nuclear Forces (INF) and Conventional Forces in Europe (CFE) treaties, as well as to the inspection of Iraq after the Persian Gulf War of 1991.

THE ARMISTICE OF 1918

After four bloody years, World War I drew to a close when Germany realized that it could no longer continue the struggle. On 4 October 1918, a newly constituted German government informed President Woodrow Wilson that it was prepared to conclude a peace agreement based on the U.S. government's Fourteen Points. The Allies debated the terms of the armistice among themselves for several weeks, and in a note of 5 November 1918, the Allies and the United States accepted the German request for peace.

The terms of the instrument of surrender called for German withdrawal from all occupied areas and from the west bank of the Rhine within thirty days. Germany would turn over a fixed number of aircraft, ships, submarines (160), trucks (5,000), locomotives (5,000), and rolling stock (150,000 cars) to the victors immediately. The armistice finally went into effect on 11 November 1918.

The armistice was not an unconditional surrender, but was based on specific terms and implied an equitable peace under the Fourteen Points, including sweeping reference to general worldwide disarmament. (Point Four called for "adequate guarantees given and taken that national armaments will be reduced to the lowest point consistent with domestic safety.") Nothing in the armistice's terms indicated that unilateral and permanent disarmament was going to be imposed upon Germany.

By and large, Germany sought to comply with the terms of the armistice, although supply and transportation shortages and domestic unrest prevented rapid troop withdrawal to east of the Rhine. The armistice was extended several times to accommodate reality; in each instance additional requirements were imposed upon Germany. In a major violation of the armistice, the Germans scuttled their fleet at the Scotland naval base of Scapa Flow in June 1919 rather than turn it over to the Allies.

NEGOTIATING THE ARMS LIMITATION CLAUSES

The Paris Peace Conference convened on 18 January 1919, with the "Allied and Associated Powers" setting as their primary goal lasting international security. In particular, they wished to establish a European state system that could not be upset by future German aggression. Consistent with this purpose, they deprived Germany of over 10 percent of its continental territory and all overseas assets and colonies. Massive reparations were imposed, and stringent limitations were placed on German armaments and on industries capable of constructing armaments.

Not all the arms control clauses were carefully crafted, however; in many instances they represented the result of hasty action and dubious compromises on the part of the Allies. The net effect, nonetheless, was to impose extensive, severe restrictions that did indeed hamstring the German military for many years.

President Wilson, who had arrived in Europe in mid-December to great acclaim, was the central player in the conference deliberations. Initially, proceedings were focused in the Supreme Council; later however, the key decisions were made by the Council of Four, which consisted of the heads of government of the United States, Great Britain, France, and Italy. On 25 January 1919, the conference unanimously adopted a resolution calling for the establishment of the League of Nations. Thereafter, commissions to draft the League Covenant and to consider various territorial questions and reparations were created. Among these was a small committee on disarmament, whose members included Marshal Ferdinand Foch of France, Winston Churchill of Great Britain, and Gen. Tasker Bliss of the United States.

Britain, motivated by domestic pressures to demobilize, advocated disarmament of Germany, while France, ironically, was initially hesitant out of concern that Allied armies would soon thereafter also be disbanded to the detriment of French security. The United States supported the British position. Initially, the Western leaders did not contemplate the permanent disarmament of Germany, but rather a onetime surrendering of arms as part of a renewal of the armistice. However, President Wilson's reluctance to use the armistice for this purpose resulted in disarmament being folded into the peace treaty process.

President Wilson spent mid-February to mid-March 1919 in the United States, during which time a drafting committee under Marshal Foch developed most of the military clauses. One especially contested issue was the size of the German army and its method of recruitment. British Prime Minister Lloyd George advocated a small professional force for Germany, thus permitting Britain to abolish conscription. Conversely, Marshal Foch favored the continuation of German conscription, which he saw as providing a powerful argument for continuing the French conscription he deemed essential. The resulting compromise provided for a German long-term professional army of only one hundred thousand men and the prohibition of conscription. Upon his return to Paris, Wilson, who favored conscription and a somewhat larger German army, unsuccessfully attempted to overturn this decision.

The configuration and duration of the control body charged with overseeing German disarmament was also a matter of controversy. The French sought to create a permanent supervisory body outside the League of Nations. The United States and

Britain opposed this position, and their view prevailed. The Inter-Allied Commissions of Control (IACC) would supervise only those terms of disarmament for which there was a specified time limit. Beyond that, verification of German compliance would be the responsibility of the League. At Paris, the Allies anticipated that the work of the IACC would last no longer than a few months.

The League of Nations and Disarmament

In April 1919, a month after agreement on Part V of the Versailles treaty—regarding military, naval, and air provisions—had been reached, President Wilson suggested that a preamble be included indicating that German disarmament was the first step toward general disarmament. He believed that the reiteration of this point, which also appeared in the League Covenant, would make the terms of the treaty more acceptable to Germany. The preamble to Part V was adopted without detailed consideration.

In a critical decision based on immediate political considerations, the peacemakers determined to place the Covenant of the League of Nations within the treaty with Germany. The Covenant, which was completed on 26 April 1919, provided in Article 8 for League involvement in seeking general disarmament. This article reflected the growing concern with the destructiveness of modern weaponry and, to a lesser extent, the influence of the international peace movement since the late nineteenth century. The Hague conferences of 1899 and 1907 had set up a predecessor to the World Court, outlawed the use of poison gas and certain other inhumane weapons, and defined certain rules of war and blockade.

In Article 8, Paragraph 1, of the Covenant, the victorious Allies in effect agreed to negotiate their own reduction of armaments in deliberations supervised by the League of Nations:

The Members of the League recognise that the maintenance of peace requires the reduction of national armaments to the lowest point consistent with national safety and the enforcement by common action of international obligations.

In refining the text of Article 8, the drafters softened the extent of disarmament required by retreating from the initial phrase "domestic safety" and replacing it with "national safety." The League Council was to formulate plans for general reductions, and League members undertook to exchange information on armaments. The private manufacture of arms was declared in paragraph 5 "open to grave objections." Article 8 contained six paragraphs and received careful consideration in the drafting process. Consequently, this article can be viewed as a serious policy statement by the Allied and Associated Powers.

Although the League established a Permanent Commission on Armaments in 1921 and sponsored negotiations throughout the interwar period, including the World Disarmament Conference in 1932, little was accomplished toward general disarmament. This failure was taken by the Germans, who overlooked their own contribution to the failure of general disarmament, as a breach of faith and justification for their own violations of the Versailles arms control clauses.

The League, Germany, and Disarmament

In the drafting of the treaty clauses concerning the disarmament of Germany, the peace negotiators disagreed over the extent to which Germany should be occupied, partitioned, and permanently disarmed. The French took a far sterner position than did the other participants, demanding separation of the left (or west) bank of the Rhine from Germany and annexation of the Saar Basin. The United States and Britain insisted that the Rhineland not be detached from Germany, but in deference to the French views agreed to permanent demilitarization.

In addition, U.S. and British leaders initially pledged, in a tripartite treaty of 28 June 1919, to come to the aid of France in the event of an unprovoked German attack. When the U.S. Senate refused to ratify the treaty and Britain also backed away from its obligations, France felt betrayed and abandoned.

The disarmament clauses of the Versailles treaty were developed to satisfy French demands for security, and reflected a degree of imprecision and undue harshness in some respects. In April, the German delegation asked for two changes—that Germany be admitted to the League immediately, and that the Allies honor their promise of general disarmament within two years. The Allied and Associated Powers refused these modifications, but in their reply reiterated support for general disarmament as contained in Article 8 and argued that German disarmament facilitated general disarmament. The failure of the Allies to carry out general disarmament in the interwar period fortified the German view that the arms control that had been unilaterally imposed on Germany was unfair and provided moral and legal justification for German rearmament.

The Versailles treaty as a whole was presented to the German delegation, which had had no role in its preparation, on 7 May 1919. It included Article 231, which assigned guilt to Germany for causing the war; provisions for German reparations for all civilian damages sustained by the Allies; the loss by Germany of territory including its colonies, Alsace-Lorraine, and Danzig and the so-called Polish Corridor; and extensive restrictions on armaments, as described below.

The German delegation's note of 29 May 1919 expressed the nation's anguish. Delegation president Count Ulrich von Brockdorff-Rantzau was "aghast" at the terms which he described as a death sentence. The proposed treaty, the Germans believed, violated the conditions under which Germany had initially accepted the armistice in November 1918. Germany offered to disarm ahead of the Allies, but deplored the reparations, war guilt, and territorial clauses agreed to at Versailles.

Replying for the victors on 16 June, French Premier Georges Clemenceau expressed to the Germans the Allies' dissatisfaction with their position. The Germans were guilty of causing the war and waging it in an inhuman manner; they must sign the treaty as it stood within five days or face further military action. Confronted with this ultimatum, Germany signed the Treaty of Versailles on 28 June 1919, but from the beginning regarded it as a diktat, imposed under duress and without moral standing. The arms control clauses, some of which the Germans might have willingly accepted and did partially fulfill, were tarnished by Berlin's view of the treaty as a whole.

ARMS CONTROL CLAUSES OF THE TREATY

The Versailles treaty limited Germany to an army of one hundred thousand men; outlawed conscription; prohibited military aircraft and submarines, and put severe limitations on surface ships; required the dismantling of fortifications in the Rhineland and at Heligoland, and elsewhere; authorized the Allies to occupy the west bank of the Rhine for at least fifteen years, and prohibited German forces from the area permanently. This formula resulted in eliminating any threat to Germany's neighbors for a decade and would have had

the same effect indefinitely if political factors and the will of the Allies had permitted permanent enforcement.

The preamble to Part V of the treaty, which contains military, naval, and air clauses, reiterated the assertion in Article 8 that the Germans were being asked to disarm as part of a larger scheme of international arms control. It read as follows: "In order to render possible the initiation of a general limitation of the armaments of all nations, Germany undertakes strictly to observe the military, naval and air clauses which follow." This third instance of the Allies linking German arms restrictions to general disarmament, the others being the written response to German objections to the treaty and the Covenant of the League, was not a carefully considered initiative. Rather, it was an afterthought designed to encourage German acceptance; later it would return to haunt Western disarmament negotiators.

Military Manpower   Part V, setting forth the terms for the disarmament of Germany, was comprised of Articles 159 through 213. Chapter I of Section I (Articles 159–163) dealt with army manpower. The German army was required to reduce its strength to one hundred thousand by 31 March 1920. The officer corps was limited to four thousand, and the general staff was to be abolished. Nonmilitary uniformed personnel such as customs officers and forest guards and coastguards were not to exceed the 1913 level.

Armaments and Munitions   In Chapter II of Section I, Part V (Articles 164–172), limits were placed upon German armaments, munitions, and materials. The restrictions applied until such time as Germany was allowed to join the League of Nations. Even then, any increase above the limits had to be approved by the League Council. Munitions and stores had to be concentrated at points known to the Allies. Arms and munitions manufacturing could occur only in Allied-approved factories. Stores in excess of limits had to be surrendered to the Allies for destruction. Germany was forbidden from importing or exporting all war material. Poison gas and related material were prohibited entirely.

Recruiting and Military Training   Chapter III of Section I, Part V (Articles 173–179) dealt with recruiting and military training. Conscription was outlawed and the army was to be staffed exclusively by long-term professionals. Enlisted men and non-commissioned officers were required to serve twelve years, and officers twenty-five years. Officers already in service and retained could not retire before the age of forty-five. Only 5 percent of personnel could be replaced per year. The rationale for this undemocratic system of military service was to limit the number of men who received military training. Members of educational establishments, veterans organizations, and recreational clubs were forbidden from engaging in military training or activities.

Demilitarization Chapter IV of Part V (Article 180) specified that all fortifications west of a line drawn fifty kilometers (30 miles) east of the Rhine had to be demolished within four months. This provision complemented Articles 42 and 43 in Part III of the treaty, which permanently prohibited both fortifications and armed forces from the Rhineland area. The Saar Basin was also demilitarized in the Annex to Part III, Section IV. Article 180 allowed for Germany's fortifications on its eastern and southern borders to be maintained in their existing state. In addition to the limitations on fortifications in this article, Article 115 in Part III, Section XIII, mandated that the fortifications on Heligoland be dismantled.

Naval Limitations Section II of Part V (Articles 181–197) contained the naval clauses of the treaty. Germany was limited to six battleships of older design, six light cruisers, twelve destroyers, and twelve torpedo boats. Submarines were prohibited. German naval personnel could not exceed fifteen thousand men, including a maximum of fifteen hundred officers. All German warships not in German ports were to be forfeited to the victors. As with army personnel, enlisted men would have to serve for twelve years and officers for twenty-five, with the same 5 percent yearly turnover restriction. The arms, munitions, and mines that Germany would surrender, retain, or destroy were also defined. Naval fortifications in the Baltic and North Sea area could not be upgraded and certain islands were demilitarized. The navy was forbidden from training merchant seamen.

Air Clauses The air clauses of the treaty are found in Section III of Part V (Articles 198–202). Military and naval air forces were banned entirely.

Until the final withdrawal of their personnel from Germany, the Allies were granted freedom of passage and landing rights. The Germans could not manufacture or import aircraft or aircraft engines. Germany was compelled to surrender specific numbers of aircraft, engines, aircraft manufacturing machinery, instruments, and aircraft armaments.

Verification and Compliance Section IV of Part V (Articles 203–210) set forth the structure and functions of the Inter-Allied Commissions of Control (IACC) that would supervise and verify German compliance with the military, naval, and air clauses of the treaty. The military, naval, and air commissions would be established in Berlin, with the right to send teams to any part of Germany. The Germans would bear the costs of commission operations, as well as of actual deliveries and destruction of arms and munitions.

The last section of Part V (Section V, Articles 211–213), included miscellaneous items. Germany was required to enact domestic legislation implementing the military, naval, and air clauses of the treaty within three months. Certain provisions of the armistice were designated as remaining in force. Finally, it was specified in Article 213 that the League of Nations would have responsibility for long-term verification of compliance. The article stated that "so long as the present Treaty remains in force, Germany undertakes to give every facility for any investigation which the Council of the League of Nations, acting if need be by a majority vote, may consider necessary."

Restrictions on Other Central Powers
The Paris Peace Conference prepared peace treaties for Germany's allies. These treaties reflected the determination of the Allies to impose long-term disarmament requirements on the lesser members of the defeated Central Powers. For the most part, their disarmament clauses paralleled those of the Versailles document. They limited the size of armies and armaments, reduced navies to insignificance, and prohibited air forces. Compulsory service was prohibited. Commissions of Control were established, with the League of Nations assigned responsibility for long-term supervision of compliance.

The Treaty of Saint Germain with Austria, signed on 10 September 1919, limited the central remnant of the former Austro-Hungarian Empire to an army of thirty thousand men. Under the terms of the

Treaty of Neuilly, signed on 27 November 1919, the Bulgarian army was limited to twenty thousand men and required to surrender most of its arms and war material. The Treaty of Trianon, signed on 4 June 1920, reduced the army of Hungary to thirty-five thousand men. The Treaty of Sèvres with Turkey, signed on 20 August 1920, was never implemented due to Turkey's domestic upheaval and Turkish-Greek fighting. It was replaced by the Treaty of Lausanne of 24 July 1923, which demilitarized the Turkish straits and opened them to all ships in peacetime and neutral ships in wartime.

The United States–Germany Treaty   Following the refusal of the U.S. Senate to ratify the Treaty of Versailles, the two nations concluded the "Treaty Between the United States and Germany Restoring Friendly Relations" of 25 August 1921. The treaty included the text of a congressional joint resolution approved by President Harding on 2 July 1921 declaring the state of war to be terminated. The bilateral treaty conferred upon the United States all the rights guaranteed under the Treaty of Versailles, but in accordance with a reservation attached prior to the favorable Senate vote of ratification on 18 October 1921. The United States was barred from participating in any treaty-related control activities without additional congressional legislation. The United States was not represented on the control commissions that supervised German implementation of the Versailles disarmament terms.

THE INTER-ALLIED COMMISSIONS OF CONTROL

Under Article 204 of the Treaty of Versailles, the Inter-Allied Commissions of Control (IACC) were specifically charged with "the duty of seeing to the complete execution of the delivery, destruction, demolition, and rendering things useless" by Germany in accordance with the disarmament clauses that had a time limit. The Commissions of Control reported initially to the Supreme Council in Paris, which consisted of the Allied heads of government or their representatives. From 1921 the IACC received instructions from the Allied Conference of Ambassadors in Paris, and from the Allied Military Committee, also in Paris, which dealt with questions concerning the execution of the Treaty of Versailles up until 1931.

On 12 September 1919, the first train departing from Paris to Berlin in five years carried the vanguard of the IACC to their assignment. The task of verifying compliance was daunting indeed. Germany still had millions of men under arms; perhaps twenty-five thousand factories capable of producing war munitions; and thousands of planes, warships, tanks, and artillery pieces in excess of permitted levels. The German military, the civilian government, and the general population were united in their contempt for the Treaty of Versailles, their sullen obstructionism tempered only by the threat of the renewal of hostilities by the Allies. Viewed in this perspective, IACC success in overseeing the demobilization of German armed forces and the massive destruction of arms and munitions, though imperfect, constitutes a substantial achievement.

Composition, Organization, and Functions   Comprising representatives of Britain, France, Italy, Belgium, and Japan, the Inter-Allied Commissions of Control (IACC) had a complement of over one thousand men, including almost four hundred officers, in 1920, although its strength was reduced thereafter. Its headquarters was in the Hotel Adlon in Berlin. The IACC conducted thousands of on-site inspections throughout Germany during the course of its existence. It also supervised the destruction by the Germans of massive quantities of small arms, heavy weapons, and munitions. A ranking IACC official claimed in 1923 that more war material had been destroyed than Germany possessed in 1914.

The IACC consisted of three component commissions: the Inter-Allied Military Commission of Control (IAMCC), the Inter-Allied Naval Commission of Control (IANCC), and the Inter-Allied Aeronautical Commission of Control (IAACC). The three bodies coordinated their activities in areas of common concern, such as factories that could produce arms or munitions for more than one branch of the German armed forces. The IACC was entitled to total freedom of movement, but was limited by German transportation arrangements. A German "peace commission" served as liaison between the IACC and the German government and military.

The Inter-Allied Military Commission of Control   The first president of the Inter-Allied Military Commission of Control (IAMCC) was Gen. Charles Nollet of France. The commission main-

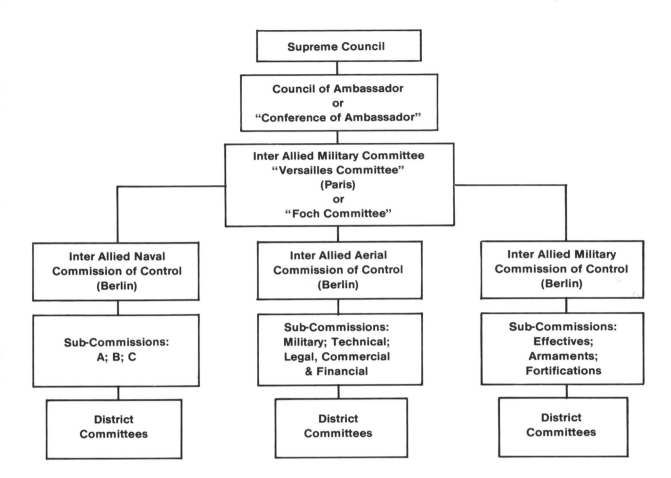

tained its headquarters in Berlin, and had six sub-commissions: (1) outside liaison; (2) fortifications; (3) effectives; (4) armaments; (5) translations and press reports; and (6) administration. The subcommission on fortifications had district committees at Kiel, Cologne, and Stuttgart.

The subcommission on effectives had the near hopeless task of verifying the demobilization of the German army down to the one-hundred-thousand-men treaty level, and keeping track of police and paramilitary organizations. (The political collapse of Germany at the end of the war had resulted in a great deal of civil strife between private, often heavily armed paramilitary groups.) It also was charged with preventing illegal military training and the emergence of a new German general staff. The subcommission had eight district committees—Berlin, Königsberg (Kaliningrad), Stettin (Szczecin) Dresden, Stuttgart, Münster, Munich, and Breslau (Wrocław). Its chief areas of activity were Berlin, Silesia, Westphalia, and East Prussia.

The subcommission on armaments, probably the most important IACC unit, had eleven district committees at locations corresponding to former German army corps headquarters: Berlin, Dresden, Munich, Stuttgart, Düsseldorf, Cologne, Frankfurt, Hannover, Stettin (Szczecin), Breslau (Wrocław), and Königsberg (Kaliningrad). There were also district committees at the Krupp munitions works in Essen, and at Münster to monitor arsenals and factories in the Rhineland. The Allies concentrated on Westphalia, where many Krupp factories were located and 70 percent of German military hardware was produced.

The armaments subcommittee required the Germans to submit detailed information on factory production and inventories as of 5 January 1920, much of which proved to be inaccurate. During the war, most German engineering, chemical, and heavy manufacturing plants were converted to war production. All were to be reconverted or destroyed. The Germans declared three thousand factories as producers of war material, but the IAMCC discovered a total of some seven thousand. This is not to say that massive destruction or conversion of factories did not occur. Krupp began destroying some heavy weapons factories as early as May 1920. The IAMCC, especially its French component, placed spies within the Reichswehr, the German army permitted under the Versailles treaty, to detect violations. Certainly large quantities of arms were never declared and remained concealed throughout the country.

The IAMCC established two hundred destruction centers and a like number of storage depots. The Germans destroyed their weapons themselves under IAMCC supervision. Scrap was sold and registered until actual meltdown. The Allied supervisors kept detailed records on arms destroyed. Munitions factories were also systematically rendered permanently inoperable. Shell presses, gun lathes, gun shrinking pits, chlorine cells, gunpowder plants, and test cites were destroyed or dismantled. Gen. Francis R. Bingham, British member of the IACC, reported in 1924 that almost seven thousand munitions factories had been converted to civilian production.

The Inter-Allied Naval Commission of Control
The Inter-Allied Naval Commission of Control (IANCC) was responsible for enforcing the limits on warships and a fifteen-thousand-man ceiling on naval personnel. Its chief was Admiral Charlton of Great Britain. Since Germany had scuttled its high seas fleet in 1919 and never approached building up to even the meager treaty limits during the period of control, the IANCC task was largely confined to overseeing the breaking up of ships under construction which would have exceeded treaty limits if launched, and the demobilization of personnel.

Substantial undetected German violations occurred, including concealment of weapons, illegal recruitment and training, and proscribed research and development at home and abroad. Nonetheless, the Naval Commission had a relatively noncontroversial existence.

The Inter-Allied Aeronautical Commission of Control
Since Germany was permitted no military aircraft whatever (under Art. 198) and no air force personnel (under Art. 199), the Inter-Allied Aeronautical Commission of Control (IAACC) had the straightforward but formidable task of observing the destruction of warplanes still in German hands after the armistice, and the demobilization of air force units. Germany eventually surrendered or destroyed some fifteen thousand aircraft, twenty-eight thousand aircraft engines, and sixteen airships, and dismantled about one million square feet of hangars. Having completed its work, the IAACC left Germany in May 1922. It was replaced by the Aeronautical Committee of Guarantee, which withdrew in 1926. Allied inspectors did not detect or prevent a wide variety of German evasions, which are described below.

The IACC AND EUROPEAN SECURITY, 1920–1927

The operations of the Commissions of Control were influenced at every turn by turmoil in Germany, tumultuous postwar relations between Germany and the Allies, and by lack of agreement among the Allies themselves. The most important control operation, the Inter-Allied Military Commission of Control, purportedly functioned from January 1920 to January 1927. In reality, the commission was inoperative from 1923 to late 1924 due to German refusal to permit French and Belgian officers to participate in inspections during the Franco-Belgian occupation of the Ruhr. Nor did significant, systematic IACC activities take place after the general inspection of 1924–1925.

Initial Operations, 1920–1922 The IACC officially began operations on 10 January 1920, and held its first meeting with the German Army Peace Commission, which served as liaison to the German military, on 29 January. In March, the monarchist Kapp putsch was defeated by a trade union general strike that resulted in a breakdown in political order. To maintain domestic peace, Germany requested that it be permitted to maintain an army of two hundred thousand. The Allies meeting at San Remo in April flatly refused, and warned Germany to reduce to conference limits or face the consequences. In June, the Supreme Council did allow an expansion of German police forces provided that they were decentralized, but also expressed dissatisfaction with the speed of overall German compliance with the disarmament provisions of the treaty and Germany's failure to enact enabling legislation.

At the Spa Conference of July 1920, the Allies met in Belgium formally with German representatives and agreed to extend the deadline for the reduction of the German army to one hundred thousand men to 21 January 1921, and granted other minor concessions. At the same time, Germany was found grossly in default on execution of many treaty provisions. Conscription had not been abolished. The army remained at about one million men. An estimated fifteen thousand artillery pieces and nine thousand planes remained to be delivered. At Spa, Germany was compelled to reiterate formally its intent to comply with basic provisions of the treaty—disarming of paramilitary forces, establishment of a long-term service army, surrender of excess arms, enactment of domestic legislation—under the threat of sanctions.

The Allies again notified Germany in December 1920 and January 1921 that it remained in default on fundamental disarmament provisions. From March to December 1921, French troops occupied portions of the Ruhr, at least in part because of German treaty violations.

Nevertheless, by April 1922 some IACC activities had begun to wind down. The Conference of Ambassadors informed the German government on 14 April that the Aeronautical Commission (IAACC) had finished its work and would be replaced by a committee of guarantee. The Allies suggested that guarantee committees might also replace the military and naval control commissions. Germany insisted that all forms of in-country control be abolished. The Allies agreed in principle late in 1922, conditional upon German compliance with a long list of treaty terms that had not yet been honored.

Period of Stalemate and Inactivity, 1923–1924

Before further negotiations for total removal of the Inter-Allied Commissions of Control could occur, control activities were curtailed by the Franco-Belgian occupation of the Ruhr in response to German nonfulfillment of reparations requirements. Germany now refused to admit IACC inspection teams that included French and Belgian officers, while the Allies insisted on complete representation. On 15 March 1923, General Nollet ordered inspections to be resumed, but the Germans refused. German chancellor Gustav Stresemann announced that military control was "over and done with." Only three inspections occurred in 1923. The Conference of Ambassadors ordered resumption in

January 1924; eight visits by inspectors in civilian clothes were made that month.

Overall, however, the Military Commission was virtually inactive between January 1923 and September 1924 except for a very few unannounced inspections. In October and November 1923, the Allies warned the Germans of grave consequences for continued noncooperation. The French, but not the British, favored the actual application of sanctions.

The stalemate continued in 1924, with the Germans contending that the IACC had finished their work, and that Article 213 provided only for League inquiries, not for permanent control. With the Allies also weary of the process, the Conference of Ambassadors decreed that there would be one last general inspection followed by the withdrawal of the IACC.

Final IACC Inspections and Withdrawal, 1924–1927

With grudging German assent, the closeout inspections occurred between 8 September 1924 and 25 January 1925. The IACC components carried out almost eight hundred separate inspections of military organizations, arsenals, the war ministry, police offices, and factories. The Germans offered no serious opposition, but pursued a policy of passive obstructionism.

The Naval Commission completed its work and dissolved on 30 September 1924. The Military Commission did not finish its part of the general inspection until 5 January 1925, and found many violations indicating German failure to comply with limits on armaments. These included the reconstruction of the general staff within the war ministry, excessive police and paramilitary forces, failure to convert factories so that they could not rapidly resume the production of munitions, and the stockpiling of gas masks for chemical warfare. The report stated that the Deutschwerke munitions firm and the Krupp works in Essen were still manufacturing war material.

The Allies, who were scheduled to evacuate the Cologne and north Rhineland area on 20 January 1925 (expiration of the five-year period established in Articles 428–429) refused to do so, citing German violations of disarmament and other terms of the treaty. There was general outrage in the German population.

At this point, Stresemann, now the German foreign minister, put forth proposals for French-

British-German security arrangements that eventually became the Locarno agreements. Stresemann, who guided Weimar foreign policy from 1923 to 1929, was a right-of-center opponent of Versailles and particularly of the disarmament clauses. He was also a realist who recognized that Germany could only achieve relief through negotiations. He had been willing to bargain the thorough closeout inspection for full and final withdrawal of Allied inspectors.

As discussions for a security pact progressed, the Allies, particularly the British, became increasingly willing to overlook German noncompliance with the disarmament clauses as set forth in the report of the general inspection. The Allies presented Germany with a bill of particulars, but never followed up with sanctions. On the contrary, evacuation of the Ruhr and the northern Rhineland occurred from July 1925 to February 1926. A special commission of the Reichswehr ministry began working out differences with the IACC.

The Locarno conference of October 1925 resulted in treaties of mutual guarantee of the French-German border and the Belgian-German border, arbitration treaties between Germany and its neighbors, Franco-Polish and Franco-Czechoslovakian mutual assistance treaties, and the decision to allow Germany to join the League of Nations. The "spirit of Locarno" lowered tensions in Europe and enhanced Allied willingness to withdraw the Inter-Allied Commissions of Control. In October 1925, it was announced that Krupp had finally begun to dismantle its artillery manufacturing plant. During the same period, French spokesmen indicated that German destruction of war production plants had been satisfactory. General Foch of the Allied Military Commission in Paris stated that the Germans had made a genuine effort to disarm, but problems remained concerning the reconstituting of the general staff, and the strength of police and paramilitary organizations.

On 25 November 1925, the Conference of Ambassadors announced that agreement had been reached with Germany on disarmament issues and that the IACC would be dissolved when they completed their tasks. Official notice was given on 1 January 1926 that all district branches except Munich and Königsberg (Kaliningrad) would be withdrawn. This small nucleus stayed behind to oversee the last controlled phase of German disarmament. IACC inspectors departed from the Krupp works in March 1926.

In December 1926 at Geneva, the Allied foreign ministers gave final approval to the termination of control operations in Germany. The departure of remaining IACC elements occurred in February 1927; its final report was filed with the League of Nations on 31 July. That report indicated that Germany had failed fully to comply with many requirements of the treaty: many arms had not been turned in, illegal paramilitary forces existed in great numbers, factories had not been converted entirely and could be put into war production on short notice, and many other deficiencies remained. The Allies chose not to act on these findings in light of the existing political thaw. Thenceforth, verification of German compliance was the responsibility of the League.

No permanent control organization was established, and after the Allies left the Rhineland in 1929 there was no inspection system for the demilitarized zone. The League never exercised its rights under Article 213 to investigate alleged German violations.

GERMAN VIOLATIONS, 1920–1927

Critics of the Versailles treaty often overlook the substantial accomplishments of the Inter-Allied Commissions of Control and the extent to which Germany really did disarm in the 1920s. At the beginning of the Nazi era, Germany posed no military threat to anyone.

According to Lt. Col. Stewart Roddie, a British member of the IACC, in 1918 Germany had 260 divisions and 20,000 guns. In 1925 it had 7 divisions and 280 guns. Over 4,500,000 small arms had been destroyed. More than 7,000 factories had been converted or razed. Germany was disarmed, said Roddie. To whatever material she had concealed she was welcome.

Nonetheless, massive arms control violations and evasions were perpetrated by the German military-industrial complex, with the moral support of the civilian government and most citizens. Some of the violations had the effect of accelerating rearmament after 1933. It is important to note that the violations of the 1920s were not solely the responsibility of the German military. Stresemann and other leaders of the Weimar Republic had considerable knowledge of the Reichswehr's clandestine operations, even though their relations with Gen. Hans von Seeckt, the chief of the army staff, were strained.

German Army Violations   The German Army, which numbered perhaps five hundred thousand men at the end of 1919 and increased in strength thereafter, was supposed to be reduced to one hundred thousand by 31 March 1920 under Article 160 of the Treaty of Versailles. The deadline was extended several times by the Allies in view of civil unrest in Germany. Accurate statistics are not available, but the Reichswehr, exclusive of paramilitary units it supported, may have been reduced to two hundred thousand by 1922.

Many demobilized soldiers went directly into official government-supported paramilitary formations such as the home militia (Volkswehren) and civic guards (Einwohnerwehren). These units evolved out of the immediate postwar "free corps" (Freikorps) and were supplied in part by the Reichswehr. They were eventually disbanded because of Allied protests, but many small arms were not recovered since members took their weapons with them as they joined other paramilitary groups. Veterans and civilians joined local paramilitary units that were often only marginally associated with the central government, as in Bavaria. These units opposed Polish incursions in the east and were used to suppress leftist uprisings throughout the nation. Although some arms were extracted from paramilitary formations, hundreds of thousands of small arms were never declared.

Paramilitary personnel, policemen, and members of veterans organizations and purported recreational clubs received on-the-job military training, and provided manpower for the Nazi movement and the Wehrmacht in the 1930s. Similarly, police forces were never reduced to 1913 levels or decentralized as required by the treaty. The existence of official and unofficial paramilitary forces that numbered in the hundreds of thousands was a grievous treaty violation, largely beyond the control of the IACC or the German government.

General von Seeckt, a determined, outspoken opponent of the Versailles treaty, was named chief of the general staff in July 1919. He became head of the Truppenamt, or troops office, in March 1920 when the general staff was supposedly abolished in accordance with Article 160. In reality von Seeckt continued the basic structure of a general staff within the Truppenamt, and it provided training for the future general staff corps. Allied complaints in 1925 had no effect.

Von Seeckt consciously designed his forces not as a small army but as the nucleus of a large army. With conscription banned by the Versailles treaty in favor of long-term enlistments, the army could choose the cream of hundreds of thousands of volunteers. Officers and noncommissioned officers, the latter proportionally overrepresented in enlisted ranks, were trained for responsibilities beyond their rank. They became the cadres for the new German army which would emerge when the Versailles restraints were cast aside. The Reichswehr augmented the number of trained veterans by releasing unauthorized numbers of men before their treaty-required twelve years were served, and replacing them with new recruits. Under von Seeckt, the army also engaged in covert weapons research and development at home and abroad.

German Navy Violations   On 21 June 1919, the Germans scuttled the high seas fleet at Scapa Flow to prevent its expropriation by the Allies. Thereafter, limited to six battleships of older design and a handful of ships in other categories, the German navy made little effort to construct an illegal fleet in the 1920s. Indeed, Germany did not build up to treaty limits. The number of battleships in service actually fell from eight to five by the 1930s.

However, the navy sought illegally to preserve the technology of submarine construction. The Admiralty maintained close ties with shipbuilders and subsidized them. Former navy officers helped design and build submarines in Holland, Finland, and Spain. Krupp formed a dummy Dutch company in Rotterdam for submarine development, with which the German navy cooperated. In 1925 this Dutch Krupp operation laid down the hulls of two U-boats. Germany also concluded secret agreements with Japan for exchange of technical information on submarine construction. The real payoff for the covert submarine program was the successful development of prototypes—the U-1 and U-24 classes in Finland and the U-25 and U-26 classes at Cadiz.

The German navy also engaged in a variety of lesser illegal activities, including the training of reservists, and retention of sea mines, small arms, artillery, and ammunition in excess of treaty ceilings. It also sponsored an illegal seaplane competition in 1926. In 1929 the German navy began construction of the first of three pocket battleships that would ultimately exceed treaty tonnage limits.

German Violation of Air Clauses   Evasion of the treaty provisions forbidding Germany's possession of a military air force occurred at a low level. Some World War I pilots retained their proficiency and instructed cadets in ostensibly civilian flying clubs and veterans organizations. The Reichswehr maintained ties with commercial aviation firms. In January 1926, Lufthansa was established as a government commercial airline monopoly. It was used extensively as a cover for covert air force testing, training, and formation of reserve units.

Germany successfully concealed the establishment of a flying center within the war ministry, which illegally disbursed funds to private aviation activities. Von Seeckt brought 180 veteran pilots into the Reichswehr in 1923, and placed air officers in units throughout the army. Significant covert army spending for aviation began in 1925. The most serious naval and air force circumvention of the treaty occurred, however, in the area of construction and research and development.

Illegal Arms Production, Research, and Development

Following the von Seeckt doctrine of building for the future, the most serious German evasion of the spirit and letter of the Versailles treaty fell in the areas of covert arms production and research and development at home and in neighboring countries. Just as he saw the one-hundred-thousand-man army as the nucleus of a future full-size establishment, von Seeckt saw the value of developing state-of-the-art prototypes of modern weapons which would permit mass production in the future. In July 1925 the firm of Koch and Kienzle (E) (the E stands for *Entwicklung,* or development), was set up in Berlin as cover for Krupp ordnance design. Krupp began producing tanks in the guise of tractors in 1926. Little weapons design or production could occur while the Commissions of Control remained in Germany, however. The thrust of the effort occurred in other countries.

Without any government master plan, the German arms industry began to relocate abroad soon after the end of the war, operating through subsidiaries and part interest arrangements or acting jointly with business associates and tolerant governments. In 1921 a weapons designer and manufacturer, Joseph Vollmer, smuggled ten tanks to Sweden, and Krupp gained secret control of a Bofors steel and cannon factory, also in Sweden.

Germany violated the air clauses in many respects during the period of control, but not to such an obvious extent as to draw protests from the Aeronautical Commission. Clandestine training of pilots and aircrew, and investment in experimental aircraft were the main transgressions. The airplane builder Ernst Heinkel established an aircraft factory at Warnemuende in 1922, which included a secret area for producing warplanes.

An organization for the design of aircraft prototypes was founded in Berlin in 1923. It assisted designer Tony Fokker, who relocated an entire aircraft factory in Holland, and also the engineer and builder Hugo Junkers in setting up a factory in the Soviet Union in 1923, and a second subsequent plant in Sweden. German aircraft development operations came to spread across the map of Europe—Rohrback in Denmark, Dornier in Switzerland, and Junkers and Heinkel in Sweden. Adm. Erich Raeder later contended that in the Weimar period the navy had already completely designed a multipurpose aircraft and a dive bomber. Some governments that acquiesced in German arms development on their soil surely came to regret it after 1939.

German Military Activities in Russia

It is quite incredible that from 1921 to 1933 two nations that would soon fight one of the cruelest wars in human history engaged in extensive military cooperation. General von Seeckt vigorously pursued military cooperation with the Soviet Union as a method of evading the Versailles restrictions. Count Brockdorff-Rantzau, who became German ambassador to Moscow, wrote in 1920 that although he was not unaware of the evils of Bolshevism, he found them less repugnant "than the consequences of the undignified helotism into which our vengeful and rapacious enemies have forced us for generations to come" (Gatzke, *American Historical Review,* 1958, p. 570).

The May 1921 Soviet-German trade agreement and Treaty of Rapallo the following year opened the door to military discussions and later large-scale circumvention of Versailles limitations. Germany was permitted to establish training facilities for tanks and aviation in Russia and would direct the construction of factories for the production of war materials. Krupp produced a large consignment of artillery shells in Russia that was delivered to Germany in 1927. Germany also engaged in chemical warfare research in Russia and built factories for the production of chlorine and phosgene. The Soviets closed down the production operation in 1925, but permitted the Germans to maintain a gas warfare training school at Torski (code-named Tomka) beginning in 1927 or 1928.

In the area of aviation, the Germans were allowed to establish an airfield at Lipetsk in 1924. Dozens of pilots trained there in the 1920s and many more later. Dutch-built Fokker fighter-trainers were smuggled by the Germans from Holland to Lipetsk. Junkers opened an aircraft factory at Fili, in the USSR, in 1924.

The German foreign ministry was always uneasy about the Reichswehr's relations with the Red Army. Stresemann feared that revelation of the activities of von Seeckt's lieutenants in Russia could destroy his careful efforts to lift the burdens of Versailles by diplomacy. Nonetheless, the German government gave tacit approval to this dangerous game.

An Appraisal of German Violations   The reality of serious German violations cannot be denied. They involved retention of a general staff apparatus, illegal training and enlistment of personnel, creation of paramilitary forces, concealment of arms and munitions, and most important, the development and manufacture of prohibited weapons and prototypes at home and abroad.

The net effect of all this, however, is in dispute. Col. Roddie, British control commission member and liaison between the German military and the British War Office, argued that violations during the 1920s were minimal. Viscount D'Abernon, British ambassador in Berlin from 1920 to 1926, did not find German evasion sufficiently serious to prevent the Allies from adopting a conciliatory approach. Conversely, Gen. John H. Morgan, a ranking British member of the Inter-Allied Commissions of Control, felt that Germany had built up a covert army under the very noses of the Allied inspectors. Most French participants and observers have agreed with Morgan.

Internal documents reveal that in 1927 the German military felt completely impotent, unable to defend the nation against even second-rate powers such as Czechoslovakia. Indeed, these documents indicate that the Allies had largely accomplished their disarmament objectives. Germany was without tanks, military aviation, heavy artillery, chemical weapons, and submarines.

Actually, the significance of German violations in the period of control lies not in the meager forces that were amassed, but in the development of cadres and weapon prototypes that permitted accelerated expansion after the decision to rearm was made.

GERMAN DISARMAMENT AND REARMAMENT, 1927–1933

The years between the end of Allied in-country control and the coming to power of Adolf Hitler offered the last chance to rescue the frayed Versailles arms control clauses and incorporate them into an international system of disarmament envisaged by Article 8 and the preamble to Part V of the treaty. Instead, Germany used the period to escalate research and development and begin semi-secret mass production of prohibited heavy weapons, while disarmament foundered on the rocks of Allied disagreements and the impasse posed by French demands for security and German insistence on equality.

Escalating German Noncompliance   Germany remained cautious with regard to openly challenging the Versailles disarmament clauses in the years following the withdrawal of the Inter-Allied Commissions of Control, particularly as long as Stresemann, who died in office in 1929, continued to guide German foreign policy. For all of its evasions, Germany was militarily powerless and Allied troops remained in the Rhineland until 1929.

However, the pace of secret illegal rearmament quickened. By 1930, Krupp was receiving additional Reichswehr funds for tractor/tank design, as were the firms of Daimler and Rheinmetall. Gustav Krupp later boasted that state-of-the-art tank design had been virtually completed in the 1920s. Krupp also tested new artillery prototypes in cooperation with Bofors facilities in Sweden, which were controlled by Krupp from 1925 to 1935, and by virtue of work done in Essen and Berlin.

In other areas, Charlottenburg Polytechnic Institute in Berlin became a center for military technical research. Work was done on ballistics, explosives, rocket propulsion, and mine warfare under the cover of academic pursuits.

Krupp began limited covert production in 1928; serious stockpiling of arms and armaments began in 1931, well before the rise of Hitler. This included tanks and artillery beyond treaty limits, and items that were prohibited—such as submarines and military aircraft. Warplanes produced in 1931 numbered 70; 221 were produced in 1932. Pilots were trained in Brunswick in the 1930s. The navy operated a limited aviation training program through the Severna company, and developed aviation equipment. German military activities in Russia—aviation, armor, and chemical warfare programs—continued unabated through the period. Not until the appearance of the openly hostile National Socialist regime in 1933 did Stalin terminate military cooperation with Germany.

Naval noncompliance and rearmament quickened in the late 1920s. Guns were taken from surplus warships for future use. The navy also concealed sea mines, small arms, and ammunition. Purportedly within the Versailles limits, Germany began construction of the first 10,000-ton pocket battleship in 1928; as launched it would exceed treaty tonnage ceilings. Masked torpedo boats were constructed, with torpedo tubes secretly stored for rapid refitting. Submarine design and production abroad continued. In 1932 the Swedish navy, in collaboration with Krupp, began the construction of three submarines.

Germany, Arms Control, and European Security, 1927–1936

The first years following the withdrawal of the Inter-Allied Commissions of Control saw some superficial relaxation of tension in Europe, with the signing of the Kellogg-Briand Pact and the conclusion of the Young Plan to regularize German finances and reparations payments. The Allies evacuated the Rhineland ahead of schedule in 1929, and the Saar in 1930. On the other hand, with the onset of the depression, the political and economic situation deteriorated within Germany; by 1930, the National Socialists were a significant force.

The Preparatory Commission for the Disarmament Conference met regularly in Geneva from 1926 to 1930. In this forum, Germany made clear its dissatisfaction with the one-sided nature of the Versailles arms control provisions and refused to accept them as permanent. France, conversely, looked to the League and its disarmament deliberations for the indefinite perpetuation of the Versailles limitations. Despite the stalemate, the Preparatory Commission completed a draft convention (with many incomplete sections) in 1930. The

World Disarmament Conference convened in 1932, but failed to break the impasse.

Burdened by inherent weaknesses, undermined by widespread German noncompliance, and discredited by lack of Allied willingness to enforce it, the Versailles disarmament regime nonetheless left Germany shackled at the time that Hitler came to power. At the beginning of the Nazi era, Germany posed no military threat to anyone. The Third Reich was able to rearm in violation of the Versailles treaty partially because of the inadequacy of Allied intelligence. A dearth of precise and accurate information on the German buildup sapped the resolve of Anglo-French policymakers. More important was the weariness and lack of political will in London and Paris that allowed Hitler to publicly and unilaterally abrogate one major element of the Versailles disarmament system after another with impunity from 1933 to 1936.

German Rearmament, 1933–1936

Adolf Hitler, who came to power in January 1933, made his intentions clear in October when Germany withdrew from both the Disarmament Conference and the League of Nations. A year later, he ordered the army to triple its official strength to three hundred thousand, shattering the one-hundred-thousand Versailles limit that constituted the most severe constraint on German rearmament. While maintaining the fiction of its nonexistence, the general staff forbidden by Versailles developed apace. In the Ruhr and Rhineland, the production of heavy weapons by Krupp and defense-related chemicals by I. G. Farben was accelerated.

Hitler also undertook naval rearmament, raising the German naval budget dramatically. He authorized the construction of the battle cruisers *Scharnhorst* and *Gneisenau,* the twenty-six-thousand-ton displacement of which exceeded Versailles limits by sixteen thousand tons. On 1 October 1933 a secret U-boat school opened at Kiel. Frames and parts of submarines that had been manufactured in Holland, Finland, and Spain were brought to Germany in violation of Article 191. The construction of twelve new submarines was authorized in early 1935 and completed by the end of the year. Naval personnel, limited to fifteen thousand by Article 183, increased to thirty-four thousand by 1935.

Hermann Göring, Hitler's minister of aviation, expedited the designing of warplanes and covert training. German pilots trained in Italy in 1933. Hitler secretly established the Luftwaffe in February 1935, which began testing bombers, camouflaged as civilian transports. The following month, Göring publicly announced the existence of the Luftwaffe and held a mass air display. Hitler then told British Foreign Secretary Anthony Eden that the Luftwaffe was the equal of the Royal Air Force, a bluff with no basis in fact.

End of the Versailles Arms Control Clauses, 1935–1936

In January 1935, the residents of the Saar voted overwhelmingly to rejoin Germany, contributing to Allied willingness to abandon other "unequal" provisions of Versailles. The following month, Britain and France approached Germany with the outline of a general settlement providing for a Locarno-like guarantee of Germany's eastern borders and providing for equality in levels of armed forces, thus abandoning Versailles. Hitler gave an evasive reply, which was followed by Göring's false claim of a powerful air force. This admission, or boast, revealing massive noncompliance with Versailles, brought no firm reaction from the Allies.

Emboldened, Hitler delivered the death blow to Part V of the Treaty of Versailles. On 16 March 1935, he announced the reintroduction of universal military service and the formation of an army of thirty-six divisions, or approximately five hundred thousand men. The Reichswehr became the Wehrmacht. The Allies protested, but took no action. Britain expressed eagerness to continue security pact negotiations. Germany erupted in national celebration: the diktat of Versailles had been overturned. The Allies and the League of Nations expressed belated and muted objections to Germany's unilateral renunciation of treaty obligations. British, French, and Italian representatives, meeting at Stresa in April, condemned the German action.

Hitler, undeterred, moved forward. On 21 May, he secretly issued the Reich Defense Law, which reorganized the armed forces, resurrected an overt general staff, and put the economy on a war production footing. Henceforth, Germany prepared for war at full capacity, without even the pretext of abiding by Versailles limitations. In October 1935 the Wehrmacht's seven infantry divisions were broken up to provide cadre for the new thirty-six-division force, and the War Academy opened publicly on 15 October.

Also on 21 May 1935, Hitler delivered a carefully crafted speech containing intimidation and concili-

ation, offering to negotiate collective security arrangements and deep cuts in armaments, assuming, of course, that Germany was treated as a sovereign equal. He emphasized the failure of the Allies to honor their own Versailles disarmament obligations. Hitler offered to conclude a naval agreement that would limit Germany to 35 percent of British tonnage. Incredibly, Britain entered into such a treaty the following month. With one stroke, Britain toppled the naval clauses of the Treaty of Versailles; legitimized Germany's past violations, including construction of submarines and oversized battle cruisers; and destroyed the front that had been created at Stresa in April. Germany, its navy having been reduced to insignificance, was now free to build warships as fast as resources permitted. The Anglo-German Naval Pact dealt a body blow to the League of Nations, which was charged with ensuring compliance with the 1919 peace treaties.

Hitler swept away the final vestige of the arms provisions of Versailles on 7 March 1936. Germany reoccupied the Rhineland in violation of Article 43, as well as the Locarno Pact of 1925. The modest German operational contingent was prepared to withdraw if confronted, but the French hesitated and asked for British support. London's attitude was expressed by Lord Lothian, who as Lloyd George's assistant at Paris had helped to draft the Allied note of 16 June 1919, which denounced Germany for causing World War I. He now observed that the Germans invading the Rhineland were only going into their own back garden. Foreign Secretary Anthony Eden told the House of Commons that the occupation of the Rhineland dealt a heavy blow to the principle of the sanctity of treaties, but did not appear to raise the threat of hostilities.

CONCLUSIONS

German circumvention of the disarmament terms of Versailles is instructive with regard to late-twentieth-century attempts to limit the capabilities of potential aggressors. For example, parallels between the efforts of the Allies to contain German war potential after World War I and those of the United Nations in curbing that of Iraq after the Gulf War are numerous. German disarmament and rearmament demonstrate the difficulty of distinguishing between civilian and military production in the automotive, aviation, electrical, and chemical fields. Hundreds of war-related factories were razed by the Inter-Allied Commissions of Control (IACC), but countless others were reconverted to war production overnight in the 1930s.

Germany made full use of offshore procurement and research and development. Holland, Spain, Finland, Sweden, Switzerland, and especially the Soviet Union tolerated or abetted German military-related activities in violation of the purposes of Versailles. Krupp, Fokker, and many other munitions firms were able to use subsidiaries abroad and cooperate with various world arms manufacturers to evade treaty purposes, evidence that successful quarantines of potential aggressors require the cooperation of all nations and international corporations.

German disarmament and rearmament also established the importance and danger of research and development, as opposed to the mere possession of weapons. German emphasis on the design of prototypes in the 1920s permitted breakout from the restrictions of Versailles in the 1930s. Similarly, Germany proved that the size of a potential aggressor's armed forces is less vital than its composition if a small army is designed in such a way that it is able to form the nucleus of a much larger force.

The effectiveness of the arms control provisions of the Treaty of Versailles and their enforcement by the IACC deserve a balanced assessment. During the period of control (1920–1927), the German armed forces and government engaged in willful evasion on a massive scale. Given the size of Germany and the degree of domestic unrest, full compliance was not feasible even had there been full cooperation from the central government. But under the supervision of a few hundred inspectors, the Germans destroyed unprecedented numbers of factories, heavy weapons, and small arms. Military aircraft and submarines really were eliminated from the national arsenal; the German fleet was reduced to insignificant proportions.

Germany posed no military threat whatever to its neighbors at the end of the period of control in 1927, or when Hitler came to power in 1933, or indeed in 1935 when Germany unilaterally abrogated the main disarmament provisions of Versailles.

Churchill later said that simple enforcement of treaty obligations could have kept Germany disarmed for thirty years. It was French policy to keep Germany disarmed forever. But lasting security based on arms control must rest on a firm political base, must have the acceptance of all parties, and

must provide mutual benefits. On 23 June 1919, the German peace conference delegation stated: "Yielding to superior force, and without renouncing in the meantime its own view of the unheard-of injustice of the peace conditions, the Government of the German Republic declares that it is ready to accept and sign the peace conditions imposed" (U.S. Department of State, vol. 13, p. 418). That the Treaty of Versailles, including its imposed arms control provisions, was a diktat was a view shared by almost all Germans. Domestic support for the treaty was thus rendered almost impossible to achieve from the outset.

The repeated pledges of the Allies that German disarmament would constitute the prelude to general disarmament further undermined the determination of the international community to enforce German disarmament indefinitely. The arms control provisions of the Treaty of Versailles and their implementation were flawed, but the larger share of blame for the inability of Europe to find security lies with the failed negotiations for normalization of Germany's status between 1920 and 1933.

BIBLIOGRAPHY

General Accounts   A number of works about the World War I armistice and the Paris Peace Conference are particularly informative on the arms control provisions of the Treaty of Versailles. These include PAUL BIRDSALL, *Versailles Twenty Years After* (New York, 1941); DAVID HUNTER MILLER, *The Drafting of the Covenant,* 2 vols. (New York, 1928); and HARRY R. RUDIN, *Armistice, 1918* (New Haven, Conn., 1944).

European diplomacy and arms control in the interwar period are dealt with in HENRY L. BRETTON, *Stresemann and the Revision of Versailles: A Fight for Reason* (Stanford, Calif., 1953); CHRISTOPHER HALL, *Britain, America, and Arms Control, 1921–1937* (New York, 1987); W. M. JORDAN, *Great Britain, France, and the German Problem, 1918–1939: A Study of Anglo-French Relations in the Making and Maintenance of the Versailles Settlement* (London and New York, 1943); LORD RIDDELL, et al., *The Treaty of Versailles and After* (New York, 1935), which includes essays on disarmament by ARNOLD J. TOYNBEE and NORMAN ANGELL; WILLIAM L. SHIRER, *The Rise and Fall of the Third Reich: A History of Nazi Germany* (New York, 1960); and HUGH R. WILSON, *Disarmament and the Cold War in the Thirties*

(New York, 1963). WESLEY K. WARK, *The Ultimate Enemy: British Intelligence and Nazi Germany, 1933–1939* (Ithaca, N.Y., 1985), covers the effect of intelligence on British policy with respect to the defense of the Versailles arms control provisions. On the Anglo-German naval pact of 1935 that erased the Versailles naval restrictions, see CHARLES BLOCH, "Great Britain, German Rearmament, and the Naval Agreement of 1935," in HANS W. GATZKE, ed., *European Diplomacy between the Two Wars, 1919–1939* (Chicago, 1972), pp. 125–151, and D. C. WATT, "The Anglo-German Naval Agreement of 1935: an Interim Judgment," *Journal of Modern History* 28 (June 1956): 155–175. Regarding the final blow to the disarmament provisions, see JAMES THOMAS EMMERSON, *The Rhineland Crisis, 7 March 1936: A Study in Multilateral Diplomacy* (Ames, Iowa, 1977).

Arms Control Provisions

The most useful and comprehensive treatment of the arms control provisions of the Treaty of Versailles is RICHARD DEAN BURNS and DONALD URQUIDI, *Disarmament in Perspective: An Analysis of Selected Arms Control and Disarmament Agreements Between the World Wars, 1919–1939,* vol. I (Washington, D.C., 1968), prepared for the U.S. Arms Control and Disarmament Agency. Also of exceptional importance is U.S. DEPARTMENT OF STATE, *Papers Relating to the Foreign Relations of the United States. The Paris Peace Conference, 1919,* 13 vols. (Washington, D.C., 1942–1947). Volume 13 contains an annotated text of the Treaty of Versailles, providing extensive information on the interpretation and subsequent implementation of the disarmament clauses, as well as other portions of the treaty.

Participants' Evaluations

For the account of the president of the Inter-Allied Commissions of Control (IACC) see C. N. E. NOLLET, *Une expérience de désarmement: cinq ans de Control militaire en Allemagne* (Paris, 1932). Three British members of the IACC wrote illuminating accounts. GENERAL JOHN H. MORGAN, *Assize of Arms: The Disarmament of Germany and Her Rearmament, 1919–1939* (New York, 1946), has an anti-German perspective. MORGAN also wrote "The Disarmament of Germany and After," *Quarterly Review* (October 1924): 415–457. LT. COL. STEWART RODDIE, *Peace Patrol* (New York, 1933), is more sanguine regarding the extent of German disarmament. Also see SIR FRANCIS R.

BINGHAM, "Work with the Allied Control Commission in Germany, 1919–1924," *Royal United Services Institute Journal* 69 (1924). *An Ambassador of Peace: Pages from the Diary of Viscount D'Abernon (Berlin 1920–1926),* 3 vols. (London, 1929) is another participant account.

Evasions and Violations

German noncompliance with the Versailles disarmament clauses is documented in the historical literature of German rearmament. FRANCIS L. CARSTEN, *The Reichswehr and Politics, 1918–1933* (Oxford, England, 1966) makes thorough use of German sources. HANS W. GATZKE, *Stresemann and the Rearmament of Germany* (Baltimore, 1954), is balanced and perceptive. HAROLD J. GORDON, *The Reichswehr and the German Republic, 1919–1926* (Princeton, N.J., 1957), is an important scholarly work. Also see EDWARD W. BENNETT, *German Rearmament and the West, 1932–1933* (Princeton, N.J., 1979); E. J. GUMBEL, "Disarmament and Clandestine Rearmament under the Weimar Republic," in SEYMOUR MELMAN, ed., *Inspection for Disarmament* (New York, 1958), pp. 203–219; EDWARD L. HOMZE, *Arming the Luftwaffe: The Reich Air Ministry and the German Aircraft Industry, 1919–1939* (Lincoln, Neb., 1976); W. M. KNIGHT-PATTERSON, *Germany from Defeat to Conquest, 1913–1933* (London, 1945); WILLIAM MANCHESTER, *The Arms of Krupp, 1587–1968* (Boston, 1968); HERBERT MOLLOY MASON, JR., *The Rise of the Luftwaffe: Forging the Secret German Air Weapon, 1918–1940* (New York, 1973); HANFRIED SCHLIEPAHKE, *The Birth of the Luftwaffe* (Chicago, 1972); RICHARD SUCHENWIRTH, *The Development of the German Air Force, 1919–1939* (New York, 1970); and JOHN W. WHEELER-BENNETT, *The Nemesis of Power: The German Army in Politics, 1918–1945* (New York, 1953). "The Fight of the Navy Against Versailles, 1919–1935," edited by CAPT. SCHUESSLER, in *Trials of War Criminals before the Nuremberg Military Tribunals,* vol. 10 (Washington, D.C., 1951), pp. 433–465, is a tract written in 1937 boasting in detail of the dozens of violations, evasions, and subterfuges perpetrated by Navy personnel, with and without approval of the central government. BARTON WHALEY, *Covert German Rearmament, 1919–1939: Deception and Misperception* (Frederick, Md., 1984), is a treatment very critical of the Versailles treaty and its arms control enforcement process, as well as of Germany. See also ANN SINCLAIR BETHEL, "The French Perceptions and Responses to German Rearmament, 1932–

1935," Ph.D. diss. (University of California, Irvine, 1990).

Important works on Russo-German military cooperation include the following: GERALD FREUND, *Unholy Alliance: Russian-German Relations from the Treaty of Brest-Litovsk to the Treaty of Berlin* (New York, 1957); HANS W. GATZKE, "Russo-German Military Collaboration during the Weimar Republic," *American Historical Review* 63:3 (1958): 565–597; GEORGE W. F. HALLGARTEN, "General Hans von Seeckt and Russia, 1920–1922," *Journal of Modern History* 21:1 (1949): 28–34; LIONEL KOCHAN, *Russia and the Weimar Republic* (Cambridge, England, 1954); ARTHUR L. SMITH, "The German General Staff and Russia, 1919–1926," *Soviet Studies* 8 (October 1956); and GEORGE H. STEIN, "Russo-German Military Collaboration: the Last Phase, 1933," *Political Science Quarterly* 77:1 (1962): 54–71.

The Washington Naval Limitation System

1921–1939

THOMAS H. BUCKLEY

See also Great Britain; Japan; Naval Arms Control Since World War II; *and* The United States. *Treaties discussed in this essay are excerpted in Volume III.*

The basis of the Washington Naval Limitation System, in existence from 1921 to 1939, was laid with the signing of the Washington Treaties of 1922, which comprised not only the Five-Power Naval Treaty but also the Four- and Nine-Power treaties on the Pacific and China. Major additions came with the two London Naval Treaties of 1930 and 1936. Minor embellishments included: the Turkish-Greek Naval Protocol of 1930, the Turkish-Soviet Naval Protocol of 1931, and the Anglo-German Naval Pact of 1935. Two failed attempts, the Geneva Naval Conference of 1927 and the abortive Italian-French negotiations of the early 1930s, also had a final impact on the characteristics of the system. As from all of the continuing endeavors to control arms, there is much to learn from the story of these first attempts to limit major weapons systems by mutual agreement.

WASHINGTON CONFERENCE, 1921–1922

The immediate origins of the Washington Conference on the Limitation of Armaments of 1921–1922 arose out of three interrelated events: (1) the failure of the United States to join the League of Nations; (2) the threatening growth of a naval con-

struction race in capital ships between the Americans, British, and Japanese; and (3) a desire on the part of the British and the Japanese to renew the Anglo-Japanese Alliance due to expire in 1921. Facets of both domestic and international politics played a role in all three activities and contributed to the calling of the conference.

The failure of the United States Senate to give its advice and consent to the ratification of the Treaty of Versailles, which included the League of Nations charter, seriously complicated the search for arms control measures in the interwar period. Steps that were then taken, such as the disarmament and demilitarization of Germany, Austria, Hungary, and Bulgaria, and the demilitarization of various islands, frontiers, and straits from Spitsbergen to the Dardanelles, largely dealt with the losers of World War I. While officials in the administration of President Warren G. Harding were disengaging from European affairs, the American people did show an interest in bringing the victors into a disarmament arrangement.

Problems in the Pacific, including the potential military use of the former German islands (the Marshalls, Carolines, Marianas) acquired by the Japanese as mandates in the Treaty of Versailles, the chaos in China that contributed to her domestic and international weakness, and the extent of Japanese ambitions—issues not definitively settled at

Versailles—coupled with a burgeoning international naval race, brought the United States into the arms control arena. It is important to note, however, that at no time did the U.S. interest officially connect itself with the League. No president, from Warren G. Harding to Franklin D. Roosevelt, was willing to align the U.S. effort with that of the League: all believed that any formal connection could bring the wrath of the isolationists down upon them at the next election.

President Warren G. Harding won the greatest election victory in U.S. history to that point in 1920 by defeating James M. Cox. He immediately announced that he would not take the United States into the League of Nations. He had, however, mentioned during the campaign that he would favor an "association of nations" that would periodically meet to find solutions to narrowly defined specific problems and that the United States would participate only in issues that it wished and would not become a member of any permanent organization, thus preserving its complete traditional freedom of action. Harding had suggested that disarmament might well serve as the subject of such a conference.

Before Harding and his newly appointed secretary of state, Charles Evans Hughes, could act, Senator William E. Borah, a Republican from Idaho, who had helped lead the fight against the League in the Senate, offered a resolution calling for a 50 percent reduction in the naval construction programs of the United States, Great Britain, and Japan. Borah's resolution struck a public chord, as many Americans wanted to lift the financial burden of arms construction after the heavy taxes of the war period. The resolution, to Harding's discomfort, temporarily moved the center of attention away from the White House.

Congress in 1916 had passed a naval act that called for the construction of 156 ships of which 16 would be capital ships (battleships and battle cruisers). With the U.S. entrance into World War I, the construction yards concentrated on the building of destroyers for use in convoy duties across the Atlantic. As a result only one of the 16 capital ships had joined the fleet; 15 remained on their stocks roughly 10 to 80 percent completed in 1921. On completion the United States would have the most modern, most powerful battle fleet in the world; however, both the British and the Japanese had accepted the U.S. challenge. While the British had the largest, most powerful navy in 1921, their construc-

tion lagged; upon completion, the U.S. program would eclipse Great Britain's historical position as the number one navy in the world. To no one's surprise, the British then announced that they would continue to match any other fleet with new construction. When in 1920 the Japanese weighed in with a proclamation that they would also push the construction of 15 new capital ships, a major naval race appeared imminent.

According to the U.S. Navy's General Board, Great Britain in 1921 had a total warship displacement of 1,753,539 long tons (to find metric tons, multiply by 1.016); the United States had 1,302,441 tons; and Japan 641,852 tons. Using the U.S. figures as a base, the ratio for all tonnage, including capital ships, was 13.5 (Great Britain): 10 (U.S.): 4.9 (Japan). In the crucial category of capital ships Great Britain had 1,015,825 tons; the United States 728,390 tons; and Japan 494,528 tons. Again using U.S. figures as a base, the tonnage ratio for capital ships was 13.9 : 10 : 6.8. Great Britain had under construction in ships of all categories—from submarines to battleships—some 182,950 tons, the United States had 747,007 tons, and Japan 707,888 tons projected or under construction. The British had just begun four capital ships totaling 172,000 tons. The United States had fifteen capital ships of 618,000 tons under construction. The Japanese had fifteen capital ships of 599,700 tons projected or under construction. Upon completion of all the capital ships, when added to those existing, the capital-ship tonnage ratio would change from 13.9 : 10 : 6.8 to 10.6 : 10 : 8.7. In a relative sense, both the United States and Japan would gain on Great Britain.

It is important to note at this point that published figures on the actual tonnage of existing ships vary by as much as 10 percent due to different standards of measurement, and there are, of course, even greater uncertainties in future projections, for no one could also predict with any degree of confidence when or how many old ships might be retired, whether any or all of the projected ships would indeed be funded or built, or whether any further programs might be added. Even with these difficulties, however, it was evident that a much smaller naval race had helped lead to World War I.

The existence of the Anglo-Japanese Alliance further complicated the situation for the United States. Originally signed in 1902 and directed against the Russians, renewed for ten years in 1911 and then aimed against German ambitions, it appeared destined for renewal in 1921. But the United States feared that the alliance would result in British support for Japanese designs in Asia that often conflicted with U.S. interests. Britain, in a pinch, might well decide that its considerable economic investments in China would find more protection in appeasing the Japanese than in agreeing with the United States. While few believed that this might lead to a U.S.-British war, Britain as a neutral in a U.S.-Japanese conflict could cause the United States maritime difficulties in the Pacific. When one added the British Royal Navy figures to those of the Japanese Imperial Navy, the numbers could only prove unsettling to the United States. Renewal of the alliance was thus not favored in Washington. The U.S. opposition found support in Canada, always fearful of an aroused United States in the event of a serious United States–British dispute.

All of these threads came together in the spring and summer of 1921. By early July the British, during an Imperial Conference, had come up with a proposal for a meeting on the Pacific and the Far East, and the Americans at the exact same time had come up with a proposal for a conference on the limitation of armaments. Secretary of State Hughes merged the two proposals and after a short time issued a call for a conference in Washington, D.C., to meet on 11 November 1921. To begin arms control discussions on the day marking the end of World War I seemed an appropriate gesture in hopes for a more peaceful world.

President Harding appointed as the U.S. delegates to the upcoming conference Charles Evans Hughes, secretary of state; Henry Cabot Lodge, the Senate Republican majority leader as well as chairman of the Senate Foreign Relations Committee; Oscar W. Underwood, the Senate Democratic minority leader; and Elihu Root, a former secretary of state under Theodore Roosevelt. The president, having noted Woodrow Wilson's failure to invite senators to the Versailles conference, had wisely decided to add prominent senators of both parties to the delegation. Lodge and Underwood proved towers of strength in the ratification debates that followed the Washington conference.

The United States Proposal

Working secretly from August through October of 1921, the delegation, closely advised by the assistant secretary of the navy, Theodore Roosevelt, Jr., developed a naval proposal. The first proposals of the General Board of the navy recommended that the U.S. fleet must equal that of Great Britain and be at least double that of Japan. Under pressure the board then recommended one million tons of capital ships for the United States and Great Britain with Japan to have 600,000 tons. A further modification dropped the totals to 820,000 apiece for Britain and the United States and 420,000 for the Japanese. The U.S. delegation rejected all of the General Board's proposals as inadequate and adopted a "stop now" standard that would involve the discontinuance of building programs in all three countries, prohibit further construction for the term of agreement, and through the scrapping of existing old battleships, establish a ratio of capital ship tonnage of five for Great Britain and the United States to three for Japan–that is, approximately 500,000 tons apiece for the United States and Great Britain with Japan scheduled for 300,000 tons. While the British and the Japanese also worked on general plans, both had decided to let the United States make an opening proposal that would form the basis of the initial discussions at the conference; each would then work their own positions into the ensuing negotiations.

Harding and Hughes had made it very clear to the naval officers that they viewed the arms treaty as a political question to be decided on the basis of political calculations. With military considerations placed in a secondary position, military advice did not become a major determinant of policy. Lodge, during the later Senate ratification debates, strongly expressed the administration's view: "It is not for technical experts to make this treaty any more than I regard it as the duty of technical experts to make the tariff bill.... The idea should be dismissed that the naval experts were to formulate the policy to be pursued or that we should ever have allowed them to do it. The policy, be it good or bad, was the policy of the government represented by the American delegates at the conference" (*Congressional Record,* 28 March 1922, p. 1677).

Neither the British nor the Japanese, and only eleven Americans, had any real conception of the content or the scope of the proposal that Secretary of State Hughes was to present so dramatically to the conference delegates at the first session on 12 November 1921. No U.S. diplomat had ever presented an international proposal in such a breathtaking manner as Hughes on that November morning. Barely settled in their seats after a perfunctory welcome by Harding, the delegates expected much of the same from Hughes. At first their expectations were well founded as Hughes droned on, but suddenly, about halfway through the speech, the secretary of state stated that rather than talk about stopping naval competition that it was time "to end it now." He called for a ten-year naval holiday based on four principles:

1. that all capital shipbuilding programs, either actual or projected, should be abandoned;
2. that further reduction should be made through the scrapping of certain of the older ships;
3. that in general, regard should be had to the existing naval strength of the powers concerned; and
4. that the capital-ship tonnage should be used as the measurement of strength for navies and a proportionate allowance of auxiliary craft prescribed.

No one in the hall missed Hughes's next words. The United States offered to scrap its fifteen capital ships under construction as well as fifteen older ones for a total tonnage of 845,740. Hughes asked Great Britain to stop construction on its four battleships and scrap nineteen others totaling 583,375 tons. He then turned to the Japanese and listed eight projected battleships and seventeen existing ones totaling 448,928 tons as their contribution to the naval scrap heap. As Charles A'Court in his *After the War: A Diary* (1922) remarked, "Hughes sank in thirty-five minutes more ships than all the admirals of the world have sunk in a cycle of centuries." The U.S. proposal would leave the United States with eighteen capital ships (500,650 tons), Great Britain with twenty-two older, more lightly armed battleships and battle cruisers (604,450 tons), and Japan with ten capital ships (299,700 tons). Replacement tonnage could not be laid down for ten years and would be limited by a total maximum capital-ship tonnage of 500,000 tons for the United States and Great Britain and 300,000 for Japan, that is, a ratio of 5:5:3. Hughes had played his trump card and stolen the lead from his opponents.

When the leading delegates arose at the next session and accepted the U.S. proposal in general, there were, of course, some details that needed tending to; every experienced diplomat knew that hard negotiations were just ahead. Two major controversies arose around the naval negotiations: the Japanese request for a higher ratio of capital ships and the French refusal to accept limitations on auxiliary vessels. Both changed the U.S. proposal in major ways.

Negotiating Capital-Ship Ratios   The Japanese rejected the 5:5:3 (or, 10:10:6) ratio in capital ships and asked for a 10:10:7 ratio. Their argument on the surface revolved around the 35,000-ton *Mutsu,* at the time a just-completed battleship listed as a ship to be scrapped under the U.S. proposal. With rhetorical tears shed by the Japanese as they described how Japanese schoolchildren had contributed their last yen toward the construction of the *Mutsu,* the U.S. delegation, recognizing that it represented a bargaining chip, at first resisted, but finally decided that by retaining the *Mutsu,* but scrapping the older 21,400-ton *Settsu,* the overall tonnage totals for the three major powers would rise but the 5:5:3 ratio would remain intact.

Within the Japanese delegation, navy minister Kato Tomasaburo, head of the delegation and former promoter of the Japanese construction program, took the broad view that Japan must first build up its industrial strength before building a great peacetime navy. Therefore, he was willing to foster a diplomatic settlement with the United States and accept the 10:10:6 ratio. Tomasaburo was opposed by Vice Admiral Kato Kanji, who wanted a powerful fleet in being—that could defeat any opponent in the initial days of a war—and thus strongly supported the 10:10:7 ratio. While the navy minister was to win this political battle over the vice admiral, naval officers, represented by the vice admiral, never willingly accepted the 10:10:6 ratio.

This seemingly minor concession to Japan, however, revealed a deeper Japanese concern that led in turn to a major addition to the naval treaty. Many in the Japanese Imperial Navy believed that a 5:5:3 ratio placed Japan in an inferior position both politically and militarily. After all, the Anglo-Japanese Alliance as well as the Versailles conference had accepted the Japanese as equals. To the navy, while the addition of a nominal 50,000 more tons of capital ship was a difference of approximately one battleship between a 10:10:6 and a 10:10:7 ratio, it appeared that that might be enough to assure victory in a defensive war against the United States. While Kato Tomasaburo accepted 5:5:3, many were rankled by the subordinate political implications of the 10:10:6, or even the 10:10:7.

In order to gain more for Japan and disarm the naval critics, the Japanese government, with Kato Tomasaburo in the lead, began to push for a clause that would prohibit the further fortification of Pacific islands by the signatories of the naval treaty. If the Japanese could not have a higher ratio of capital ships, they could make it almost impossible for any potential enemy to either build new bases or increase the power of their present ones. Over the protests of its military advisers the U.S. delegation accepted the Japanese proposals. Hughes reasoned first that no president was likely ever to talk Congress into voting the necessary funds to expand the Pacific bases and, secondly, even if that happened, the process of a buildup would appear extraordinarily threatening to the Japanese. Such action might even provoke an attack before the bases could be completed.

The French also made a serious dent in the U.S. proposal when they asked for a higher capital-ship ratio. Hughes had left both the French and Italians out of the initial proposal and had not proposed tonnage figures until after he had settled with the British and the Japanese. When Hughes suggested 175,000 tons apiece for the French and Italians, the French exploded; the Italians, meanwhile, did not actually care what they received as long as it was the same as the French. Acceptance would have left the ratios at 5 : 5 : 3 : 1.75 : 1.75, but the French demanded 350,000 tons, even more than the Japanese. The U.S. ratios, based on a rough approximation of existing naval power in 1921, did not appeal to the French, who had only 164,500 tons of capital ships. The French for decades had placed more emphasis on their land forces rather than on sea power and had not built a navy up to the level that they now believed their prestige demanded. While under the U.S. proposal the French would not have had to scrap any capital ships, they also would not have had to build any. Under the French proposal, however, the French would have had to build capital ships to raise themselves to their suggested level. That position would have not only destroyed the entire basis of the American "stop now" proposal but also have upset the 5 : 5 : 3 ratio already agreed to by the British and Japanese, for then the British would feel compelled to ask for more capital-ship tonnage to match the higher French and Italian totals in European waters; this, in turn, in a domino effect, would cause both the Americans and the Japanese to raise their totals in relation to the British.

The secretary of state found himself forced to appeal to the French prime minister, Aristide Briand, who had attended the opening sessions of the Washington conference and then returned to Paris. Hughes had privately concluded that if the French did not cooperate they would be left out of the naval treaty. Briand, unaware of the U.S. decision, rose to the occasion and instructed the French delegates to accept the U.S. proposal on capital ships. However, he then said it was impossible to accept the same ratios on auxiliary ships.

Failure to Limit Auxiliary Warships The French position on auxiliary ships led to the greatest single defect of the naval treaty: the complete absence of any limitations on the number of heavy and light cruisers, destroyers, and submarines. By treaty definition, capital ships included only battleships, battle cruisers (similar to battleships in size and guns but with less armor and higher speeds), and aircraft carriers; all other ships of lesser size and tonnage were considered auxiliary ships. Hughes had hoped to apply the same ratios to auxiliary ships as he had to capital ships, but the French decision and the resulting debates left little hope of achieving that goal. A bitter French-British debate over whether submarines were defensive weapons that all nations could build without limit (as the French insisted) or offensive weapons (as the British, still burning from their recent experiences with German U-boats, argued) destroyed all chance of any auxiliary limitations at all. In order to prevent nations from building auxiliary ships that were capital ships in everything but name, the conference did pass a resolution that no auxiliary ships could exceed 10,000 tons or have larger than 8-inch (20-cm) guns. Cursorily debated at the time, this clause was to become the center of a bitter debate over heavy and light cruisers at subsequent naval conferences.

Submarines were indeed an issue at the conference. As the conference began the United States had the largest fleet of submarines. U.S. public opinion, however, had strong feelings against the submarines as weapons of war based on their use by Germany during World War I. The 5 : 5 : 3 ratio proposed at the conference would have given 90,000 tons to the United States and Great Britain and 54,000 to Japan. Arthur Balfour of Great Britain called for their complete abolition, while France, as indicated, supported their defensive use. When the French refused to accept any ratios for auxiliary ships, all chance of total tonnage or numerical limitations for submarines disappeared. The so-called Root resolutions (named for Elihu Root) attempted to limit the legal activities of submarines in wartime to traditional international law, which regulated cruiser warfare; the resolutions also attempted to outlaw unrestricted submarine warfare. Clearly designed to mollify public opinion, the submarine rules were combined with poison-gas rules into a separate treaty on submarines and poison gas. France, in the end, refused to ratify and the Treaty Relating to the Use of Submarines and Noxious Gases in Warfare never went into effect.

Finally there was the question of aircraft carriers. Hughes had suggested 80,000 tons for the United States and Great Britain and 48,000 tons for Japan, with no figures for France and Italy in the opening proposal. After considerable negotiation over what was to become the most important category of capital ships in World War II, the United States and Great Britain accepted 135,000 tons apiece, Japan received 81,000, and France and Italy got 60,000 tons. All were higher figures than existed in 1921: the United States had 19,360 tons built or being built, Great Britain had 87,190 tons, Japan had 21,000, France had 24,230 and Italy had none. Also adopted was a 27,000 maximum tonnage limit for aircraft carriers and an 8-inch (20-cm) gun limitation. Both the United States and Great Britain got the right to convert two of their unfinished capital ships to aircraft carriers; in the case of the United States the two converted battle cruisers became the *Lexington* and the *Saratoga*. Not only were no aircraft carriers scrapped at the Washington conference, additional construction was anticipated—the significance of which was little understood at the time by the battleship admirals.

The Washington Treaties   The final result was the Five-Power (United States, Great Britain, Japan, France, and Italy) Naval Treaty signed 6 February 1922. It provided for: a ten-year naval holiday in the construction of battleships and battle cruisers; the scrapping of seventy-six capital ships built, being built, or planned; a ratio of strength between the five powers of 5 : 5 : 3 : 1.75 : 1.75 for that ten-year period; no further fortification on stipulated Pacific islands that included the Philippines, Guam, and Wake on the U.S. side (but not Hawaii), did not include Hong Kong and Singapore on the British side, and did include the Pescadores, Amoni-Òshima, the Bonins, and others belonging to the Japanese; and the construction of aircraft carriers.

The treaty did not include limitations on the numbers of auxiliary ships. There were no formal verification or inspection clauses (what later came to be called safeguards) except for a minor self-reporting requirement; nor any limitations on aircraft; nor any provisions limiting technological improvements as long as those additions did not push the total tonnage beyond 35,000 tons for individual capital ships and 10,000 tons for auxiliary ships.

The United States deliberately linked several other treaties and understandings regarding the Far East that were signed at the conference with the Five-Power Naval Treaty. Prior to and during the conference the United States had clearly indicated to both Great Britain and Japan that the United States would not ratify the naval arms control treaty until Great Britain and Japan gave up the Anglo-Japanese Alliance and Japan relaxed its aggressive attitude in the Pacific and on the Asian mainland. Unwillingness by either would lead the United States to go ahead and build its navy "second to none" and begin a naval race that neither Great Britain nor Japan wanted at that time. The decision to tie the arms control treaty to political arrangements was a major and unusual step for the United States. It is the only treaty of the Washington system in the interwar years that had such a clear linkage.

The arrangements included:

1. a Four-Power Treaty (United States, Great Britain, Japan, and France) that ended the Anglo-Japanese Alliance and provided that the four powers would jointly confer if disputes among them arose or aggression from outside threatened the peace of the Pacific area;
2. a Nine-Power Treaty (United States, Great Britain, Japan, Italy, France, Portugal, the Netherlands, Belgium, and China) in which the powers pledged to respect the sovereignty, independence, and integrity of China, as well as *(a)* give the Chinese a chance to establish a stable government and *(b)* to uphold the open door of commercial opportunity in China;
3. a Chinese Customs Treaty (again signed by all nine powers) that provided for an effective tariff rate that all powers could follow; and
4. in a series of agreements concluded outside the formal confines of the conference but not formal treaties, Japan agreed to restore Shantung to the Chinese, to sell the Japanese-owned Shan-

tung railway to the Chinese, and to withdraw its troops from Siberia.

The Harding administration rushed the treaties through the United States Senate on a tidal wave of popular opinion. Major opposition developed over the Four-Power Treaty, which isolationists called an alliance, but it passed after a bitter fight. Crucial to its passage was the fact that it was so closely linked by the Harding administration to the Five-Power Treaty, which almost no one opposed. The administration could successfully suggest that the defeat of the Four-Power Treaty might lead to serious difficulty with the naval treaty itself; the ratification of the one and not the other might cause Great Britain and Japan to hesitate, and the United States itself might face, without a strong navy, the recreation of the Anglo-Japanese Alliance. With the passage of the Four-Power Treaty, all the other treaties sailed through with little or no opposition. The Five-Power Naval Treaty was so popular that no hearings were held, there was almost no debate on the Senate floor, and the treaty was adopted, seventy-four to one, with twenty-one abstentions. It appears that almost all of those absent would have voted, with perhaps one exception, for the treaty. Those naval supporters who opposed the treaty were never able to organize and present their arguments. While more naval opposition developed in Japan than in the United States, neither there nor in Great Britain did the popular naval treaty run into serious trouble in the ratification debates.

GENEVA NAVAL CONFERENCE, 1927

In an attempt to "finish the work" of the Washington conference, President Calvin Coolidge sent out invitations on 10 February 1927 for a second naval arms control conference. Italy and France sent only observers rather than official delegates. Thus the United States, Great Britain, and Japan began to talk on 20 June, in Geneva, without official representatives of the two disgruntled powers. Neither power wanted to accept limitations on auxiliary ships that they considered as defensive vessels. Their absence, and a less than enthusiastic British response, indicated that the arguments over both the tonnage of specific cruisers, destroyers, and submarines, as well as total tonnages of each class for the three nations, would be extensive.

Ambassador Hugh Gibson presented the opening U.S. proposal which in essence extended the $5:5:3$ ratio to the three classes of auxiliary ships. United States–Japanese issues over the $10:10:7$ problem never received a chance to develop when the British spurned the U.S. cruiser proposal of 300,000 tons for the United States and a similar figure for Great Britain (with 180,000 for Japan), by asking for 600,000 tons. At a conference designed to limit tonnage, the British were calling for substantial construction. But, even worse, the British wanted to split the cruiser category into two separate classes: one would include, as provided by the Washington Naval treaty, heavy cruisers with 8-inch (20-cm) guns and limited to 10,000 tons displacement, while the second would include light cruisers with 6-inch (15-cm) guns limited to 7,500 tons displacement. In addition, the British proposed that no country be allowed to have more than fifteen of the larger cruisers in category one. The British had, as the conference began, fifteen of the 10,000-ton class either built or being built: the United States had two and the Japanese had six; in other words, the British had designed their proposals to protect their own ships and their own naval advantage.

The cruiser argument sank the Geneva conference. Neither Congress nor the president, both notoriously reluctant to ask for or spend funds, would support the building of such a massive tonnage of cruisers to match the British. Putting aside the various technical issues and the self-justifying debates over whether a 10,000-ton ship was more offensive than a 7,500-ton "defensive" ship, at the core of the dispute was the U.S. belief that it might need many more than fifteen 10,000-ton heavy cruisers if it ever had to fight a war in the great expanses of the Pacific Ocean. A larger ship would have not only greater range but more firepower when the battle came.

The conference ended with no agreements and considerable hard feelings between the United States and Great Britain. Some commentators felt that employing senior naval officers as the major negotiators in each delegation, unlike the Washington conference where civilians had control, led to insoluble technical disputes and prevented political compromise.

After the conference, the Coolidge administration then met the British challenge head on when it called for the building of fifteen 10,000-ton heavy cruisers and one aircraft carrier. The House of Representatives approved the bill 287 to 58, but the Senate, under intense pressure from arms-limitation supporters, did not give its 68 to 12 approval until almost a year later on 5 February 1929. The president, however, was authorized to suspend the construction of the ships in the event of a further arms control agreement. This, coupled with the signing of the Kellogg-Briand Treaty (1928), outlawing war as an instrument of national policy, encouraged a new president, Herbert Hoover, to begin a series of preliminary talks with the British in order to avoid a repeat of the open confrontations of the failed Geneva negotiations; discussions with the Japanese and the French were also held.

LONDON CONFERENCE, 1930

Hoover's first thoughts were delivered by Ambassador Hugh Gibson on 22 April 1929. The president, looking for a method to defuse the cruiser issue, called for the invention of a "yardstick" to measure the relative requirements of each naval power; Hughes, at Washington in 1921, had used the existing strength of each navy as the foundation of the 5 : 5 : 3 ratio. Hoover clearly wanted reductions as well as linkage of the whole process to the Kellogg-Briand Treaty. He discovered, however, that while virtually all the countries could easily accept the concept of a yardstick, it was all but impossible to devise one whose specifics would be acceptable to everyone. Neither the president nor Secretary of State Henry L. Stimson could come up with a satisfactory numerical solution.

Given the failure to find a satisfactory yardstick and the resulting neglect of political problems, the cruiser issue once again came to the forefront. Prime Minister J. Ramsey MacDonald of Great Britain suggested that while he supported an arrangement that would give the United States eighteen heavy cruisers to Britain's fifteen, he also wanted Britain to have up to forty-five light cruisers. Since the United States's desire for parity would require matching the British, and since Hoover wanted reduction, not construction, the Hoover administration was appalled.

The crux of the situation, unlike Washington in 1921, was that the United States in 1929 had almost all of its cruisers in the planning stage while most of the British cruisers were already afloat. This put Britain, not the United States, in the driver's seat when it came to U.S. demands for parity. The final preconference negotiations ended up with Britain accepting fifteen cruisers with 8-inch (20-cm) guns to twenty-one for the United States and thirty-five cruisers with 6-inch (15-cm) guns to fifteen for the United States—with the British ending up with more cruiser total tonnage, 339,000 to 315,000.

Opposition soon developed both in Paris and Tokyo. The French pointed out that their far-flung empire clearly necessitated more auxiliary vessels than the British wanted them to possess and, in addition, the obsession of the United States with numerical ratios resulted in the complete exclusion of political considerations. The Japanese weighed in with requests for a 70-percent ratio in auxiliary ships. The upcoming negotiations in London were going to be difficult.

Quite clearly, the differing demands for satisfactory ratios would dominate the conference. Each country had a rationale for its position; everything from domestic political pressures to simply different ideas about what constituted naval security for their particular circumstances complicated the quest for compromise. Hughes had successfully avoided this in 1921 by his "stop now" program based on existing strengths and the power of his surprise proposals. By 1930, however, the political atmosphere, both domestic and international, was much more threatening, a worldwide economic depression was underway, and both statesmen and naval officers more clearly saw the implications and problems of the naval ratios. Great Britain and France had vast world empires, Tokyo felt that its 60-percent ratio was an insult to its pride and place in the world, and Italy continued to want parity with France. Only the United States wanted a full continuation of further reductions, retention of the 5 : 5 : 3 ratios, and a low level of naval construction. Over nine months of constant effort had revealed that something would have to give at London in order for the Washington system to continue.

Negotiations at London   The United States held separate negotiations at the conference with both the British and the Japanese. The Japanese felt that they were being thwarted by Great Britain and the United States in an attempt to prevent them from achieving a 70-percent ratio rather than the 60-percent ratio. All were well aware that Great Britain and the United States might well make their own deal and leave Japan out.

The Senator David Reed–Ambassador Matsudaira Tsuneo compromise of March 1930 provided for a 60-percent ratio in heavy cruisers, a 70-percent ratio in light cruisers and destroyers, and parity in submarines. Matsudaira had made this arrangement without the approval of his naval advisers, who were furious, but Prime Minister Osayuki Hamaguchi came down on the side of the diplomats who feared—if the London conference failed—that a naval race might break out that Japan could not win. While Hamaguchi was successful in his demands, even fending off a naval appeal to the emperor, the naval officers now became public, major opponents of the Washington system.

France and Italy were also to present difficulties for the U.S. position. France above all wanted security against the possible rebirth of a military threat from Germany. Without mutual security guarantees the French felt that it would be impossible to sign any serious arms-limitation agreements. Neither the United States nor Great Britain displayed any willingness to enter into that particular military, political thicket. Hoover, in particular, believed that any such political-military agreement would lessen the significance of the Kellogg-Briand Treaty. Attempts by organized public opinion groups in the United States, supported by many newspapers and journals, to move the Hoover administration toward the acceptance of a consultative pact with the French failed. It is doubtful that the French would have agreed to anything short of a military guarantee, and no U.S. president in the interwar period—given the domestic isolationist climate—could have offered one. The British refused point blank.

It is clear that President Hoover refused to face the realities of the connection of politics to disarmament. One of the great strengths of the original Washington system proposed by Hughes in 1921 was that the secretary of state had tied the naval agreement to the Four-Power Treaty, which had ended the Anglo-Japanese Alliance and provided for consultation if any disputes occurred in the Pacific area; had secured treaty protection for China in the Nine-Power Treaty; and had helped convince the Japanese that it was time to leave Shantung and Siberia. In contrast, technical considerations alone drove the Hoover proposals. Disarmament was separate and distinct from political considerations; it was to be pursued for its own benefits. This had not worked at Geneva and did not work at London, but one must point out that the European political problems of 1930 were far more serious than those of the Far East in 1921, and that the complexity of the situation made it much more difficult to achieve any satisfactory political connections to arms control disputes. With each passing year in the 1930s the difficulty grew.

The Japanese came to view the London conference as a defeat, and it was to lead to a serious break between the leaders of the Japanese military and civilian leaders. Great Britain and the United States had quite clearly designed their proposals with an eye on the Japanese. The Japanese desire for a 70-percent ratio in all types of auxiliary ships (except for submarines where the Japanese wanted no numerical limits at all), including heavy cruisers, was only partially achieved; Japan was given approximately 70 percent in auxiliaries, but only 60 percent in heavy cruisers while the clause giving them parity in submarines with the United States and Great Britain would actually require a reduction in the Japanese 1930 total tonnage. The unfortunate result of these levels, which the Japanese military considered unacceptable restrictions, and a failure by the two Western powers to recognize legitimate demands on the part of the Japanese, was to contribute to the end of civilian supremacy within the Japanese government and to the rise of the militarists.

Terms of the London Treaty   Under the London Naval Treaty of 1930 all five nations (Great Britain, United States, Japan, France, and Italy) agreed to refrain from laying down the capital ship replacement tonnage (new construction of capital ships that according to the Washington agreement would become overage) from 1931 to 1936; moreover, France and Italy received exemptions that allowed them to construct 70,000 tons apiece to meet the challenge of German programs then underway. The London Naval Treaty also provided for the continuation of scrapping: the United States, Great Britain, and Japan would demolish a total of nine capital ships. The resulting ratio of capital ships planned for 1936 would stabilize at a tonnage of approximately 10 : 10 : 6, but if the twenty-year age limit of the Washington Naval Treaty were applied at that date, ten of the eighteen U.S. capital ships would be overage, sixteen of the British eighteen, and five of the Japanese nine. What this meant, of course, was that all three powers might well want to build large numbers of capital ships after 1936. Much depended on what political tensions might exist by then. Aircraft-carrier tonnage remained the same as under the Washington agreement: United States, 135,000 tons; Great Britain, 135,000 tons; Japan, 81,000 tons; France and Italy, 60,000 tons.

Limits placed on auxiliary tonnage included:

1. heavy cruisers—United States, 180,000 tons; Great Britain, 146,800; Japan, 108,400;
2. light cruisers—United States, 143,500 tons; Great Britain, 192,200; Japan, 100,450;
3. destroyers—United States, 150,000 tons; Great Britain, 150,000; and
4. submarines—United States, Great Britain, and Japan each 52,700 tons.

The United States would not reach its full heavy-cruiser tonnage until 1936. France and Italy did not, as mentioned, accept any limitations on auxiliary ships. In order to provide for the possibility of either of them constructing auxiliary fleets that might challenge the position of the three signatories, the British insisted on the inclusion of a "safety valve" clause in the treaty. Designed to continue Great Britain's two-power standard in European waters, which meant that the British fleet would be the equal of the combined French-Italian fleets, it specified that if France or Italy should build auxiliary ships that challenged the position of the three signatory powers, any one of the latter could then begin to construct ships to meet the challenge; if one signatory power built, the other two signatory powers could then construct auxiliary ships with the same proportional increases.

The submarine issue, supposedly settled by the Root resolutions of the Washington conference, surfaced again in London because the French had refused to ratify the Treaty Relating to the Use of Submarines and Noxious Gases in Warfare. When the British again called for abolition, they found that the United States now supported them against the French, who continued to claim that submarines were defensive weapons. The French position, in turn, now found support from the Japanese who also wanted parity in submarine tonnage with the United States and Great Britain. Japan did receive its parity demand, and another submarine code of conduct was passed at London. It provided that submarines had to follow the same rules of international law as surface ships and that in the event of a submarine sinking a merchant ship, it had first to place the ship's crew, passengers, and ship's papers in a place of safety.

The Ratification Process   While the London Naval Treaty found prompt approval during the ratification process in the United States, Great Britain, and Japan, a great deal more opposition developed in all three countries than the Washington system had faced in 1921. This time nationalists and naval officers were much better organized and prepared than they had been after Hughes's surprise proposals at Washington. Having lost the initiative at that time, they were determined to present their viewpoints in a much stronger fashion. Since the London Naval Treaty was building on the ratios of the Washington conference, the opponents by 1930 had almost nine years of experience and thinking to build their arguments.

While the Harding administration in 1922 had capitalized on the all but overwhelming support for the surprise proposals of Hughes by rushing the treaties through the United States Senate without any hearings or even more than a short, superficial debate on the Five-Power Naval Treaty on the Senate floor, in 1930 there were full Senate hearings before both the Committee on Foreign Affairs and the Committee on Naval Affairs. In essence, the naval officers argued that the emphasis on ratios and tonnages and parity left out other considerations such as logistics, the importance of naval bases, access to fuel, and general overall naval strategies. In particular they believed that by not insisting on a change in the no-further-fortification-of-Pacific-bases clause of the Washington Naval Treaty and also by agreeing to a further increase in the tonnage of Japanese auxiliary ships, the United States had ceded control of the western Pacific to the Japanese and made it all but impossible for the United States to defend effectively its interests in the Pacific. If the opponents had strong arguments, Hoover had the votes, and the London treaty was approved by a vote of fifty-eight to nine, a majority that easily met the constitutional requirement of two-thirds of the United States Senate present and concurring. But one must note the increase from one to nine senators voting against the Washington system from 1921 to 1930, and the fact that thirty-one senators (compared to twenty-one in 1922), for one reason or another, chose not to vote.

Similar arguments surfaced in Great Britain. Unlike Hoover, who had praised the London Naval Treaty for its accomplishments and stressed the savings of great sums of money, MacDonald was careful and cautious and described the treaty as a modest advance. Winston Churchill, in the opposition party in the House of Commons, found that the treaty left Great Britain in an inferior position; Britain needed more ships to defend its worldwide imperial commitments. The Conservatives attempted to delay ratification by sending the treaty to an investigative commission but failed to gain majority support. It was then approved.

The fight over ratification was most bitter in Japan. Prime Minister Hamaguchi insisted that support of the treaty was a governmental position and thus reflected more than just the opinion of the military. But Admiral Kanji Kato, chief of the naval staff, publicly opposed the treaty and suggested that the government had no right to agree to a treaty that was not supported by the Japanese navy staff. When the Privy Council, at first hesitant about the treaty, finally approved ratification, clearly with the emperor's approval, the treaty went into effect. But while the government had won the battle, the military had seriously eroded the government's support and within a year, after Japanese troops invaded Manchuria in 1931, the military began its 14-year dominance.

TURKO-GREEK, 1930, AND TURKO-SOVIET, 1931, NAVAL ACCORDS

At this time two minor additions to the naval arms control structure were signed: the Turko-Greek protocol of 30 October 1930 and the Turko-Soviet pact of 7 March 1931. A mini naval race between the Greeks and Turks appeared in the offing when the latter announced in 1928 that they were going to modernize the former German battleship *Goeben,* now renamed the *Yavus.* The Greeks immediately began to look into the acquisition of another former German capital ship. Premier Eleutherious Venizelos of Greece and President Mustafa Kemel Pasha of Turkey, aided by the Italians, who wanted to keep the Aegean calm, and by the recognition of all that naval funds were extraordinarily limited, came to an agreement that called for the continuation of the naval status quo until a signatory gave six months' notice of intent to alter the situation. The Turko-Soviet pact extended the continuation of the naval status quo to the Black Sea, with the same notification requirement.

LONDON NAVAL CONFERENCE, 1936

It took no special insight to predict that the next major naval conference, to be held in London from 9 December 1935 to 25 March 1936, might well run into impossible obstacles. This, the last of the great conferences, occurred after the Japanese had expanded from Manchuria into northern China, after Italy had conquered Ethiopia, and during the period in which Germany had marched into the Rhineland. The United States, more interested in the Pacific situation than in its European counterpart, still sought naval reductions, and still neglected to build its fleet up to the levels permitted by the treaties. The British, meanwhile, had demonstrated considerable disenchantment with the seemingly blind attitude of the Americans who seemed to ignore the naval needs of the British, and the Japanese by 1936 were calling for naval parity with the United States and Great Britain in all categories. Clearly, the Washington system of naval arms control was on tottering legs.

President Franklin D. Roosevelt, on entering the White House in March 1933 in the midst of the Great Depression, had found that the U.S. Navy was only built up to approximately 65 percent of the treaty limits authorized by the Washington and London arrangements. Roosevelt, a former assistant secretary of the navy who remained much interested in naval affairs, proposed using Section 202 of the National Industrial Recovery Act to authorize funds for the building of thirty-two warships (including the aircraft carriers *Yorktown* and *Enterprise*) that would total some 126,000 tons. Such construction would not only increase the strength of the navy but also reduce unemployment by putting men to work both in producing parts and in the actual construction of the ships. Roosevelt's proposal was followed by the Vinson-Trammel Act of 1934, which authorized the United States to build the navy to 100 percent of treaty strength by the end of 1942. Congress authorized this huge program, which called for the construction of 102 ships and almost 1,200 aircraft for the navy, but it did not allocate the $286 million necessary to pay for the program. Roosevelt continued to suggest to the British that he would prefer a renewal of the Washington and London treaties for another ten years with a further reduction of 20 percent over the ten-year period.

Negotiations Again   The British suggested that preliminary discussions between the United States, Great Britain, and Japan prior to the holding of any conference would allow the three major powers to explore each other's positions. These talks, beginning in 1934, indicated that the British wanted either more cruisers (approximately seventy) or a pact with the United States on the Pacific before any further reductions could be made; the United States rejected both proposals.

Before negotiations could take place, the two powers received news that the Japanese government was about to announce that before the end of 1934 it would give the required two-years notice that Japan would no longer remain in the Washington system after 1936. Prior to the denunciation, the Japanese had asked for an end to ratios and parity, but the United States continued to insist on the retention of the Washington system of quantitative levels. The Japanese called for reductions with a common upper limit of tonnage; each of the three powers could build the particular mix of vessels they wanted with no restrictions on total numbers and sizes as long as their particular mix did not exceed the common upper limit of total tonnage. The Japanese also proposed that ship construction center around the building of defensive arms and not offensive arms (identified as aircraft carriers, battleships, battle cruisers, and heavy cruisers).

Parity was totally unacceptable to the United States and Great Britain, who pointed out that Japan did not have the same worldwide commitments, nor had recent Japanese actions expressed a nonoffensive spirit. Secretary of State Cordell Hull took an especially hard line posited on the belief that it might be best just to let the Japanese go, make a naval arrangement without them, and have both the United States and Great Britain build their fleets to a full treaty level. This, supposedly, would force the Japanese to come to terms. On 9 December 1934 the Japanese, unaware of the exact specifics of Hull's words to the British but certainly aware of his hard-line approach to Japan, formally invoked the two-year notice of the termination of the treaties.

When the five naval powers met in London in 1936, neither the Americans nor the Japanese were prepared to shift their basic positions, nor were the British, French, and Italians enthusiastic about the continuation of the ratio system. The British demonstrated the most flexibility when they called for an end to ratios and categories and proposed instead that qualitative limits (the size of armaments and total tonnage of individual types of ships) be followed rather than the quantitative limits of the Washington system; France and Italy agreed and also supported the exchange of information, including a timetable of construction and characteristics of each new ship. The Americans remained absolutely opposed not only to the Japanese demand for parity but basically to any increase in Japanese numbers that did not fit the Washington system.

Faced with the uncompromising U.S. position and a just as strong position on the part of the Japanese to end what they considered the onerous restrictions of the Washington system, the conference hobbled on to its predictable conclusion. On 15 January 1936 the Japanese delegation, leaving two members as observers, left the conference and returned to Japan. Japan's demand for equality in rank with the great world powers, having met with success only twice in the first two decades of the twentieth century with the Anglo-Japanese Alliance and the Versailles conference, was not achieved again at London. The Italians also refused to sign the final treaty.

Franco-Italian Issues in the 1930s   French and Italian issues, stemming from the granting of naval equality to Italy with France at Washington in 1922, remained an irritant between the two countries throughout the early 1930s as Italy, largely on concerns of prestige, wanted to apply the capital-ship ratio established at Washington to auxiliary ships. France, concerned far more with both the German continental threat and the protection of the overseas French empire, displayed no interest in parity. Neither nation could agree at the London conference of 1930. Both the United States and Great Britain attempted to mediate, and the final result was a Franco-Italian "basis of agreement" arrangement of 1 March 1931. Concessions were made on both sides, but the naval complications raised by German naval construction, and the French and Italian response to it, prevented the consummation of any final agreement. By 1935 it was too late, as both France and Italy were building vessels in response to the deteriorating European situation.

Terms of the Second London Treaty   The final treaty, signed by the United States, Great Britain, and France, provided for qualitative limitations: new capital ships could not displace over 35,000 tons nor mount guns over 14 inches (36 cm) in caliber (but if Japan did not agree, a 16-inch limit would apply); the smallest acceptable capital-ship tonnage would be 17,500 tons; new aircraft carriers (but not old ones already afloat) could not be over 23,000 tons nor have guns bigger than 6.1 inches (15 cm); new submarines could not be over 2,000 tons nor have a deck gun of over 5.1 inches (13 cm); and merchant ships were not to be armed during peacetime. In 1937 the Japanese refused the 14-inch-gun limitation.

Other features of the treaty included a six-year holiday on the building of heavy cruisers (again dependent on the future actions of Japan in that category), a reporting procedure whereby construction information was to be exchanged, and the famous "escalator clause" whereby if nonsignatory powers built to an excessive degree, a signatory power could exceed the treaty limitations by notifying the other powers.

The submarine code, adopted at the London conference of 1930, was supposed to end since the London treaty itself was expiring, but a last-minute protocol that extended its terms was signed in November 1936 after the end of the conference. Some thirty nations, including all the major combatants of World War II, were eventually to agree to its terms.

Ratification occurred without any of the great disputes that had occurred after the previous London conference of 1930. Most unusual was the fact that a whole series of nations bilaterally joined the treaty in 1937 and 1938: Germany, the Soviet Union, Poland, Italy, Denmark, Norway, Sweden, and Finland all signed treaties with Great Britain that included small changes. The United States in effect ignored these additions, neither approving nor disapproving of the treaties.

ANGLO-GERMAN NAVAL PACT, 1935

Perhaps the most important of the pacts signed outside of the major conferences, but that still form a part of the interwar naval-limitation system, was the Anglo-German pact of 1935. Adolph Hitler suggested the negotiations that led to the agreement. It was his hope that a naval arrangement with Great Britain would in effect lead to the lifting of the final armament restrictions placed on Germany by the Treaty of Versailles. Hitler also recognized that the

construction of a large German fleet might well inspire the British to enter into a naval race with Germany that in turn would force Hitler to divert funds from Germany's more important, in Hitler's mind, ground and air buildup. The British were receptive to bringing Germany into the European ratio system at a level that would be safe for Great Britain but not too far out of line with the French and Italian positions.

Hitler declared quite early that Germany would accept a limitation of 35 percent of the British tonnage. Great Britain found this too high a figure because it would cause the French and Italians to raise their tonnage ratios in regard to the British, in order to equal the Germans, which in turn would force the British to build more, and then, of course, the Germans' 35 percent would increase even more. Moreover, Germany felt that its security requirements were at least equal to those of France or Italy. Great Britain also had to factor in the expected positions of the naval powers who were to meet at the upcoming London conference of 1936.

After some difficult negotiations in which the Germans took a determined stance, the Anglo-German pact of 1935 was signed. A "permanent" 100:35 percent total-tonnage ratio between the two powers marked the upper limit. Germany hoped to reach its 35 percent in total by 1942; this would include approximately 176,000 tons of capital ships (to Great Britain's 504,000), 40,000 tons of aircraft carriers (G.B., 111,950), 160,000 tons of heavy and light cruisers (G.B., 472,500), 53,000 tons of destroyers (G.B., 150,000), and 22,000 tons of submarines (G.B., 49,000). All but the last category fit into the 100:35 ratio.

Submarine figures require a special explanation. The Germans accepted an initial figure of 45 percent but they also received the right to build to full parity with the British, after informing the latter, if circumstances demanded. In December 1938 the Germans exercised that right.

Both the British and the Germans secured their goals. While there were those in Parliament who questioned the morality of approving of German naval construction, the pact secured a 247 to 44 vote of approval in the House of Commons. The French were extraordinarily upset and saw the agreement as breaking up the anti-German front they had attempted to establish. While the treaty did not significantly affect the rate of German naval construction from 1935 to 1939, Hitler did win a diplomatic victory in the eyes of many by securing unilateral British consent to the abolition of the Versailles naval restrictions on Germany.

The pact did provide for further minor negotiations that resulted in the Anglo-German Naval Treaty of 1937, which basically added the pertinent sections of the London conference arrangements of 1936 to the pact. In April 1939, the Germans denounced the arrangements and were therefore no longer bound by them.

ISSUES OF VERIFICATION AND COMPLIANCE

The treaties of the Washington system provided only minor safeguards. Reportage requirements on the construction of replacement tonnage did not include any organized or structured methods to verify the truthfulness and accuracy of the reported information. Consequently, in keeping with most interwar arms control agreements, each nation relied upon "national means" to verify that terms of the treaties were being honored. That is, each nation's intelligence agencies were responsible for gathering data related to compliance and, through assessment of this data, to detect evasions or violations.

Charges were raised, both before and after World War II, that all nations party to the Washington naval system had evaded some one or other of its terms. These allegations fall generally into two categories: (1) evasion of the qualitative naval terms; and (2) evasion of the nonfortification pledge regarding the Pacific islands.

Evasions of Naval Terms   No official charges of premeditated violation of naval terms appear to have been lodged during the lifetime of the Washington system. Yet informal accusations were levied and suspicions voiced, at the time and after World War II, against Japan, Germany, Italy and the United States for qualitative—unannounced technical or design—alterations that ranged from deliberate violations to discreet evasions. These qualitative alterations usually resulted in displacement over tonnage limits.

Japan was accused of evading the 1922 Washington Naval Treaty by secretly building two 68,000-ton battleships with 18-inch (45-cm) guns, *Yamato* and *Musushi,* the construction of which caught U.S. and British naval officials by surprise. It is true that the Allies did not learn of the actual size or armament of these naval behemoths until near the end of the

Pacific war; however, Western agents had heard rumors as early as the fall of 1937 that the oversized ships were planned. Contrary to accusations, neither ship was in violation of the 35,000-ton weight limit and the 16-inch- (40-cm-) gun limit since both were started in the fall of 1937 and spring of 1938 respectively, and the Washington naval restrictions had expired on 31 December 1936.

Allegations were also made that the German battleships *Bismark* and *Tirpitz* were over tonnage limits. Laid down in 1936, these ships were launched in 1939 with displacements of approximately 41,700 and 42,900 tons, respectively. Charges that these tonnages violated the Anglo-German naval pact of 1935 disregard the fact that Germany had accepted the Washington limits only "in principle" until the Anglo-German Naval Treaty of 1937, which made Germany a full-fledged party to the Washington system. And the 35,000-ton limit was raised— by employing the "escalator clause" of the 1936 London treaty—to 45,000 tons in June 1938. If the Germans were technically correct in maintaining that neither ship was in violation of treaty limits, it was only the fortuitous invoking of the escalator clause that saved Germany from deliberate violations. At the Nuremberg trials Admiral Erich Raeder was charged with hiding the fact that the *Scharnhorst,* listed at 26,000 tons, actually weighed 31,300 tons and with failing to inform the British of the true tonnages of the *Bismark* and *Tirpitz.* Since Germany's total capital-ship tonnage was less than that allowed under the 1935 pact, he was acquitted of these charges. British historian Donald C. Watt has concluded that the Anglo-German pact "was more or less faithfully observed until its denuciation in April 1939" (p. 160).

Japan, Italy and, perhaps, the United States built cruisers larger than the 10,000-ton Washington treaty limit. Japan had the most flagrant record, deliberately building three classes of oversized cruisers—the *Mogami* (12,499 tons), *Takao* (13,160 tons) and *Tone* (11,200 tons). Some of the increased tonnage, particularly in the *Mogami* class, was necessary because their great top weight seriously affected their stability. Japan's actions cannot be excused, because their original designs violated treaty limits and because a reduction of ship armaments could have brought them within the tonnage restrictions.

Between 1922 and 1934, Italy built seven cruisers that substantially exceeded the 10,000-ton limit. When the *Gorizia* was towed into Gibraltar for internal repairs in 1937, British naval experts carefully measured it and verified that the cruiser was at least 10 percent overweight. Finally, it has been suggested that the United States's nine ships of the *Brooklyn* class, and the sole *Wichita*—all listed at 10,000 tons—were also overweight. After comparing the measurements of the *Helena* (largest of the *Brooklyn* class) with Japan's *Mogami,* it has been suggested that the two weighed about the same although this has not been confirmed.

The United States Navy's insistence on increasing the gun elevation of its battleships did provoke British authorities to charge that this constituted a violation of the "spirit," if not the "letter," of the Washington Naval Treaty. This complex technical issue arose in January 1923 when Secretary of the Navy Edwin Denby requested $6.5 million from Congress to modify the turrets of U.S. battleships to raise the elevation of their guns and thus give them greater range. The British ambassador at Washington immediately denied Denby's allegation that similar alterations were currently underway on British ships or were even contemplated. The next year, when Denby again sought funds for gun elevation, the ambassador complained that such action was not permitted under terms of the treaty. Despite these British objections, the Americans proceeded and, in 1930, announced that the program had been completed. They did not announce that consequently U.S. battleships were considerably superior to British in firing distances.

Evasion of Nonfortification Pledges   Perhaps the most controversial speculation revolved, and continues to revolve, around the no-further-fortification-of-Pacific-islands clause of the Five-Power Naval Treaty. Accusations and concern grew in the 1930s as it became evident that the Japanese were in fact increasing fortifications on their Pacific islands. Japanese officials were also certain that new U.S. construction on Guam, Midway, and Wake islands was in violation of the nonfortification clause. Popular mythology has consistently held that the famous American aviator, Amelia Earhart, who disappeared while flying over the Pacific in 1937, observed Japanese fortifications and was shot down before she could report them. As late as 1973, former Secretary of State Dean Acheson could charge, in his *This Vast External Realm,* that "the Japanese . . . behind the device of an iron curtain proceeded to fortify the mandated islands" in violation of the Washington treaty.

Although on-site inspection procedures were not considered during the drafting of the 1922 treaties,

Secretary of State Hughes did seek to initiate exchange visits to areas designated as unfortified. He arranged in January 1923 for a Japanese officer to visit Guam and for the U.S. naval attaché at Tokyo to tour Japanese bases in the Pescadores Islands. Hughes urged the U.S. War and Navy departments to open other areas for mutual inspection visits as a means of "assuring a mutual confidence" among treaty nations. Neither U.S. military service liked the idea. Navy Secretary Denby responded "that there should be no question of the good faith of the signatory powers and that, in consequence, visits of inspection either to ships or to stations to verify execution of the terms of a treaty are undesirable and may be provocative of friction." More specifically, both army and navy authorities argued that Japan had more to gain from inspections than did the United States.

When in the fall of 1929 U.S. naval officers became disturbed about Japanese construction on their mandated islands and the navy changed its mind on mutual inspection visits, it was too late. The subsequent failure of diplomatic negotiations and the League of Nations Mandate Commission to persuade Japan to allow Western visitors to the mandated islands only served to convince U.S. officials that violations were taking place.

Postwar evidence shows rather clearly that the Japanese did not begin construction of military "fortifications" in the mandates until 1940. During the late 1920s and 1930s, the Japanese had built a few airfields, oil-storage depots, communications stations, and harbor facilities in the mandates, but so had the United States on Guam, Midway, and Wake. Both nations insisted that their improvements were commercial ventures aimed at stimulating economic activity on their islands, and that this was allowable under terms of the treaty—even if the improvement might have some potential military use. Obviously part of the problem stemmed from the vague, loosely worded restriction that only forbade the construction or improvement of "naval bases" and "fortifications," but said nothing about other improvements.

The Japanese, like the United States, Great Britain, and France, did have the five-year period before the Japanese attack on Pearl Harbor in 1941 to do as they wished with regard to fortification. All of them, in varying degrees, increased their fortifications in that period.

Evaluation of Compliance   Fundamentally, the countries relied on international "good faith"

and diplomatic integrity—the belief that all countries would act in essentially honorable fashion. With good faith and integrity, no formal verification measures were seen as necessary in the treaties. After all, who could hide the construction of a battleship? Indeed, that feat was impossible, but it was very possible to hide modifications such as gun elevations that might result in longer gun ranges and to build in disguised tonnage that pushed the vessel over the total tonnage limitations. The Americans and British argued over gun ranges, and it is clear that the Japanese did break the tonnage limitations.

Although evasions of the naval treaties did take place, none of these irregularities provided their beneficiaries with a significant military advantage during World War II. Japan's oversized cruisers and the United States's increased firing range provided at most only an ephemeral advantage that quickly evaporated. Even so, the evasions and allegations of evasions—both of the letter and the spirit of the Washington treaty system—do raise at least two basic points regarding compliance and verification in general.

First, all of the naval bureaucracies were obsessed with the idea of achieving "superiority." While in most instances this trait is understandable, it did work against the letter and spirit of the naval treaties. It accounted for most of the tonnage violations, as the quest for superiority actually created the 10,000-ton "treaty cruisers"—ships designed more to reach the maximum cruiser tonnage limit than to meet specific naval requirements. (What irony, for the 10,000-ton figure was originally chosen, not as an upper limit for cruisers, but as a lower limit for battleships!)

In pressing their naval architects to design the largest allowable cruisers and battleships, some naval bureaucrats overlooked—or encouraged?—technical improvements in armaments, armor, and engines that occasionally transgressed treaty restrictions. The complicity of civilian officials in these transgressions is not generally known; it is even possible that often civilian authorities were simply not informed of such design evasions.

And second, the Washington naval system did not provide for a low-level, informal resolution of complaints regarding actual or possible evasions. When British officials finally verified that some Italian cruisers were in violation of treaty limits, they could not determine a suitable method of registering their complaint. The only channel open then was an official diplomatic protest; but the British foreign office decided to avoid making their grievance known, rather than upset other very delicate negotiations then being conducted with Rome.

CONCLUSION

The 1922 Five-Power Treaty did provide that if "circumstances" (undefined) should change in such a way that the national security of any country appeared to be threatened, the signatories could again come together to discuss the situation. It also provided that if, after eight years, technological and scientific advancements presented a similar threat, the treaty powers could also reconvene. The two London conferences provided "escalator" clauses that permitted the signatory powers to exceed their quotas (upon informing the other treaty powers of their intention to commence building) should they become alarmed by the naval construction of non-signatory powers. And the 1936 London Naval Treaty called for the exchange of construction information but provided no process to verify the honesty of each nation's report.

While a formal reconvening of the Washington conference never took place either on the grounds of changed "circumstances" or technological advances, and the exchange of information proved neither inclusive nor useful, the escalator clauses were put into effect in 1936 by Great Britain, the United States, and Japan.

By late 1936, all three powers were in various stages of major construction programs that in the area of capital ships still fell technically within treaty terms. All, however, had various overage auxiliary ships, viewed by them as defensive weapons (destroyers, submarines, and cruisers), that the London Treaty of 1930 had slated for scrapping by 31 December 1936. Each felt those ships, while old, were usable. The only legal way to retain these vessels was to invoke the escalator clauses, which all three did between 1936 and 1938, with the latter decisions based on the London Naval Treaty of 1936.

With the coming of World War II, the Washington system fell into disrepute. Critics called the treaties idealistic dreams written on pieces of paper filled with self-deceptions that ultimately altered the balance of power in favor of aggressors. In their opinion, had the United States and Great Britain continued to build their ships and fortifications, they would have deterred Japan, and perhaps Germany and Italy. Certainly naval officers, both before and after the war, made that point. At the very least, others argue that the United States and Britain might have averted the early disasters of 1941–1942 in the Pacific.

The statesmen at the time, however, believed that the choice was not just the simple one of building or not building. All of the leading nations did in fact build from 1922 to 1936; it was, after all, arms control and not disarmament that was the basis of the Washington system. Rather, statesmen had to decide what degree of naval security they could gain given the constraints of the contemporary situation: a lack of funds for either ships or bases, strong public support for arms control, and the limited-threat level of the international scene until the mid-1930s. It forced them to attempt to cover security problems by a resort to diplomacy rather than construction. Each wanted to gain a better "relative" position by agreeing to arms control in the hope that the treaties would also prevent their competitors from building at higher levels.

The United States, for example, gained in the relative sense that the system achieved acknowledged parity with Great Britain and superiority over Japan; but the United States then frittered away much of that relative advantage by not even building up to the treaty limits. Great Britain gave up, on paper, a superiority it could not have maintained (actually because of the U.S. failure to build, it maintained a superiority, in fact, at a lower level of competition, throughout the treaty period) and was able to concentrate on its more important European security concerns. Japan received formal recognition of its naval control of the western Pacific, something that had informally existed since at least 1916.

The treaties attempted to capture a slice of temporary reality in the one specific area of naval arms control. Politicians of the time, like Warren G. Harding, oversold the system as one that would bring a new era of peace. But the attempt by itself could not prevent war; that is, perhaps, too heavy a burden for any arms control system. The more reasonable statesmen hoped that the treaties would be first steps toward a more stable international system, especially in the Pacific. Further steps—that is, more political arrangements to relieve tensions and resolve basic issues—were not taken, and the treaties could not stand by themselves.

BIBLIOGRAPHY

General Accounts There are a number of studies that provide an overview of the Washington treaty system. Important recent surveys include EMILY O. GOLDMAN, "The Washington Treaty System: Arms Racing and Arms Control in the Inter-War Period," Ph.D. diss., Stanford University (1989); CHRISTOPHER G. L. HALL, *Britain, America, and Arms Control, 1921–1937* (Houndsmill, England 1987); and ROBERT G. KAUFMAN, *Arms Control During the Pre-Nuclear Era: The United States and Naval Limitation Between the Two World Wars* (New York, 1990). An interesting but eclectic study that is quite critical of naval limitation is HARLOW A. HYDE, *Scraps of Paper, The Disarmament Treaties Between the World Wars* (Lincoln, Neb., 1988).

An older study, but one that reviews (vol. 3) in considerable detail all of the conferences and treaties discussed above, is RICHARD DEAN BURNS and DONALD URQUIDI, *Disarmament in Perspective: An Analysis of Selected Arms Control and Disarmament Agreements Between the World Wars, 1919–1939* (Los Angeles, 1968). For a broad survey also see, ROSEMARY RAINBOLT, "Arms Reduction Versus Arms Modernization: U.S. Nongovernmental Organizations and Arms Conferences, 1920–1935," Ph.D. diss., Carnegie-Mellon University (1988).

U.S. naval policies and policymakers are discussed in PAOLO E. COLETTA, ed., *American Secretaries of the Navy,* 2 vols. (Annapolis, Md., 1980); and ROBERT LOVE, JR., ed., *The Chiefs of Naval Operations* (Annapolis, Md., 1980). For a British view, see STEPHEN ROSKILL, *Naval Policy Between the Wars,* 2 vols. (London, 1968–1976). HERBERT O. YARDLEY, *The American Black Chamber* (Laguna Hills, Calif., 1931) tells of naval intelligence operations that broke the Japanese diplomatic code and provided information regarding their conferees instructions.

Washington Naval Conference The basic work is THOMAS H. BUCKLEY, *The United States and the Washington Conference, 1921–1922* (Knoxville, Tenn., 1970), which provides a detailed discussion of all issues, especially from the U.S. viewpoint; it may be supplemented by WILLIAM R. BRAISTED, *The United States Navy in the Pacific, 1909–1922* (Austin, Tex., 1971). A thoughtful study that looks at the decision-making process in Washington, London, and Tokyo is ROGER DINGMAN, *Power in the Pacific, The Origins of Naval Arms Limitation, 1914–1922* (Chicago, 1976). Older but still useful accounts include: HAROLD and MARGARET SPROUT, *Toward a New Order of Sea Power: American Naval Policy and the World Scene, 1918–1922* (Princeton, N.J., 1943); JOHN C. VINSON, *The*

Parchment Peace, The United States Senate and the Washington Conference, 1921–1922 (Athens, Ga. 1955); C. LEONARD HOAG, *Preface to Preparedness, The Washington Conference and Public Opinion* (Washington, D.C., 1941); and RAYMOND L. BUELL, *The Washington Conference* (New York, 1922).

Discussions of questions related to possible Japanese violations of Japan's pledge not to fortify its designated Pacific islands are found in RICHARD DEAN BURNS, "Inspection of the Mandates, 1919–1941," *Pacific Historical Review* 37 (November 1968): 445–562; and THOMAS WILDS, "How Japan Fortified the Mandated Islands," *U. S. Naval Institute Proceedings* 81 (April 1955): 401–407.

Other Conferences   Little has been printed about the ill-fated Geneva conference. See DAVID L. CARLTON, "Great Britain and the Coolidge Naval Disarmament Conference of 1927," *Political Science Quarterly* 83:4 (October 1968): 573–598. Much more has appeared in dissertations, see for example, ADOLPH B. CLEMENSEN, "The Geneva Tripartite Conference of 1927 in Japanese-American Relations," Ph.D. diss., University of Arizona (1975). For U.S. naval views of national security and naval limitation from the Washington to London conferences, see GERALD E. WHEELER, *Prelude to Pearl Harbor: The United States Navy and the Far East, 1921–1931* (Columbia, Mo., 1963).

The essential study of the first London conference is RAYMOND G. O'CONNOR, *Perilous Equilibrium: The United States and the London Naval Conference of 1930* (Lawrence, Kans., 1962). A sequel, which picks up with the second London conference, is a fine study by STEVEN E. PELZ, *Race to Pearl Harbor: The Failure of the Second London Naval Conference and the Onset of World War II* (Cambridge, Mass., 1974).

The Japanese posed a special problem during the negotiations. SADAO ASADA, "Japanese Admirals and the Politics of Naval Limitation: Kato Tomosaburo Versus Kato Kanji," in GERALD JORDAN, ed., *Naval Warfare in the Twentieth Century: Essays in Honour of Arthur Marder* (New York, 1977), and JAMES B. CROWLEY, *Japan's Quest for Autonomy: National Security and Foreign Policy, 1921–1938* (Princeton, N.J., 1966), examine the dynamics in Japanese foreign and naval policies.

DONALD C. WATT, "The Anglo-German Naval Agreement of 1935: An Interim Judgment," *Journal of Modern History* 28 (June 1956): 155–175, is the initial post–World War II study and retains value. Other useful accounts include CHARLES BLOCH, "Great Britain, German Rearmament, and the Naval Agreement of 1935," in HANS W. GATZKE, ed. *European Diplomacy Between Two Wars, 1919–1939* (Chicago, 1972): 125–151, and NICHOLAS G. PAPP, "The Anglo-German Naval Agreement of 1935," Ph.D. diss., University of Connecticut (1969).

The only published historical assessment of the Turko-Greek (1930) and Turko-Soviet (1931) naval pacts is RICHARD DEAN BURNS and SEYMOUR L. CHAPIN, "Near Eastern Naval Protocols, 1930–1931," *East European Quarterly* (March 1970): 72–87.

Controlling Chemical and Biological Weapons Through World War II

○

JOHN ELLIS VAN COURTLAND MOON

See also Arms Control Treaty Verification; Chemical and Biological Weapons and Arms Control; The Law of War; The League of Nations and Disarmament; *and* The United Nations and Disarmament. *The* Geneva Protocol on Poison Gases *is excerpted in Volume III.*

Chemical and biological warfare (CBW) is widely regarded as cruel and inhumane. This revulsion has its origins in codes and customs, traditions, and ways of thinking about the conduct and character of war stretching back into unrecorded time when today's chemical and biological weapons were inconceivable. It ultimately promoted the development of arms control measures—initially in the form of "law of war" and later as treaties—that sought to regulate or, often, prohibit CBW.

THE PROHIBITION AGAINST POISON

The prohibition regarding the use of poison in warfare is based upon a long-honored precedent. Despite violations, that prohibition has stood firm during the evolution of the law of war through three main stages: custom, definition, and codification.

Before 3000 B.C., usages of war emerged that led to generally accepted customs defining what was allowed and what was forbidden. Among the prohibited practices were the poisoning of weapons, wells, and food. These prohibitions were honored in different civilizations. In India, the *Atharva Veda* (ca. 1500–500 B.C.) and the *Law of Manu* (ca. 200 B.C.–A.D. 200) condemned the use of all poisoned weapons. The classical Greeks and Romans saw them as a violation of *ius gentium,* the law of nations. However, they did not extend this prohibition to cover the use of smoke and incendiaries, as evidenced by the Spartan siege of Platea (429 B.C.) and the Boetian siege of Delium (424/423 B.C.). The Roman attitude against the use of poison was expressed by Marcus Tullius Cicero (106–43 B.C.), who also defined the Roman concept of international law. In *De Officiis* (On Duty), Cicero cited the example of the consul Gaius Luscinnus Fabricius and the Roman Senate, who turned over a deserter to their enemy Pyrrhus. The deserter had promised to poison their enemy: "Thus they stamped with their disapproval the treacherous murder even of an enemy who was at once powerful, unprovoked, aggressive and successful." This prohibition stands out dramatically in a period when the practice of war was savage, as evidenced by the Syracusans' treatment of the vanquished Athenians after the failed siege of Syracuse (415–413 B.C.) and by the total annihilation of Carthage at the close of the Third Punic War (146 B.C.). By the end of the classical period, the prohibition against poison was a principle of customary international law.

In the Middle Ages, more attention was paid to the question of the legitimacy or "justness" of a war (*ius ad bellum*) than to the rules governing its conduct (*ius in bello*). The reason is obvious: Christianity, initially a pacifist religion, had to be reconciled to the political and military realities of a turbulent period. The just-war theory was extensively elaborated by the major Christian thinkers from Saint Augustine (A.D. 354–430) to Saint Thomas Aquinas (1225–1274). Although the three major criteria for determining the legitimacy of a war were authority, cause, and motive, attention was paid to proportionality: the conduct of war should not cause "unnecessary suffering." Thus certain practices and weapons were condemned. Philosopher and ecclesiastic John of Salisbury (d. 1180) denounced the use of poison. The Second Lateran Council (1139) condemned crossbows and longbows. Historians have argued that these weapons were banned by the Catholic church because they could be used to deliver poison-tipped bolts and arrows. Although there were reported violations of the prohibition against poisoned weapons, these violations were neither significant nor widespread. In contrast, the Byzantine armies made repeated use of an incendiary weapon—Greek fire—with which they destroyed enemy fleets.

During the Renaissance, political thinkers, especially Niccolò Machiavelli (1469–1527), challenged the established Christian concept that timeless values should govern human conduct: the belief that divine law controlled natural law, which in turn governed the law of nations, including the law of war. Machiavelli argued that *raison d'état* (reason of state) was the guide to political conduct in war and peace. Although this hardheaded approach challenged ethical conduct in statecraft, it did not change attitudes toward the use of poison, in private murder or in war. This is evident in the literature of the times: there are 123 references to poison in the works of Shakespeare, and in *Hamlet* it serves as the instrument of treachery and masked murder. Moreover, the use of poison was not accepted as a legitimate instrument of war. Despite proposals for the designing of poisoned weapons, including a design by Leonardo da Vinci (1452–1519), there is no recorded widespread use. The prohibition held even during the savage religious conflicts that dominated Europe in the sixteenth and early seventeenth centuries.

In the seventeenth century, the law of war evolved from custom to theoretical and philosophical definition. The outstanding figure in this effort was Hugo Grotius (1583–1645). In *De Jure Belli ac Pacis* (*The Law of War and Peace,* 1625), Grotius defined the practices accepted as normal under the laws of nature and nations. Although some of these practices seem barbaric by modern standards, especially regarding the treatment of the vanquished, Grotius defined a number of restraints later incorporated into the Hague and Geneva conventions. He unequivocally condemned the use of poison in war, basing his prohibition on the law of nations: "from old times the law of nations—if not all nations, certainly those of the better sort—has been that it is not permissible to kill an enemy by poison."

After the indiscriminate slaughter of the Thirty Years War (1618–1648), the savagery of warfare decreased, beginning an age of limited war that persisted throughout the eighteenth century. According to historian William Ballis, the just-war theory was stripped of its universalism and internalized by the monarchical European states, which were engaged in recurring wars against one another. Justification was based on *raison d'état,* determined by the will of the sovereign. In an age of limited warfare, it is not surprising that the prohibition against the use of poisoned weapons was largely honored, although there was a notable exception: From earliest times, human or animal corpses were used as a form of primitive biological warfare (BW) to foul wells and to spread disease; however, this practice had generally disappeared in western warfare by the eighteenth century. Another code prevailed in America. In 1763, Sir Jeffrey Amherst, the British Commander-in-chief in North America, proposed a scheme to spread smallpox by distributing infected blankets among the hostile Native American tribes in the Ohio Valley. Amherst believed that "every stratagem" was justifiable if used against those he deemed savages. Whether this scheme was implemented and whether it led to the smallpox epidemic among the Native Americans remains a matter of historical dispute.

Lord Amherst's advocacy of the use of infected blankets, if known, would have scandalized the outstanding eighteenth-century writer of *Le Droit des gens* (*The Law of Nations*) on the law of war, Emmerich de Vattel (1714–1767). Vattel, who condemned the use of poison as vigorously as Grotius, saw it as "contrary to the laws of war, and equally condemned by the law of nature and the consent of all civilized nations." He reinforced his argument against the use of poisoned weapons and the poisoning of wells by evoking the principle of deterrence and the argument of humanity. If one side violates the prohibition, the other side will retaliate.

Moreover, the use of such weapons causes useless suffering, adding to the "cruelty and calamities of war."

The explosive growth of nationalism in the nineteenth century led to a new challenge: the nationalization of ethics—that is, the belief that a nation could justifiably use any means to achieve its aims in warfare. To militarists, the doctrine of military necessity prevailed over moral considerations. Paradoxically, however, the nineteenth century saw the third stage in the evolution of the law of war: the promulgation of military codes and the conclusion of international agreements designed to define and control the conduct of war. During the American Civil War (1861–1865), Francis Lieber (1800–1872), a German-American political philosopher, drafted a code known as *General Order No. 100* (1863) for the secretary of war. Article 70 states: "The use of poison in any manner, be it to poison wells, or food, or arms, is wholly excluded from modern warfare. He that uses it puts himself out of the pale of law and usages of war." The Lieber code significantly influenced subsequent European army regulations.

Meanwhile, proposals were made for the employment of toxic weapons. During the Crimean War (1854–1856), Lord Dundonald proposed the use of shells releasing sulphur dioxide fumes to reduce the defenses of Sevastapol. During the American Civil War, Major John W. Doughty proposed the use of chlorine gas shells to Secretary of War Edwin Stanton. Lord Dundonald's proposal was rejected, and Major Doughty's was ignored. Nevertheless, the fact that such proposals were feasible justifies the concern of the major powers regarding the use of chemical poisons in warfare.

This concern resulted in action on the international level. The Declaration of Saint Petersburg (1868), signed by seventeen European powers, renounced the use in war of explosive or inflammatory bullets, claiming that "the employment of such arms would . . . be contrary to the laws of humanity." The Declaration of Brussels (1874), signed by fourteen European nations, would have specifically prohibited "the use of poison or poisoned weapons," but it was never ratified.

Despite the cynicism of some of the participants, the Hague Conference of 1899 was a greater success. The conference declaration, entitled "Laws and Customs of War on Land," was signed by twenty-four nations, including the United States and Japan. It not only repeated the ancient prohibition against "the use of poison or poisoned arms" but also dealt with the potential use of new weapons, made possible by nineteenth-century advances in synthetic chemistry: in a special convention, twenty-four signatory nations pledged "to abstain from the use of projectiles the object of which is the diffusion of asphyxiating or deleterious gases." The United States and Great Britain did not sign the special convention. The British, however, later agreed to adhere to its terms. Among the signatories were all of the other future belligerents of World War I, including Germany. The prohibition in the 1899 "Laws and Customs of War on Land" was repeated in identical language in a similar convention signed at The Hague in 1907 by the future belligerent powers of World War I.

Although the achievement of the nineteenth century in codifying the law of war was impressive, the maintenance of these restraints was threatened by the nationalization of ethics and technological advances. The argument of military necessity could also be used by any belligerent as an excuse for violating the codes of war. It was reinforced by the nationalization of the concept of the just war and bolstered by arguments derived from *raison d'état*. Nationalistic appeals to just-war doctrine were now in direct conflict with the law of war as defined by international covenants. The rules embodied in the law of war apply to both sides, irrespective of the justice of one cause as opposed to another; based on precedent and experience, the law of war appeals to a common humanity that underlies differences between combatants and their causes. This dichotomy between nationalism and the universal law of war was largely unperceived in 1899 and 1907.

At the beginning of the twentieth century, Western nations dominated the globe. Confident in the permanence of their superiority, self-congratulatory about their enlightenment, buoyed by the myth of progress, they had codified the law of war into international conventions. Regarding the harnessing of the future uses of violence as an ongoing process, they scheduled the next Hague Conference for 1915. Across this sunny prospect fell the shadow of World War I.

WORLD WAR I, 1914–1918

It was a moment of shock and terror. On 22 April 1915, shortly after 5:00 P.M., a wave of dense yellow smoke descended upon the trenches of the left flank of the Allied salient around the Belgian town of Ypres, striking two French divisions, the Eighty-seventh Territorial and the Forty-fifth Algerian. The medical officer of the First African Battalion later recalled: "I felt the action of the gas upon my respiratory system; it burned in my throat, caused pain in my chest, and made breathing all but impossible. I spat blood and suffered from dizziness. We all thought we were lost. It grieved us to see poor Cordier. He was purple, incapable of walking."

The unprepared and inexperienced soldiers had been struck by the first toxic gas in history in warfare (although harassing agents had previously been used in 1914 and 1915 by the Germans and the French). The front momentarily caved in as soldiers panicked and ran pell-mell toward Ypres. If the advancing German infantry, cautiously picking their way forward in the wake of the gas cloud, had pursued their advantage, Ypres would have fallen, and the entire salient would have been menaced. Lacking reserves and restrained by the skepticism of the high command, who regarded the use of gas as experimental, the Germans dug in after punching an eight to nine kilometer (5 mi.) gap in the Allied line. The Allied command reacted energetically. Despite at least six additional gas attacks by the Germans during the Second Battle of Ypres (22 April–24 May 1915), the line bent but held. Although the Allies could only devise makeshift means of protection, the Germans could never duplicate their success of 22 April 1915.

The gas, released from 5,730 emplaced cylinders, was chlorine, an asphyxiant that inflames the lung tissues, leading to a pulmonary edema. The victim drowns from within as the intake of oxygen is blocked by the flooding of the respiratory system. A new weapon had entered warfare, challenging the taboos against poisoned weapons. Its use, moreover, was seen by the Allies as a contravention of the Hague Convention of 1899 prohibiting the use of asphyxiating gas projectiles. Not surprisingly, Field Marshal Sir John French, commander of the British Expeditionary Force, denounced it as "a cynical and barbarous disregard of well-known usages of civilized war." In his memoirs, David Lloyd George recalled that "a feeling of anger and horror ran through the whole nation." A contemporary cartoon in the British magazine *Punch* depicted the German kaiser as a cloaked Macbeth summoning chemical poisons in his lair.

The Second Battle of Ypres is a paradigm of the issues and problems of modern chemical warfare (CW). It pits the argument of humanity against the argument of effectiveness: the belief that some weapons are too horrible to use against the belief that military necessity justifies the use of any weapon that promises decisive success. It also pits hypothesis against history: what might have been against what was.

In Second Ypres, the argument of effectiveness is based partly upon history but mainly upon hypothesis. The impact of the surprise gas attack is obvious: two divisions were temporarily routed. Although no body count was taken in the trenches, horrendous casualties were later cited: fifteen thousand of whom five thousand were fatalities. Frequently quoted, these figures are probably three times the actual losses. Ironically, the cited statistics could be used to argue the "frightfulness" of gas warfare as well as its effectiveness.

Speculation reinforces the argument of effectiveness by elaborating the consequences that could have flowed from the first success. If the Germans had moved sufficient reserves to the front, if the advancing infantry had exploited their breakthrough, the results could have been decisive. The Germans could have seized Ypres and eliminated the salient. They could have turned their forces toward the English Channel and seized the ports. In more extravagant versions, it is claimed that they could have won the war through the proper exploitation of their weapon.

Although the Germans, with the forces at their disposal, could have seized Ypres and perhaps collapsed the salient, the wider conjectures strain credulity. The massing of reserves would have alerted the Allies who, lulled by the apparent quiescence of the Ypres front, had ignored the accumulating intelligence signals prior to the launching of the German gas attack. History shows, moreover, that the Allies reacted swiftly to close the gap, that further uses of gas were less effective than the initial attack, and that General Ferdinand Foch, coordinating Allied operations in the north, commanded major units to halt any overall collapse. Foch's main concern was that the German attack could derail his planned offensive in Artois. Despite the Ypres crisis, he managed to launch his ill-fated offensive on 9 May 1915.

The Duel Between Offense and Defense

On 23 April 1915, Sir John French asked the British government to implement retaliation. Although the secretary of state for war, Lord Kitchener, had doubts regarding the morality of falling "to the level of the degraded Germans," he referred the question to the cabinet, which debated it until 18 May. Given the public fury following the reports of the German gas attack, retaliation was almost axiomatic. On 25 September 1915, the British released their first gas cloud against the German line opposite Loos, France. As at Second Ypres, the results were inconclusive. The reciprocal use of gas temporarily silenced the cries of Allied governments against the inhumanity of gas warfare.

In the protracted stalemate on the western front, the gas war became a duel between offense and defense. New means of delivery (mortars, artillery shells, projectors), new agents (phosgene, chloropicrin, hydrogen cyanide, adamsite, mustard), new protective devices (from treated gauze cloths to respirators) were devised. By the end of 1916, defense had effectively countered offense. Masks, properly utilized by trained troops, provided adequate protection against chlorine and phosgene, a respiratory agent six times more powerful than chlorine. This chemical-warfare stalemate, however, was broken on 12 July 1917 when the Germans launched their first mustard gas attack against ill-fated Ypres. Unlike the choking agents, mustard is a vesicant that attacks through the skin, temporarily blinding its victims and raising huge blisters on the sensitive, moist areas of the human body. A persistent agent, it poisons terrain for an extended period of time. Although a heavy dosage can wreck the pulmonary system, mustard gas is generally not fatal. Since the Allies failed to develop adequate defense suits, their chemical casualties multiplied during the remainder of the war. The introduction of the "king of war gases" on the battlefield increased the sufferings of Allied soldiers. But it did not break the stalemate.

Mobility returned to the battlefield in the spring of 1918. On 21 March 1918, German Field Marshal Erich Ludendorff launched the first of five massive offensives on the western front, gambling that he could defeat the British and the French before large-scale American forces were deployed. On the Somme front, the Germans drenched British artillery positions, troop concentrations, and communication lines with lachrymatory and casualty agents, seeking to neutralize counter-battery fire and to wear down troop resistance. They used mustard to deny terrain and to protect the flanks of their advances. These gas attacks were accompanied by a tornado of concentrated conventional artillery fire. It was an impressive use of combined arms. And it

scored local successes. On 7–8 April 1918, during the Battle of the Lys, a formidable preliminary bombardment prior to the launching of the German infantry attack, Armentières was drenched in mustard gas, making the city uninhabitable for the next nine days. On 25 April, gas shells helped to break up the French defense around Mount Kemmel, with mustard gas effectively paralyzing the artillery.

Whether the use of chemical shells accelerated the German breakthrough is less clear since their use in combination with conventional firepower makes it impossible for an analyst to separate the effect of gas from that of artillery fire. Even in the 21 March 1918 attack, only 20–30 percent of the German shells were gas filled. Since the use of preparatory mustard shelling partially revealed the direction of the forthcoming German thrust, surprise was lost. The British command could map out the flanks of the enemy advance. Whatever the effects of the preliminary bombardment, it was the force and the weight of the German infantry attack that swept away British resistance, smashing their hold on the Somme sector. In the succeeding phases of the Ludendorff offensive launched between 9 April and 15 July 1918, the Germans used the same combination of gas and artillery shells in the preparatory and initial stages of their assaults. When the Allies assumed the offensive in August 1918, the British carried out numerous gas attacks against the retreating enemy. By now, the Allies were supplied with mustard and the Germans were running out of it. Its use may have hampered the Allied advance.

Evaluating the Use of Gas How inhumane was the chemical warfare waged in World War I? How effective was it? The sufferings of the victims of the first gas attacks were vividly reported. Doctor J. S. Haldane and Professor H. B. Baker, who examined the casualties, graphically described the victims they observed in the hospitals: "These men were lying struggling for breath and blue in the face . . . they were suffering from acute bronchitis." In later gas attacks, preparedness and training, especially the proper use of the respirator, cut down on the sufferings of soldiers struck by respiratory agents. Sudden attacks then caught only the unwary or the unlucky. But nothing could protect soldiers against the blistering action of mustard gas. And, psychologically, the use of chemical weapons in World War I caused suffering totally out of proportion to the casualties it inflicted. It multiplied the uncertainties and anxieties of war. In addition, although the sufferings inflicted by conventional arms on soldiers were often more horrifying and their effects more lasting than those inflicted by gas, chemical weapons had another aspect often ignored by its postwar defenders: it caused large civilian casualties in towns close to the battlefield. Lille, Armentières, and Nieuport were repeatedly struck by toxic cylinder attacks or by gas shellings.

The question of humaneness revolves, at least partly, upon the issue of effectiveness. Was the use of chemical weapons militarily justifiable? Did it materially increase the chance of victory? Fritz Haber, the father of German gas warfare, saw CW as decisive. As he informed Lieutenant Otto Hahn, "It was a way of saving countless lives, if it meant that the war could be brought to an end sooner." But the German high command was skeptical. It saw the initiation of gas warfare as an experiment, not as a necessity. The decision was made, therefore, with cynical casualness. Once the Allies retaliated, the belligerents discovered that the use of gas entailed an internal cost: it degraded combat performance and complicated logistics. Until 1918, chemical warfare intensified the attritional deadlock on the western front. More suited to stalemate than to breakout, it produced casualties and helped to wear down morale. It was effective in producing local successes in the 1918 offensives, but it was not decisive; it did not bring victory to the Germans or accelcrate victory for the Allies. Several decades later, Ludwig F. Haber rendered a stinging verdict on his father's work: "Technically, poison gas was an ingenious attempt to overcome trench warfare: it was cheap to produce and capable of further development. But in practice it was, until 1918, largely a waste of effort. In that year it helped the Germans rather more than the Allies but it did not win them a battle, let alone give them victory" (pp. 279–280).

Such an indictment would have been rejected by CW champions who, at the end of World War I, continued to build hypothetical arguments regarding the potential decisiveness of chemical weapons. Besides citing the "might have beens" of World War I, they expounded the "would be" of the future. After a study of chemical operations in World War I, Lieutenant Colonel Augustin Prentiss of the U.S. Chemical Warfare Service concluded: "had the war continued for another year, the campaign of 1919 would have been largely a chemical war" (Prentiss, p. 684). Predicting that gas would certainly be used in any future conflict, the CW experts emphasized that CW preparedness was essential to national security. At the close of the war, they were convinced that gas was a proven, assimilated weapon system and that the public accepted it as such.

These expectations were defeated by the postwar backlash against chemical warfare. Once the fighting was over, it became clear that the Western public did not accept CW as legitimate. The horror of the past and future use of poison in warfare was emphasized by peace activists and by international organizations. In the reminiscences and imaginative recreations of war, gas emerged as a repellent symbol of the protracted slaughter on the western front. This revulsion found its voice in interwar treaties and in attempts to ban the future use of chemical and biological weapons through the conclusion of disarmament agreements. Throughout this period, the argument of "humanity in war" took precedence over the argument of military effectiveness.

EFFORTS TO BAN CHEMICAL AND BIOLOGICAL WEAPONS, 1919–1939

In the stillness that followed the armistice, statesmen, generals, and military theorists could reflect on the ordeal through which their nations had passed. To the victorious Allies, World War I was simply a war; to the United States, it was fought to "end all wars." Only such a goal could justify the slaughter and cost. The relief that the killing had ended was accompanied by a revulsion against war that spurred the movement toward a general disarmament. That goal was enunciated in the preamble to the Covenant of the League of Nations, which stressed the need "to promote international cooperation and to achieve international peace and security" and "the acceptance of obligations not to resort to war." Simultaneously, since the maintenance of peace remained uncertain, there was a movement toward qualitative disarmament, the renewed codification of *ius in bello,* by banning or controlling the new weapons that made total war indiscriminate.

The initiation of gas warfare at Second Ypres had been viewed in Allied countries as a violation of the law of war. For the Allies, retaliation had been justified as a military necessity. Their motivation, however, was more political than military. In a vengeful mood, the Allies retaliated without regard to the tenets of proportionality. The *ius ad bellum* overwhelmed the *ius in bello,* eroding the defenses erected to safeguard humanity against excessive use of force. The law of war, whether customary or codified, is designed to restrain the inherent psychological dynamism of combat that pushes belligerents toward excessive violence. As Karl von Clausewitz observed, each side seeks to overcome its opponent's will by escalating force. In twentieth-century total war, psychological dynamism is reinforced by technological dynamism, which creates new potentialities for violence. What was not possible before, the targeting of the nation (its civilians as well as its soldiers), now became possible. Indiscriminate weapons, so called because they erode the distinction between combatants and noncombatants, weaken the ability to make distinctions, to forego those choices upon which the maintenance of the rules of war depends.

In any protracted conflict, no law of war can survive repeated and reciprocal violations; however, in its aftermath, the rule may recover its strength. The reaction to the frightfulness of World War I was an attempt to put the genie back into the bottle: to restore and to strengthen rules against the use of certain weapons, to abolish or control new weapons that violated customs and the law of war. The movement for qualitative disarmament targeted forms of warfare regarded as inherently indiscriminate: submarine warfare, air bombardment of civilian populations, and the use of chemical and bacteriological weapons.

The Chemical Disarmament Debate

Two factors gave particular urgency to CBW disarmament. One was the fear that new chemical weapons, against which no defense was possible, would be developed. The second was the danger of escalation. In World War I, the use of harassing agents had preceded the use of casualty agents. If the war had lasted into 1919, tactical use against troops could have escalated into strategic use against urban centers. The advisory committee to the American delegation at the Washington Naval Conference (1921–1922) warned that the use of chemical bombs against population centers could lead to "the depopulation of large sections of the country, as to threaten, if not destroy, all that has been gained during the painful centuries of the past" (quoted in Brown, p. 65). Although this warning was based on highly exaggerated estimates, it was

widely believed. The development of air power placed large civilian targets within the reach of chemical weapons. Throughout the interwar period the debate, widely reported in the press, pitted the humanity argument against the effectiveness argument.

The humanity argument called for the abolition of chemical weapons. It assumed that, since no limitation was possible within a weapon system, the only hope lay in a total ban. As the American advisory committee warned: any use of CW would destroy all restraints. Arguing that no defense was feasible against aero-chemical attacks, the pro-ban advocates saw a future war in which CW was used as doomsday. Therefore, they concluded that chemical weapons should never be used in warfare.

The effectiveness argument assumed that no limitation was possible or desirable. In 1928, Lord Trenchard, chief of the British air staff, stated forcibly in a memorandum: "In a vital struggle, all available weapons have been used and always will be used" (Sir Charles Webster and Noble Frankland, *The Strategic Air Offensive Against Germany,* London, 1961, vol. 4, p. 76). Accordingly, all limits will break down and all weapons will be used to bring the war to a rapid conclusion. Implicit in this position is the belief that distinctions among weapons are artificial. As C. R. M. F. Cruttwell stated in his history of World War I when discussing the ethics of gas warfare: "there is little to choose in horror and pain between the injuries inflicted by modern war" (p. 153). Moreover, a nation stripped of a decisive weapon or unwilling to use it would place itself in mortal danger. Seeing CW as decisive, its extreme champions argued that all forms of chemical warfare should be used: tactical and strategic; harassing, incapacitating, and lethal. Invoking the humanity argument, they claimed that chemical weapons were more humane than other weapons. They marshaled the casualty figures of World War I to prove their point. The dead and wounded in battle were roughly estimated at ten million and twenty million respectively. Gas produced approximately one million casualties, one hundred thousand of which were fatalities. (Unfortunately, no civilian gas casualty figures are available.)

Some strategic thinkers and military officers proposed middle positions between two extremes. Four kinds of limitation were proposed during the interwar period: a prohibition against use, not against preparations; against strategic objectives (cities and factories), not against tactical targets (troops and other military objectives); against lethal agents, not against nontoxic agents; against offensive cw operations on foreign territory, not against an enemy invader.

Early Arms Control Efforts   The first priority of the victorious Allies was to strip Germany of arms, especially the newer weapons: submarines, aircraft, and chemical warfare equipment. The Treaty of Versailles explicitly barred "the manufacture and importation" of "asphyxiating, poisonous or other gases and all analogous liquids, materials or devices . . . by Germany." Although the treaty also called for a reciprocal "reduction of national armaments to the lowest point consistent with national safety and the enforcement by common action of international obligations," an outright ban applied only to Germany. However, on 6 February 1922, the United States, the United Kingdom, France, Italy, and Japan, in identical language, pledged themselves against the use of chemical weapons in warfare and invited "all other civilized nations" to make the same pledge. The Five-Power Naval Limitation Treaty, signed at the Washington Conference, never went into effect. France refused to ratify it because the French government objected to an accompanying provision relating to submarines.

The Geneva Protocol, 1925   The most significant step universalizing the prohibition against chemical and biological weapons was taken on 17 June 1925 when twenty-nine countries signed the Geneva Protocol:

The Undersigned Plenipotentiaries, in the name of their respective Governments:

Whereas the use in war of asphyxiating, poisonous or other gases, and of all analogous liquids, materials or devices, has been justly condemned by the general opinion of the civilized world; and

Whereas the prohibition of such use has been declared in Treaties to which the majority of Powers of the world are Parties; and

To the end that this prohibition shall be universally accepted as a part of International Law, binding alike the conscience and the practice of nations; Declare:

That the High Contracting Parties, so far as they are not already Parties to Treaties prohibiting such use, accept this prohibition, agree to extend this prohibition to the use of bacteriological methods of warfare and agree to be bound as between themselves to the terms of this declaration.

The prohibition on bacteriological weapons was tagged on at the urging of the Polish representative who argued persuasively that the horrors of bacteriological warfare would surpass chemical warfare. Forty-three nations had ratified the protocol before the outbreak of World War II. The most important holdouts were Japan and the United States, both of whom had signed. Ironically, the United States representative to the conference, billed as the Conference for the Supervision of the International Trade in Arms and in Implements of War, had played a major role in shifting the focus from export controls to the prohibition of gas warfare. Japan finally ratified the Protocol in 1970; the United States, in 1975.

The Germans had claimed that the lethal gas attack launched at Ypres had not violated the Hague declaration: the gas had been released through cylinders, not shells. To avoid future evasions based on narrow interpretations of agreements, the Geneva Protocol's definition of chemical warfare was more comprehensive than the definition of the Hague Conference. However, the protocol still suffered from a number of limitations, the most significant being the reservations that many nations attached to their ratifications. The reservations usually stated that the protocol was binding only toward other state parties and that it would, in the words of the French reservation, "cease to be binding" toward "any enemy State whose armed forces or whose allies fail to respect the prohibitions laid down in the Protocol." Since the right of retaliation was retained by major state parties (including the United Kingdom, the Commonwealth nations, France, and the Soviet Union), the Geneva Protocol was essentially a rather ambiguous "no-first-use" pledge. Another weakness of the protocol, not recognized at the time, was the restricted definition of bacterial agents. Microbiological organisms, such as viruses and ricketsias, were unknown in 1925. Years later, the scope of the prohibition was extended in the 1972 Biological and Toxin Weapons Convention.

Attempts to Strengthen the Protocol, 1926–1936   During the rest of the interwar period, repeated efforts were made to strengthen the Geneva Protocol. The League of Nations' Preparatory Commission for the Disarmament Conference (1926–1930) and the subsequent Disarmament Conference (1932–1936) wrestled with the issues unresolved by the protocol. Five major issues dominated the debates.

The first issue was the scope of the prohibition. The commission and the conference debated how comprehensive the definition of cw should be. Some states considered the use of incendiary munitions a form of cw. Others resisted a ban on the tear gasses commonly used to quell internal civil disturbances. In addition, the commission and the conference questioned whether preparedness—that is, production and possession of chemical weapons or the ingredients necessary to make them—should be banned. This question was complex because some of the chemicals used to produce chemical weapons were dual purpose, essential to the peacetime chemical industry. Banning them outright was therefore impossible. Finally, a ban on preparedness could leave a country defenseless against an unscrupulous adversary. Negotiators, therefore, struggled to distinguish between offensive and defensive preparedness in order to define the scope of "permitted activities."

The second issue was the implementation of a ban on peacetime preparations for cw and the supervision of the dismantling of chemical-weapon facilities.

The third issue was verification to prevent cheating. The negotiators debated the reliability of national intelligence, and some states proposed international inspectors. And some states, like France, proposed international inspectors to enforce compliance. The prospect of international inspectors recognized that procedures were needed to govern the investigation of allegations of noncompliance. Especially troublesome were two related problems: the determination of offensive or defensive intent of the inspected nation and the protection of the chemical-industry's legitimate secrets. Finally, the negotiators recognized that procedures needed to be established to govern the investigation of allegations of noncompliance. A number of proposals called for a permanent disarmament commission to carry out such investigations.

The fourth issue concerned what sanctions should be used against violators. Echoing the Geneva Protocol, several disarmament negotiators invoked world public opinion. Others maintained public opinion was insufficient and proposed assistance to the attacked state as well as economic and military sanctions. The issue of military sanctions, however, raised retaliation questions. If a chemical attack were launched, should the victim state retaliate in kind or by other means? Should retaliation be individual or collective?

The fifth and final issue was biological warfare, an associated problem previously submerged by concerns regarding chemical disarmament. During the Disarmament Conference negotiations, as in the negotiations which led to the 1972 Convention, bw became a separate issue. The common conviction was that it was more dangerous than cw. The Special Committee of the Disarmament Conference judged that biological-weapon research was impossible to monitor. Fortunately for those who would ban them, biological weapons were considered unreliable; they could easily boomerang on the user. Therefore, since bw was neither effective nor moral, it could be condemned outright. No negotiator at the Disarmament Conference questioned the belief that the protocol prohibited all methods of biological warfare.

Despite the daunting questions, there was an encouraging trend to the cbw disarmament efforts, a trend embodied in the British proposal of 16 March 1933. Great Britain proposed extending the prohibition against the use of chemical and bacteriological weapons to incendiaries, redefining them in sweeping terms: "The use of chemical, incendiary or bacterial weapons as against any State, whether or not a Party to the present Convention, and in any war, whatever its character, is prohibited." The proposed prohibition covered all "toxic, asphyxiating, lachrymatory, irritant or vesicant substances." Although the victim nation's right to retaliate was protected, it was hedged: "subject to such conditions as may hereafter be agreed." The prohibition against the use of biological weapons was unconditional. The draft convention prohibited peacetime preparations for chemical, biological, and incendiary warfare and set up safeguards to ensure that permitted activities were not used to mask cheating. Finally, it established procedures whereby the Permanent Disarmament Commission would investigate any allegations that the convention had been violated. Despite some reservations on the part of state parties who felt that it did not go far enough, the British draft was adopted unanimously for the drafting of the future convention.

The negotiators had come a long way, but major problems still remained: there was no consensus on sanctions, export controls, verification, or the structure of the disarmament agency. No further progress was made. On 22 January 1936, the council of the League of Nations postponed a new convocation of the Disarmament Conference.

The Italo-Ethiopian War, 1935–1936

This postponement was another indication of the decline of the League of Nations in the 1930s. Germany had withdrawn in 1933, Japan pulled out in 1935, and in 1935–36 the League failed to deal with the Italo-Ethiopian War, which saw the first large-scale use of gas since World War I. Anxious to bring the conflict to a rapid close, the Italian army launched chemical warfare attacks against unprotected Ethiopian army units and villages. The chief agent was mustard gas; the most effective means of delivery was spraying from low altitudes (100 yards, or 90 meters, above ground). The Italians justified this action as retaliation for atrocities committed by the Ethiopians, including "torture and decapitation of prisoners; emasculation of the wounded and killed; savagery towards and the killing of, noncombatants; systematic use of dumdum [expanding] bullets" (SIPRI, vol. 4, p. 180). Since Italy and Ethiopia had ratified the Geneva Protocol without reservations and since the gasing of Ethiopian troops and population centers was indiscriminate, the Italian justification was invalid under international law.

In this war, the argument of humanity was once again pitted against the argument of effectiveness. The emperor of Ethiopia, Haile Selassie, eloquently described the horror, in terms that foreshadow later descriptions of the alleged "yellow rain" attacks in Southeast Asia: "Sprayers were installed on board aircraft so that they could vaporize, over vast areas of territory, a fine, death-dealing rain. Groups of nine, fifteen, eighteen aircraft followed one another so that the fog issuing from them formed a continuous sheet.... Men and animals succumbed. The deadly rain that fell from the aircraft made all those whom it touched fly shrieking with pain. All who drank the poisoned water or ate the infected food succumbed ... in dreadful suffering" (SIPRI, vol. 4, pp. 185–186). In his account, the emperor linked modern chemical warfare with the ancient prohibition against the poisoning of water and food.

Advocates of the effectiveness argument found three military advantages to this mustard spraying: interdiction or the protection of the flanks of the advancing Italian army, the disruption of Ethiopian communications, and the demoralization of the retreating units. Some experts, like General Sir Henry Thuillier, argued that it hastened Italian victory by nine months. In itself, however, the use of gas was not decisive. It was expedient rather than necessary.

The reaction to the use of gas in the Italo-Ethiopian War was predictable. It heightened public horror of cw, raising fears regarding its strategic use in future wars. British Foreign Secretary Anthony Eden expressed this fear at the League of Nations by denouncing the Italians' violation of the Geneva Protocol as a challenge to the credibility of the League: "If a Convention such as this can be torn up, will not our people ... ask, and ask with reason ... how can we have confidence that our own folk, despite all solemnly signed protocols, will not be burned, blinded, done to death, in agony hereafter?"

Deterrence, National cw Policies, and Preparedness

Paradoxically, the survival of the Geneva Protocol would largely depend upon deterrence, not upon adherence to the principles of disarmament. Deterrence can be seen as a form of arms control based upon the threat of retaliation, not upon a treaty agreement.

France, the United Kingdom, the Commonwealth states, the Soviet Union, Italy, and Germany had ratified the protocol. Japan and the United States had not. Whereas France, Britain, the Commonwealth states, and the Soviet Union attached reservations regarding reciprocity and the right of retaliation, Italy and Germany unconditionally adhered. In each nation, there were, however, potential challenges to declaratory policy. So as nations took steps to shield themselves from gas and other toxic agents, debate continued as to whether cw preparedness would strengthen deterrence or increase the likelihood of chemical war. That issue intertwined with the intelligence question: how did the belligerents view their capability as opposed to their opponents'?

Throughout the interwar period, the United Kingdom saw itself as highly vulnerable to gas attack from the air; a concern sharpened by the fear of public panic if the Germans drenched British cities with gas bombs. A priority, therefore, was to protect the population, and by September 1939 44,000,000 gas masks had been distributed. British offensive preparations, begun only in 1938, were less impressive. They did not accelerate significantly until Winston Churchill took over as prime minister in 1940. At the beginning of World War II, the British had limited cw retaliatory capability.

Not surprisingly, since French troops had been the first victims of gas attacks during World War I, the interwar years saw the development of an extensive CW program in France and Algeria, including the designation of testing grounds and the construction of factories capable of producing major CW agents. By the outbreak of World War II, France's offensive stocks were adequate for retaliatory purposes. Significantly, the German expert, Dr. Rudolf Hanslian, was convinced that France and the Soviet Union were the best-prepared CW nations.

The Soviet Union, initially behind the Western nations, made impressive gains in CW preparations by 1939. Its infrastructure was highly developed, its defensive equipment was adequate, and its offensive capability was rumored to be the best in the world. For example, its mustard gas stocks were estimated at eight thousand tons (7,200 metric tons). Other nations believed that the Soviet Union was well prepared, but the Soviets much preferred to fight a war without chemical weapons. Their early CW preparedness efforts were jointly undertaken with the Germans (1923–1933). When this collaboration ended, the Soviets were left in the dark regarding German CW rearmament under Adolf Hitler. Despite the gains of the preceding decade, Soviet leaders were convinced that their nation was technologically inferior vis-à-vis its potential foes, especially Germany. The Stalinist purges of 1937, moreover, had weakened all branches of the Red Army, including the chemical arm. Under Marshal Mikhail Tukachevsky, CW had been integrated into offensive operations. After his execution, it was downgraded into a secondary weapon system.

In National Socialist Germany, the disarmament clauses of the Versailles Treaty had their impact. Despite furtive efforts by the Germans to circumvent the treaty, it delayed CW defensive and offensive preparedness. Defensive preparations were accelerated in 1926, but by September 1939 the German armed forces were still inadequately supplied and civil defense remained far weaker than in Great Britain. Germany was as sensitive as Great Britain to the vulnerability of its cities to gas attack. Nonetheless, when World War II began only twelve million gas masks had been distributed. Even during the war, the protection of the civilian population was never achieved. Offensive preparations, accelerated in 1938, lagged significantly, primarily because Hitler was hostile to the use of gas in warfare and the army was indifferent to its chemical arm, seeing it as counterproductive to rapid warfare.

Germany developed only a limited retaliatory capability; if a chemical war broke out, its reserves would be quickly exhausted. General Herman Ochsner, a leading German CW expert, concluded after the war: "Germany, restricted as she was in all spheres of armament, had probably been left farther behind in the field of chemical warfare than in any other" (unpublished manuscript, 1949). Since Germany started late on her rearmament, her leaders assumed that their opponents were better prepared than they were for chemical warfare.

Moreover, German military leaders had absorbed the lessons of World War I regarding the limited battlefield effectiveness of CW. Consequently, they tended to downplay the advantages of the surprise use of gas. Overestimating their enemies' capabilities, they did not realize that Germany had a potentially devastating weapon that none of her enemies possessed: nerve gas. In the late 1930s, Dr. Gerhard Schrader of I. G. Farben invented tabun (GA) and sarin (GB). These agents, first of the generation of CW toxic weapons that were to dominate the post–World War II CW preparedness effort, were far more powerful than the World War I agents. Dosages of one milligram could inflict instant death by paralyzing the voluntary muscles through the disruption of the nervous system, leading to death by asphyxia.

Germany's ally, Italy, had had more recent experience with chemical agents in combat than other nations. But spraying mustard gas in low-level attacks against defended civilian and military targets in Europe would be far more hazardous for Italian pilots than attacking unprotected targets in Ethiopia. Despite accumulated supplies of such agents as phosgene and mustard gas, Italian CW preparations in 1939 were still, according to General Ochsner, in their "infancy." British intelligence judged otherwise: they saw the Italians as prepared and highly likely to use gas in the next war.

Although Japan had not ratified the Geneva Protocol, she was a party to the Hague declarations of 1899. Until mid-1944, Japan was protected from aerial chemical attack by her geographical isolation and by the weakness of her neighbors. Although many senior Japanese military officials had no enthusiasm for chemical warfare, some well-connected officers were true believers in novel weapons. This latter group was given a freer hand to experiment than were their counterparts in other industrialized nations. Even before the "China Incident" (Japan's invasion of North China in 1937) escalated into the war in the Pacific, chemical and biological weapons were used occasionally against Chinese troops and civilians. Senior officers, however, remained skeptical regarding the results of these CBW attacks, and chemical weapons were relegated to a minor role in Japan's military strategy. Japan's CBW offensive capability was sufficient to score tactical successes against the unprotected Chinese, but it would not suffice for a chemical war against the Anglo-American powers. Moreover, although Japanese soldiers were sufficiently equipped to protect themselves against chemical attacks, Japan's civil defenses were totally inadequate.

The United States was not bound by a CW treaty. Chemical warfare advocates, led by General Amos A. Fries (chief of the Chemical Warfare Service, 1920–1929), had successfully blocked the ratification of the Geneva Protocol by the United States Senate. Despite hostile public opinion regarding gas warfare, Fries and his allies in the War Plans Division, the chemical industry, and the Congress kept alive the cause of CW preparedness and effectiveness. Citing the World War I casualty figures, they argued for the humanity of gas warfare and warned that CW unpreparedness could lead to military disaster. Occasionally, these advocates swayed their fellow officers. Even General John J. Pershing, a strong opponent of CW, warned in his final report as commander of the World War I American Expeditionary Force: "Whether or not gas will be employed in future wars is a matter of conjecture, but the effect is so deadly to the unprepared that we can never afford to ignore the question." Army support, however, was at best lukewarm and intermittent. Peyton C. March (chief of staff, 1918–1921) and Malin Craig (chief of staff, 1935–1939), were hostile to the Chemical Warfare Service (CWS). Most Army officers wanted to dismember the CWS as a separate service, scattering its parts within other branches. Most decisively, U.S. presidents from Warren G. Harding to Franklin D. Roosevelt regarded gas warfare as inhumane. Not surprisingly, therefore, at the time of Pearl Harbor the United States was unprepared, defensively and offensively, for chemical war.

Deterrence is most effective when backed by the threat of massive retaliation, a threat that ignores the rule of proportionality in war. Ironically, although none of the major belligerents of World War II could have carried out massive strategic CW operations at the beginning of the war, illusions and bluff served deterrence: each side felt that the other side was better prepared than it was for CW operations. Since policymakers did not want to use CW,

they had given it low priority in the rearmament race of the late 1930s. Additionally, the public repugnance against the use of gas and the distrust of military officers for a weapon that was unpredictable and that imposed an unwanted logistical burden acted as a check on initiation of CW. There was no major impetus from the top to force the reversal of policy that would have insured CW offensive preparedness by 1939.

CHEMICAL/BIOLOGICAL WARFARE, 1939–1945

The interwar years had been haunted by images of the Armageddon that would inaugurate the next European conflict. In 1932 British Conservative leader Stanley Baldwin warned the House of Commons that the "bomber will always get through." Scenarios of hypothetical attacks against the major cities of Europe were a favorite pastime for military speculation. Major General J. F. C. Fuller drew a terrifying picture of an opening "knock-out blow" in which London would be drenched with mustard gas: "London for several days will be one vast raving Bedlam, the hospitals will be stormed, traffic will cease, the homeless will shriek for help, the city will be pandemonium . . . the government will be swept away by an avalanche of terror" (quoted in Lord Carver, *Twentieth Century Warriors,* 1987, p. 27). In 1928, the earl of Halsbury, a chemist, had speculated on the effect of a single phosgene bomb. He predicted that "such a bomb would destroy every man, woman, and child between Regent's Park and the Thames" (Hans Lioyma, *Poisons in the Air,* p. 19). Although these doomsday claims were derided by chemical warfare experts like James Kendall and Sir Henry Thuillier, they were widely spread by the press and generally believed by the public.

When the war came and sirens sounded in London, no cataclysmic attack ravaged the city. But the expectation remained that, at some stage of the war, gas would be used. Writing in 1941, Dr. Curt Wachtel, a chemical warfare expert, predicted that it was only a matter of time. Throughout the war, anxiety persisted, momentarily heightened in crisis and fed by numerous rumors and intelligence estimates. Although concern slackened toward the close of the European war, intelligence officers still cautioned that Hitler could order a desperate "mad-dog" gas attack. Once more, history defeated expectation.

Chemical Warfare   On 2 September 1939, one day before declaring war against Germany, Great Britain and France publicly pledged that they would abide by the Geneva Protocol provided that Germany did. Germany followed suit later in the month. As the war intensified and rumors multiplied regarding enemy intentions to use gas against the Soviet Union, British Prime Minister Winston S. Churchill warned Hitler on 10 May 1942: "we shall treat the unprovoked use of poison gas against our Russian ally exactly as if it were used against ourselves." President Franklin D. Roosevelt, reacting to reports that the Japanese had used gas against the Chinese, delivered two warnings to Tokyo. His second warning, delivered on 8 June 1943, clarified retaliation doctrine while limiting United States cw policy: "I state categorically that we shall under no circumstances resort to the use of such weapons unless they are first used by our enemies." But the pledge was accompanied by a stern threat: "I want to make clear … that acts of this nature will be regarded as having been committed against the United States itself and will be treated accordingly. We promise to any perpetrators of such crimes full and swift retaliation in kind." In the decisions that accompanied and followed the declarations of their heads of government, the American and British chiefs of staff further bound policy to the imperatives of coalition warfare.

The ban against initiation, therefore, was total although conditional. Nevertheless, there were a number of violations throughout the war. Some were local incidents that were ignored because the opposing belligerent was convinced the use of gas was accidental or a desperate act of individual soldiers, unauthorized by the high command.

A far more serious challenge to the ban was the continued Japanese use of chemical weapons against unprotected Chinese opponents. However, Japanese field commanders were forbidden to use chemical weapons against the British and Americans. This policy held throughout the war, despite pressure from the Japanese army general staff for a reversal as American forces advanced toward Japan. By 1944, feeling increasingly vulnerable to air attack, Japan sought reassurances that the Allies would abide by the Geneva Protocol.

Another significant violation of accepted cw policy, which foreshadowed Saddam Hussein's use of chemical weapons against the Kurdish population in Iraq (1988), was the gassing of prisoners, especially Jews, in German concentration camps. The genocidal "final solution" against the Jewish people continued until Germany's defeat in 1945 and resulted in the deaths of an estimated six million Jews by means of gas, starvation, and other methods.

The Allies could have used either the Japanese or the German use of chemical weapons to justify a retaliatory strike. China was a member of the Allied coalition, and although Chinese claims were often open to suspicion, a number of the reported incidents were verified by outside sources. Violations were even reported subsequent to Roosevelt's 1943 declaration. Since the evidence was often contradictory and since there were policy reasons for maintaining the Allied ban, the Chinese allegations were ignored. The Jews, of course, were not a nation, not members of the Allied coalition, so their plight was easily ignored.

There were at least six instances in which the initiation of chemical warfare was discussed, only to be rejected or overtaken by events. In June and July 1940, Churchill raised the issue with his chief advisors. Confronted with the threat of invasion, fearful that the Germans might use gas in support of their invading troops, and determined to use any means in the defense of the United Kingdom, Churchill asked for a report on available chemical weapons stocks. Sir John Greer Dill, the chief of the imperial general staff, who personally favored the use of gas to repel a German invasion, replied that stocks were available for an attack but that reserves were inadequate for prolonged operations. Fortunately, the emergency passed and the occasion never arose.

According to General Ochsner, the Germans considered the use of toxic gas to counter Soviet partisan operations. Although the partisans were virtually defenseless against toxic attacks, the supreme command rejected the proposal on the grounds that it would give the Allies, who were judged better prepared for cw than the Germans, an excuse to initiate gas warfare.

In 1944, knowing that the Allies were preparing to invade continental Europe, the Germans once more considered initiating gas warfare. According to Ochsner, the tactical advantages were recognized: it would interdict certain areas, degrade Allied combat performance, complicate Allied logistics, and delay troop deployment. The resources were available; the result could have been decisive. But the Germans could expect terrible retaliation from a foe that had gained undisputed air supremacy. The German civilian population, whose civil defense preparations were still inadequate, would have paid a terrible price for a momentary military gain.

The initiation, on 12 June 1944, six days after the successful Allied landings in France, of Germany's V-weapons offensive, in which pilotless aircraft and rockets were used against civilian targets in the United Kingdom, provoked the next debate. Enraged by these indiscriminate attacks, Churchill ordered his planners to review the advantages of initiating chemical warfare against the Germans. The British chiefs of staff, despite vigorous prodding by the prime minister, ruled it out on tactical and strategic grounds. They doubted that a massive CW offensive against German cities would hasten the collapse of German resistance. They cautioned that it would create difficulties for the advancing Allied armies, and they warned that it could lead to global escalation, thereby complicating operations in the Pacific. Grudgingly, Churchill yielded, covering his retreat with a characteristic verbal sting: "clearly I cannot make head against the parsons and the warriors at the same time."

Nazi leaders also wanted to use chemical warfare to retaliate against the Allies. Seeing the use of toxic agents as justified by the devastation caused by Allied air raids, Nazi hard-liners pressured Hitler for a reversal of policy, stressing the advantages that nerve gas might confer on the German forces. Although Hitler wavered temporarily, his military advisors were adamantly opposed. Despite the desperateness of the military situation, the order was never issued.

During the last months of the war, a crucial and final debate on the use of CW took place. Germany was defeated, Japan was under constant attack from the air and the sea, and President Roosevelt, a leading opponent of chemical warfare, was dead. The U.S. Chemical Warfare Service, which had repeatedly advocated the use of gas in the Pacific, found support from the chief planning body of the army, the Operations Division, and from the army chief of staff, General George C. Marshall. The conflict in the Pacific had become "a war without mercy" (a phrase John W. Dower used to title his 1986 book). Each campaign was more costly than the last and the invasion of Japan was scheduled for November 1945. According to the Chemical Warfare Service, gas could provide a solution to the tactical nightmare presented by the fanatical resistance of an entrenched enemy that, steeled against the hopelessness of its situation, could impose staggering casualties on the Allied landing forces in the forthcoming invasion. The chief of staff to the president, Admiral William D. Leahy, however, countered Marshall's arguments for CW initiation by citing Roosevelt's pledge. The unexpectedly rapid end of the war with the dropping of the atomic bomb on the Japanese cities of Hiroshima and Nagasaki in August 1945 foreclosed the debate.

Although CW was not initiated, the Chemical Warfare Service, among others, had evolved elaborate plans for the strategic use of gas against major German and Japanese population centers. They had targeted the most "densely populated industrial cities," aiming "primarily at inflicting widespread casualties and causing substantial damage to the Axis war effort" (from an unpublished "planning paper," "Selected Aerial Objectives for Retaliatory Gas Attack on Germany," 11 March 1944). Thirty major German cities, ranging from Berlin to Lubeck, and eleven major Japanese cities, ranging from Tokyo to Tobata, were targeted. Obviously, despite claims that precision attacks were intended against industrial and military objectives, these proposed offensives constituted area gas bombing.

Biological Warfare   Every major belligerent in World War II, except Germany, also had an active biological warfare program. At the beginning of the war, British and American scientists concluded that BW was feasible. Concern was heightened by allegations that the Germans had used BW against horses in World War I and by the belief that biological weapons research had continued throughout the interwar period. Two possible threats were envisaged: sabotage and military attack. Concern continued during the war, periodically activated by rumors that the Axis powers would use every weapon when cornered. The most serious alert came seven months before the launching of the Allied invasion of France. In December 1943, the U.S. Office of Strategic Services warned that the Germans might arm their V weapons with botulinus toxin warheads. Although British intelligence was skeptical, the Allied command took precautionary measures. Fortunately, the alarm was ill founded.

Great Britain and the United States pursued a dual objective in their BW effort: defensive preparedness and the buildup of a retaliatory capability. Although many potential agents were investigated, only two were actively developed: anthrax and botulinus toxin. The deadliness and the stability of anthrax was demonstrated by British experiments, carried out in 1942 and 1943, which poisoned un-inhabited Gruinard Island off the coast of Scotland. (The contamination lasted for forty-five years.) Toward the end of the war, the United States shifted its emphasis to agents that caused brucellosis, an incapacitating disease characterized by fever and pains in the joints. Contrary to popular belief, the Allies did not develop large-scale BW capability during World War II, although research was performed, agents were developed, munitions were designed, and anthrax was stockpiled. At the end of the war in the Pacific, the most viable BW munitions were anti-plant agents designed to attack crops such as rice.

Ironically, there was only a limited BW threat to the Allies. In Germany, Hitler interdicted BW research. Experiments were performed on concentration camp inmates and a limited program was carried on without Hitler's knowledge, but German capability remained insignificant. Japan, however, did develop an active program. Hindered neither by a pledge to respect the Geneva Protocol nor by a squeamishness regarding the effects of biological weapons, Japanese Special Unit 731 launched experimental BW attacks against Chinese troops and carried out horrifying experiments on prisoners of war. Colonel Shiro Ishii, the commander of Unit 731, was a true believer, convinced that biological warfare could give Japan a unique advantage against otherwise superior opponents. Although used against unprotected targets, the BW attacks had limited effectiveness: local successes were accelerated but no decisive results were gained.

In its conclusion, a 1946 report on BW written by George Merck, the U.S. secretary of war's chief biological weapons expert, stated: "There is no evidence that our enemies at any time attempted a biological warfare attack." Although this judgment ignored the war in China, it was otherwise accurate. Axis BW capability remained slight; neither Germany nor Japan enjoyed any strategic capability against the Western Allies or the Soviet Union. Germany had no tactical capability; Japan had a limited tactical capability.

The Allies, fearing Axis BW efforts, developed more impressive programs than their enemies. But the results remained potential rather than actual. At no point during the war could the Allies have launched massive biological retaliatory strikes. If the Pacific war had lasted into 1946, the United States could have used anti-crop agents against Japanese rice production. But there were those in the U.S. military who questioned the effectiveness and the morality of such attacks.

Why Deterrence Worked   Despite violations, crises, and recurring temptations to initiate chemical warfare, deterrence held throughout World War II. The reasons were multiple. A war is often defined in its initial stages. The non-use of chemical weapons in the early European campaigns created a presumption against their use throughout the war. Second, the continuing impact of the experience of World War I on the European belligerents was considerable. Except for such atypical cases as the Italo-Ethiopian conflict, CW effectiveness was seen as questionable. The disadvantages of chemical weapons were understood by the belligerents.

The third factor was the continued unpreparedness of the belligerents for full-scale chemical warfare. Germany's CW position was inferior to that of the Allies. Japan's capability declined toward the close of the war. By 1944, the United States had the resources, but faced daunting logistical challenges in the forward deployment of chemical munitions in the Pacific. Another restraint was the inevitable delay before a decision to initiate could be implemented: extensive training, theater stockpiling, and other detailed preparations would be necessary prior to any attack. Each side, moreover, tended to see its own preparedness problems and to exaggerate the readiness of its foes. Illusion protected deterrence. Although the Allies discounted intelligence that the Germans had developed new chemical agents, they had sufficient respect for German scientific ability that they assessed Germany's initial CW capability as high. Ironically, the Germans believed that the Allies had developed the nerve gases that they held at their exclusive command.

The fourth reason was tactical. Overall, World War II was characterized by mobile warfare, in stark contrast to the western front in World War I. Only a few occasions favored initiation of CW. Additionally, tactical chemical attacks could lead to strategic retaliation, and ultimately to global chemical warfare. Throughout the war, civilian populations were held hostage by the threat of aerial chemical attack.

Finally, the pressure for the initiation of chemical warfare was never sufficient to overcome the restraints against its use. The advocates of effectiveness did not occupy positions of commanding influence in the councils of power. Churchill's interest was momentary. Roosevelt was consistently opposed. Hitler had an aversion to the use of gas in combat, having been incapacitated in a mustard-gas attack toward the close of World War I. Stalin was too fearful of German retaliation to favor initiation of cw on the eastern front. Tojo, the most powerful of the Japanese warlords, permitted cw against the Chinese but adamantly opposed its use against Anglo-American forces. With the exception of General Dill in 1940 and General Marshall in 1945, the top Allied military establishment was opposed to initiation.

The Heritage of World War II   In World War II, deterrence doctrine dominated over the humanity argument. Considerations of humanity, however, did have an impact on some policymakers, especially President Roosevelt. Generally, these considerations served more as conditioning than as causative factors. Paradoxically, the non-use of chemical weapons in the war strengthened the argument against them after the war, thereby reinforcing the humanity argument.

Except in the Chinese theater of operations, the effectiveness of chemical weapons was not tested in World War II. Moreover, because the results in China were not impressive, the effectiveness advocates have relied upon hypothetical cases. If, some have argued, the British had used gas against the feared but cancelled German invasion, it would have stopped the landing force; or, if the Germans had used nerve gas against the successful Allied landings in Normandy in 1944, the invasion of Europe would have been defeated.

The World War II experience had a significant impact upon postwar cbw planning. First, firebombing broke down all restraints against the use of incendiary weapons in war, even though these weapons had been condemned in the 1930s Disarmament Conference. Second, preparations for biological warfare encouraged the United States and other major powers to develop a significant postwar bw program. Third, the World War II experience reinforced the belief that deterrence was more effective than international agreement in preventing chemical warfare. The context in which deterrence had worked was forgotten as it was elevated to a single determining factor. Fourth, the fear of being taken by surprise was reinforced. Although there was no Second Ypres, Pearl Harbor had a pronounced effect upon American military planning. Weapons of mass destruction (chemical, biological, and nuclear) seemed ideally suited to

surprise attack. This conviction reinforced the belief that deterrence was a better shield than any treaty. Fifth, nuclear weapons took center stage. Far more convincingly than chemical weapons, hydrogen bombs embodied the threat of ultimate weapons as envisaged during the interwar period. Thus chemical warfare moved into the shadow of truly cataclysmic weapons.

CONCLUSION

From World War I to the close of World War II, cw advocates were convinced that chemical warfare was an effective means of combat. They claimed by hypothetical cases that cw could have won a battle, cut down casualties, hastened victory, or reversed the course of a campaign. Hypothesis, based on faith in the unknowable, can never be exorcised. But the historical record is clear. In World War I, the Italo-Ethiopian war, and the Sino-Japanese War (1937–1945), cw was temporarily and locally effective against certain targets and in certain tactical situations. It was used to protect the flanks of advancing armies, neutralize artillery batteries, harass troops, effect casualties, make towns uninhabitable, disrupt communications, repel attacks, and panic untrained and unprepared soldiers. Against this last target, it came closest to promising decisiveness. Here its psychological effect dominated.

In isolation, the outcomes of cw seem impressive. But military effectiveness, which should be viewed in a wider context, can be judged by two standards: external and internal. Externally, cw played a minor role in the wars in which it was used. For example, the major weapon of World War I was artillery. Only 4.5 percent of the shells expended were chemically charged. Yet 85 percent of the cw agents were fired by artillery and mortars. Accounts of the 1918 German offensives, in which gas was skillfully integrated into artillery shoots, are dominated by the crushing weight of the conventional barrages, not by the impact of gas shells. In the 1918 campaign, gas did serve as a force multiplier but only when used in conjunction with other arms. Even then, it could not counter the mass of Allied matériel and manpower accumulating against the Germans. It could harass; it could not overcome.

Internally, chemical warfare in World War I often proved more of a burden than an advantage. Once it was adopted by both sides, the weapon lost its edge. Although it was still possible to achieve surprise against the unprepared or the unlucky, the logistical burden of waging cw, the degradation of performance caused by the need to wear masks, and the psychological toll exacted upon combatants hampered overall effectiveness. Chemical warfare was a force divider as well as a force multiplier.

In World War I, cw complicated the tasks of the fighting forces, intensified the physical and psychological miseries of troops mired in the stalemate of trench fighting, and multiplied uncertainty and terror without creating a decisive breakthrough to victory. Not surprisingly, soldiers regarded gas as a curse.

The question of effectiveness is political as well as military: Is a weapon effective if it is regarded with special revulsion? Public opposition impeded the assimilation of chemical weapons into military arsenals and complicated the tasks of preparedness. It may also have radically limited the use of cw in war.

In arguing for cbw disarmament, advocates have evoked, in the words of the Geneva Protocol, the just condemnation of "the general opinion of the civilized world" against the use of this type of warfare. To the apologists, this revulsion is irrational, incomprehensible. But it is inescapable, and its causes are deep and ultimately mysterious. Although the ancient taboo against the use of poisons in warfare has not prevented the use of chemical and biological weapons, it has limited it. Mankind should not ignore a prohibition merely because it cannot completely understand it. Ultimately, this deep and lasting revulsion may provide the soundest foundation for the permanent abolition of chemical and biological weapons.

BIBLIOGRAPHY

The indispensable work, which provides a survey of the entire field of chemical and biological warfare, is the Stockholm International Peace Research Institute (SIPRI), *The Problem of Chemical and Biological Warfare: A Study of the Historical, Technical, Legal and Political Aspects of CBW, and Possible Disarmament Measures*, 6 vols. (New York, 1971–1975). Especially useful for the early phases are vol. 1: *The Rise of CB Weapons* (1971) and vol. 4: CB *Disarmament Negotiations: 1920–1970* (1971).

Law of War   A thoughtful work on the development of the law of war from the eighteenth century to the present is GEOFFREY BEST, *Humanity in Warfare* (New York, 1980). Relevant documents can be found in LEON FRIEDMAN, ed., *The Law of War: A Documentary History,* 2 vols. (New York, 1972). The legal ambiguities of the law of war are explored in MORRIS GREENSPAN, *The Modern Law of Land Warfare* (Berkeley, Calif., 1959) and in ANN THOMAS and A. J. THOMAS, *Legal Limits on the Use of Chemical and Biological Weapons* (Dallas, 1970). The question of General Amherst's "use" of infected blankets as a weapon against the Indians was first raised by Francis Parkman in *The Conspiracy of Pontiac* (1851; repr. New York, 1991), pp. 647–649. The charge is challenged by Bernhard Knollenberg in "General Amherst and Germ Warfare," *The Mississippi Valley Historical Review* (December 1954): 489–494. James Poupard and Linda A. Miller have reexamined the charge in *ASM News* 55, no. 3, 1989.

CW and Disarmament   The issues of chemical warfare and disarmament are covered in the following works: VALERIE ADAMS, *Chemical Warfare, Chemical Disarmament* (Bloomington, Ind., 1990); EDWARD M. SPIERS, *Chemical Warfare* (Champaign, Ill., 1986); EDWARD M. SPIERS, *Chemical Weaponry: A Continuing Challenge* (New York, 1989); and VICTOR A. UTGOFF, *The Challenge of Chemical Weapons: An American Perspective* (New York, 1991).

Battle of Ypres   The use of gas at the Second Battle of Ypres, from the German and French perspective respectively, is recounted and analyzed in the following works: RUDOLF HANSLIAN, "The Gas Attack at Ypres: A Study in Military History," *Chemical Warfare Bulletin* 22 (1936): 2–15, 69–80, 119–129; and JEAN J. MORDACQ, *Le drame de l'Yser* (Paris, 1933). More detached analyses are found in ULRICH TRUMPENER, "The Road to Ypres: The Beginning of Gas Warfare in World War I," *Journal of Modern History* 47 (September 1975): 460–480, and in JAMES L. MCWILLIAMS and R. JAMES STEEL, *Gas! The Battle for Ypres, 1915* (St. Catherine, Ontario, 1985). The latter work is confined to the Canadian role in the battle.

WWI Accounts   The official histories of military operations in World War I (British, French, and German) and the memoirs of the combatants contain numerous accounts of the use of chemical weapons. DOROTHY KNEELAND CLARK, *Effectiveness of Chemical Weapons in WWI* (Bethesda, Md., 1959), provides an in-depth statistical analysis of the role that cw played in combat. C. H. FOULKES, *"Gas!" The Story of the Special Brigade* (Edinburgh, 1936) is an account of the operations of the British gas brigade in World War I. Like all special pleaders, Foulkes tends to overrate the effectiveness of his weapon. LUDWIG F. HABER, *The Poisonous Cloud: Chemical Warfare in the First World War* (New York, 1986) provides the best single-volume analysis of cw operations. RUDOLF HANSLIAN, ed., *Der chemische Krieg,* 3rd ed. (Berlin, 1937), is a usefully detailed account that is partial to the German viewpoint. C. E. HELLER, *Chemical Warfare in World War I: The American Experience, 1917–1918* (Fort Leavenworth, Kans., 1985) graphically demonstrates the unpreparedness of the United States for cw combat.

Disarmament Efforts CBW disarmament efforts between the two world wars are summarized in the above cited general works. Unfortunately, there is no adequate separate study on the subject. The disarmament debates can be followed in the publications of the League of Nations. The case of chemical warfare advocates and the current state of cw technology are covered in the following works: AMOS A. FRIES and CLARENCE J. WEST, *Chemical Warfare* (New York, 1921); J. B. S. HALDANE, *Callinicus: A Defense of Chemical Warfare* (London, 1925); AUGUSTIN M. PRENTISS, *Chemicals in War* (New York, 1937); and HENRY F. THUILLIER, *Gas in the Next War* (London, 1939).

WWII Accounts Three volumes of the series *United States Army in World War II* deal with cw: LEO P. BROPHY and GEORGE J. B. FISHER, *The Chemical Warfare Service: Organizing for War* (Washington, D.C., 1959); LEO P. BROPHY, WYNDHAM D. MILES, and REXMOND C. COCHRANE, *The Chemical Warfare Service: From Laboratory to Field* (Washington, D.C., 1959); and BROOKS E. KLEBER and DALE BIRDSELL, *The Chemical Warfare Service: Chemicals in Combat* (Washington, D.C., 1966). These three works are immensely valuable from the technical point of view. On policy, FREDERIC J. BROWN, *Chemical Warfare: A Study in Restraints* (Princeton, N.J., 1968) remains indispensable. JOHN ELLIS VAN COURTLAND MOON "Chemical Weapons and Deterrence: The World War II Experience," *International Security* 8 (Spring 1984): 3–35, uses Joint Chiefs of Staff documents unavailable to Brown. There has been a great deal of speculation regarding Churchill's willingness to use BW as well as cw against German targets. See, for example, Barton Bernstein, "Churchill's Secret Biological Weapons," *Bulletin of the Atomic Scientists* 43 (1987): 46–50. This charge, however, has been vigorously refuted in R. V. Jones, *Reflections on Intelligence* (London, 1989), pp. 251–254, and Julian Lewis, *Changing Direction: British Military Planning for Post-War Strategic Defence, 1942–1947* (London, 1988), pp. 388–405.

Journalists on CBW Since CBW is a sensational subject it has attracted the attention of journalists as well as historians. Although they have succeeded in unearthing previously untapped material, the journalists whose works are listed below often fail to discriminate between their sources. The following works are to be used with care: JOHN BRYDEN, *Deadly Allies: Canada's Secret War: 1937–1947* (Toronto, 1989); ROBERT HARRIS and JEREMY PAXMAN, *A Higher Form of Killing: The Secret Story of Gas and Germ Warfare* (London, 1982); and PETER WILLIAMS and DAVID WALLACE, *Unit 731: Japan's Secret Biological Warfare in World War II* (London and New York, 1989).

Demilitarization and Neutralization Through World War II

○

ALLAN S. NANES

See also Arms Control in Antiquity; Chile and Argentina: Entente and Naval Limitation, 1902; Nuclear-Weapon-Free Zones; The Rush-Bagot Agreement: Demilitarizing the Great Lakes; *and* Switzerland. *Most of the treaties discussed in this essay are excerpted in Volume III.*

Demilitarization and neutralization are among the oldest of arms control techniques, with examples existing in antiquity. Although these two approaches do not involve precisely the same arms control and disarmament mechanisms, they have a similar objective—preventing stipulated geographical areas from becoming sources or sites of conflict. Some of these measures have been designed to reduce or eliminate "flash points," such as areas along the frontiers of aggressive, potentially hostile nations, where a minor, unpremeditated armed clash could quickly lead to a major confrontation. Fortifications and military bases in or near canals and straits, lakes and seas, and islands and "buffer" zones also have been potential sources of conflict that were removed from international contention by demilitarization or neutralization.

DEFINITIONS

Before undertaking a general survey of examples of demilitarization and neutralization—which will demonstrate the parameters of these arms control and disarmament techniques, stretching from ancient times to the onset of World War II—it is appropriate to provide a definition of these terms.

According to one commentator, the word *demilitarize* was first used at the Paris Peace Conference of 1919 to describe the regime devised for the Rhineland, which forbade Germany to have any troops or fortifications within a specified zone. The term subsequently passed into international usage with the Straits convention, which was annexed to the Treaty of Lausanne in 1923. It contains prohibitions against the maintenance of troops or other military components or fortifications in a particular geographic area during peacetime. But the concept may extend beyond such military restrictions to include a ban on the construction of strategic facilities—such as railroads, highways, and airports.

If the concept of demilitarization is broad, the objectives of specific agreements are usually quite narrow. They involve reducing the chances of an armed clash, while enhancing each country's confidence that its national security has been increased by entering into the agreement. If reciprocity is perceived to be lacking by one of the parties to a demilitarization agreement—that is, if a demilitarized frontier agreement comes to be seen as one-sided—it probably will not last very long.

This does not mean that a demilitarized zone needs to be symmetrical. Different geographical features can justify fewer fortifications and fewer

675

troops on one side of a border than another. One signatory to a frontier demilitarization may confront internal unrest that justifies the maintenance of small forces of lightly armed troops within its segment of a "demilitarized" zone. Demilitarized zones need not be mirror images of each other.

However, whatever the nature of a demilitarization proposal, whether it involves only the removal of troops or fortifications or other restrictions, historically it has been much more likely to be successful if it is entered into freely by the parties concerned and if it is designed to serve the needs of all. Imposed demilitarization has tended, at least in the years preceding World War II, to be self-defeating.

Neutralization, which may or may not involve demilitarization, usually takes place when a given expanse of territory—perhaps an entire country—has been stipulated by international agreement to be insulated from invasion by external forces. A neutralized nation, while it may be allowed military forces and fortifications, is prohibited from engaging in any international conflict or military alliances.

A unilateral declaration of neutrality, whether by legislative or constitutional action, constitutes neutralization in international law only if it is accompanied by some form of international recognition. A nation may pursue a policy of neutrality vis-à-vis belligerents, or may declare its nonalignment with competing power blocs, but neither of these self-neutralizing actions conveys the status of permanent or perpetual neutrality. Neutralization may begin with unilateral national action, but to attain permanence it normally requires the acknowledgement of other states.

Neutralization carries obligations for the state that is neutralized as well as for those states that guarantee its neutrality. The neutralized party must abstain from wars or alliances or other commitments that might lead to its involvement in hostilities. It does not have to disarm, but it is obligated to refrain from using its military forces for any purpose other than self-defense and the maintenance of internal order. It must not permit other states to use its territory for military purposes. It may have to refrain from joining customs unions or other economic alliances that might seemingly render it economically dependent on another nation or nations, and thus compromise its status should members of its joint economic undertaking become involved in hostilities. But the legal obligations of a neutralized status cannot, as a practical matter, be extended to require moral neutrality as well.

The signatories to a neutralization agreement who are themselves not being neutralized obviously act as guarantors for the nation that is. This means that they are obligated to respect the status and integrity of the neutralized state. They may be required to come to its aid if its neutral status is violated by another country. They must also forswear coercive policies aimed at the neutralized state; for example, they may be required to refrain from supporting any domestic uprising against the government of the neutralized party.

Neutralization is presumed to serve the interests of both the state being neutralized and its guarantors. The former gives up freedom of action, but gains in security. The latter believe they gain in security as well, first by removing the threat of an advantage their competitors would gain by exercising coercive power over the state being neutralized, and second by reducing the chances of a military confrontation with those competitors.

NEUTRALIZED NATIONS

In the three major examples discussed here, neutralization was generally successful only in the case of Switzerland. The neutrality of both Belgium and Luxembourg was violated during World War I.

Switzerland   The most prominent state to undergo the neutralizing process has been Switzerland, and its arrangement illustrates the advantages that both it and its guarantors gained from this arms control technique. The Swiss themselves, as early as the late fourteenth century, recognized that their mountainous topography offered advantages in seeking to escape the quarrels of their neighbors.

The city of Zürich first employed the neutralization technique when it signed a treaty in 1309 with the Austrian dukes Frederick and Leopold, to exempt the valley floor along the Lake of Zürich from any warfare. In 1393 Zürich signed a friendship pact with Austria by which each side pledged to maintain an attitude of aloofness and impartiality in the event of war. Thus, Swiss neutrality began as a process embodying parallel concepts: one, that a state or political community could remain apart from or outside an active conflict; and two, that particular segments of territory could be ruled out or exempted from military action.

Swiss neutralization through the early modern era sought to avoid involvement in the recurring wars between France and the principally German states of the Holy Roman Empire. In 1647 the Swiss felt their territorial integrity so menaced by the strife of the Thirty Years' War that they organized an army of thirty-six thousand men to defend it.

Following the 1648 Peace of Westphalia, which ended that war, the neutral status of Switzerland was generally recognized, although not guaranteed in any international instrument, and not always respected. During the Napoleonic era, from 1798 to 1815, Switzerland became involved in Europe's wars, which not only ended its unilateral neutralization but set the stage for the international guarantee that followed.

That guarantee was embodied in the Act of Paris of 20 November 1815. By its terms France, Britain, Prussia, Russia, and Austria declared "their formal and authentic Acknowledgement of the perpetual Neutrality of Switzerland; and they Guarantee to that country the Integrity and Inviolability of its Territory." (This guarantee became an integral part of the European political system; it was again specifically recognized in Article 435 of the Treaty of Versailles.)

At the Congress of Vienna, the Swiss proposed that their neutrality be enhanced by a demilitarized border to be established on the territory of their neighbors. This was not accepted by the Congress, although it was agreed that the fortress of Huningen in Upper Alsace be demolished, which the Swiss desired.

Finally, the Congress of Vienna recognized Switzerland's neutrality on the express condition that Switzerland was able to uphold it. To that end, the Swiss have maintained their unique volunteer force since 1815. The arrangement has been successful in that the Swiss were able to maintain their neutrality during World War I and World War II. Thus the neutralization of Switzerland demonstrates that this concept does not necessarily require a reduction of armaments; although it does demand that forces of a neutral state be recognized as exclusively defensive.

Belgium

The same countries that guaranteed the neutralization of the Swiss sought to impose that same arms control technique on Belgium. But in this case there was no demand for neutrality, as Belgium and Holland were united by the Congress of Vienna in 1815 to constitute a combined political and military barrier against the possibility of renewed French aggression. Unhappy under Dutch rule, the Belgians revolted in 1830, confronting the major European powers with the problem of how to preserve this desired barrier against the French while satisfying the Belgian desire for independence.

To solve the problem they drafted a treaty in 1831 stating that "Belgium . . . shall form an Independent and perpetually Neutral State. It shall be bound to observe such neutrality towards all other States." Holland was reluctant to accept Belgian independence, and it was eight years before final arrangements incorporating Belgian independence and neutrality were concluded. Again, Britain, France, Russia, Prussia, and Austria bound themselves to maintain the integrity, neutrality, and independence of Belgium.

In the years that followed, Belgium figured prominently in the relations of France, Great Britain, and Prussia. Thus in 1866, Napoleon III of France entered into negotiations with Bismarck, representing Prussia, hoping to annex Belgium as compensation for the unification of Germany. Nothing came of this, but three years later Bismarck embarrassed France by making the negotiations public. Subsequently in 1870, England concluded separate treaties with France and Prussia, providing that if either country violated Belgian neutrality, Britain would assist the other in defending it.

When the famous Schlieffen Plan became known in 1904—positing a German attack through Belgium on France—Belgium immediately undertook negotiations with Great Britain, France, and Germany hoping to guarantee its neutrality in the event of war. In 1914, when the German invasion took place, authorities in Berlin dismissed the agreement on Belgian neutrality as a "scrap of paper." This treaty violation, however, together with the strategic significance of Germany's military actions, brought Britain into World War I.

The Belgian government never had been enthusiastic about its imposed neutrality, which it regarded as an imposed limitation on its sovereignty. That sentiment was recognized in Article 31 of the Treaty of Versailles. The article abrogated the 1831 treaty, thereby terminating Belgium's neutrality. Unfortunately, military forces also failed to provide for Belgium's security, and it was quickly conquered by Germany in World War II.

Luxembourg

A very small state, the Grand Duchy of Luxembourg occupied a strategic position flanking the northeastern approaches to France by way of the Meuse and Moselle valleys. Its neutrality was guaranteed by treaty in 1867, in the wake of the war between Prussia and Austria. The same five signatories that guaranteed the neutrality of Belgium signed the treaty, but under different circumstances.

For one thing, Britain maintained that the guarantee was collective only, and that the guarantor states were not individually responsible for the defense of Luxembourg's neutrality. The other guarantor states did not share this opinion. Secondly, Luxembourg was demilitarized as well as neutralized, which was not the case with Belgium. Indeed, according to one commentator, Luxembourg may be said to have presented the only example of a demilitarized state in nineteenth century Europe.

Luxembourg was occupied in the German advance during 1914, but the occupation was concerned primarily with facilitating the rail transit of troops and supplies and did not significantly intervene in the affairs of the civilian government. Ironically, the government of the Grand Duchy did not consider its neutralization to have been violated and, therefore, did not break relations with Germany. Furthermore, Luxembourg was not a participant in the 1919 peace conference, and it did not recognize the abrogations of the 1867 treaty provided for in Article 40 of the Treaty of Versailles.

It considered its neutrality to be in force right down to the beginning if the Second World War, but formally abandoned that policy during the latter conflict.

Lesser Known Examples   In addition to Switzerland, Belgium, and Luxembourg, there have been other attempts to neutralize nations or "city-states." The city of Cracow, Poland, was declared to be a neutral city in the treaty regarding Poland signed at Vienna in 1815. It was to be under the protection of Russia, Prussia, and Austria. This neutralization lasted thirty-one years, until it was repudiated in 1846 on the grounds that the city had become a center of revolutionary activity. Cracow and its surrounding territory were absorbed under Austrian rule. Britain and France protested this breach of the Vienna treaty, but without satisfactory results.

A futile instance of neutralization was the case of Albania. Albania was created as an independent state by the Treaty of London, following the Balkan War of 1912–1913. Pursuant to that treaty, a conference of ambassadors of Britain, France, Russia, Italy,

Germany, and Austria-Hungary declared that Albania would be neutralized, and that its neutrality was guaranteed by the six powers they represented.

When World War I broke out in 1914, this declaration was effectively voided. There was no further attempt at neutralization after the war.

Finally, in 1929, in a treaty between Italy and the Holy See, Vatican City was decreed to be neutral and inviolable territory. But this provision was more significant in the context of Italian-Vatican relations than it was as a contribution to peace or arms control in any significant sense.

DEMILITARIZED AND/OR NEUTRALIZED ZONES

From earliest historical times, rulers and states have sought to protect themselves from external aggression. At first this search for security took the form of stout walls. Examples of these include the Great Wall of China, designed to keep out the Huns, Hadrian's Wall in ancient Britain, erected to keep out the Caledonians, the Scots and others, and lesser known walls, such as the Great Fence, constructed by the Bulgar conquerors of Thrace. These were expensive undertakings, as troops were required to defend and maintain the walls.

Consequently, leaders sought an alternative, less expensive method of creating protective barriers. Eventually they concluded that this security might be obtained by separating the armed forces of neighboring territories, thereby removing the possibility of provocative armed clashes—which often occurred between military forces stationed in close proximity to each other—that might escalate in a general war. A political barrier was substituted for the physical one.

Differing means were used to bring about the desired separation. Tracts of land were razed or depopulated to accomplish this purpose. (Sometimes heavily fortified areas would be used as a natural barrier for preventing raids and incursions. Julius Caesar noted both types of boundaries in his works on the Gallic wars.) An example of an uncultivated and depopulated area could be found along the border of China and Korea until the middle of the nineteenth century. No settlement was permitted in this zone under pain of death.

At least one specialist has argued that the word "frontier" in all probability never conveyed the idea of a line, but rather that of a neutral zone. J. H. Marshall-Cornwall, a British general, suggests that substituting separation by space for physical contact between armed neighbors constituted a definite, perhaps first stage, of arms control.

Along with the idea of an intervening or exclusionary zone, the idea of removing specific areas of land or sea from military operations dates from ancient times. It may have had its origin in the concept of sanctuary, by which certain temples or other sacred grounds were insulated from conflict by agreement. The famous oracle at Delphi, for example, was in this exempt category. In medieval times the high alters of churches and cathedrals were accorded the same status as sanctuaries.

But not only religious sites were respected. Even commercial arteries of common interest to neighboring states and territories might be subject to treaties that would exempt them from hostilities. While these examples may not be precise analogues for neutralization as it came to be practiced, there are nevertheless many historical instances where both land and sea areas were designated by treaty as places to be excluded from belligerent activity. All this was done, of course, with a view to limiting the geographical scope of conflict.

Armistice (Neutral) Zones

In the modern era, a particularly useful, but usually temporary, arms control technique has been the separating of opposing forces immediately following the cessation of hostilities. (Subsequent political settlements occasionally may attempt to formalize the temporary agreement by creating a demilitarized zone. Or in the case of the demilitarized zone created in the Korean armistice of 1953, the failure to reach agreement of a formal peace treaty may give durability to a temporary measure.)

One can cite a great many armistice agreements in which formerly belligerent armies were withdrawn beyond striking distance of one another. For example, in the 1859 armistice following war between Austria on the one side, and France and Sardinia on the other, it was agreed that a neutral space would be left between the two lines of demarcation of the belligerent armies. This technique could also be found in the 1871 armistice convention following the Franco-Prussian War, in which it was agreed that the two belligerent armies, and their advanced posts on either side, would remain at a distance of at least ten kilometers (6.2 miles) from the lines drawn to separate their positions. Similarly, the Treaty of Portsmouth, which ended the Russo-Japa-

nese War of 1904–1905, provided that a demarcated zone would be established to separate the forward military positions of the two powers.

The armistice that ended World War I elaborated a series of lines beyond which the German forces were to withdraw according to a predetermined schedule. As the Germans withdrew, Allied troops would occupy the ground after a set interval. After thirty-one days had elapsed, the Germans were to have evacuated all territory on the left bank of the Rhine, retiring to a neutral zone on the right bank of the river. Somewhat similar terms were set down in the Protocol of Armistice between the Allied powers and Austria-Hungary.

During the interwar years there were a number of attempts to employ neutralized zones in order to defuse frontier disputes or assist in the termination of hostilities. Results were mixed.

An attempt by the fledgling League of Nations to establish a neutral zone during a border dispute between Poland and Lithuania in 1920 came to grief when the Poles simply disregarded the zone and seized the territory in contention. But in 1921 a "zone of demarcation" was successfully established as neutral ground until a disputed border could be settled between Yugoslavia and Albania. The League Council managed to persuade both Greece and Bulgaria to withdraw their forces behind separate lines when a border war threatened in 1925.

Demilitarized Land Zones

The sporadic fighting between Chinese and Japanese troops that began with the 1931 Japanese occupation of Mukden, Manchuria, was interrupted by an armistice in 1932 and again in 1933. In the latter case a demilitarized zone was created by the Chinese troops withdrawing south and west of a line running roughly from Tientsin to Peiping (as Beijing was then called), while Japanese troops were to withdraw north of the Great Wall.

These measures resulted in the creation between Manchukuo—the Japanese puppet state in Manchuria—and China of a demilitarized zone administered by Chinese who were under Japanese influence. The zone may have ameliorated friction during the period in which hostilities were broken off, but it did not greatly improve China's fortunes.

A second instance of the use of a demilitarized zone as a part of the process of terminating hostilities occurred in 1934, when the League of Nations sought to end the protracted Gran Chaco War between Bolivia and Paraguay. A committee of the

League Assembly, in accordance with Article 15 of the Covenant, had investigated the facts of the dispute and proposed an armistice. Among their proposals was one that called for the two armies to withdraw their advanced elements at least fifty kilometers (31 miles) from the point reached on the day hostilities ceased. That would leave a gap of at least one hundred kilometers (62 miles) between opposing forces, and within that zone no military works of an offensive or defensive character were to be established, nor were the troops to be re-equipped.

The League Assembly added a provision to these proposals noting that they were purely of a military character, and were not designed to prejudice the territorial issues between the parties. Hostilities between the two countries ended in June 1935, and the creation of this demilitarized zone appears to have been a useful contribution to its termination.

Demilitarized Maritime Zones　The notion of restricting certain waters, rendering them "off-limits" to the naval forces of contesting or rival powers, also dates back to ancient times. Periclean Athens entered into an agreement with Persia in 449 B.C. whereby Athens acknowledged Persian suzerainty over Egypt and Cyprus, and in return the king of Persia agreed not to send warships into the Aegean, nor to attack Greek settlements in Asia Minor. This agreement can be pronounced a modest success, for it helped bring about a peace between Athens and the Persian Empire that lasted almost forty years.

A less successful example arose during the Peloponnesian War of 431–404 B.C., when there was an armistice between Athens and Sparta. Under its terms, the Spartans and their allies bound themselves not to navigate their own territorial waters with any warship or oared vessel of more than five hundred talents burden. This seems a major concession, but the armistice was short-lived. This provision apparently had little effect on preventing these two cities from resuming their bitter hostilities.

Those two great rivals of the ancient world, Rome and Carthage, signed at least two treaties relative to commerce and navigation that imposed restrictions on Rome's freedom of the seas. By a treaty of 348 B.C., it was agreed that neither Rome nor its allies would sail beyond a designated point in the Mediterranean unless compelled by bad weather or an enemy. In return, Carthage promised not to build any fortifications on "Latin" territory, and if its forces landed on such territory in a hostile manner, they were to withdraw "before night"—in other words, the same day. The second treaty, in 306 B.C., further restricted the reach of Rome's fleets.

After the First Punic War, the Romans sought to thwart Carthage's aspirations in Spain by attempting to exempt the Ebro River from military action. The Carthaginian general Hasdrubal agreed that Carthage would not cross the Ebro with an army. Eight years later his brother, Hannibal, did so, however, on the way to his crossing of the Pyrenees and the Alps, and his eventual invasion of Italy.

The famous Rush-Bagot agreement of 1817 between the United States and Great Britain (and later Canada) specified the demilitarization of the Great Lakes. The agreement, which will be discussed later, did not call for the removal of all warships from the lakes, as each side was permitted to retain police vessels to prevent smuggling. Over time it was amended, evaded, and almost repudiated; however, it evolved into the demilitarization of the entire United States–Canadian border. This was achieved because it came to be seen that such was in both nations' interest.

Demilitarization of the Rhineland　It was a regime imposed by the victors of World War I, through Articles 42 and 43 of the Treaty of Versailles. Germany was forbidden to maintain or construct any fortifications on the left bank of the Rhine or on the right bank west of a line drawn fifty kilometers (31 miles) east of the river. Germany was also forbidden to keep any troops in this area, permanently or temporarily, or to conduct maneuvers there, or to keep up any mobilization facilities. Article 180 of the Versailles treaty specified that any fortified works, fortresses, or field works within this zone were to be dismantled.

France, in pursuit of its security, had originally proposed that the Rhineland be detached from Germany altogether. Paris's original intention was to establish a buffer state as a guarantee against invasion. Both Britain and the United States opposed this idea and, in the end, France withdrew its demand for a separate state on the left bank of the Rhine. The French settled for the demilitarized zone described above, together with the occupation of this territory by an inter-Allied force for a period of at least fifteen years. This was supposed to serve as a guarantee that Germany would carry out the provisions of the peace treaty.

In addition, both England and the United States signed separate guarantee treaties with the French for the security of the demilitarized zone. Both treaties, however, were drawn up in such a way that neither would come into force unless the other was ratified. When the United States failed to ratify the security treaty, both pledges were nullified. No security guarantees for the Rhineland regime existed, then, until the Locarno Pact of 1925. Under its terms, Germany, France, Belgium, Italy, and Great Britain individually and as a group guaranteed the inviolability of the existing Franco-German frontiers and of the demilitarized Rhineland zone.

However, when the Nazis came to power in Germany in 1933, the existence of the Rhineland demilitarization was threatened. The Nazis argued that this one-sided demilitarization was yet another example of the unfairness of the Versailles *diktat*. Despite their bluster, few European statesmen believed the Germans would force the issue by reoccupying the Rhineland. But that is precisely what they did, on 7–9 March 1936, violating both the Treaty of Versailles and the Locarno Pact.

Adolf Hitler gambled that Britain and France would not offer armed resistance, and his reading of the situation proved to be correct. The French did not feel ready for war, even though their army vastly outnumbered the German forces; the British rejected both force and economic sanctions, calling instead for negotiations. Both allies urged America to condemn Germany's invasion of the demilitarized territory, but the United States refused to become involved. There was widespread popular support in England and France for the caution displayed by the respective governments; indeed, in England and other countries there was varying degrees of sympathy for the German position.

Thus the demilitarization of the Rhineland ended in failure. If there is a conclusion to be drawn, it is that in the absence of serving the mutual interests of the concerned parties, demilitarization (and other similar) agreements have only a slim chance of succeeding.

STRAITS AND CANALS

Control of the major straits and canals that connected key bodies of water were viewed as vital for the commerce and security of major powers during this era. Demilitarization was considered for the major examples examined here—the Turkish straits, the Strait of Magellan, the Suez Canal, and the Panama Canal.

The Turkish Straits Great-power rivalry in nineteenth century Europe often revolved around the so-called Eastern Question—the competition for power, influence, trade, and even territorial acquisition in the Middle East. A major focal point of the contest were the "Turkish" straits that connect the Mediterranean and the Black seas.

Essentially, the Russians sought to restrict passage through the straits and into the Black Sea; conversely, the other powers wanted unrestricted access to the Black Sea. Two arms control techniques—neutralization and demilitarization—were frequently employed to promote one or the other of these objectives in several political compromises regarding the straits.

Russian power in the area seemed to reach an apogee in 1833, when the czar's government, following an Egyptian victory over Turkish arms, persuaded the Turks to sign an agreement closing the Dardanelles to all foreign warships except Russian naval vessels. This treaty regime made Russia dominant in the region and rendered the Black Sea a virtual *mare clausum,* a closed sea. Known as the Treaty of Unkiar-Iskelessi, this agreement was highly unpopular with the western European powers and, predictably, they exerted heavy diplomatic pressure to change it.

The western European powers succeeded in gaining a new agreement, the Convention of the Straits, signed in London on 13 July 1841, which provided that the straits would be closed to warships of all nations so long as Turkey was at peace. But if Turkey were to become involved in a conflict, it could open the straits to foreign warships by simply inviting them in. In short, the powers put Turkey back in control by allowing it the option of reopening the straits to the world's navies if war broke out in the region.

This system lasted only fifteen years. With the Treaty of Paris of 30 March 1856, which ended the Crimean War, a new regime was instituted that not only neutralized the Black Sea but demilitarized both its Russian and Turkish shores as well. (This system is more fully developed in the Lakes and Seas section, below.)

The neutralized and demilitarized status of the straits, established by the Treaty of Paris, was designed to advance the interests of the victors in the Crimean War, particularly Great Britain, as Russia's influence over Turkey was diminished. Britain gained her objective of keeping the straits open to commercial shipping, and Britain and France together were in a position either to uphold or directly threaten Russian security. From Russia's standpoint, the restrictions of the Treaty of Paris amounted to an infringement of its sovereign rights. Czar Alexander II took advantage of the French defeat in the Franco-Prussian War to unilaterally repudiate the treaty in 1870.

Eventually a new conference of the powers was convened in London in 1871 and a new treaty, the so-called Pontus Treaty, established yet another set of rules for naval and defense policy in the straits. This time the straits were closed to all foreign warships. Both Russia and Turkey were permitted to fortify their Black Sea coasts, and no limitations were placed on the number of warships that each might maintain in the Black Sea, which was to remain open to the mercantile marine of all nations.

However, there was a significant provision that precluded egress of the Black Sea fleets through the straits. This meant that although Russia had regained the right to fortify its Black Sea coast and to maintain naval forces on that body of water, it did not regain operational access to the Mediterranean. From the British standpoint, this situation was eminently satisfactory.

During the Russo-Japanese War, the closure of the straits had a negative impact on Russia's capabilities, as her Black Sea fleet was, in effect, kept out of the war. During World War I, when England and Russia were allied, the British had reason to regret their prior policy, for Turkey simply closed the straits to commercial as well as military shipping. This blocked the shipment of supplies to Russia's southern ports—the only ones that were not icebound much of the year. Furthermore, Allied efforts to force open the straits at the Dardanelles and on the Gallipoli peninsula were bloody failures, resulting in the continuing inability of England and France to supply Russia adequately. This has been viewed as one important element leading to Russia's ultimate collapse in World War I.

Actually, under the pressures of war, a secret treaty was signed in London in 1915, which provided that Russia would obtain possession of both the straits and Constantinople. Such an arrangement would have fueled the fires of Turkish nationalism, and it seems doubtful that it could have lasted. But it never went into effect because the 1915 secret treaty was repudiated by Russia after the

revolution of 1917. Thus while the 1871 treaty was still legally in force, the political situation affecting the straits was again in flux as World War I came to an end.

This is illustrated by the difficulties attendant on reaching a settlement with Turkey. By the Armistice of Mudros (1918), which terminated Turkey's participation in the war, the straits were once again reopened. Officially, the reopening of the straits was to facilitate Allied occupation and pacification of Turkey; but it actually was employed largely to ship Allied aid to anti-Bolshevik forces in the Caucasus and Crimea. Troops from Britain, France, and Italy occupied strategic points in Turkey, and the Allies permitted Greek landings at Smyrna and elsewhere. What might have been foreseen happened; the Turks resisted and rallied to the standard of revolt raised in eastern Anatolia by Mustafa Kemal Pasha, later to be known as Kemal Ataturk.

When in August 1919 a peace treaty between Turkey and the Allies was arranged at Sèvres, the Turks were infuriated. The straits were to be internationalized, the adjoining territory demilitarized, and Allied occupation was to be permanent. The secret wartime agreements, which would have carved up much of Turkish territory, were to come into effect. Turkey was to surrender its sovereignty over practically all of its non-Turkish populations.

These onerous terms fanned the fires of indignation even higher among the Turkish nationalists, who refused to accept the Treaty of Sèvres, organized a new government, and launched a diplomatic offensive. They won Soviet disavowal of Sèvres and Italian and French withdrawals from Turkish territory, and defeated the Greeks and drove them off the Anatolian mainland. Subsequently, the major powers invited Greece and Turkey to a conference in order to draft a new treaty.

The Lausanne conference of 1922–1923 was notable because it included Turkish delegates, which meant that the settlement that emerged was the only World War I peace treaty that was negotiated rather than imposed. The first draft was rejected by the Turks, but three months later a second draft was accepted. Insofar as the straits were concerned, the Treaty of Lausanne specifically recognized the principle of freedom of navigation and transit by sea and air of the Dardanelles, the Sea of Marmara, and the Bosporus in time of peace. The same would prevail in wartime when Turkey was a neutral. If Turkey was a belligerent, she had to allow freedom of navigation to neutral merchant ships and civil aircraft, provided these did not carry contraband. Also as a belligerent, Turkey would have the right to prevent enemy vessels from using the straits. Both shores of the Dardanelles and the Bosporus were to be demilitarized, as were the islands off the entrance to the Dardanelles and all islands in the Sea of Marmara, except one known as Emir Ali Adasi.

An International Straits Commission—composed of representatives from Britain, France, Italy, and Turkey—was retained from the earlier Sèvres treaty. It was deprived, however, of calling on Allied military intervention should it decide that the security of the straits was threatened, as Sèvres provided. The Allied maritime powers that signed the Lausanne convention guaranteed the security of the straits under the general aegis of the League of Nations.

The straits commission, which reported to the Council of the League of Nations, was charged with defining the precise boundaries of the demilitarized zones and verifying the destruction of fortifications within the zones. Once these conditions were met, the demilitarization terms were to be self-enforcing; that is, the nations affected—Turkey, Greece, and Bulgaria—were responsible for continued fulfillment of their pledges. After some apparent internal dissension, the commission reported to the Council on 16 November 1925 that the initial demilitarization of the straits had been accomplished.

The commission also was engaged in carrying out the main arms control provisions of the transit terms regarding warships and military aircraft. The "right of free passage" to warships was revised at Lausanne to allow a non-littoral power to send through the straits into the Black Sea a naval force that was not greater than that of the most powerful littoral fleet. In practice this meant that each of the Allies could put warships into the Black Sea equal to the entire Russian fleet. Even if the Russian fleet was disarmed, the non-littoral powers reserved "the right to send into Black Sea, at all times and under all circumstances, a force of not more than three ships, of which no individual ship shall exceed 10,000 tons."

While the Soviets initially refused to provide the commission with figures regarding the composition of their Black Sea fleet, they later changed their mind. The decision to cooperate came about because they feared that the commission, which was charged with determining the size of the Russian fleet, might employ inprecise data and set the figure too high, thus permitting each of the Allies to send a larger naval force through the straits than accurate figures would authorize.

Thus, after overcoming temporary difficulties, the arms control measures affecting demilitarization and transit were fully operational by early 1926. During the decade the Lausanne convention was in effect, according to Richard Dean Burns and Donald Urquidi, the execution of the terms may be summarized as follows:

First, while rumors were occasionally circulated that Turkey was clandestinely remilitarizing its demilitarized zones, there is no reliable evidence that any important or systematic violations took place; *second,* the treaty was adhered to by all other Powers with only minor and relatively insignificant infractions; [and] *third,* while violations of the treaty were few and unimportant, serious difficulties did arise between the Straits Commission and the Turkish Government over the interpretation of the treaty. (Burns and Urquidi, vol. 2, p. 128)

Inherent in the demilitarization of the straits was an assumption that the League of Nations would be an effective guarantor of Turkish security, and that general disarmament would be achieved, thus reducing Turkey's strategic vulnerability. To the extent that the League's pursuit of general disarmament remained a distant hope, the Turkish government demanded its prewar right to fortify the straits.

The Turks began to sound out the other powers about a revision of the demilitarization terms, and finally in 1936 they laid before the Lausanne signatory states and the League a formal request relating to the nonfortification of the Dardanelles and the demilitarized zones. The very fact that Turkey had approached the international community in this fashion redounded to its credit, as it was in such marked contrast to the actions of Italy and Germany, which had employed force to challenge the status quo.

Consequently, when an international conference met in Montreux, Switzerland, in July 1936, it approved a new convention authorizing Turkey to proceed immediately with the fortification of the straits (as well as the Thracian frontier and the Aegean islands). The Soviet Union was interested in reducing the presence of non-littoral warships in the Black Sea and, apparently, working with the Turks succeeded in changing the Lausanne terms in this regard. And finally, the straits commission was disbanded, its functions transferred to the Turkish government. The 1936 convention was in force when World War II broke out.

Given the intimate connection of the straits with the imperial interests of Great Britain and Russia, with to a perhaps lesser extent other major European powers, and with Turkey's national security, it is not surprising that the attempts at demilitarization met with only moderate success and duration. Yet the various straits regimes were perceived as reassuring at the time, and to that extent may be said to have contributed to stability in eastern Europe.

The Strait of Magellan
Demilitarization of the Strait of Magellan in 1881 grew out of the border disputes between Argentina and Chile. Located at the southernmost tip of South America, the straits became an object of contention in 1843 when Chileans founded the town of Punta Arenas there, and subsequently claimed the Straits of Magellan, the Patagonia, and Tierra del Fuego as their own. It was not until the 1870s that Argentina was able to press its demands for a favorable settlement of the southern boundary controversy.

Negotiations between the two nations began in 1876, when the Argentinians proposed a compromise dividing the disputed territory between them and establishing the straits as a *mare liberum*. Chile, however, initially rejected the suggestion. In 1879 a tentative agreement was reached between the two protagonists, along the lines of Argentina's original suggestion that would have neutralized the strait. This time it was the Argentine congress that rejected the proposed accord.

Assisted by the mediation of two United States diplomats—General Thomas O. Osborn, minister to Argentina, and Thomas A. Osborn, minister to Chile—the Treaty of 1881 gradually took shape. On 6 June after several telegraphic exchanges, General Osborn wired his colleague the Argentine version of Article V: "The Straits of Magellan are to be neutralized forever and their free navigation insured to flags of all nations; and it will be forbidden to raise on either side of their coast fortifications or military establishments."

The Chileans countered with their version of the article: "The waters of the Straits are neutralized and free navigation therein insured to the Flags of all nations; no works of defense will be allowed to be raised that may impede . . . free passage through the canal." They were concerned that the Argentine language might impede the construction of "works

for defense which without at all threatening the free navigation of the waters of the Straits would serve as a protection and source of security" to the distant Chilean residents.

The treaty signed on 23 July 1881 contained language that conformed closely to the Chilean version. And in subsequent years Article V has withstood the test of time—there have been no charges of violations.

The Suez Canal
The interoceanic canals that were dug in the late nineteenth and early twentieth centuries were constructed primarily for reasons of commerce, but they quickly assumed strategic importance as well. Thus the Suez Canal, for example, was never demilitarized because, as J. H. Marshall-Cornwall has written, it formed such a vital link between Great Britain and its Asian dominions that "it is difficult to envisage any international pact which, unsupported by military force, would suffice to guarantee its security" (Marshall-Cornwall, p. 67). Nevertheless, an international convention signed at Constantinople in 1888 sought to neutralize the Suez Canal and immunize it from conflict. It provided that the canal would always be free and open, in war or peace, to all commercial vessels. Nor was the canal ever to be subjected to the right of blockade. Furthermore, the convention provided that the canal would remain open in time of war to the warships of combatants, and that no right of war, no act of hostility, and no act designed to obstruct its free navigation was to be committed in the canal or in its ports of access, or within a radius of three marine miles from those ports, even if the Ottoman Empire was one of the belligerents.

A Franco-British Agreement of 1904 relative to Egypt and Morocco seemed to modify the provisions set forth above, inasmuch as it recognized Britain's responsibility for protecting the Suez Canal zone. During both world wars, Britain took the position that the right of navigation of the Suez was subordinate to the necessities of defense.

In 1922 the British, having in mind a Turkish attempt during World War I to interfere with navigation in the Suez Canal, declared that the security of British imperial communications in Egypt was entirely reserved to British discretion. In so doing they were merely stating explicitly what had in fact been the case all along, namely that the canal was a key link in the worldwide power system that Britain had constructed, and she meant to keep it under her control.

The Panama Canal If the Suez Canal was vital to Britain, the Panama Canal could be said to be equally vital to the United States. After all, the canal's construction, which eliminated the long voyage around Cape Horn, not only facilitated seaborne commerce, but allowed U.S. naval vessels to be shifted far more quickly from one coast to the other should the need arise.

Nevertheless, the negotiations preceding the construction of the canal contained several gestures in the direction of neutralization and even demilitarization. Thus as early as 1850, at a time when it appeared that British interests might participate in the building and ownership of the canal, the Clayton-Bulwer Treaty between the United States and Great Britain provided that neither country would ever erect or maintain any fortifications commanding such a canal, or occupy, fortify, colonize, or assume control over Nicaragua, Costa Rica, the Mosquito Coast, or any part of Central America. Also, both parties agreed that neither would seek exclusive control over the proposed canal.

Fifty years later, when Britain no longer entertained ambitions to participate in the construction or governance of a Central American canal, the Clayton-Bulwer Treaty was superseded by the first Hay-Pauncefote Treaty, which granted the United States the sole right to construct and control the canal. The aspiration to neutralization was maintained by adopting as a basis the same rules that could be found in the Constantinople convention of 1888 for the Suez Canal. There was also a provision in Article II, paragraph 7 of the Hay-Pauncefote Treaty that no fortifications would be built commanding the canal or adjacent waters. However, that very same paragraph also stipulated that the United States could "maintain ... military police along the canal ... to protect it against lawlessness and disorder." No numerical limitation was placed on these military police. Herein lay the opening for the eventual militarization of the canal.

Within two years there was another Hay-Pauncefote Treaty that removed the nonfortification clause, but appeared to suggest that the new canal would be both demilitarized and neutralized. Thus Article III of this second treaty contained a section providing that the canal should never be blockaded, nor any right of war or act of hostility be committed within it. Once again, however, the United States was given the right to maintain military police along the canal. Furthermore, the guarantee of freedom of navigation now omitted the phrase "in time of war as in time of peace." This meant that the United States was reserving the right to close the canal to ships of any nation with which it might be at war. Moreover the treaty gave the United States the right to build, control, police, and protect the canal, seemingly opening ample avenues for U.S. militarization of the facility.

That the United States had the right to fortify canal was vigorously asserted by Theodore Roosevelt, who was its political architect. But such an assertion was unnecessary, given the Hay-Bunau-Varilla Treaty signed with the compliant government of Panama in 1903. This was the treaty by which the United States acquired the perpetual and unrestricted use, occupation, and control of the ten-mile-wide (16-kilometer) canal zone, with the right to employ its armed forces for the protection of the canal, the ships using it, and the railways and other auxiliary works that were a part of it. This treaty also gave the United States the right to fortify the canal.

Thus, from the time it opened in 1914 the Panama Canal has not been demilitarized. Rather it was considered the linchpin of any strategy for the defense both of the United States and its western hemisphere interests. As such, the canal remained fortified and garrisoned until the United States turned it over to Panama in 1977; the treaties were implemented in 1979.

ISLANDS

Åland Islands Convention of 1921 The Åland Islands Convention of 1921 is notable because it represented the first and perhaps the most successful effort of the League of Nations in the area of demilitarization. The Åland (Ahvenanmaa) Islands, an archipelago in the Gulf of Bothnia, had been a Swedish possession for hundreds of years, but were ceded to Russia following Sweden's defeat by that country in 1808–1809.

Russia, following its defeat in the Crimean War, agreed in the Treaty of Paris in 1856 not to fortify these islands, or maintain any military or naval establishment there. But Russia chafed under this obligation, and after World War I broke out she occupied the islands and constructed fortifications there. The Russian government intended to press for the removal of prohibitions she had violated as part of any postwar settlement, but her collapse rendered this moot. In the Treaty of Brest-Litovsk, the new Soviet government gave up all claims to the islands and agreed to demolish the fortifications the czarist government had built. But this, too, became moot when Germany's defeat resulted in the annulment of the Treaty of Brest-Litovsk.

In the aftermath of the war, the question of the Åland Islands became contentious. The Soviet Union was no longer interested in the islands, but Sweden and Finland were. Sweden claimed the group by virtue of its prior possession and the fact that the islands were inhabited by Swedish speakers, and Finland by virtue of the fact that as a duchy under Swedish and then Russian rule, it had administered them. Acrimony between the claimants escalated to the point that Britain felt impelled, under Article 11 of the Covenant, to bring the matter to the Council of the League of Nations in 1920. The Council thoroughly investigated the claims of the contending parties and awarded the islands to Finland in 1921, on the condition that said islands be demilitarized and neutralized, a condition, incidentally, that both claimants had accepted in advance.

This decision was confirmed by the Åland Islands Convention, signed by ten interested powers (but not the Soviet Union) in October of 1921. That convention formulated the specific rules implementing the demilitarization and neutralization policies set forth by the League. By the terms of the convention, Finland undertook not to fortify the islands. In addition, no military, naval, and air installations could be established on the islands, nor could any troops be stationed there. If exceptional circumstances demanded it, Finland could send troops into the archipelago, but they had to withdraw once order was restored. In something of an innovation, Article 4 of the convention prohibited the manufacture, import, transport, and reexport of arms in this demilitarized area. It also provided that no military, naval, or air force of any other power could enter the demilitarized zone. This prevented military overflights by other countries. Finland was permitted such flights, although its aircraft were forbidden to land on the islands except in cases of *force majeure*. Finland was also granted the exclusive right to sail "one or two light surface warships" into the island waters from time to time, which meant that it could not station any warships there permanently.

However, the agreement stated that if "important special circumstances" demanded it, Finland could send in additional warships, but the total displacement of these vessels could not exceed 6,000 tons. The Finnish government was also empowered to permit the entry of one other warship of one other nation at a time. Despite all these restrictions, the convention reaffirmed freedom of innocent passage through the territorial waters of the islands.

A special feature of the Åland Islands Convention is that it provided for neutralization as well as demilitarization. Article 6 stated that in time of war the islands would be considered a neutral zone and were not to be used, either directly or indirectly, for any purpose connected with military operations. To preserve that neutrality, Finland was given the right, in the event of war affecting the Baltic Sea, to lay mines in Åland Island waters on a temporary basis. In the event such a situation arose, Finland was to immediately refer the matter to the League of Nations.

This invocation of the League to guarantee the immunization of the Ålands in the event of war was reinforced and expanded in Article 7. Under its terms the League Council became the body with the power to decide what countermeasures would be taken if a signatory to the convention violated its terms. Thus the League, and by implication all its members, was invested with the power to enforce the convention. Going one step further, the agreement departed from the League Covenant's requirement of unanimity, and provided that the convention's contracting parties would be entitled to take any enforcement measures recommended by a two thirds vote of the Council, with the vote of the country accused of violating the convention not being counted. This provision was a significant innovation, and consumed more time and effort at the conference than the main concerns of demilitarization and neutralization.

Public reaction in Sweden and Finland to the treaty was markedly different. In Finland much of the public and many officials viewed the agreement with suspicion and misgivings from the beginning; while in Sweden it was generally viewed favorably—at least until 1938. Finnish proposals for remilitarization became particularly insistent during the mid-1930s as it became evident that the League had lost its ability to guarantee the island's neutrality. The Finns frequently urged the Swedes to join them in a campaign to seek treaty revision, but the Swedes were uninterested until late 1937 and early 1938.

In 1938 the two governments entered into talks that eventually resulted in an agreement which, granted the approval of the other signatories to the 1921 convention and interested parties, would have led to the refortification and remilitarization of the Åland Islands. Although all signatories granted their approval, the USSR, an interested party, formally announced its opposition to the proposed revisions on 31 May 1939.

In spite of the Russo-Finnish War, the subsequent German invasion of the USSR, and the Finns' reentry into the war on the side of Germany, the neutrality of the Ålands apparently was honored during World War II. Whether this was the result of the convention's demilitarization clauses is impossible to determine.

Spitsbergen Archipelago

The Svalbard [Spitsbergen] Treaty of 9 February 1920 resolved the dispute that had broken out between Norway, Sweden, Holland, and England over possession of the Arctic islands by awarding them to Norway on the condition that they be permantly defortified. The initial dispute arose in the early 1900s largely over the undefined status of the islands.

Devoid of population, for centuries the islands were considered a no-man's-land—legally, a *terra nullius*. All countries were seen as having equal commercial and economic rights, but no country had exclusive sovereign authority. The archipelago is made up of one large island (West Spitsbergen) of some fifteen thousand square miles (39,000 square kilometers) and three smaller islands of between one thousand and four thousand square miles (2,600 and 10,400 square kilometers), plus a number of islets. The main island is completely ice free for three months out of the year and, because a branch of the Gulf Stream touches the west coast of the island, it can be fairly easily reached through thin ice for an additional three months. This makes West Spitsbergen the most navigable area in the Arctic.

Early in the twentieth century large coal and iron deposits were discovered there, which brought U.S., English, and Norwegian entrepreneurs to the islands. Additionally, Spitsbergen—located 360 nautical miles north of Norway and Sweden, between Greenland on the west and Franz Josef Land on the east—began to take on strategic significance. While no military action took place there during World War I, several naval officers thought the islands would be ideal for a naval base, especially for submarines.

During the war, however, most of the economic activity on Spitsbergen ceased. The most significant events that took place were the purchase by Norway of almost all of the American-owned mines on the islands and the total withdrawal of the Russians from the area. This left Norway with the greatest interests there.

Norway's claim to the islands was advanced, almost single-handedly, by its minister to Paris, Frederik Jarlsberg, who brought the matter to the attention of the Paris Peace Conference in 1919. No objection was raised by any nation to the idea of permanently demilitarizing the islands, consequently Article 9 of the Spitsbergen Treaty read:

Subject to the rights and duties resulting from the admission of Norway to the League of Nations, Norway undertakes not to create nor to allow the establishment of any naval base in the [archipelago] . . . and not to construct any fortification in said territories, which may never be used for warlike purpose.

Thus the arms control provisions were limited to defortification and did not, properly speaking, introduce demilitarization.

Despite the lack of international supervisory machinery, the arms control provisions were apparently upheld during the interwar years. No official complaint of evasions was ever submitted and the press reported no violations of the arms control provisions. A post–World War II study by John J. Teal, Jr., noted (p. 263), "For a quarter century Norway has scrupulously honored the treaty. No fortifications have been built in Svalbard [Spitsbergen]." (During World War II, however, the Germans did attempt to establish a naval base in the islands, and in the postwar period the Americans were suspicious of Russian "economic" missions and "commercial" endeavors on the islands.)

Pacific Mandated Islands

While the Washington naval treaty (1922) was primarily concerned with the limitation of naval armaments, it also contained a provision that banned further fortification or the establishment of additional bases in certain areas of the Pacific. This provision, Article XIX, simply stated that the status quo was to be maintained with respect to the fortifications and naval bases in the Pacific Ocean of the United States, the British Empire, and Japan.

There were exceptions, of course. For the United States these exceptions were the islands adjacent to the U.S. coast, to Alaska, the Panama Canal zone, and the Hawaiian Islands. For Britain the exceptions were the islands adjacent to the coast of Canada, the Commonwealth of Australia and its territories, and New Zealand. In the case of Japan, Article XIX did not specify any exemptions. The status quo limitation was to apply, in the case of the United States, to the rest of its insular possessions in the Pacific and those it might acquire. For Britain, the limitation was to apply to Hong Kong and the insular possessions Britain might hold or acquire in the Pacific east of the meridian of 110° east longitude. In the case of Japan it was specified that the status quo was to be maintained with respect to the Kuril Islands, the Bonin Islands, Amami-Oshima, the Luchu Islands, Formosa (Taiwan) and the Pescadores, and any insular territories or possessions that Japan might subsequently acquire.

The provision that no new fortifications or naval bases were to be established could also be interpreted to mean, by implication, that naval repair and maintenance facilities could not be increased, nor could coast defenses be strengthened in the specified areas. But this did not mean that the customary repair and replacement activities of existing installations in those specified areas could not be continued.

There were charges, during the 1930s, that the Japanese had violated this provision and had sought to fortify their League-mandated islands—the Marianas, Carolines, and Marshalls—which cut across the United States' sea communications between Hawaii and the Philippines. These charges were not verified during the 1930s, nor have subsequent studies completely resolved the issue; however, the episode did raise some fundamental questions.

Records indicate that airfields, harbor improvements, communication facilities, and fuel storage depots were under construction; but were these intended for military use or, as the Japanese claimed, for commercial use? Had international inspectors conducted an on-site survey of the islands during the late 1930s, would they have been able to make the distinction?

A cursory review of Article XIX would suggest that the United States and Great Britain gained more from this status quo than did Japan. Nevertheless, when the Japanese eventually terminated the Washington treaty, their action was based essentially on their demand for naval parity, and they did not indicate any dissatisfaction with the demilitarization provisions of Article XIX.

LAKES AND SEAS

Rush-Bagot Agreement   The Great Lakes demilitarization agreement, affecting the United States, Great Britain, and later Canada, has been in existence since 1817. The agreement between the United States, Great Britain, and subsequently Canada for demilitarization of the Great Lakes, did over time evolve into the demilitarization of the entire United States–Canadian border. Mutuality of interest established by practice and precedent, but not without violations of the letter of the original agreement, made this possible.

When the War of 1812 came to an end, mutual suspicion between the combatants—the United States on one side and the British and Canadians on the other—remained high. Both sides had substantial naval forces on the Great Lakes, and the British planned to build enough additional warships to maintain supremacy. The Canadians especially feared that the United States, which had launched an abortive invasion of their territory during the war, might try again.

The United States government, which had no desire to engage in a costly naval race on the Great Lakes if it could be avoided, instructed its minister to Great Britain, John Quincy Adams, to inquire if the British were interested in a mutual demilitarization of the Great Lakes. The British proved receptive, for two reasons: first, the United States could bring superior local resources to bear if it came to an arms race; and second, the expensive warships built for the Great Lakes would be useless to the Royal Navy in supporting Britain's other interests on the high seas. The United States wanted breathing room, and the British obliged. Mutual interests were served. But the Canadians, who remained highly suspicious of U.S. acquisitiveness, were disappointed at the outcome.

Contrary to popular belief, the Rush-Bagot agreement did not remove all naval warships from the Great Lakes. Each side was permitted to retain a number of small, lightly armed ships for enforcing revenue regulations. Dismantled vessels and discarded naval installations were mothballed, not destroyed. The U.S. Congress, angered by the manner in which Britain permitted the use of British and colonial ports for the construction, provisioning, and repair of Confederate commerce raiders, actually passed a resolution authorizing termination of the agreement in November 1864. A short time later, however, notice of termination was withdrawn. It was not until 1871, when the Treaty of Washington settled a longstanding fisheries dispute, as well as the Alabama claims, that the Canadians permitted their border fortifications to fall into disrepair, and the unguarded frontier became a reality.

What is important to remember is the attitude of confidence that this long-lived and successful agreement has engendered. Canada and the United States have had their disputes over the years, and at times the relations between the two countries have soured. But the idea of resolving any such disputes between the two by military force is almost unthinkable. The basic reason for this is what one might call the habits of mind developed along both sides of the border as the result of years of demilitarization, a demilitarization that began with an agreement covering only the Great Lakes.

Demilitarization of the Black Sea, 1856–1871

With the Treaty of Paris of 30 March 1856, which ended the Crimean War, a new regime was instituted that not only neutralized the Black Sea, but demilitarized both its Russian and Turkish shores as well. That the negotiators were also concerned about the status of the Turkish straits—the entrance to the Black Sea—is expanded upon in the straits section above.

Article XI of the treaty stated: "The Black Sea is neutralized; its waters and ports thrown open to the mercantile marine of every nation, are formally and in perpetuity interdicted to the flag of war." Article XIII provided that, "the Black Sea being neutralized . . . H.M. the Emperor of all the Russias, and His Imperial Majesty the Sultan, engage not to establish or maintain upon that coast any military-maritime Arsenal." The treaty went on to limit the number and size of the warships both countries could maintain in the Black Sea.

In stark contrast to the successful Great Lakes agreement stands the attempt to neutralize and "denavalize" the Black Sea in the Treaty of Paris. The latter was doomed from the start for at least two reasons. First, just as the Black Sea was linked inextricably to the Turkish straits geographically, so its status was tied directly to the regime governing the straits at that particular time. With the straits as the focal point of European rivalries, a demilitarized regime proved impossible to maintain.

Second, the Black Sea's neutralization was imposed on Russia by the victors in the Crimean War.

The czar's government always felt that it was an illegal abridgement of Russian sovereignty, and denounced it at the first opportunity. The fate of the Treaty of Paris stands as an example of the ultimate failure of demilitarization and neutralization when such policies are forcefully imposed by the victors upon the vanquished, rather than negotiated with a sense of mutual benefits.

Yet, one analyst, Winfried Baumgart, has concluded that the "neutralization of the Black Sea through demilitarization soothed a 150-year-old Ottoman-Russian canker. Until 1871 the Black Sea remained pacified. Its neutralization is the only case in history of the pacification of an entire sea" (*The Peace of Paris, 1856*, p. 115).

BORDERS AND FRONTIER AREAS

The unfortified United States–Canadian frontier (discussed above)—an outgrowth of the Rush-Bagot agreement—is probably the best known example of a demilitarized frontier. Perhaps the next most significant example is the unfortified zone created in 1905 between Norway and Sweden.

As World War I drew to a close the new Communist government in the Soviet Union adopted the technique of demilitarization as an inexpensive means of providing a measure of security along its northern and southern borders. A rather volatile situation had developed in the Baltic territories of Estonia, Latvia, and Lithuania, as German, Russian, and indigenous forces fought for control. Eventually, these three territories gained their independence and international recognition. A somewhat similar situation occurred in Finland, resulting in the independence of that country as well. Although these countries had been under Russian rule, Estonia and Finland were able to reach demilitarization agreements with the Soviet government in 1920, while Finland and Russia concluded an additional one in 1922. Additionally, the Soviet government reached agreements with Turkey regarding its southern border and the straits.

Convention of Karlstadt

Whereas the North American Rush-Bagot agreement was reached in the aftermath of a war, the Scandinavian agreement was the product of negotiations undertaken to ward off or eliminate the possibility of conflict.

As the year 1905 began, Norway's status was that of a separate national entity, yet united with Sweden under the Swedish Crown. The Norwegians had long resented this arrangement and had demonstrated their feelings by erecting a series of fortifications that covered possible invasion routes from Sweden. In 1905 these fortifications took on added importance when the Norwegian parliament ended the union with Sweden and the Swedish parliament subsequently recognized the independence of Norway. Sweden, presumably expecting no invasion, did not fortify its side of the border. Sweden also believed that its army was sufficiently strong to defeat any attack that might come from Norway.

The idea that differences between the two Scandinavian nations might eventuate in a clash of arms may seem farfetched today, but in 1905 it did not appear out of the question. That possibility was put to rest, however, when the two nations finally signed the Convention of Karlstadt in October 1905, a month after Sweden recognized Norway's independence. This convention set the tone for the more peaceful atmosphere that has characterized relations between the two neighbors ever since.

At the outset of negotiations the Swedes demanded that the Norwegians dismantle the border fortifications, but such a blanket demand was unacceptable to Norway. Eventually, both parties agreed on the concept of a fortified zone on each side of the frontier. This zone ran for about two hundred miles (320 kilometers) north from Skagerrak and averaged only ten miles (16 kilometers) in width on each side of the border. However, given the rugged terrain along the Swedish-Norwegian frontier, this narrow barrier was more effective in deterring conflict than might have been the case had the ground been more suited to military operations. Apparently reassured by the establishment of the demilitarized zone, the Norwegians agreed to destroy three fortresses within it. One fortress, called Kongsvinger, was excluded from the zone, but could not be strengthened in buildings, armaments, or personnel. The Swedes, with no defenses in the zone, agreed to erect none.

The zone established by the Karlstadt convention was defined in strong language. It was to be perpetual; its demilitarized character was to be absolute. Military operations could not be conducted in the zone, nor originate there. No military forces were to be concentrated there except those necessary to maintain public order or assist in case of disaster. There appears to have been no evasions of this agreement over the years.

The Russo-Finnish Treaty of 1920   The 14 October 1920 Treaty of Tartu (Dorpat) between Finland and Russia demilitarized Finnish waters in the Arctic Ocean, the Gulf of Finland, and Lake Ladoga, a large body of water bordering both countries. In somewhat vague language, the two countries bound themselves to support, in principle, the neutralization of the Gulf of Finland, the Finnish Sea, and the entire Baltic, and to contribute to the realization of such measures.

The agreement stated that Finland could maintain warships or armed vessels of less than one hundred tons in the waters contiguous to her Arctic shores in unlimited numbers, and no more than 15 warships with a maximum displacement of up to two hundred tons. A number of islands in the Gulf of Finland were to be "militarily neutralized" or demilitarized, which meant that no fortifications, batteries, observation posts, and other specified categories of military installations could be maintained there. As an exception, the Finns could install observation posts on two islands. Both countries agreed not to maintain forces or offensive armaments on Lake Ladoga or its banks. But Russia was given the right to send warships into the navigable waterways of the interior by canals along the southern banks of Ladoga, or upon the southern part of the lake itself, should the canals be impeded.

With the sole exception of the limitations on offensive capabilities on Lake Ladoga, which will be discussed next, this treaty, like the one with Estonia, was heavily weighted in Russia's favor. Finnish coastal forts, whose guns commanded the approaches to the Russian naval base at Kronstadt and which could target the base itself, were dismantled. Leningrad's security was considerably enhanced. For these concessions, the Soviet Union gave up virtually nothing.

However, in a separate convention in 1922, both the Finns and the Russians, but primarily the former, gained from the establishment of a demilitarized zone on both sides of the Karelian frontier between Lake Ladoga and the Arctic Ocean. That agreement brought a measure of security for almost two decades to an area that had been the scene of considerable tension.

In October 1939 the Soviet Union demanded that the security of Leningrad be improved by a Finnish grant of additional territory on the Karelian isthmus, the allowance of a Russian naval base on the southern coast of Finland, and the cession of some islands in the Gulf of Finland. Unable to obtain much diplomatic support from abroad, the Finns resisted and war broke out on 30 November 1939. The fighting lasted for one hundred days and in the end the Russians—not without embarrassment and serious military setbacks—got their naval base and substantially more territory than they had originally demanded. With World War II on the horizon, the Soviets apparently felt that annexation offered greater security than territorial demilitarization.

The Russo-Estonian Treaty of 1920 The peace treaty between Estonia and Soviet Russia of February 1920, also signed at Tartu (Dorpat), contained a demilitarized zone drawn along the land frontier. Additionally, the large lakes Peipus and Pskov, which separated the two countries for about eighty miles (128 kilometers), were demilitarized. No armed vessels were to be permitted on those lakes, with the exception of five customs patrol boats whose armament was strictly limited.

While both parties undertook not to station troops in the zone, with the exception of those necessary to maintain order, the treaty prohibitions seemed to fall more heavily on Estonia. It consented not to construct fortifications, for example; a restriction not placed on Soviet Russia. Estonia also agreed not to establish bases or depots for the use of any vessels or airplanes in the demilitarized area; again, no such provision applied to Soviet Russia.

DEMILITARIZATION, NEUTRALIZATION, AND THE LEAGUE

One might have expected that the League of Nations, as a body charged with the responsibility of maintaining peace in the 1920s and 1930s, would have displayed great interest in fostering agreements for demilitarization and neutralization. But its record in this respect is rather mixed. On the positive side was its contribution to the success of the Åland Islands Convention.

Yet other attempts to raise the issue of demilitarization and assign the League a role in its implementation were generally met with skepticism or outright rejection. A prime example can be found in the fate that befell the memorandum of Lord Robert Cecil to the Temporary Mixed Commission for the Reduction of Armaments in 1923. The Cecil memorandum suggested that the establishment of demilitarized zones would facilitate the definition of aggression, particularly if these zones were controlled by commissioners appointed by the League.

Cecil specified zones of thirty miles (48 kilometers) at least, with no fortifications or other military installations therein. Neutral commissioners would be appointed by the League Council to reside within the zones, with powers to inspect and investigate. There was a provision to prevent the use of railways in such zones for purposes of aggression and to dismantle those railways that were constructed purely for military purposes. Cecil argued that the establishment of these zones would offer a tangible guarantee against sudden aggression. His proposal would also have permitted the establishment of a permanent international police force within those zones where there was a grave danger of hostilities between the bordering states.

This proposal was forwarded by the Temporary Mixed Commission to the League's Permanent Advisory Commission on Naval, Military, and Air Questions, where it was unanimously rejected. That opinion was based essentially on military grounds, such as the argument that the proposal put the armies of a smaller state at a disadvantage, and that it ignored the growing importance of airpower. This advice prompted the Temporary Mixed Commission to recommend to the League Assembly in rather vague and confusing language that such zones be considered as one method of dealing with extant disputes, rather than as a permanent peacekeeping mechanism.

That view found further expression in Article 9 of a draft Treaty of Mutual Assistance submitted by the League Assembly to interested governments in 1923. It provided that any contracting party might negotiate, through the League Council, with one or more neighboring countries for the establishment of demilitarized zones. It was the Council's responsibility, in cooperation with the interested parties, to make certain that any such zones did not call for unilateral military sacrifices by any such parties.

This formulation was unacceptable to many countries and was rejected in July 1924.

Yet another attempt to wrestle with the problem of demilitarized zones was advanced in 1924, in a Protocol for the Pacific Settlement of International Disputes. This protocol recommended that demilitarized zones be adopted as a means of preventing aggression and identifying as the aggressor any state that might violate them. This proposal also floundered and was eventually abandoned.

The Locarno Pact of 1925 included two provisions relative to demilitarization: one demilitarizing German territory west of a line drawn fifty kilometers (31 miles) east of the Rhine, and the other stipulating that if armed forces are assembled in the demilitarized zone, the mutual guarantees of non-aggression between Germany and France and Germany and Belgium would not apply. But the League of Nations exercised no control or supervision over the zone.

Although both the League Council and Assembly discussed demilitarization proposals on subsequent occasions, none were pushed vigorously, and none were implemented. The League's ambiguity concerning the concept was manifest. This has been attributed to the influence of the Locarno Pact, which meant the endorsement of the unilateral disarmament of Germany by Europe's principal powers, to the possible influence of Italian opposition to the whole idea, and to the widespread reluctance among League members to have the organization assume responsibility for the supervision and control of such zones. As a result, it may be fair to say that the potential value of demilitarized zones never received a fair trial during the League's existence.

AN ASSESSMENT

As one might expect, a historical assessment of demilitarized zones and neutralized territories yields quite mixed results. The demilitarized United States–Canadian border undoubtedly produced habits of mind on both sides of the forty-ninth parallel that have been conducive to the settlement of disputes around a negotiating table rather than by armed conflict. Yet it cannot be denied that this long demilitarized border developed as it did because both neighbors believed it to be in their national interest. The security of each nation was enhanced probably more than it would have been if large numbers of troops faced each other along the frontier. The same general comments would seem to apply to the neutralized Swedish–Norwegian border zone. What began as a compromise that served the interests of both states evolved into a regime that epitomized their peaceful relationship and a common predilection for employing international machinery to settle controversies. The long neutrality of Switzerland illustrates how useful that status can be, not only to the Swiss themselves but to Europe as a whole.

But if, in the period under review, there were instances of demilitarization and neutralization that both responded to national interest and promoted international understanding, there were certainly a number of instances that were failures on both counts. One of these was the Treaty of Paris of 1856 which, as we have seen, was devised more for the purpose of reinforcing England's imperial interests than for providing true demilitarization and neutralization. Rather than effecting any rapprochement between Britain and Russia, it antagonized the latter to the point where termination of the treaty's burdens became a prime object of the nation's foreign policy. Indeed, the history of the Turkish straits question in the nineteenth century is eloquent testimony of the difficulty of constructing a viable demilitarization regime when the vital interests of the parties concerned diverge rather than converge. Also, in contrast to Switzerland, whose neutrality was preserved, there was the example of Belgium, whose neutrality fell victim to Germany's view of military necessity.

Many more examples could be brought forth to illustrate that attempts at demilitarization and neutralization have rendered mixed results. Yet the fact that what has been called geographic disarmament can be traced so far back in history indicates that these techniques have been useful. One reason they were utilized so frequently in the period under review is that there is a certain practicality about them. They are relatively easy to negotiate, as the consequences of demilitarization are relatively easy to assess.

What then may we say as a final assessment of demilitarization and neutralization in the period preceding World War II? Certainly these methods were not a panacea, but neither can they be discounted. Rather, they proved valuable tools when conditions were right, and when they were employed in an equitable manner. When such arrangements were imposed on unwilling parties, they inevitably failed. However, where there was concern with the interests of the parties involved, the arrangements tended to be successful. In such cases they were sometimes able to defuse flash points and in others to help produce a climate of trust that led to long-term peace.

BIBLIOGRAPHY

General Accounts The most comprehensive general treatment, which focuses on the pre-1939 era, is Major General J. H. MARSHALL-CORNWALL's *Geographic Disarmament: A Study of Regional Demilitarization* (London, 1935). Another good treatment, which covers both the period under review and the post–World War II era, is CYRIL E. BLACK, RICHARD A. FALK, KLAUS KNORR, and ORAN R. YOUNG, *Neutralization and World Politics* (Princeton, N.J., 1968). Also useful is LOUIS B. SOHN's "Disarmament and Arms Control by Territories," *Bulletin of the Atomic Scientists* 17 (April 1961): 130–133, reprinted in ERNEST W. LEFEVER, ed., *Arms and Arms Control: A Symposium* (New York, 1962). A useful general discussion by LAURENCE W. MARTIN is "Political Settlements and Arms Control," *Current History* 42 (May 1962): 296–301.

A full treatment is provided in EDGAR W. McINNIS, *The Unguarded Frontier: A History of American-Canadian Relations* (New York, 1942). RAYMOND E. LINDGREN, *Norway-Sweden: Union, Disunion, and Scandinavian Integration* (Princeton, N.J., 1959) contains considerable material on the demilitarization of that border. The study by ANDRÉ SIEGFRIED, *Suez and Panama* (London, 1940), covers developments in the history of those crucial canals.

Specific Treaties RICHARD DEAN BURNS and DONALD URQUIDI, in their study *Disarmament in Perspective, 1919–1939* (Washington, D.C., 1968) provide an excellent discussion in Chapter 8 of Part I and all of Part II of the Russo-Finnish Treaty of October 1920, and of the demilitarization of frontiers, islands, and straits. See also HERBERT TINGSTEN, *The Debate on the Foreign Policy of Sweden, 1918–1939* (1949), which refers to the demilitarization of the Åland Islands; and JOHN J. TEAL, JR., "Europe's Northernmost Frontier," *Foreign Affairs* 29 (January 1951): 263–275, for a discussion of the Spitsbergen treaty.

Rhineland Demilitarization Studies of the Rhineland demilitarization and its termination can be found in JAMES THOMAS EMMERSON, *The Rhineland Crisis, 7 March 1936: A Study in Multilateral Diplomacy* (Ames, Iowa, 1977), and GERHARD L. WEINBERG, *The Foreign Policy of Hitler's Germany: Diplomatic Revolution in Europe, 1933–36* (Chicago, 1970). The neutralization of Belgium is fully explored by DANIEL H. THOMAS, *The Guarantee of Belgian Independence and Neutrality in European Diplomacy, 1830s–1930s* (Kingston, R.I., 1983).

The Eastern Question The always troubling "Eastern Question" is covered in two works with almost identical names, J. A. R. MARRIOTT, *The Eastern Question: An Historical Study in European Diplomacy,* 4th ed. (Oxford, 1947); and M. S. ANDERSON, *The Eastern Question, 1774–1923: A Study in International Relations* (New York, 1966). WINFRIED BAUMGART, *The Peace of Paris, 1856: Studies in War, Diplomacy, and Peacemaking* (Santa Barbara, Calif., 1981) discusses the demilitarization and "denavalization" of the Black Sea at length.

The Kellogg-Briand Pact and the Outlawry of War

JOSEPH PRESTON BARATTA

See also The League of Nations and Disarmament *and* Legal Dimensions of Arms Control and Disarmament. *The* Kellogg-Briand Pact *is excerpted in Volume III.*

"Peace has been proclaimed—that is good, that is much," declared Foreign Minister Aristide Briand of France on signing the Pact of Paris for the Renunciation of War on 27 August 1928. "But it is necessary to organize it. For settlements by force we must substitute judicial settlements. That is the work of the future."

The full organization of peace, in which peaceful means for the solution of international disputes have in practice replaced recourse to war, still remains for the future, but the Kellogg-Briand Pact (also known as the Pact of Paris) must be ranked with the League of Nations as a milestone on humanity's long, hard road toward an effective international security organization. In a 1987 judgment on the pact, international lawyer John Norton Moore argued that while the League only attempted to limit or restrict war, the Kellogg-Briand Pact formally abolished it, thus providing a "normative, substantive emphasis" lacking in the League.

SIGNIFICANCE OF THE PACT

Approved by virtually all the nations (sixty-three) of its day, the pact to renounce war "as an instrument of national policy" declared an end—in principle—to Karl von Clausewitz's tradition of "war" as "a continuation of politics by other means." The Kellogg-Briand Pact did not abolish defensive war or (very important from the point of view of international organization) war for the enforcement of collective security, but it did abolish aggressive war *as a legitimate right of the sovereign state.*

The era of "right of conquest," going back to the ancient Kurgan pastoral invasions and the first conquests of Sumerian civilization, was, after the Great War of 1914–1918, declared at an end. As Secretary of State Henry Stimson wrote in "The Pact of Paris: Three Years of Development" in a special supplement to *Foreign Affairs* (pp. iii–iv) in 1932, the League Covenant and the Kellogg-Briand Pact signal "a revolution in human thought." He continued:

Under its present organization the world simply could not go on recognizing war, with its constantly growing destructiveness, as one of the normal instrumentalities of human life. . . . So the entire central point from which the problem was viewed was changed. War between nations was renounced by the signatories of the Briand-Kellogg Pact. This means that it has become illegal throughout practically the entire world. It is no longer to be the source and subject of rights. It is no longer to be the principle around which the duties, the conduct, and the rights of nations revolve. It is an illegal thing. Hereafter when two nations engage in armed conflict either one or both of them must be wrongdoers—violators of the general treaty. We no longer draw a circle about them and treat them with the punctilios of the duelist's code. Instead we denounce them as lawbreakers.

A year later, when reviewing the Japanese invasion of Manchuria as the first real challenge to the Kellogg-Briand Pact, Stimson still took a long, positive view of the pact. Its appeal not to military enforcement but to public opinion, he wrote in the April 1933 issue of *Foreign Affairs,* laid "the basis of a system of organic law into the development of which the United States could throw its whole weight and strength" (p. 389). He and President Herbert Hoover aimed to make of the pact "a living force of law in the world" (p. 390). Hoover then signed the protocol of the World Court, which he sent to the Senate for ratification in expectation that the Court would develop by its decisions "a harmonious and effective system of international law" (p. 392). This U.S. approach to the World Court, though the Senate rejected it until 1945, when the Statute of the Court was made an integral part of the U.N. Charter, seems in retrospect to mark a high point for the full program of "outlawry, code, and court" of the original outlawrists.

Stimson himself applied the pact in settling a dispute between Russia and China in 1929 and in inducing Japan, following what it called "world-wide odium" (p. 394), to withdraw from Shanghai in May 1932. But the limits of the pact were soon evident in the Manchurian crisis. The League Assembly adopted the "Stimson doctrine" of nonrecognition of the fruits of aggression in early 1932. But when, a year later, the Lytton commission effectively found Japan the aggressor, Tokyo, rather than submit to censure, defiantly withdrew from the League. Germany and Italy soon followed and the world slid toward World War II. All of Stimson's "mobilization of an effective world opinion" (p. 391) was no match for the Axis challenge to peace.

Most diplomats, politicians, and historians have seen the lack of military enforcement powers as a fatal flaw in the Kellogg-Briand Pact. Nevertheless, even as a moral declaration, the pact continued to influence events. It set a precedent for the Saavedra Lamas Treaty of Non-Aggression and Conciliation of 1933, in which Argentina and five other Latin American countries renounced war and provided explicit measures for peaceful resolution. That treaty in turn contributed to the Pan-American movement that later brought about the Charter of the Organization of American States (1948). The pact was also interpreted authoritatively by the International Law Association at its Budapest conference in 1934, contributing to the work of legal publicists.

But most lastingly, the pact's two substantive articles—the one renouncing war as an instrument of national policy, and the other pledging recourse only to peaceful means of settlement—were by 1945 enshrined in the United Nations Charter: In Article 2, paragraph 4, members pledge to refrain from the threat or use of force, and in 2(3) they promise to settle their disputes by peaceful means. The only exceptions allowed are for collective security in Article 1(1) and defense in Article 51.

The Kellogg-Briand Pact was a major source of law for the Nuremberg and Tokyo war crimes trials in 1945–1948. "Crimes against the peace"—planning, initiating, or waging a war of aggression, a war in violation of international treaties, agreements, or assurances—were conceived by reference to the pact, as Justice Jackson made abundantly clear in his opening statement to the International Military Tribunal. He cited the pact as "the re-establishment of the principle that there are unjust wars and that unjust wars are illegal.... This pact altered the legal status of a war of aggression" (*The Case Against the Nazi War Criminals,* p. 75).

Henry Stimson, writing in his vigorous old age in 1947, also drew the connection when discussing the fundamental issue of whether the Nazis were being tried under *ex post facto* laws: "These opinions [that aggressive war has been renounced and that national leaders who launch it are responsible], in large part formally embodied in the Kellogg Pact, are the basis for the law of Nuremberg." He continued:

What happened before World War II was that we lacked the courage to enforce the authoritative decision of the international world. We agreed with the Kellogg Pact that aggressive war must end. We renounced it, and we condemned those who might use it. But it was a moral condemnation only. We thus did not reach the second half of the question: What will you do to an aggressor when you catch him? If we *had* reached it, we should easily have found the right answer. But that answer escaped us, for it implied a duty to catch the criminal, and such a chase meant war. It was the Nazi confidence that we would never chase and catch them, and not a misunderstanding of our opinion of them, that led them to commit their crimes. Our offense was thus that of the man who passed by on the other side. That we have finally recognized our negligence and named the criminals for what they are is a piece of righteousness too long delayed by fear. ... Now this [trial] is a new judicial process, but it is not *ex post facto* law. It is the enforcement of a moral judgment which dates back a generation. (*Foreign Affairs,* January 1947, pp. 183–185)

The Kellogg-Briand Pact, then, by the time of the Nuremberg trials, had led to the concept of individual responsibility for the international crime of waging an aggressive war. One difficulty with this interpretation is that the pact only declared aggressive war illegal; it did not add that such a war was criminal and hence punishable on individual political leaders and military commanders. That step was taken with the Charter of London in August 1945, agreed to by nineteen governments, not including occupied Germany. If any law bearing on the Nuremberg defendants was *ex post facto,* it was the London Charter that set up the tribunal.

But Justice Jackson argued eloquently that international law grows not only by treaties and agreements between nations but also by custom and decision, as the common law does. He cited all the precedents that had declared aggressive war a punishable crime, even though there was some fault with each of them: the Geneva Protocol for the Peaceful Settlement of International Disputes of 1924 (never ratified), the League of Nations Assembly's resolution on aggressive war of 1927 (nonbinding), and the Pan-American Conference's resolution of 1928 (not applicable to Germany).

Public opinion then settled the matter. With the revelation of Nazi offenses against their own people, prisoners, Jews, and others—horrors never before witnessed in modern war—the preponderance of opinion in Allied countries and among pensive Germans like philosopher Karl Jaspers was that the deeds listed in the London Charter were indeed crimes recognizable to any civilized person and hence punishable. Of the three categories of crimes at Nuremberg, war crimes had long been recognized by the laws or customs of war; crimes against the peace were rooted in the Kellogg-Briand Pact, the Locarno Treaty, the Hague Conventions, and many other treaties and assurances of the 1920s and 1930s; and crimes against humanity (including genocide) were the most novel, but no one was punished solely for this offense.

The international legal scholar Quincy Wright argued that a "revolution" in international law occurred between the renunciation of war in the Kellogg-Briand Pact and the first attempt to enforce it in the Nuremberg tribunal. Hitherto, only the state had been a "subject" of international law; now the individual was too. In law, what happened was a general turning away from the assumptive framework of Austinian positivism (named after the nineteenth-century English jurist John Austin), under which the Nazis had operated, back toward that of the Grotian concept of natural law (named after the seventeenth-century Dutch scholar Hugo Grotius). One of the immediate consequences was the flowering of the idea of human rights, beginning with the Universal Declaration of Human Rights in 1948.

Seven "Nuremberg principles," drafted by the U.N.'s International Law Commission, were accepted by the General Assembly in 1950. The first is that "any person who commits an act which constitutes a crime under international law is responsible therefore and liable to punishment" (*American Journal of International Law* 44 [1950]: 125). Such principles have in part grown out of the Kellogg-Briand Pact and remain latent in international law as a warning to future aggressors.

Since World War II, concerned private citizens and some governments have sustained an international effort to draft a "code of offenses against the peace and security of mankind" and to establish a permanent international criminal court on the model of the Nuremberg tribunal, as law scholars Benjamin Ferencz and Robert Woetzel recount. The International Law Commission completed a draft code of such offenses in 1954, and both the Genocide Convention (1948) and the Convention Against Terrorism (1979) call for an international criminal court as a means of enforcement. Such a court could also assist in the enforcement of international conventions on drug trafficking, hijacking, hostage taking, and crimes against diplomats.

Several nongovernmental organizations that have no direct ties to the old outlawry movement continue the same effort to strengthen the organization of peace and the rule of law: the World Peace Through Law Center, the American Bar Association's Standing Committee on World Order Under Law, the International Commission of Jurists, the International Parliamentary Union, the Campaign for U.N. Reform, the Parliamentarians for Global Action, and the World Association for World Federation, later renamed the World Federalist Movement.

The principles of the Kellogg-Briand Pact thus continue to exert a long-range impact on international organization, even if the pact itself is often forgotten among the historical curiosities of the first hopeful decade of the League of Nations. After World War II, the United States and most other national states restyled their military forces as "defense" forces, which reflected the objective of "the abandonment of the use of force" in the Atlantic Charter (1941) as well as the renunciation of war "as an instrument of national policy" in the Pact of Paris.

It was to mark a stage in the progress of international law—what Henry Stimson called a "revolution in human thought"—that the Kellogg-Briand Pact was so universally agreed to in 1928. The treaty remains in force, though no new states have adhered to it since 1932. Its principles remain powerful norms of national conduct, which have been invoked in World War II, the Korean War, and the Gulf War against Iraq.

HISTORICAL RETROSPECTIVE

Time alters our perspective on the past. As prospects for "a new world order" open up following the end of the Cold War, we will need to reassess what George Kennan called in 1951 "the legalistic-moralistic approach to international problems," exemplified by the Kellogg-Briand Pact. If "the rule of law" in international organization is a main pillar of a new world order, as both George Bush in his U.N. address of 1990 and Mikhail Gorbachev in his of 1988 have maintained, and if the pact was a "revolutionary" step toward such a rule of law, as we have argued, then the history of the pact should offer new light on the emerging order. But a positive view of the pact amounts to a virtual reversal of considered historical opinion.

Historians have reserved their harshest criticism for the pact's failure to provide any enforcement mechanism. Robert Ferrell, writing in 1952, at the beginning of the Cold War, belittled the pact for relying only on "outlawry" (public opinion) while allowing the diplomats of the day to preserve their war powers by means of the escape clause for "defense." "The Kellogg-Briand Pact was the peculiar result," he concluded, "of some very shrewd diplomacy and some very unsophisticated popular enthusiasm for peace" (p. 263). Similarly, at the peak of the Vietnam War in 1967, Robert J. Maddox looked back on the pact in an article in *Historian,* calling it a "monument to wishful thinking," an "utter vacuity," and an "ephemeral achievement." He overlooked the pact's role in setting up the Nuremberg tribunal (perhaps because it was short-lived) and concluded, "A pact without machinery was worthless" (p. 200, 218, 220).

Even historians who are better disposed to the peace movement find the Kellogg-Briand Pact wanting. Charles DeBenedetti, writing in the *Pacific Northwest Quarterly* (January 1972), found the pact's "fatal defect" in having "no credible means of enforcement" (p. 22). Warren Kuehl in *Peace and Change* (Summer–Fall 1975) saw the pact as symptomatic of American "irresponsibility" in the 1920s and 1930s (p. 84). World War II taught the lesson that "the United States bears the responsibility for maintaining world peace," he concluded, whether that meant cooperating in collective-security actions or unilaterally playing the role of world policeman. Harold Josephson concluded in a 1979 issue of *Diplomatic History* that with the coming of the war, "most internationalists gave up on the pact" (p. 387) and after the war, "most Americans accepted the concept that force was required to preserve the peace" (p. 388). This of course meant, when the U.N. Charter's Chapter VII proved a hollow threat, that general public support for U.S. and Western deterrence policy. Only Richard N. Current, among historians, has written positively about the pact since World War II. He agreed with Stimson that the pact produced a revolution in international law, even though few Americans remembered the pact itself.

LEGAL AND POLITICAL DIMENSIONS

The question of enforcement is the largest problem that must be addressed in reappraising the Kellogg-Briand Pact. Others include the broad loophole for "defensive" war; the reservations that the United States, Britain, France, and other nations made to their adherence; the meaning of "aggression"; the erosion of neutrality as a safe defense policy in an interdependent world; the ineffectiveness of the pact at the approach of World War II; what DeBenedetti called the "fatuity" of popularly directed diplomacy; and the nature of the necessary international authority in a world where war has been "outlawed." We will take up these problems one by one.

International Enforcement   Normally, as international law is observed in the great majority of cases, treaties are enforced by the national law of states parties. In case of violation of an arms limitation treaty, say, or even of an antiwar pact, there are two conceivable modes of enforcement or coercion (after exhaustion of such "peaceful means of settlement" as negotiation, inquiry, mediation, conciliation, arbitration, and adjudication): (1) collective economic sanctions, interruption of communication, suspension of diplomatic relations, and, finally, joint military operations against the offending state (commonly called "enforcement" under a system of collective security); and (2) judicial action by new world equity tribunals (competent to hear "political" cases) or by greatly expanded world organs of arbitration or adjudication whose judgments would reach directly to individuals (the "rule of law").

The first was the mode of enforcement provided in the League of Nations Covenant (notably Article 16) and subsequently in the United Nations Charter (Chapter VII). The second has only since World War II begun to be implemented at the world or regional level, as in the Nuremberg tribunal, the public reporting mechanisms for certain U.N. human rights treaties, the European Court of Human Rights, and the Inter-American Court of Human Rights. Nevertheless, the rule of law was clearly envisaged by the advocates of outlawry.

Salmon O. Levinson, a successful Chicago corporation lawyer, inaugurated the movement to outlaw war with a critical article in the *New Republic* in early 1918. His subject was the nature of the proposed postwar League to Enforce Peace. Levinson argued forcefully that to abolish war civilized nations would first have to declare war illegal and then criminal under international law, so that, like dueling, war would lose its aura of honor and finally be put down as an odious abuse. This was the minimal idea of outlawry, which some historians have only too easily ridiculed as naive and simplistic.

Levinson's full program from the beginning included subsequent establishment of a strong international code of conduct for nations, coupled with a strong international court for the peaceful resolution of disputes. But he could not resolve in his time the problem of enforcement. Levinson waivered between use of international sanctions or military forces against states, as in the proposed League of Nations, and use of interpretations or punishments reaching individuals, as in the U.S. Supreme Court, his constant analogy. Years later, he left the problem to the decision of national delegates to a convention to codify the international law against war, trusting that they would possess the wisdom to find a workable interim solution. His own recommendation was for national enforcement on war criminals, as on pirates and felons on the high seas who had violated the law of nations.

The odd and sometime comic Senator William E. Borah (Republican of Idaho) was persuaded by Levinson, Charles C. Morrison (influential editor of the *Christian Century*), and others to introduce in 1923 an important Senate resolution on outlawry, which became an antecedent to the Kellogg-Briand Pact. Borah made a fundamental contribution to the idea of enforcement by international courts with his doctrine of the role of enlightened public opinion. The "Lion of Idaho" and the leader of the "irreconcilables" against Wilson's League of Nations, Borah became chairman of the Senate Foreign Relations Committee in 1924 and spoke for a broad public.

Senator Borah opposed U.S. entry into the League of Nations and even into the World Court or the Geneva Protocol for the Pacific Settlement of Disputes, because the ultimate recourse for their enforcement was the League Covenant's Article 16, which provided for international economic sanctions and finally armed force to deter an aggressor state. To Borah—and eventually to a majority of the American people after the Senate's rejection of the League of Nations—collective security plainly meant war waged by the international community against states, not unlike that waged by the Allied and Associated Powers in World War I. International enforcement actions, then, seemed deceptive to many who hoped their security organization would preserve the peace.

In the debate on the League in 1919, as quoted in John Vinsor's biography, Borah explained that there were two types of league for the preservation of world peace:

The first is a league which would organize the moral forces of the world. The second is a league which would organize the military forces of the world. . . . Senators, you cannot establish peace by force, by repression. . . . The scheme based on force is more repulsive and destructive of human justice and human liberty and human progress than Prussianism itself. (pp. 20–21)

What Borah was looking for was an international organization that ruled by law, was popularly respected, and did not use the threat of collective force.

In the political atmosphere of the 1920s, the hopes of many internationalists that the League of Nations would actually work—that the threat of collective sanctions would induce statesmen to bring their disputes into general institutions for peaceful settlement or, if necessary, that collective use of force would halt or repulse aggression—reached a peak. The decade was marked by the Washington naval treaties, the Geneva Protocol, the disarmament conferences, and growth in League membership to fifty-eight. The hopes live on to this day, but the fears of others like Borah—that if the League worked this way, wars would actually increase—dissipated in the 1930s. Weak economic sanctions based on Article 16 were voted against Italy without appreciably slowing Mussolini's conquest of Abyssinia (Ethiopia), while the League's threat of military enforcement proved totally hollow against Japan and Nazi Germany.

Since then, international enforcement action against states has generally been rejected. The analogous warrant in the U.N. Charter, Article 42, never has been invoked, even against North Korea in 1950 (Article 39 sufficed). U.N. peacekeeping as in the Congo in 1960–1964 was based not on Article 42, but on what Dag Hammarskjöld called "Chapter VI 1/2" (no express article for the use of international forces to gain time for pacific settlement). In the Persian Gulf crisis of 1990–1991, the Security Council never invoked Article 42, and the multinational coalition force was organized by the United States without the U.N. command and authority provided by the enforcement provisions of Chapter VII. These facts about the failure of collective security by military enforcement must be borne in mind when judging the wisdom of Senator Borah in relation to that of his great antagonist James T. Shotwell, a director of the Carnegie Endowment for International Peace and leading advocate of "effective" international organization.

In his 1923 Senate resolution, Borah set out a complete program of outlawry, code, and court. It called for international agreements declaring war to be contrary to international law and a "public crime." It proposed to draft "a code of international law of peace based upon equality and justice between nations." And it urged expansion of the then existing Permanent Court of International Justice or creation of a powerful new world court "modeled on our Federal Supreme Court."

Such ideas logically implied some form of limited, federal world government in place of a league of sovereign states. Borah did not find it politic to carry the argument so far, but his irreconcilability to the League was not inconsistent with an effort to establish the conditions for the world rule of law. "Enlightened public opinion" was the first of these.

Borah's reply to the "realists" of the day was that the only alternative to the threat and use of force, national or international, was the rule of law backed by popular will.

As the U.S. Supreme Court's judgments were obeyed voluntarily, so the decisions of an international tribunal would have to be acceptable to concerned national peoples without the threat or use of military force, except as a last resort for the enforcement of the laws, as in every national state. Until such an international judicial mechanism was fully developed and reliable, public sentiment would have to be prepared by a long process of repeated appeals to it, not by periodic bouts of military enforcement. During the transition, the United States could lead by creating new forms of adjudication outside the League, toward which the Kellogg-Briand Pact was a step. The United States would still have to maintain its defenses in the meantime; neither Borah nor Secretary Kellogg were chargeable with hypocrisy for supporting the naval construction bills of the late 1920s and 1930s.

Later, after the Kellogg-Briand Pact was ratified and a movement arose to give it "teeth," which he opposed, Borah explained:

What they mean is to change the peace pact into a military pact. They would transform it into another peace scheme based upon force, and force is another name for war. By putting teeth into it, they mean an agreement to employ armies and navies wherever the fertile mind of some ambitious schemer can find an aggressor.... I have no language to express my horror of this proposal to build peace treaties, or peace schemes, upon the doctrine of force. (Vinson, p. 181)

The full implications of outlawry for the rule of law were explored in a vigorous exchange between philosopher John Dewey and political commentator Walter Lippmann in 1923. Writing in the *Atlantic Monthly* of August 1923, Lippmann saw immediately that Borah's code and court implied a "superstate." He concluded that with the world in its present state of disorder, there could be no substitute for traditional diplomacy, including the threat of force, to settle the most dangerous international controversies (pp. 247, 252).

Dewey replied in the *New Republic* of 3 October 1923 that outlawrists believed that the historical moment had arrived to urge the establishment of the world rule of law as a fundamental alternative to the diplomats' threat and use of force. Both had the power to compel settlement. "The genuine alternatives," he wrote, "are between political methods based upon a system which legalizes war, and political methods that have as their basic principle that war is a crime, so that when diplomacy and conferences cannot reach agreement the dispute shall be submitted to a court" (p. 151). Dewey did not shrink from Lippmann's clear argument that outlawry implied the political reorganization of Europe and the world. He believed, however, that a start could be made with the current generation of jurists at The Hague and international legal experts, who should be competent to draft a working code of national conduct and to devise an international court of appeal without first establishing a world legislature and the full panoply of world government.

Later, in 1927, as Secretary of State Frank B. Kellogg was preparing his diplomatic response to Foreign Minister Briand's proposal for a pact to renounce war between their two countries, C. C. Morrison published a slim book entitled *The Outlawry of War,* in which the full political implications were boldly spelled out. The "full-orbed outlawry proposal," Morrison wrote, consisted of two hemispheres: the declaration of the illegality of war, which was about to be achieved, and the organization of peace, which still remains largely to the future. The organization of peace Morrison vividly described in terms of "a political federation of the world" (pp. 32, 192–197). This little book, which briefly had an influence on events, remains a classic on the larger program of establishing the rule of law as a basis of world peace. A similar work is Lord Lothian's *Pacifism Is Not Enough* of 1935.

Secretary Kellogg's view on enforcement of the pact is instructive. In his address in November 1928, he acknowledged "the lofty ideal of a world tribunal or superstate" (Gerould, p. 125). But he argued, realistically enough, that neither the United States nor other independent nations had yet arrived at "the advanced stage of thought which will permit such a tribunal to be established." That left only the force of public opinion or enforcement under the League or other entangling alliances. The latter he rejected as "futile" in principle and politically unacceptable to the United States, so the former—"solemn pledges and the honor of nations"—was the only possible choice (p. 127).

Was this naive? That Kellogg did not regard such a pact as an immediate bulwark of U.S. national defense is shown by his support for the naval building program. What he hoped for was general public re-

jection of war throughout the international community:

If by this treaty all the nations solemnly pronounce against war as an instrument for settling international disputes, the world will have taken a forward step, created a public opinion, marshalled the great moral forces of the world for its observance and entered into a sacred obligation which will make it far more difficult to plunge the world into another great conflict. (p. 128)

Kellogg regarded his pact as "the consummation and crown" of his life's labors. As he said in his last address on the subject in 1930, his object was to negotiate "a treaty so simple and unconditional that the people of all nations could understand it, a declaration which could be a rallying point for world sentiment, a foundation on which to build world peace" (Bryn-Jones, p. 238).

Right of Self-Defense   The Kellogg-Briand Pact purported to renounce war without qualification, yet the diplomatic correspondence prior to the signing of the pact indicates clearly that virtually every signatory made an exemption for wars of self-defense. Was not "defense" a loophole so large that, as Yale law professor Edwin M. Borchard charged in 1929, the treaty could never be legally violated?

The outlawrists and Secretary Kellogg, in the absence of a strong international legal organization in their times, were not able to avoid making an exemption for the sovereign right of self-defense. Even Salmon O. Levinson privately reserved the right of self-defense for nations, as for individuals, and Senator Borah in debate went so far as to say that the Spanish-American War of 1898 had been a war of self-defense, of the sort permissible under the proposed pact. Secretary Kellogg, in his delayed December 1927 response to the original Briand proposal of April, which was evidently part of a French search for alliances, urged first that Briand's pact for the *general* renunciation of war between France and the United States be made multilateral—that is, totally abolish war. When the French counterproposed that the multilateral pact be limited to the renunciation of *aggressive* war, Kellogg vigorously protested with ironic references to the "ideal of peace" at the heart of the League of Nations, but finally had to make practical accommodations to France's and other nations' commitments to the League, the Locarno Treaty, and treaties of neutrality.

Kellogg thereafter firmly defended the implied reservation permitting war in self-defense, as decided by every sovereign state. But while the pact could not limit this right, it was limited, he believed, "before the bar of world opinion": "If [the nation going to war in self-defense] has a good case, the world will applaud it and not condemn it, but a nation must answer to the tribunal of public opinion as to whether its claim of the right of self-defense is an adequate justification for it to go to war" (Gerould, p. 124).

Years later, the world made this judgment in the case of the Nazi war criminals, and the potential for public condemnation of professed defensive wars continues to exist.

National Reservations   Once Secretary Kellogg made it clear by April 1928 that the United States understood that the multilateral antiwar pact did not impair "the right of self-defense," which was "inherent in every sovereign state" and "implicit in every treaty," the original fifteen signatory states rapidly came to an agreement (Gerould, p. 113). Their motivations doubtless were partly cynical, but the rush of acceptances is hard to explain without assuming that hardened statesmen valued the abolition of the most dangerous class of warfare. Nevertheless, most expressed reservations about the right of self-defense and about their obligations to use force under the collective security provisions of the League Covenant and the Locarno Treaty. The reservation of the British was the most extreme: "There are certain regions of the world the welfare and integrity of which constitute a special and vital interest for our peace and safety.... Their protection against attack is to the British Empire a measure of self-defence" (p. 55).

Secretary Kellogg refused to accept such statements as legal *reservations,* impairing the obligations of the treaty. To him, they were mere "understandings," explaining to other states parties how certain critical terms would be interpreted. The most he would do was to change the (nonbinding) preamble to read that in case any party resorts to war to promote its national interests, it "should be denied the benefits furnished by this Treaty" (pp. 16–19, 123–124). That is, in case of aggressive war, other states parties were no longer under an obligation *not* to go to war against the violator. He also refused to print the correspondence as reservations to the legal text.

This was an act of bold statesmanship, but most knowledgeable commentators on international law, like Edwin Borchard and David Miller, regarded the correspondence as technical reservations as much a part of the treaty as the preamble and three formal articles. The matter was settled—very imperfectly—only when the drafters of the U.N. Charter moved the renunciation of the threat or use of force and the pledge to use only peaceful means of settlement to the hortatory "Principles" of the Charter (Article 2, paragraphs 3 and 4), while stiffening the collective security obligations of all states members (Chapters VI and VII).

Aggression Defined by Public Opinion   Because of its exemption for defensive war, the Kellogg-Briand Pact was commonly regarded as a pact only against aggressive war. Yet the term "aggression" nowhere appears in the pact. The Geneva Protocol of 1924 (unratified) defined the term, and a League of Nations Assembly resolution of 1927 declared aggression a crime, but there was no general international agreement on its meaning until a U.N. resolution in 1974.

Kellogg declined to place in the pact of 1928 a definition either of self-defense or of aggression because, as he said, "no comprehensive legalistic definition could be framed in advance." Any technical definition like "firing the first shot" or "resorting to war before exhausting peaceful remedies" could easily be evaded by a nation intent on military action. Kellogg therefore thought best "simply to make a broad declaration against war" and leave it to public opinion to identify the aggressor (Gerould, pp. 124–125). This is also the solution taken in the U.N. Charter, whose drafters left the determination of aggression not to a technical definition but to a decision of the Security Council with respect to the circumstances of each case.

Neutrality Outmoded   The Kellogg-Briand Pact contained obligations that undermined the traditional law of neutrality. Although the United States was not a member of the League, the pledge in the Pact of Paris to "deny its benefits" to a state that initiated a war removed the threat that American neutrality would benefit an aggressor against the League. Quincy Wright even argued in 1933 in the *American Journal of International Law* that the United States was bound, by its continuing obligations to the remaining parties to the peace pact, to "employ any degree of coercion, including war, against primary belligerents" (p. 60). He concluded, "Neutrality posited upon isolation and impartiality has lost its legal foundation" (p. 61).

This legal view was a far cry from the usual historical one that the Kellogg-Briand Pact carried no definite obligations. Wright here was playing the role of the international legal publicist who defined "new law" with respect to "new facts in the world" (Wright, p. 57). By 1932, these new facts manifestly included rapid advances in worldwide communications and transportation and world industrial, financial, and commercial "interdependence." Secretary of State Stimson followed just this reasoning in his speech of 8 August 1932, in which he rejected U.S. neutrality in case of League sanctions against Japan. Another leading international lawyer, John Bassett Moore, protested at length the next year in favor of traditional neutrality to limit the spread of war, but he could not even explain why in 1914–1918 war quickly spread over the whole earth. World War II seems to have settled the question, except for small states, like Finland or Austria, that shelter in the lee of powerful neighbors.

Fatuity of Popularly Directed Diplomacy

Worldwide popular support and press support for the Kellogg-Briand Pact in 1928 was phenomenal. Was it "naive," "gullible," "unsophisticated," "idealistic"? No doubt the public generally had little notion of what was really required to abolish war. The leaders of outlawry had clear ideas, but in exploiting the diplomacy of the day, they achieved only the first step of their program, while code and court were indefinitely postponed. They compromised and then suffered odium for achieving only the delegitimization of aggressive war.

Historians like Charles DeBenedetti have roundly criticized Borah's "politics of preemption" (drive for the White House), which produced a mere "apolitical" antiwar treaty (DeBenedetti, pp. 28–29). But probably the cause of a *political* peace pact was lost when the Senate narrowly rejected U.S. participation in the League in 1920. If the United States had been in, collective security would likely still have proved an illusion, but a new generation of American leaders familiar with international organization might have prepared the country for the larger program of fundamentally strengthening the world body after World War II.

Failure of the Pact Through World War II

In the initial flurry of popular enthusiasm for the Kellogg-Briand Pact, extravagant claims were made for its effectiveness. James Shotwell stated that had the pact existed in 1914, World War I might have been avoided, and President Coolidge made a similar claim. In 1928 the pact (minus the "reservations" that Kellogg had refused to accept) was posted in U.S. Post Offices across the nation, creating the impression that a historic event was afoot, as it was, though it was not the immediate abolition of war. By 27 August 1928, international attention and the hopes of millions were focused on the impressive signing ceremony in the Salle d'Horloge in Paris. It is understandable why one attendee could get carried away and exclaim, "Today international war was banished from civilization" (Ferrell, pp. 219–220).

The pact, like the League Covenant and the U.N. Charter, was oversold. It had a brief influence on practical diplomacy while Henry Stimson was secretary of state, but with the rise of aggressive governments in Germany, Italy, and Japan that were determined not to renounce the threat and use of force, Secretary of State Cordell Hull and President Franklin D. Roosevelt rarely referred to the pact. By the 1930s, as Harold Josephson wrote, most internationalists had given up on it. It resurfaced only with the Nuremberg trials. Its influence on the U.N. Charter was perceptible only to international lawyers and historians of the organization like Leland Goodrich. Disappointment has led to general oblivion.

CONCLUSION

"Peace has been proclaimed," said Aristide Briand in 1928. "But it is necessary to organize it." The Kellogg-Briand Pact has fallen into the oblivion of time, but its principles—the renunciation of war as an instrument of national policy and the commitment to use peaceful means to settle international disputes—remain standards for "the work of the future."

The nature of the necessary international organization to secure the peace depends largely on the means humanity chooses to enforce such norms as the rejection of aggressive war. The 1991 Gulf War with Iraq, though victorious for the U.S.-led coalition, proved again that collective security means war. Are such enforcement actions to become a regular feature of a "new world order"? The alternative is judicial enforcement upon individuals in accordance with the world rule of law, which was once held up as an ideal by the mostly ridiculed and forgotten advocates of the outlawry of war. The key issue for them was whether the renunciation of war could rest on public opinion, somehow made strong and effective, or would have to be based on periodic use of collective force, as under the League or the United Nations.

"I have the greatest hope," Secretary Kellogg wrote after the signing of the pact, "that in the advancement of our civilization all people will be trained in the thought and come to the belief that nations in their relations with each other should be governed by principles of law and that the decisions of arbitrators or judicial tribunals and the efforts of conciliation commissions should be relied upon in the settlement of international disputes rather than war" (p. 126).

The Kellogg-Briand Pact, then, was an incomplete attempt to organize the peace on the basis of law rather than collective security. The problem for Kellogg, Borah, Levinson, Morrison, Dewey, and the other outlawrists was to guide humanity through the transition from a world where war was a regular feature to one where life's disputes were settled by the orderly and reasonable processes of the law. Considering their fewness in numbers, the volatility of public opinion, and the strength of sovereign traditions, their achievement in bringing about a near universal international agreement declaring war as an instrument of national policy illegal was magnificent.

During the transition, it is true, Kellogg was willing to permit a plea of self-defense, but he thought that flimsy claims would not stand up to the light of public opinion. The ethos of defense, he thought, would gradually reduce the incidence of wars.

The nature of an adequate international authority to keep the peace was left undefined, but there were hints in calls for an international code of conduct drawn up by judicial experts from every land, and for an international criminal court. John Dewey did not shrink from the idea of a world legislature, and C. C. Morrison dared to carry the political argument as far as a world federal government.

BIBLIOGRAPHY

Original Sources Original sources on the outlawry of war start with SALMON O. LEVINSON, "The Legal Status of War," *New Republic,* 9 March 1918, pp. 171–173. For WILLIAM E. BORAH's contribution, see his full resolution on outlawry, reprinted in vol. 3, and his ingenious political argument, which tipped the balance in the Senate, "One Great Treaty to Outlaw All War," *New York Times,* 5 February 1928. WALTER LIPPMANN's brilliant, disdainful critique, "Outlawry of War," *Atlantic Monthly,* August 1923, pp. 245–253, met an equally brillant match in JOHN DEWEY, "What Outlawry of War Is Not," *New Republic,* 3 October 1923, pp. 149–152, and "War and a Code of Law," *New Republic,* 24 October 1923, pp. 224–126. Dewey reflected on the accomplishments of the movement in "Peace, by Pact or Covenant," *New Republic,* 23 March 1932, pp. 145–147. CHARLES CLAYTON MORRISON, *The Outlawry of War: A Constructive Policy for World Peace* (Chicago, 1927), which appeared just in time for the diplomatic action, expressed the broad views of leading outlawrists. Secretary Frank B. Kellogg's speeches as he took over the leading role in outlawry, Briand's proposal, several drafts of the pact, all the diplomatic correspondence, reservations, and early interpretations are in JAMES T. GEROULD, comp., *Selected Articles on the Pact of Paris* (New York, 1929). Kellogg's authoritative exposition is "The War Prevention Policy of the United States," *American Journal of International Law* 22 (1928): 253–261, and, with WILLIAM R. CASTLE, "Outlawry of War," in *Encyclopedia Britannica* (14th ed., 1936).

These original materials can be supplemented by DAVID H. MILLER, *The Peace Pact of Paris: A Study of the Briand-Kellogg Treaty* (New York, 1928), and JAMES T. SHOTWELL, "The Pact of Paris: With Historical Commentary," *International Conciliation* 243 (October 1928): 443–532. Shotwell's leading role is reflected in his *War as an Instrument of National Policy and Its Renunciation in the Pact of Paris* (New York, 1929). LORD LOTHIAN's addresses "The Outlawry of War" (Chatham House, November 1928) and "Address at Hamburg" (30 October 1929), in JOHN PINDER and ANDREA BOSCO, eds., *Pacifism Is Not Enough: Collected Lectures and Speeches of Lord Lothian* (London, 1990), provide a valuable contemporary European view.

Early Accounts Early criticism begins with EDWIN BORCHARD's Austinian views: "The Kellogg Treaties Sanction War," *Nation,* 5 September 1928, pp. 234–236, and " 'War' and 'Peace,' " *American Journal of International Law* 27 (January 1933): 114–117. For his reflective view long afterward, see "International Law and International Organization," *American Journal of International Law* 41 (January 1947): 106–108. JOHN BASSETT MOORE, "An Appeal to Reason," *Foreign Affairs* 11 (July 1933): 547–588, takes similar negative, not to say cynical, views rooted in long experience in international affairs. For the future president's negative opinion, see FRANKLIN D. ROOSEVELT, "Our Foreign Policy: A

Democratic View," *Foreign Affairs* 6 (July 1928): 573–586. Borchard and Moore are answered in terms of principle and practical diplomacy by HENRY L. STIMSON, "The Pact of Paris: Three Years of Development," *Foreign Affairs* 11 (October 1932): special supplement; and "Bases of American Foreign Policy During the Past Four Years," *Foreign Affairs* 11 (April 1933): 383–396. See also, on the "revolution" in international law, QUINCY WRIGHT, "The Meaning of the Pact of Paris," *The American Journal of International Law* 27 (1933): 39–61.

Standard biographies round out the early account. JOHN E. STONER, *S. O. Levinson and the Pact of Paris: A Study in the Techniques of Influence* (Chicago, 1943), is basic on the founder of the movement. JOHN CHALMERS VINSON, *William E. Borah and the Outlawry of War* (Athens, Ga., 1957), succeeds in laying bare the senator's "consistent philosophy." DAVID BRYN-JONES, *Frank B. Kellogg: A Biography* (New York, 1937), is fair. HAROLD JOSEPHSON, *James T. Shotwell and the Rise of Internationalism in America* (Rutherford, N.J., 1975) is excellent. ANNE V. MEIBURGER, *Efforts of Raymond Robins Toward the Recognition of Soviet Russia and the Outlawry of War, 1917–1933* (Washington, D.C., 1958), treats the last major figure among the outlawrists.

Kellogg-Briand Pact at Nuremberg For the "enforcement" of the Kellogg-Briand Pact at Nuremberg, HENRY L. STIMSON, "The Nuremberg Trial, Landmark in Law," *Foreign Affairs* 25 (January 1947): 179–189, is fundamental, as are three articles by Quincy Wright in the *American Journal of International Law*: "The Law of the Nuremberg Trial," 41 (January 1947): 38–72; "Legal Positivism and the Nuremberg Judgment," 42 (April 1948): 405–414, and "The Outlawry of War and the Law of War," 47 (July 1953): 365–376. Chief prosecutor Justice ROBERT H. JACKSON's statements to the tribunal and his "Nuremberg in Retrospect: Legal Answer to International Lawlessness," *American Bar Association Journal* 35 (October 1949): 813–816, 881–887, are authoritative. See also Jackson's *The Case Against the Nazi War Criminals: Opening Statement for the United States of America and Other Documents* (New York, 1946). KARL JASPERS, "The Significance of the Nürnberg Trials for Germany and the World," *Notre Dame Lawyer* 22 (January 1947): 150–160, courageously accepts the international legal punishment of his countrymen for crimes against the peace, war crimes, and crimes against humanity,

just as he expects other nationals will have to in the future. BENJAMIN B. FERENCZ draws out the future implications in *An International Criminal Court, A Step Toward World Peace: A Documentary History and Analysis* (Dobbs Ferry, N.Y., 1980), as does ROBERT K. WOETZEL, *The Nuremberg Trials in International Law* (New York, 1960), and *Toward a Feasible International Criminal Court* (Geneva, 1970). An interesting survey of the history and issues of such a court is Michael P. Scharf, "The Jury Is Still Out on the Need for an International Criminal Court," *Duke Journal of Comparative and International Law* 1 (1991): 135–168.

Historical Commentary Among historians, ROBERT H. FERRELL, *Peace in Their Time: The Origins of the Kellogg-Briand Pact* (New Haven, Conn., 1952), is standard but not above slurs on the loyalty and realism of the outlawrists. ROBERT J. MADDOX, "William E. Borah and the Crusade to Outlaw War," *Historian* 29 (February 1967): 200–220, is similar, rooted in the "realistic" interpretation of international relations. The most balanced, but still negative, interpretation is HAROLD JOSEPHSON, "Outlawing War: Internationalism and the Pact of Paris," *Diplomatic History* 3 (Fall 1979): 377–390. Similar views, sympathetic yet critical toward the outlawry movement, include WARREN F. KUEHL, "The Principle of Responsibility for Peace and National Security, 1920–1973," *Peace and Change* 3 (Summer/Fall 1975): 84–93; CHARLES DEBENEDETTI, "Borah and the Kellogg-Briand Pact," *Pacific Northwest Quarterly* 73, no. 1 (1972): 22–29; J. THEODORE HEFLEY, "War Outlawed: The Christian Century and the Kellogg Peace Pact," *Journalism Quarterly* 48 (1971): 26–32; CHARLES F. HOWLETT, "John Dewey and the Crusade to Outlaw War," *World Affairs* 138 (Spring 1976): 336–355; and STEPHEN J. KNEESHAW, "The Kellogg-Briand Pact and American Recognition of the Soviet Union," *Mid-America* 56 (1974): 16–31.

The best positive view is RICHARD N. CURRENT, "Consequences of the Kellogg Pact," in GEORGE L. ANDERSON, ed., *Issues and Conflicts: Studies in Twentieth-Century American Diplomacy* (Lawrence, Kans., 1959). GARY B. OSTROWER, *Collective Insecurity: The United States and the League of Nations During the Early Thirties* (Lewisburg, Pa., 1979), provides a broad context. A positive view by an international lawyer is JOHN NORTON MOORE, "Strengthening World Order: Reversing the Slide to Anarchy," *American University Journal of International Law and Policy* 4 (Winter 1989): 1–24.

Regulating Arms Sales Through World War II

○

KEITH KRAUSE

MARY K. MacDONALD

See also Controlling the Arms Trade Since 1945; The League of Nations and Disarmament; *and* The United Nations and Disarmament. *Most of the treaties discussed in this essay are excerpted in Volume III.*

Arms have been traded between states, empires, and peoples throughout human history to achieve a variety of political, military, and economic goals. The desire to acquire or export arms is tied closely to the "self-help" nature of the current international system, in which responsibility for security and defense rests with individual states. The ability to buy and sell weapons has almost been considered by states to be a sovereign right. This, coupled with the uneven process of military technological innovation and diffusion (which produces gaps in the weaponry available to different states), generates a constant struggle between the military haves and have-nots to maintain or improve their relative position.

The same set of forces that gave rise to the arms trade also generated attempts from the beginning to regulate and control it. Seldom were these efforts undertaken because of ethical considerations or because of a general aversion to warfare and the means of waging it. Rather, the arms trade was controlled because it was in the interest of particular states (and other actors) to restrict access to weapons technologies. The two most prominent reasons for controlling the arms trade were to prevent actual or potential battlefield opponents from obtaining arms and to restrict the diffusion of new and sophisticated weapons technologies (or the knowledge required to produce them). A numerical ad-

vantage or technological monopoly that could be guarded even temporarily might provide a decisive advantage in warfare.

Only for relatively brief periods has the arms trade been uncontrolled, and it is not true (although it is widely believed) that before 1945 arms were traded as freely as other commodities. Yet, there are few examples of negotiated international agreements (either between two or several states) to control the arms trade. Most restrictions on the arms trade took the form of unilateral national legislation prohibiting the export of weapons or materials of war (contraband) to the enemy in time of war. Thus, in order to understand how and why the arms trade was regulated before 1945, one must define rather broadly what is meant by "control" or "regulation" of the arms trade. It must include not only negotiated multilateral attempts to restrict the flow of weapons across borders but also unilateral attempts by states to regulate their exports. It must include not only attempts to control the flow of actual weapons but also the proliferation or diffusion of the technologies required to produce or assemble them. It must also include tacit or indirect attempts to restrict the ability of other states to buy or produce weapons, including threats of other punishments or restrictions on trade. Powerful incentives to refrain from trading weapons or weapons-producing technologies could often be introduced without having any strict legal or treaty sanction.

We have adopted this broad approach and will survey the historical pattern of control of the arms trade, while emphasizing two particular themes: the progressive growth of legal and multilateral restrictions and the pervasive difficulties encountered in attempts to control the arms trade. Although this survey will cover a broad historical sweep, it will concentrate on the efforts associated with the League of Nations in the 1920s and 1930s, representing the most active and important multilateral attempts to control the arms trade. Throughout, the arms trade will be situated against the backdrop of the technological innovations in warfare that accelerated the arms trade and the dominant political and economic ideologies or climate that formed the setting in which arms control efforts were undertaken.

PRE-NINETEENTH-CENTURY REGULATION

Information on the arms trade itself and on attempts to control it is limited for the period before 1900 and even more so as one moves back before the nineteenth century. Nevertheless, sketchy evidence makes clear that as early as the ancient Greek period, military technological advances created a demand for the most "sophisticated" arms and armor throughout the Mediterranean. Regulation of the arms trade occurred through competition to attract (and keep) the best military engineers and technicians and to restrict the circulation of plans for their machines. During the Roman imperial period, arms production was controlled by the state and no "interstate" arms trade existed, as the laws of the Roman Empire forbade any provision of arms to "barbarians."

After the collapse of the Roman Empire, the main commercial cities on the Mediterranean traded arms and armor actively throughout Europe and the Middle East. The rivalry and struggle for supremacy between Christianity and Islam, however, triggered explicit attempts on the part of Christian rulers to restrict the diffusion of weapons to the Muslim world, especially during the Crusades. In A.D. 971, the doge of Venice prohibited the sale of arms to the Saracens, who were in nearly constant battle with various Balkan rulers. In 1179 the Third

Lateran Council prohibited the sale of arms, ships, or material for weapons (such as iron) to the Saracens, on pain of excommunication or imprisonment. This interdiction was repeated by the Fourth Lateran Council in 1215, by the Council of Lyons in 1245, and by Popes Innocent III and Benedict XI. Also at the church's insistence, the leaders of Venice and Genoa prohibited their citizens from transporting arms to Egypt, which was a prominent commercial entrepôt for trade with the "infidels." All of these efforts were of limited success in stemming the diffusion of weapons around the Mediterranean, as the church had few concrete means of punishing violators.

Within Europe the church did not exert a decisive influence over the arms trade, although individual rulers sometimes did. In fact, the earliest documented regulations of a ruler predate the church injunctions and date from Charlemagne's rule (768–814). His capitularies prohibited the export of Frankish armor, which was much in demand across Europe, from his territories, although these regulations had no effect on third parties and were intended simply to preserve Charlemagne's military advantages over his opponents.

As the European political scene slowly transformed itself between 1000 and 1500 from a medieval hierarchy under the church into a nascent system of competing (and warring) states over which the church had diminished practical influence, slowly the patchwork of religious injunctions that had governed the arms trade prior to the emergence of powerful nation-states was replaced by national policies, which were soon followed by interstate agreements between rulers. Three prominent and representative (although certainly not exhaustive) examples illustrate the nature of the interstate controls that were created. In 1315, the English king Edward II, in conflict with rebellious Scots, prohibited not only his subjects but also foreigners from supplying Scotland with weapons. In 1370 one finds the first example of "negotiated multilateral" restraints, when Edward III of England signed an agreement with rulers in the Low Countries (Flanders, Bruges, Ypres) that prohibited the supply of arms and military materials to enemies of England. A similar embargo was negotiated between the Danes and the Hanseatic cities to restrict arms exports to Sweden (with whom Denmark was at war at various times between 1448 and 1500).

With uniform military technology spanning Europe, arms exports diminished one's potential arsenal and augmented that of potential or actual enemies. Since the output of a good armorer or forger was not large, this could be a serious drain when no surplus production existed. The existence of these injunctions and agreements suggests that the political hazards of arms exports to potential enemies was recognized early, along with the general prohibition against trade with an opponent in wartime. But since most of the weapons trade of this period remained passive, responding to orders from specific princes or magistrates rather than actively seeking markets for ready-made wares, the urgency of controlling the arms trade was not great.

But the invention and perfection of cannon and firearms in the period between 1400 and 1650 was a watershed in military technology, accelerated the arms trade, and intensified efforts to control it. Modern arms were produced wherever sufficient concentrations of technological knowledge, raw materials, and market demand existed. Main production centers sprang up in northern Italy, England, Sweden, Germany, and the Low Countries (especially the city of Liège). The expansion of markets and trade that accompanied the consolidation of the state system and improvements in transportation meant that arms were at first traded with relative ease. But technological innovations meant that gaps in the weapons possessed by different states emerged, and states quickly became sensitive to the negative implications of an uncontrolled trade in weapons.

The implication for arms control was obvious: whereas previous attempts to control the arms trade had concentrated almost exclusively on the weapons themselves, now the knowledge required to produce them was equally—if not more—valuable. Systematic national control efforts thus expanded to include not only arms exports but also restrictions on the diffusion of technology. Three patterns of control and regulation manifested themselves, the most common of which were unilateral national controls on exports and the diffusion of technology.

The first type of control was defensive and was designed to protect one's limited military resources by restricting exports. This was consistent with previous types of regulations and was typified by the policies of France, Spain, and Portugal. France suffered from a shortage of armaments until the seventeenth century, despite repeated efforts to create a self-sustaining arms industry. Thus, the government imposed severe restrictions on the export of

arms, that were summed up in a 1572 regulation that incorporated previous measures:

Because the founding of cannon and ball and the gathering and manufacture of the materials for gunpowder are a sovereign right, belonging to the King alone for the safeguard and defence of the realm," no subject whatsoever was to make or seek to sell such war material without licence from those deputed to act "in the interest of the prince and of the public good. (quoted in Hale, p. 226)

As early as 1488, Spain adopted similar regulations that prohibited the export of cannon, handguns, crossbows, and a wide assortment of other arms and armor. After 1570 they were altered to incorporate a license requirement for all exports, with exports permitted only if no royal orders were pending. Both France and Spain continued to try to import English cannon through extra-legal channels to circumvent the less than wholly effective prohibitions on exports. Portugal, in its colonial policy throughout Asia, South America, and Africa, followed a papal injunction dating from 1454 that prohibited the transfer of arms to "infidels." Although ostensibly justified on religious grounds to give it greater moral authority, the measure was driven by the fact that Portugal suffered terrible shortages of weapons and was dependent upon arms imports in the fifteenth to seventeenth centuries.

The second type of control, manifested by leading producers such as Milan, Liège, and England, was driven by a desire to protect one's technological lead. This was a novel development, for most previous restrictions on the arms trade, such as Charlemagne's capitularies, had been designed to preserve available supplies for the state or ruler in the face of insufficient domestic production (one exception to this being the church's edicts against trade with the infidel). In this case, however, it was surplus production that could strengthen opponents if exported that motivated control. Milan and Liège, for example, attempted repeatedly, but with little success, to impose legal restrictions on the migration of skilled workers. Threats of imprisonment were common, and the Poles and Livonians even executed migrant military craftsmen who were headed to Russia and refused to return home. Few restrictions were imposed by their rulers on the migration of German or southern European workers, however, and they represented an ongoing source of technological knowledge for countries such as Turkey and Hungary with less arms production.

England went beyond controls on arms exports or the diffusion of technological knowledge to restrict production itself. After it was pointed out to the Privy Council that the export of guns from England ensured that "yor enimie is better fourneshed with them than or own country ships ar," Elizabeth I in 1574 ordered gun production to be limited to the amount needed "for the only use of the realm" and heavy fines were imposed for unauthorized exports (quoted in Ffoulkes, p. 74). This interdiction was reinforced by bills in 1610 and 1614, although some exports continued. In 1619 further restrictions were imposed: all sales and testing had to take place in London, and all exports had to be shipped from the Tower wharf. Some exports were maintained through the 1620s and 1630s, though the licensing system ensured that they flowed almost exclusively to the United Provinces in the Thirty Years' War. In 1660, restrictions on exports were reinforced, and the Tonnage and Poundage Act gave the sovereign the power "to prohibit the transportation of gunpowder, arms and ammunition out of the Kingdom whenever he should see cause to do so, and for such time as should be specified" (quoted in Atwater, 1939, p. 292). These laws were strengthened again in 1756 and 1793, with bans on the export of saltpeter and naval material, which were directed at restricting exports in times of crisis. Given the relatively small size of the English market, these restrictions strangled the nascent arms industry, and by the late seventeenth century, England again depended almost entirely on imports of European arms.

The third type of control was the restriction of arms exports in time of war or conflict, which was driven by the desire not to arm a potential or actual enemy. Here one finds, in addition to unilateral efforts, the only prominent examples of multilateral efforts to control the arms trade. Most multilateral arrangements were temporary and coincided with prevailing diplomatic alliances; none of them were negotiated with an eye to comprehensive regulation of the arms trade. In fact, these controls ran against the grain of existing international law, which recognized no general obligation on neutral governments to restrict arms exports to belligerents. The prevailing attitude was that it was an unqualified right of states and citizens to trade with any state (including those at war) as long as their own government was not directly involved. The influence of the nascent economic doctrine of laissez-faire was clear.

Several cases of unilateral or multilateral controls can be cited. One of the more noteworthy examples of multilateral controls was the effort of northern European states (especially Poland, Livonia, the Hanseatic League, and, to a lesser extent, England) to impose an anti-Russian arms embargo to counter Ivan IV's attempt to gain Russian access to the Baltic in the Livonian War (1558–1583). Again, religious differences were prominent, as both civil and church authorities as early as 1499 had attempted (mostly unsuccessfully) to prohibit the export of military goods (such as armor, crossbows, sulphur, copper, and saltpeter) that could be used by the Orthodox Russians against Latin Christians. The perceived threat to Europe was summed up in an oft-quoted letter from the duke of Alba to the Frankfurt Diet in 1571, in which he argued for a prohibition on exports of armor, cannon, and firearms to Ivan IV because "if one day the Muscovites succeed in acquiring the military discipline and methods of Europe, they will pose a danger for all of Christendom" (quoted in Yakemtchouk, pp. 27–28). Activity was also great in the late eighteenth century and early nineteenth. In 1775 the European powers (under English pressure) embargoed the export of arms and ammunition to the rebellious American colonies—with little success, for the French supplied large quantities of arms to the United States. During the Napoleonic Wars, a series of restrictions were implemented by the majority of combatants, but most were removed by 1816.

The British were perhaps the most energetic in imposing further restrictions throughout the following decades. As a consequence of an Anglo-Spanish accord, the British undertook in 1814 to prevent the sale of arms to Spain's rebellious American colonies. These restrictions were lifted in 1823 as Britain followed most other European powers in adopting a noninterventionist stance in the Latin American "wars of liberation." In 1823, Britain restricted all arms exports for a six-month period during the Greco-Turkish War, although this global ban was lifted after it was alleged to have brought disaster to the British arms industry. A similar embargo of 1848 restricted the export of arms that could be used against Denmark, as a consequence of treaty obligations between Britain and Denmark.

Overall, however, this period was characterized by short-term unilateral initiatives to control arms exports rather than by multilateral or bilateral initiatives. Controls were imposed by states for straightforward reasons: to protect a technological lead or safeguard scarce weapons, not to curb a practice that had devastating effects on warfare. When self-interest did not dictate restraint, states were more inclined to follow the policy articulated by Thomas Jefferson in 1793:

Our citizens have always been free to make, vend, and export arms. It is the constant occupation and livelihood of some of them. To suppress their callings . . . because a war exists in foreign and distant countries, in which we have no concern, would scarcely be expected. . . . The law of nations . . . does not require from them such an internal disarrangement in their occupations. (quoted in Atwater, 1941, p. 8)

Finally, the system of national controls was not effective in stemming the export of arms and diffusion of arms-producing technologies. Although solid evidence of ineffectiveness does not exist, since exports were illegal and undocumented, the rapid diffusion of innovations in weapons suggests that the controls on the export of weapons or technologies were not effective. At the end of the sixteenth century, for example, Sir Walter Raleigh was protesting in the House of Commons against the loss of England's technological lead in spite of export controls: "I am sure heretofore one ship of Her Majesty's was able to beat ten Spaniards, but now, by reason of our own ordnance, we are hardly matched one to one." (Hale, p. 223) National restrictions on the migration of workers were of limited utility, given the numerous references to the presence of Italian, Dutch, and German gunfounders in Russia, Sweden, Turkey, France, and Spain.

THE INDUSTRIAL REVOLUTION

Although arms were widely traded from the fifteenth century to the nineteenth, this represented a triumph of primitive capitalism and the prestige and power of modern technology more than it did a triumph of conscious state policies. The dominant mercantilist economic ethic controlled or throttled down arms production in many states, and when coupled with the drive for autarky inherent in a self-help international system, this limited the expansion of arms production and exports. Although trade and production were initially closely controlled and conducted at the behest of the state, Europe was undergoing a shift in the underlying economic ideology of trade from mercantilism to capitalism, a shift that transformed the arms trade.

The situation changed dramatically in the mid-nineteenth century, when the industrial revolution and the influence of laissez-faire economic ideas stimulated a tremendous expansion of the arms trade. Between 1858 and 1888, armaments underwent a technological revolution greater than any since the development of gunpowder and the cannon, as new technologies in metallurgy and steam power were applied systematically to warfare. Ships evolved from wind to steam power and wooden to iron (and later steel) construction. Breech-loading rifled steel cannon were perfected, which increased their accurate range threefold. Breech-loading rifled firearms with an accurate range of 2,000–3,000 feet (600–900 meters)—double or triple previous ranges—also became the norm.

Coincident with this, and by the time of the Crimean War, most major arms producers had virtually abandoned controls on arms exports, except in time of war. Sensitivity to the arms trade only arose in situations in which political or military considerations were paramount. Two examples of limited controls were the Belgian embargo on arms sales to France and Prussia during the Franco-Prussian War and the 1881 Russo-Persian accord that prohibited the export of arms and munitions across their shared border. Even in wartime, neutral states often allowed weapons to be sold to belligerents: Prussia, Belgium, and the United States, for example, adopted laissez-faire policies toward the Crimean conflict and toward others preceding World War I. Because of its geographic position and strict neutrality, Switzerland was one of the only countries that prohibited exports to belligerents in the Italian and Franco-Prussian wars. For other states, to impose a peacetime ban on the export of arms to another state would have been tantamount to a declaration of war.

Significantly, the dominant arms-producing states (Prussia, Britain, and France), permitted and even encouraged arms exports in order to guarantee the health of the arms industry, maintain the motors of technological innovation, and reduce the cost of domestic arms procurement. For example, by 1877 the dominant Prussian arms producer, Krupp, had more than twenty customers and had produced 24,576 cannon, of which 57 percent had been exported. By 1914, the firm had supplied arms to fifty-two states and 51 percent of its 53,000 cannon had gone abroad. Although Krupp assured his government that he would never sell a gun "which might some day be turned against Prussia," his customer list expanded so rapidly that it was difficult to see how this promise could be kept. The government's response was timid: the war minister, on the eve of the 1866 Austro-Prussian War, was moved to ask Krupp "whether [you] are willing, out of patriotic regard to present political conditions, to undertake not to supply any guns to Austria without the consent of the king's government"; Krupp's response was an evasive no (quoted in Manchester, p. 94). The two other major producers, Britain and France, also loosened their systems of control, with France permitting commercial exports in 1885 as part of its attempt to stimulate modern arms production. Thus, direct and indirect attempts to control the burgeoning trade met great resistance from states, and the last half of the nineteenth century saw the fewest restraints and regulations on the arms trade in modern history.

There was, however, one major exception to this pattern: the Brussels Act of 1890, a multilateral agreement signed by thirteen European states, the United States, Persia, Zanzibar, and the Congo Free State. It was designed both to suppress the slave trade and to restrict the import of arms into Africa. The Brussels Act combined two motives: the self-interested desire of colonial powers to control the continent by preserving their monopoly of military power and the broader interest expressed by states and citizens to eliminate slavery. The first interest was captured well by the British consul general in Zanzibar, who wrote in 1888:

This trade has now assumed [such] proportions that . . . unless some steps are taken to check this immense import of arms into East Africa, the development and pacification of this great continent will have to be carried out in the face of an enormous population, the majority of whom will probably be armed with first-class breech-loading rifles. (quoted in Beachey, p. 453)

The link between the slave trade and the import of arms was established by the act (Art. 8), which argued that experience demonstrated "the pernicious and preponderating part played by firearms in operations connected with the slave trade as well as internal wars between the native tribes."

The problem was of course one that the colonial powers had created themselves, for obsolete surplus weapons were being sold by traders to local rulers and increasingly sophisticated weapons (rifled breechloaders) were finding their way into Africa as a product of competition between colonial

powers for influence and control. The numbers were astonishing: more than a hundred thousand firearms a year were imported along the east coast of Africa (Zanzibar and Kenya), while just before the Brussels conference convened, six hundred thousand rifles destined for Africa were sold in Antwerp. Over time, local rulers began to purchase arms on their own in the European market, thus threatening to eliminate even the short-term advantages enjoyed by European powers.

The Brussels Act was the first significant multilateral negotiated agreement to restrict the arms trade. Its operative clauses directed signatories to prevent the import of firearms (and especially accurate and sophisticated weapons), as well as powder and ammunition, to the area between the twentieth parallel north and the twenty-second parallel south. This covered an area extending from the middle of the Sahara to present-day Namibia and Zimbabwe, including the coasts and islands of Africa. Two weaknesses of the treaty—one geographic, the other technological—are evident. The geographic limitation of the treaty was extremely difficult to enforce and did not correspond to any existing frontiers, and the rough distinction between sophisticated (breech-loading rifled percussion shell) and primitive weapons was difficult to operationalize. A continentwide total ban on firearms imports might have been considerably less difficult to enforce. Similar geographic and technological issues have bedeviled arms trade control efforts ever since.

Several other features of the Brussels Act are noteworthy, especially since they find their echo in post-1945 initiatives. First, opposition to even its limited application was great. Lord Salisbury, the British foreign secretary, was firmly opposed to any restraints on the grounds that it would be impossible to stop the trade, that other suppliers would not follow Britain's lead and that restraint would be a considerable loss to Britain's arms industry. Traders in Africa naturally sought to surmount the regulation, and the black market trade flourished (albeit at a lower volume). Britain was not the only nation initially opposed to controls, but British public opinion (which firmly linked the arms trade to slavery) manifested itself in favor of control in a series of popular meetings and protests. This is one of the first instances of public influence on arms control policy formulation.

The Brussels Act was also not ratified by all possible suppliers, and this somewhat limited its effectiveness. States such as Sweden and the United States refrained from ratification because of neutrality or (in the U.S. case) the doctrine of non-interference in foreign trade. The Act had no real multinational "verification or "operational" clauses, as it was essentially an agreement by signatories to coordinate their respective national policies and to enforce the measures of the act on their colonial territories. The signatories were also to disclose to each other information on the arms traffic, the permits granted, and the measures in place to repress the trade in these areas. In particular regions, such as Ethiopia, Djibouti, and Somalia, control measures were originally also only weakly applied.

Despite these weaknesses, the Brussels Act did have some restraining impact on the import of arms to Africa, especially into interior and sub-Saharan regions. It also stimulated legislation to control the arms trade in colonial territories and strengthened the power of colonial administrators. Finally, it gave rise to several lesser joint efforts (between Italy and Britain in Somalia; between Germany, Italy, and Britain in the Congo Basin; between France, Italy, and Britain in the Horn of Africa) to control the import of arms to particular African territories. These efforts were helped somewhat by the indirect participation of Mediterranean littoral states, such as Egypt, that had an interest in controlling the diffusion of arms beyond their borders. Most important, the act laid the basis for post–World War I initiatives to control the arms trade.

POST–WORLD WAR I YEARS

Interest in controlling the arms trade slowly grew in the period leading up to World War I, and several minor initiatives were pursued. Major suppliers began to reassert national control over the arms trade as the negative consequences of a laissez-faire policy became increasingly apparent. In 1900, Britain passed the Exportation of Arms Act (which allowed the government "to prohibit the export of arms and war materials . . . to any specific country or place whenever necessary to prevent such materials from being used against the forces of Great Britain or her allies") in order to impose an embargo on arms sales to China during the Boxer Rebellion, although the new regulations were not used until 1914. In the Treaty of Peking signed after the rebellion was suppressed, the European powers imposed upon China a temporary (two-year renewable) prohibi-

tion on the import of arms and materials for arms production. The United States, in a significant, albeit slow, shift from its policies of economic laissez-faire and diplomatic neutrality, imposed an embargo on arms exports to the Dominican Republic in 1905 and to Mexico in 1912, in an effort to curtail civil strife in both these states. European suppliers, such as France, imposed restrictions on the ability of foreigners to raise loans for arms imports.

It was in the period following World War I that the most exhaustive international efforts to control the arms trade were launched. These efforts covered the gamut of possible arms control measures, from imposed restraints in the peace treaties following the war, to negotiations on multilateral treaties in the League of Nations, to coordinated (but not negotiated) embargoes on arms transfers to zones of conflict or combatants in particular wars, to national attempts to reassert control over arms production and export policies. Most efforts explicitly addressed the transfer of weapons themselves, but some also attempted to control the transfer of machinery and materials that could be used to produce arms or to impose international restrictions on arms production. Most of these efforts find their echo in contemporary attempts to control the arms trade, both in the obstacles they face and in the measures undertaken.

All these efforts were driven by a widespread public sentiment against the arms trade and arms manufacturers. Most often, this belief took the form of crude conspiracy theories that argued that "detail upon detail, incident upon incident, illustrate how well the armaments makers apply the two axioms of their business: when there are wars, prolong them; when there is peace, disturb it" ("Arms and Men," *Fortune,* March 1934, p. 120). This made several of the efforts dramatically different from previous ones, because national policy was driven not solely by simple self-interest but by a need to respond to public pressure.

The first efforts to control the arms trade were enshrined in the Covenant of the League of Nations and in the peace treaties. As Prime Minister David Lloyd George noted, "there was not one [at Versailles] who did not agree that if you wanted to preserve peace in the world you must eliminate the idea of profit . . . in the manufacture of armaments" (quoted in *The Arms Bazaar,* Anthony Sampson, London, 1977, p. 70). This sentiment was embodied in Article 8, paragraph 5, of the League of Nations Covenant, which stated that "the manufacture by private enterprise of munitions and implements of war is open to grave objections." Article 23, paragraph 4, of the Covenant operationalized this sentiment and entrusted members of the League "with the general supervision of the trade in arms and ammunition with the countries in which the control of this traffic is necessary in the common interest." Initiatives in this regard (and in accordance with Article 8) took place for the most part under the auspices of the international conventions discussed below.

The peace treaties with Germany (Versailles, Art. 170), Austria (St. Germain, Art. 134), Hungary (Trianon, Art. 118), Turkey (Sèvres, Art. 175) and Bulgaria (Neuilly, Art. 81) all contained similar restrictions. Each explicitly prohibited "the importation . . . of arms, munitions and war material of all kinds . . . [and] the manufacture for foreign countries and the exportation of arms, munitions and war material." These punitive restrictions were intended to be merely the first step toward international disarmament and control of the arms trade, and they progressively lost their credibility as broader disarmament efforts failed.

The greatest efforts of the interwar period were undertaken under the auspices of the League of Nations. From the organization's founding until nearly the start of World War II, the problem of controlling the arms trade appeared frequently on its agenda. The League launched five major initiatives to control the arms trade: the St. Germain Convention for the Control of the Trade in Arms and Ammunition (1919); the Conference for the Supervision of the International Trade in Arms, Munitions, and Implements of War (1925); the Draft Convention for the Supervision of the Private Manufacture and Publicity of the Manufacture of Arms and Ammunition and of Implements of War (1929); the Conference for the Reduction and Limitation of Armaments (1932–1934); and statistics and information gathering (1924–1938).

The St. Germain Convention The first achievement of the League of Nations was the St. Germain Convention for the Control of the Trade in Arms and Ammunition of 1919, which explicitly built upon, and extended, the provisions of the 1890 Brussels Act. It was signed by twenty-three states (the adherence of the defeated European states was guaranteed by their peace treaties), but was not ratified by enough major arms suppliers to become effective. The concern that gave rise to the conven-

tion, as stated in its preamble, was that the accumulated surplus weapons of World War I would be dispersed to colonial territories, thus endangering peace and public order. The major purpose of the convention was to prohibit the export of arms to the areas of Africa and Asia that were under colonial control or League mandates (all of Africa, except South Africa, Algeria, and Libya; the entire Middle East and Persian Gulf region).

The convention tried to address the problem of the arms trade by prohibiting the export of specified arms and ammunition (such as artillery, bombs, grenades, machine guns, and small-caliber rifled weapons) except with a government export license for direct supply to another government. For arms having military and civilian applications (such as police revolvers), governments had the discretion to determine the intended use and need for a license. The convention also contained extensive provisions for the land and maritime supervision of arms in these areas pertaining to such aspects as their storage, manufacture, repair, and transport.

The other major provision of the convention, and the one most problematic for major producers such as the United States, was the creation of the Central International Office, under the auspices of the League (Art. V). This office had a general supervisory function and was to collect and preserve documents exchanged by the convention adherents regarding the trade in, and distribution of, the arms and ammunition specified in the convention. In addition, the contracting parties agreed to publish an annual report showing the licenses granted, as well as the quantities and destinations of the arms. Copies of the report were to be sent to the central office and the secretary-general of the League, who was responsible for publishing full statistical information on the quantities and destination of all arms exported without licenses.

This initial effort of the League of Nations failed for two main reasons. First, few states were prepared to ratify the convention until it was clear that other states would do likewise. At the meeting of the League of Nations Assembly in 1922, thirty-four states (including all the major arms producers, except the United States) declared themselves prepared to ratify the convention as soon as all other major arms producers (without exception) signified the same intention. But one major arms producer, the United States, was opposed to the convention's close association with the League (of which it was not a member) and refused to sign it. When the position of the United States became clear, there was little chance of securing the ratification of other principal producers, despite the fact that they had signed the convention. Second, the convention contained several anachronistic features that were repugnant to newly emerging states, as the language of the convention (especially Art. 4) made the subordination of colonies and mandates evident. The transition to independence that many colonies and mandate territories were undergoing made them opposed to any imposed measures that appeared to degrade their sovereignty.

The League continued its efforts to address the supervision and control of the arms trade as part of its mandate to achieve progress in the reduction of armaments. Unfortunately, headway in controlling the arms trade was then inextricably linked to progress in disarmament. Member states agreed to "full and frank" exchanges of information on the level of their armaments and created the Permanent Advisory Commission (Art. 9) to assist the league's nine-member Executive Council in executing its obligations under the first eight articles of the Covenant and to advise it on military, naval, and air questions. But members of the commission were primarily military officers and were unsympathetic to disarmament, recommending in their first report that prevailing conditions prevented the profitable consideration of arms reduction. The Assembly, consisting of all League members, then decided to create the Temporary Mixed Commission in February 1921 to submit to the Executive Council practical schemes for the reduction of arms. Thus, although the issues of arms reduction and control of the manufacture of, and trade in, arms were discussed by the Executive Council and Assembly, the majority of the work was carried out by the Temporary Mixed Commission and various conferences.

The Conference for the Supervision of the International Arms Trade

When it became apparent that the St. Germain Convention was stillborn, the Assembly instructed the Temporary Mixed Commission to revise the convention and prepare a scheme for controlling the international arms traffic, to be considered at a conference dealing with the private manufacture of arms. The commission recognized that the success of such a conference depended upon the participation of the United States, which was finally secured only after vigorous attempts at persuasion. The Conference for the Supervision of the International Trade in Arms, Munitions, and Implements of War was held in Geneva from 4 May to 17 June 1925. It was the keystone of League efforts and introduced a new element into the equation, the idea that the supervision of the trade in arms beyond the colonial areas was desirable, because of the broader deleterious international effects of the arms trade. Forty-five states participated in the conference, including some (such as the United States, Germany, and Egypt) that were not members of the League.

At the outset, it was widely accepted that the trade in arms and the private manufacture of arms were intimately linked. After World War I the private arms manufacturers had been accused of engaging in unethical and even criminal activities to promote and coerce governments into buying their wares. Among the allegations articulated by the Temporary Mixed Commission were charges of inciting arms races, bribery, the spreading of false information and propaganda, and the formation of international arms cartels. Certainly, evidence for bribery and cartels was strong, but the conclusion that wars and arms races were incited by arms merchants was largely unsupported.

While the conference president argued that its mandate pertained only to the trade in arms, some states were reluctant to separate the trade from the manufacture of arms, believing that the two were linked. France was the strongest advocate of combining the two, arguing that from both a logical and economic standpoint the private manufacture of arms should be regulated prior to the trade. Regulating the manufacture of arms would get to the source of the problem directly, since it "is the first link in the chain, while trade is only the last" and would impose control earlier, helping to eliminate the secrecy that plagued the industry. In addition, the French pointed out the discriminatory nature of controls that were placed only on the arms trade: "Trade cannot be effectively controlled . . . in a manner that will be equitable to all, if private manufacture is not, at the same time, controlled" (Conference proceedings, p. 143).

There were two converging, sometimes competing attitudes toward controlling the arms trade that manifested themselves at the conference. The first, represented primarily by Britain, France, and Italy, wanted to establish a system of control over exports to those parts of the world (primarily the colonial areas) where disturbances harmful to their interests could result from unrestricted trade. The second view, represented by such states as Norway and Sweden, stressed the need to curb the global threats to peace that might arise from an accumulation of vast stocks of surplus arms and munitions, and advocated regulating the international arms trade through the effect of publicity and a licensing system. Both views were represented in the concluding document of the conference, though the former was more fully realized in the provisions for special zones than was the second in the measures for reciprocal publicity.

The conference president also noted that international opinion demanded that the trade in arms not be regarded as simply a commercial transaction and thus escape all regulation, because it in fact had a great influence on the security of nations and individuals. But, at the same time, it was distinctly apparent that

the direct purpose of [our] Conference is therefore not the reduction in armaments ... nor even the reduction of the trade in arms.... The aim ... is not to throw any obstacles in the way of this legitimate trade, but to obviate the possibility that an illicit and dangerous traffic should compromise the good name of such legitimate trade or should hamper the success of the best efforts to create an atmosphere of peace and goodwill between nations. (Conference proceedings, p. 122)

It was only in the "special zones," where the great powers saw the arms trade as a direct threat to their interests, that any measure of control was envisaged; the legitimate trade was simply to be publicized.

The draft convention prepared by the Temporary Mixed Commission for the conference was a revision of the St. Germain Convention. It had circulated among governments prior to the conference and was found to be an appropriate basis for discussion. The preamble of the convention stated that the international arms trade "should be subjected to a general and effective system of supervision and publicity" and that a special, more effective supervision was needed in certain areas of the world. After occasionally difficult negotiations, the conference adopted a convention that had three significant provisions: a categorization of arms as the basis for different control measures, a general system of reporting and publicity for the arms trade, and a system of special zones of control.

The final convention distinguished five categories of arms, according to their inherent war-

fighting capabilities, and linked the system of regulation to these capabilities. Arms in the first category included those used primarily in wartime, such as artillery, machine guns, bombs, grenades, land and sea mines, and armored vehicles and their ammunition and component parts. Weapons with both military and peacetime applications, such as pistols and revolvers, swords and lances, and their component parts, were in the second category. Vessels of war, along with all their arms and ammunition, constituted the third category. Aircraft and aircraft engines made up the fourth. The fifth category included gunpowder and other explosives and weapons not in any of the above groups (generally meaning weapons primarily for civilian or peaceful purposes).

The convention constructed its system of supervision and publicity around these five categories. Arms in the first category were only to be exported with a license and in direct supply to a government with its consent. Only in exceptional cases (such as exports of components directly to manufacturers or of arms to rifle associations) could arms in this category be exported to private individuals. Arms in the second group required documentation from the exporting country, but only from the importing country if required by its national laws. The export of naval war vessels (the third category) was to be accompanied by detailed information, while there were few formalities or restrictions for exports in the last two categories. The virtual exclusion of aircraft from control (in part because of the difficulty in distinguishing civilian from military aircraft) unfortunately did not reflect the rapidly evolving state of military technology, in which air power played a large role.

The second set of provisions focused on the issue of publicity. The St. Germain and draft conventions had envisaged a central office to publish the information on the trade and on government licenses. The idea for such an office under the auspices of the League was one of the major objections of the United States to the St. Germain Convention. Thus, a subcommittee of the conference examined the idea and unanimously concluded that control of the trade in arms through a system of licenses and publicity could be achieved through the regular and uniform publication of the required information by the adherents to the convention without an international coordinating center. This decision was intended to keep the United States from opposing the plan, as some members of the League wanted to retain the international office. The French, for example, pointed out that the problem with simple reciprocal national publicity was the lack of coordinating measures for supervision. Furthermore, uniformity of legislative codes was important for compiling statistics but was not likely to be attained in the absence of a central information-gathering office. France also wanted a more credible source for the publication of information and believed such a source would likely have more influence with public opinion. Ultimately, however, France (and other states) accepted the limited publicity measures as a preliminary step to a general system of supervision and publicity.

In the convention that finally emerged from the conference, the general system of publicity depended on the contracting parties publishing statistical information on their foreign trade in arms in the first and second categories within two months of the end of each quarter. The proposal for a central international office was deleted. So as to achieve uniformity, trade information was to be published in a specified format found in an annex to the convention. The contracting parties also agreed to publish information on all their national statutes and regulations dealing with the export of arms and any provisions enacted to make the convention operative.

This emphasis on publicity rested on two nineteenth-century liberal-idealist notions: that what enlightened public opinion wanted was peace, and that in the long run public opinion would prevail. This sentiment found expression in the following memorandum, approved by the council in May 1920:

Publicity has for a long time been considered as a source of moral strength in the administration of National Law. It should equally strengthen the laws and engagements which exist *between Nations*. It will promote public control. It will awaken public interest. It will remove causes for distrust and conflict. Publicity alone will enable the League of Nations to extend a moral sanction to the contractual obligations of its Members. It will, moreover, contribute to the formation of a clear and indisputable system of International Law. (League of Nations, *Official Journal,* June 1920, p. 154)

The 1925 conference goal of arms trade control was based on this premise, as were many League initiatives.

The third set of provisions of the convention (a major portion of it) dealt with special zones of control, in keeping with the preamble's stated objective of imposing more-restrictive measures in those areas under colonial or mandate control. The convention thus prohibited the export of any arms, except those in the third category (naval arms), to the special zones unless they were licensed, required for lawful purposes (under the terms of the convention), and admissible by the territorial administrative authorities. This idea of special zones was analogous to that present in the Brussels Act and the St. Germain Convention, though in 1925 the special zone was not as extensive as proposed in 1919. It covered most of Africa and parts of what had been the Ottoman Empire, with the important exclusions of Egypt, Tunisia, Southern Rhodesia, Turkey, Ethiopia, Liberia, and South-West Africa, as independent or quasi-independent states that rejected imposed restrictions on their sovereignty.

But both the proposed system of publicity and the special zones encountered opposition from the non-producing states and from some states (particularly Persia) that were included in the special zones. The nonproducing states (such as Brazil or El Salvador) argued that the system of publicity threatened their security by imposing an unfair burden that arms-producing states avoided. Persia vehemently objected to being included in the special zone, unsuccessfully arguing that as a sovereign state it should be excluded from those restrictions. It eventually walked out of the conference in protest. The states contiguous with Russia (Estonia, Finland, Latvia, Poland, Romania) were also apprehensive that the system of publicity would undermine their precarious security. Russia did not attend the conference, and its neighbors were suspicious of its intentions. In the final convention, special provisions excluded these states from abiding by the publicity provisions until such time as Russia acceded to the convention.

Although it was considerably weaker than the St. Germain Convention, the convention produced by the conference never came into force. It required fourteen ratifications to come into effect, and although nineteen states signed the convention, only eight ratified it without reservation (Bulgaria, Canada, China, Egypt, Liberia, the Netherlands, Spain, and Venezuela). An additional nine ratified with a reservation, usually with the condition that it be ratified by certain other states, and these conditional ratifications prevented the convention from coming into force. Once again, the main obstacle was the United States, where in spite of considerable administration support, the Senate ignored the convention for eight years, finally ratifying it in 1934. By this time, it was essentially a dead letter.

Nevertheless, the considerable achievements of the convention should not be overlooked. Supervision of the international trade in arms was for the first time achieved through reciprocal publicity and a licensing system. The information garnered from the licensing system, including data on munitions, suppliers, and recipients, was to be published. This at least eliminated the possibility that misperceptions might again arouse the kind of fears that led to needless arms races and buildups. Even if the scale of the traffic was not affected, it was thought that the increased publicity would mollify fears and increase the sense of security.

Draft Convention for the Supervision of Private Manufacture and Publicity of Arms Trade

For many states, primarily the nonproducers, the manufacture of arms had to be taken in tandem with the trade of arms. Though the League directed the first session of the Temporary Mixed Commission to investigate the private manufacture of munitions and war material and to consider the utility of a central international office for alleviating the evil effects of the private manufacture, it first made progress on the trade in arms. The final act of the Convention for the Supervision of the International Trade in Arms and Ammunition and in Implements of War stated that it "must be considered as an important step towards a general system of international agreements regarding arms and ammunition and implements of war, and that it is desirable that the international aspect of the manufacture of such arms, ammunition and implements of war should receive early consideration by the different Governments."

The final act served to reinstate work on a separate convention on the private manufacture of arms. A special commission was appointed by the Executive Council in December 1926 to prepare a draft convention on supervising and publicizing the private manufacture of arms, ammunition, and implements of war. The basis of its work was the 1924 Temporary Mixed Commission report on the principles to be recommended as a basis for a convention on national control of the private manufacture of arms. The special commission held its first session in Geneva during March and April 1927. Subsequent sessions in 1928 and 1929 made noble attempts to reconcile the differing points of view, but could only report that "fundamental divergences" persisted.

The draft convention produced in 1929 reflected these difficulties. It adopted the weapons categories of the 1925 convention, requiring that the manufacture of all arms, save for the fifth category, could only occur under license. While it had been agreed that state as well as private manufacture had to be included in a convention, the problem was the absence of agreement on the extent of publicity for state manufacture of arms. France maintained that state supervision of state manufacture was devoid of meaning and preferred that it be excluded entirely from publicity provisions. Britain was agreeable to covering both state and private manufacture, but thought the draft's provisions for publicity were not feasible. Some states (the Netherlands and El Salvador) preferred to refer the discussions of publicity of the state manufacture of munitions to the Preparatory Commission on Disarmament. In spite of the diverging perspectives on the publicity of state manufacture, there was a general acceptance of the fact that a convention for the supervision of the manufacture of arms and ammunition would assist in making operative the 1925 convention on the arms trade, because it would place nonproducing and producing states on the same footing. The hoped-for conference on the supervision of the private manufacture of arms and ammunition was never held, but the draft was referred to the Conference for the Reduction and Limitation of Armaments.

While the League of Nations Covenant contains provisions to deal with the trade in, and manufacture of, arms, other provisions in the Treaty of Versailles (which contains the Covenant) deal with the particular case of Germany. Article 125 of the Treaty of Versailles commits Germany to abiding by agreements made by the Allied and Associated Powers respecting the trade in arms (and spirits), such as those found in the Brussels Act. The manufacture of arms is restricted to factories or locations approved by the Allied and Associated Powers (Art. 168), and arms imports and exports are strictly prohibited. The preamble to the fifth section of the Versailles Treaty also notes that the disarmament of Germany was a prelude to general disarmament. Once Germany disarmed, the treaty outlines how other nations should follow suit. When Germany first took its seat as a member of the League in 1926, Gustav Streseman, the German foreign minister, noted this, and the German representative reiterated it on every possible occasion during the work of the Preparatory Commission on Disarmament. The foundation of the German argument was the written guarantee given by the president of the Paris peace conference, Georges Clemenceau, on behalf of the Entente, that its members would disarm.

The Conference for the Reduction and Limitation of Armaments
The Conference for the Reduction and Limitation of Armaments opened in February 1932, with sixty-one states in attendance. The Preparatory Commission for the conference held six sessions between May 1926 and December 1930, when it produced a draft convention. It did not deal with the supervision of the trade in, and manufacture of, armaments, but during the plenary meetings of the conference in February 1932 a number of delegations indicated an interest in addressing the issue. Spain, in particular, proposed that a system of international and national supervision of private and state manufacture of arms be established. As a result, the conference's General Commission established the Committee for the Regulation of the Trade in, and Private and State Manufacture of, Arms and Implements of War and gave it the mandate to bring to the conference proposals to regulate the trade in, and state and private manufacture of, arms.

The administrative bureau of the conference decided in November 1932 that any articles regarding the trade in, and manufacture of, arms would be incorporated into the General Disarmament Convention, recognizing that any disarmament plan must deal with the trade and manufacture of arms. The bureau wanted the committee to examine ways to achieve equality between producing and non-producing countries, the different contracting countries and the special zones, and state and private manufacture. During the conference, there was growing support for the idea that the control of the manufacture and sale of arms was at the heart of the limitation and reduction of arms. But as the prospects for a disarmament plan dwindled, the control of the manufacture and trade in arms appeared likely to be the sole product of the conference.

The previous work of the League (such as the 1925 convention) was the starting point for the Regulation of the Trade in Arms committee on the arms trade, which also examined proposals to abolish or regulate the private manufacture of arms. The special committee became stalled on two questions: whether the private manufacture of arms should be entirely suppressed, and whether the manufacture of arms should be internationalized. The principal division was between those who favored the abolition of the private manufacture of arms (such as France, Poland, and Sweden) and those who thought simple licensing would create a sufficient degree of control (such as Britain and Italy). Turkey and Persia went so far as to recommend the internationalization of all arms manufacture. These divergent (and irreconcilable) concerns and opinions were transmitted back to the General Commission in the committee's report of June 1933, and the discussion in the General Commission was inconclusive.

There was no progress on the issue for almost a year until 1934, when the United States proposed the principle of national responsibility for the control of arms manufacture and trade by means of a licensing system and the creation of a permanent disarmament commission that would have investigative powers and be responsible for publicizing the manufacture and trade of arms and for supervising the national systems of regulation. In addition, the United States proposed that the export of arms whose use had been banned by international convention (such as chemical weapons) be prohibited. Although there was disagreement on specific measures, there was general agreement in the special committee that the private manufacture of arms should be subjected to government license and that there should be national responsibility for the manufacture of, and trade in, arms.

These measures did represent real progress, but they died by 1935, as the conference ceased to function. The technical work of the conference had been generally successful, but political difficulties and the lack of preparation of the political groundwork caused insurmountable problems. The key impediment was the inability of governments to look beyond the immediate military security of their borders toward a broader world peace based on collective security. France insisted on guarantees for its security as a prior condition to arms reduction; Britain refused to offer such commitments; since France and England had originally undertaken to disarm as a quid pro quo for the disarmament imposed upon Germany in the Versailles treaty, Germany viewed the French and British refusals to reduce armaments, ultimately, as a breach of commitment. The failure of the disarmament conferences was taken as a justification for German rearmament. Although not directly concerned with these issues, the question of control of the arms trade was inevitably bound up in the broader failure of disarmament in the interwar period.

The Statistical Work   The League did more than host conferences aimed at supervising, controlling, or publicizing the arms trade. As part of its responsibilities under the Covenant, the League engaged in ongoing statistics gathering on the military forces of various countries and on the trade in arms and ammunition. The intent was to keep public opinion informed and somehow keep states from excessive military expenditures. When the Executive Council established the Temporary Mixed Commission in 1921, it created a section within the Secretariat to serve as an information center for the commission and to facilitate the publishing and exchange of information as mentioned in the Covenant. The preparation of statistics on the arms trade was viewed as serving the overall objective of developing a disarmament plan.

Beginning in 1924, the League compiled general and statistical information on the land, naval, and air armaments of individual states in an annual publication of the Disarmament Section, the *Armament Yearbook*. A publication entitled *Statistical Information on the Trade in Arms, Ammunition, and Material of War* (later the *Statistical Yearbook*) contained information collected by the Secretariat on the import and export of arms and ammunition from both members and nonmembers of the League.

The *Statistical Yearbook* was prepared on the request of the Temporary Mixed Commission and was intended as a preliminary measure for the upcoming conference on the trade in arms. It condensed and classified published information on the international trade into an established scheme. The collaboration of governments was not seen as necessary, since most countries published information on international trade. The stated objective of the *Statistical Yearbook* was to provide all possible information on the international trade in the various arms and ammunition intended for use, then or later, in war. In September 1925, following the arms traffic conference, the Assembly passed a resolution recommending that states adopt the models proposed in the convention for the collection and presentation of national statistics and that the data in turn be supplied to the Secretariat.

In spite of the admirable intent, there were severe problems with the data, most of which stemmed from member state noncooperation. The most obvious was the lack of congruency between arms exports and imports. For example, in 1929, aggregate arms exports were recorded as almost five times greater than the aggregate import figure. The League was also never able to solve the problem of how to make the statistics truly comparable, because the national accounting systems varied from country to country. There was no agreed-upon classification of arms, so a sporting rifle in one country might be considered a weapon of war in another. The clandestine trade, by its nature, was also excluded, which meant that the exports of countries like Germany were underreported.

These problems would have been overcome had the 1925 convention taken effect, and it is worth remembering that the initial impetus for the *Statistical Yearbook* was to provide information for the conference. In that regard, the League was facilitating the supervision and control of the arms trade. Though the information contained in the volumes must be treated with reserve, it did indicate the major producing powers and to some extent importing states. Although the yearbooks generally did not compare the arms trade with the overall levels of international trade, the 1935 edition did make such a comparison, showing that the arms trade increased even as the overall levels of trade declined in 1933 and 1934.

Other Post-1918 Initiatives   Two other sets of arms control efforts developed parallel to the League of Nations initiatives: arms embargoes in specific conflicts, and the extension of unilateral national controls. Although concerted international action in the League of Nations was not successful in controlling the arms trade, some action was taken to regulate it via a series of multinational embargoes (of varying degree of comprehensiveness) in particular conflicts. The first was the 1919 China Arms Traffic Convention, in which the twelve signatories agreed to restrict arms exports to the warring factions in China until a stable central government was established. Most signatories adhered to the embargo for ten years, although Russia refused to comply with it, Italy continued to deliver arms previously contracted for, and Britain declared that the embargo did not include aircraft. The Arms Traffic Convention may have had some effect in limiting arms exports to China, but it was not terribly effective, especially with respect to aircraft with both civilian and military uses.

Three other embargo efforts under League of Nations auspices were launched in the early 1930s to control arms exports in particular conflicts, but the deteriorating international political conditions meant they had mixed results. The Chaco War (1932–1935) between Bolivia and Paraguay, which was the subject of a series of League resolutions and conciliation efforts, was perhaps the most successful example. More than thirty states eventually participated in one way or another in an arms embargo, and although it was not implemented until mid-1934, it may have had some influence on bringing the two parties to a settlement. Overall, however, the embargo proved difficult to coordinate and the two combatants managed to obtain at least some arms throughout the war.

Two other efforts, concerning the Sino-Japanese and Italo-Ethiopian conflicts, were less successful. In both cases, the aggressor was a great power, able to circumvent restrictions or to bring other political interests into play that weakened the resolve of arms exporters to implement an embargo. In the Sino-Japanese case, an arms embargo was among the many solutions discussed repeatedly in an attempt to halt or signal disapproval with the Japanese aggression in Manchuria that began in 1931. Britain imposed a temporary embargo in 1933, but few other states followed suit. None of the initiatives taken ameliorated the conflict, and condemnation of Japan for its aggression resulted in its leaving the League of Nations in March 1933. In the Italo-Ethiopian War (1934–1936), the League called upon members to prohibit the export of arms and ammunition to Italy. Most active member states participated in the sanctions, although the United States, because of its neutrality legislation, embargoed arms supplies to both belligerents, a measure that refused to discriminate between aggressors and victims. But the British and French desire to placate Italy and the fact that several states ignored the League request meant that the measure did little to resolve the conflict.

Two other efforts (albeit failed ones) that did not fall within the League ambit were also significant. The first was the 1923 Draft Convention for the Limitation of Armaments, signed by the five Central American states. Aside from the general provisions restricting military forces, it also prohibited exports of arms and ammunition from one signatory to another (Art. 5). However, it was never brought into effect, in part because of the apparent difficulties in verifying the agreement. The other

initiative, the effort to restrict arms exports to both sides in the Spanish Civil War, was equally a failure. Despite the adherence in 1936 of twenty-six states to a nonintervention convention, arms shipments to the Nationalists by Germany and Italy and to the Republicans by the Soviet Union rendered the restraint of Britain, France, and other parties moot. The Spanish debacle demonstrated clearly the extreme difficulty of imposing control on the arms trade in confrontations between great powers.

National controls over arms exports continued to erode the laissez-faire system of the pre–World War I period. Britain in 1921 established a comprehensive licensing system for arms exports (excluding aircraft). It participated in the China embargo until 1929 and restricted arms exports to the Soviet Union, Africa, and former enemy states. These regulations were strengthened after 1931, and embargoes were applied to the Sino-Japanese, Chaco, Italo-Ethiopian, and Spanish wars. Under public pressure from the "merchants of death" lobby, in 1935 the Royal Commission on the Private Manufacture of, and Trading in, Arms was established. Although Great Britain did not nationalize the arms industry, by 1939 its foreign ministry directly conducted arms and aircraft sales to certain countries, marking the restoration of government-to-government sales as the norm. France actively discouraged arms exports during the 1920s and participated in the Chinese and Ethiopian embargoes. It also nationalized its arms industry in 1936 so that no arms exports were made without the consent of the foreign ministry. Unfortunately, other states, such as Czechoslovakia and Italy, pursued a much more liberal export policy (in pursuit of foreign-exchange earnings), and the overall impact of the restrictive British and French policies was negligible. Germany, while expressly prohibited from producing and exporting arms, secretly rearmed and supported arms production and exports from Holland and Sweden, and accelerated its efforts in the mid-1930s.

United States policy was driven by several different motivations between 1919 and 1941. An early reluctance to participate in League of Nations arms trade control activities and residual Jeffersonian neutrality guaranteed the failure of League initiatives. By 1921, all regulations on arms exports had been repealed, and the government decided not to ratify the St. Germain Convention, which it had signed. Throughout the 1920s and 1930s, however, pressure increased to control arms exports to specific countries or regions, as a contribution to war prevention or conflict management. The rationale was summarized by President Warren G. Harding, who argued that the United States should not encourage arms shipments to areas of unrest or warfare.

The climate that spawned the various neutrality proposals of the 1930s also gave rise to specific proposals to restrict arms exports; this was seen by some as a means of enhancing neutrality and by others as a dangerous intervention. The first legislative proposal, the 1927 Burton resolution, authorized a prohibition on the export of arms, munitions, or implements of war to any aggressor nation. Subsequent resolutions in 1928, 1929, and 1933 revolved around the issues of presidential discretion in declaring embargoes and of whether they should be applicable to all belligerents or only to aggressors. No legislation was adopted, however, and by the early 1930s, public lobbying efforts on the arms trade concentrated on a newly established (1934) Senate committee to investigate the munitions industry, the Nye Committee. The deteriorating international political climate and rising U.S. isolationism coincided to make the Nye Committee a lightning rod for antiwar activists. Although many of the committee's recommendations were not acted upon, it did contribute to the coalescence of policy around the comprehensive system of export control that Congress finally adopted in 1935 and, indirectly, to the neutrality legislation adopted in the same year.

Together these developments in the major arms-producing states reinforced the trend toward government control of arms exports. Even if the arms industry was not to be nationalized, the political implications of its output could no longer escape scrutiny. Precisely what to do next was not apparent, since restrictions were ineffective when unilateral and were difficult to monitor. They also caused damage to domestic arms industries and inevitably involved supplier states in various wars and conflicts, in apparent violation of the principle of neutrality. The progressive pattern of increasing regulation (even if most efforts were of limited utility) suggests that over time practical measures to control the arms trade could have been achieved, but the deteriorating international situation of the late 1930s and the advent of World War II rendered moot any discussions.

CONCLUSION

Efforts to control the arms trade have a long history. In the pre-1939 period, one can find examples of controls ranging from unilateral national restraints, to informal agreements between groups of states, to multinational negotiated agreements, to agreements mandated by international organizations. The most significant multilateral efforts were those undertaken by the League of Nations, which devoted more time to addressing the international arms trade than any international organization. The centerpiece of its work, the 1925 Conference on the Supervision of the International Trade in Arms and Ammunition and in Implements of War and its resultant convention, did receive enough support to make it effective, but this support came too late. The slow slide into World War II contributed to the collapse of League efforts to address disarmament issues at a point when progress might otherwise have been achieved.

The achievements of the League in the field of control of the international arms trade were limited. But League efforts did have a considerable influence on the shape of national legislation: export controls were adopted by most major producers, and arms were increasingly exported only under license. Arms manufacture also came under greater government scrutiny or control. In addition, despite the repeated failure of moral exhortations to curtail the arms trade (beginning with the church's injunctions against trade with the infidel), the League articulated the long-standing and widely held view that trading in arms was morally problematic. Finally, the League entrenched a clear public recognition that action was needed to control the international arms trade and that concrete measures could be developed.

There are several possible reasons for the accelerating concern over the arms trade. Part of the concern arose from the fact that the arms trade was thought to be an integral aspect of arms races, which were in turn held to be the malevolent creation of the private arms manufacturers. That the private manufacture of armaments gave rise to "evil effects" was articulated in Article 8 of the League's Covenant. Publicizing the arms trade was offered as a way of preventing arms manufacturers from manipulating it for their own profit. The control of the traffic in arms was also viewed as having the potential to limit conflicts, especially in colonial areas. A number of regional conflicts, such as the one in China, gave rise to this perspective:

The control of the traffic in arms was a very effective means for limiting the area of disputes and for shortening wars. If certain disputes had assumed a very serious aspect, the reason was that the contrabands on both sides had been able to obtain arms without any control whatever on the part of responsible Governments. If the [St.Germain] Convention had been in force, these arms could not have been delivered to the belligerents. (League of Nations, *Official Journal,* 1923, p. 68)

The changing nature of warfare also played a role in spurring attempts to regulate the arms trade. Controlling the arms trade became a concern whenever states realized that technology was as important as manpower in calculating military strength. The disturbing aspect was that military strength could now be bought and transferred and was not solely dependent on a state's natural- and human-resource endowments. Arms themselves were now a factor to be counted in the balance of power. This helps account for the repeatedly demonstrated desire of great powers to control the dissemination of arms and arms production technology and for the reluctance of nonproducers to participate in discussions to control the arms trade.

But few, if any, pre–World War II attempts successfully imposed significant restraints on the arms trade. The reasons for this are not difficult to discern, and they persist today. Producer states continue to find that arms exports present tangible political and economic benefits that few are willing to forgo. More important, transfers of weapons to friends and allies represent a crucial tool in the arsenal of power and diplomacy and are considered almost a sovereign right of states. Recipient states are extremely reluctant to entertain unequal restrictions that divide the world into haves and have-nots: those who can produce the means of their defense and those that depend on others. In this pattern of success and failure and in the arguments advanced for and against controlling the arms trade, one hears the distant echo of contemporary debates.

BIBLIOGRAPHY

There is no comprehensive English-language overview of control of the arms trade before 1890, but the best source is the STOCKHOLM INTERNATIONAL PEACE RESEARCH INSTITUTE, *The Arms Trade with the Third World* (Stockholm, 1971), pp. 86–132. The best source overall is ROMAIN YAKEMTCHOUK, *Les Transferts internationaux d'armes de guerre* (Paris, 1980), pp. 11–138. Useful pre-nineteenth-century details are found in CLAUDE GAIER, *L'Industrie et le commerce des armes dans les anciennes principautés belges du XIIIme à la fin du XVme siècle* (Paris, 1973); JOHN RIGBY HALE, *War and Society in Renaissance Europe, 1450–1620* (Leicester, 1985); CARLO CIPOLLA, *Guns, Sails, and Empires: Technological Innovation and the Early Phases of European Expansion, 1400–1700* (New York, 1965); CHARLES FFOULKES, *The Gun-Founders of England* (York, Pa., 1969); THOMAS ESPER, "A Sixteenth-Century Anti-Russian Arms Embargo," *Jahrbücher für Geschichte Osteuropas* 15, no. 2 (June 1967): 180–196.

The 1890 Brussels Act receives good coverage in ROMAIN YAKEMTCHOUK, "Les Antécédents de la réglementation internationale du commerce d'armes en Afrique," *Revue belge de droit international* 13 (1977): 144–168; R. W. BEACHEY, "The Arms Trade in East Africa in the Late Nineteenth Century," *Journal of African History* 3 (1962): 451–467; and SUE MIERS, "Notes on the Arms Trade and Government Policy in Southern Africa between 1870 and 1990," *Journal of African History* 12, no. 4 (1971): 571–577.

The League of Nations period is best covered from the documents, including LEAGUE OF NATIONS, *Conference for the Control of the International Trade in Arms, Munitions, and Implements of War* (Geneva, 1925), document C.758.M.258.1924.IX, and *Proceedings of the Conference for the Supervision of the International Trade in Arms and Ammunition and in Implements of War* (Geneva, 1925), document A.13.1925.IX. The best supplements to these sources are *Survey of International Affairs* (London, various years) for the period 1920–1935; JULIA JOHNSEN, ed., *International Traffic in Arms and Munitions* (New York, 1934), a collection of materials; PHILIP NOEL-BAKER, *The Private Manufacture of Armaments,* 2 vols. (London, 1936); DENYS MYERS, *World Disarmament: Its Problems and Prospects* (Boston, 1932); SALVADOR DE MADARIAGA, *Disarmament* (New York, 1929).

Statistics from the period can be found in LEAGUE OF NATIONS, *Statistical Year-Book of the Trade in Arms and Ammunition* (Geneva, 1924–1938); a good discussion of them is NOKHIM SLOUTZKI, *The World Armaments Race, 1919–1939* (Geneva,

1941). Other material on the period is found in WILLIAM MANCHESTER, *The Arms of Krupp* (Toronto, 1964); LÉON DUPRIEZ, "Le Contrôle des armes et munitions et des matériels de guerre," *Revue de droit international et de législation comparée* (1926).

National policies are covered well in ELTON ATWATER, "British Control over the Export of War Materials," *American Journal of International Law* 33 (April 1939): 292–317, and *American Regulation of Arms Exports* (Washington, D.C., 1941); JOHN WILTZ, *In Search of Peace: The Senate Munitions Inquiry, 1934–36* (Baton Rouge, La., 1963); WILLIAM SCROGGS, "The American and British Munitions Investigations," *Foreign Affairs* 15 (January 1937): 320–329; JOSEPH C. GREEN, "Supervising the American Traffic in Arms," *Foreign Affairs* 15 (July 1937): 729–744. JOHN DICK SCOTT, *Vickers: A History* (London, 1962), contains details on the British Royal Commission, and the report itself is ROYAL COMMISSION, *On the Private Manufacture of and Trading in Arms, 1935–36,* Cmd. 5292 (London, 1936). French policy is summarized in Maurice Tardy, "La Nationalisation et le contrôle des industries de guerre," *Revue de France* (September 1938): 84–108; A. BIGANT, *La Nationalisation et la contrôle des usines de guerre* (Paris, 1939).

There are innumerable volumes in the "merchants of death" literature, many of questionable value. The most notable and useful are "Arms and Men," *Fortune,* 9 (March 1934): 52–57, 113–126; HELMUTH ENGELBRECHT and F. C. HANIGHEN, *Merchants of Death* (New York, 1934); GEORGE SELDES, *Iron, Blood, and Profits* (New York, 1934); ARCHIBALD FENNER BROCKWAY, *The Bloody Traffic* (London, 1933); A. HABARU, *Le Creusot, terre féodale: Schneider et les marchands de canons* (Paris, 1934); OTTO LEHMANN-RUSSBÜLDT, *Der blutige Internationale der Rüstungsindustrie* (Hamburg-Bergedorf, 1929).

For a discussion of U.S. neutrality legislation and its relevance to the arms trade, see JOSEPH CHAMBERLAIN, "The Embargo Resolutions and Neutrality," *International Conciliation* no. 251 (June 1929): 257–340; LESTER H. WOOLSEY, "The Burton Resolution on Trade in Munitions of War," *American Journal of International Law* 22 (July 1928): 610–614, "The Porter and Capper Resolutions Against Traffic in Arms," *American Journal of International Law* 23 (April 1929): 379–383; JAMES GARNER, "The Sale and Exportation of Arms and Munitions of War to Belligerents," *American Journal of International Law* 10 (October 1916): 749–797.

Details of specific embargoes can be found in the following sources: NOEL PUGACH, "Anglo-American Aircraft Competition and the China Arms Embargo, 1919–1921," *Diplomatic History* 2, no. 4 (Fall 1978): 351–371; MANLEY O. HUDSON, "The Chaco Arms Embargo," *International Conciliation* no. 320 (May 1936): 217–246; CHRISTOPHER THORNE, "The Quest for Arms Embargoes: Failure in 1933," *Journal of Contemporary History* 5, no. 4 (1970): 129–149; BRICE HARRIS, *The United States and the Italo-Ethiopian Crisis* (Stanford, Calif., 1964). Finally, RICHARD DEAN BURNS, *Arms Control and Disarmament: A Bibliography* (Santa Barbara, Calif., 1977), pp. 297–302, also contains valuable bibliographic information on this period.

Regulating Aerial Bombing

1919–1945

———————— ◯ ————————

LESTER H. BRUNE

See also Controlling Chemical and Biological Weapons Through World War II;
The Law of War *and* Regulating Submarine Warfare: 1919–1945. *Treaties
discussed in this essay are excerpted in Volume III.*

When President Franklin D. Roosevelt learned that Germany had invaded Poland on 1 September 1939, he publicly appealed to each warring nation "to affirm its determination that its armed forces shall in no event and under no circumstances undertake bombardment from the air of civilian populations or of unfortified cities" (*Foreign Relations of the United States,* 1939, p. 542). Within twenty-four hours, the leaders of Germany, France, England, and Poland replied, in varied fashions, that they would bomb only "military objectives."

In fact, of course, none of the belligerents adopted Roosevelt's principal intent; that is, to avoid bombing noncombatant urban areas under any circumstances. Roosevelt was motivated to seek broad protection for noncombatants partly because disarmament negotiations from 1919 to 1939 had failed to produce an agreement on a formula to discriminate between civilians who made weapons and could be classified as "military objectives" and civilians who had only domestic occupations. Without recognized limits on bombing, Roosevelt hoped the belligerents would adopt a "humanitarian" rather than a militarist approach; that is, he hoped that when in doubt, they would avoid bombing an urban area. In their responses to the president, the belligerents did not specify their acceptance of humanitarian standards. Subsequently, before World War II ended in 1945, the air forces of all belligerents had bombed cities without making a serious attempt to exclude civilians who were

not weaponmakers—the United States Air Force perhaps more extensively than any of the others.

Of the three new weapons introduced during World War I, the submarine, chemical gases, and aircraft, the bomber—though not as widely used as the former two—offered the greatest opportunity for military benefits and, concomitantly, civilian disaster. And during the interwar decades it was aerial bombardment that posed the most disturbing scenarios for future wars. Military men who paired aircraft with poison gas bombs depicted them either as the greatest future menace in war or as a most "humane" advancement, in that chemicals might put enemy forces to sleep and allow "their trenches [to] be taken without casualties on either side" (*Chicago Tribune,* 28 April 1915, in Slotten, p. 479).

Aviation alone, however, had demonstrated in World War I that it was an important strategic factor, with the bombing of factories and other war support facilities beyond the front. These aircraft stymied the efforts of international law experts who wanted to define all weapons as either combatant or noncombatant. Lacking a realistic, acceptable modern definition of "noncombatant," the "total" wars of the twentieth century allowed the entire population of a belligerent nation to become a "military objective." Subsequently, while arms control advocates sought to restrict or abolish aerial bombing, military leaders were developing plans to bomb the enemy's support infrastructure—inevitably located in urban areas. The military was also developing airplanes that could fly greater distances and carry heavier bomb loads.

Between 1919 and 1939, interwar aviation disarmament discussions touched upon every major arms control area that subsequently affected aviation and later aerospace issues: Can bombing targets be restricted? Can the quantity and quality of aerial weapons be limited? Can agreements be verified by international inspection, or is the "good faith" of signatory powers sufficient? The first of these issues received principal attention because it involved defining legitimate targets that an aircraft could bomb. The second involved questions about the compatibility of civilian and military airplanes. The third received the least attention, because verification was irrelevant until aviation restrictions had been accepted.

Between the two world wars, two important disarmament meetings dealt wholly or partly with the air weapon: the 1923 Commission of Jurists at The Hague; and the Preparatory and Plenary Sessions of the Geneva Disarmament Conference from 1926 to 1934. In addition, between 1934 and 1939 there were a host of proposals put forth, of which five shall be briefly described here.

Of these interwar attempts, the most important was The Hague Commission of 1923, which, while never ratified, set an international law standard by which future wartime aviation activities could be judged.

ANTECEDENTS

While some military men believed aviation's performance during World War I suggested that air power would be a primary factor in future warfare, many civilian observers feared that the examples they saw meant that indiscriminate aerial bombing could destroy civilization. Consequently, as part of the general post-1918 campaign to prevent another bloody war, many disarmament advocates wanted to restrict or prohibit aerial bombing. Since 1908, when H. G. Wells's novel *The War in the Air* described the horrors of airplanes dropping bombs on undefended cities, both the physical and psychological effects of air raids appeared capable of breaking any nation's will to resist. Combined with the extensive use of "poison gas" during World War I, aerial bombardment was feared during the interwar years as the means of ending civilized life.

At the beginning of World War I, aviation was as yet untested in the military arena, but during the conflict several aerial attacks were carried out on urban areas that resulted in the killing of civilians. Between 1914 and 1918, both sides used bombers or dirigibles to attack cities away from combat zones. As a result, German attacks on the British Isles killed 1,414 people and wounded 3,416; British and French raids on German cities killed 746 and wounded 1,843.

The war spawned a number of military strategists who held that in the future, bombers would carry the war far behind the trenches to the "vital centers" of an enemy nation. Aerial bombardment—much more heavily concentrated than in World War I—would, according to the new doctrine, accomplish two objectives: (1) it would destroy the enemy's industrial centers, which were providing the implements of warfare for the troops on the frontlines; and (2) it would "break the will" of an enemy populace. This new doctrine might very well be more humane, the argument went, because enemy populations subjected to brief, intense aerial bombings would most likely insist that their governments quickly end the war.

The leading super-salesmen of strategic bombing were Jan Christian Smuts and Hugh Trenchard in England, Giulio Douhet in Italy, and William Mitchell in the United States. Although Brigadier General Mitchell borrowed ideas from Smuts, Douhet, and others, as commander of the U.S. Army's air service, his position enabled him to testify to Congress, write books and articles, and stage experiments to demonstrate aviation's potential. In his testimony and writings, Mitchell advocated an air defense to protect America's "vital center," which was the industrial region located in the geographic triangle formed by Chicago, Boston, and Washington, D.C. At the same time, Mitchell organized flights of army air service planes from New York to Nome, Alaska, and orchestrated an official test demonstrating that bomber planes could sink a battleship. The latter was his most sensational feat when, on 21 July 1921, army planes bombed and sank the "unsinkable" German battleship *Ostfriesland* in just twenty-one and one-half minutes.

While Mitchell's warnings and the prophesies of other proponents of aerial bombing were intended to obtain government funds to develop aircraft, their vivid descriptions of future air raids also drew the concerns of disarmament advocates. Will Irwin's 1921 book, *"The Next War": An Appeal to*

Common Sense, emphasized chemical weapons as those most likely to inflict mass death and destruction in the future, and linked poison gas with aircraft's ability to deliver gas bombs beyond combat areas. In 1923, a *Literary Digest* article titled "Airplanes, and General Slaughter, in the Next War" summarized a *New York Herald Tribune* report. "Air squadrons," the report said, "will drop their poison gas and fire bombs upon the cities, and the country back of the lines will be reduced to ruins." A return to the Dark Ages "would not be improbable." Moreover, a British naval commander told the *Herald Tribune* that within ten years, the United States would no longer be immune to air raids. A dirigible airship, carrying bomber planes from Japan, could cross the Pacific Ocean and attack San Francisco and other American cities. Although the airship described in this 1923 article never materialized, "heavier-than-air" planes gradually developed greater range so that by the 1930s, some Americans feared a possible bombing attack by Germany or Japan—a fear that caused some West Coast hysteria following Japan's attack at Pearl Harbor. European nations that were unprotected by two oceans had more reason to fear aerial bombardment.

Thus, when the Washington Naval Conference opened on 11 November 1921, aircraft and poison gas as well as submarines and battleships were on the agenda. President Warren G. Harding had called the Washington conference because of widespread concern about an impending naval race between Great Britain, Japan, and the United States. By February 1922, the conference had succeeded in limiting battleships and aircraft carriers. A treaty to prohibit the use of poison gas was accepted but never ratified.

Yet the Washington delegates could not agree on a treaty to restrict aircraft in future wars. Although the United States and Great Britain subscribed to a 1907 agreement (reached at the Second International Peace Conference at The Hague) prohibiting the discharge of explosives from balloons and "new methods of a similar nature," the events of World War I demonstrated the need for new, more precise rules for the operation of military aircraft. At Washington, however, the Subcommittee on Aircraft reported that there was an affinity between commercial and military aviation that meant that limitations on military aircraft could handicap aviation's development as a commercial medium. The subcommittee recommended that a special panel of experts be called upon to prepare international rules for two new military technologies: aircraft and radio. The Washington delegates approved this recommendation and the Committee of Jurists and their Military and Naval Advisers convened in December 1922 at The Hague to prepare radio and aviation rules for modern warfare.

THE HAGUE COMMISSION'S RULES OF AIR WARFARE

The Hague Commission, which met from 11 December 1922 to 19 February 1923, consisted of legal, diplomatic, and military experts from the Netherlands and the five nations that met at the Washington Naval Conference: France, Great Britain, Italy, Japan, and the United States.

The Hague delegates elected John Bassett Moore, a judge of the Permanent Court of International Justice, as commission president, and under his skillful guidance, the discussions proceeded relatively quickly, enabling the commission report to be finalized in February.

Although the British delegation presented a proposal at the December meetings, a U.S. proposal became the basis for the final recommendation. This draft was modified by the Subcommittee on Aircraft and the Subcommittee on Radio, which met in January to reach an agreement on the precise wording. Moore was responsible for preparing the U.S. draft, finding compromise wording for conflicting proposals that the U.S. Army and Navy experts had been unable to reconcile before coming to Geneva. Generally, Moore used the U.S. Navy experts' concepts because they resembled those in the British draft. However, one important army proposal that Moore accepted was the proposal to prohibit the bombing of civilians for the purpose of terrorizing.

The Hague Commission's final report listed twelve Rules of Aerial Warfare and provided summations of the discussions on each article. Although the Hague Commission rules regarding the radio waves were a contribution to the use of this new technology, the concern here was only with rules pertaining to aerial warfare.

The Hague Commission's sixty-two aircraft rules covered a variety of wartime practices adapted from previous land warfare or naval warfare practices. The two critical areas of air combat for which the

Hague jurists proposed regulations related to aerial bombing and to procedures for the search and seizure of naval vessels or other aircraft.

Articles 22 through 26 of the Hague rules governed aerial bombardment. They prohibited certain bombing and restricted other bombing to defined "military objectives." Articles 22 and 23 limited the targets of aerial bombardment. First, they prohibited bombing "for the purpose of terrorizing the civilian population, of destroying or damaging private property not of a military character, or of injuring non-combatants. . . ." Secondly, they prohibited bombing to enforce "compliance with requisitions in kind or payment of contributions in money." The latter two activities had been permitted in naval warfare, but The Hague Commission adopted the stringent land-warfare prohibitions.

Article 24 of the Hague Commission recommendations defined those military objectives that could be bombed, but together with Articles 25 and 26, it also limited these targets. Defining legitimate targets of aerial bombing was more difficult than restricting the fire of army artillery or naval guns, because aircraft could fly anyplace within range to attack all types of enemy targets. In addition, the advent of new military technologies made industrial centers potential targets, because they were as essential to modern warfare as military forces in combat areas. The 1907 Hague Convention on Bombardment by Naval Forces had extended legitimate military targets to include various naval port support services, but the introduction of aerial bombardment in World War I expanded possible targets to areas such as factories producing aircraft engines, planes, ammunition, chemicals of poison gas, and other military equipment. This extended targets to urban locations where munitions plants and civilian housing were often in close proximity. Thus, bombs targeted for a factory might easily miss and hit a hospital or a school.

The new Hague rules tried to define legitimate bombing targets and also to prohibit bombing where civilians were at risk. Article 24 affirmed that legitimate military objectives included military works, military depots, factories engaged in manufacturing arms or "distinctively" military supplies, and lines of communication or transportation used for military purposes. At the same time, the Hague rules prohibited bombing cities outside the "immediate neighborhood" of combat. In the immediate neighborhood, the rules permitted the bombing of

sites and dwellings only if the "military concentration is sufficiently important to justify such bombardment" with due respect to the danger to civilians.

Articles 25 and 26 specifically prohibited the bombing of certain buildings and historic locations. The military were to take "all necessary steps" to spare buildings used for worship, art, science, charitable purposes, and medical purposes. These nonmilitary buildings were to be marked so as to be visible to aircraft, including night-flying planes. Article 26 proposed protective zones for historic monuments, which were not to be used for any type of military purpose. If a nation declared and marked such a zone, it should permit diplomats of three neutral nations to inspect the zone to verify the absence of military targets.

The "Humanitarian" Clause   The most significant section of Article 24 was designed to protect civilians. Section 3 affirmed that if military targets "cannot be bombarded without the indiscriminate bombardment of the civilian population, the aircraft must abstain from bombardment." In brief, this clause gave the benefit of the doubt to the protection of civilians.

According to the minutes and reports of The Hague Commission and based on his previously known concepts of international law, Judge Moore influenced the acceptance of this clause. The Subcommittee on Aircraft had been unable to agree on bombing restrictions in proximity to civilian targets. On 12 February, before the plenary session voted on Article 24, Moore urged the delegates to preserve some distinction favoring noncombatants as opposed to combatants. To do so was in the "interest of humanity" against the use of new weapons such as submarines, poison gases, and aircraft. This statement represented Moore's belief that international laws should uphold the highest standards possible to distinguish civilized from barbaric behavior. As in criminal law, he argued, civilized standards are not always fulfilled by human beings, but they should be in place as proper guides to promote the most desirable of human behavior in war or peace.

While the Hague experts achieved notable proposals regarding aerial bombardment, they had less success regarding aircraft's role in search and seizure of ships or aircraft. Because of the controversial role that German submarines demonstrated by attacking without warning during World War I, the

U.S. and British draft proposals had spelled out belligerent rights when an enemy visited, searched, and captured military naval vessels or aircraft. Although the Netherlands delegation rejected the premise of belligerent rights and refused to recognize Articles 49 through 60 regarding search and seizure by aircraft, the other five delegations approved them. The Dutch believed that aircraft could not carry out the formalities of search and seizure that were required for surface warships and that the rules should provide commercial vessels with greater immunity from seizure.

Subsequently, Article 49 represented the majority view that belligerent military aircraft should be able to search and seize private aircraft. Yet the delegates reported only tentative recommendations on exactly how aircraft should deal with neutral and nonmilitary belligerent aircraft. In the commission report, Articles 50 to 60 were proposed as open to future regulation. The Hague experts stated, however, that rules should protect the "lives of neutrals and non-combatants regarding the search and seizure of merchant vessels and non-military aircraft." Perhaps because there had not been much experience with aircraft in wartime search and seizure operations, the Hague experts provided no clear solution to the problem.

The Hague recommendations dealing with matters other than bombing or search and seizure represented, in general, the application of naval and land warfare rules to aircraft. These included Articles 1 to 10 on the classification of military, non-military, and public or private aircraft and their markings; Articles 11 to 17 on general principles of free passage of aircraft as applied to peace and wartime; Articles 27 to 29 relating to aircraft espionage activity; Articles 30 to 38 on military authorities' treatment of belligerents and neutral persons aboard aircraft as prisoners of war or detainees, and Articles 39 to 48, on relations between belligerent and neutral states with respect to aviation.

The last two articles of the Hague rules were called "Definitions." Article 61 defined "military" as all types of armed forces. Article 62 indicated that unless the Hague rules specified maritime law as applicable, aircraft personnel came under the laws of war and neutrality used for land troops.

In brief, The Hague Commission sought methods to restrict the use of aircraft in future wars by drawing up rules that would give military leaders greater latitude than before in bombing military targets outside the combat zone. At the same time, the Hague rules preserved the need for military planners to give careful consideration to noncombatant privileges when bombing targets were chosen. As Article 24, section 3 stated, where military objectives cannot be bombed without the indiscriminate bombing of civilians, "aircraft must abstain from bombardment." This was considered as embodying the highest standard of civilized behavior.

The Hague Rules Not Formally Adopted

Although released to the public in June 1923, The Hague Commission's rules on radio and aircraft never achieved treaty status. Someone in the State Department leaked the Hague report to the media, and the *New York Times* published a portion of it on 10 June 1923 and the full text of the rules on 24 June. This drew public attention to the report and, just before leaving on the Alaskan trip that ended in his mysterious death, President Harding announced support for the Hague rules. He stated he planned to send the agreements to the United States Senate.

The State Department prepared an international convention to formalize the Hague rules into a treaty. Following a State Department review, during which the War and Navy departments expressed support for the rules, Secretary of State Charles Evans Hughes recommended—and President Calvin Coolidge approved—plans to ask the five nations represented at The Hague to agree on a treaty.

In 1924 and 1925, the State Department contacted the five nations but, with one exception, was rebuked. Japan agreed to the convention to adopt the rules, but the four European countries gave a variety of excuses for rejecting the treaty. Italy said new technical aviation advances needed attention; France and the Netherlands suggested several changes in the proposals; Great Britain wanted further formal discussion about aerial bombings.

This was not unexpected by some Washington officials. In March 1923, the two United States naval delegates to the Hague sessions, Commander Forde A. Todd and Lieutenant Frederic W. Neilson informed their superiors that the European nations distrusted each other too much to accept bombing restrictions. Japan wanted the restrictions because it saw aerial bombing as a major hazard to its islands. The fate of the Hague rules proved that Todd and Neilson's assessment was correct.

In April 1928, the State Department's Division of Western European Affairs placed the 1923 Hague report in the dead file. The Hague rules failed to be adopted for the same reasons the Europeans failed to agree on other disarmament proposals. And there is real irony here because in the mid-1930s both France and Britain would become greatly concerned about the vulnerability of their cities to Adolf Hitler's rearming air force—and too late would seek arms control measures for protection!

Nevertheless, Judge Moore and his colleagues had proposed an aerial bombing standard commensurate with civilized behavior, an accomplishment that would influence future measures.

THE PREPARATORY COMMISSION, 1926–1930

The Hague Rules of 1923 had been rejected by European powers because their desire for peace and disarmament had become stymied by France's search for security. France built superior arms, obtained guarantees of help from other nations, and refused to recognize that Germany's Republic differed from the Kaiser's regime, using every possible method to keep Germany in an inferior status. Finally, in 1925, European diplomats hoped they had found a way to ease French concerns. The Locarno Pact was signed by the major powers in order to guarantee the existing borders between France, Belgium, and Germany.

To respond to Germany's demand for arms equality, the League of Nations admitted Germany as a member. In addition, the League members and the United States agreed to convene a Preparatory Disarmament Commission in 1926 to draft a general disarmament plan. This plan would become the basis for a treaty to fulfill Article VIII of the League Convenant, which Germany claimed was a promise that its disarmament, provided for in Part V of the 1919 Treaty of Versailles, would be matched by other nations.

The Preparatory Commission and the Geneva World Disarmament Conference of 1932 had their origin in the League of Nations' deliberations during September 1925. At that time, a resolution was approved that requested the League Council to form a "Preparatory Commission" to develop a "draft" agreement for review and approval by a general conference for the reduction and limitation of armaments. In addition to members of the League Council (Great Britain, France, Italy, and Japan), the Preparatory Commission included League delegates from Bulgaria, Finland, the Netherlands, Poland, Romania, and Yugoslavia. Non-League delegates on the commission were from Germany, the United States, and, in 1927, the Soviet Union.

While the Preparatory Commission and the Geneva conference of 1932 both would give primary attention to land warfare, the aviation issues at these meetings were a microcosm of the more lengthy discussions that examined the size of armies and the use of offensive weapons such as tanks and large mobile artillery. In terms of aircraft, the two principal issues were the limitation of civilian and military aviation and restrictions on the bombing of civilians, the latter being the primary question that the 1923 Hague rules had tried to address.

Civilian and Military Aircraft   During the Preparatory Commission meetings from 1926–1930, the delegates agreed that the quantity of military aircraft should be limited, but a major dispute arose over French insistence that civilian as well as military aircraft must be counted. Although France had undisputed dominance in military aviation at the time, Germany's Lufthansa was a leader in commercial aviation. René Massigli of France claimed that German civilian aircraft could easily be converted into military planes and that German aircraft companies had designed planes capable of quick conversion into military aircraft once Germany was released from the Treaty of Versailles restrictions. More generally, French military leaders suspected a German conspiracy to prepare an air force by using aviation social clubs, pilot training programs, races by glider planes, and other civilian sport or commercial aircraft activity. Thus, the French believed the connection between civil and military aviation was self-evident—if one desired to limit the latter, one must also limit the former.

To other aviation experts, however, the compatibility of civilian and military planes was controversial. The United States and most other nations rejected French assumptions and objected to limits being placed on commercial aviation. The United States delegate, Hugh Gibson, was willing to concede to some restrictions on pilots and aviation personnel who were interchangeable with military needs. In other respects, Gibson rejected the "impression that civil aircraft may be efficiently used for military purposes," because there is a "growing distinction between civil and military aircraft" (Tate, p. 91).

Noel Baker, a British expert, claimed that the type of plane made a difference. He argued that while passenger planes might become transport planes, commercial planes generally lacked the size, speed, and maneuverability needed for fighter aircraft. Bomber aircraft, he said, required a commercial plane's carrying capacity and distance of operation. Thus, with a few modifications, bombers and civilian planes had resemblances.

In the December 1930 final draft, the Preparatory Commission adopted a compromise on the civil-military dispute. Its proposal to the Geneva conference asked for qualitative restrictions aimed at preventing manufacturers of civilian aircraft from designing planes suitable for conversion to military needs. Article 28 said the nations should "refrain from prescribing the embodiment of military features in the construction of civil aviation," should not require civil aviation to employ persons "trained for military purposes," nor subsidize airlines "principally established for military purposes." Finally, each country should encourage economic agreements for civil aviation between nations as a means of fulfilling this article.

The Aerial Bombing Issue   After four years of consideration, the Preparatory Commission was unable to offer recommendations dealing with restrictions on the bombing of civilian targets. During the commission's third session in 1927, the German delegate, Count von Bernstorff, proposed that all aerial bombardment should be prohibited. The Germans wanted no offensive weapons to be launched from aircraft, including unpiloted airplanes that might carry explosives or incendiary gasses.

Although Herbert Hoover later expressed willingness to prohibit bombing, during the preparatory sessions his representative, Gibson, and the French delegate, Massigli, opposed Bernstorff's suggestion. The United States Air Corps possessed what at that time many considered an outstanding aircraft, the Barling bomber, and planned to use aerial bombing as its principal weapon in future warfare. Gibson did not say this, of course. When the specific German proposal was debated in 1929, Gibson stated that the question of using aircraft against civilians was a "complicated and endless problem" that was impractical to consider at the present time (Tate, p. 94).

Perhaps because France had the largest and best European aerial bombing force in 1929, Massigli argued that aerial bombs were no more indiscriminate of whom they hit than heavy artillery fired from a distance of 150 kilometers or more. He also claimed that some nations needed bombers for defensive, not offensive purposes; thereby raising the central—and unresolvable—problem that plagued many disarmament proposals at that time: How does one distinguish between "offensive" and "defensive" weapons?

Because of the controversy over the German proposal, the 1930 draft convention of the Preparatory Commission did not mention aerial bombing. Articles 25 through 28 of the commission report covered aviation but included no bombardment limitations. Its four articles limited the conversion of civilian to military aircraft and recommended limitations on the total horsepower of airplanes and dirigibles as well as the total volume of dirigibles for use by land, sea, or air forces. Article 39 of the draft convention prohibited the use of chemical and bacteriological warfare, but did not explicitly refer to aerial bombs. Presumably, though, aircraft would be prohibited from using chemical weapons.

THE WORLD DISARMAMENT CONFERENCE, 1932–1934

The Preparatory Commission's four years of negotiations did not, as intended, make the work easier for the sixty nations whose delegates convened at Geneva in February 1932. The preparatory group's 1930 draft offered few real arms reductions or aviation arms control proposals. One of the major reasons for this, of course, was the deepening French-German antagonisms—the former insisting on guarantees of security, while the latter demanded equality in armaments.

Before 1932, the French delegation continually proposed limits on German rearmament despite the need to finalize the draft in order to begin the general disarmament talks. The League of Nations Covenant obliged the victorious nations to disarm in a manner similar to that required of Germany. However, to be certain that Germany would not begin rearming, France claimed that the 1930 draft represented allied compliance with the League Covenant.

Therefore, at French insistence and over Count von Bernstorff's opposition, the Preparatory Commission approved Article 53, which stated that "the present Convention shall not affect the provisions of previous treaties" regarding other nations having agreed to limit their land, sea, and air armaments.

Bernstorff claimed that Germany had waited for twelve years in expectation of a just and equitable settlement regarding the disarmament clauses that restricted it. The draft proposal, he contended, did not fulfill the League Covenant.

In the vote on Article 53, Bernstorff was supported only by Italy, the Soviet Union, Bulgaria, and Turkey. Because the majority approved Article 53, Bernstorff announced that Germany could not accept the Preparatory Commission's draft convention.

Not insignificantly, this German opposition came in 1930, three years before Adolf Hitler took power. In Germany, Heinrich Brüning's coalition cabinet of Center-Moderate parties struggled against the depression's economic problems as well as the disorders created by street fights between extremist Communist and National Socialist (Nazi) parties. During Reichstag elections on 14 September 1930, Hitler's Nazis gained 107 seats from a previous total of 12; the Communists had 77 seats and the Socialists, 143. Center-Moderate party members lost heavily in the elections. Needless to say, the French attitude at Geneva assisted the German extremists, presaging the failure of the Geneva World Disarmament conference, which began on 2 February 1932.

Because the Geneva conference met while larger political issues were unfolding in Germany and Manchuria, the final twenty months of the conference saw proposals for aircraft limitations and bombing restrictions become part of several efforts to gain arms limitations. Thus, aviation proposals—by Herbert Hoover in June 1932, by Roosevelt and Great Britain's Ramsay MacDonald during the spring of 1933—became part of last-minute proposals by which England and the United States sought to obtain a disarmament treaty palatable to both France and Germany.

Hoover's Plan to Prohibit Aerial Bombing

President Hoover's proposal was presented to the Geneva conference by Hugh Gibson on 22 June 1932. It stated that all powers must abolish all armaments except defensive ones. In particular, Hoover asked for the prohibition of all bombing machines and aerial bombing, as well as all tanks, large mobile guns, and chemical weapons. He wanted all nations to reduce their arms and armed forces to the standard that the Treaty of Versailles had stipulated for Germany. Finally, Hoover promised that if these terms were agreed to, the United

States would relieve those participating nations of some of the war debts they owed the United States. Prior to making Hoover's proposal public, Gibson had informed French Premier Edouard Herriot that Hoover would not consider reducing the French war debts without an arms reduction.

Hoover's ideas were greeted approvingly by Italy, Germany, and the Soviet Union. Several small powers including Denmark, Sweden, and Czechoslovakia also endorsed Hoover's plan, but added clauses to limit every nation's budget for arms and to establish a permanent Disarmament Commission to act as a supervisory body.

Three nations found Hoover's proposal unacceptable, Great Britain, France, and Japan. Sir John Simon, Britain's delegate, offered a substitute proposal in August 1932 in the hope of finding areas where Britain, France, and Japan might agree with Hoover's plan. Simon's proposal prohibited aviation attacks on civilians as well as chemical and biological warfare; this would leave France's bomber squadrons and bombing plans intact. Although forty-one delegates approved Simon's partial prohibition plan, both Germany and the Soviet Union opposed it. Simon did not include Hoover's arms reduction proposal that would have given Germany arms equality. This, of course, was a critical part of Hoover's proposal, but France had totally rejected it. Both Hoover's and Simon's plans failed.

The Roosevelt-MacDonald Plan, 1933 When President Roosevelt and Prime Minister Ramsay MacDonald's proposal to ease French-German differences was offered in the spring of 1933, Hitler's rise to power in Germany had generated even greater fear in Paris than it had during the 1932 Geneva conference. Originated by MacDonald and offered as a proposal at Geneva on 16 March 1933, the plan would recognize Germany's right to arms equality, but would follow a step-by-step procedure to eliminate offensive weapons.

Because Germany objected to many parts of MacDonald's proposal, on 16 May 1933 Roosevelt sought to broaden the British plan in a message to the fifty-four states participating in the World Disarmament Conference at Geneva. Emphasizing that defensive weapons "are no longer impregnable to the attack of war planes, heavy mobile artillery, land battleships called tanks, and poison gas," Roosevelt urged the complete elimination of all offensive weapons. He argued that nations must accept the first step MacDonald requested by agreeing to reduce their offensive weapons. Then the second and third steps could be taken to carry out further disarmament. In the meantime, however, no nation should increase its existing armaments. In concluding, Roosevelt added a new step to the proposal, the acceptance by all nations of a nonaggression pact.

Although Hitler responded to Roosevelt's speech by claiming Germany would "disband the entire military establishment," if "neighboring countries" did so (*Documents in German Foreign Policy 1918–1945*, Washington, D.C., 1957, p. 452), the Geneva conference delegates never approved MacDonald's proposals. The French response was to suggest that Germany delay rearming for eight more years while all European nations internationalized their civilian and military aviation units as well as their armies and navies. This unusual suggestion was not well received by the delegates and the Geneva conference soon fell apart.

By September 1933, Hitler had consolidated his power in Germany, ignoring French suggestions to delay German rearmament. Thus, on 14 October 1933, the German delegate, Baron von Neurath, indicated that Germany would leave the conference. Without Germany, the Geneva conference met again from 29 May to 11 June 1934, but the French were less ready than ever to seek the accommodation with Berlin that British diplomats proposed.

Having missed opportunities to obtain some restriction on German armaments in 1932, France searched in vain for bilateral security agreements with England, Italy, and the Soviet Union, but none proved to be effective. On 16 March 1935, Hitler denounced the disarmament clauses of the Versailles Treaty and began to rearm Germany. On 7 March 1936, he denounced the 1925 Locarno Pact, which had guaranteed the 1919 borders, and sent German forces to occupy the Rhineland territory that they had evacuated in 1919.

EFFORTS TO RESTRICT BOMBING, 1936–1939

Following the breakdown of the World Disarmament Conference in 1934, there were a variety of attempts to obtain restrictions on aerial bombardment before war broke out in Europe in September 1939. These proposals were initiated and discussed during a period when several small conflicts were demonstrating the potential destructive power of aerial bombing, in a sort of rehearsal for World War II.

In 1935, Italy effectively used aerial bombing and machine-gun strafing when it invaded Ethiopia. During Japan's invasion of Manchuria in 1931 and China in 1937, Japanese aircraft destroyed large areas of Canton, Hangkow, Nanking, and Shanghai, although in Shanghai, Tokyo agreed to prevent the bombing of a designated sanctuary for refugees. For most Europeans and Americans, however, the destruction of Guernica by German bombers during the Spanish Civil War was the most visible example of how indiscriminate aircraft attacks could destroy a town of 10,000 and kill many of its citizens. Although Guernica was not the only Spanish city to suffer, Pablo Picasso's painting *Guernica* (1937) spread that city's message of destruction throughout the world.

Many world leaders expressed moral outrage and condemned the bombing of cities, but their words had no effect on Italian, German, or Japanese bombardment activities. They did, however, inspire additional efforts to obtain agreements on bombardment restrictions. Although none of these proposals succeeded, five of them may be instructive. These five attempts were: a 1935 air pact to extend the 1925 Locarno agreement, which guaranteed France's border from attack, to include bombing; Hitler's 1935 proposal to restrict bombing to combat zones; the Nyon Agreement to regulate the bombing of neutral merchant ships; a 1938 League of Nations resolution to separate combatant from noncombatant bombing; and President Roosevelt's 1939 appeal to the belligerents to avoid bombing open cities and civilians.

The 1935 Air Pact In February 1935, Britain and France joined in proposing that the Locarno powers should extend the 1925 pact by agreeing that if one of them was the victim of an air attack, all the other nations should use their air forces to retaliate. If approved, this use of "deterrence" might protect the French-German-Belgian borders with a threat of retaliation—but other nations did not agree.

Czechoslovakia, Poland, and France wanted the pact to include Germany's eastern borders, a situation that Great Britain and Italy would not accept. Although Hitler said he would agree to the pact for the western front, he refused to extend any agreement to Germany's eastern borders. Hitler's denunciation of the entire Locarno Pact in March 1935 ended consideration of this proposal.

Hitler's Combat Zone Restriction

In July 1935 before the Reichstag, and later in an April 1936 note to the British government, Hitler said that Germany would accept an agreement to prohibit bombing outside of any battle zone. Although the idea of preventing noncombatant deaths by limiting the use of aircraft to combat areas was appealing to some people, it ignored the fact that this limitation was a military benefit only to nations whose logistic lines needed protection behind the combat zones or whose war plans employed aviation primarily for combat support operations—such as the blitzkrieg tactic that Germany used during World War II.

Thus Hitler's suggestion was not accepted by France and Britain nor by small nations such as Belgium where, in case of war, the entire nation could become a "combat zone." In the United States, military aviation plans envisioned strategic air attacks by bombers designed to operate outside combat zones by striking at economic targets in order to break the enemy's will. Hitler apparently wanted to prevent "strategic bombing"—while allowing tactical air strikes—by offering his proposal as a means to "humanize" war by confining aerial bombardment to combat zones.

The Nyon Agreement on Merchant Ships

The fear that other European nations might become caught up in the Spanish Civil War led to the Nyon Agreement, and it inspired the League of Nations to propose another method for limiting the bombing of noncombatants as well.

When the Spanish Civil War began on 16 February 1936, the European powers organized a Non-Intervention Committee by which twenty-four nations agreed to remain neutral in the conflict. Because these nations refused to embargo arms to Spain, almost all nations, as Hugh Thomas shows, violated the nonintervention proposal. Subsequently, merchant ships in the Mediterranean were often attacked by German and Italian aircraft or submarines regardless of whether they were headed for Spanish ports or elsewhere. James Spaight, writing in *Air Power and War Rights* (1947), estimates that between 1937 and 1939, one hundred British ships were damaged or sunk in the area of Spain.

To alleviate the attacks on neutral ships, Britain and France invited ten Mediterranean powers to a meeting at Nyon, Switzerland, asking them to negotiate an agreement to prevent attacks against neutral ships. Germany and Italy refused to attend the meeting and the United States did not do so because it was not a "Mediterranean power."

Following sessions from 10 to 17 September 1937, nine European nations signed the Nyon Agreement. This pact stated that if any neutral warships on patrol witnessed an illegal air or submarine attack on a merchant ship, the neutral warship could open fire to damage or destroy the transgressing airplane or submarine.

Although, as Lawrence Fernsworth wrote in 1937, the Nyon Agreement made it look as though England and France were "getting fed up" with Hitler and Mussolini and "proclaiming their own mastery of the middle sea [Mediterranean]," the Nyon pact had no practical results. Neutral merchant vessels continued to be attacked until General Francisco Franco had defeated Spain's Republican armies in 1939. The pact's shortcoming was that it asked patrolling warships to wait until a vessel was fired upon. Waiting until the attack occurred did not save the merchant ship.

League Resolutions on Bombing, 1938

Responding to the destruction of cities in Spain, Britain's Prime Minister Neville Chamberlain outlined principles to apply to aviation warfare in a statement to Parliament on 21 June 1938. These concepts were incorporated into a League of Nations resolution that was discussed and subsequently approved by the League Assembly at Geneva on 28 September 1938. The League resolution passed during the same week that British and French leaders met with Hitler at Munich (29 September) and agreed to "peace in our time" by allowing Germany to take control of the northern part of Czechoslovakia, the Sudetenland.

The League resolution enunciated a standard for defining what were legal and illegal bombing targets. The three principles adopted by the League without dissent were: (1) the intentional bombing of civilians is illegal; (2) aviation targets aimed at must be identifiable military objectives; and (3) attacks on military targets must be "carried out in such a way that civilian populations in the neighborhood are not bombed through negligence."

These seemingly simple principles did not, however, consider the complex question of identifying which "civilians" were noncombatants. Because "total war" in the twentieth century involved many warlike functions beyond the battlefront and included those who made, transported, and in other ways handled military items, acceptable bombing restrictions had to identify methods to differentiate between civilians.

Franklin Roosevelt's Appeal, 1939   As soon as President Roosevelt learned that Germany invaded Poland on 1 September 1939 and that Britain and France had agreed to aid Poland, he dispatched a message to the governments of Great Britain, France, Italy, Germany, and Poland asking them to avoid the "ruthless bombing" that had maimed or killed "thousands of defenseless men, women, and children" during recent conflicts. The president appealed to each belligerent to "affirm its determination that the armed forces shall, in no event and under no circumstances undertake the bombardment from the air of civilian populations or of unfortified cities" (*Foreign Relations of the United States*, p. 542).

During the next week, each belligerent nation responded positively to the president. Hitler agreed "unconditionally" to approve Roosevelt's message, as did Great Britain and Poland. France approved the appeal, but stated it reserved the right to recourse if an adversary did not observe Roosevelt's restrictions. Italy was not yet at war and for that reason refused to reply.

Eventually, of course, none of these nations, nor the United States after 7 December 1941, followed the spirit of Roosevelt's appeal. Each belligerent blamed the other for being the first to violate Roosevelt's proposal.

CONCLUSION

President Roosevelt's 1939 appeal had hardly been endorsed before German aircraft bombed and strafed Warsaw, hitting not only military targets but all parts of the city, including historic buildings in areas distant from any military target. During the war, all belligerents violated Roosevelt's prescription—Germany savagely bombed Warsaw in September 1939 and English towns such as Coventry; England bombed Hamburg and Lubeck without discrimination for noncombatants; the United States did so at Dresden and Tokyo. These are but a few examples that violated Roosevelt's 1939 appeal as well as the standards set at the Hague conference of 1923. Finally, of course, the total obliteration of

Hiroshima and Nagasaki in August 1945 not only opened the world to the threat of nuclear destruction, but left aviation and aerospace weapons of the future with no civilized guidelines accepted by the nations of the world.

Between 1918 and 1945, the only rules for aviation to follow were the unapproved 1923 Hague Commission proposals. Whether their formal adoption would have made a difference is doubtful. In an atmosphere of intense nationalistic attitudes—especially the French-German hostility during these years—neither the Hague Rules of Aerial Warfare nor the efforts of the Preparatory Commission and the Geneva conference of 1932–1934 reached fulfillment.

The airplane's ability to perform "strategic bombing" attacks on what once had been clearly civilian areas made the traditional categories of civilian populations and "unfortified cities" irrelevant. This is why Hoover, MacDonald, and others wanted to prohibit *all* aerial bombing. Ideally, prohibition of all bombing made the difficulty in distinguishing between civilian and military targets moot. But this simple solution ignored the fact that if a military weapon is available, it probably will be used.

BIBLIOGRAPHY

Attitudes Toward Aerial Bombing   A general study of American attitudes toward aviation and indiscriminate bombardment is MICHAEL S. SHERRY, *The Rise of American Air Power: The Creation of Armageddon* (New Haven, 1987). Special attention to disarmament proposals is given in HUGH R. SLOTTEN, "Humane Chemistry or Scientific Barbarism? American Responses to World War I Poison Gas, 1915–1930," *Journal of American History* 77 (September, 1990): 476–498.

Between 1919 and 1939, many books and articles were written about aviation's virtues and dangers. Representative ones that were used in this essay are: "Airplanes, and General Slaughter, in the Next War," *Literary Digest* 79 (17 November 1923): 60–66; LAWRENCE A. FERNSWORTH, "Twentieth Century Piracy: The Record of the Great Powers in Spain as Seen from the Spanish Point of View," *Current History* 47 (November 1937): 59–64; WILL IRWIN, *"The Next War": An Appeal to Common Sense* (New York, 1921); WILLIAM MITCHELL, *Our Air Force: The Keystone of National Defense* (New York, 1921); HUGH THOMAS, *The Spanish Civil War* (New York,

1977); H. G. WELLS, *The War in the Air and Other War Forebodings,* Vol. 20 of *The Works of H. G. Wells* (New York, 1926).

International Regulation   MORTON W. ROYSE, *Aerial Bombardment and the International Regulation of Warfare* (New York, 1928) is a study of the aviation rules proposed at the Hague conferences of 1899 and 1907, as well as the 1923 meeting; while JOHN BASSETT MOORE, *International Law and Some Current Illusions, and Other Essays* (New York, 1924), has important essays about the purpose of international law, including details of the 1923 Hague Commission and its discussions of each article of its Rules of Air Warfare recommendations. See also LESTER H. BRUNE, "An Effort to Regulate Aerial Bombing: The Hague Commission of Jurists, 1922–1923," *Aerospace Historian* 29:3 (September 1982): 183–185. A detailed study of the Preparatory Commission from 1926 to 1930 is JOHN W. WHEELER-BENNETT, *Disarmament and Security Since Locarno, 1925–1931* (New York, 1932).

Among other early studies of aerial bombardment, the best general account is JAMES M. SPAIGHT, *Air Power and War Rights,* 3rd ed. (London and New York, 1947); MERZE TATE, *The United States and Armaments* (Cambridge, Mass., 1948) provided details of the Preparatory Commission meetings for this essay. See also PAUL W. WILLIAMS, "Legitimate Targets in Aërial Bombardment," *American Journal of International Law* 23 (July 1929): 570–581.

There are several notable documentary sources. The U.S. DEPARTMENT OF STATE, *Foreign Relations of the United States* (Washington, D.C., 1930–1956) contains many valuable documents; the LEAGUE OF NATIONS also published *Air Commission, Conference for the Reduction and Limitation of Armaments, Documents 1–17* and *Records of the Conference, Series D, Volume 3, Minutes of the Air Commission* (Geneva, 1932–1935). The text of the 1937 Nyon Agreement is in *Current History* 47 (November 1937): 113–116.

Challenges to the Official Accounts   Some Americans claimed that their army air forces avoided indiscriminate bombing during World War II; WESLEY F. CRAVEN and JAMES L. CATE, eds., *The Army Air Forces in World War II* (Chicago, 1948–1958), 7 vols., provides the official version. Official American and British accounts of their respective bombing activities have been seriously questioned by MICHAEL S. SHERRY's *The Rise of American Air Power* and by such specialized studies as RONALD SCHAFFER, "American Military Ethics in World War II: The Bombing of German Civilians," *Journal of American History* 67 (September 1980): 318–334 and his *Wings of Judgment: American Bombing in World War II* (New York, 1985); MARTIN MIDDLEBROOK, *The Battle of Hamburg: Allied Bomber Forces Against a German City in 1943* (New York, 1981); and ROBERT GUILLAIN, *I Saw Tokyo Burning* (Garden City, N.Y., 1981).

Regulating Submarine Warfare

1919–1945

JANET M. MANSON

See also The Law of War; Regulating Aerial Bombing: 1919–1945; and The Washington Naval Limitation System: 1921–1939. *Treaties discussed in this essay are excerpted in Volume III.*

As part of the negotiations at the interwar naval limitation conferences, proposals were regularly offered to abolish the submarine or to regulate its employment in warfare. These negotiations were stimulated by what many contemporaries believed to be the unlawful and immoral use of submarines by Germany during World War I. Agreements to regulate submarine warfare were achieved at the Washington Conference on the Limitation of Armaments (1921–1922), and at the London naval conferences of 1930 and 1935–1936. The submarine protocol of 1936, which sought to restrict the use of submarines, emerged from the last conference and was formally adopted by all major naval powers.

Ironically, the 1936 protocol was repudiated by those same powers once World War II began. In employing unrestricted submarine warfare, all the major belligerents relied on precedents in international law, military practice, and human experience. Thus, the submarine created a new precedent in that it became the first effective new weapon to be used more than once in World War I and World War II in violation of the laws of warfare.

A historical evaluation may be useful, in that the 1936 protocol is still legally binding on forty-eight nations, including the major belligerents of World War II. Indeed, the Geneva Convention of 1949 (article 13, section 5) has extended prisoner-of-war status to "members of crews, including masters, pilots and apprentices, of the merchant marine."

While it is probably true that the protocol is now obsolete, a "brushfire" conflict might again make it a point of contention.

SUBMARINES IN WORLD WAR I

During World War I, Germany first used submarines in violation of international law because of military considerations. Prior to the abortive attempt to use unrestricted submarine warfare in 1915, the international community assumed that submarines, like all other warships, would observe the long-established "cruiser rules" of warfare. That is to say, when a submarine encountered a merchant ship it would surface and—like surface warships—send a boarding party onto the merchant vessel in order to inspect the ship's papers to determine its destination and the character of its cargo. If contraband was discovered, the sub captain would be required by cruiser rules to either put a prize crew aboard the ship or remove the ship's crew, passengers, and papers to a place of safety prior to the vessel's destruction.

Winston Churchill, who served as Britain's first lord of the admiralty from 1911 to 1915, wrote in his *The World Crisis* (1923–1929) that he had dismissed all thought of employing submarines as commerce destroyers as "abhorrent to the immemorial law and practice of the sea" (p. 288). However, in 1913, when the Institute of International

Law convened in Oxford, England, to draft a manual of international law, a German legal scholar associated with the Admiralty challenged the international laws of war that applied to armed merchantmen. This scholar later argued that more recent naval powers such as Germany and Japan should not be bound by Anglo-American legal practice, particularly in regard to prize law. Although this opinion conflicted with views held by most German legal scholars and even by the German government—which in July 1914 adopted a prize code recognizing the right of belligerent merchant vessels to arm and defend themselves against attack—such an argument was eventually used as a partial justification for unrestricted submarine warfare.

The German admiralty's argument was soon reinforced by wartime experience—that is, by combat between armed merchantmen and submarines. The British Admiralty issued instructions in 1915 that directed armed merchantmen to attack German submarines, or U-boats, on sight. This action, combined with the use of Q-ships (warships disguised as merchantmen), resulted in heavy U-boat losses. By 1916, the German admiralty staff maintained that U-boats must be allowed to attack armed merchant vessels without warning.

German naval authorities sought the erosion of cruiser rules because they found that those rules were too dangerous and impeded effective submarine operations. Given the fragility of early submarines, the U-boats risked almost certain destruction if they attempted to apply cruiser rules of warfare when surfacing to challenge swifter and frequently more heavily armed British merchant vessels. Therefore, German naval authorities argued that submarines were not designed with such rules in mind and that, in any case, the survival of U-boats must take precedence over the laws of warfare.

Shifts in U-boat policies occurred in 1915 and 1917, when Germany adopted war zones, partially enforced by unrestricted submarine warfare, in well-defined areas around the British Isles. Broadly speaking, German war zones were analogous to British blockade measures, in as much as each belligerent sought the destruction of enemy commerce. Moreover, neither belligerent ever implemented an effective blockade, because neither had sufficient forces to do so. Germany's 1915 war zone was enacted as a reprisal in response to the British blockade of 1914, thereby escalating the war and effectively obliterating neutral rights, because the German decree, unlike British measures, made no provision for neutral commerce.

Indeed, American reaction implied that the war zone declaration could cause war with the United States—a price Germany was unwilling to pay in 1915. But by 1917, German military authorities argued that unrestricted submarine warfare was necessary to break Britain's hunger-blockade (the British Navy had effectively prevented food and other supplies from reaching German ports) and to achieve a quick victory, which by then was synonymous with the survival of the state. Thus, Germany elected to play its "last card," gambling against overwhelming odds that it could survive the Anglo-American alliance.

Just as the U-boat campaign was largely responsible for bringing the United States into the war against Germany, it also strengthened historic British-American political and economic ties. The American position was, of course, rooted in the Anglo-American legal tradition—a tradition reinforced by President Woodrow Wilson's rigid interpretation of international law. Wilson had held Germany to "strict accountability" for its submarine warfare since the destruction of the *Lusitania* in 1915, when he defended America's historic right of freedom of the seas. By 1917, he saw unrestricted submarine warfare as antithetical to American interests. Thus, Wilson chose to include in the United States' war aims the defense of freedom of the seas.

The Allied victory over Germany in 1918 signaled both the repudiation of unrestricted submarine warfare and the reaffirmation of the Anglo-American interpretation of the international laws of warfare (cruiser rules). Germany was unilaterally disarmed, according to the harsh terms of the Treaty of Versailles. Its once powerful submarine fleet was either destroyed or, in the case of a few vessels, turned over to the Allied powers for study.

Many British and American citizens equated surprise, casualty-ridden attacks by German submarines on large passenger liners such as the *Lusitania* with submarine warfare itself. Consequently, Americans were highly receptive to British pleas for the abolition of submarines. As the most powerful maritime power, Britain suffered the greatest losses on account of the German U-boat campaign and would benefit the most from abolition in the postwar period. Britain had consistently advocated this policy during the Hague conference of 1899 and the 1919 Paris Peace Conference, and would continue to pursue it at the Washington conference of 1921–1922.

WASHINGTON NAVAL CONFERENCE, 1921–1922

The experiences in World War I of unrestricted submarine warfare seemed to provide persuasive arguments for the abolition movement in the interwar period. Britain chose to defend its policy of abolition at Washington on humanitarian grounds, despite the fact that Britain was one of the nations most vulnerable to submarine warfare—an island nation with an overseas empire. Moreover, Britain had lost 12 million tons of shipping and more than twenty thousand civilians—men, women, and children—as a result of this method of warfare.

The fact that an effective submarine fleet could be built cheaply and quickly meant that the weapon was accessible to any nation. But although a cheap weapon, the submarine proved expensive to contain, as the British Navy could attest, having employed at least three thousand antisubmarine warfare (ASW) vessels in order to patrol against no more than nine to ten German submarines during the latter phases of the war. For these reasons, Britain offered to scrap its entire submarine fleet of one hundred submarines, the largest and most efficient in the world.

The United States supported the British proposal to abolish submarines, but the opposition of France, Italy, and Japan prevented any agreement on this issue. All three of these nations insisted that they needed to maintain submarine fleets for coastal defense; in addition, France argued that the weapon was necessary for colonial defenses. From the 1919 peace conference at Versailles onward, France consistently backed the use of submarines on the dubious grounds that they were the only means by which a smaller naval power could defend itself. Because the Washington conference had placed limitations on capital ship production, French authorities felt that they could not forgo submarines as well. Consequently, France maintained that since controlling the seas via submarine warfare was impossible anyway, its use of submarines would not threaten world peace.

Elihu Root, a conference delegate who served as United States secretary of state and war during the first decade of the twentieth century, introduced a series of resolutions to the effect that submarines must observe cruiser rules of warfare vis-à-vis merchantmen, allowing merchant vessels to proceed unharmed, if such observance were impossible. The resolutions were incorporated into the 1922 Washington Treaty Relating to the Use of Submarines and Noxious Gases in Warfare (or Washington Naval Treaty). Article 1 states:

The Signatory Powers declare that among the rules adopted by civilized nations for the protection of the lives of neutrals and non-combatants at sea in time of war, the following are to be deemed an established part of international law:

1. A merchant vessel must be ordered to submit to visit and search to determine its character before it can be seized. . . . A merchant vessel must not be destroyed unless the crew and passengers have first been placed in safety.
2. Belligerent submarines are not in any circumstances exempt from the universal rules above stated; and if a submarine cannot capture a merchant vessel in conformity with these rules the existing law of nations requires it to desist from attack and from seizure and to permit the merchant vessel to proceed unmolested.

The major criticism of these resolutions at the time was that they made no distinction between armed and unarmed merchant ships—did armament mean loss of immunity?

To enforce compliance, Root proposed that any person who violated these rules "shall be deemed to have violated the laws of war and shall be liable to trial and punishment as if for an act of piracy."

The Root resolutions were incorporated into the treaty (which combined restricting submarines with outlawing gas warfare) with much of the original language intact. Three of the signatories (United States, Great Britain, and Italy) ratified the treaty, but France, which had led the opposition to the resolutions, did not. Because a provision stipulated that the treaty would not become binding unless ratified by all parties, the question of regulating submarines was thus deferred until the 1930 London Naval Conference.

Conference Aftermath, 1920s   The major maritime nations often struggled to formulate a coherent arms control policy in the interwar period. Although the British government and the Board of

Admiralty were firmly in favor of the abolition of submarines, a naval staff survey conducted at that time revealed that this particular policy objective conflicted with earlier recommendations to include submarines in the naval programs of the dominions. The Admiralty Board found itself in a similar predicament at the end of the war when it advocated abolition, only to discover that this posture hindered the development of the submarine fleet. This inconsistency in policy was resolved once Britain realized that abolition was impossible, at which point the government began to seek a reduction in submarine production.

American policymakers were unable to reach a consensus after the Washington conference. They conducted a delicate balancing act during this period. In reflecting public sentiment by consistently advocating submarine abolition at arms limitations conferences, the United States also accepted the recommendations of naval experts to include submarines as part of the U.S. naval building program. Most naval experts acknowledged the value of the submarine, particularly in the event of a naval war with Japan in the Pacific; hence Plan Orange, the contingency plan for this possibility, contained provisions for the use of submarines. After 1922, when Plan Orange became the focus of naval policy, naval planners consistently maintained throughout the interwar period that the United States needed both fleet and coastal submarines. Consequently the United States Navy developed and built these types of vessels—modeled after German U-boats—right up to World War II. The U.S. submarine-building policy of the early 1920s, therefore, closely resembled that of France, which so vigorously advocated the retention of submarines for similar reasons.

Initially, United States naval leaders did not consider using the submarine as a commerce destroyer, mostly because of legal and moral considerations and, perhaps, because Germany's unrestricted submarine warfare of World War I was not decisive. Moreover, U.S. perceptions of submarine capabilities were very much colored by the British view that submarines were more effective in changing the operations of surface fleets. In this sense, the *Cressy, Hogue,* and *Aboukir* (the first British men-of-war to be attacked by a submarine) cast longer shadows than the *Lusitania.* Finally, the weight of public opinion against the use of submarines as commerce destroyers and the strict limitations on the use of submarines as commerce

destroyers in the 1922 Washington Naval Treaty were compelling reasons for this policy. One U.S. delegate at the conference, Elihu Root noted that this portion of the treaty was drafted in order to "meet public opinion with regard to [the] horrors and lawlessness of the Germans" (as quoted in Lawrence H. Douglas, "The Submarine and the Washington Conference of 1921," p. 96).

Ambivalence on submarine policy permeated the different levels of American society, thereby affecting the decision-making process in various branches of government. Even though naval leaders supported the reaffirmation of cruiser rules, they were highly critical of the provisions of the 1922 treaty, which were frequently described as ambiguous or unworkable. Most of their objections echoed those of French delegates at the Washington Naval Conference regarding the failure to deal with the problems of armed merchantmen. United States naval authorities recommended that portions of the treaty dealing with cruiser rules be scrapped, that the United States return to the status quo, and that these issues be reconsidered more carefully at a future conference on international law. Admiral William Sims, concurring with his colleagues in condemning the treaty, observed that if a nation felt compelled to use the submarine "to save itself," the power of public opinion would not prevent it from doing so (as quoted in Lawrence H. Douglas, "The Submarine and the Washington Conference of 1921," p. 97). The absence of an agreement to limit submarine production meant that there were few effective restraints on the use of submarines in future wars, and indeed, at least one expert openly speculated that this failure served to nullify the Five Power Treaty on the limitation of capital ships (signed at the Washington Naval Conference by the United States, Great Britain, Japan, France, and Italy, in which the naval powers pledged to scrap dozens of warships). However, many people believed that the force of international agreement combined with the power of public opinion would be sufficient to ensure lawful conduct, and in this sense, the fruits of the Washington Naval Conference were very much a product of its age—an age of ambivalence.

The naval powers, backed by public opinion, undoubtedly wanted to enact an effective arms control agreement in order to avoid the sort of disastrous arms race that had preceded World War I. Yet the failure to adequately address international tensions and rivalries on another level undermined the chances for a successful arms limitation agreement. Instead of defusing these rivalries, international conferences such as the Washington Naval Conference merely brought them to the surface. By 1922, Britain realized that both France and the United States intended to challenge British naval supremacy by expanding their naval fleets. Obviously, such aspirations challenged British supremacy.

RENEWED NEGOTIATIONS, 1930–1936

Issues relating to submarine warfare discussed at the Washington Naval Conference reemerged at subsequent naval conferences in 1930, 1932, and 1936. American policymakers continued their delicate balancing act by balancing public demands for submarine abolition with recommendations by naval experts to build more submarines. By 1928, on a public level, the United States had clearly reversed its policy vis-à-vis the submarine and had adopted the British view favoring abolition. This dramatic change in policy reflected two important developments: first, public opinion supported abolition over regulation of submarine warfare; and, second, Japan, Italy, France, and Great Britain initiated ambitious submarine-building programs that surpassed America's meager efforts. The Coolidge, Hoover, and Roosevelt administrations not only found it difficult to justify armament programs because of the pacifist mood of the country, but were also confronted with a widespread demand for the reduction or abolition of certain types of weaponry, particularly after the failure of the 1927 Naval Arms Conference and, in the following year, the consequent broad support for the Kellogg-Briand Pact to outlaw war. In addition, even naval experts argued that submarines were too expensive to build, given the cost of an effective antisubmarine warfare system. And, of course, many people believed that the weapon would again be misused as a commerce destroyer in another war.

The United States proposed to abolish submarines at the London Naval Conference in 1930 because of these humanitarian considerations. During this conference Secretary of State Henry L. Stimson said that the American position at the Washington Naval Conference had been based on the conclusion of naval advisers that the country needed a submarine fleet, and on the fact that the Washington conference recognized the submarine as a legitimate warship, even though it was required to observe cruiser rules. The United States, he explained, had reversed this position on humanitarian grounds, fearing that the vessel might be used again to attack merchantmen in violation of the laws of war and "the dictates of humanity." (Perhaps America's change of policy was also influenced by the fact that between 1922 and 1929 Japan had thirty-five submarines under construction, France forty-two, Italy twenty-eight, and Great Britain fourteen, while the United States had begun but three.)

France, with the support of Italy and Japan, again led the opposition to the proposal to abolish submarines. However, the London Naval Conference was able to agree this time to both the limitation of future submarine production and the adoption of rules governing submarine warfare. In addition, the conference provided for the limitation of all classes of naval vessels (including auxiliary vessels such as cruisers, destroyers, and submarines, which had been excluded from the 1922 Washington Naval Treaty).

Even though the ever cost-conscious President Herbert Hoover was satisfied with the 1930 Naval Treaty, a good many naval leaders were not. Because naval experts considered certain aspects of the 1922 Washington Naval Treaty disadvantageous to the United States, they had expected the 1930 treaty to remedy these shortcomings. In general, they had hoped that the United States would seek parity in naval strength with Britain, an increase in Pacific fortifications and naval bases, and a clarification of the rules governing submarine warfare. Naval policymakers had consistently maintained during the postwar period that Pacific bases would become crucial should war occur between the United States and Japan. An impressive group of some of the most powerful United States naval officers, including the entire general board of the navy and the chief of naval operations, complained to the Senate Foreign Relations Committee that the 1930 treaty fulfilled none of these expectations. But it was ratified nonetheless.

U.S. naval leaders unquestionably favored the enactment of rules governing submarine warfare; however, they disliked Article 22 of the 1930 London Naval Treaty, which stated that submarines must observe cruiser rules, because they found the article open to interpretation. Their primary concern—a concern voiced in the immediate post–World War I period—was that cruiser rules would simply be ignored in the future because the submarine was not designed for surface combat. One such expert, Captain H. L. Schofield, observed that

the submarine treaty was intended to limit the use of the submarine against commerce but the declarations, since the [1922 Washington Naval] Treaty, of those in high authority abroad, indicate that that benevolent intention will not be realized in any future war, because each power must, of necessity, to guard its interests, act with as much freedom as any other power acts. I, therefore, expect that the submarine in future wars will act against commerce with the same freedom and under the same laws as other vessels of war. I do not believe that any order or act of an official of the American Government will ever provoke unlimited submarine warfare. ("Some Effects of the Washington Conference," Operational Archives, Naval History Division, Washington, D.C.)

Of course, one of the most powerful arguments in favor of abolition was that submarines likely would again be used in violation of international law. When the United States advocated the abolition of all major offensive weapons at the 1932 Geneva Disarmament Conference, the submarine was listed among these weapons. Although this bold proposal failed, many of the issues discussed at the time resurfaced at the London Naval Conference of 1936.

British Prime Minister Stanley Baldwin announced in the opening speech of the 1936 London Naval Conference that Britain would continue to push for abolition, and the United States supported this proposal. However, one of the French delegates insisted that it "should be buried forever," thus ending debate on the question for the duration of the conference. The conferees were able to agree on a limitation of size and armament for the submarine, and they also adopted a *procès-verbal* regulating the use of submarines—that is, verbatim incorporation of Article 22 of the 1930 London Naval Treaty. Even though Germany was not a party to the treaty, it agreed to accede to it in November 1936 and incorporated Article 22 into the German Prize Code of 1939.

The *procès-verbal* gained general acceptance by 1939, making it both the definition for lawful submarine activity during World War II and the basis for the judgment of the Nuremberg tribunal after

the war with respect to lawful submarine activity. The *procès-verbal,* or London Protocol, was quite specific:

RULES

1. In their action with regard to merchant ships, submarines must conform to the rules of international Law to which surface vessels are subject.
2. In particular, except in the case of persistent refusal to stop on being duly summoned, or of active resistance to visit and search, a warship, whether surface vessel or submarine, may not sink or render incapable of navigation a merchant vessel without having first placed passengers, crew, and ship's papers in a place of safety. For this purpose the ship's boats are not regarded as a place of safety unless the safety of the passengers and crew is assured, in the existing sea and weather conditions, by the proximity of land, or the presence of another vessel which is in a position to take them on board.

The general acceptance of the protocol by the principal maritime nations—including the United States, Great Britain, France, Italy, Japan, Germany, and the Soviet Union—meant that cruiser rules had clearly been recognized as part of international treaty law.

But was this universal recognition sufficient to ensure observance in a future war? Germany had, after all, acceded to cruiser rules of warfare prior to World War I, yet that had not prevented the German government from arguing that submarines were unable to follow the rules during the war due to military necessity and changed circumstances.

NATIONAL SUBMARINE POLICIES

Certainly, the United States had intended to abide by the London Protocol. Article 22 of the 1930 London Naval Treaty appeared in all subsequent drafts of instructions to the United States Navy on maritime warfare, and there was apparently no dissent over these, at least immediately, among top naval officials on the issue of cruiser rules.

The German submarine policy of the interwar period was no less complicated than that of the United States or Great Britain, since it was in large part dictated by the terms of the Treaty of Versailles.

For this reason, the official view was that Germany had disarmed and, therefore, that the entire submarine fleet had been destroyed or, in the case of a few vessels, turned over to the Allied powers for study. In addition, the German government had formally acceded to the 1936 London Protocol to observe cruiser rules. So on the surface, it appeared that Germany would be unable to mount a submarine campaign in the future.

Although the Allied powers had confiscated the German submarines, they had neglected to seize the submarine construction plans that remained in German shipyards. These plans eventually became the basis for the development of the modern German submarine. But Germany, unable to use this knowledge to build its own submarines in the first few years after World War I, shared its knowledge with other countries—namely Japan, the Netherlands, Finland, and Spain. This arrangement was so successful that by the mid-1930s Germany was producing the most up-to-date submarine designs. At this point, the policy goal was to keep abreast of the latest developments in submarine technology so that this knowledge could be used at some future date to create a German U-boat arm.

Germany did not begin to rearm openly, in violation of the Treaty of Versailles, until after it left the 1932 Geneva Disarmament Conference. Afterward, the Nazi government announced plans to train officers for a new submarine department in the navy and eventually to build submarines in Germany. Hitler created the submarine department in 1934, but construction of the first U-boats did not begin until February 1935, the eve of the Anglo-German naval talks.

German policy after 1932 was to attain parity with the French Navy. Even though this demand was rejected at the 1932 World Disarmament Conference, Joachim von Ribbentrop, Hitler's special minister on disarmament, refused to open the 1935 negotiations with the British unless Germany was allowed to build up to 35 percent of the British strength in all categories of vessels, which coincided with the 1.75 ratio allotted to the French and Italians at the Washington Naval Conference. The British accepted this stipulation, as well as one in which Germany was permitted to build up to 45 percent of British submarine strength, with provisions to build up to parity under certain conditions.

The experience of the interwar arms limitations conferences demonstrates the reluctance of naval powers either to limit the production or to regulate the usage of new weapons. This reluctance, combined with the disintegration of the postwar world order, convinced those nations favoring the abolition of submarines–namely Great Britain and the United States—to retain and expand their existing fleets.

WORLD WAR II: NONCOMPLIANCE

German political and naval authorities discussed the ramifications of the submarine campaign in joint conferences after war broke out in the fall of 1939. These conferences and the decisions emanating from them resulted in the decision to engage in unrestricted submarine warfare against shipping in the Atlantic. More precisely, there was no single decision for unrestricted submarine warfare but rather a series of decisions to erode cruiser rules gradually for political reasons.

In conferences with naval authorities in the fall of 1939, Adolf Hitler and German Foreign Office officials emphasized the need to avoid conflict with neutrals, particularly the United States. Germany was especially concerned that incidents involving the United States be prevented, because unrestricted submarine warfare during World War I had brought the United States into the war—a factor that contributed heavily toward the German defeat. Despite repeated complaints from naval authorities that submarines could neither safely nor effectively follow cruiser rules, the German Navy was unable to get the rules rescinded due to political considerations. Hitler was so committed to a policy of avoiding conflict with neutral nations that soon after the war began he issued orders to the naval high command to avoid, under all circumstances, incidents with the United States.

Although Hitler was clearly sympathetic to naval demands—first for the erosion of cruiser rules of warfare, and then for unrestricted submarine warfare—he deferred until December 1941 the decision to wage unrestricted submarine warfare because he thought such a decision would—as in 1917—bring the United States into the war. He preferred to tolerate an undeclared naval war in the Atlantic in 1941 because he wanted to postpone war with the United States as long as possible.

Once the Japanese attacked Pearl Harbor in December 1941, Hitler declared war on the United States assuming that the remaining U.S. naval forces would be tied down in the Pacific, thereby giving the Germans a freer hand in the Atlantic. The declaration of war carried with it orders for unrestricted submarine warfare against U.S. ships.

Close cooperation between the U.S. Navy, the State Department, and President Roosevelt preceded the U.S. decision to engage in unrestricted submarine warfare. Clearly, the navy recommended the decision for strategic reasons, and the President approved it. The rationale for this reversal of traditional U.S. policy is scattered among various naval documents, and, as a result, no written record of discussions with Roosevelt of the decision appears in any one place. Nevertheless, Chief of Naval Operations H. R. Stark insisted that the president did discuss it with him. Of course, unrestricted submarine warfare would be a violation of neutral rights—"freedom of the seas"—and the London Protocol.

The U.S. rationale for the decision was based primarily on German and British submarine practice during the early months of World War II. U.S. Secretary of the Navy Frank Knox cited British practice. The British used unrestricted submarine warfare as a form of reprisal because of German actions in specific areas such as the Skagerrak (the strait in northern Europe that separates Denmark and Norway), and Britain anticipated underwater attacks against Japan. (However, Britain waited until Japan abandoned the rules governing submarine and air warfare before implementing unrestricted submarine warfare in the Pacific.)

Knox observed that if Japan entered the war, it was expected to do so "as a full member of the Axis" (Operational Archives, Naval History Division, Washington, D.C.). He rationalized that Japan must share the responsibility for unrestricted submarine and air warfare waged by its allies, Germany and Italy, whether or not Japan engaged in this type of activity. In any event, he assumed that the United States would adopt similar measures in the event of war and recommended that it do so.

Japan's decision to attack Pearl Harbor, plus Japanese measures taken in conjunction with the attack or immediately afterward, provided public justification for American actions—even though the decision had already been made. Admiral Chester W. Nimitz, commander-in-chief, U.S. Pacific Fleet, testified before the International Military Tribunal at Nuremberg that the December orders to implement unrestricted submarine and air warfare were justified "by the Japanese attacks on that date on U.S. bases, and on both armed and unarmed ships and nationals, without warning or declaration of war" (*Trial of the Major War Criminals Before the International Military Tribunal,* vol. 40, p. 111). He also stated that no further orders were issued to U.S. submarines during the war as reprisals, even though Japanese submarine personnel were known to commit atrocities on U.S. merchant marine survivors. Undoubtedly, the United States did not declare unrestricted submarine warfare against Germany because British naval operations had eliminated the German merchant fleet.

Nevertheless, statements contained in naval memoranda both during and after the war graphically demonstrate the dependence of the rationale for U.S. actions after Pearl Harbor on the precedent of German submarine practice. Combat situations during World War II did not lend themselves to the execution of the traditional laws of visit and search. Submarine design had not been updated since the late 1930s, and U.S. submarine losses would have been greater if Japanese forces had been more efficient.

By the end of the war, tactical considerations were deemed so important in naval planning that the General Board of the Navy cited them as the reason for abandoning cruiser rules of warfare. The board concluded that the conditions of warfare—that is, changed circumstances—had forced this fundamental change in American policy. "With war forced upon us, it was necessary, radically, to change all ideas, doctrines, training procedures and to convert a fine peace time trained submarines [sic] into one capable of waging unrestricted and unlimited warfare" (Discussion, Submarines, 20 October 1945, Operational Archives, Naval History Division, Washington, D.C.).

Actually, there were relatively few reports of Japanese "violations" of the submarine protocol. The Imperial Navy had not changed its basic policy that the submarine was to search out and sink enemy warships. Mochitsura Hashimoto, a successful submarine commander who sank, among other ships, the *USS Indianapolis,* wrote after the war that "Japanese policy was to use submarines primarily for attacking enemy naval forces" while merchant vessels "had only second priority" (p. 62).

Most U.S. naval authorities have had difficulty understanding Japan's failure to more profitably employ its submarines. Some have attributed this failure to the lack of proper strategy. Samuel Eliot Morison, writing in the *History of United States Naval Operations in World War II*, affirmed that "instead of sending most of their [submarines] to raid merchant shipping, the Japanese persisted in trying to find warships. They had no scruples about unrestricted warfare, far from it; they simply failed to replace strategic notions." Another writer has concluded that while Japan began the war with a submarine fleet larger than Germany's, it "squandered" its resources on futile searches for Allied warships, land bombardment, and supply operations. As Robert Kuenne wrote in *The Attack Submarine: A Study in Strategy* (New Haven, Conn., 1965), "These employments are evidence of a total bankruptcy of strategic doctrine concerning the submarine, and the record of the Japanese in these respects constitutes the most shameful avoidable waste of a military resource in World War II" (pp. 4–5).

The Nuremberg Decisions

Belligerents explained and justified their actions during both world wars as temporary measures calculated to obtain a speedy and secure peace. But their own populations, both civilian and military, increasingly questioned those actions when faced with destruction and loss of life so great that it threatened to annihilate the very societies and institutions the belligerents promised to preserve. This was one of the issues examined at Nuremberg when the international tribunal considered the issue of unrestricted submarine warfare after the war.

Not surprisingly, then, the tribunal weighed arguments in defense of unrestricted submarine warfare (based on the effects of antisubmarine warfare technology) against the dictates of international law (as accepted, paradoxically, by all the belligerents in the interest of preserving human life and limiting the destructiveness of war). Two German admirals, Karl Doenitz and Erich Raeder, were charged as war criminals with waging unrestricted submarine warfare. In its examination of international law and submarine practice during the war, the tribunal rendered a mixed decision. It did not hold the admirals accountable for actions against armed British merchant ships because Britain had integrated armed merchantmen into the naval services—that is, because those merchantmen had orders to report submarine positions and to ram submarines after 1 October 1939. The tribunal did find Doenitz and Raeder guilty of violating the London Protocol

of 1936, which, like the Washington Naval Conference of 1922 and the London Naval Treaty of 1930, made no provisions for sinking without warning neutral vessels in operational zones. Although such zones had been used during World War I, those accords made no exception for them.

Many American naval officers undoubtedly were concerned about the Nuremberg proceeding because it was a victor's justice, and because the charges brought against Doenitz and Raeder regarding submarine warfare necessarily focused attention on Allied submarine practices. German and Allied naval authorities pointed out that all belligerents used unrestricted submarine warfare during the war and that all felt justified in doing so in serving the interests of the state. Thus, they argued that it was hypocritical to hold the vanquished nations accountable for actions committed by both sides. Although there is merit in this argument (and the tribunal did acknowledge it to some extent), the tribunal examined German submarine practices and the responsibility of those who executed them. The tribunal observed that Admirals Doenitz and Raeder occupied important positions within the German government and, therefore, had to be held accountable, at least in part, for some of the government's atrocities.

Hence, the tribunal's decision on the topic of submarine warfare was a mixed one. It did not state that unrestricted submarine warfare was allowed by international law, but it also said, in effect, that Doenitz and Raeder could not be convicted for measures also enacted by Great Britain and the United States. Furthermore, the tribunal insisted that the 1936 London Protocol was valid and must be observed. It remains in force.

CONCLUSION

Even though unrestricted submarine warfare was practiced by all of the belligerents, usually in vast areas of the high seas during World War II, each government exercised some restraint. The British confined their use of unrestricted submarine warfare to the Skagerrak. Germany and the United States made great use of the unrestricted submarine warfare, with Germany declaring extensive war zones in the Atlantic Ocean and the United States designating the entire Pacific Ocean as a war zone. In every case, the belligerents were concerned with the effect of unrestricted submarine warfare on neutrals. The United States and Britain maintained that neutrals did not sail in areas each had designated as war zones (the Skagerrak after 8 May 1940, and the Pacific Ocean after 7 December 1941).

Although the submarine proved to be an effective weapon that operated most efficiently when used in violation of international law, it often encountered a formidable antisubmarine warfare system. The use of aircraft—combined with convoy operations and detection devices such as sonar, radar, and the High Frequency Direction Finder (not to mention decipherment of the U-boat code)—deprived U-boats of their most important advantage, concealment.

The U-boat casualty figures not only emphasize Britain's victory in a naval war in which technological development in antisubmarine warfare played a crucial role, but they also reflect Germany's desperate attempt to prevent or postpone defeat, despite tremendous human costs. The U-boat arm lost 630 vessels in all theaters of war, and another 540 U-boats were destroyed outside combat areas (in port, for instance). To be sure, submarine warfare consistently brings to the fore the role of technology in warfare and the disregard for human life, whether combatant or civilian. U-boats sank 2,840 Allied vessels, or approximately 14,333,082 BRT (British royal tons) during World War II.

Perhaps, in part, because of Japan's failure to develop an effective antisubmarine warfare system, Allied submarine forces inflicted heavy casualties on the Japanese merchant and naval fleets in the Pacific. Allied submarines sank 1,152 Japanese merchantmen, or approximately 4,886,991 tons, and destroyed 217 naval vessels, or approximately 570,508 tons. Ironically, Americans, equipped with outdated submarines ill-suited to unrestricted warfare, were responsible for the majority of these sinkings. U.S. naval authorities later acknowledged that their losses would have been greater if Japanese forces had been more efficient. In a 1946 memorandum, Lieutenant Commander C. N. G. Hendrix stated, "Our submarines in the Pacific were not up against a 'first rate' group of 'killers' as were the Germans when they tried to outwit our own efficient antisubmarine forces in the Atlantic. We might be prone to boast our successes, but it is interesting and at the same time not exactly pleasant to meditate what results would have been had we submariners been up against a real first rate antisubmarine organization" (Operational Archives, Naval History Division, Washington, D.C.).

All nations that have resorted to unrestricted submarine warfare have justified their actions on the basis of military necessity. That is, they believed that the measure was necessary because they equated winning the war with the survival of the state. This fear was given greater credence because civilian populations increasingly became the primary military target as a result of technological advances, the prevalence of a philosophy of total war, and the reluctance or refusal of the belligerents to seek a negotiated peace during World War II. These developments have seriously undermined the foundation of the laws of war, and the design and deployment of each new weapon made to destroy even larger civilian populations and territories has threatened the very basis of civilization.

Even though one of the fundamental principles of international law is that noncombatants be spared direct attack by sea, air, or on land, modern practice has demonstrated that belligerents have progressively ignored this principle. In general, the attempt to regulate war through international law has been severely weakened by advances in technology. Yet the solution to this problem would seem not to lie with technology, as some people think, but with civilization itself. Clearly, attempts might be made to limit the scope and destructiveness of warfare, in much the way the use of submarines has been circumscribed, through treaties and agreements for the international regulation of weapons of all types.

BIBLIOGRAPHY

For an overview of policies related to submarine warfare, see ERNEST ANDRADE, JR., "Submarine Policy in the United States Navy, 1919–1941," *Military Affairs* 35 (April 1971): 50–56; HOLGER H. HERWIG, *Politics of Frustration: The United States in German Naval Planning, 1889–1941* (Boston, 1976); KARL LAUTENSCHLÄGER, "The Submarine in Naval Warfare, 1901–2001," *International Security* 11 (Winter 1986–87): 94–140; J. E. TALBOTT, "Weapons Development, War Planning, and Policy: The U.S. Navy and the Submarine, 1917–1941," *Naval War College Review* (May/June 1984): 53–71; ROBERT W. TUCKER, *The Law of War and Neutrality at Sea*, Naval War College International Law Studies, no. 50 (Washington, D.C., 1957).

Secondary works on submarine policy during World War I include: KARL E. BIRNBAUM, *Peace Moves* and *U-Boat Warfare, A Study of Imperial Germany's Policy Towards the United States, April 18, 1916–January 9, 1917* (Stockholm, Sweden, 1958); R. H. GIBSON and MAURICE PRENDERGAST, *The German Submarine War 1914–1918* (London, 1931); PHILIP K. LUNDEBERG, "The German Naval Critique of the U-Boat Campaign, 1915–1918," *Military Affairs* 27 (Fall 1963): 105–118.

Secondary works on the interwar period include RICHARD DEAN BURNS, "Regulating Submarine Warfare, 1921–41: A Case Study in Arms Control and Limited War," *Military Affairs* 35 (April 1971): 56–63; THOMAS H. BUCKLEY, *The United States and the Washington Conference, 1921–1922* (Knoxville, Tenn., 1970); LAWRENCE H. DOUGLAS, "The Submarine and the Washington Conference of 1921," *Naval War College Review* 26 (March/April 1974): 86–100; GROTIUS SOCIETY, University of British Columbia, "Discussion on the Abolition of Submarines," *Grotius Society Transactions* 11 (1925): 65–78; GROTIUS SOCIETY, "Report of the Committee on the Legal Status of Submarines," *Grotius Society Transactions* 14 (n.d.): 155–174; WERNER RAHN, *Reichsmarine und Landesverteidigung 1919–1928: Konzeption und Führung der Marine in der Weimarer Republik* (Munich, Germany, 1976); STEPHEN

ROSKILL, *Naval Policy Between the Wars*, 2 vols. (London, 1968–1976).

Secondary works on the World War II period include MOCHITSURA HASHIMOTO, *Sunk: The Story of the Japanese Submarine, 1941–45* (New York, 1954); WALDO HEINRICHS, "President Franklin D. Roosevelt's Intervention in the Battle of the Atlantic, 1941," *Diplomatic History* 10 (Fall 1986): 311–332; HOLGER HERWIG, "Prelude to 'Weltblitzkrieg': Germany's Naval Policy Towards the United States of America, 1939–1941," *Journal of Modern History* 43 (December 1971): 649–668; W. T. MALLISON, *Studies in the Law of Naval Warfare: Submarines in General and Limited Wars*, Naval War College International Studies, no. 68 (Washington, D.C., 1968); JANET M. MANSON, *Diplomatic Ramifications of Submarine Warfare, 1939–1941* (Westport, Conn., 1990); SAMUEL ELIOT MORISON, *History of United States Naval Operations in World War II*, 15 vols. (Boston, 1954); JUERGEN ROHWER, "Die USA und die Schlacht im Atlantik 1941," in *Kriegswende Dezember 1941,* edited by JUERGEN ROHWER and EBERHARD JAECKEL (Koblenz, Germany, 1984), pp. 81–103; JUERGEN ROHWER, *U-Boote: Eine Chronik in Bildern* (Oldenburg, Germany, 1962).

PART

4

ARMS CONTROL
ACTIVITIES SINCE 1945

The United Nations and Disarmament

○

EDMUND PIASECKI
TOBY TRISTER GATI

See also The International Atomic Energy Agency and Arms Control; The League of Nations and Arms Control; *and the essays in Part 4,* Arms Control Activities Since 1945. *Most of the treaties discussed in this essay are excerpted in Volume III.*

The establishment of an international system to regulate armaments was envisoned as a primary task of the United Nations at its founding in 1945. Provisions in the U.N. Charter called on the Security Council (Art. 26) and the General Assembly (Art. 11, par. 1) to formulate comprehensive plans for multilateral reductions in conventional weapons and national armed forces "in order to promote the establishment and maintenance of international peace and security with the least diversion for armaments of the world's human and economic resources..." (Art. 26). But the unanticipated explosion of a nuclear weapon over Hiroshima in August 1945 and the onset of the Cold War quickly dealt a blow to the U.N.'s multilateral disarmament efforts. The organization was ill-suited to the task of controlling these deadly new weapons and paralyzed by the postwar deadlock between the United States and the Soviet Union. Despite its endorsement of several successful bilateral negotiations on nuclear arms control and the development of a radically improved relationship between the United States and Russia (formerly the Soviet Union), the U.N. has, for various reasons, been unable to assume a central role in disarmament.

The nuclear question was accorded the highest priority on the international disarmament agenda from the outset, mainly for political reasons. It re-

tains its prominence, despite the U.N.'s inability to eliminate or substantially curb the nuclear arms race. The resulting inattentiveness to conventional disarmament contributed in the interim to a burgeoning arms trade involving both developed and developing nations. Not until the 1990s did the U.N. begin to address conventional disarmament and the international trade in conventional arms.

Comprehensive plans for global disarmament were proposed soon after the U.N. began to function, but were quickly abandoned in favor of a more targeted approach. In the late 1940s and 1950s, the General Assembly appointed a number of committees, comprising member nations of the Eastern and Western blocs in Europe, to negotiate immediate reductions in nuclear and conventional forces. These talks failed, however, to make any headway on either issue. Despite its avowed goal "to be a center for harmonizing the actions of nations" (Art. 1, para. 4 of the Charter), the U.N. became, and remained until the mid-1980s, a battleground between East and West, with little progress made on either regional security or arms control issues. The U.N.'s utility was largely contingent on and subordinated to the stability of relations between the superpowers. By 1960 it was clear that agreements reached under U.N. auspices would be very limited.

The General Assembly's endorsement of the concept of general and complete disarmament in 1959 (Assembly resolution 1378, 20 November 1959), the "democratization" of U.N. disarmament negotiations to include the nonaligned states, and the U.N.'s continued preoccupation with the prevention of nuclear war, produced an overly ambitious disarmament agenda. The focus of negotiations shifted from committees appointed by the General Assembly to a succession of quasi-independent multilateral bodies based in Geneva, approved by the General Assembly but established by the opposing military blocs themselves. A notable achievement for the U.N. of these annual negotiations of the various U.N. disarmament groups was the 1968 Non-Proliferation Treaty. (Actual negotiations were conducted trilaterally among the United States, the United Kingdom, and the Soviet Union, and the outcome endorsed by the General Assembly.)

During the 1970s bilateral arms control negotiations between the United States and the Soviet Union outside the U.N. began to make concrete gains, while the General Assembly became a purely deliberative body, still ostensibly striving for total disarmament but in fact working to greater effect on partial disarmament measures, especially regarding controls on nuclear proliferation.

General Assembly efforts to encourage negotiations on a comprehensive nuclear test ban consumed an inordinate amount of the debate on disarmament. However, the waning of the Cold War in the late 1980s widened the issues under debate. Limitations on conventional weapons, especially U.N. control over international arms transfers, confidence-building measures promoting greater transparency and openness between states on defense issues, the issue of conversion of military production to meet civilian needs, and measures to reduce military budgets are expected to occupy more of the U.N. disarmament agenda in the 1990s.

Reduced attention to nuclear issues and consideration of more achievable goals is likely to lead to a less ideological, more productive debate in which the U.N. begins to achieve, albeit belatedly and on a smaller scale, its goal of harmonizing the actions of its member states in the regulation of the weapons of war. The success of U.N. efforts to disarm Iraq's nuclear, chemical, and biological weapons capabilities offers tangible evidence of this, but the political, technical, and administrative difficulties encountered in the Iraqi operation may also mean that productive debate can be translated into effective action only in exceptional circumstances.

EARLY EFFORTS

Nuclear disarmament received priority attention at the United Nations from the first session of the General Assembly. Calling the uncontrolled manufacture and potential use of such weapons an unprecedented threat to international peace and security, the General Assembly established through its very first resolution the Atomic Energy Commission (24 January 1946.) The commission was to make specific proposals for the elimination of atomic weapons and other weapons of mass destruction and help ensure that atomic energy would be used only for peaceful purposes. But conflicting United States–Soviet approaches to the problem, competing draft proposals that could not be reconciled, and growing political and ideological differences between the superpowers outside the U.N. deadlocked the negotiations after only one year.

As the originator and at that time sole possessor of nuclear weapons, the United States claimed the right to eliminate them in a way that did not compromise its military security in the face of a perceived Soviet superiority in conventional weapons. The Baruch Plan (1946) called for the establishment of an International Atomic Development Authority to promote and regulate the peaceful uses of atomic energy and establish an international system of on-site inspections and sanctions to deal with potential diversions of fissionable materials for military purposes. This was to be followed by a halt to nuclear weapons production and the destruction of existing stocks.

Privately concerned that international controls might prevent it from developing nuclear weapons as a counterbalance to U.S. capability, the Soviet Union presented the Gromyko Plan (1946), which proposed a convention to prohibit the production and use of atomic weapons and their destruction within three months of the entry into force of the plan. The proposal called for verification through solely national means (methods of monitoring the treaty-related activities of another state without intruding on its territory) and sought to preserve what the Soviets considered conventional parity between Moscow and the combined forces of the West. Negotiations in the committee went nowhere on either nuclear or conventional weapons, and the linkage established then between reductions in nuclear and conventional forces complicated arms talks for years to come.

To break the impasse and deal with this new condition, the General Assembly set up the Commission for Conventional Armaments at its second session in 1947. The commission, made up of the eleven states then seated on the Security Council, was to report within three months on methods for the regulation and reduction of armaments and armed forces under international supervision. The General Assembly called on both the Atomic Energy Commission and the Commission for Conventional Armaments to take immediate action.

The question of verification proved a stumbling block, however. The West insisted that reductions be preceded by agreement on general measures to guarantee international security and the development of a program for monitoring troop levels and stores of weapons. The Soviets argued for immediate cuts of up to one third in the existing armed forces of each permanent Security Council member (the United States, the USSR, China, France, and the United Kingdom), combined with the simultaneous destruction of all nuclear weapons. Only after agreement was reached on these points would Moscow be willing to consider the problem of international supervision. Several proposals were submitted to the Security Council, to be either defeated or vetoed, before the Soviet Union withdrew from the Commission for Conventional Armaments in 1950. (The stated reason was the commission's refusal to bar the Republic of China from participation as Moscow had requested.) Negotiations on the reduction and eventual elimination of both classes of weapons reached a standstill.

In the wake of the first successful Soviet test of an atomic weapon in 1949 and the outbreak of the Korean War a year later, the General Assembly called the resumption of multilateral arms talks imperative for the maintenance of global stability and the reputation of the U.N. as a disarmament forum. While it could do little to lessen the distrust between the superpowers, the U.N. tried to overcome the problems caused by the strict separation between the consideration of nuclear and conventional arms reductions in U.N. forums. Once the Soviet Union had achieved a nuclear capability of its own, this bifurcation in mandate was no longer considered tenable. The General Assembly consolidated the mandates of the Atomic Energy Commission and the Commission for Conventional Armaments and created the Disarmament Commission in January 1952.

The Disarmament Commission, made up of the eleven members of the Security Council and Canada, was requested to draft a treaty or treaties on three subjects: the regulation, limitation, and balanced reduction of all armed forces and all armaments; the elimination of all weapons of mass destruction; and effective international control of atomic energy. *Control* referred to enforcement of a general prohibition against atomic weapons and the development of atomic energy for exclusively peaceful purposes. Differences in perception between East and West were carried into this new forum, however, and little progress was made before the Disarmament Commission ceased to function in its original form in 1957. The West continued to insist that both sides first agree to disclose their military capabilities and submit to international verification after which they could turn their attention to reductions in conventional forces. The elimination of nuclear weapons, Western countries insisted, would come last. The Soviets argued that nuclear weapons should be considered on a priority basis and stated their conviction that the voluntary dissemination of militarily sensitive information that the West required for verification was tantamount to organized espionage.

The nuclear arms race accelerated as multilateral negotiations stumbled along: the United States successfully tested the world's first hydrogen bomb, many times more powerful than atomic fission devices, in November 1952, and that same year, the United Kingdom detonated its first atomic weapon. By August 1953 the Soviets had tested their hydrogen bomb. At the request of the General Assembly, the Disarmament Commission attempted one last time to formulate a comprehensive disarmament plan, giving the task to a subcommission consisting of Canada, France, the Soviet Union, the United Kingdom, and the United States. Debating fruitlessly through 1954, the subcommission declared itself deadlocked by autumn 1955 and turned its attention to partial disarmament measures instead. These talks were no more successful. The response of the General Assembly was to enlarge the Disarmament Commission to twenty-five members in 1957. The Soviet Union objected to this increase in Western membership and refused to participate in further talks. In 1958 the Disarmament Commission was made a universal body. (The U.N. then had eighty-two members.) The Disarmament Commission met only two more times, in 1960 and in 1965.

The U.N.'s first attempt at arms control had resulted in the creation of a disarmament body too large in size and too diverse in interests to serve as a forum for effective negotiations. Indeed, with the universalization of the Disarmament Commission, multilateralism began to impede all arms control negotiations, including bilateral ones, by denying the superpowers a forum in which they could themselves pace the negotiations. As a result, when the United States and the Soviet Union decided to seek a multilateral agreement prohibiting the militarization of Antarctica in the late 1950s, they chose to bypass the Disarmament Commission and to initiate negotiations among other interested parties outside the U.N. These negotiations were concluded successfully in 1959 with the signing by twelve states of the Antarctic Treaty, the first disarmament agreement of the postwar period. It contained unprecedented provisions for verification and represented the first practical application of the nuclear-weapon-free zone concept. The Antarctic Treaty is open to signature and ratification by any member of the United Nations.

Besides the Antarctic Treaty, the most notable arms control success of the 1950s was the establishment under U.N. auspices of the International Atomic Energy Agency (IAEA), a U.S. initiative proposed by President Eisenhower in his Atoms for Peace address to the General Assembly in December 1953. Under the original U.S. proposal, the IAEA was to receive, store, and safeguard contributions of fissionable materials from nuclear states and make such materials available to non-nuclear states for exclusively peaceful purposes. The agency was also to provide technical assistance to promote the safe use of nuclear technology in electric power production, medicine, agriculture, and related fields. In addition to winning propaganda points by sharing the benefits of its nuclear research with the developing world, the United States hoped that successful international cooperation in encouraging the nonmilitary applications of such technology would pressure the Soviet Union to drop its opposition to international monitoring and verification of disarmament agreements.

The General Assembly unanimously approved the establishment of the IAEA in 1954, largely along the lines suggested by the United States, and endorsed its statute or charter in 1956. The agency came into being in July 1957 after the statute had gained a sufficient number of ratifications. Although it functions as one of the U.N.'s sixteen specialized agencies, the IAEA, headquartered in Vienna, is technically an autonomous intergovernmental organization under the auspices of the United Nations.

General and Complete Disarmament By the end of the 1950s, it was clear that the U.N. would be unable to develop a single, comprehensive disarmament plan. In 1959 the General Assembly adopted a two-prong strategy of general and complete disarmament instead. In its resolution on the subject, the first to be sponsored by all member states, the General Assembly called the elimination of the arms race the long-term goal of U.N. disarmament efforts and recognized for the first time that partial or "collateral" short-term measures were integral to the achievement of this goal. Although general and complete disarmament was inscribed on the U.N. agenda at the request of the Soviet Union alone, both the West and developing countries strongly supported the resulting resolution. There was broad agreement that a Soviet plan for general and complete disarmament, emphasizing long-term goals, and a Western proposal from the United Kingdom, suggesting partial measures, were complementary and geared toward the same ends—the comprehensive reduction of armed forces and armaments on a global basis to the degree that each state would possess only those nonnuclear forces necessary for self-defense.

Enthusiasm for general and complete disarmament was widespread at that time because it addressed both nuclear and conventional arms and assured through balanced reductions by stages that no state could gain military advantage over another. The concept was also sufficiently vague to allow future arms negotiators to bypass the troublesome question of verification, for it stipulated that reductions were to be made "under effective international control." It also envisioned the suppression of acts of aggression through the deployment of a U.N. peacekeeping force to which states were to contribute personnel. Provisions for an International Disarmament Organization to handle verification functions and the establishment of peacekeeping machinery were contained in both the Soviet and the Western proposals.

The long-term–short-term division of U.N. disarmament policy had immediate organizational consequences. It led to a restructuring of the international disarmament machinery that would eventually convert the General Assembly from a negotiating body to a deliberative forum and that would see authority over the actual conduct of arms control talks vested in a smaller multilateral institution not under direct General Assembly control.

At the same time that the General Assembly was embracing general and complete disarmament and recognizing the special responsibility of the United States and the Soviet Union in disarmament questions, the superpowers were agreeing among themselves to remove international disarmament negotiations from General Assembly scrutiny. They did so in 1959 through the establishment of the Ten Nation Committee on Disarmament, made up of equal numbers of Eastern (Bulgaria, Czechoslovakia, Poland, Romania, USSR) and Western (Canada, France, Italy, United Kingdom, United States) states. The General Assembly endorsed this action after the fact. (This committee formed the basis of the present Conference on Disarmament, the only multilateral negotiating body for disarmament questions that reports to the General Assembly but functions under its own rules of procedure.)

The Ten Nation Committee was an improvement on the plenary Disarmament Commission in that it guaranteed a balance between East and West and limited participation to states whose participation was decisive in reaching an agreement on actual arms reductions. Its limited makeup, however, was not conducive to the discussion of partial disarmament measures, such as guarantees against nuclear proliferation, which would necessarily involve a broad range of states. These issues were being deliberated within the framework of general and complete disarmament in the General Assembly.

Discussions in the Ten Nation Committee commenced on the basis of revised Western and Soviet plans for general and complete disarmament. These plans included partial steps, such as a nuclear test ban treaty and a non-proliferation regime. Little progress was made over the next two years, however, and the Soviet bloc states walked out of the talks in June 1960. That same year, France exploded its first atomic device, and the arms race continued to accelerate.

Participation in United States–Soviet multilateral disarmament negotiations was expanded beyond the membership of the competing military blocs in Europe for the first time as a result of the McCloy-Zorin agreement of September 1961, negotiated by John I. McCloy for the United States and Valerian A. Zorin for the Soviet Union. Through the eight-point Joint Statement of Agreed Principles of Disarmament Negotiations, the superpowers accepted the concept of general and complete disarmament, including the principle of equality between partial and complete disarmament measures, as the basis of their future negotiations. Washington and Moscow also agreed to enlarge the Ten Nation Committee to form an Eighteen Nation Disarmament Committee (ENDC). The membership of the Ten Nation Committee was thus brought more in line with the general membership of the U.N. through the inclusion of eight states from the newly formed nonaligned bloc of countries (Brazil, Burma, Ethiopia, India, Mexico, Nigeria, Sweden [a neutral state], and Egypt). It was hoped that participation by more states in the disarmament mechanism would add to the legitimacy and effectiveness of the U.N. in the negotiation of truly global arms control agreements, while giving due weight to the interests of the United States and the Soviet Union.

This power-sharing arrangement worked well at first, despite the refusal of France to take its seat in the eighteen-nation committee. However, the balance of forces soon shifted. The membership of the nonaligned grew, and it became preoccupied with certain issues—especially the conclusion of a treaty prohibiting all nuclear testing—that ran counter to the interests of the superpowers.

The Work of the ENDC　The new forum was no more successful than previous bodies in negotiating a treaty on general and complete disarmament, since neither Washington nor Moscow was willing to make major concessions, especially on cutting nuclear arms. They were also unable to agree on a set of collateral measures, with the United States proposing a freeze on nuclear delivery vehicles and a halt to the production of fissionable material, and the Soviets pushing for a nonaggression pact between the military blocs in Europe and a reduction in military budgets.

Despite these failures, the Eighteen Nation Disarmament Committee was well positioned to take advantage of increased interest among the general U.N. membership and the superpowers in limited and short-term measures to halt the spread of nuclear weapons to non-nuclear states. The ENDC proved to be the most successful disarmament organ to date, making significant contributions to the negotiation of three major agreements that form the bedrock of the current nuclear non-proliferation regime: the 1963 Limited Test Ban Treaty, the 1968 Non-Proliferation Treaty, and the 1971 Seabed Treaty. A fourth agreement negotiated during this period, the 1967 Treaty of Tlatelolco, established a large nuclear-weapon-free zone in Latin America. Although the ENDC was not involved in its drafting, the treaty was endorsed by the General Assembly.

These treaties reflected the shifting focus of international efforts—from disarmament, the across-the-board reduction of arms stockpiles and the eventual elimination of entire classes of weapons, to arms control, the negotiation of limitations on the development of new weapons and on the deployment of existing ones, especially those with nuclear capability. They were drafted in response to concerns that the problem of proliferation, especially nuclear proliferation, had grown acute by the 1960s and the fear that the possession of nuclear weapons by all the permanent members of the Security Council—China conducted its first successful test explosion in 1964—would encourage other states to acquire them.

Part of the success of the ENDC can be ascribed to political factors, primarily the strong support given the work of the committee by the General Assembly and the mutually reinforcing nature of their agendas. These factors would not repeat themselves in the 1970s, when the nonaligned majority in the General Assembly began to demand its own voice in disarmament affairs. Structural arrangements were also important, particularly the inability of the General Assembly to exercise direct control over the ENDC, which had been established outside its legal purview. This limited the inclusion of extraneous political issues and General Assembly interference in the complex negotiating process. The political understanding that input from the General Assembly would be recommendatory only was further institutionalized by the leadership structure of the committee—a permanently shared co-chairmanship of the United States and the Soviet Union. More than any other development since the founding of the U.N., the power of the co-chairs to control the disarmament agenda and steer the committee toward achievable and implementable agreements—and the General Assembly's acceptance of this arrangement—was key to the rapid progress made in the field between 1962 and 1968.

Agreements reached between the superpowers themselves outside the U.N. in response to the Cuban missile crisis of 1962, beginning with the 1963 Memorandum of Understanding, or "Hot Line" agreement, also moved the international arms control agenda forward, supporting the shift from complete disarmament to arms limitation and helping to harmonize, to a greater degree than before, the goals of bilateral and multilateral negotiations.

Changes in the way the U.N. handled disarmament, and increasingly effective superpower cooperation on such questions, led to a clearer and widely accepted definition of the term *arms control* in the early 1960s. By then, arms control referred specifically to United States–Soviet negotiations, conducted either bilaterally or in multilateral settings, aimed at maintaining strategic stability between the superpowers and strengthening crisis prevention and crisis management. United States–Soviet desire to keep the consideration of these issues to themselves coincided with the view of the international community at the time. New terms were added to describe agreements on partial arms control measures requiring the participation of all states. These included *nonarmament*—preempting the development of new weapons—and *confidence- and security-building measures*—measures aimed at reducing tensions and lessening the possibility of war.

The international community as a whole at first supported this redefinition of arms control as a primarily United States–Soviet issue, believing that it would lead to serious negotiations on the topic of most concern to them, nuclear disarmament, in accordance with the concept of general and complete disarmament. However, the General Assembly soon lost patience with the slow pace of progress in this piecemeal approach and with the reluctance of the superpowers to move beyond nonarmament and confidence-building agreements like the Non-Proliferation Treaty to actual arms reductions.

The Conference of the Committee on Disarmament (CCD)

By the end of the 1960s, members of the General Assembly began to complain about stalling in the Eighteen Nation Disarmament Committee on issues of nuclear arms control. In the view of the nonaligned majority, the ENDC's failure to negotiate cuts in nuclear arms was due to the superpower monopoly over the multilateral disarmament agenda. To counter this, further enlargement of the membership of the U.N.'s negotiating forum was recommended. Using its numerical superiority in the General Assembly, the nonaligned nations forced through a vote to expand the membership of the ENDC to twenty-six in 1969—Argentina, Hungary, Japan, Mongolia, Morocco, the Netherlands, Pakistan, and Yugoslavia were added—and to change its name to the Conference of the Committee on Disarmament (CCD). The CCD was enlarged in turn to thirty-one members in 1975, with the inclusion of the German Democratic Republic, the Federal Republic of Germany, Iran, Peru, and Zaire.

The General Assembly failed to force the pace of negotiations on nuclear disarmament. Enlargement of membership simply increased tension between the relatively wealthy member states of the northern hemisphere—the economically developed North—and economically developing (formerly underdeveloped) and politically nonaligned member states, located for the most part in the southern hemisphere—the South. In addition to widening this North-South divide, increases in membership amplified East-West competition, that is, between the advanced industrialized democracies of Western Europe, North America, and Japan—the West—and the Soviet Union and its socialist allies in Eastern Europe—the East.

The nonaligned nations' effort to move the consideration of nuclear issues ahead was based on several false assumptions, not the least of which was the belief that numerical superiority could be translated into political influence and concrete agreements. The U.N. majority had also assumed that the superpowers were willing to seriously discuss nuclear disarmament in multilateral forums, even though the experience of the ENDC pointed to their preference for partial measures and a step-by-step approach. In fact, the larger CCD was less conducive to negotiating cuts in nuclear arms because United States–Soviet influence was diminished. This had serious and immediate ramifications for superpower security. Instead of bringing disarmament negotiations under the General Assembly's political control as intended, the establishment of the CCD led to ceaseless bickering between the deliberative and negotiating forums of the U.N. Attention was diverted from substantive issues to procedural matters: the General Assembly sought to gain greater influence, and the superpowers fought to retain their preeminent positions as the CCD's co-chairmen. The CCD concluded only one nuclear disarmament agreement during the nine

years of its existence, the 1971 Seabed Arms Control Treaty. (Negotiations had been initiated in the Eighteen Nation Disarmament Committee). It was more successful in dealing with non-nuclear weapons of mass destruction, because their elimination did not generate the political difficulties attached to nuclear arms reductions. The 1972 Biological Weapons Convention and the 1977 Environmental Modification Convention, which prohibited alteration of the environment for hostile purposes, were also negotiated during this period.

The superpowers now looked almost exclusively to bilateral talks, away from the now politicized multilateral realm, for further nuclear weapons agreements. They concluded no fewer than nine during the decade of the 1970s on the following subjects: expanding the Hot Line agreement and preventing nuclear accidents (1971); preventing incidents on the high seas, such as collisions or provocative overflights (1972); limiting anti-ballistic missiles and strategic offensive arms (ABM Treaty and SALT I) (1972); preventing nuclear war (1973); establishing a yield threshold on nuclear tests (1974); limiting the yield of nuclear explosions for peaceful purposes (1976); and further limiting strategic offensive arms (SALT II) (1979).

Efforts to once again initiate serious negotiations on general and complete disarmament also strained relations between the General Assembly and the CCD. Although the United States and the Soviet Union had largely ignored general and complete disarmament in the ENDC and in their bilateral negotiations, the nonaligned majority in the General Assembly never completely abandoned the idea. In declaring the 1970s the first U.N. disarmament decade in 1969, the General Assembly had dropped its insistence that negotiations on general and complete disarmament produce a single draft treaty delineating both comprehensive and partial measures. At the same time, it requested the CCD to develop a comprehensive program elaborating specific partial steps. Ongoing disagreement between the superpowers on the ordering of such steps delayed the establishment of a working group to draft a concrete agreement until 1978. In the intervening years, many nations in the General Assembly had come to support another approach to multilateral disarmament, one that called for the convening of an international conference to deal with disarmament issues. This meeting, the first special session devoted to disarmament (SSOD I), was held in 1978.

SPECIAL SESSIONS
OF THE GENERAL ASSEMBLY
ON DISARMAMENT

By the late 1970s, frustration had peaked among nonaligned nations that repeated modifications of the institutional framework for multilateral disarmament negotiations and the leadership role of the superpowers in them had resulted in neither reductions in nuclear arms nor an effective voice for the General Assembly in disarmament affairs. Reiterating calls made at the first and fifth summits of nonaligned states in 1961 and 1975, the group submitted a draft resolution to the General Assembly in 1976 recommending the convening of a special session of the General Assembly not later than 1978 to review and strengthen the role of the U.N. in promoting global disarmament. After extensive debate, members of the General Assembly had found sufficient agreement among themselves to approve the draft without resort to a roll-call vote. Adoption of the resolution without a vote did not mean, however, that consensus existed among all states regarding all its provisions.

The Soviet Union, having initiated discussions in the General Assembly in 1971 on the same topic, strongly supported the convening of a special session. Decision-making in such large bodies in the past had tended to reaffirm more radical Soviet proposals, giving absolute priority to nuclear over conventional disarmament and the negotiation of immediate cuts in nuclear forces. The United States voiced caution over the feasibility of recommendations emerging from a forum dominated by non-nuclear-weapon states but expressed the hope that the serious intent of the majority of U.N. member states could be translated into realistic and constructive dialogue. China, for its part, held the United States and the Soviet Union primarily responsible for the nuclear arms race and for implementing nuclear arms control. Beijing urged them to declare their intention not to be the first to use nuclear weapons and to remove their nuclear forces from foreign soil.

The first special session on disarmament (SSOD I), held at U.N. headquarters in New York from 23 May to 1 July 1978, adopted a final document without a vote outlining an international disarmament strategy that ensured priority consideration of nuclear disarmament in future multilateral negotiations and the abolition of joint United States–Soviet control over such negotiations. Declaring that the U.N. had the central role to play in disarmament, the General Assembly accorded itself unprecedented regulatory powers over the newly created Committee on Disarmament and upgraded the status of deliberative arms control organs under the direct control of the General Assembly.

Like other radical schemes of the 1970s, which called for the redistribution of financial and technological resources from the developed to the developing world—and the establishment of "new international orders" to lessen the control of rich countries over the global economy and the worldwide media—the final document represented an attempt by the nonaligned majority to impress its political will upon wealthier and more powerful states members. Adoption of the final document without a vote did not represent a real convergence of views but instead masked concerns from the nuclear-weapon states that their interests had not been adequately taken into account. The first special session on disarmament essentially authorized non-nuclear-weapon states to pursue negotiations on reducing arms they did not themselves possess, the elimination of which would not fundamentally affect their security.

In mandating the establishment of yet another generation of U.N. disarmament bodies, SSOD I gave little consideration to the reasons behind the successes and failures of past multilateral disarmament efforts. The General Assembly ascribed the inability of the superpowers to deal effectively with the nuclear issue in previous multilateral settings simply to a lack of political will rather than the institutional shortcomings of the U.N. system, the desire of the superpowers to deal with the issue bilaterally, or the technical challenges presented by nuclear arms control. It was clear by that time that large and especially plenary bodies were ineffective forums for the negotiation of either partial or comprehensive measures and that special provisions would have to be made for the development of suitable international verification techniques if nuclear disarmament agreements were to be concluded.

SSOD I repeated the mistakes of the past—it sacrificed effectiveness for democratization of membership and universalization of scope. The introduction of the final document retained general and complete disarmament, a concept that had brought few results in nineteen years, as the final objective of U.N. disarmament efforts and named the elimination of the threat of nuclear war as the immediate goal. The contradiction between the right of all states to participate in disarmament negotiations and the "primary responsibility" of the nuclear-weapon states remained unresolved in the declaration section of the final document, which purported to outline the principles for effective negotiation. The program of action of the final document also defined the priorities that should be pursued through negotiations, further limiting the flexibility of individual member states. Nuclear weapons were to be considered first, followed by other weapons of mass destruction, including chemical weapons; conventional weapons, including those deemed excessively injurious or having indiscriminate effects; and conventional force reductions. The concluding section of the final document, on machinery, called for another enlargement of the multilateral negotiating body on disarmament, renamed the Committee on Disarmament, to forty members, and the reestablishment of a Disarmament Commission (the original body had last met in 1965) with universal membership as a subsidiary body of the General Assembly.

The Committee on Disarmament brought together all five nuclear powers (the United States, the Soviet Union, the United Kingdom, France, and China) for the first time. Their ability to negotiate on nuclear questions among themselves was severely constrained by the institution of a chairmanship that rotated monthly among all members, including the thirty-five non-nuclear-weapon states members. The committee's adoption of a permanent agenda in 1979 further lessened the likelihood that non-nuclear issues and collateral measures would receive due consideration. There was endless debate and eventual deadlock before substantive negotiations could even begin. The Committee on Disarmament was bypassed by the superpowers—as was the CCD before it—in favor of a step-by-step, bilateral approach.

The outcome of multilateral negotiations became more and more dependent on the state of bilateral United States–Soviet relations. During the détente era of the early 1970s (and again with the advent of glasnost and perestroika in the late 1980s) effective nuclear disarmament was pursued exclusively on a bilateral United States–Soviet basis. Attempting to force the superpowers into negotiations they were not prepared to pursue seriously in a venue where they had little control over outcomes, did not make the General Assembly the center for any arms control negotiations on nuclear weapons but guaranteed that it would be peripheral.

The two multilateral arms control agreements signed in the period immediately following the first special session on disarmament were negotiated outside the authority of the Committee on Disarmament. The 1979 Agreement Governing Activities of States on the Moon and Other Celestial Bodies, which complements the 1967 Outer Space Treaty and directs that the moon and other celestial bodies be preserved for peaceful purposes only, was elaborated under the auspices of the General Assembly largely as the result of United States–Soviet cooperation. A relatively minor agreement, it has been ratified by only eight states. The 1981 Inhumane Weapons Convention was the product of a special U.N. conference convened by the General Assembly. The successful conclusion of the treaty was due to widespread support among U.N. member states for controls on weapons deemed excessively injurious or having indiscriminate effects. The convention was the first treaty to prohibit or restrict specific conventional weapons since the conclusion of the 1925 Geneva Protocol outlawing poisonous gases and bacteriological warfare and demonstrated that useful work could be accomplished outside the nuclear realm.

In an effort to promote the full implementation of SSOD I's final document, the General Assembly moved in 1979 to declare the 1980s the second disarmament decade and renewed work on a comprehensive program of disarmament based on SSOD I's program of action. The General Assembly convened a second special session on disarmament (SSOD II) from 7 June to 10 July 1982 to consider a draft comprehensive program, but sharp differences between the group of nonaligned and neutral countries (with general support from the Soviet bloc and China) and the West over the particulars of the draft precluded agreement on a final document.

Western states regarded the elaboration of strict stages in the process of general and complete disarmament, as foreseen in the draft, as overly specific and rejected as unrealistic the establishment of time frames for each stage. They also objected to attempts at converting the program into a legally binding treaty. In light of this, the concluding document of the session simply "reaffirmed the validity" of the agreement reached at SSOD I and took two small initiatives in the areas of public information and education: it authorized the establishment of a World Disarmament Campaign and the expansion of training fellowships for young diplomats and public officials originally agreed to at the previous special session.

The failure of SSOD II to significantly advance the multilateral disarmament agenda was due in part to political factors beyond the U.N.'s control. The atmosphere for negotiations on sensitive security issues had been soured by a downturn in United States–Soviet relations in the late 1970s, a sharp escalation in global military expenditures, and the outbreak of serious regional conflicts in Afghanistan, Cambodia, and Iran-Iraq. But more significant than exogenous factors were the inappropriateness of the special session as the forum for the conduct of negotiations in general and the radically different viewpoints of the nonaligned nations and the West, differences only papered over at SSOD I.

Lacking any mechanisms to encourage the formulation of a consensus view, the special session resulted in the further isolation of the West and the perpetuation of multilateral disarmament machinery geared more toward guaranteeing General Assembly dominance than the promotion of effective agreements. No common ground was found between the view of the West, which opposed the participation of states that had no technological expertise to offer or strategic security interests at stake, and the inclusive position of the majority, which recognized the right of all states to participate on an equal footing.

Three years would elapse before the conclusion of a new disarmament agreement, the 1985 Treaty of Raratonga, which established a nuclear-weapon-free zone in the South Pacific. Like the other agreements concluded since the establishment of the Committee on Disarmament (renamed the Conference on Disarmament in 1983), it was negotiated outside the U.N.'s multilateral framework through regional consultations among the states to which it was open for signature and ratification. Complementing the existing zones of peace in Antarctica and Latin America, this treaty is a significant step in the international effort to halt the spread of nuclear arms.

By the late 1980s, political tensions that had precluded the implementation of the final document of the first special session on disarmament and prevented agreement at the second special session had moderated, and the third special session on disarmament (SSOD III), held from 31 May to 25 June 1988, was for the most part free of North-South and East-West confrontation. The splintering of the nonaligned movement and the introduction of "new political thinking" in Soviet foreign policy were largely responsible for the absence of polemics and the advancement of more practical and concrete proposals. United States–Soviet cooperation was also developing well, as demonstrated by the conclusion of the Intermediate-Range Nuclear Focus (INF) Treaty in December 1987, the first disarmament agreement to mandate actual reductions in arms and the elimination of an entire class of weapons.

The change in Soviet U.N. policy was particularly significant and far-reaching. Moscow abandoned Cold War obstructionism and expressed genuine interest in upgrading the effectiveness of the U.N. in a wide range of activity connected with the maintenance of international peace and security. In the arms control and disarmament field, the Soviets put forward new ideas at SSOD III that included assigning the U.N. new tasks, such as initiating a system for reciprocal exchanges of data on conventional arms, establishing independent monitoring capability (in the form of an International Verification Agency), and developing a naval peacekeeping force. Some of the examples of Soviet "new thinking," especially regarding data exchange and verification, were largely modifications of U.S. positions that the Soviets had opposed for years.

Despite the improved atmosphere and agreement on a majority of paragraphs in a draft final document prepared by the chairman of SSOD III and the Secretariat, consensus on all items could not be reached in the time allotted. Critics of multilateral arms control charged that the failure of two successive special sessions to formulate an overall disarmament strategy acceptable to all states put in question both the value of negotiations in plenary forums and the U.N.'s role in disarmament. Supporters of the organization, and especially U.N. officials, pointed out that the items on which agreement could not be reached were simply those that had not yet been considered when time ran out—nuclear-weapon-free zones, zones of peace, the relationship between disarmament and development, nuclear capabilities of South Africa and Israel, and the role of the secretary-general in investigating the use of chemical weapons.

SSOD III saw a softening of many of the demands of the nonaligned states that had been stumbling blocks to multilateral cooperation in the past. It refocused the U.N.'s work on the achievement of practical goals and identified new areas in which it could play a vital and effective role.

The non-proliferation regime, long considered unfair by non-nuclear weapon states for "disarming the disarmed," was supported in the draft final document, and its further strengthening was termed "vital." It was agreed that the U.N.'s traditional preoccupation with the quantitative aspect of the arms race and cuts in existing superpower arsenals would have to be balanced in the future by the consideration of more qualitative measures aimed at precluding further arms buildups. SSOD III highlighted the possibilities of establishing technology control regimes to limit the proliferation of sophisticated weapons systems and of applying advances in scientific research to the development of U.N. verification capacity. The majority of U.N. member states also finally conceded at SSOD III that the relationship between disarmament and development, long an issue of intense debate and the subject of a 1987 international conference that the United States refused to attend, was not direct, or "organic," and that reductions or limitations in arms would not necessarily provide resources to meet economic and social needs.

Delegations at SSOD III agreed on the importance of achieving practical goals in disarmament efforts then under way and on the need to concentrate on tasks for which the U.N. was uniquely suited. The conclusion of a global treaty banning the manufacture and use of chemical weapons, which the Conference on Disarmament had been considering since 1980, was cited as an important endeavor that only the U.N. was qualified to negotiate. The delegations also urged the U.N. to more fully exercise its comparative advantage in developing and recommending "ancillary measures" aimed at confidence building, greater openness and transparency, and comparability in military expenditures among member states. And delegations noted that U.N. disarmament efforts were more likely to bear fruit if the organization's ongoing work in related fields such as peaceful settlement of disputes, peacekeeping, and human rights was also strengthened.

Finally, SSOD III highlighted the old problem of conventional disarmament as a "new" area in which the U.N. could make a unique contribution. It concluded that the prevention of regional conflicts in the future would necessarily take reductions in armed forces and limitations on the sales of conventional weapons. Cuts in non-nuclear forces had been too long overshadowed by the supposedly more enormous and immediate threat of nuclear annihilation, but the unchecked sales of arms to the third world and U.N. peacekeeping successes in the late 1980s demonstrated the immediacy of the conventional weapons threat. SSOD III paved the way for real progress on reductions in armed forces and in the international arms trade by declaring that nuclear and non-nuclear disarmament had to be pursued in a balanced fashion and that international oversight of arms transfers between developed and developing countries as well as among developed countries could no longer be considered taboo at the U.N.

SSOD III was hindered from making further progress by the continued insistence of the majority of third world states that disarmament is not the sole responsibility of the two major powers, that nuclear disarmament should be a high priority, and that traditional concepts of military and political security must be broadened to include the economic and social concerns of the developing world.

THE UNITED NATIONS DISARMAMENT MACHINERY

The organizational structure of U.N. arms control and disarmament bodies in place in the early 1990s was created in 1978. These bodies may be grouped according to the nature of the tasks they perform. Deliberative organs consist of the General Assembly's First Committee, which was originally mandated to consider all international peace and security questions but has focused almost exclusively on arms control and disarmament issues since SSOD I; the General Assembly plenary to which it reports; and the Disarmament Commission, which carries on the work of the First Committee when the General Assembly is out of session. The General Assembly convenes in regular session at U.N. headquarters in New York City each fall, from September through December, and the First Committee usually meets in substantive session from October through November. The Disarmament Commission meets at U.N. headquarters in the spring for four weeks, usually during May. Negotiations are the exclusive purview of the Conference on Disarmament, which meets in Geneva from late January or early February through August for a total of about twenty-four weeks. It reports annually to the General Assembly. Although it is not a policy-making organ, the Vienna-based International Atomic Energy Agency (IAEA) performs important technical functions relating to the regulation of nonmilitary uses of nuclear technology and monitors compliance with the nuclear nonproliferation regime. The director general of the IAEA makes an annual report of the agency's activities to the General Assembly, which may make such nonbinding recommendations to the IAEA as it deems appropriate.

Secretarial support services are provided by the Department for Disarmament Affairs in the U.N. Secretariat, headed by an under secretary-general. Independent research is conducted by the U.N. Institute for Disarmament Research (UNIDIR) located in Geneva, which is governed by the Advisory Board on Disarmament Studies.

The First Committee has dealt exclusively with disarmament and security-related matters since 1978, leaving the discussion of political issues like regional conflicts to the General Assembly plenary. Its agenda is still heavily weighted toward nuclear weapons questions, reflecting the general priority accorded nuclear disarmament by the U.N. Items on a comprehensive test ban, nuclear-weapon-free zones, the prevention of an arms race in outer space, and the security of non-nuclear-weapon states are perennials. Annual discussions of Israeli and South African nuclear capacity also reflect the U.N.'s longtime censure of those two countries. Among non-nuclear items on the agenda, only chemical and biological weapons have been treated thoroughly—conventional disarmament has been left to the Disarmament Commission—but the role of science and technology in disarmament, including verification, is gaining prominence in discussions.

Despite its tendency toward routine debate, the First Committee has done useful work in identifying emerging disarmament issues that may be amenable to multilateral action and requesting the secretariat to follow up with in-depth studies. Issues examined include the growth of nuclear arsenals in the post–Cold War period, the role of the U.N. in verification, and the establishment of a nuclear-weapon-free zone in the Middle East. The studies themselves, usually carried out over two years by independent expert groups appointed by the secretary-general, are international and multilateral in substance and approach, helping to compensate for the tendency of academic and research institutions to concentrate on U.S.-Soviet bilateral or regional disarmament issues and exclude the multilateral dimension. On the committee's agenda for the post–Cold War period are plans to consider a report on promoting transparency in international transfers of conventional arms and on applying financial savings from reductions in military budgets to environmental protection.

Reducing the First Committee agenda and simplifying its procedures have become important issues since SSOD I spotlighted the First Committee's role in promoting multilateral disarmament measures. The First Committee's agendas have tripled in size since the 1940s, when it was concerned with only general peace and security issues. Often it responded to the increased workload by adopting more resolutions than could possibly be acted on by member states. The First Committee has also neglected its mandate to work out practical agreements acceptable to all member states on the most divisive issues—especially nuclear weapons questions—which resulted in frequent requests for roll-call votes. As the Cold War receded and member states moved from winning votes to reaching agreements, the total number of resolutions brought to a vote in the First Committee and the General Assembly has fallen and the number of drafts adopted without a vote has increased.

As a result of negotiations carried on by successive committee chairmen, the General Assembly approved a limited six-point reform package in 1987 that sought to simplify the work of the First Committee. It recommended decreasing the number of draft resolutions sent on to the General Assembly for approval by taking action on procedural questions through what are called *decisions* and consolidating separate recommendations on a given subject into a single draft. To make deliberations more effective, the General Assembly recommended clustering related agenda items in debate and combining general debate with debate on specific items. Setting an early deadline for the submission of drafts and allocating time for informal consultations among delegations was also proposed to encourage the development of consensus texts. A more substantive recommendation aimed at cutting the committee agenda by staggering, over two to three years, the consideration of agenda items on which the committee had traditionally found little agreement, was not approved.

Overall, reform has stumbled badly on the right of any state to inscribe new items of its choice on the agenda or to call for continued attention to existing items, no matter how ineffectual actions have been in the past. There are continuing attempts to have the First Committee update its approach—the chairman of the 1990 session suggested that the agenda be reformulated to "better reflect the concerns of [all] member states as well as the changing realities in the international situation." However, the General Assembly has preferred marginal increases in efficiency to meaningful increases in effectiveness. As a result, the U.N. is poorly positioned to seize the historical opportunity offered by the end of the Cold War.

The Disarmament Commission was reestablished by SSOD I to give specialized and in-depth treatment to a selection of disarmament issues chosen by the First Committee. In theory, the outcome of the Disarmament Commission's deliberations on a particular item should be a set of widely agreed upon principles that could serve as the basis of concrete and legally binding arms control and disarmament agreements. The Disarmament Commission has not, however, had much more luck than the First Committee in reaching agreements on the most divisive issues. Because SSOD I mandated that it work by consensus, the Disarmament Commission had been unable until the late 1980s to remove from its agenda items on which little progress had been made. In what was billed as a major reform effort, the First Committee drafted and the General Assembly approved a seven-point program in 1989 that reaffirmed the broad mandate of the Disarmament Commission in its decision-making, but mandated cuts in the agenda, a cap on the number of working groups established during the session, a shortening of the length of the session, a limit on general debate, and the continuation of consultations among delegations between sessions.

Since its inception, the Disarmament Commission has regularly carried from seven to eight substantive items on its agenda for any one session. These have included the nuclear arms race and a comprehensive program for nuclear and conventional disarmament; the nuclear capability of South Africa; the role of the U.N. in disarmament; the relationship between disarmament and development;

naval armaments and disarmament; conventional disarmament; the establishment of U.N. decades for disarmament; guidelines for confidence-building measures; verification in all its aspects; reductions in military budgets; and objective information on military matters. (The last item deals with a system for the voluntary exchange of data among member states on their military expenditures.) Deliberations resulted in consensus texts on only two items—confidence-building measures and verification, both in 1988.

After the adoption of the reform proposals, the Disarmament Commission decided in 1990 to clear its agenda and take final action, without consensus if necessary, on all but the most recent item, objective information on military matters. Delegations were unable to reach agreement on two issues, the nuclear arms race and a comprehensive program for disarmament, after eleven years of debate. Limited consensus was obtained on naval armaments for the first time. (The United States, which has refused to take part in any multilateral discussions on the subject, relented somewhat and allowed the Disarmament Commission to issue a consensus statement with the understanding that the United States would not be bound by its conclusions and recommendations.) Mild consensus statements were also adopted on South Africa's nuclear capability, the role of the U.N. in disarmament, conventional disarmament, and the 1990s as the third disarmament decade. The last recommendation was approved by the General Assembly in 1990.

Owing to widespread interest, nuclear disarmament was retained on the Disarmament Commission's 1991 agenda along with objective information on military matters. Two new items were added: the regional approach to disarmament and the role of science and technology in the context of international security. All other items were dropped, in accordance with the stipulation that the Disarmament Commission should consider no more than four items per session and establish no more than one working group for each. The Disarmament Commission has also agreed to retain no item on its agenda for more than three consecutive sessions. The reforms effected by the Disarmament Commission should increase its efficiency by focusing attention on fewer items and by imposing a deadline on their consideration. Increasing its efficiency may ultimately place the Disarmament Commission at cross purposes with the First Committee, which has not agreed to time constraints or agenda limitations.

Because it operates under rules of procedure separate from those of the General Assembly, the Conference on Disarmament (CD), the international community's single multilateral forum for disarmament negotiations, has been immune to reform from the outside. Its membership has not changed since 1978, when it was established by SSOD I as the Committee on Disarmament. With the reunification of Germany in October 1990, the Conference on Disarmament now has thirty-nine members: the five nuclear-weapon states and thirty-four non-nuclear-weapon states. The non-nuclear-weapon states are roughly organized by geographic region into a Western group (Australia, Belgium, Canada, Germany, Italy, Japan, and the Netherlands), an Eastern European and "other" group (Bulgaria, Czechoslovakia, Poland, Hungary, Mongolia, and Romania), and twenty-one neutral and nonaligned states known as the Group of 21 (Algeria, Argentina, Brazil, Cuba, Egypt, Ethiopia, India, Indonesia, Iran, Kenya, Mexico, Morocco, Myanmar, Nigeria, Pakistan, Peru, Sri Lanka, Sweden, Venezuela, Yugoslavia, and Zaire). Thirty-four other states have been invited to participate as observers.

The CD still uses the permanent ten-point agenda agreed to by the Committee on Disarmament in 1979 from which it chooses an annual agenda for each session and a program of work. The ten permanent items are nuclear weapons in all aspects; chemical weapons; other weapons of mass destruction; conventional weapons; reduction of military budgets; reduction of armed forces; disarmament and development; disarmament and international security; collateral measures, confidence-building measures, and effective verification methods; and a comprehensive program of disarmament leading to general and complete disarmament under effective international control.

Unlike the Eighteen Nation Disarmament Committee, which helped produce the Limited Test Ban and the nuclear non-proliferation treaties, or the Conference of the Committee on Disarmament, which oversaw the biological weapons and environmental modification conventions, the CD has to date no major disarmament agreements to its credit. A lack of firm leadership may be partly to blame. In the interests of greater "democratization," SSOD I replaced the permanent United States–Soviet co-chairmanship of the ENDC and the CCD

with a system of monthly chairmanships in the CD, which rotate among all conference member states in English alphabetical order. This diffusion of power at the top has made it difficult for the CD to coordinate its negotiations on various nuclear and non-nuclear issues and prioritize among them.

In addition, the gradual enlargement of the Conference on Disarmament exclusively on a quota system of equitable geographic distribution rather than strategic importance has divided the membership into separate groups that often function as competing blocs. This has made politically sensitive and technically difficult negotiations, which were supposed to be insulated from outside pressures, vulnerable to the vicissitudes of both East-West and North-South relations. Finally, the increasing complexity of the negotiations themselves, the explosion of scientific and technological advances in weaponry, and the need to ensure effective verification of agreements has slowed the pace of all arms control talks, bilateral as well as multilateral.

Throughout the 1980s the CD has focused its attention on five non-nuclear items chosen from its permanent agenda: banning chemical weapons, banning radiological weapons, preventing an arms race in outer space, establishing a comprehensive program for disarmament, and concluding arrangements aimed at guaranteeing the security of non-nuclear-weapon states against the use or threat of use of nuclear weapons. It has established an ad hoc committee for each subject authorized to conduct negotiations up to but not including the final drafting of a treaty or treaties. Committees are established only with the agreement of all CD members. Inasmuch as the mandates of these bodies expire at the conclusion of each annual session, member states of the CD must agree to their reestablishment before negotiations can continue. Action within the ad hoc committees is taken by consensus.

The CD has discussed nuclear questions at length—a nuclear test ban, the cessation of the nuclear arms race and nuclear disarmament, and the prevention of nuclear war—but has been able to establish an ad hoc negotiating committee on only the first nuclear item. This committee last functioned in 1983 but was reestablished in 1991 after prolonged debate as to its mandate. The CD has, however, continually renewed the mandate of an expert advisory group on the verification of a comprehensive test ban (the Ad Hoc Group of Scientific Experts to Consider International Cooperative Measures to Detect and Identify Seismic Events), which was originally established by the CCD in 1976. The group is working on the design for a system of international data exchange to assist states in their national monitoring and compliance with a prohibition on testing. The mandate of the Ad Hoc Committee on a Nuclear Test Ban is limited to examining ways and means for establishing, testing, and operating an international seismic monitoring network based on the work of the expert group.

The failure of the CD to initiate effective and comprehensive negotiations on the nuclear issue has led to increasing frustration among nonaligned non-nuclear-weapon states and calls for far-reaching procedural and structural reforms. These states have proposed that the CD abandon its practice of establishing ad hoc negotiating committees only on a case-by-case basis and agree to the collective establishment of ten committees, one for each item on its permanent agenda. The nonaligned members have also suggested that the committees be permitted to retain their negotiating authority from session to session. Western states, particularly the United States, have resisted these moves, arguing that they will, in fact, undermine the effectiveness of negotiations by ignoring the need for unanimous agreement on the establishment and mandate of each committee. The West has also refused to consider lengthening the annual session or converting the CD into a year round negotiating forum. (Agreement was reached in 1990 on reformulating the meeting schedule from two twelve-week sessions to one ten-week and two seven-week sessions.) Differences even extend to the content of the CD's annual report to the General Assembly: the West has argued that it should be concise and factual and has emphasized points of consensus; the nonaligned non-nuclear-weapon states have insisted that it include the viewpoints of various delegations on matters of continued disagreement.

Reform of the Conference on Disarmament through enlargement of its membership has also been a contentious issue. Although agreement was reached in 1983 on adding no more than four states—two for the Group of 21, one (Vietnam) for the socialist states, and one (Norway) for the West—none of the sixteen outstanding applications for full membership has been approved. The West insists that additions to the membership be done only on a case-by-case basis with the assent of all member states, while the Group of 21 seeks guarantees that equitable geographic representation will be maintained in the future.

Largely removed from the politicized atmosphere of the central U.N. organs and the high-profile negotiations in the Conference on Disarmament, the International Atomic Energy Agency (IAEA) has been widely praised for quietly promoting the peaceful uses of nuclear technology. The agency has become a respected international authority on health and safety standards in the nuclear industry and provides training and technical assistance in the areas of plant operation and maintenance. It also conducts symposia on various research-related topics, including safe disposal of nuclear wastes, food irradiation, and nuclear medicine. With the entry into force of the Non-Proliferation Treaty in 1970, the IAEA also began implementing an extensive system of safeguards agreements with nuclear- and non-nuclear-weapon states. Through these agreements agency personnel verify through on-site inspections of nuclear facilities in signatory states that no fissionable material intended for peaceful purposes is diverted to military use. In the wake of the nuclear accident at the Soviet Union's Chernobyl power plant in 1986, the IAEA drafted the first binding international agreements on nuclear disasters. They established an early warning system and rules to govern the provision of assistance in the case of a nuclear or radiological emergency. The two treaties entered into force in October 1986 and February 1987, respectively.

The IAEA came center stage in the aftermath of the Persian Gulf War when it became the implementing agency for the elimination of Iraqi nuclear weapons capability. Under the U.N. cease-fire resolution adopted on 3 April 1991 (Resolution 687), the Security Council directed the IAEA to immediately inspect all nuclear facilities in Iraq and to submit within 45 days a plan for destroying, removing, or rendering harmless all nuclear-weapons-usable material found in the country. The Security Council further directed the agency to carry out the plan within 45 days of its approval. Within 120 days of the adoption of Resolution 687, a second plan was to be submitted detailing IAEA activities for long-term monitoring and verification of Iraqi compliance. The duration of the plan is to be determined by the Security Council.

THE U.N. AND THE DISARMAMENT OF IRAQ

International Atomic Energy Agency actions in postwar Iraq mark the first time that the agency conducted involuntary inspections as well as inspections of both civilian and military installations. Iraq was also the first sovereign state subject to unilateral disarmament measures at the direction of an international authority. Initiated in May 1991, IAEA missions to Iraq will continue on a permanent basis to guarantee the government's compliance with a long-term disarmament regime. These measures were unprecedentedly broad in scope, encompassing not only Iraqi nuclear capability but also all other weapons of mass destruction in the country, including chemical and biological systems as well as longer-range ballistic missiles.

Acting under Resolution 687, three subsequent resolutions, and three less formal statements of the president, the Security Council authorized the establishment and activities of an ad hoc investigatory mechanism in the form of a Special Commission (UNSCOM), which assisted the IAEA in disarming the Iraqi nuclear threat and oversaw the elimination of Iraq's non-nuclear mass destruction capabilities. The Council also took a hard line against Iraqi obstructionism, denouncing Baghdad's attempts to conceal its advanced nuclear program and to deny U.N. inspectors access to certain facilities and information.

The lifting of the U.N. embargo on Iraqi commercial goods, mainly petroleum products, and the easing of restrictions on Iraq's financial transactions were made contingent on Baghdad's full compliance with the disarmament program. As of June 1992, no mention had yet been made of ending the arms embargo imposed at the same time.

Empowering Resolutions   In Section C of Resolution 687, which enumerated cease-fire provisions specifically relating to Iraq's weapons of mass destruction, the Security Council defined the terms of reference of the Special Commission; ordered Iraq to declare the locations, amounts, and types of weapons of mass destruction it currently possessed; and made three unprecedentedly intrusive demands on Baghdad.

First, Iraq was to reaffirm its obligations under the Geneva Protocol and the Non-Proliferation Treaty and ratify the Biological Weapons Convention. (Baghdad deposited its instrument of ratification on 8 April 1991 in Moscow.) Second, Iraq had to agree unconditionally to the destruction, removal, or rendering harmless of all chemical and biological weapons and ballistic missiles over 150 kilometers in range; allow similar action to be taken regarding all related components and production facilities; and obligate itself not to acquire such capability in the future. Third, the Security Council required an unconditional pledge from Baghdad not to acquire or develop nuclear weapons, nuclear-weapons-usable material, or any relevant subsystem or component; to foreswear any military research, development, support, or manufacturing capability in the nuclear field; to surrender its nuclear-weapons-usable material to the IAEA; and to submit to the destruction, removal, or rendering harmless of all nuclear weapon components as well as research and production facilities.

The destruction plans for Iraqi nuclear and non-nuclear capabilities were approved by the Security Council through Resolution 699 on 17 June 1991. At the same time, the council extended the authority of the special commission to inspect relevant sites and supervise the elimination of weapons of mass destruction beyond the forty-five-day period originally approved, empowering UNSCOM to remain in the field until those tasks were completed. With concerns growing among member states regarding the costs of such operations, the Security Council also requested financial assistance for the commission in cash and kind, while holding Iraq liable for all expenditures relating to the implementation of Section C of Resolution 687.

Iraq's failure to comply satisfactorily with requests for information from UNSCOM, its refusal to open all facilities to international inspection, and its objection to the use of helicopters by the special commission moved the Security Council to take further action. In Resolution 707 (15 August 1991), the Council demanded "full, final, and complete disclosure" of all Iraqi programs relating to weapons of mass destruction "without further delay." It directed Iraq to grant immediate, unconditional, and unrestricted access to all sites and to cease immediately the concealment, transport, or destruction of any military-related item without notification to and the prior consent of the special commission. Iraq was also to make immediately available all previously denied items and allow unencumbered use by the commission of fixed-wing aircraft and helicopters.

Despite difficulties encountered in eliminating Iraq's potential to wage war with weapons of mass destruction, the Security Council was able to approve plans on 11 October for ongoing monitoring and verification in the nuclear and non-nuclear fields. Resolution 715 also reiterated previous calls for contributions in cash and kind to UNSCOM activities and requested the secretary-general to submit proposals for a mechanism to monitor future sales or supplies to Iraq of prohibited weapons, materials, or equipment.

The Investigatory Mechanism

After Iraq's unconditional acceptance on 6 April 1991 of the cease-fire conditions laid down in Resolution 687, the secretary-general established the special commission on 10 April, naming Rolf Ekeus of Sweden executive chairman and Robert Gallucci of the United States deputy executive chairman. Consisting of nineteen other experts from as many member states, the commission was given seven distinct tasks by the Security Council.

In the short term, UNSCOM was to conduct immediate on-site inspections of all declared and undeclared chemical, biological, and ballistic missile sites in Iraq. Pending agreement on the technical means of eliminating Iraq's chemical and biological capabilties, the UNSCOM was to take possession of any weapons, stocks of agents or precursors, delivery systems, equipment, or facilities it found. It was also to supervise the destruction of ballistic missiles, spare parts, and repair and production facilities. The Security Council requested the commission to assist the director general of the IAEA with inspections of declared and undeclared nuclear sites.

In the medium term, UNSCOM was to cooperate with the IAEA in planning and carrying out the destruction, removal, or rendering harmless of Iraqi nuclear weapons, components, nuclear-weapons-usable material, and facilities. It was also to assist the secretary-general in devising a plan for the future monitoring and verification of compliance by Iraq of U.N. prohibitions against the use, development, manufacture, or acquisition of non-nuclear weapons of mass destruction. Finally, in the longer term, the Security Council requested UNSCOM to work with the IAEA in devising a plan to monitor and verify the nonacquisition and nondevelopment

by Iraq of nuclear weapons, nuclear-weapons-usable material, and any related facilities.

Responsibility for the implementation of the three-phase disarmament strategy was divided between the IAEA and the Special Commission. In the initial on-site phase, the IAEA was to dispatch a series of small teams, made up of agency personnel with relevant expertise, to verify the accuracy of Iraq's declarations on its nuclear holdings and to investigate other sites identified by the Special Commission. Regarding non-nuclear capabilities, the commission was to follow a similar procedure, sending separate inspection teams to chemical, biological, and ballistic missile sites to verify declarations and conduct additional investigations. The elimination of prohibited weapons and support systems mandated in the second phase was to be supervised by additional IAEA and UNSCOM teams but would most likely be carried out by Iraqi military personnel. The concluding phase, in which long-term monitoring and verification regimes would be imposed on Iraq's nuclear and non-nuclear capabilities, was expected to be administered separately by the IAEA and the commission. However, the plan was that both bodies would continue to operate under the auspices of the Security Council.

Problems Encountered in Disarming Iraq

The ability of the Special Commission to achieve its objectives in full, on time, and under budget was hindered by a variety of factors. The noncooperative attitude of Iraqi authorities was perhaps paramount among them. From the outset, Iraq refused to completely and promptly disclose relevant information as provided under the terms of the cease-fire or to respond satisfactorily to inquiries from inspectors in the field. Baghdad denied or delayed access to certain facilities, moved or destroyed requested items, impeded free travel, and imperiled the safety and security of U.N. personnel.

Three particularly egregious examples of Iraqi noncompliance in June and September 1991 were the subjects of strongly worded statements of the president of the Security Council. All involved IAEA inspectors at sites in and around Baghdad. In the first case, a team was denied access to an army barracks for four days, while equipment inside was crated and removed. In the second, Iraqi military personnel attempted to seize the cameras of U.N. monitors and eventually drove them away from a military transport facility with small-arms fire. The third and most serious incident involved the four-day detention of a forty-three-member team that had seized highly sensitive documentation on Iraq's nuclear weapons program and refused to surrender it to Iraqi authorities on the scene.

The technical difficulties involved in locating, identifying, and safely removing hidden and dangerous materials also slowed progress. Allied bombing during the Gulf War and the destruction of facilities by Iraqi authorities themselves complicated the process. Much of the chemical stocks were damaged and leaking, contaminating surrounding areas, and unexploded ordnance presented particular hazards. Iraq's refusal to raise funds for the project through closely monitored sales of its petroleum and the unwillingness of member states to finance the operation through assessed contributions had by January 1992 placed UNSCOM in some financial difficulties. The Security Council repeatedly requested voluntary contributions from interested countries. Finally, unclear lines of authority between the Security Council and the IAEA and between that agency and UNSCOM raised questions about the viability of future attempts at involuntary disarmament. The Iraqi case may prove to be the exception and not the rule.

CONCLUSION

The 1990s represent a new frontier for multilateral arms control. There are fresh opportunities for tackling long-standing problems such as verification and nuclear and conventional weapons proliferation through nontraditional approaches. Monitoring compliance with future agreements through international means is both politically and technically more feasible, and support is growing for giving the U.N. its own intrusive and perhaps nontreaty-specific surveillance capability. At the third special session on disarmament (SSOD III), the French made a proposal to establish an international satellite monitoring system under U.N. auspices. Efforts to increase the number of weapons-supplying states abiding by voluntary restraints on their arms exports under the 1987 Missile Technology Control Regime (MTCR) and to expand these restraints to cover more weapons systems received special attention after the Persian Gulf War; it included twenty-one countries by 1992. The five permanent members of the Security Council met as the world's five major weapons exporters in July 1991 in Paris

to begin work on such a supplier control regime for the Middle East. The establishment of a U.N. registry of conventional arms transfers was proposed by the then Soviet Union, France, and the United Kingdom and gained the endorsement of the U.N. General Assembly after a U.N. expert group on arms transfers reported its findings to the Forty-sixth General Assembly in the fall of 1991. Based on data voluntarily submitted by both arms suppliers and recipients, the registry, which became operational in 1992, seeks to foster "transparency," or openness, in arms transfers. But since it cannot monitor or verify arms sales data through intrusive means, it is only a small first step toward promoting greater confidence among traditional arms importers in the third world and restraint on the part of developed country exporters.

Multilateral arms control also faces new challenges that will require rethinking of past assumptions. It may be necessary to expand the scope of existing nuclear safeguards agreements, for instance, to cover weapons-related equipment as well as nuclear material and to accommodate challenge inspections of both civilian and military installations. Enforcement measures to be taken against holdouts to and violators of broader safeguards agreements might be seriously considered. The recent experience in Iraq will be analyzed for its usefulness as a prototype for combining traditional U.N. peacekeeping arrangements with more intrusive and perhaps involuntary arms control measures aimed at preventing a recurrence of hostilities or their escalation. Finally, the very success of efforts to reduce weapons stocks in Iraq in the early 1990s also reminded the international community of the financial implications of such reductions. Loser-pays arrangements such as that imposed on Iraq to cover the destruction of its nuclear, chemical, and biological weapons and ballistic missiles may not be tenable for resource-poor states. Some equitable system of payment to meet the costs of eliminating existing stocks of weapons and ensuring that covert weapons development is not carried out must be established before rich and poor states alike will fully implement and abide by disarmament agreements in the future.

BIBLIOGRAPHY

General Surveys The United Nations has not traditionally been a subject of interest to academics, and there are relatively few secondary sources available that treat U.N. arms control and disarmament efforts in a historical and comprehensive way. A notable exception is EDWARD C. LUCK, ed., *Arms Control: The Multilateral Alternative* (New York, 1983), which takes an analytical and prescriptive approach. A more descriptive account is given in the chapter on disarmament in MOSHE Y. SACHS, ed., *The United Nations: A Handbook of the United Nations* (New York, 1977) and the update contained in MOSHE Y. SACHS, ed., *United Nations,* Volume 1 of the *Worldmark Encyclopedia of the Nations,* 7th ed. (New York, 1988). As interest in the U.N. has revived, an occasional journal article can be found exploring a particular aspect of the U.N.'s role in disarmament. For a structural analysis of U.N. efforts in this area, see PETER JONES and DEMETRIS BOURANTONIS, "The United Nations and Nuclear Disarmament: A Case Study in Failure?" *Current Research on Peace and Violence* 13, no. 1 (1990): 7–15.

International Issues Government publications are useful for arms control and disarmament issues that have been the subject of international treaties. UNITED STATES ARMS CONTROL AND DISARMAMENT AGENCY, *Arms Control and Disarmament Agreements* (1990), devotes a chapter to each of the eleven multilateral treaties in force (the Treaty of Rarotonga is excluded) as well as all the United States–Soviet bilateral agreements. It provides a brief sketch of the negotiating process leading to each and the full texts of and lists of states parties to the resulting agreements. Not unexpectedly, this work is written from an official United States perspective and places particular emphasis on United States–Soviet cooperation rather than on U.N. intermediation. A 1991 paper by KATHRYN G. SESSIONS, policy analyst at the United Nations Association of the USA (UNA-USA) on "Future Roles for the United Nations in Arms Control and Disarmament-Global Norms, Regional Innovations, and Multidisciplinary Frameworks" outlines future directions for the United Nations in this area.

The U.N. Role The United Nations has attempted to fill the information void in literature on multilateral arms control itself, publishing through the Department of Disarmament Affairs and the Department of Public Information numerous works intended for general readership as well as scholarly research. Many of these publications may not be easily obtainable outside of the U.N.'s New York headquarters, however, and provide little insight into the political aspects of the disarmament debate. *Everyone's United Nations* (1986) gives a chapter-length basic treatment of U.N. structure and function in the disarmament field. *The United Nations and Disarmament: A Short History* (New York, 1988) and *The United Nations and Disarmament: 1945–1985* (New York, 1985) offer a surprisingly comprehensive account of the development of the U.N. disarmament agenda and thematic treatment of the major subfields, both nuclear and conventional.

Specific Aspects and Treaties More in-depth treatment of particular aspects of multilateral arms control efforts can be found in the specialized literature of the Department of Disarmament Affairs. For a comprehensive annual treatment of U.N. activities in a single volume, see especially *The United Nations Disarmament Yearbook,* which covers in minute detail the work of all subsidiary bodies in the field. The journal *Disarmament: A Periodic Review by the United Nations* and the series *Topical Papers* include original submissions and the texts of discussion papers circulated at U.N.-sponsored seminars held around the world. For broad overview accounts of U.N. activity, see in particular OLU ADENIJI, "Multilateral and Bilateral Approaches to Disarmament," *United Nations Conference on Disarmament Issues: Proceedings 19–22 April 1989, Kyoto, Japan* (1989): 113–120, and YASUSHI AKASHI, "Is There Still Life after SSOD III?" *Disarmament: A Periodic Review by the United Nations* 11 (Autumn 1988): 17–22. For specific treatment of a given theme or treaty, see Ove E. Bring, "The 1981 Inhumane Weapons Convention," *Disarmament: A Periodic Review by the United Nations* 12 (1991): 157–168.

U.N. Documents The *Disarmament Facts* (previously *Disarmament Fact Sheet*) series gives very brief summations of major U.N. documents in the field as well as explanations of specific treaties and is published by the United Nations Department of Disarmament Affairs in New York. See in particular "Final Document [of the] First Special Session of the General Assembly on Disarmament 1978" (n.d.); "International Conference on the Relationship between Disarmament and Development" (No. 54, February 1988); "Arms Regulation and Disarmament Treaties" (No. 58, September 1988); "Third

Special Session of the General Assembly Devoted to Disarmament" (No. 61, January 1989); "Treaty on the Prohibition of Nuclear Weapons in Latin America (Treaty of Tlatelolco)" (No. 68, September 1989); "The Sea-Bed Treaty and its Third Review Conference in 1989" (No. 69, December 1989); and "Convention on Inhumane Weapons" (No. 71, May 1990). Also worthy of mention are two periodicals, *Disarmament Newsletter,* published quarterly by the U.N., and *Disarmament Times,* published bimonthly by the NGO Committee on Disarmament in affiliation with the U.N.

Conference Proceedings and Treaty Drafts

For the scholar, primary sources should not be ignored, and U.N. documentation in the arms control and disarmament field is voluminous. The three principal organs for the consideration of such matters (the Conference on Disarmament, the Disarmament Commission, and the First Committee of the General Assembly) maintain separate records of their proceedings. For the status of ongoing negotiations, see *Report of the Conference on Disarmament,* Official Records of the General Assembly, Supplement No. 27. (The report to the 45th session of the General Assembly [1990] carries the document symbol A/45/27. Reports to previous sessions are similarly denoted [A/44/27, etc.]). The annual CD report contains a review of procedural and reform issues as well as the "working drafts" of the chemical weapons convention and other documents. For the deliberative organs, see *Report of the Disarmament Commission,* Official Records of the General Assembly, Supplement No. 42. The First Committee does not publish a comprehensive report, but an overview of its activities can be found in the verbatim records of debate. For the 1990 session, see *Provisional Verbatim Records of the First Committee,* 1990 session, U.N. Documents A/C.1/45/PV. 1-53. Verbatim records of debate in the Conference on Disarmament and the Disarmament Commission are also kept. This information is available in abbreviated form through press releases issued by the U.N. Department of Public Information (UNDPI). For the 1991 session of the Conference on Disarmament, see UNDPI press releases beginning DCF/95 (21 January 1991). For the 1991 session of the Disarmament Commission, see UNDPI press releases DC/2359 (22 April 1991) through DC/2368 (13 May 1991).

The Baruch Plan

1946–1949

○

LENEICE N. WU

See also Critics of Arms Control and Disarmament; General and Complete Disarmament Proposals; *and* The United Nations and Disarmament. *The text of Bernard Baruch's speech of 14 June 1946 is reprinted in Volume III.*

The Baruch Plan provided the basis for the initial attempt by the United States—the only country that then possessed the atomic bomb—to establish international controls over the new weapon immediately following World War II. Named for the chief U.S. negotiator, international statesman and financier, Bernard M. Baruch, the proposal was formally under discussion from 1946 to 1949. However, the negotiations failed to achieve an international system of control.

The following essay examines the historical context of these negotiations, on both the international and domestic levels. It also outlines internal U.S. policy-making efforts that culminated in the formulation of the Baruch Plan as it was presented to the United Nations in 1946. Finally, a history of the negotiations at the United Nations, including both the U.S. and Soviet proposals for international control of atomic energy, is provided. The conclusion reviews the matrix of domestic and international, military and political considerations that contributed to the failure of these efforts.

INTERNATIONAL AND DOMESTIC SETTING

The end of World War II witnessed considerable change in international relations. The United States and the Soviet Union emerged as great powers whose systems of government were basically at odds with one another. During the period of Baruch Plan negotiations, antagonism and mistrust would grow between the two countries. Bulgaria, Czechoslovakia, Hungary, and East Germany became part of the Soviet sphere; the Truman Doctrine, which inaugurated the U.S. policy of containment toward the Soviets, and the Marshall Plan, a U.S. program to rebuild Europe through massive financial aid, were promulgated; the Berlin blockade and airlift began; and the North Atlantic Treaty Organization (NATO) was formed.

At the same time, attempts were under way to fashion a system of international order through the United Nations (U.N.), founded in 1945. Postwar conferences of ministers held in 1945 and 1946 negotiated, albeit painfully, the terms of the peace following the conflict. Thus, both international conflict and cooperation provided the context for the negotiations to control nuclear weapons.

The United States and the Bomb   Once the destructive power of the atomic bomb had been demonstrated and with the end of hostilities, there was considerable popular support for reducing the size of U.S. military manpower strength. Very soon after the atomic bombing of Hiroshima and Nagasaki in August 1945, President Harry S Truman announced that within twelve to eighteen months, 5.2 million men and women would be released from military service. Coupled with doubts regarding Soviet intentions, the dramatic reduction in the size of

U.S. armed forces served to enhance the role of the atomic bomb in the U.S. defense posture and placed a premium on it in the international negotiations.

Domestic control of atomic energy, as embodied in the Atomic Energy Act of 1946 (approved 26 July 1946), also addressed the issue of international control. The act forbade exchange of information with foreign countries on the industrial use of atomic energy until Congress declared by joint resolution that effective and enforceable international safeguards against the use of atomic energy for destructive purposes had been established. It also stated that provisions of an "international arrangement"—in the form of a treaty approved by the Senate—would take precedence over any provisions of the law that were inconsistent with the international arrangement.

The debate over domestic control may have influenced the international negotiations in both positive and negative ways. For example, the Atomic Energy Act established civilian authority over U.S. atomic energy to allay any international fear that United States policies were militaristic. The law also provided for government ownership and control over atomic materials and for government licensing of nuclear facilities—an unprecedented intrusion into private enterprise. On the one hand such control may have demonstrated the U.S. awareness of the level of danger associated with atomic energy. On the other hand, the exceptional precautions that the law took regarding the release of information may have been regarded as an attempt by the United States to maintain its monopoly over atomic energy.

The Soviet Union and the Bomb   The discovery of fission was announced in Germany in 1939, and it is believed that Soviet atomic research was probably at a comparable level. Although Soviet nuclear research ground to a halt with the German invasion of the Soviet Union in June 1941, Soviet physicist Peter Kapitza, at a conference of Soviet scientists in October 1941, concluded that developing nuclear energy for military purposes could help end the war sooner. Confronted in February 1943 with information that both the United States and Germany were pursuing work on an atomic bomb, the Soviet Union launched a program aimed at developing a similar weapon. Igor Kurschatov, who had been an avid supporter of developing atomic power in the early 1940s, was

selected to head the Soviet effort, which was relatively modest compared to the United States' Manhattan Project, the wartime effort to develop the atomic bomb. The program gradually gained momentum as the Soviet army was able to stop the German advance and launch a counteroffensive of its own. The staff grew from fifty in 1943 to one hundred the next year, and after the end of the war in 1945 other Soviet institutes were invited to participate, as well as some German scientists and technicians. By spring of 1945, work proceeded on designing an industrial reactor for producing plutonium, a major step toward developing the bomb.

Prior to the advent of the bomb, political observers concluded that the Soviets expected their role in defeating Germany would make the USSR secure in the postwar world. But once the United States demonstrated the force of this new weapon in Hiroshima, the Soviets gave high priority to developing their own weapon. Four years later, they exploded their own nuclear device.

Speculation has varied widely on the extent to which espionage may have contributed to the relatively rapid development of the Soviet bomb. One writer has summarized it as follows:

At the time it seemed to many of us that espionage must have been far and away the main reason they were able to accomplish the job so quickly, especially after the devastation that had been wreaked on them by World War II. Having since seen some excellent Russian technological progress in other fields, we are no longer quite so sure that this was the case. We should note, furthermore, that it is always easier to do something a second time, even if the only thing known from the first time is that it can be done. (Herbert York, *Race to Oblivion: A Participant's View of the Arms Race,* New York, 1971, pp. 34–35).

There are several opinions regarding what initially motivated the Soviet Union to begin developing the bomb. David Holloway has suggested that one reason may have been that the Kremlin believed, before the outcome of the war was assured, it might have to deal with a nuclear-armed Germany after the war. Or, even if Germany was no longer a threat, the Soviets might have anticipated conflict with Britain and the United States, because those two nations were conducting a joint effort to develop the bomb while purposefully excluding the Soviet Union. He concludes that the Soviet effort to develop the bomb was probably a "hedge against uncertainty."

The mere existence of the German, British, and U.S. efforts gave the Soviet program impetus, even if the government did not have a clear idea of how they would use this new destructive force. By the time the American bomb had been used, the Soviet drive to acquire the bomb was spurred on by their goal of avoiding military and technological inferiority.

DEVELOPING THE BARUCH PLAN

The atomic bomb was a weapon of unparalleled destruction that had served not only to bring World War II to a close but to introduce a new era in weapons technology. Because of its immense destructive power, future wars that might employ nuclear weapons have taken on a totally new dimension. At the same time, advances in atomic energy held out prospects for important peaceful uses, such as nuclear power or large-scale excavation projects. The processes associated with the military and peaceful uses of atomic energy were virtually the same. Traditionally, with most scientific advancements, there were efforts to share information at the international level.

But because of the destructive ability of the atomic bomb and with its attendant enhancement of national power, the United States would not share the information in the absence of an effective control system. Reconciling the drive to reap the peaceful benefits of this newly harnessed force with the need to control its destructive power would pose a tremendous challenge to the Baruch Plan negotiations.

International Activities   Several political actions occurred that were aimed at establishing a framework in which to consider the control of atomic energy. First, the Three Nation Agreed Declaration was concluded among the United States, Great Britain, and Canada, wartime partners in the development of the bomb. As agreed in Washington on 15 November 1945, the three countries declared their intent to share with all nations the scientific information associated with atomic energy for peaceful purposes. Recognizing the dilemma of reconciling the peaceful and destructive powers of atomic energy, the declaration called for withholding this information until appropriate safeguards were in place. It called on the United Nations to establish a commission to recommend a system of international control.

At the Conference of Ministers meeting in Moscow, on 27 December 1945, the Soviets agreed to these principles in the Moscow Declaration, a Soviet-Anglo-U.S. statement. The declaration also contained the text of a proposed U.N. resolution to establish a commission on controlling atomic energy; it invited France, China, and Canada to cosponsor the resolution, which was passed unanimously during the first session of the U.N. General Assembly, on 24 January 1946.

Thus, the United Nations Atomic Energy Commission (UNAEC) was established. It consisted of all members of the U.N. Security Council plus Canada, for a total of twelve countries (Australia, Brazil, Canada, China, Egypt, France, Mexico, the Netherlands, Poland, the Soviet Union, the United Kingdom, and the United States). The resolution called for the commission to be accountable to the Security Council, dominated by the United States, Great Britain, China, and the Soviet Union. This move, suggested by the Soviets, demonstrated how the efforts to share the knowledge of atomic energy for peaceful purposes would be dominated by security considerations. The Security Council also operated with a veto power for each permanent member on substantive—but not procedural—issues. The veto would play an important role in the efforts to control atomic energy.

The responsibilities of the UNAEC, as set down in Resolution I, "Establishment of a Commission to Deal with the Problems Raised by the Discovery of Atomic Energy," were as follows:

(a) For extending between all nations the exchange of basic scientific information for peaceful ends;
(b) For control of atomic energy to the extent necessary to ensure its use only for peaceful purposes;
(c) For the elimination from national armaments of atomic weapons and of all other major weapons adaptable to mass destruction; and
(d) For effective safeguards by way of inspection and other means to protect complying States against the hazards of violations and evasion. *(Documents on Disarmament 1945–1959).*

Evolution of U.S. Policy   The United States recognized the need for controlling this new force as well as keeping the public informed, to a certain extent. Shortly after the first atomic weapons were used, the Smyth Report (named for its author, Princeton physicist Henry D. Smyth) was published by the United States in an effort to make basic scientific facts associated with atomic energy available to the public. Whether or not to publish the report had been debated within the Truman administration, but in the end the government decided to publish it in order to avoid public speculation and misconceptions about atomic energy. The Smyth report was used extensively in the UNAEC deliberations.

In October 1945, President Truman listed five basic principles, based largely on the unpublished report of a committee convened at his behest by Secretary of War Henry Stimson before the end of the war. These principles comprised the primary technical and political factors that would drive U.S. policy throughout the negotiations: (1) no nation could maintain a monopoly of atomic weapons; (2) no nation could maintain or morally defend a monopoly of the peaceful uses of atomic energy; (3) there was probably no adequate military defense against atomic weapons; (4) all initial and some subsequent processes to produce fissionable materials were identical regardless of whether they were for peaceful or military use; and (5) uranium or thorium were the only raw materials available that could serve as the basis for the nuclear chain reaction required for the release of atomic energy. (Substantial deposits of the ores containing these materials are not numerous; however, lower concentrations of the ores have a wide geographical distribution.)

Further activity in U.S. policy-making took the form of a committee, convened in January 1946 by Secretary of State James F. Byrnes, to study methods of control and safeguards to protect the United States during the negotiations. The five members of the group, led by Assistant Secretary of State Dean Acheson, were drawn from military and political circles associated with developing the bomb. Acheson's committee looked to a "Board of Consultants" as a source of knowledge on the technical aspects of atomic energy. The board was led by David Lilienthal, chairman of the Tennessee Valley Authority, and included three other scientists, notably among them J. Robert Oppenheimer, the physicist who had played a major role in the Manhattan Project.

The combined efforts of these two groups resulted in a document entitled "A Report on the International Control of Atomic Energy," which came to be known as the "Acheson-Lilienthal Report." Re-leased in late March 1946, the report emphasized the technical characteristics of atomic energy that would determine the nature of an international control system. Moreover, the conferees regarded their conclusions as a foundation for discussion rather than as a final plan. The United States proposal at the UNAEC would draw heavily on the Acheson-Lilienthal report's ideas for a system of international control, with some important and distinctive modifications brought to the plan by Bernard Baruch.

THE NEGOTIATIONS

On 14 June 1946, Baruch made the opening proposal at the first meeting of the UNAEC. Although he regarded his remarks as a starting point for discussion, they came to be regarded as a definitive statement of U.S. policy—that is, "The Baruch Plan." The plan called for establishing an International Atomic Development Authority that would control or own all activities associated with atomic energy, from raw materials to military applications. It would also control, license, and inspect all other uses. In addition, it would foster the beneficial application of atomic energy for peaceful purposes and would conduct research and development in the field. Once the authority was established, existing atomic bombs would be destroyed and their manufacture would stop.

Baruch listed several activities that would be illegal: possession or use of an atomic bomb; possession or separation of atomic material suitable for use in a bomb; seizure of property owned or licensed by the authority; interference with the authority's activities; and engaging in "dangerous" projects that were contrary to or without a license by the authority.

He called for penalties to be imposed against countries that engaged in such activities. And although he recognized the importance of the veto power to the work of Security Council, he said that with respect to atomic energy "there must be no veto to protect those who violate their solemn agreement not to develop or use atomic energy for destructive purposes" (*Documents on Disarmament, 1945–1959*, p. 12).

The basic outline for the authority was based on the work of the Acheson-Lilienthal group, but the provisions for sanctions and the elimination of the veto had been added by Baruch.

Reactions to the Baruch Plan

Responses to the plan were wide ranging. One supporter called it "thoughtful, imaginative and courageous" (cited in Hewlett and Anderson, p. 582); while the Toledo *Blade* asserted there was not type large enough "to emphasize the importance of the American proposal today" (quoted in Coit, p. 585). After reading the speech, Winston Churchill praised Baruch, saying, "There is no man in whose hands I would rather see these awful problems placed than Bernard Baruch's" (quoted in Coit).

Yet the plan was criticized for several different reasons. The San Francisco *Examiner* labeled it "imbecilic," because it called for surrendering to "FOREIGN MASTERS the AMERICAN SECRET of the atomic bomb" (cited in Hewlett and Anderson). Others opposed the plan as being unfair to the Soviets and called for an immediate halt in the manufacture of atomic bombs. Some thirty senators said that the plan was "not tenable nor backed by public opinion" (cited in Coit), but Senate Foreign Relations Committee Chairman Arthur Vandenberg said the plan was "more important to the peace of the world than anything that happen[ed] here [in New York]" (cited in Coit, p. 585). By September, one survey reported that 78 percent of the American public endorsed the plan.

The issue of the veto prompted both favorable and unfavorable comments. Walter Lippmann accused Baruch of taking the United States up a blind alley with the veto provision; a joint telegram from Justice William O. Douglas, Ely Culbertson, and John Foster Dulles favored Baruch's notion of removing the veto from the decision to punish violators. The American *Daily Worker*, the U.S. Communist party newspaper, viewed the elimination of the veto as an opportunity for the United States and Great Britain to "carry the day" against the Soviet Union, asserting that Baruch "was not releasing the dove of peace; he was demonstrating a new predatory flight of the American eagle" (quoted in Lieberman, p. 309).

The Soviet Proposal

At the second meeting of the UNAEC, on 19 June 1946, Soviet Deputy Foreign Minister Andrei Gromyko presented the Soviet plan. He proposed that the first step in controlling atomic energy should be a convention outlawing the production and use of atomic weapons. After this, he called for "a system of supervision and control" to ensure observance of the agreement and sanctions against the illegal use of atomic energy.

He introduced two resolutions. The first called for the agreement to ban the use and production of atomic bombs and to destroy existing weapons within three months. The resolution also called on the parties to the agreement to pass laws within their own countries to punish violators. Gromyko's second resolution called for the formation of two committees: one for exchanging scientific information, and the second to find ways to ensure compliance with the provisions of the proposed agreement.

The only direct response to the Baruch Plan was Soviet opposition to eliminating the veto: "Attempts to undermine the principles, as established by the Charter of the Security Council, including unanimity of the members of the Security Council in deciding questions of substance, are incompatible with the interests of the United Nations.... Such attempts must be rejected" (U.S. Department of State, *Documents on Disarmament, 1945–1959,* p. 24).

Further Soviet reaction to the Baruch Plan appeared in the Soviet newspaper *Pravda,* on 24 June 1946. Calling the U.S. proposal "a product of atomic diplomacy," the newspaper focused its opposition on how the Baruch Plan proposed to make the transition to international control. It criticized the United States for continuing to manufacture bombs while the control authority was being established, asking, "Why are all other countries obliged to display blind confidence in the United States' intentions while the United States obviously distrusts not only its partners but also the international control organ?" (cited in Lieberman, p. 312).

Further Negotiations

The official U.S. reaction to the Soviet proposal was low-key. In a press conference, one member of the U.S. delegation said that he was not discouraged and characterized the Soviet proposal "by way of argument rather than a final Soviet position." (Coit, p. 591). In order to avoid an open split between the two sides at this early stage of negotiation, the U.S. delegation used anonymous stories in the press to make its point. Thus, the *New York Times* reported that according to a reliable source, the United States was not able to accept the Soviet plan because it meant giving up the United States source of military power in the absence of any of the safeguards Baruch had proposed.

The next day, another story appeared in the press that addressed the differences over the issue of the veto: another "reliable source" indicated that the

United States was willing to establish an atomic development authority outside the U.N. In this way, it was asserted, the U.N. itself would not be undermined by the elimination of the veto on atomic energy matter. The Soviets responded, also through anonymous sources in the press, by insisting on retaining the veto and keeping the authority within the U.N. system.

As the UNAEC approached the task of reconciling the two proposals, initial positions of all twelve countries were evident: nine supported the Baruch Plan, two (USSR and Poland) supported the Soviet Plan, and one (the Netherlands) was without a clear position.

Subcommittee One   Initially, the UNAEC agreed to break into a working committee of the whole, to draft a plan incorporating all the ideas suggested for the international control authority. Both the United States, noting the level of support for its proposal, and the Soviet Union reiterated their respective positions. After some debate with Gromyko over its name, a smaller group, Subcommittee One, was formed to draft possible features that a control plan might have; the members of Subcommittee One were France, Mexico, the United Kingdom, the United States, and the Soviet Union.

Subcommittee One began meeting on 1 July 1946. The day before, the United States had conducted a test of an atomic bomb at Bikini Atoll in the Pacific (9 A.M. local time, 1 July; 6 P.M. EST time, 30 June), an event that provided evidence to some of a U.S. unwillingness to relinquish its monopoly over the bomb. In addition to providing propaganda value for the Soviets, continuing the U.S. testing program may have provided more impetus for them to develop their own bomb. Another test was held 25 July. In September, however, the president postponed the next test—scheduled for March 1947—partly out of deference to the negotiations.

Over the course of Subcommittee One's deliberations, the United States presented three memoranda that provided the basis for the discussions. The first, submitted on 2 July, discussed the treaty that the United States could support. The proposed treaty included transitional stages leading to full control of nuclear activities by the authority, the end of atomic weapons, inspection, defining violations, and international control of raw materials and production facilities. The second, on 5 July, explained the functions of the proposed Atomic De-

velopment Authority and elicited some response from Gromyko in the form of questions about specific points in the U.S. proposal. The third, on 12 July, dealt with the relationship between the proposed authority and the U.N., emphasizing that the loss of the veto on atomic matters would have no effect on other U.N. matters.

The third memorandum also defined three kinds of violations and what the United States viewed as commensurate sanctions. The first kind, administrative violations, would be acted on by the authority alone. The second kind was defined as serious but not threatening to world peace. The authority's decision that a violation had occurred would be subject to review by another group, possibly the International Court of Justice. The third kind of violation was defined as the most serious, constituting a threat to world peace. These last two types of violations would be punished with sanctions, enforced by majority vote of the Security Council. The memorandum called the veto "an instrument for the protection of nations, not a shield behind which deception and criminal acts can be performed with impunity," thus defending the part of the Baruch Plan that denied veto protection to violators (U.S. Department of State, *Documents on Disarmament,* p. 39).

The discussions in Subcommittee One demonstrated some of the basic differences between the U.S. citizens and the Soviets. Gromyko insisted on outlawing atomic bombs first and was less concerned about a system of control. The United States demanded adequate control before it would give up its source of military power. The opposing positions of each country on the veto became further entrenched. Although a goal of the Americans in submitting the memoranda had been to elicit more specific responses from the Soviets, Gromyko held fast to his tenets.

The chairman of Subcommittee One, Herbert Evatt of Australia, recognized the impasse and proposed to the full UNAEC that three committees of the whole be formed to address technical questions and to leave political questions aside, in the hope of finding some source of common ground between the two sides. By majority vote the group formed Committee Two, the Scientific and Technical Committee (the only one whose formation the Soviets supported), and a Legal Committee. The most significant work occurred in Committee Two and the Scientific and Technical Committee.

Committee Two   Committee Two met first but was unable to move beyond the differences experienced in Subcommittee One and became the forum for Gromyko's outright rejection of the Baruch Plan. In sum, he said, on 24 July 1946, "The United States proposals in their present form cannot be accepted in any way by the Soviet Union either as a whole or in separate parts" (quoted in Lieberman, p. 329). He refused to give up Soviet opposition to eliminating the veto.

Harkening back to the founding of the U.N., Gromyko emphasized the importance of the issue of sovereignty in those deliberations. He addressed the American plan to consider atomic energy "as matters of international and not of national importance" (Lieberman, p. 329). He viewed this principle as a violation of Article 2, Paragraph 7 of the U.N. Charter, which called for no interference in the internal matters of member states.

The initial U.S. reaction was that the Soviet position was a tactical one from which it might ultimately seek compromise, although this conclusion proved wrong. In subsequent meetings of Subcommittee Two, supporters of the Baruch Plan called on Gromyko to articulate the characteristics of a control system that would be acceptable to the Soviets. These efforts were met with statements that labeled inspection "greatly exaggerated in importance." Asserting that inspection could not guarantee peace and security, Gromyko said that this "lies only in the genuine desire of the members of the United Nations to cooperate to that end" (quoted in Lieberman, p. 332).

The discussion continued along these lines until a breakthrough, of sorts, occurred as a result of a proposal from the Mexican delegate, Luis Padilla Nervo. He pointed out that specifics about safeguards were an essential element of a control plan, and that safeguards were largely technical questions. Therefore, he proposed, the issue of safeguards should be referred to the Scientific and Technical Committee; its findings might contribute to overcoming many of the differences they were encountering. The work of the committee would focus solely on the technical feasibility of control, ignoring the political issues.

The group agreed to the Mexican proposal, although a member of the U.S. negotiating team, John Hancock, feared it would only delay matters, a point that did not seem to displease Gromyko. Subsequent discussions in Committee Two were fruitless,

and the group finally agreed to suspend its deliberations until the Scientific and Technical Committee reported its conclusions.

Scientific and Technical Committee   The committee had begun meeting on 19 July 1946, and the framework within which the members operated proved highly successful. Forming an informal group of scientists, the committee agreed that no one in the group would represent his country; the members would simply explore the technical aspects of safeguards as individuals. Whatever conclusions they drew would be referred back to the Scientific and Technical Committee for approval. The United States provided, in addition to the technical information in the Smyth Report and the Acheson-Lilienthal Report, background information and information on the beneficial uses of atomic energy in eleven different treatises. The United States also offered to consider requests for additional information.

After the group had met seven times between 25 July and 10 August, a draft report was ready by 20 August. The group spent eight more sessions refining it. One point raised at this time was the reluctance of the United States to provide all the information that had been requested. For some this raised questions regarding U.S. intentions and sincerity and presented more of an obstacle than the lack of information did. Ultimately, the group agreed on language for the report's introduction that explained that although some information had not been provided, there was no reason "to doubt the essential accuracy of this information" that had been supplied. The report called it "an orderly extension of the pre-war science of nuclear physics. . . . [with] no apparent inconsistency with this pre-existing body of scientific fact" (quoted in Hewlett and Anderson, p. 594).

The report, finished on 3 September, embodied much of the information of the Smyth and Acheson-Lilienthal reports. In response to Committee Two's mandate, the report concluded it had been unable to find "any basis in the available scientific facts for supposing that effective control is not technologically feasible" (Hewlett and Anderson, p. 594).

Until the final meeting of the committee on 6 September, the Soviets had agreed with the group. But for the final vote on the report, a new Soviet representative, Pavel S. Alexandrov, was sent, who said he had no instructions from Gromyko on how to vote because the latter had been preoccupied with Security Council affairs. He asked for a week's delay, after which still no Soviet position emerged.

THE UNITED STATES APPROACH

Baruch and his delegation were in a quandary about what to do next. During the Scientific and Technical Committee's deliberations, the U.S. delegation had debated the advantages and disadvantages of forcing a vote on the Baruch Plan, thereby demonstrating what they viewed as Soviet recalcitrance to the world. Those in favor of forcing the Soviets' hand counseled that delay could lead to appeasement; the opposing view held that the United States should await the outcome of the foreign ministers' conference in Paris on postwar matters, before taking any precipitous action in the U.N. Baruch had chosen the latter course.

But as the work of the Scientific and Technical Committee bogged down, Baruch decided to write a letter to President Truman, seeking approval for two recommendations. First, his goal would be to force a vote in the UNAEC on the Baruch Plan at an early date, preferably before 1 January 1947, when the membership of the commission would rotate (three Baruch Plan supporters, Egypt, Mexico, and the Netherlands, would leave the commission). Second, he called for renewed efforts toward military preparedness in the field of atomic energy, in the face of the expected failure of the UNAEC.

Disarray in U.S. Policy Widespread press coverage of the views of Secretary of Commerce Henry Wallace, who was critical of the Baruch Plan, provided the backdrop for Baruch's visit to deliver his letter to the president on 18 September. Wallace's remarks, well received by a liberal audience, had explicitly and publicly undercut Baruch's position.

Wallace said that a major defect of the Baruch Plan was the U.S. insistence that other countries give up their right to explore military uses of atomic energies and turn over raw materials to an international authority, whereas the United States would not give up its weapons until a system was in place to U.S. satisfaction. If the tables were turned, he did not see how the United States could accept such an arrangement.

Furthermore, Wallace viewed the transitional stages as too vague and called for an agreement

"which will commit us to disclosing information and destroying our bombs at a specified time or in terms of specified actions by other countries, rather than at our unfettered discretion" (Hewlett and Anderson, p. 598). The United States would still have the facilities for producing weapons as well as technical knowledge to fall back on during the transition to international control. Wallace insisted that the veto was not relevant to questions of atomic energy because each nation would be free to take any action against a violator, including declaring war. He felt that the United States had unnecessarily created a barrier to achieving agreement in the negotiations by raising this issue.

To Baruch, this public display of American disunity would undermine the impact of a UNAEC vote on the Baruch Plan. At the Paris Conference of Ministers, Secretary of State James F. Byrnes had a similar reaction, complaining to Truman that the United States position at Paris had been eroded by Wallace's statements. Both public officials told Truman that they would resign if Wallace did not recant. Ultimately, Truman asked for and received Wallace's resignation on 20 September.

Over the next two weeks, at the U.N., Soviet delegates sought to bolster support for their plan by raising questions about whether Baruch represented the American people. On 24 September the London *Sunday Times* asked Soviet leader Josef Stalin whether the United States monopoly over atomic bombs posed a threat to peace. His response was that the atomic bomb was a threat of sorts, but it could not determine the outcome of a war; in the final analysis, in Stalin's view, the United States could not maintain its monopoly forever, and the use of atomic bombs should be outlawed.

Baruch felt that Wallace had been uninformed about his plan and attempted to set the record straight with him. Although he was unable to change Wallace's mind, Baruch's public statements toward this end came to form the most comprehensive description of the United States plan. He argued that there was no point setting down the details of the transition stages until there was agreement on the broad basic principles of the plan. He denied that the United States expected other countries to reveal their sources of atomic material unless the United States was prepared to do the same. Furthermore, he disagreed with Wallace's criticism of the denial of the veto with regard to sanctions and Wallace's notion that the only possible sanction should be war; rather he hoped that international law and group action could be used to punish various types of violations of the control plan.

Even after his resignation and Baruch's attempts to persuade him to do otherwise, Wallace continued to criticize the Baruch Plan openly, focusing primarily on his view that it was the hypocrisy of continued U.S. manufacture of atomic bombs that was the primary motive for Soviet actions in the United Nations. During the rest of the year, other commentators joined Wallace in calling for a halt to bomb manufacture as a gesture of goodwill and rejecting Baruch's position on the veto.

FINAL ACTIONS AT THE UNITED NATIONS

As the Wallace-Baruch affair continued in the press, the Soviets finally, on 26 September, called for a vote on the Scientific and Technical Committee's report. The group was pleased by the Soviet vote in favor of the report, but the feeling was short-lived. The Soviet representative stated that their vote was accompanied by a reservation, based on the fact that the information on which the report's conclusions were based was incomplete and therefore should be regarded as "hypothetical and conditional" (cited in Lieberman, p. 355). On 2 October, Committee Two formally accepted the report of the Scientific and Technical Committee and began hearing testimony from various experts on the nature of safeguards over the raw materials and chemical processes associated with atomic energy.

Although Committee Two's meetings were proceeding smoothly, various Soviet actions through October 1946 demonstrated to the U.S. delegation that it would not be possible to obtain an understanding between the United States and the Soviet Union, based on mutual trust and cooperation. Baruch pressed Truman for an answer to his September letter that called for an early vote on the Baruch Plan. By the time Baruch received permission in November to force a vote by the end of the year, the Baruch Plan had been rejected and Baruch's reputation had been subject to a personal attack by the Soviets in the U.N.

On 13 November, at the first plenary meeting of the United Nations Atomic Energy Commission in four months, the vote was ten in favor, two (USSR and Poland) abstaining, that the UNAEC should re-port its finding and recommendations to the Security Council by 31 December 1946. Despite various delaying tactics from the Soviets, the Americans moved closer to their goal of an early vote. On 5 December, Baruch, whose position on major elements of the plan had been reaffirmed by the administration, proposed in the UNAEC that the Baruch Plan be adopted as a recommendation to the Security Council, but he did not insist on a vote that day. On 20 December, the UNAEC rejected a Soviet proposal to postpone the vote for one week and a Polish proposal to refer the Baruch Plan to the Political and Social Committee of the U.N. General Assembly. At this point, Gromyko simply refused to participate any further, a stance he maintained through the end of the year.

On 26 December, Committee Two passed its report on safeguards and forwarded it to the Working Committee. The next day, the Working Committee discussed the Baruch Plan, one paragraph at a time. In the end, the discussion revealed one area of disagreement: the veto. The group agreed to report to the full UNAEC, with a cover letter explaining the remaining dispute, and a note that the Soviets had not participated. At the final meeting of the UNAEC, on 30 December, the group agreed to Baruch's proposal to adopt the Working Committee report and to submit it to the Security Council the next day. Ten voted for the proposal, with none opposed and with two abstentions. It had passed by a majority but without Soviet agreement. But, as so aptly characterized by one writer, it was for the United States "a hollow victory" (Lieberman, p. 358).

As originally planned, Baruch resigned shortly after the vote under the hope that by the United States having the same representative in the UNAEC and the Security Council (U.S. representative to the U.N. Warren Austin), its hand would be strengthened. The Security Council discussed the report without success until March 1947, when it passed a resolution to refer the discussions back to the UNAEC. The UNAEC provided the second report in September; their deliberations had included considering twelve Soviet amendments to the first UNAEC report, all of which had been rejected. The Security Council did not consider the second report of the UNAEC, which continued to meet through the spring of 1948. A third UNAEC report concluded that the group had reached an impasse and requested that the Security Council suspend its deliberations. In the summer of 1948, the Soviets vetoed a Security Council resolution approving all of the UNAEC reports, while a nonbinding resolution of the General Assembly nevertheless approved the majority plan. The General Assembly insisted that the UNAEC continue its negotiations, in the hope of sometime in the future being able to bring these weapons under control.

In the meantime, in September 1949, President Truman announced that there had been evidence within recent weeks of an atomic explosion in the Soviet Union. With the U.S. atomic monopoly at an end, efforts to control the destructive powers of atomic energy would take on a new dimension. In November 1949, the General Assembly agreed to suspend the work of the United Nations Atomic Energy Commission.

At the outset, several points of difference emerged that remained at issue throughout the negotiations. One of the most critical was the order in which certain events would occur. The United States, with substantial reliance on the atomic bomb as a source of its military power, was adamant in its insistence that adequate safeguards be in place before it would relinquish its weapons or the information needed to manufacture them.

The Soviets and others regarded the U.S. refusal to dismantle its nuclear arsenal and the continuation of weapons manufacture as evidence of U.S. hypocrisy, and they questioned the sincerity of U.S. intentions to relinquish the bomb. Although the United States did not appear willing to relinquish control of atomic energy, it nevertheless expected others to surrender the right to develop it through acceptance of an international control authority with very intrusive powers.

A related question focused on the extent of control to be exercised by the international authority over all phases of atomic energy. The technical characteristics of working with atomic energy, from raw materials to final product, coupled with its massive destructive power, appeared to drive the proposal for controlling it. But reconciling these concepts with national sovereignty—of both the United States and the Soviet Union—and private ownership proved an impossible task.

Finally, a major stumbling block was the proposal to eliminate the veto on matters affecting violators of the system of international control. Baruch had added this feature to the U.S. proposal, partly to avoid appearing to be a "messenger boy" for the already published proposals of the Acheson-Lilienthal Report. On the face of it, this part of the proposal alone may have given the Soviets sufficient reason to reject the Baruch Plan, because it struck at the heart of the newly created security arrangements embodied in the U.N.

CONCLUSION

Although warm to the Soviet Union as a wartime ally, Roosevelt had been careful to keep from Stalin any mention of the atomic bomb, apparently appreciating the special nature of this project. President Truman largely continued this policy, although he referred to the bomb obliquely at Potsdam, by which time Stalin was already aware, through espionage, of its existence. Signs of Soviet expansion into Eastern Europe motivated Truman to continue along this line. Indeed, the foreign policy scholar Barton Bernstein argues that Truman delayed having the Baruch Plan presented, preferring to have it done at the U.N. rather than broaching it to the Soviets sooner.

Soviet actions were responsible in part for this attitude. During the war, the United States had unwittingly given the Soviets an opportunity to become further entrenched in Germany and Czechoslovakia, by agreeing to allow the Soviet army, rather than Allied forces, to liberate Berlin and Prague. In March 1945, one month before Roosevelt's death, the Soviets began to establish a satellite regime in Poland that appeared to undercut what the United States believed the Soviets had agreed to at Yalta. By January 1946, when the U.N. General Assembly passed the resolution creating the UNAEC, "disputes over British forces in Greece and Soviet troops in Iran, as well as continuing differences over Eastern Europe and Germany, emphasized the split between the wartime allies" (Bernstein, p. 1029).

Although the Soviets claimed their actions were defensive, their build-up of ground forces, taking place as the Allies were demobilizing theirs, was regarded as aggressive. Moreover, the United States was concerned that its rapid withdrawal of troops from Europe may have created a vacuum that the Soviets could fill. Public opinion gradually endorsed Washington's mistrust of the Soviets—by the summer of 1946, polls showed that Americans did not trust the Russians and expected another war, started by the Russians, in the next twenty-five years.

The United States and "Atomic Diplomacy"

With the depth and nature of U.S. suspicions regarding Soviet intentions, it is understandable that the Truman administration would entertain the idea that the atomic bomb could be used to gain political leverage over the Soviets. The issue was debated within the administration and perhaps is best illustrated by the differences between Secretary of War Stimson and Secretary of State Byrnes. Stimson had toyed with the idea that the promise of international cooperation and control of atomic energy could be used as a lever to force the Soviets to open their society, perhaps ultimately leading to conditions for a democracy. But once the terrifying force of the new weapons had been demonstrated, Stimson cautioned Truman that if the United States tried to use its monopoly to get the Soviets to change, United States–Soviet relations would become irretrievably embittered. In Stimson's view, the need to control this terrible force, and to avoid a futile arms race, could not wait for a radical change in Soviet society.

Because of his mistrust of the Soviets, deepened by their behavior at Potsdam—a meeting attended by the United States, Soviet, and British leaders following the defeat of Germany to plan military operations against Japan, and to decide on substance and procedures for a peace settlement in Europe—Byrnes advocated a concentrated effort to develop the destructive uses of atomic energy and discouraged the notion of working with the Soviets on a system of international control. In September 1945, by the time he left for the London Conference of Ministers, the effort to arrive at a postwar arrangement for peace, Byrnes was determined, as Stimson put it, "to have the implied threat of the bomb in his pocket during the conference" (Hewlett and Anderson, p. 417). The conference adjourned after three weeks, when it could not come to any agreement, even on procedural matters. While Byrnes blamed the failure of the talks on Soviet intransigence, the outcome also may have demonstrated the futility of his strategy of "atomic diplomacy."

Many observers at the time concluded that the Soviets perceived that the United States was using the bomb for leverage, thus exercising a tremendous influence on international relations and raising doubts about U.S. intentions. A *New York Times* headline called the November 1945 signing of the Three Nation Agreed Declaration "A Further Step in Pursuit of 'Atomic Diplomacy'" (Bernstein, p. 1025). A British correspondent in the Soviet Union observed in the article that the bomb "had become an immense factor in the world's power politics," and that the real purpose of the two bombs dropped on Japan was "first and foremost, to intimidate Russia."

One U.S. policymaker confided to another that "just the naked fact" of the U.S. atomic bomb "constituted a 'threat' to the Soviet Union, unless the United States simply gave away the secret. As long as there was talk of bargaining, the bomb would be viewed by the Soviets, not irrationally, as a threat to Soviet security" (Bernstein, p. 1025).

There seems to be sufficient evidence to support this view. Truman informed Stalin of the existence of the bomb at Potsdam in July 1945. Although Stalin's public reaction was sanguine, after the conference he admonished Soviet scientists to "hurry things up" because the Americans "simply want to raise the price," that is, use the bomb as leverage to exact political gains. Indeed, the first successful Soviet test of a nuclear device in August 1949 prompted one scientist to observe that "they had knocked the trump card from the hands of the American atomic diplomats" (Herbert F. York, *The Advisors,* Stanford, Calif., 1989, p. 33).

The Timing of Information-Sharing

Other factors that influenced U.S. and Soviet nuclear policy were the role of secrecy and theories about the life span of the U.S. monopoly of the atomic bomb. Both during and after the war, U.S. policymakers continuously debated the question of whether and when to disclose information to the Soviets about the bomb, even the knowledge that the effort to develop it existed.

As early as May 1944, Niels Bohr, a notable physicist involved in developing the bomb, was urging Roosevelt to tell the Soviets early about the development of the bomb and to begin discussions with them about international control. He was motivated by the belief that the Soviets would have the bomb soon after the war and that an early approach to an international control arrangement would prevent an arms race. Bohr's plan lacked specifics, however, for such an arrangement. Although Roosevelt did not reject Bohr's suggestion—indeed, Bohr left the meeting believing he had convinced the president—Roosevelt ultimately solidified an Anglo-American agreement to maintain tight control over atomic energy, to the exclusion of the Soviets. By taking this route, Roosevelt chose to use the bomb "to help shape the peace that the Anglo-American alliance desired" (Bernstein, p. 1007). Ultimately, Bohr was watched by the C.I.A., on Roosevelt's orders, to ensure that he did not share any information with the Soviets. Truman wrestled with the question and finally informed the Soviets at Potsdam in July 1945.

Another element in the debate was the role of U.S. domestic politics and public opinion on this question, consistent with popular mistrust of the Soviets. In mid-1945, as the debate developed in the United States over domestic control of atomic energy, it became clear that in order for legislation on the issue to gain popular support, there had to be assurances that the secrets of atomic energy would not be disclosed to the Soviets. By the fall of 1945, public sentiment against disclosing atomic information to the Soviets was quite strong.

The discussions on whether or when to inform the Soviets about the bomb were driven in part by estimates regarding the life of the U.S. monopoly. The most optimistic, that is, the longest, estimate came from General Leslie Groves, the head of the Manhattan Project, who, in 1942, believed not only that it would be twenty years before the Soviets had the bomb, but also that the United States controlled the world's supply of ore. At the other extreme, in the early 1940s, some felt Soviet acquisition of the bomb would occur much sooner, in three to four years. Vannevar Bush and James Conant, two prominent scientist-administrators in Washington, held this view and counseled early disclosure and consultation with the Soviets.

Oddly enough, even the Soviets estimated in 1942 that it might take ten to twenty years to develop the bomb. But by 1945, when the Soviets were prepared for an all-out effort, the estimate changed to five years. They actually accomplished it in four years.

In the end, Groves's estimate prevailed in shaping U.S. policy. As a consequence, there was a delay in telling the Soviets about the bomb; moreover, Baruch and other officials continued to believe that the U.S. monopoly of the bomb ensured U.S. negotiating strength. Even in December 1946, Baruch asserted "America can get what she wants if she insists on it. After all, we've got it and they haven't, and won't for a long time to come" (Gerber, p. 75).

Soviet Motivation During the Negotiations

It may never be known with certainty what the Soviets' motivations were for their behavior during the negotiation of the Baruch Plan. One opinion is that they were simply stalling in order to develop their own bomb. Although this view may explain their actions in part, other factors may be considered. The powerful force that the bomb's use on Japan demonstrated has been shown to have had a major impact on Soviet efforts to develop the bomb. Their feelings of inferiority and vulnerability, in the wake of the devastation of World War II, were inevitable.

They also had been aware of U.S. mistrust in them on atomic energy matters, early in the war. Early in 1942, secret files reached the Soviet leadership that documented British, American, and German work on the bomb. In May 1942 a Soviet Air Force lieutenant who had been a student of Kurschatov—the lead physicist in the Soviet bomb effort—observed the total absence in physics journals of further information regarding the discovery of spontaneous fission. None of the names of the more prominent nuclear scientists appeared, either. Thus, he concluded, research on nuclear fission was being conducted in secret, and in a letter to Stalin, urged that the Soviets pursue their own effort to build a uranium bomb. In 1945, when Truman finally shared with Stalin the knowledge of the bomb's existence, sufficient mistrust in U.S. intentions could have developed and been carried over into the negotiations.

Finally, the Soviets perceived—rightly so, in some instances—the tendency of U.S. diplomats to use the bomb for leverage in a variety of areas. This perception only helped to contribute to an atmosphere of mistrust and recalcitrance in the negotiations. Thus, as historian Larry Gerber sums it up, "America's failure to keep Russia informed during the war about the development of the atomic bomb, the implied threat to Russia entailed in America's use of the bomb against Japan, and the slowness with which the United States acted to initiate discussions after the war on the subject of international controls all lessened the chances for agreement on atomic energy by making the Soviets wary of American intentions" (p. 70).

While some modern writers place the blame for the failure of the negotiations primarily on U.S. actions, or the lack thereof, Barton Bernstein offers a broader perspective:

Neither the United States nor the Soviet Union was prepared in 1945 or 1946 to take the risks that the other power required for agreement. In this sense, the stalemate on atomic energy was a symbol of the mutual mistrust in Soviet-American relations. The dispute over atomic energy was both a cause and a consequence of the Cold War. (p. 1044)

BIBLIOGRAPHY

Historical Treatments   General historical treatment of the early efforts to control atomic energy can be found in BERNHARD G. BECHHOEFER, *Postwar Negotiations for Arms Control* (Washington, D.C., 1961); GREGG HERKEN, *The Winning Weapon: The Atomic Bomb in the Cold War 1945–1950* (New York, 1981); JOSEPH NOGEE, *Soviet Policy Toward International Control of Atomic Energy* (Notre Dame, Ind., 1961); and GEORGE QUESTER, *Nuclear Diplomacy, The First Twenty-Five Years* (New York, 1970). The Soviet perspective is addressed in DAVID HOLLOWAY, *The Soviet Union and the Arms Race* (New Haven, 1983).

For a detailed treatment of the Baruch Plan, which contains a considerable amount of primary source material see RICHARD G. HEWLETT and OSCAR E. ANDERSON, JR., *A History of the United States Atomic Energy Commission,* vol. 1, *The New World, 1939/1946* (University Park, Pa., 1962). A more popular treatment, with slightly less detail can be found in JOSEPH I. LIEBERMAN, *The Scorpion and the Tarantula: the Struggle to Control Atomic Weapons 1945–1949* (Boston, 1970). Primary source materials may be available in government depository libraries, as well as a useful collection is the U.S. DEPARTMENT OF STATE, *Documents on Disarmament, 1945–1959,* vol. 1, *1945–1956* (Washington, D.C., 1960).

Biographies   Several biographies, including an autobiography, of Bernard Baruch have been written: BERNARD M. BARUCH, *Baruch: The Public Years* (New York, 1960), MARGARET L. COIT, *Mr. Baruch* (Boston, 1957), and JAMES GRANT, *Bernard M. Baruch* (New York, 1983). Other first-person accounts of key participants include GEN. LESLIE R. GROVES, *Now It Can Be Told* (New York, 1962); DAVID E. LILIENTHAL, *The Journals of David E. Lilienthal,* vol. 2, *The Atomic Energy Years, 1945–1950* (New York, 1964); and DEAN ACHESON, *Present at the Creation: My Years in the State Department* (New York, 1969).

Critical Assessments   Several historical assessments of the Baruch Plan have appeared, including JOSEPH PRESTON BARATTA, "Was the Baruch Plan a Proposal of World Government?" *The International History Review* 7 (November, 1985): 592–621; BARTON J. BERNSTEIN, "The Quest for Security: American Foreign Policy and International Control of Atomic Energy, 1942–1946," *Journal of American History* 60 (March 1974): 1003–1044; and LARRY G. GERBER, "The Baruch Plan and the Origins of the Cold War," *Diplomatic History* 6 (Winter, 1982): 69–95. Finally, ROBERT L. MESSER, *The End of an Alliance: James F. Byrnes, Roosevelt, Truman, and the Origins of the Cold War* (Chapel Hill, N.C., 1982) reviews the unsuccessful efforts, especially those of Byrnes, to employ "atomic diplomacy."

The Disarming and Rearming of Germany

———○———

FRANK A. MAYER

See also The Disarming and Rearming of Italy; The Disarming and Rearming of Japan; Germany; From MBFR to CFE: Negotiating Conventional Arms Control in Europe; The Versailles Treaty; *and the essays in Part 4,* Arms Control Activities Since 1945. *Treaties regarding German disarmament following World War II are excerpted in Volume III.*

When World War II ended in Europe on 8 May 1945, the victorious Allies swore that never again would they allow German soldiers, airmen, or sailors to menace the peace. Germany lay devastated. Six and one-half million Germans had lost their lives as a consequence of Adolf Hitler's war, of which three and one-half million were Wehrmacht, or military personnel. Even to the vanquished, the idea of rearming seemed unthinkable and undesirable. But on 12 November 1955, only a decade later, under an enormous replica of the symbol of German military might, the Iron Cross, a reborn West German military force, or Bundeswehr, was welcomed into existence by three of the four former allied states.

German disarmament had lasted but a brief time, only to give way to extensive rearmament brought on by the breakup of the wartime coalition and the onset of Cold War tensions in Europe. Concurrent with the emergence of a democratic West Germany was the emergence of a military system that sought to redirect and reform an antidemocratic and aggressive military tradition.

The collapse of the Cold War in 1989 brought about the long-awaited reunion of the two Germanys, symbolized by the destruction of the Berlin Wall beginning in November of that year. In 1990, the final act in the post–World War II drama was concluded with a restatement of limits on future German military policy.

IMPOSED DISARMAMENT

Allied wartime planning for peace was clearly predicated on the disarmament of the Axis powers. President Franklin D. Roosevelt's 1941 Four Freedoms included "the freedom from fear," which called for the reduction of all armaments. At the Dumbarton Oaks Conference the Allied powers agreed that the enemy states must be disarmed at the end of the war. On 11 February 1945 at the Yalta Conference, Franklin Roosevelt, Winston Churchill, and Joseph Stalin confirmed the principle of disarming Germany when they agreed that:

It is our inflexible purpose to destroy German militarism and Nazism and to ensure that Germany will never again be able to disturb the peace of the world. We are determined to disarm and disband all German armed forces; break up for all time the German General Staff that has repeatedly contrived the resurgence of German militarism; remove or destroy all German military equipment; eliminate or control all German industry that could be used for military production . . . [and to take] such other measures in Germany as may be necessary to the future peace and safety of the world.

Allied policy toward the defeated Reich was spelled out in more detail in the 15 June 1945 "Declaration" drawn up by delegates of the four victors—the United States, Britain, the USSR, and

France, known as the "Allied Representatives." The declaration stated that all German military units "shall be completely disarmed, handing over their weapons and equipment to local Allied Commanders." Separate instructions were prepared for German air and naval craft, retributive in nature. The victors sought the total demilitarization of Hitler's war machine—a demilitarization even more intense than they had sought to impose some two decades earlier.

The victors established an Allied Military Security Board (MSB) that outlawed the manufacture of any weapon system, be it "tanks, planes, submarines, surface ships, or even pistols." Arms manufacturing plants were dismantled; such companies as the Krupp Iron and Steel Works in the Ruhr were stripped of any capacity to produce artillery pieces or armored vehicles. The post–World War I example of the Versailles Treaty of 1919 that had allowed Germany a field army of 100,000 men and 4,000 officers was rejected—no military units of any kind would be permitted. Those planes, tanks, or ships that remained after the German surrender were either destroyed or confiscated as reparations. The German general staff, which the Allies saw as the evil genius behind German militarism, was abolished. Even the wearing of military decorations was forbidden, as was the teaching of military history in the defeated and divided Reich.

So complete was this policy of disarmament, that when Churchill in 1946 praised the German officers who had attempted on 20 July 1944 to assassinate Hitler, accounts of his speech were forbidden in the U.S., British, and French occupation zones in Germany. Likewise, research that had anything to do with atomic energy was banned because the MSB felt such activity could have "possible value for war purposes." The nations of Western Europe resorted to bilateral and multilateral negotiations to further implement German disarmament.

On 4 March 1947 France and Britain signed the Treaty of Dunkirk, a mutual assistance agreement that would come into force in case of German attack. Article I of the treaty prevented any infringement by Germany of disarmament practices enforced by the MSB. Belgium, France, Luxembourg, the Netherlands, and Britain later established a Western European Union, which was formalized on 17 March 1948 with the Treaty of Brussels. This was a mutual defense pact that would come into force in the event of any future German military offensive.

In 1948, the U.S., British, and French governments allowed those Germans in their zones of occupation to convoke a constituent assembly to draft a formula for a new German republic. A constitution or basic law was drafted, and on 8 April 1949 all three Western zones of occupation were merged into what became the Federal Republic of Germany, or West Germany. On 15 September 1949, the former mayor of Cologne, Konrad Adenauer, became Germany's first democratically elected chancellor since Hitler.

Particular care, however, was taken to ensure the continuity of the demilitarization provisions, as Article 139 of the new German Constitution specifically safeguarded the permanency of this policy. The Western Allies and the Federal Republic signed the Petersberg Agreement on 22 November 1949 that granted West Germany increased domestic powers but maintained the demilitarization of the Federal Republic. In the agreement, the new Bonn government declared "its earnest determination to maintain the demilitarization of the federal territory and to endeavour by all means in its power to prevent the re-creation of armed forces of any kind." Ultimate authority for ensuring the demilitarization was vested with the Allied High Commission, composed of representatives of Britain, France, and the United States.

Yet for Chancellor Konrad Adenauer and the newly formed Republic, security from Russian aggression was a paramount issue. West Germany did not form part of the area protected by the North Atlantic Treaty Organization (NATO), and there was no contractual obligation for either the nations of the North Atlantic Pact or the Western European Union to defend the Federal Republic.

THE COLD WAR AND THE SEARCH FOR SECURITY

Only months after the end of World War II and before a structure for postwar peace could be created, the Allied coalition began to unravel. Suspicions, fears, and outright hostility replaced the fragile spirit of cooperation. On 24 June 1948, another phase in the emerging Cold War unfolded in Germany when the Soviet government forbade its former allies from using land routes to supply their occupation zones in Berlin. The Berlin blockade prompted Western leaders to search for ways to deter what they perceived as a growing Soviet menace. Shifting their attention from the traditional "German threat," the Brussels Treaty signatories joined with the United States and Canada to establish the North Atlantic Treaty Organization (NATO) to balance Soviet military power in Eastern Europe. This new security focus had a direct impact, both politically and militarily, on Germany.

German fears of possible Soviet aggression were based on perceived military imbalances between the new Soviet Eastern European "empire" and the United States and its Western European allies. Postwar American forces in Europe had been reduced to 390,000 men, while England had shrunk its forces to 500,000 troops. The Soviets, in 1950, had at least twenty-two divisions in Eastern Europe (with six thousand tanks) facing three and one-half American, two and one-half British, and six understaffed French and six Benelux (Belgium, the Netherlands, and Luxembourg) divisions. In May of 1950, at the Western foreign ministers meeting in London, it was agreed that West Germany would be welcomed into the political and economic system of the West if the Federal Republic would begin to plan for its own internal security.

Adenauer acted quickly. His postwar political policy was based on a unity of interests with the West, and here was the chance to determine the initial form of German security. As his first security adviser, he chose a former general of tank troops, Gerhard Graf von Schwerin, a soldier who had the confidence of the British high commissioner, Lord Robertson. Given the title of "Advisor of the Federal Chancellor for Security Questions," Schwerin began Germany's postwar defense planning. In early June, he suggested that a possible German defense force could be created quickly if existing police forces were given adequate military training. This idea was given added weight when the American State Department published a report that showed the Soviets had already created a forty-thousand-man armed force in their German zone of occupation. Despite these developments, the idea of a German military contribution to supplement the occupation forces was acknowledged in private but denied in public.

It would take an event of major proportions to move the Western Allied powers to rethink their positions regarding German rearmament. Oddly, this event did not take place in Europe but in Asia.

The Korean War, which broke out on 25 June 1950, prompted a sudden reversal of German demilitarization policy. What had been unthinkable in May of that year—Germans once again in uniform—quickly became the goal of American military planners. English officials agreed, and urged the creation of twenty active and ten reserve German divisions. At the Allied Foreign Ministers Conference in September 1950, the United States government formally requested German forces to strengthen the defense of Western Europe. France, which earlier had rejected any notion of German rearmament, again balked and requested more time to consider the unthinkable. What aroused French fears was Washington's insistence on German divisions that would retain their national status—that is, the reestablishment of the German national army.

Adenauer recognized the need for a concrete German rearmament concept. In October 1950 Schwerin asked a group of former Wehrmacht officers to develop such a plan. Former colonel Johann A. Graf von Kielmansegg acted as secretary to the group, which included Hans Speidel, Adolf Heusinger, Admiral Friedrich Ruge, and former general staff officer Major Graf von Baudissin. Strictly speaking, such a meeting violated the demilitarization statutes of the Allies and could have brought each a sentence of life imprisonment. To avoid such an eventuality, they met in the Eifel Mountains at the Abbey Himmerod. The product of this four-day meeting was a document, "Memorandum on the Formation of a German Contingent for the Defense of Western Europe within the Framework of an International Fighting Force," or simply, the "Himmerod Memorandum." This document was to guide German and NATO military thinking throughout the Cold War era.

Its major elements included total equality for German contingents, the creation of twelve armored divisions under the command of six corps headquarters, a tactical Luftwaffe (air force), and a navy geared to coastal defense. These forces would be deployed as close to the West German border as possible. Aware of possible hostile European reactions to German rearmament, the memorandum would prevent any soldier who harbored neo-Nazi sympathies from joining the future German armed forces and called for training programs that would teach German recruits about their new role as European soldiers defending a democratic Europe. As opposed to a soldier in the kaiser's army (Reichswehr) or Hitler's force (Wehrmacht), the Himmerod soldier could look forward to being a citizen in uniform, who could enjoy the rights and privileges of a democratic state while soldiering. Another crucial concept, that of *Innere Führung,* or military code of conduct, was likewise proposed as a starting point for any postwar German military structure. It was these two concepts, that of citizen-soldier and *Innere Führung,* that became the most important innovations of the postwar German military.

The Paris government, however, was in the throws of a major dilemma. On the one hand, its war in Indochina was going badly and it needed American equipment and funds to sustain its military operations there. On the other hand, it faced American demands for German rearmament. In a move to soothe French fears and appease American demands for German troops, French Prime Minister René Pleven unveiled on 24 October 1950 a plan for a unified European army under a European defense minister, who would be answerable to a European parliament. German divisions, command structure, or defense ministers would not be allowed. Psychologically sound but militarily questionable, the "Pleven Plan" was rejected by NATO planners. Finally, in mid-December 1950, NATO offered a compromise. The French idea of a European army was accepted, as was the raising of German forces, which would be limited to only one-fifth of all other nations' forces. Events had moved quickly in Europe—just five years after the defeat of Hitler, the victors now sought soldiers, sailors, and airmen from their former enemy.

Even though Adenauer and his security advisers had serious doubts about the effectiveness of the European-army concept, the chancellor accepted it in order not to arouse French apprehensions. Besides, he wanted to show that the Federal Republic was committed to democratic principles and civilian control of any future German military organization. On 23 October 1950 Adenauer replaced the former Wehrmacht officer Schwerin with the parliamentarian Theodor Blank. Blank was the son of a cabinetmaker who had refused to join the Nazi Labor Front. After war's end, Blank emerged as a powerful union leader and a believer in a united Europe. He projected the image of one who would address the problem of rearmament from a European point of view, one devoid of any nationalistic or militaristic ideals. His fledgling staff in 1950 would become, in June 1955, a full-fledged defense ministry.

GERMAN REARMAMENT

From February 1951 to May 1952 Allied diplomats debated the European army idea, finally agreeing to a European Defense Community (EDC) Treaty on 27 May 1952. Its protocol proclaimed that an attack on one of its members would be considered an attack on a NATO member. As part of this agreement, the occupation statutes were to be revoked, the office of high commissioner abolished, and the Federal Republic of Germany was granted full sovereignty. However, the treaty also contained various parts that sought to limit Germany's military potential, as the EDC disallowed any German defense minister or any national command structure. On 19 March 1953, the German Bundestag ratified the EDC Treaty; however, the French parliament would take another two years to make known its decision.

By the beginning of 1953, Blank, working in conjunction with the Bundestag Security Committee, introduced the principle of full civilian control over the rearmament effort. The law that permitted the creation of German military forces made the minister of defense the supreme commander of the military in peacetime. Personal screening boards were established by the Bundestag to select those officers for the rank of colonel or general. Operating as an independent organ of the government, the screening agency prevented officers with antidemocratic or neo-Nazi sympathies from entering the ranks of the new German military establishment. Members of the Social Democratic Party, such as Helmut Schmidt, worked with the ruling Christian Democratic Party in supporting the concept that now sought for Germany only good citizen-soldiers.

While the German democrats tried to prepare a new military structure, France's parliamentarians failed on 30 August 1954 to ratify the EDC Treaty. Western diplomats tried to salvage the plan that would have allowed West Germany to join in the defense of Europe. They eventually decided to resurrect the old Brussels Treaty by renaming its former executive body the Western European Union, or WEU. West Germany was offered membership.

The WEU's military forces were to be placed exclusively at the service of NATO.

The German chancellor unilaterally promised never to manufacture atomic weapons. His non-nuclear pledge read:

The Federal Republic undertakes not to manufacture in its territory any atomic weapons ... defined as any weapon which contains ... nuclear fuel ... and which, by ... uncontrolled nuclear transformation of the nuclear fuel ... is capable of mass destruction ... [or] any part, device, assembly or material especially designed for ... any [such] weapon. (U.S. Senate, Committee on Foreign Relations, Subcommittee on Disarmament, *Disarmament and Security, 1919–55,* Washington, D.C., 1956, p. 510)

Additionally, the Germans promised not to manufacture biological or chemical weapons or guided missiles, magnetic mines, warships, or long-range bombers. Only at the request of NATO's supreme Allied commander, and with the approval of a two-thirds majority of the WEU member nations, was the Federal Republic later allowed to acquire missiles, submarines, and jet aircraft.

In return the Western nations, including France, on 5 May 1955 terminated their occupation of West Germany and formally recognized the Federal Republic as a sovereign state. On 9 May 1955 West Germany officially became a NATO member. For the first time in its history, the German Armed Forces would have a purely defensive role within NATO and be led by an international or NATO commander in chief.

In 1975 the Federal Republic's share of defense spending encompassed 11 percent of all NATO expenditures and by 1980 this figure had risen to 21 percent. Its twelve divisions of approximately 345,000 men were perhaps the best-equipped military forces in NATO. The Bundeswehr in 1985 comprised 60 percent of NATO's land forces, 30 percent of its combat aircraft, 70 percent of the Baltic Sea forces and 100 percent of the Baltic Sea naval air units. Germany also kept its promise not to manufacture nuclear weapons, although its defense forces did purchase weapon systems capable of delivering nuclear shells, such as the intermediate-range Pershing A missile system. Still, the Federal Republic did not break its nuclear weapon pledge because to do so would have undermined the deterrence role assigned to it by NATO.

GERMANY AND ARMS CONTROL

The imminent reappearance of a rearmed West Germany in the early 1950s did not go unnoticed by the Soviet Union. Stalin sought to undermine the EDC plan for integrating the Federal Republic into the Western defense bloc when he dispatched two diplomatic notes to the Western powers, one on 10 March and the other on 9 April 1952. In his March note he sanctioned the creation of a united but neutral Germany, with all foreign troops withdrawn from German soil. Stalin apparently even approved the creation of a small German defense force in this nonaligned Germany. The April note mentioned free elections that could take place in a united Germany. Thus, Moscow's neutralization proposal called for the reunification of East and West Germany as long as this German state remained outside any Western defense pact.

Adenauer refused Stalin's diplomatic proposals because to accept them would mean destroying his policy of integrating the Federal Republic into the EDC. Still, this decision allowed the leading German opposition party, the Social Democrats, to equate Adenauer's rearmament policy with the denial of reunification. They attacked the EDC as demanding too much of the Federal Republic in terms of taxes and troops. The rejection of the Stalin notes was said to be at the cost of national unity. Adenauer countered by claiming that Stalin was not interested in a free, democratic Germany, but in a weak, neutral nation, one susceptible to Soviet subversion and control. Germany's security needs could only be satisfied in the context of the Western security system. Adenauer and the Christian Democrats won the German general election of 1953 with this argument; however, the Social Democrats persisted in criticizing Germany's Western defense links.

On 15 May 1955, France, England, the Soviet Union, and the United States finalized the Austrian State Treaty, which ended the four-power occupation of that nation. Austria was required to pledge itself to a status of strict neutrality. The effect of the treaty in Germany was to renew efforts by the Social Democrats to champion the cause of a nonaligned Federal Republic. On 18 July 1955, the four former allied nations held a summit conference in Geneva, Switzerland. Prior to this meeting, President Dwight D. Eisenhower had publicly spoken in favor of "neutral zones" in Europe. At Geneva, the leaders of the "Big Four" discussed a British plan that proposed the "thinning out" of military forces in Central Europe.

Adenauer feared the Allies might unilaterally sacrifice Germany's security needs by adopting a policy for Germany similar to the Austrian model. On 23 July 1955, the summit leaders directed their foreign ministers to discuss the terms of a proposed German and European settlement. Although the foreign ministers met from 27 October to 15 November 1955, an agreement similar to the Austrian State Treaty failed to materialize. Moscow suddenly changed its policy of seeking a neutral Germany and demanded that France, Britain, and the United States accept the reality of two German states. According to Moscow, East Germany was a sovereign nation. This demand that the Western powers recognize this fact would later lead to the Berlin crises of 1958 and 1961. In November 1958 the Soviet leader Nikita Khrushchev threatened the freedom of West Berlin by demanding it become a "free city" and that all questions concerning access to the former German capital by the Allied powers be handled by the East German "government." In August 1961, the East German Communists built the infamous Berlin Wall in an attempt to force the Allies to recognize their power and presence in Berlin.

Although the Federal Republic by the 1970s and 1980s had become one of the key military pillars of NATO, it had repeatedly shown deference to the United States in arms control issues. For example, on 28 November 1969, West Germany signed the nuclear Non-Proliferation Treaty; the U.S. government had pressured Bonn for its signature and Germany's acquiescence satisfied Washington's demand. However, the administration of President Jimmy Carter witnessed a change in this policy of deference. The U.S. president initially advocated NATO's deployment of the Enhanced Radiation Weapon (ERW), or neutron bomb. This weapon system was to balance the large number of Soviet tanks stationed in East Germany. Bonn supported Carter's concept even though this support was heavily criticized by the left wing of the ruling Social Democratic Party and the popular antinuclear party, the Greens. When, without informing Bonn, Carter canceled ERW, West German chancellor Helmut Schmidt publicly aired what he felt was the vulnerability of Germany to such unilateral actions by the U.S. government on basic defense issues.

Schmidt was also concerned about a new category of Russian missile, the SS-20 system, which the Soviets had begun to station in Eastern Europe in the late 1970s. The highly mobile and accurate SS-20 was an intermediate-range nuclear forces (INF) weapon system of two warheads per launcher. Its targeting area was within a range of 660 to 3,400 miles (1,056 to 5,440 kilometers), that is, within range of West Germany. NATO countered with its own intermediate-range missile systems, the cruise missile and a modernized Pershing system. But to Bonn, Washington seemed oblivious to its European allies' pleas for consultation before any talks with the Soviets over such missile systems commenced, either in the Strategic Arms Limitation Talks (SALT) or the Mutual Balance Force Reduction (MBFR) sessions.

Given Germany's military stature, the German government agreed to support a December 1979 NATO decision on arms negotiations with Moscow. In what was termed a "dual track" decision, NATO was to introduce 572 Pershing II A missiles and the ground-launched cruise missile system. This decision was to be reversed if the Soviets agreed to reduce or destroy their SS-20s. NATO, and especially Germany, now had a voice in United States–Soviet arms negotiations.

President Ronald Reagan resumed the intermediate-range missile talks (INF) in early 1982. The U.S. government consulted with its NATO allies in formal sessions and also in bilateral talks with the new West German chancellor, Helmut Kohl. By April of 1987 a double-zero option had surfaced, which included the scrapping of Soviet SS-20s and Pershing IIs along with the cruise missiles as well as short-range missile systems of 300–600 miles (480–960 kilometers). In September of 1987 Kohl publicly promised to scrap the German Pershing IIA missiles if both the United States and the Soviet Union phased out their INF systems. By December of 1987, in Washington, D.C., Soviet general secretary Mikhail Gorbachev and the American president signed the INF Treaty, an arms control agreement that had been brought about by a major German contribution.

CONCLUSION

German rearmament may have enhanced the deterrent effect of NATO, but it also deterred Mutual Balance Force Reduction (MBFR) efforts to reduce conventional military forces in Central Europe. During the protracted MBFR negotiations—from the

1960s to 1980s—and other negotiations related to arms control in Central Europe, the Soviets made it quite clear that they considered the Germans, not the Americans, as posing the gravest potential threat to their security.

This attitude appeared to change in 1989. That year witnessed a truly seismic change in Europe as the Berlin Wall, one of the most prominent symbols of Cold War tensions, was breached in November and later demolished. On 16 July 1990 the Soviet Union became the last of the World War II nations to acknowledge a rearmed Germany. Gorbachev accepted a united and rearmed Germany within the NATO alliance during bilateral negotiations with Helmut Kohl in Moscow and Stavropol.

The two leaders agreed to a united German force level of 370,000 men, a reduction of all German forces of approximately 40 percent. Germany again unilaterally promised not to manufacture, possess, or control nuclear, biological, and chemical weapons, a pledge that in 1954 made acceptable its initial rearmament effort and now helps stabilize the post–Cold War arms control environment.

BIBLIOGRAPHY

English-Language Texts. OLAV RISTE, ed., *Western Security, the Formative Years: European and Atlantic Defence, 1947–1953* (New York, 1985), presents an analysis of German defense concepts prior to and following the Korean War. JAMES L. RICHARDSON, *Germany and the Atlantic Alliance: The Interaction of Strategy and Politics* (Cambridge, Mass., 1966), offers the reader a review of West Germany's responses to U.S. military strategy, such as massive retaliation. RICHARD H. IMMERMAN, ed., *John Foster Dulles and the Diplomacy of the Cold War,* (Princeton, N.J., 1990), specifically chapter 3, studies the origins of the European Defense Community. JOHN A. REID, JR., *Germany and NATO* (Washington, D.C., 1987), describes Germany's NATO contributions from 1955 to 1985. STEPHEN F. SZABO, ed., *The Bundeswehr and Western Security* (New York, 1990), studies the international and domestic forces that shaped the fundamentals of German defense policies since the 1950s. Such topics as German force levels and the INF Treaty are analyzed in depth. DONALD ABENHEIM, *Reforging the Iron Cross: The Search for Tradition in the West German Armed Forces* (Princeton, N.J., 1988), is an excellent study of the evolution of the concept of *Innere Führung*. MONTECUE J. LOWRY, *The Forge of West German Rearmament, Theodor Blank and the Amt Blank* (New York, 1990), reviews the efforts of Blank and his shadow defense ministry during the early days of the Federal Republic.

CATHERINE MCARDLE KELLEHER, *Germany and the Politics of Nuclear Weapons* (New York, 1975), analyzes the German non-nuclear pledge. The author challenges the sincerity of Germany's promise not to seek a nuclear capability, basing her study on a series of interviews with both German and American defense specialists. ROBERT MCGEEHAN, *The German Rearmament Question: American Diplomacy and European Defense After World War II* (Urbana, Ill., 1971), examines U.S. diplomatic attempts to rearm Germany. Chapter 3 offers an excellent review of the interaction between U.S., German, and French diplomats who were struggling with the difficulties of creating an acceptable German military structure. F. W. E. FURSDON, *The European Defense Community: A History* (New York, 1980), gives the reader a comprehensive analysis of the EDC.

German-Language Texts. German writers have studied the military issues thoroughly. The two volumes published by the Militärgeschichtliche Forschungsamt in 1982 and 1990 (Freiburg, Germany) represent the topic of rearmament. This Forschungsamt is one of the leading sources of military research in Germany. *Aspekte der deutschen Wiederbewaffnung bis 1955,* edited by the MILITÄRGESCHICHTLICHE FORSCHUNGSAMT (Boppard, 1975), describes Germany's rearmament efforts and offers the reader insights of HANS SPEIDEL and JOHANN A. GRAF KIELMANSEGG. ROLF STEININGER, *Wiederbewaffnung—Die Entscheidung für einen westdeutschen Verteidigungsbeitrag: Adenauer und die Westmächte 1950* (Erlangen, Bonn, and Vienna, 1989), reviews Adenauer's rearmament policies and the Western Allies' demands for German troops. ULRICH de MAIZIERE, *Führen im Frieden, 20 Jahre Dienst Für Bundeswehr Und Staat* (München, 1974), and *Wolf Graf von Baudissin, Soldat für den Frieden,* edited by PETER VON SCHUBERT (München, 1969), provide a comprehensive study of the Bundeswehr.

The Disarming and Rearming of Italy

○

E. TIMOTHY SMITH

See also The Disarming and Rearming of Germany; The Disarming and Rearming of Japan; *and* From MBFR to CFE: Negotiating Conventional Arms Control in Europe. *The* Italian Peace Treaty *is excerpted in Volume III.*

On 10 February 1947 the Allied powers of World War II and Italy signed a treaty of peace ending the state of war between them. Although the treaty reflected the optimism of the immediate postwar era, by the time it was signed, divisions between the Soviet Union and the Western powers, the United States and Great Britain, had developed into the Cold War. The treaty limitations placed on Italian armed forces reflected the hopes placed on the newly created United Nations to keep the peace. However, by 1947 the United States had begun to implement a postwar policy aimed at containing the Soviet Union in a sphere of influence in Eastern Europe.

The desire to prevent the spread of communism to Western Europe, including Italy, brought a deepening American involvement in Italy and led the Western powers to include Italy in the North Atlantic Treaty Organization (NATO). With membership in NATO, it became difficult for Italy to participate effectively in the defense of Western Europe without violating the arms limitation clauses of the treaty of peace. Ultimately, Italian reliance on the United Nations for security was abandoned and it rearmed at the urging of its NATO allies.

ITALIAN DISARMAMENT

On 3 September 1943 the Italians surrendered and signed an armistice with the Allies. Between 1943 and 1946 American goals for Italy included establishing a democratic government, keeping the Soviet Union out of occupied Italy, reducing the role of the British in the occupation, preventing an economic collapse, and gaining a nonpunitive peace treaty. Meanwhile the British, with the support of the Soviets and the French, sought to impose much harsher armistice and peace conditions.

In 1945, United States leaders prepared for the July–August Potsdam Conference and relayed the U.S. objective to bolster the Italian government and economy enough for them to withstand the threat of new totalitarianism. This reflected concern about the role of the British and the Soviets, Italy's economic conditions, and the postwar strength of the Italian Communist party. In order to assure its objectives, the United States became involved in Italian politics and came to play a major role in its economy.

The Allies agreed at the Potsdam Conference to create a Council of Foreign Ministers (CFM) to develop peace treaties for the defeated powers. The first meeting of the CFM was held in London in the fall of 1945, and subsequent negotiations continued at Paris between April and July 1946. The council drafted a treaty for Italy that was then submitted to a twenty-one-nation peace conference in Paris, held from July to October 1946. The final treaty was approved by the CFM in New York at the November–December 1946 meetings and then signed in Paris on 10 February 1947, and final ratifications were completed by September 1947.

In its efforts to write the Italian Peace Treaty, the CFM encountered several major problems before reaching a final agreement. The powers differed over reparations, the disposition of the prewar Italian colonies, and the Yugoslav-Italian border, especially the city of Trieste. In addition to those elements, which deepened suspicions among the wartime allies, the treaty also limited Italian armaments.

The history of those arms limitation clauses (Articles 49–70) demonstrate the changing U.S. perceptions about security in the postwar world. Upon the outbreak of World War II President Franklin D. Roosevelt had indicated that the United States would seek a final peace that would eliminate the use of force between nations. During the two years prior to the United States' entry into the war Roosevelt frequently discussed postwar security. His January 1941 Four Freedoms included "the freedom from fear," which called for the reduction of armaments. The August 1941 Atlantic Charter urged the establishment of a permanent system of general security.

Disarmament also figured into the Allies' postwar planning. At the Dumbarton Oaks Conference the Allied powers agreed that enemy states were to be disarmed at the end of the war. Based on the assumption of continuing cooperation among the Allies, the United States intended to rely on the newly established United Nations to protect a disarmed Italy. However, within a few years the U.S. government became convinced that Italy must rearm to meet an apparent Soviet threat to Western Europe.

The Italian Peace Treaty   As the CFM negotiations began, the United States sought to draft a treaty that would enable Italy to establish a stable economy and a democratic government. One U.S. official in Italy wrote President Harry S Truman urging that the United States and Great Britain treat Italy not as a defeated enemy but as a junior partner in the Mediterranean. The Italians themselves sought a treaty that would limit their territorial and colonial losses, avoid penalties, and assure Italian security. Noting that it was with their assistance that the Germans were ultimately defeated, the Italians requested that their military forces not be reduced. The treaty, as it was completed, did note Italian cobelligerency against Germany after the armistice, but stated in the preamble that Italy bore its "share of responsibility for the war." The Allies, after hard negotiations, reached a settlement on the Italian-Yugoslav border, created the Free Territory of Trieste, and established reparations. They turned the issue of the Italian colonies over to the United Nations.

Decisions on the terms limiting Italian armament were reached without much difficulty at the Council of Foreign Ministers' first Paris session. These clauses were aimed not at a complete disarmament of the nation but at arms reduction that would deny it the means of waging an aggressive war. Italy was to be defended by a small border force and by the U.N., allowing it to devote its resources to benefit its civilian economy.

Under the treaty, Italian fortifications were to be removed from the Franco-Italian and Italo-Yugoslav frontiers. In Sicily and Sardinia, Italy was prohibited from building any naval, military, or air force installations except for the accommodation of security forces. It was prohibited from possessing, constructing, and experimenting with atomic weapons, self-propelled or guided missiles, guns with a range of over 30 kilometers, sea mines, and torpedoes capable of being manned. It was limited to the possession of two hundred heavy and medium tanks.

The Italian fleet was reduced, with some of its vessels disarmed and converted to civilian use while others were transferred to other governments. It was expressly prohibited from acquiring battleships, aircraft carriers, and submarines. The total standard displacement of its war vessels (other than battleships) was not to exceed 67,500 tons, and its naval personnel was not to exceed 25,000 officers and men.

The Italian Army was limited to 185,000 combat and service personnel and 65,000 Carabinieri (internal security forces). Allowing for some variation in the two, the total of these forces was not to exceed 250,000. The organization, armament, and deployment of its forces, as stated in article 61 of the treaty, were "to meet only tasks of an internal character" and frontier defense. The air force was limited to 25,000 combat and service personnel, a force of 200 fighters, and 150 transport and training aircraft.

The military, naval, and air clauses of the treaty of peace could be modified, under Article 46, "by agreement between the Allied and Associated Powers and Italy or, after Italy becomes a member of the United Nations, by agreement between the Security Council and Italy." The Allies assumed that Italy would join the U.N. and, in the treaty's preamble, pledged to support Italy's application.

In the execution and enforcement of the treaty, the signatories were to rely on the British, French, Russian, and American ambassadors in Rome acting in concert. According to Article 86.2, these four were to give the Italian government "guidance, technical advice and clarification" to ensure the rapid and efficient execution of the treaty. Disputes not settled by direct diplomatic negotiations were to be referred first to the four ambassadors. If they could not resolve the problem, a commission—composed of representatives of each party and a third member selected by mutual agreement (or by the secretary-general of the U.N.)—would decide the issue by a majority vote. By the absence of strict verification clauses it is clear that no one expected any enforcement problems. Under the observation and direction of the Allied ambassadors, Italy would disarm much of its armed forces and not rebuild its military power. Many of the limits would be upheld by the Italians themselves, who, in 1947, saw no immediate need to build their military beyond the limitations established in the treaty.

As far as the United States was concerned, the main threat to Italy's stability was its weak economy. If the economy collapsed, the United States feared that the Italian Communists would seize power, thus moving Italy into the Soviet sphere of influence. Such action would disrupt all U.S. postwar plans to rebuild a democratic, stable Western Europe. According to historian Melvyn Leffler, Washington believed that if the United States lost the resources of Western Europe, the Soviets could challenge U.S. power.

At this point the limitations imposed on the Italian military were not a problem. The size restrictions were meant to keep Italy from developing an offensive capability, yet allow it to provide for internal security. In addition, under the peace treaty, Allied forces would remain in Italy until the end of 1947.

The Italians were never happy with the peace treaty, although they did accept it in 1947. Critics of the treaty argued that it was based on obsolete premises: Italy was treated as an enemy state while the big powers assumed that postwar cooperation would continue. However, by 1947 the United States was coming to view Italy as an ally, because wartime cooperation was collapsing into a cold war. Historian Martin Folly, viewing the treaty from a critical Cold War perspective, finds it the last of the Allied wartime accommodations to the Soviets. He criticizes the treaty because it imposed punitive terms upon a nation that fought on the Allied side at the end of the war, and because it penalized a nation that the British and Americans were trying to rebuild. Other historians, however, have tended to see the treaty in a more favorable light. Noting the great differences among the powers, Patricia Dawson Ward concluded it was remarkable that any treaty was actually completed. The United States and Britain had sought to limit Soviet influence in the Balkans, while the Soviets had sought to weaken Anglo-American control in Italy. Both sides failed to achieve their objectives; nevertheless, the treaty was signed and ratified.

U.S. POLICY TOWARD ITALY, 1947–1950

World events between 1947 and 1950 had a major impact on U.S. policy as Italy came to be seen as a pivotal nation between the United States' Eastern Mediterranean interests and its Western European interests. In 1948 the newly created Central Intelligence Agency (CIA) emphasized Italy's importance to U.S. security, stating that a Communist Italy would adversely affect Western Europe, the Mediterranean, and the Near East. It would give the Soviet Union bases near the Mediterranean, Greece, Turkey, and the Near East oil fields and pose a potential threat to the security of U.S. communications in these areas.

The first confrontations of the Cold War between the United States and the Soviet Union emerged in the Mediterranean and the Near East. With the breakdown of cooperation between the United States and Soviet Union, and with the veto dominating policy in the U.N. Security Council, the United States unilaterally determined that it would stop any further Soviet expansion. President Truman asked Congress to assist non-Communist forces in the Greek Civil War and issued the Truman Doctrine, pledging support to free peoples resisting subjugation by armed minorities and outside pressure. Central to the objectives of the Truman Doctrine was the stabilizing of Western Europe. U.S. leaders feared that a Communist triumph in Greece would cause communism to spread westward in a domino-like effect.

In Italy the change in United States policy led the U.S.-backed Christian Democratic party (DC) to break off its four-year cooperation with the Communist and Socialist parties. In May 1947 Italian prime minister Alcide De Gasperi formed a cabinet that excluded the two leftist parties.

U.S. efforts to provide security for Europe under the Truman Doctrine did not eliminate all danger. As U.S. economic assistance to European nations in the immediate aftermath of the war was spasmodic and limited, the general economic situation remained grave. United States officials warned that Western Europe could not achieve economic and social recovery without massive assistance. An April 1947 U.S. Army report on Italy noted that the foreign aid already extended had prevented the collapse of the Italian economy, but without substantially more assistance "it must be expected that Italy will . . . descend rapidly into political and economic chaos culminating in civil war, out of which it will emerge with a totalitarian regime." The United States Ambassador in Rome, James Dunn, emphasized the same point when he warned that the situation in Italy had reached the point of delicate balance where the struggle between the extreme Left and democratic forces might be decided by outside aid coming from democratic nations.

With those warnings—and others pointing to the same economic problems, with similar political implications, throughout Europe—the United States in June 1947 launched a major economic relief program known as the Marshall Plan, or the European Recovery Program (ERP). The ERP established a unified economic plan for Western Europe that could achieve economic and political stability, weaken the appeal of communism, and increase the well-being of the United States. The Italian government eagerly participated in the program, and in the process developed closer relationships with the other Western European nations.

Despite the massive undertaking of the ERP, the United States remained concerned about the stability of the Mediterranean region. In October 1947 the United States and Britain held talks on the Eastern Mediterranean and the Near East. These discussions highlighted the importance of Iran, Turkey, Greece, and Italy to the West. If the Soviets gained control of those nations, U.S. policymakers believed that the United States would be forced back into the Atlantic and would no longer be able to muster the political, economic, and military strength to maintain the security of that region. The United States was thus gradually becoming committed to the defense of the Mediterranean, including Italy.

The next step toward a firm commitment came on 13 December 1947, when the United States fulfilled its treaty commitments and announced the withdrawal of its occupation forces from Italy. Some observers in Washington and Rome feared that United States withdrawal would provide the Communists with the opportunity to seize control of parts of Italy. Consequently, when Truman announced the troop withdrawals, he emphasized that the United States would continue to maintain its interest in an independent Italy, warning that if it became "apparent that the freedom and independence of Italy upon which the peace settlement is based are threatened directly or indirectly, the United States, as a signatory of the peace treaty and as a member of the United Nations, will be obliged to consider what measures would be appropriate for the maintenance of peace and security." (U.S. President, *Public Papers of the Presidents of the United States,* Washington, D.C., 1963–1964, p. 510) Although no specific action was indicated, it was clear that the United States was prepared to act to prevent Italy from falling into the Soviet sphere.

Coupled with the fear of Communist actions after the withdrawal of U.S. troops was a growing fear that the Communists and Socialists might win the first election, scheduled for April 1948, to be held under the new Italian constitution. This prompted the newly established National Security Council (NSC) to consider how the United States could prevent the leftist coalition from gaining power. In a series of policy decisions, from November 1947 to the election, the NSC declared that United States policy would underwrite the preservation of democracy in Italy and hoped for Italian resistance to the spread of communism. To achieve that goal the United States declared it would use economic, political, and, if need be, military force to prevent the USSR from attacking Italy, either overtly or covertly. At the same time the NSC advocated a series of military, diplomatic, economic, and covert actions to assist the Christian Democrats in the election. These included a British-French-American proposal that Trieste be returned to Italian sovereignty, a threat to cut off United States assistance if the Communists were to win, and covert funding of anti-Communist political parties.

The election results seem to indicate success for United States policy. The Washington-backed Christian Democrats received 48.5 percent of the vote, while the Communists and Socialists together received only 31 percent. De Gasperi again became the prime minister of a government that was able to function while excluding the two leftist parties. Despite this victory, Washington continued to watch developments in Italian politics. The Communists, influential in Italian trade unions, could still disrupt Marshall Plan aid and would be a threat in the next election. This continuing concern regarding Italian security and United States postwar reconstruction efforts ultimately led Italy to join NATO.

The Decision to Include Italy in NATO   By the time of the Italian elections, Britain, France, Belgium, Luxembourg, and the Netherlands had formed the Brussels Pact, an alliance to defend those nations from aggression. Italian membership in that agreement had been discussed, but Italy was not invited to join. Western nations continued negotiations regarding a more permanent and inclusive security arrangement, ultimately creating NATO, which would include Italy. The United States, Britain, and Canada held secret discussions in Washington during March 1948 to create a security system for the North Atlantic region. In the summer of 1948 these talks expanded to include the rest of the Brussels Pact nations and culminated in the creation of NATO in April 1949.

Because Italy is not a North Atlantic nation, Italian participation was not automatically considered. There were many delays, and debates were long, as the powers discussed Italy's role in such a treaty. Moreover, the Italians were not unanimously in favor of inclusion. Public opinion in Italy tended to be neutralist, and some Italian government officials feared that the new security system would distract Western Europeans from economic and political cooperation. In addition to Italian reluctance, the other powers objected to Italian membership, based in part on their concern that the Italians would place conditions on their participation, including revision of the territorial and military clauses of the 1947 peace treaty. Only in January 1949 did the De Gasperi government openly seek NATO membership. By then Italy had become convinced that neutrality was no longer an option, and that the rearmament and defense of its territory depended on admission to the Western alliance.

Throughout the negotiations the Italians indicated that they hoped in joining NATO they would receive a more sympathetic view toward the revision of peace treaty terms. The Italian Peace Treaty was discussed during the NATO negotiations, but any suggestion of changes was rejected at that time. Many Western European leaders wanted Italy to continue to abide by the terms of the treaty so that the Soviets would not have an excuse to claim that the treaty was being violated. Also during the discussions, some U.S. officials argued that a way had to be found to increase Italian armed strength; but other Western diplomats noted that revision was not necessary because military improvements could be made within the peace treaty limitations. France favored Italy's inclusion because of geographical considerations, and U.S. diplomats held that rejection of Italian membership would strengthen the Italian Communists. Those two nations joined to pressure their more reluctant partners and, ultimately, the Western powers decided to include Italy as a charter member of the North Atlantic alliance.

ITALIAN REARMAMENT

While the United States worked to create an alliance among the Western European nations, it also initiated a policy aimed at the rearmament of Western Europe in order to withstand any Soviet military activity. In 1949 the Truman administration created the Mutual Defense Assistance Program (MDAP) to provide equipment and training to its new NATO allies. With the onset of the Korean War in 1950—and the adoption of NSC 68, a policy that emphasized the growing Soviet military threat to Western Europe—the United States' rearmament program came to overshadow the European Recovery Program in importance. In 1952 the economic and military programs were merged into the Mutual Security Administration as the United States had moved away from a security policy based on economic stability to one based on military might.

This shift in United States policy changed the Western view of the military terms of the 1947 Italian Peace Treaty. With the emphasis of U.S. policy now aimed at stopping a possible Soviet invasion of Western Europe rather than preventing subversion by internal Communist forces, the rearmament of Western Europe demanded a larger contribution by Italy's military forces so that it could play a substantial role in NATO's defense plans.

Revision of the Treaty   Within the Truman administration there had been no serious discussion of treaty revision until Italy joined NATO. The CIA concluded that the Italians were capable, with some assistance, of maintaining internal security. As the Italian role in new defensive arrangements was discussed, Washington officials sought some means of modifying the treaty limits, but still viewed substantial revision as impractical.

The Italian government, however, forcefully pressed for revision because it feared that without NATO rearmament programs—which would conflict with the 1947 treaty—their current forces would only be able to withstand an invasion for a few days. In order to obtain Security Council support for treaty revision, the Italians continued to ask for membership in the United Nations. These requests, however, were blocked by the Soviet Union until 1955, when the issue of treaty revision had become moot because of unilateral actions.

As the United States continued to develop rearmament programs during 1950, however, Truman administration officials began to pay more attention to the arms limitation clauses. A Department of State policy paper on the MDAP and the peace treaty limits concluded that, although the basic program was not in violation of the treaty, "where any variance appears, the Peace Treaty must govern." Thus while there was a growing awareness that treaty limits could cause problems, throughout 1950 United States policy held that the treaty terms should be honored, if interpreted liberally, unless revised or abrogated in time of war.

Although Italy hoped that the United States and Britain would "wink an eye" at violations, the United States was concerned with its responsibility to verify Italian conformity with the military clauses. The United States feared that any violation of Italian international obligations would give the Soviets a new justification for blocking Italian inclusion in the United Nations. Thus while U.S. diplomats worried about violations of the treaty, U.S. military officials, throughout 1950, worried that treaty limitations might keep Italy from fulfilling its requirements.

By late 1950, with the Soviets blocking the legal methods of revision, the United States, France, Great Britain, and Italy slowly moved to create a "Western revision" of the treaty. Several options were discussed within the U.S. Department of State, centering on the concept that revision was justified because of developments unforeseen during the negotiation of the peace treaty. The weakness of the United Nations, the onset of the Korean War, and the use of internal subversion by the Soviet Union, they argued, made it possible to remove the arms limitations. Historian Norman Kogan has noted that the hostility between the Soviets and Western powers actually developed during the negotiation process and that there had been no marked change in the world since the treaty's ratification. By 1947 the Cold War already had begun. Still, "unforeseen developments" would be employed as a justification. As far as the United States was concerned, though, the real reason for the revision of the treaty was the need to remove or modify the arms limitation clauses so that Italy could fulfill its defense obligations under NATO.

Soon the United States found it could no longer ignore the fact that Italy had legal treaty obligations. By the end of 1950 the Italian military was approaching treaty limits in a variety of categories. With more equipment on its way to Italy, the United States decided to stop the delivery of some MDAP items and modify some of the matériel that was set to be delivered. For example, bomb bays were closed off and some rocket launchers were removed from aircraft. By June 1951, Italy had exceeded treaty limits on ship tonnage by sixteen hundred tons, which could force the United States to cancel the 1952 naval assistance program. That same month, the Italian Air Force, limited to 350 aircraft, had received 249 planes, and another 216 were scheduled for MDAP delivery. In addition to the MDAP deliveries, there were NATO military commitments, established in a Medium Term Defense Plan, which needed to be fulfilled. The plan called on Italy to have 127,652 naval tonnage by 1954 (treaty limits were 67,500). The air force, under the plan, was to have 453 planes.

The potential violations faced by the navy and air force also faced the Italian Army. For example, Italy was allowed to possess 200 tanks under the peace treaty. By 1951 it already had 201, and under the MDAP, 118 more were to be delivered by 1953. The peace treaty limited the army to 185,000 men, yet NATO planning called for an army of 470,000. The Defense Department concluded that "Italy is prevented by the treaty limitations from effectively meeting her joint defense obligations and from making the fullest contribution to the common NATO defense effort."

In 1951 the Italian government stepped up its demands for treaty revision. The Italians sought changes in the military, territorial, and economic clauses, arguing that relations between Italy and the Allies should be dictated by the spirit of the NATO alliance rather than by the peace treaty. The Italians also argued that the revision was necessary because of the increasingly lenient attitude of the Allies toward the Germans, whose role in NATO was being seriously discussed, and the Japanese, who were completing their own treaty with the United States. They felt that the Italian treaty was an out-of-date moral sanction against a nation that had resumed its place among the free and democratic nations.

By mid-1951 serious negotiations were under way for the revision. Noting that the military limitations had been written hoping the United Nations would bring lasting peace, the United States insisted that changes in the world situation made the elimination of military restrictions necessary. Blaming the Soviets for those changes, the United States argued that the military restrictions were "incompatible" with NATO objectives.

At first, the United States suggested a revision process that would begin within NATO, while the British favored bilateral agreements between Italy and the treaty signatories. Britain was concerned with the position of Yugoslavia and hoped that a settlement on Trieste could be achieved first. The French favored a tripartite declaration suspending the military clauses, which would then be sent to the U.N. General Assembly—bypassing the Security Council—for approval.

Ultimately, a procedure was established that called for a formal Italian request to treaty signatories for revision, followed by a tripartite declaration indicating that the spirit of NATO should govern relations with Italy, and an Italian note declaring that the need to assure self-defense required revision of military clauses. A four-to-six-week interim period would allow for an attempt to settle the Trieste issue and to obtain a reply by the three powers (and others) that bilateral relations with Italy would no longer be governed by certain treaty articles.

The procedure began in September 1951 when the United States, Great Britain, and France publicly expressed agreement to an Italian request for the removal of certain restrictions that affected Italian capacity for self-defense. And again they reiterated their support for Italian admission to the U.N. In December, the Italians formally requested that the signatories agree that the spirit of the treaty's preamble was no longer valid and that it should be replaced by language that reflected the spirit of the U.N. Charter. Moreover, they argued that the political clauses of the treaty (Articles 15–18) were "superfluous" and that the military clauses (Articles 46–70)—and the relevant military annexes—restricted Italy's right to provide for its defense and as such were inconsistent with Italy's position as a member of the family of democratic nations.

The United States gave Italy a note in December relieving it of its arms limitations and other restrictions. After that action, and similiar ones from the other Western signatories of the peace treaty, the Italian government announced that it considered the revision an accomplished fact. In November, before the procedure was even complete, the United States ordered the three services to lift all restrictions on the shipment of Mutual Defense Assistance Program military equipment to Italy. With that decision, the delivery of some types of aircraft was resumed prior to the actual completion of the revision procedure.

The Italian announcement, and the resumption of deliveries under the MDAP, did not end the issue. In February 1952 the Soviet Union again vetoed an Italian application for U.N. membership, prompting Italy to tell the Russians that they had violated the peace treaty by the veto because all signatories were committed to support Italian membership. Therefore Italy no longer considered itself bound by treaty obligations to the Soviet Union.

Legally, such Soviet action was not considered to be a violation of Russian treaty obligations. Norman Kogan has written that there was nothing in the treaty granting the right to revision, and without the consent of *all* the powers there was "no right to revise." In reality there was no revision of the treaty. The Western powers simply granted the Italians, unilaterally, the authority to rearm.

CONCLUSION

Although the problem of Trieste remained until 1954, when Italy and Yugoslavia divided the area, and Italy had to wait until 1955 to enter the United Nations, the 1951 "revision" of the peace treaty did eliminate a major reminder of its defeat in World War II. Italy, at least in terms of its military forces, was a sovereign nation again. That had always been a major Italian goal. What Italy saw as an unjust peace had been revised.

However, for the Western powers, especially the United States, more was at stake than Italian prestige. The peace treaty had become an obstruction to the creation of a powerful NATO military force that could deter or contain the Soviet Union in Europe. The treaty had been based on the wartime belief that disarming the defeated powers would enhance the peace and that Allied wartime cooperation would continue into the postwar world. But the development of the Cold War prevented the United Nations from performing the role of peacekeeper, and prevented change in treaty restrictions by the means outlined in the treaty. For the United States, the development of the Cold War made it essential that Italian arms limitations be eliminated so that a rearmed Italy could participate fully in the defense of Western Europe.

Rearmament had become so important to the United States and other Western nations that they felt justified in abandoning proper legal procedures to modify earlier agreed-upon arms limitation measures. And this unilateral action would be an impediment during future arms control negotiations—such as those involving the Austrian State Treaty and Mutual and Balanced Force Reductions—that dealt with European political and military issues.

BIBLIOGRAPHY

English-Language Texts   The full 1947 Italian Peace Treaty can be found in FRED L. ISRAEL, ed., *Major Peace Treaties of Modern History, 1648–1967,* vol. 4 (New York, 1967). U.S. DEPARTMENT OF STATE, *Foreign Relations of the United States, 1945–1951* (Washington, D.C.: 1960–1985) is a multivolume collection that includes documents relating to the Italian Peace Treaty and the revision of the treaty, the European Recovery Program, the North Atlantic Treaty Organization, and the Mutual Defense Assistance Program. ROBERT C. HILDERBRAND, *Dumbarton Oaks: The Origins of the United Nations and the Search for Postwar Security* (Chapel Hill, N.C., 1990), focuses on the development of the U.N. and discusses early ideas for postwar security, including disarmament.

MARTIN H. FOLLY, "Breaking the Vicious Circle: Britain, the United States, and the Genesis of the North Atlantic Treaty," *Diplomatic History* 12 (Winter 1988): 59–77, views the treaty as the final appeasement of Soviet demands. In a different vein, PATRICIA DAWSON WARD, *The Threat of Peace: James F. Byrnes and the Council of Foreign Ministers,* *1945–1946* (Kent, Ohio, 1979), sees the treaty negotiations as a successful compromise given the onset of the Cold War. MELVYN P. LEFFLER, "The American Conception of National Security and the Beginnings of the Cold War, 1945–48," *American Historical Review* 89 (April 1984): 346–381, discusses the expansion of U.S. interests after World War II in terms of national security. JOHN L. HARPER, *America and the Reconstruction of Italy, 1945–1948* (New York, 1986) looks at the U.S.-Italian economic relationship in the immediate postwar years, while JAMES E. MILLER, *The United States and Italy, 1940–1950: The Politics and Diplomacy of Stabilization* (Chapel Hill, N.C., 1986) is the best overall study of Italian-American relations during World War II and the early years of the Cold War and focuses on the political stability of Italy.

E. TIMOTHY SMITH, *The United States, Italy and NATO, 1947–52* (New York, 1991), analyzes the decision to include Italy in NATO, the rearmament process, and the revision of the treaty—with a focus on U.S. security interests. LAWRENCE S. KAPLAN, *The United States and NATO: The Formative Years* (Lexington, Ky., 1984), is the best work on the creation of the alliance, and his *A Community of Interests: NATO and the Military Assistance Program 1948–1951* (Washington, D.C., 1980) analyzes the development of the MDAP and its close relationship to NATO. NORMAN KOGAN, "Revision of the Italian Peace Treaty," *Indiana Law Journal* 27 (1953): 334–353, is critical of the revision process for ignoring international law.

Italian-Language Texts   Several Italian diplomats and scholars have written on the Italian position after World War II. EGIDIO ORTONA, *Anni d'America: La Riconstruzione, 1944–1951,* vol. I (Bologna, 1984), discusses the Italian point of view from his diplomatic post in Washington during the negotiations on the peace treaty, NATO, and treaty revision. ROSARIA QUARTARARO, *Italia e Stati Uniti: Gli Anni Difficili (1945–1952)* (Napoli and Roma, 1986) examines U.S.-Italian postwar relations; while ANTONIO VARSORI, "La Scelta Occidentale Dell'Italia (1948–1949)," 2 pts, *Storia delle Relazioni Internazionali* (1985), pt I: 95–159, and II: 302–368, analyzes the decision by the Italians to join with the West in NATO. BRUNELLO VIGEZZI, "De Gasperi, Sforza, la Diplomazia Italiana e la Percezione della Politica di Potenza dal Trattato di Pace al Patto Atlantico (1947–1950)," *Storia Contemporanea* 16 (1985): 661–685, discusses Italian diplomacy from the peace treaty to NATO.

The Disarming and Rearming of Japan

○

MIKE M. MOCHIZUKI

See also The Disarming and Rearming of Germany; The Disarming and Rearming of Italy; Japan; *and* Unilateral Initiatives. *Article 9 of the Japanese Constitution is excerpted in Volume III.*

After defeating Japan in World War II, the United States moved decisively to demilitarize the country in accordance with the Potsdam Declaration of 26 July 1945, which articulated the surrender terms of the Allied powers. Under the command of General Douglas MacArthur, the U.S. occupation forces demobilized the Japanese military, reorganized the war and navy ministries into agencies to implement this demobilization, and dismantled what remained of the nation's military-industrial base. MacArthur also purged from public life over two hundred thousand political, military, and business professionals who were designated as responsible for steering their country on the path of military expansion. In order to uproot the political and social basis of militarism, a policy of democratization accompanied the demilitarization program. U.S. occupation officials ordered a sweeping land-reform program, promoted a labor movement independent of the state, and pushed for a deconcentration of economic power.

JAPAN'S ANTIWAR CONSTITUTION: ARTICLE 9

Perhaps the greatest legacy of the occupation for the future of Japanese defense policy was the postwar constitution. Dissatisfied with the Japanese government's limited proposals for amending the Meiji constitution of 1889, MacArthur directed his staff to write a completely new document. The U.S. draft was formally submitted to the Imperial Diet in June 1946 for approval under the amendment procedure outlined in the existing imperial constitution. After making several revisions to the original draft, the legislature approved the new constitution and the emperor promulgated it in November 1946. Taking effect six months later, the new constitution granted sovereignty to the people and relegated the emperor to a symbolic role. It established a parliamentary form of government and guaranteed basic political and social rights for citizens. The most controversial aspect of this document was Article 9, which renounced war as an instrument of national policy.

The exact origins of this article are still unclear. MacArthur himself claimed that then Prime Minister Kijūrō Shidehara had originally suggested the idea to him. Foreign Minister Shigeru Yoshida, however, believed that MacArthur was the originator. After the addition of explanatory clauses at the beginning of each of the two paragraphs as proposed by the Japanese, the final English text of Article 9 reads as follows:

Aspiring sincerely to international peace based on justice and order, the Japanese people forever renounce war as a sovereign right of the nation and the threat or use of force as means of settling international disputes.

In order to accomplish the aim of the preceding paragraph, land, sea and air forces, as well as other war potential, will never be maintained. The right of belligerency of the State will not be recognized.

Whether or not the above renunciation of "the right to belligerency" denied Japan the right to maintain military forces even for the purpose of self-defense became an issue of intense political and legal controversy.

When the cabinet, headed by Prime Minister Shigeru Yoshida, approved the postwar constitution, it gave the impression that Article 9 proscribed armed forces even for purely defensive purposes. But later MacArthur in his memoirs stated that Article 9 was not meant to prevent Japan from taking steps necessary to preserve national safety. Yoshida himself added to the controversy by distinguishing between "wars of self-defense" and "the fundamental right to defend one's country." The implication was that Article 9 renounced the former, but not necessarily the latter. Nevertheless, Japanese constitutional scholars have tended to take a more restrictive view. While acknowledging that Japan retained the right to self-defense under international law, most of them interpreted the second paragraph of Article 9 as denying Japan the right to maintain military forces even for the purpose of self-defense. More important, until Japan regained its national sovereignty in 1952, the Japanese government did not explicitly claim a right to possess self-defense forces.

THE KOREAN WAR AND LIMITED REARMAMENT

The climate for U.S. occupation policy changed dramatically after the outbreak of the Korean War in June 1950. Given the geopolitical importance of Japan for the U.S. strategy to contain Communism in Asia, the United States began to encourage Japanese rearmament and to seek the incorporation of Japan into an anti-Soviet network of alliances. In July 1950, General MacArthur ordered Prime Minister Yoshida to create a national police reserve consisting of seventy-five thousand members. He justified this policy as necessary to maintain internal security since a large portion of the U.S. forces in Japan had to be redeployed to fight in Korea. Many of the lower-ranking officers of the demobilized Imperial Army were reactivated to serve in this police reserve.

The basic framework for Japan's postwar defense policy as well as its security relationship with the United States was established as part of the peace settlement between these two countries. As early as June 1947, Hitoshi Ashida, then foreign minister in the coalition cabinet headed by the Socialist Prime Minister Tetsu Katayama, drafted his famous memorandum that urged Japan to conclude a mutual defense pact with Washington whereby the United States would be committed to defend Japan against external attack. The Ashida memorandum rested on three assumptions: that the emerging United States–Soviet split would not be resolved in the Far East, that the United States would see the defense of Japan as essential to its security interests, and that the domestic Communist movement encouraged and assisted by the Soviet Union posed a formidable threat to Japan. Given this linkage between an external Soviet threat and an internal Communist threat, Ashida proposed that U.S. forces would focus on protecting Japan from a Soviet attack while the Japanese government would deal with the domestic Communist movement by establishing a national paramilitary police force. At the time, however, Ashida did not feel that the Soviet external threat was so acute that Japan needed to rearm in order to assist the United States.

During the peace-treaty negotiations with the United States, which began formally in January 1951, Prime Minister Yoshida followed the basic thrust of the Ashida memorandum. He calculated that the best way to end the U.S. occupation at an early date and to ensure Japanese security was to agree to a bilateral security pact that included the establishment of U.S. military bases on Japanese territory. However, he resisted pressures from John Foster Dulles, then the chief U.S. negotiator, to initiate a major rearmament program that would entail an army of about 350,000 soldiers to repel a possible Soviet attack. Yoshida argued that such a course would alarm Japan's neighbors in the Asia-Pacific region, strengthen domestic opposition against the pro–United States conservative government given the pacifism of the Japanese people, contradict the peace constitution that had been imposed by the United States, and jeopardize economic reconstruction. Yoshida also felt that the U.S. military presence in Japan was adequate to deter the Soviets. Consequently, he only made a verbal commitment to develop armed forces for defense against direct and indirect attack within the limits of Japan's economic capabilities and constitution.

Both the Treaty of Peace with Japan and the Security Treaty between the United States and Japan were signed in San Francisco in September 1951. Although delegates from the Soviet Union attended the San Francisco conference, they refused to sign the peace treaty because of its linkage with the United States–Japan security pact. In order to gain U.S. Senate approval for the treaties, Dulles persuaded Yoshida to support the U.S. China policy. Japan, as a consequence, recognized the Nationalist regime in Taiwan rather than the People's Republic of China as the sole legitimate government of China.

All in all, the postwar bargain struck between Japan and the United States was balanced. Japan obtained an early termination of the occupation, a U.S. security commitment, a limited burden for military expenditures, and the economic benefits of U.S. military procurements during the Korean War and after. The United States, in turn, gained access to military bases in Japan, Japanese support of its China policy, and Japan's integration into the U.S. containment strategy.

As beneficial as this settlement was to Japan, Yoshida was criticized by both the Left and the Right. The Left led by the Japan Socialist Party argued that the U.S. bases not only violated Japanese sovereignty, but also risked Japan's involvement in a United States–Soviet conflict. They stressed that even the minimal military buildup undertaken by Yoshida violated the constitution. They advocated a total peace that included the Soviet Union and the People's Republic of China, and a policy of unarmed neutrality. The Right attacked Yoshida's policy of slow and limited rearmament and subordination to U.S. foreign policy and pushed for a revision of the "peace constitution." Insofar as the Yoshida-Dulles bargain survived during the 1950s, it was because of the political stalemate between the Left and Right, rather than a broad-based consensus behind the settlement.

After the U.S. occupation ended in 1952, Yoshida followed through on his pledge of limited rearmament. He transformed the National Police Reserve into a National Safety Force composed of 100,000 uniformed personnel and created an 8,900-man Maritime Safety Force. He also established the National Safety Agency as the government agency responsible for managing these forces. In 1953, Yoshida finally came around to stating formally that Article 9 of the postwar constitution did not prohibit armed forces for the purpose of self-defense. A year later, Japan's nascent military forces underwent another reorganization. The National Safety Forces and the National Safety Agency became the Self-Defense Forces and the Self-Defense Agency respectively, and the Self-Defense Forces assumed a three-service structure consisting of ground, maritime, and air forces. But when the upper house of the National Diet approved the legislation establishing the Self-Defense Forces in 1954, it also passed a resolution confirming that these forces would not be deployed overseas.

Ichirō Hatoyama, who followed Yoshida as prime minister in December 1954, attempted to revise the postwar settlement. He succeeded in normalizing relations with the Soviet Union, although a territorial dispute with Moscow over the islands off the Hokkaido coast blocked the signing of a formal peace treaty. His effort to revise the constitution, however, failed. Although he rallied the conservative political forces to unite by forming the Liberal Democratic Party and to adopt a platform favoring constitutional revision, Hatoyama and his successors failed to win the two-thirds majority in the Diet necessary to amend the constitution. The Japan Socialist Party mounted a vigorous campaign to defend the postwar constitution and to obstruct the rearmament effort.

REVISION OF THE SECURITY TREATY WITH THE UNITED STATES

Although Prime Minister Nobusuke Kishi shared Hatoyama's nationalistic agenda, he concentrated on revising the 1951 Security Treaty with the United States. He wanted a totally new treaty that would incorporate the notion of mutuality to the extent permissible under the postwar constitution and that would clearly obligate the United States to defend Japan. He also hoped to raise popular consciousness about defense matters through a formal treaty revision process and thereby pave the way toward the ultimate objective of constitutional revision and a truly mutual security alliance with the United States. To lay the groundwork for treaty revision, the Kishi cabinet in May 1957 adopted the "Basic Policies for National Defense," which formally articulated the objectives of preventing direct and indirect aggression and of repelling such aggression once an invasion took place. These guidelines mandated the progressive development of "effective defense capabilities necessary for self-defense, with due regard to the nation's resources and the prevailing domestic situation." The cabinet also approved Japan's first postwar defense buildup plan, which covered the 1958–1960 period, and allocated over ¥450 billion (about $1.25 billion) for this purpose, about 90 percent of which received actual Diet authorization.

In his negotiations with Washington for treaty revision, Kishi did get the United States to make explicit the implicit U.S. security guarantee in the original pact and agree to consult with Japan before using the bases for combat operations outside of Japan and making major changes in deployments. The new treaty also eliminated the reference in the 1951 document to the possible use of U.S. forces in Japan to deal with domestic disturbances provoked by an external power. The 1960 Japanese-American Treaty of Mutual Cooperation and Security, however, fell short of true mutuality because it did not obligate Japan to help defend the United States. Moreover, Tokyo resisted a U.S. proposal to commit Japan to regional defense. Despite the generally favorable terms of the revised pact for Japan, Kishi's authoritarian methods to secure Diet ratification of the treaty sparked massive protests in Tokyo. The Socialists in particular linked their advocacy of unarmed neutrality with their struggle to defend postwar democracy. This political crisis forced Kishi to cancel the scheduled visit of President Dwight D. Eisenhower to Japan and to resign as prime minister after the treaty gained formal parliamentary approval in June 1960.

Kishi's successor, Hayato Ikeda, worked to overcome the political polarization of the late 1950s by turning the nation's attention toward economic growth. As a consequence, the ruling Liberal Democratic Party soft-pedaled its defense policy and tabled its aim of revising the postwar constitution. But this emphasis on economics did not prevent Japan from gradually modernizing its Self-Defense Forces according to three additional defense buildup plans covering the periods 1962–1966, 1967–1971 and 1971–1976. Under these plans, Japan improved the quality of its armed forces by replacing obsolete U.S. equipment, acquiring modern fighter planes and

antiaircraft missiles, and developing anti-submarine defense capabilities. The number of authorized personnel in the Self-Defense Forces also grew from 152,095 in 1954 to 258,074 in 1969, while the actual number of uniformed personnel increased from 111,177 to 235,564 over the same period. Even as this military modernization and buildup took place, defense expenditures as a percentage of the gross national product (GNP) actually declined because of the rapid pace of economic growth. Whereas Japan was spending 1.78 percent of GNP on defense in 1955, this figure had dropped to 0.72 percent by 1971. Furthermore, the opposition parties thwarted repeated attempts by various cabinets to upgrade the Defense Agency into a full-fledged ministry.

DOMESTIC CONSTRAINTS ON REARMAMENT

During the 1960s and 1970s, the Liberal Democratic Party government imposed a number of constraints on its military policy. These actions were both a response to pressures from the opposition parties that continued to reflect the pacifistic sentiments of the public and an attempt to cultivate broader domestic support for the government's defense policies.

Regarding the issue of nuclear weapons, Prime Minister Eisaku Satō articulated during the routine Diet interpellations on the budget in late 1967 the three non-nuclear principles of "not possessing, manufacturing or allowing the introduction of nuclear weapons." In 1971, the Japanese House of Representatives formally approved these principles in the context of a resolution confirming the non-nuclear status of Okinawa as part of an agreement between Tokyo and Washington that returned the Ryukyu Islands to Japanese control. And in 1976, Japan ratified the Nuclear Non-Proliferation Treaty (NPT). Japan's non-nuclear status has been a matter of policy, not an issue of constitutional interpretation. Indeed, the Japanese government has maintained since 1957 that nuclear weapons would not be unconstitutional if they are defensive in nature. Because of Japan's reliance on U.S. nuclear forces to deter a nuclear threat, the third principle of not permitting the introduction of nuclear weapons has been the issue of greatest controversy and ambiguity. Tokyo has refrained from challenging Washington's "neither confirm, nor deny" policy, and has never openly asked U.S. warships to remove any nuclear weapons that may be on board before entering Japanese ports.

The Japanese government also imposed restrictions on arms exports despite the lucrative business that some Japanese military producers had enjoyed during the 1950s. In 1967, the Ministry of International Trade and Industry prohibited the export of weapon systems and ammunition to Communist-bloc countries, other countries that are belligerents, and countries that are subject to a United Nations boycott. In 1976, these restrictions were further tightened by banning all arms exports as well as the foreign sale of facilities that manufacture weapons.

Finally, during the prime ministership of Takeo Miki, the government codified its adherence to a strictly defensive military policy when it approved the National Defense Program Outline (NDPO) in 1976. Postulating a relatively stable international environment, the NDPO articulated the "standard defense force concept" under which Japan would possess a minimal defense capability "to cope effectively with situations up to the point of limited and small-scale aggression." To counter threats beyond this level, Japan would rely upon U.S. assistance and use the existing "standard defense force" as the basis for mobilizing a capability to deal with the worsening security environment. The NDPO placed an upper limit on the size of the Self-Defense Forces that closely reflected the existing authorization levels and force structure. The emphasis would now be placed almost entirely on qualitative improvements in weapon systems, logistical infrastructure, and command and control systems. At the time it approved the NDPO, the Miki cabinet also established a ceiling of 1 percent of GNP on defense expenditures. Consequently, many in Japan interpreted the NDPO as a dovish plan to maintain present force levels, not to justify a significant buildup.

In addition to the above constraints on military policy, changes in the international environment contributed to the nascent public consensus on defense issues. Although the so-called Nixon Doctrine enunciated by President Richard M. Nixon in Guam in 1969, calling for U.S. allies to bear more of the defense burden as the United States sought to withdraw from the Vietnam War, provoked some concern in Japan that the United States was withdrawing from East Asia, the overall climate of détente had a positive effect on Japan. Sino-American

rapprochement in 1971 and the subsequent normalization of Sino-Japanese relations removed a long-standing thorn in United States–Japanese relations, and the reversion of Okinawa to Japan in 1972 after nearly three decades of U.S. control settled a potentially contentious issue. United States–Soviet détente and the U.S. withdrawal from Vietnam eased Japanese anxieties that the security link with the United States could embroil Japan in an unwanted war. As a result of these developments, popular attitudes about security became more relaxed, and support for both the Self-Defense Forces and the United States–Japan Security Treaty grew steadily.

TOWARD A MORE ACTIVE DEFENSE POLICY

During the 1980s, Soviet behavior as well as U.S. pressure contributed to a more active security policy. The Soviet military buildup in Northeast Asia, the troop deployments on the "northern territories" claimed by Japan, the invasion of Afghanistan by the Soviet Union in December 1979, and the shooting down of a Korean airliner in September 1983 all had the effect of impressing both Japanese defense analysts and public at large that the Soviet Union indeed posed a military threat to Japan. Military planners in Tokyo highlighted the fact that the Soviet military had adopted a strategy of making the Sea of Okhotsk into a bastion for its nuclear ballistic-missile submarines. They argued that this strategic plan brought the Japanese archipelago within the Soviet defense perimeter and would pose an acute threat to Hokkaido during a United States–Soviet military crisis.

In this context of heightened East-West tensions, Japan began to change from a reluctant to an active U.S. ally. Diplomatically, Tokyo abandoned previous statements about an omnidirectional foreign policy and stressed its firm commitment to the Western alliance. In military terms, the government responded in a multifaceted manner: participation in joint military exercises with U.S. forces for the first time in history, formal consultation with the United States on coordinating military operations to deal with various regional contingencies, articulation of sea-lane defense out to one thousand nautical miles as a national policy objective, and the acquisition of frontline military equipment such as the

F-15 advanced fighter plane and the P-3C anti-submarine-warfare aircraft. During the mid-1980s, the government of Prime Minister Yasuhiro Nakasone promoted United States–Japanese defense cooperation by rescinding the 1-percent-of-GNP spending limit on defense, agreeing to transfer defense technology to the United States, and deciding to participate in research for America's Strategic Defense Initiative (SDI). Nakasone also stretched the concept of self-defense by arguing in the National Diet that it would not be unconstitutional if the Self-Defense Forces assisted U.S. forces operating to protect Japan before an actual attack on Japan took place.

Although the 1980s was a period of national budget austerity, the defense budget grew at an average nominal rate of 6.5 percent per year. By 1990, Japan was spending over ¥4.1 trillion ($32 billion) on its military. Some observers even estimated that Japan's defense budget had become the third largest in the world after that of the United States and the Soviet Union. But this ranking was largely an artifact of the rapid appreciation of the yen after 1985. Despite the extensive acquisition of high-technology equipment, the Self-Defense Forces still lacked basic power projection capabilities such as long-range bombers and aircraft carriers. As a percentage of GNP, defense spending again fell below the 1 percent level in 1990 after being slightly above this mark in 1987–1989. The collapse of the Soviet Union caused Japan to restrain growth in military expenditures even more and to delay long-standing procurement plans. For example, the 1991–1995 five-year defense program called for an increase of only 3 percent per year.

The Iraqi invasion and annexation of Kuwait in August 1990 shifted Japan's attention from military policy issues concerning Northeast Asia to the question of Japanese participation in United Nations security enforcement and peacekeeping activities. Although Tokyo contributed a total of $13 billion to the multinational effort against Iraqi aggression, Washington also expressed some desire for Japanese assistance with military air and sea lifts and possibly even the dispatch of minor forces to demonstrate the breadth and depth of the anti-Iraqi international coalition. The issue of deploying military forces abroad, however, cut into fundamental constitutional issues and Japan's postwar identity as a pacifist nation. To sidestep the strong domestic opposition to such deployments, the government led by Prime Minister Toshiki Kaifu opted for the development of an "international peace coopera-

tion corps" that could help in military logistics as well as humanitarian relief overseas. Stubborn resistance from the opposition parties to the participation of Self-Defense Force personnel in such a corps blocked the passage of the enabling legislation in the National Diet.

After the multinational coalition had liberated Kuwait and defeated the Iraqi forces, Kaifu did decide to dispatch Maritime Self-Defense Force minesweepers to the Persian Gulf to remove and dispose of mines. This was a historic move because it was the first time since the end of the U.S. occupation that Japan sent its military forces overseas on a nontraining mission. In the fall of 1991, the Japanese government also submitted legislation mandating the participation of Self-Defense Forces in United Nations peacekeeping operations. The National Diet finally approved the U.N. peacekeeping bill in June 1992 only after the government incorporated opposition-party demands for significant constraints on such peacekeeping activities. The new law permitted the deployment of a maximum of 2,000 members of the Self-Defense Forces to participate in noncombat support activities, including logistical support, medical assistance, and election monitoring performed as part of U.N.-led peacekeeping missions. The first such mission for the Japanese Self-Defense Forces was slated to be in Cambodia, where a Japanese citizen, Mr. Yasushi Akashi, headed the U.N. Transitional Authority for implementing the peace plan designed to end the long civil war there. Participation in more hazardous operations that might require the use of small weapons for self-defense, however, would require further legislation.

In the meantime, the government searched for ways to contribute more to international security that would be consistent with the "peace constitution" and sensitive to the pacifist sentiments of the Japanese people. For example, the Foreign Ministry proposed a strict international monitoring of arms transfers and even the linkage of economic assistance to limits on military spending and arms exports by recipient countries. These initiatives suggested that Japan was likely to use its increasing global influence to promote arms control and restraints on the use of military force.

BIBLIOGRAPHY

General JOHN K. EMMERSON, *Arms, Yen and Power: The Japanese Dilemma* (New York, 1971) and MARTIN E. WEINSTEIN, *Japan's Postwar Defense Policy, 1947–1968* (New York, 1971) are quite useful surveys of the evolution of Article 9. For a review of self-defense issues of the 1970s and 1980s, see TAKASHI INOGUCHI and DANIEL I. OKIMOTO, eds., *The Political Economy of Japan,* Vol. 2, *The Changing International Context* (Stanford, 1988) and HIDEO OTAKE, "Defense Controversies and One-Party Dominance: The Opposition in Japan and West Germany," in T.J. PEMPEL, ed., *Uncommon Democracies: The One-Party Dominant Regimes* (Ithaca, N.Y., 1990): 128–161.

For Japanese concerns with developing policies to allow greater flexibility in the employment of their fledgling military forces, see HISAHIKO OKAZAKI, *A Grand Strategy for Japanese Defense* (Lanham, Md., 1986); MIKE M. MOCHIZUKI, "Japan's Search for Strategy," *International Security* 8 (Winter 1983–1984): 152–179; and MASARU TAMAMOTO, "Trial of an Ideal: Japan's Debate over the Gulf Crisis," *World Policy Journal* 8 (Winter 1990–1991): 89–106.

Developing Article 9   TETSUYA KATAOKA, *The Price of a Constitution: The Origin of Japan's Postwar Politics* (New York, 1991), and JAMES R. VAN DE VELDE, "Article Nine of the Postwar Japanese Constitution: Codified Ambiguity," *Journal of Northeast Asian Studies* 6 (Spring 1987): 26–45, are among the more recent studies on the development of Article 9. Representative of the several earlier studies are THEODORE MCNELLY, "The Renunciation of War in the Japanese Constitution," *Political Science Quarterly* 77 (September 1962): 350–378, and TATSUO SATO, "The Origins and Development of the Japanese Constitution," *Contemporary Japan* 24: 4–6 (1956): 175–187.

For a view of the Japanese public's opinion of Article 9, see GEORGE R. PACKARD, *Protest in Tokyo: The Security Treaty Crisis of 1960* (Princeton, N.J., 1966), and NISHIJIMA YOSHIJI, "The Peace Constitution Controversy," *Japan Quarterly* 10 (January–March 1963): 18–27.

Self-Defense Forces   The early development of Japan's self-defense forces may be found in JAMES E. AUER, *The Postwar Rearmament of Japanese Maritime Forces, 1945–71* (New York, 1973); GILBERT M. BILLINGS, "Japan's Air Self-Defense Force," *Air University Review* 16 (July–August 1965): 60–71; and HIASA IWASHIMA, "Japan's Defense Policy," *Strategic Review* 3 (Spring 1975): 17–24.

The Austrian State Treaty

1955 to the Present

—————————— ◯ ——————————

STEPHEN W. YOUNG

See also Confidence-Building Measures in Europe: 1975 to the Present; Demilitarization and Neutralization Through World War II; Nuclear-Weapon-Free Zones; *and* Unilateral Initiatives. *The* Austrian State Treaty *is excerpted in Volume III.*

After seventeen years of occupation, first by Hitler's Germany and then by the four Allied powers (France, the Soviet Union, the United Kingdom, and the United States), the Austrian State Treaty liberated Austria and reestablished its sovereignty. The treaty, which was made possible by a brief thaw in the Cold War, was signed on 15 May 1955 after eight years of negotiation.

The Austrian State Treaty of 1955 was an important early example of arms control negotiations between East and West in the years following World War II. After its signing, some in the West cited the treaty as an example of the benefits of persistence and hard bargaining in negotiating with the Soviet Union. Others regarded it as another successful Soviet maneuver to weaken the West's military position. In either view, the treaty led to the withdrawal of Allied forces occupying Austria since 1945—the first Soviet pullback of its forces in Europe since the end of the war—and it placed numerous limitations on Austria's armed forces. Finally, at the insistence of the Soviets, the treaty prefaced an Austrian declaration of neutrality. The Western powers had strong reservations about Austrian neutrality, fearing it would create a military vacuum in the center of Europe and serve as an unwanted model for Germany (which the West wanted to enlist as an active ally in the Cold War). However, Austria was willing to undertake neutrality in order to regain independence, and the West could not prevent it.

BACKGROUND

On 13 March 1938, a day after German troops marched unopposed into Austria, Anschluss, or unification with Germany, was proclaimed. Anschluss was overwhelmingly confirmed in a German-controlled plebiscite on April 10, and under its terms Austrians fought in the German armed forces throughout World War II.

At the Moscow Conference of Foreign Ministers that convened in late October 1943, Soviet Foreign Minister Vyacheslav Molotov, U.S. Secretary of State Cordell Hull, and British Foreign Secretary Anthony Eden agreed that Austria was the first victim of Nazi aggression and should be liberated from German domination. Anschluss was to be considered an annexation and declared null and void. In the Moscow Declaration issued from the conference on December 1, the Allied powers called for the reestablishment of "a free and independent Austria." However, the declaration also stated, "Austria is reminded that she has a responsibility which she cannot evade for participating in the war on the side of Hitlerite Germany." This "war guilt" clause left Austria's situation ambiguous and was to be the center of debate in the negotiations to end the Allied occupation of Austria.

Soviet troops were the first to reach Austrian soil, occupying Vienna on 13 April 1945. By July 1945 the Allied powers had completed the move into their zones of occupation. The Soviet Union controlled eastern Austria, France the west, the United Kingdom the south, and the United States the north. Like Berlin, Vienna was inside the Soviet zone but occupied by all four powers; unlike Berlin, the inner core of the city was under quadripartite (four-nation) control. The United States, which wanted the United Kingdom to occupy Austria, was a reluctant participant in the occupation. In fact, the British took the initiative for much of the negotiations on Austria, as the United States considered the issue primarily a European matter.

In April 1945 the Soviet Union unilaterally formed a provisional government with limited authority over the Soviet zone of occupation. Karl Renner, a Socialist who had served as chancellor and president of the last elected Parliament in Austria, was named head of the new government and immediately set about forming a provisional regime. However, the Western powers, concerned that Renner was a Soviet pawn, delayed recognition of his government until 20 October 1945, and stipulated that national elections had to be held before the end of the year. Those elections were held 25 November 1945, and resulted in a Conservative-Socialist-Communist coalition government with Leopold Figl of the Austrian People's Party (formerly the Christian Socialist party) as chancellor. The Parliament elected Renner president.

Initially, all the decisions and actions of the Figl government had to be unanimously approved by the Allied Council, a body established by the four Allied powers to oversee the occupation of Austria. In June 1946 this system was changed to one in which Austrian laws could only be stopped by unanimous veto of the Allied powers within thirty-one days. The only exception was constitutional law, which remained subject to full-scale Allied approval. This exception was conceived to allay Soviet fears of a second Anschluss.

The Allied Council was responsible for the demilitarization and denazification of occupied Austria. Military training and activities were prohibited. Military equipment was either destroyed, removed from Austria, or controlled by the Allied powers. Military installations were dismantled or used by the occupying forces. Munitions factories were cataloged and destroyed or switched to civilian enterprises, and the production, acquisition, and development of armaments was prohibited. The process of demilitarization was essentially complete by 1947.

NEGOTIATIONS ON THE AUSTRIAN STATE TREATY

Between January 1947 and May 1955, the Allied powers met over 370 times to discuss the Austrian State Treaty. Settlement came only after an April 1955 pact between Austria and the Soviet Union in which the Soviets reduced considerably the number of economic concessions they had demanded, and Austria agreed to declare permanent neutrality after ratification of the treaty and the withdrawal of Allied forces. The Allied powers signed the treaty on 15 May 1955, and on 26 October, one day after the last occupation soldier left Austrian soil, the Austrian National Assembly passed a constitutional law proclaiming Austria's permanent neutrality.

Although the Americans had written a first draft of the Austrian State Treaty in February 1946, at the insistence of the Soviet Union negotiations among the Allied powers toward restoring Austria's sovereignty did not begin until treaties with Germany's former allies (Bulgaria, Finland, Romania, Hungary, and Italy) were concluded. Each of these countries needed peace treaties. Because the Allies considered Austria the first victim of Nazi aggression, and not a German ally, a state treaty rather than a peace treaty was needed to reestablish Austrian sovereignty.

The negotiator who worked on the state treaty faced a number of troublesome issues, the most vexing of which was the lack of a precise definition of "German assets." At the Potsdam Conference of 1945, the Allied powers agreed that Austria would pay no reparations. However, occupation powers were entitled to claim "German assets" in Austria. The Western powers understood this to mean industrial plants and other facilities built by Germany in Austria during World War II. But since "German assets" had not been specifically defined, the Soviet Union seized large properties and interests in their zone of occupation, claiming them as reparations. The Western powers, led by the United States, protested these seizures and renounced claim to all German assets in Austria. This issue remained a matter of dispute until the Austro-Soviet agreement in 1955.

Another issue that hobbled the negotiations for years was Soviet support of Yugoslavia's demand for Austrian territory and monetary payments for losses suffered during World War II. Moscow's support of this claim was based on the fact that the Allied powers had renounced Allied but not Yugoslav reparations from Austria.

In 1949, several months after Yugoslavia's Marshal Josip Tito broke with Soviet leader Joseph Stalin, the Soviet Union dropped its support of Yugoslavian claims against Austria. A treaty appeared near when the United States, at Austria's urging, agreed to accept the Soviet definition of "German assets," but then Moscow raised the question of Austrian payments for Soviet relief supplies in the immediate post–World War II period. This issue became known as the "dried peas debt" because the food supplies provided to Austrians by the Soviets were primarily leftover dried peas taken from German army rations. The issue proved insoluble because the Soviet Union refused to specify a price that would be acceptable.

For the next three years Moscow continued to introduce new issues into the negotiations that, like the "dried peas" tactic, were clearly intended to delay a treaty. For example, the Soviets cited insufficient Austrian efforts at denazification and demilitarization, and they insisted that the negotiations include discussion of U.S. and British troops in Trieste, Italy (according to the Soviets, this military presence violated the Italian Peace Treaty). These Soviet demands, coupled with the outbreak of hostilities in Korea, caused negotiations to break down in late 1950. Talks did not resume until February 1953.

Stalin's death in March 1953 initiated a power struggle among the Soviet leadership and several changes in Soviet behavior. The Soviets loosened traffic barriers around Berlin and dropped their objection to the nomination of Dag Hammarskjold as secretary-general of the United Nations. The Korean armistice agreements were signed in July. In Austria, the Soviets eased their grip on their zone, allowing East-West zonal border crossings, granting amnesty to some Austrian political prisoners, and officially ending censorship of Austrian mail, telephone communications, and telegraph messages. The Soviets also agreed to cover the ongoing costs of their occupation of Austria (thus freeing Austria from this burdensome expense); and they replaced the Soviet military high commissioner in Austria with an ambassador, following the example set by the Western powers three years earlier. Behind the scenes, the first diplomatic feelers were extended between Vienna and Moscow on Austrian willingness to declare neutrality following a treaty settlement.

Serious negotiations on the Austrian State Treaty resumed at the Berlin Conference of Foreign Ministers in February 1954. There, Soviet Foreign Minister Molotov demanded for the first time that occupation troops remain in Austria until a German peace treaty was signed. The West rejected such a linkage, and negotiations eventually broke down over this point. The Soviets also wanted the treaty to prohibit Austria from joining any military alliances and to bar the installation of foreign military bases on Austrian soil. The Western powers objected to having such a statement in the treaty itself but remained receptive to the possibility of Austrian neutrality. Figl, who had become Austria's foreign minister, unilaterally stated that in order to regain its sovereignty Austria was willing to forego military alliances and forbid foreign military bases on its soil.

At this conference, the Western powers offered to accept the Soviet version of the five treaty articles that remained in dispute, including the Soviet definition of German assets. In return, the United States, France, and the United Kingdom demanded that the Soviet Union sign the treaty immediately. The chief obstacle to the treaty was timing the withdrawal of occupation forces. The Soviets insisted that occupation forces remain in Austria until a German peace treaty was signed, or at least that the issue be put off until 1955. The Western powers refused to agree to this position, and no treaty was signed.

On 8 February 1955, Soviet Foreign Minister Molotov, in a speech to the Supreme Soviet, did an abrupt about-face: he stated that Allied troops could be withdrawn from Austria before the German question was resolved and called for a treaty "as soon as possible." Austrian Chancellor Julius Raab, who had succeeded Figl, arrived in Moscow on 12 April, and by 15 April the two sides announced the Moscow Memorandum, in which the Soviets made substantial concessions on the German assets issue and the Austrians agreed to maintain permanent neutrality. In Vienna, on 15 May, the foreign ministers of Austria and the four Allied powers signed the Austrian State Treaty.

THE AUSTRIAN STATE TREATY AND ARMS CONTROL

The Austrian State Treaty raises four issues relevant to arms control: neutrality, limitations on Austria's armed forces, Soviet motives, and the treaty's implications for the rest of the world.

Neutrality An Austrian declaration of neutrality as a solution to the problems facing the State Treaty was originally broached by the Austrians to the Soviets through India and can be traced to Stalin's call on 10 March 1952 for a German peace treaty. Stalin envisioned a unified Germany that would not join military alliances or allow foreign military bases on its soil. When the Soviet Union first publicly raised the issue of Austria's neutrality at the Berlin Conference in 1954, they proposed an agreement that, in essence, echoed Stalin's offer for Germany.

On at least one occasion, the Soviet Union demanded that the Allied powers guarantee Austrian neutrality. The Western powers were hesitant for several reasons. First, they feared that a weak, neutral Austria would create a military vacuum in the center of Europe and would be vulnerable either to external threats or to a Communist takeover from within. During the Allied occupation, Austria was prevented from establishing any armed forces other than police forces.

In fact, Western concern about a militarily weak Austria existed even before the possibility of Austrian neutrality was raised. Government documents released in the late 1970s and early 1980s indicate that as early as 1947 the U.S. State Department and the U.S. Defense Department were in serious disagreement over how to proceed on Austria. The State Department wanted a treaty as soon as possible. The Defense Department, after the Communist putsch in Czechoslovakia in February 1948, held that Austria would be unable to prevent a Communist takeover if Allied forces withdrew. Thus, the Pentagon insisted that no treaty could be signed until Austrian military forces were built up sufficiently. Eventually, President Harry Truman decided to sign the treaty while initiating secret programs to develop Austria's armed forces with the help of the U.S. government.

The Soviets, who apparently had been negotiating in earnest in 1949, then began stalling, introducing the "dried peas debt" and taking other measures designed to delay the treaty. For their part, the Western powers began a covert training program for a gendarmerie (a group of armed policemen) to form the nucleus of an Austrian army. U.S. small arms were stockpiled in the Western zones for Austrian use once Allied forces withdrew.

A unilateral decision by Austria to become neutral was acceptable to the Western powers as long as it was armed neutrality and as long as the terms were not unilaterally dictated by the Soviet Union. That, in Western eyes, would be an impingement on Austrian sovereignty. Above all, the West feared the impact Austrian neutrality might have on Germany. The Western powers, particularly the Americans and the British, were intent on rearming the Federal Republic of Germany (West Germany) and including it in a Western military alliance. A unified, neutral Austria could serve as a model for Germans coveting unification and for French leaders looking to limit the German military threat.

In fact, Austrian neutrality did not have a large impact on German rearmament. The opposition Social Democratic Party in the Federal Republic of Germany, which was against German entry in the North Atlantic Treaty Organization (NATO), cited the Austrian example as a model for Germany. But under Chancellor Konrad Adenauer's leadership, the Federal Republic's Bundestag (Parliament) was committed to military alignment with the West.

France, with some hesitation, also supported rearming the Federal Republic. A major effort in this direction began in 1952 with the proposed European Defense Community (EDC), a supranational army that would include German forces. The Soviet Union strongly opposed the EDC, especially because of Germany's expected participation, and after much debate the French Chamber of Deputies rejected the EDC in August 1954. A second attempt to rearm Germany came in the Paris Agreements of 13 October 1954, in which the British proposed inviting the Federal Republic to join NATO and become an active part of the Western military alliance. The French Chamber of Deputies ratified the Paris Agreements in December 1954, with final ratification coming on 5 May 1955—ten days before the signing of the Austrian State Treaty.

Limitations on Austria's Armed Forces The Austrian State Treaty severely restricted the types of weapons Austria's armed forces could employ. Foreign-built weapons were forbidden, and Austria was prohibited from possessing, constructing, or experimenting with nuclear, chemical, and biological weapons, self-propelled or self-guided missiles or torpedoes, long-range artillery, or submarines. The treaty also forbade the manufacture of any weapons of German design, and of German or Japanese civilian aircraft. Other clauses barred a second Anschluss with Germany and called on Austria to help prevent German rearmament.

While the Allied powers occupied Austria, the Austrian government was prohibited from establishing an army. In early drafts of the State Treaty the size of the Austrian army was limited to 53,000 men, but at the Moscow meeting of April 1955 the Soviet Union agreed to remove this restriction. In 1956, one year after the signing of the treaty, only 6,000 men were under arms; by 1957 that number had increased to 30,000. Eventually, active Austrian armed forces only slightly exceeded the originally proposed limit of 53,000, although ready reserves surpassed 240,000. (In contrast, over 200,000 Austrians died fighting in the German armed forces in World War II. The Austrian State Treaty did not place numerical limits on Austria's armaments. Thus, Austria was allowed to equip its troops with any number of tanks, combat aircraft, or other weapons systems not specifically prohibited in the treaty.

The 1955 Moscow Memorandum between Austria and the Soviet Union stated that Austria was "to adhere to a policy of permanent neutrality on the Swiss model." The type of neutrality adopted by Austria does, indeed, resemble Switzerland's in that both are based on an internationally accepted nineteenth-century legal concept that implies several responsibilities. A neutral country can maintain armed forces, but it cannot go to war except in self-defense. During time of war, neutral countries cannot aid any contending party; during peacetime, they cannot undertake political activities that may lead to war. Military alliances are prohibited. Other states are asked to recognize a country's neutral status and may not use a neutral state's territory for belligerent purposes.

Unlike Switzerland, however, Austria takes an active international role. Switzerland follows a policy of "armed neutrality" and has committed considerable resources for its self-defense, vowing to fight to the last soldier if necessary. But, while it has joined the European Free Trade Association (EFTA), Switzerland has refused to join the U.N. and has not applied for membership in the European Community (EC). While Switzerland is a Western-style, capitalist democracy, it has refrained from any alliance that might compromise its neutrality.

Austria, in contrast, joined the U.N. in 1955, and Austrian troops have participated in U.N. peacekeeping forces. In 1989 Austria applied for membership in the EC; this application came at a time when the Community was moving toward increased cooperation in political and security areas that would strain Austria's neutral position. On the other hand, Austria has never committed the resources to its own defense that Switzerland has. In fact, when Austria first announced its acceptance of permanent neutrality, Switzerland was critical of the idea, fearing a militarily weak state on its eastern border. By 1990, Austria had an active force of 42,500 with 242,000 in ready reserves from a population of over 7,500,000. Switzerland, meanwhile, had a smaller active force of only 3,500 but a ready reserve of 625,000 soldiers from a population of about 6,700,000. Switzerland had four times as many tanks and ten times the number of combat aircraft as Austria.

Soviet Motives Most observers were baffled by the sudden speed with which the Austrian State Treaty was concluded. After nearly a decade of often fruitless negotiation, Molotov announced on 8 February 1955 that the withdrawal of Soviet troops from Austria would not be linked to the ratification of a German peace treaty, and slightly more than two months later the Austrian State Treaty was ready to be signed. The Soviet move was a surprise, especially because the Soviets agreed to terms vastly more favorable to Austria and the West than they had been offered just one year earlier.

Several explanations have been put forth for the Soviet position change. The most prominent, and perhaps most widely believed, is that an Austrian State Treaty that guaranteed a neutral Austria would prevent or at least slow the rearmament of the Federal Republic of Germany. A Soviet signature on the Austrian State Treaty would show that the Soviet Union could be a reasonable negotiator and that German rearmament was not necessary. In fact, Soviet Foreign Minister Molotov found the Austrian State Treaty signing to be the appropriate time to state that the Soviets would agree to German unification if Germany also chose neutrality.

The Soviet policy change can also be seen in a wider context of the "new look" of Soviet foreign policy following Stalin's death. Nikita Khrushchev, who became the Communist Party leader in September 1953 and was the primary force behind the Soviet "new look" policy, might have reasoned that Soviet cooperation in the Austrian State Treaty would foster an East-West détente. U.S. President Dwight Eisenhower, in his "Chance for Peace" speech on 16 April 1953, specifically called for agreement on the Austrian treaty as a sign of Soviet sincerity to back up Moscow's talk of "peaceful co-operation." Khrushchev took Eisenhower at his word and made the signing of the Austrian State Treaty a part of the "new look" campaign.

The "new look" included several Soviet initiatives designed to create a more favorable world-wide image of the Soviet Union. These included the reestablishment of diplomatic relations with Yugoslavia, broken off in 1948; the establishment of de facto relations with the Federal Republic of Germany and the repatriation of German prisoners of war; the return to Finland of the Porkkala naval base, captured during World War II; and trade and aid agreements with Egypt, India, Burma, and Afghanistan.

Tied to all these efforts was a continuing Soviet effort to promote neutralism in the third world by promising undeveloped nations that a pledge of neutrality would bring them Soviet support and enable them to avoid military confrontations. It has been argued that this was a Cold War–motivated attempt by the Soviets to enable countries in Africa and Asia to develop economically without falling into the capitalist camp.

Finally, some observers have advanced the theory that Soviet agreement came from persistent Austrian efforts to negotiate a treaty. Austria, weary of what it viewed as Western delays and lack of effort, pursued its own agenda to end the long occupation by Allied powers.

Military withdrawal from Austria created difficulties for the Soviet Union. Clauses in the peace treaties with Hungary and Romania allowed the Soviet Union to station forces in those countries to maintain lines of communication with Soviet troops in Austria. A Soviet withdrawal from Austria meant that the Soviet Union had to find another way to justify its continued military presence in Romania and Hungary.

In the same period, the Soviet Union strongly protested the move to bring the Federal Republic of Germany into NATO. When Soviet objections could not prevent such a move, the Soviet Union and its Eastern bloc satellites formed the Warsaw Treaty Organization, or Warsaw Pact. An agreement outlining the Pact was signed 14 May 1955, just one day before the signing of the Austrian State Treaty. The agreement allowed the continued presence of Soviet troops not only in Hungary and Romania, but in Czechoslovakia as well. (Soviet troops were al-ready in Poland to "maintain supply lines" to East Germany.)

Historians have noted that the Soviet Union agreed to the Austrian State Treaty because, militarily and economically, it was in their best interest to do so. Militarily, a neutral Austria next to a neutral Switzerland put a wedge in the Western military bloc between north and south, effectively cutting off Italy from the Federal Republic of Germany. Limitations on Austria's armed forces virtually assured a military vacuum in the center of Europe. Economically, the Soviets had extracted almost all the value of the "German assets" in the eastern zone of Austria. The industries were becoming a liability and were dependent on resources from the British, U.S., and French zones, meaning that the Soviet zone would not have been viable as a partitioned state. Oil reserves in Austria, although still valuable, were no longer vital now that Soviet domestic oil production was sufficient.

Lastly, Soviet hopes that Austria could be converted to Communism did not materialize. In Austrian national elections, the Communist Party never received more that 5 percent of the vote and never had more than five seats in the Parliament. The largest representation the Communists ever achieved—three seats, including the Interior Ministry, key to controlling the police and internal security—was in the provisional Renner cabinet formed in April 1945. But following the poor showing of the Communists in the November 1945 elections, they were given only one seat in the new Figl cabinet. Communist-supported strikes and riots occurred in 1947 and 1950 but never seriously endangered the government. The only way to establish a Communist regime in Austria would have been through direct Soviet military intervention, and this was a risk the Soviets were apparently not willing to take.

Implications of the Treaty   The Austrian State Treaty was signed in a time of worldwide upheaval and the consolidation of the Cold War bloc system. The Federal Republic of Germany was rearming and had just joined NATO, the Soviet Union and its satellites had formed their own military alliance, and decolonization, although yet to reach its peak, had begun in Africa and Asia. The Bandung Conference of Asian and African countries took place between the signing of the Moscow Memorandum of 15 April and the signing of the Austrian State Treaty on 15 May 1955. This conference was a seminal event in the political development of the less-developed countries, and of the Non-Aligned Movement, an organization that sought to represent countries not aligned with either side in the Cold War.

The Soviet Union wanted the Austrian State Treaty to serve as a model for the world. By agreeing to neutrality, Austria was to be rewarded with an end to occupation and economic terms substantially less harsh than originally proposed by the Soviet Union. This approach held risks for the Soviets, particularly in Eastern Europe, as evidenced by Hungary's move to withdraw from the Soviet bloc in 1956 and declare itself neutral. The Soviets responded by dispatching troops to Hungary to suppress the revolt, but Hungary's attempt to follow the Austrian model did not end Soviet efforts to encourage neutralism outside its own bloc. During the Cold War, Soviet leaders apparently viewed neutrality as a reasonable option for non-Communist countries, but not for Soviet satellites.

CONCLUSION

Many of the issues that held up negotiations on the Austrian State Treaty (for example, Yugoslavian reparations, Trieste, the "dried peas debt") were manifestations of Cold War maneuvering and had no relevance to the treaty itself. It is clear that both the Soviet Union and the Western powers, particularly the U.S. Department of Defense, had strong reservations about signing any treaty on Austria. These difficulties had less to do with concern for Austria than with the implications an agreement would have on Cold War issues. In the end, the Soviet Union hoped an Austrian State Treaty would weaken the Western military alliance while demonstrating Soviet largesse. From the Western perspective, U.S. Secretary of State John Foster Dulles noted that the agreement could have troublesome implications for the Soviet Union's relations with its East European satellites. Hungary's 1956 revolt demonstrated his point.

It is most likely that the final resolution of the treaty came from a Soviet change of leadership and policy more than any negotiating tactic or Western offer. While the Austrian proposal of self-declared neutrality was the key to an agreement, it would probably not have satisfied Stalin. Historians also maintain that no agreement would have been reached had not Austria pushed its own agenda, outside of the East-West confrontation.

The Austrian State Treaty briefly showed the way for "peaceful cooperation" between East and West, opening a window of opportunity that slammed shut with the Soviet crackdown in Hungary in 1956. However, the treaty's arms control implications endured. Allied troops pulled out of Austria, marking the first Soviet withdrawal from Europe since World War II. Austria remained neutral but continued to participate in the international arena. Armaments for the Austrian army are still limited by the treaty. Whether the fall of Soviet empire and the rise of the European Community will change this remains to be seen.

BIBLIOGRAPHY

Early Accounts   SVEN ALLARD, *Russia and the Austrian State Treaty: A Case Study of Soviet Policy in Europe* (London, 1970) is a mixture of the memoirs of the Swedish ambassador to Austria and some insightful analysis into Soviet motivations. WILLIAM B. BADER, *Austria Between East and West, 1945–1955* (Stanford, Calif., 1966) focuses on events and politics in Austria itself. BLAIR G. EWING, *Peace through Negotiation: The Austrian Experience* (Washington, D.C., 1966), is an attempt to demonstrate the rewards of earnest negotiation. Other general accounts include KARL GRUBER, *Between Liberation and Liberty, Austria in the Post-War World* (New York, 1955) and GORDON SHEPARD, *The Austrian Odyssey* (London, 1957).

The official American rendering of the negotiations on the State Treaty is the U.S. Department of State's *The Austrian State Treaty. An Account of the Postwar Negotiations, Together with the Text of the Treaty and Related Documents* (Washington, D.C., no. 6437, 1957). WILLIAM LLOYD STEARMAN *The Soviet Union and the Occupation of Austria* (Bonn, 1961) is primarily a compilation of extracts from relevant documents, interspersed with text to explain ongoing events. ALFRED VEDROSS, *The Permanent Neutrality of Austria* (Vienna, 1978), offers a brief academic description of the foundations in international law of Austria's neutrality and responsibilities thereof, and a comparison to Swiss neutrality.

Recent Interpretations AUDREY KURTH CRONIN, *Great Power Politics and the Struggle over Austria, 1945–1955* (Ithaca, N.Y., 1986), is a comprehensive examination of the State Treaty, including analysis of government documents released in the late 1970s and early 1980s. An excellent summary article, including discussion of U.S. and Soviet motivations, is KURT STEINER, "Negotiations for an Austrian State Treaty," in ALEXANDER L. GEORGE, PHILIP J. FAR-LEY, and ALEXANDER DALLIN, eds., *U.S.-Soviet Security Cooperation* (New York, 1988): 46–82. A collection of essays written on the twenty-fifth anniversary of the signing of the Austrian State Treaty, including some analysis and some memories of individuals involved, can be found in ROBERT BAUER, ed., *The Austrian Solution: International Conflict and Cooperation* (Charlottesville, Va., 1982).

The Antarctic State Treaty

1959 to the Present

———————————— ◯ ————————————

CHRISTOPHER C. JOYNER

See also Confidence-Building Measures in Europe: 1975 to the Present; The Environmental Modification Convention: 1977 to the Present; From MBFR to CFE: Negotiating Conventional Arms Control in Europe; *and* Latin America. *The Antarctic State Treaty is excerpted in Volume III.*

Antarctica is the only continent completely disarmed by international agreement. All military activities, weapons tests, fortifications, and troop maneuvers are expressly prohibited on and around the continent. These extraordinary circumstances create a disarmament zone that extends northward from Antarctica to include all circumpolar islands, ice formations, and ocean space south of 60° south latitude. As a consequence, both the continent of Antarctica—covering 10 percent of the earth's land surface, or 14.3 million square kilometers (approximately 5.5 million square miles)—and the circumpolar seas of the Southern Ocean—comprising about 10 percent of the earth's ocean space, or some 27.3 million square kilometers (approximately 11 million square miles)—have formally been declared an international demilitarized zone. The 1959 Antarctic Treaty serves as the legal instrument specifically designed to keep the region free from international tensions and discord.

GEOPOLITICAL AND STRATEGIC CONSIDERATIONS

Though most states consider the geopolitical and strategic value of Antarctica to be marginal, some states view the continent as significant in terms of foreign policy considerations for at least three reasons. First, the Southern Ocean has been regarded as important to shipping, especially as it preserves free transit through the Drake Passage, the principal sea lane separating Tierra del Fuego from Antarctica. The strategic significance of this waterway turns on concern over unimpeded accessibility to the Panama Canal and the need for an alternative shipping route should the canal one day be closed to international commerce.

A second geopolitical concern relates to national claims to Antarctica. Seven states have asserted claims of national sovereignty over the continent: the United Kingdom in 1908 and 1917; New Zealand in 1923; France in 1924; Australia in 1933; Norway in 1939; Chile in 1940; and Argentina in 1946. While these claims are taken seriously by these governments, no nonclaimant government has ever acknowledged the lawful permissibility of these seven states to make claims to Antarctica, nor has any other state ever given formal recognition to the lawfulness or validity of these purported sovereign titles. Also not to be overlooked is that three of these claims overlap in large part. The claims asserted by Chile and Argentina severely encroach upon each other, and both of these are substantially overlapped by the claim of the United Kingdom. That claims by three ardent nationalist states in the region overrun and conflict with each other underscores the legal complexity and political sensitivity of the situation, as well as the latent potential for confrontation in the Southern Ocean/Antarctic region.

Third, traditional anxieties persist over geopolitical rivalries in the region. Both Argentina and Chile have long shared security concerns about their exposed southern flanks, no doubt a consideration in their respective assertions of territorial claims to Antarctica. In fact, the geopolitical thinking of both states has stressed the importance of national security, space, and projection of power southward into the maritime and resource dimensions, as well as the significance of choke points such as the Drake Passage. Not surprisingly, geopolitics has historically exacerbated antagonisms between these two Latin powers, especially their protracted controversy over legal rights to islands in the Beagle Channel and South Atlantic. Similarly, Argentina and the United Kingdom have experienced diplomatic tensions since the 1830s over their conflicting sovereignty claims to the Falkland/Malvinas Islands, as well as to South Georgia, the South Orkneys, and the South Shetlands. Anglo-Argentine-Chilean rivalry on the continent, aggravated by political squabbles over sovereign jurisdiction to these island groups, undermined political stability throughout the region until the late 1950s.

EVOLUTION OF THE ANTARCTIC TREATY

An increase in Soviet activity in the Antarctic during the 1950s prompted concerns in the United States about Soviet motivations there. A residue of Cold War anxieties, speculation in the U.S. government focused on Antarctica's potential strategic value and the possible political fallout the spillover of United States–Soviet rivalry might produce for the region. Such a development undoubtedly would complicate the already protracted sovereignty situation and overlapping claims. More disturbing, it was feared that rivalry between the United States and the Soviet Union over the south pole could precipitate an arms race in the Antarctic, ultimately leading to the implantation or testing of nuclear weapons there.

Geostrategic anxieties, especially given the increasingly active role of the Soviet Union, made interested Western governments more aware that international accommodation was essential if Cold War tensions were to be veered away from Antarctica. It was the gratifying cooperative experience of the International Geophysical Year (IGY) of 1957–

1958 that supplied the catalyst and conduit for that accommodation and laid the diplomatic foundation for negotiations that culminated in the Antarctic Treaty of 1959.

The chief lesson learned from the IGY experience was clear: political accommodation in Antarctic affairs was possible, in spite of competing national interests and the perceived high geostrategic stakes. Securing and preserving a disarmament zone throughout the Antarctic was viewed as critical for promoting successful scientific cooperation in the region.

From the outset of preliminary treaty negotiations in 1958, the need to assure that Antarctica would be used for peaceful purposes only was fixed as a priority goal. That clearly was evident in the United States' note of invitation in May 1958 to convene these discussions, and it gained significance with the explicit inclusion of the Soviet Union in the negotiation process.

THE ANTARCTIC TREATY REGIME

Largely to the credit of Ambassador Paul C. Daniels, chief of the United States delegation and chairman of the negotiating conference, the diplomatic framework hammered out between June 1958 and December 1959 produced a refined Antarctic Treaty instrument. Opened for signature on 1 December 1959, the Antarctic Treaty entered into force on 23 June 1961. Since then, that instrument has worked remarkably well, especially given that its decisions are arrived at by consensus. Treaty membership has grown from twelve parties in 1959—the "original" Antarctic Treaty Consultative Parties (ACTPS)—to forty. (See the table for a listing.) The legal regime has also been expanded into a multiple treaty system comprised of special international agreements to deal with the conservation of fauna and flora, seals, and living marine resources. Particular attention has been devoted to negotiating separate agreements for the regulation of mineral resource development and to effect comprehensive environmental protection measures. The fulcrum on which this multilateral Antarctic Treaty arrangement turns is the notion of peaceful uses only of the continent, maintained through disarmament of the Antarctic region.

Parties to the Antarctic Treaty

Countries that Signed the Antarctic Treaty in 1959

Argentina	New Zealand
Australia	Norway
Belgium	South Africa
Chile	Union of Soviet Socialist Republics
France	United Kingdom
Japan	United States

States Admitted to ATCP Status Since 1961

Poland	1977	Spain	1988
W. Germany	1981	Sweden	1988
Brazil	1983	Republic of Korea (South Korea)	1989
India	1983	Peru	1989
People's Republic of China	1985	Finland	1989
Uruguay	1985	Ecuador	1990
Italy	1987	Netherlands	1990
E. Germany	1987	Germany (United)	1990

Non-Voting Parties

Czechoslovakia	Hungary
Denmark	Cuba
Romania	Democratic People's Republic of Korea (North Korea)
Bulgaria	
Colombia	Austria
Greece	Canada
Papua New Guinea	

DISARMAMENT AND THE ANTARCTIC TREATY

The 1959 Antarctic Treaty functions to demilitarize the region. This ambition is clearly articulated in the preamble: "Antarctica shall continue forever to be used exclusively for peaceful purposes and shall not become the scene or object of international discord." This overarching security objective has become the preeminent consideration among the treaty parties—one that has repeatedly encouraged them to compromise and cooperate on potentially disruptive issues, such as legal complications arising from sovereignty claims and questions concerning access to natural resources. For example, the preamble of the 1980 Convention on the Conservation of Antarctic Marine Living Resources (CCAMLR) unequivocally reaffirms the Antarctic Treaty's premise that "[it] is in the interest of all mankind to preserve the waters surrounding the Antarctic continent for peaceful purposes only and to prevent their becoming the scene or object of international discord."

The Antarctic Treaty is a nonarmament agreement. Three provisions specifically relate to keeping the region disarmed. Article I dedicates the Antarctic area exclusively to peaceful purposes. It flatly directs that "Antarctica shall be used for peaceful purposes only." Article I goes on to assert the prohibition of "any measures of a military nature, such as the establishment of military bases and fortifications, the carrying out of military maneuvers, as well as the testing of any type of weapons." This provision aims legally at preventing the Antarctic area from becoming militarized. A notable exception exists, however, regarding actions taken for individual or collective self-defense in the western hemisphere, situations that could intrude into the area covered by the treaty—that is, south of 60° south latitude. The general provision upholding permissibility of self-defense is couched in Article 51 of the United Nations Charter, and this guarantee was intentionally preserved for the security zone created in 1947 by the Inter-American Treaty of Reciprocal Assistance (the Rio Treaty). In fact, the United States, Chile, and Argentina even attached declarations to this effect when they signed the Antarctic Treaty in 1959. The main point here is evident: the Antarctic Treaty cites as its initial reason for convening consultative party meetings the possible need to discuss measures concerning the "use of Antarctica for peaceful purposes only." This recognition forthrightly complements and highlights the fundamental intention of Article I.

A second prominent provision contributing to disarmament establishes the Antarctic as a nuclear weapons free zone. Article V bans nuclear explosions for any purpose and forbids the dumping of radioactive wastes there. In pithy language, Article V avers that "any nuclear explosions in Antarctica and the disposal there of radioactive waste material shall be prohibited." Nonmilitary, atmospheric, and subterranean nuclear tests are banned, although prohibition does not extend to the use of radioactive materials in Antarctica. Parties to the Convention on the Conservation of Antarctic Marine Living Resources (CCAMLR) are likewise enjoined to conditions of disarmament and denuclearization. Article III of CCAMLR provides in full that "the Contracting Parties, whether or not they are Parties to the Antarctic Treaty, agree that they will not engage in any activities in the Antarctic Treaty area contrary to the principles and purposes of that Treaty and that, in their relations with each other, they are bound by the obligations contained in Articles I and V of the Antarctic Treaty."

The third provision promoting disarmament throughout the Antarctic is Article VII of the Antarctic Treaty, which stipulates the right of each consultative party to appoint observers to carry out unannounced, on-site inspections. This stipulation was included in the treaty to monitor compliance with Articles I and V. It seeks to ensure that the Antarctic region is being used exclusively for peaceful purposes, absent nuclear explosions and radioactive waste disposal. As Article VII declares, "All areas of Antarctica, including all stations, installations and equipment within those areas, and all ships and aircraft at points of discharging or embarking cargoes or personnel in Antarctica, shall be open at all times to inspection by any observers designated. . . ." The inspection provision also applies to facilities and equipment used for land-based development and commercial activities in the area—for instance,

those activities associated with possible minerals exploitation.

Article VII also includes the specific right of unlimited aerial inspection. This allowance neatly reinforces the earlier stipulation in paragraph 2 that guarantees to each observer "freedom of access at any time to any or all areas of Antarctica." A proper inference also may be drawn that unlimited aerial inspection perforce entails the right of access for scientific purposes, analogous to the "open skies" policy adopted in the late 1950s by the United States. Article VII further establishes requirements for notification and exchange of information regarding expeditions to the continent, stations to be established there, and military personnel or equipment to be "introduced" by a party into Antarctica. This provision was designed to confirm the disarmament goals of the treaty arrangement. Information exchange has occurred about a broad variety of subjects, including some having perceived military relevance (for example, activities relating to logistics problems, the use and applications of nuclear equipment, and telecommunication operations). Even so, frequent information exchange and notification have served to reassure governments about the nonmilitary purposes of these activities.

The Antarctic Treaty also provides for peaceful settlement of disputes, in order to furnish legal incentives to promote restoration of peaceful uses only in the region. Article XI calls upon contracting parties to "consult among themselves with a view to having the dispute resolved by negotiation, inquiry, mediation, conciliation, arbitration, judicial settlement or other peaceful means of their own choice." Should these means fail to resolve a dispute, Article XI goes on to suggest that the dispute should be referred to the International Court of Justice for settlement, subject to consent of all the disputants. Since the Antarctic Treaty entered into force in 1961, no major dispute has been reported among the consultative parties to warrant invocation of these dispute settlement techniques.

THE ANTARCTIC DISARMAMENT PROCESS

The Antarctic Treaty unequivocally mandates that the Antarctic must remain free from any activities of a military kind, although military personnel are permitted to participate in logistics and resupply operations. Moreover, nuclear weapons are banned from the region, and rights for unlimited, unannounced, on-site inspection are guaranteed to maintain this nonmilitarized condition. That these overriding security objectives have been sustained since 1961 makes the Antarctic Treaty a conspicuous success at curbing military and geopolitical ambitions of states in the region. More accurately, this treaty instrument stands out as the most successful regional arms control agreement negotiated in the post–World War II era.

The Antarctic Treaty supplies the specific framework within which arms control, deterrence, geostrategic goals, and regulation on use of force in the south polar region has been maintained. To preserve disarmament in the Antarctic, the process must be continuously performed as a collective effort by all involved parties. Responsibility rests with governments themselves to guarantee, monitor, and coexist nonmilitarily within the Antarctic/Southern Ocean region. The Antarctic Treaty promotes trustworthy conduct and attitudes by making the behavior of members predictable; the treaty also provides for diplomatic opportunities and policy intercourse from which parties derive positive results and hence realize benefits from the relationship. What results from the treaty relationship is the evolution of institutionalized trust.

The Antarctic Treaty reserves the region for peaceful purposes only. No inference should be made, however, that states have wholly renounced the use of force in the area. They have not. The lawful use of force in the Antarctic is preserved for all states through Article 51 of the United Nations Charter; moreover, for Antarctic Treaty parties in the western hemisphere, this right is further sanctioned by the Rio Pact of 1947. Likewise, a caveat of ambiguity surrounds the use of nuclear devices in the region. Article V of the Antarctic Treaty clearly bans nuclear explosive devices, irrespective of their use for peaceful or military purposes. Still, the implications of Article V remain vague for the permissibility of operating nuclear-powered surface vessels or nuclear-armed ballistic-missile-carrying submarines in the region south of 60° south latitude. Given diplomatic difficulties in the late 1980s involving New Zealand and Japan over port visitation rights by U.S. vessels possibly carrying nuclear weapons, the potential for similar problems between these same ATCPS in Antarctic waters should not be ignored.

The degree to which the Antarctic Treaty is successful depends upon the political will of governments in general and the consultative party states in particular. If that political commitment degenerates, the demilitarized character of the Antarctic could erode. State practice since 1961 has revealed that sustained political commitment can effectively promote disarmament, that governments will pursue such policies, and that significant payoffs are available for all participants in the process. The chief challenge is to make the policy commitment worthwhile to all parties. In sum, the disarmament process only works if the parties want it to do so. The critical ingredient is stability, which is reinforced through mutual confidence.

The Antarctic Treaty merits appreciation for its preventive character. It aims to discourage activities that might produce conflict. As a consequence, the treaty contains elements that foster confidence-building: scientific exchange and peaceful cooperation are given preference over rivalry and competition; a precisely designated demilitarized zone is fixed for the region; free access to and open inspection of all facilities there is guaranteed to all governments; and special provisions are included for dispute settlement, should the need ever arise. These features are intended to promote reciprocal trust and confidence in the treaty's successful operation.

State compliance with the disarmament mandate throughout the Antarctic has clearly been met. Importantly, that success is derived neither from regulatory provisions in a treaty, nor from binding moral obligations concomitant with pledges of good-faith formal consent to those provisions. Rather, a disarmed, demilitarized condition in the Antarctic has been accomplished and sustained by the ability of the consultative party governments to articulate policy attitudes clearly with one other. These governments have communicated directly and candidly on Antarctic matters since treaty negotiations began in the late 1950s and have fostered genuine standards of reliability and trustworthiness. This self-sustaining trust and mutual confidence further promotes communication among those governments and actually reinforces and clarifies their mutual policy expectations.

One real advantage that has substantially facilitated legal compliance with disarmament in the Antarctic has been the genuine disinterest of the superpowers—or any state, for that matter—in using the region for ballistic missile bases. In fact, the emphasis on land-based ICBMS, submarine launchers, and outer space trajectories in strategic policy since the 1960s actually riveted U.S. and Soviet military attention on their homelands, and away from Antarctica. At the same time, no other governments were enthusiastic about allocating scarce military resources to the Antarctic. Little strategic advantage would be gained, and much could be lost by exacerbating greater international tension and flux in the region. Tempering and dissuading rivalry among states interested in the Antarctic has remained key to explaining the successful longevity of disarmament in that region.

Ancillary Antarctic Disarmament Agreements

The Antarctic Treaty is not alone in legally substantiating and politically sustaining disarmament throughout the Antarctic. Other international arms control instruments shore up legal obligations to sustain conditions of disarmament and demilitarization in the Antarctic because of their universal global application. The 1963 Treaty Banning Nuclear Weapon Tests in the Atmosphere, in Outer Space and Under Water stipulates that parties prohibit any nuclear explosion at any place under their jurisdiction or control, "in the atmosphere; beyond its limits, including outer space; or under water, including territorial waters or high seas." This latter reference obviously encompasses the Antarctic/Southern Ocean region. The 1971 Treaty on the Prohibition of the Emplacement of Nuclear Weapons and Other Weapons of Mass Destruction on the Sea-Bed and the Ocean Floor and in the Sub-Soil Thereof is also applicable to Antarctic ocean space. As provided for in Article I, states party to this instrument "undertake not to emplant or emplace on the seabed and the ocean floor and in the subsoil thereof beyond the outer limit of a seabed zone . . . any nuclear weapons or any other types of weapons of mass destruction as well as structures, launching installations or any other facilities specifically designed for storing, testing or using such weapons." When linked with the Nuclear Test Ban Treaty mentioned above, this agreement neatly complements the prohibitions contained in Article V of the Antarctic Treaty for the ocean space south of 60° south latitude.

Disarmament throughout the Antarctic is advanced by two other relevant international agreements. In the 1972 Convention on the Prohibition of the Development, Production and Stockpiling of Bacteriological (Biological) and Toxin Weapons and on Their Destruction, Article IV asserts in relevant part that "each State Party . . . shall, in accordance with its constitutional processes, take any necessary measures to prohibit and prevent the development, production, stockpiling, acquisition or retention of [microbial or other] agents, toxins, weapons, equipment and means of delivery . . . within the territory of such State, under its jurisdiction or under its control anywhere." The notion of "anywhere" perforce makes the convention legally relevant to the Antarctic; consequently, it would pertain to appropriate state activities there. Similarly, the 1977 Convention on the Prohibition of Military or any Other Hostile Use of Environmental Modification Techniques (ENMOD) forbids parties from utilizing military or other hostile environmental techniques against any other state party. As mandated in Article 4, each state party is charged with the responsibility of taking measures to prohibit and prevent violations of this convention "anywhere under its jurisdiction or control." Once again, because the area of application is designated as "anywhere," Antarctica and its circumpolar waters unmistakably fall within the legal ambit of this multilateral accord's jurisdiction.

Although these latter four international instruments are broad in scope, not all parties to the Antarctic Treaty, nor even all Antarctic Treaty Consultative Party governments, have signed or ratified them. But it would be improper to conclude that nonparty ATCP states are not bound by the prohibitions contained in them. To violate these provisions would in essence violate the peaceful-uses-only and disarmament provisions of the Antarctic Treaty, to which all ATCPS are formally obligated. These four arms control conventions actually serve to buttress the Antarctic Treaty's general obligation to disarm and demilitarize the region, rather than to create any new legal obligations.

Challenges to the Antarctic Disarmament Regime

The Antarctic has been formally demilitarized since 1959. Even so, prospects for the region have been complicated by several events since that time. Past success does not ensure future success. At least four main challenges to the present Antarctic Treaty system are apparent, each of which could upset the disarmament scheme in the region.

The first challenge relates to the Antarctic Treaty's possible breakdown or foundering. Two distinct scenarios suggesting the treaty's debilitation appear conceivable, albeit not likely. For one, in Article XII of the Antarctic Treaty the opportunity is given for convening a special conference to review the treaty operation thirty years after it enters into force, that is, after 23 June 1991. This proviso should neither be construed to mean that such a conference must occur in 1991 or thereafter, nor that the Antarctic Treaty expires in 1991. Neither of these presumptions is correct. The stipulation does mean, however, that such a review conference is possible if any Antarctic Treaty Consultative Party, including any of the fourteen entrants since 1961, should decide for whatever reason that a review of the treaty should be undertaken. Moreover, if such a review conference were to meet, that would not necessarily signify fatal difficulties for the treaty system. The real concern is that such a meeting might provide opportunities for disagreements to surface over suggested amendments to or modifications of the treaty—disagreements that could produce open political fissures and possibly lead to disintegration of ATCP unity and consensus. Should this come to pass, some dissatisfied ATCP state could be tempted to pursue military activities in the Antarctic. Nevertheless, prevailing opinion among ATCPS suggests that scant possibility exists that such developments will occur.

The other scenario involving treaty collapse is prompted by the competition for economic interests in the Antarctic, especially adverse political fallout from a controversy over the need for a regulatory minerals regime in the Antarctic versus formal declaration of Antarctica into the status of a "world park." In 1988 a convention to regulate Antarctic mineral resource development was opened for signature by the ATCPS. Within a year, however, that agreement was sunk when two critical governments, Australia and France, decided not to participate. Instead, they advocated establishment of an international wilderness reserve status for Antarctica, bolstered by a total ban on mining activities on the continent. This abrupt, open break with the other ATCPS touched off a political schism between pro-mining states (led by the United Kingdom, Japan, and United States) and a pro-environmentalist bloc (including Australia, France, Belgium, Italy, and New Zealand). The upshot has been the demise of the minerals agreement, superseded by new negotiations that in 1991 produced a protocol for comprehensively protecting the Antarctic environment. While comprehensive environmental protection is certainly welcome for the Antarctic, the sudden, complete reversal of priorities by two

states after six years of intense negotiations on a minerals regime could leave a residue of political bitterness and resentment among many ATCP governments. If so, that legacy of disaffection could generate negative repercussions later for Antarctic decisions, perhaps even with disruptive policy implications.

As the second major challenge to the Antarctic Treaty system, ATCP rivalries elsewhere might intensify and spill over into the Antarctic region. A stark example was the Falklands/Malvinas War between Argentina and the United Kingdom in 1982. Other geopolitical rivalries might also prick political sensitivities between ATCP states. Border disputes have historically strained relations between Argentina and Chile. Certain political tensions have encumbered relations between the Soviet Union and the People's Republic of China, Brazil and Argentina, and of course, the United States and the Soviet Union. As of 1991, however, these governments seem convinced that their interests are better served by preserving the Antarctic as a disarmed, demilitarized region.

A third broad challenge to the contemporary Antarctic Treaty system may arise from possible application of the "common heritage of mankind" notion to Antarctica and the effort by some developing states in the United Nations General Assembly to attain this end. Certain implications of this scenario are apparent: If Antarctica were established by the international community as part of the common heritage, the Antarctic Treaty Consultative Parties would lose legal justification for maintaining their access to both living and nonliving resources in the region. Under such a regime, Antarctic resources would become the patrimony of all peoples, exempt from national or corporate appropriation, and most revenues derived from exploitation would be allocated to further development opportunities of countries in the third world.

Today, attainment of such a regime is more theoretical fiction than realistic fact. The notions of common heritage of mankind and "new international economic order" have largely receded from public consideration. Changes within the Antarctic Treaty system will likely have to come from the membership itself, in particular from the ATCPS. Given U.N. General Assembly sessions since the question of Antarctica was first introduced there in 1983, that body seems more likely to produce rhetoric and nonbinding resolutions, rather than actual political or legal changes in Antarctic affairs.

There is, finally, the possibility that some government might unilaterally opt to resort to military-related activities in the Antarctic region. Reports during the late 1980s alleged that military activities may be associated with operational uses of United States Antarctic stations, and these could constitute violations of the disarmament provisions of the treaty at least in the spirit, if not in the letter of the law. Such allegations remain speculative and unsubstantiated, and may very well be politically motivated in their own right. Nonetheless, if conclusive proof were offered that some state had consciously violated the treaty's disarmament provisions, that revelation would probably undercut the credibility of that state in future Antarctic policies. It would also produce troublesome ramifications throughout the entire Antarctic Treaty system, and might even engender the emergence of new international rivalries within the region.

CONCLUSION

The geopolitical realities of the current Antarctic Treaty system are clear. The regime governing activities in the Antarctic is lawful and binding upon those states that have subscribed to it. The group of consultative parties includes the superpowers, all the acknowledged nuclear weapon states, and all the permanent members of the U.N. Security Council. Moreover, these twenty-six states represent the population of more than two-thirds of all humanity.

Since 1961, the Antarctic Treaty system has functioned exceedingly well as the institutional framework for preserving peace and stability, fostering scientific cooperation, and promoting standards for environmental preservation and conservation. The present Antarctic legal regime has well served the international community's general interests by responsibly accommodating, through legal means, geopolitical concerns in the south polar region. This is no less true of the treaty's accomplishment in preserving, through legal obligations, the disarmed, demilitarized, and denuclearized status of the Antarctic/Southern Ocean area.

The Antarctic Treaty today remains the preeminent international legal instrument embodying the twin processes of disarmament and nonnuclearization. As such, it stands out as an exemplar of international cooperation and constructive diplomacy, particularly for promoting the reduction of military activities on a regional basis. Through the Antarctic Treaty, one-tenth of the earth's surface has been formally disarmed and made subject to peaceful uses only—a fiat that has been strictly adhered to by involved governments without any reported violations. That record of achievement is one that few, if indeed any, other international arms control and disarmament agreements can claim to match.

BIBLIOGRAPHY

Demilitarization of Antarctica   Among the discussions of the arms control features of the Antarctic agreement are HARRY A. ALMOND, "Demilitarization and Arms Control: Antarctica," *Case Western Reserve Journal of International Law* 17:2 (1985): 229–284; ALAN D. HEMMINGS, "Is Antarctica Demilitarised?" in R. A. HERR, H. R. HALL, and M. G. HAWARD, eds., *Antarctica's Future: Continuity Or Change?* (Hobart, Tasmania, 1990): 225–242; and PETER J. BECK, "Antarctica As a Zone of Peace: A Strategic Irrelevance?" in R. A. HERR, H. R. HALL and M. G. HAWARD, eds., *Antarctica's Future: Continuity or Change?* (Hobart, Tasmania, 1990): 193–224.

Issues Confronting the Treaty   CHRISTOPHER C. JOYNER, "Antarctic Treaty Diplomacy: Problems, Prospects, and Policy Implications," in DAVID NEWSOM, ed., *The Diplomatic Record* (Boulder, Colo., 1990): 137–162; and M. J. PETERSON, *Managing the Frozen South: The Creation and Evolution of the Antarctic Treaty System* (Berkeley, Calif., 1988) review the nature of the changing agreement regulating the region and the possible changes in store. One area in which issues have been raised is the mining of Antarctica's mineral resources and the impact such activity would have on the environment. For additional information see CHRISTOPHER C. JOYNER, "The Antarctic Minerals Negotiating Process," *American Journal of International Law* 81 (October 1987): 888–905; CHRISTOPHER C. JOYNER and BLAIR EWING, "Antarctica and the Latin American States: The Interplay of Law, Geopolitics and Environmental Priorities," *Georgetown International Environmental Law Review* 4 (Fall 1991); PHILIP W. QUIGG, *A Pole Apart: The Emerging Issue of Antarctica* (New York, 1983); DEBORAH SHAPLEY, *The Seventh Continent: Antarctica in a Resource Age* (Washington, D.C., 1985); and FRANCISCO ORREGO VICUÑA, ed., *Antarctic Resources Policy: Scientific, Legal, and Political Issues* (New York, 1983).

Geopolitical Concerns International political considerations are examined in L. CAFLISCH and FRED TANNER, eds., *The Polar Regions and Their Strategic Significance* (Geneva, 1989); JACK CHILD, *Frozen Lebensraum: Antarctica and South American Geopolitics* (New York, 1985); CHRISTOPHER C. JOYNER, "Anglo-Argentine Rivalry after the Falklands: On the Road to Antarctica?" in ALBERTO R. COLL and ANTHONY C. AREND, eds., *The Falklands War: Lessons for Strategy, Diplomacy, and International Law* (Boston, 1985): 189–211; and WALTER SULLIVAN, "Antarctica in a Two-Power World," *Foreign Affairs* 36 (October 1957): 154–166.

Legal Implications The Antarctic Treaty's impact on international law is examined by F. M. AUBURN, *Antarctic Law and Politics* (Bloomington, Ind., 1982); W. M. BUSH, ed., *Antarctica and International Law, A Collection of Inter-State and National Documents,* 3 vols. (New York, 1982–1988); CHRISTOPHER C. JOYNER and ETHEL R. THEIS, "The United States and Antarctica: Rethinking the Interplay of Law and Interests," *Cornell International Law Journal* 20 (Winter 1987): 65–102; and CHRISTOPHER C. JOYNER and SUDHIR K. CHOPRA, eds., *The Antarctic Legal Regime* (The Hague, 1988).

Test Ban Proposals and Agreements

The 1950s to the Present

———————————— ◯ ————————————

BENJAMIN S. LOEB

See also The Non-Proliferation Treaty and the Review Conferences: 1965 to the Present; Nuclear-Weapon-Free Zones; *and* the United Nations and Disarmament. *Most of the treaties discussed in this essay are excerpted in Volume III.*

Beginning in the mid-1950s the banning of nuclear tests became one of the most persistent, yet elusive objects of arms control. Beginning with Dwight D. Eisenhower, a succession of U.S. presidents made a comprehensive test ban (CTB) a stated objective. They varied greatly, however, in the earnestness with which they pursued that objective and in the preconditions they specified. Eisenhower initiated technical discussions and tripartite (U.S.-British-Soviet) test ban negotiations, but succeeded only in achieving an informal test moratorium. President John F. Kennedy intensified the effort to reach a CTB, but after a number of concessions in U.S. verification requirements proved insufficient to satisfy the Soviets, he settled in 1963 for the multilateral Limited Test Ban Treaty (LTBT) which banned all tests except those underground. President Lyndon B. Johnson's support of further limitations on testing was primarily rhetorical. The main arms control emphasis during his administration was on negotiating the multilateral Non-Proliferation Treaty (NPT), signed in 1968. In the NPT, however, the superpowers pledged to pursue disarmament negotiations in good faith. Progress toward a CTB came to be the key criterion employed by non-nuclear-weapon states for judging compliance with this undertaking. Richard M. Nixon's administration emphasized strategic-arms negotiations over test ban negotiations, but in 1974 reached agreement with the Soviet Union on the bilateral Threshold Test Ban Treaty (TTBT) banning underground tests above 150 kilotons. In 1976, during Gerald Ford's presidency, the companion Peaceful Nuclear Explosions Treaty (PNET), with a similar limit, was negotiated. Jimmy Carter's administration resumed CTB negotiations and made rapid progress at first, but a lack of political will on both sides prevented agreement.

Intent on augmenting and modernizing the U.S. nuclear arsenal, Ronald Reagan's administration relegated a CTB to the status of "ultimate goal," emphasizing instead various problems in verifying the TTBT and PNET, which had not yet been ratified. They were ratified in December 1990, following some cooperative U.S.-Soviet endeavors regarding verification. Also in 1990, an international effort to amend the LTBT so as to ban underground tests was blocked by President George Bush, whose attitude toward a CTB was similar to Reagan's. In 1992, France joined Russia in declaring a moratorium on tests and in implying that continuation of the moratorium would depend on whether the United States followed suit. Both houses of Congress voted for a U.S. moratorium. While continuing to oppose a moratorium, the Bush administration announced a modification of its testing policy whereby it would limit the number of tests each year to six, of which no more than three would exceed thirty-five kilotons, and would mandate that tests be carried out only for safety and reliability.

The history of test ban proposals and agreements is considered at greater length below. Following the historical account is a summation of arguments that have been made for and against further test limitations.

EISENHOWER: NEGOTIATIONS BEGIN

The idea of banning nuclear tests first surfaced in 1954, following a huge U.S. test near Bikini Atoll in the Pacific. Because of a yield twice that expected—equivalent to fifteen megatons, the largest explosion ever detonated by the United States—and because of unfavorable wind conditions, the test contaminated wide areas of the Marshall Islands and showered a Japanese tuna trawler with radioactive debris. The crew of twenty-three suffered from severe radiation sickness and one crew member subsequently died. This event touched off a series of protests led by some of the world's most respected public figures. A month after the test, Prime Minister Jawaharlal Nehru of India proposed a "standstill agreement" on nuclear testing. Similar proposals soon emanated from others.

The initial U.S. government reaction to this agitation was to insist that nuclear testing was both safe and necessary. Some American scientists took issue with these contentions, however, pointing to the hazards from radioactive fallout. A spirited controversy soon arose among scientists on both sides of the fallout issue. For their part, the Soviets began including a test ban in their panoply of arms control proposals, but they linked it to visionary general disarmament schemes that had no chance of being accepted by the United States.

In 1956 Adlai Stevenson injected the nuclear testing issue into his presidential campaign against President Eisenhower, advocating a ban on large tests. Stevenson's effort to make his proposal a major campaign issue was undercut, however, when Soviet Premier Nikolai Bulganin publicly supported it in a letter to Eisenhower. In discussions at the United Nations, the United States took the position that in the absence of any agreement to eliminate or limit nuclear weapons under proper safeguards, continued testing was essential for the national interest and for the security of the free world. Eisen-

hower emphasized, however, that new precautions were being taken to minimize radioactive fallout from U.S. tests.

In 1957 the scale of international protests against atmospheric tests mushroomed. A radio appeal by Albert Schweitzer was heard in fifty countries and endorsed by the pope. American scientist Linus Pauling obtained the signatures of more than nine thousand scientists from forty-three countries to an antitesting petition. Perhaps most significant to the Eisenhower administration, a Gallup poll showed that 63 percent of the American people favored a test ban, as against only 20 percent three years earlier. In response to these pressures, the United States announced that it would consider stopping or limiting testing if verification issues could be settled.

Following the first British hydrogen-bomb test in May 1957, the Soviet Union proposed a ban on further such tests. A month later, the Soviets proposed a two- to three-year moratorium on all tests, to be supervised by an international commission utilizing unmanned instrumented detection stations ("black boxes") on the soil of the nuclear powers. President Eisenhower at first indicated that he was favorably disposed toward the Soviet offer, but he changed course after Atomic Energy Commission (AEC) scientists led by Edward Teller argued that with continued testing they could develop within seven years fallout-free battlefield weapons vital to NATO's strategy in Western Europe. They warned also that the Soviet Union could evade any moratorium by clandestine tests.

Placed on the defensive by continued international and domestic pressures for an end to tests, Eisenhower offered in August 1957 to accept a two-year moratorium on testing if it were linked to a cutoff in the further production of fissionable material. The Soviets promptly rejected this idea, perceiving it as freezing their inferiority in nuclear-weapons production.

After the Soviet Union launched *Sputniks I* and *II* in the autumn of 1957, calling into question the presumed superiority of U.S. science and technology, President Eisenhower moved to strengthen the scientific resources of his administration by establishing the President's Science Advisory Committee. This group gave Eisenhower sources of advice more disposed toward a test ban, counterbalancing negative counsel he had been getting from Lewis Strauss, who was both the AEC chairman and a presidential assistant. Secretary of State John Foster

Dulles, seeking to reverse the diplomatic embarrassments the testing issue was causing for the United States, also began to advocate greater flexibility. When the Soviet Union again proposed a three-year uninspected moratorium late in 1957, it was ultimately rejected by Eisenhower, but not until there had been an extended debate within the government.

A high-level internal debate on the test ban question continued into 1958, taking place principally before a Senate Disarmament Subcommittee chaired by Hubert Humphrey. The subcommittee provided a conspicuous sounding board for various peace groups and prominent individuals who perceived in a test ban the most practical means of starting the process of controlling nuclear arms.

In March 1958, Nikita Khrushchev, the new premier of the Soviet Union, pushed through a decree prohibiting further testing by his country, provided others did not test. While this move was transparently cynical—the Soviets had just completed a major test series and the United States was about to start one—it earned the Soviet Union much credit in world opinion. Notwithstanding, all three nuclear powers continued to test.

In April 1958 a panel of scientists headed by Cornell University physics professor Hans Bethe reported to President Eisenhower that the U.S. nuclear arsenal was sufficient to permit a test ban without endangering national security and that such a treaty would be to the nation's advantage. The president thereupon proposed to Khrushchev that the Soviet Union join Western nations in examination of the technical requirements for verification of a test ban. Khrushchev agreed, and on 1 July 1958 the Conference of Experts to Study the Possibility of Detecting Violations of a Possible Agreement on Suspension of Nuclear Tests convened in Geneva, Switzerland. Eight nations were represented, four from Eastern Europe and four from the West.

Late in August the Conference of Experts announced its conclusion: it was indeed technically feasible to set up a control system that would (1) have a "good probability" of detecting atmospheric explosions yielding as little as one kiloton if the explosions were detonated at a height below fifty kilometers (30 miles) and (2) be able to detect, and distinguish from earthquakes, underground explosions yielding as little as five kilotons. The system, which became known as the Geneva System, would have required ten ships and 160–170 land-based instrumented control posts, each to be manned by thirty to forty technicians and scientists. In addition, the system would have involved the possible dispatch of on-site inspection teams to investigate suspicious events.

Encouraged by the conference's optimistic findings, Eisenhower proposed that the three nuclear powers meet to negotiate a treaty based on the Geneva System. At the same time, reversing the stand he had taken only two years earlier in his election campaign against Stevenson, the president announced that the United States would suspend tests for a year while negotiations proceeded, provided that the Soviet Union did the same. Khrushchev promptly agreed.

After both sides rushed to complete a number of tests, the tripartite (U.S., U.K., USSR) Conference on the Discontinuance of Nuclear Weapons Tests (known as the Geneva Conference) opened on 31 October 1958. A large measure of agreement and certain differences were apparent at the outset. The differences related primarily to the control system. The main problem was that it was difficult to distinguish in all cases between the seismic signals of underground explosions and those of earthquakes, which were numerous in parts of the Soviet Union. In order to guard against Soviet cheating, the Western powers wanted mandatory on-site inspections to be conducted whenever ambiguous events were detected. Furthermore, they wanted all elements of the control system, including inspection teams, to be manned internationally and operated by majority rule. The Soviets resisted on-site inspections, claiming that they would be pretexts for Western espionage. They also wanted veto power in the control organization and insisted on having all control activities in their territory supervised and predominantly staffed by Soviet personnel.

Analysis of a U.S. test series late in 1958 indicated that the Conference of Experts had probably overestimated the ability of the Geneva System to detect and identify underground tests. U.S. studies also suggested that there were various ways to evade a test ban, such as by exploding a nuclear device in a large underground cavity to conceal its true magnitude. These findings cast a pall over the Geneva Conference, which soon bogged down over related verification issues. In order to break the deadlock, Eisenhower suggested in April 1959 that agreement be reached in phases, beginning with a ban on tests thought easy to verify without inspections—namely, those in the atmosphere up to a height of fifty kilometers. Khrushchev rejected Eisenhower's proposal as a "dishonest deal" on the basis that it would permit the United States to continue tests in nonprohibited environments. As an alternative, Khrushchev proposed that consideration be given to an earlier suggestion he said had been made by British Prime Minister Harold Macmillan—namely, that there be a comprehensive test ban monitored in part by a fixed annual quota of on-site inspections on the territory of each nuclear power. The Soviet leader's view was that this annual quota need not be large. Both Eisenhower and Macmillan agreed to explore the idea.

To fill a remaining gap in the Geneva System's capabilities, technical talks were held in June 1959 regarding the verification of high-altitude explosions. The conferees agreed, with some reservations, that such tests could be detected from five or six satellites placed in earth orbit. Eisenhower then announced in August 1959 that he was extending the U.S. test moratorium until the end of the year. Toward the end of the year, however, another tripartite technical working group, convened to consider the criteria for dispatch of inspection teams, disbanded in disagreement so profound that no report was possible. This led to an angry statement by Eisenhower condemning "politically guided" Soviet experts who had resisted every implication that the new U.S. data argued for a greater number of on-site inspections. Eisenhower also announced that the United States would no longer be bound by the voluntary test moratorium when it expired on 31 December 1959, although the U.S. would give advance notice of any intent to resume testing. In response, the Soviets repeated their pledge not to test unless "Western nations" did so.

In February 1960 the United States and United Kingdom came forward with a new proposal. It would have banned all tests deemed verifiable by the Geneva System, namely, all tests in the atmosphere and underwater, all tests in space to an altitude (unspecified) where verification was feasible, and underground tests producing signals greater than 4.75 on the Richter earthquake-magnitude scale. A joint seismic research program was to be undertaken to lower this threshold. In addition to the seismic stations posited by the Geneva System, the treaty was to be policed by annual quotas of on-site inspections, their numbers to be related to the estimated number of seismic events on the soil of each nuclear power. The formulas suggested in the proposal would have resulted in about twenty inspections each year in the Soviet Union.

The Soviet response a month later was to agree to the Western proposal, with three exceptions: the Soviets wanted to prohibit all tests in space, whether verifiable or not; to initiate the treaty with a four- to five-year moratorium on smaller underground tests; and to determine inspection quotas on a "political" basis, unrelated to the number of seismic events. Eisenhower and Macmillan promptly agreed to accept a moratorium on smaller underground tests, though only for two years. Many expected that the remaining differences could be resolved at a Big Four (United States, United Kingdom, USSR, France) summit conference scheduled to begin in Paris on 16 May.

Into this hopeful atmosphere Khrushchev hurled his dramatic announcement of 7 May 1960 that a U.S. U-2 reconnaissance plane had been downed over Soviet territory six days earlier. The Paris summit meeting then collapsed after two hours of bitter recrimination. These developments so fouled the relationships between the superpowers and between their leaders that no further progress could be made while Eisenhower was president. Notwithstanding, Eisenhower steadfastly resisted the pressures from the Pentagon and the AEC for renewed testing until the end of his term, and handed over to his successor an ongoing negotiation during which important agreements had been reached and remaining issues clearly identified. Eisenhower later said that his greatest regret about his presidency had been his failure to achieve a test ban agreement.

On 5 December 1960 the Geneva Conference adjourned to give the incoming Kennedy administration an opportunity to examine its position.

KENNEDY AND THE LIMITED TEST BAN TREATY

While in the Senate, John F. Kennedy had opposed pressures for resumption of U.S. testing during the moratorium that began in 1958, and made the need for a nuclear test ban agreement a principal personal theme. Kennedy brought with him into office a top team that was in strong agreement with his own desire for a test ban. The most important new officials involved in the test ban issue were Secretary of State Dean Rusk, Secretary of Defense

Robert S. McNamara, AEC chairman Glenn T. Seaborg, disarmament adviser John J. McCloy, and science adviser Jerome B. Wiesner.

Having requested a delay in the resumption of the Geneva Conference, Kennedy used the time for a thorough review, spearheaded by McCloy, of U.S. policy toward the negotiations. Early in March 1961 a panel of scientists headed by Bell Laboratories president James B. Fisk generally confirmed that a fully implemented Geneva System would be adequate to deter a potential violator. In addition, a team led by Kennedy's chief negotiator, Arthur H. Dean, undertook a painstaking review of all 250 Geneva Conference negotiating sessions to determine whether concessions could be made to the Soviet position without endangering U.S. security.

When the conference resumed in March 1961, the United States and United Kingdom offered again what was basically the Western 4.75 seismic magnitude threshold proposal of February 1960, but attempted to make it more palatable by offering a number of concessions. For example, they reduced slightly the number of internationally manned inspection posts proposed for location on Soviet soil, and granted the Soviet request for East-West parity in staffing the control organization. Wide differences still remained, however. One concerned a new Soviet insistence that the control organization be headed by a three-man directorate, one from the West, one from the East, and one neutral, each with veto power. The Soviets also offered to accept only three on-site inspections per year, as against a Western formula that would have required about twenty, and only fifteen inspection posts on Soviet soil, as against a Western demand for nineteen. Notwithstanding the lack of agreement, the Western side presented its proposals on 18 April 1961 in the form of a complete draft treaty, the first to be submitted by either side. Continuing their absolutist approach, the Soviets promptly rejected the draft treaty, arguing that it allowed the United States to continue to test underground.

In light of the Soviet intransigence at Geneva, Kennedy came under increasing internal pressure to resume testing. Informed by U.S. embassies around the world that reaction to such a step would be adverse, Kennedy at first ruled against it, while indicating that his patience had limits. His attitude hardened, however, when he encountered a confident and bellicose Khrushchev at their summit meeting in Vienna in June 1961. After this sobering

experience, Kennedy ordered secret preparations for resumed testing. The following month, a Gallup poll showed that the American public now favored such a step by a two-to-one margin.

A crisis over Berlin erupted during the summer of 1961, and on 13 August, East Germany closed its western border and began construction of the Berlin Wall. The Soviet Union, citing continued French tests and the international tension over Berlin, then announced on 30 August its decision to resume testing. This decision took the United States by surprise—a signal failure of U.S. intelligence. The Soviet series, which began the next day, was massive and had obviously been long in preparation. Within sixty days the Soviets conducted approximately fifty tests, exceeding in total megatonnage all preceding tests by all nations. Several of the tests were conducted high in the atmosphere and at very high yields; one of them yielded fifty-seven megatons, still the largest man-made explosion ever.

Although embittered by the Soviet action, Kennedy made one more attempt to seize the diplomatic high ground. On 2 September 1961 he and Macmillan proposed an atmospheric test ban, giving the Soviet Union a week to reply. When the Soviets rejected the offer, Kennedy announced that the United States would resume testing "in the laboratory and underground, with no fallout." The U.S. test series, a relatively modest effort, began on 15 September. Soon after, Kennedy asked the AEC to begin preparations for atmospheric testing, and on 2 November he announced that the United States intended to conduct such tests.

Kennedy committed himself to atmospheric testing with obvious reluctance, and he attempted to rein in the test series as much as possible. He directed, for example, that each test be personally approved by him, that fallout be minimized, that the test planners scale down the number of tests they were recommending, and that the series last no longer than three months. Late in November 1961 the Soviets proposed a treaty that would have banned tests in the atmosphere, in space, and underwater unconditionally and, in addition, would have banned underground tests temporarily until controls over them could be established as part of a treaty on general and complete disarmament (GCD). Considering the remoteness of any prospect for GCD, the provision on underground tests seemed tantamount to another uncontrolled moratorium. After the bitter experience with the Soviet resumption of testing in September, this was something the United States would not consider.

In January 1962 the three-power Geneva Conference, hopelessly deadlocked, terminated its work. Under the pressure of world opinion, negotiations for a test ban nevertheless resumed, being conducted after March 1962 at a newly established United Nations Eighteen Nation Disarmament Committee (ENDC) composed of five Western, five Eastern, and eight nonaligned countries. (In fact, only seventeen nations participated: France, one of the designated Western participants, refused to take part.) The neutral eight, under the goading leadership of Sweden's Alva Myrdal, were to play a very active role in the ENDC, constantly pushing East and West to negotiate and coming forward with innovative proposals of their own. U.S. participation was now coordinated by a new agency, the Arms Control and Disarmament Agency, established by Congress in September 1961 to provide more thorough research as well as better-prepared negotiators.

At the first meeting of the ENDC, the British and U.S. representatives proposed that there be a fully comprehensive treaty; that inspections for the most part be confined to seismic areas of the Soviet Union, far from sensitive industrial areas; and that each side be permitted periodic inspections of the other's test sites to assure against secret test preparations. The Soviets rejected the new proposals, insisting that any test ban should rely solely on each side's national means of detection, without any inspections.

The U.S. atmospheric test series, Operation DOMINIC, began on 25 April 1962. The series comprised forty tests, four small ones in Nevada and the remainder in the Pacific. Pursuant to President Kennedy's instructions, the total yield of the series was held to approximately twenty megatons; the Soviet series in 1961 had yielded almost ten times as much. DOMINIC was marred by a number of mishaps. In the most serious of these, a high-altitude test called STARFISH contravened predictions by AEC scientists when it left behind a new radiation belt in space, destroying the communications capability of three satellites and leading Kennedy to cancel a more powerful succeeding test. The STARFISH incident caused Secretary Rusk and other senior officials to lose confidence in the AEC testing program and added to the pressures for an agreement that would ban such tests in the future.

DOMINIC lasted some six months, twice as long as Kennedy had first instructed. Before the series ended, the Soviets began another extensive series of their own, claiming that, since the United States had tested first, they had "the right to test last."

While the tests of both countries proceeded, the atmosphere at the ENDC in Geneva was saturated with mutual recriminations. Kennedy nevertheless persisted in what seemed an almost quixotic quest of a test ban. His principal motive, as he told his associates, was to arrest the spread of nuclear weapons to additional nations, a prospect that he regarded as "the greatest possible danger." Accordingly, on 27 August 1962 the United States and the United Kingdom unveiled two new treaty proposals at the ENDC. One was for a fully comprehensive treaty, with no threshold. The other was for a limited treaty, banning tests in the atmosphere, in outer space, and underwater. Although Kennedy and Macmillan both expressed a strong preference for the comprehensive treaty, the limited one was included in case Khrushchev persisted in his opposition to inspections.

Verification of the limited treaty was to be accomplished solely by national technical means. The comprehensive treaty was also to be policed by seismic stations and on-site inspections on the soil of the nuclear powers. While the number of stations and inspections was not specified, the United States made it clear that new data from its seismic research program would allow in both cases for a lesser number than had previously been proposed. There was no negotiation over these numbers, however, since the Soviet Union promptly rejected both treaties—the comprehensive one because of its inspection requirements and the limited one because it permitted underground testing to continue.

In October 1962 the world was shaken by the Cuban missile crisis. A paradoxical effect of this brush with catastrophe was that it seemed to draw Kennedy and Khrushchev closer together. Their correspondence quickened, each expressing a desire to make progress in arms control. The world community also stepped up its pressure. In November two resolutions favoring a test ban were adopted by the U.N. General Assembly, and the neutral eight came forward with a new proposal at the ENDC. While the Soviet Union still resisted on-site inspections, it was willing now to have international personnel set up black boxes on its territory and make readings.

Progress was set back for a while by a misunderstanding over the number of on-site inspections. On 19 December, Khrushchev, in a long letter to

Kennedy, wrote that he had persuaded his Council of Ministers, as a political concession to the U.S. Senate, to accept two or three on-site inspections per year, having been informed that Ambassador Dean had told Deputy Foreign Minister V. V. Kuznetsov that this number would satisfy the United States. Kennedy wrote back that there had been a misunderstanding, that what Dean had mentioned was a minimum of eight, not three. Khrushchev later told *Saturday Review* editor Norman Cousins that while he accepted the explanation that there had been an honest misunderstanding, this incident had made him look foolish among his colleagues, and he would not allow that to happen again.

Further correspondence between the two leaders led to a brief negotiation in New York in January 1963 in a vain effort to resolve the differences about on-site inspections. In these talks the Soviets refused to budge on the number of inspections and refused to discuss at all the procedures the West proposed for conducting them. These proposed procedures were very rigorous and intrusive, involving, for example, helicopter flights covering up to five hundred square kilometers (two hundred square miles) in each inspection. Thus, even had agreement been reached on the number of inspections, there probably still would have been disagreement about the procedures.

Despite all discouragements, Kennedy persisted. In February 1963 he proposed a radical new approach toward a comprehensive treaty. The whole concept of an international control organization and of an elaborate international seismic detection system would be eliminated. Verification would be by each side's national systems, supplemented by seven black boxes on the soil of each nuclear power and up to seven inspections per year of events that, on the basis of seismic data, could not be identified as earthquakes. He further authorized U.S. negotiators to accept an on-site inspection quota of six, having by now lowered the number successively from twenty, to twelve, to ten, to eight, to seven, and now to six. The Soviets remained unyielding, however, threatening at times even to withdraw their offer of three.

In April 1963, following a suggestion by Macmillan, Kennedy and the prime minister proposed to Khrushchev that they each send senior representatives to Moscow to talk directly and privately with him, bypassing the deadlocked public negotiations in Geneva. Khrushchev assented, though in a surly

tone that offered little encouragement. (His tough public stance may well have been due to his insecurity as head of government following the setback over Cuba.) To improve the atmosphere, Kennedy directed that three scheduled tests in Nevada be postponed indefinitely. He then delivered a masterfully wrought, conciliatory speech at American University in Washington, D.C., on 10 June 1963. In it, he paid tribute to the achievements and wartime sacrifices of the Soviet people, portrayed with chilling realism the dangers of a hot war and the costs of the Cold War, and discussed the mutual interest of the two superpowers and their allies "in a just and genuine peace and in halting the arms race." Kennedy concluded by announcing the forthcoming negotiations in Moscow and by declaring that the United States would not test further in the atmosphere as long as other nations did not do so. The speech had an electric effect on the Soviet leadership. It was printed and broadcast in the Soviet media. Jamming of Western broadcasts, which had been going on for fifteen years, ceased overnight. Another straw in the wind, a sign that reasonable accommodation of differences was possible, was the signing on 20 June 1963 of a long-pending agreement to establish a private teletype link, the "hot line," between Washington and Moscow, for activation in critical situations.

When the Moscow negotiations began on 15 July 1963, Undersecretary of State W. Averell Harriman, heading the small American negotiating team, was instructed to seek first a comprehensive test ban treaty. By this time, however, it was all but certain that such a treaty was beyond reach. In addition to several indications Kennedy had received that the comprehensive treaty then being proposed by the West probably would not clear the U.S. Senate, there had been a speech by Khrushchev on 2 July repeating Soviet objections to its requirement of on-site inspections. The Soviet Union, Khrushchev said, would never "open its doors to NATO spies." He made clear, however, that he was quite willing to conclude a limited treaty. Accordingly, after ten days of often intense negotiations, closely monitored and supervised by President Kennedy, the Treaty Banning Nuclear Weapon Tests in the Atmosphere, Outer Space, and Under Water (the Limited Test Ban Treaty, or LTBT) was initialed in Moscow by the principal negotiators on 25 July 1963.

While this result was achieved in a good atmosphere and with relative speed, several contentious issues had to be resolved during the negotiations.

One was an attempt by Soviet Foreign Minister Andrei Gromyko, chief Soviet negotiator, to link the treaty with a NATO-Warsaw Pact nonaggression agreement. Harriman indicated he had no authority to negotiate such a pact on behalf of the NATO allies. Another problem was the Soviet objection to a U.S. proposal that nuclear explosions for peaceful purposes (excavating canals, etc.) be exempted from the treaty's prohibitions. Harriman was instructed to give up on this exemption in exchange for a clause permitting withdrawal from the treaty if events occurred threatening any party's "supreme interests." (It was felt that some senators might want such a withdrawal clause in view of the uncertainties introduced by China's imminent entry into the nuclear club.) Finally, there was an informal agreement that accession to the treaty did not automatically entitle a country to diplomatic recognition by other parties that had previously not recognized it.

In a television speech to the nation, President Kennedy hailed the initialed treaty, not so much for its direct contributions, which he acknowledged to be modest, but as "a first step" along the path to peace. In order to achieve a maximum impact for the treaty, he then sought Senate assent, not by a bare two-thirds majority, but by an overwhelming margin. Kennedy had previously sought to conciliate the Senate by consulting its leaders frequently about U.S. test ban policy. He now also sought to enhance the Senate's dignity and prestige by sending six senators to the signing ceremonies in Moscow on 5 August 1963, having declined Khrushchev's invitation to sign the treaty personally at a summit meeting.

Kennedy recognized that he could not win the overwhelming Senate margin he sought without the assent of the Joint Chiefs of Staff, who had expressed reservations about even a limited test ban on the eve of Harriman's departure for Moscow. Kennedy therefore agreed to four national-security safeguards that the Joint Chiefs put forward as the price for their concurrence: continued vigorous underground testing; continued readiness to resume atmospheric testing; high-level maintenance of the weapons laboratories; and improved capability to detect Soviet treaty violations.

At Senate hearings, the treaty was opposed by weapons laboratory scientists. Edward Teller, for example, voiced concern that the Soviets had gained important military advantages in their 1961–1962 high-altitude high-yield weapons tests, such as in the knowledge of weapons effects and in the ability to develop an effective ballistic missile defense. The existence of such Soviet advantages was disputed by other experts. Treaty proponents pointed to its likely effects in restraining nuclear-weapons proliferation and the hope that it would lead to a further decrease in international tensions. Polls indicated that the American public generally favored the treaty, most of all for its effect in reducing radioactive fallout from atmospheric tests.

At the conclusion of eleven days of hearings, during which it received testimony or statements from forty-four individuals or organizations, the Foreign Relations Committee recommended the treaty to the Senate by a sixteen-to-one margin. The Senate Armed Services Committee's Preparedness Subcommittee, on the other hand, which held hearings confined to the treaty's military aspects, reported on it adversely. The key moments in the floor debate occurred when Everett Dirksen of Illinois, the Republican leader, and Henry Jackson, Democrat of Washington, the senator thought to be most influential on nuclear-weapons matters, both contradicted earlier indications and announced support for the treaty.

The Senate gave its consent to ratification on 24 September 1963 by a vote of eighty to nineteen. President Kennedy signed the documents of ratification for the United States on 7 October, and three days later, following similar actions in London and Moscow, the Limited Test Ban Treaty (also widely referred to as the Partial Test Ban Treaty) went into effect.

By 1992, more than 125 nations had become parties to the treaty. While the identity of nations that had not become parties, including the People's Republic of China, Cuba, France, North Korea, and Vietnam, remained of continuing concern, the two nuclear powers among the nonsignatories, France and China, had conducted no tests in the prohibited environments since 1980.

"No other accomplishment in the White House," wrote presidential assistant Theodore Sorensen, "ever gave Kennedy greater satisfaction" (*Kennedy*, New York, 1965, p. 740). Notwithstanding, it is fair to say that the treaty did not achieve its intended effect of slowing down the arms race. Ironically, by reducing the concern about radioactive fallout, it tended to eliminate nuclear testing as a public issue and thus made the continuation of uninhibited weapons development politically respectable. Thus, in the years after the treaty went into effect, the pace of nuclear testing, albeit underground, actually quickened.

LBJ: THE TEST BAN AND NON-PROLIFERATION

After the Limited Test Ban Treaty (LTBT) went into effect, international pressure for a comprehensive test ban (CTB) continued. On 27 November 1963, five days after the assassination of President Kennedy, the U.N. General Assembly urged in a near-unanimous vote that negotiations for a CTB proceed at the ENDC "with a sense of urgency." While both superpowers voted for this resolution, each made it clear that they were still far apart on the matter of inspections. In fact, the Soviets took the occasion to withdraw their previous offer of three inspections per year.

Within the U.S. government, the mood turned against further limitations on testing. Although a CTB remained part of his stated agenda, President Lyndon Johnson seemed less intent on such a goal than Kennedy had been, preferring to expend his administration's arms control energies on the problem of nuclear-weapons proliferation and on beginning the SALT process. In Congress there was strong emphasis on the implementation of the safeguards Kennedy had negotiated with the Joint Chiefs, particularly of a vigorous underground testing program. U.S. underground testing continued at a high level throughout the Johnson years; in the five years 1964–1968, there were 140 announced U.S. tests, as against 25 by the Soviet Union.

On 30 July 1964, President Johnson issued a statement commemorating the first anniversary of the LTBT. After a passing mention that a year without atmospheric testing had left the air cleaner, the statement placed greatest emphasis on the fact that because of the safeguards the treaty had not impaired the nation's military strength. On 16 October 1964, the People's Republic of China conducted its first nuclear test, underscoring the dangers of further proliferation. During the same week, Nikita Khrushchev was removed from office, and there was a change of government in the United Kingdom. These three events, coming in such close succession, contributed to a general atmosphere of uncertainty about the international situation that added to the administration's wariness on the test ban issue.

Beginning in 1965, consideration of a CTB came more and more to be linked to the ongoing negotiations on a non-proliferation treaty (NPT). Non-nuclear-weapon states were in growing rebellion against what they considered the discriminatory aspects of an NPT; they were being asked to forgo nuclear weapons while the nuclear states continued to enhance their arsenals both quantitatively and qualitatively. In debates at the ENDC it became evident that a CTB was the one measure that the non-nuclears seemed most willing to accept as a quid pro quo for their sacrifice. Indeed, Sweden contended that a CTB would be a more effective non-proliferation measure than the NPT itself, arguing that only by forgoing their own nuclear arms race could the nuclear haves induce the have-nots to accept inferior status. In December 1965 the U.N. General Assembly adopted a resolution urging all nations to suspend tests and requesting the ENDC to continue working for a CTB.

Notwithstanding these pressures, it was decided in discussions within the government not to moderate the U.S. insistence on inspections in a CTB, knowing full well that this stand was increasingly difficult to defend on technical grounds and that it put a treaty out of reach because of the Soviet resistance to inspections. This strategy was based on a judgment by the Joint Chiefs of Staff, not counterbalanced by a strong voice from any other quarter, that continued testing was necessary for the maintenance and further development of the U.S. nuclear deterrent.

The U.S. Arms Control and Disarmament Agency (ACDA) attempted early in 1966 to soften domestic opposition to further test restrictions, recommending that favorable consideration be given to a proposal made by the United Arab Republic at the ENDC. This proposal called for a ban on all tests except those underground with a seismic magnitude below 4.75, the threshold of explosions thought to be detectable by remote seismic means. The ACDA suggestion was rejected within the Johnson administration, largely because it conflicted with the growing movement for development of a U.S. ABM system. An ABM warhead would be a high-yield device, requiring tests well above the 4.75 seismic magnitude threshold.

When the ENDC reconvened in January 1966, Sweden's Alva Myrdal came forward with a novel proposal designed to break the superpower deadlock over inspections in a CTB: if there was a suspected violation and if the country on whose territory the event occurred did not provide a satisfactory explanation, the other side could issue a "challenge for inspection." If the nation under suspicion would not then invite inspection, this could serve as grounds for abrogation of the treaty by the complaining party. In Myrdal's view, such a threat of withdrawal would be a decisive enforcement tool. Both superpowers rejected this proposal, the United States on the grounds that it was not politically sound, the Soviet Union on the grounds that it "pushed inspections." Although the idea of challenge inspections was dismissed on this occasion, more was to be heard of it in later years.

In 1967 two events abroad stiffened U.S. opposition to further test restrictions. One was the discovery of a Soviet ABM deployment around Moscow. This contributed to formulation of a U.S. national objective to develop a "complete new generation of weapons for the strategic offensive forces," with accompanying tests. There was also a felt need in the U.S. military to assess through tests the vulnerability of the Soviet ABMs to the effects of nuclear weapons. The second event was the first Chinese test of a thermonuclear weapon; this occurred on 17 June 1967.

In 1968 the relationship between further test restrictions and non-proliferation became more explicit. At the insistence of non-nuclear nations, the superpowers felt obliged to add to their joint draft of the NPT an Article VI pledging that they would "pursue negotiations in good faith on effective measures relating to cessation of the nuclear arms race at an early date." What most non-nuclear states have regarded as the touchstone for assessing compliance with Article VI was the existence of serious negotiations on a CTB. While the superpowers succeeded in resisting any mention of such a specific undertaking in the body of the NPT, they felt constrained to add to the preamble this paragraph: "Recalling the determination expressed by the Parties to the 1963 [Limited Test Ban] Treaty ... in its Preamble to seek to achieve the discontinuance of all test explosions of nuclear weapons for all time and to continue negotiations to this end."

A further concession to the non-nuclear states was a provision in the NPT that a review conference be held five years after the treaty's entry into force "with a view to assuring that the purposes of the Preamble and the provisions of the Treaty are being realized." The inclusion in this context of the preamble, with its prominent mention of a CTB, was not the superpowers' preference; it was added to the U.S.-Soviet draft treaty at the insistence of the non-nuclear states. Having made this concession, the superpowers intended to provide for only a single review conference. The non-nuclear states insisted, however, that a provision be added calling for further review conferences at additional five-year intervals if so desired by a majority of parties to the treaty, and in fact, such conferences were held in 1975, 1980, 1985, and 1990.

A more critical test lay ahead. Treaty drafts by both superpowers had contemplated an NPT "of unlimited duration." But the non-nuclear nations demurred and forced adoption of a provision requiring that a conference be held twenty-five years after the treaty's entry into force (namely, in 1995) when, by majority vote, parties to the treaty must decide whether it "shall continue in force indefinitely, or shall be extended for an additional fixed period or periods." Some parties felt that if by 1995 there has been no significant progress toward a CTB, a majority of those attending the conference might be unwilling to vote for a long-term extension of the NPT.

NIXON AND FORD: THE THRESHOLD AND PNE TREATIES

In August 1969 the ENDC was expanded from eighteen to twenty-six members and became known thereafter as the Conference of the Committee on Disarmament (CD). (It was later further enlarged to forty members.) Although a CTB was considered the most urgent item on the arms control agenda by a majority of the members of the CD, it was put aside during the early Nixon years so as not to interfere with United States–Soviet negotiations on strategic arms.

The test ban issue reemerged in 1974. Early in the year, the Soviets proposed a CTB, but only on condition that both France and China join and that verification measures be limited to national technical means. These conditions were unacceptable to the United States. In March, during pre-summit consultations conducted in Moscow by National Security Adviser Henry Kissinger, Soviet Premier Leonid Brezhnev reportedly proposed a threshold test ban. A team of U.S. experts was then sent to Moscow for technical talks.

At the Nixon-Brezhnev summit meeting in July 1974, the Soviets again proposed a multilateral CTB. Nixon rejected this, arguing that such a treaty would not be acceptable to the Senate. The two leaders then rapidly agreed on the bilateral Threshold Test Ban Treaty (TTBT). Under this treaty both nations undertook not to conduct any underground test yielding more than 150 kilotons; to keep the number of underground tests to a minimum; not to interfere with each other's means of verification; and, after the treaty was ratified, to facilitate verification by exchanging detailed data on all tests and test sites. The parties also repeated what had become a customary pledge: they would continue negotiations toward a CTB. To cover the contingency that tests designed for a yield near the 150 kiloton threshold might accidentally exceed it, there was a separate agreement that "one or two slight unintended breaches per year would not be considered a violation of the treaty."

Signing of the TTBT was one of Nixon's last official acts as president: he resigned a few weeks later. It has been thought that one of his motives in negotiating the treaty was to try to maintain the momentum of the détente process, which had begun to flag. Another motive may have been to divert attention from the mounting Watergate scandal.

Although signed on 3 July 1974, the TTBT specified an effective date of 31 March 1976. The delay was, in part, a concession to the military leaders on both sides; the U.S. military, for example, wanted to complete some high-yield tests of an ABM warhead. The delay was occasioned also by a need to deal with the problem of peaceful nuclear explosions (PNES), which were exempted from the prohibitions of the TTBT. Beginning in October 1974, negotiators tried for more than a year to reach an agreement whereby PNES of more than 150 kilotons, such as were needed for some ambitious Soviet earth-moving projects, might be permitted. They concluded that it would be too difficult to assure that no military benefits would flow from such explosions. Accordingly, it was decided that a separate treaty was needed to control PNES.

The Peaceful Nuclear Explosions Treaty (PNET) was signed by Brezhnev and President Gerald Ford in May 1976. Among other provisions, it prohibited any individual PNE that exceeded the 150 kiloton limit. The verification procedures for the PNET provided for on-site inspections under certain circumstances, the first signed treaty to do so.

President Ford delayed submitting the TTBT and the PNET to the Senate, reportedly because of a nomination challenge from California governor Ronald Reagan, who was generally critical of arms control agreements with the Soviet Union. When the treaties were finally sent to the Senate, in July 1976, the TTBT at once encountered severe criticism in hearings before the Foreign Relations Committee from those who felt that the 150 kiloton threshold, more than ten times the yield of the Hiroshima bomb, had been an unnecessary concession to weapons designers. It was noted that the previous U.S. position had been to advocate banning all tests that could be adequately verified and that recent improvement in seismic techniques had made it possible to verify by national technical means tests as small as 10 kilotons. Arms control advocates further pointed out that allowing tests as large as 150 kilotons would serve only to delay a CTB and thus contravened the obligation undertaken in Article VI of the NPT. Indeed, the first NPT review conference, in 1975, focused major attention on the lack of progress toward a CTB. In view of such criticism, the Foreign Relations Committee delayed action on the TTBT, and President Ford did not push the issue.

Ford also declined to push the promised negotiations for a CTB. The main subject of his contacts with the Soviet leadership, including a summit meeting with Brezhnev in 1974, was the limitation of strategic arms. He commented later, "You can only handle so many things on your plate at one time, and a test ban was not our highest arms control priority."

Meanwhile, the Soviet Union seemed to be adopting a more forthcoming approach to verification. In 1975 it had presented to the U.N. General Assembly a draft CTB treaty that provided for verification only by national technical means. The following year, the Soviets amended the proposal to allow for a system of voluntary challenge inspections, following the suggestion made by Sweden ten years earlier.

CARTER TRIES FOR A COMPREHENSIVE TEST BAN

With the presidency of Jimmy Carter, the focus shifted from the unratified Threshold Test Ban

Treaty back to a comprehensive test ban (CTB). In his inaugural address Carter called for an end to nuclear weapons. In his first press conference he stated his desire "to proceed quickly and aggressively with a comprehensive test ban." He repeated this theme in a speech to the U.N. General Assembly on 17 March 1977. Carter also mentioned the objective of a CTB in his early correspondence with Brezhnev, who responded positively.

When Secretary of State Cyrus Vance made his ill-fated "deep-cuts" strategic-arms reduction proposal in Moscow in late March 1977, he also proposed that the two sides open CTB discussions. This drew an affirmative response. Brezhnev hinted at the direction the discussions might take when he indicated that the Soviet Union was ready to accept "voluntary" on-site inspections in cases of doubt.

A preliminary United States–Soviet meeting on the possibility of a CTB was held in Washington in June 1977. A new round of formal tripartite (U.S., U.K., USSR) negotiations began in Geneva in October. Good progress was made in the first eighteen months, largely because of a series of Soviet concessions. It was agreed that the treaty would ban all weapons tests and that it would run for a finite period, after which there would be negotiations to determine whether it should be continued. The treaty was to be accompanied by a moratorium on PNEs until ways could be found to prevent them from adding to weapons knowledge. (This was a Soviet concession in that whereas the United States had abandoned PNEs, the Soviets still had a substantial program.) Also, the Soviets no longer required the participation of France and China. Verification was to be primarily by national technical means, supplemented by automatic, tamper-proof seismic monitoring stations (black boxes) on the territory of each nuclear party. In addition, there would be a system of challenge on-site inspections designed to ensure that any claim of a possible violation meriting an inspection would be based on serious information and that any rejection of such a claim would be similarly based, with recourse to the U.N. Security Council in cases of dispute. The United States accepted this proposal in place of its own request for a quota of mandatory inspections, in the belief that no nation would ever permit an inspection, whether termed voluntary or mandatory, in the case of an actual violation. Moreover, technical testimony had been introduced that cast doubt on the utility of on-site inspections to reveal a violation.

In spite of the large measure of agreement, certain differences remained. There was a question whether or not black boxes to be placed on the soil of any party were to be manufactured by the host country or, as the United States preferred, by the other nuclear side. The Soviets resisted the U.S. suggestion that data from black boxes should be transmitted the quickest way possible (i.e., by satellite), because they wanted a chance to examine the data before transmitting it. There was not yet an agreement on the number and location of the monitoring stations. Surprisingly, one of the most intractable issues concerned the number and location of stations on British territory. The Soviets contended that there should be ten, the same number as had been agreed on for U.S. and Soviet territories. The British were willing to accept only one. There were also a number of issues regarding the specifics of on-site inspections. These included how soon the inspection could take place, what information could be offered to justify an inspection, and what instruments inspectors might bring with them. Finally, there was no agreement on what constituted a "nuclear-weapons test explosion" (i.e., whether very-low-yield laboratory experiments were to be included).

As of spring 1978, there was a general impression, not shared by all observers, that these differences could be overcome relatively quickly if the political will to do so remained strong in all three capitals. A gradual erosion of will now ensued, however, particularly in the United States. The erosion began when President Carter became aware of the strength of opposition to a test ban. The opposition centered in the weapons laboratories, in the Joint Chiefs of Staff, and in Secretary of Energy James Schlesinger. Their stated objection to a CTB emphasized a need to conduct periodic tests in order to assure the reliability of the nuclear-weapons stockpile. During the summer of 1978, Schlesinger brought the directors of the two leading weapons laboratories, Roger Batzel of Livermore and Harold Agnew of Los Alamos, to the White House in order to make this argument directly to the president. Agnew later claimed that their representations "turned Carter around" as to the wisdom of a CTBT. Herbert F. York, who replaced ACDA director Paul Warnke as chief U.S. negotiator in January 1979, believes their chief impact was to persuade Carter that, to placate the opposition, he needed to offer certain compromises. For example, whereas his original proposal had been for a treaty of unlimited duration, with periodic reviews, he decided in September 1978 that it should lapse and be entirely renegotiated after only three years.

Shortly afterward, the president became aware that it was going to be more difficult than previously supposed to achieve his goals in SALT II, which had a higher priority for him than a CTB. As the SALT II negotiations dragged on, lagging some six months behind schedule and not reaching fruition in the form of a signed treaty until June 1979, the CTB negotiations were deemphasized for an extended period.

The political will to reach a CTB agreement was weakened further by a series of external events. One was the publicity given in August 1979 to the presence of a brigade of Soviet troops in Cuba. Another was the taking of hostages at the American embassy in Tehran in November 1979. Still another was the accession to power in Britain of Margaret Thatcher, who took a dim view of the whole CTB idea. The most damaging of all occurred in December 1979 when the Soviets invaded Afghanistan. Although the test ban negotiations continued, there was little forward movement after that date.

On 31 July 1980 the three negotiating powers submitted a progress report to the U.N. Committee on Disarmament. This report provided the general public with its first indication of how close the negotiators had come to agreement. Whether what they had accomplished would be built on further, however, depended on the results of the American election. When Ronald Reagan defeated Carter on 4 November 1980, it was clear, based on Reagan's stated positions, that the negotiations had reached at least a temporary ending. They were suspended a week after the election.

REAGAN, GORBACHEV, AND VERIFICATION

In its early days the Reagan administration took no initiative, and was generally silent, on arms control, preferring to concentrate on increasing and modernizing the U.S. nuclear arsenal. This was in keeping with President Reagan's claim that the Soviet Union had gained "a definite margin of superiority" during the 1970s. Silence was not possible on the testing issue, however, after the Soviet Union presented to the U.N. General Assembly in September 1981 a CTB proposal that was essentially an outline of the treaty that had been under negotiation during the Carter administration. ACDA director Eugene Rostow answered with a variant of what was to become the standard Reagan administration line: the United States government supported a CTB "as a long-term goal," but "international conditions . . . are not now propitious." In May 1982, Rostow admitted to the Senate Foreign Relations Committee that in discussing this issue within the government, he had "run into a profound stone wall" in the form of "whole phalanxes and battalions" of officials who believed that "given the uncertainties of the nuclear situation and the need for new weapons and modernization, we are going to need testing, and perhaps even testing above the 150-kiloton level, for a long time to come."

At a meeting of the National Security Council in July 1982, President Reagan decided formally to end U.S. participation in the CTB talks that had been suspended in November 1980. Claiming that the Soviet Union might be testing over the TTBT's 150-kiloton threshold, the administration stated that renegotiation of the verification provisions of the TTBT and PNET would have to precede any agreement on a CTB. (Although the two treaties had not been ratified, both sides had indicated that they would comply with them after the announced effective date of 31 March 1976.) While its public statements emphasized verification problems, the Reagan administration's internal guidance also stressed the need for continued testing to solve important problems in the modernization of U.S. nuclear weapons. Within a year, the administration was publicly acknowledging this rationale for continued testing.

Reagan's action in suspending the CTB talks could not have been a surprise; yet it caused a storm of protest. Resolutions were introduced promptly in both houses of Congress calling on the administration to resume the negotiations. The Senate resolution was sponsored by thirty-one members. A further source of criticism was the linkage the administration sought to establish between difficulties in verifying the TTBT and the likelihood of similar or greater difficulties in verifying a CTB. It was pointed out that it is much easier to determine whether a test has occurred at all than whether it has exceeded a specific magnitude.

The Reagan position on testing also fared poorly in the international arena. In December 1982 the United States was the only country to vote against a

U.N. General Assembly resolution calling on the Committee on Disarmament to continue consideration of CTB issues and "to take necessary steps to initiate substantive negotiations." The Soviet Union, on the other hand, was winning international favor by introducing a succession of far-reaching test ban proposals. Late in 1982 the Soviets presented a draft test ban treaty to the U.N. that would have permitted on-site inspections and exchange of seismic data. In March 1983, Premier Yuri Andropov, and a year later his successor, Konstantin Chernenko, proposed a general nuclear freeze that included a moratorium on tests of both warheads and delivery vehicles.

The movement for a bilateral freeze was achieving considerable strength in the United States as well, largely as a reaction against Reagan's harsh rhetoric about the Soviet Union ("an evil empire") and his buildup of the U.S. nuclear arsenal, both of which aroused public anxieties. In both 1983 and 1984, resolutions calling for a bilateral freeze passed the House by large majorities, only to be voted down in the Senate. For its part, the Senate, in June 1985, adopted an amendment to the defense authorization bill urging the president to submit the TTBT and PNET for ratification and to begin negotiations for a CTB.

Notwithstanding all the pressures upon it, the Reagan administration stubbornly maintained its emphasis on verifying the TTBT and PNET, refusing to be drawn into serious discussions of more stringent test limits. In February 1983, President Reagan had proposed to the Soviets that new verification protocols be added to the two treaties. Reagan had instituted a regular series of reports to Congress on "Soviet Non-Compliance with Arms Control Agreements" and in both the January 1984 and October 1984 reports he declared that the Soviet Union was "likely to have violated" the yield limit of the TTBT. This charge was denied by the Soviets and publicly questioned by a number of U.S. scientists. Even the directors of the nation's two principal weapons laboratories acknowledged there was no clear evidence of a Soviet violation. It was pointed out that because of differences in underlying geology, tests at the Soviet site produced a larger seismic signal than tests of the same size in Nevada. In January 1986 the CIA took note of this difference when it lowered by about 20 percent the multipliers used in measuring the yield of Soviet tests, all but negating the claims of Soviet violations.

Reagan proposed in a U.N. speech in September 1984 that the United States and the Soviet Union exchange visits of experts to each other's test sites as a way to resolve questions about the calibration of instruments for measuring the yield of underground tests. He expanded this offer with an invitation for Soviet experts to come to Nevada to measure the yield of a U.S. test.

After his accession to power in March 1985, Premier Mikhail Gorbachev of the Soviet Union threw his weight behind the movement for a CTB. He began by initiating a unilateral Soviet moratorium on tests to extend from 6 August 1985, the fortieth anniversary of the attack on Hiroshima, until the end of the year. He urged that the United States join in and that the moratorium be made permanent. The U.S. response was to dismiss Gorbachev's move as "a propaganda ploy" and to repeat the invitation for the Soviets to monitor a U.S. test. In November 1985, at the conclusion of his first summit meeting with President Reagan, Gorbachev declared that if a complete test ban could be negotiated, "there will be no problems from our side regarding verification." The following month, in a letter to Reagan, Gorbachev committed the Soviet Union to accept on-site inspections as part of any CTB. Reagan answered Gorbachev's letter by interposing a set of conditions that made a CTB seem a remote, almost unattainable goal: "A comprehensive test ban," the president wrote, "is a long-standing objective of the United States, in the context of achieving broad, deep, and verifiable arms reductions; substantially improved verification capabilities; expanded confidence-building measures; greater balance in conventional forces; and at a time when a nuclear deterrent is no longer . . . essential."

Congressional pressures for further test limitations continued into 1986. After both chambers had passed resolutions urging President Reagan to negotiate a CTB, the House supplemented exhortation with budgetary action. In August it passed an amendment to a defense authorization bill denying funds for tests of more than a kiloton for one year if the Soviet Union agreed to the same limit and to in-country seismic monitoring acceptable to the United States. The House rescinded this action after the administration complained that it might weaken the president's position at the upcoming Reykjavík summit. In exchange, Reagan pledged that he would submit the TTBT and PNET to the Senate after agreeable verification measures had been established and that he would then propose a step-by-step program limiting and ultimately ending nuclear testing. The House repeated its restrictive budgetary action in both 1987 and 1988. In both years similar action failed in the Senate and the House's restrictions were defeated in conference.

In March 1987 the United States again proposed to the Soviets that new verification measures be adopted as a prelude to the ratification of the TTBT and PNET, and invited Soviet scientists to observe a U.S. test scheduled for April. The Soviets rejected the invitation. In May, however, the Soviets came forward with an initiative of their own. By way of backing up previous promises to allow international inspectors into the Soviet Union, an agreement was announced between the USSR Academy of Sciences and the Natural Resources Defense Council (NRDC), a private U.S. environmental group, whereby the latter was allowed temporarily to establish three monitoring stations near the Soviet testing station at Semipalatinsk. This arrangement was followed in April 1988 by establishment of a United States–Soviet seismic program under which a number of stations in each country would continue to send seismic data to the other country.

Meanwhile, Gorbachev extended the Soviet unilateral testing moratorium three times after its initial expiration at the end of 1985: first to 31 March 1986; then, in a speech after the Chernobyl nuclear power plant accident, to 6 August 1986; then to the end of that year. In announcing the last extension, the Soviet leader stated that because the United States had conducted eighteen tests during the moratorium's first year, his military was becoming concerned about falling behind. On 18 December 1986 the Soviet Union announced that its moratorium would end with the next U.S. test. In February 1987, following a U.S. test earlier in the month, the Soviet Union conducted its first test in nineteen months.

As the Reagan administration neared its end, Gorbachev began to deemphasize his push for a CTB and to make serious efforts to resolve the Reagan administration's expressed concerns about verifying the TTBT and PNET. The Soviets doubted these concerns were genuine; early on, they had characterized them as a "sham." Indeed, administration officials, in more than one unguarded moment, acknowledged that their emphasis on verifying the TTBT had as one of its goals to stave off demands for a CTB. But Gorbachev may well have concluded that

he needed to accommodate Reagan on this point in the interest of achieving other objectives, such as an agreement on strategic arms.

The process of accommodation began at the October 1986 Reykjavík summit, where the Soviets reportedly agreed to the U.S. plan to negotiate gradual reductions in the yield of permitted tests rather than seek an immediate CTB. The Soviets insisted, however, that the ultimate goal of such negotiations be characterized as an effort to achieve a CTB. Next, in April 1987, Foreign Minister Eduard Shevardnadze proposed to Secretary of State George Shultz that each nation conduct a test on the other's territory to improve verification techniques. Then, in June 1987, at the Conference on Disarmament in Geneva, the Soviets announced readiness to open their test sites to mandatory inspection.

In September 1987 the superpowers agreed to initiate formal "stage-by-stage" test limitation negotiations by drafting new verification protocols for the TTBT and PNET. In keeping with the agreement at Reykjavík, it was announced that this first stage was to be followed by "intermediate" test ban negotiations and then by moves toward the ultimate goal of a CTB. Negotiations did not proceed beyond the first phase.

Bilateral technical talks on the verification protocols began in Geneva in November 1987. The results became evident at the Washington summit meeting in December when the two sides announced agreement on a joint verification experiment (JVE) in which each was to measure the yield of a test at the other's principal test site, the purpose being to calibrate instruments and to evaluate the accuracy of alternative verification systems. The JVE was carried out during the late summer of 1988.

BUSH: CONTINUED RESISTANCE TO A CTB

In January 1990, President George Bush approved a policy statement indicating that his administration had "not identified any further limitations on nuclear testing . . . that would be in the United States' national security interest," that no new test negotiations would be undertaken until after a "period of implementation" of the TTBT and PNET verification protocols then being negotiated, and that the administration viewed a comprehensive test ban as a "long-term objective" possible only "when we do not need to depend on nuclear deterrence."

At their summit meeting in June 1990 in Washington, Bush and Gorbachev signed the new TTBT-PNET verification protocols. This cleared the way for ratification of the two treaties, which entered into force in December 1990 after unanimous approving votes in the U.S. Senate and the Supreme Soviet. Both bodies accompanied their actions with declarations. The Senate's statement called attention to previous U.S. treaty commitments to pursue a CTB. The Supreme Soviet declared the Soviet Union's willingness to resume talks on a CTB immediately and to place an indefinite moratorium on further testing, provided the United States did the same.

The protocol to the TTBT is 107 pages long. It provides for advance notification and on-site inspection of tests above thirty-five kilotons. In addition, for tests above fifty kilotons, the verifying side is permitted to monitor the tests at seismic stations on the testing country's territory and, if it chooses, to do so utilizing a new "hydrodynamic" yield-measurement technique that the United States considered superior to seismic measurement. It involves inserting a coaxial cable into a hole alongside the buried explosive and estimating the yield by measuring the rate at which the shock wave crushes the cable.

The Soviet Union did very little testing in its last years, conducting only seven tests in 1989, one in 1990, and none in 1991. The reduced number was due in part to a February 1989 incident in which radioactive gases vented from a test at the Semipalatinsk site in Kazakhstan, causing local illnesses and leading to popular demonstrations. Following an appeal to the Kremlin by the Kazakh SSR legislature, the Ministry of Defense recommended that all testing be moved to the Arctic islands of Novaya Zemlya. But Boris Yeltsin, the president of the Russian Republic, announced his opposition to testing there, and the Nordic countries, not far to the west, also expressed concern. On 5 October 1991, USSR president Gorbachev announced a one-year testing moratorium. After the breakup of the Soviet Union, Russian president Yeltsin issued a decree supporting the one-year moratorium. He also stated that Novaya Zemlya would not be used for nuclear tests. This left all the republics in the former Soviet Union without an established testing site.

The U.S. testing program remained under pressure from those at home who urged more rapid progress toward a CTB. A month after the adminis-

tration's negative policy statement of January 1990, seventy-six House members urged Bush to reverse his stand, noting that it was inconsistent with President Reagan's 1986 pledge to negotiate further steps "immediately" after the TTBT and PNET were ratified.

More insistent pressure came from the international community. Each year from 1985 through 1990, for example, the U.N. General Assembly passed a resolution urging the superpowers to make progress toward a CTB. Then, in May 1989, President François Mitterand announced that France, never before an advocate of test restrictions, was prepared to stop testing if the United States, the United Kingdom, and the USSR did so.

The strongest international intervention was based on a provision of the LTBT which states that a conference to amend the treaty must be convened if requested by one-third or more of the parties. A proposed amendment would then enter into force if approved by a majority of the parties, including all of the "Original Parties" (the United States, the United Kingdom, the USSR). On 5 August 1988 the twenty-fifth anniversary of the signing of the LTBT, 5 non-nuclear signatories of the treaty formally proposed an amendment conference for the specific purpose of converting the LTBT into a CTB. With 40 (the required one-third) of the treaty's 119 parties having requested it, an amendment conference was indeed held in New York in January 1991. No vote was taken at the conference, because the United States and the United Kingdom had signified in advance that they stood ready to exercise their vetos to prevent adoption of an amendment. The conferees merely decided to try to meet again for the same purpose at an unspecified future date. The United States then indicated that it would not participate in or pay anything toward such a venture.

Despite its lack of tangible result, the amendment conference was significant in that it demonstrated again the isolated position of the United States, joined in this instance only by the British, in opposing further test restrictions. There were many criticisms of the U.S. position, both at the conference and in media comments. It was noteworthy that the Soviet Union joined forces with those who wanted to amend the treaty, as did several Western countries that previously had stood aside from this controversy.

Pressures on the administration to call a halt to testing mounted in 1992. France announced on 8 April 1992 that it would suspend nuclear testing for the rest of 1992, stating that it would decide whether to resume in 1993 based on whether "other nuclear powers" followed its example. Under apparent pressure from his military to resume tests, President Yeltsin made clear that whether the Russian moratorium would be renewed after it expired in October 1992 depended on the attitude of the United States. He announced that the test site at Novaya Zemlya was being made ready for "two to four tests" should the moratorium end. To keep his military at bay, Yeltsin reportedly sought some sign at his June 1992 summit meeting with President Bush that the United States would agree to additional limits on testing, but received no such concession.

On 4 June 1992 the House of Representatives approved, 237 to 187, an amendment to the fiscal year 1993 defense authorization bill that would prohibit U.S. testing for one year if Russia did not test. On 3 August 1992 the Senate voted by the surprisingly large margin of 68 to 26 for a nine-month moratorium. The Senate measure allowed for a maximum of five tests in each of the three years after the moratorium's end, but specified that no further U.S. tests could be conducted after 30 September 1996 unless Russia began testing again. Taking note of the pressures on it, the Bush administration in July 1992 reiterated its "strong opposition to a legislatively-enacted nuclear test moratorium." At the same time, the administration announced that it would henceforth test only "for the safety and reliability of our deterrent forces," that it did not anticipate conducting more than six tests in any year, and that no more than three of these would yield more than thirty-five kilotons.

THE TEST BAN DEBATE: A SUMMARY

Arguments Against a CTB   As indicated above, the anti-CTB argument most emphasized in the early years of the test ban debate was that such a treaty would not be adequately verifiable, especially if the Soviet Union continued to resist on-site inspections. The argument was reinforced by speculation about various techniques the Soviets might employ to evade detection of tests. The one taken most seriously involved detonating explosions in large cavities so that the shock wave from the explosion would be decoupled from the surrounding rock

and register on seismometers as a much smaller explosion. The verification argument received less emphasis as time went on, in view of scientific evidence about the increased capabilities of national technical means of verification and the agreements already reached by both sides to open their territories for verification purposes. The congressional Office of Technology Assessment reported in 1988 a consensus of experts that, with a battery of seismometers inside the Soviet Union, even decoupled tests could be monitored adequately down to a level of about five kilotons. Later estimates lowered this detection threshold to one or two kilotons. Tests below this level would not have military significance.

During the Carter administration, the need for testing to maintain confidence in the reliability of the U.S.-nuclear weapons stockpile became the most emphasized argument against a CTB. Test ban opponents pointed out that, over time, stockpiled weapons are subject to deterioration from corrosion and chemical changes. They cited a number of instances in which nuclear tests had uncovered serious reliability problems in the stockpile and made possible their solution. They noted further that, as weapons have to be replaced, some testing is needed to assure that the replacements are dependable. To counter such claims, test ban proponents have argued that reliability can be assured by a careful program of non-nuclear testing, replacement of suspect warheads, and remanufacture of those proven to be reliable.

Beginning in the 1980s test ban opponents have emphasized the need for tests to assure that nuclear warheads are safe—that is, that in the event of an accident they will not disperse plutonium contamination or even give rise to a very small nuclear yield. A 1990 study undertaken for the House Armed Services Committee indicated that the likelihood of such contingencies was greater than had been estimated previously. A panel of three senior physicists, headed by Sidney Drell, deputy director of the Stanford Linear Accelerator Center, recommended that completely new "safety-optimized designs . . . be studied aggressively." Another report prepared for Congress, by Ray Kidder of the Livermore weapons laboratory, commented that the course recommended by the Drell panel "would be a major and protracted undertaking requiring a very large number of tests." Kidder contended that the number of tests needed to improve safety could be minimized by a careful process of retiring some older weapons, substituting safer for less safe designs, and improvement in handling procedures. He testified in July 1992 that by means of some substitutions employing the most modern warheads, the U.S. stockpile of nuclear weapons not already scheduled for retirement could be brought up to modern standards of safety by as few as four nuclear tests over a period of no more than three years.

A companion concern to that about safety was whether nuclear weapons were secure—that is, protected from access by unauthorized persons. Substantial achievements have been made in this field by employing various controls such as permissive action links, locking devices that prevent missiles from being armed without explicit approval from high levels. It was confidently asserted that what remained to be done in the area of weapons security could be accomplished without nuclear testing.

CTB opponents also contended that tests were needed to understand the electromagnetic and other effects of nuclear explosions on critical U.S. military systems, particularly those involved in the command and control systems for the strategic forces. CTB proponents pointed out, however, that tests useful in this regard would most likely have to be conducted in the atmosphere or in space, prohibited environments under the Limited Test Ban Treaty. After the breakup of the Soviet Union, moreover, there no longer seemed to be any danger of such a concentrated attack on the United States as would threaten vital military systems.

A further argument raised against a CTB was that it would threaten the viability of U.S. weapons laboratories in that, without the opportunity to do experimental work, our scientists might gradually drift away into other employments. By contrast, it was thought that the Soviets could use government authority to retain their key laboratory personnel. The U.S. laboratories themselves seemed to refute this argument. Very likely in anticipation that a CTB might happen some day, they began to diversify their activities by taking on more work dealing with non-nuclear weapons and with high-technology civilian matters. With the breakup of the Soviet Union, it was the former Soviet laboratories that disintegrated, causing some concern that their former employees would sell their services to third world regimes intent on acquiring a nuclear weapons capability.

Within the weapons laboratories and the military, a solid core of resistance to a CTB persisted based on the perceived need to develop and test specially designed warheads to fit new weapon systems. The Reagan administration continually emphasized that testing was needed to "modernize the stockpile." Among the objectives were the development of exotic weapons such as earth-penetrating warheads designed to destroy enemy command centers, and the directed-energy weapons (such as the X-ray laser activated by a thermonuclear explosion) planned for the Strategic Defense Initiative (SDI). The demise of the Soviet Union weakened this argument for continued testing. Without the prospect of a deadly exchange with a fully armed superpower, there was clearly less need for new kinds of nuclear weapons. While there was still a felt need for a strategic defense against accidental or random launches from other parts of the world, SDI planning began to emphasize interception with non-nuclear missiles ("brilliant pebbles"). In July 1992 the Energy Department cancelled the last scheduled test of the X-ray laser.

Arguments for a CTB   A main line of argument by CTB supporters has emphasized what such a treaty would contribute in forestalling the development of destabilizing new weapons. Agreeing, for example, with test ban foes that the space-based weapons planned for SDI could not be brought into being without testing, they have cited exactly this fact as a basis for advocating a CTB. This argument had less force after the collapse of the Soviet Union diminished the likelihood that new weapons threatening to the United States would be developed or proposed.

A second principal argument offered on behalf of a CTB is that it would have a major effect in preventing further proliferation of nuclear weapons. Although non-nuclear nations may be able to develop relatively simple weapons without testing, they would find this much more difficult to do with confidence in the case of more complex fission weapons and thermonuclear weapons. During the NPT's first twenty years, failure of the superpowers to make significant progress toward a CTB was regarded as a breach of their commitments under Article VI of the Non-Proliferation Treaty. This was a contentious issue at NPT review conferences and was regarded as a threat to the NPT's extension when that question would come up for review in 1995. As the Cold War wound down and compliance with Article VI seemed to be adequately demonstrated by negotiated reductions in specific weapons, it became more likely that the NPT would be extended. The feeling remained, however, that with a CTB there would be a much stronger consensus for a long-term extension.

While a CTB seemed less essential to the NPT's future after the end of the Cold War, it was still advocated as a centerpiece of an intensified effort to strengthen the non-proliferation regime. It was contended that a CTB would be a confidence-building measure that could help to cool regional arms races, such as those between Israel and its Mideast neighbors, India and Pakistan, Brazil and Argentina, and the two Koreas. It was also noted that, if a CTB was reached by an amendment of the LTBT, several near-nuclear nations that had not signed the NPT would be bound not to test because they did sign the LTBT. Conversely, as Spurgeon M. Keeny, Jr., president of the Arms Control Association, has emphasized (*Arms Control Today*, November 1990, p. 2), "Continued testing by the nuclear powers underscores their belief in the importance and utility of nuclear weapons," a message that can have only an adverse impact on efforts to control nuclear proliferation.

A further argument offered for a CTB is that it would improve the atmosphere for negotiating other forms of arms control.

Relative Risks With the end of the Cold War, the final resistance line of test ban opponents was subsumed in a proposition put forward repeatedly by the Reagan and Bush administrations—namely, that as long as the United States depends on nuclear weapons for its security, it must be free to test such weapons. This is a hard argument to refute, since it is so unspecific and seems based on a fear of the unknown.

A possible answer may lie in the concept of relative risks. Without doubt a CTB or a low-threshold test ban involves a degree of risk. What policymakers need to decide, however, is how such risks compare with those that might be incurred in the absence of such an agreement. In the opinion of many, the latter risks, which could include a weakening of the non-proliferation regime, would be many times greater.

BIBLIOGRAPHY

Documents Basic contemporaneous documents involved in test-ban proposals and negotiations, such as statements by world leaders and by negotiators at the United Nations and disarmament conferences, are found in *Documents on Disarmament,* an annual publication issued by the U.S. Arms Control and Disarmament Agency (ACDA) since 1960. Admirable historical summations based on official sources are found in two other ACDA publications: *Review of International Negotiations on the Cessation of Nuclear Weapons Tests: 1962–1965* (1966) and *Negotiations on a Comprehensive Test Ban, 1965–1967* (1968). ACDA Annual Reports also contain some useful summations. Congressional hearings have provided valuable sources on running test ban controversies. The reader can refer with profit to *Nuclear Test Ban Treaty,* Hearings before the Senate Foreign Relations Committee, August 1963; and *To Promote Negotiations for a Comprehensive Test Ban Treaty,* Hearings before the Senate Foreign Relations Committee Subcommittee on Arms Control, May 1973—important on status of verification capabilities.

Eisenhower Period The development of arms control policy in the Eisenhower period is thoroughly reviewed in RICHARD G. HEWLETT and JACK M. HOLL, *Atoms for Peace and War, 1953–1961: Eisenhower and the Atomic Energy Commission* (Berkeley, Calif., 1989), chaps. 14, 17, and 20. ROBERT A. DIVINE, *Blowing on the Wind: The Nuclear Test Ban Debate, 1954–1960* (New York, 1978), provides a thorough discussion of the fallout controversy during the 1950s. HAROLD KARAN JACOBSON and ERIC STEIN, *Diplomats, Scientists, and Politicians: The United States and the Nuclear Test Ban Negotiations* (Ann Arbor, Mich., 1966), offers a detailed account and balanced perspective on test ban developments during the Eisenhower and Kennedy periods.

The LTBT and the Test Ban Debate The most complete consideration of events leading to the Limited Test Ban Treaty is found in GLENN T. SEABORG, *Kennedy, Khrushchev, and the Test Ban* (Berkeley, Calif., 1981), which offers an up-close perspective based on the author's diaries while chairman of the Atomic Energy Commission. RONALD J. TERCHEK, *The Making of the Test Ban Treaty* (The Hague, 1970), considers the ratification of the LTBT from the viewpoint of a political scientist. ARTHUR H. DEAN, Kennedy's chief negotiator in the tripartite negotiations in Geneva, reviews his experiences in *Test Ban and Disarmament: The Path of Negotiation* (New York, 1966). GLENN T. SEABORG, with BENJAMIN S. LOEB, *Stemming the Tide: Arms Control in the Johnson Years* (Lexington, Mass.,

1987), again based on Seaborg's diaries, is useful particularly for its account of the negotiation of the Non-Proliferation Treaty and the linkage between that treaty and the world community's advocacy of a comprehensive test ban. A participant's account of the CTB negotiations under Carter is found in HERBERT F. YORK, *Making Weapons, Talking Peace* (New York, 1987), pp. 282–323. The dissident attitude of nuclear have-nots toward the superpower arms race, including the test ban issue, is well portrayed in ALVA MYRDAL, *The Game of Disarmament: How the United States and Russia Run the Arms Race* (New York, 1976). BETTY LALL and PAUL D. BRANDES, *Banning Nuclear Tests* (New York, 1988), offers a useful summary.

The arguments on both sides in the test ban debate are reviewed and challenged at length in STEVE FETTER, *Toward a Comprehensive Test Ban* (Cambridge, Mass., 1988). Comprehensive reviews of such arguments are found as well in Committee on International Security and Arms Control, NATIONAL ACADEMY OF SCIENCES, *Nuclear Arms Control: Background and Issues* (Washington, D.C., 1985), pp. 187–223; HERBERT YORK and G. ALLEN GREB, *The Comprehensive Nuclear Test Ban,* Discussion Paper No. 84, California Seminar on Arms Control and Foreign Policy (1979); and ALAN NEIDLE, "Nuclear

Test Bans: History and Future Prospects," in ALEXANDER L. GEORGE, PHILIP J. FARLEY, and ALEXANDER DALLIN, *U.S.-Soviet Security Cooperation: Achievements, Failures, Lessons* (New York, 1988).

Discussions, often quite technical, of individual issues in the test ban debate have appeared through the years. Notable references that influenced the debate on verification were LYNN R. SYKES and JACK F. EVERNDEN, "The Verification of a Comprehensive Nuclear Test Ban," *Scientific American* (October 1982): 47–55; W. J. HANSON, "Seismic Verification of a Comprehensive Test Ban," *Science,* January 1985, pp. 251–257; and U.S. Office of Technology Assessment, *Seismic Verification of Nuclear Testing Treaties* (1988). An authoritative review of the safety issue appears in "Nuclear Warhead Safety and Nuclear Testing," *Science and Global Security* (Spring 1991): 1–14.

To follow the evolution of the test ban debate, as well as historical events, the reader is well advised to consult contemporaneous issues of *Arms Control Today* (ACT) and the *Bulletin of the Atomic Scientists.* Particularly useful is the November 1990 ACT, an entire issue devoted to the comprehensive test ban; it contains articles on both technical and political aspects, as well as a definitive chronology.

The Hot Line

Washington-Moscow Direct Communications Link, 1963 to the Present

$\bigcirc$

WEBSTER A. STONE

See also Confidence-Building Measures in Europe: 1975 to the Present; Psychological Dimensions of Nuclear Arms Control; *and* The United States Arms Control and Disarmament Agency. *The hot line agreements are excerpted in Volume III.*

Contrary to popular belief and scriptwriters, the Washington-Moscow hot line is not a red telephone atop the president's Oval Office desk. Rather, it is a group of machines located in a restricted area between the National Military Intelligence Center and the National Military Command Center. There, a code-locked door leads to a rather ordinary office suite furnished with IBM terminals, encryption machines, teleprinters, shelves of books, and framed wall posters. Within this seemingly mundane room, work occasionally requires the highest "top-secret" security classification, "Eyes Only—The President."

Referred to informally as Molink (a contraction of "Moscow link") and known formally as the Direct Communications Link, or DCL, the hot line provides the heads of the United States and Russian governments with a fast, direct, private line to each other in the event of a crisis. According to the Pentagon, the DCL serves a single, underlying purpose—"to reduce the risk of the outbreak of nuclear war," by precluding "delays, misunderstandings, and misinterpretations of actions by either side."

For a superpower to use the hot line at all conveys the most dire warning and implies, "We have a very dangerous situation on our hands." Before the advent of nuclear weaponry, enemy states frequently broke diplomatic ties (quit communicating) as tensions spiraled into crises and crises mounted into war. The unparalleled destructiveness of nuclear weapons and their speed of delivery has made mutual efforts by nuclear-armed adversaries to de-escalate crises absolutely imperative for world survival. In Thomas Schelling's words, "There is probably no single measure more critical to the process of arms control than assuring that if war should break out the adversaries are not precluded from communication with each other" (1966, pp. 263–264).

Classic definitions of arms control typically include war prevention as a primary objective. And although the United States–Russian geopolitical relationship is far different than it was during the four decades of the Cold War, the United States and Russia are still the only nuclear superpowers. As an arms control measure, the hot line maintains its purpose to decrease the chances of United States–Russian military conflicts because it ensures an open line of communication between U.S. and Russian leaders in the event of a crisis (though the hot line probably would not survive a nuclear attack).

NEGOTIATING THE HOT LINE

Though taken for granted now, communication between the two superpower leaders was not always so facile. In the late 1950s and early 1960s, the Cold War had created an ironic and perilous predicament: bombers could strike targets within hours and ballistic missiles needed only a fraction of that time, but the White House could not reach the Kremlin in a crisis. Given the immense improvements in direct dialing within the United States, no one would have believed it.

The economist and nuclear strategist Thomas Schelling is generally credited with the idea of a direct communications link. Schelling and others who got involved with promoting a hot line largely attribute the concept to popular fiction, especially Peter Bryant's *Red Alert* (which became the film *Dr. Strangelove*). "Something like a hotline was essential.... It was crucial to get information back and forth in a matter of hours. And then the same thing showed up in *Failsafe!*"

By 1961, Schelling found himself in charge of a presidential task force convened to consider, among other ideas, a hot line to Moscow. Jess Gorkin, the editor of *Parade* magazine, thought of the hot line idea himself while talking on the phone to a friend and initiated an intensive campaign for its adoption. Gorkin published an open letter in *Parade* to President Dwight Eisenhower and Premier Nikita Khrushchev, concluding with the question "Must a world be lost for want of a telephone call?" Readers responded enthusiastically, and even Soviet newspapers published Gorkin's letter. When John F. Kennedy became president, Gorkin accelerated the campaign.

Gorkin and Schelling may have lobbied for a hot line independently, but they confronted the same obstacles. The State Department and the military objected: "We don't like the idea of the president talking behind our back to the Russians." Conservatives opposed it as well; the John Birch Society proclaimed, "Washington is ideologically close enough to Moscow without making the White House a branch office of the Kremlin" (Gorkin, *I Can Tell It Now,* New York, 1964, p. 5). As for the Kremlin, it expressed interest only in proposals for general and complete disarmament. Despite some misgivings in official circles, however, the U.S. draft treaty on general and complete disarmament, submitted on 18 April 1962 to the United Nations Eighteen Nation Disarmament Committee (ENDC), proposed that "specified Parties to the Treaty would agree to the establishment of rapid and reliable communications among their heads of government and with the Secretary-General of the United Nations." In July the Soviet Union amended its draft general disarmament treaty to include a nearly identical provision. But no one actually did anything.

The hot line proposal languished through the summer of 1962; neither Kennedy nor Khrushchev seemed to take the idea very seriously. Events in October, however, would provide an inexorable catalyst.

The Cuban missile crisis clearly pointed up the woeful communication inadequacies between the U.S. and Soviet governments. Messages between Kennedy and Khrushchev took up to six hours to deliver. Secretary of State Dean Rusk described how it all went through diplomatic channels: "That would usually involve translation, coding and decoding for transmission, and delivery to the appropriate persons at the other end." Events moved so quickly that both governments resorted to public statements as the fastest way to communicate. The Soviets even gave an American Broadcasting Company reporter a message to convey.

After the crisis, the hot-line proposal became an immediate priority at the highest level of government. President Kennedy discussed it in private letters to Khrushchev. Suggesting to the premier that using a member of the American press as a vehicle for negotiating a nuclear crisis was not particularly wise, Kennedy added that the hot line would be an improvement on such unconventional methods. The United States submitted a working paper to ENDC in December 1962 on "limited measures to reduce the outbreak of war through accident, miscalculation, or failure of communication" that described some ideal features of "arrangements which could ensure the availability of prompt, dependable, and direct communications." Ordinary voice telephone was deemed a possibility but was thought subject to "inadvertent error either through lack of precision in reception or through incorrect translation." On 5 April 1963, the Soviet delegate to ENDC dismissed most of the U.S. war-risk reduction proposals as "essentially changing nothing," but he stated that his country was "ready to agree immediately, without waiting for general and complete disarmament" to the establishment of a direct communications link between the U.S. and Soviet governments. Technical talks between U.S.

and Soviet envoys began shortly after the United States welcomed the Soviet acceptance of its hot-line proposal. A memorandum of understanding specifying the technical parameters and protocols for use of the hot line was signed on 20 June 1963.

The United States–Soviet direct communications link became the first arms control agreement between the two superpowers. Press and public reaction was favorable. President Kennedy considered it a small breakthrough that portended more comprehensive arms treaties. And the agreement did appear to provide momentum toward the Limited Test Ban Treaty, which was to be signed only six weeks later.

The hot line fit into Kennedy's approach more than even he would know. As a direct and private backdoor channel, it provided a way of avoiding the diplomatic bureaucracy and became one of many innovations (such as the Situation Room, created after the Bay of Pigs) for getting fast, reliable information to the president. And if the hot line suited the president in a practical way, it also complemented his defense policy in theoretical terms. Secretary of Defense Robert McNamara's new strategy of "flexible response" emphasized matching enemy military actions step for step, but for his strategy to be successful communication would be essential.

OPERATING THE HOT LINE

The hot-line system initially agreed to was not a telephone but a teletype, with one cable routed across Europe and a backup circuit routed through North Africa. To calm the military's fears, Kennedy gave the Joint Chiefs of Staff jurisdiction over the DCL terminal instead of putting it in the White House. The Moscow terminal went to the Soviet president's two offices: one in the Kremlin and the other on the opposite side of Red Square at Communist party headquarters. Both terminals were manned by KGB specialists from the Department of Government Communications. As of the early 1990s, there was only one Moscow terminal for the hot line, in the office of the president inside the Kremlin, still operated by specialists from the Department of Government Communications; it was under direct control of the Russian president, not the KGB as before.

On 30 August 1963, the hot line became fully operational. Washington's first message, "The quick brown fox jumped over the lazy dog's back 1234567890," while it tested the equipment's alphabetic accuracy, hardly compared with the Soviet's initial, poetic transmission, a description of Moscow's setting sun. Test messages immediately began going out every even hour from Washington in English and every odd hour from Moscow in Russian. The hot line has been tested every hour of every day since 1963, and the dissolution of the Soviet Union did not alter the procedure.

Routine Operations The president may have sole discretion over official hot-line communiqués, but the Molink staff shoulders the monotonous and prodigious responsibility of continually testing the equipment to make certain the lines work properly when needed.

Five two-person teams attend the hot line around the clock on rotating eight-hour shifts. Both a professional communicator (usually a Russian-speaking sergeant who can deal with the idiosyncrasies of the equipment) and a presidential translator (an officer with professional linguistic expertise) must be on duty at all times. Studied procedures ensure that given any circumstance, someone is always ready to send or receive a message. Guaranteeing that messages will always be received is integral to the hot line's success.

Molink personnel come from all four service branches and undergo intensive training before being posted. Translators must continually hone their skills, and policy requires that they stay current on world politics by reading newspapers and magazines and by attending intelligence briefings. As one of them said, "It behooves us to know if there is a hot situation in Africa, geography of the area, what forces are involved, etc. Just in case."

The real job at Molink consists of sending and receiving test messages. Only on New Year's Day and 30 August (the hot line's anniversary) do the Washington and Moscow terminals depart from routine for one message, to send greetings.

The colonel in charge of Molink assigns his teams to come up with new messages. The messages, from 150 to 300 words long in order to simulate the length of a real message, come from the encyclopedia, Mark Twain, a first-aid manual, or whatever. "We anguish and argue over them and make sure there is no innuendo," one official has explained. For instance, a passage concerning Winnie-the-Pooh getting his head stuck in the honey jar might be considered an affront to the Russians, whose national symbol is the bear. Test messages often try to offer a slice of Americana, albeit a bland slice. Though controversy is avoided, the teams search out passages that are interesting, amusing, or challenging to translate. Puns, proverbs, poems—it has evolved into something of a mini-cultural exchange.

Test messages prepare Molink for the day when a real message comes in or out. If Boris Yeltsin sends a message to President George Bush, Molink first transmits the Russian text by "secure" line to the White House Situation Room. In this way the president can call on his National Security Council Russia expert if he so chooses. Then the on-duty team, as well as the team on call, and maybe even additional translators, meticulously translate the message and get it to the president forthwith. It is the translating that takes time: "If it's something that's so crucial, we'll get the president on the phone immediately and 'gist' it [give a rough translation] to him," Colonel Donald Siebenaler explained in 1988, when he was in charge of the hot line. For this purpose a secure phone at Molink leads directly to the White House Situation Room. From the Russian leader's lips to the U.S. president's ear, an urgent message would take well under five minutes.

Updating the Hot Line   Today, the procedures of 1963 remain intact, but now three separate links make up the hot line. Such redundancy ensures that a message will always get through. In the first strategic-arms limitations talks (SALT), the United States and Soviet Union agreed in 1971 to establish satellite hot-line links. An American commercial satellite, INTELSAT, and a Russian government satellite, MOLNIYA, each furnish a communication circuit, and the original 1963 European circuit provides the third channel. Both satellites operate simultaneously, ensuring uninterrupted communications in case one should fail. (Whenever suggestions were made to scrap the original cable, the Soviets balked. As one hot-line specialist explained, "They said, 'Ah no. That's the wedding ring, the tie that binds. And while it's old and obsolete, it's extremely reliable and inexpensive.'" Sophisticated encryption technology prevents third parties from understanding any transmitted message. The cost to operate the hot-line system is about $1.2 million per year—a Pentagon program well worth the money. In their 1971 Agreement on Measures to Reduce the Risk of Outbreak of Nuclear War, the United States and the

Soviet Union designated the hot line as the medium of choice for "transmission of urgent information, notifications, and requests for information in situations requiring prompt clarification," such as nuclear terrorism or accidents.

In 1984, hot-line technology was further modernized when the United States and the Soviet Union agreed to upgrade the system for high-speed facsimile transmission. Now, maps, charts, texts, and photographs can be sent almost instantly. The 1984 agreement also obligates both countries to review proposals periodically for additional hot-line improvements. Many wonder why the hot line is not upgraded for teleconferencing. In his 1983 "Report to Congress: Direct Communications Links and Other Measures to Enhance Stability" Defense Secretary Caspar Weinberger stated, "Because voice communication is more difficult than written material to translate, it is far more subject to misunderstanding." Printed text also provides a permanent record and time to think through a counterpart's message before responding. For both reasons, Weinberger's report states, "emergency voice communications . . . could reduce . . . ability to resolve a crisis. The same considerations apply, in heightened fashion, to the installation of video conferencing capabilities."

Wherever the president goes, he can be patched into Molink at a moment's notice. Interestingly, he does not have access to a hot line in the National Emergency Airborne Command Post (NEACP, pronounced "kneecap"), a plane intended to take the president or vice-president aloft in the event of an imminent nuclear attack. Though having a direct private line to the Russian leadership in the NEACP might be worthwhile, objections have been raised that such a communications capability might reveal the plane's location. The nuclear strategist Scott Sagan ventured that if the hot-line terminals in either capital were destroyed by a nuclear attack, "rapid and secure communications would not be possible." Sagan suggested an alternate mobile emergency hot line, since unbroken communications between adversaries is absolutely essential for terminating a nuclear war. None of the "hardened" U.S. military command centers has a hot-line terminal. Further, the hot line's satellites might not withstand the effects of nuclear explosions, and they may be subject to attacks themselves. Though technically feasible, the improvement of the hot line's ability to survive a nuclear attack would be costly. That the hot line would not survive direct nuclear attacks must give leaders in Washington and Moscow pause about launching such attacks: Could the war be stopped, once begun?

ACTUAL EMPLOYMENT OF THE HOT LINE

Though the actual number of hot-line uses is unknown—only the president is authorized to declassify that information—the Department of Defense acknowledges that Molink has been used sparingly since its inception, "but has proved invaluable in major crises."

Just before eight o'clock in the morning on 5 June 1967, Secretary of Defense Robert McNamara phoned President Lyndon Johnson's White House bedroom: "Mr. President, the hot line is up" (Johnson, *The Vantage Point,* London, 1971, p. 287). After an Israeli preemptive strike against Arab military forces, Soviet Premier Alexei Kosygin sent a hot-line message: Soviet forces would stay out of the impending Middle East conflict if the United States agreed to do likewise.

But when jets of unknown origin attacked a U.S. communications ship off the Sinai Peninsula, a U.S. carrier task force moved into the area to rescue survivors. Worried that the Soviets might misinterpret the Sixth Fleet's maneuvers as intervention, President Johnson sent a hot-line message explaining the action.

As the Six-Day War escalated, Johnson and Kosygin exchanged more messages at several crucial junctures. Referring to this episode, Robert McNamara called the hot-line "very useful" in preventing what could have become a direct United States–Soviet confrontation.

In 1971, during the India-Pakistan War, the United States warned Moscow over the hot line to pressure India for an immediate ceasefire or the United States would proceed unilaterally, an action that might produce "consequences neither of us want" (Desmond Ball, "Can Nuclear War Be Controlled?", Adelphi Paper 169, p. 22). When the United States put its nuclear forces on alert during the 1973 Arab-Israeli war, First Secretary Leonid Brezhnev responded via the hot line. The hot line was also used in 1974 during the Turkish invasion of Cyprus and in 1979–1980 because of the Soviet invasion of Afghanistan; in 1982–1984 the Soviets used it to discuss Lebanon, while the United States used it regarding Poland.

The hot line has rarely been used in noncrisis cases. For instance, during the SALT II negotiations, when President Jimmy Carter's personal letters to Brezhnev were repeatedly answered with "something that looked like it had been written by the 14th sub-secretary of the Foreign Ministry," national-security adviser Zbigniew Brzezinski recommended that the president send his letter over the hot line. It got the attention of the Soviets, who came back with something akin to "Please don't ever do that again!" The Soviets took the hot line especially seriously. Limiting the hot line's use to real crises ensures that its messages will not go unnoticed.

Not surprisingly, the hot line's success has generated similar measures around the world. The French president has his own "green line" to the Soviet leadership, as do the British. Other rival neighbors which have set up hot lines include Israel and Egypt, and North and South Korea. One of the earliest hot lines was a link between Arab and Israeli military commanders on opposite sides of Jerusalem following the 1948 cease-fire. Indian and Pakistani leaders have been connected by a hot line since their 1971 war, though it reportedly went unused during a 1986 crisis involving large military maneuvers on both sides of the international border. Even the Japanese are promoting the idea of a worldwide network of hot lines.

CONCLUSION

The superpowers seem to want more means of communicating between them. On 15 September 1987, the United States and the Soviet Union agreed to establish Nuclear Risk Reduction Centers (NRRCS), which became operational in April 1988. Referred to by some as a "warm line," the centers provide a lower-level diplomatic channel for exchanging noncrisis arms control information, such as missile-test notifications, exchange of data required by treaties and confidence-building measures, and clarification of treaty provisions. The original proposal for NRRCS outlined by Senators Sam Nunn and John Warner specified that the centers would "maintain a 24-hour watch on any events with the potential to lead to nuclear incidents." Nunn and Warner envisioned a much more expansive crisis-management role for the NRRCS than was agreed to: under their proposal the centers were to be employed for maintaining "close contact during incidents precipitated by nuclear terrorists" and "to exchange information about military activities which might be misunderstood by the other party during periods of mounting tensions."

Like the hot line, the NRRCS, one in each capital—the idea was for the Soviets to staff the Moscow center and Americans the Washington one—were to be linked by high-speed facsimile and satellite communications. Their functions would have been limited by agreement and were not intended to replace normal diplomatic communications channels or the hot line. In his 1983 Report to Congress, Defense Secretary Weinberger concluded that a crisis-control center would probably be "completely bypassed in national crisis decisionmaking." Even if it were not, Weinberger believed, such a center might exacerbate a crisis by creating a "cumbersome extra layer" of bureaucracy.

The Weinberger report also suggested the creation of a Joint Military Communications Link (JMCL), a direct line between U.S. and then Soviet national military command centers. Weinberger said that a JMCL "would allow rapid exchange of highly technical information that could be essential to understanding and therefore resolving a nuclear or other military crisis." The JMCL proposal was rejected by the Soviet Union, perhaps because Soviet leaders feared a loss of centralized political control over military involvement in crisis communications. However, in February 1992, following the end of the Cold War and the dissolution of the Soviet Union, U.S. Secretary of State James A. Baker and Russian Foreign Minister Andrei Kozyrev announced that they planned to negotiate the establishment of a ballistic missile early-warning center, which would become the first concrete defense cooperation between the United States and Russia. The proposed center would connect all NATO and Russian radar, satellite, and other early warning systems in a single location, where all the parties could monitor all ballistic missile launchings worldwide.

The hot line's simplicity and enduring importance offers a striking example and instructive lesson in managing a nuclear-armed world. As Thomas Schelling puts it, "The hot line is not a great idea, just a good one. It reminds us that arms control need not be exclusively focused on grand schemes to preserve the peace" (1966, p. 262). Even though the U.S. and Russian governments established more friendly relations than the U.S. and Soviet governments enjoyed during the Cold War, each side concluded that a direct communications link between presidents would be prudent to maintain for whatever crises might be ahead. The product of nothing more than common sense, the hot line functions as the live wire of peace.

BIBLIOGRAPHY

All of the unattributed quotations from hot line officials in this article are the result of personal interviews with the author.

The writings of THOMAS C. SCHELLING especially stress the importance of communications measures, such as hot lines, for war prevention and crisis management, including "Bargaining, Communication, and Limited War," *Journal of Conflict Resolution* 1 (1957): 19–36; "The Role of Communications in Arms Control," in EVAN LUARD, *First Steps to Disarmament* (New York, 1965); and *Arms and Influence* (New Haven, Conn., 1966).

For discussion of various United States–Soviet confidence-building agreements, including the direct communications line, see WILLIAM J. LYNN, "Existing U.S.-Soviet Confidence-Building Measures," in BARRY M. BLECHMAN, *Preventing Nuclear War: A Realistic Approach* (Bloomington, Ind., 1985); and MICHAEL M. MAY and JOHN R. HARVEY, "Nuclear Operations and Arms Control," in ASHTON B. CARTER, JOHN D. STEINBRUNER, and CHARLES A. ZRAKET, eds., *Managing Nuclear Operations* (Washington, D.C., 1987).

There is remarkably little writing on the hot line itself. The hot-line agreement and its subsequent amendments are discussed by SALLY K. HORN, "The Hotline," in JOHN BORAWSKI, ed., *Avoiding War in the Nuclear Age: Confidence-Building Measures for Crisis Stability* (Boulder, Colo., 1986). This volume includes a number of useful essays examining the importance of confidence-building measures for reducing tensions between adversary states and avoidance of "accidental" war.

For analysis and discussion of Nuclear Risk Reduction Centers and their potential role in crisis management, see RICHARD K. BETTS, "A Joint Nuclear Risk Control Center," in Blechman, *Preventing Nuclear War*; SAM NUNN, "Risk Reduction and Crisis Prevention"; and WILLIAM L. URY and RICHARD SMOKE,

"Beyond the Hotline: Controlling a Nuclear Crisis," both in Borawski, *Avoiding War in the Nuclear Age.* Ury expanded on his concepts for a crisis-management center in *Beyond the Hotline: How Crisis Control Can Prevent Nuclear War* (Boston, 1985).

For a history of the proposals and negotiations behind the United States–Soviet NRRC agreement, see John Borawski, "U.S.-Soviet Move Toward Risk Reduction," *Bulletin of the Atomic Scientists* 43 (July-August, 1987): 16–18. Senators NUNN and WARNER's original NRRC proposal and Caspar Weinberger's 1983 Report to Congress are reproduced in Blechman, *Preventing Nuclear War,* Appendices A and B.

The technical and practical aspects of implementing communications measures and crisis-management centers, including joint military communications links and high-speed embassy-capital communications links, are examined in DALE M. LANDI et al., "Improving the Means of Intergovernmental Communications in Crisis," *Survival* 26 (1984): 200–214. The usefulness and vulnerability of current hot-line technology in the event of a nuclear war are discussed in ROBERT G. LEAHY, "The Mechanics of War Termination," in STEPHEN J. CIMBALA and JOSEPH D. DOUGLASS, JR., *Ending a Nuclear War: Are the Superpowers Prepared?* (Washington, D.C., 1988).

The Non-Proliferation Treaty and the Review Conferences

1965 to the Present

○

WILLIAM EPSTEIN

See also Nuclear-Weapon-Free Zones; The Proliferation of Nuclear Weapons; *and* Test Ban Proposals and Agreements: The 1950s to the Present. *The* Non-Proliferation Treaty *is excerpted in Volume III.*

After the completion of the atomic bomb in July 1945 and its use at Hiroshima and Nagasaki the following month, the three countries involved in developing the bomb (the United States, the United Kingdom, and Canada) became preoccupied with preventing a nuclear arms race. Since the Charter of the United Nations had been signed in June 1945, before the advent of the bomb, it contained no reference to atomic weapons. The three nations therefore met in Washington, D.C., and on 15 November 1945 signed a three-power declaration on the control and use of atomic energy.

At the first session of the United Nations, which opened in January 1946 in London, the General Assembly unanimously decided, in its first resolution, to establish the United Nations Atomic Energy Commission "to deal with the problems raised by the discovery of atomic energy." The commission was charged with making specific proposals regarding the elimination of atomic weapons from national arsenals and the development of effective safeguards against violations, and to ensure that atomic energy was used only for peaceful purposes.

It was clear from the beginning of the atomic age that there was a dichotomy between military uses and peaceful uses of atomic energy. The United States, all the great powers, and indeed all the members of the U.N. wanted to promote the peaceful uses of atomic energy without disseminating the technology of the atomic bomb.

After the failure of the United States–sponsored "Baruch Plan" for the control of atomic energy, and the development of the hydrogen bomb in the early 1950s, the U.N. Atomic Energy Commission was replaced by the Disarmament Commission. The idea of a nuclear test ban was put forward as the best means of preventing the proliferation of nuclear weapons by the then three nuclear powers (the United States, the United Kingdom, and the Soviet Union) and by non-nuclear states. The development of the hydrogen bomb led to the use of the term "nuclear" to cover both atomic and hydrogen weapons. The first official proposal to stop nuclear testing was made by India on 2 April 1954, when Prime Minister Jawaharlal Nehru called for a "standstill agreement" to suspend nuclear explosions even if measures to end the production and stockpiling of nuclear weapons had not yet been undertaken.

In the meantime, in 1953 President Dwight D. Eisenhower had made his "Atoms for Peace" proposal at the U.N. for the promotion of the peaceful uses of nuclear energy under safeguards to prevent its diversion to military purposes. This initiative culminated in 1957 with the establishment of the International Atomic Energy Agency (IAEA).

On 10 May 1955 the Soviet Union became the first nuclear power to advocate a nuclear test ban when it proposed, as one of the first measures for the reduction of armaments and the prohibition of nuclear weapons, that the nuclear powers should "undertake to discontinue tests of these weapons." Thereafter, a ban on testing continued to be sought as the most effective way of stopping the further proliferation of nuclear weapons.

In 1957 a group of American scientists led by Dr. Edward Teller, who is generally regarded as the "father" of the hydrogen bomb, proposed that peaceful nuclear explosions could be undertaken for large-scale industrial purposes such as mining, oil and gas production, and the building of roads, harbors, and canals. A number of scholars believe that the idea of such peaceful nuclear explosions was invented and popularized out of fear that nuclear weapon tests would be banned.

With the development of atomic weapons by the Soviet Union (1949) and the United Kingdom (1952) and the development of the hydrogen bomb by the United States (1952), the Soviet Union (1953), and the United Kingdom (1958), there was growing international concern about such proliferation, or what was then called the "Nth country problem," to signify the unknown final number. This intensified after France developed an atomic bomb (1960) and a hydrogen bomb (1968), and China an atomic bomb (1964) and a hydrogen bomb (1967). Thus by the early 1960s there were five declared nuclear powers.

In 1958, Ireland became the first country to offer a proposal at the United Nations that was specifically aimed at preventing the spread of nuclear weapons. Three years later a resolution proposed by Ireland calling on all states, and particularly on the nuclear states, to conclude an international agreement to prevent the dissemination or acquisition of nuclear weapons was adopted unanimously.

Thereafter, the work on both a nuclear test ban and on nuclear non-proliferation proceeded as two separate but related subjects, but with the test ban given priority. The United States, the Soviet Union, and the United Kingdom, the three nuclear powers at that time who had tested both atomic and hydrogen bombs, made notable progress at the Conference on the Discontinuance of Nuclear Weapon Tests from 1958 to 1961. The conference's work was merged with other disarmament issues in the Eighteen Nation Disarmament Committee (ENDC) in 1962, with a mandate to seek agreement on a treaty for general and complete disarmament.

It quickly became clear in the ENDC that no agreement could be reached on general and complete disarmament and attention was therefore focused on a nuclear test ban as the most important and urgent step toward halting the nuclear arms race. The eight nonaligned members of the ENDC—Brazil, Burma, Egypt, Ethiopia, India, Mexico, Nigeria, and Sweden—concentrated their efforts on achieving the cessation of all nuclear-weapon tests as the best means of preventing the spread and further development of nuclear weapons, a position that almost all non-nuclear countries maintain to this day.

Early hopes for a total nuclear test ban foundered on the differences between the United States and the United Kingdom on one side and the Soviet Union on the other over the problem of verification of such a ban. The nuclear powers disagreed over the need for and the number of on-site inspections required to distinguish earthquake tremors from those produced by underground nuclear explosions.

The shock of the Cuban missile crisis in October 1962 (when the Soviet Union tried to install medium-range nuclear missiles in Cuba), and the consequent desire of the three nuclear powers to reduce tensions and improve the international atmosphere, led to their signing—on 5 August 1963—the Treaty Banning Nuclear Weapon Tests in the Atmosphere, in Outer Space, and Under Water, known as the Partial Test Ban Treaty (PTBT) or the Limited Test Ban Treaty (LTBT). The Soviet Union in effect agreed to accept the proposal of the United States and the United Kingdom to ban nuclear testing in the three environments where international verification measures were unnecessary. The treaty, however, clearly stated in Article I the determination of the parties to continue negotiations to conclude a treaty for "the permanent banning of all nuclear test explosions, including all such explosions underground," which is generally referred to as a comprehensive test ban, or (CTB). The U.N. General Assembly readily approved the PTBT and called for the urgent negotiation of a CTB.

The entry into force of the PTBT in 1963 and the explosion by China of its first atomic bomb in 1964 led the three nuclear powers and the members of the United Nations to concentrate their attention on preventing the further proliferation of nuclear weapons.

NEGOTIATIONS FOR THE NON-PROLIFERATION TREATY

In 1965 the U.N. General Assembly called for the early negotiation of a treaty by the Eighteen-Nation Disarmament Committee to prevent the proliferation of nuclear weapons. Among principles on which such a treaty should be based, according to the Assembly, were the maintenance of "an acceptable balance of mutual responsibilities and obligations of the nuclear and non-nuclear Powers," and the furtherance of nuclear disarmament.

The United States and the Soviet Union each submitted draft treaties on non-proliferation in 1965. Both drafts sought to prevent the dissemination of nuclear weapons to non-nuclear states, but the Soviet Union claimed that the U.S. draft would give the Federal Republic of Germany (West Germany) "access" to nuclear weapons through NATO or through an envisioned multilateral nuclear force. By 1967 the two powers had resolved their differences; the United States agreed not to pursue the development of a multilateral nuclear force and the Soviet Union agreed to abandon its opposition to the establishment of a nuclear planning committee in NATO. This enabled the two powers to submit separate but identical drafts of a non-proliferation treaty.

For their part, the nonaligned members of the ENDC insisted that a balance of mutual obligations would require tangible steps for halting and reversing the nuclear arms race. They urged that, in exchange for their agreeing to end the "horizontal" proliferation of nuclear weapons (the acquisition of nuclear weapons by other countries), the nuclear powers should agree to end their "vertical" proliferation of such weapons (increasing the quantity and quality of their weapons). They listed the specific steps in the following order: (a) a comprehensive nuclear test ban; (b) a complete cessation of the production of fissionable material for weapons purposes; (c) a freeze on, and gradual reduction of, nuclear weapons stocks and their means of delivery; (d) a ban on the use of nuclear weapons; and (e) security assurances to the non-nuclear states by the nuclear powers. These demands of the nonaligned states were also supported by some of the non-nuclear allies of the United States and the Soviet Union.

The two nuclear superpowers maintained that, because of their differing approaches to and priorities for arms control, it would not be possible for them to agree on mentioning the specific measures proposed by the nonaligned nations in the operative part of the treaty, but that compromise formulas were possible. After much prodding and pressure, not only from the nonaligned countries but from their own allies, the United States and Soviet Union agreed to include a provision in the operative part of the treaty (Article VI) relating to the halting and reversing of the nuclear arms race. The two nuclear powers also agreed to several amendments to strengthen the text, in particular by the addition of the phrases "in good faith" and "at an early date" in the final text of Article VI, which reads:

Each of the Parties to the Treaty undertakes to pursue negotiations in good faith on effective measures relating to cessation of the nuclear arms race at an early date and to nuclear disarmament, and on a treaty on general and complete disarmament under strict and effective international control.

The two powers also agreed to clarify the meaning of this article by stating their intentions in paragraphs 8, 10, and 11 of the preamble:

Declaring their intention to achieve at the earliest possible date the cessation of the nuclear arms race and to undertake effective measures in the direction of nuclear disarmament,
Recalling the determination expressed by the Parties to the 1963 Treaty banning nuclear weapon tests in the atmosphere, in outer space and under water in its Preamble to seek to achieve the discontinuance of all test explosions of nuclear weapons for all time and to continue negotiations to this end,
Desiring to further the easing of international tension and the strengthening of trust between States in order to facilitate the cessation of the manufacture of nuclear weapons, the liquidation of all their existing stockpiles, and the elimination from national arsenals of nuclear weapons and the means of their delivery pursuant to a treaty on general and complete disarmament under strict and effective international control.

The non-nuclear states felt that the promises of the nuclear powers to pursue negotiations to end their vertical proliferation of nuclear weapons did not constitute an adequate exchange for their binding, unqualified commitment to end horizontal proliferation, but they thought that they had pushed the nuclear powers as far as possible in this regard. They considered the treaty to be an essential measure toward the goal of nuclear disarmament and they trusted the nuclear powers to live up to their promissory commitments in the treaty. The non-nuclear states were reassured in this regard by statements of the leaders of each of the three nuclear parties, and in particular by that of British Prime Minister Harold Wilson on 5 March 1970, when he said:

We know that there are two forms of proliferation, vertical as well as horizontal. The countries which do not possess nuclear weapons and which are now undertaking an obligation never to possess them, have the right to expect that the nuclear-weapon states will fulfill their part of the bargain. (*Documents on Disarmament,* 1970, p. 82)

Even though many considered the treaty to be inherently discriminatory—in that it divided the world into nuclear "have" and "have not" states—they felt that it was a necessary step that could lead in the not too distant future to the elimination of all nuclear weapons. There were several other provisions of the treaty that the non-nuclear states felt could be improved and, in the following years, they would exert strenuous efforts toward that end.

After the final joint revised draft treaty was presented by the United States and Soviet Union in March 1968 to the Eighteen Nation Disarmament Committee, which incorporated several proposals made by the non-nuclear states, the ENDC submitted the draft treaty to the General Assembly. Following intensive discussions, and the acceptance by the nuclear powers of some further revisions to improve the text, the General Assembly, on 12 June 1968, endorsed the Treaty on the Non-Proliferation of Nuclear Weapons (known as the Non-Proliferation Treaty, or NPT). In its resolution, the General Assembly expressed the hope for the widest adherence to the NPT and singled out Article VI for special emphasis by requesting the ENDC and the nuclear powers to pursue the negotiations under that article urgently.

The three nuclear powers were unable to agree on any security assurances to include in the text of the NPT, neither "negative" assurances (not to use or threaten to use nuclear weapons against any non-nuclear state) nor "positive" assurances (to provide assistance or come to the aid of any non-nuclear state that was attacked or threatened with attack by nuclear weapons). They did, however, make declarations of intent in the U.N. Security Council to provide "immediate . . . assistance, in accordance with the Charter" to any non-nuclear party to the NPT that is the victim of an act or threat of aggression in which nuclear weapons are used.

On 19 June 1968 the Security Council adopted Resolution 255, which had been submitted by the three nuclear powers and which approved the tripartite declarations. Nearly all non-nuclear states saw these rather vague security assurances as meaningless or inadequate since they did not add anything to the existing responsibilities of the nuclear powers under the U.N. Charter.

The NPT was opened for signature on 1 July 1968. At the signing ceremony in Washington, President Lyndon B. Johnson announced that the United States and Soviet Union had agreed to hold early strategic arms limitation talks, which came to be known by the acronym SALT. The treaty entered into force on 5 March 1970.

The NPT has been hailed by a number of states and many scholars as one of the most important pacts of the nuclear era. By mid-1992, 150 states had become parties to the treaty, more than to any other arms control or disarmament treaty. Nevertheless, some 20 states still were not parties—including such near-nuclear or potential nuclear powers as Argentina, Brazil, India, Israel, and Pakistan. Following the successful conclusion of the Gulf War in 1991, however, France and China, the remaining two declared nuclear powers, announced that they would sign the NPT, and they did become parties in 1992. South Africa, which was considered to be a near-nuclear power, also decided in 1991 to accede to the treaty. Ominously, however, several states that were parties to the NPT, including Iran, Iraq, Libya, and North Korea, reportedly moved toward becoming nuclear powers. The treaty permits any party to withdraw on three months' notice.

THE NATURE AND SCOPE OF THE TREATY

During the negotiation of the Non-Proliferation Treaty, it became evident that both the nuclear and non-nuclear countries had a common interest in preventing the horizontal proliferation of nuclear weapons. Such proliferation would abort their hopes of ending the nuclear arms race and of eventually eliminating all nuclear weapons. Indeed, it would increase the risk of a nuclear war, whether that war was deliberate or a result of accident, miscalculation, panic, or desperation.

While the non-nuclear countries were willing to join with the nuclear powers in the primary objective of preventing the continued spread of nuclear weapons to other countries, their overriding purpose was to end all further proliferation of nuclear weapons, whether horizontal or vertical. Thus, they were willing to accept the discriminatory nature of the treaty as a temporary measure, not only because it would open the door to their obtaining access to the peaceful uses of nuclear energy but also because they were ready to trust the promises of the nuclear powers. The non-nuclear countries concentrated their efforts on eliminating or at least reducing the imbalance between the nuclear and the non-nuclear states. In addition, the non-nuclear states were motivated by their basic and abiding hope that if the nuclear arms race could be ended and progress could be made toward general and complete disarmament, the possibilities for receiving greater assistance for their desperately needed economic development would be vastly improved.

The Obligations of the Nuclear Parties   The Non-Proliferation Treaty imposes the following obligations on those nuclear powers party to it:

1. Not to transfer nuclear weapons or explosive devices to non-nuclear states or help them to acquire such weapons or explosive devices (Article I). This is not a burdensome obligation as no nuclear-weapon state would consider assisting in the spread of nuclear weapons to other countries. Even China and France, who decided only in 1991 to become parties to the NPT, had repeatedly stated that they would abide by its objectives. Nevertheless, there is evidence that sources of supply in all the nuclear countries have provided sensitive material to non-nuclear countries.

2. To facilitate and promote the peaceful uses of nuclear energy for non-nuclear parties (Article IV). This article has been implemented to some limited extent, but in a manner and at a level that most non-nuclear states regard as inadequate. In any case, the latter consider it to be the primary duty and responsibility of the International Atomic Energy Agency to promote and encourage the peaceful uses of atomic energy under safeguards, and they feel that the NPT merely reconfirmed and strengthened the promises made by the nuclear powers in the IAEA Statute.

3. To make the potential benefits of peaceful nuclear explosions available to non-nuclear parties (Article V). Most of the nuclear powers look with disfavor on peaceful nuclear explosions, and this article has never been implemented. Since the technology of peaceful and military nuclear explosions is practically identical, any state that can explode a peaceful nuclear device can also explode a nuclear bomb. In 1974, India exploded a peaceful nuclear device but announced that it did not intend to manufacture any nuclear weapons. The vast majority of scientists believe that peaceful nuclear explosions are neither economically feasible nor desirable.

4. Finally, the commitment to "pursue negotiations in good faith" to first halt and then reverse the nuclear arms race (Article VI). This article has traditionally been regarded as the most important part of the bargain between the nuclear and non-nuclear parties.

The Obligations of the Non-Nuclear Parties   The following obligations are imposed on those non-nuclear states party to the NPT:

1. Not to manufacture or acquire nuclear weapons or other nuclear explosive devices (Article II). This is a legally binding commitment that entered into force for each non-nuclear party when the treaty did on 5 March 1970.

2. To accept full-scope safeguards by the International Atomic Energy Agency on all their peaceful nuclear activities and facilities (Article III). This is regarded by the non-nuclear states as an onerous obligation, as the IAEA full-scope safeguards apply not only to imported nuclear materials, equipment, and technology, but also to those that are indigenously produced. The non-nuclear states also point out that Article III imposes a greater burden on them than it does on states that are not parties to the NPT and that have to accept only such safeguards as are imposed on them by the IAEA or by the nuclear supplier states, which usually apply only to the material and equipment supplied. The non-nuclear states have also claimed that it was discriminatory for them to be subjected to the IAEA safeguards, while the peaceful activities and nuclear facilities of the nuclear powers were not. As a result, the three nuclear parties to the treaty have agreed voluntarily to place some, but not all, of their peaceful nuclear reactors under IAEA safeguards.

3. Since articles IV, V, and VI set forth obligations for all parties to the treaty, the non-nuclear states

are also required to implement the obligations contained in these articles. These articles, however, have been traditionally regarded as imposing obligations on the nuclear powers.

Since the NPT contained no verification provisions to ensure that the nuclear parties were complying with their obligations under the treaty, the non-nuclear parties insisted that the following stipulations be included in the treaty text:

1. Article VIII makes provisions for amendment conferences to be held if requested by at least one-third of the parties to the treaty. However, for the amendment to enter into force, it would have to be ratified by a majority of the parties, by all the nuclear parties, and by all other parties that are members of the thirty-five-member board of governors of the International Atomic Energy Agency. This makes the amendment process very cumbersome and difficult.

2. More importantly, the article provides that a review conference may be held every five years at the request of the majority of the parties to assure "that the purposes of the Preamble and the Provisions of the Treaty are being realized." (The review conferences are considered below.)

3. Article X provides that any party may withdraw from the treaty by giving three months' notice to all other parties and to the U.N. Security Council. No party has taken advantage of this withdrawal right, but a few non-nuclear parties have hinted at some review conferences that if the nuclear powers fail to live up to their commitments under the treaty, non-nuclear parties might consider withdrawing from the treaty.

4. Again, more importantly, Article X provides that after twenty-five years a conference shall be held "to decide whether the Treaty shall continue in force indefinitely, or shall be extended for an additional fixed period or periods." This extension conference must be held in 1995. (It is considered below.)

THE NON-PROLIFERATION REGIME

The Non-Proliferation Treaty is the main pillar of a non-proliferation regime that has been carefully built up over the years. The other main components of the regime, some of which were introduced above, are reviewed here in the order in which they were developed.

The International Atomic Energy Agency
This Vienna-based organization was established in 1957, eleven years before the NPT, to promote the peaceful uses of atomic energy and to assist non-nuclear countries in the peaceful applications of nuclear energy, on condition that they do not divert any nuclear material or equipment furnished them to making nuclear weapons. The agency created a system of international safeguards to monitor compliance with this proviso. Thus the statute of the agency constituted a sort of non-proliferation bargain between the nuclear and the non-nuclear countries. (Euratom, which includes only member states of the European Community, has similar aims.) The IAEA has 112 member states, including all five nuclear powers and all Euratom members.

The Partial Test Ban Treaty   This 1963 agreement, which also predates the NPT, prohibited nuclear weapon tests in the atmosphere, in outer space, and underwater, but not underground. Underground explosions are permitted so long as they do not result in the spewing of radioactive debris or fallout outside the borders of the state conducting the test. The treaty also states that the parties seek to end "all test explosions of nuclear weapons for all time" and are determined to continue negotiations for that purpose. The treaty was concluded by the three principal nuclear powers at that time—the United States, the Soviet Union, and the United Kingdom—and by 1992 had 117 signatories, but neither China nor France had signed. Significantly, the rate of underground testing by the United States and the Soviet Union accelerated after the conclusion of the treaty. Hence the treaty, which was drawn up in the hope of curbing the nuclear arms race, has turned out to be more of an environmental and health measure than a means of arms control. While a number of other countries had by the early 1990s developed the capability to undertake nuclear tests, no other country had done so except India, which conducted one test in 1974.

The Treaty of Tlatelolco   This treaty, officially called the Treaty for the Prohibition of Nuclear Weapons in Latin America, created in 1967 a nuclear-weapon-free zone in Latin America. It prohibits the testing, production, deployment, or use of nuclear weapons by the countries of the zone. By 1992, all the countries of the area had signed the treaty except for Cuba and Guyana; twenty-three countries were full parties. In 1990 the presidents of Argentina and Brazil announced that they had jointly decided to become full parties to the Treaty of Tlatelolco. Brazil also announced the end of a secret program that had been undertaken by the military to conduct an underground nuclear test. Brazil and Chile signed and ratified the treaty but by 1992 it had not yet entered into force for them pending the completion of certain conditions; Argentina had signed the treaty but had not yet ratified it.

All five nuclear powers have signed and ratified a protocol to the treaty in which they pledge to fully respect all the provisions of the treaty and not to use or threaten to use nuclear weapons against the parties. It is the only treaty dealing with nuclear weapons to which all five nuclear powers are parties and the only one that places a legal limitation on their right to test, produce, deploy, or use nuclear weapons. Thus, the treaty has been hailed as establishing a fair balance of obligations between the nuclear and non-nuclear states, and as the model for other nuclear-free zones. Until 1985, with the signing of the Treaty of Rarotonga, it was also the only treaty to limit the use of nuclear weapons in an inhabited part of the earth.

The Nuclear Suppliers Group

In order to reduce the possibilities for nuclear weapons proliferation and to ensure to the extent possible that nuclear materials, equipment, and technology would not be diverted to the production of weapons, a number of supplier countries came together in London during 1974 and 1975 to establish rules and controls for the export of nuclear supplies. The group, which by 1992 consisted of twenty-seven supplier countries (most, but not all, of the supplier countries) including Western, Eastern, and neutral countries, prepared guidelines for restricting the export of sensitive material and equipment and urged that full-scope safeguards be applied to all nuclear exports. Australia, Canada, Sweden, and only a few other countries rigidly enforce full-scope safeguards over all their nuclear exports to non-nuclear countries. While the guidelines create useful standards for strict licensing procedures for the export of materials that can be used to develop weapons, they are not legally binding or enforceable.

The efforts of the Suppliers Group were expanded in 1977 in a meeting of both suppliers and importers called the International Nuclear Fuel Cycle Evaluation (INFCE). Sixty-six countries undertook a nonpolitical, technical, and analytical study of ways that the danger of proliferation of nuclear weapons could be minimized without jeopardizing the development of nuclear energy for peaceful purposes. After two years of study and evaluation of possible international management arrangements for elements of the nuclear fuel cycle—producing uranium from ore, using it in a nuclear reactor, and recycling the fuel—INFCE concluded that there were no feasible technical procedures or arrangements that would by themselves ensure that the military and the peaceful uses of nuclear energy could be separated or "decoupled" so as to prevent the horizontal proliferation of nuclear weapons.

Useful precautionary or ameliorative measures, according to the INFCE, include developing more effective and credible bilateral and international safeguards and establishing regional and international institutions that would have a restraining or deterrent effect on countries contemplating proliferation. It seems clear, however, that such measures would not be sufficient to prevent a nation from acquiring nuclear explosives if it possessed a nuclear power industry and if it was determined to develop an atomic or even hydrogen bomb.

The Treaty of Rarotonga

In 1985, a nuclear-weapon-free zone was created in the South Pacific. As in the Treaty of Tlatelolco, the eleven parties to the Treaty of Rarotonga agreed to prevent the testing, production, stationing, or use of any nuclear explosive device in their territories. Protocols to the treaty provide that the five nuclear weapon states shall not use or threaten to use any nuclear explosive device in or against the territory of any party to the treaty, or test a nuclear explosive device anywhere within the zone. China and the Soviet Union had signed these protocols but by 1992 France, the United Kingdom, and the United States had not.

EVALUATION OF THE NON-PROLIFERATION REGIME

The elaborate structure of the non-proliferation regime has created an international political climate in which the prospect of the further spread of nuclear weapons is looked upon with disfavor. Nevertheless, adherence to the Non-Proliferation Treaty and acceptance of IAEA safeguards do not provide any absolute guarantee that a country will not at some stage decide to "go nuclear."

The possession of either a nuclear research or a power reactor by a country does not necessarily mean that that country will make or try to make a nuclear bomb, but it does mean that the country can develop the capability to do so. Any moderately advanced country that possesses nuclear material, equipment, and technology need only build a small reprocessing plant in order to obtain the fissionable plutonium from the spent fuel of the reactor.

The NPT does not of course prevent or prohibit non-nuclear countries that are not parties from manufacturing or acquiring a nuclear weapon. Nor does it prevent or prohibit non-nuclear parties from developing a nuclear weapon capability or option; it merely prohibits them from acquiring or manufacturing the weapons themselves. The only conclusive proof that a country has joined the nuclear club is the carrying out of a nuclear test explosion. A country could therefore prepare a small stockpile of plutonium (as is believed to be the case with India and Israel, which are not parties) or of highly enriched uranium (as is reported in the case of Pakistan—a non-party—and South Africa, which became a party in 1991) without testing any explosive device and, at a time of its choosing, embark on a testing program. Even a country that is an NPT signatory could begin nuclear tests after giving the requisite three months' notice of withdrawal.

About a dozen non-nuclear parties to the NPT already possess sufficient or almost sufficient quantities of plutonium or enriched uranium, and therefore are regarded as having a nuclear weapon capability. Experts believe that another fifteen to twenty countries could either test or develop untested nuclear weapons within a year or two, if they so chose; another dozen could do so by the end of the century—if they had a sufficient motivation or incentive to embark on a purposeful program to acquire a nuclear weapon capability.

There are a number of reasons why states may wish to "go nuclear" and, for those that are already nuclear powers, to remain in the nuclear arms race. The overriding motivations are, first, the desire by a state to enhance its own military power and security—or at least to prevent its rivals from gaining military superiority; and, second, to have sufficient retaliatory capacity to discourage other nuclear powers from attacking. Great and small powers alike appear to believe that they can achieve or maintain a greater degree of independence and security if they have their own nuclear forces and do not have to rely entirely on the support or protection of other nations. In this regard, so long as the nuclear powers behave as though their security depends on their possession of nuclear weapons, it is very difficult to persuade other states that acquiring nuclear weapons would not enhance their security. This is particularly true in the case of neutral or nonaligned countries that are not allied to a nuclear power, and thus considered to be under the "nuclear umbrella" of that power.

In addition, there are a number of political and economic motivations for developing a nuclear weapons capability—to achieve or maintain great power status and prestige, that is, to "sit at the head table"; to demonstrate political and economic independence and self-reliance; and to be able to resist political or economic pressures from stronger powers, whether nuclear or non-nuclear.

Internal domestic pressures from the "military-industrial complex" and the "scientific-technological elite" are not confined solely to the nuclear powers. It is clear that equivalent pressures exist in the near-nuclear states that are not parties to the NPT and not allies of a nuclear power. Indeed, a number of scholars believe that we have been more lucky than wise in managing to avoid the nightmare world of fifteen or twenty nuclear powers that President John F. Kennedy in 1963 feared might emerge by 1975.

THE LINKAGE BETWEEN A CTB AND THE NPT

In the preamble to the Non-Proliferation Treaty the three nuclear parties recalled their determination, as expressed in the Partial Test Ban Treaty, to achieve a comprehensive test ban pact as a means of ending the nuclear arms race. The non-nuclear states have repeatedly argued that without a CTB there could be no cessation of the nuclear arms race. A CTB was additionally necessary both for nuclear disarmament and the ultimate goal of the elimination of nuclear weapons. On the other hand, according to the non-nuclear nations, if nuclear testing is not stopped, then even deep reductions of existing nuclear forces could become largely meaningless. If older nuclear weapons can be constantly replaced by new or "modernized" ones as a result of nuclear testing, then there can never be an end to vertical proliferation.

After negotiations for the Partial Test Ban Treaty were completed, President Kennedy, in a national television and radio address on 26 July 1963, drew the connection to non-proliferation: "This [Treaty] can be a step toward preventing the spread of nuclear weapons to nations not now possessing them.... This Treaty can be the opening wedge in that campaign." (*U.S. ACDA Documents on Disarmament* 1963, pp. 254–255) Later, in a message to the Eighteen Nation Disarmament Committee on 27 January 1966, President Johnson stated:

My country persists in its belief that the perils of proliferation would be materially reduced by an extension of the limited test ban treaty [PTBT] to cover underground nuclear tests. For such an extension, the United States will require only that number and kind of inspections which modern science shows to be necessary to assure that the treaty is being faithfully observed. (*U.S. ACDA Documents on Disarmament* 1966, p. 7)

Almost all non-nuclear countries regard a cessation of the nuclear arms race, which is the first obligation in Article VI of the NPT, as in effect requiring a nuclear weapons freeze, that is, a halt to the testing, production, and further deployment of nuclear weapons. They consider that Article VI gives halting the nuclear arms race priority over other measures of nuclear disarmament and that it is logical to stop the development of new nuclear weapons before proceeding to their reduction and possible elimination. As such, they regard a comprehensive test ban as the most important, feasible, and easily attainable first step to halt both the horizontal and vertical proliferation of nuclear weapons.

Deprived of the right to conduct tests, military leaders in both the nuclear and the non-nuclear countries could not be certain that new nuclear weapons would work properly, and they would have less incentive to acquire or use them. Governments, too, would be unwilling to spend the vast sums necessary to develop a stockpile of untested nuclear weapons.

In a historic Final Document adopted by consensus at the United Nations' First Special Session on Disarmament in 1978, the General Assembly recognized that the cessation of nuclear weapon testing would make a significant contribution to "ending the qualitative improvement of nuclear weapons and the development of new types of such weapons and of preventing the proliferation of nuclear weapons" (paragraph 51). In April 1980 the U.N. secretary-general submitted the report on a comprehensive nuclear test ban prepared by a group of experts at the request of the General Assembly. The conclusion of the report stated:

A comprehensive test ban could serve as an important measure of non-proliferation of nuclear weapons, both vertical and horizontal.... [It] would make it difficult, if not impossible, for the nuclear-weapon states parties to the treaty to develop new designs of nuclear weapons.... [It] would also place constraints on the further spread of nuclear weapons by preventing nuclear explosions.... (U.N. Document A/35/257, p. 40)

A study prepared in 1986 for the Council on Foreign Relations by a panel of top experts including Ambassador Gerard C. Smith, negotiator of the SALT I agreement, Brent Scowcroft, national security advisor in the Ford and Bush administrations, and James Schlesinger, secretary of defense in the Nixon and Ford administrations, concluded:

A comprehensive test ban treaty could make a significant contribution to containing proliferation.... For non-nuclear weapon states other than India abstinence from testing would mean that they could not demonstrate the achievement of a nuclear explosive capability or have full confidence that they had achieved it; and for all non-nuclear weapon states it would effectively preclude the development of improved or advanced types of explosives.... Moreover, the achievement of such a treaty ... would help preserve the viability of the Non-Proliferation Treaty by providing the most widely demanded response to the complaint that the superpowers are not meeting their obligations under that treaty to pursue nuclear arms control." (*Blocking the Spread of Nuclear Weapons,* 1986, p. 12)

A Non-Aligned Summit Conference, held in Belgrade in September 1989 and attended by more than one hundred heads of government and foreign ministers, adopted a declaration that stated, "A comprehensive nuclear test ban treaty ... is absolutely essential for the preservation of the non-proliferation regime embodied in the NPT." (U.N. document A/44/551 and S/20870, p. 22, para. 11)

Despite the massive persuasive evidence of the linkage between a CTB and the NPT, the United States in the early 1990s continued to deny that such a connection existed. The U.S. government also rejected the claim that cessation of the nuclear arms race is the first priority under Article VI of the treaty. These policies put the United States on a collision course with the nonaligned states, who constitute a large majority of the parties to the NPT, over the linkage between a CTB and the NPT. Some observers predicted that continued downgrading and postponing of a CTB by U.S. leaders would be viewed by the nonaligned states as a U.S. repudiation of its obligations under the PTBT and the NPT. That could do serious damage to the NPT.

THE NPT REVIEW CONFERENCES

The non-nuclear parties to the Non-Proliferation Treaty attach importance to the provision in Article VIII for conferences to be held every five years (if a majority of the parties concur) to review the operation of the treaty "with a view to assuring that the purposes of the Preamble and the Provisions of the Treaty are being realized." These parties had agreed in Article III to accept full-scope IAEA safeguards to ensure their compliance with the treaty; the review procedure is the only means provided in the treaty to assure the compliance of the nuclear parties. In practice, the review conferences have served merely to assess, but not to assure, the compliance of the nuclear parties.

At the review conferences of 1975, 1980, 1985, and 1990, the most noteworthy common feature was the dissatisfaction expressed by most of the non-nuclear parties with what they considered the failure of the three nuclear parties to live up to their treaty obligations. In particular, the United States, the Soviet Union, and the United Kingdom were viewed as in breach of their obligation to implement the nuclear disarmament pledges contained in Article VI and the Preamble, which deal mainly with preventing vertical proliferation. The nuclear powers, who were more interested in reducing the risks of horizontal proliferation, expressed concern at the conferences about the implementation of the provisions for promoting the peaceful uses of nuclear energy and the question of safeguards. On the whole, however, these two issues were regarded as secondary ones and did not lead to the confrontations evident over the nuclear disarmament provisions.

The non-nuclear parties did not constitute a solid bloc at any of the four review conferences. Those parties allied to either the Eastern or Western nuclear parties tended to side with the Soviet Union or the United States, the respective leaders of the two military alliances, although on secondary issues the demarcations were not always clear. On the primary disarmament issue, the non-nuclear parties who were most active in their demands and criticisms of the nuclear parties were the neutral and nonaligned states. (Throughout this essay, NNA will represent neutral and nonaligned states.)

Unlike at most conferences dealing with arms control and disarmament, there were few major differences between East and West at the review conferences. There was an evident commonality of interest among the three nuclear powers and they and their allies displayed a sense of cooperative solidarity in resisting the demands of the NNA countries. Their common overriding desire to prevent the horizontal proliferation of nuclear weapons, which they feared would undermine their nuclear monopoly and dominance, prevailed during even the darkest days of the Cold War, but tended to be less in evidence at the 1985 and 1990 reviews, when the Cold War was ending. At all four conferences, the NNA states took the lead in presenting proposals in an effort to obtain full compliance by the nuclear powers with their commitments to nuclear disarmament.

At the first review conference in 1975, attended by fifty-eight of the then ninety-six parties to the treaty, all non-nuclear parties claimed that they had lived up fully to their commitments under the NPT, but the NNA states claimed that the nuclear parties had not done so. The main proposals put forward by the NNA were: (*a*) an end to underground nuclear testing beginning with a moratorium on testing, (*b*) a substantial reduction in nuclear arsenals, (*c*) a pledge not to use or threaten to use nuclear weapons against non-nuclear parties, and (*d*) substantially increased aid to the developing countries in the peaceful uses of nuclear energy.

Several of the non-nuclear allies of the Soviet Union and the United States were sympathetic to some of these proposals and a fragile consensus was achieved on a declaration in which the nuclear powers in effect promised to try harder to meet the demands of the non-nuclear states. The NNAs, however, in an "interpretative statement" attached to the declaration, said that they stood by their political proposals and interpreted the declaration in the light of those proposals.

When the second review conference, attended by 75 of the 115 parties to the NPT, met in 1980, the NNA countries were disappointed by the failure of the nuclear parties to make progress toward the cessation of the nuclear arms race, and in particular toward a CTB, during the five-year interval. Although the SALT II Treaty had been signed by the United

States and Soviet Union in June 1979, it remained unratified and subject to considerable criticism in the United States. At the review conference, the non-nuclear parties were impressed by the opening statement of Sigvard Eklund, the director-general of the International Atomic Energy Agency, in which he said:

The non-proliferation regime can only survive on the tripod of the Non-Proliferation Treaty, effective international safeguards and a comprehensive nuclear test ban treaty. The vital third leg is still missing as it was five years ago. (Text of statement was contained in an IAEA press release at the time; it is summarized in the Final Document of the conference, NPT/CONF. II/SRI, p. 5)

A consensus was readily attainable on international cooperation in the peaceful uses of nuclear energy, and on safeguards, where all parties demonstrated some flexibility and a willingness to cooperate. However, a consensus on ending and reversing the nuclear arms race proved elusive. The nuclear powers would make no concessions on nuclear arms control measures, not even on the early establishment of a working group in the Geneva Conference on Disarmament to begin negotiating a CTB. As a result there was no agreement on a final declaration and the conference ended in failure, without even a formal reaffirmation of support for the NPT.

When the third review conference met in 1985, attended by 86 of the 130 parties to the NPT, the outlook looked gloomier than before. The international situation had deteriorated in the intervening five years and the nuclear arms race was proceeding at the fastest pace ever. Far from the nuclear powers living up to their obligations under Article VI, negotiations for several measures of nuclear arms control either had been suspended or were stalemated and, for the first time, there had been no agreement on any measure of nuclear disarmament in the preceding five years. The trilateral negotiations between the United States, the Soviet Union, and the United Kingdom for a comprehensive nuclear test ban had been suspended in 1980, and the United States refused to resume them or agree to begin multilateral negotiations in the Conference on Disarmament. Global military expenditures had escalated to some $1,000 billion a year to the detriment of world economic and development prospects, and there was the looming threat of a new, incalculable, destabilizing, and exorbitantly costly arms race in both defensive and offensive weapons in outer space.

Because of the escalating nuclear arms race, U.N. Secretary General Javier Pérez de Cuéllar struck a keynote in his message to the 1985 conference stating, "Unless the nuclear arms race between the major powers is halted and the further spread of military capability deterred, the terrible possibility of wholesale destruction will increase yet further." Referring to the commitments in Article VI he continued,

In this respect, the implementation of the treaty has been largely one-sided, to the understandable concern and profound dissatisfaction of its non-nuclear weapon parties. There must be recognition of the fact that restraint on one side cannot reasonably be demanded in the face of unlimited expansion on the other.

The Soviet Union pointed to its repeated efforts to resume negotiations for a test ban, its support for a nuclear weapons freeze and nuclear disarmament, its unilateral moratorium on nuclear testing from 5 August 1985 until 1 January 1986, and its offer to extend the moratorium if the United States agreed to stop testing also. The United States repeated that a comprehensive test ban remained a long-term goal but that a test ban would not reduce the number of nuclear weapons, and that the most urgent task was deep reductions of the existing nuclear arsenals.

Speakers from NNA countries repeated their long-standing demands made at the first two review conferences and added a call for a nuclear weapons freeze. They also urged early agreement at the bilateral United States–Soviet negotiations to end the arms race and prevent its extension into outer space. Mexico served notice that if the conference was unable to agree on a final declaration by consensus, it should proceed to adopt one or more resolutions by voting. The rules of procedure of the conference called for all decisions to be made by consensus if possible. If no consensus was obtainable, decisions could be made by a two-thirds majority vote. Obviously, if a consensus could be worked out, that would be preferable as it would reflect the support of all parties.

As was the case at the two previous reviews of the NPT, there was much discussion of safeguards against the diversion of nuclear energy from peaceful to military purposes and of the entire range of questions concerning the peaceful uses of nuclear energy. There appeared to be no serious problems, however, about reaching agreement on these subjects. As no consensus seemed likely concerning compliance with Article VI, the NNA members announced that they would cosponsor and press for a vote on three resolutions proposed by Mexican Ambassador Alfonso García Robles, a Nobel Peace laureate. The resolutions called for:

1. the resumption in 1985 of negotiations by the three nuclear powers for a comprehensive test-ban treaty;
2. a moratorium on testing pending the conclusion of a CTB treaty; and
3. a freeze on the testing, production, and deployment of nuclear weapons.

The Soviet Union, like the United States, wanted to avoid a vote and to reach a consensus final declaration, but the Soviet delegation passed the word privately that if the conference did proceed to a vote it would vote for all three resolutions, which in fact reflected basic Soviet policies.

Of the eighty-six states participating in the conference, some fifty were NNAs, about twenty were Western states, and some ten were Socialist states. Thus it seemed clear that, with the Socialist states and some Western states voting for the resolutions, they would probably be adopted by the necessary two-thirds majority. Accordingly, in order to avoid a vote, Ambassador Lewis Dunn of the United States made some concessions in an effort to reach a compromise consensus. He and Ambassador García Robles entered into negotiations with some other delegates to seek an acceptable solution.

In the final hours of the conference a compromise was worked out that made it possible to adopt, by consensus, a final declaration of some twenty-six pages. The compromise language that was included in the declaration as pertains to Article VI of the Non-Proliferation Treaty was as follows:

The Conference except for certain States . . . deeply regretted that a comprehensive multilateral Nuclear Test Ban Treaty banning all nuclear tests by all States in all environments for all time had not been concluded so far and, therefore, called on the nuclear-weapon States Party to the Treaty to resume trilateral negotiations in 1985 and called on all the nuclear-weapon States to participate in the urgent negotiation and conclusion of such a Treaty as a matter of the highest priority in the Conference on Disarmament.

The declaration also noted that certain states considered deep and verifiable reductions in existing arsenals of nuclear weapons as having the highest priority. (The "certain states" were the United States and the United Kingdom). It also noted the readiness of the Soviet Union to proceed forthwith to trilateral and multilateral negotiations to conclude a Comprehensive Test Ban Treaty.

Although both the 1975 and 1985 conferences were qualified successes, the latter meeting differed in an important respect from the former. In 1975 the NNA states could not command a two-thirds majority vote and they found it necessary to express reservations to the consensus final declaration. In 1985 the NNA states were confident they could obtain a two-thirds majority and thus were able to have their views reflected in the final declaration, while the United States and the United Kingdom found it necessary to express reservations. The 1985 conference demonstrated that voting power had shifted, or was in the process of doing so, from the nuclear powers and their allies to the NNA states. As a result of the commitment and persistence of the NNA states, the final declaration for the first time focused primarily on the disarmament aspects of the NPT and stressed the overriding importance of a CTB as having highest priority in the "cessation of the nuclear arms race at an early date" (Article VI).

The non-nuclear states considered that they had sent a clear message that the nuclear parties must abide by their treaty obligations to halt and reverse the nuclear arms race if the NPT was to endure. Thus while the Third Review Conference was considered to be a success, the NPT was given only a reprieve, not a clean bill of health.

When the fourth review conference opened in 1990, although only 84 out of 141 parties to the NPT attended (two less than in 1985), they did so with a heightened sense of the parley's importance. This would be the last review before the extension conference scheduled to take place in 1995 to decide on the future of the NPT. During the previous five years, the world had gone through historic and dramatic changes. The Cold War had ended, East and West Germany would be united in October, the

Warsaw Pact was in the process of dissolution, and NATO was going through a period of change and uncertainty. The nonaligned movement, unsure toward whom it was nonaligned, had lost much of its raison d'être. The Persian Gulf crisis had begun and had split the Arab world. The five nuclear powers, who are also the permanent members of the U.N. Security Council, appeared to be cooperating in making the Security Council function in the way it was originally intended, and the prospects for arms control and disarmament and of establishing international peace and security on a sound basis under the U.N. Charter seemed better than ever before.

While the NNA countries, the Western states, and the Socialist states all pointed to the international situation as supporting their group's position and policies on nuclear non-proliferation and the NPT, observers agreed that those positions and policies had remained the same as before, except for one new development that affected the course of the conference. In 1988, a group of six nonaligned countries had made a formal proposal to amend the PTBT and, thus, convert it into a CTB, which had received the necessary support for the convening of an amendment conference. They hoped to reach their goal before the NPT extension conference convened in 1995.

The NNA group of countries came better prepared and with greater confidence in 1990 than at the previous review conferences. They considered that they were in a stronger position to bring pressure on the nuclear parties to agree both to a CTB and to substantial measures of nuclear disarmament. They protested that despite the final declaration of the 1985 review conference, no multilateral, trilateral, or bilateral negotiations for a CTB had taken place or had even begun. As a result, the non-nuclear states had begun to lose confidence not only in the sincerity of the nuclear powers but also in the non-proliferation process itself.

Some of the NNA countries noted that the NPT had been a great success in preventing the proliferation of nuclear weapon *states* but had been an utter failure in its intended purpose of preventing the proliferation of nuclear *weapons*. Although the number of declared or acknowledged nuclear powers had remained at five, the number of strategic nuclear weapons alone possessed by the United States and Soviet Union had increased more than sixfold since the NPT was signed, to a total of some

23,000. Even if their strategic arsenals were cut by 50 percent, the two powers would still retain more than three times the number they had in 1968.

The NNA states presented their demands in four resolutions. The first contained a list of many measures to halt, freeze, and reverse the nuclear arms race with top priority given to a CTB and a moratorium on testing. The second focused on strengthening the IAEA safeguards on all exports of nuclear material, equipment, and technology. The third, which specified that the extension conference would be held in New York in 1995, called for measures to strengthen the NPT by implementing the provisions of Article VI to make possible "a significant extension of the Treaty beyond 1995." And the fourth called on all parties to negotiate in good faith at the test ban amendment conference, which would convene in New York in January 1991. Nigeria and Egypt also made separate proposals related to security assurances for non-nuclear states against nuclear threats or attack.

Except for the measures regarding peaceful uses of nuclear energy and strengthened safeguards, the United States, the United Kingdom, and their allies found little to support in any of the NNA proposals. They counterproposed that the NPT be made universal by obtaining the adherence of the states that were not parties, and that it be extended indefinitely in 1995, but they put forward no new ideas or incentives that offered any hope for achieving those goals. Their statements mainly stressed the achievement of the 1987 Intermediate-Range Nuclear Forces (INF) Treaty to eliminate an entire class of land-based intermediate and shorter-range nuclear weapons, the progress in the Strategic Arms Reduction Talks (START) negotiations, progress in the negotiations toward a convention to eliminate all chemical weapons, and advances on confidence-building and other measures. They also noted the bilateral United States–Soviet agreement on protocols to the 1974 Threshold Test Ban Treaty (TTBT) and the 1976 Peaceful Nuclear Explosions Treaty (PNET).

In response, the NNA welcomed the progress that had been made, but said that it was grossly inadequate to achieve compliance with Article VI and the Preamble of the NPT, which gave first priority to ending the nuclear arms race at an early date rather than to other measures of disarmament. They rejected the step-by-step approach to a CTB, and most of them regarded the TTBT and PNET as out of date and as tending to legitimize continued nuclear testing.

The Soviet Union supported most of the measures proposed by the NNA, including a CTB and an immediate moratorium on testing, the cessation of production of fissile materials for nuclear weapons, a nuclear freeze, the prevention of an arms race in outer space, and stronger security assurances to the non-nuclear states. But it maintained its traditional solidarity with the United States on matters relating to the NPT and in insisting on the importance of achieving a consensus on a final declaration.

Although agreement seemed possible on many issues, it became clear that a confrontation was looming on disarmament, and in particular on a CTB, which had become the main point of contention. A committee chaired by the Swedish Ambassador Carl-Magnus Hyltenius managed to produce a draft final declaration containing some 135 paragraphs, about 115 of them representing consensus. Some 15 of the unresolved paragraphs dealt with Article VI and the Preamble of the treaty. A number of compromises had been achieved, but not on a CTB.

On the last day of the conference, after many hours of discussion, Hyltenius proposed a final compromise on a CTB, which he urged the parties to accept without amendment:

The Conference further recognized that the discontinuance of nuclear testing would play a central role in the future of the NPT. The conference also stressed the significant importance placed upon negotiations, multilateral and bilateral, during the next five years, to conclude a CTB [comprehensive test-ban]. The Conference again calls for early action towards that objective, by the Conference on Disarmament, at the beginning of its first session in 1991. The Conference urges that the *ad hoc* committee on a Nuclear Test Ban be given an appropriate mandate to pursue the objective of negotiations to conclude a comprehensive nuclear test ban treaty.

The NNA states agreed to accept the chairman's compromise text without change, but the United States, to the disappointment of some of its allies, wanted some additions. Its insistence on a reference to the United States–Soviet step-by-step negotiations constituted, in effect, a rejection of the chairman's compromise and thus made agreement on a final declaration impossible.

The president of the review conference, Ambassador Oswaldo de Rivero of Peru, sought at the last minute to achieve a consensus by proposing the inclusion of a paragraph that merely summarized the differences of the two sides on Article VI and the Preamble. His proposal did not, however, mention negotiations for a CTB, which was the key point of contention. Although the Western and Eastern delegations were willing to accept the proposal, the nonaligned group was not. The conference therefore ended with no substantive final declaration nor any reaffirmation of support for the NPT, and without any request for a review conference in 1995.

The discussions at the 1990 review were on the whole more thorough and franker than in the past and the real differences among the nuclear and non-nuclear parties were clarified. Opinions of delegates and observers were divided on the failure to achieve consensus. One participant noted the special importance of this last review before the 1995 extension conference and hoped that the outcome of the review would lead the United States and United Kingdom to reconsider their attitude toward a CTB and move them toward real compliance with Article VI of the treaty. Others feared that it would serve to undermine support for the NPT and jeopardize the chances for its extension for a lengthy or even significant period of time.

U.N. secretary-general de Cuéllar addressed this concern in a statement on 25 October 1990:

The issue of nuclear weapons—and their continued testing—remains a divisive one, as the recent Fourth Review Conference on the Nuclear Non-Proliferation Treaty has shown. . . . It is of paramount importance that a viable regime for the nonproliferation of nuclear weapons beyond 1995 is agreed upon by the international community. . . . I have repeatedly underlined the desirability of a comprehensive test ban treaty and I would urge that all sides seek to make progress on this sensitive and intractable question.

THE TEST BAN AMENDMENT EFFORTS

Disappointed and frustrated by the reluctance of the Western nuclear powers even to begin negotiations for the long-promised CTB, and hoping for the support of the Soviet Union, which had consistently expressed its willingness to agree to a comprehensive test ban, a group of nonaligned states decided to take action themselves. Led by Ambassador García Robles, they received the overwhelming support of the U.N. General Assembly in 1985 to take advantage of the amendment provisions in the PTBT to convert that accord into a CTB treaty. On 5 August 1988, the twenty-fifth anniversary of the signing of the PTBT, and the eve of the forty-third anniversary of the atom bombing of Hiroshima, six parties to the PTBT—Indonesia, Mexico, Peru, Sri Lanka, Venezuela, and Yugoslavia—formally proposed to the three depositary governments (the Soviet Union, the United Kingdom, and the United States) that a conference be convened to convert the PTBT into a CTB treaty. By April 1989, more than the required one-third of the 118 parties had joined in the request, and the rather surprised and somewhat reluctant depositary governments announced that they would convene the conference in accordance with their treaty obligations.

Although only a majority of the parties, sixty, must approve and ratify an amendment in order for it to enter into force, the three nuclear powers must be included in that majority, giving them a right of veto. The Soviet Union supported the amendment but the United States and United Kingdom—who for years had blocked all attempts to begin multilateral negotiations for a CTB and had voted against the U.N. resolutions supporting the amendment efforts—announced that they would oppose the amendment, which would quickly dispose of the amendment process as a means of achieving a CTB.

The non-nuclear states believed that reason and public opinion were on their side and that the amendment initiative would eventually succeed. Their strategy was to ensure that the amendment conference would not be limited to a single session but would continue, as is customary with all arms control treaty negotiations, for as many sessions as were necessary to achieve a consensus. Their plan called for no votes to be taken until a consensus was reached, thus leaving no opportunity for a veto.

The non-nuclear states relied primarily on the linkage between a comprehensive test ban and the NPT to work to their advantage. The PTBT has a unique provision: once an amendment is ratified by the requisite majority, including the three depositaries, it becomes binding on all parties. Near-nuclear powers—such as Argentina, Brazil, India, Israel, and Pakistan—which are parties to the PTBT but not to the NPT—would all be bound by a comprehensive test ban amendment that would be enforced by a verification system. In this way, a comprehensive ban would curb both horizontal and vertical proliferation, thus providing a powerful incentive to the three nuclear parties to ratify the amendment. Another impetus for the United States and United Kingdom to reconsider their position is that continued opposition to the comprehensive ban could have a disastrous effect on the NPT renewal talks in 1995.

Despite their agreement to convene the test ban treaty conference, the nuclear powers raised many obstacles. In September 1989 a group of more than one hundred heads of government and foreign ministers from nonaligned states, meeting in Belgrade, called for "the amendment conference to convene as soon as possible in 1990." At the U.N. General Assembly session in 1989, most non-nuclear states wanted the conference to meet in New York in June 1990, before the NPT review. Following standard practice, costs would be shared on the basis of the U.N. scale of assessments, to enable the largest possible number of parties to participate.

But the three depositary states announced at the General Assembly, without consulting any other parties, that they were issuing invitations for the conference to be held in Geneva for two weeks in January 1991. The Americans let it be known that they thought all parties should share the costs equally. The General Assembly, however, voted in December 1989 to follow the nonaligned states' plan. Although the Soviet Union had joined the other depositaries in issuing the invitation for Geneva in 1991, it supported the resolution; the United States and United Kingdom cast the only negative votes.

After months of intensive consultations, a compromise was reached whereby an organizational meeting for the conference would be held in New York, from 29 May to 8 June 1990, before the NPT review conference. The amendment conference itself would be convened in New York from 7–18 January 1991. While the non-nuclear states resented what they regarded as the high-handed behavior of the depositary governments—the United States still refused to pay more than half its U.N.-scale 25 percent share of the costs for the amendment conference—they saw advantages to meeting in New York, including expanded media coverage and a larger role for the public.

U.S. representatives had expressed the fear that any meetings held before the NPT review might do damage to that treaty. Still others had suggested that if a comprehensive test ban was the price for preserving the NPT in 1991, the United States would abandon the NPT. The December 1989 issue of

Disarmament Times, a U.N.–related publication, quoted Kathleen Bailey of the U.S. Arms Control and Disarmament Agency as saying in an interview with the editor that

If the U.S. is forced to choose between its own national security and its nuclear testing program versus the survival of the NPT—which we would dearly like to see—the U.S. would choose maintenance of its own national security and therefore its own nuclear testing program.

Most American diplomats denied that the United States would abandon the NPT, and diplomats from most other countries gave little credence to that possibility. On 29 May 1989, the United Kingdom representative expressed hope at the organizational meeting for the amendment conference that the amendment initiative would be disposed of as quickly and quietly as possible: "There is no need for complex committee structure or machinery for drafting. . . . The task of the conference is a simple one, which we would like to carry out without fuss and at a minimum cost."

Nonetheless, on 25 September 1990, in a statement at the U.N. General Assembly, Soviet Foreign Minister Eduard Shevardnadze supported a CTB in some of the strongest language ever heard from a senior statesman:

As a matter of the utmost urgency, nuclear tests have to be stopped. If testing is stopped, we have a chance to survive; otherwise the world will perish. I have no doubt whatever about this. We need to tell people about this frankly, without taking refuge in all sorts of specious arguments. (U.N. Document A/45/PV. 6, p. 53)

In any case, the sponsors of the amendment initiative were determined to pursue the amendment process until a CTB was achieved. Many of them seemed convinced that by 1995 there would be both a CTB treaty and an NPT, or neither.

The Nuclear Test Ban Amendment Conference opened in New York on 7 January 1991 as scheduled. It was a historic occasion, the culmination of six years of effort by relatively small nonaligned developing third world nations seeking an end to the nuclear arms race by changing the 1963 PTBT to include a ban on all nuclear tests. This was the first time the smaller powers succeeded in pressing their views to a vote in any conference dealing with the provisions of a disarmament treaty.

The conference saw a number of other firsts. It was the first time that all parties to a multilateral nuclear disarmament treaty were able to engage in actual negotiations on the treaty. The wide participation—100 out of 117 parties—indicated the intensity of interest in a comprehensive test ban. By comparison, only 84 out of 141 parties to the Non-Proliferation Treaty took part in that treaty's 1990 review. It also was the first time that the amendment procedure had been invoked under any disarmament treaty, and the first time that the non-nuclear states had proposed a detailed verification scheme and a sanctions regime to deter violations of a nuclear disarmament treaty. Some supporters of the amendment process expressed the hope that the new developments in this conference would set precedents for future disarmament efforts.

No one expected the two-week conference to produce a CTB. Instead, the most important order of business was a vote on whether to continue the amendment work at a future date. That vote—75 to 2 to reconvene, with 19 abstentions—left the conference's two opponents, the United States and United Kingdom, once more isolated. Seven Western nations that were expected to abstain voted instead to reconvene the conference.

The conference decided that further work was needed on verification and sanctions, and authorized the conference president, Indonesian Foreign Minister Ali Alatas, to undertake consultations to achieve "progress on those issues" and to reconvene the conference "at an appropriate time."

The nonaligned states first tried to set a September 1993 deadline for reconvening the conference, and to create an intercessional working group to deal with verification and sanctions. The conference clearly would have adopted the proposal embodying these demands, but the ten sponsors (the original six conference sponsors plus the Philippines, Nigeria, Senegal, and Tanzania) decided to modify the proposal to gain wider support. As a result, seven Western parties joined in the vote to continue the conference. These included three NATO members—Denmark, Iceland, and Norway—as well as Australia, Ireland, New Zealand, and Sweden. At the end of the conference, Mexico's ambassador Miguel Marin Bosch, a leader of the amendment initiative, called the vote "an important breakthrough" in a previously solid Western front. The seven new supporters apparently saw the amendment conference as a way to increase pressure on these two nuclear powers to negotiate a total ban, possibly in the Conference on Disarmament. Cooperation between the two conferences could speed the achievement of a new treaty. In private, delegates from several other Western nations who had abstained expressed their unhappiness with the stubborn refusal of the United States and the United Kingdom to begin any negotiations for a comprehensive test ban.

The Persian Gulf War had very little impact on the conference except to keep it out of the news. But a number of U.N. representatives mentioned that a comprehensive test ban would prevent Iraq and other would-be nuclear powers from acquiring an arsenal of sophisticated nuclear weapons. Some delegates hoped that after the war, and with further progress on strategic nuclear arms control, President George Bush and the U.S. Congress would review the U.S. position. Resolutions supporting the amendment were introduced in both houses of Congress in January 1991—partly because of the impressive activity of 123 nongovernmental organizations participating in the conference.

The *New York Times,* which had originally opposed a comprehensive test ban, scolded the Bush administration for its intransigence. Additionally, it charged the U.S. delegate to the amendment conference with "gratuitously offend[ing] states that want a total test ban" when she told the conference that "consideration of testing limitations is a serious undertaking that should be conducted in a serious manner." The 27 January 1991 editorial continued: "For the U.S. to insist on testing undermines nuclear arms control and sends the wrong message to potential nuclear powers: 'Do as I say and not as I do.'"

The amendment conference sponsors felt that they had raised the comprehensive test ban once again to a top place on the international arms control agenda. They considered the continuation of the conference a victory. And they believed that with the perseverance of the conference president and activist non-nuclear states, including the seven new Western supporters, the conference could be a turning point in the long struggle to ban nuclear testing, prevent nuclear proliferation, and achieve meaningful nuclear disarmament.

They were encouraged in this belief by continuing strong support in the U.S. Congress for negotiations to achieve a CTB and for full United States participation in the amendment conference. And since the United Kingdom also conducted its tests at the U.S. testing ground in Nevada, they believed that London would follow Washington's lead.

THE 1995 CONFERENCE TO EXTEND THE NPT

The nuclear powers had at first proposed a Non-Proliferation Treaty of unlimited duration. But, as noted previously, in order to provide some assurance that the nuclear parties would comply with their obligations under the NPT, the non-nuclear parties insisted that the treaty remain in force for a fixed period, at the end of which a conference would be convened to determine whether the accord would be extended. As the representative of Mexico, Miguel Marin Bosch, stated at the fourth review conference of the NPT, "There was a close link between the limited duration of the NPT and the provisions of the eighth to twelfth preambular paragraphs and Article VI of the Treaty. That link would be of decisive importance in 1995." (Final Document of the Conference—NPT/CONF.IV/SR.14) The final compromise agreed on in Article X, paragraph 2 of the treaty reads:

Twenty-five years after the entry into force of the Treaty, a conference shall be convened to decide whether the Treaty shall continue in force indefinitely, or shall be extended for an additional fixed period or periods. This decision shall be taken by a majority of the Parties to the Treaty.

Since the NPT is the only arms control treaty that contains such a provision, the legal implications may be subject to different interpretations. Some analysis of the precise language of the text is therefore important.

Unlike the provisions regarding the review conferences and amendments to the treaty, the twenty-five-year provision does not give the depositary governments the explicit right to convene the conference for the extension of the treaty in 1995, nor does it mention where the conference should be held. Most experts believe that the depositary governments would prefer Geneva, but that the other parties would insist on U.N. headquarters in New York on the grounds that, as in the case of the Test Ban Amendment Conference, it would permit the largest number of parties to participate at lower cost, and that access to news coverage by the information media is better in New York.

The extension conference holds three options for the participants. First, they can decide that the treaty will continue in force indefinitely. Second, they can decide that the treaty will be extended for whatever fixed period can garner the support of a majority of the parties, whatever the number may be at the time, with a declared option to extend it further at the expiration of that period. Third, they can decide in 1995 on a series of additional fixed periods of whatever duration that can be agreed by a majority of the parties. Since the main purpose of the provision limiting the duration of the NPT was to provide a means of ensuring compliance with the treaty, and in particular Article VI, successive extensions could be linked to the progress achieved, otherwise there would be little sense or reason for option three. The reasons for the inclusion of the provision for successive extension periods do not appear in the records of the negotiations, but the author, who was present, clearly recalls being informed by several non-nuclear states that they had agreed to "fixed periods" so that each period could be linked or made conditional on achievement of one or more of the disarmament measures they had been advocating. They did not expect all would be agreed at one time. In any case, it would be possible to circumvent a narrow interpretation of this option by, for example, adopting resolutions or declarations at the 1995 extension conference or any review conference, declaring the intentions or views of the majority of parties, or by threatening withdrawal by parties from the treaty unless certain agreements were achieved. No doubt other devices or legal means can be found for ensuring that the will of the majority prevailed and was not defeated by legal technicalities.

At the 1990 NPT Review Conference the nuclear parties clearly indicated that they would like the NPT to be extended indefinitely. The nonaligned countries, on the other hand, emphasized that the nuclear parties must begin to meet their obligations under Article VI in order to achieve "a significant extension of the NPT beyond 1995." While there was no clarification of what was meant by "significant extension," diplomats mentioned extension periods from one to ten years in length.

The possibility exists that the 1995 meeting will yield inconclusive results. For example, fewer than two-thirds of the parties involved were present at any of the four review conferences. If this should also prove to be the case at the extension conference, it may not be easy to obtain even a simple majority of the parties for any decision concerning an NPT extension. If no specific course of action is endorsed by majority vote, it has been suggested that the treaty should continue in force until a new agreement is hammered out. This might take a long time, leaving the treaty in a sort of limbo and thereby weakening or undermining its credibility and viability.

A more prudent course would be to work with all the parties toward reaching the widest measure of agreement. A preparatory committee to decide on the organization of the extension conference (such committees are customary with almost all arms control treaty conferences) should be established as soon as possible in order to permit full consultations on all substantive and procedural questions.

The 1995 extension conference gives the non-nuclear states considerable leverage that they believe will increase as 1995 approaches. There is already some talk among the nonaligned states that, if the nuclear parties remain adamant in their opposition to a CTB, the non-nuclear states may insist that the NPT be extended for only a year or two pending the conclusion of a CTB treaty. Another option being discussed is to extend the NPT for a brief fixed period in order to amend the treaty to specify that a CTB be in place by a certain date, and possibly to fix a timetable to reach agreement on additional measures such as the cessation of production of fissile material for weapons, elaboration of a plan for a nuclear freeze followed by the phased elimination of nuclear weapons and their delivery vehicles, a ban on the threat or use of nuclear weapons, and specific security assurances to non-nuclear states. A third option is to take the United States and the United Kingdom before the International Court of Justice. If there is a confrontation on any of these issues, or if the United States follows through on its threats not to attend or not to pay its share of the costs of the next session of the test ban amendment conference, the NPT might be doomed.

In order to allay the doubts of the non-nuclear states, it may be necessary for the nuclear parties to demonstrate their commitment to the NPT and provide some assurance that its objectives will be fully realized. Without the confidence and strong support of the majority of the non-nuclear parties, the NPT cannot long endure.

THE FUTURE OF NON-PROLIFERATION

From the time of the signing of the NPT in 1968, the world community understood that, despite its importance, the NPT suffered from shortcomings, in particular as regards what some NNA countries considered its inherently discriminatory aspects. It was generally hoped and believed that these shortcomings would soon be reduced and gradually eliminated as the nuclear powers proceeded to carry out their obligations under the treaty, first to end, and then to reverse, the nuclear arms race, moving toward the ultimate goal of general and complete disarmament.

Over the years, however, the non-nuclear states became increasingly convinced that the shortcomings of the NPT were being compounded as the nuclear arms race continued to intensify and accelerate. Their experience at the successive NPT review conferences seemed to confirm their suspicions that they had been misled by the nuclear powers, perhaps deliberately. In any case, many non-nuclear states became so disillusioned and embittered that they came to distrust the whole concept of non-proliferation. The NNA parties in the 1980s and early 1990s increasingly voiced their rejection of any non-proliferation measures that discriminated between "have" and "have-not" states. Leading NNA countries repeatedly said that, in the future, the prohibition or limitation of any weapons must apply universally and equally to all countries or to none.

As a result of the perceived threat of use by Iraq in the 1991 Gulf War of nuclear, chemical, and biological weapons, and its actual use of missiles with conventional but powerful warheads, the five permanent members of the Security Council—the United States, the Soviet Union, Britain, France, and China, who are also the five nuclear powers—decided that the nuclear non-proliferation regime should be expanded to cover other weapons of mass destruction. At a meeting in Paris on 9 July 1991 they laid out plans to stop the spread of these weapons by stringent national and group controls on the export of certain equipment and materials. They also decided to establish a zone free of weapons of mass destruction first in the Middle East and then globally.

On 16 July the London summit meeting of the Group of Industrialized Nations (the G-7) adopted a similar program, with greater emphasis on strengthening the NPT. Just prior to these meetings, France and China, the only nuclear powers not yet party to the NPT, indicated that they were willing to sign. Several nonaligned nations were not impressed by this development, which they regarded merely as confirmation that all five nuclear powers were mainly interested in preserving their monopoly on nuclear weapons.

While some non-nuclear nations regarded these objectives of the five nuclear powers as commendable, others regarded them as flawed because they were aimed at preventing only the horizontal proliferation of nuclear weapons and not their vertical proliferation.

It has been proposed that the declared nuclear powers and the U.N. Security Council should agree to enter into binding legal guarantees, they would come instantly to the defense of any country that had agreed not to acquire nuclear or other weapons of mass destruction, if that country became subject to attack or threat of attack with such weapons. Such a legal commitment would replace the inadequate Security Council Resolution 255 (1968) and might help to make the expanded non-proliferation ideas of the nuclear powers more acceptable to the non-nuclear nations. It is not likely, however, that the nuclear powers would be prepared to make such onerous commitments any time soon.

The only proposals that might receive the general support of the NNA states are those that will lead to what might be called a "nonarmament" or "nonacquisition" regime (equivalent to a nuclear weapons freeze) rather than to a non-proliferation one. Examples of such regimes are the Biological Weapons Convention (1972) and the negotiations from the early 1980s to the present time (1992) for a chemical-weapons convention that would ban and eliminate all such weapons. Of course, agreements could be achieved on nonarmament or nonacquisition measures that freeze or ban the continued development or modernization of nuclear weapons if the prohibitions are universal and apply equally to all states. A CTB would come within this category.

It is also possible to envisage some additional organizations of exporting or supplier states similar to the Nuclear Suppliers Group and the Missile Technology Control Regime, which established principles and guidelines to prevent, or at least curb, the proliferation of nuclear weapons and some missile technologies. Judging from past experience, however, such export-control regimes are only partially successful. The 1986 report of the high-level panel of experts to the Council on Foreign Relations said in this connection:

The use of export controls to restrict the capabilities of non-nuclear-weapon states to make nuclear explosives can help in some cases but has significant limitations. . . . Although attempts to deny the acquisition of the requisite capabilities by other states may impede, delay, or limit the extent of such acquisition and buy time for discussion, they cannot, in most cases, prevent a sufficiently determined state from eventually acquiring them. (Smith et al., *Blocking the Spread of Nuclear Weapons,* p. 8)

For nuclear and other mass-destruction weapons, partial regimes and successes are inadequate, and only comprehensive or total prohibitions and regimes can be effective and acceptable. For such universal and total bans to be effective, it is essential that they receive the support of not only the industrialized countries but also of the third world and the NNA countries that constitute the vast majority of the community of nations.

As regards the NPT and the non-proliferation regime, India presented some new ideas at the 1988 U.N. Third Special Session on Disarmament. India is not a party to the NPT, which it regards as a discriminatory and flawed treaty, and it proposed that in 1995 the NPT be replaced by a new treaty with a legally binding commitment by the nuclear states to eliminate all nuclear weapons by the year 2010, and by the non-nuclear states not to cross the nuclear weapons threshold.

It is expected that prior to 1995, as well as thereafter, there will be many other proposals to amend, replace, improve, or strengthen the NPT. The future of the NPT will be of decisive importance not only for nuclear non-proliferation but also for the non-proliferation of other weapons of mass destruction and, indeed, of increasingly dangerous conventional weapons as well.

With the ending of the Cold War, and with the declared nuclear powers having no major power as an "enemy" that must be deterred from a nuclear attack, there is now an opportunity to end the nuclear arms race and to move rapidly toward the reduction and eventual elimination of all nuclear weapons. That is, of course, the surest and best way to end the danger of nuclear proliferation and of ridding the world of the nuclear threat.

BIBLIOGRAPHY

There is a vast literature on the Non-Proliferation Treaty and the multifaceted problems and prospects of nuclear weapons proliferation. The publications listed here represent the tip of the iceberg and in-

clude only the most important studies in English. Constraints of space have unavoidably made it necessary to omit many excellent and important works.

The Politics of Proliferation General surveys that deal with the broader political issues include JOSEPH I. COFFEY, ed., "Nuclear Proliferation: Prospects, Problems and Proposals," *The Annals of the American Academy of Political and Social Sciences* 430 (March 1977): entire issue; DAGOBERT L. BRITO, MICHAEL D. INTRILIGATOR, and ADELE E. WICK, eds., *Strategies for Managing Nuclear Proliferation: Economic and Political Issues* (Lexington, Mass., 1983); LEWIS A. DUNN and HERMAN KAHN, *Trends in Nuclear Proliferation 1975–1995: Projections, Problems and Policy Options* (New York, 1976); LEWIS A. DUNN, *Controlling the Bomb: Nuclear Proliferation in the 1980s* (New Haven, 1982); and WILLIAM EPSTEIN, *The Last Chance: Nuclear Proliferation and Arms Control* (New York, 1976).

The NPT Additional general accounts are DAVID FISCHER, *Stopping the Spread of Nuclear Weapons: The Past and the Prospects* (New York, 1992); MICHAEL P. FRY, PATRICK KEATINGE, and JOSEPH ROTBLAT, eds., *Nuclear Non-Proliferation and the Non-Proliferation Treaty* (New York, 1990); TED GREENWOOD, HAROLD A. FEIVESON, and THEODORE B. TAYLOR, *Nuclear Proliferation: Motivations, Capabilities, and Strategies for Control* (New York, 1977); ANNE W. MARKS, ed., *NPT: Paradoxes and Problems* (Washington, D.C., 1975); ALVA R. MYRDAL, *The Game of Disarmament: How the United States and Russia Run the Arms Race* (New York, 1976); GEORGE QUESTER, ed., "Nuclear Proliferation: Breaking the Chain," *International Organization* (Winter 1981): special issue; COUNCIL ON FOREIGN RELATIONS, "Blocking the Spread of Nuclear Weapons: American and European Perspectives" (New York, 1986); SADRUDDIN AGA KAHN, ed., *Non-Proliferation in a Disarming World: Prospects for the 1990s* (Geneva, 1990); MOHAMED I. SHAKER, *The Nuclear Non-Proliferation Treaty 1959–1979,* 3 vols. (New York, 1980); JOHN SIMPSON, ed., *Nuclear Non-Proliferation: An Agenda for the 1990s* (New York, 1987); and JED C. SNYDER and SAMUEL F. WELLS, JR., eds., *Limiting Nuclear Proliferation* (Cambridge, Mass., 1985).

Annual volumes that contain useful sections on proliferation and the NPT include STOCKHOLM INTERNATIONAL PEACE RESEARCH INSTITUTE, SIPRI *Yearbook of World Armaments and Disarmaments* (Stockholm, 1968/69–); UNITED NATIONS, *The United Nations and Disarmament 1945–1970* (New York, 1970), *The United Nations and Disarmament, 1970–1975* (New York, 1976), *The United Nations Disarmament Yearbooks* (New York, 1976–); and U.S. ARMS CONTROL AND DISARMAMENT AGENCY, *Documents on Disarmament* (Washington, D.C., 1960–).

Peaceful Uses and Non-Proliferation   The relationship of nuclear power to the problems of nuclear proliferation are examined in ABRAM CHAYES and W. BENNETT LEWIS, eds., *International Arrangements for Nuclear Fuel Reprocessing* (Cambridge, Mass., 1977); INTERNATIONAL NUCLEAR FUEL CYCLE EVALUATION, *Summary Volume* (Vienna, 1980); Nuclear Energy Policy Study Group, *Nuclear Power Issues and Choices* [Ford-Mitre Study] (Cambridge, Mass., 1977); WILLIAM C. POTTER, *Nuclear Power and Nonproliferation: An Interdisciplinary Perspective* (Cambridge, Mass., 1982); and ALVIN WEINBERG, MARCELO ALONSO, and JACK N. BARKENBUS, eds., *The Nuclear Connection: A Reassessment of Nuclear Power and Nuclear Proliferation* (New York, 1985).

Safeguards   Among the studies dealing with international safeguards are ZACHARY S. DAVIS and WARREN H. DONNELLY, comps., *Non Proliferation—A Compilation of Basic Documents on the International, U.S. Statutory, and U.S. Executive Branch Components of Non-Proliferation Policy* (Washington, D.C., 1990); DAVID FISCHER and PAUL SZASZ, *Safeguarding the Atom: A Critical Appraisal* [SIPRI Publication] (Philadelphia, 1985); CONGRESS OF THE UNITED STATES, OFFICE OF TECHNOLOGY ASSESSMENT, vol. 1, *Nuclear Proliferation and Safeguards* (New York, 1977); vol. 2, *Appendices* (Washington, D.C., 1977); and MASON WILLRICH, ed. *International Safeguards and Nuclear Industry* (Baltimore, Md., 1973). Other references may be found in the bibliography at the end of the IAEA essay.

The Review Conferences   The NPT review conferences have been discussed by WILLIAM EPSTEIN in INTERNATIONAL INSTITUTE FOR STRATEGIC STUDIES, "Nuclear Proliferation: The Failure of the Review Conference," *Survival* (November–December 1975): 262–269; "On Second Review of the Non-Proliferation Treaty," *Bulletin of the Atomic Scientists* (May 1981); *Reviewing the Non-Proliferation Treaty* [Background Paper No. 4] (Ottawa, March 1986); and "NPT Review: Conference a Qualified Success," *The Bulletin of the Atomic Scientists* 46 (December 1990): 45–47; and CHARLES N. VAN DOREN and GEORGE BUNN, "Progress and Peril at the Fourth NPT Review Conference," *Arms Control Today* 20 (October 1990): 8–12.

Near-Nuclear Capabilities   Listed here are assessments of the nuclear potential of individual countries, although additional items may be found in the bibliography following the "Nuclear Proliferation" essay: JOZEF GOLDBALT, ed., *Non-Proliferation: The Why and the Wherefore* (Philadelphia, 1985); GEORGE H. QUESTER, *The Politics of Nuclear Proliferation* (Baltimore, Md., 1973); and LEONARD S. SPECTOR and JACQUELINE R. SMITH, *Nuclear Ambitions: The Spread of Nuclear Weapons 1989–1990* (Boulder, Colo., 1990) provide a useful introduction to the theme.

The Terrorist Threat   Concern over the possibility that terrorists might obtain and use nuclear devices is examined by PAUL LEVENTHAL and YONAH ALEXANDER, eds., *Preventing Nuclear Terrorism: The Report and Papers of the International Task Force on Prevention of Nuclear Terrorism* (Lexington, Mass., 1987); and MASON WILLRICH and THEODORE B. TAYLOR, *Nuclear Theft: Risks and Safeguards: A Report to the Ford Foundation's Energy Policy Project* (Cambridge, Mass., 1974).

The Outer Space Treaty

1967 to the Present

—————————— ◯ ——————————

RAYMOND L. GARTHOFF

See also Arms Control and Anti-Satellite Weapons; Demilitarization and Neutralization Through World War II; Nuclear-Weapon-Free Zones; The Strategic Defense Initiative and Arms Control; *and* The United Nations and Disarmament. *The* Outer Space Treaty *is excerpted in Volume III.*

The Treaty on Principles Governing the Activities of States in the Exploration and Use of Outer Space, Including the Moon and Other Celestial Bodies (or, the Outer Space Treaty) was signed on 27 January 1967 and entered into force on 10 October 1967. It is of unlimited duration and has not been amended. The treaty covers many aspects of the activities of states in outer space, including (in Article IV) the undertaking "not to place in orbit around the Earth any objects carrying nuclear weapons or any other kinds of weapons of mass destruction, install such weapons on celestial bodies, or station such weapons in outer space in any other manner." In addition, that article prohibits "the establishment of military bases, installations and fortifications, the testing of any type of weapons and the conduct of military maneuvers on celestial bodies." The use of military personnel and any equipment or facility necessary for pursuit of peaceful purposes is permitted.

While the Outer Space Treaty is the principal document establishing arms control limitations in outer space, it is not the only one. The Limited Nuclear Test Ban Treaty (LTBT) of 1963 and the Anti-Ballistic Missile (ABM) Treaty of 1972 also include important arms control constraints against testing or deploying various weapons in outer space, and the ABM Treaty and Strategic Arms Limitation Talks (SALT) and Strategic Arms Reduction Talks (START) treaties also include commitments against interference with arms control verification monitoring

space vehicles. The Outer Space Treaty itself contains many important features regulating the peaceful uses of space.

The discussion below is divided into five parts. The first describes a series of early unsuccessful efforts to grapple with the problem of weapons in space during the years 1957 through 1963. Second is the specific question of nuclear testing in space, one element of broader negotiations on nuclear testing from 1958 into 1963. Third is an account of the background and successful negotiation in 1962–1963 of a United Nations resolution banning weapons of mass destruction in space. Fourth is the negotiation in 1966–1967 of the Outer Space Treaty. Finally, there follows a discussion of the history of the operation of the treaty since 1967, subsequent arms control agreements relating to outer space, and remaining issues concerning arms control in outer space.

FALTERING FIRST STEPS TOWARD ARMS CONTROL, 1957–1963

The first proposals for international consideration of arms control constraints in outer space were introduced by the United States, keyed to the fact that during the International Geophysical Year (1957–1958) there would be initial probes and ex-

877

plorations of outer space. On 12 January 1957, Ambassador Henry Cabot Lodge, Jr., submitted to the U.N. General Assembly a memorandum advancing several disarmament (arms control) proposals, including one calling for international inspection of all objects sent into outer space to assure they would be devoted "exclusively to . . . peaceful and scientific purposes." On 29 August 1957, the four Western members of the London U.N. Disarmament Subcommittee submitted a working paper containing the same proposal. The Soviet Union, which only two days earlier had launched the first intercontinental ballistic missile (ICBM) transiting space, reacted by promptly rejecting the proposal.

President Dwight D. Eisenhower then took the matter up with Soviet Premier Nikolai A. Bulganin, repeating the same proposal in a letter on 12 January 1958, but adding a specific proposal to cease testing of (and in effect to ban) military missiles transiting outer space. Bulganin in his reply, and the Soviet Union in a formal proposal to the United Nations on 15 March 1958, advanced a counterproposal: the Soviet Union was prepared to consider a ban on intercontinental missiles and on the use of outer space for military purposes, but only if coupled with a ban on foreign bases. The Soviet argument was that while the United States proposed banning intercontinental ballistic missiles that posed a threat to the United States, U.S. air bases and shorter-range missile bases in other countries surrounding and threatening the Soviet Union were to be maintained. The Soviets felt that if one were to be banned, the other should be banned as well.

The linkage of elimination of ICBMS transitting space and elimination of foreign bases subsumed and enveloped the less immediate issue of banning weapons stationed in outer space. The United States, soon forging ahead of the Soviet Union in ICBMS, lost interest in seeking a ban on missiles transitting space. But later proposals for assuring that outer space be used only for peaceful purposes did not make clear that they would exclude such missiles. A stalemate over this issue persisted for five years.

Two other issues compounded the stalemate. One was a confusion between assuring only peaceful uses of outer space and banning military uses of space—many of which would not involve weapons, and at least some of which (such as navigational aid) could be argued to be peaceful. The United States sought as early as September 1958 to make

this distinction by calling for separate consideration of disarmament and peaceful uses of outer space. The Soviet Union initially balked at this distinction, but the United Nations on 13 December 1958 voted—overriding Soviet opposition—in U.N. General Assembly Resolution 1348 (XIII) to create the Ad Hoc Committee on the Peaceful Uses of Outer Space, which, however, was not commissioned to debate the disarmament issue. By 12 December 1959 the Soviet Union had joined in U.N. Resolution 1472 (XIV) to create the expanded permanent U.N. Committee on the Peaceful Uses of Outer Space, still not charged with dealing with disarmament questions.

The other issue was the relationship of any arms control constraints on activities in space to other aspects of disarmament. The Soviet Union in September 1959 revived the idea of "general and complete disarmament" (GCD), and after a year or so of opposition the United States and other Western powers introduced their own competing proposals. Both Soviet and Western GCD proposals contained arms control measures banning certain activities in outer space, but there were divergences over the nature of the constraints, the stage of disarmament at which they would come into effect, and the linkage or possible separability of such constraints in relation to the general GCD package. This complex issue remained in stalemate through 1962.

There was, however, some progress in defining more discrete measures for space arms control, even if they remained mired in linkage. On 16 March 1960 the Western powers introduced a GCD plan that singled out as a first-stage measure, "joint studies" of an undertaking to prohibit nations from "[placing] into orbit or [stationing] in outer space weapons of mass destruction," albeit with a provision for on-site inspection of launchings for verification. Actual implementation, however, would remain for a second stage, which included declaration and inspection of all missile launch sites and missile launchings, along with other limitations on air, naval, and missile forces. And the Soviet proposals continued to link space, missile, and foreign base disarmament.

The first proposal delinking a ban on weapons of mass destruction stationed in orbit or space from GCD was made by President Eisenhower on 22 September 1960 to the U.N. General Assembly. Eisenhower's proposal continued, however, to condition any such agreement on "appropriate verification," which remained a major issue of contention. This proposal was not followed up, and the general disarmament talks were at that time in extended abeyance following Soviet walkout from the previous forum.

In September 1961 and April 1962 the United States under the Kennedy administration again introduced proposals for staged GCD that contained provisions for banning the placing into orbit or stationing in space of weapons of mass destruction, with provisions for advance notification and inspection of all launchings of space vehicles and missiles. Soviet proposals continued to ban (after September 1962 to limit to low levels) all strategic missiles, and to eliminate all foreign bases.

Meanwhile, several smaller nations had sought to spark negotiation of a separate ban on weapons in space. In March 1962, Canada, without advance consultation with the United States, introduced into the newly constituted disarmament talks in Geneva a proposal for a ban on weapons of mass destruction in space, without inspection. The United States opposed the proposal. A year later Mexico tabled a similar proposal, which was ignored.

Important changes in U.S. and Soviet thinking about a ban on space weapons were, however, under way in 1962–1963 and were to lead to a successful outcome. In the meantime, another aspect of arms control in space had also been developing on a separate track from 1958 to a successful conclusion in 1963.

THE LIMITED NUCLEAR TEST BAN AND OUTER SPACE, 1958–1963

The problem of verifying nuclear weapons tests at high altitudes and in outer space was one aspect of a comprehensive ban on nuclear testing addressed by experts from many nations in July-August 1958. Outer space was seen both as a possible (if unlikely) location for conducting nuclear tests, and as a medium for inspection monitoring through use of artificial earth satellites. Attention was, however, focused on testing in the atmosphere (including low and high altitudes, up to 50 kilometers, or 30 miles), and underground, not in distant outer space.

Outer space was also envisaged, for the first time, as part of a solution to disarmament on earth, with satellite sensors identified as possible contributors to verification. Verifying a ban on nuclear testing in distant outer space, however, loomed as a problem, one that not many regarded as serious in practice, but extremely difficult in principle; detection of nuclear tests conducted clandestinely on the other side of the moon or Mars or millions of miles deep in outer space could not be assured.

In negotiations over the next four years, the greatest practical difficulty and hence concern was addressed to monitoring underground testing. On 2 August 1962 the United States and Britain proposed, as an alternative to a comprehensive test ban including an international control system, a ban on tests in the atmosphere, underwater, and in outer space, relying entirely on national means of verification. While not acceptable to the Soviet Union at that time, following failure to reach agreement on a quota of on-site inspections for a comprehensive ban, the Soviet Union decided to settle for a partial ban. The Treaty Banning Nuclear Weapon Tests in the Atmosphere, in Outer Space and Under Water, more commonly called the Limited Test Ban Treaty, was signed on 5 August and entered into force on 10 October 1963.

Unrelated to that negotiation and agreement, but coincidental in time, a breakthrough was reached in the quest for a ban on deploying weapons of mass destruction in space.

THE U.N. RESOLUTION BANNING WEAPONS OF MASS DESTRUCTION IN ORBIT, 1963

From July to October 1962 the United States government wrestled with the question of a separate ban on weapons in space relying only on national technical means of verification. With President Kennedy's encouragement, a consensus in favor was reached, overcoming initial negative reactions by many to any "declaratory" arms ban. Even before a final decision to seek such a ban, the administration set the stage through a speech delivered by Deputy Secretary of Defense Roswell L. Gilpatric on 5 September 1962. Gilpatric authoritatively declared that the United States had no intention or program to place any weapons of mass destruction in orbit, and implicitly invited the Soviet Union to take a similar stand. He noted that an arms race in space would not contribute to anyone's security, and while either the United States or the Soviet Union could place weapons in space, doing so would not represent a rational military strategic move. This theme was repeated by Ambassador Albert Gore (the Senator was serving as a special U.S. representative at the U.N. General Assembly) on 3 December, and by Secretary of State Dean Rusk on 31 January 1963. Arms Control and Disarmament Agency Director William C. Foster sought to elicit Soviet interest in conversations with Soviet Foreign Minister Andrei A. Gromyko and Ambassador Anatoly F. Dobrynin in New York in October 1962 and Ambassador Semyon K. Tsarapkin in Geneva in early 1963. All were to no avail.

The Soviet leaders remained uncertain and suspicious of the new U.S. initiative. They suspected that the initiative represented an opening wedge to again raise pressure for limits on missiles transiting space, and for verification procedures that would impinge on Soviet military secrecy and missile operations. Eventually they were convinced, and on 19 September 1963 Foreign Minister Gromyko addressed the U.N. General Assembly and expressed Soviet desire and readiness to reach agreement with the United States on a ban on placing weapons of mass destruction in orbit. President Kennedy responded favorably the very next day, and Secretary Rusk confirmed with Gromyko Soviet readiness to proceed, and preference for a treaty or other formal undertaking.

President Kennedy decided that a treaty, in particular because it would involve an arms control limitation without verification except by national means, would face opposition in the Senate. He had in mind the then very recent sharp Senate debates over verification of the Limited Test Ban Treaty. Accordingly, it was decided that the best course would be a U.S. and Soviet jointly supported initiative in the U.N. General Assembly. The Soviets acquiesced. Mexico, which earlier had taken an initiative of its own, was given the opportunity to formally propose the text agreed upon by the United States and the Soviet Union.

On 17 October 1963 the U.N. adopted by acclamation General Assembly Resolution 1884 (XVIII): Stationing Weapons of Mass Destruction in Outer Space, noting and endorsing U.S. and Soviet statements of intent not to station nuclear weapons or other kinds of weapons of mass destruction in outer space. The resolution called on all states "to refrain from placing in orbit around the earth any objects carrying nuclear weapons or any other kinds of weapons of mass destruction, installing such weapons on celestial bodies, or stationing such weapons in outer space in any other manner."

Resolution 1884 was also important, indeed only possible, owing to another "arms control" provision it did *not* contain. The Soviet Union had for years sought to include a ban on satellite reconnaissance, "spying" from space. Even though Soviet Premier Nikita S. Khrushchev had conceded to President Charles de Gaulle at the abortive Paris four-power summit meeting in May 1960 that satellite observation was different from aerial overflight and permissible, the official Soviet stand remained adamantly opposed. On 9 September 1963 the Soviet U.N. representative, Ambassador Nikolai T. Fedorenko, dropped the long-standing Soviet effort to include a ban on satellite reconnaissance in a U.N. resolution on space activities.

The General Assembly also acted on a second important resolution on which agreement had been made possible by the Soviet abandonment of its attempt to outlaw space reconnaissance. On 13 December 1963 U.N. General Assembly Resolution 1962 (XVIII): Declaration of Legal Principles Governing the Activities of States in the Exploration and Use of Outer Space, was unanimously adopted. While this resolution did not include any specific arms control provisions, it helped to establish the principle of free use of space, and in particular included an undertaking to refrain from any activity that could "cause potentially harmful interference with activities of other States in the peaceful exploration and use of outer space" and to undertake appropriate consultations before proceeding with any such activity. This laid a foundation for later agreement on more explicit provisions for noninterference with national space means for arms control verification.

NEGOTIATION OF THE OUTER SPACE TREATY, 1966–1967

As noted, the Soviet Union had been ready to accept a ban on weapons of mass destruction in space in treaty form in October 1963. It was a Soviet initiative in 1966 that led to incorporation of this undertaking in the Outer Space Treaty in 1967.

President Lyndon B. Johnson had, as vice president, been charged with overseeing space affairs, and he continued to take a personal interest in this subject. On 7 May 1966 Johnson proposed conclusion of a treaty governing activities on the moon and other celestial bodies, including a provision on arms control. The U.S. proposal was to ban stationing of weapons of mass destruction, military fortifications, weapons tests, and military maneuvers on celestial bodies. It did not address outer space more generally.

The Soviet response was positive. Three weeks later, on 30 May, Gromyko also proposed a treaty including a similar ban on military installations and weapons of mass destruction on celestial bodies.

On 16 June 1966 both the Soviet Union and the United States submitted draft treaties for consideration at the forthcoming 21st U.N. General Assembly session. The U.S. draft, submitted by Ambassador Arthur J. Goldberg, covered "exploration of the moon and other celestial bodies." The Soviet draft, submitted by Ambassador Platon D. Morozov, was addressed more broadly to activities in the "exploration and use of outer space, the moon, and other celestial bodies." It extended the full range of provisions (for example, excluding claims of national sovereignty, emergency assistance to astronauts of other countries, and dedication to peaceful uses only) and included arms control prohibitions as well, to outer space as well as to celestial bodies in outer space. The provision of the Soviet draft treaty relating to arms control had been amended from Gromyko's May statement to incorporate the additional provisions in the U.S. proposal banning the testing of weapons and the conduct of military maneuvers. The provision banning the stationing in space of nuclear weapons or other weapons of mass destruction was based on the agreed U.N. General Assembly resolution of October 1963 banning the placing of such weapons in orbit around the earth as well as on the moon or other celestial bodies.

The negotiation of a treaty text was turned over to the Legal Subcommittee of the U.N. Committee on the Peaceful Uses of Outer Space. That body worked from July to September, with Ambassadors Goldberg and Morozov playing the key roles. By September agreement had been reached on most points, including the arms control provisions.

It had become clear early in these negotiations that there was wide support for the Soviet proposal to expand the scope of the treaty to outer space as well as celestial bodies. The United States had no objection to doing so, and modified its approach accordingly.

The United States initially proposed, drawing from the Antarctic Treaty of 1959, that any installations or space vehicles should be open to representatives of other countries "at all times," but in response to Soviet objections and arguments of other participants those words were dropped, and the principle of access on the basis of reciprocity and reasonable advance notice was agreed to. On Soviet initiative, military "installations" as well as bases and fortifications were banned. On American insistence, the use of military personnel was specifically allowed, and while military equipment was not explicitly mentioned, it was agreed that all necessary equipment could be used.

The Outer Space Treaty reflected the view of the United States and, by 1966, most nations, that while outer space should be reserved for peaceful purposes (as the U.N. had repeatedly held since 1958), "peaceful purposes" did not preclude use of military resources or even pursuit of military missions. There was recognition and agreement by this time that such military purposes as assistance to navigation, communications, mapping, and observation and reconnaissance were peaceful. Indeed, when it came to formulation of precise arms control constraints, the treaty did not even proscribe some weapons in space. It did not, of course, limit intercontinental ballistic missiles or any missiles transiting outer space, nor firing of earth-based or air-based weapons into space (for example, antisatellite or anti-ballistic missile weapons), nor even stationing in orbit of weapons other than nuclear weapons or other weapons of mass destruction. It did prohibit deployment of any weapons on celestial bodies.

There was no argument or even discussion of the significant provision banning the stationing in space of nuclear weapons or other weapons of mass destruction. The constraint, and even the language, embodied in the October 1963 resolution was simply carried over into the new treaty. This included the apparent redundancy of the then standard formula, referring both to "nuclear weapons" and to "any other kind of weapons of mass destruction," rather than simply to "weapons of mass destruction," nuclear or otherwise. Unknown to other countries, the redundant formula stemmed from an internal American divergence in earlier consideration of the matter in 1963. Representatives of the Joint Chiefs of Staff had favored the simple phrase "weapons of mass destruction," omitting the additional specification of nuclear weapons, because they wished to leave open the possibility later to argue that some small nuclear weapons, for such purposes as anti-satellite or anti-ballistic missile interception, were *not* "weapons of mass destruction" and therefore not banned. They wished to preserve the option of deploying such weapons in space in the future without contravening a U.N. resolution or treaty. It was not, however, their intention to make this loophole known, because that would have led to debate and probably to its rejection. The Department of State did not support the idea of such a sleight of hand approach, and Secretary of State Rusk decided the matter by standing firm for the words "any . . . nuclear weapons or any other kinds of weapons of mass destruction," to ensure that all nuclear weapons were clearly included in the ban.

Full agreement had not been reached in the Legal Subcommittee before the U.N. General Assembly opened in September. One unresolved issue remained, access to earth-based tracking stations. The Soviet Union, lacking the widespread network of friendly governments willing to provide the United States use of their territory for tracking stations, wanted to interpret "equal access to space" to mean that all countries should have equal access to and use of any tracking stations. This stand was opposed not only by the United States but by most countries. In early December the Soviet Union dropped this demand, and a fully agreed treaty text was reached in time for consideration and approval by the General Assembly.

The negotiation of the treaty was greatly facilitated by the United States, Soviet, and general international consensus agreement on legal principles and arms control constraints in the two key U.N. General Assembly resolutions of late 1963. Further compromises and mutual accommodations were made, but the essential consensus had been made three years earlier when the Soviet Union had abandoned the attempt to outlaw space reconnaissance and the United States had agreed to a ban on weapons of mass destruction in orbit with reliance only on national means of verification. The treaty did not really break new ground in any substantial way, but it was of importance because it consolidated these provisions in a solemn treaty commitment.

On 19 December 1966 the U.N. General Assembly unanimously approved Resolution 2222 (XXI), endorsing the draft Outer Space Treaty. The treaty was opened for signature in Washington, London, and Moscow on 27 January 1967.

During consideration of the treaty by the U.S. Senate, some concern was expressed over verification of the ban on orbiting nuclear weapons, but it was argued and accepted that national means provided adequate and effective means. There were no objections to the substance of the arms control or other provisions of the treaty. On 25 April 1967 the Senate gave its advice and consent to ratification by unanimous vote (88 to 0).

The treaty entered into force on 10 October 1967, and remains in effect. It has never been amended, and there have been no formal charges of violation.

ARMS CONTROL AND OUTER SPACE SINCE 1967

The Outer Space Treaty, with its undertaking "not to place in orbit around the Earth any objects carrying nuclear weapons or any other kinds of weapons of mass destruction," had scarcely gone into effect before a question was raised as to whether it was being violated. On 3 November 1967, Secretary of Defense Robert S. McNamara disclosed that the Soviet Union had been testing a fractional orbital bombardment system (FOBS). Apart from other questions (as to effectiveness, threat, countermeasures, and the like), some raised a question as to whether such a system—or even its testing—marked Soviet violation of the Outer Space Treaty. In fact, as McNamara promptly stated and other administration spokesmen confirmed, even operational deployment of such a system—on launchers on earth—would not constitute a violation, because a missile placed into space even in a potentially orbital trajectory was not technically "in orbit" unless and until there was at least one complete circle of the globe. A FOBS would return to a target on earth before completing an orbit, as would any long-range intercontinental missile. The unique feature of the new missile was that it would be placed for a time in "orbital" trajectory—gaining range and allowing an indirect approach; for example, a south polar route from Siberia to North America. In this way the new missile could circumvent existing radars, but at considerable loss in accuracy and payload over an ICBM fired on a conventional ballistic trajectory.

FOBS was not a violation, and the excitement died down. "FOBS," incidentally, is a technically accurate but potentially misleading name for the system, since the very word "orbital" did raise questions that the qualifier "fractional" did not self-evidently answer. The Soviets did not use the term: they had, in 1965, started to refer to "orbital rockets" before FOBS testing had begun, but changed to the term "global rockets" after the United States had privately questioned them (in November 1965) with reference to the 1963 U.N. resolution. Later, when FOBS was tested in 1966 and 1967, U.S. officials were able to observe and characterize the system themselves.

The second Strategic Arms Limitation Talks agreement (SALT II), signed in Vienna on 18 June 1979 by President Jimmy Carter and General Secretary Leonid Brezhnev, included a provision incorporating and expanding on the ban on orbiting weapons of mass destruction to cover fractional orbital missiles. Moreover, the ban covered not only deploying such weapons in orbit, but also the development and testing of such systems. Article IX of the treaty established a commitment "not to develop, test, or deploy . . . systems for placing into Earth orbit nuclear weapons or any other kind of weapons of mass destruction, including fractional orbital missiles." Agreement to include this provision in the SALT II Treaty was reached relatively early in the negotiations; the United States first proposed banning FOBS, and the Soviets countered by proposing incorporation of the Outer Space Treaty provision banning weapons of mass destruction in orbit. As a compromise, the treaty embraced both. This was a desirable broadening of limitations, although there had been no indication that either country was seriously inclined to resurrect ideas of space-based strategic offensive weapons. The treaty also entailed, through a separate understanding, the dismantling by the USSR of the eighteen FOBS launchers it had earlier deployed.

Although the SALT II Treaty was never ratified, it was observed from 1979 until 1986. A similar ban on FOBS is included in the Strategic Arms Reduction Talks (START) Treaty, signed in July of 1991.

Another important step in arms control in outer space, supplementing the Outer Space Treaty and the Limited Nuclear Test Ban, was reached in 1972 in the Anti-Ballistic Missile (ABM) Treaty. The ABM Treaty was signed on 26 May 1972 in Moscow, entered into force on 3 October 1972, and is of unlimited duration. Article V includes, inter alia, an obligation "not to develop, test, or deploy ABM systems or components which are . . . space-based. . . ."

While this covers only strategic anti-ballistic missile defense systems, it bans testing and development, as well as deployment, of such space-based systems or even major space-based components of such systems.

A reinterpretation of this provision by the Reagan administration in 1985 sought to justify development and testing, though not deployment, of space-based ABM systems by contending that an agreed understanding (Agreed Statement D) modified the above-cited provision if it involved ABM systems "based on other physical principles." That interpretation was rejected by the Soviet Union and by the U.S. Senate, and the Reagan and Bush administrations agreed to apply the treaty in practice in conformity with the original interpretation based on the plain language of Article V. The revised "broad interpretation" had been designed to give more leeway to the controversial Strategic Defense Initiative (SDI).

The ABM Treaty also provides in Article XII an explicit ban on interference with "national technical means" of verification, including (though not explicitly) reconnaissance satellites. Similar prohibitions were also incorporated in the expired SALT Interim Agreement of 1972 and the unratified SALT II Treaty of 1979, which would have expired in 1986.

One important area of potential arms activity, or arms control, relating to outer space remains. Anti-satellite (ASAT) weapons are not banned by any of the aforementioned arms control treaties. Certain types of potential anti-satellite systems would be banned: any involving the placing in orbit of nuclear weapons or any other kind of weapons of mass destruction, or dual-purpose anti-ballistic missile and anti-satellite systems based in space. But earth-based (land-, sea-, or air-based) anti-satellite systems, and even space-based systems not employing nuclear or other weapons of mass destruction, are not banned.

Neither the United States nor the Soviet Union proposed banning anti-satellite weapons in the negotiation of the Outer Space, ABM, SALT or START treaties. ASAT arms talks were held in 1978–1979, with inconclusive results but not without some promise.

The United States deployed two earth-based direct ascent ASAT systems during the years 1963–1975, and tested but did not deploy an air-based system in the 1980s. The Soviet Union tested and probably had a standby capability for an earth-based coorbital system since the late 1960s, although it had not tested the system since 1982. The

United States has tested but as of 1992 not deployed earth-based ABM systems with ASAT potential.

On 11 August 1981, Soviet Foreign Minister Gromyko presented to the U.N. General Assembly a draft treaty on the Prohibition of the Stationing of Weapons of Any Kind in Outer Space. Article 1 of this proposal would have broadened the Outer Space Treaty to ban all weapons from being placed in orbit. It would not have banned earth-based or air-based ASAT systems. The parties would, however, under Article 3 undertake not to destroy or disrupt any satellite (or other object) placed in orbit by any other state—so long as that object was in conformity with Article 1, that is, was not a weapon. The United States, however, rejected the Soviet proposal and made no counterproposal.

Two years later, on 19 August 1983, the Soviet Union presented a revised draft treaty directed toward a prohibition of the use of force in outer space. It included a ban on all weapons in space, and on all anti-satellite weapons wherever based. The United States, however, embarked on its SDI program, did not wish to negotiate any constraints on weapons in space or on countering objects in space.

In resuming strategic arms reductions talks in 1985, the United States reluctantly acceded to Soviet insistence on including weapons in space in the scope of negotiations, accepting the ambiguous formulation of an objective to "prevent an arms race in space." The United States continued to reject Soviet proposals to ban all weapons in space, and argued that the aim of preventing an arms race did not preclude all arms from space. The strategic arms talks (sometimes called Nuclear and Space Talks, or NST) resumed in 1985 and led to the Intermediate-Range Nuclear Forces (INF) Treaty in 1987, and a START Treaty in 1991. But the Outer Space Treaty of 1967 remains the chief agreed arms control constraint on weapons in space.

With the end of the Cold War and dissolution of the Soviet Union, there was new thinking in both Russia and the United States regarding their strategic relationship and in particular the role of strategic defenses, including possible deployment of weapons in space. In this connection, the very purposes of arms control were under reconsideration. By the early 1990s there was no proposal to amend the Outer Space Treaty provision banning the placement of nuclear and other weapons of mass destruction in space, but for the first time since the treaty had been concluded the possibility of revision and amendment was figuratively on the agenda.

BIBLIOGRAPHY

Treaty Texts and Symposiums The Outer Space Treaty and other treaties, U.N. General Assembly resolutions referred to in this entry, together with some related proposals and speeches, are located in the appropriate annual volumes of the U.S. Arms Control and Disarmament Agency titled *Documents on Disarmament* (Washington, D.C.), especially for 1967, which provides a very useful compilation of U.S., Soviet, and other official statements, as well as agreed documents. Other useful official records are *Treaty on Outer Space, Hearings Before the Committee on Foreign Relations, United States Senate, Ninetieth Congress, First Session, March 7, 13, and April 12, 1967* (Washington, D.C., 1967); and *International Cooperation in Outer Space: A Symposium,* prepared for the Committee on Aeronautical and Space Sciences (Washington, D.C., 1971), in particular, HERBERT REIS, "United Nations Committee on the Peaceful Uses of Outer Space and Its Legal Subcommittee": 247–260; and PETER S. THACHER, "Arms Control and Outer Space in the United Nations": 287–314. Both Reis as legal adviser and Thacher as science counselor, in the United States Mission to the U.N. in the 1960s, played key roles in negotiating the Outer Space Treaty and other relevant U.N. resolutions.

Analyses The principal account of the development of the 1963 U.N. Resolution banning weapons of mass destruction in orbit is RAYMOND L. GARTHOFF (a participant in the American policy process), "Banning the Bomb in Outer Space," *International Security* 5 (Winter 1980–1981): 25–40.

The principal analyses dealing in part with the Outer Space Treaty and related developments are: PAUL G. DEMBLING and DANIEL M. ARONS, "The Evolution of the Outer Space Treaty," *Journal of Air Law and Commerce* 33 (Summer 1967): 419–456; BHUPENDRA JASANI, ed., *Outer Space: A New Dimension of the Arms Race* (Cambridge, Mass., 1982): 265–329; DON E. KASH, *The Politics of Space Cooperation* (Lafayette, Ind., 1967): 95–125; WALTER A. MCDOUGALL, *The Heavens and the Earth: A Political History of the Space Age* (New York, 1985): 415–485;

PAUL B. STARES, *The Militarization of Space: U.S. Policy, 1945–1984* (Ithaca, N.Y., 1985): esp. 54–57, 66–71, 82–105, 165–168, and 229–235; and PAUL B. STARES, *Space and National Security* (Washington, D.C., 1987): 142–173.

The Soviet View   The basic Soviet source is a two-volume compilation issued by the Ministry of Foreign Affairs of the USSR, edited by a group of leading Soviet specialists headed by Professor A. S. PIRADOV, under the title *Bor'ba za mirnoye ispol'sovaniye kosmosa, 1957–1985* (*The Struggle for the Peaceful Use of Outer Space, 1957–1985*) (Moscow, 1985), 2 volumes. It provides many official Soviet statements and other materials not readily accessible.

The Seabed Treaty

1971 to the Present

○

BENNETT RAMBERG

See also The Antarctic State Treaty: 1959 to the Present; Demilitarization and Neutralization Through World War II; The Environmental Modification Convention: 1977 to the Present; *and* The United Nations and Disarmament. *The* Seabed Treaty *is excerpted in Volume III.*

The militarization of the oceans has a long history. The ancestors of today's battleships, cruisers, destroyers, and frigates were the marine-manned cargo ships and "men-of-war" galleys of the seafaring nations of ancient Crete, Phoenicia, and Greece.

In the eighteenth century, a one-man submarine called the Turtle broke the ocean's surface to sink a British frigate during the American Revolution. However, it would take more than a century for this early progenitor of the modern submarine to develop into a major weapon of war during World War I. Four decades later, during the Cold War, the submarine attained its apogee as a mobile underwater platform for launching strategic nuclear missiles.

Given the rate of technological progress during the second half of the twentieth century, the seabed afforded a last frontier for ocean militarization. At least this was the view of Arvid Pardo, Malta's ambassador to the United Nations, as he stood before the U.N. First Committee in 1967 to warn that unless the international community undertook prompt action, a new arms competition would manifest itself on the seabed. What particularly concerned Pardo was the possibility that the superpowers would extend their nuclear contest to anchored or mobile nuclear armed offensive and defensive missiles on the ocean bottom, "an environment highly resistant to the overpressures of nuclear attack." To foreclose military competition in this pristine environment, he called for the establishment

of an "international framework" to assure that the seabed would be used "exclusively for peaceful purposes."

SEABED MILITARIZATION IN THE 1960s

To what extent were Pardo's concerns justified? During the 1960s utilization of the seabed for military purposes had been limited primarily to the emplacement on the ocean bottom of fixed monitoring devices designed to track unfriendly submarines. The United States, reflecting a deep concern over Soviet submarine capabilities, was the principal user of the seabed for this purpose, and maintained an elaborate series of sonar systems in both the Atlantic and Pacific. The extent of such deployment by other states is uncertain. During the 1960s the seabed also served as a resting place for acoustical devices designed to assist submarines of several nations in accurately determining their locations. Additionally, a number of nations had the ability to moor mines on the seabed that were capable of destroying surface vessels as well as submarines.

The rather limited use of the ocean floor at the time of Pardo's address reflected in part the still primitive state of submarine technology. In the late 1960s efforts to place manned objects on the seabed were less than a decade old and still very much in the experimental stage. Pardo's concerns would have been far less significant had there not been evidence suggesting that an ocean-floor military option was being seriously explored. By the time he raised the issue in the U.N., a number of military analysts had already speculated publicly on the utility of developing such a capacity. Ballistic missiles anchored to or placed under the seabed, as well as underwater barges and mobile ocean bottom systems that crept along the ocean floor carrying ballistic missiles, were among the options discussed inside the U.S. and Soviet governments and by Western academic specialists.

However, at the time Pardo broached the seabed arms control question at the U.N., none of these alternatives had been adopted and the likelihood that they would be was remote. Policymakers in countries that had developed or were in the process of developing an underwater nuclear military capability—including the United States, Britain, France, and the Soviet Union—were convinced that mobile launching platforms of the Polaris class submarines were the optimal means by which to maintain the invulnerability of their sea-based nuclear arsenals. This does not mean that the stationary seabed nuclear option was precluded; neither were other options to utilize the environment for military purposes. Such foreclosures would have required an international agreement.

THE PRELIMINARIES TO NEGOTIATIONS

When Arvid Pardo delivered his November 1967 address, he presented his First Committee colleagues a challenge with which few were prepared to deal. Most countries either had not thought about the implications of a militarized ocean or had not ordered their preferences. To explore the matter further—along with other matters bearing on the exploitation of the ocean floor—the First Committee agreed to establish the thirty-five nation Ad Hoc Committee to Study the Peaceful Uses of the Seabed and the Ocean Floor Beyond the Limits of National Jurisdiction.

The ad hoc committee conducted sessions in March, June, and August 1968 in an effort to gather information for the Conference of the Eighteen Nation Committee on Disarmament in order that it

might intelligently consider seabed arms control. In this effort to establish an agenda, the differences that were to later divide the United States and the Soviet Union in the formal negotiations emerged. Washington called for talks that prevented "the use of [the seabed] for the emplacement of *weapons of mass destruction*," while Moscow advocated a prohibition limiting use *"for military purposes* of the seabed . . . beyond the limits of the territorial waters of coastal states"* (emphasis added). Thus the United States sought to limit seabed arms control to nuclear matters while the Soviet Union endeavored to include other issues, notably seabed-anchored sonars used to track submarines.

Differences over the scope of the prohibition marked one of three issues that required resolution. The other two involved the geographic breadth of the prohibition, and verification. The scope of the prohibition was in one respect the least difficult to resolve: the interests of only two states, the United States and the Soviet Union, required reconciliation. Only they maintained a direct strategic stake in seabed militarization. (Presumably, military allies of both had an indirect interest in the resolution of the problem as it bore on the military capability of their alliance leaders.) The United States was the principal user of the seabed for military purposes, as it maintained an elaborate series of sonar systems in both the Pacific and Atlantic oceans, at an estimated cost of $400 million to track Soviet submarines. The Soviet Union did not maintain a comparable network; its interest lay in diminishing U.S. tracking capability in order to enhance its own freedom of movement underseas. Neither superpower had placed weapons of mass destruction on the ocean floor, although both had considered the idea of placing ICBMs on or under the seabed in the mid-1960s. As late as February 1969, the U.S. Joint Chiefs of Staff were interested in keeping the option open.

Resolution of the geographic breadth of the prohibition and the means to insure compliance were more difficult issues to resolve than was the comprehensiveness of the prohibition. All conferees wanted to insure that an arms control treaty did not establish precedents that would adversely affect their claims to the ocean and the ocean floor. These nations' claims of sovereignty ranged from 3 miles to 200 miles (about 5 to 320 kilometers) off their respective shores and reflected different economic interests such as fisheries and continental-shelf mineral resources; defense and navigational considerations; and, on the part of some states, a certain amount of jingoism. In the early going, the matter of verification remained obscured by the other two issues. Later it would become a major point of contention.

As the ad hoc committee concluded its work in August 1968, it was unable to reach a consensus about the direction for seabed arms control. Still, both Washington and Moscow appeared determined to examine the issue further by agreeing, as cochairmen of the Geneva-based Eighteen Nation Committee on Disarmament (ENDC), to place the matter on the agenda. In their recommendation to the ENDC, the superpowers simply announced that under a "collateral measures" category, the "members may wish to discuss prevention of an arms race on the seabed."

The Setting for Negotiations The Conference of the Eighteen Nation Committee on Disarmament—within which seabed arms control was to be negotiated—was initially convened on 14 March 1962 as a result of private discussions between the United States and the Soviet Union the previous year following the breakdown of the Ten Nation Committee on Disarmament in 1960. The U.N. General Assembly had mandated the ENDC forum to seek general and complete disarmament under effective international control. Although it has subsequently fallen well short of this objective, at the time the seabed arms control issue was placed on the agenda, the ENDC had either negotiated or contributed to the 1963 "hot-line" agreement between Moscow and Washington, the 1963 Partial Nuclear Test Ban Treaty, and its most significant contribution, the Nuclear Non-Proliferation Treaty, signed in 1968.

As originally conceived, the ENDC was to consist of eighteen participants drawn from three blocs. Five were NATO allies—the United States, Great Britain, France, Italy, and Canada—and five were members of the Warsaw Pact—the Soviet Union, Romania, Czechoslovakia, Poland, and Bulgaria. The remaining conferees represented a geographic cross-section of the nonaligned world. Brazil and Mexico were chosen from Latin America. Asia was represented by Burma and India. Ethiopia, Nigeria, and the United Arab Republic were the representatives from the Middle East and Africa. Sweden was selected from Europe. Of the original eighteen members, France never took its seat. In 1969 the forum was enlarged by eight additional states and was renamed the Conference of the Committee on Disarmament (CCD). Argentina, Pakistan, Morocco, and Yugoslavia were the additional nonaligned participants. Two states formally associated with the Warsaw Pact and NATO, Hungary and the Netherlands, were invited to join the forum, as were two Asian allies of the superpowers, Japan and Mongolia.

In theory, each member of the committee could raise any point of arms control and disarmament. In practice, the superpowers, acting as the conference's official cochairmen, established the agenda. They also determined when the committee would convene. Customarily, the committee met six months during the year, commencing its work in late winter or early spring and concluding in August or September with one or two intervening breaks. The late summer or early fall termination date allowed the participants to return to their foreign offices to prepare for the General Assembly and Political Committee (the First Committee) sessions at the U.N. to which the CCD submitted a report.

THE NEGOTIATORY PHASES

The seabed arms control negotiation proceeded through six phases:

Phase I: The Soviet initiative, 18 March 1969 through 21 May 1969.

Phase II: The American counterpoise and the debate and critique of the superpower draft treaties, 22 May 1969 through 7 October 1969.

Phase III: The 7 October 1969 submission of the joint Soviet-American draft treaty, the critique and debate on collateral issues, and the submission of a revised joint draft treaty, 30 October 1969.

Phase IV: Discussion in the U.N. First Committee of the joint draft treaty.

Phase V: The continuation of talks in Geneva, February through April 1970.

Phase VI: The final negotiation, summer 1970.

The Initial Two Phases The formal seabed arms control negotiation began with the convocation of the Eighteen Nation Disarmament Committee's 1969 session, at which time the Soviet Union submitted a draft treaty. On the matter of military comprehensiveness, Moscow called for the prohibition of the military use of the ocean floor and subsoil. In terms of geography, its proposal was related to areas beyond the 12-mile (19-kilometer) maritime zone of coastal states. Verification would be achieved by the reciprocal opening of all installations and structures to representatives of other states party to the treaty.

At the time Moscow tendered its draft, the United States had yet to achieve an internal consensus as to its formal position on all the central issues. Beyond maintaining a commitment to denuclearization, its response to the Soviet challenge on the issues of breadth and verification was only suggestive. The United States proposed, for example, that three alternatives to resolve the geographic breadth clause be reviewed. These were a specified horizontal distance from the coastline, a depth limit, and a reference to outer limits of national jurisdiction; however, the American delegation failed to indicate its preference. As for verification, it called for some appropriate provision to be included in the agreement. The United States tentatively suggested that procedures "might" be drawn from the precedent of reciprocity, excluding the veto clause, of the Outer Space Treaty.

On 22 May 1969 the negotiations entered Phase II as the United States formally set forth its counterpoise to the Soviet submission. It called on signatories "not to emplant or emplace fixed nuclear weapons or other weapons of mass destruction or associated fixed launching platforms on, within, or beneath the seabed" beyond a 3-mile (about 5 kilometers) coastal zone. To insure compliance, the draft called for observation and consultation to resolve questions. With the two competing draft treaties before the Eighteen Nation Disarmament Committee, the stage was set for serious negotiations in an effort to find mutually, and generally, acceptable compromises.

Phase III   In Phase III of the talks, the formalization of the American position sharpened the disagreement between the United States and the Soviet Union on the issue of the comprehensiveness of the prohibition. It was apparent to all that unless one or both superpowers made concessions, no agreement could be achieved. Sweden undertook to break the apparent deadlock. In a reconciliation effort, Stockholm advocated a two-tier prohibition: beyond the 3-mile (5-kilometer) limit, all nuclear weapons and weapons of mass destruction would be banned. Beyond the twelve-mile (19-

kilometer) limit, "all weapons and . . . military bases and fortifications and other installations of a military nature, except some which are of a purely passive, defensive character—such as means of communication, navigation, and supervision" would be prohibited. Notwithstanding this and other nonaligned efforts, no reconciliation was achieved during this phase of the discussions.

However, support for a twelve-mile clause appeared to gain momentum. Several states that heretofore had not explicitly supported a particular delimitation now appeared disposed toward the application of the accord to a zone beyond the twelve-mile limit. While consensus developed on the issue of geographic breadth, dissatisfaction was growing with the verification alternatives that both superpowers had proposed. Japan, Romania, and Mexico joined the nonaligned countries that earlier had voiced objections to the Soviet advocacy of verification through reciprocity. In two working papers, Brazil argued that procedures associated with the inspection process could be used to usurp national jurisdictional rights of the coastal state over its continental shelf. As an alternative, Brazil advocated that the coastal state be directly involved in any verification activity in its jurisdiction that went beyond mere cursory observation. Brazil also proposed that consideration be given to explicitly stipulating the rights of treaty parties to submit their concerns over violations to both the U.N. Security Council and the secretary-general. As the negotiations proceeded, the reluctance of the superpowers to accommodate Brazil's concerns would prove a major point of discord.

From early September until early October 1969, discussion of the seabed question remained at a standstill as the conferees awaited the results of private bargaining between Moscow and Washington. In early October the Soviet delegation received new instructions from Moscow that reflected a turnabout—a decision to accept an accord limiting the prohibition to nuclear weapons and other weapons of mass destruction fixed to the seafloor.

The Soviet concession to the U.S. preference on this issue encouraged accommodation on the remaining central issues as well as on collateral ones. In a joint draft treaty submitted on 7 October 1969, the superpowers called for the nuclear prohibition to be measured in accordance with the provisions of the 1958 Geneva Convention on the Territorial Sea and the Contiguous Zone. The absence of any specific numerical delineation of the demarcation was apparently designed to mitigate charges that the agreement would either support or prejudice claims to the high seas and ocean floor. As for the issue of verification, the joint draft went little further than the original American proposal.

At least three other clauses of the joint draft deserve note. One required ratification by twenty-two nations, in lieu of the Soviet provision of five ratifying nations in its initial draft. (The United States never addressed itself to this matter in its draft.) In the preamble of the joint submission, a clause affirmed the determination of the treaty parties to "continue" negotiations designed to ultimately achieve a broader arms control accord. Its purpose was to placate conferees who wanted a more inclusive prohibition. Both the United States and the Soviet Union, however, were reluctant to make this intention binding, hence its location in the preamble rather than in the body of the document. This placement resulted in some consternation, particularly among the nonaligned who supported demilitarization. It provoked Sweden to tender a working paper on 16 October calling for a text article that sought a more comprehensive ban. Almost a year would pass before the superpowers would reluctantly acquiesce to this demand.

A third noteworthy clause of the U.S.-Soviet draft provided for treaty amendments. The initial Soviet proposal did not contain such a provision and, in the initial U.S. draft, amendments would have had to be ratified by a majority of the treaty's signatories. The new joint draft, however, tacked on to the original United States' provision a stipulation giving nuclear powers a veto on amendments—thus protecting them against the unforeseen consequences of majority rule.

For a number of conferees, particularly the nonaligned that supported something approaching a nearly all-inclusive prohibition, the United States–Soviet fait accompli on the issue of the scope of weapons included in an accord was a disappointment. The nonaligned felt abandoned, since the major proponent of demilitarization, the Soviet Union, had conceded. Thus, since nonaligned proponents of demilitarization did not feel that *conventional* militarization of the ocean floor was an immediate threat to their strategic interests, Sweden, India, Ethiopia, Burma, Yugoslavia, the United Arab Republic, and Nigeria reluctantly agreed to the joint proposal as the only reasonable course open to them. Most seemed to feel that a partial prohibition was better than none at all.

However, the superpower recommendations on the issues of territorial breadth and verification were another matter. As these clauses directly impinged upon the interests of every coastal nation, each had a stake in their resolution. On these matters, then, a number of the parties expressed dissatisfaction with the joint draft.

On the issue of geographical scope, Brazil, Argentina, and Pakistan voiced concern about the failure to explicitly delineate the seaward point of application. They also objected to reference to the Geneva Convention, with which a number of the conferees were not associated. Japan, the Netherlands, Sweden, Poland, and Britain expressed apprehensions about the fact that permitted superpower military deployments within the boundaries of the Geneva Convention's contiguous zone of 12 miles (19 kilometers) would allow any state, friendly or unfriendly, to place weapons in the "gap" existing where a state's territorial claim was less than twelve miles.

Dissatisfaction again was voiced by a number of states on the superpowers' terms for verification of compliance with the treaty. Virtually all the nonaligned nations, along with the Netherlands and Poland, argued that the provision was inadequate. This dissent stimulated a Canadian proposal that called for a series of graded measures ranging from discussions between concerned parties and alleged offenders, the right of facility inspection, and access to other parties such as the U.N. Security Council or the secretary-general. The proposal met with nonaligned support but drew U.S. opposition on grounds that observation of suspicious activities was sufficient.

In light of the objections to the superpowers' draft, Moscow and Washington on 30 October 1969 offered a new joint draft treaty designed to address those concerns. The document did resolve two questions: first, it allowed coastal states exclusive sovereignty over the 12-mile (19-kilometer) coastal seabed zone for military purposes, thereby eliminating the "gap" problem; and second, it removed the veto power of nuclear armed states over future amendments. However, it failed to resolve several other issues.

The draft did not deal with objections of those who wanted a superpower commitment—placed in the body of the accord rather than in the treaty preamble—to continue negotiations for broader future prohibitions. Finally, although the new treaty attempted to cope with objections to the original joint verification clause by including a stipulation allowing parties the right to refer their suspicions of violations to the Security Council, some conferees still were not content. They wanted the right to submit their concerns directly to the secretary-general and an explicit guarantee that coastal states, off whose shores verification activity might take place, would be allowed to participate.

With the presentation of this revision by the superpowers, the Geneva Committee's 1969 session came to an end. Despite superpower hopes that the new document would satisfy the apprehensions of their colleagues, their failure to resolve the above mentioned issues would require the formulation of two more draft treaties before the entire matter would be resolved. Much of these subsequent negotiations took place in New York during the United Nations' twenty-fourth session.

The Final Phases   During the First Committee's consideration of the seabed issue in Phase IV of the talks, Canada endeavored to close the differences on the issue of verification between itself, the nonaligned, and the superpowers. The Canadian paper called for nations to have the right to make direct inquiries of other nations within the region of suspected violations, or to initiate inquiries through the secretary-general if the identities of the violators were undetermined. It also allowed for inspections with cooperation of states in the region and, as a last resort, for an appeal to the Security Council. To allay concerns about the Geneva Convention, it called for verification activities to be conducted with due regard for the sovereign rights of the coastal state with respect to natural resources under international law.

Notwithstanding Ottawa's efforts, complaints arose from the nonaligned nations, notably Brazil, that Canada's proposal prejudged questions bearing on sovereign rights to economic resources on the ocean shelf. Argentina intervened with a paper of its own that attempted to minimize any prejudice to nations' claims to the ocean floor for economic exploitation. With the presentation of Argentina's paper, the seabed debate in New York concluded with a General Assembly call upon the Conference of the Committee on Disarmament "to take into account all the proposals and suggestions" made during the current session.

When the CCD reconvened in February 1970—Phase V of the negotiation—the committee found that Moscow and Washington were again at odds over verification. Resolution of this conflict required two months of private consultation. On 23 April 1970, as the spring recess approached, the United States and the Soviet Union submitted a revision of their second joint draft treaty. The document incorporated many of the suggestions offered by Argentina and Canada. However, Ottawa's call for parties to be given the opportunity to use "international good offices . . . including those of the Secretary General of the United Nations," was omitted, thereby prejudicing consensus.

As the committee entered its summer session, it concluded the final phase of the negotiation. Phase VI, however, began on a negative note as Moscow stressed its opposition to the notion of the U.N. Secretary-General participating in any verification scheme. Ambassador Roschin argued that in the past the Western powers had "tried to foist on the secretary-general political functions designed to secure the adoption of a policy corresponding to their own narrow interests." To substantiate this point, Roschin cited the Congo crisis of the early 1960s. He asserted that during that episode, then secretary-general Dag Hammarskjöld abused the authority of his office in a manner favorable to the West. The national origins of the individuals staffing the office, he concluded, would continue to provide the Western bloc with a distinct advantage.

With the notable exception of Romania, support for the Soviet position was limited to its military allies. Soviet arguments failed to convince many nonaligned nations or the American allies in attendance. Referring to the omission of a clause that would allow access to the secretary-general as a "serious weakness" or a "matter of principle," these countries took exception to the superpower position. In an effort to resolve the impasse, nine nonaligned conferees submitted a compromise formula. Rather than referring explicitly to the secretary-general, it declared that a treaty party could avail itself of "appropriate international procedures within the framework of the United Nations and in accordance with its Charter." Additionally, their recommendations included support for Sweden's efforts to have a provision mandating continued seabed arms control negotiations in the body of the treaty rather than in the treaty preamble.

On 1 September 1970 the two superpowers tendered the third, and what proved to be the final, joint draft treaty. The document included several new provisos obviously responsive to the concerns raised by the other conferees. The nine-nation compromise formula was included. An obligation that "coastal states" be explicitly informed of, and granted the right to participate in, the verification process was stipulated. It deleted portions of the earlier draft that Brazil asserted could be interpreted as prejudging questions of maritime law. Lastly, it inserted a clause calling for continued seabed arms control negotiations in a separate article (Article 5) in the body of the treaty.

With the inclusion of these provisions, the negotiations concluded with the superpowers calling upon the committee's membership to support the draft during the forthcoming General Assembly session. All delegations agreed to do so, if not explicitly then at least tacitly.

Three months later the General Assembly approved the final draft by a vote of 104 to 2 (El Salvador and Peru), with Ecuador and France abstaining. On 11 February 1971 the Treaty on the Prohibition of the Employment of Nuclear Weapons and Other Weapons of Mass Destruction on the Seabed and the Ocean Floor and the Subsoil Thereof was open for signature in Washington, London, and Moscow. On 18 May 1972 it entered into force when the United States, the United Kingdom, and the Soviet Union, along with twenty-two other nations, deposited instruments of ratification. Ultimately, eighty-nine countries signed and sixty-six ratified the treaty.

prevent an arms race on the seabed and ocean floor and subsoil and to attend review conferences every five years after the entry into force of the treaty to assure that its purposes were realized. By 1992 three such review conferences had taken place, the last occurring in Geneva in 1989. In each case the conferees concluded that the treaty continued to make a useful contribution to arms control.

How can the Seabed Treaty be properly evaluated? Did the treaty reduce the probability of war, cost of defense, or damage in the event of war— the three canonical goals of arms control identified by Schelling and Halperin? Had negotiations failed, would it have been a material setback to the United States–Soviet détente that Richard Nixon and Henry Kissinger had sought to nourish at the time?

In each regard it is doubtful that the treaty contributed much. Although deployment of seabed-based nuclear weapons was a hypothetical possibility, had deployment occurred it is unlikely that it would have increased the probability of war between the superpowers. However, the deployment of such weapons certainly would have added to the military cost of the Cold War. But the treaty probably did not save parties much money, as the mobile ballistic-missile submarine had already eliminated any need to use the seabed for nuclear purposes.

At best, the treaty made a very modest short-lived contribution toward the détente that the superpowers sought to foster at the time. And, it created one more demilitarized area under an arms control regime.

CONCLUSION

After all was said and done, the Seabed Treaty was negotiated rather rapidly. In all, three years elapsed after Malta's ambassador first raised the issue. The treaty that resulted prohibits the emplacing or emplanting on or under the seabed beyond a 12-mile (19-kilometer) zone off the coast of parties any nuclear weapon or other types of weapons of mass destruction as well as structures, launching installations, or any other facilities specifically designed for storing, testing, or using such weapons. Parties with questions of possible evasions may use observation, interparty consultation, and access to the Security Council, which is authorized to take action according to the Charter. The parties also committed themselves to negotiate further measures to

BIBLIOGRAPHY

There is only a limited amount of literature that relates to the Seabed Treaty. The basic work on the subject is BENNETT RAMBERG, *The Seabed Arms Control Negotiations: A Study of Multilateral Arms Control Conference Diplomacy,* University of Denver Monograph Series in World Affairs, vol. 15, bk. 2 (Denver, Colo., 1978); it may be supplemented by LOUIS HENKIN, "The Sea-Bed Arms Treaty—One Small Step More," *Columbia Journal of Transnational Law* 10 (Spring 1971): 61–65. The views of the treaty's "father" (Arvid Pardo) may be found in his "Who Will Control the Seabed?" *Foreign Affairs* 47 (October 1968): 123–137.

The negotiatory process has been reviewed by P. TERRENCE HOPMANN, "Bargaining in Arms Control Negotiations: The Seabeds Denuclearization Treaty," *International Organization* 28 (Summer 1974): 313–343; and BENNETT RAMBERG, "Tactical Advantages of Opening Positioning Strategies: Lessons from the Seabed Arms Control Talks, 1967–1970, *Journal of Conflict Resolution* 21 (December 1977): 685–700.

Other works that may be found useful include: EVAN LUARD, *The Control of the Sea-bed: A New International Issue* (London, 1974); HARRY N. M. WINTON, ed., *Sea-Bed 1968* (New York, 1970), 6 vols., and *Sea-Bed 1969* (New York, 1971), 8 vols.; and EDWARD WENK, *The Politics of the Ocean* (Seattle, Wash., 1972).

From SALT to START

Limiting Strategic Nuclear Weapons

○

DAN CALDWELL

See also The Anti-Ballistic Missile Treaty: 1972 to the Present; From MBFR to CFE: Negotiating Conventional Arms Control in Europe; The INF Treaty: Eliminating Intermediate-Range Nuclear Missiles, 1987 to the Present; "No First Use" Nuclear Policy; The Strategic Defense Initiative and Arms Control; *and* The Washington Naval Limitation System: 1921–1939. *The* SALT I, SALT II, *and* START *treaties are excerpted in Volume III.*

Nuclear arms are weapons of unprecedented destructive power, and their development and deployment changed world history. Concurrent with their evolution, diplomatic measures to control the likelihood of their use, their destructiveness, and their cost have been pursued. Early attempts to control nuclear weapons, such as the Baruch Plan and plans for General and Complete Disarmament, failed. By the mid-1960s, both the United States and the Soviet Union had nuclear arsenals consisting of thousands of weapons. The Cuban missile crisis of 1962 highlighted the dangers and potential for escalation to nuclear war between the two superpowers, and leaders from the two countries began to think about the possibility of limiting long-range, or "strategic," nuclear weapons. The initial negotiations to control these types of arms, the Strategic Arms Limitation Talks (SALT), were followed by the Strategic Arms Reduction Talks (START)—a process that lasted from 1969 to 1991.

TOWARD SALT, 1967–1968

In the early 1960s the leaders of the United States and the Soviet Union became quite concerned about the potential for the spread of nuclear weapons to other countries. In 1963 President John F. Kennedy made note of the possibility of ten countries developing nuclear weapons by 1970, and per-

haps fifteen to twenty by 1975. He regarded the prospect of a future president facing a world of fifteen to twenty nuclear states as posing "the greatest possible danger" (Press Conference, 13 March 1963, in *Public Papers of Presidents of the United States: John F. Kennedy, 1963*). By the mid-1960s, the United States, the Soviet Union, Great Britain, France, and the People's Republic of China had tested nuclear devices.

Soviet leaders were bothered by the fact that four of the five states that possessed nuclear weapons were hostile toward the USSR. In addition, they were concerned about the United States' proposal calling for the creation of a multilateral force of U.S. and Western European naval vessels equipped with nuclear weapons and manned by crew members from NATO countries. The Soviets strongly opposed this proposal because they believed it was simply an excuse to provide West Germany with access to nuclear weapons—a situation they greatly desired to prevent. Indelibly chiseled in the minds of Soviet citizens and leaders were, after all, traumatic memories of the horrible Soviet losses at the hands of Germany in both world wars.

For various reasons, the United States abandoned the multilateral force proposal in 1965, and this opened the way for serious discussions of the nuclear proliferation problem. As a result of discussions at the 1965 and 1967 sessions of the United Nations Eighteen Nation Disarmament Committee and informal meetings between Secretary of State Dean Rusk and Soviet Foreign Minister Andrey Gromyko, the United States and Soviet Union were able to submit identical drafts of a treaty limiting nuclear proliferation. This draft was slightly amended and then signed on 1 July 1968. Because the Non-Proliferation Treaty prevented the acquisition of nuclear weapons by West Germany, Soviet leaders viewed it as of critical importance; in fact, the Soviets apparently considered this treaty as a prerequisite for the opening of negotiations on the limitation of Soviet and U.S. strategic nuclear weapons.

In 1964 and again in 1966, President Lyndon B. Johnson proposed a policy of "building bridges with the East" in order "to search for every possible area of agreement that might enlarge the prospect for cooperation between the United States and the Soviet Union" (Speech by Lyndon B. Johnson, Arco, Idaho, 26 August 1966 in *Public Papers of Presidents of the United States: Lyndon B. Johnson, 1966, 1967*). To support this accommodative approach, the United States government, in late 1966, proposed to open negotiations with the Soviet Union to limit strategic nuclear arms. The Soviets did not respond immediately to the U.S. proposal. However, on 17 June 1967, after the People's Republic of China exploded its first thermonuclear device, the Soviets agreed to meet with the United States to discuss possible limits on strategic nuclear weapons and other issues of mutual concern. President Johnson and Soviet Premier Aleksey Kosygin met at Glassboro, New Jersey, in June 1967. Robert McNamara, who at that time was serving as secretary of defense, delivered a lecture to Kosygin on the reasons the Soviets should not deploy an anti-ballistic missile (ABM) system. After listening to McNamara, Kosygin erupted, pounding the table and exclaiming, "Defense is moral, offense is immoral!" Because of differing strategic concepts and priorities, no agreements were reached at the Glassboro summit meeting.

After the failure to limit anti-ballistic missiles at Glassboro, in September 1967 McNamara announced the U.S. government's decision to build an ABM system. Three months later, the United States also decided to proceed with the development of a new offensive technology, multiple independently targetable reentry vehicles (MIRV), which were a package of two or more warheads that could be carried on a single missile but deliverable to separate targets. In late June 1968, Foreign Minister Gromyko announced that the Soviet government was willing to discuss limitation of both offensive and defensive weapons, and three days later, on 1 July, the day that the Non-Proliferation Treaty was signed, President Johnson announced that an agreement had been reached on convening the Strategic Arms Limitation Talks. The talks were supposed to begin in Moscow or Leningrad on 30 September. A joint announcement concerning the opening and schedule of the negotiations was prepared for release on 21 August; however, the day before, Soviet and other Warsaw Pact military forces intervened in Czechoslovakia, and the U.S. government postponed the opening of SALT indefinitely.

SALT I, 1969–1972

During the 1968 presidential election, Richard Nixon promised "to restore our objective of clear-cut military superiority" (quoted in Dan Caldwell, *American-Soviet Relations,* Westport, Conn., 1981). Soon after his inauguration, however, the president indicated that his administration would seek the strategic nuclear objective of "sufficiency." President Nixon ordered his assistant for national security, Dr. Henry A. Kissinger, to conduct a comprehensive review of American strategic nuclear forces and doctrine prior to beginning strategic arms control negotiations with the Soviets. This review took almost a year to complete, and on 17 November 1969, representatives from the U.S. and Soviet governments met in Helsinki, Finland, to inaugurate the SALT I negotiations. During the ensuing thirty months, the two delegations held seven sets of formal negotiating sessions, meeting alternately in Helsinki and Vienna.

The tasks of the two delegations were difficult, for the U.S. and Soviet strategic nuclear arsenals differed in significant respects. U.S. force planners emphasized the development of technologically sophisticated, accurate missiles with relatively small (by strategic nuclear standards) payloads of one to two megatons. By contrast, the Soviet Union developed and deployed a number of different types of weapons; some were similar in design and capability to American weapons, but others were larger and had a greater throw-weight—the total weight that a missile is capable of lifting into a trajectory.

The U.S. SALT I delegation was headed by the director of the Arms Control and Disarmament Agency (ACDA), Gerard C. Smith, and consisted of representatives from a number of different government departments and agencies including the departments of State and Defense, the Central Intelligence Agency, the Joint Chiefs of Staff, and the National Security Council. President Nixon and Dr. Kissinger issued instructions to the delegation, which then presented various proposals to the Soviet negotiators.

The Soviet delegation was headed by Deputy Foreign Minister Vladimir Semenovich Semenov, a veteran foreign affairs official with little previous background in strategic matters, and consisted of more than twenty Soviet governmental officials from the military services, the Foreign Ministry, and the Soviet intelligence organization—the Committee on State Security, more commonly known in the West as the KGB. During the meetings, the Soviet delegation generally adhered to positions worked out prior to the negotiations, and was uncomfortable with the informal discussions that members of the U.S. delegation occasionally proposed. The civilian members of the Soviet delegation, including Semenov, often appeared uninformed about the military capabilities of both U.S. and Soviet weapons systems. At one point in the first round of the negotiations, Colonel General Nikolai Ogarkov, who was the second-ranking Soviet delegate and the first deputy chief of the Soviet General Staff, asked a U.S. delegate to stop talking about Soviet military hardware. Such matters, Ogarkov said, were not the concern of his civilian colleagues. Thus, many times the members of the U.S. delegation knew more about Soviet military capabilities than the civilian members of the Soviet delegation!

From the outset, the two sides favored different limitations. The Soviets wanted to concentrate on defensive weapons, particularly anti-ballistic missiles, and the Americans wanted to limit offensive systems, particularly the modern, large ("heavy") Soviet intercontinental ballistic missiles (ICBMS). Underlying the discussions of the two delegations were long-standing problems of inspection and verification, issues that had blocked previous strategic nuclear arms control agreements. In addition, the Soviet delegation repeatedly expressed its interest in discussing U.S. forces stationed in Europe, to which the Soviets referred as "forward-based systems." The Soviets argued that these systems were, in fact, "strategic," because many of them had the capability of reaching Soviet territory. The United States was insistent that these forward-based systems not be discussed at the SALT negotiations because they did not have intercontinental ranges and

because of the negative impact such discussions would have had on its NATO allies.

In late 1970, a stalemate in the negotiations developed over the forward-based systems and MIRV issues. Kissinger and Soviet Ambassador to the United States, Anatoly Dobrynin, began meeting secretly in early 1971 to discuss SALT and to exchange confidential messages between Nixon and Kosygin. These meetings were later dubbed the "back-channel negotiations," and at the time were unknown to most United States governmental officials, including the members of the U.S. SALT delegation. As a result of the back-channel discussions, the U.S. and Soviet governments in May 1971 reached a compromise formula for breaking the stalemate at the formal meetings of the two delegations: the negotiators would discuss limitations of both defensive and offensive weapons systems.

Despite the importance of the SALT negotiations to both the U.S. and Soviet governments and despite the May 1971 breakthrough, SALT could not be conducted in isolation from other aspects of United States–Soviet relations. At the end of March 1972, the North Vietnamese, supplied with military equipment from both the USSR and the People's Republic of China, unleashed a powerful attack against South Vietnam. The situation worsened for South Vietnam in April and became critical in May. Even though a United States–Soviet summit meeting was scheduled for May, President Nixon ordered the bombing of the capital of North Vietnam, Hanoi, and the mining of Haiphong and seven other North Vietnamese ports in order to prevent the fall of the South Vietnamese government. In contrast to the 1968 Soviet invasion of Czechoslovakia, however, the U.S. attack on North Vietnam did not cause a delay in the SALT negotiations.

The SALT I Agreements   Despite the predictions of a number of American Sovietologists that the United States' action in Vietnam would result in the Soviet Union canceling the Moscow summit meeting, it was held as scheduled, from 18 to 22 May 1972. The most important agreement signed at the summit was the Treaty Between the United States of America and the Union of Soviet Socialist Republics on the Limitation of Anti-Ballistic Missile Systems (or, the Anti-Ballistic Missile [ABM] Treaty). The United States and the Soviet Union agreed to deploy no more than one hundred ABM launchers at each of two sites, one at the capital and the other at least 1,300 kilometers from the capital. To insure compliance with the terms of its provisions, the treaty called for "national technical means of verification," a bureaucratic euphemism for satellite reconnaissance and the monitoring of electronic signals. Both the United States and the Soviet Union agreed not to interfere with these verification procedures nor to conceal deliberately any ABM components. Restrictions were also placed on ABM radars, and the deployment of new ABM systems based on new technologies such as lasers was prohibited. The treaty was of unlimited duration, although reviews were scheduled for every five years. Either party had the right to withdraw from the treaty on six months' notice.

The ABM Treaty also called for the establishment of a United States–Soviet Standing Consultative Commission (SCC) in order to "promote the objectives and implementation of the provisions of this Treaty" (Article XIII) by considering questions concerning compliance; by voluntarily providing information that either the United States or the Soviet Union considered necessary to insure compliance; by agreeing on the procedures for the dismantling of ABM systems and components; by considering questions concerning the interference with national technical means of verification; and by considering means to increase the viability of the SALT I agreements and to further limit strategic weapons. In essence, this commission provided a forum for Soviet and U.S. representatives to introduce and discuss issues and problems connected with the implementation of the ABM Treaty and the other SALT I accord, the Interim Agreement between the United States of America and the Union of Soviet Socialist Republics on Certain Measures with Respect to the Limitation of Strategic Offensive Arms (or, the Interim Agreement).

The Interim Agreement placed a quantitative limit on both ICBMs and submarine-launched ballistic missiles (SLBMs). The United States was limited to 1,054 ICBMs, and the Soviets to 1,618 ICBMs. Each side had the right under the agreement to deploy additional SLBMs in exchange for the dismantling of ICBMs. This was the so-called one-way-freedom-to-mix provision of the agreement. If all older ICBMs were dismantled, the United States could build up to 710 SLBMs on forty-four submarines, and the Soviets could build up to 950 SLBMs on sixty-two submarines. The USSR was limited to 308 heavy ICBMs (see the table that appears later in this article). The Interim Agreement had a duration of five years (1972–1977), and representatives from both gov-

ernments stated that they intended to replace it with a permanent agreement or treaty within this period. In essence, the Interim Agreement placed quantitative limits on the SLBMs and ICBMs of both sides without significantly restricting qualitative developments such as MIRVs.

Because the ABM agreement was a treaty, the Nixon administration was required by the Constitution to submit it to the Senate for its advice and consent. There was substantial support in the Senate for the treaty, and it was ratified by a vote of 88 to 2. Although the Interim Agreement was not a treaty, it had to be submitted to both houses of Congress for approval by a majority vote, according to the 1961 law that established the Arms Control and Disarmament Agency. During the congressional debate on the Interim Agreement, there was considerable concern over the fact that it allowed the USSR about 50 percent more ICBMs (1,054 to 1,618) and that the USSR had a superiority of four to one in deliverable payload. Supporters of the agreement noted that the United States had four times as many long-range bombers, as well as many more warheads than the USSR.

Following the signing and approval of the ABM Treaty and the Interim Agreement (which together are referred to as the SALT I agreements), four clusters of opinion emerged among high-ranking officials concerning the agreements. The first group consisted of Nixon, Kissinger, and until his resignation from the government, Ambassador Gerard C. Smith. In their memoirs, Nixon and Kissinger present the SALT I agreements as significant accomplishments representing a mutual United States–Soviet step toward increased strategic stability and the improvement of superpower relations. SALT became the underpinning of détente, and détente became the foundation of the Nixon-Kissinger grand design of U.S. foreign policy.

Within the Nixon administration itself, Secretary of Defense Melvin Laird and Chairman of the Joint Chiefs of Staff Admiral Thomas Moorer conditioned their approval of the SALT I agreements on the continued development of new strategic weapons systems: the Trident submarine and missile system; the B-1 bomber; the Washington, D.C., anti-ballistic missile site; and the submarine-launched cruise missile. The Laird-Moorer quid pro quo (their approval of the agreements in exchange for the administration's promise to support certain strategic arms programs) was not unprecedented. Military leaders had demanded and received assurances in 1963 that underground nuclear testing would continue in exchange for their support of the Limited Test Ban Treaty.

A third group of former government officials and congressmen, including Senator Henry Jackson, former Chief of Naval Operations Admiral Elmo Zumwalt, and former SALT I negotiator Paul Nitze, criticized the numerical advantages given to the Soviets by the Interim Agreement in ICBMS, SLBMS, and submarines. These critics were concerned that this quantitative difference would be translated into political advantage. They were also concerned by the 308 heavy ICBMs that the Soviets were allowed to keep according to the terms of the Interim Agreement. The fear was that the Soviets would develop and deploy up to forty warheads on each of these missiles and that U.S. land-based strategic forces would be vulnerable to attack and destruction. This "window of vulnerability" posed, in the view of these critics of SALT, a clear and present danger to American national security.

Because of his concern over what he considered the deficiencies of the Interim Agreement, and perhaps not unrelated to personal political motivations (he was actively seeking the 1972 Democratic presidential nomination), Senator Jackson introduced an amendment stipulating that any future arms control agreement "not limit the U.S. to levels of intercontinental strategic forces inferior to the limits for the Soviet Union." The Senate accepted the Jackson Amendment by a vote of 55 to 35 and then approved the Interim Agreement by a vote of 88 to 2. An action that may have been related to the Jackson Amendment was the replacement of virtually all of the top officials of the Arms Control and Disarmament Agency following the approval of the SALT I agreements. Gerard Smith, the ACDA director and the chief American SALT negotiator, resigned his positions. Fred Iklé, a strategist known to be skeptical of both arms control and Soviet foreign policy intentions, was appointed ACDA director, and U. Alexis Johnson, a career diplomat with little significant previous experience in arms control, was appointed chief negotiator.

After departing from their government positions, several former members of the U.S. SALT delegation—the fourth group—criticized the way in which Nixon and Kissinger had conducted the negotiations. Gerard Smith charged that Kissinger often did not tell him what issues were being discussed in the back-channel negotiations and that this made his job extremely difficult. Another for-

mer member of the United States delegation, Raymond Garthoff, claimed that the final negotiations on the SALT I agreements at the Moscow summit were hectic, confused, and unsuccessful in achieving U.S. objectives.

With the approval of the two SALT I agreements in August 1972, the first era in strategic nuclear arms control came to an end. In less than three years, the United States and the Soviet Union had reached significant limits on the defensive and offensive arsenals of both sides. The foundation had been laid; all that remained was to build a substantial arms control structure on this framework.

THE SECOND PHASE: SALT II

In November 1972, several months after the SALT I agreements were approved, the second phase of the negotiations began. The negotiators met in Geneva, where all subsequent SALT negotiations were held. Broadly speaking, the task at SALT I had been to impose "quantitative"—that is, numerical—limitations on the arsenals of the two sides; at SALT II the task would be to extend these quantitative limitations and, in addition, to impose "qualitative" limitations that restricted the capabilities of weapon systems. Experts realized that such qualitative limitations would be more difficult to achieve.

During the Nixon administration, SALT had become the cornerstone of détente, and détente had become the showpiece of the administration's overall approach to foreign policy. As the Watergate scandal developed, the Nixon administration attempted to divert public attention from domestic wrongdoing to the foreign policy achievements of the administration. In June 1973, Leonid I. Brezhnev visited President Nixon, and the two leaders signed an agreement on the prevention of nuclear war, as well as a communiqué pledging the two sides to reach a SALT II agreement within the year. Nixon traveled to Moscow in June 1974 hoping to conclude a SALT II agreement, but no agreement was reached. Despite these summit meetings, domestic criticism of the Nixon administration stemming from Watergate increased until, in August 1974, President Nixon resigned.

The Vladivostok Accord President Gerald R. Ford was anxious to reestablish the credibility of the presidency both domestically and internationally. Consequently, among other actions, he ordered the U.S. SALT II delegation to press forward on the achievement of a long-term (ten-year) agreement. In November 1974, Ford met Brezhnev at Vladivostok to sign an "agreement in principle," which although not legally binding constituted a listing of objectives toward which the two leaders agreed to work. The accord indicated that each side should be limited to 2,400 strategic nuclear delivery vehicles (ICBMS, SLBMS, and long-range bombers) and of this total, 1,320 could be MIRVed warheads (see the table). The new agreements were supposed to cover the period from October 1977, the date the SALT I Interim Agreement would expire, through December 1985.

When the substance of the Vladivostok Accord was made public, neither the proponents nor the opponents of SALT were satisfied. A number of arms control supporters thought that the total number of launchers and the MIRV sub-limit were too high. SALT critics, such as Senator Jackson, were concerned that the agreement—which protected the Soviet Union's missiles with large throw-weights—would threaten the survivability of U.S. ICBMS should the Soviets deploy all their authorized (1,320) MIRVed warheads.

As the arms control negotiators met in Geneva, engineers, scientists, and weapons designers in both the United States and the Soviet Union continued to develop new systems. In a sense, the SALT negotiations became an implicit race between the negotiators and the weapons designers, because a strategic arms control agreement that could have been both desirable and feasible at one point could subsequently have been negated by new technological (or "qualitative") developments. This appears to have been the case with the Vladivostok Accord. In the period following the signing of the SALT I agreements, both the United States and the Soviet Union developed, tested, and began deploying several new and more capable weapons systems that vastly complicated the SALT negotiations.

The Soviet Union began to deploy a new bomber, the Tupolov (TU)-22M (its NATO code name was Backfire), which had an estimated range of 5,500 kilometers, enough to reach the United States from the USSR and to land in friendly territory, such as Cuba, to refuel for the return trip. The U.S. SALT II delegation argued that the Backfire should count against the Soviet Union's 2,400 vehicle ceiling, a position the Soviets repeatedly rejected. The Soviets were also developing a mobile missile, the SS-16, which had the capability of reaching the continental United States.

U.S. scientists and engineers were working on a number of new weapons systems as well. Programs were under way to increase the accuracy of missiles, and work had begun on the development of a large ICBM called the Missile Experimental (MX). Research and development proceeded on a sophisticated warhead, the "maneuverable reentry vehicle" (MARV), which was designed to be not only independently targetable (like MIRVS), but also to maneuver in the last stage of its reentry, enormously complicating the problem of ballistic missile defense. Tests were also conducted on an air-launched ICBM. While all of these weapons systems were being developed and tested, President Ford requested funds for the deployment of two new systems: the B-1 bomber and the Trident submarine.

Perhaps the U.S. system that caused the greatest controversy during the SALT II negotiations was the cruise missile, a subsonic, air-breathing, long-range missile capable of extemely high accuracy. Soviet negotiators contended that these missiles, if deployed, should count against the 2,400 vehicle ceiling of the Vladivostok Accord, while U.S. negotiators rejected this position. Cruise missiles complicated the problem of verification considerably. For example, one version of cruise missiles was designed to fit into the standard torpedo tubes of submarines. Because there would be no way—short of physically inspecting all submarines and their armaments—to verify whether or not cruise missiles were on board and whether those missiles were nuclear or conventionally armed, Soviet defense planners would be forced to assume that all U.S. submarines, not just U.S. ballistic missile submarines, were "strategic launchers." In addition, because torpedo tubes could be reloaded, submarines would be counted as MIRVed launchers.

These technological issues became caught up in American domestic politics. In 1976, Ronald Reagan, Henry Jackson, George Wallace, and Jimmy Carter all were presidential candidates and each of them criticized the Nixon-Ford-Kissinger détente policy on various grounds. Reagan attacked Ford for "giving away everything and getting nothing in return from the Soviet Union" (*Washington Post,* 24 February 1976). Jackson was more specific: he criticized SALT as granting advantages to the USSR and criticized détente for placing too little emphasis on human rights. In response to these criticisms, Ford moved to the right, banned the use of the word "détente" by members of his administration, and accepted the Republican party's platform, which contained a number of specific criticisms of his détente policy. In the end, Ford narrowly defeated Reagan for the Republican nomination, only to lose the general election to Carter.

The Carter Administration and SALT II

In his inaugural address of 20 January 1977, Jimmy Carter expressed his desire to move toward the goal of eliminating nuclear weapons from the face of the earth. Within several weeks of assuming office, the president stated that he wanted to conclude a SALT II agreement quickly and to move on to other items on the arms control agenda. Along with his enthusiasm for arms control, Carter also emphasized human rights. As a gesture of support for Soviet dissidents, he wrote a personal letter to Soviet physicist and human rights activist Andrey Sakharov and received exiled Soviet dissident Vladimir Bukovsky in the White House. These actions were applauded by U.S. liberals and conservatives alike, but they deeply disturbed Soviet leaders, who charged that these activities constituted interference in Soviet domestic affairs.

Carter was anxious to make progress on "real" as opposed to "cosmetic" arms control. Consequently, he requested the National Security Council to draft a "comprehensive proposal" for making "deep cuts" in the levels established by the Vladivostok Accord. In March 1977, Secretary of State Cyrus Vance traveled to Moscow and presented a proposal that called for the following:

1. a 20 percent reduction in the total number of strategic nuclear launch vehicles allowed under Vladivostok from 2,400 to 1,800;
2. a reduction from 1,320 MIRV launchers to a level between 1,100 and 1,200;
3. a sub-limit of 550 on the number of MIRVed ICBMS allowed;
4. a cut in large Soviet heavy ICBMs from 308 to 150; and
5. a range limit of 2,500 kilometers on all cruise missiles and mobile ICBMS.

In addition, there was a limit of six on the number of missile test firings allowed per year (see Table 1). Vance was also authorized to present a fallback proposal that was much closer to the Vladivostok Accord, in the event the Soviets rejected the comprehensive proposal.

Soviet leaders rejected both U.S. proposals quickly and outright. They did so for four main reasons. First, they had been angered by President Carter's emphasis on human rights. Second, the comprehensive proposal took the Soviets by surprise. Brezhnev had expected Carter to conclude the Vladivostok Accord, as the president, through his emissary Averell Harriman, had assured him he would do. When Carter decided to present a new proposal, he did not—as had been the case with Kissinger and the "back-channel"—go over the proposal privately with the Soviets in advance. Third, they felt that the comprehensive proposal called for reductions that fell almost entirely on the Soviet side and, therefore, heavily favored the United States. Fourth, in keeping with his campaign pledge to open up the government, Carter publicly described the comprehensive proposal even before it was presented to the Soviets. In short, Soviet leaders viewed the March 1977 proposal as sabotaging plans for a quick conclusion to the SALT II negotiations. The Soviets were so angered by the comprehensive proposal that they refused even to consider the U.S. fallback proposal.

If the Soviets had rejected the "deep cuts" proposal, certain elements of the United States public did not. In the months and years that followed, the comprehensive proposal became the standard by which subsequent proposals were judged, a kind of irreducible minimum that had to be achieved in order to obtain U.S. conservatives' support, rather than simply an opening negotiating position. Following the recriminations issued by both U.S. and Soviet leaders in the aftermath of the March 1977 imbroglio, Carter and Brezhnev publicly expressed a desire to get the negotiations back on track. In May 1977, Secretary Vance and Foreign Minister Gromyko met in Geneva, where they signed an agreement banning "environmental modification," the use of climate modification techniques for hostile purposes. In addition, the two leaders discussed ways to restart the stalled SALT talks.

Of course, SALT II was not the only item on the Carter administration's foreign policy agenda. In September 1977, Carter signed the Panama Canal treaties, which granted complete control of the canal to Panama after 1999. Despite the fact that these treaties were negotiated by four different presidents and had broad support within the Congress, they did not enjoy strong public support. After investing a significant amount of political capital, the Carter administration was able to obtain the ratification of the treaties by a narrow margin.

Soviet activities throughout the world were another concern to members of the Carter administration. In July 1977, the first deployment of Cuban troops (presumably with the approval and assistance of the USSR) to the Horn of Africa was reported. The significance of this deployment was debated within the administration. To the president's assistant for national security, Dr. Zbigniew Brzezinski, "more was at stake than a disputed piece of desert. To a great extent our credibility was under scrutiny by new, relatively skeptical allies in a region strategically important to us. I believed that if Soviet-sponsored Cubans determined the outcome of an Ethiopian-Somali conflict, there could be wider regional and international consequences" (*Power and Principle: Memoirs of the National Security Adviser, 1977–1981*). Brzezinski believed therefore that this issue should be "linked" to other issues of Soviet–United States relations. This view contrasted markedly with that of Vance, who believed that SALT was so important that it should not be linked to human rights, trade, or Soviet and Cuban actions in the Horn of Africa. According to Vance, "I think it is in the interests of both nations and in the interest of world peace for us to reach a satisfactory, negotiated settlement with them. So I think it [SALT] stands on its own two feet" (in Caldwell, p. 46). The differences between Brzezinski and Vance became increasingly important and affected the course of the SALT II negotiations.

Another area over which Brzezinski and Vance disagreed was China. Brzezinski was enthusiastic about normalizing diplomatic relations with the People's Republic of China, which had begun under President Nixon in 1972, but had stalled since that time. In May 1978, Brzezinski visited China and while there made a number of anti-Soviet remarks and assured his Chinese hosts that the Carter administration had made up its mind to establish full diplomatic relations. Brzezinski's visit and undiplomatic remarks came just prior to a meeting between Vance and Gromyko concerning SALT and had a pronounced negative effect on the meeting. In December 1978, Brzezinski was able to convince President Carter that the time was right to conclude the normalization agreement, and without the knowledge of Vance, who was out of town, this decision was reached. Carter announced the full normalization of relations with China on 15 December 1978.

In retrospect, it appears that the normalization of relations with China delayed the conclusion of the SALT II negotiations by four to six months. The new Sino-American relationship was underscored at the end of January 1979 when Deng Xiaoping visited Washington. Meanwhile, Soviet and U.S. negotiators continued to work on the draft SALT II Treaty. Finally, after six and a half years of negotiations, the treaty was initialed on 18 April 1979, and was formally signed by Carter and Brezhnev in Vienna on 18 June 1979.

The SALT II agreement consisted of three parts: a treaty, a protocol, and a joint statement of principles. The treaty, scheduled to remain in effect from the time it entered into force until the end of December 1985, contained nineteen articles and was seventy-eight pages long. It placed a limit of 2,400 (to be reduced to 2,250 by the end of 1981) on the number of total strategic nuclear launch vehicles held by each side. Within this ceiling, no more than 1,320 ICBMs, SLBMs, and long-range bombers could be equipped with MIRVs or long-range cruise missiles. Within this sub-limit, no more than 1,200 ICBMs, SLBMs, and air-to-surface cruise missiles could be MIRVed, and within that sub-limit no more than 820 ICBMs could be MIRVed. In addition to these overall limits, the treaty contained the following additional qualitative limitations:

- ceilings on the throw-weight and launch-weight of light and heavy ICBMs;
- a limit on the testing and deployment of one "new type" ICBM;
- a freeze on the number of reentry vehicles on certain types of ICBMs; a limit of ten reentry vehicles on the one "new type" ICBM that each side was permitted; a limit of fourteen reentry vehicles on SLBMs; and a limit of ten reentry vehicles on air-to-surface ballistic missiles;
- a ban on the testing and deployment of air-launched cruise missiles with ranges greater than 600 kilometers (375 miles) on aircraft other than those counted as long-range bombers;
- a ban on the construction of additional fixed ICBM launchers and on any increase in the number of fixed heavy ICBM launchers, which limited the Soviet Union to 308 modern, large ballistic missiles and the United States to zero;
- a ban on heavy, mobile ICBMs, heavy SLBMs and heavy air-to-surface ballistic missiles;

- a ban on certain types of strategic, offensive weapons not yet deployed by either side, such as ballistic missiles with ranges greater than 600 kilometers deployed on surface ships;
- an agreement to exchange data on a regular basis on the numbers of weapons deployed and limited by the treaty;
- advance notification of certain ICBM test launches; and,
- a ban on ICBM systems that can be reloaded quickly.

The principal provisions of the SALT I Interim Agreement, Vladivostok Accord, U.S. comprehensive proposal, and SALT II Treaty are summarized in the table on the next page.

The second part of the SALT II agreement consisted of a protocol, scheduled to remain in effect until the end of 1981, that banned flight testing and deployment of ICBMS from mobile launch platforms; prohibited the deployment of land-based or sea-based cruise missiles with ranges greater than 600 kilometers; and banned the testing and deployment of air-to-surface ballistic missiles. The third part of the agreement consisted of a set of principles concerning the next round of SALT negotiations.

The Backfire bomber was one of the major points of contention in the SALT II negotiations. Although limits on the Backfire were not formally part of the SALT II agreement, in a letter to President Carter accompanying the treaty, Brezhnev committed the USSR to produce no more than thirty planes per year and to limit the up-grading of the capabilities of the Backfire. The U.S. State Department noted that these assurances had the same legal force as the rest of the SALT II treaty and that if the USSR were to violate these commitments, the United States could withdraw from the agreement.

Attempting to re-create President Nixon's performance when he flew by helicopter directly from Andrews Air Force Base to the Capitol upon his return from the 1972 Moscow summit, President Carter flew directly to the Capitol upon his return from the Vienna summit. Less than two hours after landing in the United States, Carter delivered a report on the summit and the SALT II Treaty to a joint session of Congress. The president noted: "SALT is not a favor we are doing for the Soviet Union. It is a deliberate, calculated move we are making as a matter of self-interest—a move that happens to serve the goals both of security and of survival, that strengthens both the military position of the United States and the cause of world peace" (*Los Angeles Times,* 19 June 1979).

When President Carter, soon after his return to Washington from the Vienna summit, submitted the SALT II Treaty to the Senate for its advice and consent, a new set of negotiations concerning SALT II began, negotiations between the executive branch and the Senate. Carter asserted, "My restraints were just as much with the Senate as they were at the bargaining table with the Soviets" (interview with Michael Charlton in *From Deterrence to Defense: The Inside Story of Strategic Policy,* 1987, p. 72). Members of the Senate believed that the task before them was of historic significance; in a 1979 press conference, Minority Leader Howard Baker called SALT II "the most important treaty this country has undertaken since World War I" (Caldwell, p. 124). Democratic Senator John Glenn agreed: "Not since Woodrow Wilson's time and the League of Nations debate has a treaty been so important, yet so contentious, as the SALT II Treaty" (unpublished press release, 17 May 1979).

Once the treaty was submitted to the Senate, four groups of thought emerged. First, some senators were irreconcilably opposed to the ratification of SALT II in the form that it was submitted to them. This group included Senators Henry Jackson, John Tower, Jake Garn, and Jesse Helms. They believed that the SALT II Treaty was not in the national security interest of the United States, and they, along with their staff members, worked hard to defeat the treaty. The second group of senators consisted of the treaty supporters and included Senators Alan Cranston, John Culver, and Gary Hart. The supporters worked closely with the Carter administration to try to win increased support for the treaty within the Senate. A third group of senators, most notably Mark Hatfield, George McGovern, and William Proxmire, believed that SALT II did not do enough to control the arms race and did not make substantial enough reductions to warrant supporting the treaty. The last group of senators, and the most critical to the fate of the treaty, were those senators who had not decided how they were going to vote on the treaty. These "undecideds" included some of the most important leaders in the Senate. Majority Leader Robert Byrd did not come out in favor of SALT II at the time that it was signed and presented to the Senate. He studied the hearings on the treaty in detail, led a delegation from the Senate to Moscow in order to meet with Soviet officials concern-

Summary of Major SALT Proposals and Agreements

	SALT I Interim Agreement (May 1972) U.S./USSR	Vladivostok Accords (November 1974)	Moscow Comprehensive Proposal (March 1977)	SALT II Agreement (June 1979)
ICBMS	1000/1409			2,400–2,250
SLBMS	710/950	2400 (total SNLVS)	1,800–2,000	(by 12/31/81)
Long-range Bombers	*			
MIRved Launchers	*	1320	1,100–1,200	1,200 for ICBM and SLBM, 1,320 including ALCM
MIRved ICBMS	*	*	550	820
MLBMS†	308	308	150	308
ALCM	*	(dispute over whether included under SNLV ceiling)	2,500-km range limit	2,500-km range limit during 3-yr. protocol < 500-km range not to count as MIRved launchers
GLCM/SLCM	*	*	2,500-km range limit	600-km range limit
Backfire Bomber	*	(dispute over whether included under SNLV ceiling)	"strict limit" on deployment to intercontinental range	statement to accompany agreement
Land-Mobile ICBMS	U.S. Unilateral Statement Favoring Ban	*	0	Protocol includes prohibition on testing.
"New" ICBMS and SLBMS	*	*	ban on new ICBMS only	one new ICBM allowed
Ballistic-Missile Flight-Test	*	*	6 per year for ICBMS 6 per year for SLBMS	
Limits on MIRVS				10 for ICBMS/ASBMS 14 for SLBMS

*not included
†USSR only

Glossary

ICBM	(land-based) intercontinental ballistic missile	MARV	maneuverable re-entry vehicle
SLBM	submarine-launched ballistic missile	MLVM	modern large ballistic missile
		MLBM	(Soviet SS-9/SS-18 type)
SNLV	strategic nuclear launch vehicle (missiles plus long-range bombers)	ALCM	air-launched cruise missile
		GLCM	ground-launched cruise missile
MIRV	multiple, independently-targeted re-entry vehicle	SLCM	sea-launched cruise missile
		ASBM	air-to-surface ballistic missile

Source: Dan Caldwell, *The Dynamics of Domestic Politics of Arms Control: The SALT II Treaty Ratification Debate* (Columbia, S.C., 1991). Reprinted by permission of University of South Carolina Press

ing the accord, and eventually came out in favor of the treaty in late October.

The Senate minority leader has played a significant role in the ratification of past treaties. During the debate on the Limited Test Ban Treaty in 1963, President Kennedy was able to obtain the support of the Senate minority leader at that time, Everett Dirksen, in order to counter Senator Jackson's criticism of the treaty. Sixteen years later, another Democratic president, Jimmy Carter, sought to convince Senator Dirksen's son-in-law and Senate minority leader, Howard Baker, to support his arms control treaty, SALT II. But this time the Democratic president was not as successful. Senator Baker had supported several previous arms control agreements and, importantly, had supported the ratification of the Panama Canal treaties. As Baker told Carter after his vote on Panama, "If I vote right many more times I'm going to lose the next election!" (Carter, p. 88). Baker was running for the Republican presidential nomination in 1979, and he viewed his stance on SALT II as key to his candidacy. For this reason as well as others, he opposed the treaty. According to Baker, "SALT II is a disaster for the deterrent effect of our weapons system. It gives us nothing of value in return, it validates Soviet strategic arms superiority, and it thus endangers national security" (Baker, *No Margin for Error: America in the Eighties,* New York, 1980, p. 192).

During the summer of 1979, three Senate committees held hearings on the SALT II Treaty. Since its creation in 1816, the Senate Foreign Relations Committee has had exclusive jurisdiction over treaties. This committee conducted hearings on the treaty for twenty-seven days from July through October. The public record of these hearings fills five volumes consisting of 2,266 pages with the testimony of eighty-eight witnesses. On 9 November 1979, after four months of hearings and one of the most exhaustive reviews of any treaty submitted to the Senate, the members of the Foreign Relations Committee by a vote of nine to six recommended the ratification of the treaty to the full Senate.

Opponents of the treaty were anxious to have a formal, public forum in which to review and criticize the treaty. Senator Jackson, a member of the Senate Armed Services Committee, convinced the chairman of the committee, Senator John Stennis, to hold hearings on the treaty. At the end of December 1979, over the objections of Chairman Stennis, the committee adopted a report denouncing the treaty as "not in the national security interests of the United States." The report specifically cited the following areas of concern: (1) certain inequalities allowed by the treaty, such as the Soviet advantage in throw-weight, the Soviet possession of modern, large ballistic missiles, the exclusion of the Backfire bomber from the formal treaty, the inclusion of Western theater nuclear forces, and the potential precedents established by the three-year protocol; (2) loopholes concerning "new types" of ICBMS; (3) the verification of the treaty; and (4) ambiguities contained in the treaty.

The third committee to hold hearings on the SALT II Treaty was the Senate Intelligence Committee, which had been created to oversee executive branch intelligence operations and to consider matters related to the intelligence capabilities of the United States. On 5 October 1979 the committee released an unclassified version of its report indicating that, in the opinion of the members of the committee, the SALT II Treaty was "adequately verifiable."

Estimates vary as to the effect of the Senate hearings on the fate of the SALT II Treaty. Opponents believed that the treaty was dead after the hearings. In contrast, Senator Cranston, known as one of the best vote counters in the Senate, estimated that shortly before the treaty was signed, the tally stood at twenty firmly opposed, ten leaning against, forty leaning heavily toward ratification, ten leaning slightly toward ratification, and twenty undecided. By the end of the summer, it appeared that the treaty supporters had won the battle. In its lead editorial of 20 August 1979, the *Los Angeles Times* stated, "It appears probable that the [SALT II] agreement will be ratified by the Senate." And politically conservative publications such as *Business Week* supported ratification. If the whole Senate had voted on the SALT II Treaty in middle to late August, it is likely the treaty would have been ratified. Such a vote was not taken because the Senate Foreign Relations Committee had not completed its hearings and its report on the treaty.

Because it appeared that the SALT II Treaty was emerging from the Senate relatively unscathed, in mid-August members of the Carter administration, legislators, and other government officials departed on scheduled vacations, leaving Washington to thousands of visiting tourists. President Carter left for a cruise down the Mississippi River on a paddlewheel steamer, the *Delta Queen.* At the end of the month, Vice President Walter Mondale and Brzezinski's deputy, David Aaron, left for China. Cyrus

Vance went to Martha's Vineyard, and Brzezinski left for his vacation home in Vermont. These vacations were interrupted by news that the Central Intelligence Agency had discovered evidence that the Soviet Union had a "combat brigade" deployed in Cuba. Surprisingly, the person who first publicly announced this discovery was Senator Frank Church, the liberal chairman of the Senate Foreign Relations Committee, who was in a tough reelection race in his home state of Idaho. Church not only announced the existence of the brigade, but also called for the removal of the Soviet troops from Cuba. On the day that the Congress reconvened in early September, Secretary Vance issued a press release saying that the United States "would not be satisfied with the status quo" (*Washington Post*, 16 October 1979). The Foreign Relations Committee then held hearings on the Soviet brigade issue, and Senator Church noted, "There is no likelihood whatever that the Senate will ratify the SALT Treaty as long as Soviet combat troops are in Cuba" (*Los Angeles Times*, 6 September 1979).

Soviet government officials contended that the brigade was not newly deployed; that, in fact, it had been in Cuba since the Cuban missile crisis of 1962. Meetings were held between Vance and various Soviet officials, but to no avail; the troops stayed in Cuba. President Carter appointed a blue-ribbon commission to study the brigade issue, and this group presented its results to the president. In an address to the nation on 1 October 1979, Carter noted, "The greatest danger to American security tonight is certainly not the two to three thousand Soviet troops in Cuba. The greatest danger to all the nations of the world . . . is the breakdown of a common effort to preserve the peace, and the ultimate threat of nuclear war. I renew my call to the Senate of the United States to ratify the SALT II Treaty" (in David D. Mewsom, *The Soviet Combat Brigade in Cuba*, 1987, p. 85).

The furor created by the Soviet combat brigade in Cuba influenced the SALT II ratification debate in several significant ways. Importantly, the crisis reversed the momentum of the Carter administration's SALT ratification effort. Whereas in the middle of August chances of ratification appeared to be very good, by the end of August the treaty was in trouble. In addition, the combat brigade issue heightened differences between Vance and Brzezinski. President Carter recognized that "Brzezinski was much more inclined to want to link the arms control efforts with the inevitable competition between us and the Soviets on extending influence" (in Michael Charlton, ed., *From Deterrence to Defense: The Inside Story of Strategic Policy* [Cambridge, 1987], p. 79). Vance, on the other hand, wanted to continue the momentum of arms control and did not want the brigade issue to slow or derail the SALT negotiations.

The debate over the brigade underscored the question of verification. Opponents of the treaty questioned the ability of the United States government to monitor the treaty adequately if the government could not even keep track of thousands of Soviet troops in Cuba. Treaty supporters noted that the task of keeping track of several thousand troops on an island of ten million people was, in fact, more difficult than keeping track of long-range missiles and bombers. The brigade crisis also had the effect of worsening United States–Soviet relations. A number of high-ranking Soviet officials believed, not without reason, that the brigade crisis, if not manufactured, was at least exploited by treaty opponents in the United States to block ratification.

A final crucial result of the crisis was the delay of the Senate's consideration of the treaty. The Senate spent most of September and October debating the brigade issue. The original schedule for consideration of the treaty called for the treaty to be submitted to the full Senate in mid-September, and floor debate would then require about another four to six weeks. This means that a final vote on the treaty would have been taken toward the end of October. As it turned out, the delay caused by the brigade issue proved critical.

On the morning of 4 November 1979, a group of several thousand Iranians stormed the U.S. embassy in Teheran and took it over. This began a 444-day-long hostage crisis, an event that dominated the last fifteen months of the Carter administration. The event was only tangentially related to SALT II: the United States operated two sites in northern Iran for the purpose of gathering intelligence on Soviet missile tests, and these were closed down early in 1979. However, the hostage crisis directly affected many Americans' evaluation of the Carter administration's handling of U.S. foreign policy, and this predominantly negative assessment had a significant influence on the SALT II debate. The hostage crisis had another important effect. On 11 April 1980 when Secretary Vance was out of town, the National Security Council met and approved a mission to attempt to rescue the U.S. hostages held in Iran. Vance had previously strongly opposed such an operation and had told President Carter that he would resign whether or not the mission succeeded. True to his word, Vance resigned following the failed hostage rescue attempt. Without Vance, there was no one who possessed sufficient influence with President Carter to counter Brzezinski's views.

At the end of December 1979, Soviet military forces entered Afghanistan. As President Carter wrote in his memoirs, *Keeping Faith,* he sent Brezhnev "the sharpest message" of his presidency on the Washington-Moscow hot line, telling him that the invasion was "a clear threat to the peace" and could make "a fundamental and long-lasting turning point in our relations." Although Carter did not want to scrap the SALT II Treaty, he recognized the reality of the situation: it meant "the immediate and automatic loss of any chance for early ratification of the SALT II treaty." Consequently, on 3 January 1980, Carter wrote to Senate Majority Leader Byrd and requested that the treaty be withdrawn from active Senate consideration.

Very early in the 1980 election campaign various candidates criticized President Carter's foreign policy initiatives. Republican nominee Ronald Reagan considered the Panama Canal treaties to be an "out and out give-away," and he said in his campaign speeches that the SALT II Treaty was "fatally flawed." In addition, the economic situation within the United States, the hostage crisis, and the Soviet invasion of Afghanistan hurt Carter's popularity with the U.S. electorate. As a result, Reagan defeated Carter in a landslide, with 489 to 49 electoral votes and 52 percent of the popular vote.

In his first news conference as president, Reagan said that the United States should be wary of the Soviets because they "have openly and publicly declared that the only morality they recognize is what will further their cause, meaning they reserve unto themselves the right to commit any crime, to lie, to cheat." Prior to his election, Reagan had publicly criticized all arms control agreements in general and SALT II in particular. He believed that SALT II had reduced American will to support a strong military posture and that it permitted the Soviet Union to open a "window of vulnerability" against U.S. land-based nuclear forces. From the first days of his administration, it was clear that Reagan was more concerned about building up U.S. military forces than reducing them. From 1981 to 1984, the average real increase in military spending was more than 7 percent. Much of this increase went to support the modernization of nuclear forces, including the MX, Trident II and Pershing II ballistic missiles, three types of cruise missiles, the B-1B bomber, and ballistic missile defenses.

Despite his opposition to the treaty, President Reagan decided not to undercut the SALT II limits as long as the Soviet Union also observed them. The Reagan administration abided by these limits until late 1986, when the United States surpassed the agreed-to number of strategic nuclear launch vehicles allowed under the treaty.

In 1979, the members of the North Atlantic Treaty Organization (NATO) had agreed that the alliance should follow a "two track" policy: it would build up NATO theater nuclear forces while engaging the Soviet Union in arms control negotiations concerning these forces. Negotiations to limit intermediate nuclear forces (INF) began under President Carter. In late 1981, the United States and Soviet Union resumed the INF talks. At the beginning of these negotiations, the United States proposed the elimination of all Soviet and U.S. INF nuclear forces (i.e., those with ranges of 1,000 to 5,000 kilometers). This proposal was referred to as the "zero option."

The prospect of the U.S. deployment of intermediate-range forces in Europe caused great concern in Europe. In October 1981, a demonstration of 250,000 people in Bonn was thought to be the largest public demonstration in West Germany since the visit to Berlin of John Kennedy in 1963. And in the United States, antinuclear activists had introduced a resolution calling for an "immediate, bilateral, verifiable" freeze in the production and deployment of nuclear weapons. By early 1982, the Reagan administration was under pressure to respond to public criticism in the United States and abroad to do something about the threat that nuclear weapons posed.

THE STRATEGIC ARMS REDUCTION TALKS (START)

In a May 1982 commencement address to his alma mater, Eureka College, President Reagan announced that the United States and the Soviet Union would resume negotiations on strategic weapons. But these meetings would be designed to achieve deep cuts in the strategic nuclear forces of both sides and would hence be renamed the Strategic Arms Reduction Talks (START). The first set of talks was held from June 1982 to December 1983 in Geneva. There was little agreement between the two sides concerning which forces would be addressed. But the talks did indicate that the Reagan administration was trying to do something to control—even reduce—the number of nuclear weapons.

In keeping with the concerns that Reagan had expressed during the 1980 presidential campaign, the U.S. negotiators at the START talks sought to reduce Soviet capabilities that were viewed as most threatening to the United States, particularly Soviet advantages in heavy missiles and throw-weight. In SALT I, the United States and Soviet Union had used launchers as the basic accounting unit; in START, the United States sought to use missiles, throw-weight, and warheads as the accounting units. This approach had serious consequences for the Soviet arsenal, which consisted mostly of land-based intercontinental ballistic missiles. Just as the SALT I Interim Agreement had sought to encourage the Soviets to deploy sea-based rather than land-based nuclear forces in the "one-way-freedom-to-mix" (from ICBMS to SLBMS) provision, the U.S. START proposal sought to encourage the Soviets to depend more heavily on submarines, bombers, and cruise missiles.

The Soviet Union, seeking to build on the SALT II Treaty, proposed percentage reductions from the SALT II limits on strategic nuclear delivery vehicles. In addition, the Soviets called for new sub-limits on MIRVs and on the total number of nuclear warheads allowed each side. Soviet negotiators rejected the United States' proposal on the grounds that it was asymmetrically disadvantageous to the Soviet Union; that it called for disproportionate reductions precisely in those weapons categories in which the Soviets had an advantage, and called for few or no limits on those weapons, such as cruise missiles and bombers, in which the United States had an advantage.

In November 1983 the United States began deploying intermediate-range nuclear forces in Europe in keeping with NATO's two-track decision. These deployments deeply concerned the Soviets because one of the systems being deployed, the Pershing II, was the most accurate intermediate- or long-range nuclear weapon in the U.S. inventory— it had a "circular error probability" (CEP) of forty-five meters. In addition, the Pershing IIs deployed in West Germany would be able to reach the Soviet Union in five minutes, giving the United States a potential first-strike capability against the Soviet

Union, possibly including Moscow itself. Once the U.S. INF deployments began and the fifth round of the START negotiations ended in December, the Soviets refused to set a date for the resumption of the negotiations. START had stalled.

Arms control analysts Michael Krepon and Alton Frye, in an article published in *American Defense Annual 1985–1986,* have accurately summarized the events of 1984: "The year 1984 appears as a blank page in the history of nuclear arms control. For the first time since SALT began in 1969, an entire year passed without any negotiations between the superpowers over the control and reduction of nuclear armaments." U.S. and Soviet spokespersons tried to place the blame on the other party for the impasse in negotiations. In addition, 1984 was an election year, and much of President Reagan's attention was devoted to running for a second term. In his campaign against former Vice President Walter Mondale, Reagan was very successful; he won 525 electoral college votes, compared with Mondale's 13, and 59 percent of the popular vote—even larger margins than he had won four years earlier. By the end of 1984, Reagan agreed to meet for the first time with Soviet Foreign Minister Gromyko. He also gave an address to the United Nations that indicated a possible change in his attitude and approach to the Soviet Union.

The Nuclear and Space Arms Talks (NST)

After a hiatus of fifteen months, in January 1985 Secretary of State George P. Shultz and Foreign Minister Gromyko signed an agreement to resume arms control negotiations on three separate but related issues: intermediate nuclear forces, strategic weapons, and defense and space weapons. Many observers questioned why the Soviet Union chose to return to the negotiations. There were several reasons. First, in March 1983, President Reagan announced that he supported an effort to develop space-based ballistic-missile defense systems that would render nuclear weapons "impotent and obsolete." The president called this new program the "Strategic Defense Initiative," although others referred to it as "Star Wars" because of its reliance on advanced technologies such as laser and charged particle beams. Many Soviets have a greater faith in the reliability and effectiveness of U.S. technology than Americans have themselves, and the Strategic Defense Initiative constituted such a case. While a number of prominent U.S. scientists questioned whether a defense of the U.S. population against a

Soviet ballistic missile attack was feasible, Soviet planners assumed the worst case—that the United States would successfully develop a workable ballistic missile defense system. In addition, President Reagan had just won one of the largest landslides in U.S. electoral history, and if they chose not to deal with him, the Soviets would have to wait at least another four years before resuming arms control talks. For these reasons, the Soviets decided to reopen negotiations.

The Nuclear and Space Arms Talks were to be conducted by a single delegation with three negotiating groups for each side. The first round of the negotiations began in March 1985, and neither the United States nor the Soviet Union had significantly changed their START positions. However, the same month that the talks opened, a new leader was named in the Soviet Union. The Politburo, the ruling body of the Soviet Communist party, selected its youngest member, Mikhail S. Gorbachev, to succeed the three elderly leaders who had died in office since November 1982. In his memoirs, Gorbachev wrote: "We believed, and still believe, that, as the eighties loomed up, major accords were just a stone's throw away for such areas as anti-satellite weapons, the arms trade, reductions in military activity in the Indian Ocean and the Middle Eastern settlement issues. Ten years ago! How much time and how many resources have been wasted on the arms race, and how many human lives have been lost!" (*Perestroika: New Thinking for Our Country and the World,* New York, 1987, p. 212). While part of Gorbachev's purpose in writing these words was undoubtedly rhetorical, he backed up his words with actions. He declared a unilateral moratorium on nuclear testing and followed this by announcing a unilateral cut of five hundred thousand troops from the Soviet military.

By the autumn of 1985, the Soviets had responded to many of the points in the U.S. proposal of the previous March. The Soviets proposed a fifty percent reduction in ballistic missiles and long-range bombers and called for a ceiling of six thousand on the number of strategic nuclear warheads on each side. No more than 60 percent of the permitted arms were to be deployed on any single leg of the triad, that is, ICBMS, SLBMS, or long-range bombers. The Soviets linked these reductions to a ban on space-based arms and called for a ban on long-range cruise missiles (those with ranges greater than 600 kilometers, or 375 miles) and a ban on new nuclear delivery systems. While these proposals were unacceptable to the United States, they did pave the way for further negotiations.

In November 1985, Reagan and Gorbachev journeyed to Geneva for their first summit meeting. According to former arms control negotiator Paul Nitze, "arms control was a primary topic of discussion. No significant progress was achieved on any of the major arms control issues, but the two leaders were able to explain to each other directly and thoroughly their views on these issues and thus reach a level of understanding that could facilitate progress in the future" (in Kruzel, p. 188). The two leaders agreed that "a nuclear war cannot be won and must never be fought" and affirmed that the two sides should continue to work toward an INF agreement and a 50 percent reduction in the strategic nuclear arsenals of their countries. And they agreed to meet again in 1986 and 1987.

In January 1986, Gorbachev made a dramatic announcement calling for a three-stage plan to achieve total nuclear disarmament by the year 2000. Gorbachev proposed that the United States and his country begin the process by reducing 50 percent of their strategic nuclear weapons and, for the first time, agreeing on zero intermediate nuclear forces in Europe. Although Gorbachev called for a different path, he and President Reagan shared a vision of the same destination, nuclear disarmament. Despite this shared goal, the Soviet Union continued to link reductions in strategic nuclear arms with limitations on space-based weapons.

The Reykjavík Summit   Reagan and Gorbachev met at Reykjavík, Iceland, on 10–11 October 1986, for what Reagan had thought would be a "base camp" en route to the summit planned for 1987. Instead, the two sides discussed some of the most dramatic and far-reaching proposals ever presented during the nuclear age.

Rather than simply discussing generalities, the Soviets presented specific proposals, marked by significant Soviet concessions, in the areas of START, INF, and nuclear testing. The Americans who were present were impressed with the Soviet proposals and were anxious to conclude an agreement that would formally oblige the Soviets to accept and implement their proposals. Consequently, negotiators from both sides met through the night of 11 October. Ambassador Nitze and Marshal Sergei Akhromeyev, the chief of the Soviet General Staff, developed the START framework, which called for a reduction to sixteen hundred of strategic nuclear launch vehicles, a ceiling of six thousand on ICBM, SLBM, and air-launched cruise missile warheads. Sea-launched cruise missiles would be limited separately from the six thousand ceiling.

On the last day of the summit, President Reagan proposed that the two sides eliminate all of their ballistic missiles within ten years. In response, Gorbachev upped the ante and called for eliminating all Soviet and U.S. strategic nuclear weapons within ten years. The two leaders also discussed their common vision of achieving total nuclear disarmament. The Soviet demand for such radical limitations were limits on the Strategic Defense Initiative. President Reagan, however, was unwilling to accept such limitations, and the most radical arms control proposals of the entire nuclear era became moot.

There was considerable reaction to the Reykjavík proposals both within and outside of the United States. U.S. military leaders had not been consulted about the possibility of eliminating all ballistic missiles and were deeply concerned about the advisability of such a proposal. Allied leaders, particularly in Europe, were concerned that the United States and the Soviet Union might reach an agreement on which they had no influence.

START, 1987–1991 In mid-1987, U.S. and Soviet negotiators presented proposals based on the less dramatic aspects of the Reykjavík discussions, and incremental progress was made. In December 1987 Gorbachev visited Washington and signed the Intermediate Nuclear Forces (INF) Treaty, which eliminated nuclear missiles based in Europe with ranges of six hundred to thirty-five hundred miles (960–5,600 kilometers), as well as those with ranges of three hundred to six hundred miles (480–960 kilometers). In addition, the United States and Soviet Union issued a statement indicating the agreed framework of the START Treaty, which called for a ceiling of six thousand total warheads on sixteen hundred launchers with a sub-limit of forty-nine hundred warheads on ballistic missiles. At the end of the Washington summit, Soviet and U.S. spokespersons indicated that the two sides were very close to concluding a START agreement and that only a few outstanding issues remained.

The most important of these outstanding issues was strategic defense. In October 1985, then National Security Affairs Adviser Robert McFarlane announced that a new "broad interpretation" of the Anti-Ballistic Missile Treaty would allow for testing of ballistic missile defense systems based on "new physical principles." Soviet officials, as well as a number of former U.S. arms control negotiators and members of Congress, insisted that the ABM Treaty specifically prohibited such testing. The Soviets insisted at the START talks that the ABM Treaty be "narrowly interpreted," thereby banning testing of new ballistic missile defense technologies, and demanded that the treaty as originally negotiated remain in effect for at least ten years. SDI remained a stumbling block to concluding a strategic arms control agreement just as it had been at Reykjavík.

At their 1988 summit meeting in Moscow, Gorbachev and Reagan were not able to narrow the U.S. and Soviet differences on the START Treaty that remained. Although negotiations continued after the summit meeting, no further progress was made during Reagan's term of office.

By the time George Bush entered office in January 1989, the START negotiations had been under way for six and a half years, about the same amount of time that had been required to conclude the SALT II Treaty. The broad outline of the framework for a START Treaty remained the same as it had been under the Reagan administration, but there were several issues, in addition to SDI, that remained contentious. Although Ambassador Nitze and Marshal Akhromeyev had tentatively agreed at Reykjavík to negotiate separate limits on sea-launched cruise missiles, little progress was made in working out the details of these limits. The United States wanted to leave this type of missile unrestricted, while the Soviet Union wanted specific limits on nuclear and conventional versions of sea-launched cruise missiles. In addition, the two sides had not worked out the final provisions for the verification of the START Treaty. Although significant new provisions for verification, including on-site inspection, surprise inspections, and a ban on coded telemetry, were part of the INF Treaty, the two sides had difficulty working out the final verification procedures for the START agreement.

A final problem with the START agreement stemmed from the implementation of another arms control treaty, the Conventional Forces in Europe (CFE) Treaty, which was signed in November 1990 by the United States, the Soviet Union, and twenty other NATO and Warsaw Pact members. After the USSR signed the treaty, the Soviet military insisted on excluding three naval infantry divisions and their weapons from the treaty's limits, on the grounds that these forces were not covered by a treaty that limited ground forces. In addition, there was evidence that the Soviets were moving some forces out of the area covered by the treaty. As long as significant issues concerning the CFE Treaty remained unresolved, there was little chance that the Bush administration would conclude a START Treaty and submit it to the Senate for ratification.

Throughout the first seven months of 1991, Secretary of State James Baker and the U.S. START delegation continued to meet with Soviet officials to discuss the unresolved problems associated with the CFE and START treaties. On 31 July 1991, using pens made out of metal melted down from SS-20 and Pershing II missiles destroyed as a result of the INF Treaty, President George Bush and Soviet President Mikhail Gorbachev signed the START Treaty. The treaty, the result of nine years of negotiations under two U.S. presidents and four Soviet leaders, was complex and lengthy; it filled 750 pages of text.

The terms of the treaty allowed for the deployment of 1,600 strategic delivery vehicles (ballistic missiles and long-range bombers) on each side and 6,000 "accountable" warheads on these systems. The counting rules of the treaty discounted some types of weapons so that each country could deploy more than the accountable limit of 6,000. For example, an American B-52 bomber carrying twenty cruise missiles was counted as carrying only ten warheads. The intent of these counting rules was to favor the deployment of non-ballistic components of each side's arsenal. Of the 6,000 accountable warheads allowed, no more than 4,900 may be deployed on ballistic missiles, and within this sublimit, no more than 1,100 warheads may be deployed on mobile ICBMS. The Soviet Union was allowed to deploy no more than 1,540 warheads on its heavy missile, the SS-18.

The START Treaty was the first arms control agreement that required both the United States and the Soviet Union to make significant cuts in their respective strategic arsenals. The treaty called for the elimination of almost 50 percent of the nuclear warheads carried by ballistic missiles. In addition, the number of Soviet heavy missiles—the component of the Soviet force that many Americans claimed had led to a window of vulnerability—was reduced from 308 to 154, halving the number of warheads on these missiles from 3,080 to 1,540. All but a few arch-conservatives agreed that the START Treaty was a significant step in the direction of greater stability.

Less than a month after the START Treaty was signed, a group of hardline Soviet government officials attempted to overthrow Mikhail Gorbachev.

The attempted coup was defeated, but a number of issues remained troublesome in the aftermath of the coup and dominated the attention of Soviet government officials: ethnic tensions in the republics of the Soviet Union that had smoldered many years ignited during the autumn of 1991; in addition, the enormous economic problems of the USSR that previous Soviet leaders had ignored became increasingly evident and painful. These factors led to the resignation of Mikhail Gorbachev and the dissolution of the Soviet government in December 1991.

CONCLUSION

The United States and the Soviet Union developed and deployed nuclear weapons in the 1940s and engaged in serious efforts to limit these weapons since the 1960s. As a result of these efforts, they signed four agreements limiting strategic nuclear forces: the two SALT I agreements of 1972 (the Anti-Ballistic Missile Treaty and the Interim Agreement on offensive forces), the SALT II Treaty of 1979, and the START Treaty of 1991. Of course, no one knows what would have happened had these agreements not been reached; however, it seems clear in retrospect that these agreements helped to stabilize the arms competition between the United States and the Soviet Union. In addition, the fear of the destruction that could have been wrought by the use of these weapons may have contributed to the forty-six year era of peace between the two superpowers.

With the end of the Soviet Union came the end of the era of United States–Soviet strategic nuclear arms control, an era that had lasted almost three decades—from the signing of the Limited Test Ban Treaty in 1963 until the disintegration of the USSR in 1991. But four of the ex-republics of the former Soviet Union—Russia, Ukraine, Byelorussia and Kazakhstan—continued to possess nuclear weapons. It may be that the future of strategic nuclear arms control will be less formal than the past. Prior to his resignation, Gorbachev exchanged with President Bush proposals for deep cuts in the arsenals of the Soviet Union and the United States. In 1992, during Russian president Boris Yeltsin's visit to Washington, he and Bush finalized these proposals. They were able to agree relatively quickly on cuts in the number of nuclear weapons possessed by both sides because, arms control analysts pointed out, both abandoned parity as the commanding tenet of arms control negotiations. It may be that such proposals will be indicative of future arms control efforts, rather than the laborious, time-consuming efforts of the 1969–1991 era.

BIBLIOGRAPHY

United States–Soviet Relations and Arms Control   Several general works address the development of strategic nuclear arms control and United States–Soviet relations throughout the 1967–1991 period. These include COIT D. BLACKER and GLORIA DUFFY, eds., *International Arms Control: Issues and Agreements,* 2d. ed. (Stanford, Calif., 1984), which is an excellent introduction to arms control and contains the texts of major agreements. ALBERT CARNESALE and RICHARD N. HAASS, eds., *Superpower Arms Control: Setting the Record Straight* (Cambridge, Mass., 1987), contains case studies of major agreements and attempts to draw a number of lessons about arms control. RAYMOND L. GARTHOFF, *Detente and Confrontation: American-Soviet Relations from Nixon to Reagan* (Washington, D.C., 1985), is a comprehensive account of the development of U.S.-Soviet relations by a former American diplomat who was once a member of the United States SALT delegation. DAVID HOLLOWAY, *The Soviet Union and the Arms Race* (New Haven, Conn., 1983), focuses on the development of nuclear weapons by the USSR. JOHN NEWHOUSE, *War and Peace in the Nuclear Age* (New York, 1989), traces the development of nuclear weapons and attempts to control them. This book is the companion volume to a television series of the same title and contains much original and interesting research.

SALT   The SALT I negotiations and agreements are the focus of a number of books. ALTON FRYE focuses on the role of Congress in arms control policy-making in *A Responsible Congress: The Politics of National Security* (New York, 1975). MORTON KAPLAN edited a collection of articles focusing on SALT I, *SALT: Problems and Prospects* (Morristown, N.J., 1973). JOHN NEWHOUSE, *Cold Dawn: The Story of SALT* (New York, 1973), is an interesting account focusing primarily on the Kissinger-Dobrynin back-channel negotiations and underrating the role of the formal negotiations. MASON WILLRICH and JOHN B. RHINELANDER edited *SALT: The Moscow Agreements*

and Beyond (New York, 1974), which contains an excellent collection of articles. Memoirs by the participants in the SALT I negotiations include: HENRY KISSINGER, *White House Years* (Boston, 1979), RICHARD NIXON, *RN: The Memoirs of Richard Nixon* (New York, 1978), and *Doubletalk: The Story of the First Strategic Arms Limitation Talks* (New York, 1980) by GERARD C. SMITH, the chief of the U.S. delegation at the SALT I negotiations.

SALT II is the principal focus of DAN CALDWELL, *The Dynamics of Domestic Politics and Arms Control: The SALT II Treaty Ratification Debate* (Columbia, S.C., 1991). WOLFGANG PANOFSKY, *Arms Control and SALT II* (Seattle, Wash., 1979) is a short but very informative analysis of the issues. STROBE TALBOTT, *Endgame: The Inside Story of SALT II* (New York, 1979), is a highly readable account of the negotiations leading to the SALT II Treaty. In *The SALT Experience,* THOMAS W. WOLFE pays particular attention to the military issues and to the Soviet and U.S. governmental organizations involved in SALT I . Memoirs that focus on SALT II include: HAROLD BROWN, *Thinking About National Security: Defense and Foreign Policy in A Dangerous World* (Boulder, Colo., 1983), ZBIGNIEW K. BRZEZINSKI, *Power and Principle: Memoirs of the National Security Adviser 1977–1981* (New York, 1983), JIMMY CARTER, *Keeping Faith: Memoirs of a President* (New York, 1982), GERALD R. FORD, *A Time to Heal: The Autobiography of Gerald R. Ford* (New York, 1979), HENRY KISSINGER, *Years of Upheaval* (Boston, 1982), and CYRUS VANCE, *Hard Choices: Critical Years in America's Foreign Policy* (New York, 1983).

START   An important factor in the START negotiations concerned the Strategic Defense Initiative (SDI). SIDNEY D. DRELL, PHILLIP J. FARLEY, and DAVID HOLLOWAY focus on SDI in *The Reagan Strategic Defense Initiative: A Technical, Political, and Arms Control Assessment* (Cambridge, Mass., 1985). MICHAEL KREPON and ALTON FRYE focus on the negotiation of START in "Arms Control," in JOSEPH KRUZEL, ed., *American Defense Annual 1985–1986* (Lexington, Mass., 1985). ROBERT SCHEER interviewed a number of members of the Reagan administration and his interviews are contained in *With Enough Shovels: Reagan, Bush and Nuclear War* (New York, 1982). STROBE TALBOTT has written two books that directly concern arms-control-making in the Reagan administration: *Deadly Gambits: The Reagan Administration and the Stalemate in Nuclear Arms*

Control (New York, 1984) and Master of the Game: Paul Nitze and the Nuclear Peace (New York, 1988). Memoirs that concern START include: MIKHAIL GORBACHEV, Perestroika: New Thinking for Our Country and the World (New York, 1987), ALEXANDER HAIG, Caveat: Realism, Reagan, and Foreign Policy (New York, 1984), PAUL H. NITZE, "Arms Control," in JOSEPH KRUZEL, ed., American Defense Annual 1986–1987 (Lexington, Mass., 1986), PAUL H. NITZE with ANN M. SMITH and STEVEN L. REARDEN, From Hiroshima to Glasnost: At the Center of Decision: A Memoir (New York, 1989), and RONALD REAGAN, An American Life (New York, 1990).

The Anti-Ballistic Missile Treaty

1972 to the Present

O

MATTHEW BUNN

See also Arms Control and Anti-Satellite Weapons; From SALT to START: Limiting Strategic Nuclear Weapons; *and* The Strategic Defense Initiative and Arms Control. *The* ABM Treaty *is excerpted in Volume III.*

The Anti-Ballistic Missile (ABM) Treaty of 1972 prohibits the United States and the Soviet Union—now replaced by Russia as the United States' principal treaty partner—from deploying nationwide defenses against strategic ballistic missiles. While neither superpower ever entirely abandoned the search for defenses against the nuclear threat, the ABM Treaty was based on a recognition by both superpowers that no foreseeable technology could provide an effective defense against the fearsome destructive power of nuclear weapons, and that building a missile defense would only force the other side to augment its offensive forces to overcome it, in order to maintain its nuclear deterrent. The resulting race between missiles and missile defenses would be expensive and potentially dangerous, would make negotiated restraints on offensive strategic forces impossible, and would undermine the predictability necessary for strategic planning.

Despite some compliance controversies—and one clear violation on the Soviet side, which will be discussed below—the ABM Treaty has been highly successful. Neither side has deployed a nationwide missile defense. While offensive forces have increased substantially since the treaty was signed, the ABM Treaty has "forestalled an explosion of offensive development on both sides," in the words of former Secretary of Defense James Schlesinger, speaking in 1985 (quoted in Bunn, p. 17). Schlesinger referred to the treaty as "the cornerstone of restraint." Today, the treaty is regarded by many as

the foundation for both the Strategic Arms Reduction Talks (START) and the accord on deeper strategic arms reductions announced by President George Bush and the Russian president, Boris Yeltsin, at their June 1992 summit. Former Secretary of Defense Harold Brown described the ABM Treaty as "the most substantive and important arms control agreement ever reached by the two superpowers" ("The SALT Negotiations: 1969–1972," in Henry Owen and John Thomas Smith II, eds., *Gerard C. Smith: A Career in Progress* [Lanham, Md., 1989], p. 67).

Since the mid-1980s, however, the ABM Treaty has been the focus of intense controversies within the United States and between the two signatories, as it places strict limits on the Strategic Defense Initiative (SDI)—better known as "Star Wars"—launched by President Reagan in 1983. The treaty's future remains a critical unresolved issue in American security policy.

THE TREATY'S HISTORY

From the dawn of the nuclear age, both the United States and the Soviet Union searched without success for an effective defense against nuclear attack. Through the 1940s and much of the 1950s, bombers posed the primary strategic nuclear threat. Both superpowers responded with large-scale air-

915

defense systems, including thousands of radar-guided missiles and hundreds of fighter aircraft.

By the late 1950s and early 1960s, however, the advent of long-range Soviet ballistic missiles forced a reevaluation of the United States air defense program. The system could not intercept intercontinental ballistic missiles (ICBMS) and was extremely vulnerable to direct ICBM attack, making it ineffective even as an anti-bomber defense. Consequently, U.S. strategic defense spending gradually shifted away from air defenses to the new problem of anti-ballistic missiles (ABMS). The former Soviet Union, however, facing a large United States bomber force as well as air threats from Europe and China, continued to maintain and upgrade its massive air-defense system.

Some preliminary research on the ABM problem had been under way since the immediate aftermath of World War II, in projects such as Thumper and Wizard. But the first large-scale program began in 1958, when the army got the go-ahead to develop the Nike-Zeus ABM missile, a long-range, nuclear-tipped interceptor.

Over the next several years, as work on Nike-Zeus advanced, the army regularly proposed rapid deployment of the system, but was rebuffed by a coalition of critics in the White House, the office of the secretary of defense, and the air force. These opponents pointed out that the system's mechanically steered radars would be overwhelmed by a large attack and were themselves vulnerable to blinding or destruction, and that the system could be overcome by potential Soviet countermeasures such as warhead-mimicking decoys and radar-reflecting chaff. Moreover, the cost of a widespread Nike-Zeus system would be extremely high, and such a deployment might provoke the Soviet Union to increase its offensive forces to overcome it. And since any missile defense would be more effective against a reduced, disorganized retaliation than against a massive, well-planned first strike, substantial missile defenses on both sides could increase the incentive to strike first in a crisis, undermining stability and increasing the risk of nuclear war. This basic troika of arguments—technical weaknesses, cost, and strategic implications—has remained the backbone of the anti-ABM case through all subsequent debates, reflecting the enduring obstacles to mounting an effective defense against a sophisticated adversary armed with the devastating destructive power of modern thermonuclear weapons.

In July 1962, Nike-Zeus scored the first in a series of test successes, intercepting an ICBM for the first time. But it was clear that Nike-Zeus was simply too primitive to handle the likely future Soviet missile threat. In 1963, the Zeus program was replaced by Nike-X, which incorporated an electronically steered "phased-array" radar, capable of simultaneously tracking many targets, and a short-range interceptor called Sprint, designed to intercept Soviet missiles inside the atmosphere. In addition, the long-range Zeus interceptor was eventually upgraded, to become the Spartan. Consideration of deployment was deferred while the more advanced system was developed.

Despite these technical advances, critics continued to raise both technical and strategic doubts. Indeed, the outlines of the missile–anti-missile race predicted by ABM opponents were already beginning to emerge. In the early 1960s, intelligence on Soviet ABM activities led to increased United States spending on decoys and other anti-defense "penetration aids," and was a significant factor in the U.S. decision to develop and ultimately deploy multiple independently targetable reentry vehicles (MIRVS) allowing each missile to deliver several warheads to separate targets. Ultimately, U.S. MIRVS drastically increased the nuclear threat to the Soviet Union, more than compensating for whatever protection its limited ABM defense could offer. The first Soviet ABM deployment around Moscow also created powerful domestic pressure for deployment of a U.S. ABM system. In this environment, then Secretary of Defense Robert McNamara and others concluded that the only way to avoid a long-term arms race in both offensive and defensive strategic arms was to negotiate an arms agreement, placing particularly strict limits on ABMS.

By the mid-1960s, the possibility of such agreed restraints on strategic arms was gaining increasing currency. Relations between the United States and the Soviet Union had warmed somewhat following the Cuban missile crisis, leading to the successful negotiation of the Limited Test Ban Treaty. The United States had deployed large offensive nuclear forces, and the Soviet Union was rapidly catching up, creating a deterrent balance in which neither side could launch a nuclear attack on the other without facing certain and devastating retaliation. Arms control proponents argued that maintaining that balance through negotiated limits on the arms competition was more likely to lead to lasting security than an unlimited race in ABMS and strategic offensive forces. At the same time, the advent of satellite reconnaissance increased confidence in the possibility of adequate verification.

The Soviet leadership first opposed limits on missile defenses. But it soon became apparent that the Soviets were involved in a debate of their own, over both ABMS and the advisability of entering negotiations on strategic arms. Eventually, Soviet leaders came to see arms control as an important means of certifying and protecting their attainment of strategic nuclear parity with the United States. And like their U.S. counterparts, Soviet officials apparently calculated that agreed limitations would better serve Soviet security in the long term than an unlimited offense-defense competition—a realization probably spurred by the clear superiority of United States ABM and MIRV technology.

But this resolution of the Soviet debate did not come until well after the United States began to press for arms talks. In December 1966, in response to continuing pressure for United States deployment of an ABM system, President Lyndon Johnson decided to include several hundred million dollars for construction of an ABM system in the following year's budget, but to withhold the funds pending an attempt to negotiate an ABM agreement with the Soviet Union. Unfortunately, at the June 1967 summit meeting in Glassboro, New Jersey, Soviet Premier Alexei Kosygin resisted Johnson and McNamara's arguments for strict ABM limitations, and no agreement to initiate strategic arms negotiations was reached. President Johnson then decided to proceed with construction of a "thin" nationwide ABM system based on Nike-X technology, dubbed Sentinel.

McNamara announced the Sentinel decision in a remarkable speech on 18 September 1967. Most of the speech was devoted to the case against deployment of a "thick" ABM system, arguing that no ABM could protect United States urban society from the devastating power of Soviet nuclear weapons, and that such a system would inevitably accelerate the arms race and destabilize the nuclear balance. Only at the end of the speech did McNamara reveal the decision to deploy a "thin" ABM system, ostensibly to defend against the developing Chinese missile threat.

The Sentinel decision, coming in the midst of increasing antimilitary sentiment provoked by the Vietnam War, launched a wave of criticism from sci-

entists and congressmen, which soon escalated into public protests. But for the moment, initial steps toward deployment went forward largely unimpeded.

On 1 July 1968, the day the Non-Proliferation Treaty was signed, President Johnson was finally able to announce that the Soviet Union had agreed to Strategic Arms Limitation Talks (SALT). But the Soviet occupation of Czechoslovakia in August, on the eve of the scheduled announcement of a summit meeting and a date for the talks, forced Johnson to postpone the negotiations, leaving the ABM issue for President Richard Nixon's administration to grapple with. The same month, United States MIRV testing began.

From the outset of his presidency, Richard Nixon abandoned his campaign call for "clear-cut military superiority" over the Soviet Union, accepting the more modest goal of "sufficiency" and thereby laying the foundation for SALT. In March 1969, after a review of the U.S. strategic posture, Nixon announced his conclusion that an ABM population defense could not be achieved, and his decision to reorient the Sentinel program to defend missile silos, under the name Safeguard. But the change of name and mission only intensified the ABM debate—particularly as the Sentinel technology was not well suited to its new role. In August 1969, the administration won Senate approval for the first phase of Safeguard by only a single vote—in part by arguing that the system was needed as a SALT bargaining chip. In October, President Nixon announced that he had agreed with the Soviet leaders to begin talks on strategic arms.

The SALT negotiations finally began on 17 November 1969, in Helsinki, Finland. Ambassador Gerard C. Smith, director of the Arms Control and Disarmament Agency, headed the United States delegation, while Ambassador Vladimir Semonov led the Soviet team. In the first rounds of talks, both sides proposed strict limits on ABM systems, but major differences over offensive limitations soon emerged. These disagreements reflected large differences in the makeup of the two sides' strategic forces, particularly the heavy Soviet reliance on large land-based ICBMS, and the Soviet desire to weigh in the balance both the strategic forces held by American allies and United States forward-based weapons on aircraft carriers and foreign bases.

With the disagreements over offensive limitations delaying progress, the Soviet Union soon switched course and proposed that the sides agree on an ABM treaty while leaving offensive forces to a subsequent negotiation. But the United States insisted on a dual agreement, hoping to use its ongoing ABM deployment program to gain Soviet concessions on offensive arms. In May 1971, Henry Kissinger, Nixon's national security adviser, and Anatoly Dobrynin, then Soviet ambassador to the United States, reached agreement in a "backchannel" negotiation that a comprehensive ABM accord would be accompanied by a more limited agreement on offensive arms, leaving more complete offensive limitations to SALT II.

A year later, on 26 May 1972, President Nixon and Soviet leader Leonid Brezhnev signed the SALT I agreements, including both the ABM Treaty and the Interim Agreement on offensive arms. The ABM Treaty banned nationwide ABM systems, while the Interim Agreement froze for five years each side's missile launchers at the level then operational or under construction. SALT I, however, did not place any limits on MIRVS, allowing a major buildup in missile warheads on both sides, or on bomber forces.

The U.S. Senate gave its advice and consent to ratification of the ABM Treaty on August 3 by a vote of 88 to 2, and both houses of Congress gave similarly overwhelming approval to the Interim Agreement, reflecting the domestic consensus in support of both accords. The agreements entered into force on 3 October 1972. Two years later, President Nixon and General Secretary Brezhnev signed a Protocol to the ABM Treaty, reducing the number of permitted ABM sites from two to one.

THE TREATY'S TERMS

The ABM Treaty's fundamental provision is its ban on nationwide missile defenses. But the basic prohibition is bolstered by a variety of restraints designed to ensure that several years of observable illegal activity would be required before either side could have such a nationwide defense in operation, preventing either side from gaining the ability to "break out" of the accord more rapidly than the other could respond. The terms of the treaty form an interlocking structure: each of the substantive articles of the accord is key to the whole, for each is carefully designed to block a potential avenue for evasion or circumvention. As a result, the ABM Treaty has enabled both sides to confidently plan their strategic missile forces in the knowledge that the other side cannot rapidly construct nationwide defenses against them.

The ABM Treaty begins with a preamble, outlining the sides' agreement that limits on ABMS would reduce pressures to build up offensive arms, contribute to chances for offensive arms control, and help reduce the risk of nuclear war.

Article I then sets out the fundamental prohibition, with each side agreeing "not to deploy ABM systems for a defense of the territory of its country and not to provide a base for such a defense."

Article II defines the ABM systems and components limited by the treaty. The term "ABM system" is defined functionally, to include any "system to counter strategic ballistic missiles or their elements in flight trajectory." The components of such a system are listed as "currently consisting of" ABM interceptor missiles, ABM launchers, and ABM radars—the most visible elements of the ABM systems of 1972. This listing, and the use of the word "currently," became controversial when the Reagan administration reinterpreted the ABM Treaty in 1985, as described in more detail below.

Article III then sets out the very limited deployments of ABM systems permitted by the accord, permitting only two ABM sites—one to defend the national capital, as the Soviet Union was then doing, and one to defend an ICBM field, the approach the United States was pursuing—each armed with no more than one hundred fixed ABM launchers. Specific restraints are also placed on the radars at each site. As mentioned above, a 1974 protocol reduced the number of permitted sites to one, which can be of either type.

With the permitted ABM defenses limited to a single site armed with only one hundred ABM launchers, the firepower and scope of the permitted defense are far too small to pose any threat to either side's offensive deterrent forces, each of which consists of thousands of ballistic missile warheads. If, on the other hand, the treaty were amended to allow a significantly larger number of deployment sites—as some have recommended in order to facilitate construction of a defense against limited strikes, such as a third world country might eventually be capable of—the much larger permitted ABM infrastructure, including more widespread ABM radars, would give either side the ability to expand its defenses much more rapidly, eroding the treaty's buffer against rapid "breakout" from the accord.

Article III bans all ABM deployments not explicitly allowed, implicitly prohibiting any deployment of

ABM systems and components other than interceptors, launchers, and radars—such as lasers or particle beams used to perform the same functions. Agreed Statement D makes this ban explicit. While the language is somewhat tortuous, both sides agreed that under this provision, future ABM components "based on other physical principles" and "capable of substituting for" ABM interceptors, launchers, and radars, could only be deployed if both parties agreed to amend the treaty to provide specific limitations on them, analogous to the treaty's limits on traditional-technology ABM components. Otherwise, the possibly superior capabilities of such new-technology systems might have undermined the specific restraints on ABM firepower contained in Article III.

Article V further limits the capabilities of the permitted ABM systems. The first paragraph of Article V prohibits development, testing, and deployment of all mobile ABM systems and components, including those that are "sea-based, air-based, space-based, or mobile land-based." This broad ban on mobile ABMs prohibiting their development beyond research, is critical to the treaty's effectiveness, for ABM systems based on mobile components would be inherently expandable beyond the single permitted site, creating a danger of rapid breakout toward a nationwide defense. Space-based ABMs, in particular, would inherently provide nationwide or even global coverage. Requiring little site preparation, mobile ABMs might be rapidly deployed once produced, further undermining the treaty's protections. Mobile ABM components would also make numerical limits on deployment more difficult to verify.

The second paragraph of Article V bans the development, testing, and deployment of multiple-launch or rapidly reloadable ABM launchers, which might otherwise have undercut the limit on defensive firepower imposed by the one-hundred-launcher ceiling. Agreed Statement E broadens that limitation to include a similar ban on multiple-warhead interceptors, which could have had a similar effect.

Article V's limits begin at the development stage. No prohibitions were placed on research, which would have been very difficult to verify. During the ABM Treaty negotiations, it was recognized that the line between permitted "research" and prohibited "development" is difficult to define. Soviet negotiators implicitly accepted the United States interpretation of "development" as a stage following

research, when prototypes or breadboard models of ABM components left the laboratory and were ready for field testing, but no formal agreed interpretation was sought. Subsequent experiments conducted in the SDI program pressed the somewhat ambiguous line between permitted research and prohibited development and testing.

Article VI addresses the possibility that non-ABM systems such as air defenses or anti-satellite (ASAT) weapons might be upgraded to serve as strategic missile defenses, thereby circumventing the accord. Article VI prohibits giving any such non-ABM components "capabilities to counter strategic ballistic missiles," or testing them "in an ABM mode." The phrase "testing in an ABM mode" was clarified in agreed interpretations negotiated in the Standing Consultative Commission (SCC) in 1978 and 1985. The treaty permits defenses against short-range tactical ballistic missiles, such as the Patriot system used to intercept Iraqi Scud missiles in the 1991 Gulf War, but under Article VI, such systems cannot be given the capability to defend against longer-range strategic missiles, or tested in an ABM mode. The line between permitted tactical defense capabilities and prohibited strategic defenses is a somewhat fuzzy one, however, creating an ambiguity that has already led to some compliance controversies, and may become a central issue as both sides pursue more capable tactical missile defenses.

The second paragraph of Article VI addresses the dual-capable technologies issue as it applies to large radars. The treaty's restraints on radars are particularly important, since large radars are the guiding eyes of traditional-technology ABM systems, and take years to build. The beginning of construction of large numbers of radars in violation of the ABM Treaty would provide ample warning of an effort to construct a nationwide missile defense. A ban on all radars that might have an ABM potential was not possible, however, since radars capable of detecting and tracking ballistic missiles are necessary for other essential purposes, such as early warning and treaty verification. (In later SDI concepts, large radars were superseded in part by difficult-to-monitor infrared sensors, creating new dilemmas—particularly as these new technologies would also have important early-warning and verification potential.)

To address these conflicting concerns, Article VI permits early warning radars, but limits future deployments of such radars to the periphery of the country and oriented outward. Located that way, an early-warning radar's coverage is almost entirely outside the country's territory, hobbling its ability to serve as a battle-manager for a missile defense. Moreover, early warning radars on the periphery of a country's territory would be especially vulnerable to attack, making it less likely that either side would rely on them as the basis for a widespread missile defense. Agreed Statement F broadens these radar restraints by prohibiting the deployment of *any* new large "phased-array" radars—a type that can be rapidly electronically steered to track large numbers of targets simultaneously, offering greater ABM potential than any other type—except as ABM radars at agreed ABM sites or test ranges, early warning radars limited by Article VI, or for space tracking and treaty verification. Phased-array radars for all other purposes are limited to a size too small to offer any significant ability to search the sky for fast-moving strategic ballistic missiles.

As described in more detail below, the Soviet Union has violated these provisions with its early-warning radar near Krasnoyarsk, but that radar is now being dismantled. Two U.S. phased-array radars, one at Thule, Greenland, and the other at Fylingdales Moor, United Kingdom, also raise serious questions of compliance with these provisions, though the issues there are more ambiguous than in the case of Krasnoyarsk—and Soviet and Russian complaints over these radars have grown muted. A number of former Soviet early-warning radars are outside Russian territory and are still being operated by the Commonwealth of Independent States, but this would not appear to violate the ABM Treaty's ban on deploying "future" early-warning radars outside each party's national territory.

Other articles address other potential avenues for circumventing the treaty's restraints. In Article IV, permitted testing of fixed, land-based ABMs is limited to agreed test ranges and a total of no more than fifteen test launchers, preventing test ranges from being used as a guise for a widespread ABM deployment. Article IX prohibits either side from deploying ABM systems and components outside its national territory, or transferring them to other states not limited by the accord. Agreed Statement G extends the "no-transfer" provision to include transfers of "technical descriptions or blue-prints specially worked out for the construction of ABM systems and their components."

Verification of the ABM Treaty depends on "national technical means" (NTM), a euphemism for photoreconnaissance satellites and other technical

intelligence systems used to collect information on treaty-limited activities. Verification is greatly facilitated by Article XII, which bars deliberate concealment of ABM activities and interference with the other party's NTM.

Article XIII established the United States–Soviet Standing Consultative Commission, to discuss measures to implement the accord, additional agreements to improve its effectiveness, and questions of compliance with the agreement. The SCC has effectively resolved many ambiguities and compliance disputes, providing an essential mechanism for reinforcing arms control agreements.

Under the terms of Article XV, the ABM Treaty is "of unlimited duration," signalling that the accord was intended to last as far into the future as either side could then predict. Either side may, however, withdraw from the treaty after giving six months' notice, if "extraordinary events related to the subject matter of this treaty have jeopardized its supreme interests." Notice must include a statement of the reasons for withdrawal. Although not specifically included in the treaty's terms, the accepted principles of international law also permit either party to withdraw or to take appropriate and proportionate responses if the other party commits a "material breach" of the accord.

Together, the provisions of the ABM Treaty have successfully prevented either side from deploying any large-scale defenses against strategic ballistic missiles. However, there are ambiguities in the ABM Treaty's provisions that are becoming more critical as ABM-related programs in both the United States and the former Soviet Union begin to come close to the boundaries. Just as the U.S. Constitution's guarantee of freedom of speech must constantly be interpreted in the age of electronic media, any agreement covering as broad and complex a technological area as ballistic missile defense will need refinement as specific technical issues arise. The ABM Treaty explicitly envisioned periodic reviews and clarification, and gave the Standing Consultative Commission (SCC) that task. There is little doubt that with superpower cooperation, the ABM Treaty could be adapted and strengthened to meet the challenges of the twenty-first century.

FROM SALT TO STAR WARS

After the ABM Treaty entered into force, both the United States and the Soviet Union continued research and development of ABM systems. The single U.S. Safeguard ABM site was completed in 1975, but was soon deactivated, as the extremely limited protection it offered was judged not to be worth the cost of continued operation and maintenance. U.S. ABM research and development continued, focused primarily on close-in defenses for hardened concrete missile silos, rather than wide-area defenses. The former Soviet Union maintained and modernized its ABM system at the permitted Moscow ABM site, and continued an active ABM development program.

During the 1970s, the Standing Consultative Commission (SCC) successfully managed the few ABM compliance and implementation issues that arose, and in 1977 conducted the first treaty-mandated ABM Treaty Review Conference, reaffirming the accord's importance. At the same time, follow-on strategic arms talks continued, and the SALT II Treaty was finally signed in 1979.

But anti-Soviet sentiment in the United States was on the rise, fueled by Soviet behavior in regional conflicts and by the rapid increase in Soviet missile capabilities as the Soviet Union followed the U.S. lead in deploying MIRVs. When the Soviet Union occupied Afghanistan in December 1979, President Jimmy Carter's administration had no choice but to ask the Senate to defer consideration of SALT II. In the same period, the potential threat to American silo-based missiles led to renewed consideration of ABMS as a possible response; but systems for this purpose never proceeded into full-scale development or deployment.

The downward trend in United States–Soviet relations contributed to the election of President Ronald Reagan and reached its nadir in the early years of his term, with the Soviet shoot-down of a civilian airliner and Reagan's description of the Soviet Union as an "evil empire." Reagan brought to the presidency a belief in the urgent need to build up U.S. military forces and a deep skepticism about arms control. Reagan had also long yearned for a defense against nuclear attack, and his advisers made no secret of their disdain for the ABM Treaty. Richard Perle, then the top arms control official in the Department of Defense, told Congress in 1982 that the treaty "was a mistake in 1972, and the sooner we face up to . . . that mistake the better" (quoted in Bunn, p. 15).

But while funding for strategic forces was significantly increased in the first years of Reagan's presidency, missile defenses remained in the background. A 1981 Defense Science Board study of the space laser concept advocated by a few senators was unenthusiastic, and air force studies flatly rejected the 1982 "High Frontier" proposal put forward by retired General Daniel Graham, a former Reagan military adviser. In 1982, the second five-year ABM Treaty Review Conference again reaffirmed the accord, albeit with far less enthusiasm than had the 1977 review.

On 23 March 1983, however, President Reagan launched the Strategic Defense Initiative (SDI), or "Star Wars," with a speech calling for an all-encompassing shield that would render nuclear weapons "impotent and obsolete."

SDI soon became the focus of intense controversy, both domestically and internationally. Some SDI advocates, particularly President Reagan, envisioned a perfect or nearly-perfect defense that would "protect us from nuclear missiles just as a roof protects a family from rain," as Reagan once put it (quoted in Bunn, p. 4). Others, recognizing that such perfection would be impossible to achieve, argued that a mix of missile defenses and offenses would provide a more stable strategic balance, and might protect against some more limited types of missile attacks. Some saw the program as a lever to force the Soviet Union to agree to reductions in its offensive forces; others saw it as a response to the substantial Soviet ABM development program. SDI critics raised many of the basic arguments of the ABM debates of the 1960s, zeroing in on the technical weaknesses, cost, and troubling strategic and arms control implications of the program. The Soviet Union angrily criticized the program as an aggressive American effort to recapture military superiority and gain the ability to attack the Soviet Union without fear of retaliation. NATO countries expressed concern over the costs and risks of an ABM race. Domestic critics, Soviet negotiators, and NATO allies all emphasized the importance of maintaining the ABM Treaty.

This controversy has remained a key focus of the debate over strategic weapons and arms control ever since. The political context has changed dramatically over the years, however. SDI was launched at a time of considerable superpower tension, and substantial domestic disagreement over defense within the United States and its NATO allies: hawkish arms control critics warned of Soviet military superiority, while demonstrations in the streets called for a nuclear freeze and opposed the deployment of intermediate-range nuclear missiles in Europe.

With Soviet leader Mikhail Gorbachev's ascension to power in 1985, superpower relations began a fundamental revolution, reaching a climax in 1989–1991 with the triumph of democratic forces in most of Eastern Europe, the unification of Germany, and the dissolution of the Soviet Union. President Bush continued to support the SDI program, though with scaled-back goals and less high-level emphasis than President Reagan gave it. In the aftermath of Iraqi short-range ballistic missile attacks in the 1991 Gulf War, Congress became more supportive of missile defenses, boosting SDI's budget and endorsing a goal of limited deployments. Russian president Boris Yeltsin, while reaffirming the importance of the ABM Treaty, has also spoken of an as-yet-undefined concept of joint missile defenses. And with the end of the Cold War, many see crises in the developing world rather than potential conflict between the United States and Russia as the key military threat the United States is likely to face—a change symbolized by the 1991 war in the Persian Gulf.

The complex ABM debate of the 1980s can be divided into three main areas: charges of widespread Soviet violations of the ABM Treaty, the Reagan administration's reinterpretation of the pact, and the link between proposals for SDI testing and deployment and the efforts to negotiate a START treaty cutting offensive nuclear arms.

A Pattern of ABM Cheating?

In the summer of 1983, the United States announced that it had detected a large radar under construction near the Soviet city of Krasnoyarsk. The Reagan administration soon charged that this radar violated the ABM Treaty, and that a variety of other Soviet activities constituted "probable" or "potential" violations. The Soviet Union struck back with a list of charges of its own, and argued repeatedly that the entire SDI program was fundamentally contrary to the purpose of the ABM Treaty.

The Reagan administration gave these charges a high public profile. Reagan administration officials and arms control critics pointed to the Krasnoyarsk radar as the prime example of what they saw as a long-standing pattern of Soviet cheating, and questioned whether the Soviet Union would abide by any arms agreement it signed. Independent studies conducted by supporters of the ABM accord, however, concluded that charges of a "pattern" of Soviet violations were unfounded—and that most of the Soviet charges against the United States had even

less merit. While the Soviet Union had pressed into several ambiguous areas, with the exception of Krasnoyarsk, the Reagan administration's charges of ABM violations rested on contentious interpretations of the available data and the treaty language. Similarly, while the Bush administration raised one new charge—that the communications link between the former Soviet Union's early-warning radars and its permitted Moscow ABM system violated the ABM Treaty—Paul Nitze, the chief negotiator of the relevant treaty provisions, dismissed this charge as "outrageously false and reckless."

The Krasnoyarsk radar, however, was an unambiguous violation of the treaty. Although never completed, it was clearly an early-warning radar, identical in design to other Soviet early-warning radars at permitted sites, and located to fill a major gap in Soviet early-warning coverage. Yet it was neither on the periphery nor oriented outward, as required by Article VI. For years, the Soviet Union claimed that the facility was not an early-warning radar but a permitted space-tracking radar. The United States rejected this explanation and demanded the radar's destruction; the issue sounded a sour note in arms control discussions through most of the 1980s. In 1988, the third ABM Treaty Review Conference collapsed in discord over the issue.

While both United States critics and supporters of the ABM Treaty agreed that the Krasnoyarsk radar was a violation of the agreement, there was great disagreement as to the radar's purpose and implications. Hawkish Reagan administration officials charged that the facility was not just an early-warning radar but potentially capable of ABM battle-management—part of a Soviet effort to gain the capability to rapidly break out of the ABM Treaty and build a nationwide missile defense. The Defense Department reportedly urged that the radar be declared a "material breach" of the ABM Treaty, and suggested that the United States take "proportionate" responses, some of which would also have violated the ABM Treaty. Supporters of the ABM accord, however, pointed to a reported CIA study that concluded the facility was "not well designed" for an ABM role, citing its extreme vulnerability to attack and the use of a radar frequency more than ten times lower than that used by modern ABM radars, which would make it very susceptible to blinding by "blackout" from nuclear blasts. Former Secretary of Defense Harold Brown summed up the treaty supporters' case in 1985: "Krasnoyarsk is an early warning radar that is located in the wrong place. I do not think it is a great threat to U.S. security because I do not think it has that much capability" (quoted in Bunn, p. 78).

By 1985, the Soviet Union had offered to halt construction at Krasnoyarsk if the United States did the same with its controversial radars at Thule and Fylingdales Moor—the Reagan administration refused, arguing that the U.S. radars were legal. In 1987, the Soviet Union ceased construction unilaterally, while Krasnoyarsk was still little more than an empty shell. In July 1988 the Soviet negotiators offered to dismantle Krasnoyarsk's "equipment"—rather than the entire structure—if the Reagan administration abandoned its reinterpretation of the ABM Treaty; later that year, the Soviets suggested turning the facility into a space research center. Finally, in September 1989, the Soviet Union agreed to dismantle Krasnoyarsk completely, without preconditions, and in October, then Soviet Foreign Minister Eduard Shevardnadze acknowledged that the radar was, "to put it bluntly, a violation of the ABM Treaty." Some 70 percent of the facility was dismantled by 1992, and local authorities have decided to turn the remainder into a furniture factory, putting an end to the only clear case of a Soviet violation of the ABM Treaty.

Why the Soviet Union chose to undertake the illegal Krasnoyarsk construction remains something of a mystery. Some Soviet officials have indicated that the illegal site was chosen because filling the same early-warning gap with a radar legally on the periphery would have required far more expensive construction in the permafrost of northeastern Siberia, far from any major roads or rail lines. Soviet leaders may have hoped that the United States would acquiesce to the "space-tracking" explanation, or may even have viewed the space-tracking provision as a genuine loophole in the accord.

The Reinterpretation of the ABM Treaty

On 6 October 1985, then National Security Adviser Robert C. McFarlane announced a reinterpretation of the ABM Treaty. Under the new "broad" interpretation, the treaty's restraints on ABM development and testing would apply only to 1972-era ABM technologies such as rocket interceptors, launchers, and radars, and not to the more futuristic technologies being developed in the SDI program. Under what came to be called the "traditional" or "narrow" interpretation, by contrast, these treaty restraints applied equally to all ABM technologies.

The "broad" interpretation was immediately denounced by the Soviet Union, many of the NATO allies, and by American experts—including all but one (Paul Nitze) of the United States negotiators of the ABM Treaty. Gerard C. Smith, the chief U.S. negotiator, called the reinterpretation "little short of a scandal," and argued that since the treaty's restraints on development and testing were critical to its protection against rapid breakout from the agreement, the reinterpretation would effectively render the treaty "a dead letter."

The Reagan administration soon attempted a partial retreat, saying that while the new interpretation was "fully justified," the issue was "moot," as the United States would respect the traditional view of the treaty for the time being. But the issue was far from moot, for the broad interpretation would enshroud the SDI program and the arms control negotiations in constant controversy for the rest of Ronald Reagan's term in office.

Reinterpretation advocates based their case on what they believed were ambiguities in the treaty's text and negotiating record. The definition of ABM *system components* in Article II, they argued, could be read as including only the components specifically listed there—ABM interceptors, launchers, and radars. Under that reading, Article V's ban on development, testing, and deployment of space-based and otherwise mobile ABM systems and components would not apply to other technologies. Supporters of the "broad" view pointed to numerous instances in the negotiating record where Soviet negotiators had resisted limits on future-technology systems, and concluded that the final text and record left enough ambiguity that the Soviet Union could reasonably claim that it was not bound to restraints on such exotic-technology systems. Therefore, they argued, the United States should not be bound either. With a few exceptions, however, reinterpretation advocates agreed that *deployment* of exotic-technology ABMs would still be prohibited under Agreed Statement D.

Critics of the reinterpretation rejected all of these arguments. They caustically pointed out that new State Department Legal Adviser Abraham Sofaer had carried out his study justifying the new view in only two and a half weeks, consulting only one of the U.S. negotiators, and no legal experts on arms control within the State Department or other agencies. They argued that the treaty language was clear on its face, defining ABM systems not by technology but by function, as systems "to counter strategic ballistic missiles or their elements in flight trajectory," and specifically indicating that the list of components is simply those that ABM systems "currently" consist of, not an exhaustive list. The language of Article V did not suggest any huge loophole of the kind suggested by reinterpretation supporters.

Moreover, critics pointed out that both parties' interpretation of the pact after it was signed—referred to as the "subsequent practice," and cited in the Vienna Convention on the Law of Treaties as the most critical indicator of a treaty's meaning, after the text itself—strongly supported the traditional interpretation. On the United States side, there were thirteen years of consistent interpretation, and there were a number of key statements on the Soviet side as well, including an authoritative statement by the chief of the Soviet General Staff specifically rejecting all of the claims raised by the broad view, even before they were raised in the United States. (Despite the central place of the subsequent practice in the law of treaty interpretation, the Reagan administration did not complete any study of this issue until nearly two years after it had announced its new interpretation.) Supporters of the traditional view argued that the negotiating record, too, supported their interpretation: the chief Soviet negotiator of Article V, for example, had confirmed to U.S. negotiators that it would cover "any type of present or future components," and U.S. negotiators had specifically inserted the word "currently" before the list of components in Article II, with Soviet agreement, to ensure that both present and future technologies would be covered.

Reinterpretation critics, particularly in the Senate, also pointed out that the statements of top Nixon administration officials during the ABM Treaty ratification hearings explicitly supported the traditional view of the accord. Sofaer, after being forced to retreat from early claims that the ratification record supported the broad interpretation (he blamed his faulty studies on "young lawyers" on his staff), argued that the president has broad latitude to disregard interpretations presented to the Senate during the ratification process, a view that became known as the "Sofaer doctrine." This undermining of the Senate's role in the treaty process provoked considerable controversy, with one 1987 Senate Foreign Relations Committee report calling the reinterpretation "the most flagrant abuse of the Constitution's treaty power in 200 years of American history."

The highly charged reinterpretation fight soon became entwined with debates over the defense budget and other treaties. Led by Senators Sam Nunn (D-Ga.), chairman of the Senate Armed Services Committee, and Carl Levin (D-Mich.), the Senate attached an amendment to the defense authorization bill in 1987 barring any SDI tests beyond the limits of the traditional interpretation. After lengthy maneuverings, including a Republican filibuster and a presidential veto, a modified version having the same effect was finally approved. Similar language has been approved with far less controversy every year since. Similarly, in 1988, the Senate attached a condition to its advice and consent to ratification of the Intermediate-Range Nuclear Forces (INF) Treaty requiring that the treaty be interpreted on the basis of the understanding shared by the Senate and executive branch at the time of ratification. While the so-called Byrd-Biden condition did not specifically mention the ABM Treaty issue, it was based on the "treaty clauses of the constitution," and both supporters and opponents made clear their understanding that it would apply to other agreements, including the ABM Treaty.

One irony of the reinterpretation debate is that it is by no means clear that even the broad interpretation would permit testing of the space-based rocket interceptors that have long been the focus of near-term SDI plans. These would appear to be "ABM interceptors," one of the ABM components specifically listed in Article II, and hence covered under any interpretation. While some reinterpretation supporters argued that interceptors that did not use nuclear weapons and were not guided by radar should be considered new technologies, this view was widely rejected—even by Paul Nitze, the only U.S. ABM Treaty negotiator who supported the broad interpretation. As of the early 1990s, any large-scale testing of lasers or particle beams seemed unlikely to occur before the twenty-first century, postponed more by budget constraints and shifting SDI emphases than by ABM Treaty restraints.

In the end, the broad interpretation was stillborn, having been rejected by a strong majority of the United States Congress, legally preventing its implementation. Nevertheless, the interpretation and future of the ABM Treaty remain major issues in strategic arms negotiations.

The ABM Treaty and Offensive Arms Reductions

The controversy over SDI and the ABM Treaty has been a central issue in arms reduction efforts throughout the Reagan and Bush administrations. In 1984 and 1985, the Soviet Union bitterly attacked the SDI program and United States ASAT development programs, and called for negotiations to ban what it called "space strike weapons." Soviet negotiators had walked out of negotiations over both intermediate-range missiles and strategic arms in late 1983, in response to the United States deployment of Pershing II and cruise missiles in Europe, and the Reagan administration saw the Soviet interest in negotiations on space weapons as a means to get the talks started again. The United States suggested talks with a broad focus that would cover all these issues, and after one or two false starts, the Soviet Union agreed.

The Nuclear and Space Talks, including START, INF, and the Defense and Space Talks (covering the future of missile defenses and the ABM Treaty) began in March 1985. The Defense and Space Talks were essentially deadlocked from the outset. The Soviet Union began the talks with what might be called a "reinterpretation" of its own, insisting that the ABM Treaty prohibited even research; over time, however, the Soviet Union fell back to a position similar to that of the traditional U.S. interpretation. Moreover, Soviet negotiators insisted that unless both sides agreed to abide by the ABM Treaty, there could be no START reductions in offensive forces. The United States, by contrast, proposed that the two sides agree on a "cooperative transition" to defenses, in which both sides would agree to reduce their offensive forces while deploying defenses well beyond the bounds of the ABM Treaty. In essence, the two sides had switched sides since the late 1960s: Now it was the Soviet Union that favored strict ABM limitations, and the United States that sought to pave the way for testing and eventual deployment. The deadlock only deepened when the United States announced the reinterpretation of the ABM Treaty in October 1985, and was apparent at the first Reagan-Gorbachev summit the following month.

United States supporters of the ABM Treaty pointed out that while the Soviet demand for a ban on SDI research was unjustifiable, the fundamental link the Soviet Union was drawing between defensive and offensive forces was the same linkage the two sides had agreed to in 1972, and still had a compelling logic. To reduce one's offensive forces while the other side was building up its defenses against them would only help the other side undermine one's offensive deterrent. In the words of a statement signed by six former secretaries of defense in 1987, it is only the ABM Treaty that "makes possible the negotiation of substantial reductions in strategic offensive forces." (The six secretaries also argued that the treaty continued to make "an important contribution to American security and to reducing the risk of nuclear war" [quoted in Bunn, p. 7].)

Critics of the treaty, by contrast, argued that by undermining the value of offensive ballistic missiles, missile defenses would encourage the Soviet Union to be more willing to bargain them away. Indeed, they argued that whatever flexibility the Soviet Union showed in the arms talks was largely a result of the U.S. pursuit of the SDI program.

The central importance of the ABM issue became even more apparent at the Reykjavík summit in October 1986. Intense expert negotiations at the summit laid the basic foundation that has since developed into the START Treaty, and Reagan and Gorbachev discussed even more visionary ideas such as the elimination of all offensive ballistic missiles and even all nuclear weapons. But the summit then collapsed in rancor over the SDI issue. Reagan insisted on freedom to test under the broad interpretation and an eventual right to deploy missile defenses, and Gorbachev called for all SDI work to be limited to the laboratory: at that moment, neither side seriously explored potential compromises.

In the months after Reykjavík, the SDI issue erupted again in the United States domestic debate. Leaks from high-level meetings indicated that the Reagan administration was considering carrying out SDI tests that would violate the traditional interpretation of the ABM Treaty, to pave the way for "early deployment" of a large-scale defense that would destroy the treaty completely. Congressional and allied reaction was strong, and it was that year that the Nunn-Levin amendment requiring compliance with the traditional interpretation was approved.

With the warming of United States–Soviet relations and the increased support for arms control after 1987, SDI's fortunes declined, and the ABM Treaty's prospects improved. The SDI issue virtually vanished from the American political agenda during 1988, and Congress dealt the program its first real decline in funding—a trend that continued in 1989 and 1990, in concert with the rapid decline in perceptions of the Soviet military threat and the consequent reductions in the overall military budget.

During that period, United States–Soviet frictions over the ABM issue also moderated considerably. In September 1989, the Soviet Union removed the greatest remaining procedural roadblock to START by announcing that it was prepared to complete a START agreement even if no agreement on the interpretation of the ABM Treaty could be reached—though the Soviet Union would consider United States violation of the traditional view as potential grounds to withdraw from START. It was at that same meeting that the Soviet Union finally agreed to dismantle the Krasnoyarsk radar, a move the United States had insisted on before it would sign START.

Nevertheless, the ABM issue lurked in the background. The Bush administration continued to give strong support to the SDI program, and to focus the program on preparing for a widespread near-term deployment of both space-based and ground-based ABM interceptors, which would require abrogating the ABM accord, or fundamentally renegotiating it in a way the Soviet Union rejected. The Soviet Union continued to indicate that violation or abrogation of the ABM Treaty would be grounds for withdrawal from START, and the Defense and Space Talks went nowhere.

THE FUTURE ABM DEBATE

The war in the Persian Gulf in early 1991 and the dissolution of the Soviet Union at the end of that year reinvigorated the SDI-ABM debate. Newscasts of Patriot rocket interceptors shooting down Iraqi Scud missiles created a widespread impression that effective missile defenses were possible and highlighted the potential threat posed by third world missiles, and the attempted Soviet coup in August 1991 raised concerns over the control of Soviet nuclear weapons. In his 1991 State of the Union address, President Bush announced that the SDI program would be refocused on a new concept, dubbed Global Protection Against Limited Strikes (GPALS). Rather than providing a partial defense against a massive Soviet attack in an effort to enhance deterrence, GPALS would be designed to provide a nearly complete defense against attacks of less than two hundred warheads. The new threats of concern were attacks by a third world country or by a mad Soviet missile commander—fears remarkably similar to the justifications for the 1960s-era Sentinel plan. GPALS would include some 1,000 space-based rockets dubbed "brilliant pebbles," 750 ground-based rockets, and tactical missile de-

fenses that could be deployed with U.S. forces and allies around the world.

Congress, also responding to the Gulf War's dramatization of the missile threat, changed direction on the SDI issue in 1991, with a measure known as the Missile Defense Act. After years of declining budgets, SDI received a billion-dollar increase over the previous year's funding. Congress approved a goal of deploying limited nationwide missile defenses, instructed the secretary of defense to prepare for a rapid deployment at the single site permitted by the ABM Treaty, and urged the president to negotiate amendments to the treaty permitting more extensive defenses. Executive-legislative disagreements over the ABM issue continued, however, as most members of Congress continued to oppose the space-based brilliant-pebbles interceptors the administration favored. Moreover, key supporters of the Missile Defense Act indicated that they favored only "modest" changes to the ABM Treaty, rather than the sweeping revisions the administration preferred.

The position of the United States' treaty partner—now a democratic Russia rather than a Communist Soviet Union—has also changed somewhat. On 29 January 1992, in a wide-ranging speech on disarmament, Russian president Boris Yeltsin reaffirmed the ABM Treaty, calling it "an important factor of maintaining strategic stability in the world," but also suggested that Russia was ready "to develop, then create, and jointly operate a global defense system, instead of the SDI system." U.S. SDI supporters were quick to claim Yeltsin's statement as an endorsement of their view. But in the U.S.-Russian discussions since then, Russian negotiators have resisted U.S. proposals to rewrite the ABM Treaty drastically and have reiterated, according to Russian defense minister Pavel Grachev, that "the process of strategic offensive arms cuts is tied into observance of the ABM Treaty" (interview in *Izvestia*, quoted in *Foreign Broadcast Information Service Daily Report, Central Eurasia*, 23 June 1992, p. 2). Russian officials have emphasized that in the near term, they are primarily interested in cooperation in treaty-permitted activities such as early warning. Any more widespread defenses, they argue, would have to be jointly developed and controlled—conditions the Bush administration made clear it will not accept. At the Washington Bush-Yeltsin summit in June 1992, the two sides issued a joint statement calling for continued high-level discussion of the ABM issue, but fundamental differences remained.

In these changed circumstances, the ABM debate continues. Critics of the treaty argue that if it was ever a useful agreement, the march of technological and political change has passed it by. They warn of the risks of limited strikes posed by the spread of ballistic missiles and uncertainties in nuclear control in the former Soviet Union, and argue that these dangers justify an urgent program to develop and deploy a GPALS system. Pointing to the Patriot, they maintain that whatever the past technological difficulties of missile defense, no fundamental technical barriers now stand in the way. They argue that to make way for the GPALS system, the ABM Treaty should either be abrogated or replaced with a new accord allowing both sides to develop and deploy widespread missile defenses, and that limited defenses such as GPALS will be compatible with arms reductions.

Supporters of the ABM Treaty disagree on all these points. Patriot's performance, some argue, may have been closer to total failure than to the near-perfect success the army initially claimed. In any case, Patriot proves nothing about SDI, as the program had no role in Patriot's development, and shooting down primitive, slow-moving, conventionally armed Scuds one at a time is a far cry from SDI's job of intercepting hundreds of fast-moving, nuclear-armed long-range missiles. Treaty supporters also argue that while missile technology is proliferating, no new countries seem likely to gain the more advanced technology needed for long-range missiles that could threaten the United States well into the twenty-first century. Moreover, they point out that a missile defense would provide no protection against other means by which a third-world fanatic might deliver a nuclear weapon, such as smuggling across United States borders. They recommend pursuing tactical defenses like the Patriot and potential successors, which are permitted by the ABM Treaty and could handle current third world missile threats. As for the risk of unauthorized missile attacks caused by potential chaos in the former Soviet Union, they point out that sophisticated safeguards such as electronic locks that prevent missiles from being armed without codes from higher authority greatly reduce the risk—and argue that safeguards improvements could reduce whatever danger remains with greater certainty and at less cost than a missile defense. Moreover, they point out that as Russia has shown few signs of agreeing to fundamentally rewrite the ABM Treaty, pursuing the GPALS program would require the United States to abrogate the accord, and would al-

most certainly mean sacrificing both START and the deeper strategic reductions agreed to at the Bush-Yeltsin summit in June 1992.

A number of developments could threaten the ABM Treaty in the years to come. As of 1992, the Bush administration continued to propose revising the treaty to eliminate or drastically loosen virtually all of its restraints, while the U.S. Congress also urged amendments, though more modest in scope. U.S.-Russian discussions of the subject continued, though Russian negotiators continued to resist any such amendment plans. At the same time, SDI officials indicated that their testing plans would collide with the traditional interpretation of the ABM Treaty by the mid-to-late 1990s and have urged Congress to remove its ban on such testing. Moreover, SDI's plans for tactical defenses include some systems that are likely to have a prohibited capability to defend against longer-range strategic missiles.

In short, the debate over the future of the SDI program and the ABM Treaty remains unresolved. This complex strategic, technical, and legal discussion is likely to continue for years to come, and to play a central role in the prospects for implementing the START agreement and the much deeper cuts in strategic arms agreed on by Bush and Yeltsin in June 1992.

BIBLIOGRAPHY

Critical Overview   An illustrated, comprehensive account that surveys all the various issues surrounding the treaty is MATTHEW BUNN, *Foundation for the Future: The ABM Treaty and National Security* (Washington, D.C., 1990). Other useful general accounts include WILLIAM J. DURCH, JR., *The ABM Treaty and Western Security* (Cambridge, Mass., 1988) and ANTONIA HANDLER CHAYES and PAUL DOTY, eds., *Defending Deterrence: Managing the ABM Treaty Regime into the 21st Century* (Washington, D.C., 1989). The essays contained in COWEN, JASANI, and STUTZLE, eds., listed below, cover many of the same issues.

Terms of the Treaty   The most authoritative unclassified account of the ABM Treaty's terms is by the chief United States negotiator, GERARD C. SMITH, "The Treaty's Basic Provisions: View of the U.S. Negotiator," in REGINA COWEN, BHUPENDRA JASANI, and WALTHER STUTZLE, eds., *The ABM Treaty: To Defend or Not to Defend?* (Oxford, England, 1987). The testing of the American SDI program clashes with Article V. For a detailed account of these issues, see MATTHEW BUNN, *Foundation for the Future: The ABM Treaty and National Security* (Washington, D.C., 1990): 90–103; and RAYMOND L. GARTHOFF's comprehensive account *Policy Versus the Law: The Reinterpretation of the ABM Treaty* (Washington, D.C., 1987).

Compliance   For a useful account of the dispute over alleged violations of the ABM Treaty, see JAMES P. RUBIN, "The Superpower Dispute Over Radars,"

Bulletin of the Atomic Scientists 43 (April 1987): 34–37; GLORIA DUFFY, *Compliance and the Future of Arms Control* (Cambridge, Mass., 1988); and MATTHEW BUNN's detailed discussion of each of the ABM charges, *Foundation for the Future: The ABM Treaty and National Security* (Washington, D.C., 1990): 74–89. RAYMOND L. GARTHOFF, "Case of the Wandering Radar," *Bulletin of the Atomic Scientists* 47 (July–August 1991): 7–9, reexamines Soviet decision making in the positioning of the Krasnoyarsk radar.

Confidence-Building Measures in Europe

1975 to the Present

○

JAMES MACINTOSH

See also Arms Control Treaty Verification; From MBFR to CFE: Negotiating Conventional Arms Control in Europe; The Hot Line: Washington-Moscow Direct Communications Link, 1963 to the Present; The International Atomic Energy Agency and Arms Control; *and* Negotiating Arms Control and Disarmament Agreements. *Most of the treaties discussed in this essay are excerpted in Volume III.*

Most analysts would agree that confidence building is an arms control–like approach employing purposely designed cooperative measures called CBMS and CSBMS. Confidence-building measures (CBMS) and confidence- and security-building measures (CSBMS) are intended to help clarify states' military intentions, to reduce uncertainties about their potentially threatening military activities, and to constrain their opportunities for surprise attack or the coercive use of military forces. However, CBMS and CSBMS do not deal directly with force reductions; that is the province of a very different type of arms control activity. The two terms—*CBM* and *CSBM*—are often used interchangeably and mean approximately the same thing.

Few believe that confidence-building agreements can prevent deliberate, premeditated attacks. However, this type of agreement can be an effective method for minimizing accidental conflicts and, perhaps most important, for improving the security relations among suspicious but not belligerent neighbors.

Much of what we know about confidence building is derived from the post-1970 arms control experience in Europe. This period has included an ongoing, multipart negotiating process and yielded a rich and varied selection of practical CBMS. It has also spawned the vast majority of conceptual explo-

rations of the confidence-building phenomenon. As a consequence, a great deal of our thinking about confidence building as a general phenomenon is closely associated with the specific European arms control experience of the last two decades. Confidence building is therefore a much more contextually bound concept and arms control approach than is frequently appreciated. This makes an examination of the European negotiating history very important. Without it, we can have little sense of the phenomenon's real meaning—or its conceptual origins and limitations.

However, because the confidence-building approach is understood primarily in terms of its European arms control context, the two sometimes become confused. Indeed, there is a tendency to treat the confidence-building concept and the CSBM agreements of the Conference on Security and Cooperation in Europe (CSCE), the principal negotiating process developing CBMS, as synonymous. This assumption, however, exaggerates the interchangeability of the confidence-building concept and specific CSCE agreements. For instance, it ignores other, non-CSCE confidence-building efforts discussed in this encyclopedia such as the Incidents at Sea Agreement (requiring the Soviet Union and the United States to avoid threatening maneuvers, simulated attacks, collisions, or disruptive behavior in international ocean areas), the Washington-Moscow Direct Communications Link, measures to prevent accidental nuclear war, and the Ballistic Missile Launch Notification agreements. These efforts all represent independent applications of the confidence-building concept that predate the CSCE or lie outside its geographic jurisdiction. As a further example of independence, the use of the term *confidence building* itself first emerged explicitly in a United Nations General Assembly resolution as early as 1955. In addition, clear functional examples of confidence building can be found in many historical international agreements. Nevertheless, it is true that confidence building has found by far its fullest practical expression in the CSCE context.

The CSCE's Vienna Document 1990 is the best example of a comprehensive confidence-building agreement. Discussed at length later in this essay, it is an elaboration of an earlier CSCE agreement negotiated in Stockholm in 1986. Not surprisingly, it includes a host of archetypical CBMs. For instance, the Vienna Document contains measures requiring states to give advance notification of a wide variety of potentially threatening military activities involving land forces of division size or larger (such as the movement or exercising of several hundred tanks; to circulate a calendar forecasting those notifiable military activities for the coming year; and to exchange detailed information annually, covering military organizations (location and structure) and equipment (such as types and numbers of tanks, artillery, and helicopters) as well as military budgets and new acquisitions. The Vienna Document also allows states to send observers to military exercises and includes several modest inspection measures. These are typical CBMs.

However, there is more to the confidence-building phenomenon than one might assume simply glancing at the Vienna Document with its list of concrete measures. There is, in particular, the question of what makes the confidence-building process actually work: how is it that states come to see each other as being less threatening as a result of adopting confidence-building agreements and using CBMs? After all, the circulation of information about neighbors cannot by itself transform perceptions from threatening to benign.

Unfortunately, the existing body of conceptual literature usually fails to identify or explain the mechanisms of confidence building. At present, most analysts agree that the implementation of specific collections of CBMs is associated somehow with the larger confidence-building process—the process of psychological transformation in decision-maker (and public) perceptions of neighboring state threats. However, the mechanism of change and the manner in which CBMs influence it have yet to be explored seriously.

For instance, does the use of CBMs initiate the transformation process or does their adoption accelerate (perhaps beyond a critical threshold) an existing but nascent process of transformation? These are very important questions that, when answered, will improve our understanding of the confidence-building phenomenon. More important, the answers will also tell us how the confidence-building approach ought to be promoted and employed in new contexts in other parts of the world.

It is reasonable to think that the CSCE experience may shed some light on these and other important conceptual issues. To understand the confidence-building phenomenon more fully, therefore, it is necessary to examine the history of the CSCE and its CBM agreements with some care. This is, after all, the preeminent example of confidence building in practice and it inevitably colors our understanding of the phenomenon. Whatever theoretical insights one might develop are almost certainly derived from this historical example.

ORIGINS OF THE CSCE PROCESS

The path leading to the Conference on Security and Cooperation in Europe and its initial regime of CBMs can be traced reliably to 1954 when the Federal Republic of Germany agreed to join the North Atlantic Treaty Organization (NATO). This effectively obliged the Soviet Union to pursue more complex multilateral security solutions in order to deal with its concerns about German revanchism. However, it would take fifteen years for circumstances to permit the superpowers and their allies to begin both the Conference on Security and Cooperation in Europe (CSCE) negotiations and the associated Mutual (and Balanced) Force Reduction (MBFR) talks. The Soviet Union was successful in gaining Western agreement to begin the CSCE negotiations, but it was obliged to accept force reduction talks with NATO (the MBFR negotiations) as the quid pro quo. Thus, each negotiation was possible only because a superpower needed the other negotiation for its own purposes.

Although it quickly developed a unique character of its own, the CSCE process was clearly the offshoot of the Soviet Union's plans in the 1964–1967 period to convene a European security conference (ESC). It was probably the emergence of the new Brezhnev-Kosygin leadership that triggered the earnest pursuit of this objective. Even before this period, however, there had been generally similar proposals, dating to at least the first plan of the Polish Foreign Minister, Adam Rapacki, in 1958. Some scholars date the origin of Soviet interest in a pan-European security conference several years earlier to 1954, the year Soviet Foreign Minister Molotov proposed a conference to deal with European collective security issues. In any event, the Warsaw Treaty Organization formally proposed a "European Security Conference," intended to discuss European collective security, in 1965, 1966, and again in 1967.

It is difficult to single out one particular goal or motivation driving the Soviet Union's European Security Conference proposals of the mid-1960s. Central to any ESC strategy was the Soviet Union's determination to neutralize the Federal Republic of Germany as a potential military threat. The formal acceptance of postwar boundaries in Central Europe would help achieve this as would the permanent separation of the two Germanys. Both would reduce the size and the resources of postwar Germany. Enmeshing the Federal Republic in European-wide security agreements would also serve this purpose. Additional undertakings to guarantee that Germany would never acquire nuclear weapons would add another dimension of perceived security in the eyes of Soviet leaders. In a related vein, the formal acceptance of the European status quo would recognize the presence of the Soviet Union's forces in East and Central Europe as well as acknowledge the Communist regimes in these regions, enshrining their buffer-state status.

From the Soviet Union's perspective, an ESC-type negotiation could also help to weaken NATO by undermining its raison d'être. A diminished threat would make NATO seem less necessary. The Soviet Union increasingly saw this as a feasible policy goal in the late 1960s, an interpretation doubtless encouraged by the departure of France from the military structure of NATO in 1966 and by aggressive German efforts to improve relations with the Soviet Union. If U.S. influence in Europe could be gradually reduced without creating instability, this too would be a welcome development.

NATO interest in the Soviet Union's European security conference idea was distinctly cool throughout the mid-1960s. There was little to gain in NATO's view from a multilateral European security conference (especially one that excluded the United States and Canada as participants) and a great deal to risk, including the health of NATO itself. Indeed, it was only when the U.S. Senate threatened to reduce unilaterally U.S. troop levels in Europe that NATO's interest in arms control was seriously engaged. After extensive internal discussions about how best to deal with the Soviet Union's initiatives, NATO produced the "Harmel Report" in 1967. This document formalized NATO's public interest in achieving stability and a détente in East-West relations. With force reduction talks under way, the U.S. Senate would never undercut the NATO position by withdrawing troops. Negotiations, therefore, would forestall any troop withdrawal for years.

This equivocal U.S. interest in and need for force reduction negotiations created a unique arms control opportunity. In addition to the domestic U.S. requirement for a visible negotiation, there was a growing interest primarily on the part of the northern European NATO states in reaching some sort of political accommodation with the Soviet Union and its allies. The Federal Republic of Germany was particularly interested in improving relations with the East. Paralleling this was the increasingly vigorous effort by the Soviet Union to persuade NATO to enter into a European security conference. The compromise was obvious although it would take several years to work out: a security conference would be traded for force reduction talks.

The Soviet-led invasion of Czechoslovakia in August 1968 temporarily disrupted the movement toward agreement on a European security conference. However, in March 1969, another Eastern proposal (the so-called Budapest Appeal) was launched, this time with more success. It spoke of organizing a conference that would deal with improved relations in the economic, scientific, and technical realms as well as the security realm for all of Europe.

There ensued a more interactive set of pronouncements beginning with several cautious NATO responses, first in April and then December 1969. Although the December statement focused on the need to pursue negotiations dealing with force reductions (MBFR) and the need to address concrete security problems associated with Germany, it also noted a number of requirements for a general European security conference. Included in that statement was an explicit reference to the possibility of developing CBMS. This was followed by another NATO statement on 27 May 1970 that spoke more positively of what would become the CSCE. The Warsaw Treaty Organization issued a statement on 22 June 1970 that corresponded quite closely to most of the emerging NATO agenda and agreed that Canada and the United States would participate in the proposed conference.

Relations between the Federal Republic of Germany and its Eastern neighbors improved significantly over the next year as did United States–Soviet relations (as exemplified by the Strategic Arms Limitation Talks). This smoothed the way for a compromise agreement creating the MBFR and the CSCE. Treaties signed by the Federal Republic of Germany with the Soviet Union (12 August 1970) and Poland (7 December 1970) were followed the next year by a treaty between the two Germanys (12 December 1971) and the Quadripartite (Four Powers) Berlin Agreement of September 1971. However, it was not until the summit meeting of May 1972 between President Richard Nixon of the United States and General Secretary Leonid Brezhnev of the Soviet Union that the linkage between the CSCE and the MBFR was finally accepted and agreement reached to pursue them both. The trade-off apparently was engineered by U.S. Secretary of State Henry Kissinger and Soviet Ambassador to the United States Anatoly Dobrynin earlier that year.

HELSINKI CONSULTATIONS, 1972–1975

The Helsinki Final Act CBMS are important more for what they led to (the Stockholm and Vienna CSBM Documents) than for any specific accomplishments of their own. They barely imposed any limits on the CSCE states and made only the most perfunctory progress toward the genuine development of confidence. In some eyes, they even bred suspicion. Nevertheless, the CSCE process and the archetypical CBMS that emerged in the Helsinki Final Act were important first steps in a much more profound process that is still unfolding in a dramatically altered Europe. Somewhere in this long process, a true transformation occurred in the way European states viewed each other and the threat they posed. Although it is difficult to date, the change appears to

have occurred during the end of the negotiations that produced the CSCE's Stockholm Document. The seeds of that transformation, however, were sown during the Helsinki negotiations. Negotiating CBMS and then living with them almost certainly played a central role in that transformation, but that role remains poorly understood to this day.

The Conference on Security and Cooperation in Europe (CSCE) process began formally on 22 November 1972 with the start of preliminary consultations in Helsinki, Finland. These discussions were intended to establish the specific subject matter of the CSCE negotiations. Their results were contained in the "Final Recommendations of the Helsinki Consultations" (the Helsinki "Blue Book"), a document that established the basic structure of the eventual Helsinki Final Act declaration. During these preparatory discussions, the Soviet Union, somewhat surprisingly, agreed to a number of concessions on CSCE subject matter that would lead inevitably to prolonged, bitter, and embarrassing (to the Soviet Union) discussions about human rights and basic freedoms. It is not clear why the Soviet Union agreed to this mandate but the decision helped to transform the CSCE into a more comprehensive and effective process than anyone could have anticipated at the time. Although the product of Soviet efforts, the CSCE certainly did not evolve in a way that reflected the interests of the Soviet Union.

The CSCE negotiations proper began on 3 July 1973, following almost six months of preparatory meetings. They continued until 1 August 1975 and involved the active participation of thirty-three European states as well as the United States and Canada. Although the negotiations were technically multilateral, conducted among thirty-five equal and sovereign states, they really involved three basic blocs—NATO, the Warsaw Treaty Organization (WTO), and the much more loosely organized neutral and nonaligned states (the NNs) such as Sweden, Austria, Yugoslavia, and Malta. In addition, there was a distinct superpower negotiating channel that sometimes bypassed the alliances. The negotiations resulted in a comprehensive document typically referred to as the Helsinki Final Act. (The term *final act* indicated that the concluding document's status was less formal than a treaty or an agreement and was not legally binding.)

This document included three basic components or "baskets" dealing with (1) "Security in Europe," (2) "Cooperation in the Fields of Economics, Science and Technology, and the Environment," and (3) "Cooperation in Humanitarian and Other Fields." It also included a commitment to discuss the implementation of the Final Act in Belgrade, Yugoslavia, in 1977. The commitment to hold follow-up meetings (FUMS) was an extremely important aspect of the Helsinki Final Act as it guaranteed a continuing and evolving process.

The principal product of the Helsinki Final Act's first "basket" was the creation of a modest collection of confidence-building measures (contained in the "Document on Confidence-Building Measures and Certain Aspects of Security and Disarmament"). There was also a commitment to discuss CBM implementation at the succeeding Belgrade CSCE Follow-Up Meeting. The CBMS were very modest and only one approached being obligatory. This principal CBM required the notification of maneuvers by CSCE states in Europe exceeding 25,000 personnel twenty-one days in advance of their conduct unless they were arranged on short notice. The notification also was to include basic information about the maneuver. Although these Helsinki CBMS were themselves very weak, they established important precedents that facilitated the development of increasingly comprehensive and constraining CBM agreements.

This combination of advance activity notification and information is perhaps the archetypical CBM and it has operated at the heart of each succeeding confidence-building agreement. The other CBMS included the voluntary invitation of observers to notifiable maneuvers; the voluntary advance notification of small-scale maneuvers; the highly discretionary advance notification of major military movements (that is, the movement of military forces from one location to another without their necessarily being involved in an exercise); and a commitment to engage in personnel exchanges. Personnel exchanges with neighbors permit military personnel to visit military bases, participate in training and educational programs, and generally develop an increased familiarity with the military establishments of neighboring states.

The fact that there would be three basic CBMS in the Helsinki Final Act (military maneuver notification, observer invitation, and discretionary military-movement notification) was largely established in the Helsinki preconference by June 1973. This is clear from the preconference's "Final Recommendations." The contention during the Helsinki conference's two years revolved mostly around what

specific figures to use as parameters in the central maneuver CBM, not whether there would be one. Toward the end of the negotiations in early 1975, the East pressed for a 40,000-person notification limit, ten days advance notification, and argued that only a 100-kilometer (60-mile) band of Soviet territory should be included in the measure's reach. The NATO position called for a 12,000-person notification trigger, forty-nine days advance notification, and a 700-kilometer (420-mile) inclusion zone within the Soviet Union. (A *notification trigger* specifies at what point a military activity must be reported in advance; it is a threshold that when crossed "triggers" the notification requirement.) The values finally accepted were 25,000 personnel, twenty-one days, and a zone of 250 kilometers, or 156 miles. This final agreement's figures were very close to the compromise proposals of the NNs.

The inclusion of CBMS in the Helsinki negotiations was not a particularly high-priority concern and came mostly as a result of NATO and NN state pressure. Officially, NATO was determined that the CSCE deal with security issues but was reluctant to permit the security component of the conference to address issues more demanding than modest information and notification CBMS. In particular, the NATO states wished to underline the difference between the CSCE and the parallel MBFR force reduction talks. This was an important constraint and more or less prescribed the permissible security-oriented subject matter of the CSCE and its CBMS. The Soviet Union and its WTO allies were even less interested in developing demanding CBMS, preferring more general political declarations. The NNs, however, saw in the CSCE the only negotiating forum in which their security interests could be pursued because they were excluded from the MBFR (as they would be from the later Conventional Forces in Europe [CFE] Agreement). Thus, they pressed for more aggressive measures although they eventually found themselves developing compromise positions to overcome East-West divisions. The NNs as a group have tended to adopt this role in succeeding CSCE security negotiations, as well.

THE BELGRADE AND MADRID MEETINGS

The Helsinki follow-up conferences—first in Belgrade in (1977–1978) and then in Madrid (1980–

1983)—were plagued by problems flowing from the seriously eroding East-West political environment, a process that began in earnest in 1975 and reached full dudgeon with the Soviet invasion of Afghanistan (1979) and the imposition of martial law in Poland (1981). The Belgrade meeting was a failure, despite the exploration of many new or expanded CBMS suggested by the neutral and non-aligned states (NNS) and NATO.

Although conducted in equally if not more contentious times, the Madrid Follow-Up Meeting eventually yielded a constructive outcome—the 6 September 1983 Concluding Document. This included what is usually called the "Madrid Mandate," a formal commitment to initiate a Conference on Confidence- and Security-Building Measures and Disarmament in Europe—what was to become the immensely successful Stockholm CCSBMDE. This new negotiation starting in January of 1984 was tasked with developing a more comprehensive and militarily significant body of verifiable, second-generation CBMS. They were to be called confidence- and security-building measures (CSBMS) in order to emphasize their more comprehensive and obligatory nature, a terminological suggestion attributed to the Yugoslav Conference on Security and Cooperation in Europe (CSCE) delegation in 1981. Whether or not the introduction of the new CSBM term was intended to signify a qualitatively more advanced form of confidence building is unclear. Some analysts suggest that the term was coined for reasons of negotiating expediency rather than conceptual need, an assessment that is probably correct. Theoretically, there are few grounds for arguing that CBMS and CSBMS differ in any fundamental way. Substantively, they address the same basic concerns in the same basic way. CSBMS are generally seen to do so, however, in a more comprehensive, compulsory, and constraining manner, making them more significant militarily. Nevertheless, there is no doubt that CSBM soon came to denote, in more professional usage, a much more comprehensive version of confidence building compared with the original Helsinki CBMS.

The Madrid FUM and the resulting Stockholm Conference were influenced strongly by the 25 May 1978 United Nations proposal of French President Valery Giscard d'Estaing that called for a two-stage security conference among CSCE states. The French president also proposed the creation of an international verification agency that would rely on satellites for arms control monitoring. It is interesting to note that Giscard d'Estaing's proposals were motivated to a significant extent by domestic politics, as he was attempting to counter the increasingly popular Socialist party leader, François Mitterand. Mitterand had proposed a generally similar European security conference in late 1977.

The new security conference was not conceived originally to be part of the CSCE-CBM process, reflecting a strong and unique French desire to separate important European security discussions from the too-broad CSCE and the too-narrow MBFR force reduction talks. The French proposal came to be called the Conference on Disarmament in Europe or CDE, an acronym sometimes used interchangeably to describe the CSCE's CSBM negotiations. It envisioned a first stage intended to develop much more extensive CBMS and a second stage that would turn to actual force reduction issues. The geographic scope of the conference was to include all of Europe, from the Atlantic coast to the Ural Mountains, the traditional dividing line between Europe and Asia within the Soviet Union. This area is usually referred to as the ATTU, an acronym for Atlantic to the Urals.

The French proposal became the subject of serious debate within NATO during late 1979 and early 1980 with the French submission of two CDE-based study papers. The main division lay between France and the United States, the latter resisting the French effort to undermine the MBFR negotiations and to weaken the status of human rights issues in the CSCE. This basic U.S.-French division has been a consistent feature of most postwar European arms control dynamics. NATO did not formally adopt the French CDE proposal but, as a practical matter, after significant changes were wrought in some of its basics, the CDE idea did become an unofficial NATO position for the CSCE's Madrid FUM. In particular, the connection between the CDE and the CSCE was emphasized and the linkage between the two stages of the negotiations—CBMS first, followed by force reductions—was obscured. The extensive list of CBMS developed by the French was also simplified and adjusted to reflect the additional thinking of some other NATO states.

In counterpoint to the French concept, the Warsaw Treaty states proposed a security conference on 15 May 1979 ("Conference on Military Détente and Disarmament in Europe"). It also spoke of two phases and was to operate independently of the CSCE. The mandate for further CBM negotiations developed at Madrid grew out of these two proposals.

The Madrid FUM began on 11 November 1980. Before the end of the year, the French proposal for a CDE had been put on the table and efforts to negotiate a workable mandate had begun. The atmosphere of the Madrid review conference was poisoned by the strong reactions to the Soviet invasion of Afghanistan and to the labor unrest in Poland; the sessions were frequently polemical in the extreme. Nevertheless, the various parties were eventually successful in blending the positive features of the two main security conference proposals to create a workable mandate for new CBM negotiations. This required a number of compromises by the Soviet Union. The Soviet effort to see nuclear, air, and naval forces included in the CDE and to ensure that North American territory was also subject to the CBMS, for instance, was eventually abandoned. President Brezhnev signalled this retreat in February 1981, but it still required two more years to complete the Madrid Mandate.

The Madrid Mandate contained the guidelines for the Stockholm Conference, and for the succeeding Vienna confidence-and-security-building-measure (CSBM) negotiation as well. It committed the CSCE states to "the negotiation and adoption of a set of mutually complementary confidence- and security-building measures designed to reduce the risk of military confrontation in Europe. . . . [These measures] will cover the whole of Europe as well as the adjoining sea area and air space. They will be of military significance and politically binding and will be provided with adequate forms of verification which correspond to their content."

STOCKHOLM CONFERENCE, 1984–1986

It is difficult to exaggerate the significance of the Stockholm Confidence- and Security-Building Measure (CSBM) Conference and its resulting Stockholm Document. A good case can be made for it being a truly transitional negotiation, the primary process that signalled the end of the Cold War for most Europeans. This view suggests that the negotiation was a facilitating—perhaps even cathartic—experience that enabled most European leaders to understand that their neighbors posed far less a threat than had earlier seemed to be the case. Less extravagant analysts will still agree that the Stockholm Document represents a significant landmark in East-West relations.

Negotiations: The First Year   This outcome could not have been guessed easily, given the difficult political environment when the negotiations began on 17 January 1984. Only several months earlier, for instance, the Soviet Union had suspended its participation in the intermediate-range nuclear forces (INF) and strategic arms (START) negotiations. Nevertheless, the Stockholm Conference managed to survive a very tough and fractious first year, countless international political crises, and the general breakdown in East-West arms control dialogue to produce the 21 September 1986 "Document of the Stockholm Conference."

During the course of the Conference on Confidence- and Security-Building Measures and Disarmament in Europe (CCSBMDE) negotiations, the three basic groups of participants—the Warsaw Treaty Organization states, the NATO states, and the Neutral and Nonaligned states—produced six distinct packages of CSBMS. Romania and Malta, acting independently, each proposed a package as well. Critical to the eventual content of the agreement was the NATO proposal of 24 January 1984. This comprehensive proposal (termed SC.1 for Stockholm Conference document 1) and its later "amplification" of 8 March 1985 touched on many of the features that would eventually appear in the completed Stockholm Agreement. Also important was the neutral and nonaligned states' (NN's) first package of proposed measures—SC.3—proposed on 9 March 1984. The neutral and nonaligned states later developed a second package of measures, SC.7, in an effort to create the basis for a compromise agreement.

The NATO package initially revolved around a demanding information measure. This measure required the annual exchange of data outlining the structure of each participating state's military forces within the Madrid Mandate's area of application (the ATTU region). Complementing the information measure was the provision for a calendar measure requiring forecasts of each state's notifiable military activities for the coming year. In addition, SC.1 called for notifications, forty-five days in advance, of a variety of military activities. The military activities of concern—those that were to be "notifiable"—were generally out-of-garrison exercises or movements involving forces of divisional size or greater. If air- or sea-movable forces were involved (for instance, paratroops or marines), a lower threshold of approximately 3,000 personnel was suggested. In addition, the NATO proposal spoke of an improved observation measure (compared with the Helsinki Final Act's rudimentary measure), the development of compliance and verification provisions (including inspections of suspect sites), and the creation of an unspecified communication system.

The first proposal of the neutral and nonaligned states (sc.3) featured a wide array of measures designed to improve significantly the original Helsinki CBMS. It was a surprisingly coherent document considering the diverse interests of the various NN states. After all, the NN group included states such as Malta and Switzerland, Sweden and Yugoslavia, each with its own special concerns; their ability to produce a mainstream compromise text touching on virtually all of the basic CBM elements was impressive. While no specific threshold figures were used in many cases (leaving them to be established during the negotiations), the intent was to reduce the notification levels of all military activities substantially and to capture series of much smaller military activities, if they represented a special threat or were conducted close to each other, geographically or temporally. sc.3 included a specific sensitivity to amphibious and airborne special forces threats and included both in proposed notification measures and thresholds. It also required advance notification of major military activities in the adjoining sea area or associated airspace if they were part of a notifiable land activity. The NNS also proposed the advance notification of large movements, rotations, and redeployments of forces. In addition, the NN proposal called for improved observation opportunities, the exchange of calendars, the notification of alerts (exercises conducted with short warning), and spoke of developing constraints on the deployment of forces necessary for conducting sustained offensive operations.

The first Soviet proposal—sc. 4—of 8 May 1984 was very different compared with the other initial proposals. It focused on so-called political measures rather than military-technical CBMS and actively resisted the sort of openness and transparency that were central in the NATO and NN packages. At odds with other interpretations of the Mandate, the Soviet Union's proposal called for an agreement on no first use of nuclear weapons, a ban on chemical weapons, the creation of nuclear-weapon-free zones, the negotiation of a nonuse-of-force treaty, and a freeze on military spending. The Soviet proposal also included some more conventional CSBMs, but these were distinctly secondary and generally

intended to constrain NATO exercise size and expand CSBM coverage to include naval activities.

The course of negotiations was difficult. Although there were many divisions over the next several years, the most significant involved the dramatic difference in basic approach adopted by NATO and the NNS on the one hand and the Soviet Union and its allies on the other. The Soviet Union's determination to see nonuse of force and no first use of nuclear weapons emerge as the central elements of the Stockholm process was guaranteed to elicit a strong negative reaction from NATO and the NNS. These two proposals were political, declaratory, and clearly intended to damage NATO. President Reagan's 4 June 1984 speech in Ireland conceded the inclusion of a nonuse of force statement in the eventual Stockholm agreement and in so doing obliged the Soviet Union to negotiate on specific, concrete measures. By the end of the summer, the Soviet Union and its allies had begun to move toward a position more consistent with that of the NATO and NN states.

During the first year of the Stockholm negotiations, a number of basic problems emerged in addition to the fundamental disagreement over the status of political measures such as nonuse of force declarations. One was the reconsideration of how to deal with naval forces and their activities. The Madrid Mandate had seemed to exclude independent naval and air activities but this issue reemerged in the first year of the Stockholm negotiations. The Soviet Union and its allies had insisted that naval forces represented a security threat to Europe and should be included in the negotiations. Although eventually resolved in NATO's favor, this issue emerged in later CSCE security discussions.

Another basic disagreement that emerged in the first year of negotiations was how to define "adequate verification." The Soviet Union resisted any serious effort to discuss a verification regime, whereas NATO pressed for on-site inspections and observations. There were also disagreements over the creation of ceilings for military exercises. The Soviet Union made a case for limiting exercises to 40,000 personnel, largely to constrain NATO, which relied on large exercises.

Negotiations: The Second Year Negotiations in the second year involved more concrete discussions of substantive differences. By early 1985, the Soviet Union and its allies were developing CSBM proposals in working papers that corresponded generally to NATO and NN proposals. It is quite likely that the emergence of Mikhail Gorbachev as General Secretary in March contributed to the change in Soviet approach. NATO put its modified proposal (SC.1 Amplified) on the table on 8 March 1985, setting the stage for a more focused negotiation, albeit one that was still likely to include disparate elements of the three basic positions. Despite some genuine evidence of progress, there still were very significant differences over verification, with the Warsaw Treaty states demonstrating a great reluctance to consider any meaningful verification provisions.

The most important development in 1985 was the creation of a workable framework that would permit the drafting of an agreement. In the autumn of 1985, building on the existing Stockholm negotiating structure that employed two working groups, the U.S. ambassador to the negotiations, James Goodby, developed a drafting arrangement that was acceptable to the various participants. After lengthy consultations in Washington, with NATO allies, and especially with his Soviet counterpart, Oleg Grinevski, Goodby fashioned a compromise that would have the two existing Stockholm working groups deal informally with various discrete components of the future agreement. Depending upon the specific day of the week, one working group would deal with nonuse of force; information exchange, verification, and communication; or constraining measures and annual forecasts. The second working group would deal with either the notification or observation measure, again depending upon the specific day. In this manner, the process of informally drafting the Stockholm Document began within the existing formal structure of the negotiations.

Events in 1985 came to a close with the submission of the neutral and nonaligned states' second major package, SC.7, on 15 November. The package of proposed measures was comprehensive and attempted to bridge some of the differences separating the Soviet Union and NATO.

The mutually agreed need to complete the Stockholm Document by September 1986 (just prior to the CSCE's Vienna Follow-Up Meeting) ought to have created more movement than occurred during the first half of 1986, but there was only desultory progress toward agreement on notification thresholds and observer measures. What was needed was something to energize the negotiations. This came

in the form of General Secretary Gorbachev's 18 April 1986 suggestion that comprehensive European conventional arms reduction talks be made a top priority. Elaborated in the so-called Budapest Appeal of 11 June, this proposal suggested that the MBFR reduction talks be expanded or replaced by talks including all of the CSCE states. This proposal quickly recast the security situation in Europe, effectively dooming the generally unproductive MBFR and putting the CSCE's Stockholm CSBM negotiations in a clearer, more focused context. NATO followed up on Gorbachev's proposal, signalling an interest in establishing a new negotiation on conventional force reductions—what would become the Conventional Forces in Europe (CFE) negotiations.

During the summer of 1986, the Soviet Union revised its position on notification thresholds (lowering them to 18,000 personnel), suggested a more flexible form of constraint that would permit large exercises once every three years, dropped the demand for the inclusion of independent air activities, and agreed to the principle of mandatory inspections, the last being a genuine breakthrough despite some uncertainty about the actual USSR position. NATO and the NNs also proposed more flexible solutions to the notification threshold and constraint measure problems, although agreement remained elusive.

When the final session of the negotiations began in August 1986, a number of difficult issues remained to be settled. The nature of the Soviet approach to inspection, for instance, was still unclear but appeared unacceptably restrictive. Also, there was still no agreement on limiting large exercises, nor was there any agreement on how to define notifiable activities. The threshold level that, once exceeded, would trigger notification also remained unsettled. The lack of agreement on what counted as a notifiable activity was critical because several other measures depended on this definition for their drafting.

Early in this last negotiating round, agreement was finally reached on a definition for notifiable activities. Although not as satisfactory in Western eyes as the original NATO "out-of-garrison" concept that captured any division-level activity outside of regular barracks areas, the compromise was still effective. It focused on division-level "concentrations" of forces as well as transfers and exercises. Parachute and amphibious activities were included, as well, but with lower numerical thresholds because of their more threatening nature. By the end of August, there was also agreement on how to constrain large exercises. Short-warning alert activities would escape this constraining provision.

As the negotiations approached their mid-September deadline, there was still no agreement on the specifics of on-site inspection nor on the exact threshold figures to use in the notification measure. NATO finally and reluctantly accepted the Soviet approach to aerial inspection (the inspected state was to supply the aircraft and pilot), seeing no prospect for a better compromise. At virtually the last minute, the negotiators finally agreed on notification thresholds (basically, activities involving 13,000 personnel or 300 tanks—levels roughly equivalent to a division) and inspection limits (each participating state was obliged to accept three inspections a year). The Document of the Stockholm Conference on Confidence- and Security-Building Measures and Disarmament in Europe was formally completed on 19 September 1986, although the negotiators actually worked until the morning of 22 September to complete the text.

Final Document   The Stockholm Document (sc.9) includes a declaration on "Refraining from the Threat or Use of Force"; "Prior Notification," entailing forty-two days' advance notification of and information about military activities involving any land force division-equivalent (13,000 troops or 300 tanks); 200 fixed-wing combat aircraft sorties (individual flights) if associated with a notifiable land force exercise; 3,000 troops in a parachute drop or amphibious landing; or transfers of a division-equivalent of land forces into the mandate region or the concentration of at least a division-equivalent of land forces within the region; "Observation," with two observers per state to be invited to any exercise or transfer involving 17,000 land force personnel or 5,000 troops if the activity is a parachute drop or amphibious landing exercise; an "Annual Calendar," with specified information about all of a state's notifiable activities to be communicated in a standard format at least one year in advance; a "Constraining Provision," where all notifiable activities involving 40,000 or more land force troops must be forecast two years in advance (none involving 75,000 or more are permitted without a two-year calendar forecast, and none involving between 40,000 and 75,000 are permitted without a one-year calendar forecast); and the "Inspection" measure that calls for on-site inspection (aerial and/ or ground) within thirty-six hours of a request, us-

ing four inspectors, and obliges no state to accept more than three inspections per year.

The true impact of the Stockholm Document is difficult to evaluate. Even viewed in narrow terms, it has played a constructive role in helping to reduce suspicion and improve confidence in Europe. Its specific CSBMS, generally speaking, have operated as intended, yielding a synergistic product of satisfying and comprehensive quality. The record of compliance has been excellent. The acceptance of on-site inspection by the Soviet Union represented a key development in arms control history, a genuine turning point.

On a broader level, there can be little doubt that the Stockholm Document's negotiation carried the CSCE states (and especially the superpowers) through a difficult political period in East-West relations. With its completion and the renewed opportunities for genuine force reduction in Europe entailed in Mikhail Gorbachev's Budapest proposals of June 1986, a whole new era of constructive conventional arms control began. Perhaps even more important, the development of the Stockholm Document and the unfolding of the larger, informal, supporting CSCE security process coincided with—and almost certainly facilitated—a significant, positive shift in perceptions and attitudes about the nature of threats posed by various European states. This is the true essence of the confidence-building process. The Stockholm Document's negotiation stands as a good example of this complex political, military, social, and psychological process. The difficulty of identifying what exactly changed—and how— underlines the fuzziness of confidence-building thinking.

However, the process did not end with the Stockholm Document. Building on the Gorbachev proposals, two new negotiations were developed in Vienna after lengthy mandate discussions. One, the Conventional Forces in Europe (CFE) negotiation, was to address force reduction by the NATO and Warsaw Treaty Organization states. The other was to extend and expand the Stockholm Document's CSBMS in the larger forum of thirty-five CSCE states.

THE VIENNA CSBM NEGOTIATIONS

It took over two years to develop the mandates, or guidelines, for the CFE and the parallel Vienna CSBM negotiations. The process began with the start of the Vienna CSCE Follow-Up Meeting (FUM) on 4 November 1986. The "Group 23" talks (so-named because the NATO and WTO states at the time numbered twenty-three) pursued a CFE mandate while the CSBM mandate was negotiated as part of the larger effort to develop a concluding document for the Vienna CSCE FUM. Many details of the two mandates were relatively clear by the end of the first year, but it took an additional year to resolve their final details. The Vienna Concluding Document authorizing the new round of CSBM negotiations was finally approved in plenary on 15 January 1989. The CFE mandate was completed the preceding day.

The Vienna CFE and CSBM negotiations themselves were concluded successfully in less than two years. Of the two, the CSBM talks proved less difficult, but their progress was frequently delayed because of the requirement that the two negotiating processes yield agreements at the same time. Given the complexities associated with the CFE talks and the general tendency to regard the CFE as being more important, it is not surprising that the Vienna CSBM negotiations languished from time to time.

The Vienna CSBM negotiations began on 6 March 1989, and the basic positions of the two alliances were presented formally on 9 March. The NATO proposal contained twelve basic elements including several dealing with the exchange of information. It also included a measure to verify the accuracy of supplied information and measures to improve opportunities for observers and inspectors. In addition, a new threshold for observations (13,000 personnel) was proposed. One of the more important proposals suggested lowering the Stockholm Document's threshold for long-term notification of large-scale activities to 50,000 personnel. Finally, an improved communication system was suggested.

In contrast, the initial Warsaw Treaty Organization package proposed establishing a 40,000 personnel ceiling for all activities (with an additional, secondary limit of only two activities per year per state involving between 25,000 and 40,000 personnel). The WTO package also included a new notification limit of 150 combat aircraft or 500 sorties as well as a permissible ceiling of 600 aircraft or 1,800 sorties for any exercise. In addition, there was a complex notification measure proposed that tried to capture, among other things, any naval activity involving twenty or more small naval combatants (1,500 tons displacement) or five or more large combatants (5,000 tons displacement or carrying aircraft). The WTO package also proposed a limit of fifty naval combatants for any activity and sought to limit exercises in areas of "intensive" maritime activity.

The WTO package also sought to extend the existing Stockholm Document measures and proposed developing a form of reduced-offensive armament zone in Central Europe, a vaguely worded variation on the nonoffensive defense theme. Finally, the WTO package spoke of military information exchanges, continued doctrine seminars, enhanced monitoring, and the development of a consultative commission and risk reduction center. Thus, on many issues there was substantial accord from the beginning.

The initial NATO and WTO positions were refined over the following year. For instance, NATO put an "amplified" version of its original package of proposals on the table on 9 June 1989. This amplification contained, among other things, several proposals dealing with information exchange including the possible creation of a military data bank.

Following up on their 9 March introductory package of proposed CSBMs on 5 July 1989, the WTO states put four major papers on the table, including one dealing with information exchange and two others calling for the notification of air activities and the notification of "sea and amphibious activities." Several more WTO working papers were circulated between July 1989 and the summer of 1990, including ones further exploring air, sea, and amphibious activities. However, due to the firm and unequivocal resistance of NATO (and particularly the United States), the Soviet Union was obliged to abandon its efforts to include maritime measures in the coalescing Vienna agreement.

NATO concern was that any maritime arms control measure would—sooner or later—lead to limits on NATO's ability to reinforce itself across the Atlantic Ocean. Sea transport has always been key to the reinforcement of NATO with North America men and matériel. The United States has an additional, more basic aversion to any measures that could constrain its freedom of movement on the high seas. It must be remembered that the Soviet Union and its successor states are great land powers while the United States is essentially a great maritime power.

The neutral and nonaligned states introduced a package of measures on 12 July 1989 that constituted a relatively narrow expansion of the original Stockholm Document. It included lowered notification ceilings and introduced broader categories of amphibious and airborne forces.

Suggesting the eventual shape of the Vienna CSBM Document, the negotiators established two main working groups on 5 May 1989. One group was assigned the responsibility of drafting information, verification, communication, and consultation measures. The second group was to deal with notification, observation, annual calendars, and limitation measures. The main new features represented in this division of responsibilities were communication and consultation, areas where the Vienna agreement was thought likely to cover new ground.

The CSCE states agreed during the CSBM negotiations in 1989 to conduct a "Seminar on Military Doctrine." The idea was to explore issues of military doctrine and shifts toward greater "defensiveness." This informal "seminar" ran from 16 January to 5 February 1990 at the Hofburg Palace in Vienna and involved top military officials from each CSCE state. It was generally considered to be successful, although most Western and some NN states remained skeptical about Soviet doctrinal revisions. However, as an educational exercise with significant opportunities for senior military officials to interact informally with each other, the seminar was judged most worthwhile. A similar military doctrine seminar was held the following year in Vienna, 8–18 October 1991. Additional seminars in the future are likely but they will probably focus on a specific subject and involve lower-ranking working groups.

After a period of considerable internal debate, on 18 May 1990 NATO put a major package of revisions and new measures on the table. Although it would not become clear for several months, one of the critical considerations in this internal debate was the degree to which the CSCE should be permitted to become formally institutionalized. Until this time in early 1990, NATO had resisted any effort to create formal CSCE bodies and institutions. The NATO package included a proposal to examine the development of a new communication system for use by the thirty-five CSCE states as well as the creation of a "mechanism for the discussion of unusual activities of a military nature." It also proposed "visits to combat air bases to observe routine activities." Also proposed was the exchange of information detailing military infrastructure upgrading.

Expanding on the 18 May 1990 proposals, NATO's 6 July 1990 "London Declaration on a Transformed North Atlantic Alliance" proposed that the "... CSCE in Paris decide how the CSCE could be institutionalized to provide a forum for wider political dialogue in a more united Europe." Among the proposals was "a CSCE Center for the Prevention of Conflict that would serve as a forum for exchanges of military information, discussion of unusual military activities, and the conciliation of disputes involving CSCE member states." This body was in fact created in the Charter of Paris for a New Europe, signed 21 November 1990.

By early summer of 1990, it was becoming clear that a credible if modest new CSBM agreement could be negotiated in time for the Paris Summit scheduled for November. It was also increasingly clear that such an agreement would be based on the Stockholm Document and would incorporate several of NATO's recently proposed information and conflict management measures. Although some participants were skeptical and many problems remained to be solved, hard work through the summer and early autumn produced substantial progress. Even the Soviet Union's insistence on including naval activities in some measures—rejected again by NATO—failed to deflect progress. A relatively comprehensive agreement—the Vienna Document 1990—was completed by 17 November 1990.

Not surprisingly, the 1990 Vienna CSBM Document resembled the Stockholm Document in many ways. It retained a reference to the declaration on refraining from the threat or use of force and included very similar prior notification, observation, and calendar measures. The constraining provisions' terms were simplified in the Vienna Document 1990 with the double ceiling replaced by a single threshold figure of 40,000 troops. Thus, states were expected not to conduct large military activities unless they had been announced at least two years in advance. This measure also noted the expectation that the number of alert activities should be kept to a minimum. The Stockholm Document's verification measure was replaced by a more complex measure in the Vienna Document. The replacement measure, entitled "Compliance and Verification" deals with two types of verification activity. The first, inspection, is very similar to the previous agreement. The second, evaluation, however, is new and is tied closely to the information measure, which is also new. The evaluation part of the compliance and verification measure was intended to permit an evaluation of the accuracy of officially supplied military information. It worked on the basis of a quota system for each state that obliged one mandatory evaluation visit each year per sixty reporting units (a unit being a brigade/regiment or its equivalent) deployed by that state. However, no state was obliged to accept more than fifteen visits per year. As was the case with many of the measures in these two CSBM documents, there were numerous lesser qualifications and exceptions dealing with special cases, small states, limits on how many visits one was obliged to accept from the same country, and so on.

Directly associated with the evaluation portion of the compliance and verification measure, the information measure was a key addition. It required all participating states to submit a detailed annual accounting of their military forces. This report was to detail the military organization, manpower, and major weapon and equipment systems of each state. This information was to include command organization down to and including the level of brigade/regiment; designation and subordination of each unit; its peacetime location; its authorized personnel strength; and the number and type of major combat systems. In addition, this measure required the submission of annual data detailing plans to deploy major weapon and equipment systems in the region. Further, the participating states were obliged to exchange information each year itemizing defense expenditures. This amounted to a significant collection of data to be exchanged annually.

The remaining new measures include "Risk Reduction," which required consultation and cooperation in the event of unusual military activities and hazardous incidents of a military nature; "Contacts," a modest measure requiring participating states to invite visitors to an air base at least once every five years; "Communications," which established a direct communications network linking CSCE capitals; and an "Annual Implementation Assessment."

Compared to previous CSBM agreements, the comprehensiveness of the Vienna Document's information, calendar, and notification CSBMS was striking. Although it allowed for the further reduction of thresholds (which probably was not necessary) and the expansion of aircraft coverage to include independent air activities in the future, the information and notification dimension of the Vienna CSBMS was already advanced. The harmonization of information requirements was one of the few obvious remaining areas in this basic category requiring attention (particularly if the information was to be consistent with that contained in the CFE Treaty). The area of greatest weakness in the Vienna

CSBM agreement was "constraints." Other than encouraging smaller exercises and requiring two years of advance notification, there were few true constraints built into the agreement, particularly as they related to force activation on short notice. The observation and inspection measures were not as well developed as they might have been, but they establish respectable, if modest, standards.

VIENNA DOCUMENT 1992

Upon completion of the Vienna Document 1990, work began almost immediately on an extension of the existing agreement. The negotiation was intended to add several new CBMS to the increasingly elaborate Stockholm-Vienna CSBM structure before the CSCE Helsinki Follow-Up Meeting of March 1992 and its reexamination of European security processes. This Vienna CSBM negotiation was conducted, along with its CFE counterpart, in an atmosphere of increasing cooperation but also confusion and uncertainty, due to the rapid dissolution of the Cold War European security structure, which made the negotiation of new agreements much more complicated.

For instance, the unification of Germany, effective on 3 October 1990, altered NATO's defense position fundamentally, particularly when combined with major unilateral Soviet force withdrawals and the reductions of the CFE Treaty. Further altering the security landscape, the Warsaw Treaty Organization passed into history on 31 March 1991. During the 1990–1991 Vienna CSBM negotiations, the Soviet Union also underwent a series of dramatic transformations, including the abortive 19 August 1991 coup. Ultimately the former Soviet Union developed into Russia and eleven new successor states, which all became members of the CSCE. This, of course, was in addition to four other CSCE additions: Albania and the three new Baltic states (Lithuania, Estonia, and Latvia). Equally profound in terms of complicating the negotiations was the disintegration of Yugoslavia and the civil war that engulfed the emergent Croatia during 1991.

The negotiating process in Vienna was able to move forward, however, despite these transformations and disruptions. Indeed, once a disagreement was resolved in the parallel CFE negotiations about the proper way to count several Soviet divisions (the "resubordination dispute"), progress was relatively rapid. However, it was not until the beginning of the thirteenth round of CSBM negotiations in early November 1991 that real headway was made. The British, acting for the NATO states, presented two CSBM proposals on 21 November 1991. The first measure proposed a reduction in the existing Vienna Document 1990 notification and observation thresholds while the second outlined a new CSBM, one that required the prior notification of activities upgrading low-strength military formations and combat units. The latter proposal sought to address a loophole in the existing Vienna Document that left low-strength formations and units—in principle, the basis for a significant cumulative mobilization of forces—unreported and unconstrained. Shortly thereafter, on 27 November 1991, the Soviet Union introduced a constraint measure that limited military activities to 40,000 personnel or 800 tanks or 1,500 armored combat vehicles. It also proposed limits for exercises: six per year, but only two per year if they exceeded 25,000 personnel or 400 tanks.

In addition to the traditional approach with blocs developing and then presenting packages of proposed CSBMS, amorphous groups of NATO, NN, and former Warsaw Treaty states also developed individual measures during the 1991 negotiations. For instance, on 11 December 1991, the United Kingdom and Bulgaria proposed a CSBM that would permit invited aerial observation in situations of unusual military activity. Also important was a Polish information measure proposal that drew on the efforts of many CSCE participants over the course of several months.

With the March 1992 Helsinki Follow-Up Meeting looming and the associated need to develop ideas for the post-Helsinki generation of conventional arms control negotiations becoming more pressing, there was less and less time and interest available to devote to the Vienna CSBM negotiations. However, with a major push, the Vienna negotiators were able to prepare the revised text by 25 February 1992. Despite the accelerated schedule, the agreement proved to be a respectable elaboration of the two earlier CSBM documents. Perhaps more important, it opened the door on several dimensions of European military activity that can support further confidence-building efforts. In particular, the additions to the existing Vienna Document 1990 "information" and "contacts" measures may facilitate future efforts to control the destabilizing introduction of some new military technologies and capabilities.

The Vienna Document 1992 built directly on the 1990 version of the CSBM document. The first main measure, the annual exchange of military information, included a new reporting requirement for both low-strength and nonactive units (such as regiments) and formations (such as divisions) expected to receive significant extra personnel for a period of more than 21 days. This additional requirement obliged states to supply the same sort of information about major weapon systems and personnel that they did for normal-strength combat units and formations. A second major addition to the information measure was a new requirement to report "data relating to major weapon and equipment systems." This sub-measure obliged all participating states to supply additional information (including accurate photographs) about a wide range of major weapon systems and equipment including tanks, armored combat vehicles, armored infantry fighting vehicles, anti-tank guided missile launcher vehicles, armored vehicle launched bridges, combat aircraft, and helicopters. The required information ranged from whether or not a tank possessed night vision equipment, additional armor, or a snorkel for crossing water to more basic items such as gun calibre, national nomenclature, and unladen weight.

The "risk reduction" section of the Vienna Document 1990 acquired a new component in the 1992 CSBM agreement. A provision entitled "voluntary hosting of visits to dispel concerns about military activities" expanded the risk reduction function significantly, formalizing a voluntary approach to the clarification of ambiguous or threatening military activities. This sub-measure created a mechanism for the voluntary invitation of ground or air observations to dispel concerns. The "contacts" portion of the Vienna Document was likewise strengthened by the addition of a new provision requiring the "demonstration of new types of major weapon and equipment systems." This CSBM obliges CSCE states to provide an informative demonstration of any major system such as a tank, rocket launcher, or helicopter when it is first introduced into the European portion of the CSCE region, whether the system is developed indigenously or purchased abroad. Combined with the expanded information measure, the Vienna Document 1992 established a firm groundwork for containing the introduction of arms-race instabilities in Europe.

The Vienna Document 1992 lowered several thresholds for notification and observation. In the case of the notification of military activities, the personnel threshold was dropped from 13,000 to 9,000 and the tank threshold from 300 to 250. The threshold for triggering an invitation to observe an activity was dropped from 17,000 to 13,000 personnel. For amphibious and parachute exercises, the observation threshold fell to 3,500 from 5,000. The existing 1990 "constraining" measure was recast to impose additional limits on larger notifiable military activities. For instance, no state is allowed to conduct more than one activity involving more than 40,000 troops more than once every two years. Further, CSCE states are limited to six smaller activities a year, only three of which can involve between 25,000 and 40,000 troops. As before, activities involving more than 40,000 troops must be announced formally more than two years in advance. Finally, the "compliance and verification" measure was amended to clarify responsibilities and to permit multilateral inspection teams.

SUMMARY OF THE CSCE CONFIDENCE-BUILDING REGIME

The Vienna Document 1992 revisions addressed several existing problems, particularly with low-strength and inactive formations. They further refined the Vienna Document 1990's information requirements, notification thresholds, and constraints on large exercises. Constraining short-warning activities, however, remained a problem due to the role played by rapid mobilization in some CSCE states' defense plans.

Thus, by 1992, the CSCE security environment was structured by a comprehensive collection of CSBMs. The Stockholm Document of 1986 provided the basic framework with its original CSBMs, while the two Vienna Documents (1990 and 1992) added new CSBMs or refined existing ones. Collectively, the CSCE confidence-building regime encompasses the following measures:

- *Annual exchange of military information* requires the submission of information detailing land force organization, unit location, manpower, and major weapon and equipment systems organic to formations. It includes nonactive and low-strength formations and combat units. Additional requirements include information on military budgets and new weapon-system deployments;

- *Risk reduction,* employing the Conflict Prevention Centre (a CSCE forum in Vienna with a small technical staff), entails consultation regarding unusual military activities, cooperation regarding hazardous incidents, and voluntary hosting of visits to dispel concerns about military activities;

- *Contacts* enhance openness and transparency through invitations to visit air bases, expanded military exchanges, and the demonstration of new types of major weapon and equipment systems;

- *Prior notification of certain military activities* requires notice 42 days in advance of exercises, concentrations, and movements of at least 9,000 troops or 250 battle tanks (or 3,000 troops if the activity is an amphibious or parachute assault exercise);

- *Observation of certain military activities* must be invited for land force exercise activities within the region, and for transfers from outside the region, of at least 13,000 troops or 300 tanks or 3,500 amphibious or parachute assault troops;

- *Annual calendar* requires extensive information about notifiable military activities scheduled for the following year;

- *Constraining provisions* limits notifiable major activities of more than 40,000 troops or 900 tanks to one per two years and smaller exercises (13,000 to 40,000 troops or 300 to 900 tanks) to six per year. Of these six activities per year, only three may be over 25,000 troops or 400 tanks;

- *Compliance and verification* provides for short-warning inspections of troubling sites and activities (limit of three received inspections per year for each state) as well as evaluation visits to confirm the information measure's data (maximum of fifteen received visits per year for each state);

- *Communications* establishes an efficient and direct communications network for CSCE use in distributing notifications, clarifications, and requests; and

- *Annual implementation assessment* mandates an annual assessment of compliance.

Collectively, this package of CSBMs, as embodied in the Vienna Document 1992, covers a wide range of potential security concerns and does so in a comprehensive and synergistic fashion. It also provides the basis for further elaboration and extension in succeeding confidence-building negotiations.

CONCLUSION

The confidence-building concept has become increasingly concrete as the security negotiations of the CSCE have provided four successive agreements—the Helsinki Final Act of 1975, the Stockholm Document of 1986, the Vienna Document 1990, and the Vienna Document 1992. Although other negotiating fora have also provided examples of confidence building, the Conference on Security and Cooperation in Europe remains the preeminent source of practical insight. Each new agreement has provided the basis for the next agreement's elaboration and invention. This process will surely continue within the context of the post-Helsinki security environment, focusing increasingly on destabilizing sub-regional military relationships and on containing the destabilizing effects of new military technology.

Despite this positive and very constructive future, it is surprising how little we understand of the underlying processes that make confidence building "work." Although we may feel confident that the Helsinki and Stockholm negotiations—and their agreements—contributed to the transformation of East-West security relations, we still do not know how and to what extent this is true. Most analysts, understandably, have concentrated on developing new, more effective CBMS. Few have probed the underlying process of transformation. The further development of the confidence-building approach will almost certainly depend upon more attention being paid to both concrete measures and the underlying processes that those measures animate.

BIBLIOGRAPHY

The literature on confidence building is difficult to divide along a conceptual/regional application dimension. Although a chapter, article, or book may focus on some conceptual issues, it will almost always also include a discussion of practical application issues for one or more regions such as Europe or Northeast Asia. Thus, clear categories are difficult to distinguish.

Conceptual Treatments   A largely conceptual exploration of confidence building can be found in JAMES MACINTOSH, *Confidence (and Security) Building Measures and the Arms Control Process: A Ca-*

nadian Perspective, (Ottawa, 1985, rev. 1992). One of the earliest useful discussions of confidence building is JOHAN JORGEN HOLST and KAREN ALETTE MELANDER, "European Security- and Confidence-Building Measures," *Survival* 19 (July–August 1977): 146–154. See also HOLST, "Confidence-Building Measures: A Conceptual Framework," *Survival* 25 (Jan.–Feb. 1983): 2–15. An excellent collection of articles will be found in JONATHAN ALFORD, ed., *The Future of Arms Control: Part III, Confidence-Building Measures* (London, 1979). Other works combining conceptual discussions and assessments of European CBM application include: KARL E. BIRNBAUM, ed., *Confidence-Building in East-West Relations,* (Laxenburg, 1983); *Comprehensive Study of the Group of Government Experts on Confidence-Building Measures,* U.N. Document A/36/474 (New York, 1981); and F. STEPHEN LARRABEE and DIETRICH STOBBE, eds., *Confidence-Building Measures in Europe,* (New York, 1983). More recent works include Y. BEN-HORIN, R. DARILEK, M. JAS, M. LAWRENCE, A. PLATT, *Building Confidence and Security in Europe: The Potential Role of Confidence- and Security-Building Measures,* RAND/R-3431-USDP (1986); CARL C. KREHBIEL, *Confidence- and Security-Building Measures in Europe: The Stockholm Conference* (New York, 1989); ROLF BERG and ADAM-DANIEL ROTFELD, *Building Security in Europe—Confidence-Building Measures and the CSCE,* (New York, 1986); and R. B. BYERS, F. STEPHEN LARRABEE, ALLEN LYNCH, eds., *Confidence-Building Measures and International Security,* (New York, 1987).

Negotiations   Works examining the CSCE negotiating experience begin with the excellent history by JOHN BORAWSKI, *From the Atlantic to the Urals—Negotiating Arms Control at the Stockholm Conference* (Washington, D.C., 1988). See also KARL E. BIRNBAUM and BO HULDT, eds., *From Stockholm to Vienna: Building Confidence and Security in Europe,* (Stockholm, 1987); JOHN BORAWSKI, STAN WEEKS and CHARLOTTE E. THOMPSON, "The Stockholm Agreement of September 1986," *Orbis* 30 (Winter 1987): 643–662; RICHARD DARILEK, "Building Confidence and Security in Europe: The Road To and From Stockholm," *Washington Quarterly* 8 (Winter 1985): 131–140; JONATHAN DEAN, *Meeting Gorbachev's Challenge: How to Build Down the NATO -Warsaw Pact Confrontation* (New York, 1989); JONATHAN DEAN, *Watershed in Europe: Dismantling the East-West Military Confrontation*

(Lexington, Mass., 1987); JAMES E. GOODBY, "The Stockholm Conference: Negotiating a Cooperative Security System for Europe," in the excellent book by ALEXANDER L. GEORGE, PHILIP J. FARLEY, and ALEXANDER DALLIN, eds., *U.S.-Soviet Security Cooperation: Achievements, Failures, Lessons* (New York, 1988); MARILEE FAWN LAWRENCE, *A Game Worth the Candle: The Confidence- and Security-Building Process in Europe—An Analysis of U.S. and Soviet Negotiating Strategies* RAND P-7264-RGS (1986); and JOHN J. MARESCA, *To Helsinki: The Conference on Security and Cooperation in Europe, 1973–1975* (Durham, N.C., 1985; new ed. 1987).

Good annual overviews of the CSCE-CSBM negotiations are to be found in Stockholm International Peace Research Institute, *SIPRI Yearbook: World Armaments and Disarmament* (annual). The best on-going source of information about CSCE-CSBM negotiations (and all other arms control negotiations and initiatives) is INSTITUTE FOR DEFENSE AND DISARMAMENT STUDIES, *The Arms Control Reporter* (Brookline, Mass., annual with monthly updates); a related monthly source of great detail is the *ViennaFax,* also from the institute.

The UNITED NATIONS DEPARTMENT FOR DISARMAMENT AFFAIRS has produced a number of good confidence-building studies looking at European as well as Asian and Maritime applications; for instance, see "Confidence and Security-Building Measures: From Europe to Other Regions," *Disarmament,* Topical Papers 7 (New York, 1991); "Confidence and Security-Building Measures in Asia," *Disarmament* (1990); and "Naval Confidence-Building Measures," *Disarmament,* Topical Papers 4 (New York, 1990). *Disarmament: A Periodic Review by the United Nations* provides frequent material on confidence building in Europe and other regions. The UNITED NATIONS INSTITUTE FOR DISARMAMENT RESEARCH (Geneva) also produces research publications that deal with confidence building; for instance, see IGOR SCHERBAK, "Confidence-Building Measures and International Security—The Political and Military Aspects: a Soviet Approach," *UNIDIR/91/36* (New York, 1991).

The Environmental Modification Convention

1977 to the Present

○

ARTHUR H. WESTING

See also The Antarctic State Treaty: 1959 to the Present; The Law of War; *and* The Seabed Treaty: 1959 to the Present. *The* Environmental Modification Convention *is excerpted in Volume III.*

The Convention on the Prohibition of Military or Any Other Hostile Use of Environmental Modification Techniques (the Enmod Convention) was signed at Geneva on 18 May 1977. The United Nations secretary-general, the depositary thereof, accepted the requisite twenty ratifications, and the convention entered into force on 5 October 1978. Although negotiated under the auspices of what is now the Conference on Disarmament (Geneva) and nurtured by the United Nations General Assembly, by mid-1992 the Enmod Convention had acquired only fifty-five sovereign parties, a modest 29 percent of the potential total. Moreover, included among the parties are only three of the five permanent members of the United Nations Security Council—the United Kingdom, the United States, and the Russian Federation.

Analyzed here is the prohibition to which a state agrees by becoming a party to the Enmod Convention, and how this prohibition complements other environmental components of the law of war. Setting the stage for such an analysis is an examination of the panoply of environmental considerations in relation to war.

WAR AND THE ENVIRONMENT

The pursuit of war is almost unavoidably damaging to the environment, particularly so within the the-ater of operations. Three levels of wartime environmental damage can be readily distinguished: (*a*) unintentional damage; (*b*) intentional damage; and (*c*) intentionally amplified damage.

Unintentional Environmental Damage The often profligate employment of high-explosive munitions against enemy personnel and matériel and the major reliance by ground forces on heavy off-road vehicles can be especially disruptive of local habitats and the creatures that depend upon them. The construction of fortifications, base camps, and lines of communication add to the environmental disruption. Battle-related activities can also lead to considerable amounts of local air and water pollution. In addition, food, feed, and timber are often heavily exploited by armed forces in time of war, both within the theater of operations and beyond. Environmental impacts of these sorts are generally unintentional (that is, ancillary, incidental, or collateral) aspects of war. As common and as serious as these impacts might be, actions leading to them do not fall within the domain of the Enmod Convention.

Intentional Environmental Damage The pursuit of war often involves the intentional destruction of field or forest as a specific means of denying to the enemy the benefits of such components of

947

the environment. These benefits include access to water, food, feed, and construction materials, as well as access to cover or sanctuary. More subtle denial (or barrier) operations are also frequently accomplished by the emplacement of mines. Crop destruction and forest decimation operations can have a substantial environmental impact, however, such actions do not necessarily fall within the domain of the Enmod Convention.

Intentionally Amplified Environmental Damage

Under certain conditions it is possible to manipulate one component or another of the environment for hostile military purposes in a way that is intended to result in the release of dangerous pent-up forces. This third level of environmental impact—often referred to as environmental warfare—has the potential to fall within the domain of the Enmod Convention.

Environmental warfare might well be defined as the manipulation of the environment for hostile military purposes, in which the hostile manipulation involves a relatively modest expenditure of triggering energy leading to the release of a substantially greater amount of directed destructive energy. Hostile manipulations of the environment could, at least in principle, involve any of the following five domains: (a) the biota (flora and fauna); (b) the land (including fresh waters); (c) the ocean; (d) the atmosphere; and (e) celestial bodies and space. Each of these five environmental domains is discussed in turn below.

The Biota (Flora and Fauna)

There exist perhaps 15 million square kilometers (about 6 million square miles) of cropland, both annual and perennial. The land supports some 40 million square kilometers (16 million square miles) of tree-based (forest) ecosystems, some 30 million square kilometers (12 million square miles) of grass-based (prairie) ecosystems, and almost 10 million square kilometers (4 million square miles) of lichen-based (tundra) ecosystems; and the ocean supports huge expanses of alga-based (marine) ecosystems. These diverse terrestrial and oceanic ecosystems are all exploited by humans, who could not survive without the continued harvesting of trees, livestock, fish, and other renewable natural resources. These ecosystems additionally provide a series of more subtle and indirect—though equally crucial—services that keep the planet habitable.

It is more or less readily possible to alter the biotic component of the environment for hostile purposes in a number of ways, among them: (a) by applying chemical poisons (herbicides); (b) by introducing exotic living organisms, including microorganisms; (c) by incendiary means; and (d) by mechanical means.

As one prime example of environmental warfare involving the biota, forests were devastated by the United States during the Vietnam conflict (the Second Indochina War of 1961–1975) by far-reaching aerial (and ground) application of herbicides, by massive bombing, by the extensive use of large tractors, and—to a lesser extent—by fire. Killing the trees (the autotrophic component) of a forest ecosystem leads to substantial damage to that system's wildlife (the heterotrophic component) and also to its nutrient budget, the latter via soil erosion and nutrient dumping (the loss of nutrients in solution). Substantial recovery from such unbalancing of the system must be measured in decades. Prairie and tundra ecosystems are similarly exposed to hostile action. Tundra ecosystems are especially vulnerable to disruption and are also particularly slow to recover. Among other effects, destruction of the tundra vegetation could lead to disruption of the underlying permafrost, thereby perhaps converting the attacked region into a morass in summer.

Bacteriological warfare agents could do serious long-term damage to ecosystems if disruptive exotic (nonindigenous) microorganisms are employed and then become locally established. For example, if *Bacillus anthracis,* the causative agent of the deadly disease anthrax, were to be used for hostile purposes in a previously uninfected area, it might become a permanent addition to the local microbiota.

Marine ecosystems could readily be damaged if offshore oil wells, large tankers, or other offshore or near-shore oil facilities were attacked with a resulting release into the water of large amounts of oil, thereby inter alia precluding important aspects of human utilization of those ecosystems for many years. An example of such an assault on the environment was provided by the Persian Gulf War of 1991, in which Iraq (for no immediately apparent military gain) released huge amounts of oil into the Persian Gulf off the Kuwaiti coast, resulting in substantial severe damage of several years' duration to local marine flora and fauna. Similarly, the destruction of nuclear reactors (whether land-based or shipboard) would release radioactive contaminants that could prevent human utilization of marine resources in the region of attack for decades.

The Land (Including Fresh Waters)

Land (also referred to as the lithosphere) covers almost 150 million square kilometers of the earth's surface (that is, 60 million square miles, or 29 percent of the global surface). Of the total land area, almost 16 million square kilometers (6.4 million square miles; circa 11 percent) is continuously ice covered, much of this represented by Antarctica. Perhaps 18 million square kilometers (7.2 million square miles; circa 12 percent) is desert. On another 8 million square kilometers (3.2 million square miles; circa 5 percent) at least one stratum of the soil remains frozen the year round (a condition referred to as permafrost). And 2 million square kilometers or more (.8 million square miles; circa 1.5 percent) is accounted for by rugged mountainous terrain. Much of the remaining land, circa 105 million square kilometers (42 million square miles; circa 71 percent), is found largely in the Northern Hemisphere and supports virtually the entire global human population and its cultural artifacts.

Successful manipulation of the land for hostile purposes would depend for the most part upon the ability to recognize and take advantage of local instabilities or pent-up energies, whether natural or anthropogenic. Some mountainous landforms, for example, are at least at certain times prone to soil and rock avalanches (landslides), and some arctic or alpine sites are prone to snow avalanches; under the right conditions, either could be initiated with hostile intent. The hostile manipulation of permafrost was referred to in the section above on biota. In addition, a number of important rivers flow through more than one country. They can provide the opportunity for upstream nations to divert or foul the waters in order to deny their use to downstream nations, a major calamity in arid regions.

Many of the nations of the world are increasingly becoming more highly developed and heavily industrialized. Enormous damage to the human environment could be accomplished by attacks on nuclear or hydrological facilities, whether such attacks are intended or not. Therefore, the dangerous forces that have become ever more likely to be released over wide areas in a future war (whether overtly or via sabotage) now include radioactive gases or aerosols from nuclear facilities and impounded waters from hydrological facilities.

Turning to the radioactive threat, the human environment now contains about 195 civilian, nuclear power-plant clusters in thirty-one countries (altogether, approximately 482 separate plants, of which nearly 420 are currently in operation), plus a number of nuclear-fuel reprocessing plants and nuclear-waste storage sites. Nuclear facilities represent a relatively recent threat, since all of them have been constructed since World War II—and more than 80 percent of them since 1970.

The possibility exists that a destroyed nuclear facility will contaminate a large surrounding area with iodine-131, cesium-137, strontium-90, and other radioactive debris—an area that would be measurable in hundreds or thousands of square kilometers. The most heavily contaminated inner zone would become life threatening; an outer zone of lesser contamination would become health threatening; and a still greater zone beyond would become agriculturally unusable. A radioactively polluted area such as this would defy effective decontamination. Its degraded status would recover only slowly, over a period of many decades, as has been demonstrated by the Pacific test islands and other test sites. The Chernobyl accident of April 1986 suggests very well the disruption to the human environment that could be expected from damage to or destruction of a nuclear facility.

Turning to the threat of flooding, the human environment now contains more than 777 dams, scattered throughout seventy countries, that are at least 15 meters (about 50 feet) high and impound over 500 million cubic meters (600 million cubic yards) of water; in fact, more than 522 of these (in sixty-three countries) each impound over 1,000 million cubic meters (1,200 million cubic yards). Most (more than 90 percent) of the huge hydrological facilities of concern here have been constructed since World War II—and more than 60 percent of them since 1970. It is obvious that a substantial proportion of those many hundreds of huge impoundments now scattered throughout the world would make eminently suitable military targets; and it is additionally obvious how devastating the downstream effects could be on the human environment.

Indeed, the breaching of dams for the purpose of releasing impounded waters has been spectacularly successful in past wars, including both World War II and the Korean War of 1950–1953. An example from World War II demonstrates well how tempting such targets can be. In the same operation in May 1943 the Allies destroyed two major dams in the Ruhr Valley of Germany: the Möhne and the Eder. The breaching of these two containment structures had released only on the order of 120 million cubic meters (144 million cubic yards) of water each, resulting in a vast amount of damage: (a) 125 factories were destroyed or badly damaged, 25 bridges were completely destroyed and 21 more were badly damaged, a number of power stations were destroyed, numerous coal mines were flooded, and various railroad lines were disrupted; (b) some 6,500 cattle and pigs were lost, and 3,000 square kilometers (1,200 square miles) of arable land were ruined; and (c) 1,300 German lives were lost as well as those of unnumbered slave laborers.

Finally, for the most devastating example of intentional military flooding, one must turn to the Second Sino-Japanese War of 1937–1945. In order to curtail the Japanese advance, the Chinese in June 1938 dynamited the Huayuankow dike of the Huang He (Yellow River) near Chengchow. This action resulted in the drowning of several thousand Japanese soldiers and stopped the Japanese advance into China along this front. In the process, however, the floodwaters also ravaged major portions of Henan, Anhui, and Jiangsu provinces. Several million square kilometers of farmland were inundated, with crops and topsoil destroyed. The river was not brought back under control until 1947. The flooding also inundated some eleven Chinese cities and more than four thousand villages. At least several hundred thousand Chinese (and possibly many more) drowned, and several million were left homeless. Indeed, this act of environmental warfare appears to have been the most devastating single act in all human history, in terms of numbers of lives claimed.

It becomes clear that the release of dangerous forces from nuclear or hydrological facilities—whether the intended or unintended result of hostile action—would now constitute one of the gravest threats to the human environment in any major war of the future.

The instigation of earthquakes or the awakening of quiescent volcanoes remains as yet beyond human reach.

The Ocean   The ocean comprises the bulk of the hydrosphere (the remainder found within "land" and "atmosphere"). The Ocean covers just

over 360 million square kilometers (144 million square miles) of the earth's surface (that is, 71 percent of the global surface). Of the 189 nations in the world in 1992, 150 border on the ocean (and of those 150 coastal nations, 46 are island nations).

A number of hostile manipulations of the ocean have been suggested as future possibilities—including those that might alter its acoustic or electromagnetic properties for purposes of disrupting underwater communication, remote sensing, navigation, and missile guidance—but these are not as yet within human capabilities. Tsunamis (seismic sea waves or tidal waves) occasionally cause enormous damage to coastal life and structures, but it has not been possible to generate them for hostile purposes. Diversion of the ocean currents also remains impossible. The hostile destruction of ships or other offshore (or near-shore) facilities containing dangerous forces (whether radioactive or otherwise poisonous) was referred to in the section above on biota.

The Atmosphere   The earth's atmosphere extends upward many hundreds of kilometers, but it becomes extraordinarily thin beyond approximately 200 kilometers (120 miles). It is divided into: (a) the lower atmosphere, which extends upward to about 55 kilometers (33 miles) and represents more than 99 percent of the total atmospheric mass; and (b) the upper atmosphere, which is found in the range of approximately 55–200+ kilometers up (33–120+ miles) and represents less than 1 percent of the total atmospheric mass.

The lower atmosphere consists of: (a) the troposphere (circa 0–12 kilometers up, or about 0–7.2 miles; circa 87 percent of the total atmospheric mass); and (b) the stratosphere (circa 12–55 kilometers up, or 7.2–33 miles). The stratosphere, in turn, can be divided into: (a) the lower stratosphere (circa 12–30 kilometers up, or 7.2–18 miles); and (b) the upper stratosphere (circa 30–55 kilometers up, or 18–33 miles). The troposphere is turbulent (windy) and contains clouds, whereas the stratosphere is essentially quiescent and cloudless. The lower stratosphere contains an ozone layer (circa 20–30 kilometers up, or 12–18 miles), which provides a partial barrier to solar ultraviolet radiation.

The upper atmosphere consists of: (a) the mesosphere (circa 55–80 kilometers up, or 33–48 miles); and (b) the ionosphere, or thermosphere (circa 80–200+ kilometers up, or 48–120+ miles).

The ionosphere is distinguished by its ionized (electrified) molecules, which serve to deflect certain radio waves downward, thereby making possible long-distance, amplitude-modulated (AM) radio communication.

As to the lower atmosphere, two sorts of hostile manipulations were pursued by the United States during the Vietnam War. First, various chemical substances were released into clouds over enemy territory in a massive attempt to increase rainfall so as to make enemy lines of communication impassable; however, this operation had very little, if any, success. Second, unspecified substances were introduced into the troposphere over enemy territory in order to render enemy radars inoperable, although the results of these efforts have never been made public. (Indeed, it is these atmospheric manipulations during the Vietnam War, together with the biotic manipulations alluded to earlier, that appear to have been the original impetus for drafting the Enmod Convention.) During the Persian Gulf War of 1991, Iraq set fire to many hundreds of Kuwaiti oil wells (as noted earlier, this was done for no immediately apparent military gain). Immense amounts of soot and poisonous fumes were discharged into the troposphere, with deleterious effects of several years' duration on the health of the local human population as well as on the local biota. (Damaged oil wells also produced numerous lakes of oil.) Whether local-weather patterns were influenced by these discharges remains unclear. Regarding further hostile possibilities for the lower atmosphere, it has been suggested that it may become possible to temporarily disrupt the ozone layer above enemy territory for the purpose of permitting injurious levels of ultraviolet radiation to reach the ground (perhaps by the controlled release of a bromine compound from orbiting satellites). Control over winds, for example the creation or redirection of hurricanes, remains as yet beyond human reach.

As to the upper atmosphere, it is conceivable that means could be devised in the future to manipulate the ionosphere for hostile purposes—specifically, to alter its electrical properties in such a way as to disrupt enemy communications.

Celestial Bodies and Space   "Celestial bodies" refers to the moon and other planetary satellites, the planets, the sun and other stars, asteroids, meteors, and the like. "Space" refers to all of the vast region beyond the earth's atmosphere (that is, to the region above the ionosphere) and thus, for practical purposes, begins about 200+ kilometers (120+ miles) above the earth's surface.

It appears not to be possible to manipulate the celestial bodies for hostile purposes, although the suggestion has been made that some day it might be within human grasp to redirect asteroids to strike enemy territory. It also appears not to be possible to manipulate outer space for hostile purposes.

THE ENMOD CONVENTION

The Enmod Convention prohibits its parties from engaging among themselves in the hostile use of environmental modification techniques that would have "widespread, long-lasting or severe effects as the means of . . . damage" (Article I.1). An environmental modification technique is for these purposes defined as "any technique for changing—through the deliberate manipulation of natural processes—the dynamics, composition or structure of the earth, including its biota, lithosphere, hydrosphere and atmosphere, or of outer space" (Article II).

Strengths of the Enmod Convention   The Enmod Convention has helped significantly to establish the recognized importance of incorporating environmental considerations into the progressive development of the law of war. Despite its several shortcomings, the value of the Enmod Convention is thus quite considerable. More generally, the Enmod Convention is important because it adds to the modest number of multilateral arms control and disarmament treaties currently in effect.

Weaknesses of the Enmod Convention   One weakness of the Enmod Convention is the absence of definitions of the operative criteria of "widespread, long-lasting or severe." It is true that a set of informal definitions was provided by the drafters in which it was suggested that *widespread* referred to an area of at least several hundred square kilometers and that *long-lasting* referred to a period of time measured in months (the word *severe*, however, was not similarly qualified).

A second, and far more important, weakness of the convention is the inclusion of the very notion of a threshold below which the prohibition does not apply (Article I.1). Even if satisfactory definitions of the threshold criteria could be established in principle, the problem would remain of establishing in practice whether they had been breached. Moreover, by establishing a threshold, the convention thereby actually condones military preparations for, and the very perpetration of, environmental modifications for hostile purposes. Despite considerable opposition during the drafting process, the threshold provision was included in the Enmod Convention at the insistence of the United States.

A third substantial weakness of the convention is that its prohibition refers to actions carried out with a "deliberate" intent to change natural processes for hostile purposes (Article II). Deliberate hostile intent would be difficult to establish in the absence of an admission by the perpetrator. Moreover, even such an environmentally devastating action as nuclear war would not readily fall within the purview of the convention because the environmental modifications might well be considered as being unintended collateral effects.

A fourth weakness of the Enmod Convention that has been pointed out by some critics is that the complaint procedure ultimately depends upon the U.N. Security Council, in which any of the five permanent members can exercise its power of veto over an attempted investigation or other action (Article V).

Recommendations for Amending the Enmod Convention

The first shortcoming—the lack of operative definitions—would be difficult to eliminate, but could be reduced by incorporating a set of definitions into the convention. The second shortcoming—that a breach requires the surpassing of a threshold—could readily be purged from the convention (this would, of course, also obviate the need for definitions). The third shortcoming—the required demonstration of hostile intent—could readily be replaced in the convention by the notion of reasonable expectation. The fourth shortcoming—ultimate dependence upon the U.N. Security Council as the arbiter of alleged breaches—could be ameliorated if the convention called upon the Security Council to consider relevant actions to be procedural rather than substantive (thereby eliminating the veto power).

It is clear from the records of the original negotiations, as well as from those of the subsequent review conference, that the Enmod Convention would become more attractive to the community of nations if these several weaknesses—especially the inclusion of a threshold—were rectified. Indeed,

from 1989 to mid-1992 the Enmod Convention gained only two new parties.

COMPLEMENTARY TREATIES

Of the various other multilateral treaties that serve to constrain one or more aspects of environmental war, three stand out with particular clarity: (*a*) the Geneva Protocol of 1925, which prohibits the use in war of chemical and bacteriological agents, with 126 or more sovereign parties as of mid-1992 (67 percent of the potential total), among them, all five permanent members of the U.N. Security Council; (*b*) Protocol I of 1977, additional to the Geneva Conventions of 1949 on the protection of victims of international armed conflicts, with 112 or more sovereign parties as of mid-1992 (59 percent of the potential total), among them, only two of the five permanent members of the U.N. Security Council—China and the Russian Federation; and (*c*) Protocol II of 1977, additional to the Geneva Conventions of 1949 on the protection of victims of noninternational armed conflicts, with 102 or more sovereign parties as of mid-1992 (54 percent of the potential total), among them, only three of the five permanent members of the U.N. Security Council—China, France, and the Russian Federation.

The Geneva Protocol of 1925

The Geneva Protocol of 1925 prohibits its parties from resorting to chemical or bacteriological warfare. A widely accepted interpretation of what qualifies here as chemical warfare (although one not shared by the United States) includes both the use of antipersonnel and of antiplant (herbicidal) chemicals. A universally accepted interpretation of what qualifies as bacteriological warfare includes the use of the entire panoply of microorganisms (including viruses). Therefore adherence to the Geneva Protocol of 1925 would preclude some specific acts of environmental warfare outlined earlier involving manipulations of the biota.

Protocols I and II of 1977

Protocol I of 1977 (applicable to international wars) prohibits its parties from causing the release of "dangerous forces" through attacks on "dams, dykes and nuclear electrical generating stations" (Article LVI.1); it also forbids the destruction of "objects indispensable to the survival of the civilian population," such as agricultural areas and drinking-water sources (Article

LIV.2). Additionally included is a general admonition against the use of methods or means of warfare that would cause "widespread, long-term and severe damage" to the natural environment—no matter whether the impact was intended or merely to be expected (Articles XXXV.3 and LV.1).

Protocol II of 1977 (applicable to noninternational wars) prohibits its parties from causing the release of "dangerous forces" through attacks on "dams, dykes and nuclear electrical generating stations" (Article XV); it also forbids the destruction of "objects indispensable to the survival of the civilian population," such as agricultural areas and sources of drinking water (Article XIV).

Thus, adherence to Protocols I and II of 1977 would preclude various specific acts of environmental war alluded to earlier involving manipulations of the biota, land, ocean, and atmosphere.

CONCLUSION

Control over the forces of nature for the achievement of military aims has been a human fantasy throughout history. The ancient Greeks envied Zeus his ability to hurl thunderbolts. Moses was said to have been able to control the Red Sea so as to drown the Egyptian forces that were pursuing the Israelites (as described in Exodus 14:27–28).

Today, those pent-up forces in the human environment that are most readily subject to release for tactically useful hostile military purposes include especially (*a*) the potential energy of the water that is held back by levees or dams; and (*b*) the decay-emitted energy of radioactive elements contained within nuclear facilities. The future could conceivably bring the manipulation of such forces of nature as hurricanes, earthquakes, tsunamis, or volcanoes.

There is no denying that as human capabilities for environmental damage and destruction increase, the chances for human survival shrink apace. One obvious way to reverse this suicidal (genocidal) trend is to prevent the deliberate decimation of the environment for hostile purposes. Such prevention would require formal commitment by the nations of the world via treaty participation, and—equally crucial—widespread support by the peoples of the world in order to ensure that such commitment be honored.

Four general approaches are available for limiting environmental damage in the pursuit of war: (*a*) targeting restrictions; (*b*) regional (geographi-cal) restrictions; (*c*) weapon restrictions; and (*d*) methodological restrictions. The Enmod Convention, despite its weaknesses, is a valuable addition to the laws of war because it serves to reinforce the notion of the fourth of these approaches. Perhaps even more valuable, it serves to reinforce the need to incorporate environmental concerns per se into the corpus of arms control and disarmament activities.

BIBLIOGRAPHY

Environmental Warfare and Enmod   In ARTHUR H. WESTING, ed., *Environmental Warfare: A Technical, Legal and Policy Appraisal* (London and Philadelphia, 1984), ERNÖ MÉSZÁROS analyzes techniques for manipulating the atmosphere (pp. 13–23); HALLAN C. NOLTIMIER analyzes techniques for manipulating the geosphere (pp. 25–31); RICHARD A. FALK examines the evolution of international law in relation to environmental disruption by military means (pp. 33–51); JOZEF GOLDBLAT presents a thorough legal analysis of the Enmod Convention (pp. 53–64); and ALLAN S. KRASS provides a definitive exploration of the question of verification (pp. 65–81). The Enmod Convention, including its annex, is reproduced on pages 93–96. Moreover, the CONFERENCE OF THE COMMITTEE ON DISARMAMENT (now, the CONFERENCE ON DISARMAMENT), Geneva, the drafter of the Enmod Convention, established a series of four so-called understandings in explanation and amplification of the convention, which are reproduced on pages 97–98; these understandings, along with the entire treaty, are also reproduced in Volume III of this encyclopedia.

The Negotiating Process   For an outline of the negotiations that led to the Enmod Convention, see "Convention on the Prohibition of Military or Any Other Hostile Use of Environmental Modification Techniques," *United Nations Disarmament Yearbook* 1 (1976): 179–190. For the United States' position on the Enmod Convention at that time, see JOSEPH MARTIN, JR. and FRED C. IKLÉ, "United States Discusses Disarmament Issues in U.N. General Assembly Debate," *Department of State Bulletin* 76 (1977): 17–29; and CYRUS R. VANCE, "United States Signs Convention Banning Environmental Warfare," *Department of State Bulletin* 76 (1977): 633–634. It should be noted that the idea of the convention originated with the Soviet Union: VIKTOR ISRAELYAN,

"New Soviet Initiative on Disarmament," *International Affairs* [Moscow] (11) (November 1974): 19–25.

Critical Analysis   During the period of its adoption, the Enmod Convention and the steps that led to its formulation were subjected to a number of scholarly examinations, including JOZEF GOLDBLAT, "Environmental Warfare Convention: How Meaningful Is It?" *Ambio* [Stockholm] 6 (1977): 216–221; GEORGES FISCHER, "Convention sur l'interdiction d'utiliser des techniques de modification de l'environement à des fins hostiles," [Convention on the prohibition of the utilization of techniques to modify the environment for hostile purposes]. *Annuaire Français de Droit International* [Paris] 23 (1977): 820–836; LAWRENCE JUDA, "Negotiating a Treaty on Environmental Modification Warfare: the Convention on Environmental Warfare and Its Impact upon Arms Control Negotiations," *International Organization* 32 (1978): 975–991; JERRY MUNTZ, "Environmental Modification," *Harvard International Law Journal* 19 (Winter 1978): 384–389; and

CHARLES R. WUNSCH, "Environmental Modification Treaty," *A.S.I.L.S. International Law Journal* 4 (1980): 113–131.

Review Conference   The Enmod Convention calls for a minimum of one review conference (Article VIII) that was held in September 1984. For an outline of the negotiations, see "Review Conference of the Parties to the Convention on the Prohibition of Military or Any Other Hostile Use of Environmental Modification Techniques," *United Nations Disarmament Yearbook* 9 (1984): 453–468, which also reproduces the final declaration on pages 463–465 (additionally reprinted in "Review Conference Held on Environmental Modification Convention," *Department of State Bulletin* 84 [2092] [1984]: 49–50). For a brief report, see "Environmental Modification Ban Faithfully Observed, States Parties Declare," *U.N. Chronicle* 21(7) (1984): 27–28. A second review conference was scheduled for September 1992, upon the initiative of the U.N. General Assembly (Resolution 46/36.A of 6 December 1991).

The INF Treaty

Eliminating Intermediate-Range Nuclear Missiles, 1987 to the Present

○

JANNE E. NOLAN

See also Confidence-Building Measures in Europe: 1975 to the Present; From MBFR to CFE: Negotiating Conventional Arms Control in Europe; From SALT to START: Limiting Strategic Nuclear Weapons; *and* Russia and the Soviet Union. *Treaties discussed in this essay are excerpted in Volume III.*

The U.S.-Soviet agreement to eliminate intermediate-range (500 to 5,000 km, or 312 to 3,120 mi.) nuclear missiles, known as the INF Treaty, was signed on 8 December 1987 and ratified by the U.S. Senate on 27 May 1988. The agreement was the culmination of a protracted domestic and international debate about the role of U.S. nuclear weapons in Europe and, more generally, about the basic legitimacy of United States–Soviet arms control agreements. As the first agreement between the two sides to eliminate—rather than simply reduce or constrain—an entire class of weapons, the INF Treaty is popularly believed to be a major arms control success story.

The INF Treaty owes its genesis to a decision taken by the North Atlantic Treaty Organization (NATO) in the last months of the administration of President Jimmy Carter to deploy new nuclear weapons in Europe. In the effort to counter the growing superiority of Soviet nuclear forces targeted against Western Europe, especially the three-warhead SS-20 missile that began to emerge in 1976, the NATO alliance agreed in 1979 that 108 Pershing II and 464 ground-launched cruise missiles (GLCMS) would be deployed in five European countries—the Federal Republic of Germany (West Germany), Belgium, Great Britain, the Netherlands, and Italy.

To temper opposition from European publics and from the Soviet Union, the NATO members also agreed that these new deployments would be accompanied by arms control negotiations. This so-called dual-track decision was to form two parallel and complementary approaches to the quest for nuclear stability and a credible U.S. nuclear umbrella in Europe. Limitations on European-based weapons were to be pursued after the conclusion of the second Strategic Arms Limitation Talks agreement (SALT II)—an accord that subsequently was never submitted for ratification and was replaced under the Reagan administration by the Strategic Arms Reduction Talks (START).

The declaration of United States–Soviet strategic parity in the late 1970s, codified in SALT II, had focused attention on the military balance in Europe. U.S. and Soviet parity in the strategic balance, accompanied by increasing nuclear and conventional force disparities in the European theater, meant that the U.S. nuclear guarantee to Europe was seen by some strategists as no longer credible. Based on a strategy of "flexible response," U.S. deterrence in Europe required the ability to respond and counter any level of Soviet military aggression. Without European-based weapons of sufficient range and accuracy to reach targets in the Soviet Union, according to this argument, the only way to counter Soviet military advances in the region would be to resort to strategic forces, a situation that might inhibit U.S. leaders in a crisis and cause them to question whether to honor the United States' commitment to European security. The INF systems were intended to redress this imbalance, and to allay European concerns about the U.S. commitment to the collective security of the alliance.

Upon taking office in January 1981, the administration of President Ronald Reagan questioned whether it was bound by the 1979 Carter dual-track agreement; moreover, some Reagan officials hoped that the United States could embark on a full-scale rearmament program before engaging in any discussion of arms control in Europe or elsewhere. Hard-line critics of the Soviet Union and arms control made up most of the new president's cabinet, many of them veterans of the highly successful anti–SALT II lobby, the Committee on the Present Danger. In addition to INF negotiator Paul Nitze, the committee's former chairman, members included Undersecretary of Defense for Policy Fred Iklé, U.S. Arms Control and Disarmament Agency (ACDA) Director Eugene Rostow and his successor, Kenneth Adelman, and Assistant Secretary of Defense for International Security Policy Richard Perle, among others. The new administration's platform pledged to restore U.S. superiority over the USSR, a promise underscored by an unprecedentedly ambitious military modernization program and harsh rhetoric about the Soviet Union's hegemonial ambitions, disregard for human rights, and record of "cheating" in arms control agreements.

In the first phase of INF-policy formulation, differences in opinion among Reagan advisers about how to proceed revealed the disparate preoccupations of hard-liners, including Secretary of Defense Caspar Weinberger and Perle, along with career foreign policy officials, including Secretary of State Alexander Haig, Assistant Secretary of State for European Affairs Lawrence Eagleburger, and the State Department's Director of the Bureau of Politico-Military Affairs Richard Burt.

For some, proceeding with the dual-track decision not only represented excessive accommodation of pacifist trends in Europe; domestic credibility also could be undercut. Although Weinberger and Perle had substantive as well as political objections to the dual-track decision, mostly they objected to the idea that they were being pressured to honor an agreement forged by a prior administration they saw as discredited. By contrast, Haig, Eagleburger, and Burt believed that European views had to be taken into consideration for the alliance support of the INF deployments to survive. U.S. indifference to European views not only risked European refusal to proceed with the force-modernization program, they argued, but it could damage NATO cohesion for years to come.

When the Reagan administration resolved to pursue INF negotiations in late 1981, it was clear that this was a reluctant political concession to NATO needed to ensure the scheduled deployments, not an enthusiastic embrace of arms control. By the early 1980s, the support of the NATO allies for U.S. deployments of nuclear-tipped missiles to Europe was clearly on the wane. Growing European peace movements had unified around their opposition to the missiles, and the Soviet Union employed an aggressive propaganda campaign designed to capitalize on this sentiment and to sow dissent within the NATO alliance. The allies began pressuring the Reagan administration about INF as early as January 1981, when West German Chancellor Helmut Schmidt, facing a domestic peace movement and a fractious parliament, stated publicly that the United States had to give Europe a binding assurance that negotiations on INF would resume without delay. When the case for arms control was made by European governments, especially conservative leaders like Prime Minister Margaret Thatcher of Britain, the seriousness of the peace movements and their effects on the stability of NATO were difficult to ignore.

NEGOTIATIONS

The administration submitted its first formal INF proposals to the Soviet Union in December 1981. President Reagan had revealed the new U.S. negotiating posture, in what was to become known as the "zero option," in a speech on 18 November. According to this concept, the United States offered to cancel the impending missile deployments in return for Soviet elimination of all intermediate-range missiles deployed in Europe and Asia.

The zero option was aimed at appeasing European opinion while buying time to ensure that the deployments proceeded on schedule. As crafted by Assistant Secretary of Defense Perle, this bold proposal was seen as a way to outmaneuver the Soviet Union politically and to defuse the European antinuclear movement, providing maximum appeal to public opinion. For President Reagan, the zero option demonstrated the new administration's determination to replace traditional, incremental arms control measures with a more radical approach that could achieve deeper reductions in armaments.

The State Department had been pressing for a more cautious proposal that would allow U.S. deployments to go forward "at the lowest possible equal level." But critics of this view, including Perle, argued that allowing any number of Soviet missiles to remain was militarily unsound. Accepting a notional level of 600 warheads, for example, overlooked that the Soviets would still have nuclear superiority in Europe, according to this view.

The U.S. proposal, as expected by the hard-liners, was instantly rejected by the Soviet Union. Trading prospective deployments for forces in place, the Soviets argued, was unprecedentedly one-sided and inequitable. This opinion was shared by many analysts in the United States and Europe, who believed that the U.S. proposal was intended to sabotage any prospects for arms control. As Haig in his *Caveat* later argued, "It was absurd to expect the Soviets to dismantle an existing force of 1,100 warheads, which they had already put into the field at a cost of billions of rubles, in exchange for a promise from the United States not to deploy a missile force that we had not yet begun to build and that had aroused such violent controversies in Europe" (p. 229).

The decision to adopt the zero option ensured that the INF negotiations would be controversial. The proposal met opposition among Reagan advisers and from elements of the military. Aside from its dubious negotiability, the zero option was a contravention of the alliance agreement in 1979 that new nuclear forces in Europe were needed, regardless of the level of Soviet forces, to link U.S. and European security firmly. Many experts argued that deployment of the highly capable Pershing II missile, in particular, was vital as a symbol of the U.S. nuclear commitment.

The Soviet Union countered with a proposal for staged reductions in European-based forces, including French and British forces and U.S. air- and sea-based nuclear-capable forces committed to NATO's defense. Although the West has always insisted that only U.S. and Soviet land-based systems be included in the negotiations, the Soviet Union maintained that any system capable of targeting Soviet territory should be counted.

In the effort to forestall an obvious stalemate in the talks that could exacerbate political problems in Europe, the United States modified its INF negotiating position several times between February 1982 and October 1983 to allow some Soviet INF systems to remain and to permit a smaller deployment of U.S. forces to go forward. The much publicized July 1982 "walk in the woods" proposal discussed by U.S. INF negotiator Paul Nitze and his Soviet counterpart, Yuli Kvitsinsky, for instance, would have reduced the number of SS-20 missiles to 75, canceled the Pershing IIs, and limited cruise missile deployment to 300 warheads. The proposal also would have limited both sides' nuclear-capable aircraft in Europe to 150 and limited Soviet deployments of the SS-20 in the Far East. The plan was ultimately rejected by both governments.

In March 1983, the United States advanced an interim proposal that called for equal levels of U.S. deployments and Soviet reductions, to result in an equal number of missiles and warheads on each side ranging from zero to a total of 572. The Soviets again refused, countering with an offer to reduce Soviet SS-20 missiles to the level of French and British nuclear forces (calculated at 140), on the condition that the United States would cancel its ground-launched cruise missile (GLCM) and Pershing II deployments. Regardless of the formulation of U.S. proposals, the Soviet Union would not concede the legitimacy of any new U.S. deployments.

From 1981 to 1983, the negotiations were carried out against a backdrop of deteriorating U.S.-Soviet relations. Despite the twin pressures of European skepticism about the zero option and a growing sense of urgency about the effects of peace movements on the stability of NATO governments, the Reagan administration was not disposed to take Soviet INF-negotiating proposals very seriously. The United States seemed convinced that the Soviet Union was intent only on generating opposition in Europe to the scheduled deployments and was not sincere about arms control. In September 1983, relations worsened when the Soviets shot down a Korean civilian airliner that had strayed into Soviet airspace, incurring bitter denunciation from the United States and forestalling congressional amendments on behalf of arms control.

By November 1983, there was nothing in Geneva to provide a pretext for stopping the scheduled deployments. Faced with a fundamental stalemate over U.S. resolve to proceed, the Soviets walked out of the negotiations on 23 November 1983, the day after the first Pershing missiles arrived in Germany. Two weeks later, the Soviets broke off the Strategic Arms Reduction Talks (START) as well.

As the relationship between the United States and the Soviet Union grew increasingly strained, prospects for any kind of agreement seemed remote. The period 1982–1985 was a time of turbulence for the Soviet government, with three changes in leadership in three years. Soviet presidents Yuri Andropov and Konstantin Chernenko did little more than replicate the hard-line policies of Leonid Brezhnev, showing no flexibility in arms control. Despite sporadic demarches to the Soviet government from the West, such as a declaration by NATO defense ministers in December 1984 that NATO was willing to suspend missile deployments if an equitable deal could be struck, no breakthroughs on INF were believed possible until after Mikhail Gorbachev assumed control of the Soviet government in early 1985.

The ascendance of Secretary General Mikhail Gorbachev as the leader of the Warsaw Pact transformed United States–Soviet relations, ushering in a new era of conciliation and making highly publicized, radical arms-limitations proposals the new currency of arms control. From the beginning, Gorbachev stunned the world by proposing a number of ambitious disarmament plans, proposals designed to appeal to international public opinion but which the U.S. quickly dismissed as propaganda ploys. Against this backdrop, the INF negotiations reopened in Geneva on 12 March 1985, part of a new series of arms control talks that included negotiations on strategic arms and defensive weapons.

Beginning in mid-1985, the two sides moved progressively away from the seemingly non-negotiable zero option. The United States began pressing for global limits on INF systems, while the Soviets countered with proposals for moratoria on further U.S. and Soviet INF deployments. Negotiators were divided over a number of issues, including verification, British and French nuclear forces, and the permitted number of SS-20s the Soviets could deploy outside of Europe. Because of their mobility, SS-20s deployed west of the Urals posed dangerous implications for Europe because they could be moved back in a crisis and aimed at European targets. If INF reductions in Europe simply resulted in the Soviets redeploying their SS-20s east of the Urals, moreover, the security of U.S. allies in Asia could be reduced.

The Soviets were receptive when the United States proposed another interim INF formula in the fall, setting a limit of 100 INF warheads deployed in Europe on each side, with an additional 100 Soviet warheads permitted in Asia and 100 U.S. warheads within the United States. Gorbachev had agreed to delink French and British forces from the INF balance earlier in the year. By the time of the U.S.-Soviet summit in Reykjavík, Iceland, in October 1986, the two sides were prepared to engage in discussions of a wide range of arms limitations. They agreed in principle to eliminate all INF systems from Europe, to freeze shorter-range nuclear systems, to limit Soviet warheads to 100 (equivalent to 33 MIRVed SS-20s) deployed east of the Ural Mountains, and to allow the United States no more than 100 Pershing IIs and GLCMs deployed or stored on its own territory.

A formal INF agreement at Reykjavík was forestalled by sudden Soviet insistence that progress in INF be linked to progress in the negotiations on strategic and space weapons, at that point foundering over a dispute about the U.S. commitment to the 1972 Anti-Ballistic Missile Treaty. Negotiations resumed in February 1987, however, when the Soviets dropped this last precondition. In March, the United States presented a draft treaty that incorporated the basic framework of the Reykjavík discussions and put forward a comprehensive INF-verification proposal. A prior U.S.-verification package, which required each side to agree to permit "anywhere, anytime" challenge inspections without any restrictions, had to be modified to get Soviet agreement and domestic support.

In the final stages of the INF negotiations, the terms were irrevocably altered by the Soviet Union's unconditional adoption of a "double-zero" option—that is, eliminating all INF systems in Europe and all SS-20s in Asia. This global ban eliminated the 200 missiles the superpowers would have retained under the prior formulation. Gorbachev raised the stakes even further by proposing to eliminate all shorter-range nuclear forces (SRINF), missiles with ranges of 500 to 1000 kilometers (312 to 625 mi.). The Soviets had about 100 such systems deployed in Europe and Asia, while the United States had none.

Confronted by sudden and unexpected Soviet acceptance of its own proposals, the United States had to face for the first time the domestic and international controversies associated with an agreement to ban U.S. missiles in Europe and with the far-reaching verification schemes it had put forward in 1986, which required unprecedented Soviet access to Western military installations. The United States had little choice but to accept, and on 8 December 1987, Secretary General Gorbachev and President Reagan signed the INF Treaty in Washington, D.C.

TERMS OF THE INF TREATY

The INF Treaty requires the United States and the Soviet Union to eliminate all deployed and nondeployed intermediate-range missiles, shorter-range missiles, their launchers, support facilities, and operating bases worldwide. Intermediate-range missiles are defined as those with ranges between 1,000 and 5,500 kilometers (625 and 3,437 mi.); short-range intermediate missiles (a subgroup of INF missiles) have ranges of between 500 and 1,000 km (312 and 625 mi.). The treaty is of unlimited duration, but, like the majority of international treaties, it contains a withdrawal clause. If either party decides that its "supreme interests" are in jeopardy, it can withdraw by giving six months' notice. The signatories are forbidden from activities that would conflict with the treaty's intent, such as transferring missiles in these categories to other countries.

The United States and the Soviet Union agreed to eliminate a total of 2,695 intermediate- and short-range missiles, with disproportionate reductions imposed on the Soviet Union. The Soviets agreed to eliminate 1,836 missiles: 650 SS-20s, 170 SS-4s, 6 SS-5s, 726 SS-12s, 200 SS-23s, and 84 SSC-X-4s. The United States agreed to eliminate 859 missiles: 247 Pershing IIs, 442 ground-launched cruise missiles (GLCMS), and 170 Pershing Ias. The INF Treaty does not require the destruction of any nuclear warheads, but it does require the removal of more than 2,000 warheads from deployed missiles, which are to be returned to superpower stockpiles or recycled.

At least as important as the treaty itself are the two attached protocols: missile elimination and on-site inspection procedures. The treaty spells out a specific timetable for the elimination of INF systems—in two phases within three years—to be completed by 1 June 1991. This timetable was accompanied by detailed stipulations showing precisely how the missiles, their launchers, and other support equipment would be removed.

Verification provisions, based primarily on on-site inspections, are contained in a separate protocol. The treaty requires on-site inspections within the United States and the Soviet Union; at U.S. bases in Belgium, Italy, the Netherlands, Britain, and West Germany; and at Soviet bases in what were then East Germany and Czechoslovakia. The protocol on verification also spells out inspection rules and guidelines for on-site inspections that were to be carried out during the first three years the missiles were being removed and for ten years thereafter. On-site inspections were designed to verify inventories, to witness elimination of weapons and facilities, to monitor missile-production facilities, and to conduct "challenge" inspections on short notice. Such "challenge" inspections allow officials to arrive at designated entry points—Washington, D.C., and San Francisco in the United States and Moscow and Irkutsk in the former Soviet Union—and announce which of the designated facilities they intend to inspect, which they must reach within nine hours for the inspection to be valid. Twenty challenge inspections are allowed within the first three years after the treaty is in effect, fifteen inspections in the next five years, and ten in the final five years.

The treaty includes a standard prohibition against interference with national technical means of verification, such as photoreconnaissance satellites. It also establishes the Special Verification Commission both to resolve questions relating to compliance and to adopt measures to "improve the viability and effectiveness of this Treaty." Finally, an accompanying Memorandum of Understanding (MOU) provides a detailed list of the locations of all U.S. and Soviet missiles, launchers, and facilities subject to the agreement.

POLITICAL IMPACT OF THE TREATY

Although the INF agreement elicited widespread support from the European and U.S. publics, a number of disagreements among Reagan administration officials, NATO members, congressional representatives, and private analysts over the treaty's merits surfaced during the ratification debate. Despite the relatively modest scope of the agreement, affecting less than 5 percent of total U.S. nuclear forces, the agreement quickly became a lightning rod for critics of U.S.-Soviet rapprochement. For these conservative critics, the treaty's ratification spelled the end of the Reagan era.

Despite mixed reactions, NATO governments supported the treaty's provisions, in deference to U.S. pressure and European public opinion. Chancellor Kohl, for example, previously a conservative opponent of the zero option, endorsed the INF Treaty as sound policy. Prime Minister Thatcher told U.S. audiences that the agreement had Britain's full support; and French President François Mitterand, who had earlier also voiced misgivings, now said he "rejoiced" in the treaty's conclusion.

The United States forestalled allied actions that could have imposed delays on the treaty's conclusion, such as linking NATO acceptance of the missile ban to a declaration stating that no further nuclear reductions could occur without Soviet reductions in conventional forces. The administration claimed that quick resolution of INF issues would pave the way toward an agreement on strategic forces, which Reagan purportedly hoped to sign at the May 1988 summit, a promise which proved popular among European leaders.

The very nature of the zero option, however, which had never been accepted by officials or experts for its substantive merits, invited controversy. Critics raised doubts about the treaty's effect on NATO security: zero missiles meant that the United States and Europe were still "decoupled"; the elimination of U.S. missiles heightened the significance of East-West disparities in short-range (less than 500 km, or 312 mi.) nuclear and conventional forces; and SS-20s in Asia minus compensating U.S. systems could exacerbate the nuclear threat to Asian allies. These allies, according to this view, were being blackmailed into an agreement that would leave them even more vulnerable to superior Soviet conventional and shorter-range nuclear forces.

Domestically, the most vocal criticism of the INF Treaty came from the conservative wing of the Republican party. Former President Richard Nixon and his former Secretary of State Henry Kissinger expressed opposition. Several former Reagan advisers, including Perle, testified in Congress against the wisdom of the zero option. The American Security Council, a prodefense lobby, collected over 1,000 signatures from retired military personnel for a petition opposing INF, while the Conservative Caucus published full-page newspaper advertisements with a picture of Reagan and Gorbachev next to pictures of Neville Chamberlain and Adolph Hitler.

Conservatives found a voice in the 1988 presidential campaign, in which all the Republican candidates, except for Vice President Bush, were initially vitriolic in their attacks on the treaty. Having to tread a fine line between loyalty to the president and his own political ambitions, Bush staked his future with Republican moderates who favored the agreement. Other candidates, including Congressman Jack Kemp (R-N.Y.) and Senate Minority Leader Robert Dole (R-Kans.), joined the conservative critique of the Reagan accord. A hard-line Republican administration having to defend itself against its own party created a dilemma for Reagan political strategists, who were anxious to contain the potential damage to Republicans in an election year.

President Reagan, ever conscious of the power of public opinion, took his case for INF directly to the American people. In a televised network interview in November 1987, Reagan excoriated right-wing critics of the pact. Accusing them of believing that "war is inevitable," Reagan said they were "ignorant of the advances that have been made in verification" (*Congressional Quarterly,* 5 December 1987, p. 2967). Although he continued to caution at other times that the Soviets were still "our adversaries," he had clearly parted company with many of his old supporters.

For most Americans, the sudden thaw in U.S.-Soviet relations in late 1987, epitomized by the appearance of Gorbachev on U.S. television in November shaking hands with Reagan, changed public opinion toward the Soviet Union and galvanized attention to and support for the INF Treaty. A CBS/*New York Times* poll just prior to the conclusion of the INF agreement reported that U.S. citizens favored Gorbachev by a margin of two to one, and that two-thirds supported the emerging treaty (*Congressional Quarterly,* 5 December 1987, p. 2987). By the time of the Senate ratification debate, the public seemed to be overwhelmingly lined up behind INF. According to a poll conducted by the Daniel Yankelovich Group in March 1988, 77 percent of Americans approved of the treaty (*Americans Talk Security,* March 1988, pp. 30–31).

The treaty also had the support of the military. In testimony on 4 February 1988 before the Senate Foreign Relations Committee, Joint Chiefs of Staff (JCS) Chairman Admiral William J. Crowe stated that "The JCS have unanimously concluded that, on balance, this treaty is militarily sufficient and effectively verifiable. In turn, they strongly recommend its rat-ification by the U.S. Senate" (*Arms Control Today,* April 1988, p. 6). Crowe emphasized the military risks of failing to ratify the agreement, including the proliferation of more advanced missiles in Europe.

In Congress, the Senate Armed Services, the For-eign Relations, and the Intelligence committees each approved the treaty by a majority vote, but each also issued detailed reports raising questions about certain elements of the agreement. A major controversy involved the administration's verifica-tion proposals. Having assumed that the Soviets would never agree to the stringent on-site verifica-tion measures it initially proposed, the administra-tion had overlooked the domestic complexities associated with reciprocity; that is, allowing Soviet inspectors to have free access to Western military installations "anywhere, anytime." U.S. and Allied armed forces, intelligence agencies, defense indus-tries, and even the communities that the Soviets could be expected to visit raised strident objec-tions.

The revisions required in the verification propos-als to make them domestically acceptable created the appearance of U.S. retreat, which INF critics duly exploited. The restriction of short-notice inspec-tions to designated areas, critics charged, would al-low the Soviets to cheat and was therefore useless. As Perle argued, "The last place the Soviets would choose to hide missiles is in the relatively few areas that we would be permitted to inspect. . . . Some-thing like 99.999 percent of Soviet territory would be off limits to U.S. inspectors" (*Congressional Quarterly,* 5 December 1987, p. 2971).

Another major outstanding congressional issue concerned the Senate's authority for treaty ratifica-tion. A decision by the administration in 1985 to reinterpret unilaterally the meaning of the 1972 ABM Treaty, based on a reexamination of the nego-tiating record, had provoked a bitter feud between the administration and key Democrats, notably the new chairman of the Senate Armed Services Com-mittee, Sam Nunn (D-Ga.). Claiming that the review revealed fundamental errors of interpretation, the administration attempted to free itself of the legal obligation to abide by key ABM Treaty restraints. This decision was adopted without Senate consul-tation and was seen by many senators as negating their constitutional responsibilities regarding treaty making.

The ABM controversy practically guaranteed that the Senate's authority for treaties would emerge as an issue in the INF debate. After complicated par-liamentary maneuvering, the Senate adopted an amendment to the INF-ratification resolution reaf-firming that no president could repudiate or alter a treaty without Senate approval. Crafted by several members of the Senate Foreign Relations Commit-tee led by Senator Joseph Biden (D-Del.), the "Biden Condition" stipulated that the Constitution required that the interpretation of a treaty should be derived from the "shared understanding" be-tween the executive branch and the Senate of the treaty's text at the time of ratification.

The campaign to defeat the treaty in the Senate was led by a minority of conservatives that included Dan Quayle (R-Ind.), Steve Symms (R-Idaho), Alan Simpson (R-Wyo.), Jesse Helms (R-N.C.), Malcom Wallop (R-Wyo.), and Ernest Hollings (D-S.C.), the only Democrat to vote against the pact. They fash-ioned numerous "killer amendments"—measures which, had they been approved, would have re-quired returning to the negotiating table. These in-cluded a proposal to invalidate the treaty on the grounds that Gorbachev was not legally the head of the Soviet government, a provision which would al-low either side to withdraw from the treaty within fifteen days of discovering a "material breach" of the treaty's terms, and countless maneuvers to link INF approval to the record of past Soviet misdeeds. All of the amendments were soundly defeated.

The protracted debate in the Senate threatened to leave Reagan at the Moscow summit of May 1988 without a ratified treaty. When the summit delega-tion left on 25 May, White House Chief of Staff How-ard Baker stayed behind, in the hopes that he could rush to Moscow with a concluded treaty before the summit was over. On 26 May, with the summit in session, Senate Majority Leader Robert Byrd (D-W.Va.) stopped the threatened filibuster, and Baker left for Moscow with the ratified treaty in hand. On 1 June 1988, the Soviet Union and the United States exchanged instruments of ratification and put the treaty into force.

VERIFICATION
AND COMPLIANCE

The exchange of ratification documents on 1 June 1988 included several items relating to verification. These included a Protocol on Inspections, specify-ing the types of monitoring arrangements that the two sides had agreed to use to verify compliance with the agreement; a Protocol on Elimination, which spelled out how and when prohibited missiles and support equipment would be destroyed; and a Memorandum of Understanding (MOU), providing data of each side's INF missiles, launchers, associated equipment, and facilities. All sites listed in the MOU, except production facilities, would be subject to inspections, which the United States insisted on excluding to protect technological and manufacturing secrets.

The INF-verification regime represented a major new departure in U.S.-Soviet arms control practices. For the first time ever, each side was to be allowed direct access to the other's operational nuclear-missile bases and support facilities. While national technical means (NTM) of verification remained a vital element of the provisions, it was the unprecedented scope of the on-site–inspection measures that posed the most significant challenges for implementation.

Neither the United States nor the Soviet Union had much operational experience with on-site verification prior to this agreement. It was clear from the outset that new bureaucratic resources would be required to implement these ambitious measures. After much interagency wrangling over who would be in charge, the White House decided to apportion key verification tasks among several government agencies in an effort to defuse potential political frictions posed by the multiple jurisdictions upon which INF verification potentially impinged.

The administration consolidated the authority for on-site inspections under a new umbrella organization, the On-Site Inspection Agency (OSIA), created in January 1988. Since the OSIA was designated as a constituent agency of the Department of Defense, it was stipulated that the director be appointed by the secretary of defense, but a principal deputy director would also be appointed by the director of the Arms Control and Disarmament Agency. Two deputy directors, in turn, were selected from the Department of State and the Federal Bureau of Investigation to oversee international negotiations and counterintelligence, respectively. In its first year, the OSIA employed about one hundred uniformed personnel, drawn from each of the armed services, and a small number of civilians from various other elements of the executive branch. Two hundred inspectors had to be retained and trained almost immediately, including Russian linguists, missile operations experts, and other kinds of technical experts needed to staff the inspection teams.

Five types of inspection were required, including *baseline,* to insure that the data contained in the MOU were complete and accurate; *close-out,* to confirm that treaty-limited items had actually been removed from a designated base; *elimination* inspections, to confirm that restricted equipment was destroyed according to treaty specifications; follow-up, or so-called *quota* inspections of such facilities, allowing further inspections of bases for thirteen years after the completion of the baseline inspections; and *portal monitoring,* allowing each party to monitor continuously one former INF base on the other's territory. The first three kinds of inspections were completed within the first three years after the INF Treaty entered into force, (June 1988–June 1991). The latter two can continue for an additional ten years, until 2001.

Beginning on 1 July 1988, and for sixty days thereafter, twenty teams of U.S. inspectors carried out 115 baseline inspections in the Soviet Union, East Germany, and Czechoslovakia, while twenty Soviet teams conducted thirty-one inspections at the declared facilities in the United States, Belgium, West Germany, Italy, the Netherlands, and Great Britain. The inspection teams had access to all sites listed in the MOU except missile-production facilities, accounting for almost 6,000 treaty-limited items on the Soviet side and 2,000 for the United States. Conducted successfully, these inspections helped to smooth out inspection procedures and to cement relations between the U.S. and Soviet inspection authorities.

By far, the most dramatic inspections were those conducted by inspectors who witnessed the destruction of the other side's INF inventory, including the disassembly, crushing, or launching of missiles, launchers, and support equipment. These first elimination inspections occurred at a Soviet facility in August 1988. In all such inspections, observers counted the equipment to be destroyed, witnessed its elimination, and inspected the items after their destruction was complete. At the close of the initial three-year period, the United States had conducted 130 elimination inspections, and the Soviets had conducted 94. The final phase occurred on 1 June 1991, when U.S. forces in southern Germany destroyed the last Pershing II missiles in Europe.

Short-notice "challenge" inspections to ensure continuing confidence in INF Treaty compliance are permitted until 2001. All sites listed in the MOU, except missile-production facilities, are subject to challenge inspections. As noted above, in the first three years of compliance, each side was allowed twenty challenge inspections per year, subsequently phasing down to fifteen inspections per year for the next five years, and to ten per year for the final five years.

The provision to allow continuous monitoring of the portals outside one missile-production plant on each side stemmed from a U.S. concern that the Soviet SS-20 INF missile had a second-stage that is difficult to distinguish from the first stage of the SS-25 ICBM, a system not covered by the INF Treaty. As a result, the United States insisted on monitoring the Votkinsk Machine Building Plant, a facility where the banned SS-20s had been produced and which was continuing production of the SS-25. The Soviets, in turn, monitored the Hercules Plant Number 1 in Magna, Utah, which previously assembled the Pershing II missiles.

The ambitious scope of the INF on-site–verification regime had led many to doubt that it could be successfully implemented, certainly without major controversies. Anticipating chronic disputes over the many details of the regime, a Special Verification Commission (SVC) was established in 1988 to resolve any questions that might arise relating to treaty obligations and compliance. From June 1988 through June 1991, the SVC met ten times to discuss implementation and compliance issues. They ranged from who should bear the costs of different inspections to more significant compliance problems, such as allegations that the Soviets had deliberately concealed SS-25 missile canisters exiting Votkinsk to impede U.S. monitoring.

According to an OSIA official, the INF-verification regime has functioned "flawlessly." Compared to any preceding treaty, controversies about compliance certainly have been minimal. Of the few issues that have been raised, the United States charged in early 1990 and again in 1991 that seventy-two Soviet SS-23 shorter-range INF missiles deployed in Eastern Europe should have been declared in the initial MOU. The Soviets claim that the missiles were transferred to their Eastern European clients before the INF Treaty was signed in December 1987. In a February 1990 report on Soviet compliance with arms control treaties, the Bush administration fell short of accusing the Soviets of a treaty violation but called this incident an act of bad faith. The United States also questioned whether the USSR had failed to declare the existence of SS-4 and SS-5 missile-transporter vehicles as items to be limited by the treaty. As in the case of the SS-23s, the United States raised questions about this equipment but declined to charge the Soviet Union with a violation formally.

The status of the SS-23s deployed in East Germany, Czechoslovakia, and Bulgaria became a contentious issue in July 1991 as the U.S. Senate geared up for the ratification of the Strategic Arms Reduction Treaty (START). Secretary of State James Baker, appearing before the Senate Foreign Relations Committee, was asked by Senator Helms whether these East European missiles were evidence of Soviet noncompliance. That same day, Baker sent a cable to Moscow asking for clarification about when the missiles were transferred and if they were nuclear-capable. Although Helms seemed convinced that a serious violation had occurred, the Bush administration tried to deflect the significance of this charge. As Supreme Allied Commander in Europe John Galvin stated, the presence of the SS-23s in Eastern Europe should not be seen as evidence of Soviet cheating: "I'm not saying there are no problems; I'm saying the problems can be resolved" ("NATO Commander Calls Concerns Resolvable," *Washington Times,* 26 July 1991).

The OSIA mandate would suggest it was established to oversee the INF Treaty regime, and thus could be subject to dismantlement after 2001. But the OSIA, far from disbanding, has used its successes in the INF process to press for a broader role in implementing future arms control regimes. Given the growing importance of on-site inspections for a number of impending initiatives, the chances are good that OSIA will continue to expand its size and jurisdiction in the coming years. As of August 1991, the agency had 475 employees and had received formal authority to monitor the Conventional Forces in Europe Treaty and the Threshold Test Ban Treaty, both submitted for ratification in 1991. In addition, officials were optimistic that the agency would play key roles in the START Treaty, the Chemical Weapons Convention, and the destruction of Iraqi nuclear, chemical, and missile sites as stipulated by United Nations Resolution 647.

CONCLUSION

The INF Treaty, perhaps more than any other single international agreement, owes its success to a powerful and extraordinarily popular U.S. president who staked his personal prestige on the accord's success. As the most conservative and anti-Soviet president since Richard Nixon, Ronald Reagan's credibility as the champion of this agreement had an inestimable impact on the outcome of the treaty debate. The "zero option" was the product of Ronald Reagan's unique approach to arms control. Like his vision of the Strategic Defense Initiative, the zero option seemed simple, innovative, and bold. Reagan may have been the only official in his administration who believed that the zero option was a sincere and negotiable proposal, and, as it turns out, he is the only one to have been proven correct.

If any lessons are to be drawn from this experience for other treaties, however, one must consider the remarkable influence of the sweeping changes that were occurring in the Soviet Union. Minus the ascendance of Mikhail Gorbachev and his willingness to accede to even the most stringent U.S. demands, the INF Treaty might have still been languishing in the shadows of SALT and START. The peculiar convergence of events that account for the success of the INF Treaty would be difficult to replicate. Under different circumstances, it is difficult to imagine that the inherent liabilities of the zero option might not have resulted in the negotiations' failure.

The negotiation and ratification of the INF Treaty reveal how much the character of the arms control process changed in the 1980s. What had once been largely the domain of secret diplomacy between the two superpowers was transformed into an overt struggle for international public opinion. It was a new game, in which appeals for public support for proposals often preceded their introduction at the negotiating table. Neither U.S. nuclear objectives nor NATO's security concerns were decisive in setting the terms of the INF accord. In fact, none of the issues that the original dual-track decision in 1979 had set out to solve was resolved, and the role of nuclear weapons in Europe, though vastly diminished as a result of the demise of the Warsaw Pact, remains open to controversy.

Nevertheless, the INF Treaty was the first arms control agreement to eliminate an entire class of nuclear-tipped weapons.

BIBLIOGRAPHY

Primary Sources   The best primary sources on the INF Treaty are the congressional hearings held prior to ratification. See, for instance, U.S. CONGRESS, COMMITTEE ON FOREIGN RELATIONS, *The INF Treaty,* Report and Hearings, 6 vols., 100th Congress, 2d session, (Washington, D.C., 1988); and U.S. CONGRESS, COMMITTEE ON ARMED SERVICES, *NATO Defense and the INF Treaty,* Report and Hearings, 4 vols. 100th Congress, 2d session (Washington, D.C., 1988).

General Sources   General reference sources about the treaty's provisions include ARMS CONTROL ASSOCIATION, "Summary and Text of the INF Treaty and Protocols," *Arms Control Today,* INF supp., 18 (January–February 1988); Office of Public Affairs, U.S. ARMS CONTROL AND DISARMAMENT AGENCY, *Understanding the INF Treaty* (Washington, D.C., 1988).

Evolution of the Negotiations   The most authoritative and detailed account of the evolution of the INF negotiations can be found in STROBE TALBOTT, *Deadly Gambits* (New York, 1984). Other sources include FREDERICK DONOVAN and JAMES GOODBY, "Choosing Zero: Origins of the INF Treaty," *Pew Program in Case Teaching and Writing in International Affairs,* Case #319 (1988); STROBE TALBOTT, "The Road to Zero," *Time* (14 December 1987): 18–30; and PAT TOWELL, "Soviet Offer Breaks Logjam on Euromissiles," *Congressional Quarterly* (7 March 1987): 427–430, and "Conciliation Colors the Pre-Summit Picture," *Congressional Quarterly* (5 Dec. 1987): 2967–2971. On Soviet behavior and motives in INF, see JONATHAN DEAN, "Gorbachev's Arms Control Moves," *Bulletin of Atomic Scientists* 43 (June 1987): 34–40.

On the lessons of the INF Treaty for future arms limitations, see JOYCE P. KAUFMAN, "U.S.-Soviet Arms Control and Politics," *Arms Control* 8 (December 1987): 278–294; WILLIAM B. VOGELE, "Tough Bargaining and Arms Control: Lessons from the INF Treaty," *Journal of Strategic Studies* 12 (September 1989): 257–272.

Security Aspects   On the security aspects of the INF accord, see GRAHAM ALLISON and ALBERT CARNESDALE, "Can the West Accept *Da* for an Answer?" *Daedalus* 116 (Summer 1987): 69–93; LYNN DAVIS, "Lessons of the INF Treaty," *Foreign Affairs* 66 (Spring 1988): 720–734; JONATHAN DEAN, *Watershed in Europe: Dismantling the East-West Military Confrontation* (Lexington, Mass., 1987); MICHAEL R. GORDON, "Dateline Washington: INF: A Hollow Victory?," *Foreign Policy* 68 (Fall 1987): 159–179; RICH-

ARD PERLE, "What's Wrong with the INF Treaty?," *U.S. News and World Report* (21 March. 1988): 46; JANE M. O. SHARP, "Understanding the INF Debacle: Arms Control and Alliance Cohesion," *Arms Control* 5 (September 1984): 96–127; and JAMES A. THOMSON, "The LRTNF Decision: Evolution of U.S. Theatre Nuclear Policy, 1975–1979," *International Affairs* 60 (Autumn 1984): 601–614.

Ratification of the Treaty   The ratification of the INF Treaty is discussed in JOSEPH R. BIDEN, JR. and JOHN B. RITCH, "The Treaty Power: Upholding a Constitutional Partnership," *University of Pennsylvania Law Journal* 137 (1989); JANNE NOLAN, "The INF Treaty Ratification Debate," in MICHAEL KREPON, ed., *Treaty Ratification* (forthcoming); SUSAN F. RASKY, "Senate Rebuffs Foes of the Missile Treaty," *New York Times* (21 May 1988): A3; JANET HOOK, MACON MOREHOUSE, and PAT TOWELL, "Senate Votes 93–5 to Approve Ratification of INF Treaty," *Congressional Quarterly* (28 May 1988): 1431–1435.

Verification   The INF verification regime has been examined in detail in several works. See OWEN GREENE and PATRICIA LEWIS, "Verifying the INF Treaty and START," in FRANK BARNABY, ed., *A Handbook of Verification Procedures* (New York, 1990): 215–263; EDWARD J. LACEY, "On-Site Inspection: The INF Experience," and JAMES R. BLACKWELL, "Contributions and Limitations of On-Site Inspection in INF and START," both in LEWIS A. DUNN, ed., with AMY E. GORDON, *Arms Control Verification and the New Role of On-Site Inspection* (Lexington, Mass., 1990), pp. 3–14 and 95–119, respectively.

Official Sources   For official sources, see, for example, U.S. ACDA, *Annual Report on Soviet Noncompliance with Arms Control Agreements* (15 February 1991); testimony of OSIA Director Roland Lajoie before the House Foreign Affairs Committee, subcommittee on Arms Control, International Security and Science, 2 March 1989, and his interview, "Insights of an On-Site Inspector," *Arms Control Today* 18 (November 1988): 3–10; and AMY F. WOOLF, "On-Site Inspections in Arms Control: Verifying compliance with INF and START," Congressional Research Service, report 89–592 F, 1 November 1989. On the financial costs of verification regimes, see CONGRESSIONAL BUDGET OFFICE, *U.S. Costs of Verification and Compliance Under Pending Arms Treaties,* September 1990.

From MBFR to CFE

Negotiating Conventional Arms Control in Europe

O

P. TERRENCE HOPMANN

See also Arms Control Treaty Verification; Confidence-Building Measures in Europe: 1975 to the Present; Critics of Arms Control and Disarmament; *and* Negotiating Arms Control and Disarmament Agreements. *Most of the treaties discussed in this essay are excerpted in Volume III.*

On 17 July 1992 the first two major conventional disarmament agreements of the post–World War II period entered into force, calling for limitations on conventional armaments and personnel of all members of the North Atlantic Treaty Organization (NATO) and the former Warsaw Treaty Organization (WTO), including all states of the former Soviet Union west of the Ural Mountains, except the Baltic countries.

The first of these agreements, called the Treaty on Conventional Forces in Europe (CFE), limited five major categories of weapons in the arsenals of the twenty-nine signatory states. This treaty was originally signed by twenty-two states at the Paris Summit Conference on 19 November 1990, but its entry into force was delayed by the momentous events surrounding the breakup, first of the WTO, and then of the Soviet Union itself. The Paris summit included the thirty-four member states of the Conference on Security and Cooperation in Europe (CSCE), and its goal was no less than to recognize formally the end of the Cold War. The CFE Treaty was a crucial element in that endeavor. The Charter of Paris for a New Europe, adopted by the full CSCE on 21 November 1990, reflected the new spirit of cooperation:

With the ending of the division of Europe, we will strive for a new quality in our security relations while fully respecting each other's freedom of choice in that respect. Security is indivisible and the security of every participating State is inseparably linked to that of all the others. We therefore pledge to co-operate in strengthening confidence and security among us and in promoting arms control and disarmament.

The CFE Treaty was signed by twenty-two of the thirty-four members of the CSCE, including all sixteen members of NATO and the six remaining members of the Warsaw Pact, which at the time was on the verge of disintegration. The treaty called for parity of conventional military forces between the two Cold War alliances in five categories of weapons systems: each side was thus limited to twenty thousand main battle tanks, thirty thousand armored combat vehicles (ACVS), twenty thousand artillery pieces, sixty-eight hundred combat aircraft, and two thousand helicopters.

The agreement covered the entire continent of Europe stretching, in Charles de Gaulle's classic phrase, "from the Atlantic to the Urals." Furthermore, no single country could have more than about one-third of the total forces allowed in the area, which provided an especially important limitation on Soviet forces. In the event that its former Warsaw Pact allies had disarmed, the USSR would not have been free to fill the quota allotted to the entire Warsaw Treaty Organization.

Another unique feature of the CFE Treaty was that it required the destruction of all weapons over treaty limits, except for 750 tanks and 3,000 armored combat vehicles on each side, which could be converted to civilian uses. The verification system that was created to assure compliance with the treaty was one of the most far-reaching in the history of disarmament negotiations. These verification procedures included:

1. an exchange of data about the quantity and location of forces that would remain after reductions;

2. extensive on-site monitoring of the process of destroying or converting to civilian use equipment that was scheduled for reduction;

3. a large number of permitted on-site inspections to assure that residual force levels were not being exceeded (including the possibility of challenge inspections if one suspected a specific violation); and

4. a joint consultation mechanism to mediate any disputes that might arise about the implementation of the treaty.

The second agreement, known as CFE 1A, was signed at the Helsinki CSCE Summit on 10 July 1992. Unlike the main CFE Treaty, this agreement was politically rather than legally binding, and it limited the personnel of all twenty-nine signatories located in Europe from the Atlantic to the Ural Mountains to specific national thresholds. It also called for an extensive information-exchange regime in which, within forty months, comprehensive data were to be exchanged on all armaments and personnel held by each country within the limitation zone broken down to the level of the regiment, brigade, or even smaller units.

The signature of this second agreement and the decision that both would enter into force one week later was appropriately described by the United States ambassador, Lynn Hansen, as bringing "down the curtain on a whole era of arms control" (*International Herald Tribune,* 7 July 1992, p. 4). These agreements represented a major step forward on the road to reducing the armaments that remained in Europe as a deadly legacy of the Cold War. Essentially, the forces of the two blocs were reduced to parity in their major weapons categories. Throughout most of the postwar period the Soviet Union and its allies in the Warsaw Pact held a quantitative superiority in armaments and troops relative to the members of NATO. Although this imbalance was partially offset by some qualitative advantages on the NATO side, it had forced NATO to adopt several tactical doctrines that were potentially dangerous and destabilizing.

First, NATO had pursued a policy known as "flexible response"—that is, it would reply to potential Warsaw Pact aggression with whatever force was necessary to halt it. If that aggression could not be halted with conventional forces, NATO would use nuclear weapons. The potential "first use" of nuclear weapons became a central element of NATO's effort to deter a Warsaw Pact attack. NATO leaders feared that their numerically inferior conventional forces might be overrun by the more numerous forces of the Warsaw Pact, forcing them to resort to nuclear weapons.

Second, NATO had followed a policy of "forward defense" throughout most of the Cold War period. This meant that NATO would concentrate a large amount of military firepower at the geographical border between the two blocs, especially in central Germany. While this was a desirable policy from the point of view of deterrence, it did not address the possibility of Warsaw Pact forces penetrating the forward defenses.

This concern led NATO to move in the decade of the 1980s to a doctrine known as the "Follow-on Forces Attack," or FOFA. In this instance, at the outbreak of a conflict, NATO would attack the second echelon of Warsaw Pact forces, especially Soviet forces in Poland and the western military districts of the USSR, to prevent them from reinforcing frontline troops and breaking through into the NATO rear areas. This required a large number of weapons in the NATO arsenal that were basically offensive in nature. Even though the doctrine was essentially defensive, the offensive nature of the weapons caused them to appear provocative to the Soviet Union.

The CFE Treaty would shift this entire balance. For the first time the European members of NATO would have a numerical superiority over the combined forces of the entire Soviet Union, at least in their forces deployed west of the Ural Mountains, and an even larger numerical advantage to the Russian Federation, the formal successor to the USSR as a party to the treaty. When the treaty is fully implemented, scheduled for November 1995, Russia will have had to cut 4,595, or 42%, of its battle tanks; 35% of its ACVs, 24% of its field artillery; 17% of its combat aircraft; and 14% of its combat helicopters, for an overall reduction of 29% of its military hardware in these five categories. At the same time, total scheduled NATO cuts only amounted to 12.5% of their forces, with the largest cut being of 21% in tanks. (These figures are based on data exchanged at the time of signature of the CFE Treaty, 19 November 1990, as updated to account for the breakup of the Soviet Union as of 5 June 1992, as provided to the author by the United States delegation to CFE. NATO data include the forces of the former East Germany, which were included as part of German forces following the reunification of Germany, thereby enabling NATO to take a large portion of its reductions by eliminating armaments formerly belonging to East Germany.)

These reductions made a surprise attack from the east against Western Europe virtually unthinkable. The treaty, combined with other agreements that make military movements and maneuvers observable by Western specialists, made it practically impossible for Russia or any other republic of the former Soviet Union to amass the forces necessary to engage in full-scale aggression without alerting Western intelligence analysts well in advance. This would make war less likely and was intended to increase a sense of mutual confidence among all states on the continent of Europe.

Furthermore, NATO no longer needed to rely on the first use of nuclear weapons to offset the Warsaw Pact's conventional forces. Forward defense would become far less risky and provocative, as well as much easier to achieve, due not only to the dissolution of the Warsaw Pact and the Soviet Union but also to the large number of Russian forces withdrawing from Central and Eastern Europe. Finally, FOFA became largely obsolete, since the remaining Russian forces had few reserves available in the European regions of the USSR to reinforce the central front, and since forces stationed east of the Urals were largely irrelevant to this strategy. In short, as a consequence of these agreements, and the dramatic political events in Europe that they reflected, the military and political role of NATO could be entirely revised.

As significant as these accomplishments were, they came as the result of a long and difficult process of negotiations lasting almost two decades. Throughout most of this period, prospects for agreement seemed bleak, and had it not been for the dramatic political changes that occurred on the European continent starting in 1989, it is unlikely

that they could have been consummated. In 1986, the negotiations seemed hopelessly bogged down in technicalities and debates about peripheral issues. In order to understand both the significance of the progress made in 1989–1992 and indeed, of the CFE agreements themselves, it is useful to retrace some of that negotiating history.

THE POLITICAL CLIMATE

Throughout the protracted negotiations on conventional arms reductions in Europe, nations were confronted with a dilemma: Which needed to come first—arms control or political cooperation? Many analysts believed that a positive outcome of the negotiations depended upon a major change in the overall political relations among the participants. This approach has been characterized by J. David Singer as the "tensions-first" hypothesis, which suggests that political differences among adversaries must be resolved prior to negotiating on disarmament. Proponents of this point of view argue that armaments are largely a symptom of underlying political tensions, and that arms may not be reduced or eliminated as long as these tensions remain unresolved.

An alternative view maintains that armaments may be a partial consequence of political conflicts, but that armaments themselves are also an important contributing factor in creating tensions. Some analysts have noted that these two factors may reinforce each other in a vicious cycle. For example, Inis Claude in *Swords into Plowshares* (1963) observed, "The truth is that this is a circular problem, in which causes and effects, policies and instruments of policy, revolve in a cycle of interaction and are blurred into indistinguishability" (p. 298). In this conception, the negotiation process and the external international environment may change more or less in tandem.

When the negotiations on Mutual and Balanced Force Reductions (MBFR) opened in October 1973, a period of détente had begun in East-West relations. The SALT I Treaty, signed in 1972, signaled the first major attempt to bring strategic nuclear arms under control. New negotiations between the nuclear superpowers on a wide range of arms control issues were paralleling developing relationships in other areas. Trade was beginning to increase as the United States expanded its grain sales to the Soviet

Union, and cooperation was developing in other spheres such as medicine and space exploration. In this context, a reduction of conventional weapons in Europe seemed a natural complement to the emerging spirit of cooperation.

Of special significance was a series of "Mansfield resolutions"—introduced in the U.S. Senate by Senator Mike Mansfield—proposing major withdrawals of U.S. ground troops from Western Europe. Mansfield justified this action on the grounds that Europe had recovered economically from World War II and had reached the point that Europeans no longer needed to depend on a large U.S. force for their defense, especially in a period of East-West détente, when the Soviet threat was perceived to be reduced significantly. Rather than unilaterally make these reductions, U.S. and NATO leaders pushed for negotiations with the Soviets with the hope of either forestalling passage of the Mansfield resolutions or assuring that any U.S. troop reductions would be more than matched by Soviet reductions.

The long and often divisive MBFR, and subsequent CFE negotiations, were very much entwined in the politics of East-West relations in Europe. These relations deteriorated after the NATO decision to deploy new intermediate-range nuclear forces in Europe and after the Soviet invasion of Afghanistan in 1979, virtually eliminating the slim hopes for successful MBFR negotiations. A new round of détente, however, followed the arrival to power of Mikhail Gorbachev in the Soviet Union, including agreements on confidence- and security-building measures, and the Intermediate-Range Nuclear Forces (INF) Treaty was signed in 1987. In that atmosphere, conventional arms control negotiations were restructured as the CFE negotiations superseded the MBFR negotiations in 1989.

The final negotiations on CFE took place during the dramatic changes that occurred in Eastern Europe in late 1989, which led to the removal of Communist regimes in those countries and eventually to the disappearance of the Warsaw Pact as one of the two blocs participating in the negotiations and to the disintegration of their dominant superpower. These events certainly complicated the final phase of negotiations, based as they were on the effort to achieve parity between the two competing alliances in Europe. However, they also created the kind of political climate in which the maintenance of large conventional armies in Central Europe lost much of its rationale. In this respect, the eventual agreements reached in CFE were both a reflection of the improved political climate and an important foundation for a new security regime in Europe.

MBFR NEGOTIATIONS, 1973–1989

Interest in conventional arms reductions had been evident well before the opening of the Mutual and Balanced Force Reductions (MBFR) negotiations. NATO had initially proposed conventional force reduction negotiations at its ministerial meeting in 1967, following a report by Belgian foreign minister Pierre Harmel. In March 1969, the Warsaw Pact's Consultative Committee proposed convening a general conference to consider questions of European security and political cooperation. For some time thereafter the Warsaw Pact promoted negotiations on general security issues in Europe, whereas NATO insisted on a more restricted negotiation dealing with concrete military reductions. At the summit meeting between U.S. President Richard M. Nixon and Soviet General Secretary Leonid Brezhnev in May 1972, a compromise was reached to hold separate but parallel negotiations. The CSCE would deal with the broad political issues, while MBFR meetings would concentrate on force reductions in Central Europe.

The MBFR negotiations opened in Vienna on 30 October 1973. They sought to reduce conventional forces in a zone of Central Europe surrounding East and West Germany—the most likely point for the outbreak of a military confrontation in Central Europe. This area included, in the West, the Federal Republic of Germany, Belgium, the Netherlands, and Luxembourg, and in the East, the German Democratic Republic, Poland, and Czechoslovakia. So-called direct participants in these negotiations included these seven countries, plus other countries having forces stationed in this zone, that is, the Soviet Union, the United States, and Canada. (France, which also had troops stationed in West Germany, refused to participate in MBFR or even to acknowledge officially the presence of its troops there.) All other members of NATO and WTO were permitted to attend as "indirect participants," though Portugal and Iceland chose not to participate on the NATO side.

The central objective of these negotiations was to establish a stable military balance in Central Europe, to limit rising defense costs for all participants, and to reinforce the political détente that was then developing in Europe. In the West, it was widely perceived that the conventional military balance in Central Europe dramatically favored the Eastern bloc. If war were to break out in Central Europe, this would present NATO with an unacceptable dilemma. Should the Warsaw Pact achieve rapid success with conventional forces by penetrating deeply into Western Europe, NATO might be forced to choose between acquiescing in WTO gains or responding with tactical nuclear weapons. It was largely due to this concern that NATO leaders insisted on maintaining the right to use nuclear weapons first in Europe—even in an outbreak of conventional warfare.

Resolving this dilemma by increasing NATO conventional forces in Europe was deemed impractical for several reasons. First, political détente developed in Europe, making it difficult to justify force increases to European publics and political leaders at a time of reduced political tension. Of greatest significance was the fact that the two Germanys accepted one another's borders, and these borders were also ratified by the four occupying powers—the United States, the Soviet Union, Great Britain, and France. The status of the four-power occupation of Berlin and West Germany's access rights to that city were also clarified, making a war over Berlin appear to be less likely than at any time since the Berlin Wall was erected in 1961. Second, the pressure generated by the Mansfield resolutions in the United States made U.S. troop increases virtually unthinkable. Unilateral force reductions were a far more likely prospect than a unilateral buildup. Therefore, a rational non-nuclear defense policy could only be achieved—as NATO members saw it—through asymmetrical force reductions that brought WTO, and especially Soviet, conventional forces closer to the levels of NATO.

On the WTO side, the incentives for troop reductions were far less obvious. It was probably true that the Soviets feared a unilateral withdrawal of U.S. troops from Central Europe, especially if withdrawn U.S. troops might be replaced by increases in the West German Bundeswehr. Indeed, Soviet fear of the United States was never as profound as Soviet concern about a revived German threat. The Soviet and Eastern European economies, moreover, were clearly already in considerable disarray during the early 1970s, and this too might have provided an incentive for reductions.

Of course, the USSR refused to acknowledge for many years WTO's conventional superiority. While this may have been partially a result of deliberate distortion, it probably also reflected a realistic assessment of the nature of the Central European military balance. Even at this time, the Soviets were concerned about the reliability of the military forces of their WTO "partners"—partners whose commitment was more the result of coercion than of enthusiasm. In addition, the Soviets were far more aware than many Western defense analysts of the qualitative deficiencies in much of their military equipment when compared with that of their Western counterparts. Finally, Soviet forces in Eastern Europe were clearly intended to preserve the integrity of the Warsaw Pact, following unsettling events in virtually all member countries, especially Hungary in 1956 and Czechoslovakia in 1968. Therefore, Soviet military leaders undoubtedly believed that they needed to maintain a double margin of security to defend against simultaneous threats from the West and from centrifugal forces within their own bloc.

Obstacles to Agreement   Different assessments of the nature of the conventional balance in Europe, and therefore of the requirements for a stable security system, plagued the MBFR negotiations. Each side brought to bear its own definition of security in Central Europe, making a common formula difficult to discover. The result was that soon after the negotiations opened in 1973, differences emerged between the NATO and Warsaw Pact positions along five primary lines.

First, there was disagreement about the major criteria for reductions, with NATO arguing for parity between the two blocs while WTO favored equal percentage reductions on both sides. Specifically, NATO proposed a "common ceiling" of ground soldiers in the Central European zone of seven hundred thousand on each side. This would have required far larger reductions by WTO than by NATO. By contrast, WTO called for reductions in phases, amounting to about 17 percent on each side over the period of the agreement. This would have preserved the preexisting ratio of forces in Central Europe at lower levels, thereby retaining WTO numerical superiority.

Second, there was disagreement about the scope of the reductions; that is, about what types of forces were actually to be reduced. NATO's original proposal called for reductions of troops only, plus one Soviet tank army with about seventeen hundred main battle tanks. NATO reductions could be achieved by thinning out existing forces throughout the region. NATO argued that reductions of troops would cut the number of soldiers that could be rapidly deployed in a conflict in Central Europe, whereas reductions of equipment would be both difficult to verify and meaningless, since equipment could be rapidly transported into the region in the event of a crisis. Furthermore, reductions limited to personnel would enable the United States to withdraw troops across the Atlantic, leaving behind stored equipment that would be available in a crisis should the United States have to rapidly reinforce its military presence in Europe. This was seen by the West as a necessary compensation to NATO to make up for the geographical disparity. This disparity was seen as favoring WTO, because Soviet forces would only have to withdraw back into the USSR whereas U.S. forces would have to be withdrawn across the Atlantic Ocean.

Conversely, WTO insisted that reductions should be taken across the board, affecting troops and all of their associated equipment, including aircraft, helicopters, artillery, tanks, armored personnel carriers, tactical nuclear weapons, chemical weapons, and all light weapons carried by these troops. Thus the preexisting "correlation of forces" would be maintained between NATO and WTO at lower levels, without affecting the overall force balance, which the East argued had preserved the peace in Europe since 1945.

Third, NATO argued that the force ceilings should apply collectively to each alliance as a whole, whereas WTO sought subceilings on each country within the region. NATO favored a collective ceiling for several reasons. First, it did not want to have any one country singled out for "punitive" limitations, especially the Federal Republic of Germany. Second, it wanted to preserve its freedom to revise the mix of national forces within the NATO structure in Western Europe. It wanted, also, to preserve the option for countries to increase their forces to compensate for any country that reduced its forces because of domestic pressures. Thus NATO wanted each alliance to determine for itself—without interference—how its internal defense structure would be maintained, so long as the overall ceiling was not exceeded.

By contrast, WTO favored individual national ceilings that would be equally proportional across the board. That is, each country with forces in the region would be required to reduce its forces by the agreed percentage figure, for example, by 17 percent each. This was clearly intended to ensure that West Germany participated fully in any reductions undertaken by NATO, and to avoid a situation in which the United States withdrew most of its forces under pressure from the Mansfield resolutions, perhaps leaving West Germany as the dominant military power on the Western side in Central Europe. As noted above, the Soviets saw the U.S. presence in Europe as a stabilizing factor on balance, in contrast to the potential revanchist forces within West Germany.

A fourth issue involved the phasing of reductions. NATO proposed that reductions take place in two phases. The first phase would consist only of reductions of Soviet and U.S. forces, amounting to sixty-eight thousand Soviet soldiers and thirty thousand Americans. In the second phase, all other countries with troops in the zone would participate in the reductions. For NATO this had the advantage of being a rapid response to U.S. domestic pressure, while also bringing about a reduction in the most dangerous component of Warsaw Pact forces—Soviet troops.

By contrast, WTO proposed a three-phased reduction, with all countries participating fully in all three. In the first phase, each alliance would reduce its forces by twenty thousand soldiers, along with corresponding armaments. In the second phase, each alliance would reduce its troops and armaments by 5 percent, with a 10 percent across-the-board reduction coming in the third phase. Furthermore, WTO insisted that all countries commit themselves to the specific nature of their reductions in all three phases prior to the beginning of reductions. Once again, this proposal was designed to assure that all NATO countries participated fully in the reductions process. WTO particularly wanted to avoid an agreement that might end after the implementation of the first phase, which would leave U.S. and Soviet forces reduced and German forces untouched.

A fifth issue concerned so-called associated measures intended to enhance confidence, assure verification, and prevent circumvention of the agreement. NATO proposed three kinds of associated measures:

1. Confidence-building measures (CBMs) would include prior notification of military activities such as maneuvers outside of normal garrisons; this

would be legally binding under an MBFR treaty, unlike the politically binding agreements on CBMS that were being negotiated in the CSCE.

2. Specific provisions for verification by aerial and on-site inspections would establish force levels prior to reductions and assure thereafter that reductions were actually undertaken.

3. Noncircumvention provisions would assure that forces withdrawn from the MBFR zone in Central Europe would not be redeployed on either the northern or the southern flank of Europe. Countries such as Norway, Turkey, and Greece were especially insistent upon the necessity of such provisions in an MBFR agreement.

The Warsaw Pact made no initial proposals along these lines. For many years it maintained that the nature of the associated measures depended entirely on the nature of the agreements reached. It argued, therefore, that agreement had to be achieved on the substantive issues contained in the first four points before associated measures could be designed that were "appropriate" to the level and scope of reductions actually agreed upon.

Early Concessions Throughout the early years of the negotiations, substantial progress was made in reducing many of these differences. The first major concessions were offered by NATO in December 1975. NATO proposed adding air units to ground troops, with an overall ceiling of nine hundred thousand, and a subceiling of seven hundred thousand on ground troops alone. In addition, it made a "one time only" offer to withdraw about one thousand tactical nuclear warheads plus fifty-four nuclear-capable F-4 aircraft and thirty-six Pershing I missiles from Europe, if the Warsaw Pact agreed to NATO's troop proposals plus a reduction of one tank army with seventeen hundred tanks. Thus NATO introduced some of its equipment into the negotiations, with a proposal that would have reduced those forces that each side perceived to be its adversary's most threatening.

The next major concessions were proposed by WTO in June 1978. First, WTO accepted the Western proposal of equal troop ceilings of nine hundred thousand soldiers, with seven hundred thousand from ground units and two hundred thousand from air units. In addition, it accepted a two-phase reduction, with the first confined to Soviet and U.S. forces alone; however, it insisted that there be a general advance commitment by the indigenous European countries to take reductions in the second phase.

The next step became one of specifying the present troop strengths in the affected zone in order to calculate the reductions required to reach the agreed common ceiling. The Warsaw Pact accepted official NATO data that indicated the presence of 791,000 Western ground personnel in the zone, requiring a reduction of 91,000 soldiers to reach the common ceiling. Reciprocally, it asked NATO to accept official Warsaw Pact data that indicated the presence of 805,000 Eastern ground troops in the zone, requiring reductions of 105,000 soldiers to reach the ground-manpower ceiling. NATO data, however, suggested that there were 940,000 Eastern soldiers stationed in the zone, requiring reductions almost two and one-half times greater than those acknowledged by the Warsaw bloc.

Indeed, from this time on much of the focus of the Vienna negotiations turned to an effort to resolve this data dispute. Various efforts were made to see if the differences could be accounted for by differing definitions of "ground troops" or by other systematic errors in the data. For the next decade, MBFR talks were paralyzed because of the inability to resolve this dispute.

Negotiations Stumble Along, 1979–1980
Substantial activity in MBFR took place in 1979, as the ill-fated SALT II Treaty was completed and as NATO deliberated the deployment of new intermediate-range nuclear forces in Europe. In April 1979 the Warsaw Pact moved closer to the NATO position on phasing by indicating that initial force reductions could be "approximately proportional" to present troop holdings by each country. Without accepting this proposal, NATO replied by assuring WTO that all participating NATO countries would take "significant" cuts in their force levels.

In June 1979 the Warsaw Pact accepted the NATO proposal for selective armaments reductions to accompany an agreement that would focus primarily on military manpower. It called for a reduction of 1,000 Soviet tanks in three separate divisions, combined with a reduction of 250 mechanized infantry combat vehicles with anti-tank rockets and anti-aircraft capabilities, in exchange for U.S. reductions of tactical nuclear warheads, F-4 aircraft, and Pershing missiles as proposed by NATO. It also insisted that European countries agree to similar highly selective equipment reductions. Although this was slightly different from the NATO proposal of December 1975, the differences had been substantially reduced.

By the summer of 1979, then, NATO and WTO had largely bridged the gap on the substantive issues. There was agreement on a common ceiling of nine hundred thousand combined ground and air forces on each side in Central Europe. Reductions would be primarily in manpower, accompanied by few and selective armaments reductions. Ceilings would be collective for each alliance, but all countries would participate in reductions. Reductions would take place in two phases, with the first consisting solely of Soviet and U.S. forces and the second committing all European participants to reduce as well.

The major obstacle to agreement remained the data dispute about the forces present in Europe prior to reductions. NATO insisted that these be agreed upon prior to a treaty, since verification would be most effective in counting forces withdrawn rather than in verifying the residual ceilings. In addition, there had been little concrete discussion of NATO's proposals on confidence-building measures, verification procedures, and noncircumvention provisions. Had the political constellations been in proper order, agreement might have been reached at this stage.

But decisive political commitment was not forthcoming in 1979; indeed, the negotiations began to unravel by the end of that year. First, a series of unilateral moves that seemed intended to facilitate agreement actually may have detracted from success over the long run by purporting to resolve the armaments issues outside of the negotiations. In October 1979 Brezhnev offered to withdraw unilaterally up to twenty thousand soldiers and one thousand main battle tanks from East Germany to the USSR. In other words, the USSR would now do unilaterally what it had intended to do as part of an MBFR agreement in its proposals of June 1978. At its ministerial meeting in December 1979, NATO proposed to withdraw unilaterally one thousand tactical nuclear warheads from West Germany, in addition to withdrawing one warhead for each of the 572 "modernized" INF warheads to be deployed beginning in 1983. This in effect meant that NATO's compromise proposal on armaments introduced in December 1975 now would be accomplished through unilateral reductions. From that time on MBFR focused exclusively on personnel, which

eventually made it irrelevant to the primary threats to stability in Europe.

Second, under pressure to consummate a "quick and dirty" agreement as a "sweetener" to complement the "bitter pill" of the INF deployment decision, NATO adopted at its 1979 ministerial meeting a watered-down MBFR proposal designed to achieve rapid, if only symbolic agreement. Under this proposal, phase-one reductions would be about 44 percent of the amount previously proposed, amounting to a Soviet reduction of thirty thousand troops and a U.S. reduction of thirteen thousand troops. The initial agreement would contain only a vague outline for a second-phase agreement, although the goal of a common, collective ceiling in which all countries would make "significant" reductions was maintained. Less than two weeks after NATO announced this proposal for a "quick and dirty" agreement, Soviet forces entered Afghanistan and virtually all arms control negotiations entered into a deep freeze, also awaiting the outcome of the 1980 presidential election in the United States.

Diplomatic Malaise, the 1980s Throughout most of the 1980s MBFR was derided in arms control circles as a process that droned on with little or no chance for success. The negotiations seemed hopelessly bogged down in a difficult and highly technical debate about data on force size and definitions of different categories of forces. Since the newly elected Reagan administration took a dim view of arms control in general, and of MBFR in particular, there was little or no high-level interest in stimulating the negotiations. After labor unrest in Poland during 1980 led to the imposition of martial law in that country, it became evident that the Soviet Union also had little interest in an agreement that might require it to withdraw a substantial portion of its forces from Poland or other Eastern European countries.

Furthermore, as the talks proceeded many Western governments and their delegates in Vienna—who had virtually all been replaced since the negotiations opened in 1973—began to lose sight of the original rationale for NATO's positions. Why, many wondered, should NATO insist on restricting reductions to troops alone, as it had since the 1975 offer to trade Soviet tanks for U.S. nuclear weapons had been dropped from NATO proposals in 1979, when in fact the threat to NATO stemmed more from the offensive firepower represented by highly mobile Soviet tanks, artillery, and armored personnel carriers (which transported infantry rapidly into battle)? Long after the Mansfield resolutions had slipped into the past, it was difficult to remember the importance that NATO had attached to an agreement that would provide an orderly way for the United States to withdraw conventional troops from Europe. Why, also, had NATO insisted on restricting the negotiations to a limited area in Central Europe surrounding the two Germanys, when the major threat to NATO came from a Warsaw Pact offensive doctrine that called for frontline troops in Eastern Europe to open up holes in the NATO defenses through which highly mobile follow-on, or second echelon, forces—stationed in the USSR's western military districts—would be sent to achieve the final victory? These second echelon forces were not even covered in the MBFR negotiations.

The negotiations, furthermore, had increasingly appeared to be devising a special arms control regime for Germany, which the Bonn government resented. Warsaw Pact proposals seemed designed to limit the Bundeswehr more than other European forces. By the 1980s Germans on both sides of the Berlin Wall hoped that memories of the two world wars had receded. Thus they viewed with dissatisfaction MBFR's apparent attempt to single them out from the other European states as the primary locus of reductions.

In short, the entire NATO position seemed to have lost its rationale and yet, in the hostile atmosphere that characterized the mid-1980s, NATO could not bring itself to fundamentally reassess its position. Therefore, diplomats in Vienna continued to dispute fine points that few perceived as having any real relevance to threats to the security of Central Europe.

Despite this malaise, there was an attempt in 1983 by several Western European delegations, led by the Federal Republic of Germany, to try to break the logjam on data. Confronted with mounting demonstrations and domestic political pressure against the imminent implementation of the NATO decision to deploy 572 intermediate-range nuclear missiles in Europe, most of them in West Germany, they sought to stimulate some progress in the MBFR talks. Instead of agreeing about data on Warsaw Pact forces at the outset and then determining the number that had to be reduced to reach the nine-hundred-thousand ceiling, they were willing to agree upon the ceiling at the outset, followed by adequate verification to determine whether or not

each alliance had actually achieved the common ceiling. They felt that this would enable the Soviets to save face and at the same time back away from their unrealistically low data on their forces in the zone. The Soviets could then make the reductions necessary to reach the agreed-upon ceiling by whatever means they chose, and NATO would verify that they had reached the required level.

While the United States balked at this approach, the Soviets showed some interest. Indeed, in 1983 the Warsaw Pact had agreed for the first time to accept permanent observation posts to count troops as they departed and entered the zone and to allow some on-site inspections of forces remaining in the zone. But agreement with the United States was still not reached on force reduction.

After a hiatus in the negotiations following the December 1983 decision of the German Bundestag to accept intermediate-range nuclear missiles in Germany, NATO two years later made yet another attempt to reach agreement on very modest reductions by incorporating some features of the earlier West German proposal. At that time, NATO suggested initial token reductions of only 5,000 U.S. troops and 11,500 Soviet troops, even below the minimal levels proposed in 1979. But this would be accompanied by a freeze on forces of NATO and the Warsaw Pact in the zone. During subsequent years both sides could conduct as many as thirty annual on-site and aerial inspections of the other's forces, both to verify the freeze and, more importantly, to try to establish an accurate data base that might make it possible at a later stage to negotiate an agreement that would achieve parity of conventional troops. The Soviets rejected this approach, arguing that its verification requirements were excessive in light of the extremely modest reductions the proposal envisaged.

Gorbachev's Proposals, 1986–1988 Shortly after becoming general secretary of the Soviet Communist Party, Mikhail Gorbachev introduced proposals that would sound the death knell of MBFR, while at the same time breathing new life into the European conventional arms control negotiations. In April 1986 he proposed to break the stalemate in MBFR with a phased reduction in ground and air forces, including conventional and nuclear weapons that were deployed from the Atlantic to the Urals. He acknowledged at the same time—a first for a Soviet leader—that there were important asymmetries of conventional forces in Europe that might reasonably be considered as threatening by NATO. He also suggested that the side with the larger forces ought reasonably to take a larger share of the reductions, which would be verified by on-site inspections.

These proposals were formalized in a Warsaw Pact meeting in Budapest during June 1986, in what became known as "the Budapest Appeal." This program called for new negotiations, under the auspices of the CSCE, involving all twenty-three members of NATO and the Warsaw Pact. Consistent with the geographical scope of the latest round of CSCE negotiations—especially those on confidence- and security-building measures (CSBMS) at the Stockholm Conference on Disarmament in Europe where all thirty-five members of the CSCE were currently involved—these negotiations would cover all of Europe from the Atlantic to the Urals. The United States and the Soviet Union would initially reduce their forces by between 150,000 and 200,000 troops along with their associated armaments, including tactical aircraft and nuclear weapons. There would be a subsequent reduction of 25 percent of NATO and WTO forces. A third phase of reductions would include the neutral and nonaligned countries within the CSCE. A ban on chemical weapons would also be imposed. Finally, military forces on both sides would be deployed in such a way as to reduce fears of surprise attack.

The initial NATO response to this proposal was cautious, due largely to the inclusion of tactical nuclear weapons. However, success at the Stockholm conference in September 1986, followed by the summit between President Ronald Reagan and General Secretary Mikhail Gorbachev in Reykjavík, Iceland, during October 1986, created a positive context for new negotiations. By December a NATO high-level task force on conventional arms control recommended a negotiating position along the lines proposed by Gorbachev. At their December meeting NATO's foreign ministers proposed two parallel negotiations covering the Atlantic to the Urals (ATTU) region—one consisting of all thirty-five CSCE countries dealing with CSBMS, as a follow-up to the Stockholm agreement, and the other comprising all NATO and WTO countries aimed at achieving the stability of conventional forces in Europe.

Subsequent discussions about a mandate for new negotiations occurred in connection with the CSCE follow-up meeting that was taking place simultaneously in Vienna. Three major differences emerged in these discussions:

1. France wanted the states to interact independently, rather than having the negotiations occur on a bloc-to-bloc basis;
2. The Soviets wanted to exempt some parts of the Transcaucasus military district within the ATTU from reductions, and NATO argued for corresponding exemptions for some parts of Turkish territory; and
3. NATO wanted to focus on ground forces alone, whereas WTO wanted to include air forces, naval forces in European waters, chemical, and nuclear weapons.

The discussions on a new mandate for negotiation were long and difficult, although it subsequently became clear that these initial talks succeeded in resolving some of the most difficult problems that were to confront the negotiations. They were certainly aided by Gorbachev's announcement, at the United Nations in December 1988, of his unilateral withdrawal of some 240,000 troops, including 10,000 tanks, 8,500 artillery pieces, and 800 combat aircraft from the ATTU.

A new mandate was thus signed at the Palais Liechtenstein in Vienna on 10 January 1989. This mandate specified that the participants would be twenty-three states negotiating individually, even though all belonged to NATO or WTO. It would apply to all "conventional armaments and equipment of the participants based on land within the territory of the participants in Europe from the Atlantic to the Urals" (*Arms Control Today,* March 1989, pp. 18–19). Nuclear weapons were to be excluded, but systems capable of being used with both nuclear and conventional warheads or bombs would be included. Naval forces and chemical weapons were also not to be discussed, as preferred by NATO. Finally, all territory of the USSR west of the Ural River and the Caspian Sea would be included, although a small portion of Turkey bordering Iraq and Syria was exempted from reductions. Information exchange and on-site inspections would be utilized for verification of the agreement. In short, the agreement would seek

to strengthen stability and security in Europe through the establishment of a stable and secure balance of conventional armed forces, which include conventional armaments and equipment, at lower levels; the elimination of disparities prejudicial to stability and security; and the elimination, as a matter of priority, of the capability for launching surprise attack and for initiating large-scale offensive action.

When agreement on a mandate for the conference on Conventional Forces in Europe (CFE) had been completed, MBFR became obsolete. It held its final formal meeting on 2 February 1989.

Though few participants mourned its passing, it should not be forgotten that MBFR, all cynicism about it notwithstanding, had made an important contribution to European security. It provided a continuing East-West dialogue of European military issues for almost sixteen years. Much of the groundwork that it laid greatly facilitated the rapid conclusion of the negotiations in CFE. Moreover, without the expertise in many countries that had been created through participation in MBFR, and the shared working experience of many delegations in Vienna over the years, it is unlikely that a complex negotiation like CFE could have been completed in less than two years. The importance of MBFR in building a new security order in Europe may well be more widely recognized in years to come.

NEGOTIATING THE CFE TREATY, 1989–1990

The negotiations on Conventional Forces in Europe began in Vienna on 9 March 1989, under very different conditions from those that surrounded MBFR. Several of these conditions were critical to its rapid success.

First, the geographical area was expanded to include all of Europe from the Atlantic to the Urals. Perhaps the major obstacle to agreement in MBFR had been the so-called geographical asymmetry—the fact that the United States would be withdrawing its troops across the Atlantic, whereas the USSR would only be withdrawing from East Germany, Poland, and Czechoslovakia back into Soviet territory. By contrast, in CFE the Soviets would be forced either to withdraw their troops east of the Urals or to demobilize them. If Soviet forces could be moved far back from the front lines, a substantial mobilization would be required by them prior to any aggressive action. The high level of activity that this mobilization would generate would provide NATO with an early warning of a possible attack. This extended warning time would make a Soviet surprise attack virtually impossible, and it would give NATO ample time to call up reserve units in Europe or to transport reinforcements to Europe from North America.

An additional political advantage of the extended geographical area was that Germany was not the center for reductions. They had not liked the fact that MBFR singled out German territory as the primary locus of reductions, and that Warsaw Pact proposals in MBFR appeared to be designed to limit the Bundeswehr more than any European forces, East or West. Nor were they pleased with the fact that countries in the zone, especially the two Germanys, would have to reduce forces, whereas countries outside the zone, that is, the USSR, the U.S., Great Britain, and Canada would only have to withdraw their forces from the zone. In CFE, even before German reunification became an issue, the two Germanys were treated as equals among the twenty-three NATO and WTO countries. Furthermore, Soviet forces on Soviet territory were being reduced, not just withdrawn, as were French and British forces in the West; consequently, Germany would not be the only major military power in Europe taking reductions.

The price that CFE had to pay to achieve these advantages was that some aspects of verification became even more complicated in the expanded area than they had been in the smaller MBFR zone. It is not surprising, therefore, that these verification issues turned out to constitute some of the major obstacles to reaching and then to implementing a CFE agreement.

Second, CFE included more countries among the participants. The distinction in MBFR between "direct" and "indirect" participants was abolished, and all members of NATO and WTO were full participants in the negotiations. Perhaps most important on the NATO side was the inclusion of France. This represented a new direction for French arms control policy under the leadership of President François Mitterand; France, for the first time, assumed full responsibility for its own forces in Europe. French refusal to participate in MBFR had always been a source of embarrassment to NATO, since it was well known that France had about fifty thousand soldiers stationed in West Germany. Not only did CFE bring France into closer harmony with other European states in matters of continental security, it also enhanced French integration into the political structures of NATO, which had been weakened ever since France withdrew from the integrated NATO military command in 1966.

In addition to French participation, other countries were given a central role in the process. MBFR had long debated the status of Hungary and Italy, although this issue had been shifted to the back burner from the very beginning of negotiations in 1973. Similarly, the interests of so-called flank states, like Norway in the north and Turkey, Greece, Bulgaria, and Romania in the south, could be better considered within the CFE framework than within MBFR.

Third, the shift in focus away from troops and toward equipment was itself a major step forward. In the initial negotiations, NATO had focused on troop reductions because of the pressure generated by the Mansfield resolutions and because of concern with the large numbers of Soviet forces in Eastern Europe. By the 1980s these two factors had largely disappeared. NATO's concerns had shifted to the surprise-attack potential presented by highly mobile Soviet armor, artillery, and infantry units near the front lines, supported by a second echelon of highly mobile forces in the western military districts of the USSR. MBFR did little to resolve the first threat except to move the Soviet manpower further back, although the possibility of stationing equipment in Eastern Europe might enable the Soviets to send in manpower reinforcements and become battle-ready with little advance warning. And, of course, MBFR did nothing at all about the second-echelon threat since it did not cover any Soviet territory.

Paradoxically, throughout the 1980s NATO had continued to argue in Vienna for reductions of manpower only, and against reductions of armaments (which the Warsaw Pact favored throughout), even though virtually no one was convinced any longer of the rationale for this position. NATO did not want to appear to be making a major concession to the Eastern position, yet at the same time most experts realized that only armaments reductions would actually contribute to a significant reduction of the Soviet threat. CFE, of course, gave NATO a face-saving way out of this dilemma by enabling it to adopt a new mandate focusing on armaments, without having to appear to be making a direct concession to its adversaries in MBFR.

Opening Negotiating Positions Largely as a result of the revised conference mandate, and of the improved political climate in Europe that it reflected, the initial positions presented in CFE by the two sides were far more similar to one another in overall structure, although they still differed on details.

The initial NATO proposal called for equal ceilings for each bloc in the ATTU region in three categories of armaments: 20,000 main battle tanks, 16,500 artillery pieces, and 28,000 armored combat vehicles. In addition to overall limits, the NATO proposal called for three sublimits: (1) no one country could possess more than 30 percent of the forces of both blocs in the ATTU (termed the "sufficiency rule"); (2) there were far lower limits on the number of armaments that could be stationed on the territory of another country, that is, by the United States, Great Britain, and Canada in West Germany and by the USSR in Poland, Czechoslovakia, and East Germany; and (3) four geographical subzones were proposed for each alliance, creating more or less concentric circles around Central Europe.

The first of these sublimits was largely intended to force the USSR to take substantial reductions, although it also assured some countries that West Germany would not play too large a role in NATO defenses in Europe. The second sublimit was intended to ensure that Soviet forces were withdrawn in substantial numbers from Eastern Europe, while also assuring participants that the United States would make significant withdrawals from Germany. The third sublimit was intended to maintain a military balance not only in Europe as a whole but in subregions as well. Interestingly, NATO's "central zone" was identical to the old MBFR zone surrounding Germany. A separate zone was also created for the western military districts of the USSR plus Hungary to guard against massing second echelon forces near the presumed front line in Central Europe. Finally, a special zone was created for the "flank states" to avoid creating imbalances between Soviet and NATO forces on either the southern or northern borders of Europe. This would guard against troops withdrawn from Central Europe being redeployed to these flank areas.

The Warsaw Treaty Organization opened with a proposal for a three-phase reduction. Phase one would require both sides to reduce 10 to 15 percent below the level of the alliance with the lower force levels, including personnel and the most destabilizing armaments, such as tanks, combat aircraft, combat helicopters, armored vehicles, and artillery. It also proposed sublimits within three zones, including a central zone that added Hungary and Denmark to the MBFR zone, a flank zone in both the north and the south, and a "rear zone" extending in both directions from the central zone to the

Urals in the east and to Iceland, the U.K., and Portugal in the west. The second phase would entail reductions by both alliances by another 25 percent, including equipment that was "organic" to these units. Thus far, the Soviets' proposal in many ways resembled their MBFR position, although calling for more dramatic reductions. The third phase would entail a restructuring of the remaining forces into defensive postures. This was an entirely new proposal within the formal negotiations, although the idea had been widely discussed in both East and West academic and policy circles for many years.

Subsequently, the Warsaw Pact accepted a number of the NATO proposals, including the sufficiency rule, the limit on stationed forces in the zone, and precise levels of zonal limitations. NATO responded rapidly to these moves with some concessions of its own. Following a meeting at Kennebunkport, Maine, on 20–25 May 1989 with President Mitterand of France, President George Bush announced a proposal that would accept the inclusion of combat aircraft and helicopters in the reductions as proposed by WTO, and he suggested that these be reduced to a common ceiling about 10 to 15 percent lower than current NATO holdings. He also proposed that there be a limit on U.S. and Soviet forces stationed in Europe at 275,000 on either side. These proposals were adopted by a NATO summit in Brussels on 29–30 May 1989 and were then presented in Vienna.

Agreement had thus been reached indicating that five categories of armaments would be limited, including tanks, artillery, armored combat vehicles, attack aircraft, and combat helicopters. There was also agreement to limit personnel, at least on the forces of the two superpowers stationed on the territory of other European countries. From that point on, much of the subsequent discussion turned to more technical issues, especially to the development of precise definitions for each of the five categories of treaty-limited equipment (referred to as TLES), as well as attempting to bridge the relatively small differences in ceilings proposed by each of the two alliances.

Disintegration of the Warsaw Pact While these technical discussions were under way in Vienna, the political underpinnings of the negotiations received another dramatic jolt. In late fall of 1989, the Warsaw Pact fell apart as a functioning alliance. Country after country in Eastern Europe

overthrew Communist regimes in a series of mostly bloodless revolutions and, to the surprise of many observers, the Soviet Union stood by and watched its empire collapse. This, of course, provided the clearest possible signal to the world that the Gorbachev regime was truly different from its predecessors. The earlier Brezhnev Doctrine—which was asserted during the Czechoslovakian intervention (1968) as the right of the USSR to use force to defend socialism within the bloc—was completely abandoned by Gorbachev. Dramatic pressures for democratization and a more liberal economy were also sweeping the Soviet Union. The most dramatic single moment occurred on 9 November 1989, when the Berlin Wall was breached and for all practical purposes the division of Germany was ended.

As a consequence of these dramatic and unforeseen events, much of the CFE mandate had become an anachronism by early 1990. Most fundamentally, the mandate had sought to achieve parity between the two Cold War alliances. But when the Cold War and the postwar division of Europe disappeared, and when one of the Cold War alliances was in shambles, parity itself became a far less meaningful concept. The negotiations had excluded the neutrals and nonaligned, but this concept too became less meaningful, because it is difficult to define neutrality in the absence of two opposing blocs. In one sense the ultimate irony was that by the end of 1990 the Soviet Union had become Europe's largest "nonaligned" country, having no allies left on the continent.

These events had a curious effect on the negotiations themselves. On the one hand, the possibility existed of suspending CFE to create a mandate more appropriate to the new political order in Europe. On the other hand, momentum had been achieved in a rapidly progressing negotiation, and after years of frustration and stalemate in MBFR, almost all countries were reluctant to forego the consensus already achieved in CFE.

The decision was made to, in effect, plunge ahead as if nothing had changed. The concept of parity between the two alliances would be preserved, and WTO would continue to meet and, at least, coordinate positions on political matters largely for the sake of the negotiations themselves. At the same time, the representatives of several countries, especially Poland, the Czech and Slovak Federal Republic (CSFR), Hungary, and East Germany changed either their personnel or their political loyalties overnight. On many issues the Soviet Union found itself isolated, as the new democracies of Central Europe identified far more with the West in terms of their security interests than they did with their former Warsaw Pact ally. Some of the new governments even began to talk, at least privately, of a desire to become formal members of NATO, though most agreed to refrain from pressing their requests out of fear of threatening the Soviet Union.

In October 1990 one of the member countries of the CFE negotiations ceased to exist when the German Democratic Republic was formally incorporated into the Federal Republic of Germany. As part of this process, Chancellor Helmut Kohl of West Germany and President Gorbachev had agreed in July 1990 that the USSR would withdraw completely from Germany by 1994 and that a reunited Germany would accept a limitation on its active personnel within CFE at 370,000 troops.

The final phases of the negotiation process were thus in many ways bizarre, certainly quite unique in the history of international negotiations. NATO and WTO continued to negotiate a treaty based on parity of opposing military forces, even though the political basis of hostility between them had all but vanished. It is perhaps fortunate that most of the major substantive issues had been settled before the events in Eastern Europe occurred, or it perhaps would have been difficult to pull the negotiations back together. Yet since the focus after mid-1989 had become largely technical, the negotiation approach was more one of problem solving than distributive bargaining.

The Final Phase   The resolution of the many complex technical issues, however, was not easy. Precise numerical limits had to be fine-tuned. Common definitions had to be established for each category of armaments. This proved to be difficult with respect to armored combat vehicles, due to the many varieties of such vehicles, and combat aircraft, since issues about the role of trainers and of "defensive" fighter interceptors presented problems for the negotiators. Finally, issues of verification continued to present a series of very troublesome problems due to the magnitude of the tasks involved and the relative lack of experience on all sides with on-site verification of such large quantities of equipment in such a vast geographical region.

Beyond these technical difficulties one other substantive issue remained, namely the role of person-nel in the reductions. This issue was more or less settled bilaterally by the United States and the Soviet Union in August 1990 when they agreed to rescind their earlier agreement to limit their own personnel in the region. This, in effect, pushed discussion of personnel off to a follow-up negotiation, dubbed CFE 1A.

In September 1990 Soviet CFE negotiator Oleg Grinevsky startled negotiators when he made a last-ditch effort to restructure the negotiations to reflect the new political realities. If a country left its alliance, he suggested, then the remaining alliance members should be free to fill that country's quotas for treaty-limited equipment. This, in effect, would have allowed the Soviet Union to fill the quotas of all countries that might choose to leave WTO formally. Although this proposal received no support from other delegations, it clearly reflected the concerns of the Soviet military leaders with their impending isolation. It also undoubtedly caused them to redouble their efforts to create a sufficiency rule that would ensure their defensive viability after the inevitable disintegration of WTO.

Pressure to resolve these few political questions as well as the many technical issues continued to mount throughout 1990. The summit conference of the thirty-four members of the Conference on Security and Cooperation in Europe was scheduled for 19–21 November 1990 in Paris. President Bush had declared that he would not attend unless a CFE treaty was ready for signature. By early October, under pressure to attend the summit, Bush ordered his negotiators to make a dramatic push to resolve the stickiest remaining problems. Since the large forum in Vienna was not an efficient mechanism for this kind of rapid bargaining, the president attempted to have these issues resolved in a marathon session in New York between Soviet and U.S. negotiators. It was in these sessions that most of the major provisions of the verification regime were negotiated and many other differences were narrowed in matters of definitions and agreed limits. It was also at this session that the sufficiency rule was established. Approximately one-third of all treaty-limited equipment (TLE) for the entire region could be possessed by any one country. Thus the USSR would be permitted, for example, to hold 13,300 of the 40,000 tanks allowed in the ATTU as a whole in both East and West. Sufficient progress was thus made in the bilateral negotiations that President Bush agreed to attend the November summit.

Table 1:   Force Limitation in the CFE Treaty

TLE	In ATTU	In Each Alliance	In One Country	Sufficiency Rule In ATTU	Alliance
Tanks	40,000	20,000	13,300	33%	67%
Artillery	40,000	20,000	13,700	34%	68%
ACVS	60,000	30,000	20,000	33%	67%
Aircraft	13,600	6,800	5,150	38%	76%
Helicopters	4,000	2,000	1,500	38%	75%

The rapid bargaining during this endgame phase, however, resulted in a number of ambiguities and uncertainties that were to haunt negotiators in the months after the treaty was signed. In addition, this meeting brought to the fore in Vienna the concern among most of the other twenty CFE delegations that too many issues with implications for all twenty-two CFE states were now being resolved bilaterally by the two superpowers. From this time forward in CFE the European states began caucusing among themselves without either superpower present, and a distinctly "European" perspective on CFE in particular and on the structure of European security in general began to emerge on the continent.

The CFE Treaty limited five categories of conventional armed forces stationed on "the entire land territory of the States Parties in Europe from the Atlantic Ocean to the Ural Mountains." All ground-based systems, including naval aviation, were to be included, although no naval forces based at sea were covered under the agreement (see Tables 1, 2, 3, and 4).

In addition to these overall limitations, the CFE Treaty places sublimits on the three categories of ground equipment within each of the four zones contained in the original NATO proposal. There are also sublimits on each of three different categories of armored combat vehicles (ACVS). Only certain

percentages of the TLE may be in active units, so that the rest must be held in storage; however, no equipment may be stored in either the northern or the southern flank areas.

As noted previously, the treaty made no formal limitations on personnel, although it called for follow-up negotiations concerning reductions in personnel to be completed before the Helsinki meeting of the CSCE in March through July 1992. Two politically binding statements were added, however, regarding personnel. First, all parties agreed not to increase the total peacetime authorized personnel during the period of the follow-up negotiations. Second, Germany issued a unilateral statement reflecting the Kohl-Gorbachev agreements concerning German reunification, in which Germany agreed to reduce the personnel of a united Germany to 370,000 ground, air, and naval soldiers within three to four years following the entry into force of the treaty.

The CFE Treaty was to be implemented in a series of stages. The process began at the time of signature, when each country was to submit a summary of its current holdings (summarized in Tables 2, 3, and 4 above). The accuracy of these unilateral declarations was to be determined through a series of inspections during the first 120 days following the entry into force of the treaty, which eventually took

Table 2:   NATO Reductions Mandated by CFE

TLE	CFE Limit	Declared	Cut	Percentage of Holdings
Tanks	20,000	25,091	5,091	20%
Artillery	20,000	20,620	620	3%
ACVS	30,000	34,666	4,666	13%
Aircraft	6,800	5,939	0	0%
Helicopters	2,000	1,733	0	0%

Table 3:   WTO Reductions Mandated by CFE

TLE	CFE Limit	Declared	Cut	Percentage of Holdings
Tanks	20,000	33,191	13,191	40%
Artillery	20,000	23,702	3,702	16%
ACVS	30,000	40,950	10,950	27%
Aircraft	6,800	8,372	1,572	19%
Helicopters	2,000	1,631	0	0%

place on 17 July 1992. These data were then to form the baseline against which reductions would be measured. Reductions were scheduled to begin 14 November 1992 and to be completed over the next three years, with most reductions being accomplished by destroying equipment or in some cases converting equipment to civilian uses. Twenty-five percent of the reductions were to be accomplished in the first twelve months, 60 percent after twenty-four months, and the full amount within thirty-six months after the reductions began (November, 1995). How each alliance would distribute its reduction was to be determined within each alliance. Thus, for example, the Warsaw Pact countries held a difficult meeting in early November, 1990, shortly before the treaty was signed, to determine how to divide remaining forces after permitting the Soviets to retain most of the forces permissible to them under the sufficiency rule.

The verification process for the CFE Treaty was extensive, intrusive, and far more complex than that entailed in any previous arms control agreement. It began with information sharing among all parties, not only about data for force levels but also about the structure and organization of forces and their peacetime locations. This would be followed by three categories of inspections. The first are mandatory inspections not subject to quota, which primarily concern the observation of the actual re-duction of TLES. Other forms of inspection are subject to quotas. The basic location of these inspections is determined by declared "objects of verification" (OVS), which are any sites at which units at the brigade or regiment level (or their equivalent) or larger are present possessing any treaty-limited equipment. The second level of verification is thus mandatory inspections in which every country agrees to allow inspections of 20 percent of its OVS (its "passive" quota) during the initial 120 days, 10 percent of OVS in each of the three years during which reductions are being made, 20 percent during a "validation period" after reductions have been completed, and 15 percent per year during each subsequent year that the treaty is in force. The third form of verification is "challenge" inspections, where states may demand the right to inspect areas outside of the OVS, where TLE is suspected of being held. There is also a quota to these challenge inspections, which may be refused provided that a state presents satisfactory evidence that it does not have TLES stationed in the suspected area.

Differences that might arise in interpretation of the treaty or with respect to suspected violations were to be handled by a Joint Consultative Group, patterned after the Standing Consultative Commission created for strategic nuclear weapons under the SALT I Treaty. This group would be comprised of members from all participating states and must

Table 4:   USSR Reductions Mandated by CFE

TLE	CFE Limit	Declared	Cut	Percentage of Holdings
Tanks	13,300	20,694	7,544	36%
Artillery	13,700	13,828	653	5%
ACVS	20,000	29,348	9,348	32%
Aircraft	5,150	6,445	1,295	20%
Helicopters	1,500	1,330	0	0%

make decisions on the basis of consensus. It was thus more a forum for negotiating differences than for adjudicating violations. There was also a provision calling for periodic review conferences to update the treaty. Finally, a state could withdraw from the treaty if events have "jeopardised its supreme interests" or "if another State Party increases its holdings in battle tanks, armoured combat vehicles, artillery, combat aircraft, or attack helicopters . . . which are outside the scope of the limitations of this Treaty, in such proportions as to pose an obvious threat to the balance of forces within the area of application." This provision was obviously intended to guard against a Soviet buildup east of the Urals that might eventually be moved into the European theater, although it also could be interpreted as applying to any U.S. military buildup outside Europe that might have threatened the USSR.

In short, the CFE Treaty called for the most dramatic reductions of existing military forces ever formally agreed to in the history of disarmament negotiations, and it also created a regime of information exchange, inspections, and continuing dialogue that surpassed any prior arms control agreement. The rapidity with which such a complex negotiation could be completed was both a reflection of the long years of groundwork laid throughout the MBFR process and of the positive and rapid evolution of political relations in Europe in 1989–1990.

FROM THE PARIS SUMMIT TO THE HELSINKI SUMMIT

No sooner was the CFE Treaty signed at the Paris summit than important differences began to appear regarding Soviet intentions for implementing the treaty. Basically three issues arose.

First, the USSR had withdrawn large quantities of equipment east of the Urals in the weeks immediately before the treaty was signed, and many in the West believed that their data reported at the time of signature reflected the number of tanks they had planned to withdraw prior to signature, even though fewer than planned may have actually been taken out by 19 November 1990. The treaty required materials that are withdrawn after the treaty was signed to be destroyed, but no such provision applied to equipment withdrawn before the treaty's signature. Much of the ensuing debate hinged on

just when this equipment was actually moved east of the Urals, a difficult point to establish with much certainty. Many observers believed that the discrepancy was as high as ten thousand tanks with smaller differences in all other categories of treaty-limited equipment except helicopters.

This action was viewed in many countries as a deliberate effort by the Soviet military leaders to undermine the spirit of the CFE Treaty, but there was little that could be done since most of the withdrawals had occurred prior to the treaty's signature, and it was difficult to prove how much had in fact been withdrawn after 19 November 1990. Furthermore, much of the equipment moved east of the Urals was stored in the open where it could be observed and where in many cases it was slowly being allowed to rust. Consequently, in the opinion of many Western analysts, this equipment did not represent a militarily significant threat to NATO's interests.

A second issue concerned the number of "objects of verification," or OVs. In their negotiations in New York during October 1990 when this principle was agreed upon, some Soviets told U.S. delegates that the USSR had 1,560 OVs. Assurances were given that the number of OVs to be declared at the time of signature would be at least 1,300. Yet when the data were exchanged at the time of signature, the USSR listed only 895 OVs. One hypothesis was that the Soviets may have reduced the number of divisions holding TLE by removing all TLE from units that possessed only small quantities of these armaments. Once these TLE were shifted to other units, their former units no longer constituted an OV since they no longer possessed TLE. This reorganization of a number of units significantly reduced the number of Soviet OVs. Indeed, Western analysts largely acknowledged the truth of Soviet claims in this regard, but this still created a problem since the quota for the number of passive inspections in any given year was determined by a percentage of the number of OVs possessed by each country. Thus by reducing their OVs to somewhere between 57 percent and 69 percent of the number anticipated by NATO during the negotiations, the Soviets were also able to reduce the number of inspections they would be required to accept.

Again, while this greatly irked NATO officials, they acknowledged that there was little that could be done about it. Many analysts have passed this episode off as an inevitable consequence of the hurried endgame negotiations required to meet

President Bush's deadline for acceptance of his invitation to the Paris summit.

The third and militarily most significant issue concerned Soviet units that were excluded from the declared data. First, naval infantry units were excluded by the Soviets on the grounds that they constituted naval units not covered by the treaty at NATO's insistence. NATO countered that all TLE in land-based units was to be covered under the treaty regardless of the official designation of the service within which they were organized. This may well have been a ploy by the Soviet military to open up discussions of naval arms control in future negotiations. Second, strategic rocket forces were excluded on the grounds that their major function was internal security, namely guarding Soviet strategic weapons from unauthorized use. In this instance, NATO interests seemed to coincide with those of the USSR in assuring that Soviet nuclear weapons would not fall into the hands of possible dissident groups. Third, and most serious, was the Soviet restructuring of army units into "coastal defense units" based at Kalingrad, Murmansk, and Sevastapol. NATO maintained that these remained land-based units possessing TLEs, and as such they should be included under the agreement.

Many Western analysts viewed these various issues as ominous, not primarily because of their immediate military significance, but because of what they seemed to indicate about Soviet intentions regarding implementation of the CFE Treaty. Perhaps most serious was the impression that the Soviet military was not pleased with the extensive cuts required of their forces by CFE and that they had the power to ignore the Moscow government and undermine an agreement. Virtually all Western delegations agreed that the Soviet diplomats in Paris were taken by surprise when informed of the reflagging of the coastal defense units. It also appeared likely that these moves were made without the acquiescence, or perhaps even without the knowledge, of the Soviet Foreign Ministry. Indeed, this may have been one of the most important factors prompting the resignation of Soviet Foreign Minister Eduard Shevardnadze just a few weeks later, in protest against the resurgence of antidemocratic forces in the Soviet government. He had personally been a major figure in moving the CFE negotiations toward agreement, and he had become the personal target of many senior military officers who were opposed to the large reductions imposed on them by the treaty.

It took almost seven months of additional negotiations after the treaty was signed before these disputes were resolved to the satisfaction of all parties. On 14 June 1991, the Soviet government presented to the other signatory states a "legally binding" statement concerning how it would comply with the terms of the CFE Treaty. This statement was the outgrowth of a series of negotiations held primarily on a bilateral basis. Of special significance was a visit by General Mikhail Moiseyev, chief of the Soviet General Staff, to Washington during 20–23 May 1991. Although Moiseyev first tried to present a tough stand, he soon was persuaded that Washington was not prepared to give in on the issue of coastal defense units, though it was amenable to a compromise. Thus he indicated his willingness to count both naval infantry units and coastal defense units against treaty limits, but in a statement outside the treaty itself. Final details of this statement were worked on between Foreign Minister Alexander Bessmertnykh and Secretary of State James Baker in Lisbon on 1 June 1991.

In its statement of 14 June, the USSR first agreed to destroy some 14,500 treaty-limited armaments that had been moved east of the Urals. This satisfied the West's first concern. Next, the Soviet Union agreed to reduce its armaments in units that it acknowledged were covered by the CFE Treaty in order to compensate for TLEs in the naval infantry and coastal defense units. As the statement notes:

Forty months after entry into force of the Treaty and thereafter ... the holdings of the Union of Soviet Socialist Republics of battle tanks, armoured combat vehicles and pieces of artillery shall be less than its maximum levels of holdings, as notified in accordance with Article VII of the Treaty, by the number it will have in Coastal Defense forces and Naval Infantry within the area of application of the Treaty.

Specifically this meant that the USSR would have to reduce its tanks in other units by 933, its armored combat vehicles by 1,725, and its artillery by 1,080 below the levels permitted under the treaty. In other words, the Soviets maintained that these two units were not covered by the treaty, while covering them de facto by the agreement to reduce other forces by equal amounts. The Soviets further agreed to freeze their forces in all three categories including the strategic rocket forces at present levels and to restrict the strategic rocket forces to armored personnel carriers. Following the Soviet statement, U.S. Ambassador James Woolsey declared, "Resolution of this dispute should now allow all Signatories to proceed towards ratification and implementation of this historic agreement."

At an extraordinary meeting of the CFE signatory states on 14 June 1991, this Soviet statement was accepted by all parties to the treaty. Although all other parties also accepted this accord, there was some resentment among European delegations that the dispute was resolved largely on a bilateral basis. Several of the new democracies in Central Europe were especially concerned that some provisions of the internal agreement that had been reached among the former Warsaw Treaty Organization on dividing up the reductions among themselves might be affected in ways that hurt their interests. This concern, however, was by no means great enough for them to block the agreement. The resolution thus made it possible for all countries to proceed with ratification and implementation of the CFE Treaty.

The resolution of these allegations about treaty violations should have made it possible to move quickly to ratification and implementation of the treaty. However, an abortive military coup d'etat in the Soviet Union in August 1991 changed the schedule yet one more time. In the months following the coup attempt, Boris Yeltsin replaced Mikhail Gorbachev at the helm in Moscow, and the Soviet Union began to disintegrate. Indeed, by the end of 1991, all of the former republics had declared their independence and their desire to enter the United Nations and the CSCE as independent and sovereign states. This obviously presented several severe complications for the CFE Treaty, since obligations that applied to the entirety of the Soviet Union were no longer relevant, and the force entitlements needed to be divided among the successor states.

The first problem arose concerning the three Baltic republics of Estonia, Latvia, and Lithuania, the first states to be recognized as independent. They demanded that all Russian forces be withdrawn from their territory right away. Since they would be able to afford only very small armies of their own, they did not want to be placed under the CFE regime. They also refused to grant permission to CFE signatories to inspect Russian troops on their territories on the grounds that this would constitute de facto recognition of their right to be there. In a special meeting of the Joint Consultative Group on 18 October 1991, the Soviet Union issued a political declaration indicating that its weapons based in the Baltic states would be withdrawn rapidly, but that in the interim they would count against the Soviet Union's aggregate weapons total under the CFE Treaty.

The second and more serious problem arose in late 1991 and early 1992 when the Soviet Union itself disintegrated and was replaced by the much looser Commonwealth of Independent States (CIS). The issue immediately became one of how to divide the obligations of the Soviet Union among the eight successor states whose territory fell within the reductions zone. The most contentious debate was between the Russian Federation and Ukraine. For example, in the important category of tanks, with an overall limit of 13,150 agreed to by all former WTO states in Budapest in November 1990, the Russians initially proposed retaining 8,800, allowing only 2,800 for Ukraine and 1,125 for Belarus, whereas the Ukrainians proposed that they receive 4,800 tanks in comparison to 5,888 for Russia and 2,000 for Belarus.

Many months of intense discussions ensued, including a CIS meeting in Kiev on 20 March 1992 and two meetings in Brussels on 3 April and 8 May 1992 of the High Level Working Group of the North Atlantic Cooperation Council, a newly formed group intended to bring the CIS into closer cooperation with NATO. The outcome was an agreement on the division of forces reached among the CIS states at Tashkent, Uzbekistan, on 15 May 1992. The results (see Table 5) reflect fairly significant Russian concessions to Ukraine regarding tanks and artillery, while Russia retained a significant advantage in ACVs, which had not been contested by Ukraine.

These limits, as well as a number of other technical issues that followed from the breakup of the Soviet Union, were formally resolved at a second extraordinary conference of the CFE members, held following a NATO ministerial meeting in Oslo on 5 June 1992. This agreement removed all obstacles to ratification, and the way was paved for the CFE Treaty to enter into force at the Helsinki CSCE summit in early July. Indeed, within the next few weeks instruments of ratification were deposited by all the CIS states that had not ratified the CFE Treaty earlier, except Armenia and Belarus (whose presidential declaration of ratification was not accepted by the other states in the absence of a parliamentary decision), and by the few remaining NATO countries that had not previously ratified.

With the entry into force of CFE approaching, pressure increased on negotiators who remained in Vienna throughout the late spring and early sum-

Table 5:   Division of CFE Limits Among the CIS Agreed to at Tashkent

Country	Tanks	ACVS	Artillery	Aircraft	Helicopters
Russia*	6,400	11,480	6,415	3,450	890
Ukraine	4,080	5,050	4,040	1,090	330
Belarus	1,800	2,600	1,615	260	80
Moldova	210	210	250	50	50
Kazakhstan*	0	0	0	0	0
Georgia	220	220	285	100	50
Armenia	220	220	285	100	50
Azerbaijan	220	220	285	100	50
TOTAL	13,150	20,000	13,175	5,150	1,500

*These limits apply only to the territory of Russia and Kazakhstan located in the reduction zone west of the Ural River and Caspian Sea.

mer of 1992 to complete a so-called CFE 1A agreement on personnel reductions to accompany the armament reductions already agreed upon. There were several issues of disagreement in this negotiation.

First, the Germans placed such a high priority on reaching an agreement that an agreement for its own sake seemed more important than the content of that agreement; this created some tensions with other parties to the negotiation. While being ultimately flexible about the outcome, these parties also preferred to reach the most comprehensive and binding agreement possible, in contrast to the other parties, many of which preferred a looser outcome. Having agreed to limit themselves to 370,000 personnel under arms in the "2 + 4" talks on the reunification of Germany in July 1990, the Germans wanted to avoid being "singularized" as the only European state with a limit on their military personnel. In order to minimize this stigma, the Germans preferred a legally binding treaty, in contrast to most other participants.

The opposition to this stance was led by the United States, which feared that this agreement could not be verified with sufficient precision to survive Senate ratification hearings. The last thing that President George Bush's administration wanted in an election year was to submit a treaty to the Senate that would leave the administration vulnerable to the charges that Reagan and Bush had leveled against President Jimmy Carter during the 1980 campaign about the SALT II Treaty, namely that it was "fatally flawed" and "unverifiable." Therefore, this German objective of a legally binding agreement was not achieved, though they were able

to obtain a politically binding agreement that was signed by the twenty-nine heads of state at the Helsinki summit.

Second, most of the major powers in the negotiations wanted the agreement to be based on unilaterally declared personnel ceilings, in which each country would set its own ceiling without regard to the explicit approval of the others so long as these limits were not outrageously high. This approach was opposed most vigorously by those states bordering the former Soviet Union, especially Poland, Hungary, the Czech and Slovak Federal Republic, and Turkey. The three Central European countries were especially concerned that this might result in excessively high ceilings being set by most countries, while they preferred an agreement that would mandate reductions on the part of most states. The other participants were less concerned about this issue; even though the ceilings might be high, the others felt that budgetary pressures, especially in the light of the mandated equipment reductions, would inevitably require countries to reduce personnel far below their declared limits. This latter position prevailed in the final agreement.

Third, the Russian Federation held to old Soviet positions for a long time, namely that personnel in paramilitary forces and in units not possessing TLES in the CFE Treaty should be excluded from the CFE 1A agreement altogether. This position met with universal opposition. The major breakthrough in the negotiations came late in the spring of 1992, when the Soviets agreed to include all forces except those in paramilitary units. This compromise, however, failed to gain Polish and Turkish support until the final days before the Helsinki summit. Their opposition was complicated by the fact that these two countries proposed opposite solutions to the problem. Turkey favored the right of countries bordering on states with large numbers of paramilitary forces to increase their own units, whereas Poland, with the support of Hungary, wanted these forces included in limitations. At the last minute, Poland and Turkey gave up on these objections in order not to scuttle the entire agreement.

Fourth, the United States placed its primary emphasis upon obtaining a comprehensive information exchange about all forces in the CFE zone, including paramilitary forces and forces not containing TLES. Although the Russian Federation initially opposed this proposal, after considerable delay it accepted this trade-off: paramilitary forces would be included in the comprehensive information exchange at the same time that they would be excluded from the personnel ceilings. Indeed, it was this compromise that led the United States, Great Britain, and a number of other key countries to drop their insistence on including paramilitary forces in the personnel limitations.

The negotiations on CFE 1A reached a furious pace between the Oslo extraordinary meeting of CFE on 5 June 1992 and 6 July, the eve of the Helsinki summit. Prior to that time, the major negotiations had been conducted in three bilateral sets of conservations, between the Germans and the Russians, the Russians and the United States, with Germany and the United States coordinating their bilateral approaches to the Russians. Later the British and French were brought into this small group of key states, and in the final weeks Poland and Turkey were included as the major skeptical parties. Finally, an agreement was initialed in Vienna on 6 July 1992.

The CFE 1A Treaty was duly signed by all heads of state during the Helsinki summit at the third extraordinary conference of the twenty-nine CFE states on 10 July 1992. National personnel limits were spelled out in the body of the text, including limits of 250,000 personnel in Europe for the United States; 1,450,000 for the Russian Federation; 345,000 for Germany; 450,000 for Ukraine; 530,000 for Turkey; 325,000 for France; and 260,000 for the United Kingdom. Virtually all ceilings were larger than actual personnel deployments at the time of signature.

The treaty included an extensive information exchange that would gradually provide more detailed, comprehensive, and disaggregated data during the forty months that the CFE Treaty was put into force, concluding with data on all full-time military personnel down to the brigade/regiment or equivalent level. Stabilizing measures were adopted that required prior notification of any increases in unit strength, of reserve call-ups, or of force reorganization. Finally a section on "verification/evaluation" (a compromise between a German desire for verification and a U.S. preference for evaluation) called for providing data on personnel levels in connection with all inspections visits mandated under the CFE Treaty. The CFE 1A agreement would give inspectors access to units on inspection sites, for purposes of verifying personnel figures, including access to those units not possessing TLE under the CFE Treaty.

In the extraordinary conference at Helsinki, in addition to adopting the CFE 1A agreement, the eight successor states to the Soviet Union also signed the CFE Treaty, which had been modified to take into account many technical and legal issues resulting from the breakup of the USSR. At the same time, all twenty-nine signatories agreed that the CFE Treaty and the CFE 1A agreement would enter into force provisionally one week later, on 19 July 1992. The provisional entry into force was necessitated by the lack of official ratification by Armenia and Belarus, which was anticipated to come during the first 120 days, when initial inspections were to verify the baseline data prior to actual commencement of reductions.

Finally at Helsinki the CSCE Follow-on Conference, with its membership increased to fifty-two (although Yugoslavia was suspended from the summit), also adopted a mandate for new security negotiations in Europe, to be known as the CSCE Forum for Security Cooperation. This new forum was scheduled to begin meeting in Vienna on 22 September 1992, effectively replacing CFE as the primary locus for all future European negotiations on conventional arms control and confidence- and security-building measures. Unlike CFE, this forum would include all CSCE members, and all states would participate individually without reference to any military blocs or alliances.

Although the new mandate produced a lengthy list of items for immediate action, it was apparent that there was little prospect for reaching agreement on further significant measures of "hard arms control" in Europe, at least until the CFE Treaty and

1A agreement had been fully implemented in late 1995. The major focus of the new forum would likely be on the harmonization of the CFE provisions with regard to those CSCE states that were not CFE signatories. Although some negotiators hoped to be able to accommodate all CSCE states within the CFE framework, this appeared to be extremely difficult. Chaos in the Balkan region made the participation of most former Yugoslav republics unlikely in the short-term future. Dependence upon large militia and reserve forces would make it difficult to apply many CFE provisions to states such as Sweden and Switzerland. Finally, some states, such as Malta and Cyprus, seemed to show little interest in participation in CFE, and the inclusion of the latter would almost certainly be vetoed by Turkey in any event.

Other items mentioned in the CSCE mandate included further measures on confidence- and security-building beyond those adopted in Vienna in 1992; cooperation regarding non-proliferation and arms transfers; regional measures of arms control; cooperation in conversion from defense to civilian production; and cooperation in force planning and in the development of defense doctrine. Indeed, a goal-oriented security dialogue among the states of Europe was among the most hopeful provisions adopted at the Helsinki summit.

CONCLUSION

The political changes that swept across Europe during the period from 1989 through 1991 changed the European security situation fundamentally. Throughout the entire period of negotiation, both CFE and CFE 1A were caught in a constant struggle to avoid falling hopelessly behind the events that swirled around them. In the final analysis both were transitional agreements: they simultaneously constituted the concluding military agreements of the Cold War, and indeed, even of World War II with regard to the status of Germany, while also laying the foundation for a new European security regime. The political changes in Central and Eastern Europe were reinforced in the military realm by these two agreements. The fear of a massive surprise attack by one country upon others was largely removed from the realm of possibility.

New threats to European security, however, seemed to emanate from the potential disintegration of nation-states, ethnic rivalries within states, migration of populations across state boundaries,

and chaos resulting from the economic perils of the transition from centrally planned economies to market economies throughout Central and Eastern Europe. Yet these issues would inevitably fall into the realm of the political institutions evolving within the CSCE and other European institutions, including the European Community, the Council of Europe, the Western European Union, and a drastically revised North Atlantic Treaty Organization, all of which would likely replace formal arms control negotiations as the focal point for discussion of future European security issues.

The success of the CFE and CFE 1A negotiations was a major reflection of the dramatic reduction of tensions in Europe, and the agreements undoubtedly contributed reciprocally to reducing tensions by eliminating almost all military potential for massive surprise attack. Whether the reduction of the military threat could be converted into effective mechanisms to reduce the threats emanating from political and economic causes, however, remained to be seen. But CSCE and MBFR/CFE, which started out as separate and independent negotiations with very different mandates, converged in the summer of 1992. Together they offered the potential basis for a new security regime in Europe that could replace the Cold War tensions and conflicts with a new era of cooperation.

BIBLIOGRAPHY

Background to European security issues in the 1960s and early 1970s, leading up to the opening of MBFR and CSCE, can be found in ROBERT E. HUNTER, *Security in Europe*, 2d ed. (Bloomington, Ind., 1972); WOLFGANG KLAIBER, *Era of Negotiations: European Security and Force Reductions* (Lexington, Mass., 1973), and OLGA SUKOVIC of the Stockholm International Peace Research Institute, *Force Reductions in Europe* (New York, 1974).

Analyses A detailed analysis of the events leading up to MBFR and the early years of those negotiations, emphasizing technical military issues, may be found in JOHN G. KELIHER, *The Negotiations on Mutual and Balanced Force Reductions: The Search for Arms Control in Central Europe* (New York, 1980). A more comprehensive view of the broad range of security and arms control issues in Europe in the early years of the MBFR negotiations is found in JOSEPH I. COFFEY, *Arms Control and Eu-*

ropean Security: A Guide to East-West Negotiations (New York, 1977). See also J. DAVID SINGER, Deterrence, Arms Control, and Disarmament: Toward a Synthesis of National Security Policy (Columbus, Ohio, 1962). Western European views of the early years of the negotiations are presented in an edited volume by JONATHAN ALFORD of the British International Institute for Strategic Studies, Arms Control and European Security (New York, 1984). A German view is presented persuasively by LOTHAR RUEHL in MBFR: Lessons and Problems (London, 1982).

Surveys Perhaps the best overall survey of European security and arms control issues through the mid-1980s, with a special emphasis on MBFR, is found in a book by the former U.S. ambassador to MBFR: JONATHAN DEAN, Watershed in Europe: Dismantling the East-West Military Confrontation (Lexington, Mass., 1987). Ambassador Dean has also written numerous excellent articles on MBFR, of which the most important is probably "MBFR: From Apathy to Accord," International Security 7 (Spring 1983): 116–139.

The relationship between arms reductions and confidence-building measures is treated in F. STEPHEN LARRABEE and DIETRICH STOBBE, eds., Confidence-Building Measures in Europe (New York, 1983). The Institute for East-West Security Studies has also produced a comprehensive anthology of articles on all aspects of conventional arms control in Europe: ROBERT D. BLACKWILL and F. STEPHEN LARRABEE eds., Conventional Arms Control and East-West Security (Durham, N.C., 1989).

The relationship between conventional arms control and nuclear weapons in Europe is treated in DAVID SCHWARTZ, NATO's Nuclear Dilemmas (Washington, D.C., 1983); JOHN D. STEINBRUNER and LEON V. SIGAL eds., Alliance Security: NATO and the No-First-Use Question (Washington, D.C., 1983); P. TERRENCE HOPMANN, "The Path to No-First-Use: Conventional Arms Control," World Policy Journal 1 (Winter 1984): 319–337; and P. TERRENCE HOPMANN and FRANK BARNABY eds., Rethinking the Nuclear Weapons Dilemma in Europe (London, 1988).

Ongoing Sources The CFE negotiations have been completed too recently to have been covered in any published books. The negotiation process has been reported in several sources, however, including The Arms Control Reporter and ViennaFax, published by the Institute for Defense and Disarmament Studies in Cambridge, Massachusetts; BASIC Reports from Vienna, published by the British American Security Information Council in Washington, D.C.; and the monthly Arms Control Today, published by the Arms Control Association in Washington, D.C.

An early monograph covering the CFE negotiations has been written by IVO H. DAALDER, The CFE Treaty: An Overview and an Assessment (Washington, D.C., 1991). The text of the CFE Treaty was published at the time of signature in Paris on 19 November 1990 by the United States Information Agency.

Technical Assessment A technical assessment of the CFE's possible impact on military stability in Europe, written before the final conclusion of the CFE treaty, is found in JOSHUA M. EPSTEIN, Conventional Force Reductions: A Dynamic Assessment (Washington, D.C., 1990).

Anti-Satellite Weapons and Arms Control

JOHN PIKE

ERIC STAMBLER

See also The Anti-Ballistic Missile Treaty: 1972 to the Present; The Outer Space Treaty: 1967 to the Present; *and* The Strategic Defense Initiative and Arms Control. *Most of the treaties discussed in this essay are excerpted in Volume III.*

Satellites provide important support services to military forces on earth and, therefore, contribute significantly to the stability of the strategic balance. The importance of military space systems in times of both war and peace led to the development of ambivalent policies on the part of the United States and the former Soviet Union. From the late 1950s on, each country sought to acquire anti-satellite (ASAT) weapons to reduce the combat effectiveness of the other's satellites. Each country also, at various times, sought to undertake arms control negotiations to reduce the threat posed by the other's anti-satellite weapons (ASATS).

The policy dilemma was in trying to decide which threat was greater—that posed by an opponent's military satellites to one's own terrestrial military forces, or that posed by an opponent's ASATS to one's own military satellites supporting terrestrial military forces. Concern about the threat from an opponent's military satellites—that is, their capacity to provide information for launching a preemptive or first strike—was the basis for the development of ASAT systems; concern about the threat produced by an opponent's ASATS to one's own military satellites was the basis for proposing ASAT arms control measures.

As of 1992 there were no limitations or controls on the testing or deployment of anti-satellite weap-ons. The 1967 Outer Space Treaty precludes the stationing in orbit of nuclear weapons, but places no limits on other types of ASAT weapons. The 1972 Strategic Arms Limitation Talks (SALT I) agreement prohibited attacks on satellites used for verification, but placed no limits on the acquisition of systems for conducting such attacks. Negotiations for controlling ASAT weapons were held in the late 1970s, but proved inconclusive.

The case for controlling or limiting ASATS has been complicated by the fact that the technology required to intercept satellites in space is quite similar to that needed to intercept ballistic missiles or their warheads. Therefore, the development or deployment of anti-missile weaponry leads to the development of ASAT capability. Given the relatively small numbers of critical military satellites in orbit, even a modest anti-missile capability could constitute a significant ASAT capability. The prospects for ASAT arms control measures, consequently, are inextricably tied to the status of limitations placed on anti-missile systems. And during the 1980s, the ASAT arms control debate was closely tied to the debate over the Strategic Defense Initiative (SDI).

In 1983 the Soviet Union proposed a moratorium on the testing of anti-satellite weapons. Despite objections from the Reagan administration, the United States Congress responded favorably to this initiative. The informal moratorium has remained in place since 1985.

Neither the United States nor Russia, in the early 1990s, had the capacity to pose a significant threat to their respective rival's satellites. The operational Russian ASAT had significant limitations and was of doubtful military utility. The United States had deployed several ASAT systems in the past, and developed several more, but lacked an operational system as of 1992. During the Cold War, neither superpower regarded anti-satellite weapons as a high priority. With the Cold War's end, the utility of anti-satellite weapons may be called into further doubt.

ASAT MISSIONS

The growth of interest in anti-satellite systems in the 1980s resulted from the increased use of satellites to directly support military forces on earth, both in low-level conventional conflicts and as part of plans for the conducting of a protracted nuclear war. Although military satellites themselves are not lethal devices, they provide information that may increase the effectiveness of military forces by enabling improved targeting and damage-assessment capabilities. Communication, navigation, weather, and other satellites serve to supply the information needed to increase the combat potential of terrestrial weapon systems. These satellites also provide early warning of a nuclear attack as well as support for retaliatory forces; thus, these satellites are a critical component of a strategic deterrence posture.

Both the United States and the former Soviet Union have been dependent on military satellites, and both countries have consequently had an interest in reducing the vulnerability of these vital devices. As the well-respected authority Paul Stares points out, arguments claiming that anti-satellite weapons are destabilizing stem from the threat they pose to satellites supporting strategic deterrence. He notes in "Reagan and the ASAT Issue" in the Summer 1985 *Journal of International Affairs* that "the destruction or disruption of early warning and strategic communication satellites could, at least in theory, facilitate a first strike and reduce the retaliatory options of the attacked state" (p. 92).

Scenarios presented during the peak of the United States–Soviet ASAT debate, in the early to mid-1980s, focused on a first-strike attack on the full range of reconnaissance, navigation, early warn-

ing, and communication satellites. Such a planned assault would disrupt an initial retaliation and greatly reduce subsequent retaliatory efforts. These scenarios placed great emphasis on the initiation of hostilities and a general nuclear exchange, and had very negative implications for crisis stability.

At that time, however, neither the United States nor the Soviet Union had a strategic force that could come close to conducting a credible first strike. There were, in the early 1990s, approximately 150 Russian satellites in orbit, 90 percent of which were used by the military. At the same time, the United States ASAT system under development would provide only 60 to 75 interceptors; however, Defense Department officials claimed that this number would be sufficient to destroy the most important Russian satellites and their backups.

Yet in the absence of an effective "sky-sweeping" ASAT capability, it is difficult to imagine a plausible scenario for the use of counterforce, first-strike weapons. Communication, navigation, and targeting satellites could be used to coordinate surviving strategic forces, which would continue to be used in selective countervalue strikes as part of the "inter-war bargaining process," thereby effectively negating the strategic aim of the first strike.

Thus, there would be powerful incentives for a belligerent to launch a "sky-sweeping" ASAT campaign at the outset of a general war. At the same time, such action would virtually guarantee that the ensuing conflict would involve massive exchanges, with little prospect for control or damage limitation. It is the prospective loss both of command-and-control facilities and of attack characterization capabilities that would make a persuasive case for unleashing one's strategic forces, which might otherwise remain dormant, at the outset of a general war.

U.S. ASATS

The United States first started work on ASATs in the 1950s. Fortunately, the threat that these systems were intended to counter—that of orbiting nuclear weapons—failed to materialize. These early nuclear-armed ASATs, moreover, had major operational limitations, in that detonation of an ASAT's nuclear warheads would damage U.S. satellites as well as intended enemy satellites.

Because of the limitations of early guidance systems, these anti-satellite weapons could be counted on to place a warhead only within a few miles of a target, which meant that the weapon required nuclear warheads to make sure the target was destroyed. High-altitude nuclear tests in the early 1960s demonstrated, however, that the electromagnetic pulse from an explosion would be lethal to satellites over a much longer range. A 1962 test, for example, set off burglar alarms and darkened streetlights across Hawaii, hundreds of miles away, and disabled several U.S. satellites that happened to be in its vicinity.

The sensitive electronics on satellites proved to be particularly vulnerable to nuclear explosions in space. The military utility of indiscriminate anti-satellite weapons was discounted, since these weapons threatened to do as much or more damage to friendly satellites as they did to intended targets. When the threat of orbiting nuclear weapons did not materialize, the U.S. ASAT systems were dismantled.

Early ASAT Efforts

During the late 1950s and early 1960s several air-launched ASAT systems were tested by the United States. These systems tests grew out of ongoing efforts to develop strategic air-launched ballistic missiles and did not result in operational systems; but, these tests were indicative of an early and abiding interest in ASAT weapons.

Project Bold Orion, an ASAT tested by the air force beginning in October 1959, was launched by rockets from a B-47 bomber. In the two HiHo tests in 1962, the navy launched rockets from an F-4 fighter. Interestingly, both the Bold Orion and HiHo ASAT test programs of the early 1960s used the Altair rocket motor as a second stage, the same rocket upper stage as the later miniature homing vehicle ASAT. The U.S. Army's Nike Zeus ASAT was originally developed as part of an anti-ballistic missile (ABM) system. After years of research it became clear that the Nike Zeus ASAT would be largely ineffective as an ABM. According to Paul Stares, writing in his 1985 text *The Militarization of Space: U.S. Policy, 1945–1984,*

The U.S. Army's proposal to convert the Nike Zeus missile to the ASAT role in November 1957 and later in January 1960 marked the beginning of an almost symbiotic relationship between ABM and ASAT research and development. This was inevitable given the similar requirements and methods to detect, track and intercept both missiles and satellites. Moreover, the possession of exoatmospheric ABM missiles by definition provided a limited ASAT ca-

pability or certainly a system that could be transformed into one with relative ease (pp. 117–118).

The first successful U.S. space anti-satellite intercept took place on 23 May 1963, from Kwajalein Island in the Pacific Ocean. Throughout Project MUDFLAP, or Program 505 as it became generally known, at least eight Nike Zeus ground-launched missiles were fired from 1963 until 13 January 1966.

The U.S. Air Force, not to be outdone, also tested and deployed several Thor rockets that were modified for the anti-satellite mission. This capability grew out of the 1962 Operation Dominic series of high-altitude nuclear tests. These nuclear-tipped ASATs became operational on Johnston Island in the Pacific in 1964 and could intercept a target at a much greater range than the Nike Zeus. The system, according to the 14 October 1963 issue of *Aviation Week and Space Technology,* consisted of "a thrust-augmented Douglas Thor-Delta with three strap-on solid rockets, a combination giving the high acceleration needed to intercept satellites in near earth orbit" (p. 25).

The Program 437 Thor system was tested at least sixteen times from 1964 to 1970, prior to its retirement in 1976. This system could have been restored to operational status on six months' notice, since the booster components were stored as part of the U.S. capability to resume nuclear testing in the event of the demise of the Limited Test Ban Treaty (LTBT).

Analyst Frank Leary, writing in the June 1969 issue of *Space/Aeronautics,* claimed that "Program 437 . . . laid the technological groundwork for the Sentinel, Spartan, Sprint and Safeguard [ABM systems]" (p. 44). Both the Nike Zeus and Thor ASAT systems would have utilized nuclear warheads to destroy their targets. This, coupled with the complexity of their launch procedures, resulted in a limited capability with severe operational constraints. "The respective advantages of the two systems," Stares wrote in *The Militarization of Space,* "were that the Nike Zeus could react more quickly due to its solid propellant, while the Thor missile could be fired against targets at higher altitudes" (p. 81). Following the retirement of the Thor program, United States' emphasis shifted to non-nuclear kinetic "kill" mechanisms.

Air-Launched Miniature Vehicle Program

The air-launched miniature vehicle (ALMV) was the primary U.S. ASAT effort of the early 1980s. This weapon, launched from an F-15 fighter aircraft by a small two-stage rocket, carried a heat-seeking miniature homing vehicle (MHV) that could destroy its target by direct impact at high speed. The F-15 could also bring the ALMV under the ground track of its target, as opposed to a ground-based system, which requires a target satellite to overfly its launch site.

An operational force was planned to ultimately number more than one hundred interceptors. However, by 1986 the program, initially expected to cost $500 million, was projected to require $5.3 billion to complete. In an attempt to limit costs, the air force scaled back the MHV program by two-thirds in 1987. Subsequently, the Reagan administration canceled the program in 1988 after encountering technical problems with its homing-guidance system, as well as testing delays and significant additional cost increases.

Kinetic-Energy ASAT   The army's kinetic-energy (KE) ASAT was the Pentagon's main satellite-attack weapon under research and development in the early 1990s. As with the air force's air-launched project, this ground-based interceptor would destroy satellites by homing in on and colliding with them. The three-stage missile would extend a sheet of Mylar, known as a "kill enhancement device," which would strike the target and render it inoperative without shattering the satellite. This interceptor, however, would only be able to reach satellites in low earth orbit, up to ranges of several thousand kilometers. The technology is similar to the anti-ballistic missile (ABM) "hit-to-kill" interceptor, which was first tested successfully in the 1984 homing overlay experiment (HOE), and subsequently in the exoatmospheric reentry vehicle interception system (ERIS) tests, conducted under the Strategic Defense Initiative (SDI) anti-missile program.

The army has plans to start flight-testing its missile in late 1996—seven flight tests would include two actual interceptions of inactive U.S. satellites in orbit, the other five tests would involve close passes to orbiting satellites. Deployment is scheduled to begin in June 1998. According to Defense Department estimates, the KE ASAT could be built and operated for twenty years for $2–2.5 billion.

The nearest-term ASAT for the United States, in the early 1990s, was the mid-infrared advanced chemical laser (MIRACL) located at the White Sands testing range in New Mexico. Originally an SDI proj-

ect, the laser has been sought by the Pentagon to be adapted for use against satellites. In addition to MIRACL, the Pentagon has been working on two other directed-energy, ground-based ASATs based on excimer and free-electron lasers. Both technologies could be operational in the late 1990s. The directed-energy systems, in contrast to the KE ASAT, would have the ability to destroy large numbers of satellites in a very short period of time.

SOVIET ASATS

In 1968 the Soviet Union began testing a new type of anti-satellite weapon, launched atop a rocket known as the SL-10—a modified version of the SS-9 intercontinental ballistic missile (ICBM). The rocket would place a multiton satellite into low earth orbit, and this interceptor satellite would maneuver within striking range of its target. When the interceptor came within a few miles of its target, a small explosive charge would be detonated, showering the enemy satellite with shrapnel. Delicate satellites could be readily destroyed by this type of explosion. The system has been tested a total of twenty times since 1968. From 1968 to 1971, an interceptor was tested that used an active radar to direct it to the target within two orbits after launch. It achieved a 70-percent success rate in seven tests.

In 1976 the Soviets began testing an active radar interceptor that could attack targets in orbits that were somewhat different from that of the initial orbit of the interceptor. Interceptors using radar-homing have demonstrated a 30-percent failure rate, and subsequent tests using a heat-seeking sensor failed in six attempts, including the last Soviet ASAT test in June 1982.

Continued testing of the two-orbit radar interceptor has yielded a 66-percent success rate in three tests since 1976. The system had only marginal effectiveness as it required the intended target satellite to fly over the Baikonur launch facility before an interception could be attempted. With a maximum vertical range of 1,500 kilometers (about 900 miles), it was unable to reach most major U.S. satellites.

Under any plausible arms control agreement, the Russians would retain a certain residual ASAT capability in such systems as their Galosh anti-ballistic missile (ABM), and in some of their manned and unmanned spaceflight systems.

ARMS CONTROL EFFORTS

The sporadic character of ASAT weapon development has been matched by equally sporadic efforts at negotiating controls or limitations over their development. The Soviets ceased temporarily the testing of the co-orbital system at the end of 1971 and conducted no tests over the next four and a half years, including during the period of the Strategic Arms Limitation Talks (SALT). U.S. concern over the Soviet Union's activities in space at this time was quite minimal. In 1970 the operational readiness of Program 437 was reduced from twenty-four hours to thirty days.

According to Paul Stares's account in *The Militarization of Space,* several individuals within the Defense Department at this time believed "that a tacit arrangement could be reached with the Soviet Union whereby space would remain a sanctuary for the unhindered operation of their respective military space systems" (p. 172). Also, some observers attributed this test pause to a decision by the Soviets to abandon their ASAT program, and this perception may have contributed to the 1975 deactivation of the U.S. nuclear-armed ASAT.

In an article comparing U.S. and Soviet military space programs written for the Spring 1985 issue of *Daedalus,* Stares noted that:

by 1976, the increasing military use of space on the part of the Soviets had become a source of concern to the United States. . . . The resumption of Soviet satellite interceptor tests in 1976 was the primary catalyst for the United States' reconsideration of the usefulness of anti-satellite weapons. While the new Soviet tests were not markedly different from the earlier series (and if anything had an inferior performance), the tenor of U.S.–Soviet relations had changed significantly. . . . As a result, President Gerald Ford in one of the last acts of his administration authorized the development of a new U.S. anti-satellite system. While the ostensible rationale was to counter the indirect threat from Soviet military satellites—especially ocean reconnaissance satellites—the real reason appears to have been an unwillingness to accept any imbalance in U.S.–Soviet ASAT capabilities. (pp. 134–135)

The interest of President Jimmy Carter's administration in negotiating limitations on ASATS was initially hampered by the fundamental asymmetry between the Soviet and U.S. arsenals. The Soviets had an ASAT of some description, and the United States did not. President Carter announced in a March 1977 press conference that he had decided to pursue a two-track strategy. On the one hand, he approached the Soviets about foregoing "the opportunity to arm satellite bodies and also to forego the opportunity to destroy observation satellites." At the same time, he sought to develop a United States capability that could be traded for the Soviet destruction of their co-orbital system.

The air-launched miniature vehicle (ALMV) ASAT was the solution to this problem. Largely based on previously developed "off-the-shelf" technology, it was a near-term option, one that could be quickly developed, which could be "traded" for the existing Soviet ASAT should negotiations succeed, or subsequently upgraded in the event the negotiations failed. Other, more capable systems seemingly were rejected on the basis of cost and the time needed to develop them.

The United States and the Soviet Union conducted three negotiating sessions in 1978 and 1979 concerning ASATS. During these negotiations, the Soviets initiated a test pause, which lasted from May 1978 to April 1980. The Soviets advocated a permanent test ban, while the U.S. delegation called for a one-year test moratorium. These talks were discontinued when the Carter administration decided to concentrate its arms control efforts on ratification of the SALT II agreement. They were never resumed because of the general deterioration of United States–Soviet relations following the Soviet intervention in Afghanistan in December 1979. The Soviet test pause ended when it became clear that the United States had little interest in resuming the talks.

The Reagan Administration   In August 1981 the Soviets submitted a draft treaty to the United Nations prohibiting weapons in space. However, there were a number of problematic elements in this effort. Soviet Foreign Minister Andrey Gromyko, in his cover letter for the 1981 draft, characterized it as little more than an extension of the 1967 Outer Space Treaty, which banned the deployment in space of nuclear and other weapons of mass destruction. He noted that the 1981 draft would prohibit outer-space stationing of those kinds of weapons that are not covered by the definition of weapons of mass destruction. This treaty would not have restricted the testing, development, and deployment of ground-based or air-launched ASATS.

President Ronald Reagan's administration held that a treaty banning the possession of ASATs could not be verified; for this reason, the administration attested, it had little interest in the negotiations. The administration's major concern was that relatively few U.S. satellites would have to be neutralized in order to seriously impair the U.S. strategic posture. National security would be threatened if even a few ASATs escaped the verification process. Consequently, no further action was taken on the Soviet draft.

Next, on 18 August 1983, Soviet Premier Yuri Andropov proposed a moratorium on the testing of ASATs during the course of a meeting with a delegation of United States senators. He called for a "complete prohibition of the testing and development of any space-based weapons for hitting targets on Earth, in the air or in outer space." Furthermore, he committed the USSR "not to be the first to put into outer space any type of antisatellite weapon" as long as other countries "refrain from stationing in outer space antisatellite weapons of any type" (Dusko Doder, "Andropov Urges Ban on Weapons to Attack Satellites," *Washington Post,* 19 August 1983, p. 1).

On 22 August 1983, the Soviets introduced a revised draft treaty at the United Nations substantially different from the 1981 draft, banning the use of force in space and all testing of ASAT systems. It also called for the dismantling of existing ASAT systems. Apart from any other considerations, the scope of the new proposals seemed to suggest a serious Soviet interest in dealing with the major issues posed by the space weapons competition.

Recognizing the shortcomings of the Soviet proposal, the Union of Concerned Scientists, a prominent private arms control group, convened a panel of leading experts to prepare an alternative draft ASAT treaty. Its proposal generated considerable congressional interest in the issue. As the Reagan administration remained unresponsive to the Soviet initiatives, members of Congress began to apply pressure to begin negotiations and to halt testing. The first congressional action to place limits on the ASAT program was the passage of the Tsongas amendment put forward by Senator Paul Tsongas of Massachusetts in 1983, which prohibited in-space tests of the ASAT unless the president made certain certifications relating to progress on negotiating an agreement with the Soviets on ASAT limits and also the need for such tests. Similar language was passed again in 1984.

The administration's position was clarified in a report submitted to Congress on 31 March 1984, which stated:

No arrangements or agreements beyond those already governing military activities in outer space have been found to date that are judged to be in the overall interest of the United States and its Allies. The factors which impede the identification of effective ASAT arms control measures include significant difficulties of verification, diverse sources of threats to U.S. and Allied satellites and threats posed by Soviet targeting and reconnaissance satellites which undermine conventional and nuclear deterrence. . . . Until we have determined whether there are, in fact, practical solutions to these problems, we do not believe it would be productive to engage in formal international negotiations.

In 1985 President Reagan submitted certifications to Congress, permitting the first and only test of the F-15 miniature homing vehicle (MHV) device against an object in space on 13 September of that year.

Starting in fiscal year 1985, Congress began to cut the administration's requests for MHV funding by substantial amounts. Congressional ASAT opponents felt that preventing complete testing of the MHV device could preserve the chance to negotiate an ASAT agreement with the Soviet Union. It was hoped by many, including Congressman George Brown of California, that a moratorium would "provide a window of opportunity to explore a mutual and verifiable ban on ASATs" (*Congressional Record,* 8 May 1984, p. E2005).

Congressional opposition to ASATs, as well as the administration's support for the program, was closely linked to the ongoing debate over the Strategic Defense Initiative (SDI) anti-missile program. Both sides viewed the ASAT testing-and-deployment debate as a crucial testing ground for the impending debate over testing and deployment of SDI. From 1985 through 1988, Congress successfully imposed language prohibiting ASAT tests against objects in space until and unless the Soviet Union retested its ASAT device. The MHV program was finally canceled in December 1988.

Representative Brown introduced an amendment to the fiscal year 1989 Defense Department authorization bill that would have created a permanent ASAT test ban, but this measure was narrowly defeated. Following the defeat of the permanent ban, the Defense Department attempted to give renewed momentum to the development of a U.S. ASAT. On 6 March 1989, the Defense Acquisition

Board approved programs for the development of both kinetic-energy and directed-energy ASATs and selected the army to manage the kinetic-energy ASAT program. The Defense Department proceeded to request $208 million for the rejuvenated program in fiscal year 1991, an increase of 181 percent over the previous year's level.

Critics questioned the rush to develop new ASAT systems at a time when momentous changes were occurring in the Soviet Union, changes that made the likelihood of a "space" war negligible. Congressional opposition to ASATs took the form of attempts to reduce funding levels, rather than efforts to prevent testing, which would not begin for several years. Senator John Kerry introduced an amendment in August 1990 for FY 1991 Defense Authorization designed to reduce funding for ASATs to the previous year's level. This effort was unsuccessful. The army ASAT program was funded at $51 million for fiscal year 1993. Congressional action was successful, however, in placing a one-year ban on testing of the mid-infrared advanced chemical laser (MIRACL) against objects in space.

The Bush Administration

Although the Soviets had not conducted an ASAT test since 1982, President George Bush's administration maintained its insistence that the Soviet co-orbital system was indeed operationally capable. According to General Colin Powell in Defense Department appropriations hearings for fiscal year 1991, "lack of a U.S. ASAT capability—in real military terms—remains a serious warfighting deficiency" (U.S. Congress. Senate. *Hearings Before a Subcommittee of the Committee on Appropriations on H.R. 5803/S. 3189*, pt. 1, p. 207).

The president's national security advisor, Brent Scowcroft, reaffirmed the status of the ASAT program as one of the administration's top priorities. In a letter dated 22 June 1990, Scowcroft claimed, "It is essential for the U.S. to develop an operational ASAT system to deter the Soviets from exploiting their space control and space-based targeting capabilities." He went on to say that the "Soviet ability to target our forces from space alone constitutes a compelling rationale for deploying a U.S. ASAT system" (*Congressional Record,* 3 August 1990, p. S12031).

Advocates of a U.S. ASAT system argued that it was needed to counter this perceived Soviet ASAT threat, as well as to effect the destruction of an opponent's satellites in the event of hostilities. The chief of naval operations stated in response to congressional inquiry in hearings for Defense Department Appropriations for fiscal year 1991 that

even in a climate of improving relations it is not clear that an ASAT test ban treaty and elimination of the co-orbital ASAT would enhance our overall security posture. . . . Of greater concern for maritime operations than an end to the announced ASAT test moratorium is the combination of a robust Soviet space-based surveillance, tracking, and targeting capability, and the lack of a demonstrated U.S. ASAT capability, which affords a sanctuary for Soviet satellites. (U.S. Congress. Senate. *Hearings Before a Subcommittee of the Committee on Appropriations on H.R. 5803/S. 3189,* Part 3, p. 441)

The fundamental incompatibility of these two rationales has been repeatedly alluded to by members of Congress and other critics of continued ASAT development. A deterrence mission cannot coexist with the plan to use ASATs early in a conflict to disable enemy observation satellites. The administration has expressed a desire for space control. According to Army Secretary Stone, "the current U.S. national space policy recognizes that a space control capability is a key element of America's national security space posture. Space control requires an integrated combination of space surveillance, anti-satellite capabilities and satellite survivability/endurance."

These notions seemed increasingly anachronistic in the post–Cold War era, yet in the early 1990s they still appeared to be driving the U.S. ASAT program.

CONCLUSION

The future of the United States' anti-satellite capability has remained tied to the status of ballistic-missile defenses. Even if the U.S. Army kinetic-energy ASAT program, ongoing in the early 1990s, were to be discontinued, the establishment of an anti-ballistic missile (ABM) site at Grand Forks, North Dakota, as projected in Defense Department plans for the Global Protection Against Limited Strikes SDI program, would provide inherent anti-satellite capabilities. ASAT arms control efforts are not likely to be successful until the future of strategic defenses has been resolved.

Advocates of the continued need for ASATs have argued that the potential use or purchase of satellite intelligence services by third countries justifies the United States' continued efforts to develop anti-satellite weapons. The Chinese satellite reconnaissance program was cited as one possible reason for the resumption of Soviet ASAT testing in 1976. France has been developing its own reconnaissance satellite, Helios, which could be launched in 1994; and Israel reportedly has also been working on intelligence satellites. By the early twenty-first century, a number of other countries, including Brazil, India, and Japan, could also possess military reconnaissance satellites that could constitute attractive targets for an opponent's ASAT system.

The proliferation of military space systems may be matched by the proliferation of anti-satellite capabilities. While the development of a highly competent ASAT system has proven a challenge for the United States, less-sophisticated weapons capable of threatening a handful of low-altitude reconnaissance satellites might eventually prove to be within reach of any space-faring country.

Fortunately, much of the technology required for developing an ASAT is under the supervision of the Missile Technology Control Regime (MTCR). But achieving multilateral arms control agreements on anti-satellite weapons will prove at least as challenging as did the U.S.-Soviet ASAT arms control effort.

BIBLIOGRAPHY

General Accounts　MARCIA S. SMITH, *Space Activities of the United States, Soviet Union, and Other Launching Countries/Organizations, 1957–1984* (Washington, D.C., 1985), prepared by the Congressional Research Service, provides a general survey of space activities. Several books and articles focusing on military activities in space relate in various ways to the ASAT issue. Among these are the essays in WILLIAM J. DURCH, ed., *National Interests and the Military Use of Space* (Cambridge, Mass., 1984); and PAUL B. STARES, *The Militarization of Space: U.S. Policy, 1945–1984* (Ithaca, N.Y., 1985) and *Space and National Security* (Washington, D.C., 1987).

Also, see STARE's useful essay, "U.S. and Soviet Military Space Programs: A Comparative Assessment," *Daedalus* 114 (Spring 1985): 127–145, which has examined the programs of the superpowers.

Anti-Satellite Weapons　ASPEN STRATEGY GROUP, *Anti-Satellite Weapons and U.S. Military Space Policy* (Lanham, Md., 1986), provides an overview of the issues. Among articles that have focused on specific topics are those by ASHTON B. CARTER, "The Re-

lationship of ASAT and BMD Systems," *Daedalus* 114 (Spring 1985): 171–189 and "Satellites and Anti-Satellites: The Limits of the Possible," *International Security* 10 (Spring 1986): 46–98; KURT GOTTFRIED and RICHARD NED LEBOW, "Anti-Satellite Weapons: Weighing the Risks," *Daedalus* 114 (Spring 1985): 147–170; and JOHN PIKE, "Anti-Satellite Weapons," *FAS Public Interest Report* 36 (November 1983) for the Federation of American Scientists.

The Reagan administration's position is discussed in PAUL B. STARES, "Reagan and the ASAT Issue," *Journal of International Affairs* 39 (Summer 1985): 81–94.

ASAT and Arms Control　The literature on this theme is scattered and is usually found in essay, briefing, or report form. A Stockholm International Peace Research Institute (SIPRI) volume that collects the views of several individuals is BHUPENDA JASANI, ed., *Space Weapons—The Arms Control Dilemma* (London and Philadelphia, 1984). These essays include WALTER SLOCOMBE, "Approaches to an ASAT Treaty," pp. 145–155; KURT GOTTFRIED, "An ASAT Test Ban Treaty," pp. 131–144 (includes a copy of the Union of Concerned Scientists' proposed treaty); DONALD KERR, "Implications of Anti-Satellite Weapons for ABM Issues," pp. 107–125; JOZEF SCHEFFERS, "Why Anti-Satellite Warfare Should Be Prohibited," pp. 77–82; and MARCIA SMITH, "Satellite and Missile ASAT Systems and Potential Verification Problems Associated with the Existing Soviet Systems," pp. 83–91.

Other useful items include UNION OF CONCERNED SCIENTISTS, *Anti-Satellite Weapons: Arms Control or Arms Race?* (Cambridge, Mass., 1983), which has appended the UCS's proposed treaty; U.S. CONGRESS, OFFICE OF TECHNOLOGY ASSESSMENT, *Anti-satellite Weapons, Countermeasures, and Arms Control* (Washington, D.C., 1985); GRAY, COLIN S., ed. *American Military Space Policy: Information Systems, Weapons Systems and Arms Control* (Cambridge, Mass., 1982). WILLIAM J. DURCH, "Verification of Limitations on Antisatellite Weapons" in WILLIAM C. POTTER, ed., *Verification and Arms Control* (Lexington, Mass., 1985): 81–106, provides an excellent summary of the basic issues; while BORIS MAYORSKY, "The USSR Initiative in the Struggle for Peace in Outer Space," in NANDASIRI JASENTULIYANA, ed., *Maintaining Outer Space for Peaceful Uses: Proceedings of a Symposium Held in The Hague, March 1984* (Tokyo, 1984): 290–297, justifies the Soviet's 1980s proposals.

Chemical and Biological Weapons and Arms Control

◯

CHARLES C. FLOWERREE

See also Arms Control Treaty Verification; Controlling Chemical and Biological Weapons Through World War II; The Law of War; *and* Science, Technology, and Arms Control. *Most of the treaties discussed in this essay are excerpted in Volume III.*

In contrast to the worldwide revulsion over chemical warfare that was in evidence after World War I, at the close of World War II there was little publicly voiced concern over chemical and biological weapons. Although nerve gas had been invented in the 1930s and its use posed a constant threat during World War II, the atomic bomb had since its advent overshadowed all other weapons. The earliest debates in the United Nations (U.N.) thus focused on attempts to bring under control fissionable materials that could be used to manufacture atomic weapons.

Other weapons were not entirely ignored, however, and in 1948 a commission was established to set out tasks for the U.N. in the area of arms control. This commission produced a definition of weapons of mass destruction that included atomic and radiological as well as chemical and biological weapons. *Chemical-warfare agents* are substances, whether gaseous, liquid, or solid, intended for use in warfare because of their direct toxic effects on people, animals, or plants. *Biological-warfare agents* are living organisms, whatever their nature, or infective material derived from them, that are intended to cause disease or death in man, animals, or plants and whose effectiveness depends on their ability to multiply in the person, animal, or plant attacked. In the World War I era the term *bacteriological* was used to describe these agents. However, at that time microorganisms such as viruses and rickettsias were not known. *Biological* is therefore a more inclusive term. Toxins constitute a special category of chemical agents that are produced by living organisms such as microbes, animals, and plants, but that do not reproduce themselves. Chemical and biological agents can be weaponized for delivery by various means such as bombs, rockets, missiles, and artillery shells.

Although the Japanese used chemical weapons in China in the late 1930s and early 1940s, and other belligerents stockpiled them during World War II, they were not integrated into military planning for various reasons, including doubts about their effectiveness, fear of retaliation, and aversion to gas warfare by military and political leaders. The Japanese also experimented with biological agents in combat in China, but this proved almost as damaging to their own forces as to the Chinese. The British conducted some experiments with anthrax on their own territory, but biological agents did not appear on the battlefields after their use by the Japanese.

In the 1950s and 1960s both the United States and the Soviet Union developed large stockpiles of various types of weapons and integrated them into their military planning. The U.S. stockpile reached a total of some thirty thousand tons of chemical warfare agents, in filled munitions and bulk storage, before production was halted in 1969. In 1987 the Soviets disclosed that they had accumulated stocks totaling fifty thousand tons (unspecified as to type or whether in filled munitions or bulk storage). Some Western observers believed that this figure was too low. U.S. military estimates had ranged as high as three hundred thousand tons prior to the Soviet announcement.

Both the U.S. and Soviet stockpiles included lethal nerve agents that attack the respiratory system, as well as older types such as the blistering agent mustard used in World War I. In the early 1970s the United States developed a safer form of packaging nerve agents called the binary system, in which two relatively nontoxic substances, called precursors, are held in separate canisters until the delivery vehicle is projected toward the target, whereupon the precursors mix and react to form the lethal agent. After many failed attempts to get congressional approval, production of 155-mm binary shells began in December 1987, but it was halted in the summer of 1990.

During the 1960s and 1970s there were minor stirrings of interest in chemical weapons among some third world countries. Iraqi interest seems to have been influenced by the Egyptians, who reportedly used agents such as mustard and phosgene, as well as the tear gas CS, during their intervention in the Yemen civil war from 1963 to 1967. Future Iraqi president Saddam Hussein had fled to Egypt in 1959, where he completed his schooling and developed close ties with President Abdel Nasser and the Egyptian military before returning to Iraq in 1963. In January of the following year the Iraqi Chemical Warfare Corps was founded. The fruits of Iraq's efforts in the chemical-warfare field were displayed in its war with Iran, when Iraqi forces used chemical weapons on the battlefield from late 1983 until the cease-fire in 1988.

The Iraqis did not use chemical weapons against coalition forces during the Gulf War of 1991, perhaps because they feared retaliation or because the tactical situation did not present opportunities for effective employment of such weapons. A shortage of munitions was not a factor, however. After Iraq's defeat the U.N. created the Special Commission on Iraq under Security Council Resolutions 687 and 707, which gave the commission authority to inventory and supervise the destruction of Iraq's weapons of mass destruction and ballistic missiles. The Iraqi chemical arsenal proved to be considerably

larger than anticipated. An official of the special commission stated in November 1991 that U.N. inspectors had found forty-six thousand pieces of filled munitions, including bombs of three types—155-mm artillery shells filled with mustard, 122-mm rockets filled with nerve agent, and mortar shells filled with tear gas (CS). (A later newspaper account said that the U.N. inspectors had raised their estimate of the total of filled munitions to one hundred thousand, of which about half had been destroyed.) Unspecified quantities of mustard and the nerve gas sarin plus two to three thousand tons of precursor agents were found in bulk storage. Thirty warheads for Scud missiles loaded with chemical-warfare agents were also found—sixteen containing nerve gas and fourteen containing alcohol with canisters of the binary precursor DF nearby. There was no evidence that any of these warheads had been test-fired, and experts doubted that the Iraqis had mastered the technique of delivering liquid-filled warheads via ballistic missiles.

Another country whose interest in chemical weapons blossomed in the 1980s was Libya, whose purported pharmaceutical plant at Rabta was identified by Western intelligence as a facility capable of manufacturing chemical agents on a large scale. By the late 1980s some Western intelligence estimates held that more than twenty countries possessed a chemical-weapons capability or were moving to acquire one. The most likely possessors outside Europe and North America included Iran, Syria, Egypt, Israel, North Korea, and China. Iraq had a demonstrated capability.

THE 1925 GENEVA PROTOCOL

For many years the only arms control measure related to chemical and biological weapons was the 1925 Protocol for the Prohibition of the Use in War of Asphyxiating, Poisonous, or Other Gases, and of Bacteriological Methods of Warfare, generally known as the Geneva Protocol, which prohibited their use, if not their possession. One indication of the relative lack of concern about these weapons, in the United States at least, was President Harry S Truman's 1951 withdrawal of the protocol from consideration by the Senate, where it had languished since 1925, when heavy lobbying by the Army Chemical Corps had helped prevent its ratification.

In the U.N. the first high-profile debate on chemical and biological weapons occurred in 1952, when the Communist North Koreans accused the United States of using bacteriological weapons in the Korean War. The North Koreans and their sympathizers rejected a U.S. proposal for an international investigation of the charges. Instead, the Communist countries pursued the issue in the U.N. Security Council, where the Soviet Union introduced a resolution calling on all U.N. members to ratify the Geneva Protocol, a measure clearly aimed at the United States, which at the time was the only permanent member not to have done so. On 26 June 1952 the Soviet resolution was rejected by a vote of 1 to 0, with 10 abstentions, including the United States, the United Kingdom (U.K.), and France. The United States declared that it was unwilling to prohibit the use of any weapons of mass destruction unless those weapons could be controlled by a disarmament agreement containing adequate safeguards.

After the Korean charges, concern about the use of chemical and biological weapons faded into the background as the U.N. wrestled with other security issues. The Vietnam War brought about a resurgence in attention to the issue as the Communist countries put the spotlight on U.S. use of herbicides to clear the heavy undergrowth that hampered operations against the Vietcong guerrilla forces. They contended that this use, together with U.S. employment of riot-control agents such as tear gas in certain circumstances, constituted chemical warfare in violation of the Geneva Protocol.

In 1966 the Hungarian delegation in the U.N. General Assembly introduced a resolution that would have made the use of any chemical and bacteriological weapons, including herbicides and riot-control agents, an international crime. The United States maintained that the Geneva Protocol did not apply to nontoxic gases and chemical herbicides and, together with Canada, Italy, and the United Kingdom, introduced major amendments to the Hungarian resolution. In its final form the resolution called for "strict observance by all states of the principles and objectives" of the protocol, condemned "all actions contrary to those objectives," and invited all states to accede to the protocol.

Thereafter, interpretation of the Geneva Protocol remained a contentious issue both in the U.N. and at the Conference of the Committee on Disarmament (CCD) in Geneva. In his foreword to a U.N. report on chemical weapons (1 July 1969), Secretary-General U Thant recommended a clear affirmation by the member nations that the proto-

col covered the use in war of all chemical and biological weapons, including tear gas and other harassing agents. It was apparent from the debates in the U.N. and the CCD that the majority of nations agreed with the secretary-general's interpretation. At the 1969 session of the General Assembly, the twelve nonaligned members of the CCD, joined by nine other nations, introduced a resolution condemning as contrary to international law the use in international armed conflict of all chemical and biological agents. The resolution passed by a vote of 80 to 3, with Australia, Portugal, and the United States voting against, and thirty-six nations abstaining, including France and the United Kingdom. The United States reaffirmed its position that the protocol did not apply to riot-control agents and herbicides, and maintained that it was inappropriate for the General Assembly to interpret treaties by means of a resolution.

U.S. Ratification   In the meantime, President Richard Nixon announced on 25 November 1969 that he would resubmit the Geneva Protocol to the Senate for consent to ratification. In a report to the Senate on 11 August 1970 Secretary of State William Rogers made clear that the administration still adhered to the position that the Geneva Protocol did not apply to the use in war of riot-control agents and herbicides and recommended that it be ratified with a reservation of the right to retaliate in kind if an enemy state violated the protocol.

The Senate Foreign Relations Committee, however, did not accept the administration's position regarding riot-control agents and herbicides. The gap between the Senate's position and that of the administration was finally bridged by a compromise developed under the Ford administration. President Gerald Ford issued an executive order stating that use of both riot-control agents and herbicides would be subject to specific restraints. The military would abide by the same regulations applicable to the domestic use of herbicides, and that use would be limited to the control of vegetation within U.S. bases and installations or around their immediate defensive perimeters. Riot-control agents would be used only in defensive military modes to save lives. Examples given included controlling prisoner-of-war riots, rescuing downed aircrews, avoiding civilian casualties in instances when civilians were being used to mask or screen enemy attacks, and protecting convoys in areas outside the combat zone from civilian disturbances, terrorists, and paramilitary organizations.

The Geneva Protocol was ratified by President Ford on 22 January 1975 and the U.S. instrument of ratification was deposited on 10 April 1975, two months short of fifty years since it had been signed in Geneva.

Confirmed and Alleged Violations   There have been several alleged as well as confirmed violations of the 1925 Geneva Protocol in the years after World War II.

The Iran-Iraq War As early as 1981 Iran began to claim that Iraq was using chemical weapons against its troops. Subsequent analysis, however, suggests that Iraq's first use of agents other than tear gas took place in the latter part of 1983. During the rest of the war the Iraqis employed mustard and nerve gases mainly in situations in which the Iranian forces were superior numerically. Chemical weapons thus served as a force multiplier for the Iraqis in tactical situations, but they were not a decisive factor in the outcome of the war.

Until 1988 chemical weapons were used sparingly, but in that final year of the war the Iraqis employed them more frequently, particularly in attacks on rear areas such as airfields and command-and-control facilities in Iranian territory. The incident that attracted the most world attention was Iraq's use of lethal gas in March 1988 against its Kurdish citizens who inhabited the town of Halabja, where heavy fighting with Iranian forces had taken place.

During the Iran-Iraq War the U.N. undertook investigations into reported use of chemical weapons at a rate of one a year from 1984 to 1987, and then carried out four separate investigations in 1988, including the Halabja incident. These investigations established conclusively that despite Iraqi denials, Iraq had indeed used chemical weapons. In some instances the investigators were able to provide considerable detail on the circumstances of the use and the kinds of agents employed. Iraq suffered relatively minor penalties for these violations of the Geneva Protocol, to which it was a party. At first the Security Council merely condemned the use of chemical weapons in the conflict, but after the U.N. investigation in 1987, Iraq's culpability was firmly established. In 1984 the United States, and later some other industrialized nations, embargoed all shipments of certain chemical-weapon precursors to Iraq.

Egypt and Libya The first use of chemical weapons in the post–World War II period occurred during the civil war in Yemen. From 1963 to 1967 the Egyptian air force and Egyptian president Gamal Abdel Nasser's Elite Guard reportedly used such chemical agents as phosgene and mustard as well as cs, a tear gas. Although the information concerning this use was sketchy at the time, the most credible coming from a Red Cross observer, subsequent information has corroborated the earlier reports. For example, according to an article by William Claiborne in the *Washington Post* (17 August 1990), during the 1990 confrontation over Kuwait, "a senior [Egyptian] army intelligence official . . . acknowledged that Egyptian troops . . . used chemical weapons against royalist forces" in Yemen. During the 1960s Egypt was aligned with the Soviet Union, which was in all likelihood the source of the agents employed by Egyptian forces.

Another instance of minor use of chemical weapons occurred during the fighting between Libya and Chad during the period 1986–1987. On 11 December 1986 a Chadian government statement, repeated in a letter to the U.N. secretary-general, stated that Libya had used napalm and toxic gas in a skirmish with Chadian forces. There were a few other reports in subsequent months, the most widely believed of which was that Libya had countered with chemical agents during Chad's September 1987 attack on the Maaten-as-Sara air base. In that same month the United States sent some two thousand gas masks to Chad. A senior State Department official was quoted as saying, "We believe chemical weapons have been used, but don't think very extensively" (as quoted in Gordon M. Burck and Charles C. Flowerree, *International Handbook on Chemical Weapons Proliferation*, 1991, p. 269).

"Yellow Rain" Beginning in the latter half of the 1970s, reports from various foreign observers in Southeast Asia painted a disturbing picture of mountain tribesmen in Laos, the H'Mong, being sprayed with a toxic substance disbursed by aircraft.

In 1977 two French doctors who were treating H'Mong tribesmen at the Ban Vinai refugee camp in Thailand told Western journalists that some of the refugees had been afflicted by chemical poisoning. The victims reportedly suffered various symptoms including nausea, vomiting, dizziness, convulsions, fever and chills, diarrhea, and internal bleeding as a result of exposure to the clouds of vapor, and some were reported to have died. According to the H'Mong, the clouds showed a range of colors including red, brown, blue, gray, black, and white, as well as yellow. They also told of leaves and bark dotted with yellow spots following the air attacks—hence the phrase "yellow rain," which was what the phenomenon came to be called. A Laotian pilot who defected in 1979 said he had engaged in attacks on H'Mong villages in which he dropped bombs that released clouds of smoke above normal altitudes, where they could not reach his or other Laotian aircraft. He said he was given a postflight medical examination after these operations.

Following the Vietnamese invasion of Kampuchea (Cambodia) in 1978, similar reports began to be received from that country. There were reports of artillery shells as well as projectiles launched by hand-held weapons that produced clouds of various colors. A number of dying victims were said to have exhibited gruesome symptoms associable with toxin poisoning. By 1980 there were reports of the use of chemicals by Soviet forces fighting in Afghanistan.

Although these reports were received with some skepticism in the West, they were too numerous and persistent to be ignored. In the United States the Carter administration sent an assistant secretary of state to Laos to express U.S. concern over the possibility that chemical warfare was being waged against the H'Mong and Cambodian forces and to urge that these actions, if occurring, be stopped. In addition, a team of physicians was sent to Thailand to examine the alleged victims and to make a judgment as to the cause of their maladies. The team concluded that at least two, and possibly three, agents may have been used: (*a*) a nerve agent, (*b*) an irritant or riot-control agent, and (*c*) an agent that could not be identified from the variety of signs and symptoms that were being reported by some of the victims.

In early 1980 the United States made public a compilation of the hundreds of unevaluated reports relevant to the possible use of chemical warfare agents in Southeast Asia and Afghanistan. At the 1980 U.N. General Assembly a group of Western nations introduced a resolution calling for an on-site U.N. investigation of the situation in the light of these reports. It was adopted after a bitter debate in which the Soviet Union and its sympathizers expressed strenuous opposition. A team of experts from several member nations was dispatched to Southeast Asia the following year and again in 1982. Although the team was able to conduct some interviews of refugees in Thailand, it was rebuffed in its attempts to visit the scenes of the alleged incidents in Laos, Cambodia, and Afghanistan. In its report to the General Assembly the team described its frustration and said it could not find direct evidence to prove that chemical or toxin weapons had been used. However, the experts added that they could not disregard the circumstantial evidence suggesting the possible use of "some sort of toxic chemical substance in some instances" (GA Document A/37/259, 1 December 1982).

In the meantime, the U.S. government had been making efforts to pin down the exact substances that may have caused the symptoms observed in the alleged victims. None of the evidence seemed to match precisely the symptomatology that had come to be associated with exposure to known chemical agents. Finally, in 1981 a leaf sample was obtained from Laos containing yellow spots like those that had been reported by the H'Mong. The sample was sent to a laboratory in Minnesota for identification. The laboratory subsequently identified the spots from the leaf sample as a highly toxic mycotoxin known as tricothecene. The following year the U.S. government reported that blood and urine samples from sixteen alleged victims in Southeast Asia showed the presence of tricothecene mycotoxins, as did vegetation samples and two gas masks recovered from Afghanistan. In September 1981, in a speech delivered in Berlin, U.S. Secretary of State Alexander Haig said that lethal mycotoxins, probably the kind that had been used for many years in Laos, had been discovered at the site of a chemical attack in Kampuchea.

These findings were vigorously attacked by non-government critics in succeeding years. Among the critics' reasons for finding fault with the allegations were (*a*) the government's failure to find spent chemical munitions after reported attacks; (*b*) the finding of dense, heterogeneous pollen assemblages in dried yellow rain spots, difficult to explain as chemical munitions; (*c*) the insufficiency of controls regarding possible natural occurrences of the toxins, and (*d*) the fact that the interviews in the refugee camps had been done with H'Mong who had said in advance that they had been victims or witnesses of chemical attacks. The critics found it hard to believe that the military advantage gained by a state through the use of chemical and toxin agents would outweigh the risk of international opprobrium a state would incur upon strong evidence that it was violating international agreements banning the use of such weapons.

One of the most persistent and vocal of the critics was Matthew Meselson, a professor of natural sciences at Harvard University. He observed that the yellow spots presented as evidence of tricothecene mycotoxins closely resembled the feces of honey bees. Furthermore, Asian honeybees were known to make massive cleansing flights, leaving swaths of yellow fecal spots on the vegetation near their nests. To test this thesis Meselson and two colleagues went to a national park in Thailand in March 1984 to observe the behavior of the bees. During their visit they observed several cleansing flights and once were caught in a shower produced by one of these flights. Their subsequent analysis of the samples from Thailand and those that had been presented as evidence of toxin warfare against the H'Mong convinced them that "yellow rain" was in fact "a phenomenon of nature, not of man" (Thomas D. Seeley, Joan W. Nowicke, Matthew Meselson, Jeanne Guillemin, and Pongthep Akratanakul, "Yellow Rain," *Scientific American,* September 1985, p. 137).

This finding seemed to clinch the critics' case. They argued that the manner in which the government had pursued the issue of chemical and toxin warfare in Southeast Asia was flawed and politically motivated. The government, on the other hand, continued to maintain that its investigations, corroborated by intelligence, showed conclusively that Vietnamese and Lao forces supplied by the Soviet Union had deliberately used various types of chemical and toxin weapons in attempting to drive the H'Mong out of their mountain strongholds. The president's annual reports to Congress on Soviet noncompliance with arms control agreements continued to find that the USSR had been involved in the production, transfer, and use of tricothecene mycotoxins for hostile purposes in Laos, Cambodia, and Afghanistan in violation of its legal obligation under international law as codified in the Geneva Protocol of 1925 and the Biological Weapons Convention of 1972. Later reports stated that the U.S. government had no confirmed evidence of the use of lethal agents in these areas since 1984.

A middle ground in the yellow rain controversy is represented by the belief of some specialists in chemical- and biological-warfare issues that some sorts of agents were used in Southeast Asia between the mid-1970s and the early 1980s, but not necessarily the lethal chemical and toxin agents that have been cited. One hypothesis is that the North Vietnamese had access to large quantities of riot-control agents and herbicides supplied by their al-

lies during the Vietnam War or perhaps captured from U.S. forces, and that these could have been used against the H'Mong. Alternatively, since Soviet military doctrine envisaged the use of smoke of different colors to mask operations and this smoke reportedly had toxic properties, it is possible that the colored clouds seen by the alleged victims were produced by military smoke dispensers. It is not likely that the controversy will ever be settled unless the United States or the successor governments to the former Soviet Union make public convincing evidence supporting their respective cases.

THE BIOLOGICAL AND TOXIN WEAPONS CONVENTION

Following the debates on the alleged use of biological and chemical weapons in Korea and Vietnam, the United Nations eventually undertook serious efforts to grapple with the problem of banning these weapons entirely. In 1960 a separate disarmament body was established in Geneva—initially composed of ten nations, then re-created in 1962 as the Eighteen Nation Disarmament Committee (ENDC) with the addition of several nonaligned countries. The ENDC's agenda included as priority issues a comprehensive nuclear test ban as well as a ban on biological and chemical weapons (regarded as a single issue). However, the committee's initial focus was on nuclear issues and a comprehensive program for disarmament.

The first significant step toward the elimination of chemical and biological weapons occurred in 1968, when the U.N. Disarmament Commission decided to put these weapons on its formal agenda and suggested that the secretary-general study their effects. The secretary-general's report drew on the opinions of a group of experts appointed by him, and was released on 1 July 1969. The report, entitled "Chemical and Bacteriological (Biological) Weapons and the Effect of Their Possible Use," concluded that "were these weapons ever to be used on a large scale in war, no one could predict how enduring the effects would be, and how they would affect the structure of society and the environment in which we live."

The British were particularly active on the biological-weapons issue, presenting a paper in the U.N. Disarmament Commission in 1968 concerning microbiological methods of warfare, and in the same year presenting arguments in the Geneva Disarmament Committee supporting the view that biological and chemical weapons should be dealt with separately in the committee's future work. They followed up with a draft convention introduced in 1969 banning the production, possession, transfer, and use of biological weapons as well as the research, equipment, and delivery systems associated with them. The Soviet Union, on the other hand, did not wish to separate biological and chemical weapons and a couple of months after the British draft had been tabled, the Soviets introduced their version.

The British, along with the United States and other Western countries, saw the elimination of chemical weapons as a much more difficult problem than that of biological weapons. The Western countries did not wish to give up the option of using chemical weapons (which, unlike biological weapons, were viewed as having military utility) without assurances that their destruction and nonproduction could be adequately verified. It was thought that a much simpler regime could suffice for the control of biological weapons. This assessment was reflected in President Nixon's announcement on 25 November 1969 (at which time he also forswore the first use of chemical weapons) that the United States was renouncing bacteriological or biological methods of warfare and that he was ordering the closing of all facilities engaged in the production of these agents for offensive purposes, and the destruction of stockpiles of biological weapons and agents. Several other countries followed suit. Canada, Sweden, and the United Kingdom announced that they had no biological weapons nor plans to produce them. Nevertheless, it was widely agreed that unilateral actions could not substitute for a binding international agreement.

Negotiations   In Geneva the expanded disarmament committee, now named the Conference of the Committee on Disarmament (CCD), was still debating how to proceed to elaborate a convention banning biological weapons. The Soviet Union and its supporters, including most of the nonaligned nations, were holding out for a treaty that would deal with both chemical and biological weapons. The Western participants, however, held that biological weapons presented a less intractable problem than chemicals and completion of an agreement banning them should not await the completion of a prohibition on chemical weapons.

The stalemate in the CCD continued through the 1970 session, but on 30 March 1971 the Soviet Union and its allies changed their position and introduced a revised draft dealing only with biological and toxin weapons. It then became possible for the U.S. and Soviet representatives, the permanent cochairmen of the committee, to work together to develop an agreed-upon draft. On 5 August 1971 the cochairmen submitted separate but identical drafts to the committee for approval. The CCD draft was endorsed by the U.N. General Assembly on 16 December.

Neither France nor the People's Republic of China participated in the negotiations, China not being a CCD member and France refusing to take its seat because of its objection to United States–Soviet cochairmanship. The French representative in the U.N. abstained in the vote on the resolution, explaining that the convention, though a step forward, might weaken the Geneva Protocol's ban on the use of chemical weapons. China's representative attacked the convention as a "sham," and criticized it for not dealing with chemical weapons.

President Nixon submitted the convention to the Senate on 10 August 1972, calling it "the first international agreement since World War II to provide for the actual elimination of an entire class of weapons from the arsenals of nations" (*Arms Control and Disarmament Agreements*, 1982 ed., United States Arms Control and Disarmament Agency, Washington, D.C., p. 131). The Senate, however, did not consider giving its consent to ratification until the issue of the applicability of riot-control agents and herbicides to the Geneva Protocol had been decided. As previously noted, the Ford administration eventually forged a compromise solution to this problem late in 1974, following which the Senate quickly gave unanimous approval to both measures. The president then signed the two instruments of ratification on 22 January 1975. After the requisite number of nations had deposited their instruments of ratification, the Biological and Toxin Weapons Convention (BWC) entered into force on 26 March 1975.

Major Provisions   The text of the convention, officially called the "Convention on the Prohibition of the Development, Production and Stockpiling of Bacteriological (Biological) and Toxin Weapons and on Their Destruction," was brief and uncomplicated, consisting of a preamble and fifteen articles. Article I, the basic prohibition, committed the states party never to develop, produce, stockpile, or otherwise acquire or retain microbial or other biological agents or toxins in quantities that have no justification for peaceful purposes, nor to possess weapons, equipment, or means of delivery for such agents for hostile purposes. Articles II through IV enjoin the parties to destroy or convert to peaceful purposes, and not to transfer to any recipient whatsoever, any prohibited items in their possession, and to take necessary measures within their constitutional processes to insure that these provisions are observed within the territory of the state or under its control. Other articles provide for handling complaints about compliance through consultations among the parties, with ultimate recourse to the U.N. Security Council when an issue cannot be resolved by the parties. There are also provisions for assistance to parties that may be endangered by violations of the convention and for exchanges of scientific and technical information relating to biological agents. The text includes a call for good-faith negotiations to reach agreement on a convention banning chemical weapons.

The Afterlife of the BWC The earliest actions taken in response to the completion of the BWC were statements by the United States, the United Kingdom, and the Soviet Union that they were in compliance with its provisions. On 4 March 1975 the U.S. representative to the CCD confirmed that the entire U.S. stockpile had been destroyed and biological-warfare facilities had been converted to peaceful purposes. A few days later, on 18 March, the U.K. representative reported to the committee that his government had met its obligations under the treaty. The British, however, still maintained two facilities geared to defense against biological and toxin warfare. The relevant Soviet statement made on 24 June 1975 was not specific about any actions taken to destroy weapons or facilities. It merely asserted that the Soviet Union had adopted legislation, ratified by a decision of the Presidium of the Supreme Soviet on 11 February 1975, assuring compliance with the provisions of the convention and stating that the Soviet Union did not possess any bacteriological (biological) agents, or toxins, weapons, equipment, or means of delivery falling within the provisions of Article I of the convention.

There were few public expressions of concern about the provisions of the convention or its application over the next few years. At the 1978 special session of the U.N. General Assembly devoted to disarmament, the BWC was one of the few measures to receive unreservedly favorable notice in the final document. Privately, however, concerns were being

expressed by some states, and these concerns received more attention as the 1980 review conference drew near. The most serious concern was over what many regarded as the inadequacy of the provisions for assuring compliance. Another concern, particularly among the nonaligned states, was the slow pace of negotiations on a chemical-weapons convention. Lurking in the background was the fear that new technological developments, such as recombinant DNA techniques, might spark renewed interest in biological weapons.

The Sverdlovsk Incident Reports began appearing in the European press in 1979 about an accident that was said to have occurred in April of that year at a military facility in Sverdlovsk, USSR (which has reverted to its pre-1917 name of Ekaterinburg) engaged in biological-weapons research. The accident reportedly involved the release of anthrax spores into the atmosphere, causing deaths numbering in the thousands. On 17 March 1980 the U.S. government privately asked the Soviet Union for an explanation of these reports, which, if true, could have implicated the Soviet Union in a violation of the Biological and Toxin Weapons Convention. The first review conference of the convention was then taking place in Geneva. The Soviet government reacted swiftly to the charges. On 20 March the Soviet Foreign Ministry, in an unusual move, telephoned Western correspondents in Moscow, stating that the Soviet Union rejected any implication that it was guilty of noncompliance with the BWC. Through diplomatic channels, the Soviet government told the United States that there had been an outbreak of gastric anthrax in Sverdlovsk in April 1979 caused by contaminated meat. The following day in Geneva the U.S. and Soviet representatives publicly stated their countries' positions on the alleged incident.

The Soviet explanation did not satisfy the U.S. government, which reportedly had been interested for some time in a secure military installation in Sverdlovsk; that facility shared many of the characteristics of the former U.S. biological warfare facility at Fort Detrick, Maryland. In a report issued in June 1980, the House Intelligence Committee concluded on the basis of hearings in which representatives of the Central Intelligence Agency, the State Department, and the Arms Control and Disarmament Agency, along with a Soviet émigré, Mark Popovsky, testified that the anthrax epidemic in Sverdlovsk was of the inhalation variety and was linked to an explosion at a military facility there "long suspected of housing biological warfare activities" (U.S. Congress, House, "Soviet Biological Warfare Activities," June 1980).

The two countries held to their positions over the following years. The Soviets emphasized that anthrax is endemic to the region—between 1936 and 1968 there had been 159 outbreaks of anthrax poisoning of animals as a result of infected soil. Shortly after the incident became public knowledge, a Northwestern University professor who had arrived in Sverdlovsk with his family in May 1979 reported that he was able to travel around the city and nearby areas in the company of friends and never saw or heard any evidence that anything unusual had happened. Nevertheless, the U.S. government continued to be dissatisfied with the Soviet explanation. The president's annual reports to the Congress on Soviet noncompliance with arms control treaties regularly listed the Sverdlovsk outbreak as a violation of the BWC. The 1990 report stated: "We continue to be dissatisfied with Soviet explanations regarding an outbreak of anthrax in Sverdlovsk in 1979. We have raised the issue repeatedly since March 1980, and have been told that the outbreak stemmed from the consumption of contaminated meat. However, based on information available to the U.S., we concluded that the outbreak occurred as a result of an accidental release of anthrax spores from a prohibited BW [biological weapons] facility."

Once again there were objections to the government's position in some private circles. Most of the known efforts to determine exactly what happened in the April 1979 incident consisted of unofficial or semiofficial contacts between scientists of the two countries. The U.S. government chose not to use the consultation and complaint procedures of the BWC, but made several private demarches to the Soviet government. If the United States had taken the issue to the Security Council, it would undoubtedly have evoked a Soviet veto.

The most widely publicized of the nongovernment contacts was the visit to the United States in April 1988 of three Soviet health officials led by Dr. Pyotr Bugasov, a Soviet deputy minister of health. These officials gave many details of their version of the incident. Bugasov said that local authorities were forced to establish roadblocks and conduct a house-to-house search for suspect meat, slay three hundred street dogs, burn more than thirty contaminated buildings, and bury the victims of the meat

poisoning in sealed coffins. Only fourteen people who consumed the meat survived; another sixty-six perished after a swift but agonizing illness.

While many U.S. experts found the Soviet explanation plausible and consistent with what is known about experiences with human and animal anthrax, government officials who attended the briefings remained skeptical. Even those inclined to believe the Soviet version were troubled by the gaps that still remained in the accounts that the Soviets provided. A lengthy Soviet scientific paper on the incident that was said to be in its final stages of preparation in 1988 had yet to appear in 1992. In the skeptics' view some elements of the Soviet account remained puzzling, such as why only one child became ill or why in some houses only one person was affected. (Dr. Bugasov explained the latter by saying that the Soviet custom was to give the largest piece of meat to the working member of the household.) It was noted that the benign view of the Sverdlovsk scene that had been given by the visiting Northwestern University professor was at odds with the picture of the extensive measures described by the Soviet health officials.

Journalists of the former Soviet republics, no longer censored, have included among their investigations the events at Sverdlovsk in 1979. Between March 1990 and the end of 1991 some dozen articles appeared, most of them in *Izvestiya* and *Literaturnaya Gazeta,* in which physicians and ordinary citizens who were in Sverdlovsk at the time of the incident gave their version of the events. All of them suggested that the outbreak of anthrax was of the inhalation variety and not the type resulting from the ingesting of contaminated meat. One man, who said he had been a security officer for the region, stated flatly that the problem had originated at the military facility suspected of engaging in biological-warfare research, and that the largest number of people affected had been military personnel. There is the possibility that these reports are merely examples of sensational journalism. President Boris Yeltsin gave an interview in *Literaturnaya Gazeta* in May 1992 in which he admitted that there had been an accident at the military biological-weapons installation in Sverdlovsk involving the release of anthrax spores that affected people in the area. Previously he had revealed that the Soviet Union had had an offensive biological-warfare program. In June a group of U.S. scientists was allowed to visit Sverdlovsk and found evidence of the inhalation of anthrax in the preserved tissues of forty-two of the sixty-four victims they identified from tombstones. Questions remained as to the past role of the military facility and the exact nature of the material suspected of having been released.

Review Conferences   As of 1991 three review conferences (REVCON) have examined the performance of the BWC.

First REVCON, March 1980   When representatives of the states party to the BWC convened in Geneva on 3 March 1980, there were widely differing views about how seriously to treat the concerns that had been voiced about the shortcomings of the BWC and about how to deal with them. The issue that consumed most of the efforts of the REVCON was the possibility of amending the convention to incorporate effective verification provisions.

Sweden came to the REVCON armed with a proposal to amend the convention to establish a permanent consultative committee comprised of representatives of the parties, which would serve as a mechanism for conducting fact-finding investigations of alleged violations. With such a mechanism in place, a request for an investigation by the Security Council would arise only when the fact-finding procedures had failed to resolve the question. An additional element of the Swedish proposal would have made a request to the Security Council a procedural matter, thus depriving the permanent members of the option of using their veto rights. Many nonaligned states, distrustful of the Security Council as a body that would look after their vital interests, also professed to be concerned about the effectiveness of the convention's complaint procedures and supported the Swedish proposal.

The Soviet Union and its allies vigorously opposed the proposal, however, arguing that it would not be wise to amend a treaty that was functioning well. Most Western countries wished to see the procedures regarding the handling of complaints strengthened, but did not think amending the treaty was the way to proceed. They were convinced that the Soviets and their allies would not agree to an amendment and they did not wish to see the BWC regime weakened by a fundamental disagreement of this sort. Perhaps as importantly, they shared with the Soviets a desire not to set a precedent that might result in the amendment of the Nuclear Non-Proliferation Treaty (NPT) under pressure from the nonaligned states.

After two weeks of wrangling, the British proposed language for the conference report acceptable to all sides. The British solution was to interpret the phrase in Article V, "through appropriate international procedures within the framework of the United Nations" (in reference to consultations among the parties) as implying the possibility of establishing a committee of experts to look into any allegations of violations of the convention. Eventually it was agreed to include in the final declaration a sentence stating that the procedures under Article V "include, *inter alia,* the right of any State Party subsequently to request that a consultative meeting open to all States Parties be convened at expert level."

The final declaration of the REVCON commented on each of the articles of the convention, even if only to note with satisfaction that there had been no problems in the area the article addressed. Concerning the commitment under Article IX for the states parties to negotiate in good faith to complete a chemical-weapons convention, the final declaration, while taking note of the progress reports that had been submitted on the bilateral United States–Soviet negotiations begun in 1977, expressed deep regret that negotiations had not yet produced a comprehensive prohibition of chemical weapons.

Second REVCON, September 1986   In the years after the first REVCON, developments in DNA technology caused increasing concern, and the yellow rain and Sverdlovsk questions lent a certain degree of urgency to the effort to strengthen the consultation and compliance procedures of the BWC. Since the same objections to amending the convention still remained, the focus of efforts at the second REVCON was on the less drastic approach of developing confidence-building measures (CBM).

The Soviet Union, which was showing more openness to the concept of intrusive verification under the policies established by General Secretary Mikhail Gorbachev, emerged as a champion of the idea of amending the BWC by adding a legally binding verification protocol. The United States, however, continued to be reluctant to embark on this course, mainly because it had strong doubts about the feasibility of verifying the nonproduction and destruction of biological weapons through on-site inspections and other standard techniques. It was concerned about the ease with which a biological-weapons program could be hidden under the cloak of legitimate research in the field of microbiology.

Many other states were willing to lay the question of a biological-weapons verification regime aside until the chemical-weapons negotiations that were then under way produced a regime that could serve as a model. The U.S. reluctance in this area did not prevent the REVCON from moving ahead on other issues. Likewise, the festering issues of yellow rain and Sverdlovsk, although they were raised, were not allowed to hamper the work of the conference.

In the realm of confidence-building, the conference agreed in the final declaration on the following voluntary measures:

1. Exchange of data, including name, location, scope and general description of activities, on research centres and laboratories that meet very high national or international safety standards established for handling, for permitted purposes, biological materials that pose a high individual and community risk or specialize in permitted biological activities directly related to the convention.
2. Exchange of information on all outbreaks of infectious diseases and similar occurrences caused by toxins that seem to deviate from the normal pattern as regards type, development, place, or time of occurrence.

In addition, publication of results of biological research directly related to the convention, and promotion of contacts among scientists engaged in biological research related to the convention were encouraged. The modalities for effecting these exchanges were entrusted to an ad hoc group of experts that met in Geneva in April 1987 to fulfill this task.

Expanding on the interpretation of Articles V and VI agreed to at the first REVCON, the conference made it clear that when a state party requested a consultative meeting at expert level, such a meeting should be promptly convened and should consider any problem that may arise in relation to the objectives or application of the convention.

In addition to the previously mentioned exchanges of data on research centers and laboratories and on outbreaks of infectious diseases, the 1986 REVCON called on the parties to implement two further measures to reduce suspicions and ambiguities and to strengthen confidence in the BWC regime: (1) encouragement of publication of the results of biological research directly related to the convention; and (2) active promotion of contacts between scientists engaged in biological research

related to the convention, including exchanges for joint research.

The 1986 REVCON noted the increasing importance of the provisions of Article X (exchanges) in the light of scientific and technological developments, and urged the parties to take "specific measures within their competence for the promotion of the fullest possible international co-operation in this field through their active intervention." Some of the measures listed in the final declaration were:

- transfer and exchange of information concerning research programmes in bio-sciences;
....
- active promotion of contacts between scientists and technical personnel on a reciprocal basis, in relevant fields;
- increased technical co-operation including training opportunities to developing countries in the use of bio-sciences and genetic engineering for peaceful purposes;
....
- encouraging the co-ordination of national and regional programmes and working out in an appropriate manner the ways and means of co-operation in this field.

The conference also called for "greater co-operation in international public health and disease control." The United Nations, its specialized agencies, and other international organizations were envisaged as the mechanisms through which these various cooperative measures would be realized.

Third REVCON, September 1991 By the time the third REVCON appeared on the horizon, interest in the BWC had grown considerably among experts and organizations interested in arms control. One reason was the information coming from Western intelligence agencies that some ten countries had developed active programs aimed at acquiring an offensive biological-weapons capability. Concern on this score was further heightened with the outbreak of the Gulf War, as it was widely believed that Iraq was one of the countries developing such weapons. A milk plant said to be a cover for biological-weapons research was bombed by U.S. aircraft during the fighting, although the U.S. claims were met with skepticism in many quarters. Nevertheless, the prospect of countries like Iraq acquiring biological weapons spurred renewed interest in strengthening the BWC.

Each of the three BWC review conferences was held in a different political climate. The first had taken place at a time of high United States–Soviet tension in the wake of the invasion of Afghanistan. The second occurred at the beginning of a thaw in these relations and of greater Soviet cooperation in arms control matters. The third REVCON occurred as the Soviet Union was dissolving and as splits were beginning to be more pronounced along North-South lines, rather than East versus West as in the past. This latter factor somewhat soured the atmosphere at the REVCON—it began with a bitter dispute over the chairmanship of the conference, in which a former East bloc country, Hungary, was pitted against one from the South, Argentina.

Many nongovernment groups were active in the year prior to the REVCON, preparing proposals to be considered by the parties. Seminars were organized by the NGO (Nongovernment Organizations) Committee for Disarmament in Geneva, the Quaker U.N. Office, also in Geneva, and by the government of the Netherlands. The Stockholm International Peace Research Institute (SIPRI) published a volume of essays under the rubric "Views on Possible Verification Measures for the Biological Weapons Convention," and the U.N. Institute for Disarmament Research published a similar work.

The most ambitious undertaking by an NGO was a set of proposals developed by a group of experts under the sponsorship of the Federation of American Scientists (FAS). Two studies were prepared by this group. The first, dated October 1990, gave proposals for actions to be taken at the REVCON. It included an assessment of each article of the convention to determine whether it needed further interpretation or whether some action could be taken under it that would contribute to strengthening the treaty regime. A second document dated February 1990, titled "Implementation of the Proposals for a Verification Protocol to the Biological Weapons Convention," presented the elements that would have to be included in a verification protocol. The FAS group saw progress toward the adoption of a verification protocol as a two-step process. The first step would be for the REVCON to call for a series of meetings at expert level to draw up a draft proposal for such a protocol, which would then be submitted to the states parties to serve as a basis for subsequent negotiations.

The FAS proposal for a verification protocol, or other variations of it, did not fare well at the REVCON, largely as a result of U.S. opposition, which continued to be based on skepticism about the feasibility of verifying activities related to research and development of biological weapons. The compromise that emerged was to establish an ad hoc group of government experts to identify and examine potential verification measures from a scientific and technical standpoint. The group began meeting in early 1992 to draw up a consensus report expressing all views, preferably before the end of 1993. A special conference of states parties would be convened by the depositary states (the United States, United Kingdom, and presumably Russia as successor state to the Soviet Union) if requested by a majority of the parties. This conference would decide on any further action.

The request for information on high-level containment research facilities in each state party, which had been one of the measures agreed to at the second REVCON, had not elicited wide response. In part this was attributable to the fact that many less-developed countries were not sure of what information was required, or did not feel that they were required to respond if there were no high-level containment facilities on their territory. The third REVCON, taking note of this fact, prepared a simplified form for responding. There were, for example, boxes labeled "nothing to declare" and "nothing new to declare" that could be checked off by parties.

The conference also elaborated on the confidence-building measures relating to exchanges that had been adopted in 1986. These included:

- exchanges of data on research centers and laboratories, information on national biological-defense research and development programs and outbreaks of infectious diseases and similar occurrences caused by toxins;
- encouragement of publication of results and promotion of the use of knowledge gained from research; and
- declaration of legislation, regulations, and other measures taken by the parties to implement the BWC, of past activities in offensive- and/or defensive-biological research and development programs, and of vaccine production.

The conference recognized that the revised procedures and reporting requirements would place greater demands on the U.N. Department of Disarmament Affairs (DDA), which would be receiving and distributing the information generated by the parties. It therefore requested in its final declaration that the secretary-general allocate the necessary resources to the DDA office in Geneva "to assist in the effective implementation of the relevant decisions of the Third Review Conference, in particular of the confidence-building measures."

The sharp divide between North and South also had consequences for substantive issues. One casualty was a proposal that had been long sought by many countries for some sort of continuing body to oversee the functioning of the convention between review conferences. Prior to the opening of the REVCON it was generally believed that such a proposal would be adopted without difficulty, and the compromise that ended the dispute between Argentina and Hungary for the presidency of the conference gave the chairmanship of this "intersessional" body to Hungary. However, the hangover from the battle for the presidency made the representatives of countries from what used to be called the third world unwilling to reach an understanding on the proposed body that was strongly favored by most of the developed nations. Moreover, representatives of the developing countries saw in it the makings of a body that might end up dictating "instructions" to the states parties.

The Final Document included a recommendation that a fourth review conference be held not later than 1996, and that conferences to review the operation of the convention be held at least every five years.

THE CHEMICAL WEAPONS CONVENTION

Following the completion of the Biological and Toxin Weapons Convention, the Conference of the Committee on Disarmament began to consider the chemical-weapons problem. At first there was no organized effort to begin drafting a text. Members of the committee merely expressed their views on the subject. The United States and Soviet Union displayed no interest in moving toward the drafting of a multilateral treaty. Their summit communiqué of 1974 had called for a bilateral effort, and even though the two countries did not seem ready to move down this path, neither were they ready to work on an agreement in the committee. Other countries, however, were not so reticent. Both the Japanese and the British offered draft outlines of a treaty. Other countries, including Sweden, Canada, and the Netherlands, contributed to the discussion with concrete proposals and comments on the British and Japanese drafts.

The United States, while welcoming the Japanese and British drafts and other proposals, took a more restrained approach to the idea of embarking on multilateral negotiations in the committee. On 21 March 1972 the U.S. delegation tabled a comprehensive work program (CCD/360) which set forth detailed considerations concerning major categories of chemical agents and precursors as well as possible ways of defining those substances. It also dealt with the scope of a possible convention, its verification, and international consultative arrangements to review its implementation. The U.S. delegation expressed the hope that its work program would contribute to the "essential work of exchanging ideas and studying intensively all the issues relating to possible prohibitions of chemical weapons" (CCD/392).

This formulation indicated clearly that the United States did not believe the time was ripe for multilateral negotiations. Instead, it wanted to initiate a process of exposing the problems that would have to be dealt with whenever the committee got around to elaborating a chemical-weapons convention (CWC). Subsequently, workshops were organized under the auspices of the committee to deal with specific problems of a technical nature, such as developing standards of toxicity to be applied to a future ban.

Bilateral United States–Soviet Negotiations, 1977–1980 With the change of administrations in the United States in 1977 came a more active interest in arms control negotiations. In March 1977 President Jimmy Carter sent Secretary of State Cyrus Vance to Moscow with proposals for a range of negotiations including a ban on chemical weapons. The Soviets were receptive to the proposals and shortly thereafter chemical-weapons negotiations began in Geneva, with the representatives of the two countries to the CCD heading their respective delegations. These negotiations continued until the summer of 1980 when, as a result of the deterioration of the political climate, they were suspended.

Although the bilaterals did not come close to producing an agreement, considerable progress was made in some areas, providing a basis for subsequent negotiations. The two sides submitted their final report to the Conference on Disarmament (CD) in July 1980.

The areas in which agreement was reported included the following:

- the scope of the convention: that the parties would oblige themselves never to develop, produce, or otherwise acquire, stockpile, or retain super-toxic lethal, other lethal, or other harmful chemicals, or precursors of such chemicals;
- definitions of basic terms, including: (*a*) "chemical weapons," (*b*) "super-toxic lethal chemicals," (*c*) "other lethal chemicals," (*d*) "other harmful chemicals," and (*e*) "nonhostile purposes";
- a prohibition on transfers of chemical weapons to others;
- time frames for destruction of stockpiles and dismantling production facilities: eight years after entry into force for stockpiles and ten years for production facilities;
- a limitation of one metric ton on the quantity of super-toxic lethal chemicals that could be produced for peaceful purposes, such as research on protective measures; and
- verification based on a combination of national and international measures, which would include the establishment of a consultative committee.

There was no agreement on the specifics of verification, such as on-site inspections and the functions of the consultative committee. These elements were to remain major sticking points in the years to come. Other areas in which there was no agreement included the extent to which irritants and toxins should be covered, the concise definition of the term "means of production," and the timing and content of national declarations pertaining to chemical-weapons stocks and means of production and the time for beginning destruction.

Multilateral Negotiations   Following the 1978 U.N. General Assembly's Special Session on Disarmament, a new forty-nation committee, the Conference on Disarmament (CD) was established, superseding the CCD. Since the nuclear powers were unwilling to allow the committee to become involved in negotiations on nuclear weapons, chemical disarmament was left as the most important issue with which it might deal. However, even in this area the CD found itself constrained, as the United States and Soviet Union were reluctant to permit it to become fully engaged while they were attempting to negotiate a bilateral agreement. Not until 1980 was the CD permitted to form a chemical-

weapons working group, and even then the group's mandate was very restricted.

In June 1982 the Soviet Union submitted a paper, "Basic Provisions of a Convention on the Prohibition of the Development, Production and Stockpiling of Chemical Weapons and on Their Destruction." It spelled out the positions that had been taken by the Soviets since consideration of the chemical-weapons issue began in the old CCD. It envisaged a BWC-type convention with verification based on cooperation and consultations, and provided for the possibility of lodging a complaint of noncompliance with the Security Council. Some proposals appeared to have been included for propaganda purposes, such as a reference to the non-stationing of binary weapons on the territories of other states, and a pitch to third world interests in a section headed "Promotion of Development Goals."

In 1983 the United States, which had previously been the most reluctant to see the CD become involved in conducting negotiations on a treaty, agreed to participate in a working group with an expanded mandate authorizing it to elaborate a draft CWC although not the definitive treaty text. At the opening of the 1983 session, the United States submitted "Detailed Views on the Contents of a Chemical Weapons Ban." In expanded outline form, covering twenty-four pages, it dealt with the elements that should be included in an eventual convention under the headings: "Scope of Prohibition"; "Declaration/Destruction"; "Verification and Assurance"; and "Other Provisions."

The following year, George Bush, as vice president, presented a complete draft treaty for consideration by the CD. It contained many of the now-familiar elements that had long been discussed in the CD and its predecessors. The draft treaty was based on the paper presented the year before and incorporated ideas presented by many other delegations. It included many features that had already been incorporated into what was known in the CD as the "rolling text," a regularly updated draft of the eventual convention that recorded agreed-upon language as well as alternative formulations in cases where there was not universal agreement. The treaty would prohibit development, production, stockpiling, acquisition, retention or transfer of chemical weapons, and incapacitating agents and their precursors. It would also ban the use of chemical weapons. Destruction of weapons and elimination of facilities would be accomplished within ten years of the treaty's entry into force. Verification of compliance with these provisions would be accomplished by a combination of national and international measures that would be tailored to the particular items to be verified:

- declared weapons and facilities would be monitored by systematic international on-site verification;
- destruction of stockpiles would be verified by continuous monitoring with on-site instruments and continuous presence of international inspectors;
- chemical-weapons production facilities would be monitored by on-site instruments and periodic international on-site inspection;
- production of commercial chemicals that could also be used in the manufacture of chemical weapons would be monitored by systematic international on-site verification and data exchange; and
- suspected sites and facilities owned or controlled by the governments of treaty parties would be monitored by a special "anywhere, anytime" on-site inspection procedure that would be established to permit treaty parties unimpeded access to the suspect locations.

The most controversial new element introduced by the U.S. draft was the concept of "anywhere, anytime" challenge inspection. It provided that whenever a state party or group of parties detected an activity that might be construed to be a violation of the convention, the state on whose territory the activity was taking place would be obliged to permit a prompt, internationally conducted on-site inspection to determine whether a violation had indeed occurred.

At first there was wide resistance to the idea. Third world countries as well as the Soviet Union were wary of giving what was seen as a blank check to international inspectors to look into their sensitive military facilities. Soviet opposition began to soften in 1986, and in the spring of 1987 the Soviet representative said his government agreed in principle with "quick challenge" inspection of suspected chemical-weapons sites. Most of the other delegations came around to similar positions and for a while challenge inspection no longer seemed to be a major obstacle to the completion of the convention. As it turned out, however, the issue had not been disposed of, as will be discussed below.

The CWC, as it has evolved, is probably the most complicated arms control measure ever undertaken, as it impinges on one of the world's basic industries as well as on sensitive national security interests. The version of the text in 1992 runs to some two hundred pages, including detailed provisions for destroying chemical weapons and production facilities, the order of destruction and disposition of discovered war munitions, the criteria for determining toxicity, definitions of "precursors," reports on the production of certain chemicals, and many other details. It also incorporates provisions for assistance and protection against chemical-weapons attack for parties, sanctions against violators, and economic and technological development for parties.

One of the most complicated and distinctive features of the CWC is the international body (Organization for the Prevention of Chemical Weapons, or OPCW), which would oversee the functioning of the treaty regime and compliance with its provisions. It would also maintain records and make reports to the parties, conduct inspections, and serve as the point of receipt for complaints lodged by one party against another.

The elements that have been agreed upon in order to satisfy the desire for full representation by all states without sacrificing efficient operation are: (1) a consultative committee to which all parties would belong, (2) an executive council of forty members charged with continuous oversight of the functioning of the convention, and (3) a technical secretariat to carry out day-to-day activities such as conducting inspections and receiving reports and complaints.

While there has been general agreement on the shape of the international authority, negotiators have had to wrestle with many thorny issues relating to the distribution of power among its components and their specific functions. These issues have included the composition of the Executive Council, how decisions will be made, and how the organization will be financed. For a time another stumbling block to achievement of the convention was the U.S. position that chemical-weapons states would have the right to retaliate in kind to chemical-weapons attacks, and to retain 2 percent of their current stockpiles until all "chemical-weapons-capable" states had subscribed to the convention. On 13 May 1991, however, President Bush issued a statement dropping these proposals and calling for the completion of the convention within one year. At the same time he promised that the United States would make new proposals for resolution of the challenge inspection issue. These new proposals, which were introduced at the CD in July 1991 under the sponsorship of the United States, the United Kingdom, Japan, and Australia, substantially modified the "anywhere, anytime" concept by giving the challenged state more time in which to respond and a say in how the inspection would be conducted—by aerial observation, for example, or by the establishment of perimeter observation posts. Although proponents of strong verification measures have not been happy with this new formulation, the committee agreed to go along with a modified version that took into account some of their concerns. One of those concerns expressed by delegations was about the role of the Executive Council—whether it should decide when an inspection takes place and whether it should make a judgment on the results. It was eventually agreed that the council could stop an investigation within twelve hours of its initiation by a three-fourths vote of the members and that, following an investigation, the council could address concerns about compliance that might be raised by either party.

Other contentious issues have been (1) the composition of the Executive Council—how many members and which countries would belong; (2) the extension of the industry-monitoring regime to "chemical-weapons-capable" countries; (3) whether export controls should continue after the convention enters into force; and (4) destruction schedules for stocks and for the elimination or conversion of chemical-weapons manufacturing facilities.

The negotiators made a determined effort to resolve the outstanding issues in the summer of 1992. Although not all participants were happy with some of the necessary compromises, a final version of the convention was adopted in August.

OTHER MEASURES TO CONTROL CHEMICAL WEAPONS

Attempts to Control Proliferation   Worldwide attention to the threat of the proliferation of chemical weapons began to grow in the 1980s, reaching a peak with the confirmed use of mustard and nerve gases by Iraq in its war with Iran. Many factors may contribute to the decisions of countries to embark on chemical-weapons programs. Among these could be a desire to counter a perceived threat from a neighbor, the ready availability and relative cheapness of necessary materials for creating a chemical-weapons capability as compared with nuclear weapons, as well as psychological, moral, and cultural factors.

Export Controls   Watching these ominous developments, the industrialized countries came to the conclusion that they could not wait for the achievement of a chemical-weapons convention to slow or halt the spread of chemical weapons. One of their first actions was to look at the possibility of controlling the export of critical materials to countries that might have an interest in developing a chemical-weapons capability.

Shortly after the first U.N. report was issued on the use of chemical weapons in the Iran-Iraq War in 1984, the United States placed a ban on the export of eight chemical precursors to Iraq and urged its allies to do likewise. The following year an informal group representing several developed countries met to try to coordinate their export-control policies with respect to materials related to chemical weapons. The Australians offered their embassy in Paris as the venue for the group's meeting and took a leading role in its work, causing it soon to be dubbed the "Australia Group." The member nations differed markedly in their procedures governing the export of chemical products, but over the years the Australia Group has achieved considerable success in getting agreement on a standardized list of chemicals that would be subject to controls. In 1991 the group, composed of twenty countries plus the European Community, represented as such, agreed to place export controls on fifty chemicals having a potential for dual-purpose use as chemical-weapons precursors. Their export is not banned, but government approval is required before they may be shipped to countries not members of the group.

The impact of export controls on the spread of chemical weapons is severely limited. No matter how careful a country may be in its effort to insure that a chemical on the control list is intended only for legitimate use, there are often ways that a determined proliferator can circumvent controls through the setting up of dummy companies, transshipments, and other ruses. In addition to precursor chemicals, manufacturing equipment may be involved. Several examples have been uncovered in recent years, most notably a suspected chemical-weapons plant at Rabta in Libya, which was constructed with materials initially consigned to a bogus pharmaceutical plant in Hong Kong.

An additional weakness of export controls is the suspicion they arouse among the developing nations, which often see them as representing an effort by the industrialized nations to limit the availability of vital materials needed for their economic development. Nevertheless, in the absence of a worldwide regime to which the majority of nations subscribe, the industrialized nations see export controls as vital to slowing the spread of chemical weapons.

Sanctions   Related to export controls as an interim measure to limit proliferation are sanctions against countries that use chemical or biological weapons or attempt to create a capability for manufacturing them. Sanctions also have substantial limitations. To be effective they must inflict penalties on the offending state, must not be easily circumvented, and their application must be coordinated among the various supplier nations. In the United States, disagreement developed between the legislative and the executive branches over the degree of automaticity with which sanctions should be applied when a nation or a foreign commercial firm violates the accepted norms. Congress was interested in making the imposition of sanctions relatively automatic, while the executive branch wished to be free to consider in each case whether sanctions would harm important foreign policy interests involving a particular country or group of countries. After more than a year of sparring, a sanctions bill was passed and signed into law in December 1991. It provided for the imposition of sanctions against foreign persons and governments that knowingly and materially contribute to the efforts of another country to acquire the capability to develop, produce, stockpile, deliver, or use chemical or biological weapons. A wide range of possible sanctions are specified, such as denial of economic or military assistance, breaking of diplomatic relations, denial of landing rights, and the like. The president could waive these sanctions in instances when U.S. national security would be jeopardized by their imposition.

The Paris Conference of January 1989

Iraq's use of chemical weapons in the Iran-Iraq War stimulated an initiative by the United States for an international conference to consider the growing threat of chemical warfare and to reaffirm the commitment of the world community to the 1925 Geneva Protocol. At the U.N. General Assembly in September 1988 President Ronald Reagan made a call for such a conference to be held at the foreign ministers level. France offered to be the host, citing its role as the depositary power for the Geneva Protocol.

Interest in the conference, which opened in Paris on 7 January 1989, was heightened by the discovery of a suspected chemical-weapons plant in Libya. Representatives of 149 countries attended, and at the conclusion of the conference on 11 January they unanimously approved a communiqué that:

- reaffirmed the commitment of the parties to the Geneva Protocol;
- called for a strengthening of the ability of the United Nations to take action in event of alleged violations of the protocol;
- called on all nations to exercise restraint and responsible action "in accordance with the purpose of the present declaration"; and
- urged a redoubling of efforts to conclude a convention on the prohibition of the development, production, stockpiling, and use of all chemical weapons and on their destruction.

The Canberra Government-Industry Conference Against Chemical Weapons   In September 1989 the Australian government organized a conference for representatives of industry and government to discuss areas of concern to the chemical industry under a worldwide ban on chemical weapons and to explore ways of stimulating progress in the Geneva negotiations aimed at achieving such a ban. Some 375 delegates from sixty-six countries met in Canberra from 18 to 22 September.

The most significant achievement was the adoption of a collective statement by representatives of the global chemical industry recording "their willingness to work actively with governments to achieve a global ban on chemical weapons . . . and their willingness to continue their dialogue with governments to prepare for the entry into force of an effective Chemical Weapons Convention (CWC) which protects the free and non-discriminatory exchange of chemicals and transfer of technology for economic development and the welfare of all people" (News release, Australian Ministry of Foreign Affairs and Trade, 22 September 1989). Industry representatives, many of whom had served as unofficial consultants to their national delegations, agreed to meet periodically in Geneva to coordinate the industry-wide response to the emerging convention.

In the summary conference statement, Chairman Gareth Evans, the Australian minister for foreign affairs and trade, placed heavy emphasis on promoting the achievement of a CWC, and touched only obliquely on efforts, such as export controls, aimed at arresting proliferation. His report did, however, identify "a number of measures in support of the objectives of the convention which both governments and industry are either implementing, or have indicated a willingness to consider in advance of its coming into effect." The conference took note of the fact that some countries were adapting existing national measures to the convention framework, or adopting other measures which would assist in its implementation. The conference report also noted that preparations for the implementation of the convention would entail specific actions by government and industry, and cited "the need for industry to apply its code of responsible care so as to ensure, amongst other things, the compatibility of its activities with objectives of the convention including the objective, shared with governments, of non-diversion of its products for the manufacture of chemical weapons" (both quotations from Australian Overseas Information Service, "Australia Background; Chemical Weapons Conference," Canberra, 18–22 September 1989," Washington, D.C., Embassy of Australia).

The United States–Soviet Bilateral Agreement of 1990

In September 1989, at a meeting at the foreign minister level in Jackson Hole, Wyoming, the United States and the Soviet Union signed a "Memorandum of Understanding" in which the two sides agreed to embark upon a bilateral verification experiment and data exchange. The first phase of the exchange was completed on 31 December 1989, as provided in the memorandum, and was followed up in mid-1990 with initial visits to chemical-weapons storage facilities in both countries. More thoroughgoing data exchanges and visits were to be undertaken at a later date when the two sides agreed that the completion of the chemical-weapons convention was imminent.

Events moved rapidly in late 1989 and early 1990. At the Malta summit in December 1989, President Bush offered to halt binary production if the Soviets would agree to the proposals he had made at the

U.N. in September. He had suggested that the United States and Soviet Union begin cutting their stockpiles by 20 percent of current U.S. levels while continuing to work to complete the CWC. U.S. binary production would continue, however, within the established limits. Once a treaty went into effect, the United States would destroy 98 percent of its stockpile during the first eight years. The remaining 2 percent would be destroyed during the following two years only if nations capable of building chemical weapons joined the treaty, a condition that the United States dropped in May 1991.

A cessation of U.S. binary production had been a major Soviet condition for progress on a bilateral agreement to reduce stockpiles, and the Bush offer at Malta made it possible to move rapidly toward an agreement along the lines of his earlier proposal. By the time of the Washington summit at the end of May 1990, a bilateral agreement was ready for signing, albeit after some strenuous last minute negotiating and with the details of a verification protocol still to be worked out.

The agreement, signed 1 June 1990, provided for the following, as reported in the *Chemical Weapons Bulletin* (Federation of American Scientists, Washington, D.C., June 1990):

- cessation of production of chemical weapons upon entry into force;
- reduction of chemical-weapons stockpiles so that by no later than 31 December 2002 each party would have no more than five thousand agent tons; or reduction of their stockpiles to not more than five hundred agent tons no later than the eighth year after a CWC enters into force;
- cooperation regarding methods and technologies for the safe and efficient destruction of chemical weapons;
- cooperation in developing, testing, and carrying out appropriate inspection procedures; and
- cooperation in efforts to insure the conclusion of the multilateral convention at the earliest date and to implement it effectively.

Detailed provisions to implement the inspection measures remained to be worked out, but the parties pledged to attempt to complete this task by 31 December 1990. Each party was to begin destruction of its chemical weapons by no later than December 1992.

Some progress toward completing a verification protocol to the agreement was made over the next year, but after the breakup of the Soviet Union, these efforts came to a halt and the agreement was suspended. Because of technical, economic, and political problems, the Russian Republic's efforts to create a capability for the safe destruction of chemical weapons lagged markedly, making it impossible to meet the destruction schedule in the bilateral agreement.

CONCLUSION

The U.N. Conference on Disarmament completed its work on the CWC in the summer of 1992. However, there were some states that were not committed to adhering to the convention, among them some of the more worrisome. Another concern was the problem of destroying chemical weapons in an environmentally sound manner, particularly in Russia, where no plans were in place for destroying the large chemical-weapons stockpile inherited from the Soviet Union. In addition, in the absence of a chemical-weapons convention, proliferation of these weapons continued to be a concern.

The arms control regime for biological weapons will be faced with revolutionary advances in the field of microbiology, which could lead to the development of new agents with greater military appeal than heretofore. The ability of the Biological and Toxin Weapons Convention to serve as a bulwark against a resurgence of interest in these weapons will depend in large measure on the degree of commitment by the parties to the measures that have been proposed at the review conferences for strengthening the convention.

BIBLIOGRAPHY

A multilateral arms control agreement prohibiting biological weapons has been in existence since 1972, while chemical weapons arms control has been in flux since that time. As a result, accounts of the effort to achieve a chemical weapons convention are less complete and more speculative than those relating to the Biological Weapons Convention. Also, for chemical weapons there is a wide range of issues outside the multilateral negotiations that are germane to the overall effort to control these weapons: bilateral United States–Soviet negotiations, efforts to control the export of critical chemicals, problems of the safe destruction of chemical weapons, use of chemical weapons in warfare since World War II, and their proliferation.

General Reading   The Stockholm International Peace Research Institute (SIPRI) has published a series of monographs on a wide range of issues dealing with chemical and biological warfare under the rubric *The Problem of Chemical and Biological Warfare: A Study of the Historical, Technical, Military, Legal and Political Aspects of CWB, and Possible Disarmament Measures,* 6 vols. (Stockholm and New York, 1971–1975) and the SIPRI *Chemical and Biological Warfare Studies* ("Scorpion" Series), vols. 1–13 (Oxford, 1985–1991). Also see FREDERIC J. BROWN, *Chemical Warfare: A Study in Restraints* (Princeton, N.J., 1968); ERHARD GEISSLER, *Biological and Toxin Weapons Today* [SIPRI] (Oxford and New York, 1986); UNITED NATIONS, *Chemical and Bacteriological (Biological) Weapons and the Effects of Their Possible Use: Report of the Secretary General* (New York, 1969); and MATTHEW MESELSON and JULIAN PERRY ROBINSON, "Chemical Warfare and Chemical Disarmament," *Scientific American* 242 (April 1980): 38–47.

Historical Background   For an account of the evolution and afterlife of the Biological Weapons Convention, see NICHOLAS A. SIMS, *The Diplomacy of Biological Disarmament: Vicissitudes of a Treaty in Force, 1975–85* (New York, 1988); and BAREND TER HAAR, *The Future of Biological Weapons* (Westport, Conn., 1991). Efforts to control chemical weapons may be found in L. F. HABER, *The Poisonous Cloud: Chemical Warfare in the First World War* (Oxford and New York, 1986) and CHARLES C. FLOWERREE, "The Politics of Arms Control: A Case Study," *Journal of International Affairs* 37 (Winter 1984): 269–282.

Chemical-Weapons Negotiations   Specific aspects of the negotiations for a multilateral convention banning chemical weapons may be found in the following volumes of the SIPRI, Scorpion Series: vol. 2, *Chemical Warfare Arms Control Disarmament* (Oxford, 1987); vol. 11, *National Implementation of the Future Chemical Weapons Convention* (Oxford and New York, 1990). A thorough examination of the genesis and dynamics of the negotiations on the chemical weapons convention through 1991 is contained in a case study by CHARLES C. FLOWERREE and RICKI ABERLE, *Multilateral Negotiations for Chemical Weapons Ban* (Washington,

D.C., 1991). For the verification aspects of chemical weapons arms control, see MICHAEL KREPON, *Verification of a Chemical Weapons Convention: A Guide to the Perplexed* (Washington, D.C., 1992) and JOHN G. TOWER, JAMES BROWN, and WILLIAM K. CHEEK, eds., *Verification: The Key to Arms Control in the 1990s* (New York, 1990), Part IV. Essays on what happens after the conclusion of negotiations of a convention are contained in BRAD ROBERTS, ed., *Chemical Disarmament and U.S. Security* (Boulder, Colo., 1992).

Proliferation of Chemical Weapons   An examination of all aspects of chemical proliferation with analyses of the capabilities for chemical warfare of thirty-nine countries may be found in GORDON M. BURCK and CHARLES C. FLOWERREE, *International Handbook on Chemical Weapons Proliferation* (Westport, Conn., 1991). Also see TREVOR FINDLAY, ed., *Chemical Weapons and Missile Proliferation—With Implications for the Asia-Pacific Region* (Boulder, Colo., 1991); ELISA D. HARRIS, "Stemming the Spread of Chemical Weapons," *Brookings Review* 8 (Winter 1989/90): 39–45; and TERRY M. WEEKLY, "Proliferation of Chemical Warfare: Challenge to Traditional Restraints," *Parameters, U.S. Army War College Quarterly* 19 (December 1989): 51–66.

Chemical Weapons in the Iran-Iraq War
Many books and articles have been written on the war but few focus on the role of chemical weapons. A detailed military analysis of the use of chemical weapons by Iraq may be found in GORDON M. BURCK and CHARLES C. FLOWERREE, *International Handbook on Chemical Weapons Proliferation* (Westport Conn., 1991), pp. 85–137. Also see THOMAS L. MCNAUGHER, "Ballistic Missiles and Chemical Weapons: the Legacy of the Iran-Iraq War," *International Security* 15 (Fall 1990): 5–34.

Strategic and Political Aspects   See BRAD ROBERTS, *Chemical Disarmament and International Security,* Adelphi Papers No. 267 (London, 1992); JULIAN PERRY ROBINSON, "Salient Features of the Current Chemical Warfare Situation," in ENRICO JACCHIA, ed., *Chemical Weapons and Arms Control: Views from Europe* (Rome, 1983); *Report of the President's Chemical Warfare Review Commission* [G.P.O.] (Washington, D.C., 1985); W. SETH CARUS, *Chemical Weapons in the Middle East,* Policy Focus

No. 9, Washington Institute for New East Policy (Washington, D.C., 1988); and ELISA D. HARRIS, "Chemical and Biological Arms Control: The Role of the Allies," in FEN OSLER HAMPSON, HARALD VON RIEKHOFF, and JOHN ROPER, eds., *The Allies and Arms Control* (Baltimore, 1991), pp. 75–94.

Manufacturing and Technical Aspects   GORDON M. BURCK, "Chemical Weapons Technology and the Conversion to Civilian Production," *Arms Control* [London] 11 (1990): SIPRI Scorpion Series, Vols. 4 and 5, *The Chemical Industry and the Projected Chemical Weapons Convention* (Oxford and New York, 1986) and Vol. 9, *Non-Production by Industry of Chemical-Warfare Agents: Technical Verification under a Chemical Weapons Convention* (Oxford, 1988).

Strengthening the Biological Weapons Convention   Reports of the FEDERATION OF AMERICAN SCIENTISTS Working Group on Biological and Toxin Weapons Verification, *Proposals for the Third Review Conference of the Biological Weapons Convention* (Washington, D.C., 1990) and *Implementation of the Proposals for a Verification Protocol to the Biological Weapons Convention* (Scheduled for publication in *Arms Control* [London] in 1992); also SIPRI Scorpion Series, Vol. 10., *Strengthening the Biological Weapons Convention by Confidence-Building Measures* (Oxford, 1990), and Vol. 12, *Views on Possible Verification Measures for the Biological Weapons Convention* (Oxford, 1991); NICHOLAS A. SIMS, *The Diplomacy of Biological Disarmament: Vicissitudes of a Treaty in Force, 1975–85* (New York, 1988); and BAREND TER HAAR, *The Future of Biological Weapons* (Westport, Conn., 1991).

Alleged Use of Chemical and Biological Weapons in Southeast Asia and Afghanistan   For official U.S. government views see U.S. DEPARTMENT OF STATE, *Chemical Warfare in Southeast Asia and Afghanistan, Report to the Congress from Secretary of State Alexander M. Haig Jr.* (Washington, D.C., March 1982) and U.S. DEPARTMENT OF STATE, *Chemical Warfare in Southeast Asia and Afghanistan: An Update, Report from Secretary of State George P. Shultz* (Washington, D.C., November 1982). For a popular account supporting the government's view see JANE HAMILTON-MERRITT, "Gas Warfare in Laos: Communism's Drive to Annihilate a People," *Read-*

ers' Digest (October 1980): 81–88; and STERLING SEA-GRAVE, *Yellow Rain: A Journey Through the Terror of Chemical Warfare* (New York, 1981). Views critical of the government's position may be found in ELISA D. HARRIS, "Sverdlovsk and Yellow Rain: Two Cases of Soviet Noncompliance?" *International Se-*

curity 11 (Spring 1987): 41–95; and THOMAS D. SEE-LEY, JOAN W. NOWICKE, MATTHEW MESELSON, JEANNE GUILLEMIN, and PONGTHEP AKRATANAKUL, "Yellow Rain," *Scientific American* 253 (September 1985): 128–137.

Controlling the Arms Trade
Since 1945

○

KEITH R. KRAUSE

See also Budgetary Limitations on Military Expenditures; Latin America; The Middle East; *and* Regulating Arms Sales to 1945.

For the first forty years after World War II, measures to restrict or control the global trade in weapons were slow to gain prominence on the international arms control and disarmament agenda. Although numerous partial proposals had been advanced or launched, these gained few adherents and had no appreciable impact on the volume or sophistication of the weapons traded. Yet the global arms trade has arguably played as large a role in post-1945 world politics (in terms of wars fought and lives lost) as the nuclear arms race between the superpower blocs, and the change since 1945 in the "international military system" has been unprecedented. With the end of the Cold War, a number of initiatives to control the arms trade were launched, some of which rapidly bore fruit. The United Nations, for example, has since 1990 mandated the imposition of five arms-transfer embargoes (in the context of various conflict-resolution efforts), more than in the previous forty years. This article will discuss the various proposals to control the arms trade and explore some of the reasons it has resisted international controls in spite of its importance. It will begin with an overview of the development of the global arms trade since 1945 and the different national regulations and policies governing arms transfers, review the history of post-1945 control initiatives, and analyze the problems with and future prospects for controls on the arms trade.

One of the reasons that initiatives to control the arms trade have failed is that consensus on the nature of the "problem" to be solved has not been achieved. To begin, there is disagreement over whether the arms trade is a global problem that can only be tackled with broad international treaties and agreements to restrict the transfer of certain types of weapons, or a regional problem directly connected with particular conflicts. Although most analysts accept that arms transfers must be evaluated in their specific regional contexts (since a transfer of sophisticated fighters that appears "normal" in the Middle East may be highly destabilizing in Latin America), it is difficult to establish discriminatory controls. Since the sale of arms is often a test of a patron-client relationship, the refusal to supply one ally with weapons that another had already received would be perceived as a major diplomatic and political snub. Likewise, there is no agreement over whether the arms trade contributes to regional conflicts (in which case controlling it would reduce friction), or is merely a reflection of them (in which case the underlying insecurities need to be addressed first).

There are also different possible justifications for controlling the arms trade, none of which is shared by all suppliers and recipients. Perhaps the broadest justification is the desire to make war less likely, or less destructive should it occur, by restricting the volume and sophistication of weapons acquired by states. But often arms transfers have been justified precisely as a means to make war less likely, by creating a military balance or stalemate between states

1021

that might otherwise go to war. Many states (especially in the developing world) also view attempts to control the arms trade with suspicion: they regard controls as a means for military "have" powers to freeze a particular global distribution of military power, or to maintain an existing technological lead by restricting the access of "have not" powers to modern weapons. The reluctance of states such as China and India to agree to multilateral arms-transfer controls signals their unwillingness to accept a position of possibly permanent military inferiority, and there is little doubt that many of the initiatives that will be discussed in this essay have been designed by supplier states to maintain their technological lead. Finally, it is often argued that limits on the arms trade could save money by reducing spending on armaments or on the military as a whole. But expenditures on arms imports are actually only a small percentage (usually less than one-third) of total military expenditure in most states, and there is no guarantee that the money saved would be devoted to nonmilitary purposes. Limits on overall military expenditures might have a more direct economic benefit, although attempts to analyze the impact of military spending on economic growth and development have not produced clear evidence of a negative link.

Despite these debates, the arms trade has assumed such proportions (and prominence in public debates) that a number of serious measures for control have been actively pursued. These include efforts to increase transparency of the arms trade through the establishment of a United Nations arms transfer register, initiatives to reduce the overall volume of arms transfers to the developing world, attempts to restrict arms deliveries to specific zones of conflict (such as the Middle East), measures to prevent the proliferation of unconventional weapons or weapons of mass destruction (such as ballistic missiles or chemical and nuclear weapons), and proposals to enhance national control over illegal (black-market) weapons transfers. Not all of these proposals require actual reductions in the volume or sophistication of weapons transferred, and in some cases the goals sought could be achieved with controls that simply regulated the flow of arms to particular states or regions. Some measures (such as the U.N. register) are quantitative and focus on the numbers of weapons being transferred; others (such as the Missile Technology Control Regime) are qualitative and focus on particular technologies or systems.

To discuss this range of initiatives, this essay will adopt a broad definition of *control* that includes all measures designed to restrict, regulate, or moderate the international flow of weapons. In this sense, states almost always exercise some restraint over their arms transfers, since few countries trade weapons as freely as goods such as bananas or televisions, and seldom do they export arms without any consideration of the possible consequences. Thus this essay will discuss not only proposals for global negotiated multilateral restraints, but also regional, bilateral, tacit, and imposed restrictions or regulations. It will begin with a discussion of unilateral or national controls, discuss local or regional arrangements, and then examine global or multilateral initiatives.

GLOBAL ARMS TRANSFERS: AN OVERVIEW

To evaluate or understand proposals to control the arms trade, one must have some sense of its scope and character. Between 1963 and 1988, arms transfers more than quadrupled in real terms, from about $12 billion to more than $50 billion dollars per year (constant 1988 dollars). This growth in the importance and volume of the arms trade in the post-1945 period was a consequence of three major developments. The first was the Cold War rivalry between the superpowers, which resulted in massive transfers of weapons by the Americans and Soviets to their respective allies in Europe in the 1950s, and after 1955 in competitive transfers to friends and clients in the developing world. The second was the process of decolonization, one consequence of which was the establishment and equipping of modern armed forces in a large number of newly independent states in Africa and Asia. The third trend was the reestablishment and expansion of the European arms industries. As Britain, France, and Germany (and later Italy, Czechoslovakia, and Spain) rebuilt their arms industries after World War II, they found that to produce sophisticated modern weapons at the technological frontier (and to compete with the United States and the Soviet Union), they had to export large quantities of arms. These states (so-called second-tier producers) rely heavily upon arms exports for the well-being and survival of their arms industries, and are thus reluctant to agree to quantitative limitations of their arms transfers.

Table 1:   Global Arms Deliveries, 1963–1988, Four-Year Averages (million constant 1988 dollars)

Country	1963–1966	1967–1970	1971–1974	1975–1978	1979–1982	1983–1986	1987–1988*
United States	4,842	8,575	10,751	11,039	10,099	11,885	14,536
Soviet Union	4,415	4,614	8,312	12,951	23,978	21,339	22,219
France	481	507	1,450	2,512	4,202	4,833	2,340
Britain	557	402	1,071	1,613	2,707	1,705	1,447
West Germany	360	329	475	1,373	1,730	1,838	1,125
Italy	74	76	295	817	1,284	1,067	381
Czechoslovakia	449	379	531	1,161	1,167	1,250	1,045
Poland	412	445	443	856	1,125	1,304	957
Other Industrial	444	565	1,010	1,859	2,369	2,538	1,762
Other East European	22	46	240	370	997	1,634	1,242
China	223	491	916	280	680	1,535	2,738
Developing World	310	48	156	1,448	2,961	3,044	2,543
Total	12,589	16,475	25,649	36,282	53,297	53,972	52,333

*Average for the two-year period 1987–1988 only; also note that, due to rounding, a given total may not be the exact sum of its column in this and the following tables.
Source: United States Arms Control and Disarmament Agency, *World Military Expenditures and Arms Transfers* (Washington, D.C.: ACDA, various years).

Table 2:   Regional Distribution of Arms Imports, 1963–1987

Region	1963–1967	1968–1972	1973–1977	1978–1982	1983–1987	(% popul. 1982)
Africa	4.2	3.6	11.3	18.7	12.3	(9.8)
East Asia	28.7	34.6	15.6	10.7	11.5	(35.1)
Latin America	3.1	3.6	4.8	6.8	7.4	(8.1)
Middle East	9.2	16.6	33.6	37.5	37.8	(3.1)
North America	3.0	3.5	2.0	1.7	1.5	(5.6)
Oceania	2.0	1.4	0.9	1.0	1.5	(0.5)
South Asia	6.8	4.3	4.0	3.9	7.3	(20.4)
NATO Europe	20.3	18.3	10.2	8.7	7.4	(7.1)
Warsaw Pact	19.1	11.2	14.7	8.3	10.4	(8.2)
Other Europe	3.6	2.7	2.8	2.7	2.4	(2.0)
Developed	41.7	28.9	25.7	19.5	20.9	(23.8)
Developing	58.3	71.1	74.3	80.5	79.1	(76.1)

Regions are classified as follows:
Oceania: Australia, New Zealand, Fiji, Papua New Guinea.
Africa: does not include Egypt.
Middle East: Egypt to the Persian Gulf, Iran and Cyprus.
Latin America: Mexico south, all Caribbean states.
North America: Canada and the United States.
South Asia: Afghanistan, India, Pakistan, Nepal, Bangladesh, Sri Lanka.
East Asia: Mongolia, both Koreas, both Chinas, Japan, and from Burma to Indonesia.
Other Europe: Albania, Austria, Finland, Ireland, Malta, Spain, Sweden, Switzerland, Yugoslavia.
Developed: all of NATO, except Greece and Turkey; all of the Warsaw Pact except Bulgaria, Japan, Australia, New Zealand, Finland, Austria, Ireland, Sweden, and Switzerland.
Developing: all others.

Source: ACDA, *WMEAT*, various years.

Table 3: Top Ten Arms Recipients, Selected Years (percentage of world total)

	1963	1972	1982	1988
West Germany	14.6	6.5		
Indonesia	7.4			
Italy	6.8			
India	5.8		3.5	6.6
Egypt	4.7	5.3	4.0	
East Germany	4.1	3.3		
Iraq	3.3		14.8	9.5
Poland	3.2			
Soviet Union	2.9			
South Vietnam	2.8	15.4		
North Vietnam		11.6		3.1*
Iran		5.1	3.3	4.1
South Korea		3.4		
Israel		2.9	2.0	3.9
Syria		2.7	5.4	2.7
Poland		2.5		
Saudi Arabia			6.7	6.2
Libya			6.7	
Cuba			3.5	3.5
Algeria			2.5	
Afghanistan				5.3
Angola				3.3
TOTAL	55.6	58.6	52.4	48.1

*Includes former South Vietnam.

Source: ACDA, *WMEAT*, various years.

Throughout the 1980s, an annual average of about $52 billion worth of arms was bought and sold. Although more than 40 states acted as suppliers, the majority of the arms (more than 75 percent) was exported from the leading industrial world arms producers—the United States, the former Soviet Union, Britain, France, and Germany. On the recipient side, about 120 states imported significant quantities of arms in the late 1980s, and about 80 percent of those weapons were delivered to the developing world, particularly the Middle East. The preceding tables provide a snapshot of global arms deliveries from major suppliers and show how these deliveries are distributed by recipient region. The top ten arms recipients at different points in the 1963 to 1988 period are also listed. Together these tables illustrate that the arms trade is not a "global" phenomenon, but rather one that is concentrated among a few states. The top five suppliers account for three-quarters, and the top ten recipients for about half, of total arms transfers.

These tables also illustrate, however, that arms transfers are not exclusively restricted to these few states. Weapons deliveries from many lesser suppliers can play a large role in particular regional conflicts and wars (such as Brazilian and North Korean transfers to the Persian Gulf during the Iran-Iraq War), and global measures to limit the overall arms trade are unlikely to be effective unless lesser producers are also included.

EVOLUTION OF NATIONAL CONTROL SYSTEMS

The most basic controls on the arms trade are the unilateral export controls applied by supplier states, virtually all of which have formal decision-making procedures for arms transfers. Overall policy is expressed either in a government guideline that can be changed by executive decision, or by a legal framework. The United States, for example, has congressional reporting requirements for all arms exports greater than $50 million, and major sales are widely discussed and debated. In France, however, government agencies work closely with defense firms to find markets and cultivate clients, and although final approval rests with a political committee—the Commission interministérielle pour l'étude des exportations de matériels de guerre, or the Inter-ministerial Commission for the Study of War Equipment Exports (CIEEMG)—the initiation of sales occurs primarily on a bureaucratic or commercial level, not a political one. In Canada, export decisions are made within a policy framework publicly explained by the government in 1986, but individual export decisions are seldom debated publicly; in Brazil, until the early 1990s arms exports were pursued with almost no political restraint or oversight being exercised.

In general, the procedures in most states include a licensing requirement for all arms exports (based on a "munitions list") and a government approval process that includes high-level representation from the foreign ministry, defense department, intelligence community, arms control agencies, and other interested bodies. The United States is somewhat unusual in that, as stated above, large export deals must also have congressional approval (or not be vetoed by Congress). Most transactions are government-to-government deals, meaning that an arms firm sells its wares to its national government, which in turn makes a deal with a recipient state. Of course, in most cases the decision-making procedures incorporate political and economic factors that may promote arms transfers, and there is no necessary element of restraint in the regulation policies of many suppliers. But all states are (most of the time) conscious of the potentially harmful consequences of arms transfers, and have forgone particular deals that would be controversial or destructive. One can, however, distinguish four broad categories of national control systems, as determined by the weight given by states to political, commercial, or ethical considerations.

The first type of system is represented by the United States and (until 1991) the Soviet Union (since the future position of the successor states is unclear). Because of their large domestic markets for arms, neither the U.S. nor the Soviet defense industries have depended on arms transfers for their well-being, since only about 15 percent of total production was exported (although exports were important for particular weapon systems). This meant that the dominant factors governing arms-transfer decisions were foreign policy considerations: arms were supplied to friends and clients, and not to states that were potential adversaries or were aligned on the opposing side in the Cold War. In many cases (such as Soviet arms supplied to Egypt in the 1960s, or American arms supplied to Egypt after 1979), both superpowers exercised restraint over the types of weapons they supplied clients, attempting to prevent them from obtaining a potentially destabilizing military advantage in a region. Finally, both the United States and the Soviet Union have, since the early 1960s, been reluctant to export military technology to assist clients in building their own defense industries, a stance that reflects concern over maintaining their military technological lead. This concern is reflected in many U.S. arms-transfer control policies of the late twentieth century (such as the Missile Technology Control Regime, which will be discussed below).

The second type of system is represented by France, Britain, and to a lesser extent Italy and Spain and other smaller industrialized producers such as Belgium. The decision-making structure of these producers, and the actual policies they pursue, reflect the relatively strong influence of economic factors and the concomitant weak influence of other political or military considerations. These states exported around 40 to 50 percent of their arms production throughout the 1980s, and their industries depended on either high levels of exports or on state subsidies in order to maintain production. Their export regulation mechanisms hence have tended to emphasize commercial or economic considerations, only rejecting sales when strong political pressures are present. France, for example, sold about $7 billion in advanced weapons to Iraq during the Iran-Iraq War, only to face its own weapons in the 1991 Persian Gulf War. Until 1989, Poland and Czechoslovakia also appeared to follow similarly unrestrained policies (within the overall framework of Warsaw Pact alignments). Their post–Cold War policies were not yet clear as of 1992. Overall, this group of states had not until the early 1990s been concerned with trading away their technological lead, and had participated extensively in coproduction and licensed production arrangements with developing-world arms producers. There were some moves, however, within the European Community (EC) to harmonize national policies in order to achieve greater control over arms exports. With the creation of the single market in 1993, it may become more difficult to control unauthorized weapons or technology transfers out of the "leakiest" states in the EC. The debate is between countries such as Germany and the Netherlands, which would like tight coordination of national policies at the EC level, and France and Britain, which want to retain some national autonomy in order to pursue independent national security policies. It is not clear, however, whether greater coordination would result in lower levels of arms exports from this second group of states.

The third type of system, made up of the "voluntary restricters," temper their export policy with what could be called "ethical" considerations. Japan, Germany, Sweden, Canada, Finland, and Switzerland all fall into this category. Japan does not in principle allow the export of goods that could be used by military forces directly in combat. Sweden shuns involvement in "areas of conflict," and Canada does not (in principle) export arms to countries under threat of hostilities or that have a persistent record of human rights violations. Frequent breaches of these policies (such as the Canadian sale of armored vehicles to Saudi Arabia, or the German sale of chemical-weapons equipment to Libya, or the Swedish sale of explosives to India) often create scandals and illustrate the pressure to export that these states face. But these suppliers could export more arms if they chose to do so, and their policies are an important element of restraint in the global arms market.

The fourth category includes developing-world arms producers, many of which have pursued rather promiscuous arms-export policies. Throughout the Iran-Iraq War, for example, Chile and Brazil sold hundreds of millions of dollars of weapons to both sides in the conflict. North Korea appears to have delivered surface-to-surface missiles to Iran, in the face of considerable international opposition. China, too, has been relatively indiscriminate in its arms-transfer policy and has been the most reluctant participant in multilateral discussions on controls. For most of these states, encouragement of arms exports is a matter of state policy, both because of the perceived economic benefits this brings, and because of a perception that exports garner some political influence (or at least a higher international profile). Developing world producers are extremely susceptible to fluctuations in demand, however, and many saw their sales drop dramatically in the early 1990s. Some, such as Brazil and Argentina, have also come under pressure from states such as the United States to implement more restrictive arms-transfer policies.

PARTIAL AND REGIONAL EFFORTS TO CONTROL THE ARMS TRADE

A range of partial initiatives to control the arms trade to specific countries, regions, or conflicts has been launched in the post-1945 period, although most of them have been confined to either the Middle East or Latin America. Efforts at regional limitations have been absent from Africa and Asia, with the exception of the United Nations embargo against South Africa (discussed below), and the embargo against India and Pakistan during their 1965 war. Some of the initiatives that were launched were simple supplier embargoes; others grew out of recipient states' arms control initiatives. All were temporary, however, and none evolved into a system of formal multilateral controls on arms transfers. A brief review of these initiatives does illustrate some of the complexities and problems that regional-based arms transfer controls face.

Middle Eastern Efforts Since 1950   The first postwar attempt to create a regional control system for arms transfers was the 1950 Tripartite Declaration of Britain, the United States, and France, the three dominant powers in the Middle East.

They built upon the temporary U.N. embargo on arms transfers to the Arab-Israeli conflict that lasted from 29 May 1948 to 11 August 1949, and they established the Near Eastern Arms Coordinating Committee (NEACC) as a consultative committee to regulate their arms deliveries to the region. Until 1955 these states were the sole arms suppliers to the region, and hence they were able to orchestrate their arms deliveries in order (as the declaration noted) to suppress the nascent arms race between Israel and its Arab neighbors. In addition, the colonial powers wished to maintain their political influence in the region and to push Arab states to participate in a regional defense arrangement that was directed at the Soviet Union. But the tripartite agreement had two major flaws: it was a supplier condominium that generated active resentment among the Arab Middle Eastern states, and it excluded one major potential supplier. These flaws meant that when the Soviet Union entered the picture with a 1955 arms deal with Egypt, using Czechoslovakia as the supplier state, the informal agreement collapsed. Within a few years, Arab states such as Syria, Iraq, and Egypt were major clients of Soviet arms, and a regional arms race had been unleashed.

States continued, however, to pay at least lip service to the idea of restraining arms exports to the Middle East. Between 1956 and 1958, the Soviet Union made restraint proposals, suggesting on one occasion that the four major powers (the tripartite powers plus the Soviet Union) should refuse to deliver arms to the Middle East, and in another case, linking this to the withdrawal of foreign troops from the region. These proposals were unacceptable to the Western powers. After the 1967 Arab-Israeli War, the United States advocated that arms exports to the region be made public and reported to the United Nations, as a prelude to reaching some understanding, in the words of Secretary of State Dean Rusk, "that the arms-supplying nations will not themselves be responsible for a major renewal of an arms race in the Middle East" (quoted in SIPRI, *The Arms Trade with the Third World,* 1971, p. 112). A similar goal was reiterated in 1971, but control of arms transfers to the region became (after 1967) bound up with the overall question of a Middle East peace settlement. Until some (albeit limited) progress on a broader settlement of the Middle East conflict was achieved with the convening of multilateral talks in 1991, no progress on limiting arms transfers to the region was possible.

Proposals that followed the 1991 Gulf War will be dealt with below.

Although it cannot be considered a formal control arrangement, the American relationship with Egypt, Israel, and (to a lesser extent) Jordan since the 1973 Middle Eastern war does represent a conscious policy of regulation of arms transfers as a means of reducing the risk of war between the parties. For some analysts, the 1978 Camp David accords between Israel and Egypt constitute a successful case of regulating arms transfers to enhance regional security, although it should be noted that regulation did not mean *restraint*. The United States replaced Israeli airfields removed from the Sinai, granted both parties a large military aid package after the deal was signed ($3 billion to Israel, $1.5 billion to Egypt), and has measured subsequent arms deliveries to each side against the arsenal of the other side, in order to maintain rough parity. This arrangement does not depend on the narrow "control" of arms transfers, but upon an understanding that the United States will not deny arms to either party for what are considered its legitimate security needs. One should not overstate the argument, but this case does demonstrate the potential importance of tacit, informal arrangements and the need for regional actors' acceptance of the control arrangements.

Latin America, 1961–1985

A similar supplier-led attempt to create a regional arms-transfer control regime was the U.S. effort to slow the introduction of advanced (supersonic) fighter planes to Latin America in the 1960s. Because these states depended on the United States for virtually all their arms supplies, informal controls were already in place when President Lyndon Johnson decided in 1965 to delay the introduction of supersonic F-5 aircraft until at least 1969. In the absence of acute regional conflicts, U.S. policy was concerned mainly with preventing the perceived waste of scarce financial resources on unnecessary arms. But although Argentina and Venezuela appeared willing to accept the U.S. restraints, Peru was not, and it acquired the supersonic French Mirage 5 in 1969. The United States maintained the embargo on sales of the F-5 until 1973, by which time Argentina, Brazil, Colombia, and Venezuela had also purchased French planes. By 1975 Venezuela, Chile, Argentina, and Brazil had also purchased the F-5, giving six states possession of supersonic planes, and a minor arms race had occurred in the absence of acute regional

tensions. The result of this and subsequent supply restrictions was that Latin American states diversified their arms acquisitions, making any kind of unilaterally imposed controls unlikely to succeed.

Some indication of possible recipient cooperation in control has, however, manifested itself in Latin America on several occasions. In 1958 Costa Rica proposed that the Latin American members of the Organization of American States (OAS) agree not to purchase arms from suppliers outside the hemisphere (that is, from suppliers other than the United States and Canada) and in return, that the United States (or any other potential arms producer in the region) pledge not to supply arms except with the approval of a technical "inter-American" commission established under OAS auspices. This broad proposal would have made Latin American states entirely dependent upon the United States, and it was rejected by those states that wanted to link regional arms control to global disarmament efforts. In 1974 a more independent proposal was launched with the Ayacucho Declaration. This initiative, which was signed by Argentina, Bolivia, Chile, Colombia, Ecuador, Panama, Peru, and Venezuela, committed the signatories to restrain their arms imports. It was nonbinding, however, and has had no discernable effect on arms acquisition policies (although Latin America has continued to be a region of low arms imports). Follow-on meetings and proposals (including Peruvian president Alan García Pérez's 1985 call for a regional freeze on arms acquisitions) were also tied to broader discussions of limitations on Latin American military expenditures, weapons arsenals, and other specific arms control measures.

The Persian Gulf, 1980–1988

The Iran-Iraq War was an important case study for supply-side controls of arms transfers, for it involved many attempts by major suppliers to restrict the flow of arms to both combatants. The overall failure of these efforts to halt the fighting highlights the difficulties encountered by less than comprehensive multilateral arms-transfer controls. When the war began, the arsenals of both sides were almost entirely composed of weapons purchased from the five major arms suppliers, which suggested that supply restrictions could be effective in ending the war. Western states adopted a relatively neutral stance, and the United States and other Western arms suppliers suspended arms transfers to both belligerents. The Soviet Union suspended arms shipments to Iraq when the war broke out (this suspension even included weapons already contracted for). By 1982, however, the Soviet Union had resumed arms supplies to Iraq, apparently out of fear that Iraq might lose the war, and by 1984 Western states were tacitly supporting Iraq with weapons supplies (mostly from France).

In 1984 the United States launched "Operation Staunch" in an attempt to solicit cooperation from allies to stop the flow of arms to Iran. More than forty approaches were made to twenty states about arms deliveries to Iran, and although Operation Staunch was widely violated, it did restrict the delivery of major weapon systems to Iran and forced it to turn to suppliers such as North Korea and China for arms. In July 1987 the United Nations became seized with the issue as international pressure to end the war mounted. Security Council Resolution 598, which called for a cease-fire and return to international boundaries, did not mention an arms embargo, although it called on the Security Council to "consider further steps to ensure compliance with [this] resolution." This was widely understood to mean an arms embargo, and since Iraq accepted the resolution, the threat to implement an embargo was directed at Iran. The United States led the effort to tighten Western controls and win Soviet and Chinese acceptance of an embargo, and although no formal agreement was reached, the threat of an embargo did loom large (the threat included a leak, in February 1988, of a document claiming to be a draft embargo resolution supported by the five permanent members of the Security Council). One year later, on 18 July 1988, Iran accepted the cease-fire terms of Resolution 598 and the fighting ended.

One should not, however, conclude that the threatened embargo played a major role in ending the war. Both combatants turned to other suppliers for arms when their major sources were cut off. Iraq bought weapons from up to eighteen different states between 1980 and 1983, including France, the Soviet Union, Egypt, China, Poland, Italy, West Germany, Brazil, Czechoslovakia, and Saudi Arabia. Iran obtained weapons from about twenty different suppliers, including North Korea, Vietnam, West Germany, Libya, China, Taiwan, Chile, Syria, and Israel. By 1984 forty states had supplied weapons to the war; by 1985 fifty-three states had been implicated in one way or another. This illustrated the role that minor suppliers could play in overturning

any less than unanimously supported initiatives to control the arms trade to particular conflicts.

BILATERAL INITIATIVES: THE U.S.-SOVIET CONVENTIONAL ARMS TRANSFER (CAT) TALKS

Perhaps the most sustained and high-level attempt to control the arms trade was the United States–Soviet Conventional Arms Transfer (CAT) talks, which grew out of President Jimmy Carter's unilateral initiatives to throttle down U.S. arms transfers. In the early 1970s, and especially after the 1973 oil price increases, global arms transfers increased dramatically as the newly rich oil states went on massive arms buying sprees from all major suppliers. Global arms transfers between 1967 and 1970 averaged $16 billion a year; between 1971 and 1974 they had risen to 25 billion (constant 1988 dollars). Much of this increase was concentrated in the Middle East, which accounted for one-third of global arms transfers in the 1973 to 1977 period. By 1976 this change had given rise to a perception in some quarters that U.S. arms-transfer policy was out of control and that open-ended arms transfers could endanger U.S. interests by entangling the United States or its allies in a regional conflict, by reducing its technological lead, or simply by effecting a loss of political control over the arms-transfer process. As one State Department official described it: "[Secretary of State] Henry [Kissinger] used to hand weapons out like hostess gifts. We would think we had sales to Country X sealed off and then Kissinger would come back from some trip and tell us he had just agreed to supply another billion or so in arms" (quoted in Stephanie G. Neuman and Robert E. Harkavy, eds., *Arms Transfers in the Modern World*, p. 171).

Soon after entering office, the Carter administration followed one of its campaign promises and announced a comprehensive arms-transfer restraint policy that had both a unilateral and a multilateral dimension. President Carter in a statement on 19 May 1977 affirmed that underlying the policy was a belief that arms transfers should be regarded "as an exceptional foreign policy implement, to be used only in instances where it can be clearly demonstrated that the transfer contributes to our national security interests." This marked a radical departure from the previous policy of using arms exports relatively widely as a foreign policy tool to gain influence around the world. Specific policy changes included commitments to:

1. reduce the dollar volume of transfers
2. forswear development of weapon systems solely for export
3. prohibit coproduction agreements for major weapon systems
4. tighten regulations on the retransfer of equipment
5. refuse to introduce more advanced weapon systems into a region
6. abstain from using government personnel abroad to promote U.S. weapons.

These unilateral initiatives were implicitly tied to the success of the Carter administration's promotion of the CAT talks, which began in early 1977. The United States first approached its European allies (Britain, France, and Germany) about participating in formal discussions, but the Europeans demurred on the grounds that they wished to see prior evidence of Soviet willingness to participate. Many analysts interpreted this reluctance as self-serving, based on a desire to maintain the large volume of exports needed for the health of European arms industries.

United States–Soviet talks began in late 1977 and proceeded through four rounds. By the end of the second round, both sides had agreed on the urgency of limiting international transfers of conventional arms, and the Soviets appeared willing to pursue serious negotiations. At that point, however, a major dispute over strategy arose in the U.S. government. The Arms Control and Disarmament Agency (ACDA) argued that the CAT talks should focus on global and technical issues, such as developing lists of weapons or technologies that both sides would agree not to transfer outside of their alliances, in order to build a basis for future progress on the more controversial political dimensions of the problem. Secretary of State Cyrus Vance and chief CAT negotiator Leslie Gelb wanted to focus on the regional and political aspects of conventional arms transfers, and to embed these discussions in the larger context of the Soviet-American détente relationship. It was decided that the latter approach would be pursued, and in the third round of discussions the United States suggested establishing working groups to develop guidelines for particular regions (Latin America and sub-Saharan Africa). When the Soviets responded by suggesting that discussions include East Asia and the Persian Gulf, the Carter administration split, with some officials (including National Security Adviser Zbigniew Brzezinski) advocating that the United States walk out of the talks if other regions were raised. The talks were suspended after no progress was made on this issue in the fourth round. On top of this, the unilateral U.S. restraints were riddled with exceptions and were coming unravelled. The attempt to lower the dollar volume of transfers was subject to curious accounting, some top-line weapons continued to be exported as they entered into service with U.S. forces, and coproduction agreements continued to be signed—all of which could be seen as violations of the CAT talks. By early 1980, the Carter restraint policy was effectively dead, although the Soviets continued to raise the issue for several years.

Although the divisions in the Carter administration were directly responsible for the failure of the CAT talks, that failure must be seen against the backdrop of the deteriorating United States–Soviet relationship. As long as conventional arms control negotiations were treated as a political exercise associated with détente, they could not remain immune from political vicissitudes. On the technical level, however, the CAT talks did make some progress. Both sides agreed on some military and technical criteria by which to judge particular types and quantities of arms, on standards by which to judge states' eligibility to receive arms, and on procedures for applying these criteria to specific regions (even if they could not discuss particular regions). These areas of agreement illustrated that it was possible for major suppliers to develop cooperatively the kinds of technical and formal restrictions that would be necessary to implement multilateral controls on the arms trade. This may serve as an important precedent, as the end of the Cold War and superpower competition in the developing world has changed the political conditions sufficiently that broader controls on the arms trade have become conceivable.

MULTILATERAL INITIATIVES IN THE UNITED NATIONS

The most prominent control efforts concerning the arms trade in the multilateral arena have focused on the establishment of a United Nations register of conventional arms transfers. But for the first two decades after World War II, the issue of controlling the arms trade did not appear on the United Nations agenda, as its efforts were directed toward other arms control and disarmament measures. The first specific proposal concerning the arms trade was made in 1965 by Malta, in the First Committee of the General Assembly. The Maltese draft resolution of 30 November mandated the Eighteen Nation Disarmament Committee to develop proposals for "the establishment of a system of publicity" of the global arms trade under U.N. auspices. This was the genesis of what became, in 1991, the United Nations Register of Conventional Arms. The 1965 proposal itself failed (with a vote of 18 in favor, 19 against, and 39 abstentions), but even the earliest debates highlighted the main arguments for and against a register.

On the positive side, advocates of a register argued that the publicity that it would provide might reduce tensions and build confidence between states by making transparent their military holdings. In addition, some argued that it might deter regimes that would otherwise devote large amounts of scarce resources to armaments by pointing a public spotlight at their activities. Here the analogy with the activities of groups such as Amnesty International in agitating against government abuses of human rights has often been cited. Finally, a register would arguably help create a standard international data base on international armaments that could contribute to a range of other arms control and confidence-building activities. On the negative side, opponents of a register argued that it discriminated against non-arms-producing states by making transfers to these states public without any concomitant transparency of domestic production and consumption. In addition, they suggested that support for a register might be a political tactic designed to avoid measures that might actually address the arms trade more directly. Finally, it was not clear that states would voluntarily submit data to a register, or that the register would add any new information to what is already publicly available (although it should be noted that information on the arms trade was, until the mid-1970s, sparse).

The issue of a register was raised again in 1967 by Denmark in an informal way in the General Assembly, and in 1968 by Denmark, Iceland, Malta, and Norway via a draft resolution. Although by then several other states seemed to support a register,

the trenchant opposition expressed by developing countries such as India and Egypt ensured that no concrete action was taken. The issue lay dormant until 1976, when the Japanese raised it in the General Assembly in the form of a proposal that the secretary-general solicit the views of different countries on the international arms trade. This effort was amended to include arms production as well as transfers, but it was defeated on a procedural point by a group of countries led by India. In 1978, at the special session of the General Assembly on disarmament, many states raised the issue of the arms trade and suggested both a U.N. study and register. The final document (General Assembly Resolution S-10/2) called for negotiations to limit conventional arms transfers and consultations between suppliers and recipients on this issue. Following on this, West Germany, Italy, Britain, and Japan raised the specific issue of a register between 1981 and 1983 in different United Nations forums, and by the late 1980s a certain amount of momentum had been created around the issue.

The direct efforts that culminated in the 1991 register resolution began in 1989, when the United Nations General Assembly adopted a resolution (A/RES/43/75) mandating the secretary-general to initiate a study by governmental experts on the arms trade. Several conferences were held and studies commissioned, and on 9 September 1991 the experts' group submitted *Study on Ways and Means of Promoting Transparency in International Transfers of Conventional Arms* to the General Assembly (document A/46/301). The report discussed the different dimensions of the international arms trade, surveyed previous attempts to control it, and considered the possible modalities of measures to increase transparency. It endorsed the idea of a register as a means to promote transparency, although it recognized the obstacles this would face. Greater transparency in arms transfers was advocated as potentially increasing confidence and security between states, providing an "early warning signal" for dangerous arms buildups, reinforcing the defensive character of military structures, and representing a possible step toward more concrete supplier and recipient restraint and regional arms control measures.

By the time this report was tabled, the initiative to create a register had gathered widespread support among the industrialized states. On 14 March 1989 the European Parliament passed a resolution calling on the Commission of the European Community to publish an annual report on arms exports from EC member states. In August 1990 Soviet foreign minister Eduard Shevardnadze suggested that limiting international arms transfers was "a means of building a new model of security" (quoted in SIPRI *Yearbook* 1991, p. 220); while NATO secretary-general Manfred Wörner suggested NATO member states should examine enhanced controls on the proliferation of new military technologies. In 1991 British prime minister John Major promised British support for a U.N. arms-transfer register (a position supported by the European Community); Japanese prime minister Toshiki Kaifu pledged to introduce the register resolution at the U.N.; and France agreed (as part of a comprehensive initiative that included adherence to the Non-Proliferation Treaty) to the register, and suggested monitoring of unusual weapons buildups. As a result, movement toward a register was relatively swift, and on 9 December 1991 the General Assembly passed a resolution (46/36L) mandating the establishment of the Register of Conventional Arms.

The resolution was cosponsored by about forty states, with 150 votes in favor, none against, and 2 abstentions. China was, however, notably absent from the deliberations (and was not counted in the vote). The final resolution was drafted by the European Community and Japan, and the main negotiations occurred between the EC/Japan and six representatives of the nonaligned movement. A larger informal group of about fifteen "like-minded states" (including Canada, Australia, the Nordics, and the East Europeans) also had some input in the main negotiations.

Although the 1991 Gulf War perhaps accelerated the momentum toward a register, there were two underlying changes that made it possible. First, the end of the Cold War eliminated arms transfers as a means of superpower competition in the developing world. As the locus of political confrontation shifted from the East-West conflict to the North-South conflict, Northern states as a group manifested a collective interest in preventing the spread of weapons that might someday be used against them. Second, states were able to find a compromise on the most thorny issue that had doomed previous efforts: the expansion of the register to include domestic weapons holdings and procurement. In its final form, the resolution mandated the register to include not only data on international arms transfers, but also information on military

holdings and domestic procurement or production. This measure helped bridge the gap between the arms-producing sponsors and the nonaligned states, many of whom had objected that a register was discriminatory as long as arms-producing states were immune to the same transparency they wished to impose on others. The resolution did, however, equivocate somewhat on the issue, as the mechanisms by which production and military holdings are to be reported remained undecided in mid-1991, and the register is intended to operate at the outset with only data on arms transfers.

The register itself requests states to submit data annually on the number of items imported and exported according to the following equipment categories:

1. battle tanks (weighing more than 16.5 metric tons with a main gun of 75-mm or larger caliber)
2. armored combat vehicles (including transport, lightly armed, and anti-tank vehicles)
3. large caliber artillery systems (including multiple rocket launchers, and all weapons with a caliber of 100-mm or more)
4. combat aircraft (including all ground attack, air defense, or multi-role aircraft equipped with destructive weapons)
5. attack helicopters (including those equipped with anti-armor, air-to-ground, or air-to-air guided weapons)
6. warships (all vessels displacing more than 850 metric tons armed for military use)
7. missiles or missile systems (including all guided missiles with a range of 25 kilometers or more, or their launching vehicles)

The information is also to include the name of the supplying or receiving state. The resolution also directs the secretary-general to review the operation of the register using these categories, in order to expand or improve the coverage, and to make provisions for the inclusion of similar data on military holdings and arms production.

While these data may appear detailed, there are some significant omissions. First, small arms and ammunition are not included (and this covers some sophisticated portable weapons), primarily because of reporting difficulties, although in local conflicts these kinds of weapons can play a large role, especially as electronic miniaturization increases the lethality of portable weapons (such as anti-aircraft missiles). Second, there is no requirement to specify the type or sophistication of the weapons transferred. Since the same model of tank or aircraft can be supplied in many variants and with significantly different armaments and capabilities, the register information by itself will not be sufficient for observers to assess the relative military capabilities of states. But together with other publicly available information, the register should allow a good picture to be built up over time of regional and national military capabilities. Finally, the mere passing of a U.N. resolution establishing a register does not guarantee its success, and its ultimate value will depend on the voluntary cooperation of U.N. member states, which will probably turn on the issue of comprehensiveness. The precedent set by the U.N. mechanism for registering military expenditures is not, however, a good one, as few states submit information and little public attention is paid to it.

Action at the United Nations concerning the arms trade has not been exclusively confined to the arms-transfer register, and a wide range of lesser measures have been taken against specific states. The most noteworthy was the arms embargo against South Africa, which was mandated by a 1963 resolution (181) of the Security Council urging member states to halt the sale and shipment of all arms, ammunition, and military vehicles to South Africa (the embargo call was expanded in Resolution 182 to include equipment and materials for the manufacture and maintenance of arms). In 1977 the embargo was made mandatory (Resolution 418), and a call for renewed adherence was contained in Resolution 558 (1984). Although numerous breaches have been reported, the embargo has been widely adhered to. In 1966 a similar embargo was instituted against Rhodesia.

The end of the Cold War triggered more active involvement of the United Nations in a range of conflict-resolution efforts, many of which have included calls for an arms embargo. During the Iraq-Kuwait conflict, several resolutions (661, 687, and 700) imposed an arms embargo against Iraq. Transfers to Yugoslavia were prohibited under Resolution 713 (25 September 1991), which attempted to enforce a cease-fire in its civil war (the European Community had already imposed its own arms embargo). The agreement of the Paris Conference on Cambodia (23 October 1991) to end the Cambodian civil war also called for "an immediate cessation of all outside military assistance to all Cambodian parties" (Article 10), to be enforced by the United Nations Transitional Authority in Cambodia (UNTAC). U.N. attempts to mediate an end to the civil war in Somalia included a call to all member states to suspend arms deliveries (Resolution 733 of 23 January 1992). The export of arms and military equipment to Libya was prohibited by Security Council Resolution 748 (31 March 1992) as an enforcement measure against the Libyan refusal to hand over two accused terrorists (in connection with the bombing of a Pan American airliner over Lockerbie, Scotland, in December 1988). Finally, the U.N. General Assembly passed a resolution in 1991 (Resolution 46/36H, adopted without a vote) calling on all states to establish an administrative machinery to eradicate the illicit trade in arms. The duration of these measures is unspecified, but the wide range of embargoes that have been implemented suggests a renewed role for the United Nations in this field.

MEASURES TO CONTROL THE TRADE IN SPECIFIC TECHNOLOGIES

There are at least four arms control "regimes" dealing with specific technologies that directly concern the arms trade, and that might form the basis for broader or more comprehensive measures. Two of them, the Missile Technology Control Regime (MTCR) and the system of export controls over sophisticated technologies conducted under the umbrella of the Western states' Coordinating Committee for Multilateral Export Controls (COCOM) are specifically directed at arms transfers; two others, the nuclear non-proliferation regime and the ongoing negotiations toward a chemical weapons convention (CWC), indirectly concern the arms trade. All of these efforts are supplier-side qualitative controls and do not enjoy unqualified support among possible arms recipients. Although expanded supplier controls on specific types of technologies are the most likely future measures against the arms trade, a brief overview of these existing programs will illuminate the difficulties this type of control will face.

The Missile Technology Control Regime
The most high-profile set of controls on specific technologies is the (MTCR), established in 1987 by the United States, Britain, Canada, France, Japan, Italy, and West Germany, in response to a growing concern about the proliferation of ballistic-missile

technologies. About twenty states in the developing world now possess some type of ballistic missile; thirteen to sixteen states possess weapons with a range greater than 200 kilometers; and approximately five states may be able to produce missiles by the year 2000. The MTCR grew out of discussions in the Group of Seven (G-7) industrialized states' summits and was originally designed to restrict the export of technologies that could be used to deliver nuclear weapons (although it is also directed at thwarting potential conventional missile threats against its members). It prohibited the export by MTCR members of missile systems (or related technologies) with a range greater than 300 kilometers and a payload greater than 500 kilograms. By 1991 ten additional Western states had joined the regime, and several others (including the Soviet Union) were actively exploring membership. In addition, members have been investigating the feasibility of expanding the regime to include missiles with a shorter range and payload, especially since the most widely distributed missile, the Soviet-made Scud, has an unmodified range of 300 kilometers, just outside the current control threshold.

The technical aspects of the MTCR are quite daunting. Restricted items are listed in two categories, with different degrees of control. Category one items include complete rocket systems, individual stages, solid or liquid fuel rocket engines, reentry heat shields, guidance systems, thrust vector controls, and warhead arming and firing mechanisms. These items are the most sensitive, and MTCR member states have agreed (according to a White House fact sheet of 16 April 1987) that "there will be a strong presumption to deny such transfers," and that transfers will only be authorized with the assurance that the item will not be modified or re-transferred for possible use in a nuclear-weapons delivery system. Items in category two include a wide range of materials (covering sixteen sub-items and several pages) that are components or subsystems of the first category, and particular caution is exercised with transfers of these technologies. Such items include (to give some sense of the technical detail involved) detailed specifications on particular chemical compounds that could be used in rocket fuel; descriptions of sophisticated machinery that could be used to spin or weave high-strength composite materials (such as carbon fibers or ceramics); minicomputers, microcircuits, and electronic systems that could be used at low or high temperatures or that have been radiation hardened;

software that could be used to design or simulate rocket systems; and precision guidance equipment (compasses, gyroscopes, and accelerometers of a specified accuracy). The technical specifications of the systems to be restricted are detailed, in an attempt to distinguish between military and civilian systems. These guidelines, which concern only ballistic missiles, illustrate well the complexities that will be involved in agreements to restrict the proliferation of other weapons technologies.

Opinions on the success of the MTCR are mixed. Although it appears to have slowed or halted missile development programs in Egypt, Argentina, India, and Iraq (including the joint Argentinian-Egyptian-Iraqi Condor II project, which was to have produced a 1000-kilometer (600-mile) range missile with a 500-kilogram (1,100-pound) payload, and which was cancelled in 1991), it enjoys only limited membership (China, North Korea, Israel, and India, for example, are not members). It also has no real enforcement mechanisms and, despite its technical detail, does not cover all systems that could contribute to a ballistic-missile capability. Leaving this aside, there are two noteworthy features of the MTCR that make it a possible future precedent for arms-transfer controls. First, it is not a formal treaty, but a voluntary agreement to harmonize national export-control policies. It thus has a flexibility that treaties often do not have. New members are admitted only with the agreement of existing members, who must be satisfied that a state is willing and able to adhere to the regulations. Second, the inducement for membership is the access to civilian technology (especially for space and satellite programs) that would otherwise be denied to nonmembers. In this sense, the "membership rules" of the MTCR can be compared to those of a street gang: in joining, one agrees not to supply lethal objects to nonmembers, not to use them against fellow members, and to trade them freely among the gang! Although not all members make their specific national regulations available, the U.S. regulations are public (see bibliography) and can be used as a guide to the current state of the MTCR.

Western Technology Transfer Controls During the Cold War, the North Atlantic Treaty Organization (NATO) states, plus Japan, developed a comprehensive set of technology export restrictions under the auspices of the Coordinating Committee for Multilateral Export Controls (COCOM). COCOM restrictions covered military goods, nuclear technologies and "civil goods" considered dual-use technologies (having both a civilian and a military application). Technologies on these lists, which were negotiated secretly among member states, were embargoed to all states on the approved blacklist, consisting of the Warsaw Pact states and close allies of the Soviet Union. Its targets were clear, although there were frequent disputes between the United States and western Europe on the inclusion of certain technologies that might have military applications, with the Europeans in general favoring more liberal restrictions in an attempt to encourage trade with the Soviet Union.

The COCOM was, like the MTCR, an informal harmonization of national policies; its main goal was to slow the diffusion of advanced military technologies to the Soviet Union and Warsaw Pact, and hence to maintain the West's lead in critical defense sectors. It was not expected to stop the flow of technologies, many of which could (given sufficient time) be copied or independently discovered. With the end of the Cold War, attention has been focused on the possibility of transforming the COCOM into a North-South technology transfer regime, or of creating a new COCOM-like entity. The controls in such a regime could harmonize the existing regimes on nuclear and chemical weapons and ballistic missiles, or they could deal with technologies not covered by these regimes (such as military electronics and communications systems, computers and guidance systems, and advanced-materials technologies).

As of 1992 no formal system of North-South military technology transfer controls was in place, although there were many informal consultations and proposals. There are, however, a number of obstacles in the way of establishing a North-South COCOM. First, the supplier-side nature of such a regime would be resented by the military have-nots in the South. Second, it would be difficult to draw a clear black-and-white distinction among states to be blacklisted, and technology controls that admit different degrees of restriction would be more difficult to implement. Third, unlike the East-West situation of relative economic autonomy, North-South economic relations are complex and interdependent, and include a wide range of civilian technology transfers. The dual-use nature of many modern technologies (such as high speed computers and precision lathes) make attempts to distinguish between purely military and civilian technologies almost impossible. Under the old COCOM, if a technology could have a significant military application, its export was restricted; a similar measure in the North-South context would not be acceptable to many Northern states and would create tremendous resentment in the South if it were seen as preventing economic development. Finally, the trend toward increased military coproduction and licensed production, and perhaps even genuinely "international" production (with components for a final product produced in many different countries), will make COCOM-like regulations difficult to achieve.

The Nuclear Non-Proliferation Regime Although it stands by itself as an arms control measure, the nuclear non-proliferation regime can also be regarded as a measure of control of the arms trade. Efforts to restrict the proliferation of nuclear weapons have been conducted under the umbrella of the Non-Proliferation Treaty (NPT), which was signed in 1968 and came into force in 1970; other elements of the regime include the informal restraints of the London Suppliers' Group; the NPT-mandated activities of the International Atomic Energy Agency (IAEA), and regional arrangements (such as the Tlatelolco and Rarotonga treaties, creating nuclear-free zones in Latin America and the South Pacific). The NPT pledged those signatories that did not possess nuclear weapons not to acquire them, and nuclear weapons states eventually to disarm. In return, a comprehensive system of supervision and safeguards on the trade in nuclear technologies was established under the IAEA, which permitted the peaceful exploitation of nuclear energy and trade in necessary technologies.

These efforts will not be discussed in detail; what is worth noting is that the diffusion of nuclear-weapon technologies has not been entirely halted. At least three states in the developing world are on or across the nuclear-weapons threshold (Israel, India, Pakistan) and several others (among them Brazil, Argentina, Iraq, Iran, South Africa, and South Korea) have at one point pursued a nuclear-weapons program. The efforts of a United Nations special commission (UNSCOM) to dismantle Iraq's nuclear-weapons program after the Persian Gulf War uncovered a wide range of unexpected activities and highlighted several loopholes in the non-proliferation system. The regime is unable to thwart completely a determined state's efforts to acquire nuclear weapons. Until the more radical nuclear-weapons reductions treaties of the early 1990s were in place, states in the developing world were also able to accuse Northern countries of implementing a discriminatory regime that allowed them to proliferate unchecked (via the growth in their arsenals), while preventing other states from acquiring nuclear weapons. Similar criticisms are leveled at other attempts to control specific weapons technologies monopolized by a few states.

Chemical Weapons   As of 1992, the number of states that possessed chemical weapons was estimated at between ten and twenty-five, and efforts to control their further proliferation have focused on two forums: the chemical weapons convention (CWC) negotiations under the United Nations Conference on Disarmament, and the "Australia Group" of supplier states. The draft chemical weapons convention has been under negotiation since 1980 and (if and when completed) it will prohibit the production and procurement of chemical weapons and implement strict safeguards against the trade in weapons materials and technologies. In the absence of a CWC, the main mechanism for controlling this trade has been the Australia Group, which is not a formal treaty or institution but an agreement among the twenty-three participating states to harmonize progressively their export regulations on chemical feedstocks that could be used to produce weapons.

The major obstacle to completion of a CWC concerns the degree of intrusiveness of any verification system, which would require large numbers of inspectors with relatively free access to major industrial complexes in all countries. Developing states are concerned that (as in the NPT case) the treaty not be used to hamper possible civilian uses of the technologies. From the perspective of the arms trade, the problem is unlikely to be the trade in chemical weapons (which are not normally transferred between states). The primary difficulty, however, is that several of the chemicals that would need to be controlled are not in themselves weapons, but merely precursors that can, with relatively unsophisticated techniques, be used as the basis for producing weapons. Crude chemical weapons can also in principle be produced by almost any state that possesses an advanced chemical industrial plant (to produce pesticides or pharmaceuticals, for example). Thus the problem of controlling chemical weapons highlights the link between the arms trade and arms production: controls on the trade in chemicals are unlikely to succeed unless they are coupled with a comprehensive system of monitoring and verification of possible production.

OTHER INITIATIVES TO CONTROL THE ARMS TRADE

In the aftermath of the 1991 Gulf War, many states and multilateral forums took up the issue of controlling the arms trade, although by 1992 most of the action had been confined to declaratory measures. The first concrete proposal was launched by Canada in February 1991. It called for a United Nations–sponsored world summit to condemn the proliferation of conventional weapons and weapons of mass destruction and kick off a series of individual negotiations in appropriate multilateral forums, to be followed up by a concluding conference in 1995 that would mark the completion of a comprehensive network of non-proliferation regimes. Specific Canadian proposals concerning the arms trade included calling for a meeting of major arms exporters to encourage greater transparency, restraint, and consultations; a proposed information-exchange system; and a suggested commitment from the states that had signed the Conventional Forces in Europe (CFE) Treaty not to retransfer treaty-limited items to regions of tension. In April 1991 British Prime Minister Major pledged British support for a U.N. arms-transfer register (a position supported by the European Community). Japanese Prime Minister Kaifu pledged in May to introduce the register resolution at the U.N. in the fall. France, as part of a comprehensive initiative that included adherence to the NPT, also agreed in June to the register idea and suggested monitoring of unusual weapons buildups. Finally, after some months of internal debate, President Bush announced on 29 May a comprehensive plan to control arms proliferation and destabilizing weapons buildups in the Middle East. Various international organizations also seized the issue in June and July 1991:

- The Organization of American States (OAS) adopted a resolution calling for a halt to proliferation of weapons of mass destruction, and for the exercise of sensitivity in transfers of arms and military technologies to regions of conflict or arms buildups.
- The G-7 summit issued a declaration on arms proliferation and agreed to increase consultation,

transparency, and action against egregious arms buildups.

- The Conference for Security and Cooperation in Europe (CSCE) adopted a declaration encouraging transparency and restraint in arms transfers.
- The European Community leaders declared their support for a stronger nuclear non-proliferation regime, early agreement on a chemical weapons convention, and measures to harmonize their national arms export policies and to restrain conventional arms transfers.
- The Harare Commonwealth summit "underlined the need to . . . curb the build-up of conventional weapons beyond the legitimate requirements of self-defence" (Conference Communique, item 15).

The most important initiative was that pursued by the permanent five (P-5) members of the Security Council. On 8–9 July they met in Paris to discuss measures to control the arms trade, with special reference to the Middle East. At a follow-on meeting on 17–18 October, the P-5 established common guidelines for arms exports to all regions, agreed to exchange information on transfers to the Middle East, supported U.N. efforts to establish an arms trade register and (perhaps most important in the long run) agreed to meet at least once a year to pursue these issues. The guidelines for arms transfers that the P-5 adopted included consideration of whether the transfer meets legitimate self-defense needs or is an appropriate response to potential threats, and a pledge to avoid transfers that might prolong or aggravate existing conflicts, increase tensions, introduce destabilizing military capabilities to a region, contravene international embargoes, undermine recipients' economies, or support terrorism. Seen in the most optimistic light, the P-5's actions could mark the beginning of an informal supplier arms-transfer control regime. Certainly by early 1992 the P-5 had become the main focus for concrete action to control the arms trade, eclipsing the CSCE, the U.N., and the G-7.

THE FUTURE OF ARMS-TRANSFER CONTROLS: PROBLEMS AND PROSPECTS

Several issues confront future attempts to control the arms trade, and a quick summary of them will serve as a provisional conclusion to a rapidly evolving issue area. The first concern is the changing nature of the arms trade, which vastly complicates the task of controlling it. Three main shifts are significant: the shift in trade from finished weapon systems toward components and technologies that have a variety of uses; the increase in the number of states in the developing world that have some (usually minimal) arms-production capabilities (including maintenance, assembly, and upgrading expertise); and the move toward genuinely transnational arms production (in which technology and components for finished weapons flow between a number of firms and states). All three imply that simple limitations on the transfer of items such as tanks, missiles, and aircraft will not deter a determined recipient, who will have multiple sources for different components and may be able to assemble them into a usable weapon. Further, these changes mean that the degree of technical detail required in any multilateral agreement to control technologies is enormous, as is illustrated by the annex to the Missile Technology Control Regime (MTCR), or by the draft chemical weapons convention.

The second issue concerns the most appropriate forums in which to develop control regimes. To date, most initiatives have evolved in an ad hoc fashion and have emerged from existing multilateral institutions (such as the MTCR emerging from the G-7 economic summits). The disadvantages of such arrangements are that: 1) they do not usually include all the relevant suppliers (Germany, for example is not one of the P-5); 2) they do not include recipient states, and 3) they result in global measures that may not be appropriate in particular regional contexts. The difficulties in controlling the arms trade are so great that it is unlikely much further progress can be made without the participation of arms recipients. Since their concerns primarily revolve around regional security issues, controls on the arms trade will have to be dovetailed with other initiatives to address regional conflicts. In the Middle East, for example, discussions of arms control (and by implication, arms transfers) have become part of the broader peace effort. In other regions of the world, controls on arms transfers could be part of peacekeeping and confidence-building measures. Here the problems of controlling arms transfers, controlling arms production, and regional arms restraints (on the model of the Conventional Forces in Europe Treaty) are inseparable. Controls on transfers that do not ultimately lead to regional controls on weapons arsenals will fall short of the goal of enhancing security.

Further, although few states in the developing world are able to produce large quantities of weapons, the ones that can are sufficiently important (Israel, India, China, North and South Korea, Brazil, Egypt) that neighboring states will not accept controls on arms transfers that do not also protect them against uncontrolled buildups of arms from domestic production.

The third set of concerns revolves around possible new measures to control the arms trade and military expenditures. One proposal was raised in 1980 by the Brandt Commission report (Independent Commission on International Development Issues), which suggested a tax on arms transfers that would be levied by arms suppliers and devoted to development assistance. Another set of proposals under more active consideration would link foreign aid and international lending decisions to an evaluation of the military expenditures and arms acquisition policies of recipient states (either to punish high spenders or to reward low spenders). The first suggestion for this linkage goes back to 1968, when the Tunisian delegate in the U.N. debate over a transparency resolution suggested that the U.N. might refuse development assistance to any nation that spent more than 5 or 6 percent of its budget on armaments. Such a linkage would be a major departure from the current practice of donor countries and lending institutions, which have explicitly treated human and development needs separately from the security policies of states. This measure would also be discriminatory because it would only affect states that receive foreign aid or international loans; most Middle Eastern and several major South Asian states would not come under serious pressure. Other related inducements could include the withholding of most favored nation (MFN) trade status from high spenders on arms. Finally, some analysts have suggested that supplier states consider substituting security guarantees, peacekeeping forces, and conflict-resolution mechanisms for arms transfers. If the goal is to increase the security of friends and allies, in the post–Cold War world arms transfers may be the wrong means to achieve it.

This last set of concerns raises the suspicion that, in the final analysis, a focus on controlling the arms trade as a means to build confidence and security might be misplaced. On one level, arms transfers are only one part of a larger problem of global military spending, which is itself triggered by the many unresolved conflicts and insecurities around the world. On a deeper level, arms transfers are woven into the fabric of international relations and are an inevitable product of a self-help system in which states must look to their own devices for security and survival. Hence until other mechanisms for achieving security and resolving conflicts are devised, the trade in weapons and instruments of destruction is unlikely to disappear.

BIBLIOGRAPHY

General Works Overviews of this topic, most of which discuss proposals for future controls, are numerous. The most important single source is THOMAS OHLSON, ed., *Arms Transfer Limitations and Third World Security* (New York, 1988), which contains chapters on different regions and initiatives. A historical survey of most efforts can be found in STOCKHOLM INTERNATIONAL PEACE RESEARCH INSTITUTE (SIPRI), *The Arms Trade with the Third World* (Stockholm and New York, 1971); and from a legal perspective see JOST DELBRÜCK, "International Traffic in Arms—Legal and Political Aspects of a Long Neglected Problem of Arms Control and Disarmament," *German Yearbook of International Law* 24 (1981): 114–143. Data in this article are derived from the annual publication of the UNITED STATES ARMS CONTROL AND DISARMAMENT AGENCY, *World Military Expenditures and Arms Transfers* (Washington, D.C.), and much useful information is contained in the chapters of the annual *SIPRI Yearbook* devoted to arms transfers and arms production.

Among the most accessible articles on the topic are HERBERT WULF, "Arms Transfer Control: The Feasibility and the Obstacles," in SAADET DEGER and ROBERT WEST, eds., *Defence, Security, and Development* (New York, 1987), pp. 190–206; UNITED NATIONS, *Transparency in International Arms Transfers*, U.N. Disarmament Topical Papers no. 3 (New York, 1990); KEITH KRAUSE, "Constructing Regional Security Régimes and the Control of Arms Transfers," *International Journal* 45 (Spring 1990): 386–423; MICHAEL BRZOSKA, "The Arms Trade—Can It Be Controlled?" *Journal of Peace Research* 24 (December 1987): 327–331; MICHAEL BRZOSKA, "Third World Arms Control: Problems of Verification," *Bulletin of Peace Proposals* 14:2 (June 1983): 165–173; RAIMO VÄYRYNEN, "Curbing International Transfers of Arms and Military Technology," *Alternatives* 4 (July 1978), 87–113; and JANNE NOLAN, "The Global Arms Market After the Gulf War: Prospects for

Control," *The Washington Quarterly* 14 (Summer 1991): 125–138.

Regional Studies　For an overview of national regulation of arms exports, see IAN ANTHONY, ed., *Arms Export Regulations* (Oxford, 1991). On specific countries see FREDERIC S. PEARSON, "'Necessary Evil': Perspectives on West German Arms Transfer Policies," *Armed Forces and Society* 12 (Summer 1986): 525–552; FREDERIC S. PEARSON, "The Question of Control in British Defence Sales Policy," *International Affairs* [London] 59 (Spring 1983): 211–238; S. SCOTT-MORRISON, "The Arms Export Control Act: An Evaluation of the Role of Congress in Policing Arms Sales," *Stanford Journal of International Studies* 14 (Spring 1979): 105–124; JO L. HUSBANDS, "How the United States Makes Foreign Military Sales," in STEPHANIE G. NEUMAN and ROBERT HARKAVY, eds., *Arms Transfers in the Modern World* (New York, 1979) pp. 155–192; EDWARD A. KOLODZIEJ, *Making and Marketing Arms: The French Experience and its Implications for the International System* (Princeton, N.J., 1987); JOHN W. LEWIS, HUA DI, and XUE LITAI, "Beijing's Defense Establishment," *International Security* 15 (Spring 1991): 87–109. On the effort to establish a common policy within the European Community, see HARALD BAUER, MICHAEL BRZOSKA, and WILFRIED KARL, "Coordination and Control of Arms Exports from EC Member States and the Development of a Common Arms Export Policy," working paper 54 of the Institut für politische Wissenschaft, Forschungsstelle Kriege, Rüstung und Entwicklung (Institute for Political Science, Unit for the Study of Wars, Armaments, and Development), University of Hamburg, prepared for the European Parliament, Directorate General for Research, 1991; SAFERWORLD FOUNDATION, *Regulating Arms Exports: A Programme for the European Community* (London, 1991). Canadian regulation and recent international efforts are discussed in KEITH KRAUSE, "Arms Transfers and International Security: The Evolution of Canadian Policy," in FEN OSLER HAMPSON and CHRISTOPHER MAULE, eds., *Canada among Nations, 1992* (Ottawa, 1992), pp. 283–301.

For brief discussions of the Latin American and tripartite initiatives, see JOHN STANLEY and MAURICE PEARTON, *The International Trade in Arms* (New York, 1972), pp. 196–221. For more detail see PAUL JABBER, *Not by War Alone: Security and Arms Control in the Middle East* (Berkeley, Calif., 1981); and AUGUSTO VARAS, "Regional Arms Control in the South American Context," in THOMAS OHLSON, ed., *Arms Transfer Limitations and Third World Security* (Oxford, 1988), pp. 175–185. On the Iran-Iraq War see KEITH KRAUSE, "Transferts d'armements et gestion des conflits: le cas de la guerre Iran-Irak," *Cultures & conflits* 4 (hiver 1991/92): 13–40.

Control Efforts　On the Conventional Arms Transfer (CAT) talks see JO L. HUSBANDS, "The Arms Connection: Jimmy Carter and the Politics of Military Exports," in CINDY CANNIZZO, ed., *The Gun Merchants: Politics and Policies of the Major Arms Suppliers* (New York, 1980), pp. 18–48; BARRY BLECHMAN and JANNE NOLAN, *The U.S.-Soviet Conventional Arms Transfer Negotiations* (Washington, D.C., 1987); CONGRESSIONAL RESEARCH SERVICE, *Changing Perspectives on U.S. Arms Transfer Policy,* a report for the Subcommittee on International Security and Scientific Affairs, Committee on Foreign Affairs, House of Representatives, 97th Congress, 1st session (Washington, D.C., 1981); and COMPTROLLER GENERAL OF THE UNITED STATES, *Arms Sales Ceiling Based on Inconsistent and Erroneous Data* (Washington, D.C., 1978).

On the history of U.N. efforts to create an arms register, see MARY MACDONALD, "Arms Control Phoenix: Building Transparency through an Arms Transfer Register," Ph.D. diss., Queen's University, Kingston, Ontario, 1991. The report of the U.N. "experts group" is available as the *Study on Ways and Means of Promoting Transparency in International Transfers of Conventional Arms,* report of the Secretary-General to the United Nations General Assembly, A/46/301, 9 September 1991. The register itself was established by U.N. General Assembly Resolution 46/36L (9 December 1991), "General and Complete Disarmament: International Arms Transfers. Transparency in Armaments." Concerning the embargo against South Africa, see SIGNE LANDGREN, *Embargo Disimplemented: South Africa's Military Industry* (New York, 1989).

For good overviews on ballistic missiles and the MTCR see STEVE FETTER, "Ballistic Missiles and Weapons of Mass Destruction: What Is the Threat? What Should Be Done?" *International Security* 16 (Summer 1991): 5–42; MARTIN NAVIAS, *Ballistic Missile Proliferation in the Third World* (London, 1990); AARON KARP, "Ballistic Missile Proliferation," in Stockholm International Peace Research Institute (SIPRI), *SIPRI Yearbook, 1990* (Oxford and New York, 1990) pp. 369–391; ROBERT SHUEY, *Missile Proliferation: A Discussion of U.S. Objectives and Policy*

Options, report 90–120F of the Congressional Research Service (Washington, D.C., 1990); and JANNE E. NOLAN, *Trappings of Power: Ballistic Missiles in the Third World* (Washington, D.C., 1991). U.S. regulations in place at time of writing can be found in "Foreign Policy Controls on Equipment and Technical Data Used in the Development of Nuclear-Capable Missiles: Revisions," *Federal Register* (56 FR 29425), 56:124, 27 June 1991.

On nuclear and chemical weapons see ASPEN STRATEGY GROUP, *New Threats: Responding to the Proliferation of Nuclear, Chemical, and Delivery Capabilities in the Third World* (Lanham, Md., 1990); JOHN SIMPSON, "The Nuclear Non-Proliferation Regime as a Model for Conventional Armament Restraint," in THOMAS OHLSON, ed., *Arms Transfer Limitations and Third World Security,* pp. 227–240; HAROLD MÜLLER, "Prospects for the Fourth Review of the Non-Proliferation Treaty," *SIPRI Yearbook 1990,* pp. 553–586; KATHLEEN BAILEY, *Doomsday Weapons in the Hands of the Many: The Arms Control Challenge of the '90s* (Urbana, Ill., 1990). On the activities of the "Australia Group" and the chemical and biological weapons convention negotiations, see the relevant sections in annual editions of the *SIPRI Yearbook.* On a more academic level, see ROGER K. SMITH, "Explaining the Non-Proliferation Regime: Anomalies for Contemporary International Relations Theory," *International Organization* 41 (Spring 1987): 253–281; and TREVOR MCMORRIS TATE, "Regime-Building in the Non-Proliferation System," *Journal of Peace Research* 27 (November 1990): 399–414. On the overall issue of controlling the trade in military technology see JANNE E. NOLAN, *Trappings of Power: Ballistic Missiles in the Third World* (Washington, D.C., 1991).

General and Complete Disarmament Proposals

○

ALESSANDRO CORRADINI

See also Nongovernment Organizations in Arms Control and Disarmament; Russia and the Soviet Union; Transnational Peace Movements and Arms Control: The Nineteenth and Twentieth Centuries; *and* The United Nations and Disarmament. *Most of the treaties discussed in this essay are excerpted in Volume III.*

Up to the beginning of the twentieth century, general disarmament was essentially a subject for philosophical and moral reflections. Until then disarmament usually meant the punitive elimination or reduction of the armaments of a country defeated in war. Or occasionally it might have meant the neutralization or demilitarization of a nation or a specific zone. In any event, agreements on armaments, whether bilateral or unilateral, were still few and limited in scope. There were no permanent structures for the maintenance of international peace and security. The legitimacy of war as an instrument of national policy was hardly questioned. Under the circumstances, general disarmament found no place in the realm of international politics.

PROPOSALS OF THE INTERWAR PERIOD

When, however, late in World War I, statesmen began to consider ways to establish a collective security system to maintain the peace, proposals for general disarmament could no longer be denied serious consideration, particularly in view of the fact that the arms race in pre-1914 Europe had been a major cause of tension, finally leading to a tragic ordeal. Yet the very proposition of freeing the world from the threat and burden of armaments implied such a radical change in interstate relations

that only a leader of great vision moved by idealistic fervor could face the challenge with a sense of urgency. Shortly before the United States entered the war, President Woodrow Wilson chose to follow that course.

In his "Peace Without Victory" address of January 1917, considering the conditions for a just and lasting settlement of World War I, President Wilson stressed the need for a "covenant of cooperative peace," a peace made secure by the "organized major force of mankind," which would act as the guarantor of the settlement. Within this context, he viewed the question of armaments as "the most immediately and intensely practical question connected with the future fortunes of nations and of mankind."

A year later, in the fourth point of his Fourteen Points, President Wilson called for "adequate guarantees given and taken that national armaments will be reduced to the lowest point consistent with domestic safety." This was a proposal of unprecedented scope and a watershed in the history of international efforts for disarmament.

The disarmament provisions of the Covenant of the League of Nations (Arts. 8 and 9) and the other relevant clauses of the Treaty of Versailles (Part V, Preamble) ultimately fell short of the goal set in Point Four. Taken together they still constituted, however, a strong international commitment to disarmament. The general reduction of national armaments was recognized to be a precondition of peace and security; security was related to the enforcement by common action of international obligations; a general reduction of the armaments of all nations was envisaged; and the Council of the League was called upon to formulate plans accordingly. Indeed, it was the very essence of the Covenant, as F. P. Walters has said, "that States should renounce their right to be the sole judges of their own armaments" (*A History of the League of Nations*, p. 218).

The League of Nations   On the basis of these principles, for more than ten years—from the beginning of the 1920s to 1933—the League sought to make decisive progress toward disarmament, and it was by the test of disarmament that public opinion judged the League. Yet formal discussion about general and complete disarmament (GCD) began only in 1927 when a Soviet delegation, headed by Maksim Litvinov, joined in the preparations for a world disarmament conference under the auspices of the League.

The Assembly and the Council of the League soon discovered that disarmament was more than a technical question and that the implementation of agreed disarmament principles was closely connected with a whole series of complex political and security problems. The fact that the United States was not a member of the League, due to the failure on the part of the Senate to consent to the ratification of the Covenant, made the task of the Council and the Assembly even more difficult. Not surprisingly, their debates in the early years of the League centered upon the question of drastic reductions of armaments in Europe and the ultimate relationship between disarmament and security.

Efforts on the latter question led to the adoption, by the Fifth Assembly, of the Protocol for the Pacific Settlement of International Disputes, better known as the Geneva Protocol of 1924, a document built on the association of three components: arbitration, mutual security, and disarmament. The Protocol would reinforce the Covenant by making arbitration compulsory with regard to the settlement of international disputes and by specifying the use of enforcement measures to be taken against an aggressor, that is, a state that did not submit to arbitration or other peaceful settlement. The signatories of the Protocol would further agree to take part in a disarmament conference, open to all countries, to be convened in Geneva. The Protocol itself was made dependent on the outcome of such a conference.

Discussions that took place in the League Council in 1925 showed that the Protocol, accepted by the Assembly and signed by several states, including France, had failed to gain the support of other countries, notably the United Kingdom and the Commonwealth, required to bring it into force. However, the idea of holding a disarmament conference, possibly at an early date, was not abandoned.

The Preparatory Commission   Support came from the signatories of the Locarno agreements of October 1925—Belgium, France, Germany, Great Britain, and Italy—which pledged themselves to cooperate in the work relating to disarmament already undertaken by the League of Nations and to seek its realization in a general agreement. Two months later, the Council established the Preparatory Commission for the Disarmament Conference, which met for the first time in May 1926. All the states then in the Council were included, plus the United States, whose absence from the League—although mitigated by repeated signs of unofficial collaboration—limited the scope of the United States' initiatives; Germany, which was to become a member of the League in 1926; and the Soviet Union, which was to join it in 1934. Progress in the commission was painfully slow. The Soviet Union brought to Geneva a plan for GCD without delay, which contrasted with the more limited and gradual goals supported by the other members. Also the French position—that disarmament could not be the basis, but must be the result of an effective system of international security—was not easily reconciled with that of other members of the committee who held more businesslike, pragmatic views. Finally, by the end of 1930, qualified agreement was reached on a draft convention for consideration by the Conference for the Reduction and Limitation of Armaments.

The "World" Disarmament Conference   The conference opened in Geneva, in February 1932, under the presidency of Arthur Henderson of the United Kingdom. It brought together sixty-one members and nonmembers of the League—until then the largest and most representative gathering in the history of disarmament. Their task was to reach agreement on a general disarmament treaty embracing all states and all categories of forces and weapons and, at the same time, strengthen the collective security system of the League. Full technical preparations for this difficult task had been made by the commission. There existed, however, serious doubts as to whether the political preparation of the conference had been such as to ensure ultimate success.

Already in the early weeks after its opening, due to the fact that a number of participants submitted proposals of their own and revived their old supporting arguments, the conference was obliged to put aside the draft convention and open discussion on a series of competing plans. The qualitative approach to disarmament, implying the elimination or reduction of weapons designed for attack rather than for defense, came also to dominate the work of the conference. This approach, although not ignored in earlier negotiations, had reappeared at the conference with unprecedented vigor.

The main subjects that the conference addressed were: (*a*) measures for strengthening the League's system of collective security; (*b*) reduction of the strength of armed forces; (*c*) limitation of land, naval, and air armaments; (*d*) limitation and publicity of national defense expenditures; (*e*) prohibition of chemical, incendiary, and bacteriological warfare; (*f*) control of arms manufacture and trade; (*g*) exchange of information on military forces and armaments; (*h*) international verification of disarmament agreements; and (*i*) moral disarmament.

With regard to the reinforcement of collective security, progress was made in two directions. First, the conference participants agreed substantially on measures that should be taken for a consultation of states in the event of a breach, or threat of a breach, of the Kellogg-Briand Pact of 1928. Second, agreement was reached on a draft undertaking not to resort to force, to be signed by all European states. Various participants strongly expressed the hope that this undertaking would subsequently assume a universal character.

As to the results achieved in dealing with the substantive problems of disarmament, it was difficult to draw a balance. The reason, as Arthur Henderson wrote in his *Preliminary Report on the Work of the Conference,* was that the results could not be measured by the proposals made and the decisions taken, as political events constantly outran those proposals and decisions, "which served rather as landmarks of what might have been achieved at a given moment than as evidence of effective progress" (pp. 55–56).

Of the many difficulties inherent in the political situation prevailing during the conference, the question of German armaments and Germany's claim to "equality of rights" dominated. The issue reached a critical point in July 1932, when Germany announced that it could not collaborate any longer in the work of the conference until the principle of equality of rights had been definitely recognized. By the end of the year, France, Germany, Italy, and the United Kingdom, with the help of the United States, had arrived at a formula they hoped would resolve the question. The aim of the conference, the four powers agreed, should be to conclude a convention in which Germany should possess equality of rights in a system that could provide security for all nations; second, all European states should solemnly reaffirm that they would never, under any circumstances, attempt to settle their differences by a resort to force.

On this basis, Germany returned to the conference, but not for long. The Germans continued to demand equality in armaments. Their claims found some support in the West, but the prevailing view remained that nothing should be done that would weaken the diplomatic or military position of France, the "central protective force" on the continent of Europe (Winston Churchill, *The Second World War,* vol. 1, p. 76). In the course of 1933, a French plan, accepted by Britain and Italy, suggested that armaments should be stabilized at the existing levels for a four- or five-year period. Germany, now under the control of Hitler, rejected the plan and left the disarmament conference and the League of Nations. This event precipitated the breakdown of the conference and the setting aside of all plans for world disarmament as nations gradually prepared for war.

On 3 September 1939, two days after the outbreak of World War II, President Franklin D. Roosevelt, speaking to the American people, pointed out that the unfortunate events in Europe in recent years had their roots in the use or threat of force, and that a peace should be sought "which will eliminate, as far as it is possible to do so, the continued use of force between nations."

FROM THE ATLANTIC CHARTER TO THE UNITED NATIONS

In the midst of World War II, before the United States entered into the war, President Roosevelt and Prime Minister Winston Churchill drafted principles on which their two countries and all the peoples of the world could build a better future. In their Atlantic Charter, issued on 14 August 1941, they stated their belief that "all the nations of the world, for realistic as well as spiritual reasons must come to the abandonment of the use of force." They further envisaged the establishment of "a permanent system of general security" as well as practicable measures to "lighten for peace-loving peoples the crushing burden of armaments."

These principles were further developed at subsequent Allied meetings. Thus, at the Moscow Conference of 19–30 October 1943, the governments of the United States, the United Kingdom, the USSR, and China, in the Declaration on General Security, recognized the need to establish at the earliest possible date a "general international organization" based on the principle of the "sovereign equality" of states for the maintenance of international peace and security and to bring about "a practical general agreement with respect to the regulation of armaments in the post-war period." The next stage came in 1944 at the Dumbarton Oaks Conference, held at the Washington, D.C., estate by that name, with the adoption of a draft charter of the United Nations.

The Charter of the United Nations, adopted on 26 June 1945, at San Francisco, set the maintenance of international peace and security as the first and overriding purpose of the organization (Art. 1, par. 1). It stipulated that all member states shall refrain in their international relations from the threat or use of force against the territorial integrity or political independence of any state, or in any other manner inconsistent with the purposes of the United Nations (Art. 2, subpar. 4). It established that the General Assembly may consider the general principles of cooperation in the maintenance of international peace and security, including the principles governing "disarmament and the regulation of armaments" (Art. 11, par. 1). It made the Security Council responsible for formulation of plans to be submitted to the member states for the establishment of a system for "the regulation of armaments" (Art. 26). It envisaged the establishment of a Military Staff Committee to advise the Security Council on military requirements for the maintenance of international peace and security as well as "the regulation of armaments, and possible disarmament" (Art. 47).

While these provisions were not intended to make disarmament the centerpiece of the U.N. Charter security system, they were flexible enough to provide useful instruments for dealing with the question as required. Above all, the Charter, with its emphasis on the principle of the nonuse of force,

with its specific clauses on the pacific settlement of disputes, on the removal of threats to the peace, and on the suppression of acts of aggression, provided disarmament with a strong underpinning. If the member states were willing to cooperate in the common interest, disarmament could at any moment move to center stage.

PURSUING GCD WITHIN THE U.N. FRAMEWORK

Only weeks after the signing of the Charter of the United Nations, the world entered the atomic age. This event was bound to give disarmament greater urgency and an enhanced place in international politics. Thus the very first resolution adopted by the United Nations—Resolution 1 (Session I) of 24 January 1946—was a resolution on disarmament. By it the General Assembly dealt with the problems raised by the discovery of atomic energy and established a United Nations Atomic Energy Commission (UNAEC) to make specific proposals for the elimination from national armaments of atomic and of all other major weapons adaptable to mass destruction. Later that year, in Resolution 41 (Session I), the U.N. Assembly not only reaffirmed the urgent necessity that nuclear and other weapons of mass destruction be prohibited under international control but also recommended that practical measures be adopted by the Security Council for the general regulation and reduction of armaments and armed forces.

During the 1950s, following the dissolution of UNAEC, which from 1946 to 1949 had dominated the disarmament scene, disarmament was pursued mainly under the item entitled "Regulation, Limitation, and Balanced Reduction of All Armed Forces and All Armaments." Up to 1955, under that item of the U.N. agenda, several disarmament schemes were formulated by both East and West and many resolutions were adopted by the General Assembly, but they did not offer real opportunities to develop concrete agreements.

The 1950s was a period of events of great consequence, including the Korean War, the development of thermonuclear weapons by the United States and the Soviet Union, West Germany's affiliation with NATO, the establishment of the Warsaw Treaty Organization and in 1957, the launching of the first Sputnik by the Soviet Union. The first summit of the postwar period was held in Geneva, in

July 1955. Each of the four participants—France, the Soviet Union, the United Kingdom, and the United States—submitted disarmament proposals, one of them being President Dwight D. Eisenhower's Open Skies proposal, but there was no real meeting of minds. As a matter of fact, the positions of the two major powers hardened shortly after the summit. Then, in 1959, the Soviet Union revived the idea of general and complete disarmament.

GCD Unanimously Endorsed by General Assembly

On 18 September 1959, Premier Nikita Khrushchev addressed the General Assembly of the United Nations and proposed a plan for general and complete disarmament. He called for an end to the waging of war. The essence of the Soviet proposal, he stated, was that all states "should divest themselves of the means of waging war." He further stressed that the development of the international situation as a whole depended to a large extent on the future course of relations between the United States and the Soviet Union.

The proposed GCD plan was organized in three stages and aimed at eliminating within four years, under international control, all armed forces and armaments. The plan, the premier held, was the best means of solving the problem of disarmament, because it would completely eliminate the possibility of a state gaining military advantages of any kind. By the end of the disarmament process, states would be allowed to retain only strictly limited police (militia) contingents—of a strength agreed upon for each country—equipped with light firearms and intended solely for the maintenance of internal order and the protection of their citizens' personal safety.

Concerning the control of the disarmament process, the Soviet leader proposed the creation of an international control organ in which all states would participate and the setting up of a system "which could be operated in conformity with the stages in which disarmament was carried out." He summed up the Soviet position on this question by saying: "We are in favor of geniune disarmament under control, but we are against control without disarmament." He further made clear that, since "a certain time" would be required in which to work out so broad a disarmament plan, the settlement of a question "so acute and currently ripe for solution as that of discontinuing nuclear weapon tests for all time" should not be delayed. Finally, Khrushchev added that if there should be no readiness on the part of the Western powers to embark upon GCD without delay, the Soviet Union was prepared to come to terms on appropriate partial measures relating to disarmament and the strengthening of security.

The General Assembly also had before it a three-stage plan for comprehensive disarmament submitted on 17 September 1959 by Selwyn Lloyd, the foreign secretary of the United Kingdom. The plan, which was based on the principle of balanced stages toward the abolition of all nuclear weapons and the reduction of all other weapons to levels which would rule out the possibility of aggressive war, was the basis for the Western position when GCD negotiations started the following year.

France proposed that, in any disarmament program, high priority be given to measures prohibiting first the development and then the manufacture and possession of all vehicles for the delivery of nuclear devices. It was likewise necessary to provide for control—not control without disarmament, which France rejected just as it rejected disarmament without control, but "control of disarmament," the aim of which, at every stage, was to dispel mistrust by giving each state the certainty that the others were faithfully fulfilling their obligations.

The United States representative declared that his government unreservedly supported the greatest possible amount of controlled disarmament and welcomed in particular Soviet willingness to seek progress through limited steps. In Washington, Secretary of State Christian Herter's comment was that "if it were practicable and if it could safely be done, the type of disarmament that Mr. Khrushchev has spoken about is a highly desirable thing for mankind. From that point of view it must be taken very seriously" (*New York Times,* 23 September 1959).

Among the nonaligned countries, India held that the Soviet premier's statement fell into two distinct parts. One was a proposal for disarmament that had some common features with the earlier plans for the limitation and balanced reduction of all armaments; the other, India emphasized, was an entirely different proposal—a proposal for a warless world. This was the kind of thing that disarmament alone could not bring about. As the world could not survive in the context of modern war, India stated, war must be outlawed. Yugoslavia thought that negotiations were in themselves the surest way to assess the practicability of the Soviet proposal. In a situation where "realism" had served to increase international tension, the proposal should be given a trial, on the understanding that in later stages negotiations should focus on what was practicable.

Sweden stated that, while the schedule of transforming a heavily armed world into a completely disarmed world in a period of four years seemed utopian, perhaps the length of the period was not an essential feature of the scheme. Moreover, Mr. Khrushchev himself had taken into account the probability that a more limited program for disarmament might have greater chances to be carried out and had expressed the willingness of the Soviet government to seek agreement on appropriate limited measures of disarmament and security, listing those which in its view were the most important.

On 20 November 1959, the General Assembly unanimously adopted Resolution 1378 (Session XIV), a resolution that had the unique feature of being cosponsored by all the members of the United Nations. In the preamble, the General Assembly considered that "the question of general and complete disarmament is the most important one facing the world today." In the operative part, the assembly called upon governments "to make every effort to achieve a constructive solution of this problem," and expressed the hope "that measures leading towards the goal of general and complete disarmament under effective international control will be worked out in detail and agreed upon in the shortest possible time." No time frame was set for the task, however. The negotiations were to take place in the Ten Nation Committee on Disarmament, a new negotiating body on whose composition agreement had been reached before the convening of the 1959 session of the General Assembly.

The Ten Nation Committee on Disarmament convened in Geneva in March 1960. Its deliberations were short lived. Canada, France, Italy, the United Kingdom, and the United States, on one side, and Bulgaria, Czechoslovakia, Poland, Romania, and the Soviet Union, on the other, tried to come to grips with GCD, but from the very beginning there was no meeting of minds. The five Western members concentrated their efforts on preliminary security measures and on limitations and reductions of armaments, although GCD was proclaimed to be the final goal. The five Eastern members, on the other hand, saw the task of the committee as that of elaborating a comprehensive and detailed GCD plan. The talks ended with the withdrawal of the five Eastern European delegations.

The U.S.–Soviet Joint Statement of Agreed Principles   Many heads of government and chiefs of state, including Premier Khrushchev, attended the 1960 session of the General Assembly. Principles and directives for future negotiations were considered and several draft resolutions were submitted, but none was able to command the joint support of all the main powers. On the other hand, private consultations were initiated between the United States and the Soviet Union with the purpose of finding a basis for disarmament negotiations. They were continued in 1961, in Washington, Moscow, and New York, and on 20 September a joint statement containing agreed principles as a basis for multilateral disarmament negotiations was issued by the United States and the Soviet Union, for circulation to all members of the United Nations at the 1961 General Assembly session.

In the "Joint Statement of Agreed Principles for Disarmament Negotiations," as negotiated by John J. McCloy for the United States and Valerian A. Zorin for the USSR, the Soviet Union and the United States stated that the goal of negotiations was to achieve agreement on a program which would ensure that

1. Disarmament would be general and complete and war would no longer be an instrument for settling international problems, and that reliable procedures for the peaceful settlement of disputes and effective arrangements for the maintenance of peace in accordance with the principles of the Charter of the United Nations would be established.
2. States would have at their disposal only such non-nuclear armaments, forces, facilities, and establishments as were agreed to be necessary to maintain internal order and protect the personal security of citizens, and states would support and provide agreed manpower for a United Nations peace force.
3. The disarmament program would be implemented in an agreed sequence, by stages, until it was completed, with each measure and stage carried out within specified time limits and in such a balanced manner as not to create advantages for any state or group of states.
4. All measures of GCD would be balanced, so that at no stage of the implementation of the treaty could any state or group of states gain military advantage.
5. All disarmament measures would be implemented from beginning to end under strict and

effective international control, which would provide firm assurance that all parties were honoring their obligations.

6. For the purpose of implementing disarmament measures under strict and effective international control, an international disarmament organization including all parties to the treaty would be created within the framework of the United Nations and be assured unrestricted access without veto to all places as necessary for the purpose of effective verification.

7. Progress in disarmament would be accompanied by measures to strengthen institutions for maintaining peace and settling international disputes by peaceful means, including the obligation of states to place at the disposal of the United Nations agreed manpower necessary for an international peace force to be equipped with agreed types of armaments.

8. States participating in the negotiations would seek to achieve and implement the widest possible agreement at the earliest possible date and efforts would continue without interruption until agreement upon the total program had been achieved.

On the subject of verification, Mr. McCloy and Mr. Zorin, in an exchange of letters, further clarified the position of the respective governments. The letters showed that there was disagreement between the two sides on how far verification should go. The position of the United States government was that verification must ensure not only that agreed limitations and reductions had taken place, but also that the retained armed forces and armaments did not exceed agreed levels at any stage. The Soviet Union considered the verification of retained armed forces and armaments a form of espionage.

President John F. Kennedy, in his address to the General Assembly on 25 September 1961, invited the Soviet Union to go beyond agreement in principle to reach agreement on actual GCD plans. The United States GCD program, he said, would move to bridge the gap between those who insisted on a gradual approach and those who talked of the final and total achievement. In his words:

It would create machinery to keep the peace as it destroys the machinery of war. It would proceed through balanced and safeguarded stages designed to give no state a military advantage over another. It would place the final responsibility for verification and control where it belongs—not with the big

Powers alone, not with one's adversary or one's self, but in an international organization within the framework of the United Nations. It would assure that indispensable condition of disarmament—true inspection—and apply it in stages proportionate to the stage of disarmament. It would cover delivery systems as well as weapons. It would ultimately halt their production as well as their testing, their transfer as well as their possession. It would achieve, under the eyes of an international disarmament organization, a steady reduction in force, both nuclear and conventional, until it has abolished all armies and all weapons except those needed for internal order and a new United Nations peace force.

All this would require "new strength and new roles for the United Nations."

On 20 December 1961 the General Assembly, by unanimously approved Resolution 1722 (Session XVI), welcomed the Joint Statement of Agreed Principles and endorsed the agreement that had been reached on the composition of the negotiating body, the Eighteen Nation Disarmament Committee (ENDC), whose membership would be: Brazil, Bulgaria, Burma, Canada, Czechoslovakia, Ethiopia, France, India, Italy, Mexico, Nigeria, Poland, Romania, Sweden, USSR, United Arab Republic, United Kingdom, United States. The General Assembly recommended that the committee should undertake urgent negotiations with a view to reaching agreement on GCD under effective international control, on the basis of the Joint Statement.

ENDC Negotiations The ENDC opened in Geneva on 15 March 1962. France decided not to participate in the negotiations. During the first session two basic documents were considered: the "Draft Treaty on General and Complete Disarmament Under Strict International Control" submitted by the Soviet Union on 15 March, and the "Outline of Basic Provisions of a Treaty on General and Complete Disarmament in a Peaceful World" submitted by the United States on 18 April. These documents were amended from time to time during the period 1962–1964. The main emphasis of the Soviet plan was on the completion of the disarmament process within a fixed, short period of time as a means of achieving increasing equality between the two sides at each successive stage of the disarmament process. The United States plan was designed to reduce progressively armaments and forces without altering the positions and pattern of armaments as they existed at the beginning of the process within each military establishment.

Both drafts envisaged a disarmament process to take place in three stages. The USSR draft involved a four-year program with fifteen months for each of the first and second stages; the United States draft provided for two stages of three years each, to be followed by a third stage the duration of which would be fixed at the time the treaty was signed. In the course of the negotiations, the USSR agreed to extend the program from four to five years with a first stage of two years.

Both plans made the transition from one stage to the next dependent on the completion of previous disarmament measures and the readiness of inspection machinery for the subsequent measures. The United States plan also contained requirements that, for the transition to the second stage, all "other militarily significant States" would have to adhere to the treaty and that, before the third stage, certain rules of international conduct would have to be adopted. From the very beginning there was disagreement between the two sides about major aspects of their respective plans, particularly with regard to nuclear disarmament, verification, military bases, and measures to reinforce the peace.

Concerning conventional disarmament, both plans provided for the reduction, in stages, of the armed forces and conventional armaments of the two major powers. In spite of differences between the two powers about the scope of the reductions to be carried out at each stage, the conventional area was not a major source of disagreement.

On the other hand, there were deep divergencies on the question of military bases. The Soviet Union proposed the total liquidation of all foreign military bases in the first stage and, as a first step during the first stage, the liquidation of all foreign bases in Europe. This liquidation of bases was linked by the Soviet Union to the elimination of nuclear delivery vehicles. The United States provided for a reduction of agreed military bases in the second stage; the remaining ones would be retained until the last stage. The United States further opposed any distinction between foreign and domestic bases.

With regard to nuclear disarmament, the USSR's original draft provided for the complete elimination of vehicles for delivering nuclear weapons and the cessation of the production of such vehicles in the first stage. Subsequently, at the 1962 General Assembly's session, the USSR amended its proposal to permit the USSR and the United States to retain,

on their own territories, a limited number of intercontinental, anti-missile, and anti-aircraft missiles until the end of the second stage. The total elimination of nuclear weapons and fissionable material for weapons purposes and the discontinuance of their production would take place during the second stage.

The United States plan provided in the first stage for cutting off production of fissionable materials for weapon purposes and for transferring, for peaceful uses, agreed quantities of weapon-grade uranium-235 already produced and stockpiled. The number of vehicles carrying nuclear weapons would be reduced by 30 percent in the second stage, stocks of nuclear weapons would be reduced by an agreed percentage, and the production of nuclear weapons would be subject to agreed limitations. The total elimination of such weapons would take place in the third stage.

Both sides agreed on the need to verify what was being reduced, destroyed, or converted to peaceful uses as well as to control the cessation of production of armaments. In addition, the United States stressed the need to verify remaining quantities of armaments and forces and to ensure that undisclosed, clandestine forces, weapons, or production facilities did not exist. To meet these requirements, the United States suggested a system of progressive zonal inspection whereby the amount of inspection in any country's territory would be related to the amount of disarmament undertaken and to the degree of risk arising from possible clandestine activities. The USSR was opposed to the inspection of remaining stocks of armaments for security reasons and, in particular, to the zonal system, as it would disclose the defense system of a country.

The United States draft provided for a number of measures to keep and reinforce peace during and after the disarmament process. The United States stressed that no GCD agreement could be reached without prior agreement on peacekeeping machinery as a means to fill the gap created by disarmament. According to the United States plan, peace observation corps would be established in the first stage. At the start of the second stage, a United Nations peace force would come into existence; during the remainder of that stage the jurisdiction of the International Court of Justice would become compulsory and measures would be adopted against indirect aggression and subversion. The USSR draft provided for contingents from member states with non-nuclear weapons to be made available to the Security Council, under Article 43 of the United Nations Charter, during and following the disarmament process. The USSR opposed the United States approach on the ground that it created supranational institutions contrary to the United Nations Charter.

At its 1962 session, the General Assembly reviewed the ENDC negotiations and unanimously reaffirmed, in Resolution 1767 (Session XVII), the need for the conclusion, at the earliest possible date, of a GCD agreement. The resolution also recommended that urgent attention should be given "to various collateral measures intended to decrease tension and to facilitate general and complete disarmament."

In the ENDC, discussion centered mainly on the new Soviet proposal, whereby the USSR and the United States would retain a limited number of missiles until the end of the second stage of disarmament. The Western states held that the USSR proposal, as they understood it, taken either alone or in the context of other measures, would, if implemented, create a grave imbalance in favor of the USSR.

The USSR stated that it would consider specific proposals regarding the number of vehicles to be retained and measures of implementation, provided they were in accordance with the criterion that the number must be minimal so as not to serve aggressive plans. The USSR also stated that it accepted that the remaining missiles at the launching pads would be subject to control. These pads should not be more numerous than the remaining missiles and should be liquidated at the end of the second stage, together with the missiles themselves.

On 14 August 1963, the United States submitted draft treaty articles on nuclear disarmament measures in the first stage. These dealt, among other things, with: (*a*) a cutoff of production of fissionable materials for weapons purposes; (*b*) transfer of fissionable material to peaceful purposes; (*c*) the non-proliferation of nuclear weapons; (*d*) the conclusion of a comprehensive test ban treaty, a measure that could be put into effect before the conclusion of a general disarmament treaty. The United States said it was ready to consider a transfer of fissionable material to peaceful uses larger than that which would be requested of the USSR—for example, sixty tons as against forty tons. The cutoff and the transfer, as a combined step, would not need to await agreement on the first stage of GCD.

The USSR rejected the United States proposal for the cutoff of production of fissionable material and transfer of some quantities to peaceful uses as contributing to neither the elimination nor reduction of the danger of nuclear war, and as leaving intact nuclear-weapons stockpiles, which could even increase, because further production of weapons from accumulated stocks of fissionable material would not be specifically banned.

At the General Assembly in 1963, Foreign Minister Gromyko submitted a revised Soviet plan whereby the USSR and the United States would retain on their own territories limited contingents of intercontinental, anti-missile, and anti-aircraft missiles and their warheads, not only until the end of the second stage as previously proposed, but until the end of the third stage. The number of delivery vehicles to be retained would be minimal so as to prevent their use as a means of waging war or carrying out aggression.

Resolution 1908 (Session XVIII), which was adopted unanimously on 27 November 1963, recommended that the ENDC resume its negotiations on GCD without delay. The resolution also urged the ENDC once again to seek agreement on measures that could serve to reduce international tension, lessen the possibility of war, and facilitate agreement on GCD.

In 1964, the ENDC focussed on the USSR's revised proposal on the elimination of nuclear delivery vehicles, as put forward by Mr. Gromyko, which was soon referred to as the "nuclear umbrella" proposal. In promoting its own proposal, the Soviet Union maintained that the principle of retaining the relative balance between nuclear and conventional armaments as it existed at the beginning of the disarmament process—which the Soviet Union regarded as the core of the United States position on disarmament—was contrary to the objective of achieving equal security through disarmament, as stipulated in the Joint Statement of Agreed Principles.

The United States, supported by Canada, Italy, and the United Kingdom, held that the revised USSR plan, while representing a step forward, would rapidly alter the existing mixture of conventional and nuclear armaments, and therefore the balance of power, in favor of the USSR.

The basic difference of approach between the United States and the USSR regarding the question of the elimination of nuclear delivery vehicles led the nonaligned members of the ENDC to suggest that the matter be referred for detailed study to a working group. However, no decision on the terms of reference of the working group was ever taken.

GCD as the Ultimate Goal of Disarmament Negotiations

In subsequent years, while GCD remained on the ENDC agenda, other disarmament issues received growing attention by that body. The General Assembly also put decreasing emphasis on GCD in its resolutions. Increasingly, member states came to acknowledge that GCD was a long-term program—a goal that could be realized at some indefinite point well into the future, rather than within a precise time frame.

For its part the General Assembly helped to keep the goal in view by including each year an item entitled "general and complete disarmament" on its agenda. Under that item it considered a wide variety of subjects covering not only concepts aimed at dealing more effectively with the overall problem, but also with many specific disarmament issues, particularly new ideas that were not established as separate items on the agenda.

Among the more noteworthy initiatives put forward to foster a comprehensive disarmament approach was the 1969 request by the General Assembly, as originally proposed by Secretary-General U Thant, that the Conference of the Committee on Disarmament (CCD), the successor to the ENDC, work out a comprehensive program of disarmament under effective international control, which would provide the conference with a guideline to chart the course of its future work and its negotiations. In the relevant resolution, 2602 E (Session XXIV), the Assembly clearly stated that "the ultimate goal is general and complete disarmament." In 1969, and in subsequent years, the nonaligned countries strongly supported this position.

In 1978 the General Assembly, at its first special session on disarmament, adopted a Final Document in which it drew up a broad program of action with a view to facilitating the achievement of more concrete results. Also the Final Document clearly set out GCD as the ultimate goal of disarmament efforts.

The present multilateral disarmament negotiating body, the Conference on Disarmament (CD), has a permanent agenda (a basis for annual agendas) that contains an item entitled "Comprehensive Program of Disarmament Leading to General and Complete Disarmament Under Effective International Control." The question has been under consider-ation for over a decade, and efforts have been made to work out a document containing agreed objectives, principles, priorities, and measures of a comprehensive program. While progress has been achieved, the document still contains a large number of brackets, thereby signifying that the content is still the object of disagreement.

It must also be mentioned that the goal of GCD has been affirmed in the preamble of practically every multilateral disarmament accord that has been concluded since the beginning of the 1960s. It has been affirmed also in some bilateral agreements between the United States and the USSR, notably the Anti-Ballistic Missile Treaty of 26 May 1972 and the Treaty on the Limitation of Strategic Offensive Arms (SALT II) of 18 June 1979. In addition, Article VI of the Treaty on the Non-Proliferation of Nuclear Weapons (1968) establishes that the parties to the treaty undertake "to pursue negotiations in good faith on effective measures relating to cessation of the nuclear arms race at an early date and to nuclear disarmament, and on a treaty on general and complete disarmament under strict and effective international control."

CONCLUSION

The development of an international commitment to disarmament after World War I was to a very large extent the outgrowth of Woodrow Wilson's fervent drive for peace. A "covenant of cooperative peace" and the reduction of national armaments "to the lowest point consistent with domestic safety" were his priority goals. He succeeded in establishing the League of Nations as the foundation of the peace treaties of 1919. With regard to disarmament, he showed appreciation of the ideas and interests of the European states and made some concessions dictated by their national security concerns. Nevertheless, he succeeded in conferring legitimacy on general disarmament.

Up to 1933, the League of Nations was actively engaged in promoting general disarmament, thus seeking to give substance to the principle that states are not the sole judges of their own armaments. In accordance with the Covenant of the League of Nations, the reduction of armaments by international agreement was an essential part of the League's peace plan. In 1925, the League agreed in principle to the convening of a disarmament conference open to all states.

The Conference on the Reduction and Limitation of Armaments finally met in Geneva, under the auspices of the League, early in 1932, at a time when Europe and the world were approaching a state of crisis. Thus the conference met and operated under conditions that in no way offered hope of ultimate success. The collapse of the conference, in 1934, marked the end of all disarmament efforts by the League of Nations.

The Charter of the United Nations, born out of the suffering and destruction of World War II, was built on the principle that members shall refrain from the threat or use of force in their relations. Thus, the "sovereign equality" of member states as declared by the Charter (Art. 2, subpar. 1) implies that, states being equal, no state is allowed to impose its will upon another by the use of force.

The United Nations has provided a very fertile ground for disarmament initiatives, either comprehensive or limited. Practically every aspect of disarmament has been the object of deliberations by the General Assembly and its subordinate bodies.

When in 1959 Premier Khrushchev presented the Soviet plan for GCD, the United Nations unanimously endorsed that goal and called upon its members to pursue it earnestly. Most of the talks took place in a multilateral negotiating forum—the ENDC—operating within the United Nations framework, and composed of members from East, West, and the nonaligned countries. In spite of the composition of the negotiating body, in the bipolar world of the 1960s the Soviet Union and the United States unavoidably dominated its work. Only the two major powers submitted GCD draft agreements for consideration by the ENDC. Nevertheless, the GCD talks had wide implications.

As Arthur H. Dean, who for long periods represented the United States at the ENDC, has written: "The discussions—at Geneva, at the United Nations, and in confidential diplomatic conversations— were a necessary means whereby the nations of the world could become educated on disarmament questions and the ground could be broken for concrete agreements. This was a continuing process carried on in a comparatively normal diplomatic manner and with an avoidance of crisis. No hurriedly summoned *ad hoc* or summit conference, meeting for a limited time ... could have duplicated the work that was accomplished in this way" (*Test Ban and Disarmament: The Path of Negotiation,* 1966, pp. 23–30). Thus, even though, in the view of the United States government, GCD was

hardly a practical proposition for negotiation under the then existing conditions, continued discussions had a favorable impact and helped to promote the search for a more peaceful and more stable world.

The United States' position throughout the negotiating process was that GCD implied—as President Kennedy had stated at the United Nations in 1961—creating machinery to keep the peace while the machinery of war was being destroyed. It is a position that goes far back to the early disarmament efforts of the League of Nations and has found well-grounded support in theoretical studies.

Since the 1960s, when the United Nations endorsed the goal of GCD, peace has undoubtedly been strengthened and some important measures of disarmament have been adopted. As a matter of fact, some of the major obstacles that the United States and the Soviet Union encountered in the GCD talks of the 1960s no longer exist today or, at least, have been reduced to manageable proportions. For instance, even when stringent criteria of national security are applied, it can no longer be said that verification is an unsurmountable obstacle to disarmament. A large number of agreements—from the Non-Proliferation Treaty (NPT) to the Intermediate-Range Nuclear Forces Treaty (INF) and the Conventional Forces in Europe (CFE) Treaty—provide evidence that satisfactory solutions to the problem can be found.

As to the role of the United Nations in a disarming world, the disagreements of the past no longer exist. There is in fact a consensus that, in order to confront and master the problems of our time, a new sense of responsibility for peace must be developed, and that the United Nations must play a leading role in the promotion of international peace and security in all its aspects.

Undoubtedly, there is still a long way to go. Even in the vastly improved situation of the early 1990s, a GCD plan with precise timetables, to be embodied in a formal legal document for general adoption, is not practicable. Comprehensive measures of disarmament have, however, finally entered the realm of the possible, as evidenced by the INF, CFE, and START treaties and by the unilateral drastic measures of nuclear arms reductions announced by the United States on 27 September 1991, which the Soviet Union was promptly prepared to match, as stated on 5 October 1991.

Thus all options, including GCD, must be kept open. At a time when nations face unprecedented challenges of regional as well as global dimensions, the vision of a world free from the threat and burden of armaments can help them in their efforts to find better ways to organize their security.

BIBLIOGRAPHY

General Surveys For general surveys dealing with GCD and related questions in the interwar years and after World War II, see SALVADOR DE MADARIAGA, *Disarmament* (New York, 1929); FRANCIS P. WALTERS, *A History of the League of Nations* (London, 1952); PHILIP J. NOEL-BAKER, *The Arms Race: A Programme for World Disarmament* (London, 1958); ARTHUR LARSON, ed., *A Warless World* (New York, 1963); ARTHUR H. DEAN, *Test Ban and Disarmament: The Path of Negotiation* (New York, 1966); ALVA MYRDAL, *The Game of Disarmament* (New York, 1982); and JOSEPH S. NYE, JR., GRAHAM T. ALLISON, and ALBERT CARNESALE, eds., *Fateful Visions: Avoiding Nuclear Catastrophe* (Cambridge, Mass., 1988).

Initial Proposals A review of the U.S. and USSR's initial proposals is found in MARION H. MCVITTY's *A Comparison and Evaluation of Current Disarmament Proposals as of March 1, 1964* (New York, 1964); while ARNOLD WOLFERS and others explored Washington's position in *The United States in a Disarmed World: A Study of the U.S. Outline for General and Complete Disarmament* (Baltimore, 1966). Early U.S. critics of GCD included SIDNEY HOOK, "The Political Aspects of General and Completed Disarmament," and AMRON H. KATZ, "The Technical Aspects of General and Complete Disarmament," in JAMES E. DOUGHERTY and JOHN F. LEHMAN, JR., eds., *The Prospect of Arms Control* (New York, 1965): 153–163 and 58–82, respectively. Differing views were collected in "Controversy Over 'General and Complete Disarmament' and International Arms Control: Pro & Con," *Congressional Digest* 43 (August–September 1964): 193–224.

Subsequent Proposals Subsequent queries, searching to see if GCD were still alive, include DAVID KRIEGER, "Toward a World Disarmament Community," *Bulletin of Peace Proposals* 4:2 (1973): 183–192; and ADAM ROBERTS, "Is General and Complete Disarmament Dead?" *War/Peace Report* 13 (February 1973): 16–19. Efforts by the U.N. and USSR to convene a World Disarmament Conference during the late 1960s and early 1970s, which were opposed by the U.S., is reviewed by HOMER A. JACK, "A World Disarmament Conference," *Disarmament* 11 (September 1966): 11–15, and NICHOLAS A. SIMS, "U.N. Deadlocks and Delaying Tactics: The First Three Years of the Soviet Proposal for a World Disarmament Conference, 1971–1974," *Millenium* 4 (Autumn 1975): 113–131.

Records of Negotiations Records of the final negotiations during the interwar years may be found in LEAGUE OF NATIONS, *Records of the Conference for the Reduction and Limitation of Armaments* (1932–1933); and LEAGUE OF NATIONS, CONFERENCE FOR THE REDUCTION AND LIMITATION OF ARMAMENTS, *Preliminary Report on the Work of the Conference prepared by the President, Mr. Arthur Henderson* (1935). The records of the post–World War II negotiations are located in the CONFERENCE OF THE EIGHTEEN NATION COMMITTEE ON DISARMAMENT, *Verbatim Records* (1962–1964); CONFERENCE OF THE EIGHTEEN NATION COMMITTEE ON DISARMAMENT, *Documents* (1962–1964); UNITED NATIONS, DEPARTMENT OF POLITICAL AND SECURITY COUNCIL AFFAIRS, *The United Nations and Disarmament: 1945–1970* (1970); UNITED NATIONS, DEPARTMENT OF POLITICAL AND SECURITY COUNCIL AFFAIRS, *The United Nations and Disarmament: 1970–1975* (1976); and the UNITED NATIONS, DEPARTMENT FOR DISARMAMENT AFFAIRS, *The United Nations Disarmament Yearbook,* an annual publication from 1976 on.

The Law of War

○

W. HAYS PARKS

See also The Environmental Modification Convention: 1977 to the Present; Legal Dimensions of Arms Control and Disarmament; *and* Medieval Arms Control Movements and the Western Quest for Peace. *Most of the treaties discussed in this essay are excerpted in the* Regulating and Outlawing Weapons and War *section of Volume III.*

While arms control has long emphasized techniques that have as their objective the prevention of military conflict, it also has been concerned with minimizing violence in the event of war. It is at this point that arms control connects with international law generally, and with the law of war specifically.

The law of war is that part of international law that regulates the conduct of armed hostilities. It is sometimes termed "the law of armed conflict" or the "international humanitarian law of armed conflict." The latter term is appropriate with respect to those law of war treaties that protect war victims, such as prisoners of war, but is somewhat of a misnomer when applied to those portions of the law that authorize the destruction of property or the taking of life.

There are differences and similarities between the law of war and human-rights law. The law of war is highly codified and fairly specific, while human-rights law represents basic but general principles. The purpose of human-rights law is to guarantee to individuals at all times the enjoyment of certain prescribed fundamental rights, and to protect individuals from social evils such as arbitrary treatment. The law of war obligates nations to make reasonable efforts to limit the suffering of noncombatants, while authorizing the taking of life, destruction of property, and in certain cases the imposition of limitations on individual rights. Human-rights law applies both in peace and war, while the law of war applies only in war. Derived from a common origin,

the law of war has evolved over several centuries, while the human-rights law originated with the Universal Declaration on Human Rights of 1948.

DEVELOPMENT OF THE LAW OF WAR

In its original form the law of war was divided into two segments. In the "just-war" tradition developed by religious and secular sources through the Middle Ages, *ius ad bellum* addressed the morality and legality of going to war, while *ius in bello* dealt with the conduct of combatants during hostilities, providing limited protection for innocent civilians and other noncombatants in the hands of a belligerent. *Ius ad bellum* was supplanted in the twentieth century by the Kellogg-Briand Pact (or the Pact of Paris) of 1928 for the renunciation of war, the Charter of the United Nations, regional treaties such as the Charter of the Organization of American States, and mutual defense agreements. The basis for the *ius ad bellum* and modern treaty law is the same, however, in the emphasis of each on self-defense and condemnation of acts of aggression.

The law of war is an effort by nations to reduce destruction and suffering in war to that which is necessary for the accomplishment of legitimate military objectives. The purposes of the law of war are three: (1) to protect both combatants and noncombatants from unnecessary suffering; (2) to safeguard certain fundamental human rights of persons who fall into the hands of the enemy, particularly prisoners of war; the wounded, sick, and shipwrecked; and civilians; and (3) to facilitate the restoration of peace.

As a former Nuremberg prosecutor commented, one may be an optimist or a pessimist about the law of war. A pessimist looking over a battlefield would observe the hospitals and other civilian property damaged or destroyed, and conclude that the law of war is a failure. An optimist would observe the same scene and point to the undamaged hospitals and other civilian property that would have been damaged or destroyed but for the law of war. As is true of all international law, the success of the law of war is highly dependent upon good-faith respect for treaty obligations by nations.

History   Today's law of war is derived from the ancient code of chivalry, the writings of clergy and international lawyers, and the practice of nations. While many of its basic concepts are consistent with tenets found in each of the world's great religions, the law of war is primarily the product of European, Christian thinking and development.

The works of the Spanish theologian and philosopher Francisco Suárez (1548–1617), the Italian jurist and Oxford professor Alberico Gentili (1552–1610), the Dutch theologian and publicist Cornelius van Bynkershoek (1673–1743), the German jurist Samuel von Pufendorf (1632–1694), and the Swiss philosopher Emmerich von Vattel (1714–1767), among others, contributed greatly to the development of the law of war. But it is the Dutch jurist Hugo Grotius (1583–1645) who is most frequently associated with the birth of the law of war as it is known today. His *De iure belli ac pacis (On the Law of War and Peace),* published in 1625, provided the basic foundation for the law of war.

Others followed. *Elements of International Law* (1836) and *History of the Law of Nations* (1845) by the American international lawyer and diplomat Henry Wheaton (1785–1848) were valuable contributions to the field. But two wars in the mid-nineteenth century were the catalyst for movement of the law of war from philosophical consideration into a recognizable practice of nations.

In 1859 Jean-Henri Dunant, a citizen of Geneva, came upon the aftermath of the battle of Solferino between Austrian and French-Italian forces. Moved by the suffering of those who remained wounded and dying on the battlefield, Dunant published *Un Souvenir de Solférino (A Memory of Solferino)* in 1862, in which he proposed the establishment of civilian relief agencies for the care of the wounded. He also suggested the promulgation of an international agreement to protect the medical services and the wounded from intentional attack.

Dunant was not the first to act. The humanitarian work of the English nurse Florence Nightingale (1820–1910) during the Crimean War (1853–1856) undoubtedly served as a precedent for Dunant's ideas. Others were of like mind. In the American Civil War (1861–1865), for example, philanthropist George H. Stuart formed the U.S. Christian Commission at a Young Men's Christian Association convention in New York in November 1861. The work of its 4,859 clergy and lay members preceded that of the International Committee of the Red Cross (ICRC) in venturing upon the battlefield to provide aid and comfort to wounded and dying combatants of both sides. But it was Dunant's publication of *Un Souvenir de Solférino* that planted the seed for the formal codification of the law of war. A Geneva conference the following year led to the founding of the ICRC, and one in 1864 adopted the Convention for the Amelioration of the Condition of the Wounded in Armies in the Field. That convention was replaced by the Geneva Conventions of 1906, 1929, and 1949, the last being the one presently in effect.

An important phase in the birth of the modern law of war came during the American Civil War. Faced with the problems of guerrilla warfare, President Abraham Lincoln tasked Dr. Francis Lieber (1798–1872) with the preparation of a law of war code for Union forces. Lieber, a Berlin-born veteran of the 1815 campaign against Napoléon and a professor of law at Columbia College in New York, prepared two documents. One addressed the issue of guerrillas and the law of war. The second, adopted by the Union army in 1863 as "General Orders, No. 100," became the first modern statement of the law of war adopted by a government. Popularly known as the Lieber Code, it bridged the gap between the philosophy of the law of war and the military art of war, serving as a practical guide for commanders in the field in describing the rights and obligations of belligerents. The Lieber Code was a principal source for much of the law of war as it was to exist over the next century.

At the turn of the century two international peace conferences were held at The Hague to develop multilateral treaties on several law of war subjects.

The first conference (1899), attended by representatives from twenty-six nations, failed in its attempt at general disarmament, but produced two conventions and three declarations relating to the law of war. The second (1907), attended by forty-four nations, revised the two 1899 law of war conventions and adopted ten new conventions, many of which remain in effect today. The significance of the Hague International Peace Conferences lies in the meeting of governments to codify the law of war.

With the exceptions of a 1925 Geneva conference that restricted the use of chemical and biological weapons, 1929 and 1949 conferences to update and expand the 1864 and 1906 Geneva Conventions for the protection of war victims, and a 1954 Hague conference to further delineate protection for cultural property in time of war, there occurred a hiatus of almost three-quarters of a century in the codification of the law of war. Following conferences of government experts sponsored by the International Committee of the Red Cross (ICRC) in 1971 and 1972, Switzerland hosted the Diplomatic Conference on the Reaffirmation and Development of International Humanitarian Law Applicable in Armed Conflicts, held in Geneva between 1974 and 1977. That conference, attended by more than one hundred nations, eleven national liberation movements, and fifty-one public and private organizations granted observer status, produced two treaties intended to supplement the four 1949 Geneva Conventions for the protection of war victims: Additional Protocol I, which applies in international armed conflict, and Additional Protocol II, which provides minimal standards of conduct for internal armed conflicts that meet its threshold.

The 1974–1977 diplomatic conference eschewed discussion of modern weapons except in general terms, but adopted a resolution calling upon the United Nations to host a separate conference with a view to reaching agreement on prohibitions or restrictions on the use of certain conventional weapons. Acting on that request, the United Nations General Assembly convened a conference that met in Geneva between 1978 and 1980. Eighty-five nations attended. The conference produced the 1980 Convention on Prohibitions or Restrictions on the Use of Certain Conventional Weapons Which May Be Deemed to Be Excessively Injurious or to Have Indiscriminate Effects. That treaty contains an "umbrella" of general provisions and three protocols addressing munitions with nondetectable fragments (a weapon conferees acknowledged did not exist),

land mines and booby traps, and incendiary weapons. Despite its treaty's title, the conference found no weapon to be illegal or indiscriminate per se, and provided no protection for combatants from existing weapons.

BASIC PRINCIPLES OF THE LAW OF WAR

The law of war constitutes a balancing—often delicate—between "military necessity" and "unnecessary suffering." Military necessity was defined by the Lieber Code as "those measures which are indispensable for securing the ends of the war, and which are lawful according to the modern law and usages of war" (Sec. 1, para. 14). Other definitions describe military necessity as "that principle which justifies those measures not forbidden by international law which are indispensable for securing the complete submission of the enemy as soon as possible" (Department of the Army, Field Manual 27–10, *The Law of Land Warfare* [Washington, D.C., 1976], para. 3, p. 4) and "such destruction, and only such destruction, as is necessary, relevant, and proportionate to the prompt realization of legitimate military objectives" (Myres S. McDougal and Florentino P. Feliciano, *Law and Minimum World Public Order,* New Haven, Conn., 1961, p. 72). When read together, they provide an accurate description of the principle.

The war-crimes tribunals following World War II reinforced that which is stated in each of these definitions; that is, that military necessity does not authorize wanton destruction or other violation(s) of the law of war.

The principle of unnecessary suffering is not as well defined, except in those acts that are specifically prohibited in the various law of war treaties. It may be characterized as a violation of either of two general law of war concepts: (1) that of noncombatant immunity from intentional acts of violence, and (2) that of discrimination in the use of violence. Violation of either concept would constitute unnecessary suffering, as neither the direct attack of noncombatants (military wounded, sick, or shipwrecked; medical personnel; and civilians not taking part in hostilities) nor the indiscriminate use of force can be justified by the principle of military necessity.

Unnecessary suffering takes on a third dimension in the proscription contained in Article 23 of the

Annex to the Hague Convention Respecting the Laws and Customs of War on Land (Hague Convention IV), signed on 18 October 1907. Subparagraph (*b*) prohibits the killing or wounding of an enemy "treacherously," that is, through a perfidious act such as feigning surrender before recommencing combatant acts. Subparagraph (*e*) prohibits the employment of "arms, projectiles, or material of a nature to cause superfluous injury." Article 35, paragraph 2, of the 1977 Additional Protocol I to the 1949 Geneva Conventions adds "methods of warfare" to this list, while using the terms *unnecessary suffering* and *superfluous injury* synonymously.

The term *superfluous injury* is the more descriptive in understanding the concept of unnecessary suffering as it is applied to the employment of weapons against combatants; it also illustrates the difficulty of applying the law of war. The law of war recognizes the legitimacy of the taking of life in combat. But while a weapon intended for use against an individual combatant may take his or her life, it may not be designed with the intent of producing a wound that would be superfluous to the enemy combatant's incapacitation.

The classic example of a weapon that causes superfluous injury is a barbed spear. A spear without barbs will incapacitate an enemy soldier; the barbs do not enhance the probability of incapacitation, but serve to aggravate the wound as the spear is removed, thereby causing superfluous injury or unnecessary suffering. The concept is sound; it recognizes that all wars end, and weapons that cause superfluous injury needlessly extend the suffering of combatants beyond the war.

As the delegates to the 1978–1980 United Nations conventional-weapons conference discovered, however, great difficulty occurs in the practical application of such laws. The treaty produced by that conference prohibits a nonexistent weapon and provides protection to the civilian population only in the employment of lawful weapons. While a number of weapons were examined, no restriction was placed on the use of any existing weapon against combatants. In the history of the law of war, with the exceptions of the 1899 Hague Declaration Concerning Expanding Bullets (Declaration IV), and the first-use restriction on chemical weapons found in the 1925 Geneva Protocol for the Prohibition of the Use in War of Asphyxiating, Poisonous or Other Gases, and of Bacteriological Methods of Warfare, no weapon having legitimate military value has been found to cause superfluous injury or unnecessary suffering, or has otherwise been prohibited.

Subparagraph (*a*) of Article 23 of the Annex to Hague Convention IV prohibits the use of poison or poisoned weapons, a form of unnecessary suffering long proscribed in the practice of nations. It reflects the balancing of military necessity and unnecessary suffering: a retreating commander deliberating whether to authorize the poisoning of wells to deny their use to his advancing enemy must take into account the fact that his recapture of the territory would require the use of those same wells. The use of poisoned weapons relates to the concept of superfluous injury, applied in the same manner as it was with regard to the barbed spear; poison aggravates the wound rather than improving incapacitation effects. (The prohibition on poison is not considered applicable to chemical weapons.)

A third but subordinate principle is that of proportionality. This concept does not limit a belligerent's use of a preponderance of military power against his opponent's military forces. It is used in general terms in three ways: (1) in ensuring that a peacetime act in self-defense is proportionate to the threat; (2) in requiring that a reprisal be proportionate to the original wrong that prompted the reprisal; and (3) in weighing the military value of a weapon against the suffering it causes.

A fourth way in which proportionality has been used is in weighing the value of an attack against the cost in terms of collateral civilian casualties and damage to civilian objects. This concept, emerging in the late twentieth century, describes the balancing between military necessity and unnecessary suffering rather than serving as a separate, distinct principle.

The classic example of a violation of the concept of proportionality, for example, is the destruction by artillery barrage of a village with a civilian population of five hundred and no military objectives, solely to neutralize a single enemy sniper or machine-gun position on the edge of that village. Such destruction would constitute willful and wanton destruction, which is prohibited by the law of war.

Beyond this example, application of the concept of proportionality is fraught with difficulties, not the least of which is determining which party to the conflict has the primary responsibility for separating military objectives from the civilian population and civilian objects. Other difficulties include the value of destruction of a particular target (which may vary) and the degree of knowledge an attacking commander may have of the presence of civilians in the vicinity of a target. These issues will be discussed in the section on targeting. The foregoing suggests that while the concept of proportionality has merit, it offers difficulty in practical application.

The codified and uncodified law of war is focused on particular areas, including the protection of war victims; means and methods of warfare; targeting (related to the conduct of hostilities); and war crimes. A brief discussion of each follows. Other areas that will not be addressed include the law of neutrality and of naval warfare.

PROTECTION OF WAR VICTIMS

Although the Annex to Hague Convention IV of 1907 contains provisions relating to prisoners of war, in the aftermath of World War I the scope of the Geneva law was expanded beyond the protection for military wounded and sick (and medical personnel and establishments caring for them) to include prisoners of war. The 1949 Geneva diplomatic conference sought to benefit from the experience of World War II to improve upon the two 1929 Geneva Conventions for the wounded and sick and prisoners of war, while promulgating new conventions for the protection of military wounded, sick, and shipwrecked at sea, and civilians. The four 1949 Geneva Conventions for the protection of war victims address these topical areas.

Additional Protocol I of 1977 developed protection for civilian medical personnel and establishments equal to that in the 1949 conventions for military medical personnel and establishments, while attempting a more practical formula for the protection of medical aircraft and enhanced means for identification of medical transportation.

The four 1949 Geneva Conventions are among the most widely accepted treaties in force today, with 169 signatories (out of 174) party to them; there are more nations party to these four conventions than there are members of the United Nations. National implementation remains uneven, however, and is virtually nonexistent in some states.

The 1949 Geneva Conventions contain a number of common provisions. Each opens with an obligation on the part of the parties "to respect and to ensure respect" for each of the conventions "in all circumstances." This provision in part is a repudia-

tion of the "just-war" tradition, which holds that combatants not fighting for a just cause are not entitled to the same protection as those fighting for such a cause. Under the 1949 Geneva Conventions, all legitimate combatants are entitled to equal treatment regardless of the "justness" of their cause, or the degree to which an enemy nation is adhering to its obligations under the Geneva Conventions. Unlike the case in other areas of the law of war, adherence to the 1949 Geneva Conventions is not dependent upon reciprocity.

The conventions apply to "all cases of declared war or of any other armed conflict which may arise between two or more of the High Contracting Parties, even if the state of war is not recognized by one of them." This provision seeks to avoid the confusion that exists frequently over whether a state of war formally exists, and aligns the conventions with the historic practice of nations entering armed conflict without a formal declaration of war except under extraordinary circumstances. (For example, the United States has declared war only five times in its history, and no nation has issued a formal declaration of war since 1948.)

The four conventions set the duration of their application, generally until the cessation of active hostilities and/or repatriation or release of the war victims protected by the particular convention; encourage special agreements between parties to a conflict to provide further protection under circumstances not contemplated by the treaty; deny to any person the authority to renounce the protection provided by that convention to him or her (in order to protect a war victim from being coerced to renounce his or her Geneva Convention rights); and prohibit the persons or objects that are the subject of the treaty from being the object of medical experimentation, torture, reprisal, or collective punishment. Each convention sets forth specific offenses that are regarded as "grave breaches," or major violations of each convention.

A critical aspect of the law of war is that it is neutral; that is, it creates rights commensurate with the responsibilities it imposes; that it favors neither party to a conflict, nor defensive over offensive actions (or vice versa). Examples will be provided in examining each of the 1949 Geneva Conventions, and in the discussion of targeting below.

Protection for Military Wounded, Sick, and Shipwrecked
The first two of the four 1949 Geneva Conventions are the Convention for the

Amelioration of the Condition of the Wounded and Sick in Armed Forces in the Field and the Convention for the Amelioration of the Condition of Wounded, Sick and Shipwrecked Members of Armed Forces at Sea. They are referred to here as the first and second Geneva Conventions.

The first convention's lineage can be traced back to the 1864 Geneva Convention for the Amelioration of the Condition of the Wounded in Armies in the Field. The 1949 convention provides protection from intentional attack for combatants who are *hors de combat,* or "out of action," due to wounds or illness. Protection for the sick as well as the wounded was added in the 1929 Geneva Convention in recognition that more combatants fall victim to disease than to the lethal instruments of war, a historical fact that has been borne out in most conflicts in the twentieth century. The second convention was added in 1949, following the great naval battles of World War II, to provide humanitarian protection for the wounded, sick, and shipwrecked at sea. With the exception of its additional provisions regarding hospital ships, the second convention carefully parallels the first.

These two conventions also provide protection to permanent medical personnel (to include chaplains attached to the military); administrative and logistical personnel who normally would be combatants so long as they are assigned full-time to perform their duties in support of medical units; medical units and installations (permanent or temporary); medical transportation; and part-time medical support personnel during the time that they are performing their medical support duties. Additional Protocol I of 1977 extends to civilian medical and religious personnel and civilian medical installations and equipment the same protection as that provided the military by the first and second conventions. Certain civilian relief organizations are entitled to similar protection, provided they have gained the consent of the parties to the conflict to perform their humanitarian duties. Movement of the latter on or about the battlefield without close coordination with military authorities may place them at undue risk, due to the fluidity and uncertainty of the combat environment.

The balancing requirement of the law of war is reflected in the language of the first convention in that it provides protection for medical units unless they are used to commit, outside their humanitarian duties, "acts harmful to the enemy" (Art. 21). This includes any act in which the protected medical status is used to gain a military advantage over an opponent, such as using a military ambulance to carry out a reconnaissance mission. Similarly, combatants are *hors de combat* and protected from intentional attack so long as they refrain from engaging in hostile acts; a wounded combatant who continues to fight may be very courageous, but obviously relinquishes any protection from hostile acts being directed at him or her. This "balancing" does not prevent medical personnel from carrying personal weapons (such as a pistol or rifle) to protect themselves and their patients from persons (civilian or military) who might be intent on criminal activities.

Provisions for hospital ships also reflect this balancing. Hospital ships are protected from intentional attack so long as they are not used to commit acts harmful to the enemy. As hospital ships carry no weapons except some small arms for internal discipline, their most obvious act harmful to the enemy would be their use as vessels for the gathering and/or transmission of intelligence. Recognizing this, the second convention contains an express prohibition, in Article 34, on hospital ships utilizing encrypted communications equipment. While this provision may be archaic in modern times of encryption of most military communications (and the ease of interception of unencrypted communications), it represents the concern of nations that an enemy may use the humanitarian provisions of the Geneva Conventions to seek to gain some advantage over its opponent. For this reason, an enemy has a right to visit and search hospital ships or land-based medical units and facilities (if it can gain access to the latter) to confirm compliance with the Geneva Conventions.

In an age of "beyond-visual-range" or "over-the-horizon" weapons that may mistake a hospital ship for a combatant vessel, proposals have been proffered, but not adopted as of 1992, to permit hospital ships to carry defensive protection from unintentional attack by such weapons. One possibility involves equipping hospital ships with obscurant devices, such as a chaff dispenser. This defensive technique would enable a false radar image to be projected, in this case through the launching of chaff, drawing a missile away from the hospital ship. Another would be to install "close-in" weapon systems, such as a small-caliber (25-mm to 30-mm), rapid-fire point defense gun to engage a missile at close range as a last resort. While there are logical arguments on behalf of each proposal, equally practical concerns have been expressed against any device that may change the traditional character or appearance of the unarmed hospital ship—yet another example of the friction that exists in writing and implementing a law of war that is entirely neutral.

Medical aircraft operate under similar balancing constraints. These aircraft are protected from intentional attack because they perform humanitarian duties. But combatant forces view with suspicion enemy aircraft operating in their vicinity, even if an aircraft is identified as bearing the Red Cross or Red Crescent, indicating that it is a medical aircraft. Although the 1949 Geneva Conventions prohibit the use of the distinctive emblem of the Red Cross or Red Crescent for unauthorized (non-humanitarian) purposes, and abuse is rare, this is not regarded as adequate assurance for opposing forces. Protection for medical aircraft is assured only if they operate at heights, times, and on routes specifically agreed upon between the belligerents concerned. A medical aircraft also must obey any summons by an enemy to land so that it may be inspected to ensure its compliance with its humanitarian duties. These provisions have proved impractical in practice, and have become all the more so on the modern battlefield, where incompatibility of communications equipment and electronic warfare (such as the jamming of enemy communications) is routine.

In an effort to rectify this problem, Additional Protocol I of 1977 established a modified regime for protection of medical aircraft, depending in part upon the distance of the aircraft from areas of hostile activity. However, as this new regime remains highly dependent upon the consent of an opponent, it is not regarded as having made any substantial improvement to what perhaps may be an irresolvable problem. Unlike hospital ships, however, under Protocol I a medical aircraft may carry encrypted communications equipment so long as its use does not include the collection or transmission of intelligence.

Some intelligence gathering and transmission of information by a medical aircraft may benefit its humanitarian mission without resulting in an act harmful to an enemy. For example, a medical aircraft returning from a mission with wounded on board may send an abbreviated message describing the wounds of its passengers to expedite their handling and treatment at the hospital. This abbreviated message, even if not encrypted, may appear so if intercepted by an enemy force. A medical-evacuation aircraft lifting off from a contested site may draw enemy fire; his passing that information to another medical-evacuation aircraft approaching the site so that the in-bound aircraft can try a different, safer approach is a form of gathering and transmission of intelligence. Obviously, this provision remains subject to interpretation.

Fratricide or "amicicide"—the accidental destruction of friendly forces due to misidentification—is an age-old problem in war. Medical units and transportation, including hospital ships, have suffered enemy attacks in twentieth-century combat more through misidentification than malice aforethought, notwithstanding use of the two recognized distinctive emblems of the Red Cross and Red Crescent (the latter used by Moslem nations).

Moreover, Israel employs the Mogen David Adom, or Red Shield of David. Although not formally recognized by any nation or in any law of war treaty, former foes have attested that protection was afforded Israeli Defense Force units and transports displaying the Red Shield of David when it was recognized. There are obvious potential identification problems at a distance or in subdued lighting, as the red shield would be indistinguishable from a blue shield on a white background—Israel's national insignia. Iran utilized a third authorized emblem, the Red Lion and Sun, until 1981. Efforts to establish a single emblem for all nations have been unsuccessful.

To facilitate identification of medical units and transports, Additional Protocol I of 1977 offered a number of additional means of identification, to include electronic identification through the Secondary Surveillance Radar (SSR) system specified in Annex 10 to the 1944 Chicago Convention on International Civil Aviation, methods to increase infrared detection of the distinctive emblem, special radio signals, and a special marker featuring a flashing blue light. Each signal was intended to facilitate identification rather than establish the user's status as a unit or transport entitled to protection from direct attack. A 1990 review conference of experts hosted by the International Committee of the Red Cross (ICRC) revealed that some of the means proposed in 1977 were approaching obsolescence (such as voice communication), while others were plagued by practical or technical difficulties; a flashing blue light appears white at a distance, cannot be seen through fog or dust, and could be mistaken for a gun shot or an enemy laser, for example. However, ICRC aircraft repatriating Iraqi and Coalition prisoners of war following the 1991 Persian Gulf War successfully used electronic signals to enhance their identification, providing a limited confirmation that this area may yet prove of value.

The protections provided medical personnel, units, and equipment (including hospital ships and medical aircraft) are balanced by an obligation by parties to a conflict to search for, come to the aid of, and recover wounded, sick, shipwrecked, and dead enemy personnel from the battlefield during and after hostilities. Wounded and sick are treated according to medical priority only. This is the fundamental reason for the first and second conventions, which lay out a regime for the collection and care of wounded and sick once they fall into enemy hands.

The first and second conventions apply to wounded and sick military personnel only, and provide protection from intentional attack for military medical personnel, establishments, units, and transportation. The 1949 Geneva Convention Relative to the Protection of Civilian Persons in Time of War, or the fourth convention, provides limited protection for wounded and sick civilians, and civilian medical personnel and establishments, while the Annex to Hague Convention IV also provides protection from intentional attack for civilian hospitals. Additional Protocol I of 1977 provides more detailed protection for civilian medical personnel, transportation, and establishments in an effort to reconcile the protection for the civilian medical establishments and personnel with that provided the military.

While there has been some suggestion that a military force bound by Protocol I has an affirmative obligation to care for wounded and sick civilians in its area of operations, others believe that an obligation arises only when the military force is operating in an area where civilian health-care capabilities have ceased to exist. Still others question whether a military commander incurs any obligation unless he is an occupying power and local health care no longer is available. If a civilian receives treatment from the military, of course, medical treatment must be made available on the basis of medical priority only.

Protection for Prisoners of War
Enemy wounded and sick also are prisoners of war, and are protected by the Convention Relative to the Treatment of Prisoners of War, or the Third Geneva Convention of 1949. The history of prisoners of war prior to the twentieth century is not a happy one. Prisoners of war routinely were put to the sword, sold into slavery, held for ransom, or permitted to die through malnourishment, inadequate medical care, or other neglect or brutality by a captor. While twentieth-century practice on occasion has matched the brutality seen in conflicts in earlier times, overall care steadily has progressed.

Care   The Annex to Hague Convention IV of 1907 contains a limited number of provisions regarding care for prisoners of war. The Geneva Convention Relative to the Treatment of Prisoners of War was first promulgated in 1929. Japan and the Union of Soviet Socialist Republics were not parties to this treaty during World War II, resulting in a number of instances of egregious abuse and mixed treatment. British and United States personnel captured by German forces generally received treatment consistent with the 1929 Geneva prisoner-of-war convention, while Russian prisoners of war in German hands (and vice versa) suffered a variety of abuses, including summary execution. The 1949 Convention was intended to profit from the lessons learned in that conflict.

The capture of an enemy combatant transforms the relationship between enemies into one that is unique and fraught with friction. The captor who a moment before had the lawful right to kill his enemy now accepts an obligation not only to care for his captive but to protect him or her from the dangers of hostilities, spiriting his prisoner away from the battlefield to a safe site of internment as expeditiously as reasonably possible under the circumstances. In turn, the prisoner of war is protected by his captor so long as he makes no effort to escape or harm his captor. This unique relationship may be summarized in the following prisoner-of-war rights and responsibilities:

Rights	Responsibilities
Humane treatment	Respect of internal
Safeguards from hostilities	discipline
No torture	No illegal actions that do
No reprisals or collective	not facilitate escape
punishment	No violence to life
No criminal liability for	or limb against captor
escape attempts	
involving illegal actions	
that do not incur	
violence to life	
or limb	

The prisoner of war must be cared for by his captor according to the minimum standards set forth in the regime established by the third convention. That treaty holds a captor responsible for his prisoners of war from the moment of capture until their repatriation, to include their feeding, clothing, shelter, and medical care. The standard is not a difficult one: the prisoner of war is entitled to the same quality and quantity of food and care afforded a soldier in the captor's own forces. (Captured military medical personnel are not prisoners of war but "retained personnel." If they are not released, however, they are entitled to the same treatment as a prisoner of war, as are most civilians who accompany the armed forces in the field in time of war.) The regime established within the third convention sets forth authorized labor, prisoner-of-war rates of pay (now somewhat dated), authorized labor, and bases for punishment of a prisoner of war and incarceration for offenses committed as a prisoner of war.

Physical and mental torture, as well as threats and acts of violence, are prohibited. Women prisoners of war must be treated with all regard due their sex, and in all cases benefit from treatment as favorable as that provided male prisoners of war. Other third-convention prohibitions are not as clear. For example, a provision in Article 13 protects prisoners of war from "insults and public curiosity." When coupled with the prohibition on torture and/or threats, clearly this provision would prohibit forcing a prisoner of war to make an involuntary, videotaped statement. But what about a voluntary statement? Or a news photograph showing a number of prisoners of war surrendering, being processed or fed, or engaged in a sports activity in a prisoner-of-war camp? One apparent answer would be that photographing such activities would be prohibited if identification of individual prisoners of war might place the families of those prisoners at risk from their own government. But the fact that there are prisoners of war, and that they are receiving treatment consistent with the third convention, is a newsworthy item subject to publication. This illustrates how the innocent ambiguity of some third-convention provisions requires skillful but good-faith balancing of competing interests.

Accountability Accountability for prisoners of war is a national responsibility. To ensure full accountability, the third convention directs a capturing nation to establish a bureau to collect information from prisoners of war that may be transmitted back to the prisoner's national authorities. This information is passed from the captor nation to the prisoner's national authorities through the Central Prisoners of War Information Agency, established under Article 123. Such an agency may be established in a neutral country, though the general practice has been for nations to avail themselves of the services offered in this regard by the International Committee of the Red Cross (ICRC). The degree of accountability may be illustrated by the information a prisoner of war is obligated to give his or her captor (left column) when compared with the information the captor is expected to supply regarding prisoners of war in its hands.

Prisoner of war must give	Captor must give
Full name	Full name
Rank	Rank
Serial number	Serial number
Date of birth	Date of birth
	Place of birth
	Nation for which prisoner was fighting
	First name of father
	Maiden name of mother
	Name and address of person to be informed (next of kin)
	Address to which correspondence for prisoner may be sent

Additional information may be collected to distinguish one prisoner of war from another, such as physical description (hair and eye color, height, weight, distinguishing marks), blood type, photograph, fingerprints, and/or deoxyribonucleic acid (DNA) typing. Post–third convention conflicts have revealed a failure on the part of some nations to provide even rudimentary identification for their military personnel, whether in the form of an identification card or tag, or serial number. A prisoner-of-war serial number may be assigned by a captor to complement or serve in place of a military serial number.

Accountability can be difficult, given the myriad of ways in which an enemy soldier may fall into the hands of his enemy—and be processed once captured. Thus, able-bodied prisoners of war enter one processing chain, while prisoners of war who are wounded enter a different, medical process, eventually to return to the former. While accountability has suffered in some conflicts, new automated processes hold some hope for increased adherence with the accountability provisions of the third convention. In the 1991 Gulf War, for example, an unprecedented 99.99 percent accuracy was achieved in accounting for the 69,820 Iraqi prisoners of war captured by French, British, and United States forces, due to an automated Prisoner of War Information System developed by the U.S. Army. A disparity may continue to exist from nation to nation, but automation should tend to facilitate accountability in future conflicts.

Under the third convention, the captor is obligated to account for his prisoners of war, and may take necessary and reasonable measures to prevent a prisoner's escape—including the use of deadly force. Recognizing that many nations impose an obligation on their personnel to make reasonable efforts to escape if captured, the third convention walks a delicate but specific line in limiting punishment that may be imposed upon a prisoner of war who is unsuccessful in attempting escape.

Discipline The third convention authorizes two forms of punishment for prisoners of war. Disciplinary punishment, which can include a fine (taken from up to 50 percent of a prisoner's pay), discontinuance of certain privileges (such as denial of tobacco products), fatigue duties not exceeding two hours daily, or an enhanced form of confinement, may be awarded for minor infractions, such as violation of prisoner-of-war camp rules and regulations. It is the only punishment authorized for an unsuccessful escape attempt not involving violence to life or limb, or illegal acts not facilitating

escape. Judicial punishment is more formal in its manner of imposition and more severe in degree, and may include imprisonment or death if military personnel of the captor would be subject to the same punishment for the same offense(s).

The distinction in punishment recognizes a prisoner of war's obligation to attempt escape, limiting the punishment that may be imposed upon him or her for that effort, but does not condone illegal acts that would not facilitate escape or would entail violence to life or limb. Thus a prisoner of war who steals a bicycle or civilian clothing would have committed an act or acts that are illegal, but that were intended to facilitate his or her escape. The recaptured prisoner of war would be subject to disciplinary punishment only for his unsuccessful effort. Theft of some other object as a "souvenir" of his time as a prisoner of war is ordinary theft, for which the prisoner would be prosecuted in the same manner as military personnel in the captor's armed services. Enemy prisoners of war in United States custody, for example, are subject to prosecution by court-martial under the U.S. Uniform Code of Military Justice for such offenses. Similarly, if the escaping prisoner of war assaults or murders a soldier or civilian in order to obtain the bicycle upon which he intends to make his escape, he has used violence to life and limb for which he may face judicial punishment if he does not make successful his escape. The fact that he may commit an act of murder in killing an enemy soldier while attempting escape again indicates the unique relationship upon which a prisoner of war embarks once in the hands of his captor.

Collective punishment of prisoners of war is prohibited; the fact that one attempted or made good his or her escape does not permit the punishment

	Disciplinary Punishment	Judicial Punishment
Prisoner attempting escape	yes	no
Prisoner planning escape	yes	no
Prisoner using illegal act not involving violence that facilitates escape	yes	no
Prisoner using violence to facilitate escape	yes	yes
Prisoner using illegal act not involving violence that does not facilitate escape	yes	yes
Prisoner not participating in escape planning or attempt	no	no

of all, although the captor may inflict disciplinary punishment on prisoners of war who assisted in the escape. By way of summary, the table lists the forms of punishment, if any, a prisoner of war may suffer if he or she attempts an escape, or is in a prisoner-of-war camp where escape is attempted.

Release and Repatriation All wars end, at which time troops withdraw, demobilize, and return home. Prisoners of war are entitled to release during the hostilities or, failing that, repatriation after the cessation of active hostilities.

During hostilities, medical personnel who fall into enemy hands are to be retained only insofar as the state of health, the spiritual needs, and the number of prisoners of war require. Medical personnel whose retention is not indispensable are to be released and returned to their national authorities as soon as possible and military requirements permit. Regrettably, this provision has not been widely observed in twentieth-century conflicts.

Seriously wounded or sick prisoners of war are to be returned to their military authorities after their captor has provided adequate medical care to make them fit for travel. Able-bodied prisoners of war and wounded or sick prisoners of war or retained personnel not previously released are entitled, under Article 118, to release and repatriation "without delay after the cessation of active hostilities." This phrase is sufficiently ambiguous, however, that prisoners of war often have been detained for extended periods of time following the end of a conflict.

The precise terms of repatriation are subject to negotiation and agreement between the parties to the conflict who have prisoners of war in enemy hands. Repatriation may occur with or without outside assistance, such as that sometimes provided by the International Committee of the Red Cross (ICRC).

There have been occasions in which prisoners of war have declined repatriation. While a prisoner of war is entitled to repatriation, it may not be imposed involuntarily. To ensure the voluntariness of his or her decision, representatives of the ICRC frequently are called upon to interview prisoners of war privately.

Protection for Civilians

A primary reason for the law of war is to protect noncombatants from the effects of hostilities—a concept that has its roots in medieval Europe's "Peace of God" efforts, which are discussed in Udo Heyn's essay in Section 3. In particular, civilians are protected from intentional harm so long as they do not take part in hostilities. The principle is sound and entirely consistent with military efficiency. A military commander does not wish to expend finite resources on personnel and objects that do not pose a threat to his mission. Application of this simple principle is complicated by the degree to which some civilians in industrialized societies engage in activities that are essential to a nation's defense or military force's mission or, at the lower end of the conflict spectrum, the degree to which a guerrilla force uses the civilian population to conceal its identity or accomplish its mission.

A civilian who is not engaged in any activity connected to the national defense or to military activities as such clearly is protected by the law of war from intentional attack. This norm establishes unequivocal protection for 95 percent or more of a nation's population, and is consistent with general historic practice. Similarly, civilian objects are protected from intentional damage or destruction so long as they are not being used for military purposes, or no military advantage can be achieved by their destruction. (Injury to civilians and/or damage of civilian objects incidental to military operations will be discussed in the section on targeting.)

But what about a civilian who is an aircraft-maintenance technician for a fighter squadron, or employed in a similar position of considerable value to his nation's armed forces or national defense? During World War II, for example, a number of civilian scientists engaged in operational research that was critical to the Allied anti-U-boat campaign and the combined bomber offensive against Germany. Military personnel engaged in such activities are legitimate targets. May a nation convert what normally is a military function into a civilian position in order to protect its incumbent from attack?

Similar questions arise with regard to civilian objects that may also serve a military purpose; for example, most highway networks used for everyday traffic are constructed with funding provided by the federal government because the highways are essential to national defense. Regrettably, no law of war treaty adequately addresses these problems in a way that may offer meaningful protection to those civilians not engaged in acts harmful to enemy forces, or to civilian objects.

Notwithstanding the risk to combatants engaged in combat, civilians traditionally have suffered the most in war. The greatest number of civilian deaths during World War II are not attributable to military operations, but to abuse of the civilian population by military forces occupying enemy territory. The Geneva Convention Relative to the Protection of Civilian Persons in Time of War, or the fourth convention, was prepared in the aftermath of the massive abuse of civilian populations during World War II by occupation forces.

An occupying power has an obligation to continue to care for the civilian population of occupied territory with the same responsibilities as those held by the government it replaced. It must provide such essentials as health care, food, and water, and attend to other matters necessary for the survival of the civilian population. The occupying power incurs this responsibility to the degree that those services have ceased to exist. Thus, if the civilian hospitals remain open to the public, an occupying power incurs no obligation to establish new health services provided existing facilities are adequate. Many of these services may be continued simply by permitting the agencies that previously existed to continue their functions.

With that responsibility comes commensurate authority as to control of the population and appropriation of property. An occupying power may exercise the latter for purposes that support its military mission (as any military force may do, including destroying property if there is an absolute military necessity for doing so) or to the extent necessary in its role as the occupying power. The occupying power simultaneously is obligated to protect certain property within its control, such as cultural property, and to discipline its own forces to prevent destructive acts.

The occupying power owes a special responsibility to the civilian population, and the fourth convention endeavors to prevent recurrence of the abuses that occurred during World War II. Individual or mass forcible transfers, as well as deportation of civilians from occupied territory, is expressly prohibited, as is the taking of hostages, reprisals, and collective punishment. Nor may an occupying power require citizens of occupied territory to serve in its armed forces, or to transfer its own citizens into the occupied territory. Special attention is provided for the protection of families and children.

Civilians may be detained for security purposes. In this regard the provisions for the care of prisoners of war are duplicated in large measure for civilian internees as to standards for food, clothing, housing, medical and religious support, labor, and discipline against civilian internees. An occupying power incurs the same obligation for accountability for civilian internees as a captor has for enemy prisoners of war.

MEANS AND METHODS OF WARFARE

Notwithstanding the adage that "all's fair in love and war," the right to adopt means of injuring the enemy is not unlimited. While there is a sense of fairness, generally the concept has been affected most by military necessity, military efficiency, and common interests of parties to a conflict. The following four areas illustrate the regulation of means and methods of warfare.

Deception　Stratagems and ruses involve acts to deceive an enemy of one's intentions. Deception, defined as those measures designed to mislead enemy forces by manipulation, distortion, or falsification of evidence to induce them to react in a manner prejudicial to their interests, is recognized as legitimate by the law of war, with certain exceptions. Perfidious acts that invite the confidence of an adversary to lead him to believe that he is entitled to, or is obliged to accord, protection under the law of war, are prohibited. Examples are feigning an intent to surrender or negotiate under a flag of truce in order to carry out an attack, or use of the distinctive emblems of the Red Cross and Red Crescent for other than humanitarian purposes.

Environmental Protection　There has been an expression of international concern over certain acts that threaten to do permanent damage to the environment. The 1977 Convention on the Prohibition of Military or Any Other Hostile Use of Environmental Modification Techniques, known as the ENMOD Convention, prohibits engaging in military or any other hostile use of environmental-modification techniques that have widespread, long-lasting, or severe effects as the means of destruction or injury to another nation. The 1977 Protocol I Additional to the 1949 Geneva Conventions prohibits means and methods of warfare that are intended to or may be expected to cause widespread, long-term, and severe damage to the natural environment, thereby prejudicing the health or survival of the population. The terms of the two treaties are not synonymous. Neither the ENMOD Convention nor the 1977 Protocol I was intended to restrict conventional battlefield damage, such as that caused by artillery, armor, or air power.

Chemical Weapons

Following the widespread use of chemical weapons in World War I, there was a movement to banish them from the battlefield. The 1925 Protocol for the Prohibition of the Use in War of Asphyxiating, Poisonous or Other Gases, and of Bacteriological Methods of Warfare, is an absolute prohibition of the use of chemical weapons. However, the treaty does not prohibit the possession of chemical weapons.

Not eager to trust their security exclusively to the written word, many nations possess chemical weapons with a reservation to the treaty retaining the right to use chemical weapons if another nation uses them first. The effectiveness of the deterrent is corroborated by the fact that chemical-weapon use since 1925 usually has been by a nation against an opponent incapable of responding in kind.

The prohibition on chemical-weapons use has created the appearance of an anomaly, in that a nation may use nonlethal chemical weapons, such as riot-control agents, to quell a civil disturbance against its own citizens within its own borders, but may not use them in an international armed conflict. As a result, some nations have retained the right to use riot-control agents on the battlefield where their use would lead to a saving of lives, such as to control rioting prisoners of war, or where civilians are being used by an enemy to mask or screen attacks (in violation of the law of war). Use of riot-control agents remains limited and under strict control, as the use of a riot-control agent may lead an opposing force to believe that lethal chemical agents are being used, and to escalate the level of the conflict by responding with lethal chemical weapons.

For more than a decade, the nations of the world have sought a way to prohibit the possession (and use) of chemical weapons. On 26 August 1992, the United Nations Conference on Disarmament produced its Draft Convention on the Prohibition of the Development, Production, Stockpiling and Use of Chemical Weapons and on Their Destruction, providing for a comprehensive ban of chemical weapons; that document was to be submitted to the United Nations General Assembly for signature and ratification or accession by member nations.

Use of biological weapons also is prohibited by the 1925 Geneva Protocol, as its title suggests. Interest in a comprehensive ban on biological weapons increased in the 1960s. The subject was easier to address, as biological agents are difficult to control and pose as much a threat to a user as to a potential victim. Negotiations by the United States, United Kingdom, and Soviet Union led in 1972 to the Convention on the Prohibition of the Development, Production and Stockpiling of Bacteriological (Biological) and Toxin Weapons and on Their Destruction. It prohibits any possession of biological agents except for small quantities for antidotal purposes.

Nuclear Weapons

The destructive power of nuclear weapons appears to be in direct conflict with the basic law of war concept of discrimination (discussed below), making nuclear weapons illegal per se. However, nuclear weapons never have been classified by any international organization as illegal, and their legality has been confirmed by the many arms control agreements that have been accepted and enforced by international agencies. The issue is one of the law of war staying current with technology, or recognizing nuclear weapons as *lex specialis,* or a special category of law. Nonetheless, United Nations General Assembly Resolution 24 (1968), adopted unanimously, lists three law of war concepts that are applicable to nuclear weapons: (1) that the right of the parties to a conflict to adopt means of injuring the enemy is not unlimited; (2) that it is prohibited to launch attacks against the civilian population as such; and (3) that distinction must be made at all times between persons taking part in the hostilities and members of the civilian population, to the effect that the latter be spared as much as possible.

Nuclear-policy statements made by nuclear powers as to the possible employment of nuclear weapons necessarily must be read as statements of deterrence, which have been successful, rather than as being statements of actual employment intent.

TARGETS

The law of war regarding targeting is divided into issues of the intentional attack of specific individuals and objects, and injury to innocent persons or damage to civilian objects incidental to legitimate combat operations (frequently called "collateral injury" or "collateral damage").

The subject area is derived from the principle of discrimination; that is, the necessity for distinguishing combatants, who may be attacked, from noncombatants, against whom an intentional attack may not be directed, and legitimate military objectives from civilian objects. Although this is a major part of the foundation on which the law of war is built, it remains one of the less codified portions of the law. While there are provisions in Protocol I of 1977 dealing with targeting and military operations in general, they have yet to be tested in combat to determine their feasibility. Those provisions were not applicable in the 1991 Gulf War, for example, as Iraq and the major Coalition members were not parties to Protocol I.

As a general principle, the law of war prohibits the intentional destruction of civilian objects not imperatively required by military necessity, and the direct, intentional attack of civilians not taking part in hostilities. As the basic principle is consistent with the efficient use of military force, nations generally take these proscriptions into account in developing and acquiring weapon systems, using them in combat, and matching available forces and weapon systems to selected targets.

Legitimate targets may be attacked wherever they are located; the presence of civilians will not render a target immune from attack. The legitimacy of a target that is not clearly a military object as such will depend upon a variety of circumstances, including its use at the time or its potential use. Generally, however, legitimate targets have fallen into the following categories:

I. Military
  A. Equipment
  B. Units, bases
II. Economic
  A. Power supplies
  B. Industry (war supporting/import/export)
  C. Transportation
    1. Equipment
    2. Lines of communication (roads, bridges, railroads, airports)
    3. Petroleum, oil, and lubricants
III. Command and control
IV. Geographic (such as a critical mountain pass)
V. Personnel
  A. Military
  B. Civilians taking part in hostilities

An uncodified but similar provision is the concept of "proportionality," previously discussed in several different contexts. In the context of targeting and the concern for collateral civilian casualties, the concept of proportionality prohibits military action in which the negative effects (such as collateral civilian casualties) outweigh the military gain. This balancing may be done on a target-by-target basis, but also may be weighed in overall terms against campaign objectives.

The concept of proportionality acknowledges the unfortunate inevitability of collateral civilian casualties and collateral damage to civilian objects when noncombatant civilians and civilian objects are commingled with combatants and military targets, even with reasonable efforts by the parties to the conflict to minimize collateral injury and damage.

There are several reasons for this. One is the fact that in any modern society, many objects intended for civilian use also may have military purposes, such as roads, railroads, and bridges. The same is true with major utilities; for example, microwave towers for everyday, peacetime civilian communications can constitute a vital part of a military command and control system, while electric power grids may be used simultaneously for military and civilian purposes. When objects are used concurrently for civilian and military purposes, they are liable to attack if there is a military advantage to be gained in their attack. ("Military advantage" is not restricted to tactical gains, but is linked to the full context of war strategy.)

In order to minimize collateral injury to innocent civilians and damage to civilian objects, the law of war imposes specific obligations.

Historically, and from a common-sense standpoint, the primary responsibility for protection of the civilian population rests with the party controlling the civilian population. This is accomplished through separation of military objects from the civilian population, evacuation of the civilian population from the vicinity of immovable military objects, and development of air-raid precautions (such as air-raid shelters). Throughout World War II, for example, both Axis and Allied nations took each of these steps to protect their respective civilian populations from the effects of military operations.

An attacker must exercise reasonable precautions to minimize collateral injury to the civilian population or damage to civilian objects, consistent with mission accomplishment and allowable risk to his attacking forces. The law of war is not a suicide pact in which a nation is expected to expend its military force on frivolous acts of courage to minimize incidental injury to innocent civilians; the standard is one of reasonableness. The defending party must exercise reasonable precautions to separate the civilian population and civilian objects from military objectives, and avoid placing military objectives in the midst of the civilian population. A defender is expressly prohibited from using the civilian population or civilian objects (including cultural property) to shield legitimate targets from attack.

Injury to innocent civilians and damage to civilian objects occur in war, in large measure due to the friction in war between opposing forces. Under the circumstances, a variety of things can occur that may cause collateral damage and injury that is beyond the control of either an attacker or a defender. Combatant force assumes criminal liability for collateral damage or injury only when there is willful and wanton disregard for the safety of the civilian population. Where injury or death of innocent civilians occurs as a result of combat operations, a commander's decision is judged on the basis of the information reasonably available to him at the time, rather than what may become known after the event. This recognizes the "fog of war" in which combat operations are conducted.

WAR CRIMES

Nations have an affirmative obligation to conduct their combat operations in accordance with the law of war, and to discipline those under their control who fail to follow the law. This is not unusual, as military forces depend upon discipline for battlefield success.

The shortcoming comes when a nation intentionally elects to violate the law of war. While many conflicts have been excessively brutal, history has proved that little is gained by violation of the law of war; in essence, there has been negative gain from negative actions.

Where a violation of the law of war occurs, a nation is expected to take prompt action to investigate and bring to justice those who committed the offense. There is no strict liability on the part of a military commander for offenses committed by his or her subordinates. Criminal liability occurs if a commander orders or permits the offense to be committed, or knew or should have known of the offense(s), had the means to prevent or halt them, and failed to do all that he was capable of doing to prevent the offenses or their recurrence.

While war crimes include a variety of traditional offenses, such as refusal to grant quarter (that is, refusal to permit a unit or individual(s) to surrender under any circumstances), the four 1949 Geneva Conventions for the protection of war victims specify a number of offenses as grave breaches, or major felonies. These include torture of protected persons, medical experimentation, and murder.

BIBLIOGRAPHY

General Works For a general background on the law of war and its development, see GEOFFREY BEST, *Humanity in Warfare* (New York, 1980), and WILLIAM V. O'BRIEN, *The Conduct of Just and Limited War* (New York, 1981). The Lieber Code is covered in RICHARD SHELLY HARTIGAN, *Lieber's Code and the Law of War* (Chicago, 1983).

Other useful texts are MORRIS GREENSPAN, *The Modern Law of Land Warfare* (Berkeley, Calif., 1959); MICHAEL HOWARD, ed., *Restraints on War: Studies in the Limitation of Armed Conflict* (Oxford and New York, 1979); FRITS KALSHOVEN, *The Law of Warfare: A Summary of its Recent History and Trends in Development* (Leiden, Holland, 1973); SIR HERSCH LAUTERPACHT, ed., *Oppenheim's International Law,* 7th ed., 2 vols., (London, 1969); JEAN S. PICTET, *Development and Principles of International Humanitarian Law* (Boston, 1985); and JULIUS STONE, *Legal Controls of International Conflict: A Treatise on the Dynamics of Disputes and War-law.* (New York, 1954).

Documents Law of war treaties may be found in ADAM ROBERTS and RICHARD GUELFF, eds., *Documents on the Laws of War,* 2d ed. (Oxford and New York, 1989) and the more comprehensive work by DIETRICH SCHINDLER and JIRI TOMAN, eds., *The Laws of Armed Conflicts: A Collection of Conventions, Resolutions and Other Documents,* 3d rev. ed. (Boston, 1988). THE INTERNATIONAL COMMITTEE FOR THE RED CROSS (ICRC) and the HENRY DUNANT INSTITUTE have produced a substantial bibliography of references on the law of war in *Bibliography of International Humanitarian Law Applicable in Armed Conflict,* 2d. rev. ed. (Geneva, 1987).

Analysis The 1949 Geneva Conventions for the protection of war victims are analyzed in four volumes put out by the ICRC under the general editorship of JEAN S. PICTET entitled, respectively, *Commentary on the Geneva Convention for the Amelioration of the Condition of the Wounded and Sick in Armed Forces in the Field* (Geneva, 1952), *Commentary on the Geneva Convention for the Amelioration of the Condition of the Wounded, Sick and Shipwrecked Members of Armed Forces at Sea* (Geneva, 1960), *Commentary on the Geneva Convention Relative to the Treatment of Prisoners of War* (Geneva, 1960), and *Commentary on the Geneva Convention Relative to the Protection of Civilian Persons in Time of War* (Geneva, 1958). Similar analysis has been provided of the 1977 Protocols by the International Committee of the Red Cross in CLAUD PILLOUD, JEAN DE PREUX, YVES SANDOZ, BRUNO ZIMMERMANN, PHILIPPE EBERLIN, and SYLVIE-S. JUNOD, *Commentary on the Additional Protocols of 8 June 1977 to the Geneva Conventions of 12 August 1949* (Geneva, 1987), and MICHAEL BOTHE, KARL JOSEF PARTSCH, and WALDEMAR A. SOLF, *New Rules for Victims of Armed Conflicts: Commentary on the Two 1977 Protocols Additional to the Geneva Conventions of 1949* (Boston, 1982).

The best treatment of prisoners of war is contained in HOWARD S. LEVIE, *Prisoners of War in International Armed Conflict* (Newport, R.I., 1978) and its companion volume, *Documents on Prisoners of War* (Newport, R.I., 1979). The issue of repatriation is covered in CHRISTIANE S. DELESSERT, *Release and Repatriation of Prisoners of War at the End of Active Hostilities: A Study of Article 118, Paragraph 1 of the 3rd Geneva Convention Relative to the Treatment of Prisoners of War* (Zürich, Switzerland, 1977).

Civilians and occupation law are discussed in DORIS A. GRABER, *The Development of the Law of Belligerent Occupation, 1863–1914* (New York, 1968); and GERHARD VON GLAHN, *The Occupation of Enemy Territory: A Commentary on the Law and Practice of Belligerent Occupation* (Minneapolis, 1957). An excellent analysis of one facet of World War II occupation is ALEXANDER DALLIN, *German Rule in Russia, 1941–1945: A Study of Occupation Policies,* 2d. rev. ed. (Boulder, Colo., 1981). A general history is RICHARD SHELLY HARTIGAN, *The Forgotten Victim: A History of the Civilian* (Chicago, 1982). An interesting modern treatment of occupation law in practice is MEIR SHAMGAR, ed., *Military Government in the Territories Administered by Israel, 1967–1980* (Jerusalem, 1982).

There is a wealth of material on war crimes. The best reference (in addition to the ICRC/Henry Dunant bibliography previously referred to) is JOHN R. LEWIS, ed., *Uncertain Judgment: A Bibliography of War Crimes Trials* (Santa Barbara, Calif., 1979). To endeavor to list a few of the titles would do an injustice to the many works that exist in this subject area.

Targets and targeting are discussed by M. W. ROYSE in *Aerial Bombardment and the International Regulation of Warfare* (New York, 1928), JAMES M. SPAIGHT in *Air Power and War Rights,* 3d ed. (London and New York, 1947), HANS BLIX, "Area Bombardment: Rules and Reasons," *British Yearbook of International Law* 49 (1978): 31–69, and W. HAYS PARKS, "Air Power and the Law of War," *Air Force Law Review* 32 (1990): 1–225. Aerial bombing during World War II has long been a source of debate. For a view that is critical of the United States' concern for the laws of war and that emphasizes the moral and ethical dimensions of that topic, see RONALD SCHAFFER, *Wings of Judgment: American Bombing in World War II* (New York, 1985). That work's bibliography contains citations to other aspects of the debate.

"No-First-Use" Nuclear Policy

○

FEN OSLER HAMPSON

See also The Hot Line: Washington-Moscow Direct Communications Link, 1963 to the Present; The Open Skies Negotiations; *and* The Strategic Defense Initiative and Arms Control.

Most observers credit the beginnings of the debate over "no-first-use" with the publication of the now-famous article "Nuclear Weapons and the Atlantic Alliance," by McGeorge Bundy, George F. Kennan, Robert S. McNamara, and Gerard Smith, in *Foreign Affairs* in 1982. In point of fact, its origins are to be found some thirty years earlier at the dawn of the nuclear age, when the United States government found itself divided over the question of whether to proceed with the development of the hydrogen bomb. Then, as now, the debate was marked by controversy over the broader moral purpose and meaning of nuclear weapons. Then, as now, there were those who shared the conviction that weapons of mass destruction can serve no positive national purpose either politically or militarily. Then, as now, the no-first-use pledge was seen as a way to get military planners to renounce the first use of nuclear weapons and to completely reorient the nation's strategy in the direction of regular forces and strengthened conventional capabilities. Then, as now, the figure of George Kennan loomed large among the advocates of no-first-use.

The underlying elements of continuity in repeated calls for a no-first-use policy with regard to nuclear weapons should not obscure some of the key elements in this debate. In the early years, the idea of no-first-use was linked to the proposals for the development of an international control mechanism over nuclear weapons. When the idea resurfaced in the early 1980s, no-first-use was directed at the North Atlantic Treaty Organization (NATO) and at reorienting its long-standing policy of "flexible response" away from its traditional reliance on nu-

clear weapons toward weapons of final resort. Since then, the idea has been expanded into a comprehensive no-first-use declaratory policy that would cover not just NATO but all U.S. strategic and tactical nuclear forces, including those deployed at sea.

In reviewing the origins and history of the debate over no-first-use, it is useful to focus on the arguments of the proponents and critics of no-first-use. Whether the debate over the years has had much impact on the strategic thinking and various twists and turns in military nuclear strategy is questionable; its advocates did not carry the day. Nevertheless, with the ending of the Cold War and the dismantling of the Warsaw Pact, NATO's declaratory policy has been altered to reflect these new geostrategic realities and transformed into what amounts to a de facto no-first-use nuclear policy. Moreover, progress in superpower arms control is bringing about a corresponding shift in nuclear policy at the strategic level, leading to 50-percent reductions in strategic warheads under the strategic arms reduction talks (START) agreements, which, if followed by additional cuts, would further diminish the strategic and military importance of nuclear weapons.

NO-FIRST-USE AND ATOMIC WEAPONS

The debate over the development of the hydrogen bomb in 1949–1950 in a real way marked the beginning of the debate about the desirability of relying on "first use" of weapons of mass destruction. With the discovery in September 1949 by U.S. weather reconnaissance aircraft that the Soviet Union had detonated an atomic weapon, an intense debate began in the United States about the feasibility and desirability of constructing a "superbomb," or thermonuclear weapon. The Soviet atomic explosion came as a shock to the U.S. government, even though members of the scientific community had predicted in 1945 that it would take the Soviets no more than four to five years to build a weapon of their own. In fact, the Soviet test came exactly four years and six weeks after the first U.S. test of an atomic weapon at the Alamogordo test site in New Mexico. The Soviets were clearly not the "technologically backward nation" many had thought them to be (York, p. 42).

Confronted with the end of U.S. atomic monopoly, a number of options were discussed. The Joint Chiefs of Staff immediately asked for more fissionable material to build up the nation's stockpile of atomic weapons, while a special committee of the National Security Council recommended an accelerated fission-weapons program. Others such as James Conant, who was a member of the General Advisory Committee of the Atomic Energy Commission (AEC), suggested a buildup of U.S. conventional forces in Europe to address the growing Soviet threat. David Lilienthal, the chairman of the AEC, called for a sweeping review of U.S. strategic policies and a revival of the Baruch Plan for the international control of atomic energy, which had been presented in June 1946 and subsequently abandoned in the deepening spiral of mistrust between the United States and Soviet Union in the aftermath of World War II. Finally, another AEC commissioner, Admiral Lewis L. Strauss, along with director Ernest O. Lawrence and Dr. Luis Alvarez of the University of California Radiation Laboratory in Berkeley, argued in favor of the development of a "superweapon" (the H-bomb) that would be many more times powerful than atomic or fission weapons as a deterrent to Soviet aggression and entry into the nuclear age. This last option was eagerly endorsed by Senator Brian McMahon, chairman of the Joint Committee on Atomic Energy of the United States Congress.

At the request of Strauss, the matter was taken up for discussion by the General Advisory Committee of the AEC, which had been created by the Atomic Energy Act of 1946 and whose chairman was J. Robert Oppenheimer, former director of the Los Alamos Laboratory, which had built the first atomic bomb. Oppenheimer had grave doubts about the wisdom and feasibility of proceeding with the superbomb. The committee heard testimony from General Omar Bradley, chairman of the Joint Chiefs of Staff, who wanted to move quickly ahead with development of the H-bomb, and from George Kennan, chief of the Policy-Planning Staff of the State Department, who favored another attempt at international control of atomic energy. Kennan's own views were subsequently elaborated in an internal memorandum he prepared for Secretary of State Dean Acheson, entitled "International Control of Atomic Energy," which was completed on 20 January 1950. The text consisted of seventy-nine double-spaced typewritten pages and was a wide-ranging discussion of the arguments for and against international control and prohibition of atomic weapons, as well as the question of whether to proceed with the development of the superbomb. It was in this memorandum that the idea of a no-first-use nuclear policy, intended to be the first step toward a system of international control of atomic weapons, emerged.

In Kennan's view, the crucial question for the United States was:

Are we to rely upon weapons of mass destruction as an integral and vitally important component of our military strength, which we would expect to deploy deliberately, immediately, and unhesitatingly in the event that we become involved in a military conflict with the Soviet Union? Or are we to retain such weapons in our national arsenal only as a deterrent to the use of similar weapons against ourselves or our allies and as possible means of retaliation in case they are used? According to the way this question is answered, a whole series of decisions are influenced, of which the decision as to what to do about international control of atomic energy and the prohibition of the weapons is only one. (*Foreign Relations of the United States,* vol. 1, p. 29)

Kennan's answer was that "barring some system of international control and prohibition of atomic weapons . . . *some* weapons of mass destruction must be retained in the national arsenal for purposes of deterrence and retaliation." He offered two alternatives: one in which nuclear weapons would be central to U.S. war plans and employed "forthwith and unhesitatingly at the outset of any great military conflict," and one in which nuclear weapons would be regarded as essentially "superfluous to our basic military posture—as something which we are compelled to hold against the possibility that they might be used by our opponents." Kennan then went on to spell out the implications of this second alternative—"only the minimum should be required *for the deterrent-retaliatory purpose*" (emphasis added).

Kennan explained that the "deterrent-retaliatory" function was at best a temporary expedient because the objective would be "to divest ourselves of this minimum at the earliest moment by achieving a scheme of international control." It was clear that he preferred this second alternative but recognized that "any discussion of the military implications of a decision not to rely on the atomic bomb . . . brings up the subject of limitation of conventional armaments" (p. 31). Conventional-arms control, he said, was a vastly more complex undertaking than atomic-arms control, but that political—as opposed to military—means would have to be found to get the Soviets out of Central Europe; thus, the two should not be linked. Moreover, Kennan also believed that for both ideological and practical reasons the Soviets sought to avoid nuclear war themselves and therefore, the United States should begin to reorient its own strategy away from reliance on first-use of nuclear weapons. Although he recognized that military planners were opposed to such a reorientation in U.S. nuclear strategy, "an imperfect system of international control" would be far less dangerous:

If, as I understand to be the case at the present moment, we are not prepared to reorient our military planning and to envisage the renunciation, either now or with time, of our reliance on "first use" of weapons of mass destruction in a future war, then we should not move closer than we are today to international control. To do so would be doubly invidious; for not only would we be moving toward a situation which we had already found unacceptable, but we would meanwhile be making that situation even more unacceptable by increasing our reliance on plans incompatible with it. (p. 35)

Kennan based his conclusion on the conviction that "it would be difficult . . . to hold and develop such weapons at all, to keep them in their proper place as an instrument of national policy" (p. 37). For Kennan, weapons of mass destruction failed to meet any of the traditional criteria for warfare:

Warfare should be a means to an end other than warfare, an end connected with the beliefs and the feelings and the attitudes of people, an end marked

by submission to a new political will and perhaps to a new regime of life, but an end which at least did not negate the principle of life itself. (p. 39)

To those who argued that the difference between conventional and nuclear weapons was only one of degree, he retorted with the words of Shakespeare in *Troilus and Cressida:*

Take but degree away—untune that string
And hark what discord follows:

. . . .

Then everything includes [itself] in power—
Power into will, will into appetite,
And appetite, a universal wolf,
So doubly seconded with will and power,
Must make perforce a universal prey,
And last eat up himself. (1.3.109–124)

Kennan believed that the United States was in grave danger of "hypnotizing" itself into the belief that nuclear weapons "serve some positive national purpose." He argued:

Even if we were to conclude today that "first-use" would not be advantageous, I would not trust the steadfastness of this outlook in a situation where the shadow of uncontrolled mass destruction weapons continues to lie across the peoples of the world. Measured against this alternative, an imperfect system of international control seems to me less dangerous. (pp. 39–40)

Kennan's views were not shared by his superiors. Secretary of State Dean Acheson believed that the Soviets would build their own H-bomb, regardless of what the United States did, and that therefore the United States should proceed with the development of the H-bomb in order to prevent Soviet monopoly over this new technology.

Although the AEC recommended against the development of the H-bomb in its report to President Harry S Truman on 9 November 1949, this recommendation was opposed by civilian and defense leaders, including the powerful and influential Joint Committee on Atomic Energy of the U.S. Congress, chaired by Senator McMahon. On 18 November, President Truman directed a special committee of the National Security Council to study the matter further. The committee's report was delivered to the president on 31 January 1950. The committee recommended continued development of all atomic weapons, including the H-bomb, and a major review of United States strategic policy. The president accepted both of the committee's recommendations. As Samuel Wells notes in "Sounding the Tocsin: NSC-68 and the Soviet Threat" (*International Security* 4, 1979), the debate and subsequent decision to proceed with development of the H-bomb "marked the final stage in forging a consensus among national security policymakers in favor of an atomic strategy" (p. 119).

The Soviet Union

In the 1950s the Soviet Union was the first country to raise the idea of no-first-use in an international forum. At the 1955 Geneva summit meeting, the Soviet Union proposed a reduction of armaments and a prohibition on nuclear weapons, suggesting that pending such a convention, France, Britain, the USSR, and the United States would agree not to be the first to use nuclear weapons against any country. The United States later proposed that parties should not use nuclear weapons unless they were confronted with a conventional attack that could not be stopped with conventional forces. However, the Soviets rejected this proposal.

In 1982 the Soviet Union formally pledged itself to a no-first-use declaration, with the provision that its own nuclear-employment policies would take into account whether other countries followed its own example. This followed earlier declarations by the Soviet Union that it would not use nuclear weapons against any state which does not have nuclear weapons. The United States, France, and Great Britain had also announced that they would not use nuclear weapons against any state which is a party to the Non-Proliferation Treaty and does not possess nuclear arms (Blackaby, Goldblat, and Lodgaard, pp. 9–10).

The Atlantic Alliance

In the early 1980s, no-first-use was resurrected by George Kennan and several other former senior U.S. officials—Robert McNamara, who had served as secretary of defense under Presidents John F. Kennedy and Lyndon Johnson; McGeorge Bundy, national security adviser to Kennedy and Johnson; and Gerard Smith, a U.S. negotiator in SALT I and former head of the U.S. Arms Control and Disarmament Agency. Much had changed in public attitudes since the 1950s when Kennan first expressed his concerns about the political and military utility of nuclear weapons. The 1980s were marked by a groundswell of public op-

position to deterrence and the growing involvement of churches, lawyers, doctors, academics, and peace activists in discussions about the finer points of nuclear strategy. The level of interest and public concern was unparalleled, even when compared to the Cuban missile crisis of 1962, the Middle East crisis of 1973, or the Soviet invasion of Afghanistan in 1979 when superpower tensions were running high.

Unquestionably, the decision by the new administration of President Ronald Reagan in 1981 to embark on the biggest military buildup in peacetime U.S. history fueled this debate. So, too, did the announcement of several major new strategic programs, such as the MX intercontinental ballistic missile and the B-1 strategic manned bomber, and acceleration of such existing programs as the Trident submarine and missile. Underlying these concerns, however, was a growing sense that the arms race was moving to a qualitatively new and more dangerous phase, which, in the words of Randall Forsberg, was brought on by the deployment of weapons systems that would "increase the pressure on both sides to use nuclear weapons in a crisis, rather than risk losing them in a first strike" (quoted in Tucker, p. 62).

The 1982 *Foreign Affairs* article was a seminal contribution to this debate, although in many ways the key arguments merely echoed those that Kennan had so forcefully advanced some thirty years earlier. The authors declared:

It is time to recognize that no one has ever succeeded in advancing any persuasive reason to believe that any use of nuclear weapons, even on the smallest scale, could reliably be expected to remain limited. Every serious analysis and every military exercise, for over 25 years, has demonstrated that even the most restrained battlefield use would be enormously destructive to civilian life. . . . Any use of nuclear weapons in Europe, by the Alliance or against it, carries with it a high and inescapable risk of escalation into the general nuclear war which would bring ruin to all and victory to none. (Bundy et al., p. 757)

Because of the uncontrollable nature of nuclear war, the authors argued that it was essential to widen the firebreak between conventional and nuclear war—a firebreak that had been weakened over the years by the deployment of a wide variety of short- and medium-range nuclear weapons in the European theater by both NATO and the Soviet

Union. "To keep the firebreak wide and strong," they asserted, "is in the deepest interest of all mankind." And thus "it seems timely to consider the possibilities, the requirements, the difficulties, and the advantages of a policy of no-first-use" (p. 757).

The authors made it clear that they were not advocating a withdrawal of the United States' nuclear umbrella from Europe, nor were they advocating any sort of unilateral move to a "minimum" nuclear deterrent posture: "In the absence of agreement on both sides to proceed to very large-scale reductions in nuclear forces, it is clear that large, varied, and survivable nuclear forces will still be necessary for nuclear deterrence" (p. 764). In their opinion, an effective no-first-use policy would require a reassessment and possible buildup of NATO's conventional-force capabilities and a change in its attitude—and especially in the U.S. attitude—toward reduced reliance on nuclear weapons. The authors concluded that the "only nuclear need of the Alliance is for adequately survivable and varied *second strike* forces" (p. 764). No-first-use would not contribute to a significant weakening of NATO's nuclear deterrent capabilities, because "as long as the weapons themselves exist, the possibility of their use will remain" (p. 766).

The authors could not have anticipated the intensity of the reaction to their article: it became a debate that quickly carried over to the other side of the Atlantic. The first broadside attack came from four prominent Germans: Karl Kaiser, director of the German Society for Foreign Affairs in Bonn; Georg Leber, a Social Democrat and vice-president of the West German Bundestag; Alois Mertes, a Christian Democrat and member of the Bundestag Foreign Affairs Committee; and General Franz-Josef Schulze, commander in chief of Allied Forces Central Europe from 1977 to 1979. Their indictment was blunt: "The advice of the authors to renounce the use of nuclear weapons even in the face of pending conventional defeat of Western Europe is tantamount to suggesting that 'rather Red than dead' would be the only remaining option for those Europeans then still alive" (Kaiser et al., p. 1165). They expressed concern that no-first-use would lead to "acceptance of further growth of Soviet nuclear superiority below the intercontinental level" and that this would put "unimaginable" pressure on the governments of Western Europe, should the Soviets try to flex their military muscle. No-first-use would also feed the fires of the European peace movement, which might compromise "the capability of democratic majorities to define and implement security policy in the future" (pp. 1167–1168).

The spectrum of opinion in Western Europe on no-first-use nevertheless ranged quite broadly across the entire political spectrum. Some groups, like elements of the Social Democratic Party (Sozialdemokratische Partei Deutschlands, or SPD) in Germany or the Labour Party in Britain and sections of the peace movement, came out in support of unconditional, unilateral no-first-use. Other defense experts, while generally considering no-first-use to be a good idea in principle, doubted whether NATO would be able to muster the political will and requisite financial resources to build up its conventional forces to compensate for reduced reliance on nuclear weapons. Others viewed no-first-use as part of a long-term security strategy for Europe that would be achieved through arms control and would eventually cover both nuclear and conventional weapons. Still others argued in favor of options that would raise the nuclear threshold short of outright declaration of a no-first-use policy (Krell et al.).

Some U.S. defense analysts suggested that no-first-use might even be counterproductive, producing an effect the exact opposite of the one intended. According to John Mearsheimer, a political scientist at the University of Chicago, a buildup of conventional forces by NATO in response to a no-first-use policy might well be perceived by the Soviets as threatening and as a preparatory step for launching an offensive attack against their own forces in Eastern Europe, thus creating a prescription for disaster such as appeared in the world in 1914. Mearsheimer also argued that no-first-use might create the "false illusion" that nuclear weapons would never be used in a European conflict and that the problem would remain unless, and until, nuclear weapons were eliminated altogether or radically reduced in numbers and eliminated from Europe.

NO-FIRST-USE IN A CHANGING WORLD

The world has changed greatly since the early 1980s, when a no-first-use policy for NATO was first put forward; in many ways, the debate has been superseded by the dramatic turn of events that came at the end of the decade. If 1989 was the year of revolution in Eastern Europe, marking the end of the Soviet empire, 1990 was the year of German reunification, marking the formal end of the post-war division of Europe. The Cold War effectively ended with German reunification, the Gorbachev revolution, and the breakup of the Soviet Union itself and the emergence of the new Commonwealth of Independent States (CIS) in 1991.

At the NATO summit in July 1990, in response to pressure from the allies, NATO decided to modify its long-standing doctrine of flexible response to reflect a reduced reliance on nuclear weapons, by declaring that nuclear weapons would only be used as "truly weapons of last resort" (London Declaration, NATO *Press Communique,* 6 July 1990, p. 5). NATO also committed itself to reduce the role of substrategic nuclear systems of shortest range and to propose the reciprocal elimination of all nuclear artillery shells from both NATO and the Warsaw Pact. In effect, NATO was moving to a de facto no-first-use regime. The intention was, as the London Declaration said, to "profoundly alter the way we think about defense," in accordance with the principle that "in the new Europe, the security of every state is inseparably linked to the security of its neighbors." The summit's formal declaration also specified NATO's commitment to extend its hand to the East by inviting Gorbachev to attend a NATO meeting and establishing a formal liaison between the Warsaw Pact countries and NATO; to modify NATO's defensive doctrine and strategies and replace "forward defense" with a new concept of "defensive defense"; and expand NATO's commitment to arms control and gradually to construct new CSCE institutions for the whole of Europe.

These commitments helped pave the way for the historic July 1990 summit meeting in Stavropol between German chancellor Helmut Kohl and Soviet president Mikhail Gorbachev, at which the Federal Republic of Germany and the Soviet Union agreed on eight points that would terminate four-power (Britain, France, the United States, and the Soviet Union) rights at the time of unification and restore Germany's full sovereignty and prerogatives under the Helsinki Final Act. The Soviets also received assurances that NATO would not station forces or extend its military structures into the territory of the German Democratic Republic, that the size of the Bundeswehr would be limited to 370,000 troops after unification, and that the new united Germany would not have weapons of mass destruction.

These dramatic political developments and changes to NATO declaratory policy also reflected an evolutionary process of arms control, which had seen a gradual downgrading of the nuclear component in NATO forces in Europe. Progress came first in intermediate-range nuclear weapons; on 8 December 1987, President Reagan and General Secretary Gorbachev signed the Intermediate-Range Nuclear Forces (INF) Treaty banning all such U.S. and Soviet land-based forces. This treaty was also historic because of its extensive verification provisions, which would allow, for a period of thirteen years, on-site inspections to monitor missile-production sites of each country.

On 19 November 1990 the culmination of several years of negotiations ended with the signing of two significant arms control agreements: under the umbrella of the Conference on Security and Cooperation in Europe (CSCE), the twenty-two states of the NATO Alliance and the crumbling Warsaw Pact Organization signed the Treaty on Conventional Armed Forces in Europe (CFE) and an accompanying declaration of nonaggression; the thirty-four members of the CSCE also agreed to a new package of confidence- and security-building measures (CSBMS) known as the Vienna Document 1990. The CFE agreements impose equal aggregate numbers of major equipment systems (tanks, armored combat vehicles, artillery pieces, combat aircraft, and attack helicopters) on both sides, and the reduction process, for which the treaty allowed forty months, was to be subject to rigorous inspection without any right of refusal. It was also agreed that a follow-up negotiation, which would be expanded to include the thirty-four members of the CSCE, should aim in the next two years at defining additional measures to limit the personnel strength of the conventional armed forces.

Reductions in nuclear and conventional forces in Central Europe, the further development of a series of confidence-building measures within the framework of the CSCE, and the startling political developments in 1989–1990 that dramatically changed the political map of Europe effectively reduced the risks of a surprise attack and war in Europe. Not only did NATO move to a de facto no-first-use regime, but the political and military pressures of the past, which might have led to a first use of nuclear weapons in the unlikely event of war, were greatly reduced with the withdrawal of Soviet forces from Eastern Europe, easing tensions in East-West relations, and the dissolution of the Warsaw Pact as a formal military alliance.

NO-STRATEGIC-FIRST-USE

Some would argue that these developments, important as they are, do not obviate the need for a no-first-use nuclear policy, because as long as there are nuclear weapons in the world, there will always be the risk that they might be used. After the START agreement, which will reduce strategic offensive nuclear weapons by approximately 50 percent, the United States and the republics of the former Soviet Union would still possess some 12,000 strategic nuclear warheads between them. In fact, even after implementing START-mandated reductions, both nuclear powers will have deployed more strategic warheads than they had at the outset of strategic arms negotiations back in the late 1960s.

In an important article entitled "Back from the Brink" (August 1986 issue of the *Atlantic* magazine), an eminent group of persons, including the authors of the original *Foreign Affairs* article, proposed that "the United States should base its military plans, training programs, defense budgets, weapons deployments, and arms negotiations on the assumption that it will not initiate the use of nuclear weapons" (Bundy et al., p. 35). Unlike some of the earlier proposals, no-first-use was urged not just for NATO but for all U.S. forces deployed around the world. Central to this formulation was a policy of no-strategic-first-use for the United States, namely, "a commitment not to initiate the use of American nuclear weapons based on the U.S. mainland or at sea." Under this policy, the United States would forego the deployment of the MX missile and the Trident D-5 missile and opt for a drastically reduced strategic arsenal. No-strategic-first-use would "significantly alter targeting criteria and the forces needed to destroy these targets. . . . Changes in targeting would reduce the requirement for systems designed to destroy hard targets" (p. 41).

Under an assumption of no-strategic-first-use, the United States would not require the capability to destroy large numbers of Soviet "hard" targets, because "only a disarming first strike could possibly catch Soviet missiles in their silos." The logic behind the argument was essentially the same as that of earlier proposals: "The fundamental problem with the current first-use policy," the authors declared, "is that it misconstrues the nature of nuclear weapons. It assumes that nuclear weapons can fulfill conventional war-fighting roles. But even their most limited use carries an unacceptable risk of escalation to general nuclear war" (p. 40).

The consequences of no-strategic-first-use policy are profound indeed. First, it would lead to greatly reduced numbers of strategic nuclear weapons and very different nuclear targeting requirements. Over the years, the United States' nuclear arsenals have evolved to provide greater flexibility in targeting and "limited" nuclear options through the deployment of a wide range (as well as numbers) of different kinds of weapons systems. Thus, if Russia were to launch a limited nuclear attack against U.S. forces, the United States would—in theory—be able to respond at some level short of a major nuclear exchange. Some argue that based on what we know about the strategic doctrine of the former Soviet Union, the Russians would never resort to limited nuclear attacks; if they were to launch an attack against the United States, it would be a massive one. Thus, a U.S. counterattack would simply be an attack against empty silos. Moreover, to the extent that the United States possesses a vulnerable first-strike force, it would simply encourage the Russians to launch a massive preemptive attack in a crisis. Either scenario is extremely hypothetical. But each has profound implications for the kind of forces that would be required to perform each set of missions. For those who believe in the possibility of a limited nuclear war, counterforce options may be essential and deep cuts in strategic nuclear forces beyond a certain level therefore deemed undesirable because they would limit targeting flexibility. But if this possibility is not realistic, as others contend, then this capability is not necessary and deep cuts are not only possible but indeed desirable. The proponents of no-strategic-first-use side with the latter viewpoint. In the current political climate these scenarios seem even more arcane and far-fetched than they did during the height of the Cold War and the topic of no-strategic-first-use is even more compelling.

Second, important moral questions are raised by a no-strategic-first-use policy. Faced with a limited nuclear attack or the prospects of war where the use of nuclear weapons seemed imminent, which would be the morally defensible position: a retaliatory attack on cities or an attack against the adversary's military forces? Most would opt for the second on the grounds of just-war theory and the innocence of noncombatants, although in practice the distinction may be somewhat blurred because of the collateral damage and the civilian casualties that would result from the use of nuclear weapons even in very small numbers (cf. Nye). To the extent that a flexible and relatively swift retaliatory capability provides this option (i.e., to attack an adversary's military forces rather than his cities), most would argue that this is an option worth retaining— at least until one can abolish nuclear weapons or replace them with something that would preserve deterrence but would be less catastrophic if deterrence failed. As Ashton B. Carter points out, the problem with deep cuts leading

to a "minimum deterrent" of a few hundred warheads deliberately targeted in such a way as to punish an enemy by attacking his cities rather than to remove the threat of his military power by attacking his military forces ... is that minimum deterrence in this sense is morally objectionable. Such an arsenal can only invite violation of the strictures on proportionality and discrimination that Western thinkers long ago established to counter the natural temptation, having decided to resort to force, to use all the force at hand. (p. 241)

Advocates of no-strategic-first-use have not specified how deep strategic nuclear reductions would go or what targets would be the subject of a retaliatory attack in the event nuclear weapons were used. But it is unquestionably the case that such a policy would have profound implications for U.S. strategic policy and the requirements for deterrence, which are already being challenged to the core by the dissolution of the Soviet Union and the elimination of the communist threat to U.S. interests. The burden of proof has therefore fallen on the critics rather than on the supporters of no-strategic-first-use.

CONCLUSION

Although much has changed since no-first-use was initially put on the Atlantic Alliance agenda, the fundamental questions about nuclear weapons have not changed since George Kennan first posed them some forty years ago: "Are we to rely upon weapons of mass destruction as an integral and vitally im-

portant component of our military strength? . . . Or are we to retain such weapons in our national arsenal only as a deterrent to the use of similar weapons against ourselves or our allies and as possible means of retaliation in case they are used?" In the 1990s, political logic began to dictate an affirmative answer to the second one that effectively repudiated much of the Cold War logic and thinking about nuclear weapons.

As the Soviet threat receded, did it still make sense to rely on nuclear weapons in U.S. national military plans to the extent that we did during the Cold War? Against what possible array of threats should nuclear weapons be retained as a means of deterrence? Since Kennan first advanced the idea, proponents of no-first-use have argued that the sole function of nuclear weapons is to act as a deterrent to their use by another nation and that a no-first-use posture would greatly change both the size and composition of nuclear forces by eliminating tactical and counterforce weapons and by bringing about reductions in nuclear weaponry. Much progress has been achieved in meeting these goals, both unilaterally and via joint measures in arms control. NATO's shift to a de facto no-first-use policy was the result of changing political and military circumstances brought about by the disintegration of the Soviet empire in Eastern Europe. Arms control and the rush of political developments have also brought about corresponding reductions in the size and composition of nuclear and conventional forces, thus raising the nuclear threshold and diminishing the likelihood of war in Central Europe. Ironically, at the very time a no-first-use policy for NATO became feasible and practicable (if in all but name), its value appeared to be diminishing because of dramatically changed political circumstances that altered the geopolitical map of Europe and the Eurasian continent.

Nonetheless, large numbers of nuclear weapons continue to remain in the strategic arsenals not just of the republics of the former Soviet Union but other nuclear-weapons states, and the membership of the nuclear club is growing as other states seek to acquire a nuclear-weapons capability. As long as there are nuclear weapons in the world, and as long as states perceive these weapons as having some military value, there will be influential voices who will argue that no-first-use is one way to diminish their importance and reduce the risks of nuclear war.

BIBLIOGRAPHY

The Debate   Renewal of the no-first-use debate began with McGeorge Bundy, George F. Kennan, Robert S. McNamara, and Gerard Smith, "Nuclear Weapons and the Atlantic Alliance," *Foreign Affairs* 60 (1982): 753–765. Kennan's early memo may be found in the U.S. Department of State, *Foreign Relations of the United States,* vol. 1 (Washington, D.C., 1950), pp. 22–45. Frank Blackaby, Jozef Goldblat, and Sverre Lodgaard, "No-First-Use of Nuclear Weapons—An Overview," in their *No-First-Use* (London, 1984), provides a useful survey of the issue. See also Herbert F. York, *The Advisors: Oppenheimer, Teller, and the Super Bomb* (San Francisco, 1976).

A critical response came promptly from Karl Kaiser, Georg Leber, Alois Mertes, and Franz-Josef Schulze, "Nuclear Weapons and the Preservation of Peace: A German Response," *Foreign Affairs* 60 (1982): 1157–1170; and John Mearsheimer, "Nuclear Weapons and Deterrence in Europe," *International Security* 9 (1984–1985): 19–56. Other Europeans were not so unsympathetic; see Gert Krell, Thomas Risse-Kappen, and Hans-Joachim Schmidt, "The No-First-Use Question in West Germany," in John D. Steinbruner and Leon V. Sigal, eds., *Alliance Security: NATO and the No-First-Use Question* (Washington, D.C., 1983).

Strategic Nuclear Weapons Debate   The advocates of no-first-use extended their scope to include strategic nuclear weapons in McGeorge Bundy, Morton H. Halperin, William W. Kaufmann, George F. Kennan, Robert S. McNamara, Madelene O'Donnell, Leon V. Sigal, Gerard C. Smith, Richard H. Ullman and Paul C. Warnke, "Back from the Brink," *Atlantic,* August 1986, pp. 35–41.

This shift prompted responses from U.S. critics of the no-first-use idea, including Richard K. Betts, "Compound Deterrence vs. No-First-Use: What's Wrong Is What's Right, *Orbis* 28 (1985): 697–718; and Robert W. Tucker, *The Nuclear Debate: Deterrence and the Lapse of Faith* (New York, 1985). Two other writers wondered if following this policy would shift targeting away from the enemy's military targets toward the cities and thus raise a new set of ethical issues; see Ashton B. Carter, "Emerging Themes in Nuclear Arms Control," *Daedalus* 120 (1991): 233–250; and Joseph S. Nye, Jr., *Nuclear Ethics* (New York, 1986).

Nuclear-Weapon-Free Zones

○

JOHN R. REDICK

See also Africa; Australia and New Zealand; Demilitarization and Neutralization Through World War II; Latin America; The Middle East; *and* Scandinavia. *Most of the treaties discussed in this essay are excerpted in the* Demilitarization, Denuclearization, and Neutralization *section of Volume III.*

The term *nuclear-weapon-free zone* (NWFZ) lacks an authoritative and empirical definition, although it has been the object of considerable international attention, discussion, and study. Implicit in the term, however, are the following generally accepted elements: (1) nuclear weapons may not be manufactured or produced in the zone; (2) importation of nuclear weapons into the zone by a nation within the zone is prohibited; (3) nuclear-weapon states may not station or store nuclear weapons within the borders of any nation within the zone; and (4) nuclear-weapon states should supply a guarantee, preferably in the form of a formal pledge, neither to use, nor threaten to use, nuclear weapons against the nations forming the zone. In other words, production, importation, or storage of nuclear weapons is prohibited within a NWFZ, and external respect and support are required. Other principles often identified with establishment of a NWFZ are: the initiative for creation of a zone should be indigenous to the states in the region, the zone should be composed of all militarily significant states in the region, and the zone should include effective measures for verification to assure compliance with the agreement.

Nuclear-weapon-free zones, as arms control measures, are a part of the non-proliferation regime, which is defined as those rules, norms, arrangements, organizations, and treaties that have been established to prevent or retard the spread of nuclear weapons. The non-proliferation regime was established gradually, following the failure of post–World War II efforts—such as the Baruch Plan of the late 1940s—to control and eliminate nuclear weapons. At the heart of the non-proliferation regime are the Non-Proliferation Treaty (NPT) and International Atomic Energy Agency (IAEA) safeguards.

The NPT is a global agreement that seeks to limit the number of nuclear-weapon states to those five that existed at the time the treaty came into force (1970): the United States, Great Britain, France, the USSR, and China. Under the NPT, nuclear-weapon states are prohibited from assisting other nations in obtaining nuclear weapons, and non-nuclear-weapon states pledge not to acquire such weapons and to subject their entire nuclear program to the system of accounting and inspection applied by the Vienna-based IAEA.

Nuclear-weapon-free zones complement or parallel the NPT. They may be distinguished from the NPT by their regional scope and by their more stringent prohibitions (i.e., no nuclear-weapon bases). Moreover, the NPT specifically acknowledges the importance of NWFZS in Article VII, which states: "Nothing in this treaty affects the right of any group or states to conclude regional treaties in order to assure the total absence of nuclear weapons in their respective territories."

EARLY PROPOSALS

Nuclear-weapon-free zones have been proposed, beginning in the mid-1950s, for nearly every major region of the world. One of the first proposals—for a central Europe NWFZ—was placed before the

United Nations Disarmament Commission in 1956 by the Soviet Union. The following year Poland, supported by the USSR, Czechoslovakia, and East Germany, submitted what is often referred to as the first substantial NWFZ proposal, the Rapacki Plan, which also called for a zone prohibiting nuclear weapons in central Europe. In 1962 Poland reintroduced the Rapacki Plan at the Eighteen Nation Disarmament Committee (ENDC) in Geneva and, in 1963, modified it (calling for a freeze of nuclear weapons at existing levels) with the submission of the Gomulka Plan. The proposals were found unacceptable by Western nations that viewed them as prejudicial to their security interests.

In addition to supporting the Central Europe proposal, the Soviet Union, in 1959, advanced a series of plans for denuclearization of the Nordic area (Denmark, Sweden, Norway, and Finland), the Balkans, and the Middle East. In 1963 the Soviets also submitted a proposal for a NWFZ in the Mediterranean area. The Soviet programs were put forward at the U.N. and other international fora. Similar plans were advanced by other nations, including Romania (1957 and 1959) and Bulgaria (1958) with respect to the Balkans. In 1961 Sweden proposed a NWFZ for the Nordic area, and this was followed by similar proposals by Finland in 1963 and 1965.

In 1957, the Soviet Union proposed the establishment of a NWFZ for the Pacific area. This plan was endorsed, at the time, by both India and the People's Republic of China. In the South Pacific some Australian political leaders advocated a NWFZ in the early 1960s, but the real momentum leading to a treaty did not begin until the mid-1970s. In Africa, stimulated by French nuclear tests in the Sahara, a U.N. General Assembly resolution calling for a NWFZ was passed as early as 1961. In 1964, the Organization of African Unity reinforced this by calling on all nations to respect Africa as a NWFZ. Finally, and most significantly, in Latin America in 1963, the presidents of Bolivia, Brazil, Chile, Ecuador, and Mexico issued a joint declaration for a NWFZ—an initial step that led to the signing of the Treaty for the Prohibition of Nuclear Weapons in Latin America (Treaty of Tlatelolco) in 1967.

As the aforementioned suggests, numerous proposals for NWFZS were discussed and advanced for many geographic areas during a particularly active decade beginning in the late 1950s. Cold War politics, and the fear that this tension could escalate into a nuclear war, clearly stimulated interest in NWFZS. The Soviet Union's proposals for NWFZS were generalized and opportunistic, having as a primary objective the removal of U.S. nuclear bases situated near Soviet borders. The Soviets were particularly adept at utilizing NWFZ proposals for advancing other foreign-policy objectives (such as securing a non-nuclear Germany and preventing the installation of U.S. intermediate-range missiles elsewhere) and for purely propaganda gains in nonaligned countries.

In contrast, the United States frequently found itself in the uncomfortable position of opposing NWFZ proposals as potentially disruptive to its security arrangements. The many Soviet proposals for NWFZ in this early period had the result of forcing the United States to define its criteria for support of zones: (1) the initiative for the zone must originate within the area concerned; (2) the zone should include all states in the area whose participation is deemed important (i.e., militarily significant nations); (3) creation of the zone should not disturb existing military arrangements; and (4) the NWFZ agreement should include provisions for controlling alleged violations. These U.S. criteria have remained generally constant for more than two decades.

In contrast, Soviet criteria for support of NWFZS were less extensive and based primarily on two considerations: (1) the readiness of other nuclear-weapon states to respect the nuclear-weapon-free status of the region, and (2) the completeness and effectiveness of the obligations of the parties to the NWFZ. While many NWFZ proposals in this earlier period were advanced and resisted due to Cold War politics, the situation differed in other regions. Nuclear-weapon-free zone proposals for Africa, Latin America, and Scandinavia were advanced by the indigenous nations, with the objective of keeping nuclear weapons out of their areas and preventing their regions from being targeted by nuclear-weapon states. For example, factors affecting support by African nations for a NWFZ in their area were: opposition to British, French, and U.S. military bases in northern Africa; the French nuclear tests in the Sahara; and a particular concern regarding the growing nuclear capacity of South Africa.

For Latin America a variety of motives prevailed, but a principal catalyst was the 1962 Cuban missile crisis in which Latin American nations found themselves helpless bystanders as a nuclear war between the U.S. and the Soviet Union threatened to break out in their own region. In Scandinavia a NWFZ proposal enjoyed a measure of support from all of the states in the region, also owing to a desire to minimize danger of nuclear conflict in the region. Progress was hindered, however, by differing political relationships: two nations being NATO members (Norway and Denmark), one neutral (Sweden), and the other linked to the Soviet Union (Finland).

NWFZs IN NON-POPULATED AREAS

While early NWFZ proposals were affected by U.S.-Soviet rivalry, progress was achieved in denuclearizing three nonpopulated areas: Antarctica, outer space, and the seabed. For these three regions, multilateral agreements exist that include, as part of their requirements, a prohibition of nuclear weapons in a specific area or environment.

The Antarctic Treaty has been described as the forerunner to all NWFZ agreements owing to its precedent-setting provisions demilitarizing a significant area. The treaty was signed in 1959 and entered into force in 1961. The purpose of the treaty is to assure that the continent is used exclusively for peaceful purposes and to set a framework for continued scientific research by interested nations in the area. Article 1 provides that the continent will be limited to peaceful purposes and all measures of a military nature are prohibited. Article 5 prohibits any nuclear explosions or disposal of nuclear wastes subject to possible future international agreements. Taken together, the provisions of Articles 1 and 5 are generally interpreted as establishing the continent as a de facto NWFZ. Another innovative element of this early agreement is a verification system whereby the contracting parties may conduct aerial inspections and have complete access at all times to all areas and installations. In 1990, there were twenty-five parties to the Antarctic Treaty.

After nearly ten years of discussion in the U.N. General Assembly and in the Geneva-based multilateral disarmament sessions, the Outer Space Treaty was signed and entered into force in 1967. As the name implies, the objective was to assure that the exploration and utilization of space would be carried out in a peaceful, cooperative fashion. The substantive treaty provisions relevant to NWFZs include: prohibition of the placement in earth orbit, on the moon or other celestial object, or to otherwise station in space, nuclear or other weapons of mass destruction; and prohibition of use of the moon and other celestial bodies for military bases

or installations, or the testing of military weapons of any kind (Art. 4). As of 1990, ninety-one nations had signed the treaty, and a total of sixty-three had ratified the agreement.

The objective of the Seabed Treaty is to prevent the introduction of nuclear weapons onto the seabed beyond territorial waters. The treaty, initially advanced by Malta in 1967 in the U.N. General Assembly, was signed in 1971 and entered into force in 1972. Article 1 prohibits parties from placing nuclear weapons or weapons of mass destruction on the ocean floor beyond 12 miles, or 19.2 kilometers (the "seabed zone"). The extent of the territorial seas was a divisive issue during the negotiations, with some nations defining it as 3 miles (4.8 kilometers) and others as much as 200 miles (320 kilometers). For purposes of the treaty, 12 miles was defined as the "seabed zone" not subject to the restrictions of the treaty. Verification procedures (Art. 3) include individual observations undertaken by parties using their own means, followed by consultations with other parties in the event of a suspected violation. A serious violation not resolved by consultation is referred to the U.N. Security Council.

Article 5 of the Seabed Treaty calls for continued efforts by the parties to negotiate further agreements assuring the complete demilitarization of the seabed and ocean floor. Article 7 required a review conference to be held five years after the treaty's activation to assess the success of the agreement. The first such conference occurred in 1977, followed by two similar sessions in 1983 and 1989. Eighty-nine nations have signed and sixty-six have ratified the agreement; a fourth review conference was scheduled for 1996.

EXISTING NUCLEAR-WEAPON-FREE ZONES

There are also two treaties that have been designed specifically to meet the regional desires of nations who do not wish to become involved in any nuclear conflict. These treaties involved Latin America and the South Pacific.

Treaty for the Prohibition of Nuclear Weapons in Latin America (Treaty of Tlatelolco) The Treaty of Tlatelolco was signed in 1967; by 1992, it had been ratified by twenty-seven Latin American states of which twenty-three are full parties. The Latin American NWFZ was the first established in a populated region. The full parties to Tlatelolco include several nations, such as Mexico, Colombia, and Peru, which have small, but growing nuclear programs.

Under the provisions of Tlatelolco, the parties pledge to keep their territories free of nuclear weapons; not to test, develop, or import such weapons; to prevent foreign-controlled nuclear weapon bases from being established in the region; and to negotiate IAEA safeguards. Four Latin American nations—Argentina, Brazil, Chile, and Cuba—are not full parties to the treaty. Argentina signed, but did not ratify, whereas Cuba neither signed nor ratified. Brazil and Chile technically ratified the agreement but, under the complex ratification arrangements of the treaty, their adherence is conditional in that it will not come into force until the treaty is ratified by all Latin American nations.

In addition, for the treaty to come into force, two additional protocols must be signed and ratified by non-Latin American nations. One was designated for those nations having territorial interests in the Americas (Great Britain, France, the Netherlands, and the United States). Such states were asked to pledge "to apply the status of denuclearization in respect to warlike purposes" for their territories within the geographic zone of the treaty. Protocol I has been ratified by the United States, Great Britain, and the Netherlands, and has been signed, but not ratified, by France.

Protocol II applies to the nuclear-weapon states and requires them "not to use or threaten to use, nuclear weapons against the Contracting Parties of the Treaty for the Prohibition of Nuclear Weapons in Latin America." The nuclear-weapon states also pledge not to engage in any activities that might lead to violations of the treaty obligations by the Latin American parties (i.e., not to introduce nuclear weapons to the region via bases, etc.). The five known nuclear-weapon states all ratified Protocol II: the United States, the Soviet Union, Great Britain, France, and China. While no reservations to protocol ratification are permitted, several non-Latin American countries have included certain "interpretive declarations" with their ratification that have included points considered unacceptable to some Latin American nations. These differing interpretations continue to complicate the efforts to bring Argentina and Brazil fully into the treaty.

The treaty's control system was established under Article 12 and is outlined in Articles 13–18. The goals of the control system are overseen by an organization based in Mexico City, the Agency for the Prohibition of Nuclear Weapons in Latin America (OPANAL), and the IAEA, which applies international safeguards. OPANAL is comprised of three elements: a general conference, at which all parties are represented and that meets every two years; a council of five members elected by the general conference for four-year terms, which meets periodically in Mexico City; and a secretariat, under the leadership of a general secretary, which coordinates the work of the two bodies and serves as the official spokesman of OPANAL.

A critically important element of the Tlatelolco control system is Article 13, which provides that a nation shall negotiate bilateral safeguards agreements over its nuclear programs. All Tlatelolco parties concluded safeguards agreements, with the exception of several small Caribbean nations having no nuclear facilities. The question of the type of safeguard agreements to be negotiated, however, has become an issue to some countries such as Argentina and Brazil. These nations, which refused to enter the Non-Proliferation Treaty (NPT), also objected to the fact that the Tlatelolco Treaty establishes a NPT-type safeguards system. Argentine and Brazilian officials argued that the IAEA should have a safeguards system uniquely designed to the requirements of Tlatelolco parties, including protection of industrial secrets and other proprietary information.

The control system also mandates (Art. 14) that obligatory semi-annual reports be made by the Tlatelolco parties to OPANAL, pledging that no activities in violation of the treaty have occurred. In addition, the general secretary may require special reports (Art. 15) from the parties on events related to compliance with the treaty. A particularly innovative element of the control system provides for the undertaking of "special inspections" (Art. 16) in the territory of any party suspected of a treaty violation. Special inspections may be administered either by the IAEA or the secretariat, under the direction of the council. Parties agree to cooperate with the inspections, providing full and free access to all areas. To date no party has availed itself of the inspection-by-demand provision, but its potential activation provides an additional dimension to the Tlatelolco Treaty.

The Latin American NWFZ exists within the boundaries of the twenty-three parties to the agreement. As noted earlier, Tlatelolco has a complex ratification procedure that reflects the creativity of the father of the treaty, Alfonso García Robles, the Mexican diplomat who was awarded the Nobel Peace Prize in 1982 for his efforts. Under the terms of the treaty, (Art. 28, par. 1), the NWFZ comes into full effect when ratified by all Latin American states and when accompanying protocols are ratified by nuclear-weapon states and countries having territorial interests in the Americas. All parties, however, have the right to waive any or all of the requirements of Article 28, paragraph 1, thereby allowing the treaty to come into force for each of their national territories.

As Argentina and Brazil have a clear nuclear-weapon potential, their relationship to the Tlatelolco Treaty is one of critical importance to the future of the Latin American NWFZ. Brazil ratified but did not choose to waive Article 28, paragraph 1; consequently, the treaty is not in force for Brazil. Argentina signed, but did not ratify, Tlatelolco. Its traditional concerns have centered on retaining its rights under the treaty to detonate underground (so called "peaceful") nuclear devices, the type of safeguards arrangements, protection of industrial secrets, and the "interpretations" expressed by nuclear-weapon states when signing and ratifying Protocol II. In a dramatic reversal of policy, however, Argentina and Brazil jointly announced, in November 1990, their intent to undertake initiatives to permit the Treaty of Tlatelolco to come into full force for their territories. On 12 February 1992, on the occasion of the twenty-fifth anniversary of the signing of the Treaty of Tlatelolco, Argentina and Brazil proposed some amendments to the treaty. These amendments, considered technical in nature and not prejudicial to the objectives of the treaty, have been endorsed by Chile, and are expected to be approved by all Tlatelolco parties.

Assuming Argentina, Brazil, and Chile join the Tlatelolco regime, Cuba would remain the lone Latin American holdout. Cuban opposition to any form of cooperation with the treaty had not appreciably altered since the early phases of the negotiating process, until the early 1990s. Cuban demands have, in the past, included the return of the Guantanamo military base and the removal of U.S. nuclear weapons alleged to exist in the Caribbean area (a charge denied by the U.S.). The U.S.-Soviet rapprochement, followed by the collapse of the Soviet Union as well as considerably reduced Russian financial and political support, softened Cuban opposition to the treaty. Cuba's growing isolation, and the decision by Argentina and Brazil to ratify the treaty, all contributed to a Cuban announcement in 1992 to ratify Tlatelolco (following completion of Argentine and Brazilian ratification).

A final remaining obstacle to full implementation of the Latin American NWFZ is the failure of France to complete ratification of Protocol I. French reticence has generally been attributed to its concern that adherence would set a precedent adversely affecting its continued nuclear-testing program in the South Pacific region. France, however, announced a moratorium on all nuclear testing in 1992, as well as its intent to ratify Protocol I.

The Latin American NWFZ has made a significant contribution toward the broadly shared objective of preventing further proliferation of nuclear weapons. It has done this both through its accomplishments within the Latin American region, and by its capacity as a model for similar initiatives in other regions, such as the South Pacific. While, as noted above, there remain clear shortcomings, the zone is supported by most Latin American nations and appears to be progressing toward universal regional adherence.

The South Pacific Nuclear-Free-Zone Treaty (Treaty of Raratonga)

The Raratonga Treaty was signed on 6 August 1985 (the fortieth anniversary of the bombing of Hiroshima). It entered into force on 11 December 1986, upon ratification by the eighth South Pacific state. As of 1992 there were eleven South Pacific parties to Raratonga, and two nuclear-weapon states had ratified treaty protocols. Raratonga is the second NWFZ established in a populated area and is closely modeled on Tlatelolco (although having certain important distinctions). The two most militarily significant Raratonga parties are Australia and New Zealand. Other parties include the Cook Islands, Fiji, Kirbati, Nauru, Niue, Papua New Guinea, Western Samoa, the Solomon Islands, and Tuvalu.

The incentive for creation of a NWFZ in the South Pacific was the desire by the regional nations to pressure France to cease its underground nuclear-testing program on Mururoa Atoll in the Tuamoto Archipelago and to prevent radioactive-waste disposal in the region. The first concerted action for creation of a zone was a resolution introduced by nine South Pacific nations and passed by the U.N. General Assembly in 1975. While the concept elicited much regional interest, it was not until the coming to power of the Labour party in Australia in

1983 that a NWFZ assumed real political force. At that point Australia, with the support of New Zealand, encouraged creation of a working group of the South Pacific Forum (a regional intergovernmental coordinating mechanism) to negotiate the main provisions of the agreement.

The South Pacific NWFZ comprises a large oceanic area, one continent (Australia), and many islands. None of its parties is a near-nuclear-weapon state, that is, none of them has the nuclear capability necessary for the rapid development of nuclear weapons. By contrast, the Latin American zone covers a large land area, inclusive of some ocean. Within the Latin American region, but not yet fully part of the zone, are nations considered potential nuclear-weapon states. The principal provisions of the Raratonga Treaty are analogous to Tlatelolco: the complete prohibition of the acquisition, manufacture, testing, and stationing of nuclear weapons in the region. In addition, Raratonga relies on the IAEA to verify that nuclear materials and facilities in the region are not used for nuclear weapons, as does Tlatelolco. While Tlatelolco's language suggests IAEA safeguards apply to all facilities, Raratonga is explicit in stating that safeguards shall "be equivalent in its scope and effect to an agreement required in connection with the NPT" (Art. 8, Annex 2, par. 1).

Another similarity between the two treaties is the provision for special inspections under specific circumstances (if a prohibited act is suspected). The manner in which this would be undertaken, however, highlights a difference between the agreements. Raratonga does not set up a separate secretariat as does Tlatelolco but instead relies on the South Pacific Forum. Specifically, Raratonga permits the director of the secretariat of the South Pacific Forum, at the request of a party, to call a meeting that, with support of two-thirds of the parties, may result in authorization of a special inspection.

Both Tlatelolco and Raratonga leave it to the individual parties to decide on port visits by foreign ships that may carry nuclear weapons. Raratonga's language on this point is explicit, whereas Tlatelolco's is more implicit (and was reaffirmed by the United States in its ratification of Protocol II).

Distinct differences exist in certain areas between the two NWFZs. As noted earlier, Tlatelolco is, at best, ambiguous regarding so-called "peaceful" nuclear explosions (i.e., underground nuclear explosion testing alleged to have no military intent), leading to differing interpretations on this point between some Latin American and protocol parties. Raratonga has no such ambiguities: it specifically bans nuclear explosions, whether deemed weapons or "peaceful." Raratonga also includes a provision forbidding parties to dump radioactive waste anywhere in the zone, or to permit dumping in their territorial seas, and calls for a regional convention specifically prohibiting dumping in the region. The concern of South Pacific nations on this point is due to possible Japanese interest in establishing a waste-disposal facility in the area. Tlatelolco is silent on the issue of waste disposal. Other distinctions include the withdrawal period (Tlatelolco requires three months' advance notice; Raratonga, twelve months) and nuclear-export provisions. On the latter point, Raratonga requires, as a condition for nuclear exports or cooperation, that the recipient state accept NPT-type safeguards. Tlatelolco has no such requirement.

Raratonga also includes three protocols for non-regional nations to guarantee the nuclear-weapon-free status of the zone. Protocol I commits nations with territories in the South Pacific (United States, France, United Kingdom) to apply the treaty's basic non-proliferation prohibition to their territories in the zone. Protocol II calls for all the nuclear-weapon states not to contribute to any act that violates the treaty or its protocols, nor to use or threaten to use nuclear explosives against any party. Protocol III forbids the signatories from testing nuclear explosives anywhere within the zone.

China and the Soviet Union have adhered to the relevant protocols, whereas the United States, the United Kingdom, and France have not. The French refusal rises directly from its intent to continue its nuclear testing program in French Polynesia. France does not wish to test nuclear devices in France and, consequently, views its South Pacific testing program as a required component of its independent nuclear force. France's moratorium on all nuclear testing, announced in 1992, drew strong approval from Raratonga parties. Although the Raratonga Treaty meets traditional U.S. requirements for support of a NWFZ, the failure of the United States to give its support apparently derives from a desire not to offend France, and to avoid encouraging further movements opposed to nuclear weapons in the South Pacific region.

The South Pacific NWFZ has considerable importance as an arms control mechanism due to several factors. First, while not all nuclear-weapon states have adhered to the agreement, the treaty will help prevent the stationing of nuclear weapons in the region. Given the clear expression of support by the regional states for the zone, it is highly unlikely any nuclear-weapon state will seek to introduce nuclear weapons in territories it may control in the region.

Second, the Raratonga Treaty has particular merit as a contribution to the peace and security of regions adjoining the South Pacific, notably Indonesia, Malaysia, and the Southeast Asian area. While Australia is not generally considered a near nuclear-weapon state, it has the potential resources and technological skill to develop a nuclear arsenal, should it so choose. The fact that Australia, an NPT party, has fully embraced a regional NWFZ sends an important message to potential rivals such as Indonesia.

Third, the South Pacific zone may serve to stimulate similar initiatives in adjoining areas. In this regard, the Association of South East Asian Nations (ASEAN), an intergovernmental coordinating body that is somewhat similar to the South Pacific Forum, has followed the progress of Raratonga closely and may seek to establish a similar zone in its region.

POTENTIAL NUCLEAR-WEAPON-FREE ZONES

A number of regions have been proposed for creation of future NWFZs. This section describes the current status and prospects for the most serious proposals.

Central Europe   The Rapacki and Gomulka plans, proposed by Poland for a NWFZ in central Europe, were considered unacceptable by the Western powers, and serious discussion ended by 1964. The Rapacki and Gomulka plans included components for freezing and reducing both nuclear as well as conventional armaments. These plans were eventually succeeded by the Vienna Conference on Mutual Force Reductions begun in 1973 and other associated measures in central Europe. The signing of the 1987 Intermediate-Range Nuclear Forces (INF) Treaty by the United States and the USSR eliminated a whole class of nuclear-delivery vehicles that were largely European-based. The Treaty on the Reduction of Conventional Armed Forces in Europe (CFE), signed in November 1990 by sixteen NATO

and six Warsaw Treaty Organization countries, was yet another important step in the creation of a new post–Cold War, European security system. Continued East-West negotiations affecting nuclear weapons in Europe have, in effect, been overtaken by the pace of change in the former Soviet Union and new disarmament initiatives undertaken by the U.S., its NATO allies, and Russia. On 27 September 1991, President Bush declared the U.S. would unilaterally remove and destroy all ground- and naval-launched nuclear weapons from Europe, while retaining a limited air-mounted nuclear capability for NATO. On 5 October 1991, President Gorbachev declared that the Soviet Union would eliminate short range ground- and naval-launched nuclear warheads in Europe and elsewhere, and proposed further U.S.-Soviet negotiations to limit air-launched nuclear weapons. On 17 October 1991, the NATO Ministry of Defense announced a decision to reduce, by 50 percent, free-fall nuclear weapons (i.e., those lacking guidance and propulsion systems) deployed in the U.S. and Belgium, Netherlands, West Germany, Italy, and Turkey. Following the demise of the USSR in 1991, Russia and the three other republics with nuclear weapons on their soil declared their intent to withdraw all tactical nuclear weapons and send them to Russia for dismantling. Three of the four republics (Russia, Belarus, and Ukraine) border on Europe and, consequently, this action impacted on the process of eliminating nuclear weapons from central Europe.

Middle East   In 1974 Iran formally proposed that the U.N. General Assembly consider the question of the establishment of a Middle East NWFZ. The proposal drew the strong support of Egypt, which suggested three basic principles that have continued to frame most discussions of a Middle East NWFZ: (1) states of the region should refrain from producing, acquiring, or possessing nuclear weapons; (2) nuclear-weapon states should refrain from introducing nuclear weapons into the region or using nuclear weapons against any state in the region; (3) an effective international safeguards system, affecting both the nuclear-weapon states and the states within the region, should be established.

In 1974, a resolution calling for a Middle East NWFZ was passed by the U.N. General Assembly. While Israel initially opposed the General Assembly action, by 1980 it shifted tactics and allowed the resolution to be adopted without a vote. Israel's posture, however, has been that a Middle East NWFZ can only be achieved as a result of direct negotiations between the states of the region. Arab nations have been unwilling to enter into direct discussions for this objective unless broader issues between Israel and the Arab states can be resolved.

In 1984 the principal supporters of the U.N. resolution introduced a variation in its text emphasizing the central role of the U.N. in establishment of a zone and requesting the secretary general to seek views of all parties regarding implementation of the resolution. This request was incorporated into subsequent resolutions adopted by the General Assembly the following year.

In 1988 Egypt again sought to give momentum to the concept by introducing a new proposal at the U.N. Special Session on Disarmament. The Egyptian proposal called on all regional and nuclear-weapon states to declare publicly their intent not to introduce nuclear weapons into the area; stated that the secretary general should appoint either a personal representative or group of experts to work with regional states to explore the parameters of a model draft treaty; and maintained that the IAEA should prepare a study regarding verification and inspection measures that would be necessary for an effective Middle East NWFZ.

The Egyptian proposal, pursued in the IAEA and the 1988 regular sessions of the General Assembly, did help stimulate some useful results. These included a 1989 IAEA technical study on how safeguards might be applied to a Middle East NWFZ and a formal General Assembly resolution calling for the secretary general to commission an expert study on establishment of a zone. The study, which was to take into consideration the views and suggestions of member states (as requested by the 1984 General Assembly resolution), was completed and approved by the forty-fifth U.N. General Assembly in 1990. Following the Persian Gulf War in 1991, U.S. President Bush announced (29 May 1991) a Middle East Arms Control Initiative which, among other things, called on the states in the region to implement a verifiable ban on the production and acquisition of weapon-usable materials and to adhere to the NPT. The proposal would place all nuclear facilities in the region under IAEA safeguards and supports eventual establishment of a Middle East NWFZ.

The U.N. expert study, the Persian Gulf War, and President Bush's Middle East Arms Control Initiative suggest that achievement of a Middle East NWFZ will require both the will of the states in the region (bitter enemies divided by a legacy of wars) and the active involvement of major nonregional nations. Among the measures deemed necessary to achieve a zone are the following: consensus between the states in the region that there will be no test of a nuclear explosive device; reaffirmation of support for the NPT by all current Middle East parties to that agreement; a considerably enhanced and more effective IAEA safeguards system applied to their nuclear programs; acceptance by Israel of safeguards on its principal nuclear facilities; an agreement that there will be no attacks on nuclear facilities; and strong security assurances by the nuclear-weapon states neither to threaten nor to attack states in the zone with nuclear weapons.

Such activities can serve as part of a series of confidence- and security-building measures (CSBMS), including negotiations among the regional states and active leadership by the nuclear-weapon states. Realization of a Middle East NWFZ would also have to be pursued in concert with regional initiatives to control biological and chemical weapons and missile-delivery systems.

Africa   In 1960 the French government tested its first nuclear-explosive device in the Sahara, an event that served as a catalyst for an initiative by eight African nations to create a NWFZ in the region. The following year, fourteen African states proposed, and the U.N. General Assembly approved, a resolution calling for Africa to be considered a denuclearized zone and for all U.N. members to refrain from conducting nuclear tests in Africa. In 1964, the summit conference of the heads of state of the Organization of African Unity (OAU) approved a declaration on the denuclearization of Africa, in which they declared their readiness to undertake an agreement not to produce or acquire nuclear weapons, and called for all non-African nations to respect the declaration. In 1965 the U.N. General Assembly again passed a resolution calling for denuclearization of the region, which gained nearly unanimous support including that of all nuclear-weapon states except France.

For the next nine years there was little formal activity to create an African NWFZ. In 1974, however, twenty-six African nations reintroduced the resolution in the U.N. General Assembly. The resolution was unanimously endorsed. France gave its support, having shifted its nuclear testing from the Sahara to islands in the Pacific region. The General Assembly again passed a resolution in 1975 under the leadership of Nigeria. In 1976, however, the initiative assumed a new dimension due to the concern by African nations regarding the nuclear-weapons capability of South Africa. Since that point, the issue of creating a NWFZ in Africa has essentially merged with the issue of South African nuclear-weapons development; progress has been minimal. Studies carried out under the auspices of the U.N. Institute for Disarmament Research (UNIDIR) and the U.N. Disarmament Commission have contributed to the widespread perception by African nations of a South African nuclear-weapon program, with the possible cooperation of Israel.

The impasse, however, began to show signs of change in 1988 when the South African president stated that his nation might consider signing the NPT, thereby placing its entire nuclear program under IAEA safeguards. The gradual dismantling of apartheid in South Africa, which began in 1988, helped to reduce tensions between South Africa and its neighbors. In addition, the agreement between South Africa and its regional neighbors signed in late 1988, focusing on Angola and Namibia, and the withdrawal of Cuban forces from the area, significantly contributed to South Africa's sense of security. On 10 July 1991, the South African government acceded to the NPT, and the following September concluded the required full-scope safeguard agreement with the IAEA to cover its entire nuclear program. In addition, the front-line black African nations of Mozambique, Angola, and Zimbabwe have ratified the NPT, thus removing additional obstacles to the creation of a sub-Saharan NWFZ in Africa.

Southern Asia   The 1974 Indian test of a so-called peaceful nuclear explosive (PNE) was quickly followed by a Pakistani proposal in the U.N. General Assembly for creation of a South Asia NWFZ. Pakistan maintained that most of the necessary conditions for a zone already existed since all states in the region had made unilateral declarations not to acquire, develop, or manufacture nuclear weapons; moreover, they opposed foreign introduction of nuclear weapons into the area and continued to be strong supporters of multilateral efforts for effective nuclear disarmament.

India objected to the Pakistani proposal and each year thereafter has opposed General Assembly resolutions supporting such a zone. India argued that the proposal was flawed because it was not the result of prior consultations and agreement among the countries in the area. India also questioned the validity of Southern Asia as a subregion of Asia and the Pacific. India, instead, argued that a NWFZ makes little sense due to the existence of a nuclear weapon state (China) in Asia, nuclear testing in the Pacific, the presence of foreign military bases (such as the U.S.-administered Diego Garcia Island in the Indian Ocean), and the presence of nuclear weapons on U.S., British, and Russian naval vessels in the area.

Despite broad support among U.N. member nations, the South Asian NWFZ proposal has remained stalled due to India's opposition. Pakistan's proposal for a NWFZ represents one of many nuclear-arms-control initiatives that it has suggested to India at various times, including bilateral NPT ratification; joint acceptance of full-scope IAEA safeguards; a bilateral inspection arrangement of all nuclear facilities; and mutual pledges not to develop nuclear weapons. India has viewed the Pakistani proposals as a means of restraining India's nuclear-weapon program while buying time to proceed with its own program. Further, some Indian policy-makers do not wish to acknowledge Pakistan as being on an equal footing, while they continue to view China as a potentially significant nuclear threat.

A South Asian NWFZ will probably occur only as a result of a series of successful confidence-building measures between India and Pakistan. A tentative first step was taken in 1988 when the two nations signed an agreement not to attack each other's nuclear installations. In the early 1990s several events occurred that tended to undercut India's unyielding nuclear policy. These included the collapse of its ally of nearly thirty-five years, the Soviet Union, the adherence of China, France, and South Africa to the NPT, and the agreement by Argentina and Brazil to join the Latin American NWFZ and accept full-scope IAEA safeguards. The U.S. called on India to engage in a five-nation (U.S., Russia, China, India, and Pakistan) regional discussion that might lead to agreement on a NWFZ in South Asia. While India did not agree, and its bilateral relations with Pakistan are periodically tense, many observers believe that a regional NWFZ agreement may yet prove possible, assuming continued support for the concept by the nuclear-weapon states.

Other Areas   As noted earlier, NWFZ have been proposed for many regions, but few have generated much political momentum. Those which could possibly develop in the future include the Balkans, the Nordic area, and Southeast Asia. A Balkans NWFZ, which might be comprised of Albania, Bulgaria, Romania, Yugoslavia, and possibly Greece and Turkey, was proposed by Romania in 1957. In 1963 the Soviet Union reiterated the earlier Romanian proposal for convening a conference to establish a Balkan-Adriatic NWFZ.

In the 1968 Conference of Non-Nuclear Weapon States, Bulgaria, Yugoslavia, and Romania proposed the convening of a conference to consider establishing a NWFZ in the Balkans; Romania repeated the proposal at the 1978 United Nations Special Session on Disarmament. The failure of the Balkan nations to pursue the NWFZ objective by either convening such a meeting or introducing a proposal as a U.N. General Assembly item (the traditional manner of encouraging international discussion and building support for a NWFZ), as well as the breakup of Yugoslavia, suggests a regional agreement is not likely.

The Nordic area has been the object of a number of NWFZ proposals. In 1961 the Swedish foreign minister, Öster Undén, presented a proposal for such a zone. Finland, under President Urho Kekkonen, vigorously pursued the concept throughout the 1960s, although it gained only limited official acceptance from the other regional nations. While the Nordic area has not been marked by sharp antagonisms, differing political relationships exist between the area states and nations outside the area. These differing political relationships have tended to inhibit plans for a Nordic NWFZ. Finland's foreign policy has tended to be one of prescribed neutrality due to its relationship with the Soviet Union, as outlined in the Russo-Finnish Agreement of Friendship, Cooperation, and Mutual Assistance in 1948. Sweden has remained carefully neutral, whereas Denmark and Norway have been part of NATO.

The Soviet Union supported the concept of a Nordic NWFZ, whereas the United States has opposed it as disturbing its existing military relationships. In the 1990s, with the collapse of the Soviet Union and the Warsaw Pact, dramatic reductions in nuclear weapons, the withdrawal of most nuclear weapons from central Europe, and the gradual reorientation of NATO, the rationale for a separate Nordic NWFZ became less compelling.

A Southeast Asian NWFZ could evolve from the Association of South East Asian Nations (ASEAN), composed of Thailand, the Philippines, Singapore, Malaysia, and Indonesia. ASEAN's focus has been primarily in the area of trade, although there have been indications of growing regional security cooperation. Singapore, Malaysia, and Indonesia have traditionally been part of the nonaligned nations, whereas Thailand and the Philippines have had limited defense ties with the United States. A South Asian NWFZ modeled after the Raratonga Treaty remains a distinct possibility.

ZONES OF PEACE

The concept of a zone of peace encompasses a nuclear-weapon-free zone but is more extensive. As is true of the NWFZ concept, zones of peace lack a precise definition. A 1981 United Nations study of regional disarmament identified several elements that characterize the zone-of-peace concept: removal of the zone from interference by extrazonal states and from the global arms race; maintenance of regional peace and security by political cooperation and military restraint among the regional nations; promotion of regional cooperation in the economic and political fields; and respect and support on the part of extrazonal states for the zone. In other words, a zone of peace is more comprehensive and flexible than a NWFZ since, in addition to disarmament, it includes positive measures of cooperation in other areas. Moreover, in the disarmament area, zones of peace refer to non-nuclear measures as well, such as conventional arms control and removal of foreign military bases.

Indian Ocean Zone of Peace   Zone-of-peace proposals initially were rooted in the efforts of the nonaligned nations. The first proposal was made by Ceylon (Sri Lanka) at the Cairo nonaligned nation meeting in 1964 calling for a zone of peace (which emphasized denuclearization) in Africa, the Indian Ocean, and the South Atlantic. In 1970 Sri Lanka proposed an Indian Ocean zone of peace at the Lusaka nonaligned-nation meeting. In the following year, the U.N. General Assembly, again on the initiative of Sri Lanka, declared the Indian Ocean a zone of peace. The resolution also called on all nations (notably the U.S. and USSR) to enter into consultations with the littoral states of the Indian Ocean to halt the further escalation and expansion of their military presence in the Indian Ocean and to eliminate from the area all bases, military installations, logistical supply facilities, and nuclear weapons and weapons of mass destruction.

The proposal was overwhelmingly supported, although four of the five nuclear-weapon states (United States, Great Britain, USSR, and France) abstained. In subsequent years, the Soviet Union shifted its position to support the resolution, whereas the United States, and Great Britain have opposed it. The Indian Ocean Zone of Peace is not tightly defined. It does not specify prohibition of nuclear weapons in the territories of the littoral states of the Indian Ocean but, instead, is directed toward discouraging nuclear activities by the nuclear-weapon states in the Indian Ocean. In the view of its supporters, the concept includes elimination of foreign nuclear bases in the Indian Ocean (such as Diego Garcia), but is unclear as regards transit of nuclear weapons on ships through the ocean.

In 1979 the littoral and hinterland states of the Indian Ocean agreed to the principles of a zone of peace. They also agreed to convene a conference on the Indian Ocean to include all affected nations, with the objective of establishing a zone of peace. An Ad Hoc Committee on the Indian Ocean including Security Council Permanent Members, littoral nations, and other major maritime users was to undertake the preparations. Due to a lack of agreement among the members of the Ad Hoc Committee, to date the proposed conference has been continuously postponed.

South Atlantic Zone of Peace

While the concept of a South Atlantic zone of peace dates from the 1960s, since the Falkland/Malvinas conflict in 1982 there has been greater interest. In 1985 the president of Brazil, José Sarney, initiated discussion of the zone, suggesting that continued naval military buildup in the region would inevitably result in the proliferation of nuclear weapons in the region. In the following year the Brazilian president sent messages to the heads of state of nine countries in the South Atlantic area (Latin America and Africa) stressing their shared interest in the region's peace, security, and economic and social development.

On the initiative of Brazil, with fourteen regional cosponsors, the forty-first U.N. General Assembly in 1986 passed a resolution declaring the Atlantic Ocean in the regions between Africa and South America should be a zone of peace and cooperation. The resolution included specific reference to the nonintroduction of nuclear weapons or other weapons of mass destruction into the region. In an accompanying statement, the Brazilian foreign minister drew a direct connection between the South Atlantic zone-of-peace proposal and the treaties of Tlatelolco and Raratonga, as well as the continued effort to create an African NWFZ.

Argentina, owing to the disastrous war in the South Atlantic, cosponsored the proposal. African nations viewed the proposal with favor due to their concern with South Africa and the situation in Namibia. The resolution was passed with only one dissenting vote, that of the United States. The U.S. opposition was due to the fact that the resolution did not apply to the territories of the littoral and hinterland states of the South Atlantic and could be interpreted as imposing restrictions on naval access to, and activity in, the South Atlantic. The proposal was supported by China, the Soviet Union, and the United Kingdom, with France abstaining. (France joined in support of the resolution in 1989.)

In 1988 Brazil hosted a meeting of States of the Zone of Peace and Cooperation of the South Atlantic. Attended by twenty-one nations from Africa and Latin America, the meeting helped generate continued interest by the regional states, which have, subsequently, sponsored annual General Assembly resolutions endorsing the zone.

In contrast to the Indian Ocean zone, the geographical scope of the proposed zone has not been precisely defined, nor have the sponsors called for formal multilateral negotiations leading to an international treaty establishing a zone. The preference of the regional nations for a more flexible and gradual approach is derived, in part, from the difficulty in establishing an Indian Ocean zone of peace. The acceptance of non-proliferation agreements in the early 1990s by three littoral states (the Treaty of Tlatelolco by Argentina and Brazil, and the NPT by South Africa) enhanced the prospects for eventual realization of the objectives of the South Atlantic zone.

CONCLUSION

Nuclear-weapon-free zones have made a useful contribution to efforts to extend the influence of arms control and disarmament. In nonpopulated areas the direct impact, however, is minimal: only in the Antarctic area are the restrictions apparently fully effective. Efforts to ban nuclear weapons from other nonpopulated regions such as space, or the oceans, have met partial success.

In populated areas, the Latin American and South Pacific NWFZ treaties are genuine accomplishments, despite certain limitations. While neither zone is, as yet, fully effective, the Tlatelolco and Raratonga treaties have contributed significantly to the peace and security of their regions.

The effectiveness of future NWFZS as arms control and disarmament mechanisms will depend on how such arrangements respond to certain basic issues. There must be a generally accepted understanding among the parties as to what constitutes a nuclear weapon. In the view of most experts, the distinction between a so-called peaceful nuclear-explosive device and a nuclear weapon is meaningless, and the prohibition must be complete, applying to any nuclear explosive device. In addition, the ban must extend to stationing of nuclear weapons within the zone, even if under the control of a nuclear-weapon state.

The question of transit of nuclear weapons through the territory of a zone is subject to differing interpretations. Both Tlatelolco and Raratonga permit movement of nuclear weapons, under the control of a nuclear-weapon state, through the territory of a party. Tlatelolco, for example, has been interpreted as leaving the matter to the sovereign decision of each party. While some nations view this as a substantial weakness, most authorities believe such latitude to be a practical necessity and as not compromising the basic objectives of a NWFZ.

The respect and support of nuclear-weapon states is fundamental to the effectiveness of a NWFZ. Tlatelolco and Raratonga have sought this support in the form of formal protocols that the nuclear-weapon states are requested to sign and ratify. These protocols constitute a nonuse or negative guarantee by the nuclear-weapon states that they will not use, or threaten to use, nuclear weapons against a party. While desirable, such formal guarantees by all nuclear-weapon states are not a requirement for substantial progress on a NWFZ agreement. France's failure, for instance, to ratify protocols for both Tlatelolco and Raratonga did not prevent the establishment of a NWFZ in either region, comprised of the territories of those parties that have chosen to accede to the agreement. In other words, while the support of all nuclear-weapon states is highly desirable for the complete effectiveness of the zone, the timing and even the nature of this support may vary without necessarily compromising the effectiveness of the zone.

An adequate system of verification and control is essential for a NWFZ to be an effective arms control and disarmament mechanism. Such a system must assure confidence among states within the zone and among nations outside the region. The nature of the verification procedures may vary from region to region. The Tlatelolco and Raratonga treaties rely on IAEA safeguards to verify the nondiversion of nuclear material to nuclear-explosive devices. The safeguards applied under Raratonga are identical to those of the NPT (full-scope), whereas Tlatelolco does not clearly specify the scope of the IAEA safeguards. Parties to NWFZS may also institute additional verification procedures, including arrangements for performing special inspections (as in the case of Tlatelolco). Alternatively, existing regional or international organizations may be employed for some verification activities.

The termination of the protracted Cold War and the dramatic improvement in East-West relations significantly decreased the probability of a global nuclear conflict in the 1990s. Continued progress toward reductions in nuclear weapons, and a halt in nuclear testing, will enhance prospects for international peace and security. An improved international climate enhances opportunities for regional confidence-building initiatives, especially NWFZS. In such a climate, nuclear-weapon states are less inclined to deploy nuclear weapons to the remaining troubled regions, and they are more likely to offer binding guarantees of support for indigenous nuclear-weapon-free zone arrangements.

BIBLIOGRAPHY

General Studies The definitive international study of NWFZS is United Nations Special Report of the Conference on the Committee on Disarmament, *Comprehensive Study of the Question of Nuclear-Weapon-Free Zones in All Its Aspects,* U.N. Doc. A/10027, Add.1 (New York, 1976). A more recent U.N. study, though focused on the Middle East, is also an excellent general source of information: Report of the Secretary General, *Establishment of a Nuclear-Weapon-Free Zone in the Region of the Middle East,* U.N. Doc. A/45/435 (New York, 1990). Other sources for general information on NWFZS include: U.N. DEPARTMENT OF PUBLIC INFORMATION, *Nuclear-Weapon-Free Zones (New York, 1977);* DAVID PITT and GORDON THOMPSON, eds., *Nuclear-Free*

Zones (New York, 1987); G. DELCOIGNE, "An Overview of Nuclear-Weapon-Free Zones," *International Atomic Energy Agency Bulletin* 24:2 (June 1982). One of the best overviews of NWFZS is K. G. M. GRAHAM, "Nuclear-Weapon-Free Zones as an Arms Control Measure," Ph.D. diss., Victoria University of Wellington, New Zealand (1983). *The United Nations Disarmament Yearbook* is also an excellent annual source of information on NWFZS.

Particular Regions The most useful published material on nuclear-weapon-free zones is devoted to particular areas or regions. For the Latin American nuclear-weapon-free zone, the following publications are particularly useful: ALFONSO GARCÍA ROBLES, *The Denuclearization of Latin America* (Washington, D.C., 1967); ALFONSO GARCÍA ROBLES, *The Latin American Nuclear-Weapon-Free Zone,* (Muscatine, Iowa, 1979); H. GROS ESPIELL, "The Non-Proliferation of Nuclear Weapons in Latin America," *International Atomic Energy Agency Bulletin* 22 (August 1980): 81–85; JULIO CÉSAR CARASALES, "The Future of Tlatelolco 20 Years After Its Signature," and ANTONIO STEMPEL PARIS, "OPANAL and the Treaty of Tlatelolco," both of which appeared in *Disarmament* XI (Winter 1987/1988): 74–84, 86–91, respectively; JOHN R. REDICK, "The Tlatelolco Regime and Non-Proliferation in Latin America," *International Organization* 35 (Winter, 1981): 103–134; JOHN R. REDICK, "Latin America: Reducing the Threat of Nuclear Proliferation," *Wisconsin International Law Journal* 5 (June 1987): 79–107.

The text of the Treaty of Raratonga may be found in an excellent study authored by WARREN H. DONNELLY, *Two Approaches to Establishing Nuclear-Weapon-Free Zones: A Comparison of the Treaties of Tlatelolco and Raratonga,* Congressional Research Service, Library of Congress (Washington, D.C., 1987). Other studies on the South Pacific include: RODERIC ALLEY, *Nuclear-Weapon-Free Zones: The South Pacific Proposal,* (Muscatine, Iowa, 1977); PAUL F. POWER, "The South Pacific Nuclear-Weapon-Free Zone," *Pacific Affairs* 59 (Fall 1986): 455–475; GREG FRY, "The South Pacific Nuclear-Free-Zone: Significance and Implications," *Bulletin of Concerned Asian Scholars* 18 (April–June 1986): 61–72; and DAVID MCDOWELL, "The Treaty of Raratonga," *Disarmament* XI (Winter 1987/1988): 93–104.

In respect to the proposed Middle East NWFZ, the principal document is the United Nations study cited above. See also MOHAMED SHAKER, *Establish-ment of a Nuclear-Free Zone in the Middle East* (paper presented at the International Meeting for the Establishment of Nuclear-Free Zones, Berlin, 20–23 June 1988, issued by the Congressional Research Service, Library of Congress). An IAEA study is also of particular value, *Technical Study on Different Modalities of Applications of Safeguards in the Middle East* (29 August 1989). See also ZACHARY DAVIS and WARREN H. DONNELLY, *A Nuclear-Weapons-Free Zone in the Middle East: Background and Issues,* (Washington, D.C., 1992).

The African NWFZ is discussed in WILLIAM EPSTEIN, *A Nuclear-Weapon-Free Zone in Africa?* (Muscatine, Iowa, 1977). The Scandinavian area is covered in OSMO APUNEN, "Nuclear-Weapon-Free Zones, Zones of Peace and Nordic Security"; KALEVI RUHALA and PAULI JARVENPAA, "A Nordic Nuclear-Free Zone: Prospects for Arms Control in Northern Europe"; and YURI KOMISSAROV, "The Future of a Nuclear-Weapon-Free Zone in Northern Europe," in the FINNISH INSTITUTE OF INTERNATIONAL AFFAIRS, *Yearbook of Finnish Foreign Policy, 1978* (Helsinki, 1979). For the Balkans area see PERI PAMIR, "The Quest for a Balkans Nuclear-Weapons-Free-Zone," in DAVID PITT and GORDON THOMPSON, eds., *Nuclear-Free Zones* (New York, 1987). An excellent source of background information regarding recent nuclear disarmament measures, as they affect Europe, is STEPHEN W. YOUNG, RONALD J. BEE, and BRUCE SEYMORE II, *One Nation Becomes Many: The ACCESS Guide to the Former Soviet Union* (Washington, D.C., 1992).

The South Asian area has been the subject of several Pakistani proposals that are well documented in various United Nations resolutions reported in the annual publication, *United Nations Disarmament Yearbook*.

Zone-of-Peace Proposals Zone-of-peace proposals are discussed in an excellent recent study, EDMUNDO FUJITA, *The Prevention of Geographical Proliferation of Nuclear Weapons: Nuclear-Weapon-Free Zones and Zones of Peace in the Southern Hemisphere,* (Geneva, 1989). The Indian Ocean zone-of-peace proposal is contained in documents available from the United Nations, especially those of the Ad Hoc Committee on the Indian Ocean, as reported in the *United Nations Disarmament Yearbook*. The South Atlantic zone-of-peace proposal is less well documented, the best source being the FUJITA study and the original U.N. General Assembly documentation.

Preventing Accidental War

○

LAURA S. HAYES HOLGATE

See also Confidence-Building Measures in Europe: 1975 to the Present; The Hot Line: Washington-Moscow Direct Communications Link, 1963 to the Present; "No First Use" Nuclear Policy; The Open Skies Negotiations; *and* The Strategic Defense Initiative and Arms Control. *Most of the treaties discussed in this essay are excerpted in Volume III.*

In the nuclear age, the perception that nuclear war is unthinkable as a purposeful policy has drawn many individuals to feel that an accidental war—war not intended yet sparked by an accident or misunderstanding—is the more likely route to a nuclear exchange. A handful of diplomatic and in some cases military efforts has resulted in the effort to reduce the possibility of an accidental war. Although many of these arrangements focus on superpower, and hence nuclear, relations, the concern for accidental war predates the nuclear age. Throughout the seventeenth, eighteenth, and nineteenth centuries there was concern for the potential for wars through misperception or accident. It was thought, however, that traditional diplomatic means—rather than specific agreements—could deal with that possibility.

History holds few instances of accidental wars. The advent of nuclear weapons, however, has greatly raised the stakes of accidental war, primarily because of the immensely destructive nature of the weapons and the heightened concern due to the premium placed on striking first—in order to ensure survival or to preempt an attack. The pressure for haste may prevent leaders from waiting for clarification of uncertainties or from communicating with rival leaders. Knowing that the other side is under similar pressures compounds the incentive to attack preemptively. The combination of ambiguity and pressures for haste could prompt a nuclear exchange even when rivals strongly desire to avoid a war; similar logic applies to conventional forces as well.

One approach to reducing these tensions has been to make each side's forces more survivable against an enemy's first strike, thereby reducing the incentive to "use them or lose them" and affording each side the opportunity to consider a situation carefully before taking irreversible action. Diplomatic efforts to prevent accidental war are the flip side of the same coin. Hence, many of these efforts consist of measures to increase the time available for judgment in a crisis, to increase information available to leaders, and to improve communication in times of tension. This article traces some of the most significant attempts to codify these principles through agreements and action.

THE HOT LINE AGREEMENT

The 1962 Cuban missile crisis—in which a U.S. blockade caused the Soviet Union to remove missiles from Cuba—was an all-too-realistic demonstration of the potential for escalation in a crisis and the dangers of misperception, miscommunication, and lack of information. In circumstances in which neither side had sought war, the United States and the Soviet Union came perhaps as close as they ever have to nuclear war. Shaken by the experience, leaders of both nations took up serious negotiations on the basis of proposals advanced earlier that year at the United Nations Eighteen Nation Disarmament Conference. From these wide-ranging approaches to the question of disarmament, the superpowers eventually agreed to negotiations of a measure to improve communications between their leaders.

This 1963 agreement, officially known as the Memorandum of Understanding between the United States of America and the Union of Soviet Socialist Republics Regarding the Establishment of a Direct Communications Link, became known as the Hot Line Agreement. The popular image of a red telephone connecting Washington and Moscow belies the actual mechanism of teletype machines connected by dedicated lines and backed up by radio connections. This print-based technology was chosen because it was felt that instantaneous communication by voice could reveal more than was intended or create difficulties of inaccurate translation. The process of drafting written responses was intended to increase the care taken with messages sent over this system, thereby avoiding impetuous or thoughtless statements.

The Hot Line Agreement improved upon the sometimes improvised and unreliable lines of communication used by President John F. Kennedy and Soviet Premier Nikita Khrushchev during the Cuban missile crisis. Improved communications are understood to prevent war by allowing national leaders to make their intentions clear to each other in a timely and accurate fashion. Critics argue that such communications would only be the source of disinformation tactics and could be used to lull the enemy with reassuring messages while taking hostile action. Although such a scenario could occur in the case of intentional war, these concerns would not apply when leaders genuinely wished to avoid war. In such cases, the hot line could be used to clarify actions that could be perceived as hostile, as occurred in its most discussed use during the 1967 Arab-Israeli war, in which U.S. and Soviet leaders depended on the hot line to clarify an accidental Israeli strike on a U.S. naval vessel stationed near Soviet ships.

Apparently British and French leaders also have thought the idea of direct communication with the Kremlin is a good one. They subsequently established London-to-Moscow and Paris-to-Moscow direct, secure communications links. India and Pakistan, too, have established a similar communications system.

The Hot Line Agreement, and subsequent agreements upgrading the technological capabilities to include facsimile transmission and satellite links, encountered little opposition in the United States. In contrast to later arms control efforts, these measures remained relatively free from politicization and have generally operated quietly in the background of superpower politics.

ACCIDENTS MEASURES AGREEMENT

The best known result of the Strategic Arms Limitation Talks (SALT) is the Anti-Ballistic Missile (ABM) Treaty. These negotiations also included discussions aimed at preventing accidental war. The 1971 Accidents Measures Agreement was negotiated in discussions held parallel to the main talks on limiting weapons and reflected the similarities and differences in U.S. and Soviet approaches to the problem of accidental war. U.S. proposals tended to stress the technical details of military operations, while the Soviets preferred sweeping political pledges.

The Accidents Measures Agreement sought to reduce the likelihood of nuclear accidents and to arrange procedures to minimize the chance of war should such accidents occur. Its articles committed each side to improve procedures to prevent unauthorized or accidental nuclear explosions, reflecting a need felt by both sides to increase the safety and security of their nuclear operations. Despite Soviet reluctance to reciprocate, the United States described its precautions in a fair amount of detail, feeling that reassuring the Soviets, and possibly helping them improve their own security procedures, was worth the price of any advantage the Soviets might glean from the information.

Both sides pledged to notify each other immediately of possible unauthorized or accidental detonation of a nuclear weapon as well as to provide for notification in cases where unidentified triggers of early warning systems or signs of interference threatened war between the two nations. The U.S. and the USSR also agreed to constraints on military activities by requiring advance notification of missile test launches in the direction of the other party. This provision reflected a mutual concern that missile tests could be interpreted as the opening volley in a nuclear exchange. Discussions also revealed a common interest in measures, that each nation could undertake to reduce potential misinterpretations in cases of unexplained nuclear incidents. These agreements should be recognized as promises to take action in ways each nation would determine for itself. No provisions were made for verification of these promises. The agreement was signed in Washington, D.C., on 30 September 1971.

The sides were unable to agree on measures to address provocative attacks by other nuclear powers. The United States perceived Soviet attempts to establish cooperative measures to prevent and react to such attacks as damaging to U.S. relations with nuclear allies Britain and France, and especially to the planned but still secret opening to China. The United States also blocked several Soviet overtures to include other nations in the agreement for similar reasons. France and Britain, however, established similar bilateral understandings on accidents measures with the USSR in 1976 and 1977, respectively.

BASIC PRINCIPLES AGREEMENT

Eight months after the Accidents Measures Agreement was signed, President Richard M. Nixon traveled to Moscow to join Soviet Premier Leonid Brezhnev in signing the ABM Treaty, in addition to the less well-known Basic Principles Agreement (BPA). This 1972 statement was a general document meant to codify the terms of the U.S.-Soviet détente. The BPA reflects the great importance placed by Soviet diplomats on general statements of principle. The generality of the BPA permitted both sides to express their own conceptions of détente without addressing the significant inconsistencies between those conceptions. Negotiated under the shadow of Vietnam, the Soviet efforts to establish "peaceful coexistence" as the basis of U.S.-USSR relations seemed to Nixon hypocritical in light of Soviet support of so-called wars of national liberation around the world. Nevertheless, Nixon acquiesced to the Soviet phrase while inserting his own loaded language calling on the Soviets to eschew "efforts to obtain unilateral advantage" and to "exercise restraint" in the practice of foreign policy. This ambiguity enabled each side to feel that its point of view had been legitimized by the agreement. Little effort was made on either side to translate these general pledges into operational guidelines for be-

havior, and the nebulous agreement was difficult to implement.

The Soviets nevertheless saw the BPA as an important achievement, owing primarily to its phrases committing the U.S. to achieving "normal relations" with the Soviet Union on the basis of "equality." Soviet leaders interpreted these agreements as formal acknowledgment of Soviet strategic parity with the United States and as commitments by the Americans to treat the Soviet Union as a political and diplomatic equal. Such interpretations were not shared or intended by U.S. leaders, who continued to reject the notion of the Soviet Union as a superpower peer and who placed little importance on the BPA itself.

AGREEMENT ON THE PREVENTION OF INCIDENTS AT SEA

The May 1972 Nixon-Brezhnev summit also produced a more concrete agreement designed to ease the operational consequences of superpower rivalry. Throughout the 1960s and early 1970s, U.S. and Soviet naval commanders had engaged in harassment such as buzzing enemy ships with aircraft, aiming guns at vessels, nudging or "shouldering" hostile ships, and an occasional game of "chicken," in which two rival ships threaten to ram each other, turning aside at the last possible moment. These incidents, whether inadvertent or instigated for political signaling purposes, posed dangers both of injuring vessels or personnel and of provoking an actual military engagement between the superpowers. One set of international guidelines already existed to prevent collisions at sea, known collectively as the "Rules of the Road." The idea of a bilateral agreement to reduce dangerous incidents, however, originated in a 1967 U.S. proposal that was ignored until the Soviets in 1970 suggested opening negotiations the following year.

An unusually well-prepared and high-level U.S. team arrived in Moscow with instructions to clarify and expand the Rules of the Road—a change from most earlier negotiations, in which the Americans tended to listen to the Soviet proposals before offering their own. The Soviet negotiators included several high-ranking naval officers, indicating a clear interest in the talks, and perhaps freeing them from some political restrictions. The delegations' seriousness and preparation facilitated rapid progress, with the major disagreement being limited to Soviet proposals for a "distance formula" restricting how close aircraft and ships could approach enemy vessels. The United States refused to accept such a formula, fearing excessive constraints on its surveillance activities, and the Soviets eventually dropped their demand in exchange for promises of future discussions of the distance issue. Both nations agreed to limit their negotiations to only surface ship and aircraft activities, leaving submarine operations unfettered.

The resulting document, Agreement on the Prevention of Incidents at Sea (INCSEA), serves several purposes. In regulating dangerous maneuvers, it reaffirms the Rules of the Road and requires ships to give each other wide berths, particularly during aircraft takeoffs and landings. To restrict other types of harassment, INCSEA forbids simulated attacks, the shining of searchlights on bridges, buzzing by aircraft, and other hazardous activities. Communication at sea has been increased by using international signals to indicate operations and intentions and through prior notification of marine activities that present a danger to nearby ships or aircraft (for example, missile testing or naval exercises). Most important, INCSEA establishes channels for regular consultation and for an information exchange about dangerous incidents, perhaps preventing political escalation by permitting concerns to be addressed between the militaries themselves.

Signed in 1972 with relatively little controversy or publicity, INCSEA has been considered successful, contributing to a reduction of dangerous incidents from over one hundred per year in the late 1960s to forty in 1973. Despite several more hostile incidents during the early 1980s, the 1984 review meetings in Moscow indicated continued acknowledgment of INCSEA's success by naval officers on both sides.

AGREEMENT ON PREVENTION OF NUCLEAR WAR

The second Nixon-Brezhnev summit in June 1973 in Washington, D.C., was the occasion for signing the Agreement on the Prevention of Nuclear War (APNW). In the complex negotiations for this agreement, the Soviets again raised the issues of pledg-

ing nonuse of nuclear weapons against each other and of cooperating to prevent nuclear provocation by other nuclear powers. The United States continued to resist these notions, given their disastrous implications for NATO strategy, which included the option of first use of nuclear weapons, and for U.S.-China relations. The United States was extremely wary of any agreement that would give the impression of joint superpower domination of the rest of the world. U.S. Secretary of State Henry Kissinger was eventually able to redirect the negotiations toward provisions to avoid nuclear war, such as renouncing the use of force in diplomacy and pledging to consult in situations that contain the risk of nuclear war. The two nations further agreed to consult with each other in situations that posed a risk of nuclear war.

Like the BPA and the Accidents Measures Agreement, the APNW lacked specific guidelines for behavior in any particular case, and few, if any, efforts were made to translate the agreement into operational reality. The ambiguities and generalities of the BPA and the APNW were broad enough to encompass two widely divergent views of the purposes of crisis-prevention agreements. While both sides shared an interest in reducing the likelihood of nuclear war for its own sake, the U.S. and the USSR differed in their conceptions of the effects of the agreements on superpower behavior in third world conflicts. Nixon and Kissinger hoped to constrain Soviet involvement in these "wars of liberation" by focusing on the perceived potential for escalation to nuclear war, including these "wars" in the definition of actions that should be avoided. The Soviets, however, saw the agreements to ease nuclear tensions as making the world safer for their activities in the third world by reducing the threat that the West would react to those activities with nuclear weapons. Despite these fundamental differences, the agreements were hailed as important evidence of détente and of nuclear-war prevention.

THE HELSINKI ACCORD

The Conference on Security and Cooperation in Europe (CSCE) was an ambitious multilateral assembly that sought to set the terms for interstate behavior and to establish a framework for continuing East-West contact. The CSCE was to legitimize and codify the European post–World War II status quo as well as establish guidelines for its peaceful evolution. Originating in a Soviet proposal and subsequent Warsaw Pact–NATO dialogue in the early 1970s, the thirty-five-nation negotiations opened with a ministerial meeting in Helsinki in June 1973 and continued in an intricate arrangement of committees and subcommittees in Geneva from 1973 to July 1975, when the Final Act, the Helsinki accord, was signed in Helsinki. These wide-ranging agreements covering a vast number of issues are divided into three "baskets": Basket I contains ten standards for international behavior and some limited military confidence-building measures (CBMS); Basket II includes measures for cooperation on economic, scientific, and environmental issues; and Basket III holds the well-known and controversial agreements on human rights as well as educational and cultural exchanges.

In contrast to Soviet enthusiasm—and in particular, that of Premier Brezhnev—for a CSCE agreement recognizing its Eastern European satellites and other existing boundaries, the U.S. reaction was lukewarm at best. Nixon and Kissinger saw in CSCE an easy way to satisfy Soviet demands in exchange for more concrete gains in other areas of concern, such as in the strategic-arms limitation efforts, which they viewed as the central definition of the U.S.-Soviet relationship. This lack of interest was reflected in the low profile taken by the U.S. delegation. The United States wanted to conclude the CSCE quickly and at times angered the Europeans by seeming to undercut their leverage. As détente began to fade in early 1975, however, the U.S. joined its European allies in a tough negotiating stance to exact several Soviet concessions and to pave the way for the summit in July of that year.

Those elements of the Helsinki accord dealing more broadly with improving superpower relations and decreasing tension in Europe may contribute in a general way to preventing accidental war, but the most relevant aspects of the agreement are the CBMS in Basket I. These measures provide for prior notification of major military maneuvers of 25,000 or more troops in Europe and in the westernmost 250 kilometers (150 mi.) of the USSR. Other agreements provide for the voluntary invitation of observers from the other side to military exercises. Such agreements are intended to reduce the possibility of disguising a surprise attack in a military exercise or of mistaking an exercise for an attack. This three-week advance notice would clarify intentions and, it was hoped, deter the use of military maneuvers for political intimidation, as had happened in Czechoslovakia in 1968.

President Gerald R. Ford encountered much public hostility when he announced his departure for Helsinki to sign the Final Act in July 1975. The administration's downplaying of the CSCE negotiations left both the public and Congress unprepared for a major East-West agreement. As it was a political agreement, the accord had no legal standing and therefore was not subject to Senate ratification, but the perception was that the United States was giving up much in terms of recognition of Soviet concerns while receiving little in return. The terms of the accord are not legally binding and contain no verification measures. The Soviets did in fact receive the recognition they desired from the CSCE at the signing of the Final Act, but the West would have to rely on promised unilateral actions of states in the Soviet bloc to see the results of its desires for improved human rights. These actions would not be immediately forthcoming.

As for the CBMS, the notification measures functioned reasonably well, with the Soviets making proper notification for all major exercises, with the notable exception of the 1981 maneuvers near the Polish-Soviet border coincident with Soviet pressure on Polish leaders to suppress the Solidarity movement. The voluntary invitations to opposing military observers were issued more frequently by NATO than by the Warsaw Pact. Despite this spotty record of compliance, the Helsinki accord established several important principles, among them the concept that less secrecy and less unilateralism in military operations were beneficial to the security of the European continent as a whole.

THE STOCKHOLM CONFERENCE

The Helsinki accord spawned several subsequent review meetings, at which several of its provisions—including the military CBMS—were criticized as overly voluntary and lacking verification measures or consequences of noncompliance. A 1983 meeting in Madrid mandated a special independent multilateral conference—to begin in Stockholm in January 1984—to negotiate militarily significant, binding, verifiable measures to create not only political confidence (as in the Helsinki accord) but military confidence. These measures were renamed "confidence- and security-building measures" (CSBMS) and were to be proposed to the next Helsinki review meeting in Vienna in November 1986. Begun during a period of chilly U.S.-Soviet relations, the significant achievements of the Stockholm conference reflected the improvement in superpower politics during the mid-1980s.

The NATO alliance presented the first proposals, consisting of provisions for the exchange of military information on a yearly basis; the forty-five-day advance notification of larger-scale military exercises; the observation of all prenotified activities by all other states; verification by national technical means (e.g., satellite and aircraft reconnaissance, ground- and sea-based radar) and on-site inspections; and improved means of communication in urgent situations. Many of these ideas were echoed in the proposals of the neutral and nonaligned nations as well as in plans submitted independently by Romania. In contrast to these specific agreements for positive action, the Soviet proposals consisted of exhortations to avoid certain activities, such as declarations of nuclear no-first-use, creation of a nuclear-and-chemical-weapons-free zone in Europe, a freeze of military budgets, and pledges to nonuse of force in international relations. The Soviets also called for the improvement of the Helsinki accord's CBMS. These last two proposals found support because they essentially had already been agreed to in the Madrid document establishing the Stockholm conference. The other Soviet suggestions, perceived as unnegotiable or propagandistic, found little support.

As the negotiations neared the November 1986 deadline, nations' positions began to be clarified. Significant areas of dispute included the definition of a notifiable military activity, enforced observation, the inclusion of air and naval activities, on-site inspection, information exchange about force location, and force ceilings for military exercises. The Soviet position on these disagreements reflected the premium placed on secrecy as the foundation of security, in contrast to the relative openness of the West. The Soviets were also concerned that the CSBMS would apply to exercises on Soviet territory, but not to any military actions taken on U.S. territory. The Soviets sought to compensate for this perceived imbalance by pushing for measures that would constrain Western activities more than their own. Such measures included mandatory notification only for high levels of troop activity (so that fewer maneuvers would be notified and observed) and limits on the size of forces involved in military

exercises (since NATO land-force exercises tended to be larger than Warsaw Pact activities).

Some of these disputes were resolved by promises to address them in later discussions, while others were eased through intervention from President Ronald Reagan and Soviet Premier Mikhail Gorbachev as the two superpowers moved toward a new era of détente. The Soviets eventually accepted nearly all of the Western proposals but added amendments meant to reduce their impact on Soviet actions. The NATO allies made some concessions, including dropping the proposal for initial declaration of the structure and location of military forces, agreeing to include American-troop transits through Europe in the definition of actions requiring notification, and accepting some constraints on military operations. The CSBMS agreed to at Stockholm accomplished several improvements on the Helsinki CBMS, such as:

1. requiring notification for smaller maneuvers as defined both by manpower and by force structure and equipment;
2. extending notification requirements to a larger set of military activities, from alerts to parachute drops;
3. including observers from all nations in all notifiable exercises above a certain level;
4. sharing annual forecasts of military activities;
5. requiring two years' notice for exercises of 75,000 troops or more and at least one year's notice for exercises involving 40,000 troops; and
6. imposing mandatory on-site inspection and detailed verification measures.

The agreement also reaffirmed the United Nations Charter's principle of nonuse of force. These CSBMS are expected to reduce the possibility of accidental war by increasing communication and clarifying intentions. If followed, they will increase the predictability of military operations and reduce their threatening nature. The strict verification measures insure that noncompliance will be obvious and will permit a swift response, if desired.

AGREEMENT ON THE PREVENTION OF DANGEROUS MILITARY ACTIVITIES

The 1989 Agreement on the Prevention of Dangerous Military Activities (PDMA) originated in several incidents of dangerous Soviet reactions, such as the shooting down of Korean Airlines Flight 007 in 1983 and the fatal shooting of a U.S. army officer by Soviet troops in East Germany in 1985, to inadvertent actions by Americans and others. These events contributed to the strains on the superpower relationship and could have led to an escalation of hostilities in certain circumstances. Warming United States–Soviet relations in the mid-1980s coincided with domestic political changes within both countries—*glasnost* and *perestroika* in the Soviet Union and the 1986 Defense Reorganization Act in the United States—to loosen some of the barriers to the direct participation of military officers in political affairs. Until this point, Soviet suggestions for widening the few direct military-to-military contacts had been rebuffed by the United States. But as part of the third Reagan-Gorbachev summit in December 1987 in Washington, the chairman of the Joint Chiefs of Staff and the chief of the Soviet General Staff took part in a historic first-ever meeting between the highest-ranking military officers of the two nations. Soviet interest in a wide range of military-to-military contacts to further the superpower détente met with U.S. insistence that resolution of U.S. concerns about dangerous Soviet military activities take precedence over any large-scale military exchanges. After several high-level meetings, an agenda for military-to-military negotiations was set. Topics included the Soviet assumption that any territorial incursions were potentially hostile; dangerous use of lasers by Soviet military personnel against U.S. military personnel; Soviet attempts to draw Western aircraft into Soviet territory with communications decoys; and ground rules for operations of the two militaries in close proximity in dangerous regions such as the Persian Gulf.

A joint working group was established to explore further the issues of dangerous military activities and to make recommendations. The two delegations met several times between October 1988 and June 1989, and after each side dispelled initial doubts about the seriousness of the other, the combination of a press blackout and overlapping interests resulted in rapid progress on several issues of concern. Some areas of dispute were deemed better handled in other fora, such as the Law of the Sea negotiations and multilateral CSBM discussions, with the PDMA talks focusing on inadvertent activities. The final agreement contained measures to improve military-to-military communication in times of crisis; to create areas of "special caution" where both militaries were operating side by side in areas of heightened tension; to avoid dangerous use of

lasers; to avoid interfering with command and control networks by jamming; and to treat accidental territorial incursions as potentially harmless rather than automatically threatening. These commitments took the form of an executive agreement signed in June 1989.

The PDMA resembled the INCSEA in its efforts to include direct military contacts in the resolution of potentially dangerous incidents, and it set out specific procedures for addressing certain inadvertent or dangerous actions by each nation's armed forces. The PDMA also created training guidelines designed to help Soviet and American military personnel avoid dangerous actions. While its first priority was to prevent loss of lives and property, the PDMA also sought to avoid or contain accidental military incidents before they engender a crisis and perhaps a war.

THE PARIS SUMMIT

At the November 1990 summit of the CSCE in Paris, several additional CSBMs were agreed to, and a Conflict Prevention Center (CPC) was established as a mechanism to support the implementation of these CSBMS. Located in Vienna, the CPC's principal task is assisting the Council of Foreign Ministers in reducing the risk of conflict. CSBMs agreed to at the Paris summit include a mechanism for consultation and cooperation in regard to unusual military activities, annual exchange of military information, a communications network, annual implementation assessment meetings, and cooperation regarding hazardous incidents of a military nature. Overshadowed by other summit business—German unification and the Conventional Forces treaty—the Paris summit's CSBMs nonetheless offer some steps toward transparency and consultation, perhaps easing potential conflict as the institutions of NATO, the Warsaw Pact, and the European Community come to terms with the post–Cold War world.

OTHER WAR PREVENTION MEASURES

While most efforts to prevent accidental war have focused on the superpower, and in some cases the European, context, other efforts have been pursued in the United Nations and in regional contexts. U.N. efforts to apply the CBM concept to global politics encountered severe differences of opinion about the usefulness of these types of measures and skepticism on the part of many nonaligned nations who saw the CBM approach as a distraction from the larger problem of nuclear disarmament. Discussed in the U.N. General Assembly, in a Special Session on Disarmament, in the U.N. Disarmament Commission (now the Conference on Disarmament), and in the Security Council, CBMS were defined so differently by the various participants that no agreement was possible.

Latin America has had a long history of military cooperation compared to Europe, primarily in the form of ad hoc, joint military exercises. While such activities can improve confidence among regional enemies, the frequent involvement of the United States or the Soviet Union in these exercises can undermine their usefulness for building trust among Latin American nations by creating an atmosphere of opposing military blocs. Expansion and formalization of these types of arrangements have been proposed to ease tensions in the region and to prevent inadvertent actions from escalating to war.

India, one of the major critics of the CBM approach, concluded a series of CBMS with one of its regional rivals, Pakistan, in April 1991. These agreements provide for military overflights and landing facilities in each other's territory as well as prior notification of troop movements and military exercises. They are the result of a set of discussions intended to improve overall relations between the two nations, long involved in confrontation and competition for influence.

CONCLUSIONS

Some have doubted the importance of agreements to prevent accidental war, pointing out that few wars have ever begun by accident. Sometimes derided as "arms control junk food," the war-prevention elements of these agreements have maintained a relatively low profile. Skeptics would attribute this unobtrusiveness to insignificance, but defenders note that lack of publicity has permitted these measures to operate without the controversy, fanfare,

and politicization accorded better-known arms-reduction treaties like SALT and START. Since CBMS and related approaches to preventing accidental war do not engender debates among bean-counters or intra-service rivalries, these approaches can be permitted to operate in areas where true mutual benefits can arise from military cooperation. Some military resistance has naturally been expressed to several proposals for preventing accidental war, but in each case, the gains in information, safety, and security have seemed to outweigh the costs of secrecy and freedom of operation. As the world moves away from superpower confrontation and toward a future of disintegration and unrest, accidental war may become more likely, and the creation of methods of avoiding it more important.

BIBLIOGRAPHY

The literature regarding this topic is quite limited. The basic articles include KURT M. CAMPBELL, "The US-Soviet Agreement on the Prevention of Dangerous Military Activities," *Security Studies* 1, no. 1 (Autumn 1991): 109–131; ALEXANDER L. GEORGE, "The Basic Principles Agreement of 1972: Origins and Expectations," in ALEXANDER L. GEORGE, ed., *Managing U.S.-Soviet Rivalry* (Boulder, 1983): 107–118; and SEAN M. LYNN-JONES, "A Quiet Success for Arms Control: Preventing Incidents at Sea," *International Security* 9 (Spring 1985): 154–184. THOMAS C. SCHELLING, *Arms and Influence* (New Haven, 1966) showed early concern with the problem of accidental war.

Other useful accounts may be found in JOHN BORAWSKI, ed., *Avoiding War in the Nuclear Age* (Boulder, 1986). Also see ALEXANDER L. GEORGE, PHILIP J. FARLEY, and ALEXANDER DALLIN, eds., *U.S.-Soviet Security Cooperation* (New York, 1988). A regional perspective may be found in VICTOR MILLÁN, "Regional Confidence-Building in the Military Field: The Case of Latin America," in MICHAEL A. MORRIS and VICTOR MILLÁN, eds., *Controlling Latin American Conflicts* (Boulder, 1983): 89–98.

Naval Arms Control Since World War II

○

RONALD O'ROURKE

See also Chile and Argentina: Entente and Naval Limitation, 1902; Regulating Submarine Warfare: 1919–1945; The Rush-Bagot Agreement: Demilitarizing the Great Lakes, 1817 to the Present; *and* The Washington Naval Limitation System: 1921–1939. *Most of the treaties discussed in this essay are excerpted in Volume III.*

Naval arms control, which was at the center of the arms control process in the 1920s and 1930s, has been at the periphery of that process since the end of World War II. A major question for arms control in the 1990s is whether naval forces and operations will reemerge as a major agenda item for arms control negotiators.

Some arms control analysts object to the term "naval arms control" as an unfortunate carryover from the interwar negotiations on naval armaments. They argue that the term implies a separation between naval and other forces in the arms control process that is analytically inappropriate in an era in which long-ranged aircraft and missiles have greatly increased the potential scope of interaction between naval and land-based forces. Rather than "naval arms control," these analysts prefer designations such as "naval forces in the arms control process." Despite its detractors, however, "naval arms control" remains the most common phrasing, and for that reason it is used here.

Naval arms control proposals can be divided into three broad categories:

1. *Naval confidence-building measures* (CBMS), including proposals for the exchange of information on naval doctrine, forces, and programs, and measures to provide prior notification of naval exercises and on-board observation of those exercises;

2. *Constraints on naval operations,* including provisions of "incidents at sea" agreements as well as proposals for limits on the number or scope of naval exercises, and limits or bans on naval forces in certain sea areas and on the activities of naval forces in certain sea areas; and

3. *Naval force structure constraints,* including proposals for measures analogous to those of the 1920s and 1930s—limits on the number and size of warships, and limits or bans on weapons, notably sea-launched cruise missiles and nonstrategic naval nuclear weapons.

This categorization is not as neat as it might at first appear. Some analysts prefer to exclude CBMS, naval or otherwise, from their definition of arms control. Naval CBMS are sometimes combined with proposed constraints on naval operations under the term naval confidence- and security-building measures (CSBMS). Other analysts argue that certain proposed CBMS would amount in practice to de facto constraints on operations, or that certain proposed constraints on operations would amount in practice to de facto constraints on force structure. Still other experts prefer to treat certain proposals, such as constraints on naval nonstrategic nuclear weapons, as categories unto themselves. All these categories, moreover, ignore other forms of arms control, such as agreements on strategic nuclear weapons, regional nuclear-weapon-free zones, and demilitarized zones of peace, which can have an important effect on naval forces and operations but which are not naval arms control agreements per se. All of these limits on terminology must be kept in mind during discussions of naval arms control.

AT THE PERIPHERY, 1946–1985

For a period of forty years following the end of World War II, the topic of naval arms control was essentially moribund.

In the early years, this in part reflected the lack of meaningful arms control activity in general. From the 1960s onward, it reflected the fact that arms control activities were dominated by negotiations over other issues, including strategic nuclear weapons, nuclear testing and nuclear proliferation, shorter-ranged land-based nuclear weapons, chemical and biological weapons, and conventional forces in Europe. Naval forces, because they were neither inherently weapons of mass destruction nor directly linked to the tense East-West military confrontation in Europe, were considered low-priority topics for arms control.

The Soviets, from the late 1950s onward, included in their wide-ranging disarmament schemes proposals that could affect naval forces but did not place any particular sustained emphasis on naval arms control. Nuclear weapons, which were apparently viewed by the Soviets as the only military forces capable of destroying the socialist system, appeared to be their top priority. Perhaps more important, the Soviets in the 1960s began a major buildup of their naval forces, the object of which was to attain a blue-water fleet that could be deployed worldwide. Naval arms control could have interfered with this planned buildup.

The United States during this period, with few exceptions, showed very little interest in naval arms control, not only because naval forces did not appear to pose a pressing arms control issue, but because of the navy's experience with the naval limitation agreements of the 1920s and 1930s. These agreements came to be viewed very negatively after World War II by the U.S. Navy and many U.S. policymakers as having failed to help prevent the outbreak of war. And worse, they were seen as having seriously reduced the readiness of United States naval forces to prosecute the war when it began. This negative assessment—which some analysts argue was supported more by conviction than by fact—

prompted the navy and its political allies to oppose the entire concept of naval arms control.

This is not to say, however, that the period 1946 to 1985 witnessed no arms control agreements affecting naval forces directly or, more often, indirectly. Indeed, there were several. The following summary, in roughly chronological fashion, emphasizes the more important features of these agreements as they affect naval operations.

The 1954 protocols to the Brussels Treaty of 1948 limited the displacements of West Germany's surface ships and submarines, and contained prohibitions for the West German navy relating to certain kinds of naval mines. These provisions have been relaxed over the years.

The Antarctic Treaty of 1959 demilitarized the Antarctic region south of 60 degrees south latitude. Advance notification is required for ship expeditions to Antarctica, and ships visiting the continent are subject to inspection by designated observers. The treaty does not, however, otherwise affect the exercise of rights under international law regarding operations on the high seas in its zone of application. One naval arms control proposal that has been discussed in the United Nations seeks to extend the demilitarization provisions of the treaty to the waters within the treaty's zone of application.

The Limited Test Ban Treaty (LTBT) of 1963 prohibited underwater nuclear tests. The 1967 Treaty for the Prohibition of Nuclear Weapons in Latin America, also called the Treaty of Tlatelolco, established a nuclear-weapon-free zone for Latin America with provisions, not in force as of 1991, for extending the zone of application to substantial adjoining portions of the Atlantic and Pacific Oceans. The Seabed Treaty of 1971 prohibits implanting or emplacing nuclear weapons or other weapons of mass destruction on the seabed and ocean floor and in the subsoil thereof.

The 1972 United States–Soviet Agreement on the Prevention of Incidents On and Over the High Seas, commonly called the Incidents at Sea Agreement, established operational constraints for the two sides' naval forces when they are operating in proximity to one another. Many analysts ascribe the successful implementation of this agreement to its administration by the professional leadership of the two sides' navies, thereby partially shielding the agreement from changing East-West political currents. The agreement has served as a precedent for similar bilateral agreements between the Soviet Union and several other Western countries. Some analysts have proposed broadening these bilateral agreements into a multilateral incidents at sea accord. Further provisions affecting the operations of U.S. and Soviet naval forces were established by the Ballistic Missile Launch Notification Agreement of 1988 and the Agreement on the Prevention of Dangerous Military Activities of 1989.

The Anti-Ballistic Missile (ABM) Treaty of 1972 prohibits sea-based ABM systems or components. The SALT I agreement of 1972 on strategic nuclear weapons placed numerical limits on ballistic missile submarines and launchers for submarine-launched ballistic missiles (SLBMS). The SALT II agreement of 1979 placed additional indirect limits on SLBM launchers. It also limited the number of reentry vehicles per SLBM, and indirectly limited the number of SLBMS with multiple reentry vehicles. The agreement prohibited ballistic missiles with ranges of more than six hundred kilometers (375 miles) on vessels other than submarines, and extended the provisions of the Seabed Treaty to prohibit ballistic or cruise missile launchers in territorial waters, including inland waters. The agreement was never ratified, but its provisions were generally followed. The START agreement of 1991 on strategic nuclear weapons placed further indirect limits on SLBM reentry vehicles.

The United Nations Convention on the Law of the Sea of 1982 established rules for innocent passage through territorial waters, transit passage through international straits, and for exclusive economic zones at sea. The treaty requires sixty parties for it to enter into force, and the United States and Britain—major maritime powers—were among those who elected not to become signatories. United States nonparticipation, however, is primarily due not to the provisions relating to passage but to those on seabed economic mining. The convention is regarded by many arms control analysts, especially within the United Nations, as significant for having established a maritime legal regime that formed an important foundation for pursuing further proposals for naval arms control.

The South Pacific Nuclear-Free-Zone Treaty of 1985, also known as the Treaty of Rarotonga, prohibits the South Pacific parties from stationing nuclear explosives in their own territories. It does not, however, affect the exercise of rights under international law regarding freedom of the seas. The Soviet Union and China signed protocols to the treaty prohibiting the use, or threat of use, of nuclear explosives against parties to the treaty, and prohib-

iting nuclear testing within the treaty's zone of application. The United States, the United Kingdom, and France, however, have declined to sign both these protocols and a third extending other provisions of the treaty to themselves.

The Stockholm document of 1986, the final document of the 1984–1986 Stockholm Conference on Confidence- and Security-Building Measures and Disarmament in Europe (CCSBMDE) of the Conference on Security and Cooperation in Europe (CSCE), required prior notification of certain naval activities functionally related to military activities on the ground in Europe. Its terms included amphibious exercises, ship-to-shore gunfire, and ship-to-shore naval support activities.

It should also be noted that in the late 1970s, the United States and the Soviet Union engaged in discussions on freezing or otherwise limiting their naval forces in the Indian Ocean, which at the time was a low-priority naval operating area for both countries. But these Naval Arms Limitation Talks, as they were called, produced no agreement, and events in Southwest Asia soon made the Indian Ocean/Persian Gulf region a much more important operating area for the U.S. Navy.

RENEWED DEBATE, 1986–1990

In 1983, a year after the U.N. Convention of the Law of the Sea was opened for signature, the United Nations initiated a study on the competition in naval arms. The publication of the study in 1986 created an opportunity for a renewed debate on naval arms control. This opportunity was taken up by the Soviets, who had written to the U.N. secretary-general in 1984 expressing their readiness to pursue the issue.

In 1986, the Soviets began to argue in favor of making naval forces a full-fledged item on the East-West arms control agenda. Over the next four years, Soviet leader Mikhail Gorbachev and other Soviet officials publicly issued a wide array of proposals for naval arms control. These proposals pulled naval arms control out of moribundity and engendered a lively debate on the topic in the United States, Europe, the East Asia–Pacific region, and the United Nations. Numerous conferences and symposiums were held, and a wealth of books, reports, articles, and papers were produced, exploring most aspects of the issue. By 1990 it appeared that naval forces and operations might well develop into a major arms control agenda item. Indeed, some analysts believed that it was only a matter of time before formal negotiations on the topic would commence.

Soviet Proposals

The Soviets during this period took advantage of numerous public forums to make their naval arms control proposals, and put out such a large number of them that it became difficult to keep track of them all. In summary, the Soviets proposed:

- exchanging information on naval forces and doctrines
- adding new provisions to the 1972 United States-Soviet Incidents at Sea Agreement
- requiring prior notification of naval exercises
- permitting official on-board observers for naval exercises
- limiting the number, scale, and geographic extent of naval exercises
- banning, freezing, reducing, or otherwise limiting naval forces and activities—especially antisubmarine forces and nuclear-armed naval platforms—in a number of sea areas, international straits, and major shipping lanes
- withdrawing Soviet forces from the Soviet base at Cam Ranh, Vietnam in exchange for the United States withdrawing its forces from U.S. bases in the Philippines
- banning or limiting sea-launched cruise missiles, especially long-range, nuclear-armed designs
- banning or limiting nonstrategic naval nuclear weapons generally
- scrapping one hundred of their attack submarines in exchange for the United States eliminating five to seven of its aircraft carriers.

The Soviets officially tabled several of their proposals at the Confidence- and Security-Building Measures (CSBMS) talks of the Vienna meeting of the Conference on Security and Cooperation in Europe (CSCE) in 1989. The Soviets during this period also called for integrating naval forces into the talks on limiting conventional forces in Europe, and for convening a multilateral conference on Asian security issues that would take up naval forces as one of its primary topics. Soviet proposals in several cases dovetailed with Soviet support for demilitarized zones of peace and regional nuclear-weapon-free zones.

Soviet Motives

The Soviet decision in 1986 to begin placing more emphasis on naval arms control was apparently motivated by a number of factors. One appears to have been a desire to score propaganda points and put the United States on the diplomatic defensive. The Soviets shifted rapidly from one naval arms control proposal to another, at times seeming to care more about generating an effect on public opinion than on producing a sustained debate on specific proposals. Some of the Soviets' proposals, moreover, were structured in a way that many analysts in the West considered blatantly one-sided and of little potential value.

While the Soviets were issuing their proposals, they were also reducing the amount of time that Soviet naval forces spent on distant deployments. This was apparently an economy measure, but the Soviets may have hoped that the combination of naval arms control proposals and reduced overseas Soviet naval deployments would raise doubts in the United States and elsewhere about the need for a large U.S. Navy, for its continued forward deployment of naval forces, and for its network of overseas bases supporting forward naval operations. By encouraging a reduction in U.S. naval forces and operations, the Soviets may have hoped to use their proposals on naval arms control as a means of loosening linkages between the United States and its overseas allies and restricting the ability of the United States to influence events in the third world.

The Soviets undoubtedly viewed naval arms control as an option for reducing the naval advantage of the United States and its allies, just as the United States and its European allies viewed negotiations on conventional forces in Europe as a means of neutralizing the Soviets' numerical advantages in that sphere. By 1986, the Soviets may have concluded that naval arms control was either the best way or in some cases the only way to reduce or neutralize certain developing Western naval threats. By this time, the Reagan administration's program for building a six-hundred-ship fleet was well underway. The U.S. Navy was expanding its deployment of the Tomahawk sea-launched cruise missile, and the navy and its supporters were forcefully arguing the merits of the navy's new maritime strategy, which called for using naval forces in an offensive (forward) manner in any major war with the Soviets.

It is also possible that the Soviets began emphasizing naval arms control at this time as a means of facilitating reductions in Soviet defense spending and of dealing with the approaching obsolescence of many older Soviet warships. The Gorbachev government, which came to power in 1985, appears to have had fewer illusions than its predecessors about the difficulties facing the Soviet economy and about the burden placed on that economy by defense programs. In the late 1970s, the Soviets began to produce a new generation of technologically sophisticated warships and by the mid-1980s it probably became clear to Soviet leaders that these warships, although much more capable than their predecessors, could not be built in the same large quantities as those built in the 1950s and 1960s. Facing the prospect of having to scrap large numbers of older warships without one-for-one replacements, the Soviets may have viewed naval arms control as a means of trading the aging units of the Soviet fleet for something on the Western side before these older ships disappeared from the Soviet fleet due to obsolescence and lack of funds.

Some Soviet naval arms control proposals, particularly those relating to expanding the Incidents at Sea Agreement and to restricting naval operations in certain areas, may have been motivated by a genuine desire to reduce naval operations as a potential source of friction and crisis. United States and Soviet naval forces carried nuclear weapons and they operated with more independence from central control than did other kinds of military forces. In spite of the apparent success of the 1972 Incidents at Sea Agreement, U.S. and Soviet naval operations in the 1980s, including a U.S. Navy program for asserting navigation rights in the littoral waters of, among other places, the Black Sea and the Sea of Okhotsk, led to disputes and tense encounters at sea.

The U.S. Response　The United States' response to the Soviet proposals was slow in coming and almost entirely negative. From 1986 to 1988, the Reagan administration for the most part ignored Soviet naval arms control initiatives, perhaps out of a hope that the Soviets would lose interest and allow the topic to fade back into obscurity. When the administration did begin to articulate its views on the topic, it soon became clear that those views were broadly consistent with those of the U.S. Navy, which was strongly opposed to the concept of naval arms control. Its basic position was that the United States, as a maritime power separated from

allies (and potential military theaters) by two oceans, relies on maritime activities and freedom of navigation under international law to protect its security and trade interests and saw little merit in Soviet or other proposals for any naval arms limitations or additional constraints on its naval activities. The United States' position at this time was so strongly negative that it was characterized by some as the "just-say-no" policy, a tongue-in-cheek reference to the rhetoric of the Reagan administration's anti-drug policy.

In 1990, the Bush administration altered its public statements on naval arms control to make it clear that United States policy was not one of rejecting naval arms control in principle, but rather of rejecting specific naval arms control proposals. The difference, though subtle, suggested that the United States in theory might support certain naval arms control proposals, provided they could be shown to be in the United States' interest. In early 1991 the administration, in response to a direction from Congress, published its first report on naval arms control. The report was largely negative in tone, but did endorse some minor naval confidence-building measures (CBMS), such as continued exchange visits of naval leaders and reciprocal port visits.

Congress began holding hearings on naval arms control in 1989. The topic was by no means at the top of Congress' crowded defense and arms control agenda, but interest began to grow slowly. By the end of 1990, three different subcommittees had held hearings on the topic. At the last of these hearings, held in 1990 before a subcommittee of the Senate Armed Services Committee, the subcommittee chairman, Senator Edward Kennedy, identified three areas in arms control as worthy of further investigation: (1) naval CBMS; (2) a ban or limit on naval nonstrategic nuclear weapons; and (3) a United States–Soviet bilateral limit on attack submarines. This was the first major attempt to lend some structure and direction to the United States' debate on naval arms control, which until then had been rather amorphous.

Later that year, the Senate Armed Services Committee, in its report on the fiscal year 1991 defense budget, directed the Department of Defense to write a report on the three naval arms control areas highlighted in the hearing, and on any other naval arms control proposals of potential interest as well. The committee also took the extraordinary step of urging the Soviet government to follow the United

States' example of annually publishing its long-term naval construction plans and other related data.

Outside of the United States government, numerous private individuals and organizations, many of them supportive of certain naval arms control proposals, began to participate in the general debate on the topic. These individuals and organizations probably accounted for most of the United States participants at international naval arms control conferences held during this period, and their papers form a major part of the global literature that was developed on the topic. The proposal for a United States–Soviet bilateral attack-submarine limit was developed by some of these individuals (and by some of their West European counterparts).

The central issue in the debate over naval arms control during this period was whether the United States should maintain its steadfast opposition to entering into formal discussions, or agree to engage the Soviets in negotiation. The administration officials and other opponents of naval arms control pressed their standard position that geographically the United States was a maritime-oriented power, while the Soviet Union was a land-oriented power. Consequently, strong naval forces and maximum freedom of operation at sea were much more critical to U.S. security, and any agreement limiting United States and Soviet naval forces or operations would be inherently more disadvantageous to the United States and its allies. The United States shouldn't allow itself to be stampeded by the Soviets into negotiations or agreements that could undermine U.S. security. Thus, even proposed Soviet naval CBMs were not as harmless as they appeared. Moreover, engaging the Soviets on naval CBMs would give them an opportunity to draw the United States into more extensive talks on naval forces. (This became known as the "slippery slope" argument.) Steadfast opposition to naval arms control negotiations was not as politically costly as naval arms control advocates made it out to be, since the United States was by no means the only country cool to the idea.

United States advocates of naval arms control negotiations argued that even though the United States was a maritime nation, the securing of naval agreements in its interest was possible. If the United States and its allies were currently superior to the Soviets at sea, then limitations on naval forces and operations could lock that superiority into place. Supporters maintained that steadfast oppo-

sition to naval arms control negotiations was politically unsustainable, because it made the United States look unreasonable in international diplomacy. Moreover, some of the Soviet-proposed naval CBMs would not necessarily damage U.S. interests. Engaging Moscow on these proposals would put Washington in a more reasonable diplomatic position and relieve pressure to engage the Soviets on some of their more extensive and less attractive proposals. The slippery slope argument was simply untenable because it implied that the United States had no control over the scope of a negotiation or the activities of its negotiators.

Allied and International Response Some U.S. allies in Europe were very supportive of the United States' position on naval arms control. Others, while not necessarily enthusiastic about naval arms control, expressed some curiosity about the topic and searched for proposals, particularly CBMs, that could reasonably be supported. And two European allies, Iceland and to a lesser extent Norway, came out in support of more extensive forms of naval arms control. As a group, however, the NATO allies generally supported the U.S. position. Prior to the 1989 revolutions that brought down their Communist governments, the countries of Eastern Europe generally supported the Soviet position on naval arms control. After the revolutions, however, some of these countries expressed concern about agreements that might result in a reduction in the United States' or its allies' naval presence in the region.

Canada, which at this time was contemplating a naval buildup program, did not appear enthusiastic about naval arms control in general, but nevertheless explored proposals for agreements relating to the Arctic, an important operating area for U.S. and Soviet submarines. Japan, which maintained very cool relations with the Soviets and was in the middle of its own naval buildup, showed little interest in the idea. As in the United States' case, lack of interest at the official government level in all these countries did not deter many private individuals and private organizations from exploring the issue and coming out in favor of various proposals.

At the United Nations, many member countries supported the idea of beginning negotiations of some kind on naval forces. It was in this forum that the United States tended to appear the most isolated diplomatically on the topic.

ISSUES AND PERSPECTIVES, 1986–1990

To a large degree, the positions of the Soviet Union, the United States, and other countries on the merits of naval arms control reflected differing strategic cultures rooted in contrasting geographic and military circumstances. The Soviets, with a strong tradition as a continental power and fleets that are tied fairly closely to separate military theaters, were more inclined to think of naval forces as integral elements of various regional military balances. A country with limited overseas interests, the Soviet Union also tended to think of its naval forces more exclusively in terms of the East-West competition. And since it was a country with exposed borders and a history of invasion by hostile foreign powers, it tended to equate military stability with predictability.

In contrast, the United States, with a strong tradition as a maritime power and a history of shifting naval forces from one region to another, considered naval forces as globally deployable assets separate from individual regional military balances. As a country with extensive overseas interests, the United States considered its naval forces not only in connection with the East-West competition, but also as a major tool for defending U.S. interests in third world situations having little or nothing to do with the Soviets. And lastly, the United States usually considered military stability in terms of deterrence, which depends on the ability of one's forces to survive an opening blow and respond in an effective manner. In the case of naval forces, unpredictable movement is a major contributor to survivability. Thus, in the area of naval forces, the United States tended to equate stability with the idea of avoiding predictability of movement. These three basic differences in strategic culture go a long way toward explaining why the Soviet and U.S. approaches to naval arms control were so difficult to reconcile.

American allies in Europe would depend on United States naval power in an East-West war to secure the sea lines of communication linking the United States to its European allies. And some of these countries have fairly strong naval forces and important overseas interests of their own. Other European countries, however, have very limited naval forces and overseas interests and, in the case of the Scandinavian countries, a geographic position that put them in the middle of the United States–Soviet naval competition. This variation in national circumstances helps explain the somewhat differing positions on naval arms control adopted by the European governments. The debate on naval arms control in European countries also tended to treat the topic in a more multilateral context, in contrast to the U.S. debate, which focused more on proposed bilateral measures with the Soviets. The wide support in the United Nations for negotiations on naval arms control during this period probably reflected in large part the fact that most member countries have limited coastal naval forces or none at all, and little or no land-based means for countering hostile naval forces.

Naval Arms Control in Europe   Since the Soviets, as mentioned earlier, regarded naval forces as integral to a region's overall military balance, they viewed the military situation in Europe as one of offsetting asymmetries, with their advantage in ground forces being offset by what they saw as NATO's advantage in naval (and tactical air) forces. Accordingly, the Soviets proposed that naval forces be included in the Conventional Forces in Europe (CFE) negotiations, and suggested that even if naval forces were excluded from those negotiations, the Soviet view of the equitability of any proposed CFE accord would be influenced by the regional naval equation.

The United States and its European allies approached the regional military situation and the CFE talks from a different perspective. In their view, the central purpose of the talks was to reduce the specific threat posed by forces that can rapidly seize and occupy territory. Naval forces by themselves cannot do that, so the United States and its allies were primarily interested in discussing ground forces. The United States and its NATO allies saw a different set of offsetting asymmetries in the European theater. They emphasized that the Soviet Union is connected to the potential battlefield in Europe by road and rail networks, while the United States is separated from its allies by the Atlantic Ocean. The United States and its European allies consequently argued that superior U.S. and allied naval forces simply offset the Soviets' advantage in having a road and rail network connecting them to the battlefield, and that naval superiority thus constituted a prerequisite to an equitable overall military balance in the European theater. Accordingly,

NATO in 1989 successfully opposed the inclusion of naval forces in the mandate for the CFE talks.

The mandate of the confidence- and security-building measures talks of the Vienna meeting of the Conference on Security and Cooperation in Europe (CSCE) included the waters around Europe and consequently naval activities in those waters that had a direct functional link to military operations on the ground. The naval arms control measures formally proposed by the Soviets at the CSBM talks in 1989, however, appeared intended to cover naval forces carrying out essentially independent activities on the high seas. The United States and allied countries opposed the expansion of the mandate of the CSBM talks to include such operations.

Naval Arms Control in the East Asia–Pacific Region

The U.S. military presence in the East Asia–Pacific region is heavily weighted toward naval forces. Its forward-deployed naval units played an important role in maintaining stability in the region independent of the Soviet military threat. As a consequence, the challenge for advocates of naval arms control in this region was to devise a regional naval arms control scheme that would be equitable to the United States from an East-West perspective and not create a power vacuum that could upset regional stability. This did not prove easy. Many of the symposiums on naval arms control held in the period 1986–1990 were held in this region, but with few concrete results.

Dispute over nuclear weapons, however, led to a diplomatic impasse between the United States and New Zealand in the second half of the 1980s on the issue of visits by U.S. warships. Antinuclear sentiment also found expression in the aforementioned South Pacific Nuclear-Free-Zone Treaty.

Naval CBMS

Western advocates of naval confidence-building measures (CBMS) during this period argued that by helping to reduce East-West military tensions, naval CBMS could release U.S. naval forces for use in third world operations. They also argued that naval CBMS could be advantageous to the United States and its allies. Geographic limits on exercises, for example, could reduce Soviet proficiency in the kinds of mid-ocean interdiction operations they might attempt in an East-West conflict. Given the less open nature of the Soviet system, advocates argued, advance notification and observation of exercises might benefit the West more than the Soviets. And as mentioned earlier, it was argued that opening talks with the Soviets on CBMS would reduce pressure for the United States to engage the Soviets in broader talks on naval forces.

Some opponents of naval CBMS believed they were unnecessary. They argued that movements of naval forces in international waters are readily observable by ships, aircraft, and other means, and that prior notification of exercises was already provided through several existing forms of notification. Management of at-sea naval tensions was adequately taken care of by incidents at sea agreements, the 1989 United States–Soviet agreement on the prevention of dangerous military activities, and the United States–Soviet Nuclear Risk Reduction Centers. CBMS are directed at reducing the chances of a surprise attack. But using naval forces for a surprise attack would only make sense if one planned to follow it up with a ground operation to seize and occupy land territory, and ground forces were covered by the Conventional Forces in Europe (CFE) talks.

Other opponents believed that CBMS could force the United States and Western naval forces into more predictable or otherwise dangerous deployment patterns, reducing uncertainty for Soviet military planners and thereby weakening deterrence, and reduce the readiness of United States and Western naval forces to operate in potential wartime areas. Naval CBMS, it was argued, could encourage a Soviet perception that NATO could not secure the Atlantic sea lanes, which itself could be destabilizing. And as mentioned earlier, it was feared that entering into talks on naval CBMS could draw the United States and its allies into broader talks on naval forces.

Constraints on Naval Operations

Soviet-proposed constraints on naval operations included antisubmarine warfare-free zones, sanctuaries for ballistic missile submarines, minimum naval stand-off distances from certain shores, and limits on naval force levels in a variety of sea areas around the Soviet periphery. The Soviet proposals in this area were discussed in Europe to some degree, but in the United States they were judged to be inherently one-sided in favor of the Soviets and received little attention.

Limiting or Banning Sea-Launched Cruise Missiles

The idea for limiting or banning sea-launched cruise missiles (SLCMS), particularly long-range, nuclear-armed, land-attack SLCMS, was probably the single most prominent item in the 1986–1990 debate on naval arms control. Indeed, SLCMs had been an arms control issue since the late 1970s. The focus of the debate was the nuclear-armed, land-attack variant of the U.S. Navy's Tomahawk SLCM, which the United States began deploying in the mid-1980s, and an analogous Soviet weapon, the SS-N-21 nuclear-armed land-attack SLCM. The Soviets attempted several times to have these weapons included in the United States–Soviet talks on strategic nuclear weapons; but the United States resisted. In the end, SLCMs were more or less excluded from the strategic nuclear arms control process and thereby became an issue for naval arms control.

Western advocates of a limit or ban on these weapons insisted that the United States, because of its huge coastal populations, was proportionately more vulnerable to an attack by nuclear-armed SLCMs than the insular Soviet Union. These weapons, they argued, were also destabilizing because they could fly in under radar detection and could thus be used in a nuclear first strike. They also insisted that limiting or banning SLCMs would be advantageous to the West because the Soviet navy relied more heavily than United States and Western naval forces on SLCMs for its strike capability.

Opponents countered that U.S. naval forces would destroy any Soviet ship attempting to put itself in a position to launch a SLCM attack against the United States. They also argued that the slow speed and limited number of nuclear-armed, land-attack SLCMs made them unsuitable for use in a first strike, and that in the wake of the Intermediate-Range Nuclear Forces (INF) agreement eliminating ground-launched cruise missiles from Europe, the nuclear land-attack variant of the Tomahawk would play an increasingly important role in buttressing nuclear deterrence. Sea-launched cruise missiles, they argued, were important because they dispersed the Navy's striking power away from the Navy's aircraft carriers, which are limited in number and vulnerable to attack. Limiting or banning SLCMs, they affirmed, would also reduce U.S. naval capabilities for operations in the third world.

Devising an adequate verification regime for a limit or ban on SLCMs is a very difficult problem. This is particularly true of the Tomahawk, which comes in both nuclear and conventional variants of virtually identical outward appearance and which can be fired from launchers that are suitable for other kinds of weapons as well. Many of the writings on naval arms control produced during the late 1980s focused on SLCMs and in particular on the problem of verifying compliance with a limit or ban. Advocates of a ban or limit on SLCMs proposed numerous schemes to accomplish this objective; however, opponents insisted that these ideas were either inadequate or, because of their intrusiveness, would impose unacceptable constraints on naval operations.

At the 1987 Washington summit, the United States and the Soviet Union agreed to seek a mutually acceptable resolution of the SLCM issue. At a summit three years later, the two sides agreed, in parallel with the START treaty on strategic nuclear weapons but not as part of it, to make annual, politically binding declarations of their planned deployments of nuclear-armed SLCMs with ranges of more than 600 kilometers, the number not to exceed 880, and to refrain from producing or deploying nuclear SLCMs with multiple, independently targetable warheads.

Limiting or Banning Naval Nonstrategic Nuclear Weapons
Nonstrategic naval nuclear weapons, often referred to as tactical naval nuclear weapons, comprise all naval nuclear weapons other than strategic submarine-launched ballistic missiles. The category includes not only nuclear-armed SLCMs, but nuclear-armed bombs, depth charges, torpedoes, rockets, and missiles.

In general, Western advocates of a ban or limit on these weapons during the late 1980s argued that the Soviets could use naval nuclear weapons to fight on even terms with technologically more advanced United States and allied naval forces. The result might be the destruction of both fleets, but this would be to the Soviets' advantage, since naval forces are more critical to Western than to Soviet security. The Soviets might also perceive only a limited risk that nuclear war might spread from sea to land. Limiting or banning these weapons would also reduce the risk of a peacetime nuclear accident at sea and the potential risks of any serious United States–Soviet naval incident. It would reduce the shipboard bureaucratic and training work load associated with deploying nuclear weapons at sea, and release scarce magazine space on ships for conventional weapons that are much more likely to be used, especially in third world operations. Lastly, it would reduce or eliminate the problems experienced by the United States with New Zealand and other countries on port calls by U.S. ships resulting from the United States' policy of neither confirming nor denying the presence or absence of nuclear weapons aboard its warships.

Opponents countered that these weapons will be needed to help buttress deterrence in Europe and underscore the United States' commitment to NATO as ground-based nuclear weapons are reduced in Europe. Limiting or banning these weapons would also leave Japan and Korea more open to attack by Soviet land-based nuclear weapons, and lessen confidence in the U.S. security commitment to the East Asian–Pacific region. Indeed, reducing or eliminating these weapons could create regional nuclear power vacuums that might encourage states to embark on nuclear-weapon programs of their own. The Soviets were not likely to begin a nuclear war at sea because they recognized the probability of nuclear combat spreading to land. The administrative burden of nuclear weapons is not that onerous, and the issue of port calls by U.S. warships can be handled on a case-by-case basis; the diplomatic impasse with New Zealand was an isolated case.

In the West, advocates of a limit or ban on these weapons came to include prominent figures such as Paul Nitze, a senior United States foreign policy adviser and arms control negotiator, and retired Admiral William J. Crowe, a former chairman of the U.S. Joint Chiefs of Staff. In 1990, the Bush administration stated that in theory, it would be willing to consider negotiations on naval nonstrategic nuclear weapons, provided that two conditions were met: First, the negotiations would have to address all nuclear weapons capable of threatening ships at sea, including nuclear-armed antiship weapons on land-based maritime bombers. Second, one would have to be able to envision beforehand an adequate and operationally acceptable verification regime for all these weapons.

The Soviets at one point indicated that they might agree to include in negotiations the nuclear antiship weapons on their land-based bombers. As with the discussion over limiting SLCMS, however, verification became a major point of debate. Advocates argued that adequate and operationally acceptable verification regimes for these weapons were possible, particularly with the kinds of intrusive, on-site verification measures that the Soviets began to accept in the latter 1980s in other areas of arms control. Opponents argued, as in the debate on SLCMS, that these schemes were either inadequate or so intrusive as to impose an unacceptable constraint on naval operational flexibility. Since even a small number of clandestine nuclear weapons fired at

U.S. aircraft carriers could tilt a war at sea decisively in the Soviets' advantage, even an extremely low level of Soviet cheating, they argued, would be significant.

In September 1991, as part of a broad unilateral initiative to reduce nuclear weapons, U.S. President George Bush announced that the United States would remove all nonstrategic naval nuclear weapons from its surface ships and submarines, destroy about half of these weapons, and store the remainder on land. Upon completion of the removal of these weapons, the United States would also suspend its policy of neither confirming nor denying the presence of nuclear weapons aboard these ships and submarines. The administration explained that it had made this decision in view of reduced East-West tensions and the declining military utility of these weapons. However, the administration also reserved the right to load the stored weapons back aboard the ships and submarines if future conditions warranted.

In October 1991, Soviet President Mikhail Gorbachev responded with a similar broad unilateral initiative to reduce nuclear weapons. As part of this initiative, Gorbachev announced that the Soviets would likewise remove nonstrategic naval nuclear weapons from its ships and submarines, destroy some of these weapons, and store others on land. Gorbachev also proposed that the United States and the Soviet Union reach agreement on the elimination of all these weapons. In light of the disintegration of the Soviet Union in December 1991 and the subsequent dispute between Russia and Ukraine over possession of the Black Sea fleet, the status of nonstrategic nuclear weapons in the ex-Soviet navy as of 1992 remained unclear.

Naval Force Structure Constraints The Soviets' proposal for scrapping large numbers of their submarines in exchange for a reduction in the U.S. aircraft carrier fleet was greeted in the United States as a one-sided proposal. The scrapped submarines, it was judged, would be obsolete boats on the verge of retirement, while the carriers were important not only to the East-West military competition, but to United States naval operations in the third world as well.

The force-structure constraint that received more attention at this time was proposed not by the Soviets, but by some United States and Western naval analysts. This was the idea for a bilateral United States–Soviet (or, in some versions, NATO–Warsaw

Pact) limit on attack submarines. Advocates of this proposal argued that since each side's attack submarines were directed in large part against the other side's military forces, a negotiated reduction in submarine force levels would be equitable to both sides. The Soviets would face a reduced attack-submarine threat to their ballistic missile submarines while retaining a sufficient attack-submarine force for self-defense. The United States and its allies would face a reduced Soviet attack-submarine threat to the sea lines of communication, and would retain a sufficient attack-submarine force for non-Soviet-oriented naval operations in the third world. Moreover, advocates argued, this proposal, unlike many other naval arms control proposals, could be adequately verified by national technical means with little difficulty.

The Reagan administration came out against the proposal, arguing that it would benefit the Soviets more than the United States. It would leave the United States with insufficient numbers of attack submarines for naval operations in the third world, and would harm the U.S. submarine-construction industrial base. Perhaps the more important barrier to any negotiation on this proposal, though, was lack of Soviet enthusiasm. This was not the sort of proposal the Soviets had in mind when they began raising the topic of naval arms control, and they turned down many opportunities to engage United States and Western naval analysts on this idea.

CONCLUSION

The ending of the Cold War raises a question as to whether the active debate on naval arms control begun in 1986 will continue into the 1990s and beyond. To some analysts, the lessening of East-West tensions increases the chances of arriving at naval arms control agreements. Such agreements, they argue, can have value in helping rationalize the post–Cold War U.S. and ex-Soviet naval build-downs and in codifying and stabilizing the new era of reduced military tensions. For other analysts, however, the ending of the Cold War reduces the apparent need for naval arms control. With both the U.S. and ex-Soviet fleets poised to decline in size, with the ex-Soviet fleet spending more time in its home waters, and with the focus of United States military planning shifting to operations in the third world, these analysts question the existence of a pressing problem to be addressed by naval arms control.

Has the time for naval arms control come or has it passed? The proposals that energized the naval arms control debate of 1986–1990 were intended to address concerns arising out of the military tensions of the Cold War. There may still be value in pursuing these proposals in the post–Cold War era. But if naval arms control is to retain its saliency in the 1990s and beyond, it may have to incorporate new proposals and ideas that address the emerging security concerns of the post–Cold War era. One possibility, which would address the already strong post–Cold War concern over the proliferation of advanced weapons in the third world, would be to limit exports of certain naval equipment, such as modern attack submarines, advanced cruise missiles, and advanced naval mines, to the third world. Another possibility, which would address concerns over the highly militarized nature of the former Soviet economy, would be to assist the former Soviet republics in converting their naval shipyards and related naval production facilities over to civilian uses.

BIBLIOGRAPHY

Overviews For book-length treatments made since the late 1980s of the various issues in naval arms control, see RICHARD FIELDHOUSE, ed., *Security at Sea: Naval Forces and Arms Control* (Oxford and New York, 1990), a publication of the Stockholm International Peace Research Institute's Project on Naval Forces and Arms Control; J. R. HILL, *Arms Control at Sea* (Annapolis, Md., 1989); and BARRY M. BLECHMAN, et al., *Naval Arms Control: A Strategic Assessment* (New York, 1991). An earlier version of this study was published in 1990 by the Henry L. Stimson Center, Washington, D.C., under the title *The U.S. Stake in Naval Arms Control*. The first two of these, Fieldhouse and Hill, contain extensive bibliographies. For somewhat older surveys of the topic, reflecting the debate as it developed by the 1970s, see GEORGE H. QUESTER, ed., *Navies and Arms Control* (New York, 1980), issued by the Aspen Institute for Humanistic Studies and the Aspen Arms Control Consortium; and BARRY M. BLECHMAN, *The Control of Naval Armaments: Prospects and Possibilities* (Washington, D.C., 1975), issued by the Brookings Institution Studies in Defense Policy.

International Debate For documents and analyses reflecting the international debate on naval arms control since the latter half of the 1980s, see UNITED NATIONS, DEPARTMENT FOR DISARMAMENT AFFAIRS, *The Naval Arms Race* (New York, 1986), Study Series 16, Report of the Secretary-General, U.N. document A/40/535; UNITED NATIONS, DEPARTMENT FOR DISARMAMENT AFFAIRS, *Naval Confidence-Building Measures* (New York, 1990), Disarmament Topical Papers 4; papers from United Nations seminars held in Helsingör, Denmark, 13–15 June 1990, and Varna, Bulgaria, 4–6 September 1990; and SVERRE LODGAARD, ed., *Naval Arms Control* (Oslo, Norway, 1990), issued by the International Peace Research Institute, Oslo, comprised of papers from the 52d Symposium of the Pugwash Conference on Science and World Affairs, "Naval Forces: Arms Restraint and Confidence Building," held in Oslo, Norway, on 23–26 June 1988.

Debate in the United States   For items reflecting the debate in the United States on naval arms control since the late 1980s, see UNITED STATES DEPARTMENT OF DEFENSE, *Report on Naval Arms Control* (Washington, D.C., 1991), submitted to Senate Committee on Armed Services and House Committee on Armed Services, April 1991; JAMES L. LACY, *Naval Arms Control: The Backdrop of History; The Baroque Debate: Public Diplomacy and Naval Arms Control, 1986–1989; Within and Beyond Naval Confidence-Building: The Legacy and the Options; Between Worlds: Europe and the Seas in Arms Control* (Santa Monica, Calif., 1990). Respectively, these publications comprise RAND notes N-3120-USDP, N-3121-USDP, N-3122-USDP, and N-3123-USDP;

prepared by the RAND Corporation for the U.S. undersecretary of defense for policy; each includes a bibliography; See also WILLIAM H. NELSON, *Three Issues in Naval Arms Control* (Newport, R.I., 1991), Report 2-91, 1 May 1991, of the Strategy and Campaign Department, Center for Naval Warfare Studies, U.S. Naval War College, which includes bibliography; UNITED STATES CONGRESS, SENATE, COMMITTEE ON ARMED SERVICES, *Approaches to Naval Arms Control* (Washington, D.C., 1990), which includes hearings before the Subcommittee on Projection Forces and Regional Defense, 101st Congress, 2d Session, 8 and 11 May 1990; and UNITED STATES CONGRESS, HOUSE OF REPRESENTATIVES, HOUSE COMMITTEE ON FOREIGN AFFAIRS, *Arms Control in Asia and U.S. Interests in the Region* (Washington, D.C., 1991), which includes hearings before the Subcommittee on Asian and Pacific Affairs, 101st Congress, 2d Session, 31 January and 13 March 1990.

Sea-Launched Cruise Missiles   For items reflecting the debate on sea-launched cruise missiles, on which there is an extensive specialized literature, see ROBERT J. LEMPERT, *Cruise Missile Arms Control* (Santa Monica, Calif., 1989), RAND Corporation R-3792-FF/RC, which includes a bibliography; and "Sea-Launched Cruise Missiles and Arms Control: Policy Focus," *International Security* 13 (Winter 1988/1989): 168–202, which includes articles by Linton Brooks, Rose E. Gottemoeller, Henry C. Mustin, and Theodore A. Postol.

The Open Skies Negotiations

○

ANN M. FLORINI

See also Arms Control Treaty Verification; Confidence-Building Measures in
Europe: 1975 to the Present; *and* "No First Use" Nucler Policy. *Treaties discussed
in this essay are excerpted in Volume III.*

Open Skies refers to a proposal that allows participating countries to fly over each other's territory in
order to build confidence that no untoward or
threatening activities are going on below. It was first
put forward by President Dwight D. Eisenhower in
1955 and was intended to allow the United States
and the Soviet Union to overfly each other, but the
negotiations went nowhere. In 1989, President
George Bush revived the idea, expanding it to include all members of NATO and the Warsaw Pact. On
24 March 1992, after three years of negotiation during which the political relations of the parties were
completely transformed and the Warsaw Pact disappeared, the Open Skies Treaty was signed.

THE 1955 PROPOSAL

In mid-1955 the Cold War was enjoying its first
thaw. With the signing of the Austrian State Treaty
on 5 May 1955, the Soviet Union had agreed to withdraw its troops from Austria and leave that country
neutral. The United States, Great Britain, and France
then invited the USSR to participate in a four-power
summit that July. The Soviets agreed and simultaneously made new disarmament proposals at the
United Nations that moved significantly closer to
the Western position on many issues.

In this relatively optimistic atmosphere, Nelson
Rockefeller, special assistant to the president, convened a meeting of academics and other experts to
consider what proposals the U.S. might make at the
summit and thereafter. Meeting over several days at

the Quantico marine base in Virginia, the group
concluded that a prime aim should be to test the
seriousness of the new Soviet attitude toward reducing armaments.

Although in 1955 the U.S. possessed clear military superiority over the Soviet Union, experts were
warning that the Soviets could catch up within a few
years if agreement was not reached on arms control
measures. The USSR had tested a thermonuclear device in 1953. The Quantico panel concluded that
the U.S. should put forward a proposal to determine whether the Soviets would be willing to accept the type of intrusive inspection that would be
needed for any disarmament agreement to be verified. At the time, two years before the launch of
Sputnik ushered in the satellite age, the United
States had few means of gathering information on
Soviet military activity, and aerial inspection was believed to be an essential component of verification.
If the Soviets rejected a proposal to allow overflights, the experts felt, this would indicate that the
Soviets were not serious about disarmament, and
the U.S. should then take steps to maintain its military superiority.

Within the U.S. bureaucracy, the idea of Open
Skies encountered substantial resistance. Secretary
of State John Foster Dulles initially objected, in part
because he did not want the United States to put
forward *any* specific propositions during the summit and in part because the proposal was initiated
by Nelson Rockefeller, his political rival, rather than
by the Department of State. Nonetheless, after the
opening days of the summit had seemed to indicate

that the United States did not have any new ideas at this critical time in international affairs, President Eisenhower decided to proceed with the Open Skies proposal. On 21 July 1955, Eisenhower, speaking "principally to the Delegates from the Soviet Union," proposed a two-part arrangement, to begin immediately:

To give to each other a complete blueprint of our military establishments, from beginning to end, from one end of our countries to the other; lay out the establishments and provide the blueprints to each other.

Next, to provide within our countries facilities for aerial photography to the other country—we to provide you the facilities within our country, ample facilities for aerial reconnaissance, where you can make all the pictures you choose and take them to your own country to study; you to provide exactly the same facilities for us and we to make these examinations, and by this step to convince the world that we are providing as between ourselves against the possibility of great surprise attack, thus lessening danger and relaxing tensions.

Likewise we will make more easily attainable a comprehensive and effective system of inspection and disarmament, because what I propose, I assure you, would be but a beginning.

The immediate Soviet reaction was mixed. Premier Nikolai Bulganin, the ostensible head of the delegation, initially responded positively, saying that the proposal seemed to have real merit. Nikita Khrushchev's response more accurately foreshadowed the eventual Soviet response, rejecting the proposal as a bald espionage plot. By August, Bulganin was condemning aerial photography as useless because it would not prevent the two countries from being able to hide virtually anything in their respective vast territories. The Soviets emphasized two specific objections: an arrangement on aerial photography should follow, not precede, an arms-reduction agreement, and the U.S. proposal would not allow the Soviets to overfly U.S. forces and installations located in other countries.

Although the summiteers did not agree on Open Skies, they did agree to try to develop a comprehensive system of disarmament, working under the auspices of a United Nations Disarmament Commission (UNDC) subcommittee, whose members included the four summit powers, plus Canada. As soon as this subcommittee began meeting in late August 1955, the United States submitted a plan for implementing Open Skies. In addition to unrestricted (although monitored) aerial reconnaissance, the plan called for an exchange of blueprints of military facilities. It also incorporated a previous Soviet proposal to establish ground control posts to monitor troop movements at key locations. Under the plan, each country would use its own planes and sensors to conduct overflights, and each flight would have aboard a representative of the country being overflown.

Despite continued Soviet objections to the plan, the U.S. persisted. In December 1955 a nearly unanimous U.N. General Assembly passed a resolution calling on the subcommittee to continue working on a comprehensive disarmament agreement, with special emphasis on Open Skies. The Soviet bloc voted against the resolution, and Khrushchev vociferously rejected Open Skies in a speech at the end of the month.

In 1956 the U.S. took a new approach, suggesting that techniques of aerial and ground observation be tested in a large test area (20,000–30,000 square miles) containing no sensitive military installations, except for units stationed in the area specifically for the experiment. The Soviet Union objected once again that the proposal was not connected to any concrete measures of disarmament.

Nonetheless, an apparent shift in Soviet thinking on Open Skies soon emerged. In a letter dated 17 November 1956, Chairman Bulganin told President Eisenhower that the USSR was willing to consider using aerial photography in Europe. Shortly thereafter, in February 1957, the U.S. revealed a new disarmament policy with a new role for Open Skies. Rather than a necessary precondition for comprehensive disarmament, Open Skies would instead serve as a tool for preventing surprise attack.

With these new proposals, Open Skies took on an entirely different hue. The discussions began to center upon setting up regional inspection zones. Through the spring of 1957, the two sides traded proposals on defining a test zone in Europe, but they reached no agreement. Canada, which had strongly supported Open Skies from the beginning, had previously suggested to the U.S. that the Canadian Arctic might serve as one of the test sites for Open Skies. In August 1957, on behalf of Canada, France, Britain, and the U.S., Secretary of State Dulles presented a new set of proposals to the UNDC subcommittee. He proposed that the United States, Canada, and the Soviet Union be entirely open to inspection. As a fallback, these three countries' territories north of the Arctic Circle, along with the

Arctic possessions of Denmark and Norway, could form an inspection zone. In either case, the Soviets would also have to agree to accept one of two inspection zones in Europe defined in the U.S. proposal.

The Soviets responded angrily to the proposals for new zones, charging that "the object of the United States proposal is the collection of reconnaissance data; that it would not result in an improvement but rather in a deterioration of the international situation; and that its real purpose is to contribute to the preparation of aggressive war, not to the removal of the threat of war" (Disarmament Commission Official Records, 1957–1958). When the U.S. tried again in April 1958, this time in the U.N. Security Council, to promote the idea of an arctic test zone for Open Skies, the Soviet Union again opposed it as an espionage plot of little value in preventing surprise attack.

The substantial differences between the U.S. and Soviet views of how an aerial inspection system might work emerged clearly at a conference on preventing surprise attack, in November and December 1958. Although Open Skies was not on the agenda, the Soviet Union did repeat its proposal for a European zone to be subject to both aerial and ground inspection, adding implementation details that differed greatly from Western versions. Under the Soviet proposal, each country would be photographed only by its own nationals, albeit accompanied by representatives of the other side, and data processing and interpretation would be carried out at a joint center. Like the Open Skies discussions, the surprise-attack conference led nowhere.

By the end of the decade, Open Skies seemed both unattainable and obsolete. The first U.S. spy satellites were in orbit by 10 August 1960, which provided complete aerial coverage of the vast Soviet empire, and within a few years the Soviets orbited their own "spies-in-the-sky." Other issues soon took precedence in the disarmament negotiations and the Open Skies concept seemed lost to history.

OPEN SKIES REKINDLED

After lying dormant for three decades, the Open Skies proposal suddenly gained new life in the spring of 1989. The story of its revival bears striking resemblance to the history of Open Skies in the 1950s. Once again, the United States sought to test Soviet intentions with a sweeping proposal for increased openness and once again, the Soviet response appeared to be largely conditioned by fears of espionage. Their differences reflected disagreements over the types of measures needed to build confidence.

The differences between 1955 and 1989 are also significant. The original Open Skies proposal represented, in part, an effort to determine whether arms control verification was even feasible—a less urgent task in the late 1980s after twenty years of experience with arms control. The 1989 proposal was a more purely political test of intent as well as an effort to recapture political momentum. In 1989 the USSR, under President Mikhail Gorbachev, was scoring one propaganda victory after another by suggesting far-reaching arms control measures, in marked contrast to the slow pace of President George Bush's administration regarding arms control. Within the NATO alliance, a divisive debate that threatened to dominate the upcoming NATO summit in late May was raging over the modernization of short-range nuclear forces (SNF). At the same time, Gorbachev's policy of glasnost, or openness, appeared to offer new opportunities for a fundamental transformation of U.S.-Soviet relations.

The decision to revive Open Skies flowed out of discussions in the U.S. National Security Council over ways to test the depth of the Soviet commitment to glasnost, in particular the Soviets' professed willingness to accept any means of verification, no matter how intrusive, on a reciprocal basis and to put forward a significant U.S. proposal that might divert attention from the NATO-SNF debate. It originated early in 1989 with Robert Blackwill, the president's special assistant for European and Soviet affairs, and was soon approved, despite some resistance within the NSC, by Brent Scowcroft, President Bush's national security adviser.

Even in this age of extraordinarily capable spy satellites, aerial overflights of the kind envisioned by the Open Skies plan still have some significant advantages, many of which are technical and economic. Satellites are generally far more expensive because they must be lighter, more reliable, and able to observe from a much greater distance than aircraft. They generally travel in fixed and easily predicted orbits, thus allowing an observed country the time to hide activities of interest before the satellite passes overhead. Although it is possible to shift satellites to different orbits, doing so depletes the fuel needed to keep them in orbit. The types of sensors they carry cannot be changed once the satellite is launched. Aircraft, however, are cheaper and more flexible, able to change routes and sensors as needed. But aircraft have one key flaw: the amount of territory they can cover in a single flight is limited. Thus, satellites and aircraft could serve complementary, rather than competing, roles.

Even before it was made public, the proposal received encouragement from Canada, which had learned of the proposal through informal contacts. On 4 May 1989, Canadian Prime Minister Brian Mulroney and Foreign Minister Joe Clark met privately with President Bush, making a number of crucial suggestions that Bush incorporated into the proposal. Among these was a recommendation that Open Skies be expanded to include the members of NATO and the Warsaw Pact as well as the superpowers.

Bush made the proposal public in his first foreign-policy speech as president, a commencement address on 12 May 1989 at Texas A&M University. He called for consideration of "a broader, more intrusive, and radical" version of Open Skies, one that "would include allies on both sides." Bush argued that "such surveillance flights, complementing satellites, would provide regular scrutiny for both sides. Such unprecedented territorial access would show the world the meaning of the concept of openness."

The proposal failed to reap many propaganda points at home. Within the United States, pundits and the media dismissed Open Skies as an unimaginative resurrection of a dated idea. Most assumed, incorrectly, that the advent of satellites had rendered aerial reconnaissance obsolete.

The reaction from abroad was more positive. The Canadian government was the first to respond, releasing a statement by Prime Minister Mulroney on 12 May supporting the proposal, followed in early June by a *New York Times* op-ed article by Foreign Minister Clark. Although the other NATO allies had not been informed in advance, at the NATO summit at the end of May, the allies welcomed the initiative and promised careful study and consultations.

Allied acceptance of Open Skies had two causes. First, the proposal was the first positive sign of U.S. leadership on arms control from the new Bush administration. Second, Open Skies represented a means by which the allies could observe Soviet-bloc countries directly, rather than having to rely on U.S. statements based on closely held and rarely shared data from U.S. spy satellites. Virtually all NATO members have at least some technical capability for aerial reconnaissance, although sophisticated sensors and the ability to process information are not uniformly available. Yet, as of 1989, only France planned to launch its own spy satellite in the near future; and it would be substantially less capable than those operated by the United States.

The first official Soviet response came in the form of a letter from Gorbachev delivered to Secretary of State James Baker by Soviet Foreign Minister Eduard Shevardnadze at their ministerial meeting in Jackson Hole, Wyoming, on 22–23 September 1989. The letter generally favored Open Skies, but it expressed certain concerns that foreshadowed what later proved to be serious obstacles to agreement on the proposal. Gorbachev stressed the need to rule out any chance that information from Open Skies overflights could be used to the detriment of the security of the observed country. He argued that all parties should have full equality of access to information, regardless of geographical and/or technological differences among the parties, an implicit reference to the much larger size and less-sophisticated technology of the Soviet Union. The letter also mentioned the need for "agreed constraints." Gorbachev suggested that these concerns might be addressed by establishing a multinational pool of aircraft and sensors and by sharing with all parties all the data gathered during overflights.

Despite these reservations, Shevardnadze indicated that the USSR would participate in the first round of negotiations, to be held in Ottawa. At their Malta summit in early December, Bush and Gorbachev confirmed that both countries would actively participate in the Open Skies talks.

The NATO position, formulated during the fall of 1989, differed markedly from Gorbachev's suggestions. As finally agreed on in December, the NATO basic-elements paper laid out a proposal for a highly intrusive and flexible Open Skies regime, with virtually no constraints other than "those imposed by flight safety rules or international law." It called on all countries to accept a large number of overflights of their territory, up to several overflights a month of larger countries, and at least one per quarter year for even the smallest countries. The only restriction on sensor technology prohibited "devices used for the collection and recording of signals intelligence." The paper permitted the sharing of data within an alliance, but it made no mention of the possibility of sharing data across alliances. Nothing was said about establishing a common pool of aircraft or sensors.

Open Skies raised unprecedented operational questions. How well could air-traffic controllers cope with Open Skies overflights with flight plans outside normal air corridors filed only hours before a flight? How much time would be needed for a host country to inspect the aircraft to check for forbidden sensors? To test possible procedures, on 6 January 1990, a month before Open Skies negotiations were to begin, Canada conducted a three-hour test overflight of Hungary. The plane, a Canadian C-130, crossed three air-traffic control corridors, flying over several Hungarian and Soviet military installations. The plane carried no sensors. Several Hungarian and Canadian officials, including the head of the Hungarian Air Force, were aboard. The test demonstrated the feasibility and safety of short-notice aerial inspections of the type envisioned under Open Skies. Canada invited Warsaw Pact countries, including the USSR, to undertake a similar flight over Canada. In January 1992 Hungary conducted a reciprocal overflight of Canada.

The Negotiations   By the time the negotiations formally opened in February 1990, the European security system had changed beyond recognition. The collapse of Communist regimes throughout Eastern Europe drastically affected the agenda of security issues for both NATO and the Warsaw Pact. The first subject for discussion in Ottawa was German reunification, which dominated the opening days of the Open Skies talks, taking advantage of the presence of all the relevant foreign ministers. The political transformation of Europe also changed the nature of the negotiations, initially intended to be bloc-to-bloc. For the first time, the Eastern European members of the Warsaw Pact refused to support the Soviet position on a number of key issues.

Because of the Soviet policy of glasnost, the changes that the Soviets had allowed in Eastern Europe, and the drastic improvement in East-West relations, most Western analysts and negotiators hoped for a speedy and successful conclusion to the talks. Two rounds were scheduled, first in Ottawa in February and then in Budapest in April and May, a session at which organizers hoped a treaty would be signed one year to the day after Bush revived Open Skies.

But as the negotiations opened, striking differences emerged between the Soviet and Western views of what an Open Skies regime should look like. NATO, with U.S. prodding, was fairly well unified in its call for a simple, flexible approach with as few restrictions as possible. The Soviets argued for a far more restricted regime to prevent possible adverse uses of the information gathered from overflights. The other Warsaw Pact countries supported the Soviet position on a few issues and the NATO position on most others. The differences fell into four categories.

Aircraft and Sensors   NATO argued that each country that wished to conduct an overflight of another country should be free to use whatever aircraft and sensors, except signals intelligence (SIGINT) sensors, it had available. The host country would be given several hours to inspect the aircraft prior to the overflight to ensure that it did not contain SIGINT equipment. The Soviets, however, were not satisfied that an inspection would be adequate. They suggested that a common fleet of aircraft be operated by mixed crews or that the host country provide the plane and crew. They also expressed concern over the advantages that would accrue to the more technically advanced West if no other restrictions were placed on the sensors that could be used on Open Skies overflights, and they argued that all participants in Open Skies should have access to the same sensors. The other members of the Warsaw Pact generally shared this view, but they were willing to include far more sophisticated sensors than was the USSR, so long as the Warsaw Pact members would have equal access to sensor technology.

At the Budapest round of talks, NATO modified its stance on sensors to appeal to the Eastern Europeans. NATO agreed to relax export controls so that all participants could buy commercially available technology equivalent to whatever the West would use in Open Skies. Although the Soviets, then isolated, continued to call for a sensor package limited to relatively low-resolution cameras, they did indicate that very low resolution radar might also be acceptable.

Data Distribution   The NATO position would leave the use of Open Skies information up to the country that conducted the overflight and would allow the sharing of data only within an alliance. The Soviets wanted to give all participants access to all data to ensure that the information collected was not too sophisticated. The Eastern Europeans agreed, for such a provision would allow the Eastern European countries to see data that NATO had collected on the Soviet Union and on other Eastern European countries. Once NATO agreed to provide access to comparable sensor technology, most Eastern European countries dropped their support for data sharing.

Quotas   The United States insisted that if Open Skies were truly to build confidence, each participant would have to accept enough overflights to cover its territory so that other nations could reassure themselves about military facilities and activities. The U.S. offered to accept one overflight a week and argued that the USSR should accept 2.4 times as many, being 2.4 times as large. The Soviets proposed drastically lower numbers: a total of thirty per year per alliance, with no single country having to accept more than half of these. At Budapest, the USSR increased the number of overflights it would accept to twenty-five, but with strict limits on the length (five hundred kilometers, 300 miles) and duration (the flight could last much longer, but the sensors could only operate for a total of three hours) of any single overflight.

With the dissolution of the Warsaw Pact, the quota issue has become extremely complicated. In addition to the matter of passive quotas (the number of overflights of its territory each participant must accept), negotiators have to resolve the thorny problems of how many overflights each participant may conduct and what other nations it may overfly. Originally, Open Skies was to allow members of one alliance to overfly members of the other. Several of the former Warsaw Pact members have now indicated that they wish to be able to overfly each other.

Territory   NATO proposed that all territory of all participating nations be opened for overflight, except for air-traffic safety restrictions. The Soviets proposed three categories of restrictions that would have closed off a substantial portion of their territory and wanted the right to overfly U.S. bases overseas in countries not participating in Open Skies, such as Japan and the Philippines.

From the U.S. perspective, the Soviet proposals would greatly reduce the confidence-building value of Open Skies. The chief U.S. ambassador, John Hawes, argued that "Open Skies is intended as a serious confidence-building measure, that is, one in which international confidence derives from the substance of what the regime produces, and not

solely or even primarily from the symbolism or novelty of the fact that the regime exists at all," and that the proposed Soviet restrictions on sensor capability, territory, numbers of overflights, and control of aircraft were so great that, if accepted, Open Skies "would not increase confidence" (Hawes, pp. 8–9).

The Soviet position reflected several factors, particularly Soviet military resistance to a program that they feared could affect Soviet security and concerns about overlap with aerial inspections to be conducted as part of the Treaty on Conventional Forces in Europe. In addition, although Gorbachev's restatement of support in principle for Open Skies at the U.S.-Soviet summit in June 1990 indicated that Open Skies still enjoyed high-level political support in the USSR, the Soviet domestic political situation and the CFE and START negotiations left the leadership little time to concern itself with Open Skies.

The NATO allies other than the United States and the Warsaw Pact members other than the USSR were, for the most part, willing to accept compromises between the U.S. and Soviet positions, although on most issues they were closer to the U.S. than to the Soviet position. For these states, even a somewhat restricted version of Open Skies would provide a substantial improvement in their ability to gather information about the other participating nations.

After Budapest: Links to CFE   The Open Skies negotiations were substantively closely linked with the talks over reductions of conventional forces in Europe (CFE). In 1989, when expectations were high that an Open Skies accord could be rapidly concluded, many Western officials believed that the Open Skies provisions could simply be transferred to provide the anticipated aerial-inspection protocol (AIP) of CFE. The AIP would be a verification measure intended to help detect possible noncompliance with the CFE limits on numbers of various types of military equipment, a much clearer goal than the vague confidence-building aim of Open Skies. With the failure to reach agreement at Budapest, negotiators decided to suspend the talks until the CFE Treaty was completed, given that similar issues arose in both sets of talks and that CFE, a higher priority for most participants, was likely to divert attention from Open Skies for several months.

The CFE I Treaty was signed in November 1990 at a Paris summit of all twenty-two NATO and Warsaw

Pact members. But for many of the same reasons that Open Skies had faltered, the parties were unable to include an aerial-inspection component in the CFE verification provisions and agreed instead to put off discussion of aerial inspection to the 1991 round of CFE negotiations. The summit did issue a joint declaration in which the participants reaffirmed "the importance of the 'Open Skies' initiative and their determination to bring the negotiations to a successful conclusion as soon as possible."

Open Skies Becomes a Reality With the CFE negotiations resolved, attention returned to Open Skies, which now seemed more important than ever. Because the CFE Treaty failed in the end to include an aerial-inspection component, Open Skies was seen as a potentially important source of verification of the CFE Treaty. This view was reinforced in late 1990, shortly before the CFE Treaty was signed, when the Soviet Union shipped substantial quantities of military equipment east of the Ural Mountains as a means of removing the equipment from CFE limitations. The verification regime of the CFE Treaty did not apply east of the Urals, but an Open Skies treaty would cover all of Soviet territory, allowing Europeans to monitor the moved equipment.

By April 1991, the NATO allies had agreed to several modifications of their positions on Open Skies, such as sharing raw data, limiting sensors to those available to all participants, and allowing an observed nation to insist on use of its own aircraft (but only if the observed nation also paid the costs). NATO continued to insist, however, that sensors be good enough to be militarily useful, that all territory of all participants could be overflown without restriction, and that military bases of Open Skies participants in third countries would not be included. In August, the Soviets agreed to meet in Vienna in September for renewed discussions. Despite the intervening coup attempt in the USSR, the meeting opened on September 9 for one week, but the Soviet delegates had not yet received new instructions reflecting the changed political situation in their country. When the meeting reconvened on November 5, it was clear that the Soviets were prepared to make significant concessions, including acceptance of full territorial coverage and willingness to accept a much larger number of overflights. Even the dissolution of the Soviet Union in late December did not break the momentum. The Russian Federation took over the Soviet seat, and Ukraine and Belarus joined the talks as independent states.

In this optimistic atmosphere, negotiators set a target date of 24 March 1992, to coincide with the CSCE ministerial meeting in Helsinki. Although some technical and cost issues had to be deferred, the 100-page treaty was completed and signed on schedule. In final form, the treaty permitted the use of reasonably capable sensors: optical equipment with resolution as good as thirty centimeters and infrared sensors with resolution of fifty centimeters, which is adequate to recognize most military equipment, and synthetic aperture radar with resolution of three meters, adequate to locate possible concentrations of military equipment. It also called for fairly short notice. A party wishing to conduct an overflight must provide no less than seventy-two hours' notice, and on arrival it must submit a route plan to the host country. The actual flight can begin no sooner than twenty-four hours after submission of the flight plan. There are no territorial restrictions. All parts of all participating countries can be overflown. In addition, the treaty includes procedures by which members can agree to upgrade the permitted sensor capabilities or add new types of sensors. The treaty also establishes an Open Skies Consultative Commission (OSCC) to review implementation of treaty terms.

The treaty covers a remarkable geographic scope. Signatories include all NATO members, all the non-Soviet members of the former Warsaw Pact, and four of the successor states to the Soviet Union: Russia, Ukraine, Belarus, and Georgia. All other CSCE members are eligible to join, with the consent of the existing parties (or later at the discretion of the OSCC). The treaty will enter into force sixty days after ratification by twenty signatories, including all the major parties.

CONCLUSION

Although Open Skies is somewhat more restricted in terms of sensor capabilities than the regime originally envisaged by the United States in 1989, it is still a major accomplishment. The terms add up to a remarkably flexible and intrusive regime, one that goes far beyond any previous confidence-building measures. Open Skies may help to stabilize relations among new nations in a volatile part of the world and could provide a model for confidence-building measures elsewhere. It could serve as the basis of a verification component for a wide range of possible arms control agreements. It could even fairly easily be adapted for environmental monitoring. Open Skies may not have received the attention of some of the more glamorous arms control negotiations, but it may prove to be among the most significant security treaties of the late twentieth century.

BIBLIOGRAPHY

President Eisenhower's 1955 proposal is discussed by JANE BOULDEN, "Open Skies: The 1955 Proposal and its Current Revival," *Dalhousie Law Journal* 13, no. 2 (1990); and W. W. ROSTOW, *Open Skies: Eisenhower's Proposal of July 21, 1955* (Austin, Texas, 1982). The 1989 proposal is examined by JOHN H. HAWES, "Open Skies: From Idea to Negotiation," *NATO Review* 38, no. 2 (1990): 6–9; and JONATHAN B. TUCKER, "Back to the Future: The Open Skies Talks," *Arms Control Today* (October 1990): 20–24.

The various aspects of Open Skies are reviewed in MICHAEL SLACK and HEATHER CHESTNUTT, eds., *Open Skies: Technical, Organizational, Operational, Legal, and Political Aspects* (Toronto, 1990) and in PETER JONES, "Open Skies: A New Era of Transparency," *Arms Control Today* 22, no. 4 (May 1992): 10–15. The arms control aspects of the Open Skies concept are examined in ALLEN V. BANNER, ANDREW J. YOUNG, and KEITH W. HALL, *Aerial Reconnaissance for Verification of Arms Limitation Agreements: An Introduction* (New York, 1990); and PETER JONES, "CFE Aerial Inspections and Open Skies: A Comparison," in HEATHER CHESTNUTT and MICHAEL SLACK, eds., *Verifying Conventional Force Reductions in Europe: CFE I and Beyond* (Toronto, n.d.).

The Strategic Defense Initiative and Arms Control

DOUGLAS C. WALLER

See also The Anti-Ballistic Missile Treaty: 1972 to the Present; Anti-Satellite Weapons and Arms Control; Negotiating Arms Control and Disarmament Agreements; Russia and the Soviet Union; *and* The United States. *The* Anti-Ballistic Missile Treaty *is excerpted in Volume III.*

For two years President Ronald Reagan had faced hardly any opposition as he launched the largest U.S. military buildup in peacetime history. Indeed, it was a buildup supported by a Congress and an American public humiliated by a failed 1980 Tehran rescue of U.S. hostages and convinced that the Soviet military had overtaken the United States. But by 1983, the pendulum had begun to swing back. Americans had become alarmed concerning the loose talk about nuclear war coming out of the Reagan administration. Congress had become restive over soaring Pentagon budgets. A grass-roots nuclear-freeze movement calling for a superpower halt to the nuclear-arms race was building momentum across the country. To regain the initiative, Reagan took to the airwaves on 23 March 1983 to plead for higher defense spending and to denounce a nuclear-freeze resolution then being considered by the U.S. House of Representatives. But tucked into the end of the president's nationwide address was a message about which only a handful of his advisers had been given advance warning.

"Let me share with you a vision of the future which offers hope," Reagan began. "What if free people could live secure in the knowledge that their security did not rest on the threat of instant U.S. retaliation to deter a Soviet attack; that we could intercept and destroy strategic ballistic missiles before they reached our own soil or that of our allies?" Beginning that night, the president announced, the United States would launch a massive research and development project with the aim of making nuclear weapons "impotent and obsolete." The idea was to erect an anti-ballistic-missile shield over the United States "to achieve our ultimate goal of eliminating the threat posed by strategic nuclear missiles."

The announcement stunned Congress and even the Pentagon. For more than three decades, the United States had ultimately relied on the threat of massive nuclear retaliation to deter a Soviet nuclear attack. This standoff became known as Mutual Assured Destruction (MAD). A U.S. retaliatory response to a Soviet nuclear attack would be so devastating that it would be suicidal for the Kremlin to ever strike first. Over the years, nuclear weapons and strategies had been refined by the two superpowers. Both sides had the capability to deliver nuclear weapons with pinpoint accuracy, threatening the other's missile silos and hardened military targets. U.S. nuclear deterrence had been extended to United States allies in Asia and Europe. Moscow and Washington had developed a variety of response options, such as limited nuclear strikes to destroy selected military targets. But ultimately, any type of nuclear conflict between the superpowers would lead to an all-out, all-consuming nuclear war—a reality that had left U.S. presidents of the nuclear age uneasy.

Ronald Reagan proposed to change that reality with the Strategic Defense Initiative (SDI). Political opponents and most of the scientific community ridiculed the notion of comprehensive ballistic-missile defenses as pie in the sky. Cynics quickly dubbed the program to research the idea "Star Wars," and the name stuck. But the president was determined. The White House launched an unprecedented effort to militarize space, not only with anti-ballistic missiles to shoot down Soviet rockets, but also with anti-satellite weapons to attack Soviet satellites. The 1972 Anti-Ballistic Missile (ABM) Treaty, which restricted the development of ballistic-missile defenses, came under withering attack from defense conservatives who saw the accord as a relic of failed arms control. During the next eight years, from 1984 to 1991, more than $20 billion was spent on the research and development of space weapons. Today, SDI bears little resemblance to Reagan's vision of a massive research effort to build comprehensive missile defenses. The Soviet empire is no longer the monolithic military threat of Reagan's day. With the public-relations success of the U.S. Army's Patriot anti-missile system in the Persian Gulf War, President George Bush, who was never particularly enamored of the Reagan vision, has redirected SDI to explore limited defenses against accidental or third world ballistic-missile launches. Nevertheless, Star Wars has been and continues to be one of the most controversial United States defense programs ever undertaken—in part, because of its impact, direct or perceived, on the arms control process.

HISTORY OF MISSILE DEFENSES

Intercontinental ballistic missiles (ICBMs) can speed nuclear warheads thousands of miles across the ocean to their targets in just a half-hour. Almost from their inception, defense technologists have searched unsuccessfully for weapons to shoot them down. In the late 1950s the U.S. Army experimented with the Nike-Zeus anti-ballistic-missile system for a nationwide defense, but the Eisenhower and Kennedy administrations took a dim view of the program, questioning its effectiveness. In 1959, the Defense Department launched the Ballistic Missile Boost Intercept program (BAMBI) to investigate whether Soviet ICBMs that had been launched could be destroyed by interceptors based on satellites in space. The BAMBI program was canceled four years later. During the remainder of the 1960s and early 1970s the Defense Department researched and developed a variety of ground-based, nuclear-armed

missile interceptors: Sprint, Spartan, Sentinel, and Safeguard. The Soviet Union also developed a crude interceptor-missile system known as Galosh. But by 1967, Defense Secretary Robert McNamara had concluded that a ballistic-missile defense system to protect U.S. cities from a full-scale Soviet nuclear attack was not feasible and proposed instead a partial ABM system to defend against a Chinese or accidental Soviet nuclear launch. Two years later, the Nixon administration proposed an ABM system to defend only U.S. Minuteman ICBMs in their silos.

By 1972, both superpowers had reluctantly come to the realization that they would never be able to deploy comprehensive ballistic-missile defenses that could alter the reality of MAD. Any attempt to do so would only fuel an expensive and dangerous offensive-defensive arms race that would never end. In May, Moscow and Washington signed a treaty on the limitation of anti-ballistic missile systems (ABMS).

The ABM Treaty became the cornerstone of U.S.-Soviet strategic-arms control, the first permanent, bilateral nuclear accord the superpowers had signed. Under the treaty, the two sides agreed not to deploy an ABM system to defend the territory or any region of their nations. Both countries also agreed not to develop, test, or deploy ABM systems or components that were sea-, air-, space-, or mobile land-based. Missiles used to attack airplanes could not be upgraded to defend against ballistic missiles. Likewise, radars could be deployed along each country's periphery to warn of a strategic nuclear attack, but could not be deployed farther inland to direct ballistic-missile defenses. Finally, ABM systems or their components could not be deployed abroad or transferred to other countries.

There were exceptions to the treaty. One was a very limited, fixed land-based system of no more than one hundred ABM launchers, which each country could deploy. The USSR placed a one-hundred-missile "Galosh" system around Moscow. The United States deactivated its ABM system at Grand Forks, North Dakota, in 1975 for cost reasons and because of the system's questionable effectiveness. Each side could develop and deploy shorter range anti-tactical ballistic missiles. The treaty did not ban anti-satellite weapons. Both countries had been testing ground-based anti-satellite missiles since the mid-1960s. The treaty also allowed each side to continue anti-ballistic-missile research.

During the 1970s and early 1980s, the Soviet Union conducted extensive research into laser and particle-beam technology, although U.S. intelligence analysts still cannot agree on how much progress the Soviets actually made in this research and how militarily useful it was. The Moscow ABM system was based on fairly antiquated technology and would be largely ineffective against a concentrated United States attack. The Pentagon warned that the Moscow ABM system could be expanded and the Soviet Union's extensive air-defense network could be easily converted to anti-ballistic-missile defenses. In addition, conservatives charged that the Kremlin was building a massive network of underground shelters. But cooler heads concluded that the bomb shelters were largely a waste of money and would not protect the Soviet Union from the devastation of nuclear war. The Central Intelligence Agency did not see much evidence that Soviet air defenses would be converted to ballistic-missile defenses or that the Moscow ABM system would be expanded. About the best that could be said for the Galoshes ringing Moscow were that they gave Soviet units operational training that U.S. soldiers did not get.

For its part, the United States conducted a modest yet hardly insignificant research program. All told, less than $1 billion was spent annually on ballistic-missile-defense research, primarily on nuclear and conventionally armed rockets that would intercept Soviet warheads as they reentered the Earth's atmosphere. Some research was conducted into exotic technologies such as lasers, but critics were justified in pointing out that the work was scattered among a number of agencies and services and lacked focus or direction.

Throughout the 1970s, conventional wisdom held that the Pandora's box of anti-ballistic missiles was best left closed by the ABM Treaty. Most scientists viewed ballistic-missile defenses as a dangerous pipe dream. The political mainstream agreed; only the fringe Right advocated a ballistic missile shield. But a handful of military officers and researchers in the nation's federal weapons laboratories remained convinced that advances in rocket, laser, sensor, and computer technologies would make such defenses possible by the end of the twentieth century. By 1980, political conservatives had convinced many in Washington and across the country that arms control had weakened United States national security by failing to contain the expanding Soviet nuclear arsenal. Ballistic-missile defense advocates now insisted that United States technology and Yankee ingenuity could accomplish

what arms control had not—the elimination of the danger of nuclear war. Surely a national security policy that relied on mutual assured survival (the destruction of missiles) was more moral and humane than mutual assured destruction (the destruction of people). All that was needed was someone to give the idea political respectability, someone with the political will to ignore skeptics and begin a bold new military research program. That person was Ronald Reagan.

THE STRATEGIC DEFENSE INITIATIVE

Reagan launched his Strategic Defense Initiative with hardly any consultation among the scientific and defense communities. That was just as well as far as SDI proponents were concerned. If the president had taken a traditional approach—requesting feasibility studies from the Defense Department or a blue-ribbon scientific panel before deciding to launch the program—SDI would never have gotten off the ground. The Pentagon was lukewarm to the idea. The scientific community was flatly opposed.

Instead, Reagan relied on the advice of only a few decidedly partisan scientists, such as Dr. Edward Teller, a missile defense enthusiast at the Lawrence Livermore National Laboratory in Livermore, California, and one of the fathers of the hydrogen bomb. Making claims his own Livermore scientists would later complain were inflated, Teller convinced Reagan that directed-energy weapons such as Excaliber, the nuclear-pumped, X-ray laser being researched at Livermore, could be sent in space to zap Soviet missiles as they left their silos. Reagan had no technical or scientific background nor any aides offering objective scientific advice. White House science aide Dr. George Keyworth, who was more Star Wars advocate than adviser, did not broach the new initiative with the White House Science Council before the 23 March speech. Senior Defense and State Department officials were likewise kept in the dark or given only a few days' notice. National Security Adviser Robert McFarlane privately expressed doubts that a defense shield could ever be erected but went along with SDI as a bargaining chip that might be traded away for deep cuts in Soviet strategic weapons. The Joint Chiefs of Staff were likewise privately skeptical. The Strategic Defense Initiative thus began with no serious scientific review but with the advocacy of the one person who mattered: the president of the United States.

The Defense Department and defense contractors, however, quickly closed ranks behind Reagan's proposal. The administration formed the Defense Technologies Study team, chaired by the former head of the National Aeronautics and Space Administration (NASA), James Fletcher, to map out a long-term research program to develop ballistic-missile defenses. The Fletcher panel recommended a massive research effort limited only by the pace of technology. By the beginning of 1984, the Strategic Defense Initiative Organization (SDIO) was chartered to manage the program. Over the next six years the organization proposed to spend $33 billion to determine the feasibility of ballistic-missile defenses, making SDI the largest military research program the Pentagon had ever undertaken.

The "Layers" of the Shield

The shield the Strategic Defense Initiative Organization envisioned erecting was breathtaking, nothing less than a nearly leakproof astrodome that would keep Soviet nuclear warheads from landing on U.S. military and civilian targets. Such a defense is commonly called an "area defense." The shield—or "architecture"—SDI planners hoped to erect would consist of layers of anti-ballistic missiles and laser weapons, with each layer successively thinning out the attacking Soviet force.

The first layer would be the boost-phase defense, which would destroy Soviet missiles shortly after they left their silos. During the boost phase, a typical Soviet ICBM will spend three to five minutes traveling to an altitude of about 200 kilometers (120 miles) before its boosters burn out and its warheads are dispensed. Shooting down Soviet missiles during their boost phase would be critical to making the astrodome shield work. The reason for this has largely to do with the target and numbers. A large bright exhaust plume that can be easily spotted and tracked by space-based sensors trails a launched missile. However, single warheads speeding through space are more difficult to spot and track. Each missile also contains as many as ten warheads. If one shot can kill the missile, the defense destroys ten warheads. If the missile survives and dispenses its warheads, the defense has to expend ten shots to kill ten warheads. The boost-phase defenses would have a large number of Soviet strategic missiles to shoot down: then calculated to be

more than 1,300 land-based ICBMs and 900 submarine-launched ballistic missiles. But the number of targets the other layers of the defense would face would be in the tens of thousands if the boost phase did not thin out the Soviet missile force.

But the boost-phase defense must work quickly and from great distances. An orbiting battle station thousands of miles away has just three to five minutes to destroy the missile. SDI researchers planned to deploy space-based sensor satellites that would detect and track Soviet missile launches, feeding information on their positions to battle stations that would destroy the rockets. These satellites would have passive sensors such as infrared detectors that would pick up the radiation from the missiles' exhaust plumes.

Two types of weapons were being considered for the boost-phase kill: kinetic-energy weapons and directed-energy weapons. Kinetic-energy weapons are rockets or projectiles that would collide with the missiles or warheads at very high speeds, destroying them on impact. Under the SDI program, research began on space-based kinetic "kill" vehicles—tiny rockets fired from orbiting battle stations. But the Strategic Defense Initiative Organization faced a major hurdle: building a small lightweight rocket that could travel fast enough to reach the Soviet booster before it burned out.

Directed energy weapons could reach the target much quicker but they would also be exceedingly more difficult to build. A variety of lasers were being investigated. A laser produces a coherent beam of light that SDI scientists hoped could be made powerful enough to burn a hole through a Soviet missile's skin or disable the missile with a shock wave. The laser's light may be visible to the naked eye, or may consist of infrared or ultraviolet radiation or X rays. The lasing occurs when more molecules or atoms are in an excited, higher energy state than are in a lower energy state. When the excited molecule drops to a lower energy state it emits radiation. Chemical hydrogen-flouride or deuterium-flouride lasers produce radiation through chemical reactions. Excimer lasers use an excited dimer, or a two-atom molecule, whose laser radiation is produced by a pulsed electrical discharge. Free-electron lasers produce an intense radiation beam by passing electrons through a magnetic field. A nuclear explosion could pump an X-ray laser beam. SDI also began intensive research into particle-beam weapons that fire subatomic particles at the speed of light. These particles—protons, electrons, neutral atoms, heavy ions—pass through the missile's skin and destroy the electronic systems inside.

The next stage of flight is the post-boost phase. After the last booster burns out and is jettisoned, the rest of the missile consists of a post-boost vehicle, or "bus," that houses the warheads. The bus carries the warheads for about ten minutes to an approximate apogee of 1,200 kilometers (720 miles) above the earth, firing its thrusters to adjust the trajectory and releasing warheads that speed to their targets. The bus is more difficult to destroy than the missile because it is a smaller target for the satellite sensors to track and emits less heat. But if the kinetic- or directed-energy weapons of the boost-phase defenses could not shoot down the missile, the bus was their next-best target before it released warheads.

After they are released by the bus, the warheads spend approximately twenty minutes in flight before they reenter the earth's atmosphere. During this midcourse phase of flight the defenses have the most time to find and destroy the warheads. But the defenses face two other problems. The sensors have more difficulty finding the small warheads, which emit little telltale energy speeding through cold, black space. Also, the defenses may have to track and destroy thousands of warheads, an enormous task by itself but one made more difficult for the kinetic-kill vehicles and directed-energy weapons because thousands of decoys and bits of debris may be traveling with the warheads. The defense does not want to waste its firepower on decoys and debris.

The final layer of the defense is the terminal phase, when the Soviet warheads reenter the atmosphere about 100 kilometers (60 miles) above the United States. Ground-based radars and optical sensors based on patrolling planes would have an easier time spotting and tracking them. Friction from the atmosphere would heat up the warheads, which would be traveling up to 25,600 kilometers (16,000 miles) per hour, while lighter-weight decoys would slow down because of air drag.

But the problem at this point is time. The defense has only ten seconds to destroy the warheads with high-speed and highly accurate ground-based rocket interceptors before the warheads strike their targets. Actually, they have less than ten seconds. Because these Soviet warheads might be salvage-fused (set to detonate if struck during flight), the defense must intercept them at high altitudes so

that the nuclear explosions will not do unacceptable damage to cities on the ground. Two types of conventionally armed interceptors had begun to be developed for the mission: an exo-atmospheric reentry interception system (ERIS) to destroy Soviet warheads in the late midcourse phase, and a high endo-atmospheric defense interceptor (HEDI) to destroy warheads at an altitude of 13 to 48 kilometers (8 to 30 miles).

The defense must be coordinated. Computerized sensors that identify and track missile launches also must pass that information to space-based battle stations, where the targets must be divided up and engaged. Sensors must then identify missiles that have been destroyed and pass along to ground-based radars and airborne optical scanners information on the warheads that have escaped and are heading their way. Ground and airborne sensors then must direct the ground-based interceptors that home in for the final kill. An elaborate battle-management system directed by sophisticated computers would have to be erected.

The Strategic Defense Initiative was only concerned with the ballistic-missile threat. Even if that threat was eliminated, the Soviets still had low-flying, nuclear-armed cruise missiles and bombers in their arsenal that could devastate the United States. The Reagan administration later began an air defense initiative to contend with those threats.

Amazing Breakthroughs?   The Reagan administration planned four phases of its Strategic Defense Initiative. Phase 1, the research phase, would last through the early 1990s, when SDI would explore different ballistic-missile defense options so that a future president could decide whether to begin full-scale engineering development of a system. The Soviets could be expected to keep pace with their own strategic defense program. Phase 2 would begin in the early 1990s with full-scale engineering development and the testing of prototype weapons. The 1972 ABM Treaty would be abrogated by this time. During the third phase, the United States and Soviet Union would begin deploying incrementally their defenses, negotiating arms control agreements along the way to reduce each side's offensive nuclear forces. Even the administration admitted that this transition phase was fraught with dangers, particularly if one side jumped ahead of the other in developing defenses. At one point Reagan even floated the possibility of sharing strategic-defense technology with the Soviets to smooth the transition. Pentagon officials expressed their consternation and the president quickly abandoned the idea. The final phase, Phase 4, would be mutually assured survival, when both superpowers had functioning astrodome shields.

When that day would come was anybody's guess. The strategic defense being considered was so massive—outside estimates put its eventual cost as high as $1 trillion—that the Strategic Defense Initiative Organization could only guess that the astrodome would be decades away. Yet SDIO had barely begun Phase 1 when its leaders and senior Reagan administration officials began claiming incredible breakthroughs in research that had speeded up the timetable. A prototype ground-based rocket developed by the army had already intercepted a test warhead high in the atmosphere. The SDIO released videotapes of a chemical laser shooting through the skin of a stationary mock-up of a Titan booster causing a spectacular explosion. "The barriers we saw to progress are crumbling," Defense Secretary Caspar Weinberger announced. A little more than a year after the program began, SDI's director, Lieutenant General James Abrahamson, proclaimed that his scientists had already resolved the question of whether strategic defenses could be effectively deployed: they could. According to Abrahamson, the only question now was "when, how fast and at what cost."

Abrahamson's scientists actually had concluded no such thing. The Strategic Defense Initiative had indeed made commendable progress. Disparate ballistic-missile defense projects among the various armed services had been brought together under one management team. Among the approximately two thousand contracts the SDIO issued were a number of innovative research efforts in universities and small businesses. Yet as the SDI program matured, its scientists began to realize that strategic defenses faced enormous technological hurdles. Chemical lasers weighed too much to be launched into space and had operational problems in destroying Soviet missiles in the boost phase. X-ray lasers and neutral particle-beam weapons also had operational problems as weapons. Engineers were having difficulty designing kinetic-kill vehicles small enough to be placed on orbiting satellites yet with engines powerful enough to speed them to the Soviet missiles within minutes of their launch.

Ground-based interceptors could be built to attack incoming warheads, but they could not yet be built cheaply. The experimental interceptor the army successfully tested cost more than $10 million. For the defense, SDI would have to mass-produce thousands of ground-based interceptors for as little as $1 million apiece. SDI would require a massive new launch capability to orbit the thousands of kinetic-kill vehicles, sensors, and lasers needed for the space-based portion of the defense. As many as five thousand space-shuttle flights would be needed to put 200 million pounds (90 million kilograms) of hardware into space. Launch costs, by 1986, were as high as $3,000 per pound. To keep space-based defenses from being prohibitively expensive the cost had to be slashed to $400 per pound, requiring a revolution in the way NASA conducted business.

SDI scientists also faced two fundamental problems with strategic defenses: discrimination and survivability. With its successful interception of a test warhead, the army had already demonstrated that a bullet could hit a bullet. The problem was finding the bullet. During the midcourse phase, the Soviet buses could release tens of thousands of decoy warheads. Satellite sensors would be overwhelmed trying to sort them out so kinetic-kill vehicles wouldn't be wasted on decoys. Therefore, for strategic defenses to be effective, battle stations had to be orbited in space to attack missiles in their boost phase before the warheads and decoys were released.

But the space-based battle stations would be vulnerable to counterattack. SDI scientists began grappling with a host of countermeasures the Soviets might take, such as fast-burn boosters that would shorten the time kinetic-kill vehicles had to attack missiles after they were launched. Space mines could be orbited to sneak up to battle stations and explode. Anti-satellite rockets like the ones being developed by the U.S. Air Force for F-15 jet fighters could be launched to knock out orbiting stations. Directed-energy weapons that might make good ballistic-missile defense weapons became even better anti-satellite weapons. Soviet space-based lasers or particle-beam weapons used for ballistic-missile defense could just as easily turn their sights on U.S. space-based stations. SDI scientists soon discovered that pop-up X-ray lasers that the Soviets might launch and explode would prove particularly deadly to space-based defenses. Satellite survivability was so nettlesome a problem, some SDI scientists worried that it could only be solved by each side signing agreements not to attack the other's defenses—an unlikely possibility.

SDI AND ARMS CONTROL

From its inception, the Strategic Defense Initiative appeared to be on a collision course with arms control programs and advocates. The 1972 ABM Treaty allowed SDI research. Its prohibition on deploying ABM systems did not immediately constrain SDI, because the program would not be able to deploy anything until the late 1990s. But SDI managers wanted to begin development and testing of space-based strategic defenses by the early 1990s and by everyone's reading, the treaty clearly banned that kind of activity. In 1985, the administration set out to change the reading.

On 6 October 1985, National Security Adviser Robert McFarlane dropped the bombshell during a televised appearance on NBC's *Meet the Press*. According to McFarlane, the ABM Treaty permitted development and testing of space-based defenses SDI had in mind because they were based on exotic technologies that did not exist when the accord was signed. For the previous month, Pentagon and State Department lawyers had been reviewing the secret record of the U.S.-Soviet negotiations on the treaty to determine its effect on SDI. The lawyers argued that the Nixon administration had tried but failed to get the Soviets to agree to limit the development and testing of future ABM systems based on exotic technologies. Therefore, the treaty did not ban either side from developing and testing such systems.

But Nixon administration diplomats who negotiated the treaty insisted that both Washington and Moscow wanted the development of future systems based on exotic technologies banned and the accord did just that. A strict interpretation of the ABM Treaty was the only legal one, they argued. The reading of the treaty concocted by the Reagan administration was "absurd as a matter of policy, intent, and interpretation," complained John Rhinelander, who served as the legal adviser to the ABM Treaty negotiations. If Congress accepted this broad interpretation, the ABM Treaty would be rendered "a dead letter," warned its chief United States negotiator, Ambassador Gerard Smith.

Congress was in no mood to do that. Conservative Democrats who had gone along with the SDI program, like Georgia senator Sam Nunn, the powerful Armed Services Committee chairman, flatly opposed any tinkering with the treaty's interpretation. Faced with a revolt on Capitol Hill that threatened SDI itself, the Reagan administration quickly backed down. The White House announced it would adopt the broad reading of the accord as the correct and legal one. But SDI research would continue to comply with the traditional or "strict" interpretation. The administration, however, reserved the right to adopt the broad interpretation in the future. A confrontation with Congress had been sidestepped.

But one remained with the Soviets. Moscow believed the U.S. SDI program was a thinly disguised effort to acquire a first-strike capability. With an effective shield in place, the United States could launch a nuclear attack on the Soviet Union, then use its strategic defenses to parry any retaliatory blow. The Kremlin scoffed at U.S. professions of benign intent, including Reagan's offer to share strategic defense technology; the Americans would not even share their dairy technology at the moment, Mikhail Gorbachev complained. The Soviet general secretary had ambitious plans to revitalize the ailing Russian economy. The last thing he wanted was a costly new strategic-defense arms race with the United States, which the Soviet Union could never win.

Moscow launched an intensive propaganda campaign to derail the U.S. SDI program. Gorbachev proposed that the superpowers cut their nuclear arsenals by one half in exchange for restricting SDI to laboratory research. Reagan countered with his so-called 5-2-6 proposal. Both sides would confine themselves for five years to the research, development, and testing of strategic defenses (that Reagan still argued was permitted by the ABM Treaty) in order to determine if they were technically feasible. Then if either side decided to deploy an ABM system, it must offer to negotiate within two years a plan to share the benefits of strategic defense and eliminate offensive ballistic missiles. If no agreement was reached in two years, either side could deploy its ABM system after giving six months' notice.

On 11 October 1986, Reagan and Gorbachev met in Reykjavík, Iceland, for what the White House billed as a "preparatory" session in advance of a full-blown summit later in Washington in December 1987. But Gorbachev had his own agenda—reining in the U.S. "Star Wars" program. The Soviet leader was prepared to trade away a major part of his strategic nuclear arsenal in exchange for a cap on SDI. After two days of nearly round-the-clock negotiations, the two countries had agreed to sweeping reductions. Intermediate-range nuclear forces would be eliminated in Europe and held to one hundred warheads worldwide. Strategic nuclear weapons would be cut in half within five years. During the next five years all ballistic missiles would be eliminated. But in exchange for these deep cuts, Gorbachev demanded that both sides strictly abide by the ABM Treaty and that the U.S. SDI program be scaled back to only laboratory research and testing. Reagan balked and the negotiations collapsed.

The Reagan administration had argued for increased SDI funding as a bargaining chip to force reductions in Soviet nuclear weapons. In the aftermath of Reykjavík, however, SDI appeared to be more an obstacle to arms reduction than a bargaining chip. Reykjavík undercut another rationale for SDI, as far as the program's critics were concerned. Gorbachev was willing to dismantle half his nuclear arsenal in exchange for SDI's dismantlement. SDI critics doubted a strategic defense could ever be erected that would shoot down even half the Soviet nuclear force. An arms-reduction treaty, therefore, could accomplish what SDI could not—without costing the American taxpayer hundreds of billions of dollars. The administration rejected that logic and continued to press for higher SDI budgets.

Not until it became obvious in later years that SDI would not be receiving the funding needed for a crash effort to deploy strategic defenses would Moscow soften its antipathy toward the program. Although it would never accept the broad interpretation of the ABM Treaty, the Soviet Union would eventually agree to deep reductions in strategic nuclear arms without a scale-down of SDI as quid pro quo. But the Soviet Union was quick to stipulate that if the United States ever veered from the strict interpretation of the ABM Treaty and began testing and developing space-based weapons, Moscow would withdraw from a strategic arms-reduction treaty.

NEAR-TERM DEPLOYMENT

The Strategic Defense Initiative Organization mapped out a program restrained only by the pace of its technological development. Congress funded a program constrained by budget realities. SDI received the lion's share of the military research budget, but it never got all it wanted. In fiscal year 1985, the Reagan administration requested $1.78 billion. Congress approved $1.4 billion. In fiscal year 1986,

the administration asked for $3.72 billion, a 166 percent increase in the SDI budget. Congress appropriated $2.76 billion, a 97 percent increase. For fiscal year 1987, the administration had requested $4.8 billion, a 74 percent increase. Congress approved only a 16 percent increase, to $3.2 billion.

"Star Wars" advocates were worried. The SDI budget had nearly tripled since its inception, but the program appeared to be losing political momentum as Congress each year curbed even more the large funding increases its managers had planned. Congress and the American people like instant gratification. The fruits of SDI's research would be reaped too far into the future to compel large funding increases for the present. SDI's timetable was slipping. The program's supporters feared that slippage would continue unless SDI produced something definable, such as strategic defense hardware around which Congress and the American public could rally. The solution: deploy a limited strategic defense quickly, "while the political will to do so undeniably exists," Teller and other proponents urged the president.

Reagan at first resisted. "To deploy systems of limited effectiveness now would divert limited funds and delay our main research," he argued. But with a growing number of congressional moderates becoming increasingly skeptical that an astrodome defense would ever be erected, the administration decided that an early deployment of partial defenses was the only way to keep SDI from becoming a permanent research project.

By the end of 1986, SDI's managers had begun quietly reorganizing the program toward a near-term deployment. Millions of dollars were transferred from the directed-energy projects, whose weapons would take decades to develop, to ground- and space-based rocket interceptors that could be built much sooner. A crash program was instituted to build heavy-lift launchers to put hardware in space early. Systems engineers began planning a partial defense that could be deployed as early as 1995. The deployment of directed-energy weapons would be postponed. A 1995 early deployment would have only a token force of space-based kinetic-kill vehicles, little or no capability to intercept warheads in the midcourse phase, and approximately one thousand ground-based interceptors produced on a hurry-up schedule. An early deployment would be far less expensive—$60 billion, according to initial SDI projections, compared with as much as $1 trillion for an astrodome shield. But instead of the president's vision of a nearly leakproof defense, the 1995 defense would be able to destroy less than one-fifth of the Soviet strategic missile force.

The Search for a Mission   The Defense Department believed it had a compelling case for a near-term deployment of strategic defenses. The Joint Chiefs of Staff mandated that the limited defense deployed in "Phase 1" be aimed at the missiles the Soviets would use in a first strike, such as the highly accurate SS-18 that would be targeted at U.S. ICBMs. Though the Phase 1 defense would not be 100 percent effective, it would nevertheless ensure the survivability of the United States retaliatory force and thus deter a Soviet attack in the first place. Moreover, Phase 1 would so complicate Soviet strategic planning, Moscow would be forced to do one of two things: Either it would scrap its ballistic-missile force and concentrate on strategic bombers and cruise missiles, which were less threatening to the United States because they were not first-strike weapons; or, Moscow would be compelled to negotiate arms control agreements reducing its offensive force and to move toward a greater reliance on strategic defenses itself. Either way, U.S. security would be enhanced.

Congress was not convinced. The program's critics questioned whether a near-term defense was technically feasible even if the money were available to pay for it. It would likely be the next century before NASA or the air force would have an affordable launch capability to put all the weapons and sensors in space, even for an early deployment. SDIO had to find a way to mass-produce low-cost, ground-based interceptors that would have to sit dormant for years and be ready to fire at a moment's notice. Space-based interceptors likewise faced major technological hurdles. The battle stations housing these interceptors would be vulnerable to counterattack. Critics argued that by the time the United States had the space stations in orbit, the Soviets would likely have developed countermeasures to render them useless, such as fast-burn rocket boosters that would shorten the time of their missiles' boost phase. The space-based interceptors would not be able to reach their targets before the boosters had burned out and the missiles had dispensed their warhead buses.

Even more serious, an early deployment threatened to leave the United States stranded with an imperfect defense that the Soviets had bested with

countermeasures. Rather than enhancing stability, the early deployment would end up making the superpowers' strategic relationship more unstable, with the Soviets able to knock out U.S. defenses and still launch a first strike. To prevent this from happening, SDIO must quickly follow an early deployment with more sophisticated technologies such as directed-energy weapons that would counter the countermeasure. Administration officials insisted that SDI research would be structured to do just that. But congressional critics and many of the program's own scientists were skeptical. If SDI began early deployment, all available resources would be poured into the first phases of defenses, and research into far-term technologies such as directed-energy weapons would be shortchanged. In fact, by 1987 the program's budgeters were beginning to do just that, critics charged.

The federal budget was another problem. Congress was struggling to contain soaring deficits. SDI's early estimates of $60 billion in near-term deployment costs were soon revised upward to as high as $150 billion. Though a near-term deployment would be far less expensive than an astrodome defense, Congress was not thrilled about the lower price tag.

By the time Reagan left office in early 1989, America's military program for space was adrift. The president's original vision of an astrodome defense that would make nuclear weapons obsolete was now a distant memory. Plans for early deployment were dead. The SDI organization produced more scaled-down versions of Phase 1 defenses, but even these plans became victims of tight budgets and slipping schedules for when the first defenses could be deployed. Shackled by congressional restrictions on testing, the air force canceled its program to develop anti-satellite rockets fired from F-15s, leaving only a scaled-down research into ground-based ASATs being conducted by the army.

Desperate for a mission that could garner political support, the administration considered a proposal by Senator Nunn to erect an Accidental Launch Protection System (ALPS). To protect against accidental or unauthorized launches or a missile attack by a country other than the Soviet Union, Nunn called on the administration to consider deploying just one hundred anti-missile interceptors, which it was allowed to do under the ABM Treaty. Defense contractors rushed in with estimates of $5–8 billion for a one-hundred-interceptor defense system.

But even ALPS had its problems. It would be decades or more before any third world nation had the capability to build ICBMs that might threaten the United States. Washington had simpler means to preempt their development than sophisticated ballistic-missile defenses. The most immediate third world missile threat—being that of Iraq—was put out of action with cruise missiles and conventional bombers. Moreover, Pentagon officials had to admit that the chance of an accidental or unauthorized Soviet launch was remote. And if it occurred, even the mistaken launch of just one heavy Soviet ICBM, packed with as many as ten warheads and perhaps one hundred decoys, could overwhelm a one-hundred-interceptor defense. Though the Pentagon continued to investigate a global system to protect against accidental launches, Nunn soon backed off with his proposal when defense contractors began lobbying for an ALPS with more inteceptors than the one hundred allowed by the ABM Treaty. The senator was not prepared to sanction any substantial renegotiation or abrogation of the treaty.

The Strategic Defense Initiative Organization shifted course again. Space-based battle stations packed with ten interceptors each had a nagging vulnerability problem. They were also expensive. Scientists at the Lawrence Livermore Laboratory had the answer: "brilliant pebbles." Instead of deploying several hundred space-based battle stations and their equally vulnerable sensor satellites, why not individually orbit thousands of autonomous interceptors in low-earth orbit (500 kilometers—300 miles—or less) that would not rely on large satellites? The interceptors, nicknamed brilliant pebbles, would be the ultimate smart weapon. Roughly one meter (approximately 1 yard) in length and weighing 50 kilograms (110 pounds), the brilliant pebble would have ultraviolet and infrared sensors plus a tiny high-speed computer to identify and select targets and to guide the interceptor in for the kill. Small solar panels and batteries would allow each interceptor to remain in orbit up to ten years, while a laser communications system would link it to a ground-based command center.

Best of all, brilliant pebbles theoretically would solve the survivability and cost problems. It would be much more difficult to shoot down thousands of small interceptors than hundreds of large battle stations. Brilliant-pebbles advocates claimed that the 4,600 space-based interceptors envisioned for a Phase 1 defense could be produced for as little as $1 million apiece, making the space-based defense

about $14 billion cheaper than one that depended on large battle stations.

Brilliant pebbles had its skeptics. Even with the tremendous advances over the past decade in microminiaturization, outside analysts doubted that all that sensing and computing capability could be crammed into such a tiny interceptor that would orbit in space for up to a decade. The Pentagon does not have a good track record for building cheap, smart weapons. Brilliant pebbles would also add to a growing problem of space litter. The U.S. Space Command now tracks more than 7,000 objects in space, from working satellites to space junk (spent-rocket bodies, inactive payloads, fragments of engines that have blown apart). Adding 4,600 interceptors to already crowded orbits would increase the chances of space collisions with commercial and military satellites. By the summer of 1990, the Senate voted to freeze the funding for brilliant pebbles. The cap was lifted only after intense lobbying by the Pentagon.

SDI AFTER THE COLD WAR

But the Pentagon was not able to change international realities. Gorbachev had freed Eastern Europe. The two Germanys were reunited. The Warsaw Pact had been dissolved. The Soviet Union itself was on the verge of collapsing as a democracy movement grew within. Conventional-force reduction agreements could barely keep up with the convoys of Soviet tanks unilaterally pulling out of Eastern Europe. Washington and Moscow then joined in an unprecedented alliance in the Middle East to incur sanctions against Iraqi dictator Saddam Hussein's invasion of Kuwait. White House Chief of Staff John Sununu even visited the Kremlin to advise its leaders on how to organize a democratically elected executive branch.

The breakup of the Soviet Union in 1991 rendered the strategic nuclear threat against the United States almost nonexistent. The defense industry in the new Commonwealth of Independent States that replaced the Soviet Union practically ground to a halt. The Russian Republic's new president, Boris Yeltsin, promised drastic cuts in the old Soviet nuclear arsenal and reached out to the West for aid to convert his country to a market economy. The other republics began trucking their nuclear weapons to Moscow for destruction. Weapons design bureaus began looking for ways to retool to serve civilian industry. By 1992, the United States and the Commonwealth of Independent States were forging close ties. SDI critics asked, why spend hundreds of billions of dollars to render obsolete nuclear weapons that are not likely to be used in the first place?

The Bush administration appeared to have the same doubts much earlier. Within months of assuming office, President Bush scaled back the long-term growth in SDI's budget that the Reagan administration had proposed. Congress moved to cut more. In a post–Cold War world, both Congress and the administration began drastic reductions in the overall defense budget. An expensive program like Star Wars could not hope to escape those cuts. For fiscal year 1991, Congress whittled SDI's budget down to less than $3 billion—the second year in a row that SDI spending decreased instead of increased. Funding for an army program to develop ground-based anti-satellite weapons was almost cut in half, with more budget reductions likely in the future. Perhaps more telling, Congress halted funding for SDI's nuclear directed-energy weapons program, once the crown jewel of Star Wars. Dr. Teller's claim that nuclear-pumped lasers in space could shoot down Soviet missiles had played a key role in Reagan's decision to launch the Strategic Defense Intitiative. But after spending $1.5 billion over five years on X-ray laser weapons, SDI still had little hope of producing a workable one. "You can safely say this represents the demise of Star Wars," California Democratic Congressman George Brown told the *Washington Post*. "The centerpiece is no longer being considered."

Star Wars proponents were not ready to throw in the towel. Even the Bush administration was prepared to carve out a hefty share of the shrinking Pentagon budget for SDI. For fiscal year 1992 it requested $5.2 billion for strategic-defense research. Congress approved $4.15 billion. The administration came back the next year with a request of $5.4 billion for fiscal 1993. The "Star Warriors" believed they had a valuable new ally: the Patriots of Desert Storm.

For more than two decades, the army had struggled to field the Patriot missile, originally built as an air-defense system to shoot down enemy planes. In the mid-1980s, the army upgraded the Patriot system, which consists of ground-based interceptor missiles, radars, and computer controls, to attack short-range ballistic missiles an enemy would fire in a ground war. During the Persian Gulf War, United States Patriot missiles engaged Soviet-supplied Scud

missiles Iraq fired at Saudi Arabia. When Saddam began firing Scuds at Tel Aviv, the Pentagon rushed Patriot batteries to Israel. The Patriots became one of the heroes of the Desert Storm conflict. Their interception of the Israeli-bound Scuds became the key to keeping Israel out of the war. Star Wars proponents immediately touted the Patriot as positive proof that strategic defenses worked.

That was not quite the case. The Patriot performed moderately well in the Persian Gulf. But the system employed fairly rudimentary anti-ballistic-missile technology that was up against an even cruder, slow-moving Scud missile of 1960s vintage. Iraqi Scud crews could guarantee their missiles would hit a city but not a target much smaller. They also launched their Scuds singly or in small volleys, so the Patriot batteries were never overwhelmed. The Patriots would have much more difficulty intercepting sophisticated Soviet missiles, particularly ones employing countermeasures. Intercepting Soviet ICBMS and warheads required technology even more sophisticated than the Patriot's. Ironically, SDIO had once turned down an army request for help with Patriot funding believing its technology was inferior to what strategic defense scientists wanted to develop.

Bush nevertheless was convinced that the Patriot's performance in the Persian Gulf could help politically resuscitate SDI. On 29 January 1991, in the State of the Union address before Congress, he announced that SDI's mission would again change. Instead of defending against a large-scale Soviet attack, SDI would be reoriented to "providing protection against limited ballistic missile strikes—whatever their source." "Let us pursue an SDI program that can deal with any future threat to the United States, to our forces overseas and to our friends and allies," Bush said. At least fifteen developing nations were building ballistic missiles, by the CIA's count, with some, such as Iraq, also conducting research into chemical and nuclear weapons. SDI would defend against future attacks from those nations as well as an accidental launch by the Soviets.

The new concept was dubbed GPALS, for Global Positioning Against Limited Strikes. About one-fourth of the 4,600 brilliant pebbles planned for a Phase 1 defense would be deployed under GPALS. The ground-based interceptors would be in the 750 to 1,000 range and would be backed up by mobile anti-tactical ballistic missiles (ATBMS) like the Patriot that could be rushed to foreign countries to protect

U.S. forces or allies. GPALS would cost about $41 billion, far less than the $55 billion SDIO estimated for full deployment of brilliant pebbles under Phase 1.

Whether strategic defenses have finally found a home with GPALS remains to be seen. A Congress tightfisted when it comes to defense budgets does not appear in the mood for a $41-billion weapons system to combat a distant threat. Capitol Hill is adamant about preserving the ABM Treaty, which would have to be abrogated to deploy GPALS. Critics continue to question whether the United States is really in any danger from third world ballistic missiles. "If Third World and terrorist weapons emerge as a threat to the United States, they are far more likely to be delivered by aircraft, ships sailed into our harbors, or packing crates smuggled across our borders than by ballistic missiles," Harold Brown, the Carter administration's secretary of defense, pointed out.

Star Wars advocates, however, can be counted on to lobby hard for GPALS. Beginning in the 1980s, a wide-ranging, indeed wrenching, debate over whether there is a technological solution to the threat of nuclear war has taken place in the United States. The debate has yet to be resolved. SDI has lurched from one mission to another. Opponents have managed only to slow the program, not kill it. Perhaps it is inevitable that the search for a technological quick fix will continue. Reagan cannot be faulted for wanting to render nuclear arms obsolete. But billions of dollars worth of research have yet to alter the inescapable fact that the horror of nuclear war, like that of all wars, can only be avoided by people agreeing not to fight one in the first place.

BIBLIOGRAPHY

Historical Overview For a general survey of space activities and early efforts to develop a ballistic-missile defense system, see ASHTON B. CARTER and DAVID N. SCHWARTZ, eds., *Ballistic Missile Defense* (Washington, D.C., 1984); PAUL B. STARES, *Space and National Security* (Washington, D.C., 1987); and U.S. CONGRESS, *Military Space Programs: An Unclassified Overview of Defense Satellite Programs and Launch Activities* (Washington, D.C., 1990). Another useful source is OFFICE OF TECHNOL-OGY ASSESSMENT, *Ballistic Missile Defense Technologies* (Washington, D.C., 1985).

Critical Overview The writings on SDI are voluminous. For critical overviews and bibliography see PHILIP M. BOFFEY et al., *Claiming the Heavens: The New York Times Complete Guide to the Star Wars Debate* (New York, 1988); DOUGLAS C. WALLER, JAMES T. BRUCE III, and DOUGLAS M. COOK, *The Strategic Defense Initiative, Progress and Challenges: A Guide to Issues and References* (Claremont, Calif., 1987); and SIDNEY D. DRELL, PHILIP J. FARLEY, and DAVID HOLLOWAY, *The Reagan Strategic Defense Initiative: A Technical, Political, and Arms Control Assessment* (Cambridge, Mass., 1985). A debate between supporters and critics is contained in JAMES A. ABRAHAMSON, RICHARD N. PERLE, RICHARD L. GARWIN, and CARL SAGAN, "SDI: Vision or Delusion?" *Issues in Science and Technology* (Winter 1988): 82–92. For an interesting look at some of the individuals involved in the SDI program, see WILLIAM J. BROAD, *Star Warriors: A Penetrating Look into the Lives of the Young Scientists Behind Our Space Age Weaponry* (New York, 1985).

Early Deployment The views of those arguing for early deployment of an SDI system may be found in GREGORY CANAVAN and EDWARD TELLER, "Strategic Defence for the 1990s," *Nature* (19 April 1990): 699–704. A broader look is provided by STEVEN A. HILDRETH, *The Strategic Defense Initiative: Issues for Phase 1 Deployment* (Washington, D.C., Congressional Research Service, 1990) and AMY F. WOLF, *Accidental Launch Protection System: Requirements and Proposed Concepts* (Washington, D.C., Congressional Research Service, 1989). One of the latest weapons to be explored by the SDI program is examined in JOHN D. MOTEFF, *Brilliant Pebbles: Implications for the Strategic Defense Initiative* (Washington, D.C., Congressional Research Service, 1990).

Countermeasures Countermeasures that might be employed against an SDI system are examined in OFFICE OF TECHNOLOGY ASSESSMENT, *Anti-Satellite Weapons, Countermeasures, and Arms Control* (Washington, D.C., 1985) and MARCIA S. SMITH, *ASATs: Anti-Satellite Weapon Systems* (Washington, D.C., Congressional Research Service, 1991).